Frommer's

South America

2nd Edition

by Shawn Blore, Shane Christensen, Alexandra de Vries, Eliot Greenspan, Haas Mroue, Neil E. Schlecht & Kristina Schreck

Here's what the critics say about Frommer's:

"Amazingly easy to use. Very portable, very complete."
—*Booklist*

"Detailed, accurate, and easy-to-read information for all price ranges."
—*Glamour Magazine*

"Hotel information is close to encyclopedic."
—*Des Moines Sunday Register*

"Frommer's Guides have a way of giving you a real feel for a place."
—*Knight Ridder Newspapers*

WILEY
Wiley Publishing, Inc.

D0067535

Published by:

Wiley Publishing, Inc.

111 River St.
Hoboken, NJ 07030-5774

ISBN 0-7645-5625-8

Editors: Myka Carroll Del Barrio and John Vorwald
Production Editor: Suzanna R. Thompson
Cartographer: Elizabeth Puhl
Photo Editor: Richard Fox
Production by Wiley Indianapolis Composition Services

Front cover photo: Machu Picchu, Peru
Back cover photo: Dancers in Salvador, Brazil

For information on our other products and services or to obtain technical support, please contact our Customer Care Department within the U.S. at 800/762-2974, outside the U.S. at 317/572-3993 or fax 317/572-4002.

Wiley also publishes its books in a variety of electronic formats. Some content that appears in print may not be available in electronic formats.

Manufactured in the United States of America

5 4 3 2

Contents

8 Ecuador   482

by Haas Mroue

9 Peru   559

by Neil E. Schlecht

10 Uruguay   669

by Shane Christensen

11 Venezuela   687

by Eliot Greenspan

12 Difficult Destinations: Antarctica & Colombia   751

by Kristina Schreck

Appendix: Useful Terms & Phrases   764

Index   773

List of Maps

About the Authors

A native of California, **Shawn Blore** (Brazil) has lived and worked in a half dozen countries and traveled in 40 more (but who's counting?). Now a resident of Vancouver, Shawn is an award-winning magazine writer and the author of *Vancouver: Secrets of the City* and co-author of *Frommer's Brazil* and *Frommer's Portable Rio de Janeiro*.

To do Argentina right, **Shane Christensen** (Argentina, Uruguay) moved in with a Porteño family, committed himself to a rigorous steak-only diet, searched Buenos Aires for the perfect tango partner, and added a rich Argentine accent to his Mexican-learned Spanish. With his nascent Argentine credentials, he roamed the country's far corners, finding that no place in South America offers such geographic diversity and cultural distinction. A California native, Shane has written extensively in South America, Western Europe, and the United States for the Berkeley Guides, Fodor's, and *The Wall Street Journal*.

Alexandra de Vries (Brazil) made her first journey to Brazil at the ripe old age of 1 month. (Alas, few of her food reviews from that trip survive.) In the years since, Alexandra has returned many times to travel, explore, and live in this amazing country. Alexandra co-writes *Frommer's Brazil* and *Frommer's Portable Rio de Janeiro* about her all-time favorite place to visit.

Eliot Greenspan (Venezuela) is a poet, journalist, and travel writer who took his backpack and typewriter the length of Mesoamerica before settling in Costa Rica in 1992. Since then, he has traveled almost ceaselessly around Latin America, writing articles and guidebooks to feed his travel habit. He feels particularly at home in the neotropics—in its rain and cloud forests, on its rivers, and under its seas. Eliot is the author of *Frommer's Costa Rica* and *Frommer's Belize* and co-author of *Frommer's Cuba*.

Haas Mroue (Argentina, Bolivia, Chile, Ecuador) is a freelance travel writer based in the United States. His short stories, poems, and travel pieces have appeared in a variety of publications, including *Interiors Magazine,* the *Michigan Quarterly Review,* the *Literary Review,* National Geographic guides, Fodor's, Berlitz, and Britannica.com. He's the author of *Frommer's Memorable Walks in Paris* and *Frommer's Paris from $90 a Day,* and is a contributor to *Frommer's Argentina & Chile, Frommer's Gay & Lesbian Europe,* and *Frommer's Europe from $70 a Day.*

Neil E. Schlecht (Peru) first trekked to Machu Picchu in 1983 as a college student spending his junior year abroad in Quito, Ecuador. The author of a dozen travel guides (including *Frommer's Peru* and *Spain For Dummies*), as well as articles on art and culture and art catalogue essays, and a photographer, he has lived for extensive periods in Brazil and Spain. He now resides in northwestern Connecticut.

Kristina Schreck (Antarctica, Chile, Colombia) has traveled extensively throughout Latin America and has lived and worked in Argentina and Chile for 8 years. She is the former managing editor of *Adventure Journal* magazine and is co-author of the first edition of *Frommer's Argentina & Chile*. Kristina currently resides in Santiago and the Andes, where she works year-round for Ski Portillo (and although she thinks it is the greatest ski resort in the world, to be fair, she asked an independent, impartial source to edit the Chile skiing coverage in this guide).

An Invitation to the Reader

In researching this book, we discovered many wonderful places—hotels, restaurants, shops, and more. We're sure you'll find others. Please tell us about them, so we can share the information with your fellow travelers in upcoming editions. If you were disappointed with a recommendation, we'd love to know that, too. Please write to:

Frommer's South America, 2nd Edition
Wiley Publishing, Inc. • 111 River St. • Hoboken, NJ 07030-5774

An Additional Note

Please be advised that travel information is subject to change at any time—and this is especially true of prices. We therefore suggest that you write or call ahead for confirmation when making your travel plans. The authors, editors, and publisher cannot be held responsible for the experiences of readers while traveling. Your safety is important to us, however, so we encourage you to stay alert and be aware of your surroundings. Keep a close eye on cameras, purses, and wallets, all favorite targets of thieves and pickpockets.

Other Great Guides for Your Trip:

Frommer's Argentina & Chile

Frommer's Belize

Frommer's Brazil

Frommer's Costa Rica

Frommer's Peru

Frommer's Portable Rio de Janeiro

Frommer's Star Ratings, Icons & Abbreviations

Every hotel, restaurant, and attraction listing in this guide has been ranked for quality, value, service, amenities, and special features using a **star-rating system.** In country, state, and regional guides, we also rate towns and regions to help you narrow down your choices and budget your time accordingly. Hotels and restaurants are rated on a scale of zero (recommended) to three stars (exceptional). Attractions, shopping, nightlife, towns, and regions are rated according to the following scale: zero stars (recommended), one star (highly recommended), two stars (very highly recommended), and three stars (must-see).

In addition to the star-rating system, we also use **seven feature icons** that point you to the great deals, in-the-know advice, and unique experiences that separate travelers from tourists. Throughout the book, look for:

Finds	Special finds—those places only insiders know about
Fun Fact	Fun facts—details that make travelers more informed and their trips more fun
Kids	Best bets for kids and advice for the whole family
Moments	Special moments—those experiences that memories are made of
Overrated	Places or experiences not worth your time or money
Tips	Insider tips—great ways to save time and money
Value	Great values—where to get the best deals

The following **abbreviations** are used for credit cards:

AE	American Express	DISC	Discover	V	Visa
DC	Diners Club	MC	MasterCard		

Frommers.com

Now that you have the guidebook to a great trip, visit our website at **www.frommers.com** for travel information on more than 3,000 destinations. With features updated regularly, we give you instant access to the most current trip-planning information available. At Frommers.com, you'll also find the best prices on airfares, accommodations, and car rentals—and you can even book travel online through our travel booking partners. At Frommers.com, you'll also find the following:

- Online updates to our most popular guidebooks
- Vacation sweepstakes and contest giveaways
- Newsletter highlighting the hottest travel trends
- Online travel message boards with featured travel discussions

What's New in South America

ARGENTINA

Many readers will wonder how Argentina's economic crisis has affected the tourism industry and the rest of the country. First, prices have been slashed across the board, from hotels and restaurants to airfares, attractions, and shopping. Argentina has become a bargain for foreign travelers. Also, with growing recognition that tourism provides oxygen for the struggling economy, travelers to Argentina are catered to in a way they never were in the past. You should be aware, however, that many hotels and other establishments have introduced different prices for foreigners than for Argentines; confirm prices before agreeing to the service, and realize that high inflation and volatile exchange rates will limit the accuracy of rates quoted here.

This economic crisis is popularly viewed as the worst in Argentina's history, and everyone feels it. Poverty has skyrocketed, young people can't find jobs, and some children face malnutrition as families struggle to get bread on the table. One result is an increase in crime, particularly in the big cities, and travelers should take extra precautions when visiting Argentina.

BUENOS AIRES Travelers will find Buenos Aires far cheaper than at any time in recent memory, and quality hotels, restaurants, shops, and tourist attractions are all open for business. Due to the economic crisis, however, travelers should avoid walking alone and should not take taxis off the streets. Call a radio taxi or *remise* (private, unmetered taxi), instead.

THE ARGENTINE LAKE DISTRICT San Martín's new restaurant, **La Pierrade,** Mariano Moreno and Villegas (© **02972/421421**), is the height of romance with a beautiful stone fireplace and plump red pillows. Specials include deer carpaccio and a variety of Patagonian pâtés.

Bariloche's luxurious **Llao Llao Hotel & Resort,** Avenida Bustillo (© **02944/448530;** www.llaollao. com), now offers extensive spa packages at its lovely new spa. The treatment rooms have breathtaking views of the mountains and the lake.

BOLIVIA

The recent unrest has not prevented adventurous visitors from visiting this enchanting country. But because most of the recent protests have been in and around La Paz (including the roads to Lake Titicaca), the focus of many travelers has shifted south to Sucre and even Cochabamba. Be sure to check your country's travel warnings before your trip to Bolivia as the security situation is constantly changing.

PLANNING YOUR TRIP Lloyd Aéreo Boliviano (LAB; © 0800-4321; www.labairlines.com) now offers daily nonstop flights to Santa Cruz from Miami, with immediate connections to La Paz and Cochabamba. Unfortunately, the airline still operates an aging fleet of Boeing 727s on its domestic routes, and delays are common.

SUCRE   Sucre's newest hotel is very charming and very affordable. **Hotel La Posada,** Calle Audiencia 92 (*© 0104/6913-427;* Laposadahostal@ entel.bo), boasts an excellent restaurant with an outdoor seating area in its delightful courtyard.

POTOSI   Finally, a comfortable and modern hotel in Potosí: The **Hotel Cima Argentum,** Av. Villazon 239 (*© 0102/6229-538;* www.hca-potosi. com), not only has attractive (and heated) rooms, but it also boasts an excellent restaurant and a friendly, efficient staff.

COCHABAMBA   The newest resort in all of Bolivia is located a 30-minute drive from the center of Cochabamba. Nestled against verdant hills and overlooking a small lake, the romantic **Hacienda De Kaluyo Resort,** Camino La Angostura, Tarata (*© 0104/4576-594;* www.kaluyo.com), offers a great getaway for both active travelers and those looking for rest and relaxation. The property includes an open-air gym, a handsome restaurant, and an adjoining 19th-century chapel—perfect for weddings.

The newest restaurant in Cochabamba is **Casa de Campo,** Av. Uyuni 618 (*© 0104/4243-937*), a huge and vibrant eatery specializing in local cuisine. It's the best place in town to try the slightly spicy and aromatic traditional chicken stew, *picante de pollo.* Come here for a boisterously fun evening with the locals.

BRAZIL

The biggest news has been the presidential election of left-of-center candidate Luiz Inácio Lula da Silva. Lula, as he is universally known, is an impressive figure: a bear of a man with the charisma of JFK and a true-life rags-to-riches story to rival any in America. Although not all Brazilians agree with Lula's policies, everyone took pride in the fact that the country could elect a left-wing candidate without provoking a meltdown in the economy, foreign intervention, or a domestic coup d'état. The huge celebration at Lula's January 2003 inauguration was really for Brazil itself, where democracy at last seems to have taken firm root.

RIO DE JANEIRO   Accommodations   Recently taken over by the excellent Windsor hotel chain, the **Miramar Palace Hotel,** Av. Atlântica 3668, Copacabana (*© 0800/232-211* or 021/2521-1122; www.windsor hoteis.com), offers luxury beachfront accommodations at reasonable rates.

Dining   New in downtown Rio is **Cais do Oriente,** Rua Visconde de Itaboraí 8, Centro (*© 021/2233-2531*). This former warehouse has been gloriously restored and emerged as a stunning restaurant and bar venue; the kitchen serves up an interesting mix of Asian and Mediterranean dishes.

Over the past couple of years Leblon has cemented its reputation as *the* diner's destination in Rio. The epicenter is a 4-block stretch on the upscale Rua Dias Ferreira, home to the trendiest of Rio's new restaurants. New kid on the block **Zuka,** Rua Dias Ferreira 233 (*© 021/3205-7154*), does up cleverly inventive dishes. Across the street you'll find **Carlota,** Rua Dias Ferreira 64 (*© 021/2540-6821*), chosen by *Condé Nast Traveller* as one of the 50 most exciting restaurants in the world. Nearby is Rio's top sushi spot, **Sushi Leblon,** Rua Dias Ferreira 256 (*© 021/2512-7830*).

After Dark   For lovers of Brazilian music, Lapa remains the place to go, even more so now thanks to two extraordinary new music venues. The **Centro Cultural Carioca,** Rua do Teatro 37, Centro (*© 021/2242-9642;* www.centroculturalcarioca.

com), hosts local musicians as well as big names who specialize in samba, MPB, choro, and gafieira. In a renovated warehouse on Lapa's edge, **Rio Scenarium,** Rua do Lavradio 20 (© **021/2233-3239**), is crammed with antiques, centered on a stage and dance floor visible from all three floors. It's the perfect setting for traditional Brazilian samba and choro.

If you just want a nice little bar to hang out with some friends, check out **Devassa,** Rua General San Martin 1241, Leblon (© **021/2540-6087**). This new bohemian bistrolike bar attracts a good-looking crowd that seems to enjoy the casual atmosphere and the delicious microbrews on tap.

SÃO PAULO Accommodations Builders just can't seem to get enough of São Paulo and new luxury hotels are springing up left and right. Most notable of these is the **Unique,** Av. Brigadeiro Luis Antônio 4700 (© **011/3055-4700;** www.hotel unique.com.br), an extraordinary hotel with gorgeous rooftop views and rooms featuring the cleanest of clean white-on-white decor and a plethora of room gadgets.

More discrete but just as luxurious is the **Emiliano,** Rua Oscar Freire 384, Cerqueira César (© **011/3069-4369;** www.emiliano.com.br). It's top-flight treatment all the way, from the welcome massage to the minibar stocked according to your preferences and a personalized selection of pillows, carefully fluffed and placed on your Egyptian cotton sheets.

Dining The gourmet capital of Brazil, São Paulo offers some outstanding restaurants, including the gorgeous **Figueira Rubaiyat,** Rua Haddock Lobo 1738, Jardins (© **011/ 3063-3888**), which is built around a magnificent centenary fig tree with a glass expansion wrapping around the trunk to let in lots of natural light.

The menu specializes in a la carte meats and seafood, most of it freshly grilled.

After Dark The latest hit on São Paulo's club scene is **Azucar,** Rua Mario Feraz 423, Itaim Bibi (© **011/ 3078-3130**). Salsa, merengue, and other Latin beats get the crowd going. For a night of barhopping, the Vila Olimpia neighborhood has recently emerged as the São Paulo destination. Packed with clubs and bars, it's always busy, even on weeknights. The more popular bars concentrate along the **Rua Prof. Atilio Innocenti.**

SALVADOR Accommodations Pestana Bahia, Rua Fonte do Boi (© **071/453-8005;** www.pestana. com), is positively buzzing after its extensive makeover. Set on an outcrop overlooking Rio Vermelho, its privileged location guarantees all 430 units an ocean view, and the amenities are outstanding.

Porto da Barra's newest budget hotel, **Village Novo,** Av. Sete de Setembro 3659 (© **071/267-4362;** www.villagenovo.com), is housed in a 125-year-old heritage mansion. Village Novo offers a number of beautiful rooms at very reasonable rates.

Dining The latest eatery by a longtime darling of Salvador foodies, **Caranguejo da Dadá,** Av. Otavio Mangabeira 940 (© **071/363-5151**), is located out in Patamares beach. Overlooking the ocean, the bar and restaurant are perfect for a casual afternoon snack or as a fine dinner destination in itself.

For years, one of the best fine-dining restaurants in Salvador has been the **Trapiche Adelaide,** Praça do Tupinambás 2, Av. Contorno, Comércio (© **071/326-2211;** www. trapicheadelaide.com.br). New chef Luciano Boseggia has given the menu a definite Italian twist with a hint of French influence, and the results are excellent.

MANAUS   Riverboats now dock at the brand-new **Hidroviaria do Amazonas (Riverboat Terminal),** in the middle of downtown at Rua Marquês de Santa Cruz 25 (© **092/621-4359).** The terminal features a bar and churrascaria, **Choppicanha Bar and Grill** (© **092/631-1111),** on a deck with a view of the broad Amazon River. Downstream of downtown by the Ceasa port, the new **Peixaria Moronguêtá,** Rua Jaith Chaves s/n (© **092/615-3362),** serves fresh local Amazon fish in an astonishing variety of ways.

For those looking to explore the rainforest in depth, the best option is the new suite of kayak descents offered by **Amazon Mystery Tours,** Av. Djalma Batista 385, Sala 103 (© **092/ 633-7844;** www.amazon-outdoor. com). Amazon Mystery has the skills and experience to bring you deep into the rainforest, make your time there safe and fun, and then get you back to town again.

For a more luxurious rainforest experience, there's a new lodge with lots of space, **Amazonat** (©/fax **092/ 633-3227;** www.amazonat.com.br). Located 160km (98 miles) east of Manaus, Amazonat is surrounded by walking trails that you are free to roam on your own; there is a lake with a beach for swimming and an orchid park with more than 1,000 specimens to explore.

CHILE

The Chilean tourism industry has lost a lot of business to neighboring Argentina over the past 2 years, after the devaluation of the Argentine peso. However, worldwide interest in Chile continues to grow wildly, mostly because Chile offers wonderful landscapes and adventure-travel opportunities that are incomparable to its Andean neighbor. As a result, the country's tourism infrastructure continues to improve.

The bad news is that the reciprocity entry fee for first-time visitors from the United States has risen sharply to $100, but it's good for the life of the visitor's passport.

It's comical how fast telephone numbers in Chile change; have your hotel help you find any updated numbers.

PLANNING YOUR TRIP By Plane   United Airlines, in the face of its recent bankruptcy, has pulled out of Chile completely. **Delta** has entered the scene, usually offering the lowest fares to Santiago, via Atlanta. Great news for Canadians: **Air Canada** now offers nonstop service from Toronto to Santiago.

The total overhaul of the portion of the Panamericana Highway that runs from Puerto Montt to the north of Chile is finished at last, meaning that hundreds of tollbooths dot its length at highway exits and entrances. Prices range from 30¢ to $5.

SANTIAGO   Accommodations The hotel industry is stagnant, keeping prices down. Don't be afraid to investigate rates for hotels that might seem well beyond your budget as these hotels often advertise incredible bargains, especially for multiple-day stays.

Santiago now has South America's first **Ritz-Carlton,** El Alcalde 15 (© **800/241-3333** from the U.S., or 23/629619; www.ritzcarlton.com), which opened in May 2003.

THE CENTRAL VALLEY   Viña del Mar's newest lodging option is the **Hotel del Mar,** Av. San Martín 199 (© **600/700-6000;** www.casino.cl), which abuts the grand, classic casino. Its beautiful seaside views and a sumptuous indoor pool and gym are draws, but this hotel needs to work out a few bugs in its service. Great location nonetheless.

Chile's wine industry has seen unbelievable growth and an unprecedented improvement in quality over the past few years. The new **Hotel Santa Cruz Plaza,** Plaza de Armas 286, Santa Cruz (© 72/821010; www.hotelsantacruzplaza.cl), in the heart of the Colchagua Valley, serves as an excellent jumping-off point to sample the wonderful varieties Chile has to offer. The Hotel Santa Cruz will organize day tours with the **Ruta del Vino,** or you can just rent a car and explore at your own pace.

THE CHILEAN LAKE DISTRICT Pucón's new **airport** (no phone), minutes from the center of town, is now operational, saving you from the tedious 1½-hour drive from Temuco. **LanChile** (© 600/600-4000; www.lanchile.com) jets arrive from Santiago on Friday and Sunday, in high season only.

The **Airesbuenos International Hostel,** General Lagos 1036 (©/fax 63/206304; www.airesbuenos.cl), opened in one of Valdivia's most beautiful historical mansions. In addition to private rooms with en-suite bathrooms, there are bunk beds for $8.50 for those traveling on a tight budget.

There are two notable additions to the vibrant restaurant scene in Puerto Varas. **Kika's,** Walker Martínez 584 (© 65/234703), serves distinctive cuisine blending old German favorites with local ingredients, such as grilled Patagonian venison with sauerkraut. Its wine list is made up entirely of award-winning Chilean vintages. **Mediterráneo,** Santa Rosa 068, on the corner of Portales (© 65/237268), serves up imaginative Chilean-Mediterranean fusion dishes in a great location with a view of the water.

Also, a deluxe hotel has opened in Puerto Montt. The sleek seven-story **Gran Pacífico,** Urmeneta 719 (© 65/482100; Reservas@hotelpacifico.cl),

towers over the city's harbor and offers breathtaking views from its Art Deco rooms, which come with large-screen TVs and small marble bathrooms.

THE CARRETERA AUSTRAL A convenient, scenic, and very comfortable way to travel from Puerto Montt to Chaitén has just begun: catamarans that make the trip in 4 hours. **Catamaranes del Sur** (© 02/482308; www.catamaranesdelsur.cl) operates three times a week and costs $40 one-way, $72 round-trip.

ECUADOR

Ecuador is booming—and it's not only the Galápagos that are getting all the attention.

QUITO The old town is getting safer and new restaurants are opening up. Right on the lovely Plaza de la Independencia, you'll find the grand **Mea Culpa** (© 02/2951-190). Be sure to call ahead for reservations and request a table by the window overlooking the plaza. A few minutes by taxi up the hill, you'll find the most spectacular view in the city at **Café Mosaico,** Manuel Samaniego N8-95 and Antepara (© 02/2542-871). Here, the crème de la crème of Ecuadorian society can be found sipping coffee, nibbling on cheesecake, and taking in the sumptuous views of Old Town.

CUENCA This lovely pedestrian-friendly city boasts two beautiful new hotels. First to open was **Mansión Alcázar,** Calle Bolívar 12-5 and Tarquí (© 07/823-918; www.mansionalcazar.com), an oasis of elegance and tranquillity right in the heart of the historic downtown. The incredible back garden even has a resident hummingbird. Steps from the main plaza in one of the finest colonial buildings in the city, you'll find **Hotel Santa Lucía,** Antonio Borrero 8-44 and Sucre (© 07/828-000; www.santa

luciahotel.com). The hotel has already received the city's most prestigious architectural award for the meticulous renovation and preservation of a historical building.

GUAYAQUIL Ecuador's largest city has been practically a huge construction site since the mayor began his ambitious plan of turning his drab metropolis into a vibrant tourist attraction. There are new museums, shopping areas, restaurants, and cafes sprouting in safe and attractive neighborhoods. Don't miss a stroll up the steps to the attractive **Cerro Santa Ana** neighborhood, and a visit to the new lighthouse at the top of the hill with a spectacular view of the river and the entire city.

Best of the city's new restaurants is **Lo Nuestro**, Av. Estrada 903 and Higueras (✆ **04/2386-398**), serving not only Ecuadorian cuisine but also dishes unique to Guayaquil (think lots of bananas, fresh seafood, and tropical fruit).

THE GALAPAGOS ISLANDS Aerogal (✆ **800/2376-425**; aerogal@ andinanet.net), short for AeroGalápagos, began service last year from Quito and Guayaquil to the island of San Cristóbal in the Galápagos, giving Tame a run for its money. Its clean and comfortable planes and professional crew have an enviable on-time record.

There's also now a truly luxurious resort in Ecuador—and in the Galápagos, no less. The **Royal Palm Hotel** (✆ **800/528-6069** in the U.S., or 05/5527-409; www.royalpalmhotel. net) is destined to become one of the most celebrated new resorts in South America. It sits on 200 lush tropical hectares (500 acres) and offers personalized service and unique day excursions to the outlying islands. The views from its drop-dead gorgeous villas are breathtaking.

PERU

Peru had a rough time of it during the first couple of years of Alejandro Toledo's administration, with strikes by public workers and several cabinet reorganizations, but international interest in Peru continues to grow. The recent discoveries of still more "lost" Inca cities has added to the fascination of Machu Picchu and given a fresh jolt to the appeal of the Inca Trail and Peru's ancient ruins. Simmering unrest and widespread dissatisfaction among Peruvians, and discord in neighboring Bolivia (which some observers expected to spill over to Peru), have so far not affected travel in any part of the country.

PLANNING YOUR TRIP **United Airlines** no longer flies to Lima from the United States or Canada. Contrary to some published reports, **AeroContinente** has not resumed international service from Miami to Iquitos.

The world's highest train, the eternally problematic, on-again, off-again **Ferrocarril Lima-Huancayo** (which travels from Lima to Huancayo in the Central Highlands) is apparently up and running again—but that's not necessarily reason to believe it will be by the time you hit Peru. For the meantime, the schedule for one of the Americas' most impressive train trips is just one round-trip per month (during the 3rd or 4th week of the month) between April and October. The round-trip cost is US$30 per person for the 10-hour journey. The train departs downtown Lima at the **Desamparados station,** Jr. Ancash 201 (✆ **01/441-2222**), just behind the Government Palace. A train schedule is posted at www.incasdelperu.org/ StatusoftheTrain.htm. For additional information, visit **www.ferrovias peru.com.pe** and make reservations at reservas@fcca.com.pe.

LIMA   All that glitters is apparently not gold. The famed **Museo de Oro del Perú (Gold Museum)**, for decades the most popular attraction in Lima, has been determined to be one of the biggest museum frauds ever uncovered. The National Institute of Culture and the Tourism Protection Bureau declared just about everything in the museum—about 7,000 pieces, much of it purportedly pre-Columbian gold artifacts—to be complete and utter fakes.

CUSCO   Lima has long been Peru's preeminent museum city, but Cusco has added an important archaeological museum, the **Museo de Arte Precolombino,** Plaza de las Nazarenas s/n (© **084/233-210**), to its stately attractions. Taking advantage of the vast collection of pre-Columbian works belonging to the Rafael Larco Herrera Museum in Lima, this new addition in the San Blas district occupies a onetime Inca ceremonial court and later colonial-era mansion, and displays nearly 500 pieces dating from 1250 B.C. to A.D. 1532 representing the Nasca, Moche, Huari, Chimú, Chancay, and Inca cultures.

THE SACRED VALLEY OF THE INCAS   The spectacular narrow-gauge train from Cusco to Machu Picchu has new names, prices, and categories for its services, including the introduction of a top-flight luxury service, the **Hiram Bingham,** which includes brunch, afternoon tea, a guided tour of the ruins, and cocktails and dinner on the return trip. It's the way to go if money is no object. Check **www.perurail.com** for the latest details and rates. Helicopter travel to Machu Picchu has been suspended indefinitely, although the Hiram Bingham train should suffice for bragging rights.

The Peruvian government, seeking to limit numbers of trekkers on the Inca Trail, has finally begun to strictly enforce the new regulations adopted in 2001. All trekkers must still organize their treks through an approved local agency that provides guides and porters, but the price of hiking the trail has steadily risen. To guarantee a spot with an agency (which must request a trek permit for each trekker), trekkers must make a reservation and pay entrance fees at least 15 days advance, and at least 1 month in advance during the peak months (May–Sept). It's now nearly impossible to show up in Cusco and quickly organize an Inca Trail trek, even though some first-come, first-served spots may be available.

PUNO/AREQUIPA   Train service from Arequipa to Puno is now available by charter only, although it may be reinstated sometime in the near future. The train from Arequipa to Colca Canyon also no longer is in service. For updates, visit **www.perurail.com**.

URUGUAY

The major news in Uruguay is the currency devaluation, which, as with Argentina, has made the country more affordable. Punta del Este, the historic favorite of jet-setting Argentines, is slightly quieter as a result of the ongoing economic crisis next door. This means better bargains in shops, and friendlier rates at hotels and restaurants.

VENEZUELA

Venezuela's political situation continues to be tense, and the economy is in steep decline. This has led to a drastic drop in tourism. Caracas continues to be relatively inhospitable, but brave souls venturing farther afield will find wonderful adventures, abundant wildlife, deserted beaches, and real bargains (thanks to an artificially fixed exchange rate, tight currency restrictions, and a thriving black market).

PLANNING YOUR TRIP

INATUR (© 0800/462-8871 or 0212/576-9032; www.inatur.gov.ve) is the new national tourism institute. Its main office, located on the 35th floor of the Torre Oeste (West Tower) of the Parque Central (near the Caracas Hilton), is open weekdays during business hours.

In January 2002, the government fixed the official exchange rate at 1600Bs to the U.S. dollar. It also made it virtually impossible for Venezuelan citizens and businesses, as well as tourists, to exchange bolivares for dollars. This has led to a thriving black market, where the real exchange rate hovers around 2500Bs to the dollar at press time.

There is an airport departure tax of 48,500Bs, paid in either bolivares, or the current official exchange in dollars. This fee is sometimes included in the airline ticket price, so be sure to ask before paying twice.

CARACAS After several years of sitting in mothballs, the Pico El Avila **Teleférico** (© 0212/793-5129) is finally open again. This modern cable car system stretches from the Maripérez station on the northern edge of the city 3.4km (2 miles) to the top of El Avila. The restoration and reopening of the tramway section down to the coastal city of La Guaira is still far off.

The luxurious **Four Seasons Caracas** (www.fourseasons.com), near the Altamira metro station, has been shut down for over a year, due to legal wrangling. But the fancy new **JW Marriott Hotel,** Avenida Venezuela and Calle Mohedano, El Rosal (© 0212/957-2222; www.marriott.com), is filling the void.

Finally recovering from the disastrous mudslides and devastation of the 1999 Vargas tragedy, the coastal area near the Simón Bolívar International Airport in Maiquetia now boasts a few hotel options for those wanting a quick overnight, without having to brave the traffic, madness, and insecurity of Caracas. Among the choices are the **Hampton Inn & Suites,** Avenida La Armada, Urbanización 10 de Marzo (© 800/426-7866 in the U.S., or 0212/331-7111 in Venezuela; www.hamptoninn.com), located just 2 minutes from the airport terminals. For a more upscale option, try the recently restored **Hotel Olé Caribe,** Avenida Intercomunal, El Playón Macuto (© 0212/331-1133; www.hotelolecaribe.com).

The **American Book Shop,** has moved into new, more spacious digs at Centro Plaza, Nivel Jardín, Avenida Francisco de Miranda, Los Palos Grandes (© 0212/286-2230).

ISLA DE MARGARITA Conferry (© 0212/782-8544, or 0295/261-6397 for current ferry schedules and fares) has finally opened regular express service between La Guaira (just outside of Caracas) and Margarita, although it only runs on Tuesday and Thursday.

The beachside restaurant **Bahia** in the Bella Vista section of Porlamar has closed.

In the Sambil mall, **A Granel** (© 0295/260-2491) is a popular new restaurant and cafe that often features live jazz or bolero groups.

LOS ROQUES NATIONAL PARK

All visitors to Los Roques must now pay a one-time 15,000Bs entrance fee for the national park, good for the duration of your stay.

Banesco (© 0237/221-1265) has opened a branch office on Gran Roque, but it is of limited use to travelers, as it does not have an ATM and will not change money. However, it will do in a pinch if you need a cash advance off of your credit card.

MERIDA, THE ANDES & LOS LLANOS The somewhat upscale (at least for Mérida) **Hotel Tisure** has closed. However, the folks at **Natoura Adventure Tours** are nearing completion on a very comfortable new hotel **Posada Casa Sol** (© 0274/252-4164; www.posadacasasol.com) just a few blocks away.

CANAIMA, ANGEL FALLS & THE GRAN SABANA The new and comfortable **Waku Lodge** (© 0286/962-0559; www.canaimatours.com) is set right on the banks of the Canaima lagoon, with excellent views across the water and toward several waterfalls.

1

The Best of South America

by Shawn Blore, Shane Christensen, Alexandra de Vries, Eliot Greenspan, Haas Mroue, Neil E. Schlecht & Kristina Schreck

Whether you're an archaeology buff, an outdoor adventurer, or a partyer in search of a good time, South America presents so many diverse travel options that it'll make your head spin. We'll help you plan a memorable trip, starting with our highly opinionated lists of the best experiences the continent has to offer.

1 The Most Unforgettable Travel Experiences

- **Visiting Iguazú (Iguaçu) Falls:** One of the world's most spectacular sights, Iguazú boasts more than 275 waterfalls fed by the Iguazú River, which can (and should) be visited from both the Argentine and the Brazilian sides. In addition to the falls, Iguazú encompasses a marvelous subtropical jungle with extensive flora and fauna. See "Iguazú Falls" in chapter 4 and "Iguaçu Falls" in chapter 6.

- **Traveling the Wine Roads of Mendoza:** Less commercialized than their European and North American counterparts, Mendoza's wineries are free to visit and easily accessible along roads known locally as *los Caminos del Vino*. There are about 80 wineries that formally offer tours and tastings. Be sure to try the region's famed Malbec. See "Mendoza" in chapter 4.

- **Walking in the Sun's footsteps on the Isla del Sol:** The Incas trace their roots from Manco Capac and Mama Ocllo, the children of the Sun. Supposedly, the Sun stepped forth onto the Sun Island in Lake Titicaca to give birth to the first Incas. Nowadays, on the northwestern tip of the Sun Island, you can walk right up to rock formations that look like footsteps, which according to legend, were left here when the Sun came down to Earth to drop off Manco Capac and Mama Ocllo. See "Lake Titicaca" in chapter 5.

- **Celebrating Carnaval in Rio:** The biggest party in the world. Whether you dance it out on the streets, watch the thousands of participants in their elaborate costumes in the samba parade, or attend the fairy-tale Copacabana Palace ball, this is one event not to miss! See "Rio de Janeiro" in chapter 6.

- **Observing red macaws at sunset:** The sunset over the red rock formations in the Chapada dos Guimarães north of Cuiabá in Brazil is a magical experience in itself. Even more special is the view of scarlet macaws working the thermals off the sheer cliffs in the warm glow of the setting sun. See "The Pantanal" in chapter 6.

• **Exploring the madcap streets of Valparaíso:** The ramshackle, sinuous streets of Valparaíso offer a walking tour unlike any other. Valparaíso could be called the penniless older brother of San Francisco, California, and part of the fascination here is touring the faded remains of this once-thriving port town. Antique Victorian mansions and colorful tin houses line terraced walkways that wind around precipitous hills—to get to the top, there are a handful of 1900s funiculars. Sweeping views and atmospheric restaurants and cafes can be found at every turn, but Valparaíso's bars, which seem to have authored the word "bohemian," are what have brought this city notoriety. See "Around Santiago & the Central Valley" in chapter 7.

• **Sailing past the islands and fiords of southern Chile:** Quietly sailing through the lush beauty of Chile's southern fiords is an experience that all can afford. There are two breathtaking trajectories: a 3-day ride between Puerto Natales and Puerto Montt, and a 1- to 6-day ride to the spectacular Laguna San Rafael Glacier. Backpackers on a shoestring (as well as those who need spiffier accommodations) all have options. These pristine, remote fiords are often said to be more dramatic than those in Norway. Farther south, a small cruise line takes passengers through Tierra del Fuego and past remote glaciers, peaks, and sea-lion colonies, stopping at the end of the world in Puerto Williams. See "The Chilean Lake District" in chapter 7.

• **Watching blue-footed boobies dance for love in the Galápagos:** Birds are usually shy, especially during mating season. But in the Galápagos Islands, where wild animals have no fear of humans, you can watch male blue-footed boobies spread their wings, lift their beaks, and dance wildly in a performance known as "sky pointing," all in hope of attracting a mate. If the female likes what she sees, she'll do the same. It's a scene right out of a *National Geographic* documentary. See "The Galápagos Islands" in chapter 8.

• **Floating on Lake Titicaca:** Lake Titicaca, the world's highest navigable body of water, straddles the border between Peru and Bolivia. To locals, it is a mysterious and sacred place. A 1-hour boat ride from Puno takes you to the Uros floating islands, where communities dwell upon soft patches of reeds. Visitors have a rare opportunity to experience the ancient cultures of two inhabited natural islands, Amantani and Taquile, by staying with a local family. You won't find any cars or electricity here, but there are remarkable local festivals. The views of the oceanlike lake, at more than 3,600m (12,000 ft.) above sea level, and the star-littered night sky alone are worth the trip. See "Puno & Lake Titicaca" in chapter 9.

• **Gazing upon Machu Picchu:** However you get to it—whether you hike the fabled Inca Trail, hop aboard one of the prettiest train rides in South America, or zip in by helicopter—Machu Picchu more than lives up to its reputation as one of the most spectacular sites on earth. The ruins of the legendary "lost city of the Incas" sit majestically among the massive Andes, swathed in clouds. The ceremonial and agricultural center, never discovered or looted by the Spanish, dates from the mid-1400s but seems even more ancient. Exploring the site is a thrilling experience, especially at sunrise, when dramatic rays of light creep over the mountaintops. See "The Sacred Valley of the Incas" in chapter 9.

• **Visiting Punta del Este in summer:** As *Porteños* (residents of Buenos Aires) will tell you, anyone who's anyone from Buenos Aires heads to Punta del Este for summer vacation. The glitzy Atlantic coast resort in Uruguay is packed with South America's jet set from December through February and offers inviting beaches and outstanding nightlife. See "Punta del Este" in chapter 10.

• **Enjoying the splendor of Angel Falls:** From the boat ride through rapids in a dugout canoe, to the steep hike from the river's edge to the base of the falls, to a swim in the cool waters at the foot of this natural wonder and back again, this is an amazing experience, with spectacular views and scenery throughout. See "Canaima, Angel Falls & the Gran Sabana" in chapter 11.

• **Riding El Teleférico in Mérida, Venezuela:** The world's highest and longest cable car system will bring you to the summit of Pico Espejo at 4,765m (15,629 ft.). If you've ever wanted to get into thin air without the toil of actually climbing there, this is the way to go. Go early if you want the best views. But be careful: The effects of altitude can be felt, whether or not you actually climb. See "Mérida, the Andes & Los Llanos" in chapter 11.

2 The Best Small Towns & Villages

• **San Martín de los Andes, Argentina:** City planners in San Martín had the smart sense to do what Bariloche never thought of: limit building height to two stories and mandate continuity in the town's Alpine architecture. The result? Bariloche is crass whereas San Martín is class, and the town is a year-round playground to boot. The cornucopia of hotels, restaurants, and shops that line the streets are built of stout, cinnamon-colored tree trunks or are Swiss-style, gingerbread confections that all seem right at home in San Martín's blessed, pastoral setting. Relax, swim, bike, ski, raft, hunt, or fish—this small town has it all. See "The Argentine Lake District" in chapter 4.

• **The Isla del Sol, Bolivia:** There are actually several small villages on the Sun Island, but in total, only a few thousand people live here. There are no cars and barely any telephones. At rush hour, things get very chaotic: You may have to wait a few minutes while the locals herd their llamas from one end of the island to the other. Spend a day here, and you'll feel as if you have taken a trip back in time. See "Lake Titicaca" in chapter 5.

• **Porto de Galinhas, Brazil:** This village of three streets in a sea of white sand is the perfect spot to learn to surf. You'll never get cold, while steamed crab and fresh tropical juices between waves do wonders to keep you going. See "Recife & Olinda" in chapter 6.

• **Morro de São Paulo, Brazil:** situated on a green lush island just a boat ride away from Salvador, this sleepy village offers some of the best laidback beach life on the northeast coast of Brazil. Car-free and stress-free, Morro de São Paulo offers the perfect mix of deserted beaches, watersports, and fun nightlife in an idyllic setting. See "A Side Trip from Salvador" in chapter 6.

- **San Pedro de Atacama, Chile:** Quaint, unhurried, and built of adobe brick, San Pedro de Atacama has drawn Santiaguinos and expatriates the world over to experience the mellow charm and New Age spirituality that waft through the dusty roads of this town. San Pedro hasn't grown much over the past 10 years—it has simply reinvented itself. Its location in the driest desert in the world makes for starry skies and breathtaking views of the weird and wonderful land formations that are just a stone's throw away. See "The Desert North" in chapter 7.

- **Pucón, Chile:** Not only was Pucón bestowed with a stunning location at the skirt of a smoking volcano and the shore of a glittering lake, it's also Chile's self-proclaimed adventure capital, offering so many outdoor activities that you could keep busy for a week. But if your idea of a vacation is plopping yourself down on a beach, Pucón also has plenty of low-key activities, and that is the real attraction here. You'll find everything you want and need without forfeiting small-town charm (that is, if you don't come with the Jan–Feb megacrowds). Timber creates the downtown atmosphere, with plenty of wood-hewn restaurants, pubs, and crafts stores, blending harmoniously with the forested surroundings. See "The Chilean Lake District" in chapter 7.

- **Baños, Ecuador:** This is the perfect place to get away from it all. Baños is only about 3 hours from Quito, but it feels like it's on a different planet. This tiny little town sits right below an active volcano, and the lush green countryside serves as a fantastic backdrop. Most people come here to relax or enjoy outdoor activities, such as rafting or hiking. The weather is almost always perfect—never too hot or too cold. See "Baños" in chapter 8.

- **Ollantaytambo, Peru:** One of the principal villages of the Sacred Valley of the Incas, Ollanta (as the locals call it) is a spectacularly beautiful place along the Urubamba River; the gorge is lined by agricultural terraces, and snow-capped peaks rise in the distance. The ruins of a formidable temple-fortress overlook the old town, a perfect grid of streets built by the Incas, the only such layout remaining in Peru. See "The Sacred Valley of the Incas" in chapter 9.

- **Colonia del Sacramento, Uruguay:** Just a short ferry trip from Buenos Aires, Colonia is Uruguay's best example of colonial life. The old city contains brilliant examples of colonial wealth and many of Uruguay's oldest structures. Dating from the 17th century, this beautifully preserved Portuguese settlement makes a perfect day trip. See "A Side Trip to Colonia del Sacramento" in chapter 10.

- **Mérida, Venezuela:** Nestled in a narrow valley between two immense spines of the great Andes Mountains, this lively college town is a great base for a wide range of adventure activities. Its narrow streets and colonial architecture also make it a great place to wander around and explore. See "Mérida, the Andes & Los Llanos" in chapter 11.

- **Canaima, Venezuela:** This isolated indigenous village sits on the edge of a black-water lagoon fed by a series of impressive waterfalls. The lagoon and its rivers offer access to even more spectacular waterfalls, including the world's tallest, Angel Falls, as well as the region's distinctive tabletop mesas, or *tepuis*. See "Canaima, Angel Falls & the Gran Sabana" in chapter 11.

3 The Best Outdoor Adventures

- **Discovering Iguazú Falls by raft:** This is a place where birds like the great dusky swift and brilliant morpho butterfly spread color through the thick forest canopy. You can easily arrange an outing into the forest once you arrive in Iguazú. See "Puerto Iguazú & Iguazú Falls" in chapter 4.

- **Raging down the Mendoza River:** Mendoza offers the best white-water rafting in Argentina, and during the summer months, when the snow melts in the Andes and fills the Mendoza River, rafters enjoy up to class IV and V rapids. Rafting is possible year-round, but the river is colder and calmer in winter months. See "Mendoza" in chapter 4.

- **Biking the most dangerous road in Bolivia:** The 97km (60-mile) road that descends nearly 1,800m (6,000 ft.) from the barren high-plateau area of La Paz to the lush tropical area of Los Yungas is considered one of the most dangerous roads in the world. It's unpaved, narrow, and carved out of the edge of a cliff (without any guardrails). The road recently has become a popular mountain-biking challenge. The views are unbelievable, but don't stare at them too long—you have to keep an eye out for speeding trucks coming at you from the other direction. See "La Paz" in chapter 5.

- **Horseback riding in the Pantanal:** The world's largest flood-plain is best explored cowboy-style on horseback. Spend some time quietly observing the many large bird species and every now and then take off on a fast gallop through the wetlands, startling alligators and snakes underfoot. See "The Pantanal" in chapter 6.

- **Hang gliding in Rio:** Running off the edge of a platform with nothing between you and the ground 800m (2,624 ft.) below requires a leap of faith, but once you do, the views of the rainforest and beaches are so enthralling that you almost forget about the ground until your toes touch down on the sand at São Conrado beach. See "Rio de Janeiro" in chapter 6.

- **Kayaking the Brazilian Amazon:** Perhaps the best way to really get in touch with the rainforest is by good old sea kayak. Drifting down an Amazon tributary, you have the time to observe the rainforest, to search the trees for toucans, macaws, and sloths, and to scout the water for anaconda and caiman. On daytime hikes, you explore and swim in rarely visited Amazon waterfalls. To truly make like a researcher, you can hoist yourself 60m (197 ft.) into the treetops, and spend some time exploring the rainforest canopy. See "Manaus & the Amazon" in chapter 6.

- **Trekking in Torres del Paine:** This backpacking mecca just keeps growing in popularity, and it's no wonder. Torres del Paine is one of the most spectacular national parks in the world, with hundreds of kilometers of trails through ever-changing landscapes of jagged peaks and one-of-a-kind granite spires, undulating meadows, milky, turquoise lakes and rivers, and mammoth glaciers.

The park has a well-organized system of *refugios* and campgrounds, but there are also several hotels, and visitors can access the park's major highlights on a day hike. See "Patagonia" in chapter 7.

- **Snorkeling in the Galápagos:** The sea lions in the Galápagos are a curious bunch. Once you put on a snorkeling mask and flippers, these guys will think you're one of the gang and swim right up to you. When you aren't playing with sea lions, you'll have the chance to see hammerhead sharks, penguins, sea turtles, and some of the most colorful fish in the world. See "The Galápagos Islands" in chapter 8.

- **Hiking the Inca Trail:** The legendary trail to Machu Picchu, the Camino del Inca, is one of the world's most rewarding ecoadventures. The arduous 42km (26-mile) trek leads across phenomenal Andes mountain passes and through some of the greatest natural and man-made attractions in Peru, including dozens of Inca ruins, dense cloud forest, and breathtaking mountain scenery. The trek has a superlative payoff: a sunset arrival at the glorious ruins of Machu Picchu, laid out at your feet. See "The Sacred Valley of the Incas" in chapter 9.

- **Exploring the Peruvian Amazon:** More than half of Peru is Amazon rainforest, and the country has some of the richest biodiversity on the planet. Cusco is the gateway to the southeastern jungle and two principal protected areas, Tambopata and the Manu Biosphere Reserve. Manu is the least accessible and least explored jungle in Peru, with unparalleled opportunity for viewing wildlife and more than 1,000 species of birds, but it's not easy or cheap to get to. Iquitos leads to the accessible northern Amazon basin, with some of the top jungle lodges in the country. Ecotravelers can fish for piranhas and keep an eye out for pink dolphins, caiman, and tapirs. One of the best jungle experiences is viewing the dense forest from the heights of a rickety canopy walkway. See "The Southern Amazon: Manu & Tambopata" and "Iquitos & the Northern Amazon" in chapter 9.

- **Scuba diving in Los Roques, Venezuela:** Los Roques offers much of the same coral, marine life, and crystal clear waters as the rest of the popular Caribbean dive destinations, but it's still virtually undiscovered. There are only two dive operations on the islands, and plenty of dive sites to go around. **Sesto Continente** (ℂ/fax **0212/ 632-9411;** www.scdr.com) has the best equipment and the most experience diving the archipelago. See "Los Roques National Park" in chapter 11.

- **One-stop adventure travel from Mérida, Venezuela:** With a half dozen or so peaks 4,500m (15,000 ft.) and above, raging rivers, and a couple of very competent adventure tour outfitters, you can go climbing, trekking, mountain biking, white-water rafting, horseback riding, canyoneering, and even paragliding out of Mérida. You may need a couple weeks to do it all, but both **Arassari Treks** (www.arassari.com) and **Natoura Adventure Tours** (www.natoura. com) can help you come up with an adventure package to fit your budget, skill level, and time frame. See "Mérida, the Andes & Los Llanos" in chapter 11.

4 The Most Intriguing Historical Sites

- **Manzana de las Luces,** Buenos Aires: The Manzana de las Luces (Block of Lights) served as the intellectual center of the city in the 17th and 18th centuries. This land was granted in 1616 to the Jesuits, who built San Ignacio— the city's oldest church—still standing at the corner of Bolívar and Aslina streets. Worth a visit to see the beautiful altar. See p. 98.

- **Teatro Colón,** Buenos Aires: The majestic Teatro Colón, completed in 1908, combines a variety of European styles, from the Ionic and Corinthian capitals and French stained-glass pieces in the main entrance to the Italian marble staircase and exquisite French furniture, chandeliers, and vases in the Golden Hall. The Colón has hosted the world's most important opera singers. See p. 100.

- **Tiwanaku,** Bolivia: The Tiwanaku lived in Bolivia from 1600 B.C. to A.D. 1200. Visit the Tiwanaku archaeological site, which is about 2 hours from La Paz, and you'll see proof of some of the amazing feats of this pre-Columbian culture. The stone-carved Sun Gate could gauge the position of the sun. The technologically advanced irrigation system transformed this barren terrain into viable farmland. The enormous and intricately designed stone-carved monoliths found here give testament to the amazing artistic talents of these people. Much here still remains a mystery, but when you walk around the site, it's exciting to imagine what life must have been like here for the Tiwanaku. See "La Paz" in chapter 5.

- **Brasília,** Brazil: Built from scratch in a matter of years on the red soil of the dry cerrado, Brasília is an oasis of modernism in Brazil's interior. Marvel at the clean lines and functional forms and admire some of the best modern architecture in the world. See "Brasília" in chapter 6.

- **Pelourinho,** Brazil: The restored historical center of Salvador is a treasure trove of baroque churches, colorful colonial architecture, steep cobblestone streets, and large squares. See "Salvador" in chapter 6.

- **San Pedro de Atacama, Chiu Chium,** and **Caspana,** Chile: The driest desert in the world has one perk: Everything deteriorates very, very slowly. This is good news for travelers in search of the architectural roots of Chile, where villages such as San Pedro, Chiu Chiu, and Caspana boast equally impressive examples of 17th-century colonial adobe buildings and the sun-baked ruins of the Atacama Indian culture; some sites date from 800 B.C. Highlights undoubtedly are the enchanting, crumbling San Francisco Church of Chiu Chiu and the labyrinthine streets of the indigenous fort Pukará de Lasana. See "The Desert North" in chapter 7.

- **Chiloé Island,** Chile: Chiloé's historical appeal is in large part derived from the fact that many citizens live much as they did 200 years ago, tilling fields with an ox and a plow, plying the coves with rickety wooden fishing skiffs, and hand-knitting sweaters to keep out the cold. Chiloé is home to a rare display of antique ecclesiastical architecture in the form of hundreds of 17th- and 18th-century wooden churches, two dozen of which were recently named a World Patrimony by UNESCO. See "Chiloé" in chapter 7.

- **Quito's Old Town,** Ecuador: When you walk around old Quito, you will feel as if you have stepped back in time. The oldest church here dates from 1535, and it's still magnificent. La Compañia de Jesús only dates from 1765, but it is one of the most impressive baroque structures in all of South America. It's rare to find a city with so many charming colonial-style buildings. When you wander through the streets, it really seems as if you are walking through an outdoor museum. See "Quito" in chapter 8.

- **The Nasca Lines,** Peru: One of South America's great enigmas are the ancient, baffling lines etched into the desert sands along Peru's southern coast. There are trapezoids and triangles, identifiable shapes of animal and plant figures, and more than 10,000 lines that can only really be seen from the air. Variously thought to be signs from the gods, agricultural and astronomical calendars, or even extraterrestrial airstrips, the Nasca Lines were constructed between

300 B.C. and A.D. 700. See "Lima" in chapter 9.

- **Cusco,** Peru: Cusco is a living museum of Peruvian history, with Spanish colonial churches and mansions sitting atop perfectly constructed Inca walls of exquisitely carved granite blocks that fit together without mortar. In the hills above the city lie more terrific examples of Inca masonry: the zigzagged defensive walls of Sacsayhuamán and the smaller ruins of Q'enko, Puca Pucara, and Tambomachay. See "Cusco" in chapter 9.

- **Colonia del Sacramento,** Uruguay: An easy day trip from either Buenos Aires or Montevideo, Colonia del Sacramento is a World Heritage City with the best preserved colonial artistry in the region dating from the 17th century. See "A Side Trip to Colonia del Sacramento" in chapter 10.

- **Iglesia de San Francisco,** Caracas: This is the church where Simón Bolívar was proclaimed El Libertador in 1813, and the site of his massive funeral in 1842—the year his remains were brought back from Colombia, some 12 years after his death. Begun in 1575, the church shows the architectural influences of various periods and styles, but retains much of its colonial-era charm. See p. 705.

5 The Best Museums

- **Caminito,** Buenos Aires: At the center of La Boca lies the Caminito, a short pedestrian walkway that is both an outdoor museum and marketplace. Each day, tango performers dance alongside musicians, street vendors, and artists. Surrounding the street are shabby metal houses painted in dynamic shades of red, yellow, blue, and green, thanks to designer Benito Quinquela Martín. See p. 95.

- **Museo Nacional de Bellas Artes,** Buenos Aires: This museum contains the world's largest collection of Argentine sculptures and paintings from the 19th and 20th centuries. It also houses European art dating from the pre-Renaissance

The Best of Sensuous South America

Your trip will not be complete until you indulge in at least one of the following uniquely South American experiences:

- **Dance the tango in Argentina:** Top Al Pacino and Gabrielle Anwar in *Scent of a Woman* with the creation of your own tango dance, preferably in one of the seedier tango salons of Buenos Aires where it all started. See "Tango: Lessons in the Dance of Seduction & Despair" on p. 118.
- **Get high in Bolivia:** With the world's highest capital city, highest commercial airport, and highest navigable lake, Bolivia's air is so thin, it will make your head spin. But Bolivia is also home to the infamous coca leaf, a perfectly legal, extremely nutritious source of energy and an antidote to altitude sickness. To learn the complete history of the coca leaf (and for free samples), stop in at the **Coca Museum** in La Paz. See p. 183.
- **Be the girl (or boy) from Ipanema:** Rio may have other beaches but Ipanema is still the one with the best people-watching. Grab a spot, and food, drink, and eye-candy will come to you. See "Rio de Janeiro" in chapter 6.
- **Feel the beat in Brazil:** At night the historic heart of Salvador comes alive with music. Most impressive of all are the Afro blocos, the all-percussion bands that create such an intense rhythm with their drums that it sends shivers down your spine. See "Salvador" in chapter 6.
- **Soak in Chilean hot springs:** The volatile Andes not only builds volcanoes; it also produces steaming mineralized water that spouts from fissures, many of which have been developed into hot springs, from rock pools to full-scale luxury resorts. Most hot springs seem to have

period to the present day. The collections include notable pieces by Manet, Goya, El Greco, and Gauguin. See p. 100.

- **Malba-Colección Constantini,** Buenos Aires: This stunning new private museum houses one of the most impressive collections of Latin American art anywhere. Temporary and permanent exhibitions showcase names like Antonio Berni, Pedro Figari, Frida Kahlo, Candido Portinari, Diego Rivera, and Antonio Siguí. Many of the works confront social issues and explore questions of national identity. See p. 99.

- **Casa Nacional de la Moneda,** Potosí: Silver was discovered in Potosí in the 16th century. During the next few hundred years, Potosí would become one of the most important cities in the Spanish empire. The exhibits at this museum, which was originally a mint, do an excellent job of explaining both the history of Potosí and the process of turning raw silver into money. See p. 214.

- **Museu de Arte Sacra,** Salvador: When you walk into this small but splendid museum, what you hear is not the usual gloomy silence but the soft sweet sound of been magically paired by nature with outdoor adventure spots, making for a thankful way to end a day of activity. The Lake District is a noted "hot spot," especially around Pucón. See "The Chilean Lake District" in chapter 7.

- **Moisturize naturally in Ecuador:** In the cooler months, a light mist, known as the *garúa*, falls over the highlands of Santa Cruz Island in the Galápagos. Walking around the spectacular grounds at the **Royal Palm Hotel** (© **800/528-6069** in the U.S., or 05/5527-409), nestled on 200 lush hectares (500 acres), your face will be gently sprayed with a sweet, tropical mist that is cool, soothing, and the purest moisturizer Mother Nature can offer. See p. 557.
- **Stand beneath the condor's wings in Peru:** Colca Canyon is the best place in South America to see giant Andean condors, majestic birds with wingspans of up to 3.5m (12 ft.). From a stunning lookout point nearly 1,200m (4,000 ft.) above the canyon river, you can watch as the condors appear, slowly circle, and gradually gain altitude with each pass, until they soar silently above your head and head off down the river. A truly spine-tingling spectacle, the flight of the big birds may make you feel quite small. See "Arequipa" in chapter 9.
- **Stroke a 3.6m (12-ft.) anaconda in Venezuela:** There's no guarantee you'll wrangle an anaconda—many lodges frown on direct contact—but you can get awfully close. Try a stay at **Hato El Cedral** (© 0212/781-8995; www.hatocedral.com); sightings of the large anaconda here are common, particularly in the dry season. If you're lucky, you'll see a "mating ball," several males and one female entwined in a writhing ball of anaconda lust. See p. 743.

Handel. It's a small indication of the care curators have taken in assembling and displaying one of Brazil's best collections of Catholic art—reliquaries, processional crosses, and crucifixes of astonishing refinement. The artifacts are shown in a former monastery, a simple, beautiful building that itself counts as a work of art. See p. 296.

- **Museu de Arte Moderna,** Rio de Janeiro: It's impossible to miss the MAM. It's a long, large, rectangular building lofted off the ground by an arcade of concrete struts, giving the structure the appearance of an airplane wing. Inside

are walls of solid plate glass that welcome in both city and sea. Displays present the best of contemporary art from Brazil and Latin America. See p. 256.

- **Museo Arqueológico Padre Le Paige,** San Pedro de Atacama: This little museum will come as an unexpected surprise for its wealth of indigenous artifacts, such as "Miss Chile," a leathered mummy whose skin, teeth, and hair are mostly intact, as well as a display of skulls that show the creepy ancient custom of cranial deformation practiced by the elite as a status symbol. The Atacama Desert is the driest in the world, and this climate has produced some of the best-preserved artifacts in Latin America, on view here. See p. 437.

- **Fundación Guayasamín,** Quito: Quito is most famous for being a city of historical wonders. But this modern art museum proves that the city is also moving forward. Oswaldo Guayasamín is one of Ecuador's best-known modern artists, and this museum has an impressive collection of his often-chaotic work. He used his art to express his hatred for the totalitarian regimes of many Latin American countries in the 1970s. His work is extremely moving and powerful. See p. 505.

- **Museo de la Nación,** Lima: Lima is the museum capital of Peru, and the National Museum traces the art and history of the earliest inhabitants to the Inca Empire, the last before colonization by the Spaniards. In well-organized, chronological exhibits, it covers the country's unique architecture (including scale models of most major ruins in Peru) as well as ceramics and textiles. See p. 583.

- **Monasterio de Santa Catalina** and **Museo Santuarios Andinos,** Arequipa: The Convent of Santa

Catalina, founded in 1579, is the greatest religious monument in Peru. More than a convent, it's an extraordinary and evocative small village, with Spanish-style cobblestone streets, passageways, plazas, and cloisters, where more than 200 sequestered nuns once lived (only a handful remain). Down the street at the Museo Santuarios Andinos is a singular exhibit: Juanita, the Ice Maiden of Ampato. A 13- or 14-year-old girl sacrificed in the 1500s by Inca priests high on a volcano at more than 6,000m (20,000 ft.), "Juanita" was discovered in almost perfect condition in 1995. See p. 648 and p. 649.

- **Museo de Arte Contemporáneo de Sofía Imber,** Caracas: Occupying 13 rooms spread out through the labyrinthine architecture of Caracas's Parque Central, the permanent collection here features a small but high-quality collection of singular works by such modern masters as Picasso, Red Grooms, Henry Moore, Joan Miró, and Francis Bacon, as well as a good representation of the conceptual works of Venezuelan star Jesús Soto. See p. 706.

6 The Best Festivals & Celebrations

- **Carnaval,** Argentina, Brazil, and Uruguay: The week before the start of Lent, Mardi Gras is celebrated in many towns in Argentina, although to a much lesser extent than in neighboring Brazil. In addition to Rio's incredible party, Salvador puts the accent on participation: The action is out on the streets with the *blocos,* flatbed trucks with bands and sound systems leading people on a 3-day dance through the streets. Carnaval is celebrated throughout Uruguay with

a passion topped only by Brazil. Montevideo spares no neighborhood parades, dance parties, and intense Latin merrymaking. See chapters 4, 6, and 10.

- **Festival of the Virgen de la Candelaria,** Bolivia and Peru: The Virgen de la Candelaria is one of the most beloved religious icons in Bolivia. On February 2, parades and parties erupt in Copacabana in her honor. The festivities, which are some of the liveliest in Bolivia, combine a mixture of Catholic and ancient local influences. Puno, perhaps the epi-center of Peruvian folklore, imbues its festivals with a unique vibrancy; their celebration of the Virgin is one of the greatest folk religious festivals in South America, with a 2-week explosion of music and dance, and some of the most fantastic costumes and masks seen anywhere. See "Lake Titicaca" in chapter 5 and "Puno & Lake Titicaca" in chapter 9.

- **A soccer game at Maracanã stadium,** Brazil: Nothing can prepare you for a game at the largest stadium in the world. Up to 100,000 fans sing, dance, and drum for hours in one of the biggest parties in town. See "Rio de Janeiro" in chapter 6.

- **New Year's Eve,** Brazil and Chile: Join up to a million revelers on Copacabana Beach for one the largest celebrations in Brazil; fireworks, concerts, and the religious ceremonies of the Afro-Brazilian Candomblé make for an unforgettable New Year's Eve. In Chile, Valparaíso rings in the new year with a spectacular bang, setting off a fireworks display high above the city's shimmering bay for the throngs of visitors who blanket the hills. Pablo Neruda used to spend New Year's here, watching the exploding sky from his home high on a cliff. The yearly event is absolutely hectic, so come early and plan on staying late. See "Rio de Janeiro" in chapter 6 and "Around Santiago & the Central Valley" in chapter 7.

- **Dieciocho,** Chile: Chile's Independence Day (Sept 18), followed by Armed Force's Day (Sept 19), constitute 2 days of hearty celebration. The hub of the Dieciocho celebration is the *fonda,* a circus-like tent surrounded by tiny stands selling empanadas, *chicha* (fermented apple juice), and other typical treats popular during this holiday. Inside the *fonda,* live bands play music for revelers to dance the *cueca,* the Chilean national dance. Nearly all drivers, it seems, decorate their cars with flags, and in the main plaza of every town, citizens string flags across streets. See "Planning Your Trip to Chile" in chapter 7.

- **Inti Raymi,** Ecuador and Peru: June 24 to 29, the fiestas of San Pablo, San Juan, and Inti Raymi (a sun festival celebrating the summer solstice) all merge into one big holiday in the Otavalo area. For the whole week, local people celebrate with big barbecues, parades, traditional dances, and bonfires. In Peru, it takes over Cusco and transforms the Sacsayhuamán ruins overlooking the city into a majestic stage. See "Otavalo & Imbabura Province" in chapter 8 and "Cusco" in chapter 9.

- **Caracas International Theater Festival,** Venezuela: Each year, this festival brings together scores of companies from around the world and across Venezuela for a 2-week celebration of the theater arts. Performances are held in a variety of theaters around Caracas, as well as in the streets and plazas. This is the premiere theater festival in Latin America. See "Caracas" in chapter 11.

7 The Best Hotels

- **Alvear Palace Hotel,** Buenos Aires (© **0800/44-HOTEL** local toll-free, or 011/4808-2100): Decorated in Empire- and Louis XV–style furnishings, this is the most exclusive hotel in Buenos Aires. Luxurious guest rooms and suites have chandelier lighting, feather beds, silk drapes, and beautiful marble bathrooms;

service is sharp and professional. See p. 105.

- **Los Notros,** Perito Moreno Glacier, near Calafate ((℄ **011/4814-3934**): Location—in this case, the view spanning one of Argentina's great wonders, the Perito Moreno Glacier—is everything at Los Notros hotel. Impeccable rooms come with dramatic views of the electric-blue tongue of the glacier, making this lodge one of the most upscale, unique hotels in Argentina. See p. 158.

- **El Hostal de su Merced,** Sucre ((℄ **0104/6442-706**): Sucre is one of the most historic cities in Bolivia, so it makes sense to stay in a historic hotel. El Hostal de su Merced is housed in an elegant 300-year-old mansion. All the rooms have charming antiques, crystal chandeliers, and lace curtains. See p. 210.

- **Copacabana Palace,** Rio de Janeiro ((℄ **0800/211-533**): Fred and Ginger didn't dance just anywhere when they went "flying down to Rio." The Copacabana Palace is Brazil's most famous hotel, standing beautiful on the country's most famous beach. See p. 273.

- **Hotel Tropical de Manaus** ((℄ **0800/150-006**): The Tropical Hotel in Manaus is without a doubt the hotel in town. Set in its own piece of rainforest on the banks of the Rio Negro, the hotel is built in an elegant colonial style. Rooms are spacious and the amenities are top-notch; archery lessons, a zoo, wakeboard lessons, a wave pool, a salon, and more await you in the middle of the Amazon. See p. 365.

- **Hotel Explora,** San Pedro de Atacama and Torres del Paine ((℄ **2/206-6060** in Santiago): Few hotels have generated as much press in Latin America as the two all-inclusive Explora lodges in San Pedro de Atacama and Torres del Paine. A dynamite location has helped, of course, but great service, cozy rooms with out-of-this-world views, interiors that are equally elegant and comfortable, and guided outdoor trekking, horseback-riding, and biking excursions are what really put these hotels above par. The lodges were designed by several of Chile's top architects, built of native materials, and decorated with local art. All-inclusive packages are pricey, but you won't need to spend anything once you're there. See p. 439 and p. 478.

- **Hotel Antumalal,** Pucón ((℄ **45/441011**): This low-slung, Bauhaus-influenced country inn is one of the most special places to lodge in Chile. Located high above the shore of Lake Villarrica and a sloping, terraced garden, the hotel literally sinks into its surroundings, offering a cozy ambience and number-one view of the evening sunset. A warm welcome and a room with no lock are all part of making you feel at home, and the chic, retro decor is a welcome relief from the cookie-cutter style of many hotels. See p. 445.

- **La Mirage Garden Hotel & Spa,** Otavalo ((℄ **800/327-3573** in the U.S., or 06/915-237): This luxurious hotel is one of Ecuador's finest. The manicured gardens make this place feel like a mini-Versailles, while the rooms are all palatial-style suites. Ancient Ecuadorian treatments are the specialty at the spa. See p. 525.

- **Royal Palm Hotel,** Santa Cruz, Galápagos ((℄ **800/528-6069** in the U.S., or 05/5527-409): This is the most luxurious resort in all of Ecuador and its restaurant is arguably one of the finest in the country. The villas are truly sumptuous, each with a private Jacuzzi and an enormous bathroom with hardwood floors. Large windows open up to the lush tropical landscape and the awesome stretch of the Pacific in the distance. See p. 557.

- **Hotel Antigua Miraflores,** Lima (© 01/241-6116): This charming midsize hotel, occupying a gracious century-old mansion, is full of Peruvian touches. The house is tastefully decorated, lined with colonial Peruvian art, but laidback, built around a leafy courtyard. It's a peaceful respite within the hubbub of Miraflores and the rest of Lima. See p. 586.

- **Hotel Monasterio,** Cusco (© 084/ 241-777): Carved out of a 16th-century monastery, itself built over the foundations of an Inca palace, this Orient Express hotel is the most dignified and historic place to stay in Peru. With its own gilded chapel and 18th-century Cusco School art collection, it's an attraction in its own right. Rooms are gracefully decorated with colonial touches, particularly the rooms off the serene first courtyard. See p. 608.

- **Belmont House,** Montevideo (© 2/600-0430): A boutique hotel in Montevideo's peaceful Carrasco neighborhood, Belmont House offers its privileged guests intimacy and luxury close to the city and the beach. Small elegant spaces with carefully chosen antiques and wood furnishings give this the feeling of a private estate. See p. 677.

- **Conrad Resort & Casino,** Punta del Este (© 42/491-111): This resort dominates social life in Punta del Este. Luxurious rooms have terraces overlooking the two main beaches, and there's a wealth of outdoor activities from tennis and golf to horseback riding and watersports. See p. 684.

- **Jungle Rudy Campamento,** Canaima (©/fax 0286/962-2359 in Canaima, or 0212/693-0618 in Caracas; www.junglerudy.com): The accommodations here are decidedly rustic—no television, air-conditioning, or telephones. However, the setting, on the banks of the Río Carrao above Ucaima Falls, is spectacular. If you can land no. 9, you'll be able to say you stayed in the same room as Prince Charles. See p. 749.

8 The Best Local Dining Experiences

- **Grilled meat in Argentina:** Widely considered the best *parrilla* (grill restaurant) in Buenos Aires, **Cabaña las Lilas** (© 011/ 4313-1336) is always packed. The menu pays homage to Argentine beef cuts, which come exclusively from the restaurant's private *estancia* (ranch). The steaks are outstanding. See p. 110.

- *Salteñas* **in Bolivia:** In almost every town in Bolivia, the locals eat salteñas for breakfast. These delicious treats are made with either chicken or beef, spiced with onions and raisins, and all wrapped up in a doughy pastry shell. Most people buy them from vendors on the street. See "Bolivian Breakfast" on p. 192.

- **Street food in Brazil:** Whether you want prawns, chicken, tapioca pancakes, coconut sweets, or corn on the cob, it can all be purchased on the street for next to nothing. Indulge—don't be afraid to try some of the best snacks that Brazil has to offer. See chapter 6.

- **Prawns on Ilhabela:** Ilhabela has the most succulent, sweet, and juicy prawns in all of Brazil. Enjoy them grilled, sautéed, or stuffed with cheese—they're as good as they come. See "São Paulo" in chapter 6.
- **Fish in the Pantanal:** Anywhere in the Pantanal you can try the phenomenal bounty of the world's largest floodplain. Paçu, dourado, and pintado are just a few of the region's best catches. See "The Pantanal" in chapter 6.
- **The Mercado Central in Santiago:** The chaotic, colorful central fish-and-produce market of Santiago should not be missed by anyone, even if you are not particularly fond of seafood. But if you are, you'll want to relish one of the flavorful concoctions served at one of the market's simple restaurants. Hawklike waitresses guard the market's passageways awaiting hungry diners and shouting "Hey, lady! Hey, sir! Eat here!"—but **Donde Augusto** is a good bet. See p. 400.
- **Fresh fruit drinks in Ecuador:** The tropical coastal climate in Ecuador is perfect for growing fruit. Almost every restaurant offers a wonderful selection of fresh local fruit, including pineapple, orange, passion fruit, coconut, blackberry, banana, and a variety of typical Ecuadorian fruits such as *guarnaba* and *naranjilla*, which don't even have English names. It's common to serve fruit in the form of a drink. See chapter 8.
- ***Ceviche* in Peru:** Peruvian cuisine is one of the most distinguished in the Americas. Though cooking varies greatly from Andean to coastal and Amazonian climes, there are few things more satisfying than a classic Peruvian ceviche: raw fish and shellfish marinated in lime or lemon juice and hot chile peppers, served with raw onion, sweet potato, and toasted corn. It's wonderfully refreshing and spicy. The perfect accompaniment is either *chicha morada*, a refreshment made from blue corn, or a pisco sour, a frothy cocktail of white grape brandy, egg whites, lemon juice, sugar, and bitters—akin to a margarita. See chapter 9.
- **Ice cream in Mérida:** Heladería Coromoto holds the Guinness world record for the most ice cream flavors. Be adventurous and sample a scoop of smoked trout, garlic, beer, avocado, or squid ice cream. The count currently exceeds 700 flavors, with roughly 100 choices available on any night. See p. 740.

9 The Best Markets

- **San Telmo antiques market,** Buenos Aires: The Sunday market is as much a cultural event as a commercial event, as old-time tango and *milonga* dancers take to the streets with other performers. Here you will glimpse Buenos Aires much as it was at the beginning of the 20th century. See p. 95.
- **The Witch Doctors' Market,** La Paz: This is one of the most unusual markets in South America. The stalls are filled with llama fetuses and all sorts of good-luck charms. Locals come here to buy magic potions or small trinkets that will bring them wealth, health, or perhaps a good harvest. You'll be sure to find unique gifts here for all your friends at home. See p. 187.

• **Mercado Adolpho Lisboa,** Manaus: This is a beautiful iron-and-glass copy of Paris's now demolished market hall in Les Halles. It's a great place to see fruits and fish fresh from the Amazon, but it's not for the squeamish. Vendors cut and clean the fish on the spot; some of the chopped-in-half catfish still wriggle. A short walk downstream, you can watch Amazon riverboats load up on supplies at the Feira do Produtor. See p. 363.

• **Ver-o-Peso Market,** Belém: This 1899 market hall is a vast waterside cornucopia, with just about every product grown or made in the Amazon available for purchase. Stroll into the blue Gothic building and you're in an Amazon Fish World, with dozens of outrageously strange Amazon fish laid out before you on ice. Outside under the canopies there are hundreds of species of Amazon fruits. The love-starved and sexually bereft can seek out the traditional medicine kiosks, where every potion and bark-derived infusion seems to heighten allure, potency, and fertility.

• **Mercado Central,** Santiago: It would be a crime to visit Chile and not sample the rich variety of fish and shellfish available here, and this vibrant market is the best place to experience the country's love affair with its fruits of the sea. Nearly every edible (and seemingly inedible) creature is for sale, from sea urchins to the alien-looking and unfamiliar piure, among colorful bushels of fresh vegetables and some of the most aggressive salesmen this side of the Andes. See p. 400.

• **Feria Artesanal de Angelmó,** Puerto Montt: Stretching along several blocks of the Angelmó port area of Puerto Montt are rows and rows of stalls stocked with arts and crafts, clothing, and novelty items from the entire surrounding region, even Chiloé. This market is set up to buy, buy, buy! and it imparts little local color, but chances are you'll find yourself here before Temuco, which is more off the beaten path. Be sure to bargain for everything. See p. 462.

• **Otavalo,** Ecuador: Otavalo is probably one of the most famous markets in South America for good reason: You won't find run-of-the-mill tourist trinkets here. The local people are well known for their masterful craftsmanship—you can buy alpaca scarves, handwoven bags, and a variety of other exquisite handmade goods. See "Otavalo & Imbabura Province" in chapter 8.

• **Pisac,** Peru: Thousands of tourists descend each Sunday morning on Pisac's liveliest handicrafts market, which takes over the central plaza and spills across adjoining streets. Many sellers, decked out in the dress typical of their villages, come from remote populations high in the mountains. Village officials lead processions around the square after Mass. Pisac is one of the best spots for colorful Andean textiles, including rugs, alpaca sweaters, and ponchos. See "The Sacred Valley of the Incas" in chapter 9.

• **Mercado del Puerto,** Montevideo: The Mercado del Puerto (Port Market) takes place afternoons and weekends, letting you sample the flavors of Uruguay, from small empanadas to enormous barbecued meats. Saturday is the best day to visit, when cultural activities accompany the market. See p. 677.

• **Hannsi Centro Artesanal,** El Hatillo (© 0212/963-7184; www.hannsi.com.ve): This huge indoor bazaar has everything from indigenous masks to ceramic wares to woven baskets. The selection is broad and covers everything from trinkets to pieces of the finest craftsmanship. Most of the major indigenous groups of Venezuela are represented, including the Yanomami, Guajiro, Warao, Pemón, and Piaroa. See p. 708.

10 The Best of South America Online

• **http://lanic.utexas.edu:** The University of Texas Latin American Studies Department's database features an extensive list of useful links for every country in South America.

• **www.southamericadaily.com:** This is a good daily news site, with good links.

• **www.turismo.gov.ar:** This attractive site is best for official visitor information about the country, with maps and tips about places off the beaten track.

• **www.andesweb.com:** This great website offers complete information about skiing and snowboarding in Argentina and Chile. You can find full descriptions of resorts and related information such as weather conditions, ski rental, and general travel information.

• **www.boliviabiz.com:** Log on to this site for information about Bolivia's best hotels, tour operators, and museums.

• **www.brazil.org.uk:** Log on for information on Brazil's history, government, environment, and tourism, plus lots of links.

• **www.chile.com:** Chile's largest and most comprehensive website, featuring everything from regional and travel information, hotel and car rentals to a guide to investment. The majority is in Spanish; however, the English section has very complete information.

• **www.chilevinos.com:** Every aspect of the Chilean wine industry is covered at this website, such as winemaker and winery profiles, grape-growing updates, a glossary, a chat room, and online ordering. The only thing this site doesn't have is an English edition. If you can't get through the lingo, head to www.winesofchile.com.

• **www.ecuadorexplorer.com:** Great source of information about all things Ecuadorian.

• **www.peru.org.pe:** The recently revamped PromPerú website has detailed sections on Peruvian history, festivals, trip planning, and outdoor "adrenaline rushes," as well as a stock of photo and video images and audio files. Also check out **http://gci275.com/peru** ("Peruvian Graffiti"), a website by an American journalist and former resident of Peru. It's an engaging compendium of Peruvian history, politics, media, and culture, as well as the latest news, from a very personal perspective. It's an interesting place to start to get a handle on a complicated nation.

• **www.turismo.gub.uy:** The Uruguayan Ministry of Tourism's website is chock full of information about the country, including promotional specials for travelers and links to local media.

2

Introducing South America

by Shawn Blore, Shane Christensen, Alexandra de Vries, Eliot Greenspan,
Haas Mroue, Neil E. Schlecht & Kristina Schreck

Many outsiders may think of South America as a third-world land of poverty and political instability. And historically, this impression hasn't been far from the truth. But although the economy here is still rocky, South America is now beginning to come into its own, both politically and socially. The military dictatorships and guerrilla wars that plagued this region in the 1970s and 1980s are largely things of the past, and a new respect for traditional culture and indigenous people is beginning to ease social tensions—though there's still a long way to go. These social advances are great news for travelers, who are beginning to take notice. The increasing popularity of adventure and archaeological tourism has translated into more visitors for South America, and we expect to see still more in the years to come.

1 South America Past & Present

It has been said that 57 million people were living in the Americas when Columbus landed here in 1492. The arrival of the Europeans in this isolated area of the world brought many problems for the local people. With their gunpowder and horses, the Europeans had a distinct military advantage and were able to destroy powerful empires. They also introduced foreign diseases, such as smallpox, measles, and typhus, which wiped out entire communities. But what a boon for the Spanish crown—explorers discovered precious "jewels" here, including corn, potatoes, chocolate, and of course, gold and silver. Thus began the age of colonialism. Amazingly, 400 years after the Spanish conquest of South America, millions of indigenous people have managed to hold on to their pre-Columbian past. That's what makes South America so unique. Visitors can explore the ruins of old Inca palaces, hike along Inca trails, witness colorful local celebrations that honor the sun or Pachamama (Mother Earth), and visit museums filled with amazing artifacts—gold chest plates, alpaca ponchos, tightly woven textiles, hand-carved silver figurines, wonderfully descriptive ceramic jugs—that give testament to the rich cultural heritage that existed here before the arrival of the Spanish.

In this section, we'll give you a little bit of background on the history and culture of the countries we cover in this guide. See the individual country chapters for more on both subjects.

ARGENTINA
A LOOK AT THE PAST
Several distinct indigenous groups populated the area now called Argentina well before the arrival of the Europeans. The Incas made inroads into the highlands of the Northwest. Most other groups were nomadic hunters and fishers, such as those in the Chaco, the Tehuelche of Patagonia, and the Querandí and Puelche

(Guennakin) of the pampas. Others (the Diaguitas of the Northwest) developed stationary agriculture.

In 1535, Spain—having conquered Peru and being aware of Portugal's presence in Brazil—sent an expedition headed by Pedro de Mendoza to settle the country. Mendoza was initially successful in founding Santa María del Buen Aire, or Buenos Aires (1536), but lack of food proved fatal. Mendoza, discouraged by Indian attacks and mortally ill, sailed for Spain in 1537; he died on the way.

Northern Argentina (including Buenos Aires) was settled mainly by people traveling from the neighboring Spanish colonies of Chile and Peru and the settlement of Asunción in Paraguay. Little migration occurred directly from Spain; the area lacked the attractions of colonies such as Mexico and Peru, with their rich mines, a large supply of Indian slave labor, and easy accessibility. Nevertheless, early communities forged a society dependent on cattle and horses imported from Spain, as well as native crops such as corn and potatoes. Pervasive Roman Catholic missions played a strong role in the colonizing process. The Spanish presence grew over the following centuries, as Buenos Aires became a critical South American port.

The years 1806 and 1807 saw the first stirrings of independence. Buenos Aires fought off two British attacks, in battles known as the *Reconquista* and the *Defensa*. Around this time, a civil war had distracted Spain from its colonial holdings, and many Argentine-born Europeans began to debate the idea of self-government in the Buenos Aires *cabildo* (a municipal council with minimal powers established by colonial rulers). On July 9, 1816, Buenos Aires officially declared its independence from Spain, under the name United Provinces of the Río de la Plata. Several years of hard fighting followed before the Spanish were defeated in northern Argentina. But they remained a threat from their base in Peru until it was liberated by General José de San Martín (to this day a national hero) and Simón Bolívar from 1820 to 1824. Despite the drawing up of a national constitution, the territory that now constitutes modern Argentina was frequently disunited until 1860. The root cause of the trouble, the power struggle between Buenos Aires and the rest of the country, was not settled until 1880, and even after that it, continued to cause dissatisfaction.

Conservative forces ruled for much of the late 19th and early 20th centuries, at one point deposing from power an elected opposition party president through military force. Despite the Conservatives' efforts to suppress new social and political groups—including a growing urban working class—their power began to erode. In 1943, the military overthrew Argentina's constitutional government in a coup led by then army colonel Juan Domingo Perón. Perón became president in a 1946 election and was reelected 6 years later. He is famous (although by no means universally applauded) for his populist governing style, which empowered and economically aided the working class. His wife, Eva Duarte de Perón (popularly known as Evita), herself a controversial historical figure, worked alongside her husband to strengthen the voice of Argentina's women. In 1955, the military deposed Perón, and the following years were marked by economic troubles (partly the result of Perón's expansive government spending) and social unrest, with a surge in terrorist activity by both the left and the right. While Perón was exiled in Spain, his power base in Argentina strengthened, allowing his return to the presidency in 1973. When he died in 1974, his third wife (and vice president), Isabel, replaced him.

The second Peronist era abruptly ended with a March 1976 coup that installed a military junta. The regime of Jorge Rafael Videla carried out a campaign to weed out anybody suspected of having Communist sympathies. Congress was closed, censorship imposed, and unions banned. Over the next 7 years, during this "Process of National Reorganization"—a period known as the *Guerra Sucia* (Dirty War)—the country witnessed a level of political violence that affects the Argentine psyche today: More than 10,000 intellectuals, artists, activists, and others were tortured or executed by the Argentine government. The mothers of these *desaparecidos* (the disappeared ones) began holding Thursday afternoon vigils in front of the Presidential Palace in Buenos Aires's Plaza de Mayo as a way to call international attention to the plight of the missing. Although the junta was overturned in 1983, the weekly protests continue to this day.

ARGENTINA TODAY

Public outrage over the military's human rights abuses, combined with Argentina's crushing defeat by the British in the 1982 Falkland Islands war, undermined the dictatorship's control of the country. An election in 1983 restored constitutional rule and brought Raul Alfonsín of the Radical Civic Union to power. In 1989, political power shifted from the Radical Party to the Peronist Party (established by Juan Perón), the first democratic transition in 60 years. Carlos Saúl Ménem, a former governor of a province of little political significance, won the presidency by a surprising margin.

A strong leader, Ménem pursued an ambitious but controversial agenda with the privatization of staterun institutions as its centerpiece. Privatization of inefficient state firms reduced government debt by billions of dollars, and inflation was brought under control. After 10 years as president—and a constitutional amendment that allowed him to seek a second term—Ménem left office. Meanwhile, an alternative to the traditional Peronist and Radical parties, the center-left FREPASO political alliance, had emerged on the scene. The Radicals and FREPASO formed an alliance for the October 1999 election, and their candidate defeated his Peronist competitor.

President Fernando de la Rua, not as charismatic as his predecessor, was forced to reckon with the recession the economy had suffered since 1998. In an effort to eliminate Argentina's ballooning deficit, de la Rua followed a strict regimen of government spending cuts and tax increases recommended by the International Monetary Fund. However, the tax increase crippled economic growth, and political infighting prevented de la Rua from implementing other needed reforms designed to stimulate the economy. With a heavy drop in production and steep rise in unemployment, an economic crisis loomed.

The meltdown arrived with a run on the peso in December 2001, when investors moved en masse to withdraw their money from Argentine banks. Government efforts to restrict the run by limiting depositor withdrawals fueled anger throughout society, and Argentines took to the streets in sometimes violent demonstrations. De la Rua resigned on December 20, as Argentina faced the worst economic crisis in its history. A series of interim governments did little to improve the situation, as Buenos Aires began to default on its international debts. On January 1, 2002, Peronist President Eduardo Duhalde unlocked the Argentine peso from the dollar, and the currency's value quickly tumbled.

Argentina's economic crisis has severely eroded the population's trust in government. Increased poverty, unemployment surpassing 20%, and inflation hitting 30% have made it difficult for ordinary Argentines to smile on their fortunes. One result has been massive emigration, particularly among younger Argentines, to Italy, Spain, and other destinations in Europe and North America. But despite these profound economic troubles, the country is not as bad off as some would have it. Argentina retains a large middle class with a healthy standard of living, and the country is rich in natural resources, human capital, and tourist infrastructure.

BOLIVIA
A LOOK AT THE PAST

Lake Titicaca, the birthplace of the Incas, is one of Bolivia's most sacred and historic sites. But the history of Bolivia begins thousands of years before the arrival of the Incas. The Tiwanaku culture, which eventually spread to the area from northern Argentina and Chile all the way up to southern Peru, was one of the most highly developed pre-Columbian civilizations. From 1600 B.C. to 100 B.C., the Tiwanaku made the important move of domesticating animals, which allowed them to become more productive farmers. From 100 B.C. to A.D. 900, the arts flourished in the Tiwanaku culture. But it wasn't until A.D. 900 to 1200 that the Tiwanaku became warriors and set out to dominate the area that is now Bolivia. A drought destroyed the heart of the Tiwanaku region in the 13th century, and when the Incas swooped down from Peru around 1450, the Tiwanaku had broken up into small Aymara-speaking communities. The Quechua-speaking Incas dominated the area until the arrival of the Spanish in 1525.

Bolivia proved to be the crown jewel of the Spanish empire. As early as 1545, silver was discovered in southern Bolivia. Over the next 200 years, Potosí, home of Cerro Rico (the "rich hill," which was the source of all the silver), became one of the largest and wealthiest cities in the world. Getting rich quickly was the name of the game for most European settlers in Bolivia. Other than the development of Potosí and transportation systems to deliver the silver to the rest of the world, much of Bolivia remained neglected. Indigenous men were forced to work in the mines, often for no pay. This was only the beginning of a system of inequality and sharp class distinctions that to this day exist in Bolivia.

Not surprisingly, the first rumblings for independence arose in the area of Chuquisaca (present-day Sucre, which was then the administrative capital of Potosí). The first revolutionary uprising took place in Chuquisaca in 1809, but Bolivia did not win independence until August 6, 1825.

The age of the republic did not bring much glory to Bolivia. In the next 100-plus years, Bolivia lost its seacoast to Chile in the War of the Pacific (1879–83); in 1903, after a conflict with Brazil, Bolivia was forced to give up its access to the Acre River, which had become a valuable source of rubber; and in the Chaco War (1932–35), Bolivia surrendered the Chaco region, which was believed to be rich in oil, to Paraguay. The high price of silver in the late 19th century and the discovery of tin in the early 20th century kept Bolivia afloat.

After the Chaco War, which drained Bolivia's resources and caused a great loss of life, the indigenous people began to distrust the elite ruling classes. In December 1943, the proworker National Revolutionary Movement (MNR) organized a revolt in protest of the abysmal working conditions and inflation. This was the beginning of the MNR's reign of power. In 1951, the MNR candidate, Victor Paz Estenssoro, was elected president, but a military junta denied him power. In 1952, the MNR, with the help of peasants and miners, staged a successful revolution. The MNR managed to implement sweeping land reforms and nationalize the tin holdings of the wealthy. Under the reign of Estenssoro, the government also introduced universal suffrage and improved the educational system.

The MNR managed to hold on to power until a coup in 1964. For the next 20 years, Bolivia became a pawn in the Cold War between the United States and the Soviet Union. A series of military revolts brought power to both leftist and right-wing regimes. In 1971, Hugo Bánzer Suárez became president with the support of the MNR, and instituted a pro-U.S. policy. In 1974, because of growing opposition, he set up an all-military government. He was forced to resign in 1978. In the coming years, a series of different leaders were unable to deal with the problems of high inflation, growing social unrest, increased drug trafficking, and the collapse of the tin market. Victor Paz Estenssoro returned to power in 1985. He kept the military at bay and was able to create economic stability. Finally, in 1989, Jaime Paz Zamora, a moderate, left-leaning politician, was elected president; he worked to stamp out domestic terrorism, bringing a semblance of peace to the country. In 1993, a mining engineer, Gonzalo Sánchez de Lozada, was elected president. He worked successfully to reprivatize public business, an effort that actually helped the economy. In 1997, Hugo Bánzer Suárez returned to power. He worked with the United States to eradicate coca growing, with much opposition from local farm workers. The late 1990s marked another period of social unrest for Bolivia, with frequent strikes that paralyzed the nation.

BOLIVIA TODAY

President Gonzalo Sánchez de Lozada was elected president in 2002, but his cooperation with the United States in eradicating coca growing (and thus causing much unemployment) turned most of the country against him. When he signed a deal to export Bolivian gas to the United States and Mexico and transport it via Chile, popular protests swept the nation. Bolivians felt that the president wasn't protecting their interests, and that the exporting of Bolivian gas would benefit the elite and do nothing for the average citizen. In late 2003, the anger erupted in violent demonstrations in La Paz and El Alta, the neighboring city. Thousands of peasants flocked to the city from rural areas to participate in the revolt. The situation deteriorated quickly and more than 70 people were killed by the police. The airport in La Paz was closed for a week and the situation spiraled out of control. On October 17, 2003, more than a quarter of a million protesters rallied in La Paz's Plaza de San Francisco, near the Presidential Palace, demanding the president's resignation. Later that day, Gonzalo Sánchez de Lozada stepped down and fled to Miami; Vice President Carlos Mesa was appointed president. Things returned to normal very quickly in La Paz. But the situation in general remains unstable, with a weak economy and the restlessness of the peasants leaving a big question mark for the future of Bolivia.

BRAZIL
A LOOK AT THE PAST

At the time of the Europeans' arrival in 1500, there were between one million and eight million indigenous people in Brazil, speaking nearly 170 different languages. The Europeans were seeking pau-brasil, a type of wood that could be processed to yield a rich red dye. Coastal Indians were induced to cut and sell timber in return for metal implements such as axes. It was an efficient system, so much so that within a little more than a generation, the trees—which had by then given their name to the country—were all but nonexistent.

But the Portuguese colony soon found a better source of income in sugar, the cash crop of the 16th century. Sugar cane grew excellently in the tropical climate of northeast Brazil. Turning that cane into sugar, however, was backbreaking work, and the Portuguese were critically short of labor. So the Portuguese began to import slaves from West Africa. Brazil was soon one leg on a lucrative maritime triangle: guns and supplies from Portugal to Africa, slaves from Africa to Brazil, sugar from Brazil back to Europe. Within a few decades, colonial cities such as Salvador and Olinda were fabulously rich.

Gold was soon uncovered in what would later be Minas Girais, while diamonds were found in the interior in Bahia. In addition to the miners, the other main beneficiary of the Minas gold rush was Rio de Janeiro, the major transshipment point for gold and supplies. In recognition of this, in 1762, the colonial capital was officially transferred to Rio. It would likely have remained little more than a backwater colonial capital had it not been for Napoléon. In 1807, having overrun most of western Europe, the French emperor set his sights on Portugal. Faced with the imminent conquest of Lisbon, Portuguese Prince Regent João (later King João VI) fled to his ships, opting to relocate himself and his entire court to Brazil. In March 1808, the king and 15,000 of his nobles, knights, and courtiers arrived in the rather raw town of Rio. When the king returned to Portugal in 1821, Brazilians—among them the king's 23-year-old son, Pedro—were outraged at the prospect of being returned to the status of mere colony. In January 1822, Pedro announced he was remaining in Brazil. Initially, he planned on ruling as prince regent, but as the year wore on, it became clear that Lisbon was not interested in compromise, so on September 7, 1822, Pedro declared Brazil independent and himself Emperor Pedro I.

Brazil in this period was a deeply conservative country, with a few very wealthy plantation owners, a tiny professional class, and a great mass of slaves to cultivate sugar or Brazil's new cash crop, coffee. Though the antislavery movement was growing worldwide, Brazil's conservative landowning class was determined to hold on to its slaves at all costs. In the 1850s, under heavy pressure from Britain, Brazil finally moved to halt the importation of slaves from Africa, though slavery wasn't officially outlawed until 1888. Seeking a new source of labor, in 1857 Brazil opened itself up to immigration. Thousands poured in, mostly Germans and Italians, settling themselves in the hilly, temperate lands in the south of Brazil.

When reformist army officers and other liberals staged a coup in 1889, the 57-year rule of Pedro II (son of the 1st emperor) came to an end. The republic that took its place had many of the same ills of the old regime. Corruption was endemic, rebellions a regular occurrence. Finally, in 1930, reformist army officers staged a bloody coup. After several days of fighting, a military-backed regime took charge, putting an end to the Old Republic and ushering in the 15-year reign of the fascinating, maddening figure of Getúlio Vargas.

Vargas began his time in office as a populist, legalizing unions and investing in hundreds of projects designed to foster the industrial development of the country. When the workers nonetheless looked set to reject him in renewed elections, Vargas tore up the constitution and instituted a quasifascist dictatorship, complete with a propaganda ministry that celebrated every action of the glorious leader Getúlio. In the early 1940s, when the United States made it clear that Brazil had better cease its flirtation with Germany, Vargas dumped his fascist posturing, declared war on the Axis powers, and sent 20,000 Brazilian troops to take part in the invasion of Italy. When the troops came home at war's end, the contradiction between the fight for freedom abroad and the dictatorship at home proved too much even for Vargas's political skills. In 1945, the army removed Getúlio from power in a very quiet coup. In 1950, he returned, this time as the democratically elected president, but his reign was a disaster, and in 1954, he committed suicide.

In 1956, Juscelino Kubitschek (known as J. K.) took office, largely on the strength of a single bold promise: Within 4 years, he would transfer the capital from Rio de Janeiro to an entirely new city located somewhere in Brazil's vast interior. The site chosen in Brazil's high interior plateau (the *sertão*) was hundreds of miles from the nearest paved road, thousands from the nearest airport. Undaunted, J. K. assembled a team of Brazil's top modernist architects—among the best in the world at the time—and 4 years later, the new capital of Brasília was complete.

Democracy, unfortunately, did not fare well in the arid soil of the sertão. In 1964, the army took power in a coup, ushering in an ever more repressive military dictatorship that would last for another 20 years. For a time,

no one complained much. Thanks to massive government investment, the economy boomed. São Paulo, which had been little more than a market town in the 1940s, exploded in size and population, surpassing Rio to become the heart of Brazil's new manufacturing economy. These were the days of the Brazilian "economic miracle."

In the early 1970s, however, the party came to an end; it became clear that much of the "miracle" had been financed on easy international loans, many of which were invested in dubious development projects. As discontent with the regime spread, the military reacted with stronger repression. The 1980s were even worse. Inflation ran rampant, while growth was next to nonexistent. Austerity measures imposed by the International Monetary Fund left governments with little money for basic infrastructure—much less social services—and in big cities such as Rio and São Paulo, *favelas* (shantytowns) spread while crime spiraled out of control. In the midst of this mess, the army began a transition to democracy. In 1988, Brazil held its first direct presidential election in more than 2 decades.

In 1992, Fernando Henrique Cardoso (or "FHC," as he was often called), was elected president for two terms. Under his governance, Brazil settled down to something approaching normality: Inflation was reined in, crime decreased dramatically, and the army remained safely back in the barracks. At the end of 2001, the Argentine economy went into free fall, but under FHC's leadership Brazil managed to avoid getting sucked into the vortex.

BRAZIL TODAY

In the 2002 presidential elections, Brazilians shocked and impressed both themselves and the world by electing leftist candidate Luiz Inácio

Lula da Silva ("Lula" for short), a charismatic trade unionist with a rags-to-riches story. Born into a poverty in the northeast, Lula left school to work as a shoeshine boy, then got a job in a São Paulo factory, rose to the head of the metal workers union, and, in the dying days of Brazil's dictatorship, welded together Brazil's disparate leftist factions into a formidable political force called the Workers Party. Lula was a close second in three consecutive elections before finally grasping the brass ring in 2002, the first democratically elected leftist ever to hold power in Brazil.

Hopes for Lula's first term in office have been enormous. Confounding the expectations of the financial markets and right-wing critics, Lula has proved to be a pragmatic moderate. Having reassured the financial community, however, Lula now faces the challenge of fulfilling at least some of the expectations of his own supporters. The issue of land reform, in particular, is likely to become the defining issue of Lula's first term, with the Landless Workers Movement (MST) putting enormous pressure on Lula to break up at least some of Brazil's large estates and redistribute the land to the rural poor.

CHILE
A LOOK AT THE PAST

Chile's history as a nation began rather inconspicuously on the banks of the Mapoche River on February 12, 1541, when the Spanish conquistador Pedro de Valdivia founded Santiago de la Nueva Extremadura. At the time, several distinct indigenous groups called Chile home, including the more advanced northern tribes (which had already been conquered by the Incas), the fierce Mapuche warriors of the central region, and the nomadic hunting and gathering tribes of Patagonia. In Spain's eyes, Chile did not hold much interest because of its lack of riches such as gold, and the country remained somewhat of a colonial backwater until the country's independence in 1818, which was led by the son of an Irish immigrant, Bernardo O'Higgins. Spain did, however, see to the development of a feudal landowning system whereby prominent Spaniards were issued a large tract of land and an *encomienda,* or a group of Indian slaves, that the landowner was charged with caring for and converting to Christianity. Thus rose Chile's traditional and nearly self-supporting hacienda, known as a *latifundio,* as well as a rigid class system that defined the population.

Chile experienced an economic boom in the early 20th century in the form of nitrate mining in the northern desert, a region that had been confiscated from Peru and Bolivia after the War of the Pacific in 1883. Mining is still a huge economic force, especially copper mining, and Chile's abundant natural resources have fostered industries in petroleum, timber, fishing, agriculture, tourism, and wine.

Chile enjoyed a politically democratic government until the onset of a vicious military dictatorship, led by General Augusto Pinochet, who took power from 1973 to 1990. In 1970, voters narrowly elected the controversial Dr. Salvador Allende as Chile's first socialist president. Allende vowed to improve the lives of Chile's poorer citizens by instituting a series of radical changes that might redistribute the nation's lopsided wealth. Although the first year showed promising signs, Allende's reforms ultimately sent the country spiraling into economic ruin. On September 11, 1973, military forces led by General Augusto Pinochet and supported by the U.S. government toppled Allende's government with a dramatic coup d'état, during which Allende took his own life. Upper-class Chileans celebrated the coup as an economic and political salvation, but nobody was prepared for the brutal repression that would haunt Chile for the next 17 years. Most disturbing were the series of tortures and "disappearances" of an estimated 3,000 of Pinochet's political adversaries, including activists, journalists, professors, and any other "subversive" threats. Thousands more fled the country.

Pinochet set out to rebuild the economy using free-market policies, which was later dubbed the "Chilean Miracle," but the miracle did nothing to address the country's high unemployment rate, worsening social conditions, and falling wages. In a pivotal 1988 "yes or no" plebiscite, 55% of the voting public said no to military rule, and Patricio Alywin was democratically elected president of Chile.

CHILE TODAY

Today, the Chilean economy is considered one of the (if not *the*) strongest economies in Latin America. Chile still suffers from an unhealthy dose of classism; however, the country boasts a larger middle class than its neighbors Peru and Bolivia, with about 30% of the population living under the poverty level. Politically, Chile is on its third democratically elected president, the left-leaning Ricardo Lagos. Even today, the country remains divided over the legacy of Pinochet, and many wish the whole controversy would just go away. Pinochet is currently under fire both nationally and internationally for his crimes; however, he is now so old and frail that many believe prosecution before his death is unlikely.

ECUADOR
A LOOK AT THE PAST

Before the Spanish arrived in Ecuador in 1533, a group of diverse cultures lived in various areas throughout the country. Archaeologists believe that many indigenous groups can trace their roots all the way back to the Mayas in Mexico. Many of these cultures, including the Valdivia, Machalilla, and Chorrera, may not have left any written records, but the highly sophisticated pottery, beautifully designed artwork, and gold masks that have been unearthed in Ecuador prove that these cultures were highly developed. By the 16th century, the Incas had conquered the highland areas of the country of Ecuador. Cuenca, in southern Ecuador, was the second-most important city in the Inca Empire. In 1526, when the Inca leader Huayna Capac died, he divided the empire between his two sons. Huáscar gained control of Cusco and Peru, while Atahualpa inherited control of Cuenca and Ecuador. This split led to a war for dominance, which weakened both sides. Because of this conflict, when the Spanish arrived in the mid–16th century, they didn't have much trouble defeating the Incas.

The indigenous cultures had a hard time under Spanish rule. Newly introduced diseases decimated the local population, and the Spanish system of encomienda (forced labor) broke the spirit and the health of the local people. Ecuador wasn't rich in natural resources and, therefore, wasn't of great value to the Spanish. In the 300 years before independence, Ecuador split its time between belonging to the viceroyalty of Peru to the south and to the viceroyalty of New Granada in Bogotá to the north.

Ecuador declared independence in 1820, but the independence forces weren't able to defeat the Spanish royalists until the Battle of Pichincha on May 24, 1822. At that time, Ecuador became a part of Gran Colombia, which consisted of Colombia and Venezuela. In 1830, Ecuador seceded from Gran Colombia and became its own separate republic. The rest of the 19th century was marked by political instability. Conflicts flared between the Conservatives, led by Gabriel García Moreno, and the Liberals, led by Eloy Alfaro. The Conservatives sided with the Catholic Church and Ecuadorians of privilege, while the Liberals fought for social reforms.

At the end of the 19th century, Ecuador was getting rich off cocoa exports, and the economy was booming. Later in the early 20th century, when the demand for cocoa decreased, political unrest ensued. In 1925, the military seized power from the former procapitalist leaders. The 1930s were a time of uncertainty for Ecuador: From 1931 to 1940 a total of 12 different presidents spent time at the helm. In 1941, war erupted between Ecuador and Peru over land in the Amazon basin region. In an attempt to settle the dispute, Ecuador signed the Protocol of Rio de Janeiro in 1942 and surrendered much of the disputed land to Peru.

The post–World War II era was a time of prosperity for Ecuador. The country became one of the world's leaders in banana exports. From 1948 to 1960, there were three freely elected presidents who were all able to serve their full terms. In 1952, President José María Velasco implemented social reforms, including improvements in both the schools and the public highways. But in 1960, when Velasco was again elected president, he was faced with a failing economy, and he was unable to hold on to power. During the next 10 years, a series of military juntas controlled the country.

The economy rebounded in the 1970s. Ecuador became the second-largest oil-producing nation in South America, after Venezuela. The oil boom led to an increase in public spending and industrialization. But by the 1980s, when the oil bubble began

to burst, the country was again faced with serious economic troubles, including inflation and an insurmountable international debt. In 1986, the price of oil collapsed, and in 1987, an earthquake partially destroyed one of Ecuador's major pipelines. Rodrigo Borja came to power in 1988. In an attempt to alleviate his country's problems, he increased the price of oil while severely cutting back on public spending. But that wasn't enough—inflation soared, and civil unrest increased. In 1992, in a conciliatory move, the government ceded a large region of the rainforest to the indigenous people. In 1995, Ecuador again disputed its border with Peru in the Amazon area; it wasn't until 1998 that it finally settled with Peru and secured its access to the Amazon. The 3-year war proved to be a drain on the economy. In 1997, a national protest with overwhelming support of all the Ecuadorian people succeeded in ousting the corrupt President Abdalá Bucaram. The national congress appointed a new president and reformed the constitution. But again, low oil prices and the devastating effects of El Niño brought the economy to its knees.

ECUADOR TODAY

On July 12, 1998, the mayor of Quito, Jamil Mahuad, was elected president. His biggest success was negotiating a peace treaty with Peru over the country's borders in the Amazon, but he was unable to turn the economy around. His popularity reached a low point on January 9, 2000, when he announced his decision to eliminate the sucre, the national currency, and replace it with the U.S. dollar. On January 21, 2000, the military and police "failed" to quell chaotic nationwide protests. Mahuad was forced to resign, and his vice president Gustavo Noboa became president. Noboa continued on the course of dollarization, and in September 2000, the U.S. dollar became the official currency of Ecuador. This move helped to decrease the country's international debt, but it hasn't been able to stem the inflation problem, and many Ecuadorians are still suffering economically under this policy. In the meantime, the government is trying to strengthen its oil business to bolster the economy. In February 2001, Ecuador made a deal with an international consortium to invest $1.1 billion to build a crude-oil pipeline, with the aim of increasing foreign investment in Ecuador.

After Lucio Gutierrez was elected president in 2002, the economic situation began steadily improving. The situation with Colombia, however, remained volatile. In January 2002, as the Colombian government failed to make peace with the Marxist guerrilla group FARC, Ecuador began to send troops to its border with Colombia to prevent the spread of hostilities to Ecuador and to protect the country from the very dangerous business of narcotics trafficking. At press time, the situation remains very tense and travel near the Colombian border is discouraged.

PERU
A LOOK AT THE PAST

Over the course of nearly 15 centuries, pre-Inca cultures settled along the Peruvian coast and highlands. By the 1st century B.C., during what is known as the Formative or Initial Period, Andean society had created sophisticated irrigation canals and produced its first textiles and decorative ceramics. Another important advance was labor specialization, aided in large part by the development of a hierarchical society.

Though Peru is likely to be forever synonymous with the Incas, who built the spectacular city of Machu Picchu high in the Andes, that society, in place when the Spanish conquistadors arrived at the end of the 15th century, was merely the last in a long line of pre-Columbian cultures. The Inca Empire (1200–1532) was short-lived, but it remains the best documented of all Peruvian civilizations. The Incas' dominance was achieved through a formidable organization and highly developed economic system. They laid a vast network of roadways, nearly 30,000km (20,000 miles) total across the difficult territory of the Andes, connecting cities, farming communities, and religious sites. Their agricultural techniques were exceedingly skilled and efficient, and their stone-masonry remains unparalleled.

By the 1520s, the Spanish conquistadors had reached South America. Francisco Pizarro led an expedition along Peru's coast in 1528. Impressed with the riches of the Inca Empire, he returned to Spain and succeeded in raising money and recruiting men for a return expedition. In 1532, Pizarro made his return to Peru overland from Ecuador. After founding the first Spanish city in Peru, San Miguel de Piura, near the Ecuadorian border, he advanced upon the northern highland city of Cajamarca, an Inca stronghold. There, a small number of Spanish troops—about 180 men and 30 horses—captured the Inca emperor Atahualpa. The emperor promised to pay a king's ransom of gold and silver for his release, but the Spaniards, having received warning of an advancing Inca army, executed the emperor in 1533. It was a catastrophic blow to the Inca Empire.

Two years later, Pizarro founded the coastal city of Lima, which became capital of the new colony, the viceroyalty of Peru. The Spanish crown appointed Spanish-born viceroys the rulers of Peru, but Spaniards battled among themselves for control of Peru's riches, and the remaining Incas continued to battle the conquistadors. Pizarro was assassinated in 1541, and the indigenous insurrection ended with the beheading of Manco Inca, the last of the Inca leaders, in 1544. The Inca Tupac Amaru led a rebellion in 1572, but he met the same fate. Over the next 2 centuries, Lima gained in power and prestige at the expense of the old Inca capital of Cusco and became the foremost colonial city of the Andean nations.

By the 19th century, grumbling over high taxes and burdensome Spanish controls grew in Peru. After liberating Chile and Argentina, José de San Martín set his sights north on Lima in 1821 and declared it an independent nation the same year. Simón Bolívar, the other hero of independence on the continent, came from the other direction. His successful campaigns in Venezuela and Colombia led him south to Ecuador and finally to Peru. Peru won its independence after crucial battles in late 1824.

After several military regimes, Peru finally returned to civilian rule in 1895. Landowning elites dominated this new "Aristocratic Republic." In 1941, the country went to war with Ecuador over a border dispute (just one of several long-running border conflicts). Though the 1942 Treaty of Rio de Janeiro granted the area north of the Marañón River to Peru, Ecuador would continue to claim the territory, part of the Amazon basin, until the end of the 20th century.

Peru's recent political history has been a turbulent mix of military dictatorships, coups d'état, and several disastrous civilian governments, engendering a near-continual cycle of instability. The country's hyperinflation, nationwide strikes, and two guerrilla movements—the Maoist Sendero Luminoso (Shining Path) and the Tupac Amaru Revolutionary Movement (MRTA)—produced violence and terror throughout the late 1980s and early 1990s. Meanwhile, Peru's role on the production end of the international cocaine trade grew exponentially.

With the economy in ruins and the government in chaos, Alberto Fujimori, the son of Japanese immigrants, became president in 1990. Fujimori campaigned on promises to fix the ailing economy and root out terrorist guerrillas, and in 1992, his government succeeded in arresting key members of both the MRTA and the Shining Path (catapulting the president to unprecedented popularity). Fujimori became suddenly authoritarian, however, shutting down Congress in 1992, suspending the constitution, and decreeing an emergency government (which he effectively ruled as dictator). He was reelected in 1995.

Most international observers denounced Peru's 2000 presidential election results, which were announced after Fujimori's controversial runoff with Alejandro Toledo, a newcomer from a poor Indian family. Public outcry forced Fujimori to call new elections, but he escaped into exile in Japan and resigned the presidency in late 2000 after a corruption scandal involving his shadowy intelligence chief, Vladimiro Montesinos. Toledo, a former shoeshine boy and son of an Andean sheepherder who went on to teach at Harvard and become a World Bank economist, won the election and became president in July 2001, formally accepting the post at Machu Picchu.

PERU TODAY

Peru remains a society dominated by elites. Toledo labeled himself an "Indian rebel with a cause," alluding to his intent to recognize and his support for the nation's Native Andean populations, or *cholos*. To both Peruvians and the international community, Toledo offered an encouraging symbol of hope. However, Toledo's Peru got off to a rough start in 2001. There were reports of the Shining Path guerrilla terrorist group resurfacing after years of inactivity, and a year-end blaze in downtown Lima ripped through illegal fireworks booths, killing 300 people and leaving many hundreds homeless. A couple years into Toledo's presidency and his hopeful *Perú Posible,* the results Peruvians were hoping for largely have not been achieved. Peru continues to be beset by economic and political difficulties, highlighted by a series of education and public worker strikes in 2003.

URUGUAY
A LOOK AT THE PAST

In 1516, a surprised Spanish sailor discovered the area of what would become Uruguay and was followed by Ferdinand Magellan, who in 1520 anchored outside present-day Montevideo. Despite the Spaniards' success in making the journey from home, they were less successful settling in the area, due to resistance from the Charrúa Indians who inhabited the land. Not until the early 17th century, as Spain competed with Portugal for South American territory, did Spanish colonization begin to take hold. Colonia del Sacramento was founded by the Portuguese in 1680. Not to be outdone, the Spanish responded by establishing Montevideo after the turn of the century.

Uruguay's history until the beginning of the 19th century was marked by colonial struggle for the Argentina-Brazil-Uruguay region. In 1811, José Gervasio Artigas initiated a revolt against Spain. The war lasted until 1828, when Uruguay earned its independence from Brazil, to which it had been annexed by the Portuguese. Argentine troops assisted the

Uruguayan fighters in defeating the Brazilians, and Uruguay adopted its first constitution by 1830. Political instability dominated the rest of the century, as large numbers of immigrants arrived from Europe. By 1910, the population reached one million.

Uruguay experienced significant political, economic, and social progress under the two presidencies of José Batlle y Ordoñez, who in the early 20th century created what many considered a model social-welfare state. Life seemed to be getting better and better for Uruguayans, who achieved their first World Cup victory in 1930 and again in 1950. By the 1960s, however, Uruguay's charmed reputation as the "Switzerland of South America" was shattered by corruption, high unemployment, and runaway inflation. The instability of Uruguay's economy paved the way for military government, which seized control in 1973 and was responsible for the detention of more than 60,000 citizens during its time in power.

Civilians resumed control of the government in 1984, when Colorado Party leader Julio María Sanguinetti won the presidency. His tenure in office was focused on national reconciliation, the consolidation of democratic governance, and the stabilization of the economy. Violations under the military regime were controversially pardoned in order to promote reconciliation, and a general amnesty was given to military leaders charged with human rights abuses.

URUGUAY TODAY

The National Party's Luis Alberto Lacalle held the presidency from 1990 to 1995, during which time he reformed the economy in favor of trade liberalization and export promotion. He brought Uruguay into the Southern Cone Common Market (Mercosur) in 1991 and privatized inefficient state industries. Julio María

Sanguinetti was reelected in 1995, continuing Uruguay's economic reforms and improving education, public safety, and the electoral system. The economy tripped at the end of the century, however, when low commodity prices pounded the country's agricultural-based export market and landed Uruguay in recession. In 2001, the recession deepened following Argentina's economic crisis, and Uruguay has continued to struggle with the misfortunes of its bigger neighbor.

VENEZUELA
A LOOK AT THE PAST

The area we call Venezuela has been inhabited for more than 15,000 years. The earliest indigenous residents were predominantly nomadic; these peoples, decedents of the Carib, Arawak, and Chibcha tribes, left few traces and no major ruins. The most significant archaeological evidence left behind are some well preserved, although largely undeciphered, petroglyphs found in various sites around the country.

In 1498, on his third voyage, Christopher Columbus became the first European to set foot in Venezuela. One year later, Amerigo Vespucci and Alonso de Ojeda, leading another exploration to the New World, dubbed the land Venezuela, or "Little Venice," in honor of (or perhaps making fun of) the traditional indigenous stilt-houses along Lake Maracaibo, which called to mind the namesake city.

Lacking readily apparent gold and silver stores, Venezuela was never a major colonial concern for the Spanish crown. The first city still in existence to be founded was Cumaná, established in 1521. Caracas, the current capital, was founded in 1567. For centuries, the colony was governed from afar by Spanish seats in Peru, Colombia, and the Dominican Republic. The relative isolation and low level of development encouraged a certain amount of autonomy. Perhaps this is why Venezuela figured so prominently in the region's independence struggle.

Venezuela's struggle for independence from Spanish rule began in the early 19th century and took nearly 2 decades to consolidate. The principal figure in the fight was Simón Bolívar, El Libertador—a Venezuelan-born aristocrat considered the "Father of Venezuela" and the person most responsible for ending Spanish colonial rule throughout South America. Taking over in the wake of Francisco de Miranda's death, Bolívar led a series of long and bloody campaigns. In 1819, in the city of Angostura (currently Ciudad Bolívar), the rebel forces declared the independence of Gran Colombia, comprised of the current states of Panama, Colombia, Ecuador, and Venezuela. Still, Royalist forces held on, and fighting continued for several more years, culminating in the decisive 1821 Battle of Carabobo. Nevertheless, both Bolívar's good fortune and the fledgling nation were short-lived. By 1830, El Libertador had died a poor and pitiful figure, and Gran Colombia had dissolved into separate nation states, including present-day Venezuela.

Over the next century or so, Venezuela was ruled by a series of strongman dictators, or *caudillos,* whose reigns were sometimes interspersed with periods of civil war and anarchy. One of the most infamous dictators was General Juan Vincente Gómez, who ruled from 1908 until his death in 1935. In addition to his cruelty and suppression of dissent, Gómez is best known for having presided over the first period of discovery and exploitation of Venezuela's massive oil reserves. Venezuela quickly became the world's number-one exporter of crude oil. However, there was little trickledown, and most of the wealth generated went to international oil companies and a small local elite.

By 1945, the opposition, led by Rómulo Betancourt, was able to take power and organize elections, granting universal voting rights to both men and women. In 1947, Rómulo Gallegos, the country's greatest novelist, became the first democratically elected president of Venezuela. However, the new democracy was fragile, and Gallegos was overthrown in a military coup within 8 months.

The subsequent military dictator, Colonel Marcos Pérez Jiménez, rivaled Gómez in brutality but will forever be remembered as the architect of modern Venezuela. Pérez Jiménez dedicated vast amounts of oil money to public works projects and modern buildings. In 1958, Pérez Jiménez himself was overthrown and a more stable democracy instituted. Back in the spotlight, Rómulo Betancourt became the first democratically elected president to finish his term. For decades, Venezuela enjoyed a relatively peaceful period of democratic rule, with two principal parties amicably sharing power.

But Venezuela's almost sole dependence on oil revenues, modern ebbs and flows in international crude prices and production, and internal corruption and mismanagement all took their toll. In 1992, there were two unsuccessful coup attempts, one led by a brash paratrooper, Lieutenant Colonel Hugo Chávez Frías. Chávez spent several years in prison, but was not out for the count. In 1993, President Carlos Andrés Pérez was found guilty of embezzlement and misuse of public funds, was impeached, and spent more than 2 years under house arrest. More economic woe and political turmoil ensued, and in December 1998, Hugo Chávez was elected president in a landslide.

VENEZUELA TODAY

Soon after assuming power, Chávez orchestrated a series of maneuvers, including the dissolution of Congress and the drafting of a new constitution, which have granted him far-reaching powers. Chávez's flamboyant populism and leftist rhetoric have given him a relatively strong base of support among the poorer classes, but he has faced constant and fierce opposition from much of the political, business, and academic classes, not to mention an overwhelmingly hostile press. Moreover, labor disputes are increasing, and the president's popularity is declining. Far from delivering the worker's paradise and social equality promised, Venezuela is mired in a severe economic crisis marked by massive capital flight, sharply declining GDP, and high inflation. Venezuela today is a country bitterly divided, predominantly along class lines, although the political and economic situation has become so dire that Chávez has stirred the ire of many across the entire social spectrum. An attempt by opposition groups to force a recall election dragged its way through the judicial system for more than 2 years; at press time, the National Electoral Council had just rejected the effort and Venezuela's U.N. ambassador resigned in protest. The legal and political wrangling has led to a series of demonstrations and the ever-increasing polarization of Venezuelan society.

2 A South American Cultural Primer

It's estimated that 310 million people live in South America. The population is extremely diverse, and it would be difficult to generalize about the cultural makeup of the continent. But it is safe to say that of all the different people who live here, a large majority can trace their roots back to Spain, Portugal, Africa, or South America itself. Because of the Spanish and Portuguese influence, mestizos (people of both Amerindian and either Spanish or Portuguese ancestry) are also in the majority. From the late 19th century through 1930, the look of South Americans began to gradually change. Millions of Italians emigrated mainly to Brazil, Argentina, and Uruguay. Significant numbers of Germans, Poles, Syrians, Lebanese, and Japanese began to settle here as well.

THE CULTURAL MAKEUP OF SOUTH AMERICA
ARGENTINA

To understand how Argentina's European heritage impacts its South American identity, you must identify its distinct culture. Tango is the quintessential example—the sensual dance originated in the suspect corners of Buenos Aires's San Telmo neighborhood, was legitimized in the ballrooms of France, and was then reexported to Argentina to become this nation's great art form. Each journey you take, whether into a tango salon, an Argentine cafe, or a meat-only *parrilla*, will bring you closer to the country's true character.

But beyond the borders of Argentina's capital and largest city, you will find a land of vibrant extremes—from the Northwest's desert plateau to the flat grasslands of the pampas, from the rain-forest jungle of Iguazú to the towering blue-white glaciers of Patagonia. The land's geographic diversity is reflected in its people; witness the contrast between the capital's largely immigrant population and the indigenous people of the Northwest. Greater Buenos Aires, in which a third of Argentines live, is separated from the rest of Argentina both culturally and economically. Considerable suspicion exists between *Porteños*, as the people

of Buenos Aires are called, and the rest of the Argentines. Residents of the fast-paced metropolis who consider themselves more European than South American share little in common with the indigenous people of the Northwest, for example, who trace their roots to the Incas and take pride in a slower country life.

BOLIVIA

Bolivia has the highest percentage of indigenous people in all of South America. The country is twice as big as France, but its population is only 8.8 million (about the same as New York City's). And because of the country's rugged vastness, its indigenous groups have remained isolated and have been able to hold on to their traditions. In the rural highlands, lifestyles still revolve around agriculture and traditional weaving. It is also common to see people all over the country chewing coca leaves, a thousands-year-old tradition that is believed to give people energy. The customs of the indigenous people are in full flower not only in rural areas but in cities such as La Paz as well. In addition, Bolivians all over, particularly in rural highland areas, are known for their love of traditional music. It is a testament to the tenacity of Bolivian traditions that millions of Bolivians still speak Aymara, a language that predates not only the Spanish conquest of Bolivia but also the Inca conquest. Millions more speak Quechua, the language of the Incas. In fact, only half the population speaks Spanish as their first language. Of course, in the cities there are many mestizos, and most people speak Spanish.

Almost all Bolivians today are Roman Catholic, though traditional indigenous rituals are still practiced, even by devout Catholics. In the 18th and 19th centuries, a distinct "Mestizo Baroque" movement developed, where mestizo artists used indigenous techniques to create religious art. Even today, the mixture of the two influences is evident throughout Bolivian society. In Copacabana, where the Virgin of the Candelaria is one of the most revered Catholic symbols in all of South America, you can climb Calvario, the hill that looms over the cathedral, and receive blessings or have your coca leaves read by traditional Andean priests.

BRAZIL

Modern Brazil's diverse population is a melting pot of three main ethnic groups: the indigenous inhabitants of Brazil, the European settlers, and the descendants of black slaves from Africa. Within Brazil the blending of various cultures and ethnic groups varies from region to region. Rio de Janeiro's population is comprised largely of people of mixed European and African heritage. In Salvador, more than any other area of Brazil, the people are mostly of African descent. Many of the freed slaves settled in this area, and the African influence is reflected in the food, religion, and music. In the Amazon, the cities are populated by migrants from other parts of Brazil, while the forest is predominantly populated by *caboclos* (a mixture of European and Indian ethnicities) and indigenous tribes, many of which maintain their traditional culture, dress, and lifestyle. European immigrants mostly settled the south of Brazil, with a few notable exceptions, such as the large Japanese and Middle Eastern communities of São Paulo.

Brazil remains the largest Roman Catholic country in the world, though Catholicism is perhaps stronger as a cultural influence than a religious force; many Brazilian Catholics see the inside of a church only once a year. Meanwhile, evangelical Protestant churches are growing fast, and African religious practices such as Candomblé remain important, particularly in northern cities such as Salvador.

Brazil is well known for its music. Local sounds encompass much more than samba and bossa nova, with Brazilian artists playing everything from rap, funk, jazz, and rock to regional rhythms such as the swinging afro-axé pop in Salvador and the fast maracatu in the Northeast. The cultural center of Brazil is São Paulo and its rich theater and film scene is begrudgingly envied even by Cariocas (Rio residents). Rio remains the center of Brazil's sizable television industry.

CHILE

About 95% of Chile's population is mestizo, a mix of indigenous and European blood that includes Spanish, German (in the Lake District), and Croatian (in southern Patagonia). Other nationalities, such as Italian, Russian, and English, have contributed a smaller influence. Indigenous groups, such as the Aymara in the northern desert and the Mapuche in the Lake District, still exist in large numbers, although nothing compared to their size before the Spanish conquest. It is estimated that there are more than a half million Mapuches, many of whom live on poverty-stricken *reducciones,* literally "reductions," where they continue to use their language and carry on their customs. In southern Chile and Tierra del Fuego, indigenous groups such as Alacalufe and Yagan have been diminished to only a few remaining representatives, and some, such as the Patagonian Ona, have been completely extinguished. One-third of Chile's 15 million residents live in the Santiago metropolis alone.

Until the late 1800s, the Roman Catholic Church exerted a heavy influence over all political, educational, and social spheres of society. Today, although more than 85% of the population claims faith in the Catholic religion, only a fraction attends Mass regularly. The church has lost much of its sway over government, but it still is the dominant influence when the government deals with issues such as abortion and divorce. It is estimated that less than 10% of Chileans are Protestants, mostly Anglican and Lutheran descendants of British and German immigrants, and fewer are Pentecostal. The remaining percentage belongs to tiny communities of Jewish, Mormon, and Muslim faiths.

Chile is a country whose rich cultural tapestry reflects its wide-ranging topography. From this range of cultures and landscapes have arisen some of Latin America's most prominent poets and writers, notably Nobel Prize winners Pablo Neruda and Gabriela Mistral, as well as contemporary writers Isabel Allende and José Donoso. Despite an artistically sterile period during the Pinochet regime, when any form of art deemed "suspicious" or "offensive" (meaning nothing beyond safe, traditional entertainment) was censored, modern art has begun to bloom, and even folkloric art and music are finding a fresh voice. Chile is also known for theater, and visitors to Santiago will find dozens of excellent productions to choose from. The national Chilean dance is the *cueca,* a courtship dance between couples that is said to imitate the mating ritual between chickens! The cueca is danced by couples who perform a one-two stomp while flitting and twirling a handkerchief.

ECUADOR

About 25% of the Ecuadorian population is indigenous, and more than 55% of the population is mestizo. An additional 10% of Ecuadorians are Afro-Ecuadorian, descendants of African slaves who were forced to work in the coastal areas. Caucasian, Asian, and Middle Eastern immigrants account for the remaining 10%. During the cocoa boom of the late 19th century, many Ecuadorians moved from the heavily populated highland areas to work on the fertile coast. In the past 100 years, there has also been a significant migration of people from the rural highlands to the major cities. El Oriente (the eastern, Amazon basin region of Ecuador) remains the least populated area in the whole country; only 3% of the population lives here.

In the highland areas, the local people have managed to hold on to their traditional culture. It's very common to see people still celebrating ancient holidays such as Inti Raymi—a festival welcoming the summer solstice. In Otavalo, in the northern highlands, the people still wear traditional clothing, and they have also kept their artisan traditions alive. The finest handicrafts in the country can be found here.

Because of the Amazon basin's isolated location, the locals here were able to escape domination by the Spanish, and managed to maintain thousand-year-old rituals and customs. Some groups never had contact with "the outside world" until the 1960s and 1970s. Visitors to the Ecuadorian jungle who are taken to Amazonian villages will find that the people here live very much as their ancestors did thousands of years ago.

When it comes to modern art in Ecuador, it's been hard for artists to break from the old colonial mode. Oswaldo Guayasamín is one of Ecuador's most important modern artists. Some of his most famous pieces are expressions of outrage at the military governments in South America in the 1970s.

Music in Ecuador is still strongly influenced by the large traditional Andean population in the country. If you head to any local festival in the Andes, you can be assured that you will find groups of colorfully dressed men playing drums and reed instruments.

PERU

Peru's 27 million people are predominantly mestizo and Andean Indian, but there are also significant minority groups of Afro-Peruvians (descendants of African slaves, confined mainly to a coastal area south of Lima), immigrant Japanese and Chinese populations that are among the largest on the continent, and smaller groups of European immigrants, including Italians and Germans. Their religion is mainly Roman Catholic, though many people still practice pre-Columbian religious rituals inherited from the Incas.

Peru has, after Bolivia and Guatemala, the largest population by percentage of Amerindians in Latin America. Perhaps half the country lives in the *sierra*, or highlands, and most of these people, commonly called *campesinos* (peasants), live in either small villages or rural areas. Descendants of Peru's many Andean indigenous groups who live in remote rural areas continue to speak the native languages Quechua (made an official language in 1975) and Aymara or other Amerindian tongues, and for the most part they adhere to traditional regional dress. However, massive peasant migration to cities from rural highland villages has contributed to a dramatic weakening of indigenous traditions and culture across Peru.

Indigenous Amazonian tribes in Peru's jungle are dwindling in number—today, the population is less than two million. Still, many traditions and languages have yet to be extinguished, especially deep in the jungle—though most visitors are unlikely to come into contact with groups of unadulterated, non-Spanish-speaking native peoples.

Amerindian—Altiplano and Andina (highland)—music, is played on wind instruments such as bamboo panpipes and *quena* flutes, as well as *charangos* (small, bright-sounding, guitarlike instruments), among others. For many, this *música folklórica* is the very sound of Peru, but there are also significant strands of *música criolla* (based on a mix of European and African forms, played with guitar and *cajón*, a wooden box used as a percussion instrument), bouncy-sounding *huayno* rhythms played by *orquestas típicas*, and Afro-Peruvian music, adapted from music brought by African slaves.

Peru has one of the richest handicrafts traditions in the Americas. Many ancient traditions, such as the drop spindle (weaving done with a stick and spinning wooden wheel) are still employed in many regions. Terrific alpaca wool sweaters, ponchos, and shawls; tightly woven and brilliantly colored blankets and tapestries; and many other items of great quality are on display throughout Peru.

URUGUAY

There are 3.3 million Uruguayans, 93% of whom are of European descent. About 5% of the population is of African descent, and 1% is mestizo. The majority of Uruguayans are Roman Catholic. Most live in the capital or one of only 20 other significant towns. Uruguay enjoys high literacy, long life expectancy, and a relatively high standard of living. Despite Uruguay's recent economic troubles, this middle-income nation remains largely sheltered from the pervasive poverty and extreme socioeconomic differences characterizing much of Latin America.

Uruguay has a rich artistic and literary heritage. Among the country's notable artists are the sculptor José Belloni and the painter Joaquín Torres-García, founder of Uruguay's Constructivist movement. Top writers include José Enrique Rodó, a famed essayist; Mauricio Rosencof, a politically active playwright; and journalist Eduardo Galeano.

VENEZUELA

Venezuela has a population of approximately 24 million people, some 80% of whom live in a narrow urban belt running along the Caribbean coast and slightly inland. Venezuela is a young country, with an estimated half the population under 20 and around 70% under 35. Almost 70% of the population is mestizo, or a mix of Spanish, European, indigenous, and African ancestry. Another 19% are considered white, and 10% are black. While indigenous peoples make up only about 1% of the population, their influence and presence are noticeable. Venezuela has more than 20 different indigenous tribes totaling some 200,000 people. The principal tribes are the Guajiro, found north of Maracaibo; the Pémon, Piaroa, Yekuana, and Yanomami, who live in the Amazon and Gran Sabana regions; and the Warao of the Orinoco Delta.

More than 90% of the population claims to be Roman Catholic, although church attendance is relatively low and Venezuelans are not considered the most devout of followers on the continent. There is a growing influx of U.S.-style Protestant denominational churches, as well as small Jewish and Muslim populations. The country's indigenous peoples were an early target of Catholic missionary fervor, although their traditional beliefs and faith do survive. One of the most interesting religious phenomena in the country is the cult of María Lionza, a unique syncretic sect that combines elements of Roman Catholicism, African voodoo, and indigenous rites.

Although Venezuela has its fair share of European-influenced colonial and religious art, its most important art, literature, and music are almost all modern. Jesús Soto is perhaps the country's most famous artist. A pioneer and leading figure of the kinetic art movement, Soto has major and prominent works in public spaces around Caracas. Novelist, essayist, and one-time president of Venezuela, Rómulo Gallegos is the defining literary figure in Venezuela. One important literary figure from the revolutionary era is Andrés Bello, a poet, journalist, historian, and close friend of Simón Bolívar. Venezuelans love to dance, and no one has been getting them up and moving longer and more consistently than Oscar D'León. Alternately known as El Rey (The King), El León (The Lion), and El Diablo (The Devil) of salsa, D'León has been recording and performing live for more than 30 years, and he shows no sign of slowing down.

3 Doing Business in South America

When Christopher Columbus landed in the Americas in 1492, he brought with him thousands of years of European traditions. In the next few hundred years, because of the Spanish influence, the business climate in South America would prove to be distinctively European. If you're accustomed to doing business in North America or Europe, you'll find that the culture in South America is very similar. However, there are some minor differences. Here are some tips to help you feel like a local.

GREETINGS, GESTURES & SOCIAL INTERACTION

South Americans are very affectionate. In most countries, they greet acquaintances with at least one kiss on the cheek, repeating the ritual when saying goodbye. (The number of kisses varies from country to country, and even from city to city. Observe the natives and take your cue from them.) As a general rule, however, men do not greet other men in this manner; instead, they shake hands. Businesspeople are aware that North

Americans and Brits often prefer handshakes, so don't be surprised if a colleague immediately offers you a hand instead of a cheek.

You should also note that punctuality is usually not taken very seriously here. It's not unusual to wait around for a half-hour before your meeting begins; a major exception is São Paulo, South America's largest business city, where punctuality is the rule. It's also common, especially in stores and travel agencies, to wait for your host to finish a long-winded personal conversation before attending to you.

If you're trying to negotiate with indigenous people, you should understand that they are not accustomed to excessive bargaining. Yes, you can definitely talk people into decreasing the asking price, but it's considered rude to continue bargaining once the seller has told you that he won't go any lower. Also, it's fine to call indigenous people *indígenas,* but they may be offended if you call them Indians *(indios).* You should also always ask permission before taking their photograph; sometimes they will only say yes if you offer them a *propina* (tip).

You probably already know that in Spanish *hola* means hello and *adiós* means goodbye. But in most Spanish-speaking countries, businesspeople greet each other with *"Buen día"* or *"Buenos días"* from the morning until noon (*"Bom dia"* in Brazilian Portuguese), *"Buenas tardes"* from noon until nightfall (*"Boa tarde"*), and *"Buenas noches"* in the evening (*"Boa noite"*). Please note that Brazilians particularly appreciate it if you are aware of the differences between Spanish and Portuguese. Do not assume that you will be able to speak to people in Spanish in Brazil, although in communities close to the border (such as Foz de Iguaçu) or in larger tourist destinations, you'll likely find some people who speak Spanish.

In South America, lunch is the main meal of the day. If you want to have an important business meeting over a meal, you should always suggest a power lunch instead of a power dinner. Even in most large cities, businesses (except for restaurants) still have a tendency to close down in the middle of the day, so if you're trying to reach someone, it's best to try early in the morning or late in the afternoon (usually after 3pm).

DRESSING FOR CULTURAL SUCCESS

In general, South Americans take fashion very seriously. Jeans and casual clothes are considered inappropriate for business meetings. In large cities, men still overwhelmingly wear suits, although chinos and button-up shirts are slowly working their way into the office environment. Fortunately, women should not feel obligated to wear skirts—a nice pair of slacks is considered perfectly acceptable.

Modesty is generally not an issue here, unless you plan on visiting Catholic churches. Even if you visit religious sites, however, no one will be offended by the sight of shorts or a tank top, as long as they're not sloppy. When it gets hot in the tropical coastal areas, you will want to wear light clothes. At night, especially, it's not uncommon to see people wearing extremely flimsy outfits, although in Chile, plan to dress sharply for dinner, especially at upscale restaurants.

3

Planning Your Trip to South America

The country chapters in this guide provide specific information on traveling to and getting around individual South American countries. In this chapter, we provide you with region-wide tips and general information that will help you plan your trip.

1 Entry Requirements at a Glance

The passport and visa information in this section is for quick reference; see individual country chapters for complete details about the entry requirements for your destination.

Due to concern about parental abductions, there are **special requirements for children** visiting many foreign countries, including Brazil, Chile, Colombia, and Venezuela. If you are a lone or single parent or a guardian, you must bring a copy of the child's birth certificate and a notarized consent document from the parent(s). For single parents, a decree of sole custody or a parental death certificate will also do. Ask your airline what's required when you book the ticket; also check the State Department's **"Foreign Entry Requirements"** page at http://travel.state.gov/foreignentryreqs.html. **Single Parent Travel Forum** also has a helpful FAQ section at http://www.singleparenttravel.net.

ARGENTINA Citizens of the United States, Canada, the United Kingdom, Australia, New Zealand, and South Africa must have a passport to enter the country. No visa is required for citizens of these countries for tourist stays of up to 90 days. For more information concerning longer stays, employment, or other types of visas, contact the Argentine embassy or consulate in your home country.

BOLIVIA Visas are not required if you're a citizen of 45 designated countries, which include the United States, the United Kingdom, Canada, Australia, New Zealand, South Africa, France, Germany, and Switzerland. You will be granted entry for 30 days. You can easily extend the visa for an additional 60 days by visiting an Oficina de Migración in Bolivia.

BRAZIL Citizens of the United States, Canada, Australia, and New Zealand require a visa to visit Brazil. British nationals and holders of an E.U. passport do not require a visa, but do need a passport valid for at least 6 months and a return ticket. A number of visa types are available; cost, processing time, and documentation requirements vary.

CHILE Citizens of the United States, Canada, the United Kingdom, Australia, and New Zealand do not need a visa to enter Chile. However, citizens of the following countries must pay a fee upon arrival: United States, $100; Canada, $55; and Australia, $33. Visitors to Chile are given a tourist visa that allows a stay for up to 90 days. To renew this visa, visitors must either cross the border into Argentina and return (for another 90-day visa), or pay $100 at an immigration or provincial government office for a 30-day extension.

ECUADOR   Visas are not required if you're a citizen of the United States, the United Kingdom, Canada, Australia, New Zealand, South Africa, France, Germany, or Switzerland for stays of up to 90 days.

PERU   Citizens of the United States, Canada, the United Kingdom, South Africa, New Zealand, and Australia do not require visas to enter Peru as tourists. Citizens of any of these countries conducting business or enrolled in formal educational programs in Peru do require visas. Tourist cards, distributed on arriving international flights or at border crossings, are good for stays of up to 90 days. Keep a copy of the tourist card for presentation upon departure from Peru. A maximum of three extensions of 30 days each, for a total of 180 days, is allowed.

URUGUAY   Citizens of the United States, Canada, and the United Kingdom do not need visas to enter Uruguay for stays up to 3 months. Citizens of Australia must apply for a visa from a Uruguayan consulate. For more information in Australia, contact ℂ **02/6273-9100.**

VENEZUELA   Citizens and residents of the United States, Canada, the United Kingdom, Australia, and New Zealand who enter by air or cruise ship are issued a free tourist card valid for 90 days upon arrival. You can extend your tourist card for up to 120 days at the Caracas office of the national immigration agency, **Dirección de Identificación y Extranjería** (**DIEX**; ℂ **0212/483-2070;** www. onidex.gov.ve). You will have to present your tourist card upon departure.

If you are arriving by air, there is no need to obtain a tourist card in advance. However, if you plan on arriving by land or by sea, you might try to get one ahead of time from your nearest Venezuelan embassy or consulate. Tourist cards are free, although you may be charged between $20 and $40 for a tourist card depending on the processing fees and policies of your local embassy or consulate. I've also heard reports that you may face an arbitrary charge of between $3 and $10 at some of the border crossings along the Colombian and Brazilian borders.

PASSPORT INFORMATION

Allow plenty of time before your trip to apply for a passport; processing normally takes 3 weeks but can take longer during busy periods (especially spring). And keep in mind that if you need a passport in a hurry, you'll pay a higher processing fee. When traveling, safeguard your passport in an inconspicuous, inaccessible place like a money belt and keep a copy of the critical pages with your passport number in a separate place. If you lose your passport, visit the nearest consulate or embassy of your native country as soon as possible for a replacement.

To apply for a passport, residents of the United States can download passport applications from the U.S. State Department website at http://travel. state.gov, or call the **National Passport Agency** at ℂ **202/647-0518.** Canadian residents should visit www.ppt. gc.ca or call ℂ **800/567-6868.**

British citizens should contact the **United Kingdom Passport Service** at ℂ **0870/521-0410** or search the website at www.ukpa.gov.uk. Residents of Ireland can call ℂ **01/671-1633,** or visit www.irlgov.ie/iveagh.

Australian citizens should contact the **Australian Passport Information Service** at ℂ **131-232,** or visit www. passports.gov.au. Residents of New Zealand should call the **Passports Office** at ℂ **0800/225-050** or 04/ 474-8100, or log on to www.passports. govt.nz.

2 Customs

For information about what you can bring with you upon entry, see the "Customs" section in individual country chapters.

WHAT YOU CAN BRING HOME

Returning **U.S. citizens** who have been away for at least 48 hours are allowed to bring back, once every 30 days, US$800 worth of merchandise duty-free. You'll be charged a flat rate of 4% duty on the next US$1,000 worth of purchases. Be sure to have your receipts handy. On mailed gifts, the duty-free limit is US$200. With some exceptions, you cannot bring fresh fruits and vegetables into the United States. For specifics on what you can bring back, download the invaluable free pamphlet *Know Before You Go* online at **www.cbp.gov**. (Click on "Travel," then on "Know Before You Go! Online Brochure.") Or contact the **U.S. Customs & Border Protection (CBP),** 1300 Pennsylvania Ave. NW, Washington, DC 20229 (© **877/287-8667**), and request the pamphlet.

For a clear summary of **Canadian** rules, write for the booklet *I Declare,* issued by the **Canada Border Services Agency** (© **800/461-9999** in Canada, or 204/983-3500; www.cbsa.gc.ca). Canada allows its citizens a C$750 exemption, and you're allowed to bring back duty-free one carton of cigarettes, 1 can of tobacco, 40 imperial ounces of liquor, and 50 cigars. In addition, you're allowed to mail gifts to Canada valued at less than C$60 a day, provided they're unsolicited and don't contain alcohol or tobacco (write on the package "Unsolicited gift, under $60 value"). All valuables should be declared on the Y-38 form before departure from Canada, including serial numbers of valuables you already own, such as expensive foreign cameras. *Note:* The $750 exemption can only be used once a year and only after an absence of 7 days.

U.K. citizens returning from **a non-E.U. country** have a customs allowance of: 200 cigarettes; 50 cigars; 250 grams of smoking tobacco; 2 liters of still table wine; 1 liter of spirits or strong liqueurs (over 22% volume); 2 liters of fortified wine, sparkling wine or other liqueurs; 60cc (ml) perfume; 250cc (ml) of toilet water; and £145 worth of all other goods, including gifts and souvenirs. People under 17 cannot have the tobacco or alcohol allowance. For more information, contact HM Customs & Excise at © **0845/010-9000** (from outside the U.K., 020/8929-0152), or consult their website at www.hmce.gov.uk.

The duty-free allowance in **Australia** is A$400 or, for those under 18, A$200. Citizens can bring in 250 cigarettes or 250 grams of loose tobacco, and 1,125 milliliters of alcohol. If you're returning with valuables you already own, such as foreign-made cameras, you should file form B263. A helpful brochure available from Australian consulates or Customs offices is *Know Before You Go.* For more information, call the **Australian Customs Service** at © **1300/363-263,** or log on to www.customs.gov.au.

The duty-free allowance for **New Zealand** is NZ$700. Citizens over 17 can bring in 200 cigarettes, 50 cigars, or 250 grams of tobacco (or a mixture of all three if their combined weight doesn't exceed 250g); plus 4.5 liters of wine and beer, or 1.125 liters of liquor. New Zealand currency does not carry import or export restrictions. Fill out a certificate of export, listing the valuables you are taking out of the country; that way, you can bring them back without paying duty. Most questions are answered in a free pamphlet available at New Zealand consulates and Customs offices: *New Zealand*

Customs Guide for Travellers, Notice no. 4. For more information, contact **New Zealand Customs,** The Customhouse, 17–21 Whitmore St., Box 2218, Wellington (© **04/473-6099** or 0800/428-786; www.customs.govt.nz).

3 Money

Inflation has been a perennial thorn in the economies of every South American nation. Ecuador has responded to this problem by befriending the U.S. dollar—in Ecuador, the U.S. dollar is the official currency. In other South American countries, you can expect the local currency to fluctuate while you're there, usually resulting in a better exchange rate for foreigners. You can usually use U.S. dollars for all transactions without much problem. Because of inflation, hotels generally quote their rates in dollars.

Note that most vendors prefer small bills and exact change. It's almost impossible to find someone who has change for a large bill. Many ATMs give out money in multiples of one or five, so try to request odd denominations of money. For larger sums, try to withdraw in a multiple of 500 instead of 1,000, or 550 instead of 600.

CARRYING MONEY

ATMs Automated teller machines in South America are linked to a network that most likely includes your bank at home. Using ATMs is a great way to obtain local currency without having to go through a middleman at a bank or an exchange office. **Cirrus** (© **800/424-7787;** www.mastercard.com) and **PLUS** (© **800/843-7587;** www.visa.com) are the two most popular networks; check the back of your ATM card to see which network your bank belongs to and use the toll-free numbers or check the websites to locate ATMs in your destination. Be sure to check the daily withdrawal limit before you depart, and if you don't have a four-digit personal identification number (PIN), request one. Keep in mind that many banks impose a fee every time a card is used at an ATM in a different bank; on top of this, the bank from which you withdraw cash may charge its own fee.

TRAVELER'S CHECKS In South America, most vendors prefer cash and credit cards over traveler's checks *(cheques de viajeros),* although many hotels happily accept them. You can exchange traveler's checks at *casas de cambio* (money-exchange houses), usually for a significant fee. Many banks will not exchange traveler's checks, and those that do often have long lines. Note that in some countries, the American Express offices won't exchange even their own traveler's checks.

If you'd still like to use traveler's checks, you can buy them at almost any bank. **American Express** offers U.S. dollar denominations of $10, $20, $50, $100, $500, and $1,000. You'll pay a service charge ranging from 1% to 4%. You can also get American Express traveler's checks by calling © **800/221-7282;** by using this number, Amex gold and platinum cardholders are exempt from the 1% fee.

Visa (© **800/732-1322**) offers traveler's checks at Citibank locations nationwide, as well as several other banks. The service charge ranges from 1.5% to 2%; checks come in U.S. dollar denominations of $20, $50, $100, $500, and $1,000. AAA members can obtain Visa checks without a fee at most AAA offices or by calling © **866/339-3378. MasterCard** also offers traveler's checks. Call © **800/223-9920** for a location near you.

If you opt to carry traveler's checks, be sure to keep a record of their serial numbers, separately from the checks, of course, so that you're ensured a refund in case of an emergency.

CREDIT CARDS   Credit cards are a safe way to carry money. They provide a convenient record of all your expenses, and they generally offer relatively good exchange rates. You can also withdraw cash advances from your credit cards at any bank, provided you know your PIN (note that you'll start paying hefty interest on the advance the moment you receive the cash). Keep in mind that credit card companies try to protect themselves (and you) from theft by limiting the funds you can withdraw away from home. It's therefore best to call your credit card company before you leave and let them know where you're going and how much you plan to spend.

Visa, MasterCard, American Express, and Diners Club are all commonly accepted in South America. Your credit card company will likely charge a commission (1% or 2%) on every foreign purchase you make, but don't sweat this small stuff; for most purchases, you'll still get the best deal with credit cards when you factor in things like ATM fees and higher traveler's check exchange rates.

IF YOUR WALLET IS LOST OR STOLEN   Be sure to tell all of your credit card companies the minute you discover your wallet has been lost or stolen, and file a report at the nearest police precinct. Your credit card company or insurer may require a police report number or record of the loss. Most credit card companies have an emergency toll-free number to call if your card is lost or stolen; they may be able to wire you a cash advance immediately or deliver an emergency credit card in a day or two. Emergency numbers for each country are listed in the "Money" section of each individual country chapter.

Identity theft or fraud are potential complications of losing your wallet, especially if you've lost your driver's license along with your cash and credit cards. Notify the major credit-reporting bureaus immediately; placing a fraud alert on your records may protect you against liability for criminal activity. The three major U.S. credit-reporting agencies are **Equifax** (© **800/766-0008;** www.equifax.com), **Experian** (© **888/397-3742;** www.experian.com), and **TransUnion** (© **800/680-7289;** www.transunion.com). Finally, if you've lost all forms of photo ID call your airline and explain the situation; they might allow you to board the plane if you have a copy of your passport or birth certificate and a copy of the police report you've filed.

WORKING WITH THE LOCAL CURRENCY

In most countries in South America, you can use American dollars without much of a problem. But if you're traveling in rural areas, it's always useful to have the local currency on hand. A list of currencies for all the countries in this guide follows. See "South American Currency Conversions," below, for comparisons of all these currencies to U.S., Australian, Canadian, and New Zealand dollars and the British pound.

ARGENTINA   The official Argentine currency is the **peso,** made up of 100 centavos. It was pegged to the U.S. dollar until the country's economic meltdown in late 2001, when it quickly devalued. Money is denominated in notes of 2, 5, 10, 20, 50, and 100 pesos; and in coins of 1, 2, and 5 pesos and 1, 5, 10, 25, and 50 centavos.

BOLIVIA   The Bolivian unit of currency is the **boliviano** (Bs). You'll find coins with values of 1 and 2 bolivianos. Otherwise, all the currency is paper, in denominations of 2, 5, 10, 20, 50, and 100. It's very hard to make change, especially for a 100Bs note.

BRAZIL   In an attempt to rein in inflation, the Brazilian government

South American Currency Conversions

	U.S. $1	CAN $1	U.K. £1	AUS $1	N.Z. $1
Argentine peso	2.87	2.15	4.77	1.97	1.71
Bolivian boliviano	7.70	5.80	13.10	5.50	4.75
Brazilian real	3.00	2.15	4.68	1.92	1.72
Chilean peso	645.00	484.34	1,071.09	442.31	381.39
Ecuadorian dollar	1.00	1.30	0.60	1.40	1.60
Peruvian nuevo sol	3.50	2.70	6.00	2.50	2.20
Uruguayan peso	27.80	20.93	46.36	19.18	16.64
Venezuelan bolívar	1,600.00	1,171.00	2,546.72	1,052.32	932.62

introduced a new currency in 1994, the **real** (R$). It was stable for several years, then devalued by almost 50% in 1999, after which it remained stable for most of 2000. In 2002, international speculation in advance of the presidential elections sent the real into a tailspin, arriving at a record low of nearly R$4 to the U.S. dollar. When it became clear that the new socialist president, Lula da Silva, actually planned to follow a quite conservative monetary policy, the real settled back around R$3 to the U.S. dollar. Prices stabilized, even going down for the first time in years. You can find real coins in denominations of R$1 and 1, 5, 10, and 50 centavos. Bank notes are available in forms of R$1, R$5, R$10, R$50, and R$100.

CHILE The unit of currency in Chile is the **peso,** which comes in notes with denominations of 1,000, 2,000, 5,000, 10,000, and 20,000. There are currently six coins in circulation in denominations of 1, 5, 10, 50, 100, and 500; however, it's unusual to be issued 1 peso or even 5 pesos. Chileans commonly call 1,000 pesos a *luca.*

ECUADOR The official unit of currency in Ecuador is the **U.S. dollar.** You can use both American and Ecuadorian coins, divided into 100 cents. Otherwise, all the currency is in

the paper form of American dollars, in denominations of $1, $5, US$10, $20, $50, and $100.

PERU The Peruvian currency is the **nuevo sol,** abbreviated "S/" and usually referred to simply as the *sol* or *soles.* Bank notes are issued in 10, 20, 50, 100, and 200 soles. Visitors are advised to be very careful of counterfeit bank notes. A sol is divided into 100 centavos, with coins in denominations of 5, 10, 20, and 50 centavo coins. U.S. dollars are also widely accepted across Peru for many commercial transactions.

URUGUAY The Uruguayan unit of currency is the **peso uruguayo** ($U). The peso comes in coin denominations of 1, 5, 10, 50, 100, 200, and 500 pesos; and bank notes of 50, 100, 200, 500, 1,000, 5,000, and 10,000.

VENEZUELA The Venezuelan unit of currency is the **bolívar,** popularly referred to as *bolos,* and abbreviated as "Bs." Paper bills come in denominations of 5, 10, 20, 50, 100, 500, 1,000, 2,000, 5,000, 10,000, 20,000, and 50,000 bolivares. There are coins of 5, 10, 20, 50, 100, and 500 bolivares. There are even coins for céntimos (fractions of a bolívar), but the currency has devalued so much in recent years that all coins are virtually meaningless and increasingly rare.

4 When to Go

South America is a huge continent (it crosses both the equator and the Tropic of Capricorn), and climatic conditions vary widely. In June, when it's freezing cold at the southern tip of Argentina, it's hot and humid in Venezuela. You can take into account, however, that more than 75% of the continent sits south of the equator, which means that winter usually lasts from June through September and summer from December through March. In high-altitude cities such as Quito, you can expect cool weather year-round; in the Amazon basin region—in the center of the continent, from Ecuador to Brazil—the weather is hot and humid year-round.

In general, the high season for travel in South America lasts from June through September, from mid-December through mid-January, and during Carnaval, which takes place the week before Ash Wednesday. The ski season in Chile and Argentina reaches its peak in July and August.

HOLIDAYS, CELEBRATIONS & EVENTS

Many of the holidays and festivals in South America correspond to Catholic and indigenous celebrations. (Sometimes they are a mixture of both.) The whole continent seems to turn into one big party zone during Carnaval, usually in February or March. During the solstices and equinoxes, many indigenous groups, which historically have worshipped the sun, organize traditional celebrations throughout South America.

SOUTH AMERICA CALENDAR OF EVENTS

February

Carnaval. Generally celebrated during the week before the start of Lent, the liveliest Carnaval festivities are held in Argentina, Uruguay, and, most famously, Brazil. In Salta, Argentina, citizens throw a large parade, which includes caricatures of public officials and "water bomb" fights. In Uruguay, Montevideo is the center for the main events, including parades, dance parties, and widespread debauchery. In Brazil, it's the party to end all parties—all life comes to a halt for 4 days of nonstop singing, dancing, drinking, and general over-the-top merrymaking. If you're going to Brazil, mark your calendar for February 5 to February 9, 2005, and February 25 to February 29, 2006.

Festival of the Virgen de la Candelaria. Lively festivities are held in honor of one of the most beloved religious symbols in Bolivia and Peru. In Copacabana, Bolivia, the home of the Virgin, the celebration includes parades and dancing in the street. In Puno, Peru, it's one of the largest and most colorful folk religious festivals in the Americas, with abundant music and dance troupes, many in fantastic costumes and masks. February 2.

Festival de la Canción (Festival of Song), Viña del Mar, Chile. This gala showcases Latin American and international performers during a 5-day festival of concerts held in the city's outdoor amphitheater. The spectacle draws thousands of visitors to an already packed Viña del Mar, so plan your hotel reservations accordingly. Late February.

April

Festival Internacional de Teatro (Caracas International Theater Festival). This festival brings together scores of troupes and companies from around the world and across Venezuela for a 2-week celebration of the theater arts. Performances are held in a variety of theaters (and a plethora of languages) around Caracas, as well as in the streets and plazas. Begun nearly 30 years ago, this is the premiere theater festival in Latin America. For more information, contact the **Ateneo de Caracas** (© **0212/573-4400**). Early to mid-April.

Semana Santa, Uruguay. During Holy Week, Uruguay shuts down. In Montevideo and the smaller cities, you'll find gaucho-style barbecues all over the place. During this time, there are also parades, where you'll be able to hear local folk music. Wednesday through Friday before Easter.

June

Gaucho Parade, Salta, Argentina. The parade features music by folk artists and gauchos dressed in traditional red ponchos with black stripes, leather chaps, black boots, belts, and knives. June 16.

Inti Raymi (Festival of the Sun). This Inca Festival of the Sun— the mother of all pre-Hispanic festivals—celebrates the winter solstice and honors the sun god with traditional pageantry, parades, and dances. In Argentina, celebrations take place in towns throughout the northwest on the night before the summer solstice (around June 20). In Peru, it draws thousands of visitors who fill Cusco's hotels; the principal event takes place on June 24 at the Sacsayhuamán ruins and includes the sacrifice of a pair of llamas. General celebrations continue for several days. In Ecuador, Inti Raymi merges with the fiestas of San Pablo and San Juan to create one big holiday from June 24 to June 29 in the Otavalo area.

August

Independence Day, Bolivia. To celebrate this holiday, Bolivians flock to Sucre, where the leaders of the Bolivian independence movement signed the declaration of independence in 1825. For several days before and several days afterward, there are colorful parades, fireworks, and all sorts of celebrations here. If you can't make it to Sucre, you'll find people partying throughout the country, especially in Copacabana. August 6.

September

Virgen del Valle, Isla de Margarita, Venezuela. The patron saint of sailors, fishermen, and all other seafarers is honored with street fairs and a colorful blessing of the fleet procession. September 8 to September 15.

Independence Day and **Armed Forces Day,** Chile. Chile's rich cultural heritage comes to life with plenty of drinking, dancing, rodeos, and military parades. This holiday can stretch into a 3- to 4-day weekend, and the best place to witness celebrations is in the Central Valley south of Santiago. September 18 and 19.

October

El Señor de los Milagros (Lord of the Miracles), Lima, Peru. Lasting nearly 24 hours and involving tens of thousands of participants, many of whom are dressed in purple, this procession celebrates a Christ image painted by an Angolan slave that survived the 1746 earthquake and has since become the most venerated image in the capital. October 18.

November

All Souls' Day and **Independence Day,** Cuenca, Ecuador. The city celebrates both the Day of the Dead and its independence day with parties, art shows, parades, dances in the streets, and food festivals. November 2 and 3.

December

Santuranticuy Festival, Cusco, Peru. Hundreds of artisans sell traditional carved Nativity figures and saints' images at one of the largest

⌒Tips Packing Tips

Regardless of where you're traveling in South America, the sun is always very strong, so be sure to bring **sunblock** (including some for your lips), **sunglasses,** and a **wide-brimmed hat.** Showers can be a bit grimy, so you may want to consider throwing in an old pair of flip-flops.

If you're traveling in the Andes (parts of Venezuela, Ecuador, Peru, Bolivia, Chile, and western Argentina), be prepared for cold weather. **Layers** are the name of the game here. It can get hot during the day and very cold at night. We recommend a lightweight sweater or sweatshirt, a T-shirt, a fleece jacket, and a windbreaker. Many hotels don't have heat, so be sure to bring flannel or heavy pajamas. At night, you may need a hat and gloves.

Contrary to popular belief, it does get cold in Buenos Aires, Santiago, and Montevideo, especially from June through September. Be sure to bring a **jacket** with you if you're traveling in Argentina, Uruguay, and Chile.

The Tropic of Capricorn cuts its way through northern Chile, northern Argentina, and Paraguay, and through Brazil to São Paulo and Rio de Janeiro. The areas north of here and east of the Andes are considered tropical climates, and **lightweight clothing** is essential. In general, no one will be offended if you wear shorts or sleeveless tops in these areas. Because it can get chilly at night and it often rains, you should be sure to pack a light sweater and rain jacket. **Sport sandals,** such as Tevas, will also come in handy.

If you're heading to the Galápagos, waterproof sandals will be your best friends. During the cooler months from June through September, you should also consider bringing a **wet suit.** The snorkeling is great this time of year, but the water can be mighty frigid.

Most toiletries are available in all large cities. The exception is **tampons;** be sure to bring enough from home to last you through your trip. For some reason, the **toothpaste** in South America can be of poor quality, so bring your own from home. Except in the most rural areas, **film** and **batteries** are easy to find in South America. It can be difficult, however, to find common medicines in South America. We recommend packing a **mini–medicine kit,** just in case. Because food and waterborne illnesses are one of the most common ailments to affect travelers in this area, be sure to bring medicine to treat diarrhea and vomiting. Pain relievers (particularly acetaminophen or paracetamol and ibuprofen) and cold medication are also recommended. Taking multivitamins and vitamins such as super bromelain, which aids in the digestion of parasites, can also help you stay healthy. If you're traveling to the jungle or coastal area, mosquito repellent with DEET is imperative.

handicrafts fairs in Peru in Cusco's Plaza de Armas. December 24.

New Year's Eve, Rio de Janeiro, Brazil. The Copacabana beach is ground zero for an event that attracts more than one million people. The 9.6km (6 miles) of sand are jam-packed with New Year's revelers, and the entertainment never stops, with concerts and performances all night long leading up to the best fireworks display in the world. The evening is also an important one in the African Candomblé religion; it's the night to make an offering to the sea goddess Yemanjá. Candomblé followers, all dressed in white, offer small boats loaded with flowers, candles, mirrors, jewelry, and other pretty trinkets to the sea in a candlelit ceremony with music and dancing. The sight on the beach is truly spectacular. December 31.

5 Travel Insurance

Check your existing insurance policies and credit card coverage before you buy travel insurance. You may already be covered for lost luggage, canceled tickets, or medical expenses. The cost of travel insurance varies widely, depending on the cost and length of your trip, your age, health, and the type of trip you're taking, but expect to pay 5% to 8% of the cost of the vacation itself.

TRIP-CANCELLATION INSURANCE Trip-cancellation insurance helps you get your money back if you have to back out of a trip, if you have to go home early, or if your travel supplier goes bankrupt. Allowed reasons for cancellation can range from sickness to natural disasters to the State Department declaring your destination unsafe for travel. (Insurers usually won't cover vague fears, though, as many travelers discovered who tried to cancel their trips in Oct 2001 because they were wary of flying.) In this unstable world, trip-cancellation insurance is a good buy if you're getting tickets well in advance—who knows what the state of the world, or of your airline, will be in 9 months? Insurance policy details vary, so read the fine print—and especially make sure that your airline is on the list of carriers covered in case of bankruptcy. A good resource is **"Travel Guard Alerts,"** a list of companies considered high-risk by Travel Guard International (see website below). Protect yourself further by paying for the insurance with a credit card—by law, consumers can get their money back on goods and services not received if they report the loss within 60 days after the charge is listed on their credit card statement.

For information, contact one of the following recommended insurers: **Access America** (© 866/807-3982; www.accessamerica.com); **Travel Guard International** (© 800/826-4919; www.travelguard.com); **Travel Insured International** (© 800/243-3174; www.travelinsured.com); and **Travelex Insurance Services** (© 888/457-4602; www.travelex-insurance.com).

MEDICAL INSURANCE For travel overseas, most health plans (including Medicare and Medicaid) do not provide coverage, and the ones that do often

---

Tips Medical Insurance Warning

Under U.S. law, insurance companies are not required to cover any medical expenses incurred in countries on the U.S. State Department's Travel Warning List, even if their policies indicate they will over out-of-country medical expenses. Some supplemental carriers (such as the ones listed in this chapter) will sell travelers coverage for these areas. You can view the Travel Warning List on the State Department's website at **http://travel.state.gov/warnings_list.html.**

require you to pay for services upfront and reimburse you only after you return home. Even if your plan does cover overseas treatment, most out-of-country hospitals make you pay your bills upfront, and send you a refund only after you've returned home and filed the necessary paperwork. As a safety net, you may want to buy travel medical insurance, particularly if you're traveling to a remote or high-risk area where emergency evacuation is a possible scenario. If you require additional medical insurance, try **MEDEX Assistance** (① **410/453-6300;** www.medexassist. com) or **Travel Assistance International** (① **800/821-2828;** www.travel assistance.com; for general information on services, call the company's Worldwide Assistance Services, Inc., at ① **800/777-8710**).

LOST-LUGGAGE INSURANCE
On international flights (including U.S. portions of international trips),

baggage coverage is limited to approximately $9.05 per pound, up to approximately $635 per checked bag. If you plan to check items more valuable than the standard liability, see if your valuables are covered by your homeowner's policy, get baggage insurance as part of your comprehensive travel-insurance package, or buy Travel Guard's "BagTrak" product. Don't buy insurance at the airport, as it's usually overpriced. Be sure to take any valuables or irreplaceable items with you in your carry-on luggage, as many valuables (including books, money, and electronics) aren't covered by airline policies.

If your luggage is lost, immediately file a lost-luggage claim at the airport, detailing the luggage contents. For most airlines, you must report delayed, damaged, or lost baggage within 4 hours of arrival. The airlines are required to deliver luggage, once found, directly to your house or destination free of charge.

6 Health & Safety

STAYING HEALTHY
For general information about health issues in South America, log on to the **Centers for Disease Control and Prevention**'s website at **www.cdc.gov/ travel**. In addition to the recommendations below, the CDC advises visitors to South America to protect themselves against hepatitis A and B. Consult your doctor for more information about these vaccinations.

BEFORE YOU GO
It can be hard to find a doctor you can trust when you're in an unfamiliar place. Try to take proper precautions the week before you depart to avoid falling ill while you're away from home. Amid the last-minute frenzy that often precedes a vacation, make an extra effort to eat and sleep well.

Pack prescription medications in their original labeled containers in your carry-on luggage. Also, bring along

copies of your prescriptions in case you lose your pills or run out. Carry written prescriptions in generic form, in case a local pharmacist is unfamiliar with the brand name. If you wear contact lenses, pack an extra pair or your glasses.

If you worry about getting sick away from home, you may want to consider **medical travel insurance** (see "Travel Insurance," above). Be sure to carry your identification card in your wallet.

If you suffer from a chronic illness, consult your doctor before your departure. For conditions such as epilepsy, diabetes, or heart problems, wear a **Medic Alert identification tag** (① **888/633-4298;** www.medicalert. org), which will immediately alert doctors to your condition and give them access to your records through Medic Alert's 24-hour hot line.

Contact the **International Association for Medical Assistance to Travelers (IAMAT;** ① **716/754-4883** or,

> ## ⓘ *Tips* Medical Warning
>
> The U.S. State Department's Office of Medical Services warns people suffering from the following ailments to exercise caution when traveling to high-altitude destinations such as La Paz, Lake Titicaca, Cusco, and Machu Picchu: sickle cell anemia, heart disease (for men 45 or over or women 55 or over who have two of the following risk factors: hypertension, diabetes, cigarette smoking, or elevated cholesterol), lung disease, and anyone with asthma and on the maximum dosage of medication for daily maintenance, or anyone who has been hospitalized for asthma within a year of their intended trip. It's best to talk with your doctor before planning a trip to a high-altitude destination in South America.

in Canada, 416/652-0137; www.iamat.org) for tips on travel and health concerns in the countries you're visiting, and lists of local, English-speaking doctors. The United States **Centers for Disease Control and Prevention** (© 800/311-3435; www.cdc.gov) provides up-to-date information on necessary vaccines and health hazards by region or country.

GENERAL AVAILABILITY OF HEALTH CARE

Not surprisingly, most of the best hospitals and healthcare centers are in the big cities, but service varies widely. If you do get sick, it's best to contact your home country's consulate or embassy. They all have health departments with staff who can recommend the best English-speaking doctors and hospitals in the area.

COMMON DISEASES & AILMENTS

DIETARY DISTRESS It's unfortunate, but many travelers to South America do suffer from some sort of food or waterborne illness. Symptoms vary widely—from minor cases of diarrhea to debilitating flulike illnesses. To minimize your chances of getting sick, be sure to always drink bottled or boiled water and avoid ice. In high altitudes, you will need to boil water for several minutes longer before it is safe to drink. If you don't have

access to bottled water, you can treat it with iodine or chlorine, with iodine being more effective. You can buy water purification tablets at pharmacies and sporting-goods stores. You should be careful to avoid raw food, especially meats, fruits, and vegetables. If you peel the fruit yourself, you should be fine.

If you do suffer from diarrhea, it's important to keep yourself hydrated. Many pharmacies sell Pedialyte, which is a mild rehydrating solution. Drinking fruit juices or soft drinks (preferably without caffeine) and eating salted crackers are also good remedies.

TROPICAL ILLNESSES Yellow fever, which is transmitted by mosquitoes, exists in the forests of remote jungle areas of South America, mainly in Brazil. You can easily get vaccinated against the disease. After you receive the vaccine, you will receive a certificate, which is good for 10 years.

In the rural, tropical areas of Ecuador, Venezuela, Brazil, Bolivia, Peru, and Colombia, there is a small risk of contracting **malaria.** Mosquitoes carrying malaria cannot survive in altitudes over 1,500m (5,000 ft.), so if you're traveling in the Andes, you won't have to worry about this disease. To protect yourself, wear mosquito repellent with DEET, wear long-sleeved shirts and trousers, and use mosquito nets. You can also take anti-malaria drugs before you go; consult your doctor about the pros and cons of such medications.

Dengue fever, transmitted by an aggressive daytime mosquito, is also a risk in tropical areas. As with malaria, the best prevention is to avoid mosquito bites; there is no vaccine available to protect you from infection.

BUGS & BITES   Snakes, scorpions, and **spiders** rarely bite without provocation. Keep your eyes open and never walk barefoot. If you're in the jungle or rainforest, be sure to shake your clothes and check your shoes before putting them on.

For most travelers, **disease-carrying mosquitoes** will prove to be the most dangerous creatures you encounter. To protect yourself from bites, always wear mosquito repellent and a long-sleeved shirt and trousers. As an extra precaution, check to see whether your hotel offers mosquito netting (or bring your own). Still water is also a source of disease. If you're drawing water from a spring or freshwater source, always be sure to purify it before you drink it.

The chances of contracting **rabies** while traveling in South America are slim. Most infected animals live in rural areas. If you are bitten by an infected cat or dog, wash the wound and get yourself to a hospital as quickly as possible.

HIGH-ALTITUDE   HAZARDS
Altitude sickness is the most common ailment affecting people who travel to high-altitude areas such as Quito, Cusco, or La Paz. Common

symptoms include headaches, nausea, sleeplessness, and a tendency to tire easily. The most common remedies include taking it easy, abstaining from alcohol, and drinking lots of bottled water. To help alleviate these symptoms, you can also take the drug acetazolamide; consult your doctor for a prescription.

The **sun** can also be very dangerous in high altitudes. Be sure to bring plenty of high-powered sunblock and a wide-brimmed hat. Don't let the cold weather fool you—even when it's cold, the sun can inflict serious damage on your skin.

STAYING SAFE

Millions of travelers visit South America without any problems. But as in any foreign destination, you should always keep your wits about you. Before you depart, check for travel advisories from the **U.S. State Department** (www. travel.state.gov), the **Canadian Department of Foreign Affairs** (www.voyage. gc.ca), the **U.K. Foreign & Commonwealth Office** (www.fco.gov.uk/travel), and the **Australian Department of Foreign Affairs** (www.dfat.gov.au/ consular/advice).

Once you're there, keep some common-sense safety advice in mind: Stay alert and be aware of your surroundings; don't walk down dark, deserted streets; and always keep an eye on your personal belongings. Theft at airports and bus stations is not unheard of, so be sure to put a lock on your luggage. See the individual chapters in this book for more specific safety advice.

7 Specialized Travel Resources

FOR TRAVELERS WITH DISABILITIES

Except for the most modern and upscale hotels in major cities, most buildings in South America are not well equipped for travelers with disabilities. Where elevators exist, they are often tiny. Many cities in South American streets are crowded and narrow. In the Andes, the high altitude and steep hills slow everyone down.

Nevertheless, a disability shouldn't stop anyone from traveling. There are more resources out there than ever before. Some of the best include **Moss-Rehab** (www.mossresourcenet.org), which provides a library of accessible-travel resources online; the **Society for Accessible Travel and Hospitality** (© 212/447-7284; www.sath.org; annual membership fees: $45 adults, $30 seniors and students), which offers a wealth of travel resources for all types of disabilities and informed recommendations on destinations, access guides, travel agents, tour operators, vehicle rentals, and companion services; and the **American Foundation for the Blind** (© 800/232-5463; www.afb. org), which offers a referral resource for the blind or visually impaired that includes information on traveling with Seeing Eye dogs.

Also check out the quarterly magazine **Emerging Horizons** ($15 per year, $20 outside the U.S.; www. emerginghorizons.com); **Twin Peaks Press** (© 360/694-2462; http:// disabilitybookshop.virtualave.net/blist 84.htm), offering travel-related books for travelers with special needs; and *Open World Magazine,* published by SATH (see above; subscription: $13 per year, $21 outside the U.S.).

Many travel agencies offer customized tours and itineraries for travelers with disabilities. **Flying Wheels Travel** (© 507/451-5005; www.flying wheelstravel.com) offers escorted tours and cruises that emphasize sports and private tours in minivans with lifts. **Accessible Journeys** (© 800/846-4537 or 610/521-0339; www.disability travel.com) caters specifically to slow walkers and wheelchair travelers and their families and friends.

FOR GAY & LESBIAN TRAVELERS

Most countries in South America are Catholic and conservative. However, in most large cities, there is a thriving underground gay community. To avoid offending local sensibilities or inviting possible verbal harassment in other parts of the continent, we recommend being discreet.

Many agencies offer tours and travel itineraries specifically for gay and lesbian travelers. For information regarding gay and lesbian travel in Ecuador and the Galápagos, contact **Zenith Ecuador Travel** at www.zenith ecuador.com. For travel in Argentina, Chile, and Uruguay, try **Pride Travel** at www.pride-travel.com. **Above and Beyond Tours** (© 800/397-2681; www.abovebeyondtours.com) is the exclusive gay and lesbian tour operator for United Airlines. **Now, Voyager** (© 800/255-6951; www.nowvoyager. com) is a well-known San Francisco–based gay-owned and -operated travel service.

The International Gay and Lesbian Travel Association (IGLTA; © 800/ 448-8550 or 954/776-2626; www. iglta.org) is the trade association for the gay and lesbian travel industry, and offers an online directory of gay- and lesbian-friendly travel businesses; go to their website and click on "Members."

Other excellent resources include *Out and About* (© 800/929-2268 or 415/644-8044; www.outandabout. com), which offers guidebooks and a newsletter ($20 per year for 10 issues); the *Damron* guides (www.damron. com), with separate, annual books for gay men and lesbians; and *Spartacus International Gay Guide* (www. spartacusworld.com), a good, annual guidebook for gay men.

FOR SENIORS

In most South American cultures, there is a deep respect for the elderly. Usually, if you ask for a senior discount, vendors will be happy to help you out. So don't be shy about asking for discounts, but always carry some kind of identification, such as a driver's license, that shows your date of birth. Also, mention the fact that you're a senior when you first make your travel reservations. All major airlines and many hotels offer discounts for seniors. In most cities, people over 60 qualify for reduced admission to theaters, museums, and other attractions, as well as discounted fares on public transportation.

Members of **AARP** (formerly the American Association of Retired Persons), 601 E St. NW, Washington, DC 20049 (℮ **888/687-2277**; www. aarp.org), get discounts on hotels, airfares, and car rentals. AARP offers members a wide range of benefits, including *AARP: The Magazine* and a monthly newsletter. Anyone over 50 can join.

Many reliable agencies and organizations target the 50-plus market. **Elderhostel** (℮ **877/426-8056**; www.elder hostel.org) arranges study programs for those 55 and over (and a spouse or companion of any age) in more than 80 countries around the world. Most courses last 2 to 4 weeks abroad, and many include airfare, accommodations in university dormitories or modest inns, meals, and tuition. **ElderTreks** (℮ **800/741-7956**; www.eldertreks. com) also offers small-group tours to off-the-beaten-path or adventure-travel locations, restricted to travelers 50 and older. **INTRAV** (℮ **800/456-8100**; www.intrav.com) is a high-end tour operator that caters to the mature, discerning traveler (not specifically seniors) with trips around the world that include guided safaris, polar expeditions, private-jet adventures, and small-boat cruises down jungle rivers.

Although many of the specialty books on the market are U.S.-focused, some do provide good general advice and contacts for the savvy senior traveler. Recommended publications offering travel resources and discounts for seniors include the quarterly magazine *Travel 50 & Beyond* (www.travel50 andbeyond.com); *Travel Unlimited: Uncommon Adventures for the Mature Traveler* (Avalon); and *101 Tips for Mature Travelers,* available

from Grand Circle Travel (℮ **800/ 221-2610** or 617/350-7500; www.gct. com).

FOR FAMILIES

Family values are very important in South America, so if you're traveling with your whole family, you can expect locals to welcome you with open arms. Children are treated with the utmost respect. When you take your kids out to eat, the staff will shower them with attention and make special provisions if your kiddies aren't up to eating exotic food. Rice, potatoes, and chicken are on almost every menu, so you won't have to worry about looking for a McDonald's.

South America is also great for children because the wildlife-watching opportunities are tremendous. Bring your kids to the jungle, and they will be eternally grateful to you for letting them get close to caimans and monkeys. In the Galápagos, swimming with sea lions will be an experience that your children will not soon forget. It's also a good idea to teach your children some South American history before your trip. They will be more willing to visit old cathedrals and museums if they understand the value of what they're seeing.

You can find good family-oriented vacation advice on the Internet from sites like the **Family Travel Network** (www.familytravelnetwork.com), an award-winning site that offers travel features, deals, and tips; **Traveling Internationally with Your Kids** (www. travelwithyourkids.com), a comprehensive site offering sound advice for long-distance and international travel with children; and **Family Travel Files** (www.thefamilytravelfiles.com), which offers an online magazine and a directory of off-the-beaten-path tours and tour operators for families.

Familyhostel (℮ **800/733-9753**; www.learn.unh.edu/familyhostel) takes the whole family, including kids ages 8 to 15, on moderately priced domestic and international learning vacations. Lectures, field trips, and sightseeing are guided by a team of academics.

FOR STUDENTS

You'd be wise to arm yourself with an **International Student Identity Card (ISIC)**, which offers substantial savings on rail passes, plane tickets, and entrance fees. It also provides you with basic health and life insurance and a 24-hour help line. The card is available for $22 from **STA Travel** (© **800/ 781-4040;** www.sta.com), the biggest student travel agency in the world. If you're no longer a student but are still under 26, you can get a **International Youth Travel Card (IYTC)** for the same price from the same people, which entitles you to some discounts (but not on museum admissions). (**Note:** In 2002, STA Travel bought competitor **Council Travel** after it went bankrupt. It's still operating some offices under the Council name, but it's owned by STA.)

Travel CUTS (© **800/667-2887** or 416/614-2887; www.travelcuts. com) offers similar services for both Canadians and U.S. residents. Irish students should turn to **USIT** (© **01/ 602-1600;** www.usitnow.ie).

FOR WOMEN

Besides the general safety advice offered in each country chapter, women traveling alone in South America should have few problems. Yes, in many cultures here, men have a very macho attitude, and women traveling alone can expect to get intense stares, catcalls, or even be followed for a few blocks by men asking for a date. But for the most part, these men are harmless. A simple

"Déjame en paz" ("Leave me alone") will send the message that you're not interested.

There have been sporadic, unconfirmed reports of tour guides attacking single women travelers. It's always worth it to pay a few extra dollars to arrange a tour with a reputable travel agency. Talk to your fellow travelers and find out if they have had any problems. If you are attacked, contact the police immediately and notify your embassy. Safety specialists at your embassy will be able to assist you and hopefully work with the police to track down the assailant.

Several websites offer women advice on how to travel safely and happily; a good one to check out is **Journeywoman** (www.journeywoman.com), a "real life" women's travel information network where you can sign up for a free e-mail newsletter and get advice on everything from etiquette and dress to safety. If you'd rather not travel alone, consider **Women Welcome Women World Wide** (5W; © **203/259-7832** in the U.S.; www.womenwelcome women.org.uk), which works to foster international friendships by enabling women of different countries to visit one another (men can come along on the trips; they just can't join the club). It's a big, active organization, with more than 3,500 members from all walks of life in some 70 countries.

Two books worth checking out are *Safety and Security for Women Who Travel,* by Sheila Swan Laufer and Peter Laufer (Travelers' Tales, Inc.), which offers common-sense advice on safe travel; and *A Journey of One's Own: Uncommon Advice for the Independent Woman Traveler* by Thalia Zepatos, a very good resource.

8 Planning Your Trip Online

SURFING FOR AIRFARES

The "big three" online travel agencies, **Expedia.com, Travelocity.com,** and

Orbitz.com sell most of the air tickets bought on the Internet. (Canadian travelers should try expedia.ca and

Travelocity.ca; U.K. residents can go for expedia.co.uk and opodo.co.uk.) Each has different business deals with the airlines and may offer different fares on the same flights, so it's wise to shop around. Expedia and Travelocity will also send you **e-mail notification** when a cheap fare becomes available to your favorite destination. Of the smaller travel agency websites, **SideStep** (www.sidestep.com) has gotten the best reviews from Frommer's authors. It's a browser add-on that purports to "search 140 sites at once," but in reality only beats competitors' fares as often as other sites do.

Also remember to check **airline websites;** you can often shave a few bucks from a fare by booking directly through the airline and avoiding a travel agency's transaction fee. But you'll get these discounts only by booking online: Most airlines now offer online-only fares that even their phone agents know nothing about. For airlines that fly to and from your destination, see "Getting There," below.

Great **last-minute deals** are available through free weekly e-mail services provided directly by the airlines. Most of these are announced on Tuesday or Wednesday and must be purchased online. Most are only valid for travel that weekend, but some can be booked weeks or months in advance. Sign up for weekly e-mail alerts at airline websites.

SURFING FOR HOTELS & RENTAL CARS

Shopping online for hotels is generally done one of two ways: by booking through the hotel's own website or through an independent booking agency (or a fare-service agency like **Priceline;** www.priceline.com). These Internet hotel agencies have multiplied in mind-boggling numbers of late, competing for the business of millions of consumers surfing for accommodations around the world. This competitiveness can be a boon to consumers who have the patience and time to shop and compare the online sites for good deals—but shop they must, for prices can vary considerably from site to site. And keep in mind that hotels at the top of a site's listing may be there

---

Frommers.com: The Complete Travel Resource

For an excellent travel-planning resource, we highly recommend **Frommers.com** (www.frommers.com), voted Best Travel Site by *PC Magazine*. We're a little biased, of course, but we guarantee that you'll find the travel tips, reviews, monthly vacation giveaways, bookstore, and online-booking capabilities thoroughly indispensable. Among the special features are our popular **Destinations** section, where you'll get expert travel tips, hotel and dining recommendations, and advice on the sights to see for more than 3,500 destinations around the globe; the **Frommers. com Newsletter,** with the latest deals, travel trends, and money-saving secrets; our **Community** area featuring **Message Boards,** where Frommer's readers post queries and share advice (sometimes even our authors show up to answer questions); and our **Photo Center,** where you can post queries and share money-saving tips. When your research is done, the **Online Reservations System** (www.frommers.com/book_a_trip) takes you to Frommer's preferred online partners for booking your vacation at affordable prices.

for no other reason than that they paid money to get the placement.

Of the "big three" sites, **Expedia** may be the top hotel booking choice, thanks to its long list of special deals and "virtual tours" or photos of available rooms so you can see what you're paying for (a feature that helps counter the claims that the best rooms are often held back from bargain booking websites). Running a close second is **Travelocity,** which posts unvarnished customer reviews and ranks its properties according to the AAA rating system. Also reliable are **Hotels.com** and **Quikbook. com**. An excellent free program, **Travel-Axe** (www.travelaxe.net), can help you search multiple hotel sites at once, even ones you may never have heard of.

For booking rental cars online, the best deals are usually found at rental-car company websites, although all the major online travel agencies also offer rental-car reservations services. **Priceline** (www.priceline.com) works well for rental cars, too; the only "mystery" is which major rental company you get, and for most travelers the difference between Hertz, Avis, and Budget is negligible.

Be sure to **get a confirmation number** and **make a printout** of any online booking transaction.

9 The 21st-Century Traveler

INTERNET ACCESS AWAY FROM HOME

Travelers have any number of ways to check their e-mail and access the Internet on the road. Of course, using your own laptop—or even a PDA or electronic organizer with a modem—gives you the most flexibility. But even if you don't have a computer, you can still access your e-mail and even your office computer from cybercafes.

WITHOUT YOUR OWN COMPUTER

It's hard nowadays to find a city that *doesn't* have a few cybercafes. Although there's no definitive directory for cybercafes—these are independent businesses, after all—two places to start looking are at **www.cybercaptive.com** and **www.cybercafe.com**.

Aside from formal cybercafes, most **youth hostels** nowadays have at least one computer you can get to the Internet on. And most **public libraries** across the world offer Internet access free or for a small charge. Avoid **hotel business centers,** unless you're willing to pay exorbitant rates.

Most major airports now have **Internet kiosks** scattered throughout their gates. These kiosks, which you'll also see in shopping malls, hotel lobbies, and tourist information offices around the world, give you basic Web access for a per-minute fee that's usually higher than cybercafe prices. The kiosks' clunkiness and high price means they should be avoided whenever possible.

To retrieve your e-mail, ask your **Internet service provider (ISP)** if it has a Web-based interface tied to your existing e-mail account. If your ISP doesn't have such an interface, you can use the free **mail2web** service (www. mail2web.com) to view and reply to your home e-mail. For more flexibility, you may want to open a free, Web-based e-mail account with **Yahoo! Mail** (http://mail.yahoo.com) or **Fastmail** (www.fastmail.fm). (Microsoft's Hotmail is another popular option, but Hotmail has severe spam problems.) Your home ISP may be able to forward your e-mail to the Web-based account automatically.

If you need to access files on your office computer, look into a service called **GoToMyPC** (www.gotomypc. com). The service provides a Web-based interface for you to access and manipulate a distant PC from anywhere—even a cybercafe—provided your "target" PC is on and has an always-on connection to the Internet (such as with Road Runner cable). The service offers top-quality security, but if you're worried about hackers, use your own laptop rather than a cybercafe to access the GoToMyPC system.

WITH YOUR OWN COMPUTER

Major ISPs have **local access numbers** around the world, allowing you to go online by simply placing a local call. Check your ISP's website or call its toll-free number and ask how you can use your current account away from home, and how much it will cost.

If you're traveling outside the reach of your ISP, the **iPass** network has dial-up numbers in most of the world's countries. You'll have to sign up with an iPass provider, who will then tell you how to set up your computer for your destination(s). For a list of iPass providers, go to www.ipass.com and click on "Individual Purchase." One solid provider is **i2roam** (✆ **866/811-6209** or 920/235-0475; www.i2roam.com).

Wherever you go, bring a **connection kit** of the right power and phone adapters, a spare phone cord, and a spare Ethernet network cable. Most business-class hotels throughout the world offer dataports for laptop modems; **call your hotel in advance** to find out what the options are.

USING A CELLPHONE

The three letters that define much of the world's **wireless capabilities** are GSM (Global System for Mobiles), a big, seamless network that makes for easy cross-border cellphone use.

If your cellphone is on a GSM system, and you have a world-capable multiband phone such as many (but not all) Sony Ericsson, Motorola, or Samsung models, you can make and receive calls across much of the globe,

from Andorra to Uganda. Just call your wireless operator and ask for "international roaming" to be activated on your account. Unfortunately, per-minute charges can be high—usually from $1 to $5.

That's why it's important to buy an "unlocked" world phone from the get-go. Many cellphone operators sell "locked" phones that restrict you from using any other removable computer memory phone chip (called a **SIM card**) card other than the ones they supply. Having an unlocked phone allows you to install a cheap, prepaid SIM card (found at a local retailer) in your destination country. (Show your phone to the salesperson; not all phones work on all networks.) You'll get a local phone number—and much, much lower calling rates. Getting an already locked phone unlocked can be a complicated process, but it can be done; just call your cellular operator and say you'll be going abroad for several months and want to use the phone with a local provider.

For many, **renting** a phone is a better bet. (You'll have little to no luck with this in Bolivia, Brazil, or Ecuador, however.) While you can rent a phone from any number of overseas sites, including kiosks at airports and at car-rental agencies, we suggest renting the phone before you leave home. That way you can give loved ones and business associates your new number, make sure the phone works, and take the phone wherever you go—especially helpful for overseas trips through several countries, where local phone-rental agencies often bill in local currency and may not let you take the phone to another country.

Phone rental isn't cheap. You'll usually pay $40 to $50 per week, plus airtime fees of at least a dollar a minute. The bottom line: Shop around.

Two good wireless rental companies are **InTouch USA** (✆ **800/872-7626;**

Online Traveler's Toolbox

Veteran travelers usually carry some essential items to make their trips easier. Following is a selection of online tools to bookmark and use.

- **Foreign Languages for Travelers** (www.travlang.com). Learn basic terms in more than 70 languages and click on any underlined phrase to hear what it sounds like.
- **Intellicast** (www.intellicast.com) and **Weather.com** (www.weather. com). Give weather forecasts for all 50 states and for cities around the world.
- **Mapquest** (www.mapquest.com). This best of the mapping sites lets you choose a specific address or destination, and in seconds, it will return a map and detailed directions.
- **Universal Currency Converter** (www.xe.com/ucc). See what your dollar or pound is worth in more than 100 other countries.

www.intouchglobal.com) and **Road-Post** (© **888/290-1606** or 905/272-5665; www.roadpost.com). Give them your itinerary, and they'll tell you what wireless products you need. InTouch will also, for free, advise you on whether your existing phone will work overseas; simply call © **703/222-7161,** or go to http://intouch global.com/travel.htm.

For trips of more than a few weeks spent in one country, **buying a phone** becomes economically attractive, as many nations have cheap, no-questions-asked prepaid phone systems. Once

you're in your destination, stop by a local cellphone shop and get the cheapest package; you'll probably pay less than US$100 for a phone and a starter calling card. Local calls may be as low as 10¢ per minute, and in many countries incoming calls are free.

True wilderness adventurers should consider renting a **satellite phone.** A satphone is more costly than a cellphone but works where there's no cellular signal and no towers. You can rent satellite phones from RoadPost (see above); InTouch USA offers a wider range of satphones but at higher rates.

10 Getting There

Buenos Aires, Santiago, Lima, and São Paulo receive the greatest number of international flights to South America. If you're planning to explore the whole continent, you might consider starting off at one of these gateways and hooking up there for connecting flights to less-serviced destinations. See the individual country chapters for more detailed information.

TO ARGENTINA

The following carriers offer service to Ezeiza Ministro Pistarini Airport in Buenos Aires:

From the U.S. & Canada Air Canada, Aerolíneas Argentinas, American, LanChile, and United

From the U.K. & Europe Aerolíneas Argentinas, Air France, Alitalia, British Airways, Iberia, KLM, and Lufthansa

From Australia & New Zealand Aerolíneas Argentinas, LanChile, and Qantas

TO BOLIVIA

The following carriers fly to El Alto Airport in La Paz:

From the U.S. & Canada American, LAB, and TACA

From the U.K. & Europe American (via Miami), Varig (via São Paulo)

From Australia & New Zealand Aerolíneas Argentinas (via Buenos Aires)

TO BRAZIL

The following carriers fly to either Guarulhos Airport in São Paulo or Antonio Carlos Jobim Airport (Galeão) in Rio de Janeiro:

From the U.S. & Canada Air Canada, American, Continental, Delta, TAM, United, Varig, and VASP

From the U.K. & Europe Aerolíneas Argentinas, Air France, Alitalia, British Airways, Iberia, KLM, Lufthansa, TAM, Varig, and VASP

From Australia & New Zealand Aerolíneas Argentinas (via Buenos Aires) and LanChile (via Santiago)

TO CHILE

The following carriers fly into Santiago's Aeropuerto Arturo Merino Benítez:

From the U.S. & Canada Air Canada, American, Delta, LanChile, and Lacsa

From the U.K. & Europe Air France, British Airways, KLM, LanChile, and Lufthansa

From Australia & New Zealand LanChile and Qantas (code-share), and Aerolíneas Argentinas

TO ECUADOR

The following carriers offer service to Quito's Aeropuerto Internacional Mariscal Sucre:

From the U.S. & Canada American, Continental, Copa (via Panama), LanChile/LanEcuador, and Taca (via San José)

From the U.K./Europe Avianca, American (via Miami), Continental (via Houston or New York), Iberia, and KLM

From Australia & New Zealand American (via Los Angeles and Miami)

TO PERU

The following carriers fly into Lima's Aeropuerto Internacional Jorge Chávez:

From the U.S. & Canada Air Canada, American, Continental, Lan-Chile, LanPeru, and United

From the U.K./Europe American (via Miami), Iberia, KLM, and United (via Miami or New York)

From Australia & New Zealand American (via Los Angeles and Miami), LanChile (via Santiago or Los Angeles), and United (via Los Angeles)

TO URUGUAY

The following airlines fly into Montevideo's Carrasco International Airport:

From the U.S. & Canada Aerolíneas Argentinas, American, United, and Varig

From the U.K./Europe Aerolíneas Argentinas, American, United, and Varig

From Australia & New Zealand Aerolíneas Argentinas and LanChile

TO VENEZUELA

The following carriers offer service to the Simón Bolívar International Airport (Maiquetía) in Caracas:

From the U.S. & Canada American, Continental, Delta, Lacsa, and Mexicana

From the U.K./Europe Air France, Air Europe, Alitalia, American, British Airways, Iberia, KLM, and Lufthansa

From Australia & New Zealand American (via Los Angeles and Miami), and LanChile (via Santiago)

GETTING THROUGH THE AIRPORT

With the federalization of airport security, security procedures at U.S. airports are more stable and consistent than ever. Generally, you'll be fine if you arrive at the airport **2 hours** before an international flight; if you show up late, tell an airline employee and she'll probably whisk you to the front of the line.

Bring a **current, government-issued photo ID** such as a driver's license or passport. Keep your ID at the ready to show at check-in, the security checkpoint, and the gate.

The TSA has phased out **gate check-in** at all U.S. airports, and **E-tickets** have made paper tickets nearly obsolete. Passengers with E-tickets can still beat the ticket-counter lines by using **airport electronic kiosks** or even **online check-in** from their home computers. Online check-in involves logging on to the airline's website, accessing your reservation, and printing out your boarding pass—and the airline may even offer you bonus miles to do so. If you're using a kiosk at the airport, bring the credit card you used to book the ticket or your frequent-flier card; print out your boarding pass from the kiosk and simply proceed to the security checkpoint with your pass and a photo ID. If you're checking bags or looking to snag an exit-row seat, you will be able to do so using most airlines' kiosks; again, call your airline for up-to-date information. **Curbside check-in** is also a good way to avoid lines, although a few airlines still ban curbside check-in; call before you go.

Security checkpoint lines are getting shorter, but some doozies remain. If you have trouble standing for long periods of time, tell an airline employee; the airline will provide a wheelchair. Speed up security by **not wearing metal objects** such as big belt buckles. If you've got metallic body parts, a note from your doctor can prevent a long chat with the security screeners. Keep in mind that only **ticketed passengers** are allowed past security, except for folks escorting passengers with disabilities or children.

Federalization has stabilized **what you can carry on** and **what you can't**. The general rule is that sharp things

are out, nail clippers are okay, and food and beverages must be passed through the X-ray machine—but that security screeners can't make you drink from your coffee cup. Bring food in your carry-on rather than checking it, as explosive-detection machines used on checked luggage have been known to mistake food (especially chocolate, for some reason) for bombs. Travelers in the U.S. are allowed one carry-on bag, plus a "personal item" such as a purse, briefcase, or laptop bag. Carry-on hoarders can stuff all sorts of things into a laptop bag; as long as it has a laptop in it, it's still considered a personal item. The Transportation Security Administration (TSA) has issued a list of restricted items; check its website, www.tsa.gov, for details.

Airport screeners may decide that your checked luggage needs to be searched by hand. You can now purchase luggage locks that allow screeners to open and re-lock a checked bag if hand-searching is necessary. Look for Travel Sentry certified locks at luggage or travel shops and Brookstone stores (you can buy them online at www.brookstone.com). These locks, approved by the TSA, can be opened by luggage inspectors with a special code or key. For more information on the locks, visit www.travelsentry.org. If you use something other than TSA-approved locks, your lock will be cut off your suitcase if a TSA agent needs to hand-search your luggage.

FLYING FOR LESS: TIPS FOR GETTING THE BEST AIRFARE

Passengers sharing the same airplane cabin rarely pay the same fare. Here are some ways to keep your airfare costs down.

- Passengers who can book their ticket **long in advance,** who can **stay over Saturday night,** or who **fly midweek** or **at less-trafficked hours** will pay a fraction of the full fare. If your schedule is flexible, say so, and ask if you can secure a cheaper fare by changing your flight plans.

- You can also save on airfares by keeping an eye out in local newspapers for **promotional specials** or **fare wars**, when airlines lower prices on their most popular routes. You rarely see fare wars offered for peak travel times, but if you can travel in the off-months, you may snag a bargain.
- Search **the Internet** for cheap fares (see "Planning Your Trip Online," earlier in this chapter).
- Try to book a ticket **in its country of origin.** For instance, if you're planning a one-way flight from Johannesburg to Bombay, a South Africa–based travel agent will probably have the lowest fares. For multileg trips, book in the country of the first leg; for example, book New York–London–Amsterdam–Rome–New York in the U.S.
- **Consolidators,** also known as bucket shops, are great sources for international tickets. Start by looking in Sunday newspaper travel sections; U.S. travelers should focus on the *New York Times, Los Angeles Times,* and *Miami Herald.* For less-developed destinations, small travel agents who cater to immigrant communities in large cities often have the best deals. *Beware:* Bucket shop tickets are usually nonrefundable or rigged with stiff cancellation penalties, often as high as 50% to 75% of the ticket price, and some put you on charter airlines, which may depart at inconvenient times and experience delays. Several reliable consolidators are worldwide and available on the Net. **STA Travel** (www.sta.com) is now the world's leader in student travel, thanks to their purchase of Council Travel; it also offers good fares for travelers of all ages. **FlyCheap** (© 800/FLY-CHEAP; www.fly cheap.com) is owned by package-holiday megalith MyTravel and so has especially good access to fares for sunny destinations. **Air Tickets Direct** (© 800/778-3447; www. airticketsdirect.com) is based in Montreal and leverages the currently weak Canadian dollar for low fares; it'll also book trips to places that U.S. travel agents won't touch, such as Cuba.

- Join **frequent-flier clubs.** Accrue enough miles, and you'll be rewarded with free flights and elite status. It's free, and you'll get the best choice of seats, faster response to phone inquiries, and prompter service if your luggage is stolen, your flight is canceled or delayed, or if you want to change your seat. You don't need to fly to build frequent-flier miles—**frequent-flier credit cards** can provide thousands of miles for doing your everyday shopping.

Travel in the Age of Bankruptcy

Airlines go bankrupt, so protect yourself by **purchasing your tickets with a credit card,** as the Fair Credit Billing Act guarantees that you can get your money back from the credit card company if a travel supplier goes under (and if you request the refund within 60 days of the bankruptcy). **Travel insurance** can also help, but make sure it covers against "carrier default" for your specific travel provider. And be aware that if a U.S. airline goes bust midtrip, a 2001 federal law requires other carriers to take you to your destination (albeit on a space-available basis) for a fee of no more than $25, provided you rebook within 60 days of the cancellation.

11 Escorted Tours, Package Deals & Special Interest Vacations

Before you start your search for the lowest airfare, you may want to consider booking your flight as part of a travel package such as an escorted tour or a package tour. What you lose in adventure, you'll gain in time and money saved when you book accommodations, and maybe even food and entertainment, along with your flight.

ESCORTED TOURS

Escorted tours are structured group tours with a group leader. The price usually includes everything from airfare to hotels, meals, tours, admission fees, and local transportation.

Some people love escorted tours. They let you relax and take in the sights while a bus driver fights traffic for you; they spell out your costs up front; and they take you to the maximum number of sights in the minimum amount of time with the least amount of hassle. On the downside, you often have to pay a lot of money upfront, and your lodging and dining choices are predetermined. Escorted tours can be jam-packed with activities, leaving little room for individual sightseeing or adventure. They also often focus only on the heavily touristed sites, so you miss out on the lesser-known gems.

If you do choose an escorted tour, you should ask a few simple questions before you buy: What is the **cancellation policy?** How busy is the **schedule?** What are the **size** and **demographics** of the group? What's included in the **price?** What **type of room** will you be staying in? If you're traveling alone, what is the **single supplement?**

PACKAGE DEALS

Package deals are not the same thing as escorted tours. With a package tour, you travel independently but pay a group rate. For popular destinations such as Ecuador, Peru, or Brazil, they are a smart way to go because they can save you a lot of money. In many cases,

a package that includes airfare, hotel, and transportation to and from the airport will cost you less than just the hotel alone would have, had you booked it yourself. That's because packages are sold in bulk to tour operators—who resell them to the public at a cost that drastically undercuts standard rates.

The quality of packages, however, varies widely, so be sure to shop around. Questions to ask: What are the **accommodations choices** available and are there price differences? What **type of room** will you being staying in? Also, look for **hidden expenses:** Ask whether airport departure fees and taxes are included in the total cost.

TOUR OPERATORS SPECIALIZING IN SOUTH AMERICA

Organizing a trip to South America can be a royal pain, especially if you don't speak Spanish or Portuguese. These tour companies have connections throughout the whole continent, and their staffs can make all of your travel arrangements for you. Here is a list of some of the best tour operators.

- **Abercrombie & Kent, Inc.** (© 800/554-7016; www. abercrombiekent.com) is the most upscale tour company arranging trips to South America. The company's tours will take you to the best parts of Patagonia, the Galápagos, Peru, Ecuador, Chile, and Argentina.
- **Kon-Tiki Tours & Travel** (© 877/ 566-8454; www.kontiki.org) is run by an American and Peruvian couple. The company specializes in trips throughout South America, including general highlights, and cultural and spiritual tours. You can choose from more than 30 different itineraries in Peru, Argentina, Bolivia, Brazil, Ecuador, and Chile. Prices include guides and airfare.
- **Ladatco Tours** (© 800/327-6162; www.ladatco.com) specializes in

package tours to South and Central America. The company offers Carnaval specials, as well as air-only packages.

- **South American Expeditions** (© 800/884-7474; www.adventure sports.com/asap/travel/exped) offers adventure, cultural, off-the-beaten path, and women-only tours to Ecuador and Peru.
- **Tara Tours Inc.** (© 800/327-0080; www.taratours.com) is one of the most experienced agencies offering package tours to South America. Tours are personalized based on your interests; some of the specialties here include archaeology and spiritual journeys. In general, the company's package tours are great deals.
- **Condor Journeys and Adventures** (© 01700/841-318; www.condor journeys-adventures.com) is a British company that offers tour packages and active vacations throughout South America.
- **Journey Latin America** (© 020/8747-8315; www.journeylatin america.co.uk) is one of the premier British travel agencies offering trips to South America. The company can arrange airfare and tour packages throughout the whole continent.
- **Adventure Associates Pty Ltd.** (© 02/9389-7466; www.adventure associates.com) is the best source in Australia for high-end package tours to South America and Antarctica.

SPECIAL INTEREST VACATIONS

Here's a list of companies offering educational and volunteer opportunities in South America.

- **AmeriSpan** (© 800/879-6640 or 215/751-1100; www.amerispan. com) helps students arrange programs that combine language study, travel, and volunteer opportunities, throughout South America.
- **Amigos de las Américas** (© 800/231-7796 or 713/782-5290; www. amigoslink.org) is always looking for volunteers to promote public health, education, and community development in rural areas of Latin America.
- **Earthwatch Institute** (© 800/776-0188 or 978/461-0081; www. earthwatch.org) supports sustainable conservation efforts of the earth's natural resources. The organization can always use volunteers for its research teams in South America.
- **Habitat for Humanity International** (© 229/924-6935, or check the website for local affiliates; www.habitat.org) needs volunteers to help build affordable housing in more than 79 countries in the world, including most countries in South America.
- **Spanish Abroad, Inc.** (© 888/722-7623 or 602/778-6791; www. spanishabroad.com) organizes intensive language-study programs throughout Latin America.

12 Getting Around

In general, the roads in South America are often in very poor condition. But there is an enormous network of bus lines, and if you have the time, patience, and a butt of steel (the roads are bumpy and the seats are lumpy), you can travel easily by bus from one country to another. Because car-rental agencies don't allow cars to be taken across international borders, it's very difficult to drive around the continent. There is also no reliable international train service. All in all, flying makes a lot of sense, especially if you're short on time.

See individual country chapters for complete details on getting around within each country.

BY PLANE

LanChile offers the most comprehensive service in South America. Besides flying to most major cities in Chile and Peru, the airline also offers flights between Argentina, Brazil, Bolivia, Ecuador, Uruguay, and Venezuela. **Grupo Taca, Aerolíneas Argentinas,** and **Varig** also have several international routes.

If you plan on traveling between Chile, Argentina, Uruguay, and Brazil, you should consider buying a **Mercosur Air Pass.** The pass allows you to make two stopovers in each country, with a total maximum of 10 stopovers. The pass is good for 7 to 30 days. Prices are based on mileage covered. You must buy the air pass outside of South America, and your initial flight must be on Aerolíneas Argentinas, American, Continental, Delta, LanChile, TAM, United, or Varig. For more information, contact **Globotur Travel** at © **800/998-5521** or visit www.globotur.com.

LanChile and American Airlines have joined forces to create the **Visit South America Airpass,** which allows you to travel between Argentina, Bolivia, Brazil, Colombia, Chile, Ecuador, Peru, Venezuela, and Uruguay. You must purchase a minimum of three flight segments, but you can only travel for 60 days or less. Again, fares are based on distance traveled. You must buy the pass in your home country. Contact **LanChile** (© **800/735-5526;** www.lanchile. com) or **American Airlines** (© **800/433-7300;** www.aa.com) for more information.

BY BUS

It's possible to travel from Venezuela all the way to the tip of Argentina by bus. In fact, for most South Americans, buses are the main method of transportation. However, it's hard to find direct international routes. Usually, you take a bus to the border, where you must switch to a bus owned by a company in the country you have just entered. From there, you may have to take a bus to the largest nearby city, where you then can switch to a bus to your final destination. It's not the most efficient way to travel, but it's certainly cheap and a great way to see the countryside.

13 The Active Vacation Planner

Many outdoor activities can be arranged easily and cheaply upon arrival in South America. Local operators will have everything you need and can arrange guides and even companions. The nonprofit **South American Explorers** (www.samexplo.org) is a great resource if you're in Lima, Cusco, or Quito. The offices here can provide useful information about the quality of most outfitters throughout the continent.

BIRD-WATCHING Over 3,100 species of birds either live or migrate through South America. Some of the rarest birds in the world live in and near the jungles of the Amazon rainforest. The jungle areas of Brazil, Peru, and Ecuador are among the best bird-watching spots in the world. The Galápagos Islands in Ecuador are also a birder's paradise—albatrosses; penguins; flightless cormorants; red-footed, blue-footed, and masked boobies; and the short-eared owl are just some of the rare birds that you'll see here. Peru's Manu Biosphere Reserve is also impressive: With more than 1,000 bird species recorded here, it has the highest concentration of birdlife on earth.

CLIMBING Many a mountaineer has traveled to South America to scale some of the highest peaks in the world. The snowy peaks of Patagonia offer some of the most challenging climbs on the continent. But you don't have to head all way down south. In Ecuador, you can climb the glacier-covered Cotopaxi, which at 5,804m (19,347 ft.) is the highest active volcano in the world.

DIVING   The Galápagos Islands, off the coast of Ecuador, offer some of the most exciting diving in the world. You'll have the opportunity to see schools of hammerhead sharks, as well as exotic underwater life. Serious divers should consider booking a special diving cruise around the islands. The Caribbean coast off of Venezuela is also a popular dive spot.

MOUNTAIN   BIKING   The 8,050km-long (5,000-mile) Andes mountain range offers some excellent mountain-biking opportunities. From Ecuador down to Patagonia, you'll find mountain-biking outfitters galore. But be careful: The roads are often poorly maintained. Some routes are narrow and open onto steep precipices. It's important to rent a high-quality bike that can deal with the conditions. The South American Explorers Club advises bikers to use Kona, Trek, or Cannondale brand bikes. Cheaper bikes may not be able to survive the rough terrain.

RIVER RAFTING   The Amazon is the world's second-longest river, and running it or one of its many tributaries is one of the great thrills in South America. The wildest parts run through Ecuador, Peru, and Brazil. And in central Chile, as the water rages down from the Andes to the Pacific, you'll find some of the wildest white-water rafting anywhere.

SKIING   July and August are prime ski season in South America. The ski areas in Chile and southern Argentina are considered the Alps of South America. In Argentina, the glitterati head to Bariloche, while Chileans consider the ski resorts Valle Nevado (east of Santiago) and Portillo to be sacred ground.

SURFING   It's been said that some of the longest breaks in the world exist off the coast of Peru. But small beach towns that cater to the surfing set dot the whole Pacific coast of South America. The Galápagos Islands have also begun to attract serious surfers to their windy shores. Not surprisingly, the Pacific can get quite cold—be sure to bring a wet suit. For warmer waters, surfers should head to the Caribbean coast of Venezuela. Henry Pitter National Park in Venezuela has become a hot spot.

SWIMMING, SNORKELING & OTHER   WATERSPORTS   The Atlantic coast of South America offers wonderful watersports opportunities. Punta del Este in Uruguay is one of the premier South American beach resorts. From December through March, the Argentine elite come here to sail, swim, water-ski, or just get close to the sea. The warm Caribbean waters off of Venezuela are also great for snorkeling, water-skiing, and windsurfing. The Pacific Coast isn't as enticing, but visitors to the Galápagos will find that the snorkeling there is out of this world.

14 Recommended Reading

Paul Theroux's *Old Patagonian Express: By Train Through the Americas* (Houghton Mifflin, 1997) provides a beautifully written account of his travels throughout South America. If you're interested in a scholarly read, pick up John Charles Chasteen's *Born in Blood and Fire: A Concise History of Latin America* (W.W. Norton & Company, 2000). The book only begins with the arrival of the Europeans in the Americas, but it gives a good overview of the diverse regions of Latin America.

ANTARCTICA Antarctica has produced some of the most dramatic adventure stories in history, and surely the most riveting is *Endurance: Shackleton's Incredible Voyage* by Alfred Lansing (Carroll & Graf, 1999), which recounts Ernest Shackleton's failed attempt to reach the South Pole. Other adventure tales include *Antarctica: Both Heaven and Hell* by Reinhold Messner (Mountaineers Books, 1992), who skied across Antarctica in 1989 and 1990; and *A First Rate Tragedy: Robert Falcon Scott and the Race to the South Pole* by Diana Preston (Houghton Mifflin, 1998).

ARGENTINA For a review of the country's history, try Nicolas Shumway's *The Invention of Argentina* (University of California Press, 1993). Argentine historians Jorge B. Rivera and José Gobello are instrumental in helping demystify modern Argentina. Their books are difficult to find in English; if you read Spanish, try Gobello's *Crónica General del Tango* (Editorial Fraterna, 1980). Jorgelina Corbatta offers the best account of Argentina's "dirty war" under the military dictatorship from 1976 to 1983 in *Narrativas de la Guerra Sucia en Argentina* (Ediciones Corregidor, 1999).

Jorge Luis Borges sits at the top of Argentine fiction writers; read *Collected Fictions* (Penguin, 1999) for an overview of his work. Manuel Puig's *Kiss of the Spider Woman* (Vintage, 1991) and Julio Cortázar's *The Winners* (New York Review Books, 1999) are good picks for more contemporary Argentine writing.

BOLIVIA *The Fat Man from La Paz* (Seven Stories Press, 2000), edited by Rosario Santos, is a collection of contemporary short stories by Bolivian writers. The stories provide readers with a vivid picture of life in Bolivia.

Che Guevara spent his last days on the run in Bolivia. There are several books detailing his journey. One of the best accounts is the *Complete Bolivian Diaries of Che Guevara and Other Captured Documents* (Cooper Square Press, 2000) by Ernesto Guevara and Daniel James.

Herbert S. Klein's *Bolivia: The Evolution of a Multi-Ethnic Society* (Oxford University Press, 1992) does an excellent job of delving into the government, economics, and history of Bolivia. Klein also touches on art, architecture, and societal relations.

For more information about the sophisticated pre-Inca Tiwanaku culture, your best bet is Alan L. Kolata's *The Tiwanku: Portrait of an Andean Civilization* (Blackwell Publishing, 1993).

BRAZIL There is no single good general history covering Brazil from 1500 to the present. *Colonial Brazil,* edited by Leslie Bethell (Cambridge University Press, 1983), is a scholarly but readable account of Brazil under the Portuguese, while Peter Flynn's *Brazil: A Political Analysis* covers political history from the birth of the first republic to the close of the second dictatorship. For a fascinating introduction to a whole range of topics in Brazil, pick up the excellent anthology *Travelers' Tales: Brazil,* edited by Annette Haddad and Scott Doggett (1997). *Tristes Tropiques* (Penguin, 1992) is a classic work of travel writing by the great French anthropologist Claude Lévi-Strauss.

Until he passed away in 2001, Bahian novelist Jorge Amado was considered a serious candidate for the Nobel Prize. His greatest novels revolve around the colorful characters of his beloved Bahia, and include *Dona Flor and Her Two Husbands* (Avon, 1998) and *Gabriela, Clove and Cinnamon* (Bard Books, 1998). In a previous generation, Joaquim Maria Machado de Assis wrote fiercely ironic novels and short stories, many set in Rio towards the end of the 19th century. His works available in English include *The Epitaph of a Small Winner*

(Noonday Press, 1990). Brazil's greatest social realist is Graciliano Ramos. His masterpiece *Barren Lives* (University of Texas Press, 1971) is considered to be one of Brazil's finest novels.

CHILE A quick, comprehensive guide to all things Chilean, Susan Roraff and Laura Camacho's *Culture Shock! Chile* (Graphic Arts Center, 2002), explains Chilean etiquette and culture. For history and a look into the Pinochet legacy that came to define modern Chile, try the following books: *A History of Chile, 1808–1994* by Simon Collier and William F. Sater (Cambridge University Press, 1996); *A Nation of Enemies: Chile Under Pinochet* by Pamela Constable and Arturo Valenzuela (W.W. Norton & Company, 1993); and *Chile: The Other September 11* by Ariel Dorfman, et al. (Ocean Press, 2002).

Chile boasts two literary Nobel Prize winners, Gabriela Mistral and Pablo Neruda; however, most North Americans are probably most familiar with the Chilean export Isabel Allende, whose popular novels such as *Of Love and Shadows* (Bantam, 1998) and *House of the Spirits* (Bantam, 1989) have been made into major motion pictures. English translations of Neruda's exceptional poetry are usually available, such as the classics *Canto General* (University of California Press, 2000) and *The Heights of Machu Picchu* (Noonday Press, 1999), but it is less common to find English versions of Mistral's works.

COLOMBIA John Hemmings's *The Search for El Dorado* (Phoenix Press, 2001) gives readers insight into the history and conquest of Colombia by the Spanish. For a general overview of Colombia's economy, government, history, geography, destinations, people, and more, try *Colombia, a Country Study Guide* by USA International Business Publications, which is updated yearly and aimed at businesspeople. To understand the political crisis and never-ending civil war in Colombia, try *Colombia: Fragmented Land, Divided Society* by Frank Safford and Marco Palacios (Oxford University Press, 2001); *The Making of Modern Colombia: A Nation in Spite of Itself* by David Bushnell, Georg Wilhelm, and Friedrich Hegel (University of California Press, 1993); or *Bandits, Peasants, and Politics: The Case of "La Violencia"* by Gonzalo Sánchez (University of Texas Press, 2001).

Colombia's—and all of South America's—premiere literary figure is Nobel Prize–winner Gabriel García Márquez, known for novels such as *Love in the Time of Cholera* (Penguin, 1994) and *One Hundred Years of Solitude* (Harperperennial Library, 1998), both of which are widely available. *Vivir para Contarla,* the first volume of his three-part autobiography, is now available in English as *Living to Tell the Tale* (Alfred A. Knopf, 2003).

ECUADOR Ecuador and the Galápagos Islands have captured the imagination of many North American and British writers. Herman Melville's *Las Encantadas* (Fawcett Publications, 1967) is a collection of various pieces from the 19th century that provide descriptions of the islands themselves, the inhabitants, and the whalers who passed through the area. Kurt Vonnegut's *Galápagos* (Delta, 1999) is a hilarious story about human evolution. It starts off with a story about a small group of people who are shipwrecked and forever stuck on a small isolated island in the Galápagos. It then follows the evolution of these people for a million years into the future.

If you're interested in learning about how Charles Darwin formed his theory of evolution, you should pick up Darwin's *Voyage of the Beagle* (Penguin, 1989) or his *Origin of Species* (Grammercy, 1998). Michael H. Jackson's *Galápagos: A Natural History* (University of Calgary Press, 1994) is the best authority on the natural history of plants and animals in the Galápagos.

For a quick, simple, and concise history of Ecuador, try reading *In Focus Ecuador: A Guide to the People, Politics, and Culture* (Interlink Pub Group, 2000) by Wilma Roos and Omer Van Renterghem. Linda Newson's *Life and Death in Early Colonial Ecuador* (University of Oklahoma Press, 1995) looks at the native people living in Ecuador in the 16th century and discusses how they were affected by both the Inca and Spanish conquests.

PERU Perhaps the classic work on Inca history is *The Conquest of the Incas* by John Hemming (Harvest Books, 1973), a very readable narrative of the fall of a short-lived but uniquely accomplished empire.

Mario Vargas Llosa, Peru's most famous novelist and a perennial candidate for the Nobel Prize, was nearly elected the country's president back in 1990. *Aunt Julia and the Scriptwriter* (Penguin, 1995) is one of his most popular works; *The Real Life of Alejandro Mayta* (Noonday Press, 1998) is a dense meditation on Peruvian and South American revolutionary politics that blurs the lines between truth and fiction; and *Death in the Andes* (Penguin, 1997) is a deep penetration into the contemporary psyche and politics of Peru. Another side of the author is evident in the small erotic gem *In Praise of the Stepmother* (Penguin, 1991).

URUGUAY Lawrence Weschler reports on Uruguay's "dirty war" in *A Miracle, A Universe* (University of Chicago Press, 1998). Uruguayan journalist Eduardo Galeano examines the consequences of colonialism and imperialism in *Open Veins of Latin America* (Monthly Review Press, 1998).

Blood Pact & Other Stories (Curbstone Press, 1997) is one of the few collections of beloved writer Mario Benedetti available in English. A good place to start with José Enrique Rodó's essays is *Ariel* (University of Texas Press, 1988).

VENEZUELA Perhaps no piece of literature is as closely associated with Venezuela as Sir Arthur Conan Doyle's 1912 *The Lost World* (Doherty, Tom Associates, 1997), which is set in an area modeled after Venezuela's Amazonas region. *The Lost World* has spawned numerous imitators and literary offspring, and has served as the model for a host of films, including *Jurassic Park.*

Anyone with even the slightest interest in Venezuelan literature should start with Rómulo Gallegos's 1929 classic *Doña Bárbara* (English translation by Robert Malloy; Smith Peter, 1990), a tale of love and struggle on the Venezuelan plains. Gallegos was a former president and is widely considered the country's principal literary light. Also of interest are Gabriel García Márquez's *The General in His Labyrinth* (Penguin, 1991), a fictional account of Simón Bolívar's dying days, and Isabel Allende's *Eva Luna* (Bantam, 1989), which is set in a town based on the Venezuelan city of Colonia Tovar.

4

Argentina

by Shane Christensen & Haas Mroue

First the numbers: Argentina is the world's eighth largest country, covering more than a million square miles. To the north, it is bordered by Bolivia, Paraguay, Brazil, and Uruguay (the latter directly northeast of Buenos Aires). The Andes cascade along Argentina's long western border with Chile, where the continent's highest peaks stand.

Now the visuals: The polychromatic hills and desert plateau of the Northwest are as far removed from the bustling activity of Buenos Aires as is the frigid scrubland of Patagonia from the dazzling waterfalls and subtropical jungle of Iguazú. The land's diversity is reflected in its people: Witness the contrast between the capital's largely immigrant population and the indigenous people of the Northwest. For us, Argentina's cultural and geographic diversity make this South America's most fascinating travel destination.

But Argentina has another, less sunny legacy—one of political upheaval, economic avarice, and military repression—from the free-spending populism of Juan and Eva Perón to the human rights abuses suffered during the government's late-1970s *Guerra Sucia* (Dirty War). An economic nose dive brought on by upper-class greed and unchecked corruption has led to widespread looting and riots. The peso has been devalued and the country is limping along in fiscal uncertainty—a shocking state of affairs for a land so fertile, so rich in natural resources. But even amid this latest existential crisis, Argentines cling fast to a national self-image of a bold, joyful, reflective people, whose economic troubles will eventually work themselves out. As long as their woes don't interfere with a night out among friends.

1 The Regions in Brief

Many people who spend at least a week in Argentina choose between exploring Buenos Aires with an excursion to Iguazú Falls, and going south to the Lake District and Patagonia. Buenos Aires requires at least several days to appreciate and absorb the city's sophisticated grandeur (and partisan that we are, we think a week is better). To see the spectacular falls of Iguazú from both the Argentine and Brazil sides, you need at least 2 full days. If you choose to head south to the Lake District and Patagonia, you can do it in a week, but you'd spend a good chunk of that time just getting down there. It's better to allot 2 weeks and allow time to savor the distinctive landscape.

BUENOS AIRES & THE PAMPAS Buenos Aires, a rich combination of South American energy and European sophistication, is a city of grand plazas and boulevards. Take time to wander its impressive museums and architectural sites, stroll along its fashionable waterfront, and immerse yourself in its dynamic culture and nightlife. A thick Argentine steak in a local *parrilla* (grill), a visit to

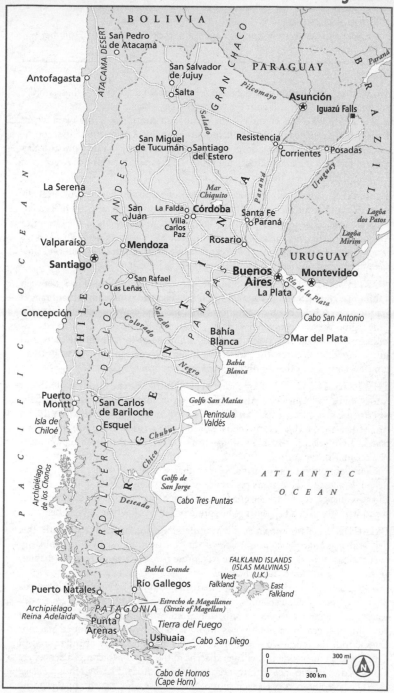

Argentina

BOLIVIA

San Pedro
de Atacamá

ATACAMA DESERT

San Salvador
de Jujuy

Salta

GRAN CHACO

PARAGUAY

Pilcomayo

Antofagasta

Asunción

Iguazú Falls

Salado

San Miguel
de Tucumán

Santiago
del Estero

Resistencia

Corrientes

Posadas

La Serena

ANDES

Mar
Chiquito

La Falda

Córdoba

San
Juan

Villa
Carlos
Paz

Santa Fe

Paraná

Paraná

Uruguay

Lagôa
dos Patos

Valparaíso

Mendoza

Rosario

Lagôa
Mirim

Santiago

URUGUAY

San Rafael

Las Leñas

Buenos
Aires

Montevideo

La Plata

Río de la Plata

Concepción

CHILE

Salado

Colorado

PAMPAS

Cabo San Antonio

Bahía
Blanca

Mar del Plata

Negro

Bahía
Blanca

PACIFIC OCEAN

Puerto
Montt

San Carlos
de Bariloche

Esquel

Isla de
Chiloé

Chubut

Chico

Golfo San Matías

Península
Valdés

Archipiélago
de los Chonos

CORDILLERA DE LOS ANDES

ARGENTINA

Golfo de
San Jorge

Deseado

ATLANTIC

OCEAN

Cabo Tres Puntas

Bahía Grande

FALKLAND ISLANDS
(ISLAS MALVINAS)
(U.K.)

West
Falkland

East
Falkland

Puerto Natales

Río Gallegos

Archipiélago
Reina Adelaida

PATAGONIA

Estrecho de Magallanes
(Strait of Magellan)

Punta
Arenas

Tierra del Fuego

Ushuaia

Cabo San Diego

Cabo de Hornos
(Cape Horn)

| 0 | | 300 mi |
| 0 | | 300 km |

Shameless Plug

For more in-depth coverage of Argentina, pick up a copy of *Frommer's Argentina & Chile.*

---

a San Telmo antiques shop, a dance in a traditional tango salon—these are the small experiences that will connect you to the city's soul.

The heartland of the country is the pampa, an enormous fertile plain where the legendary gauchos roamed. It includes the provinces of Buenos Aires, southern Santa Fe, southeastern Córdoba, and eastern La Pampa. The pampas today contain many of the major cities, including the capital. One-third of Argentines live in greater Buenos Aires.

MISIONES   This small province in the Mesopotamia enjoys a subtropical climate responsible for the region's flowing rivers and lush vegetation. The **Iguazú Falls** are created by the merger of the Iguazú and Paraná rivers at the border of Argentina, Brazil, and Paraguay. In this chapter, we explore Iguazú Falls, and we review lodging and dining on the Argentine side of the border. You can find similar information on the Brazilian part of the falls in chapter 6.

NORTHWEST   The Andes dominate the Northwest, with ranges between 4,800m (16,000 ft.) and 6,900m (23,000 ft.). The two parallel mountain ranges are the Salto-Jujeña, cut by magnificent multicolored canyons called *quebradas*. This region is often compared with the Basin and Range regions of the southwestern United States, and can be visited from the historic towns of **Salta** and **Jujuy.** For space reasons, the Northwest is not included in this guide, but you can find coverage of the region in *Frommer's Argentina & Chile.*

THE LAKE DISTRICT   Argentina's Lake District extends from Junín de los Andes south to Esquel—an Alpine-like region of snowy mountains, waterfalls, forests, and glacier-fed lakes. **San Martín de los Andes, Bariloche,** and **Villa La Angostura** are the chief destinations, but this isn't an area where you stay in one place. Driving tours, boating, skiing—you'll be on the move from the moment you set foot in the region.

Considering the enormous, flat pampa that separates Buenos Aires from the Lake District, and the region's proximity to Chile, many visitors opt to include a trip to Chile's Lake District while here. To avoid the crowds, we highly recommend that you plan a trip during the spring or fall (see "When to Go," below).

PATAGONIA   Also known as the Magellanic Region or the Deep South, this dry, arid region at the southern end of the continent has soared in popularity over the past 5 years. We discuss the Argentine part of Patagonia in this chapter, and the Chilean part of it in chapter 7.

Vast, open pampa, the colossal Northern and Southern ice fields, and hundreds of glaciers characterize Patagonia, as well as the jagged peaks of the Andes as they reach their terminus, emerald fiords, and wind, wind, wind. Getting here is an adventure—it usually takes 24 hours if coming directly from the United States or Europe. But the journey pays off in the beauty and singularity of the region. **El Calafate** is a tourist-oriented village adjacent to the Perito Moreno Glacier, where visitors stand face-to-face with its tremendous wall of ice. **El Chaltén** is a village of 200 whose numbers swell each summer with those who come to marvel at the towers of mounts Fitz Roy, Cerro Torre, and Puntiagudo. This is the second most-visited region of Argentina's Los Glaciares National Park and possibly its most exquisite, for the singular nature of the granite spires here that shoot up, torpedo-like, above huge tongues of ice that descend from the Southern Ice Field.

TIERRA DEL FUEGO Even farther south than the Deep South, this archipelago at the southern tip of South America is, like Patagonia, shared by both Chile and Argentina. The main island, separated from the mainland by the Strait of Magellan, is a triangle with its base on the Beagle Channel. Tierra del Fuego's main town is **Ushuaia,** the southernmost city in the world. Many use the city as a jumping-off point for trips to Antarctica or sailing trips around Cape Horn.

2 Planning Your Trip to Argentina

VISITOR INFORMATION

IN THE U.S. The Argentina Government Tourist Office is located at 12 W. 56th St., New York, NY 10019 (© **212/603-0443;** fax 212/315-5545); and 2655 Le Jeune Rd., Penthouse Suite F, Coral Gables, FL 33134 (© **305/442-1366;** fax 305/441-7029).

IN CANADA Basic tourist information can be obtained by the Embassy of Argentina in Ottawa (see "Entry Requirements," below).

IN THE U.K. Contact the Embassy of Argentina in London (see "Entry Requirements," below) or consult Argentina's Ministry of Tourism website (see below).

ONLINE

- **www.embajadaargentina-usa.gov:** Up-to-date travel information from the Argentine embassy in Washington, D.C.
- **www.sectur.gov.ar:** This Ministry of Tourism site has travel information for all of Argentina, including a virtual tour of the country's tourist regions, shopping tips, links to city tourist sites, and general travel facts.
- **www.mercotour.com:** A Spanish-language travel site focused on adventure and ecological excursions, with information on outdoor activities in both Argentina and Chile.
- **www.argentinatravel.com:** This promotional site advertises vacation packages, accommodations, transportation, and *estancia* (ranch) stays.

ENTRY REQUIREMENTS

Citizens of the United States, Canada, the United Kingdom, Australia, New Zealand, and South Africa require a passport to enter the country. No visa is required for citizens of these countries for tourist stays of up to 90 days. For more information concerning longer stays, employment, or other types of visas, contact the embassies or consulates in your home country.

ARGENTINE EMBASSY LOCATIONS

In the U.S.: 1718 Connecticut Ave. NW, Washington, DC 20009 (© **202/238-6460;** www.embajadaargentina-usa.gov)

In Canada: Royal Bank Center, 90 Sparks St., Suite 910, Ottawa, ON K1P 5B4 (© **613/236-2351;** fax 613/235-2659; www.argentina-canada.net)

In the U.K.: 65 Brooke St., London W1Y 4AH (© **020/7318-1300;** fax 020/7318-1301)

In Australia: John McEwan House, Level 2, 7 National Circuit, Barton, ACT 2600 (© **02/6273-9111;** fax 02/6273-0500; www.argentina.org.au)

In New Zealand: Sovereign Assurance Building, Level 14, 142 Lambton Quay, Wellington (© 04/472-8330; fax 04/472-8331; www.arg.org.nz)

CUSTOMS

Travelers coming from countries not bordering Argentina are exempt from all taxes on traveling articles and new articles up to $300, and an additional $300 for goods purchased at Argentine duty-free shops.

MONEY

The official Argentine currency is the **peso,** made up of 100 **centavos.** Money is denominated in notes of 2, 5, 10, 20, 50, and 100 pesos and coins of 1 peso and 1, 5, 10, 25, and 50 centavos. Argentina ended its parity with the dollar in January 2002. At press time, the exchange rate was 2.87 pesos to the dollar.

Prices have fallen across the board with the peso's devaluation, and Argentina has become a bargain for foreign visitors. Often, prices are less than half of what they were before the economic crisis. Prices in this chapter continue to be quoted in dollars, but realize that high inflation and volatile exchange rates will limit their accuracy. Prices in Buenos Aires are typically higher than in the rest of Argentina.

CURRENCY EXCHANGE   U.S. dollars are widely accepted in Buenos Aires and can be used to pay taxis, hotels, restaurants, and stores. Do keep some pesos on hand because you might run into spots where you'll need them. U.S. dollars are less useful in rural areas (and places to exchange money less common), so plan ahead. You can convert your currency in hotels, at *casas de cambio* (money-exchange houses), at some banks, and at the Buenos Aires International Airport. Change American Express traveler's checks in Buenos Aires at **American Express,** Arenales 707 (© 011/4130-3135); it is difficult to change traveler's checks outside the capital. We recommend that you carry sufficient pesos (or purchase traveler's checks in pesos) when you venture into small-town Argentina.

ATMs   ATMs are easy to access in Buenos Aires and other urban areas, but don't bet on finding them off the beaten path. Typically, they are connected to **Cirrus**

Telephone Dialing Info at a Glance

- **To place a call from your home country to Argentina,** dial the international access code (011 in the U.S., 0011 in Australia, 0170 in New Zealand, 00 in the U.K.) plus the country code (54), the city or region's area code, and the local number.
- **To make long-distance calls within Argentina,** dial a 0 before the city or region's area code. Note that tariffs are reduced from 10pm to 8am.
- **To place an international call from Argentina,** add 00 before the country code. Holders of **AT&T** credit cards can reach the money-saving USA Direct from Argentina by calling toll-free © 0800/555-4288 from the north, or 0800/222-1288 from the south. Similar services are offered by **MCI** (© 0800/555-1002) and **Sprint** (© 0800/555-1003 from the north, or 0800/222-1003 from the south).
- Dial **110** for **directory assistance** (most operators will speak English) and **000** to reach an **international operator.**

(© 800/424-7787) or **PLUS** (© 800/843-7587) networks. Many ATMs also accept Visa and MasterCard, less often American Express and Diners Club.

CREDIT CARDS   If you choose to use plastic, Visa, American Express, Master-Card, and Diners Club are the commonly accepted cards. However, bargain hunters take note: Some establishments—especially smaller ones—don't like pay-ing the fee to process your credit card and will give you a better price if you pay cash. Credit cards are accepted at most hotels and restaurants except the very cheap-est ones. You cannot use credit cards in many taxis or at most attractions (museums, trams, and so on). To report a lost or stolen **MasterCard,** call © 0800/555-0507; for **Visa,** © 0800/666-0171; for **American Express**, call © 0810/555-2639.

WHEN TO GO

PEAK SEASON   The seasons in Argentina are the reverse of those in the Northern Hemisphere. Buenos Aires and the Lake District are ideal in fall (Mar–May) and spring (Sept–Nov), when temperatures are mild and crowds have yet to descend. The beaches and resort towns are packed with vacationing Argentines in summer (Dec–Mar), while Buenos Aires becomes somewhat deserted. (You decide whether that's a plus or a minus—hotel prices usually drop here in summer.) Plan a trip to Patagonia and the southern Andes in their sum-mer, when days are longer and warmer. Winter (June–Aug) is the best time to visit Iguazú and the Northwest, when the rains and heat have subsided; but spring (Aug–Oct) is also pleasant, as temperatures are mild and the crowds have cleared out.

CLIMATE   Except for a small tropical area in northern Argentina, the coun-try lies in the temperate zone, characterized by cool, dry weather in the south, and warmer, humid air in the center. Accordingly, January and February are quite hot—often in the high 90s to more than 100°F (35°C–40°C)—while win-ter (about July–Oct) can be chilly.

PUBLIC HOLIDAYS   Public holidays are New Year's Day (Jan 1); Good Friday; Easter; Veterans' Day (Apr 2); Labor Day (May 1); First Argentine Government (May 25); Flag Day (June 20); Independence Day (July 9); Anniversary of the Death of General San Martín (Aug 17); Columbus Day (Oct 12); Feast of the Immaculate Conception (Dec 8); and Christmas (Dec 25).

HEALTH CONCERNS

Life in Argentina presents few health issues. Argentina requires no vaccinations to enter the country, except for passengers coming from countries where cholera and yellow fever are endemic. Some people who have allergies (especially respi-ratory ones) can be affected by air pollution in the city and the high level of pollen during spring. Because motor vehicle crashes are a leading cause of injury among travelers, walk and drive defensively. Avoid nighttime travel if possible and always use your seat belt.

Most visitors find that Argentine food and water is generally easy on the stom-ach. Water and ice are considered safe to drink in Buenos Aires. Be careful with food from street vendors, especially in dodgy neighborhoods of Buenos Aires and in cities outside the capital. Beef is a staple of the Argentine diet, and in early 2001, Argentine cattle farmers had discovered traces of foot-and-mouth disease among their herds. As a result, the United States banned importation of Argen-tine beef. The situation, however, has improved. The E.U. has lifted its restric-tions on fresh beef from Argentina; the United States still bans Argentine fresh boneless beef, but allows thermal processed (cooked) meat. The main concern for the United States is the threat of foot-and-mouth disease entering the country and infecting livestock. To be safe, anyone who has visited a farm or ranch or gone hiking in the Argentine countryside should inform the Animal and Plant Health Inspection Service (APHIS) inspector at the airport upon return to the United States. The APHIS inspector will advise you of any precautions you should take.

The medical facilities and personnel in Buenos Aires and the other urban areas in Argentina are very professional and comparable to the U.S. standards. Argentina has a system of socialized medicine, where basic services are free. Private clinics are inexpensive by Western standards.

ALTITUDE SICKNESS If you visit the Andes, ascend gradually to allow your body to adjust to the high altitude, thus avoiding altitude sickness. Altitude sickness, known as *soroche* or *puna,* is a temporary yet often debilitating affliction that affects about a quarter of travelers to the northern *altiplano,* or the Andes, at 2,427m (7,872 ft.) and up. Nausea, fatigue, headaches, shortness of breath, and sleeplessness are the symptoms, which can last from 2 to 5 days. If you feel as though you've been affected, drink plenty of water, take aspirin or ibuprofen, and avoid alcohol and sleeping pills. To prevent altitude sickness, acclimatize your body by breaking the climb to higher regions into segments.

AUSTRAL SUN The shrinking ozone layer in southern South America has caused an onset of health problems among its citizens, including increased incidents of skin cancer and cataracts. If you are planning to travel to Patagonia, keep in mind that on "red alert" days (typically Sept–Nov), it is possible to burn in *10 minutes.* If you plan to be outdoors, protect yourself with strong sunblock, a long-sleeved shirt, a wide-brimmed hat, and sunglasses.

MALARIA & OTHER TROPICAL AILMENTS The Centers for Disease Control and Prevention (www.cdc.gov) recommends that travelers to northwestern Argentina take malaria medication, but we have not heard of any incidents of malaria. Cholera has appeared from time to time in the Northwest, but such tropical diseases do not seem to be a problem in the sultry climate of Iguazú.

GETTING THERE
BY PLANE
Argentina's main international airport is **Ezeiza Ministro Pistarini** (EZE; ℂ **011/ 4480-9538**), located 42km (26 miles) outside Buenos Aires. You will be assessed a departure tax of approximately $31 upon leaving the country. For flights from Buenos Aires to Montevideo, Uruguay, the departure tax is $5. Passengers in transit and children under 2 are exempt from this tax. However, visitors are advised to verify the departure tax with their airline or travel agent, as the exact amount changes frequently.

FROM THE U.S. & CANADA Argentina's national airline, **Aerolíneas Argentinas** (ℂ **800/333-0276** in the U.S., or 011/4340-3777 in Buenos Aires; www.aerolineas.com.ar), flies nonstop from Miami and New York's JFK. **American Airlines** (ℂ **800/433-7300** in the U.S., or 011/4318-1111 in Buenos Aires; www.aa.com) flies nonstop from Miami and Dallas–Fort Worth. **United Airlines** (ℂ **800/241-6522** in the U.S., or 0810/777-8648 in Buenos Aires; www. united.com) flies nonstop from Miami and Washington, D.C. (Dulles Airport). Approximate flight time from Miami to Buenos Aires is 9 hours. **Air Canada** (ℂ **888/247-2262** in Canada, or 011/4327-3640 in Buenos Aires; www. aircanada.ca) flies from Toronto to Buenos Aires via Santiago, Chile.

FROM THE U.K.   **British Airways** (© 0845/773-3377 in the U.K., or 011/4320-6600 in Buenos Aires; www.britishairways.co.uk) flies nonstop from London Gatwick to Buenos Aires; approximate flight time is 13 hours. **Iberia** (© 0845/601-2854 in the U.K., or 011/4131-1000 in Buenos Aires; www.iberia.com) connects through Madrid.

FROM AUSTRALIA & NEW ZEALAND   **Aerolíneas Argentinas** (© 1800/22-22-15 in Australia; www.aerolineas.com.ar) flies from Sydney, with a stop in Auckland. Approximate flight time from Sydney is 16 hours.

GETTING AROUND
BY PLANE

The easiest way to travel Argentina's vast distances is by air. **Aerolíneas Argentinas** (© 0810/222-86527; www.aerolineas.com.ar) connects most cities and tourist destinations in Argentina, including Córdoba, Jujuy, Iguazú, and Salta. Its competitors, **LAPA** (© 0810/777-5272 in Buenos Aires; www.lapa.com.ar) and **Southern Winds** (© 0810/777-7979; www.sw.com.ar), serve roughly the same routes. By American standards, domestic flights within Argentina are expensive. In Buenos Aires, domestic flights and flights to Uruguay travel out of **Jorge Newbery Airport** (© 11/4514-1515), 15 minutes from downtown.

If you plan to travel extensively in Argentina, consider buying the **Airpass Visit Argentina,** issued by Aerolíneas Argentinas, available for non-Argentine residents. You must purchase the pass in your home country; it cannot be purchased once in Argentina. This pass offers discounts for domestic travel in conjunction with your international ticket. Those traveling to Argentina with Aerolíneas Argentinas can purchase unlimited flight coupons for $40 to $145 each, depending on the destination. If you arrive in Argentina on an eligible airline other than Aerolíneas Argentinas, the price for each coupon (with a minimum purchase of three) is $54 to $169. No flight segment can be flown twice in the same direction; the pass is valid for 3 months. For more information, contact the Aerolíneas office in your home country or try **www.aerolineas.com.ar**.

BY BUS

Argentine buses are comfortable, safe, and efficient. They connect nearly every part of Argentina as well as bordering countries. In cases where two classes of bus service are offered (*común* and *diferencial*), the latter is more luxurious. Most long-distance buses offer toilets, air-conditioning, and snack/bar service. Bus travel is usually considerably cheaper than air travel for similar routes. Many travelers would likely prefer a slightly more expensive 2-hour flight to a 20-plus-hour bus ride. But taking a long-distance bus in South America is a singular cultural experience, so you might want to try it.

Among the major bus companies that operate out of Buenos Aires are **La Veloz del Norte** (© 011/4315-2482), serving destinations in the Northwest including Salta and Jujuy; **Singer** (© 011/4315-2653), serving Puerto Iguazú and Brazilian destinations; and **T. A. Chevallier** (© 011/4313-3297), serving Bariloche.

BY CAR

Argentine roads and highways are generally in good condition, with the exception of some rural areas. Most highways have been privatized and charge nominal tolls. In cities, Argentines drive exceedingly fast, and do not always obey traffic lights or lanes. When driving outside the city, remember that *autopista* means motorway or highway, and *paso* means mountain pass. Don't drive in rural areas at night, as cattle sometimes overtake the road to keep warm and are nearly impossible to see. Wear your seat belt; it's required by Argentine law, although few Argentines actually wear them. U.S. driver's licenses are valid in greater Buenos Aires, but you need an Argentine or international license to drive in most other parts of the country. A car that uses gasoil (as the name implies, a hybrid fuel of gas and oil) is the cheaper option fuel-wise, about 15% cheaper than unleaded gas.

The **Automóvil Club Argentino (ACA),** Av. del Libertador 1850 ((© **011/ 4802-6061**), has working arrangements with International Automobile Clubs. The ACA offers numerous services, including roadside assistance, road maps, hotel and camping information, and discounts for various tourist activities.

CAR RENTALS   Many international car-rental companies operate in Argentina with offices at airports and in city centers. The major companies are **Hertz** ((© **800/654-3131** in the U.S.; www.hertz.com), **Avis** ((© **800/230-4898** in the U.S.; www.avis.com), **Dollar** ((© **800/800-3665** in the U.S.; www.dollar.com), and **Thrifty** ((© **800/847-4389** in the U.S.; www.thrifty.com); see "Buenos Aires," below, for locations in the capital. Car rental will cost about $50 per day for an intermediate size vehicle, including unlimited miles and 21% tax (ask for any special promotions, especially on weekly rates). Check to see if your existing automobile insurance policy (or a credit card) covers insurance for car rentals; otherwise, purchasing insurance should run you an extra $10 a day.

TIPS ON DINING

Argentines can't get enough beef. While exporting some of the finest meat in the world, they still manage to keep enough of this national treasure at home to please natives and visitors alike. However, in 2001, Argentina reported an outbreak of foot-and-mouth disease, the virus that aggressively swept through Great Britain's cloven-hooved livestock. Several countries, including the United States, banned the import of fresh Argentine beef. The situation has improved markedly since then (see "Health Concerns," above). I wouldn't warn against eating Argentina's world-renowned beef, but if you're truly concerned, check the National Center for Infectious Diseases website at www.cdc.gov for latest safety information.

Tips **Late-Night Dining**

In Argentina, meal times are, on average, later than English-speaking travelers may be used to. Dinner frequently does not begin until after 9pm, and restaurants stay open until well past midnight.

The Argentine social venue of choice is the *asado* (barbecue). Families and friends gather at someone's home and barbecue prime ribs, pork, chicken, sausages, sweetbreads, kidneys—the list goes on. You can enjoy this tradition while eating out; many restaurants are referred to interchangeably in Spanish as parrillas or *parrilladas,* with open-air grills and, occasionally, large spits twirling animal carcasses over a roaring fire. For the full experience, ask for the *parrillada mixta* (mixed grill), which includes many of the items mentioned above. And don't forget the *chimichurri* sauce—an exotic blend of chile and garlic—to season your meat. A note on steaks: You can order them *bien cocida* (well done), *a punto* (medium rare), or *jugosa* (rare, literally "juicy").

But vegetarians exhale: Argentina offers some great alternatives to the red-meat diet. One of the imprints Italians have left on Argentine culture is a plethora of pasta dishes, pizzas, and even *helados* (ice cream), reminiscent of

Italian gelato. In addition, ethnic restaurants are springing up throughout Buenos Aires, stretching beyond traditional Spanish, Italian, and French venues to Japanese, Indian, Armenian, and Thai. Ethnic dishes come to life with fresh meats, seafood, and vegetables—the products of Argentina's diverse terrain. If you're just looking for a snack, try an *empanada,* a turnover pastry filled with minced meat, chicken, vegetables, or corn and varying a bit by region.

BEVERAGES

An immensely popular afternoon custom is the sharing of *mate,* a tea made from the *yerba mate* herb. In the late afternoon, Argentines pass a gourd filled with the tea around the table, each person sipping through a metal straw with a filter on the end. The drink is bitter, so you might opt to add some sugar. *Mate* is such an important part of daily life in Argentina that if people plan to be out of the house at teatime, they tote a thermos with them.

Argentina boasts a few wine-growing regions; the best known is Mendoza, but Salta and La Rioja also produce impressive vintages. Malbec is the best Argentine red wine and is an engaging companion to any *parrillada mixta.* The Torrontes grape, a dry white wine, has won various international competitions as well.

TYPICAL ARGENTINE DISHES

Look for some of these favorites on your menu:

- *Bife de chorizo:* Similar to a New York strip steak, but twice as big. Thick and tender, usually served medium rare.
- *Bife de lomo:* Filet mignon, 3 inches thick. Tender and lean.
- *Buseca:* Stew with sausages.
- *Locro criollo:* Beef stew with potatoes.
- *Milanesa:* Breaded meat filet, sometimes in a sandwich.
- *Panqueques:* Either dessert crepes filled with *dulce de leche* (caramel) and whipped cream, or salted crepes with vegetables.
- *Provoletta:* Charbroiled slices of provolone cheese served at a parrilla.

TIPS ON SHOPPING

Porteños (as residents of Buenos Aires are called) consider their city one of the fashion capitals of the world and, even if it's not Milan, Buenos Aires boasts many of the same upscale stores you would find in New York or Paris. (The wealthiest Argentines still fly to Miami for their wardrobes.) Do not expect to find a city full of indigenous textiles and crafts as you would elsewhere in Latin America; Hermès, Louis Vuitton, Versace, and Ralph Lauren are more on the mark in wealthy districts such as Recoleta or Palermo. The European boutiques sell much better quality clothes than their Argentine counterparts, with the exception of furs, wool, and some leather goods, which are excellent across the country. Keep your receipts for invoices over 70 pesos from stores participating in tax-free shopping; you should be able to get a refund of the 21% value-added tax (abbreviated IVA in Spanish) when you leave the country. Forms are available at the airport.

FAST FACTS: Argentina

American Express Offices are located in Buenos Aires, Bariloche, Salta, San Martín, and Ushuaia. In Buenos Aires, the Amex office is at Arenales 707 (© 11/4130-3135).

Business Hours Banks are open weekdays from 10am to 3pm. Shopping hours are weekdays 9am to 8pm and Saturday 9am to 1pm. Shopping centers are open daily from 10am to 8pm. Some stores close for lunch.

Electricity If you plan to bring a hair dryer, radio, travel iron, or any other small appliance, pack a transformer and a European-style adapter, since electricity in Argentina runs on 220 volts. Note that most laptops operate on both 110 and 220 volts. Luxury hotels usually have transformers and adapters available.

Embassies In Buenos Aires: **United States,** Av. Colombia 4300 (© 11/4774-5333); **Australia,** Villanueva 1400 (© 11/4777-6580); **Canada,** Tagle 2828 (© 11/4805-3032); **New Zealand,** Echeverría 2140 (© 11/4787-0583); and the **United Kingdom,** Luis Agote 2412 (© 11/4803-6021).

Emergencies The following emergency numbers are valid throughout Argentina. For an ambulance, call © **107;** in case of fire, call © **1100;** for police assistance, call © **101.**

Hospitals The best hospitals in Buenos Aires are **British Hospital,** Perdriel 74 (© 11/4309-6400); **Sanatorio San Lucas,** Belgrano 369, San Isidro (© 11/4742-8888); and **Mater Dei,** San Martin de Tours 2952 (© 11/4809-5555). All have English-speaking doctors on staff.

Internet Access Cybercafes have begun to pop up on seemingly every corner in Buenos Aires, and are found in other cities as well, so it won't be hard to stay connected while in Argentina. Access is reasonably priced (usually averaging $1–$2 per hour) and connections are reliably good.

Language Argentina's official language is Spanish, but it's easy to find English-speakers in major hotels, restaurants, and shops—particularly in the big cities. Many working-class Argentines speak little or no English, and it's also much less common in rural areas.

Liquor Laws The official drinking age in Argentina is 18.

Maps Reliable maps can be purchased at the offices of the Automóvil Club Argentino, Av. del Libertador 1850, in Buenos Aires (© **11/4802-6061** or 11/4802-7071).

Newspapers & Magazines Major local papers are *Clarín* (independent), *Página* (center-left), and *La Nación* (conservative). The *Buenos Aires Herald* is the (quite good) local English newspaper. The *International Herald Tribune* is widely available at news kiosks around the country. Some hotels in Buenos Aires will deliver a *New York Times* headline news fax to your room; inquire when booking or checking in.

Post Offices/Mail Post offices are generally open Monday through Friday from 8am to 6pm and Saturday from 8am to 1pm. Airmail postage for a letter weighing 7 ounces or less from Argentina to North America and Europe is $1. Mail takes on average between 10 and 14 days to get to the U.S. and Europe.

Restrooms Public facilities are generally very good; you can duck into hotel lobbies, restaurants, cafes, and shopping centers.

Safety Petty crime has increased significantly in Buenos Aires as a result of Argentina's economic crisis. Travelers should be especially alert to pickpockets and purse snatching on the streets and on buses and trains. Violent crime has increased in the suburbs of the capital and in Buenos Aires Province. Take care not to be overly conspicuous, walking in pairs or groups when possible. Avoid demonstrations, strikes, and other political gatherings. In Buenos Aires, do not take taxis off the street; you should call for a radio taxi or *remise* (private, unmetered taxi) instead. Take similar precautions when traveling in Argentina's other big cities.

Smoking Smoking is a pervasive aspect of Argentine society, and you will find that most everyone lights up in restaurants and clubs. You can, however, request a nonsmoking table in a restaurant, and you will usually be accommodated.

Taxes Argentina's value-added tax (IVA) is 21%. You can recover this 21% at the airport if you have purchased local products totaling more than $200 (per invoice) from stores participating in tax-free shopping. Forms are available at the airport.

Telephone & Fax Domestic and international calls are expensive in Argentina, especially from hotels (rates fall 10pm–8am). Direct dialing to North America and Europe is available from most phones.

Public phones take either phone cards (sold at kiosks on the street) or coins (less common). Local calls cost 20 centavos to start and charge more the longer you talk. Telecentro offices—found everywhere in city centers—offer private phone booths where calls are paid when completed. Most hotels offer fax services, as do all telecentro offices.

For tips on dialing, see the "Telephone Dialing Info at a Glance" box on p. 82.

Time Zone Argentina does not adopt daylight savings time, so the country is 1 hour ahead of Eastern Standard Time in the United States in summer and 2 hours ahead in winter.

Tipping A 10% tip is expected at cafes and restaurants. Give at least $1 to bellboys and porters, 5% to hairdressers, and leftover change to taxi drivers.

Water In Buenos Aires, the water is perfectly safe to drink. But if you are traveling to more remote regions of Argentina, it's best to stick with bottled water for drinking.

3 Buenos Aires ★★

The elegance of Europe and the spirit of South America live side by side in Buenos Aires. Founded by immigrants along the shores of the Rio de la Plata, Buenos Aires built its identity on Spanish, Italian, and French influences, which appear in the grand boulevards, expansive parks, magnificent architecture, and ever-changing fashion of Argentina's beautiful capital. Take a walk through neighborhoods like Recoleta and Belgrano, for example, and you'll be convinced you're still in the Old World. Even *Porteños,* as residents of Buenos Aires are called, characterize themselves as more European than South American.

If Buenos Aires has a European face, its soul is intensely Latin. This is a city where the sun shines brightly, where people speak passionately, where family and friendship still come first. It is a city where locals go outside to interact, lining the streets, packing cafe terraces, and strolling in parks and plazas. Visit the historic neighborhoods of San Telmo and La Boca, where the first immigrants

Buenos Aires

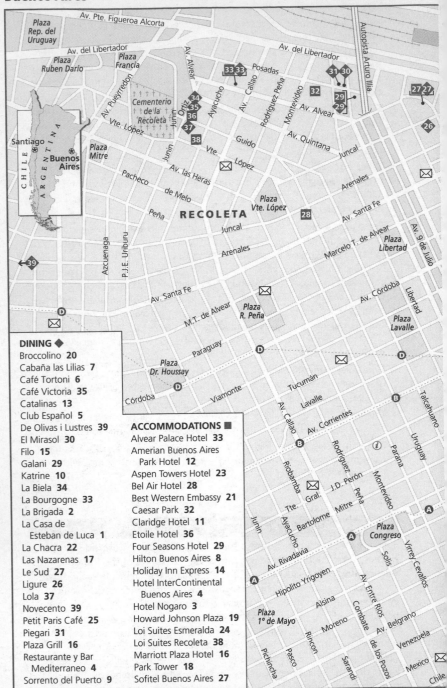

DINING ◆
Broccolino **20**
Cabaña las Lilias **7**
Café Tortoni **6**
Café Victoria **35**
Catalinas **13**
Club Español **5**
De Olivas i Lustres **39**
El Mirasol **30**
Filo **15**
Galani **29**
Katrine **10**
La Biela **34**
La Bourgogne **33**
La Brigada **2**
La Casa de
  Esteban de Luca **1**
La Chacra **22**
Las Nazarenas **17**
Le Sud **27**
Ligure **26**
Lola **37**
Novecento **39**
Petit Paris Café **25**
Piegari **31**
Plaza Grill **16**
Restaurante y Bar
  Mediterraneo **4**
Sorrento del Puerto **9**

ACCOMMODATIONS ■
Alvear Palace Hotel **33**
Amerian Buenos Aires
  Park Hotel **12**
Aspen Towers Hotel **23**
Bel Air Hotel **28**
Best Western Embassy **21**
Caesar Park **32**
Claridge Hotel **11**
Etoile Hotel **36**
Four Seasons Hotel **29**
Hilton Buenos Aires **8**
Holiday Inn Express **14**
Hotel InterContinental
  Buenos Aires **4**
Hotel Nogaro **3**
Howard Johnson Plaza **19**
Loi Suites Esmeralda **24**
Loi Suites Recoleta **38**
Marriott Plaza Hotel **16**
Park Tower **18**
Sofitel Buenos Aires **27**

Information
Post office
Subway

0   0.25 mi
0   0.25 km

Padre Mujica

Estación
Retiro

Av. del Libertador

*Darsena
Norte*

PARQUE NATURAL
Y RESERVA ECOLOGICA
COSTANERA

Av. Ramos Mejía
San Martín
Av. E. Madero
Av. Amartida Argentina

18

Plaza
Libertador
Gral.
San Martín

17

16 16

15

Av. Maipú
Florida

M.T. de Alvear

24

23

Paraguay

Córdoba

14

13

12

10

MICROCENTER

Av.

Viamonte

21 20

22

11

San Martín

Lavalle

Tucumán

Florida

Maipú

Esmeralda

Suipacha

Av. Corrientes

Sarmiento

Tte. Gral. J.D. Perón

Reconquista

25 de Mayo

Av. Leandro N. Alem

Av. Rosales

**PUERTO
MADERO**

9

8

Av. Macacha
Guemes

*Parque
Mujeres
Argentinas*

Av. de los Italianos

Av. E. Madero

Av. Alicia Moreau

de Justo

Av. de la Rábida

B

B

B

D C

SAN NICOLAS

Av. Pte. Roque Saenz Peña
(Diagonal Norte)

Libertad

Cerrito

C. Pellegrini

Bartolome Mitre

Rivadavia

*Plaza
de Mayo*

A

A

D

E

A

Balcarce

Defensa

Bolívar

Perú

Moreno

Av. Belgrano

Av. Paseo Colón

Av. Ing. Huergo

Azopardo

7

6

A

5

4 4

MONSERRAT

Rivadavia

Av. de Mayo

A

Hipólito Yrigoyen

Alsina

Av. J.A. Rocha (Diagonal Sur)

3

E

Chacabuco

Piedras

Venezuela

Mexico

Chile

Santiago del Estero

Salta

Lima

Av. 9 de Julio

Bernardo de Irigoyen

Tacuari

C

C

E

San José

Av. Belgrano

**SAN
TELMO**

Av. Independencia

Estados Unidos

Carlos Calvo

Humberto Iº

2

*Plaza
Dorrego*

1

Balcarce

Av. San Juan

Autopista 25 de Mayo

Pte. Luis Saenz Peña

Av. Independencia

arrived, and you will find working-class Argentines living alongside the city's oldest tango salons. Stand in Plaza de Mayo, the historic center of Buenos Aires where citizens gather in pivotal moments, to gain a sense of the city's political and social dynamism. And walk along the revived harbor of Puerto Madero to see where Argentina reaches out to the rest of the world.

While exploring Buenos Aires, you will find a city of contradictions. Great wealth exists alongside considerable poverty. The economy has continued to falter, but hotels and restaurants remain inexplicably busy. *Porteños* seem self-assured, although the population is intensely image-conscious and uncertain about the future. And Buenos Aires defines Argentina, yet has little to do with the rest of the country. All these elements demonstrate the complexity of a city searching for identity among its South American and European influences.

This search has become more prominent as ordinary Argentines reel from the country's economic meltdown of late 2001. Middle-class citizens watched their savings disappear in the wake of sharp currency devaluations, ending the peso's decade-long parity with the dollar and with it the illusion that Argentina was a rich nation. Weekend shopping, eating out, clubbing, and traveling to other countries—routine for many *Porteños* in the 1990s—ceased to be possible for everyone but the very rich. Homelessness, malnutrition, and street crime have risen as a result of ongoing economic troubles, and foreign travelers must exercise greater caution than they did in the past. But one of the few upsides of the country's financial woes, besides the fact that Argentina is a much, much cheaper country to visit now, is an increased recognition among Argentines that tourists provide oxygen for the economy. Do not let Argentina's economic situation keep you away: Buenos Aires remains a fascinating and welcoming city to visit.

ESSENTIALS
GETTING THERE
BY PLANE   International flights arrive at **Ezeiza International Airport** (© 11/ 4480-0224), located 34km (21 miles) west of downtown Buenos Aires. You can reach the city with several shuttle companies and *remise* services; you will see official stands with exact fares in the airport once you clear Customs. Taxis from the airport to the center of town cost about $11 to $15.

Domestic airlines and flights to Uruguay use **Jorge Newbery Airport** (© 11/ 4514-1515), located only 15 minutes from downtown. Inexpensive taxis and *remises* cost about $5 to $10 to get you to and from the city center. At both airports, only take officially sanctioned transportation and do not accept transportation services from any private individuals. **Manuel Tienda León** (© 11/4314-3636) is the most reliable transportation company, offering buses and *remises,* to and from the airports.

BY BUS   The **Estación Terminal de Omnibus,** Av. Ramos Mejía 1680 (© 011/ 4310-0700), located near Retiro Station, serves all long-distance buses.

BY CAR   In Buenos Aires, travel by *subte* (subway), *remise,* or radio taxi is easier and safer than driving yourself. Rush-hour traffic is chaotic, and parking is difficult. If you do rent a car, park it at your hotel and leave it there.

ORIENTATION
Although Buenos Aires is a huge city, the main tourist neighborhoods are concentrated in a small, comparatively wealthy section near the Río de la Plata. The "microcenter," which extends from Plaza de Mayo to the south and Plaza San Martín to the north, and from Plaza del Congreso to the west and Puerto Madero to the east, forms the city center. San Telmo, La Boca, Puerto Madero, Recoleta,

and Palermo surround the microcenter. The city layout is fairly straightforward, where *avenidas* signify two-way avenues and *calles* one-way streets, while *diagonales* cut streets and avenues at 45-degree angles. Each city block extends 100m (328 ft.), and building addresses indicate the distance on that street.

The **microcenter** includes Plaza de Mayo (the political and historic center of Buenos Aires), Plaza San Martín, and Avenida 9 de Julio (the widest street in the world). Most commercial activity is focused here, as are the majority of hotels and restaurants. Next to the microcenter, the riverfront area called **Puerto Madero** boasts excellent restaurants and nightlife as well as new commercial areas. Farther south, **La Boca, Monserrat,** and **San Telmo** are the historic neighborhoods where the first immigrants arrived and *milonga* and tango originated.

The city's most strikingly European neighborhood, **Recoleta,** offers fashionable restaurants, cafes, and evening entertainment amid rich French architecture. It's home to the city's cultural center as well as the Recoleta Cemetery, where key personalities such as Evita are buried. To the northwest, **Palermo** is a neighborhood of parks, mansions, and gardens—perfect for a weekend picnic or evening outing. Another similarly wealthy neighborhood, **Belgrano,** lies farther west.

STREET MAPS   Ask the front desk of your hotel for a copy of "The Golden Map" and "QuickGuide Buenos Aires" to help you navigate the city and locate its major attractions. You can purchase driving maps from the **Automóvil Club Argentino,** Av. del Libertador 1850 (© **11/4802-6061** or 11/4802-7071).

GETTING AROUND

The Buenos Aires metro—called the subte—is the fastest, cheapest way to get around. Buses are also convenient, though less commonly used by tourists. Get maps of metro and bus lines from tourist offices and most hotels. (Ask for the "QuickGuide Buenos Aires.") All metro stations and most bus stops have maps.

BY METRO   Five subte lines connect commercial and tourist areas in the city Monday through Saturday from 7am to 8pm and Sunday and holidays from 8am to 8pm. The flat fare is 70 centavos, with tickets purchased at machines or windows at every station. You can also buy a subte pass for 7 pesos, valid for 10 trips. Line A connects Plaza de Mayo to Primera Junta. Line B runs from near Puerto Madero (Av. Leandro N. Alem) to Federico Lacroze. Line C travels between the city's train stations, Retiro and Constitución. Line D runs from Congreso de Tucumán to Catedral. Line E links Bolívar with Plaza de los Virreyes. Although the subte is the fastest and cheapest way to travel in Buenos Aires, it gets crowded during rush hour and hot in summer.

Neither the Recoleta nor Puerto Madero neighborhoods have subte access. Most of Puerto Madero, however, can be reached via the L. N. Alem subte. (It's a 5- to 20-min. walk, depending on which dock you're going to.)

BY BUS   One hundred forty bus lines operate in Buenos Aires 24 hours a day. Local buses, called *colectivos,* are mostly used by city workers. The minimum fare is 75 centavos and goes up depending on distance traveled. Pay your fare inside the bus at an electronic ticket machine, which accepts coins only. Many bus drivers, provided you can communicate with them, will tell you the fare for your destination and help you with where to get off.

BY TAXI   Like busy bees, thousands of black-and-yellow cabs crowd the streets of Buenos Aires. Fares are relatively inexpensive, with an initial meter reading of 1.22 pesos increasing 15 centavos every 200m (654 ft.) or each minute. *Remises* and radio taxis are much safer than street taxis and only a bit more expensive. To request a taxi by phone, consider **Taxi Premium** (© **11/4374-6666**), which is used by the Four Seasons Hotel, or **Radio Taxi Blue** (© 11/4777-8888), contracted by the Alvear Palace Hotel.

BY CAR   Driving in Buenos Aires is like warfare: Never mind the lane, disregard the light, and honk your way through traffic. It's far safer, and cheaper, to hire a *remise* or radio taxi with the help of your hotel or travel agent. If you must drive, international car-rental companies rent vehicles at both airports. Most hotels offer parking for a small fee.

The main offices in Buenos Aires are **Hertz**, Paraguay 1138 (© 011/4816-8001); **Avis**, Cerrito 1527 (© 011/4307-5944); **Dollar**, Marcelo T. de Alvear 449 (© 011/4315-8800); and **Thrifty**, Av. Leandro N. Alem 699 (© 011/4315-0777). Expect to pay about $50 per day for an intermediate-size car, including unlimited miles and 21% tax. Add another $10 per day if you require insurance.

ON FOOT   Buenos Aires is a walker's city. The microcenter is small enough to navigate by foot, and you can connect to adjacent neighborhoods by catching a taxi or using the subte. If you have several days in Buenos Aires, it makes sense to slice your time into segments for walking tours—so spend a day in the microcenter, for example; an evening in Puerto Madero; another day in La Boca and San Telmo; and another day in Recoleta and Palermo. Plazas, parks, and pedestrian walkways are omnipresent in the city center.

VISITOR INFORMATION

Obtain tourist information for Argentina from the **Tourism Secretariat of the Nation**, Av. Santa Fe 883, 1059 (© 0800/555-0016 toll-free, or 11/4312-1132). The office is open weekdays from 9am to 5pm, but the toll-free information line is available daily from 8am to 8pm. There are branches at Ezeiza International Airport and Jorge Newbery Airport as well, open daily from 8am to 8pm.

The central office of the **City Tourism Secretariat**, responsible for all visitor information on Buenos Aires, is located at Av. Sarmiento 1551, on the fifth floor (© 11/4372-3612 or 11/4313-0187), and is open weekdays from 9am to 5pm. Additional city tourism branches, which have maps and hotel, restaurant, and attraction information, are found at J. M. Ortiz and Quintana in Recoleta, Galerías Pacífico, Puerto Madero, the central bus terminal, and Caminito. Most are open Monday through Friday from 10am to 5pm. The center on Caminito in La Boca is open Saturday and Sunday from 10am to 5pm.

FAST FACTS   It's easier to exchange money at the airport, your hotel, or an independent money-exchange house rather than an Argentine bank. **American Express**, in a building next to Plaza San Martín at Arenales 707 (© 011/4312-1661), offers the best rates on its traveler's checks and charges no commission. It offers currency exchange for dollars only, and is open Monday through Friday from 9am to 6pm. ATMs are plentiful in Buenos Aires. You can have money wired to **Western Union**, Av. Córdoba 917 (© 0800/800-3030; www.westernunion.com).

For **police** assistance, call © 101; in case of **fire**, © 100; for an **ambulance**, © 107; for an English-speaking **hospital**, © 011/4304-1081.

You never have to venture more than a few blocks to find a **post office**, open Monday through Friday from 10am to 8pm and Saturday until 1pm. The main post office *(Correo Central)* is at Av. Sarmiento 151 (© 011/4311-5040).

Unless you are calling from your hotel (which will be expensive), the easiest way to place calls is by going to a branch of **Telecentro**, the country's telecommunications company, found on nearly every city block. Private booths allow you to place as many calls as you like, after which you pay an attendant. A running meter gives you an idea what the call will cost. Most telecentros also have fax and Internet capabilities.

WHAT TO SEE & DO

Buenos Aires is a wonderful city to explore and is fairly easy to navigate. The most impressive historical sites are located around Plaza de Mayo, although you will certainly experience Argentine history in neighborhoods such as La Boca and San Telmo, too. Don't miss a walk along the riverfront in Puerto Madero, or an afternoon among the plazas and cafes of Recoleta or Palermo. Numerous sidewalk cafes offer respite for weary feet, and there's good public transportation to carry you from neighborhood to neighborhood.

Your first stop should be one of the city tourism centers (see "Visitor Information," above) to pick up a guidebook, city map, and advice. You can also ask at your hotel for a copy of "The Golden Map" and "QuickGuide Buenos Aires" to help you navigate the city and locate its major attractions.

NEIGHBORHOODS TO EXPLORE
La Boca

La Boca, on the banks of the Río Riachuelo, developed originally as a trading center and shipyard. Drawn to the river's commercial potential, Italian immigrants—mainly from Genoa—moved in, giving the neighborhood the distinct flavor it maintains today.

At the center of La Boca lies the **Caminito** ☆☆☆, a pedestrian walkway (and a famous tango song) that is both an outdoor museum and a marketplace. Surrounding the cobblestone street are shabby metal houses painted in dynamic shades of red, yellow, blue, and green, thanks to designer Benito Quinquela Martín. Today, many artists live or set up their studios in these multicolored sheet-metal houses. Along the Caminito, art and souvenir vendors work side by side with tango performers—this is one place you won't have to pay to see Argentina's great dance. Sculptures, murals, and engravings—some with political and social themes—line the street. This Caminito "Fine Arts Fair" is open daily from 10am to 6pm.

To catch an additional glimpse of La Boca's spirit, walk 4 blocks to the corner of calles Del Valle Iberlucea and Brandsen. **Estadio de Boca Juniors**—the stadium for Buenos Aires's most popular *club de fútbol* (soccer club), the Boca Juniors—is here. Go on game day, when street parties and general debauchery take over the area. For information on *fútbol* games, see the *Buenos Aires Herald* sports section. Use caution in straying too far from the Caminito, however, as the less patrolled surrounding areas can be unsafe. *Warning:* Avoid La Boca altogether at night.

San Telmo

Buenos Aires's oldest neighborhood, San Telmo originally housed the city's elite. When yellow fever struck in the 1870s—aggravated by substandard conditions in the area—the aristocrats moved north. Poor immigrants soon filled the neighborhood, and the houses were converted to tenements, called *conventillos.* In 1970, the city passed regulations to restore some of San Telmo's architectural landmarks. With new life injected into it, the neighborhood has taken on a bohemian flair, attracting artists, dancers, and numerous antiques dealers 7 days a week.

After Plaza de Mayo, **Plaza Dorrego** is the oldest square in the city. Originally the site of a Bethlehemite monastery, the plaza is also where Argentines met to reconfirm their Declaration of Independence from Spain. On Sundays from 10am to 5pm, the city's best **antiques market** ☆☆☆ takes over the square.

You can buy leather, silver, handicrafts, and other products here along with antiques, and tango and *milonga* dancers perform on the square.

San Telmo is full of tango clubs, one of the most notable **El Viejo Almacén** ⟨ (at Independencia and Balcarce). During the day, you can appreciate the club as a landmark: An example of colonial architecture, it was built in 1798 and was a general store and hospital before its reincarnation as the quintessential Argentine tango club. Make sure to go back for a show at night (see "Buenos Aires After Dark," later in this chapter). If you get the urge for a beginner or refresher tango course while you're in San Telmo, look for signs advertising lessons in the windows of club.

Palermo

Palermo is a neighborhood of parks filled with magnolias, pines, palms, and willows, where families picnic on weekends and couples stroll at sunset. Designed by French architect Charles Thays, the parks take their inspiration from London's Hyde Park and Paris' Bois de Boulogne. Take the metro to Plaza Italia, which lets you out next to the **Botanical Gardens** ⟨ (© 11/4831-2951) and **Zoological Gardens** ⟨ (© 11/4806-7412), open dawn to dusk. Stone paths wind their way through the botanical gardens, where a student might escape hurried city life to study on a park bench. Flora from throughout South America fills the garden, with over 8,000 plant species from around the world represented. Next door, the city zoo features an impressive diversity of animals, including indigenous birds and monkeys, giant turtles, orangutans, and a polar bear and brown bear habitat.

Parque Tres de Febrero ⟨⟨, a 400-hectare (1,000-acre) paradise of trees, lakes, and walking trails, begins just past the Rose Garden off Avenida Sarmiento. In summer, paddleboats are rented by the hour. Nearby, small streams and lakes meander through the **Japanese Garden** ⟨⟨ (© 11/4804-4922), where children can feed the fish (*alimento para peces* means "fish food") and watch the ducks. Small wood bridges connect classical Japanese gardens surrounding the artificial lake. A simple restaurant offers tea, pastries, sandwiches, and a few Japanese dishes such as sushi and teriyaki chicken. The garden is open daily from 10am to 6pm (till 7pm in summer); admission costs $1.

Recoleta

The city's most exclusive neighborhood, La Recoleta wears a distinctly European face. Tree-lined avenues lead past fashionable restaurants, cafes, boutiques, and galleries, many housed in French-style buildings. Much of the activity takes place along the pedestrian walkway Roberto M. Ortiz, and in front of the Cultural Center and Recoleta Cemetery. This is a neighborhood of plazas and parks, a place where tourists and wealthy Argentines spend their leisure time outside. Weekends bring street performances, art exhibits, fairs, and sports.

The **Recoleta Cemetery** ⟨⟨⟨ (no phone), open daily from 10am to 5pm, pays tribute to some of Argentina's historical figures and is a lasting place where the elite can show off its wealth. Once the garden of the adjoining church, the cemetery was created in 1822 and is the oldest in the city. You can spend hours wandering the grounds that cover 4 city blocks, adorned with works by local and international sculptors. More than 6,400 mausoleums form an architectural free-for-all, including Greek temples and pyramids. Some seem big enough to be small churches. The most popular site is the tomb of Eva "Evita" Perón, which is always heaped with flowers and letters from adoring fans. To prevent her body from being stolen again, she has been buried in a concrete vault 8m (27 ft.) underground. Many other rich or famous Argentines are buried here as well, including a number of Argentine presidents of the 20th century, various

Evita Perón: Woman, Wife, Icon

Eva Duarte de Perón, widely known as Evita, captured the imagination of millions of Argentines because of her social and economic programs for the working classes. A mediocre stage and radio actress, she married Colonel Juan Perón, a widower, in 1945 and helped in his charismatic presidential campaign. Her own rags-to-riches story endeared her to the people, whom Evita greeted as *los descamisados* (the shirtless ones).

Once Perón took office, Evita created the Eva Perón Foundation, which redirected funds traditionally controlled by Argentina's elite to programs benefiting hospitals, schools, elderly homes, and various charities. In addition, she raised wages for union workers, established nationwide religious education, and successfully fought for women's suffrage. When Evita died of cancer in 1952, the working classes tried to have her canonized. This effort was blocked, however, by anti-Peronistas and members of the nation's elite. Her body was stolen in 1955 following a coup against Juan Perón, and for the next 19 years was hidden in Italy and Spain. Her remains returned to Argentina in 1974 thanks to efforts by Juan Perón's third wife, Isabel, who hoped to be repaid in support from the masses. Evita finally landed in the Recoleta Cemetery, one of the only bodies allowed there from a nonelite family.

You will find that even today there is considerable disagreement among Argentines over Evita's legacy. Members of the middle and lower classes tend to see her as a national hero, while many of the country's upper classes believe she stole money from the wealthy and used it to embellish her own popularity.

literary figures, and heroes of the war for independence. As any Argentine will tell you, it's important to live in Recoleta while you're alive, but even more important to remain here in death. How to get a space? You're in luck if your family already owns a plot; otherwise, you can buy space for about $20,000 per square meter—if someone is willing to sell. Guided tours of the cemetery take place the last Sunday of each month at 2:30pm from the cemetery's entrance.

Adjacent to the cemetery, the **Centro Cultural La Recoleta** *ƒ* holds permanent and touring art exhibits along with theatrical and musical performances. Designed in the mid–18th century as a Franciscan convent, it was reincarnated as a poorhouse in 1858, serving that function until becoming a cultural center in 1979. The first floor houses an interactive children's science museum where it is "forbidden not to touch." Next door, **Buenos Aires Design Center** features shops specializing in home decor.

Plaza de Mayo *ƒ*

Juan de Garay founded the historic core of Buenos Aires, the Plaza de Mayo, in 1580. The plaza's prominent buildings create an architectural timeline: the Cabildo, Pirámide de Mayo (Pyramid of May), and Metropolitan Cathedral are vestiges of the colonial period (18th and early 19th c.), while the seats of national and local government reflect the styles of the late 19th and early 20th century. In the center of the plaza, you'll find palm trees, fountains, and benches. Plaza de Mayo remains the political heart of the city, serving as a forum for protests. The mothers of the *desaparecidos*, victims of the military dictatorship's war against leftists, have demonstrated here since 1976. You can see them march every Thursday afternoon at 3:30pm.

The Argentine president, whose actual residence is located in a suburb, goes to work every day at the **Casa Rosada (Pink House)** ⋒⋒⋒. It is from a balcony of this mansion that Eva Perón addressed adoring crowds of Argentine workers. You can watch the changing of the guard in front of the palace every hour on the hour, and around back is a small museum (✆ 11/4344-3802) with information on the history of the building and of the nation. It's open Monday through Friday from 10am to 6pm; admission is free.

The original structure of the **Metropolitan Cathedral** ⋒⋒ (✆ 11/4331-2845) was built in 1745; it was given a new facade with carvings telling the story of Jacob and his son Joseph and was designated a cathedral in 1836. Inside lies a mausoleum containing the remains of General José de San Martín, South American liberator regarded as the "Father of the Nation." (San Martín fought successfully for freedom in Argentina, Peru, and Chile.) The tomb of the unknown soldier of Argentine independence is also here.

The **Cabildo** ⋒, Bolívar 65 (✆ 11/4334-1782), was the original seat of city government established by the Spaniards. Completed in 1751, the colonial building proved significant in the events leading up to Argentina's declaration of independence from Spain in May 1810. Parts of the Cabildo were demolished to create space for Avenida de Mayo and Diagonal Sur. The remainder of the building was restored in 1939 and is worth a visit, although the small museum inside is not particularly interesting (museum open Tues–Fri 12:30–7pm, Sun 2–6pm; admission $1). The Cabildo is the only remaining public building dating from colonial times.

A striking neoclassical facade covers the **Legislatura de la Ciudad (City Legislature Building),** at Calle Perú and Hipólito Irigoyen, which houses exhibitions in several of its recently restored halls. The building's watchtower has more than 30 bells. In front of the Legislatura, you'll see a bronze statue of Julio A. Roca, considered one of Argentina's greatest presidents.

Farther down Calle Perú stands the enormous **Manzana de las Luces (Block of Lights)** ⋒⋒, Calle Perú 272, which served as the intellectual center of the city in the 17th and 18th centuries. This land was granted in 1616 to the Jesuits, who built **San Ignacio**—the city's oldest church—still standing at the corner of calles Bolívar and Aslina. San Ignacio has a beautiful altar carved in wood with Baroque details. Also located here is the **Colegio Nacional de Buenos Aires;** Argentina's best-known intellectuals have gathered and studied at the National School, and the name "block of lights" recognizes the contributions of its graduates, especially in achieving Argentina's independence in the 19th century. Tours are usually led on Saturday and Sunday at 3 and 4:30pm and include a visit to the Jesuits' system of underground tunnels, which connected their churches to strategic spots in the city (admission $2). In addition to weekend tours, the Comisión Nacional de la Manzana de las Luces organizes a variety of cultural activities during the week, including folkloric dance lessons, open-air theater performances, art expositions, and music concerts. Call ✆ 11/4331-9534 for information.

Puerto Madero

Puerto Madero became Buenos Aires's first major gateway to trade with Europe when it was built in 1880. But by 1910, the city had already outgrown the port. The Puerto Nuevo (New Port) was established to the north to accommodate growing commercial activity, and Madero was abandoned for almost a century. Urban renewal saved the original port in the 1990s with the construction of a riverfront promenade, apartments, and offices. Bustling and business-like during the day, the area attracts a fashionable, wealthy crowd at night. It's lined with elegant restaurants serving Argentine steaks and fresh seafood specialties, and there is a popular cinema showing Argentine and Hollywood films.

Plaza San Martín & Environs

Plaza San Martín ⟨⟩⟨⟩, a beautiful park at the base of Calle Florida in the Retiro neighborhood, acts as the nucleus of what's considered the city's *microcentro*. In summer months, Argentine businesspeople flock to the park on their lunch hour, loosening their ties, taking off some layers, and sunning for a while amidst the plaza's flowering jacaranda. A monument to General José de San Martín towers over the scene. The San Martín Palace, one of the seats of the Argentine Ministry of Foreign Affairs, and the elegant Plaza Hotel face the square.

Calle Florida ⟨⟩⟨⟩⟨⟩ is the main pedestrian thoroughfare of Buenos Aires and a shopper's paradise. The busiest section, extending south from Plaza San Martín to Avenida Corrientes, is lined with boutiques, restaurants, and record stores. You'll find the upscale Galerías Pacífico fashion center here (see "Shopping," below).

Avenida Corrientes ⟨⟩ is a living diary of Buenos Aires's cultural development. Until the 1930s, Avenida Corrientes was the favored hangout of tango legends. When the avenue was widened in the mid-1930s, it made its debut as the Argentine Broadway. Today, Corrientes, lined with cinemas and theaters, pulses with cultural and commercial activity day and night.

MUSEUMS

El Museo Histórico Nacional ⟨⟩⟨⟩   Argentine history from the 16th through the 19th century comes to life in the former Lezama family home. The expansive Italian-style mansion houses 30 rooms with items saved from Jesuit missions, paintings illustrating clashes between the Spaniards and Indians, and relics from the War of Independence against Spain. The focal point of the museum's collection is artist Cándido López's series of captivating scenes of the war against Paraguay in the 1870s.

Calle Defensa 1600. ✆ 11/4307-1182. Free admission. Tues–Sun noon–6pm. Closed Jan. Metro: Constitución.

Malba-Colección Constantini ⟨⟩⟨⟩⟨⟩   The stunning Museo de Arte Latinoamericano de Buenos Aires (Malba), which vaguely resembles New York's Museum of Modern Art, houses the private art collection of Eduardo Constantini. One of the most impressive collections of Latin American art anywhere, temporary and permanent exhibitions showcase names like Antonio Berni, Pedro Figari, Frida Kahlo, Candido Portinari, Diego Rivera, and Antonio Siguí. Many of the works confront social issues and explore questions of national identity. In addition to the art exhibitions, Latin films are shown Tuesday through Sunday at 2 and 10pm. This wonderful museum, which opened in late 2001, is located in Palermo.

Av. Figueroa Alcorta 3415. ✆ 11/4808-6500. Admission $1; free admission Wed. Wed–Mon noon–8pm.

Museo Nacional de Arte Decorativo ⟨⟩   French architect René Sergent, who designed some of the grandest mansions in Buenos Aires, envisioned and developed this museum. The building's 18th-century French design provides a classical setting for the diverse decorative styles represented within. Breathtaking sculptures, paintings, and furnishings round off the collection. The **Museo de Arte Oriental** displays art, pottery, and engravings on the first floor of the building.

Av. del Libertador 1902. ✆ 11/4801-8248. Admission $1. Mon–Fri 2–8pm; Sat–Sun 11am–7pm.

Museo Nacional de Bellas Artes 𝒜𝒜   This building that formerly pumped the city's water supply metamorphosed into Buenos Aires's most important art museum in 1930. The museum contains the world's largest collection of Argentine sculptures and paintings from the 19th and 20th century. It also houses European art dating from the pre-Renaissance period to the present day. The collections include notable pieces by Renoir, Monet, Rodin, Toulouse-Lautrec, and van Gogh.

Av. del Libertador 1473. ℂ 11/4803-0802. Free admission. Tues–Sun 12:30–7:30pm.

OTHER ATTRACTIONS

Among the other attractions is the **Café Tortoni,** long a meeting place for *Porteño* artists and intellectuals. For a full review, see p. 116, and for information on the cafe's tango shows, see "Buenos Aires After Dark," later in this chapter.

Basílica y Convento de San Francisco 𝒜   The San Roque parish is one of the oldest in the city. A Jesuit architect designed the church in 1730, but a final reconstruction in the early 20th century added a German baroque facade, along with statues of Saint Francis of Assisi, Dante, and Christopher Columbus. Inside, you'll find a tapestry by Argentine artist Horacio Butler along with an extensive library.

Calle Defensa and Alsina. ℂ 11/4331-0625. Free admission. Metro: Plaza de Mayo.

Biblioteca Nacional 𝒜   Opened in 1992, this modern architectural oddity stands on the land of the former Presidential Residence in which Eva Perón died. With its underground levels, the library's 13 floors can store up to five million volumes. Among its collection, the library stores 21 books printed by one of the earliest printing presses, dating from 1440 to 1500. Visit the reading room—occupying two stories at the top of the building—to enjoy an awe-inspiring view of Buenos Aires. The library also hosts special events in its exhibition hall and auditorium.

Calle Aguero 2502. ℂ 11/4807-0885. Free admission. Mon–Fri 9am–9pm; Sat–Sun noon–8pm.

Congreso 𝒜   The National Congress towers over Avenida de Mayo, with its occupants presumably keeping a watchful eye on the president's Casa Rosada down the street. The capitol building, built in 1906, combines elements of classical Greek and Roman architecture and is topped with an immense central dome modeled after its counterpart in Washington, D.C. Today, the building cannot hold its entire congressional staff, which has spilled over into neighboring structures.

Plaza Congreso was designed in 1910 to frame the congress building and memorialize the centennial of a revolutionary junta that helped overthrow Spanish rule in Argentina. Stroll around the square and its surroundings to see a number of architectural landmarks, theaters, sidewalk cafes, and bars.

Plaza Congreso. Not open to the public. Metro: Congreso.

Teatro Colón 𝒜𝒜𝒜   Buenos Aires's golden age of prosperity gave birth to this luxurious opera house, which has hosted Luciano Pavarotti, Julio Bocca, Maria Callas, Plácido Domingo, Arturo Toscanini, and Igor Stravinsky. The project took close to 80 years to complete, but the result is spectacular. The majestic building, completed in 1908, combines a variety of European styles, from the Ionic and Corinthian capitals and French stained-glass pieces in the main entrance to the Italian marble staircase and French furniture, chandeliers, and vases in the Golden Hall. In the main theater—which seats 2,500 in orchestra seats, stalls, boxes, and four rises—an enormous chandelier hangs from the domed ceiling painted by Raúl Soldi. The theater's acoustics are world renowned. In addition to hosting visiting performers, the Colón has its own philharmonic orchestra, choir, and ballet company. Opera and symphony seasons last from April to November. Guided tours, which let you view the main theater, backstage, and costume and stage design workshops, take place hourly between 11am and 3pm weekdays and from 9am to noon Saturday. Call ⓒ 11/4378-7130 for information.

Calle Libertad 621 or Calle Toscanini 1180. ⓒ 11/4378-7100. Admission $5. Metro: Tribunales.

SPECTATOR SPORTS & OUTDOOR ACTIVITIES

GOLF   Argentina has more than 200 golf courses. Closest to downtown are **Cancha de Golf de la Ciudad de Buenos Aires,** Av. Torquinst 1426 and Olleros (ⓒ **11/4772-7261**), 10 minutes from downtown with great scenery and a 71-par course; and **Jockey Club Argentino,** Av. Márquez 1700 (ⓒ **11/4743-1001**), in San Isidro, which offers two courses (par 71 and 72) designed by Allister McKenzie.

HORSE RACING   Over much of the 20th century, Argentina was famous for its thoroughbreds. It continues to send prize horses to competitions around the world, although you can watch some of the best right here in Buenos Aires. Races take place at two tracks: **Hipódromo de San Isidro,** Av. Márquez 504 (ⓒ **11/4743-4010**), and **Hipódromo Argentino de Palermo,** Av. del Libertador 4205 (ⓒ **11/4778-2839**), in Palermo. Check the *Buenos Aires Herald* for race information.

POLO   Argentina has won more international polo tournaments than any other country, and the **Argentine Open Championship,** held late November through early December, is the world's most important polo event. There are two seasons for polo: March through May and September through December, held at the **Campo Argentino de Polo,** Avenida del Libertador and Avenida Dorrego (ⓒ **11/4576-5600**). Tickets can be purchased at the gate. Contact the **Asociación Argentina de Polo,** Hipólito Yrigoyen 636 (ⓒ **11/4331-4646** or 11/4342-8321), for information on polo schools and events. **La Martina Polo Ranch** (ⓒ **11/4576-7997**), located 60km (37 miles) from Buenos Aires near the town of Vicente Casares, houses more than 80 polo horses, as well as a guesthouse with a swimming pool and tennis courts.

SOCCER *(FUTBOL)*   One cannot discuss *fútbol* in Argentina without paying homage to Diego Armando Maradona, Argentina's most revered player and one of the sport's great (if fallen) players. Any sense of national unity dissolves when Argentines watch their favorite clubs—River Plate, Boca Juniors, Racing Club, Independiente, and San Lorenzo—battle on Sunday. Passion for *fútbol* could not run hotter, and you can catch a game at the **Estadio Boca Juniors,** Brandsen 805 (ⓒ **11/4362-2260**), in San Telmo, followed by raucous street parties. Ticket prices start at $10 and can be purchased in advance or at the gate.

SHOPPING

Except for European boutiques in Recoleta, fantastic bargains abound—particularly for leather goods, antiques, and Argentine wines. There is a 19% value-added tax (VAT, or IVA in Argentina) on sales items. Keep receipts for invoices over 70 pesos; you should be able to get a refund of the VAT upon departure from the country.

BY NEIGHBORHOOD

MICROCENTER Calle Florida, the pedestrian walking street in the micro-center, is home to wall-to-wall shops from Plaza San Martín past Avenida Cor-rientes. The **Galerías Pacífico** mall is located at Calle Florida 750 and Avenida Córdoba (© **11/4319-5100**), with a magnificent dome and stunning frescoes painted by local artists. Over 180 shops are open Monday through Saturday from 10am to 9pm and Sunday from noon to 9pm, with tango shows held on weekends at 8pm. As you approach Plaza San Martín, you find a number of well-regarded shoe stores, jewelers, and shops selling leather goods.

RECOLETA Avenida Alvear is Argentina's response to the Champs-Elysées, and—without taking the comparison too far—it is indeed an elegant, Parisian-like strip of European boutiques and cafes. Start your walk from Plaza Francia and continue from Junín to Cerrito. Along Calle Quintana, French-style man-sions share company with upscale shops. Nearby **Patio Bullrich,** Av. del Liber-tador 750 (© **11/4814-7400**), is one of the city's best malls. Its 69 elegant shops are open daily from 10am to 9pm.

AVENIDA SANTA FE Popular with local shoppers, Avenida Santa Fe—which the city tourist office likens to Madrid's Gran Vía—offers a wide selection of clothing stores and more down-to-earth prices. You will also find bookstores, ice cream shops, and cinemas. The **Alto Palermo Shopping Center,** Av. Santa Fe 3253 (© **11/5777-8000**), is another excellent shopping center, with 155 stores open daily from 10am to 10pm.

SAN TELMO & LA BOCA These neighborhoods offer excellent antiques as well as arts and crafts celebrating tango. Street performers and artists are omnipresent. Both should be visited during the day and avoided at night.

SHOPPING A TO Z

Almost all shops in Buenos Aires accept credit cards. However, you will often get a better price if you offer to pay with cash, and you won't be able to use credit cards at outdoor markets.

Antiques

Throughout the streets of San Telmo, you will find the city's best antiques shops; don't miss the antiques market that takes place all day Sunday at Plaza Dorrego (see "Markets," below). There are also a number of fine antiques stores along Avenida Alvear in Recoleta, including a collection of boutiques at **Galería Alvear,** Av. Alvear 1777.

Galería El Solar de French Built in the early 20th century in a Spanish colonial style, this is where Argentine patriot Domingo French lived. Today, it's a gallery, with antiques shops and photography stores depicting the San Telmo of yesteryear. Calle Defensa 1066. Metro: Constitución.

Pallarolls Located in San Telmo, Pallarolls sells an exquisite collection of Argentine silver and other antiques. Calle Defense 1015. Metro: Constitución.

Art

Galería Ruth Benzácar This avant-garde gallery, in a hidden underground space at the start of Calle Florida next to Plaza San Martín, hosts exhibitions of local and national interest. Among the best-known Argentines who have appeared here are Alfredo Prior, Miguel Angel Ríos, Daniel García, Graciela Hasper, and Pablo Siguier. Calle Florida 1000. © **11/4313-8480.** Metro: San Martín.

Fashion

Most Argentine clothing stores do not offer the same quality as European names. You will find the city's top fashion stores along Avenida Alvear and Calle Quintana in Recoleta, including **Versace** (Av. Alvear 1901), **Polo Ralph Lauren** (Av. Alvear 1780), and **Emporio Armani** (Av. Alvear 1750).

Ermenegildo Zegna   The famous Italian chain sells outstanding suits and jackets made of light, cool fabrics. If you've landed in Buenos Aires without your suit, this is among your best options. Av. Alvear 1920. ✆ 11/4804-1908.

Escada   You can find casual and elegant selections of women's clothing combining quality and comfort in this boutique shop. Av. Alvear 1516. ✆ 11/4815-0353.

Jewelry

The city's finest jewelry stores are in Recoleta and inside many luxury hotels. You can find bargains on gold along Calle Libertad, near Avenida Corrientes.

Cousiño Jewels   Located along the Sheraton hotel's shopping arcade, this Argentine jeweler features a brilliant collection of art made of the national stone, the rhodochrosite, or Inca Rose. In the Sheraton Buenos Aires Hotel, Av. San Martín. ✆ 11/4318-9000. Metro: Retiro.

H.Stern   This upscale Brazilian jeweler, with branches in major cities around the world, sells an entire selection of South American stones, including emeralds and the unique imperial topaz. It's the top jeweler in Latin America. In the Marriott Plaza hotel, Calle Florida 1005. Metro: San Martín. ✆ 11/4318-3083.

Leather

Argentina is famous for its leather—particularly raw leather—and there are a number of excellent shops in Buenos Aires selling everything from clothing, wallets, and purses to luggage, saddles, and shoes. You can usually find better values here than abroad, but do pay close attention to the quality of craftsmanship—especially in lesser-known stores—before making your purchase.

Casa López   Widely considered the best *marroquinería* (leather goods shop) in Buenos Aires, Casa López sells an extensive range of Argentine leather products. There is also a shop in the Patio Bullrich Mall. Marcelo T. de Alvear 640. ✆ 11/4312-8911. Metro: San Martín.

El Nochero   All the products sold at El Nochero are made with first-rate Argentine leather and manufactured by local workers. Shoes and boots, leather goods and clothes, and native silverware (including *mate* gourds) decorate the store. Posadas 1245, in the Patio Bullrich Mall. ✆ 11/4815-3629.

Louis Vuitton   The famous Parisian boutique sells an elite line of luggage, purses, and travel bags. It's located alongside Recoleta's most exclusive shops. Av. Alvear 1751. ✆ 11/4813-7072.

Rossi & Caruso   This store offers the best leather products in the city and is the first choice for visiting celebrities—the king and queen of Spain and Prince Philip of England among them. Products include luggage, saddles and accessories, and leather and chamois clothes, purses, wallets, and belts. There is another branch in the Galerías Pacífico mall. Av. Santa Fe 1601. ✆ 11/4811-1965. Metro: Bulnes.

Markets

The **antiques market in San Telmo** ⊛, which takes place every Sunday from 10am to 5pm at Plaza Dorrego, is a vibrant, colorful experience. As street vendors sell their heirlooms, singers and dancers move amid the crowd to the music of tangos and *milongas*. Among the 270-plus vendor stands, you will find antique silversmith objects, porcelain, crystal, and other antiques.

Plaza Francia's Fair, at avenidas del Libertador and Pueyrredón, offers ceramics, leather goods, and arts and crafts amid street musicians and performers. It's held Sunday from 9am to 7pm.

Wine Shops

Argentine wineries, particularly those in Mendoza and Salta, produce some excellent wines. Stores selling Argentina wines abound, and three of the best are **Grand Cru,** Av. Alvear 1718, **Tonel Privado,** in the Patio Bullrich Shopping Mall, and **Winery,** which has branches at L. N. Alem 880 and Av. Del Libertador 500, both downtown.

WHERE TO STAY

Hotels in Buenos Aires often fill up in high season, so book ahead. The best hotels are found in Recoleta and the microcenter; the Hilton in Puerto Madero is close to the center. Recoleta is more scenic and not quite as noisy as the microcenter. Prices listed below are rack rates in high season; discounts are almost always available for weekends and low season, and may even be available in high season. Check-in time is generally 3pm; checkout is at noon. Most hotels charge about $5 a night for valet parking. (Self-parking is not really an option; we definitely do *not* recommend trying to park on the street.) Note that there are no convenient metro stops in Puerto Madero or Recoleta.

Buenos Aires accommodations have improved in recent years, following a series of renovations among many of the city's high-end hotels. These hotels offer in-room safes, cable TV, direct-dial phones with voice mail, and in-room modem access. Luxury hotels also offer twice-daily maid service with nightly turndown. Most hotels in this chapter, except for a couple of the least expensive, fall in these categories.

Prices have fallen so dramatically as a result of the currency devaluation that some hotels cost two to three times less than they did before December 2001. However, certain hotels are charging higher rates for foreigners than Argentines, and for overseas versus local bookings. Consider contacting the hotel beforehand and ask for a confirmed rate in writing.

PUERTO MADERO
Expensive

Hilton Buenos Aires 𝒜𝒜   The Hilton opened in mid-2000 as the first major hotel and convention center in Puerto Madero, and since then has contributed markedly to the growth of this redesigned port area. The Hilton lies within easy walking distance of some of the best restaurants in Buenos Aires, and is an excellent choice for steak and seafood gourmands. The strikingly contemporary hotel—a sleek silver block hoisted on stilts—features a seven-story atrium with more than 400 well-equipped guest rooms and an additional number of private residences. Spacious guest rooms offer multiple phone lines, walk-in closets, and bathrooms with separate showers and bathrooms. Those staying on the executive floors receive complimentary breakfast and have access to a private concierge. Next to the lobby, El Faro restaurant serves California cuisine with a focus on seafood. The hotel has an impressive on-site pool and fitness center, and the staff can also arrange access to golf, tennis, and other recreational activities. Although the Hilton is not the city's most intimate hotel, it is one of the newest and best regarded, with an excellent location in fashionable Puerto Madero.

Av. Macacha Güemes 351, 1106 Buenos Aires. © **11/4891-0000.** Fax 11/4891-0001. www.buenos.hilton.com. 418 units. From $150 double; from $300 suite. AE, DC, MC, V. **Amenities:** Restaurant; bar; modern gym with open-air pool deck; concierge; business center and secretarial services; room service; babysitting; laundry service; dry cleaning; executive-level floors. *In room:* TV, dataport, minibar, hair dryer, safe.

RECOLETA
Very Expensive
Alvear Palace Hotel 🏵🏵🏵   Located in the center of the upscale Recoleta district, the Alvear Palace is the most exclusive hotel in Buenos Aires and one of the top hotels in the world. European by design, the Alvear reflects the Belle Epoque era in which it was created, combining Empire- and Louis XV–style furniture with exquisite French decorative arts. The elegant lobby acts as a sort of who's who among Argentina's elite, and the illustrious guest list has included names like Antonio Banderas, Catherine Deneuve, Claudia Schiffer, Donatella Versace, the Emperor of Japan, George Soros, Helmut Kohl, Nelson Mandela, Shimon Peres, Ted Turner, and Warren Christopher, to name a few. Recently renovated guest rooms combine luxurious comforts, such as chandeliers, Egyptian cotton linens, and silk drapes, with modern technical conveniences like touch-screen telephones that control all in-room functions. More than half of the individually decorated guest rooms are suites, and all come with personal butler service, cellphones, fresh flowers and fruit baskets, and daily newspaper delivery. Guests are further pampered with large marble bathrooms containing Hermès toiletries, and most have Jacuzzi baths. The formal hotel provides sharp, professional service, and the excellent concierge staff goes to great lengths to accommodate guest requests. The Alvear Palace is home to one of the best restaurants (La Bourgogne, p. 111) in South America, and also offers an excellent, if expensive, Sunday brunch and afternoon tea in L'Orangerie.

Av. Alvear 1891, 1129 Buenos Aires. © **11/4808-2100.** Fax 11/4804-0034. www.alvearpalace.com. 210 units, including 85 "palace" rooms and 125 suites. From $410 double; from $475 suite. Rates include luxurious buffet breakfast. AE, DC, MC, V. **Amenities:** 2 restaurants; bar; small health club and spa with massage; concierge; elaborate business center; shopping arcade; room service; laundry service; dry cleaning. *In room:* A/C, TV, dataport, minibar, hair dryer, safe.

Four Seasons Hotel 🏵🏵🏵   In 2002, the Four Seasons took over what was already one of the city's most luxurious properties, promising to make it even better. There are two parts to this landmark hotel: the 12-story "Park" tower housing the majority of the guest rooms, and the French-Rococo "La Mansión" with seven elegant suites and a handful of private event rooms. A French-style garden and a pool separate the two buildings. The hotel's restaurant, Galani (p. 112), serves excellent Mediterranean cuisine in a casual environment. Spacious guest rooms offer atypical amenities like walk-in closets, wet and dry bars, stereo systems, and cellphones. The large bathrooms, with separate bathtubs and showers, display so much marble you'll wonder if it took an entire Italian quarry to furnish them. People staying on the club floors enjoy exclusive check-in and checkout; additional in-room amenities including a printer, fax machine, and Argentine wine; and complimentary breakfast and evening cocktails. The attentive staff will assist you in arranging day tours of Buenos Aires, as well as access to golf courses, tennis, boating, and horseback riding. The Four Seasons welcomes families with children, offering them bedtime milk and cookies.

Posadas 1086/88, 111 Buenos Aires. © **11/4321-1200.** Fax 11/4321-1201. www.fourseasons.com/buenosaires. 165 units (7 suites in La Mansión). $250 double; from $300 suite. AE, DC, MC, V. **Amenities:** Restaurant; lobby bar; health club w/heated outdoor pool, exercise room, massage, and sauna; concierge; multilingual business center; room service; babysitting; laundry service; dry cleaning; club-level rooms. *In room:* A/C, TV/VCR, dataport, minibar, hair dryer, safe.

Expensive

Caesar Park *⟨R⟩ Overrated*   This classic hotel sits opposite Patio Bullrich, the city's most exclusive shopping mall. Guest rooms vary in size and amenities, but all have been tastefully appointed with fine furniture and elegant linens, marble bathrooms with separate bathtubs and showers, and entertainment centers with TVs and stereos. Larger rooms come with a fresh fruit basket on the first night's stay. The art collection in the lobby and on the mezzanine is for sale, and there are a few boutique shops on the ground level. Although the hotel, part of a larger international chain, is a member of The Leading Hotels of the World, service is formal and not particularly warm.

Posadas 1232/46, 1014 Buenos Aires. ⟨C⟩ 11/4819-1100. Fax 11/4819-1121. www.caesar-park.com. 170 units. $180 double; from $400 suite. Rates include buffet breakfast. AE, DC, MC, V. Free valet parking. **Amenities:** Restaurant; 2 bars; small fitness center w/indoor pool and sauna; concierge; business center; room service; laundry service; dry cleaning. *In room:* A/C, TV, dataport, minibar, hair dryer, safe.

Loi Suites Recoleta *⟨R⟩⟨R⟩*   Part of a small local hotel chain, the new Loi Suites Recoleta is a contemporary hotel with spacious rooms and personalized service. A palm-filled garden atrium and covered pool adjoin the lobby, which is bathed in various shades of white. Breakfast and afternoon tea are served in the "winter garden." Although the management uses the term "suites" rather loosely to describe rooms with microwaves, sinks, and small fridges, the hotel does in fact offer some traditional suites in addition to its more regular studio-style rooms. Loi Suites lies just around the corner from Recoleta's trendy restaurants and bars, and the staff will provide information on city tours, upon request.

Vicente López 1955, 1128 Buenos Aires. ⟨C⟩ 11/5777-8950. Fax 11/5777-8999. www.loisuites.com.ar. 112 units. From $200 double; from $300 suite. Rates include buffet breakfast. AE, DC, MC, V. Parking $4. **Amenities:** Restaurant; indoor pool; exercise room and sauna; small business center; room service; laundry service; dry cleaning. *In room:* A/C, TV, dataport, minibar, fridge, hair dryer, safe.

Moderate

Etoile Hotel *⟨R⟩ Value*   Located in the heart of Recoleta, steps away from the neighborhood's fashionable restaurants and cafes, the 14-story Etoile is an older hotel with a Turkish flair. Although it's not as luxurious as the city's other high-end hotels, it is not as expensive either—making it a good value for Recoleta. Colored in gold and cream, guest rooms are fairly large—although they're not really "suites," as the hotel describes them. Executive rooms have separate sitting areas, large tile-floor bathrooms with whirlpool baths, and balconies. Rooms facing south offer balconies overlooking Plaza Francia and the Recoleta Cemetery.

Roberto M. Ortiz 1835, 1113 Buenos Aires. ⟨C⟩ 11/4805-2626. Fax 11/4805-3613. www.etoile.com.ar. 96 units. $80 double; from $115 suite. Rates include buffet breakfast. AE, DC, MC, V. Free parking. **Amenities:** Restaurant; rooftop health club w/indoor pool and exercise room; concierge; executive business services; room service; laundry service; dry cleaning. *In room:* A/C, TV, minibar, hair dryer.

MONSERRAT

Moderate

Hotel InterContinental Buenos Aires *⟨R⟩⟨R⟩⟨R⟩*   The InterContinental is one of the capital's newer luxury hotels. Despite its modernity, this luxurious tower hotel was built in one of the city's oldest districts, Monserrat, and decorated in the Argentine style of the 1930s. The marble lobby is colored in beige and apricot tones, with handsome furniture and antiques inlaid with agates and other stones. Guest rooms continue the 1930s theme, with elegant black woodwork, comfortable king beds, marble-top nightstands, large desks, and black-and-white photographs of Buenos Aires. The marble bathrooms have separate showers and bathtubs and feature extensive amenities. Business rooms, "Six Continents" rooms, and various suites offer even more luxuries. The lobby's Café de las Luces, in which you might catch a glimpse of an evening tango performance, resembles the colonial style of the famous Café Tortoni. An inviting courtyard adjacent to the lobby looks out on one of the oldest churches in the city. The Restaurante y Bar Mediterráneo (p. 114) serves healthy, gourmet Mediterranean cuisine. Stop by the Brasco & Duane wine bar for an exclusive selection of Argentine vintages.

Moreno 809, 1091 Buenos Aires. (11/4340-7100. Fax 11/4340-7119. www.interconti.com.ar. 312 units. $110 double; from $210 suite. AE, DC, MC, V. Metro: Moreno. **Amenities:** Restaurant; wine bar and lobby bar; health club w/indoor pool, exercise room, massage, and sauna; concierge; business center; room service; laundry service; dry cleaning; executive-level floors. *In room:* A/C, TV, dataport, minibar, hair dryer, safe.

Inexpensive
Hotel Nogaro ✦ *(Finds)* Hotel Nogaro's grand marble staircase leads to a variety of guest rooms noteworthy for their comfort and quietness. Deluxe rooms boast hardwood floors and high ceilings, and small but modern bathrooms with whirlpool tubs in the suites. Standard rooms, while smaller, are pleasant, too, with red carpeting, large closets, and a bit of modern art. The hotel is a good bet for people who want to stay slightly outside the city center, although you should not walk in Monserrat at night. The staff will arrange sightseeing tours upon request.

Av. Julio A. Roca 562, 1067 Buenos Aires. (**11/4331-0091.** Fax 11/4331-6791. www.nogarobue.com.ar. 140 units. From $40 double; from $45 suite. Rates include buffet breakfast. AE, DC, MC, V. Metro: Monserrat. **Amenities:** Restaurant; business center; room service; babysitting; laundry service. *In room:* A/C, TV, minibar.

MICROCENTER
Very Expensive
Park Tower ✦✦✦ One of the most beautiful, and expensive, hotels in Buenos Aires, the Park Tower is connected to the Sheraton next door. The hotel combines traditional elegance with technological sophistication and offers impeccable service. Common areas as well as private rooms feature imported marble, Italian linens, lavish furniture, and impressive works of art. The lobby, with its floor-to-ceiling windows, potted palms, and Japanese wall screens, contributes to a sense that this is the Pacific Rim rather than South America. Tastefully designed guest rooms are equipped with 29-inch color TVs, stereo systems with CD players, and cellphones. Guests also have access to 24-hour private butler service. The hotel boasts three restaurants: Chrystal Garden, serving refined international cuisine; El Aljibe, offering Argentine beef from the grill; and Cardinale, for Italian specialties. The lobby lounge features piano music, a cigar bar, tea, cocktails, and special liquors.

Av. Leandro N. Alem 1193, 1104 Buenos Aires. (**11/4318-9100.** Fax 11/4318-9150. www.luxurycollection. com/parktower. 181 units. From $300 double; from $420 suite. AE, DC, MC, V. Metro: Retiro. **Amenities:** 3 restaurants; snack bar and piano bar; 2 pools; putting green; 2 lit tennis courts; fitness center w/gym, wet and dry saunas, and massage; concierge; business center and secretarial services; room service; laundry service; dry cleaning. *In room:* A/C, TV/VCR, minibar, hair dryer, safe.

Sofitel Buenos Aires ✦✦ The Sofitel opened in late 2002, the first in Argentina. This classy French hotel near Plaza San Martín joins two seven-story buildings to a 20-story neoclassical tower dating from 1929, with a glass atrium lobby bringing them together. The lobby resembles an enormous gazebo, with six Fikus trees, a giant iron and bronze chandelier, an Art Nouveau clock, and Botticcino and black San Gabriel marble filling the space. Adjacent to the lobby you will find an elegant French restaurant, Le Sud (p. 115), and an early-20th-century-style Buenos Aires cafe. The cozy library, with its grand fireplace and dark woods, offers guests an enchanting place to read outside their rooms. These rooms vary in size, mixing modern French decor with traditional Art Deco styles.

Narrow corridors and smallish bedrooms give this the feeling of a small boutique hotel; ask for one of the "deluxe" rooms or suites if you're looking for more space. Rooms are light-filled and decorated in beiges, yellows, and blacks; beautiful marble bathrooms have separate showers and bathtubs and feature Roger & Gallet amenities. Rooms above the eighth floor enjoy the best views, and the 17th-floor suite, "L'Appartement," covers the whole floor. Many of the staff members, dressed in chic French uniforms, speak Spanish, English, and French.

Arroyo 841/849, 1007 Buenos Aires. ⓒ **11/4909-1454.** Fax 11/4909-1452. www.sofitel.com. 144 units. From $240 double; from $340 suite. AE, DC, MC, V. **Amenities:** Restaurant and cafe; bar; indoor pool; fitness center; concierge; business center; room service; laundry service. *In room:* A/C, TV, dataport, minibar, hair dryer, safe.

Expensive

Marriott Plaza Hotel 𝕒𝕒𝕒   The historic Plaza was the grande dame of Buenos Aires for most of the 20th century, and the Marriott management has maintained much of its original splendor. (The hotel still belongs to descendants of the first owners from 1909.) The intimate lobby, decorated in Italian marble, crystal, and Persian carpets, is a virtual revolving door of Argentine politicians and foreign diplomats. The hotel hosts international conferences and is popular with business executives. The veteran staff offers outstanding service, and the concierge will address needs ranging from executive business services to sightseeing tours. Although the quality of guest rooms varies widely (some still await renovation), all are spacious, well appointed, and now include cellphones. Twenty-six overlook Plaza San Martín, some with beautiful bay windows. The Plaza Grill (p. 115) remains a favorite lunch spot for Argentine politicians and international executives and offers a reasonably priced multicourse dinner menu, as well. The hotel's health club is one of the best in the city.

Calle Florida 1005, 1005 Buenos Aires. ⓒ **11/4318-3000.** Fax 11/4318-3008. www.marriott.com. 325 units. From $200 double; from $300 suite. Rates include buffet breakfast. AE, DC, MC, V. Metro: San Martín. **Amenities:** 2 restaurants; cigar bar; excellent health club w/outdoor pool, exercise room, massage, and sauna; concierge; business center; salon; room service; laundry service; dry cleaning. *In room:* A/C, TV, minibar, coffeemaker, hair dryer, safe.

Moderate

Amerian Buenos Aires Park Hotel 𝕒𝕒 *(Finds)*   Without question, one of the finest hotels in the city, the modern Amerian is a good bet for tourists as well as business travelers. The warm atrium lobby looks more like California than Argentina, and the highly qualified staff offers personalized service. The soundproofed rooms are elegantly appointed with wood, marble, and granite, and all boast comfortable beds, chairs, and work areas. The Argentine-owned hotel is just blocks away from Calle Florida, Plaza San Martín, and the Teatro Colón.

Reconquista 699, 1003 Buenos Aires. ⓒ **11/4317-5100.** Fax 11/4317-5101. www.amerianhoteles.com.ar. 152 units. From $100 double; from $200 suite. Rates include buffet breakfast. AE, DC, MC, V. Metro: Florida. **Amenities:** Restaurant; pub; exercise room; sauna; concierge; business center; room service; laundry service; dry cleaning. *In room:* A/C, TV, hair dryer, minibar.

Aspen Towers Hotel 𝕒𝕒   Built in 1995, the Aspen Towers is one of the city's newer and more refined hotels. Its 13-floor tower is contemporary in design, with a light-filled atrium lobby, elegant restaurant, and inviting rooftop pool. Guest rooms are small but classically decorated, with faux-antique furniture and soft-colored linens. All rooms feature marble bathrooms with whirlpool baths— something you're unlikely to find anywhere in the city at this price. The hotel is popular with Brazilians, Chileans, and Americans, and lies within easy walking distance of downtown's attractions.

Paraguay 857, 1057 Buenos Aires. © **11/4313-1919.** Fax 11/4313-2662. www.aspentowers.com.ar. 105 units. $75–$100 double. Rates include buffet breakfast. AE, DC, MC, V. Metro: San Martín. **Amenities:** Restaurant and cafe; rooftop pool; exercise room; sauna; concierge; business center; room service; laundry service; dry cleaning. *In room:* A/C, TV, minibar.

Claridge Hotel ⟨ℛ⟩

While no longer the capital's most luxurious hotel, it certainly remains among the most well known. From the grand entrance with its imposing Roman columns to the elegant lobby with its English hunt-club theme, the Claridge seems far removed from the bustling city life outside. Wood paneling, wrought-iron lamps, and dark furniture lend the hotel a sense of tranquillity, if not modernity. Even the staff moves at a more relaxed pace, although service remains attentive and professional. Guest rooms are spacious, tastefully decorated, and equipped with all the amenities expected of a luxury hotel. The Claridge restaurant offers a good-value executive menu for those with little time to linger over a meal. This country-style restaurant serves carefully prepared international food and an inviting breakfast buffet. Because it occasionally hosts conventions, the Claridge can become very busy.

Tucumán 535, 1049 Buenos Aires. © **11/4314-7700.** Fax 11/4314-8022. www.claridge.com.ar. 165 units. $190 double; from $290 suite. Rates include buffet breakfast. AE, DC, MC, V. Metro: Florida. **Amenities:** Restaurant; bar; health club w/heated outdoor pool, exercise room, massage service, and sauna; concierge; business center; room service; laundry service; dry cleaning. *In room:* A/C, TV, hair dryer, minibar, safe.

Loi Suites Esmeralda ⟨ℛ⟩

Previously a Comfort Inn, this Loi Suites (part of a small local chain) lies 3 blocks from Plaza San Martín and the pedestrian walking street, Calle Florida. Spacious rooms can accommodate up to six people, making this a good choice for families traveling with children. Renovated in 2001, rooms are decorated in soft whites with kitchenettes and microwaves, and all come with cellphones (only pay for calls, no rental fee). The hotel also offers complimentary access to a gym and swimming pool located off property. A more upscale Loi Suites is in Recoleta.

Marcelo T. de Alvear 842, 1058 Buenos Aires. © **11/4131-6800.** Fax 11/4131-6888. www.loisuites.com.ar. 103 units. $120 double; $205 suite. Rates include buffet breakfast. AE, DC, MC, V. Metro: San Martín. **Amenities:** Restaurant; bar; room service; laundry service. *In room:* A/C, TV, dataport, minibar, safe.

Inexpensive

Bel Air Hotel ⟨ℛ⟩ *(Finds)*

Opened in late 2000, the inexpensive and intimate Bel Air is as close as Buenos Aires comes to having a boutique hotel. Although the lobby and building's exterior are more extravagant than the rooms, guests can look forward to comfortable, quiet accommodations. Superior rooms are bigger than standards and only slightly more expensive, while suites have separate sitting areas. Certain rooms contain showers only. Next to the lobby, Bis-a-Bis restaurant and bar features window-side tables, great for people-watching along the fashionable Arenales Street. The majority of the hotel's guests hail from Peru, Chile, and Columbia. The hotel provides airport transfers upon request.

Arenales 1462, 1061 Buenos Aires. © **11/4021-4000.** Fax 11/4816-0016. www.hotelbelair.com.ar. 76 units. $40 double; from $50 suite. Rates include buffet breakfast. AE, DC, MC, V. No parking. Metro: San Martín. **Amenities:** Restaurant; bar; gym; business center; room service; laundry service; dry cleaning. *In room:* A/C, TV, dataport, minibar.

Best Western Embassy *(Kids)*

Although the owners may be exaggerating when they call this an "all-suites" hotel, guest rooms (available in five categories) do have kitchenettes. Some also have separate living areas and bedrooms, and rooms facing Avenida Cordoba come with balconies. Renovated in 1998, the hotel is convenient and comfortable, offering decent if limited service. Don't be alarmed by the talking elevators.

Av. Córdoba 860, 1054 Buenos Aires. © 11/4322-1228. Fax 11/4322-2337. 80 units. From $62 double. Rates include buffet breakfast. AE, DC, MC, V. Metro: Lavalle. **Amenities:** Cafe; fitness room; sauna; business center; room service; laundry service. *In room:* A/C, TV, minibar, hair dryer.

Holiday Inn Express This simple, convenient hotel enjoys a great location next to Puerto Madero. Although there is no room service, concierge, or bellhops, the hotel is friendly, modern, and inexpensive. Guest rooms have large, firm beds, ample desk space, and 27-inch cable TVs; half of them boast river views. Coffee and tea are served 24 hours, and the buffet breakfast is excellent.

Av. Leandro N. Alem 770, 1057 Buenos Aires. © 11/4311-5200. Fax 11/4311-5757. www.holiday-inn.com. 116 units. From $75 double. Children under 18 stay free in parent's room. Rates include buffet breakfast. AE, DC, MC, V. Metro: L. N. Alem. **Amenities:** Deli; exercise room; whirlpool; sauna; business center. *In room:* A/C, TV.

Howard Johnson Plaza *Value*   Having taken over from Courtyard by Marriott, this new Howard Johnson's is an excellent choice for business travelers who don't require many special services. It has a great location off Calle Florida near Plaza San Martín, although there is no direct street access to the hotel (making it cumbersome to get to if you have lots of luggage). Guest rooms resemble studio apartments, with king- or queen-size beds, sleeper chairs, large desks and dressers, and well-appointed bathrooms. Each room has two phones, and local calls and Internet use are free—a rarity in Buenos Aires. There's a small, airy cafe adjacent to the lobby. There are four function rooms available for business and social events.

Calle Florida 944, 1005 Buenos Aires. © 11/4891-9200. Fax 11/4891-9208. www.hojoar.com. 77 units. $75 double. Rates include buffet breakfast. AE, DC, MC, V. Metro: San Martín. **Amenities:** Restaurant; business services; laundry service. *In room:* A/C, TV, minibar, hair dryer, safe.

WHERE TO DINE

Buenos Aires offers world-class dining, with a variety of Argentine, Italian, and international restaurants. With the collapse of the peso, fine Argentine dining has become marvelously inexpensive, as well. You've heard that Argentine beef is the best in the world; parrillas serving the choicest cuts are ubiquitous. (It is said that when Argentines go on a diet, they limit themselves to eating only meat.) Many kitchens have an Italian influence, and you'll find pasta on most menus. The city's most fashionable neighborhood for eating out is Las Cañitas in Old Palermo, also called "Palermo Hollywood." A row of excellent Argentine and ethnic restaurants, shops, and bars teem with young, hip *Porteños* convinced they're in New York's SoHo. Additional top restaurants line the docks of Puerto Madero—with the majority focused on seafood. The microcenter and Recoleta offer many outstanding restaurants and cafes as well. Cafe life is as sacred to *Porteños* as it is to Parisians.

Porteños eat breakfast until 10am, lunch between noon and 2:30pm, and dinner late—usually after 9pm. Many restaurants require reservations, particularly on weekends. Executive lunch menus are offered most places at noon, but dinner menus are a la carte. There is sometimes a small "cover" charge for bread and other items placed at the table. In restaurants that serve pasta, the pasta and its sauce are priced separately. Standard tipping is 10% in Buenos Aires, more for exceptional service. When paying by credit card, you will often be expected to leave the *propina* (tip) in cash, since many credit card receipts don't provide a place to include it. Many restaurants close between lunch and dinner, and remain closed on Monday nights.

PUERTO MADERO
Expensive
Cabaña las Lilas ARGENTINE   Widely considered the best parrilla in Buenos Aires, Cabaña las Lilas is always packed. The menu pays homage to

Argentine beef, which comes from the restaurant's private *estancia* (ranch). The table "cover"—which includes dried tomatoes, mozzarella, olives, peppers, and delicious garlic bread—nicely whets the appetite. Clearly, you're here to order steak: The best cuts are the rib eye, baby beef, and thin skirt steak. Order sautéed vegetables, grilled onions, or Provençal-style fries separately. Service is hurried but professional; ask your waiter to match a fine Argentine wine with your meal. And make reservations well in advance.

Alicia Moreau de Justo 516. © 11/4313-1336. Reservations recommended. Main courses $8–$12. AE, DC, V. Daily noon–midnight. Metro: L. N. Alem.

Katrine ★★★ INTERNATIONAL   One of the top dining choices in Buenos Aires, Katrine (named after the restaurant's Norwegian chef-owner, who can be found almost every day in the kitchen) serves exquisite cuisine. Yet for such an exclusive restaurant, the dining room is surprisingly loud and festive. You won't go wrong with any of the menu choices, but a couple of suggestions include marinated salmon Scandinavian-style, followed by shrimp with vegetables and saffron, or thinly sliced beef tenderloin with portobello mushrooms, onions, and a cabernet sauvignon reduction. All of the pasta dishes are excellent, too. Katrine's modern dining room and outdoor terrace overlook the water. Service is outstanding.

Av. Alicia Moreau de Justo 138. © 11/4315-6222. Reservations recommended. Main courses $8–$15. AE, DC, MC, V. Mon–Fri noon–3:30pm and 8pm–midnight; Sat 8pm–12:30am. Metro: L. N. Alem.

Moderate
Sorrento del Puerto ★★ ITALIAN   The only two-story restaurant in Puerto Madero enjoys impressive views of the water from both floors. When the city decided to reinvigorate the port in 1995, this was one of the first five restaurants opened (today there are more than 50). The sleek modern dining room boasts large windows, modern blue lighting, and tables and booths decorated with white linens and individual roses. While an outdoor patio accommodates only 15 tables, the inside is enormous. Upstairs, you will see some of the brick columns and steel beams that formed part of the original dock house. People come here for two reasons: great pasta and even better seafood. Choose your pasta and accompanying sauce: seafood, shrimp scampi, pesto, or four cheeses. The best seafood dishes include trout stuffed with crabmeat, sole with a Belle Marnier sauce, Galician-style octopus, paella Valenciana, and assorted grilled seafood for two. A three-course menu with a drink costs $7. Sorrento has a second location in Recoleta at Posadas 1053 (© **11/4326-0532**).

Av. Alicia Moreau de Justo 430. © 11/4319-8731. Reservations recommended. Main courses $5–$9. AE, DC, MC, V. Mon–Fri noon–4pm and 8pm–1am; Sat 8pm–2am. Metro: L. N. Alem.

RECOLETA
Expensive
La Bourgogne ★★★ *Moments* FRENCH   The only Relais Gourmand in Argentina, Chef Jean Paul Bondoux serves the finest French and international food in the city. *Travel & Leisure* rated La Bourgogne the best restaurant in South America, and *Wine Spectator* gave it the distinction of being one of the "Best Restaurants in the World for Wine Lovers." Decorated in elegant pastel hues, the formal dining room serves the city's top gourmands. Meals are served slowly and deliberately, with the expert waitstaff guiding you through the impeccable list of wines. To begin your meal, consider a warm *fois gras* scallop with honey wine sauce, or perhaps the succulent *ravioli d'escargots*. Examples of the carefully prepared main courses include *chateaubriand béarnaise*, roasted salmon, veal steak,

and lamb with parsley and garlic sauce. The kitchen's fresh vegetables, fruits, herbs, and spices originate from Bondoux's private farm. Downstairs, **La Cave** offers a slightly less formal dining experience, with a different menu but from the same kitchen as La Bourgogne. Wine tastings are offered Thursdays in the restaurant's wine cellar; contact La Bourgogne directly for details.

Av. Alvear 1891 (Alvear Palace Hotel). © 11/4805-3857. Reservations required. Jacket and tie required for men. Main courses $7–$12. AE, DC, MC, V. Mon–Fri noon–3pm and 8pm–midnight; Sat 8pm–midnight. Closed Jan. Free valet parking.

Lola *(Overrated)* INTERNATIONAL   Among the best-known international restaurants in Buenos Aires, Lola recently completed a makeover, turning its dining room into one of the city's brightest and most contemporary. Like the Palm in New York and Washington, caricatures of major personalities adorn the walls, and fresh plants and flowers give Lola's dining room a springlike atmosphere. A French-trained chef offers creative dishes such as chicken fricassee with a leek sauce, grilled trout with lemon grass butter and zucchini and, for those who have failed to exhaust their craving for Argentine beef, tenderloin stuffed with Gruyère cheese and mushrooms. The chef will prepare dishes for those with special dietary requirements. Although Lola remains among the city's most famous restaurants, some feel that its quality has slipped in recent years due to a number of management changes.

Roberto M. Ortiz 1805. © 11/4804-5959 or 11/4802-3023. Reservations recommended. Main courses $7–$12. AE, DC, MC, V. Daily noon–4pm and 7pm–1am.

Moderate

El Mirasol ARGENTINE   One of the city's best parrillas, El Mirasol serves thick cuts of fine Argentine beef. Your waiter will be happy to guide you through the selection of cuts, among which the rib eye, tenderloin, sirloin, and ribs most often find their way to the dinner plate. Like a Morton's of Chicago, El Mirasol serves steaks as a featured item, with potatoes, vegetables, and other accouterments appearing only as separate side-dish orders. The best dessert is an enticing combination of meringue, ice cream, whipped cream, *dulce de leche*, walnuts, and hot chocolate sauce. The wine list pays tribute to Argentina malbec, sirah, merlot, and cabernet sauvignon. El Mirasol, which is frequented by business executives and government officials at lunch and a more relaxed crowd at night, remains open throughout the afternoon (a rarity in a city where most restaurants close between lunch and dinner).

Posadas 1032. © 11/4326-7322. Reservations recommended. Main courses $5–$10. AE, DC, MC, V. Daily noon–2am.

Galani MEDITERANNEAN   This elegant but informal bistro inside the spectacular Four Seasons Hotel serves Mediterranean cuisine with Italian and Asian influences. The executive lunch menu includes an antipasto buffet with seafood, cold cuts, cheese, and salads, followed by a main course and dessert. From the dinner menu, the aged Angus New York strip makes an excellent choice, and all grilled dishes come with béarnaise sauce or *chimichurri* and a choice of potatoes or seasonal vegetables. Organic chicken and fresh seafood join the menu, along with a terrific selection of desserts. Live harp music often accompanies meals, and tables are candlelit at night. Enjoy an after-dinner drink in Le Dôme, the split-level bar adjacent to the lobby featuring live piano music and occasional tango shows.

Posadas 1086 (in the Four Seasons Hotel). © 11/4321-1234. Reservations recommended. Main courses $5–$8; fixed-price lunch $10. AE, DC, MC, V. Daily 7–11am, noon–3pm, and 8pm–1am.

Piegari 🐸🐸 ITALIAN Piegari has two restaurants located across the street from each other, the more formal focused on Italian dishes, and the other (Piegari vitello e dolce) specializing in steaks and desserts. While both restaurants are good, visit the main Piegari for outstanding Italian cuisine, with an emphasis on seafood and pastas. Homemade spaghetti, seafood risotto, pan pizza, veal scallops, and black salmon ravioli are just a few of the mouthwatering choices. Huge portions are made for sharing, and an excellent Argentine wine list accompanies the menu. If you decide to try Piegari vitello e dolce instead, the best dishes are the short rib roast and the leg of Patagonian lamb.

Posadas 1042. ℭ 11/4328-4104. Reservations recommended. Main courses $7–$15. AE, DC, MC, V. Daily noon–3:30pm and 7:30pm–midnight.

Inexpensive
Café Victoria 🐸 CAFE Perfect for a relaxing afternoon in Recoleta, the café's outdoor patio is surrounded by flowers and shaded by an enormous *romero de India* tree. Sit and have a coffee or enjoy a complete meal. The three-course express lunch menu offers a salad, main dish, and dessert, with a drink included. Afternoon tea with pastries and scones is served daily from 4 to 7pm. The cafe remains equally popular in the evening, when live music serenades the patio and there's excellent people-watching. This is a great value for the area; the Recoleta cemetery and cultural center are located next door.

Roberto M. Ortiz 1865. ℭ 11/4804-0016. Main courses $3–$5. AE, DC, MC, V. Daily 7:30am–11:30pm.

La Biela 🐸🐸🐸 CAFE Originally a small sidewalk cafe opened in 1850, La Biela earned its distinction in the 1950s as the rendezvous choice of race car champions. Black-and-white photos of these Argentine racers decorate the dining room, so large you may well need glasses to see from one side to the other. Today, artists, politicians, and neighborhood executives (as well as a fair number of tourists) all frequent La Biela, which serves breakfast, informal lunch plates, ice cream, and crepes. The outdoor terrace sits beneath an enormous 19th-century Gum tree opposite the church of Nuestra Señora del Pinar. It is said that you have not seen Buenos Aires until you stop for a coffee or whisky at La Biela, and indeed this thoroughbred Argentine has become one of the city's cultural landmarks. Sip an espresso and watch the crowd.

Quintana 600. ℭ 11/4804-0449. Main courses $3–$5. V. Daily 7am–3am.

PALERMO
Moderate
De Olivas i Lustres 🐸🐸 *Moments* MEDITERRANEAN Located in Palermo Viejo, this magical restaurant is one of our favorites in Buenos Aires. The small, rustic dining room displays antiques, olive jars, and wine bottles, and each candlelit table is individually decorated—one resembles a writer's desk, another is sprinkled with seashells. The reasonably priced menu celebrates Mediterranean cuisine, with light soups, fresh fish, and sautéed vegetables the focus. The breast of duck with lemon and honey is mouthwatering; there are also a number of *tapeos*—appetizer-size dishes that let you sample a variety of the chef's selections. For 28 pesos each, you and your partner can share 15 such dishes brought out individually (a great option provided you have at least a couple of hours). Open only for dinner, this romantic spot offers soft, subtle service.

Gascón 1460. ℭ 11/4867-3388. Reservations recommended. Main courses $3–$5; fixed-price menu $8. AE, V. Mon–Sat 7:30pm–1:30am. Metro: Scalabrini Ortiz.

Novecento ✴✴✴ INTERNATIONAL With a sister restaurant in SoHo, Novecento was one of the pioneer restaurants of Palermo's Las Cañitas neighborhood. Fashionable Argentines pack the New York–style bistro by 11pm, clinking wine glasses under a Canal Street sign or opting for the busy outdoor terrace. Waiters rush to keep their clients happy (and glasses full), with appetizer dishes like salmon carpaccio and steak salad. The pastas and risotto are mouthwatering, but you may prefer a steak *au poivre* or a chicken brochette. Other wonderful choices include filet mignon, grilled Pacific salmon, and penne with wild mushrooms. Top it off with an Argentine wine. This is *the* place to see and be seen if you're out for a bite.

Baez 199. © 11/4778-1900. Reservations recommended. Main courses $4–$7. AE, DC, MC, V. Daily 8pm–2am. Metro: Olleros.

MONSERRAT
Moderate

Club Español ✴✴ SPANISH This Art Nouveau Spanish club, with its high, gilded ceiling and grand pillars, bas-relief artwork, and original Spanish paintings, boasts the most magnificent dining room in Buenos Aires. Despite the restaurant's architectural grandeur, the atmosphere is surprisingly relaxed and often celebratory; don't be surprised to find a table of champagne-clinking Argentines next to you. Tables have beautiful silver place settings, and tuxedo-clad waiters offer formal service. Although the menu is a tempting sample of Spanish cuisine—including the paella and Spanish omelets—the fish dishes are the chef's best.

Bernardo de Irigoyen 180. © 11/4334-4876. Reservations recommended. Main courses $4–$8. AE, DC, MC, V. Daily noon–4pm and 8pm–midnight. Metro: Lima.

Restaurante y Bar Mediterráneo ✴✴ MEDITERRANEAN The Inter-Continental hotel's exclusive Mediterranean restaurant and bar were built in colonial style, resembling the city's famous Café Tortoni. The downstairs bar, with its hardwood floor, marble-top tables, and polished Victrola playing a tango, takes you back to Buenos Aires of the 1930s. A spiral staircase leads to the elegant restaurant, where subdued lighting and well-spaced tables create an intimate atmosphere. The menu is light, healthy, and delicious. Mediterranean herbs, olive oil, and sun-dried tomatoes are among the chef's usual ingredients. Carefully prepared dishes might include shellfish bouillabaisse; black hake served with ratatouille; chicken casserole with morels, fava beans, and potatoes; or duck breast with cabbage confit, wild mushrooms, and sautéed apples. Express menus (ready within minutes) are available at lunch.

Moreno 809. © 11/4340-7200. Reservations recommended. Main courses $6–$9. AE, DC, MC, V. Daily 7–11am, 11:30am–3:30pm, and 7pm–midnight. Metro: Moreno.

MICROCENTER
Expensive

Catalinas ✴✴✴ MEDITERRANEAN/INTERNATIONAL This is Argentina's most recognized international restaurant. Since 1979, Galician-born Ramiro Rodríguez Pardo has impressed gourmands from Argentina and abroad, his kitchen defined by culinary diversity and innovation. The colorful yet classic dining room—adjacent to the Lancaster Hotel—has three open salons, each painted by one of Argentina's most famous "plastic" artists: Polesello, Beuedit, and Rovirosa. A Venetian crystal chandelier shines on the center dining room, created by the same artist who arranged the chandeliers in the lobby of New York's Plaza Hotel. Tables are large, decorated with white linens, fresh flower arrangements, and porcelain. A three-course, prix-fixe menu, including two bottles of Argentina's finest wines, is offered at lunch and dinner—an excellent value for such an elegant restaurant. The menu changes seasonally but always includes impeccable lobsters, T-bone steaks, and steaks of Patagonian tooth fish (which grow to more than 200 lb.). Pardo's grilled lamb chops, sprinkled with rosemary and fresh savory, are famous throughout Argentina.

Reconquista 850. (℃ **11/4313-0182.** Reservations recommended. Main courses $7–$10; fixed-price menu $15. AE, DC, MC, V. Mon–Fri noon–3pm and 8pm–1am; Sat 8pm–1am. Metro: San Martín.

Le Sud *⟨⟨* FRENCH/MEDITERANNEAN   Executive Chef Thierry Pszonka earned a gold medal from the National Committee of French Gastronomy and gained experience at La Bourgogne before opening this gourmet restaurant in the new Sofitel hotel. His simple, elegant cooking style embraces spices and olive oils from Provence to create delicious entrees, such as the stewed rabbit with green pepper and tomatoes, polenta with Parmesan and rosemary, and spinach with lemon raviolis. Le Sud's dining room offers the same sophistication as its cuisine, a contemporary design with chandeliers and black marble floors, tables of Brazilian rosewood, and large windows overlooking Calle Arroyo. Following dinner, consider a drink in the adjacent wine bar.

Arroyo 841/849 (in the Sofitel Buenos Aires). (℃ **11/4131-0000.** Reservations recommended. Main courses $10–$20. AE, DC, MC, V. Daily 6:30–11am, 12:30–3pm, and 7:30pm–midnight. Metro: San Martín.

Plaza Grill *⟨⟨* INTERNATIONAL   For nearly a century, the Plaza Grill dominated the city's power-lunch scene, and it remains the first choice for government officials and business executives. The dining room is decorated with dark oak furniture, 90-year-old Dutch porcelain, Indian fans from the British Empire, and Villeroy & Boch china place settings. Tables are well spaced, allowing for intimate conversations. Order a la carte from the international menu or off the parrilla—the steaks are perfect Argentine cuts. Marinated filet mignon, thinly sliced and served with gratinéed potatoes, is superb. The "po parisky eggs" form another classic dish—two poached eggs in a bread shell topped with a rich mushroom-and-bacon sauce. The restaurant's wine list spans seven countries, with the world's best Malbec coming from Mendoza.

Calle Florida 1005 (in the Marriott Plaza Hotel). (℃ **11/4318-3070.** Reservations recommended. Main courses $7–$10. AE, DC, MC, V. Daily noon–4pm and 7pm–midnight. Metro: San Martín.

Moderate
Broccolino *⟨* ITALIAN   Taking its name from New York's Italian immigrant neighborhood—notice the Brooklyn memorabilia filling the walls and the mural of Manhattan's skyline—this casual trattoria near Calle Florida is popular with North Americans (Robert Duvall has shown up three times). Many of the waiters speak English, still a rarity in much of the city, and the restaurant has a distinctly New York feel. Three small dining rooms are decorated in quintessential red-and-white checkered tablecloths, and the smell of tomatoes, onions, and garlic fills the air. The restaurant is known for its spicy pizzas, fresh pastas, and above all its sauces (*salsas* in Spanish). The restaurant also serves 2,000 pounds per month of baby calamari sautéed in wine, onions, parsley, and garlic.

Esmeralda 776. (℃ **11/4322-7652.** Reservations recommended. Main courses $3–$5. No credit cards. Daily noon–4pm and 7pm–1am. Metro: Lavalle.

La Chacra *⟨* ARGENTINE   Your first impression will be either the stuffed cow begging you to go on in and eat some meat, or the open fire spit grill glowing through the window. Professional waiters clad in black pants and white dinner jackets welcome you into what is otherwise a casual environment, with deer horns and wrought-iron lamps adorning the walls. Dishes from the grill include sirloin steak, T-bone with red peppers, and tenderloin. Barbecued ribs and suckling pig call out from the open-pit fire, and there are a number of hearty brochettes. Steaks are thick and juicy. Get a good beer, or at least an Argentine wine, to wash it all down.

Av. Córdoba 941. ⓒ 11/4322-1409. Main courses $4–$6. AE, DC, MC, V. Daily noon–1:30am. Metro: San Martín.

Las Nazarenas ⓡ ARGENTINE   This is not a restaurant, an old waiter will warn you; it's an *asador*. More specifically, it's a steakhouse with meat on the menu, not a pseudo-parrilla with vegetable plates or some froufrou international dishes for the faint of heart. You have two choices: cuts grilled on the parrilla, or meat cooked on a spit over the fire. Argentine presidents and foreign ministers have all made their way here, a pilgrimage to Argentina's great culinary tradition. The two-level dining room is handsomely decorated with cases of Argentine wines and abundant plants. Service is unhurried, offering you plenty of time for a relaxing meal.

Reconquista 1132. ⓒ 11/4312-5559. Reservations recommended. Main courses $4–$6. AE, DC, MC, V. Daily noon–1am. Metro: San Martín.

Ligure ⓡⓡ *Finds* FRENCH   Painted mirrors look over the long rectangular dining room, which since 1933 has drawn ambassadors, artists, and business leaders by day and a more romantic crowd at night. A nautical theme prevails, with fishnets, dock ropes, and masts decorating the room; captain's wheels substitute for chandeliers. Portions are huge and meticulously prepared—an unusual combination for French-inspired cuisine. Seafood options include the Patagonian tooth fish sautéed with butter, prawns, and mushrooms, or the trout glazed with an almond sauce. If you're in the mood for beef, the chateaubriand is outstanding, and the bife de lomo can be prepared seven different ways (pepper sauce with brandy is delightful, and made at your table).

Juncal 855. ⓒ 11/4393-0644 or 11/4394-8226. Reservations recommended. Main courses $4–$6. AE, DC, MC, V. Daily noon–3pm and 8–11:30pm. Metro: San Martín.

Inexpensive

Café Tortoni ⓡ *Moments* CAFE   This historic cafe has served as the artistic and intellectual capital of Buenos Aires since 1858, with guests such as Jorge Luis Borges, Julio de Caro, Cátulo Castillo, and José Gobello. Waiters gaze over the cafe's antique tables and their occupants with sphinxlike serenity, just as the eyes of the great poets whose photographs line the walls have watched so many come and go. Come in for coffee, or even a simple meal (the food is not the point), and feel Argentine history surround you. The Tortoni is a cultural tradition; there are a number of social events here, including evening tango shows in the back room.

Av. de Mayo 825/9. ⓒ 11/4342-4328. Main courses $3–$7. AE, DC, MC, V. Mon–Thurs 8am–2am; Fri–Sat 8am–3am; Sun 8am–1am. Metro: Av. de Mayo.

Filo ⓡ *Finds* PIZZA   Popular with young professionals, artists, and anyone looking for cause to celebrate, Filo presents its happy clients with mouthwatering pizzas, delicious pastas, and potent cocktails. The crowded bar has occasional live music, and tango lessons are offered downstairs a few evenings per week.

San Martín 975. ⓒ 11/4311-0312. Main courses $2–$5. AE, MC, V. Daily noon–4pm and 8pm–2am. Metro: San Martín.

Petit Paris Café ⓡ SNACKS/AFTERNOON TEA   Marble-top tables with velvet upholstered chairs, crystal chandeliers, and bow tie–clad waiters give this cafe a

European flavor. Large windows look directly onto Plaza San Martín, placing the cafe within short walking distance of some of the city's best sights. The menu offers a selection of hot and cold sandwiches, pastries, and special coffees and teas. Linger over your coffee as long as you like—nobody will pressure you to move.

Av. Santa Fe 774. (℃) 11/4312-5885. Main courses $2–$4. AE, DC, MC, V. Daily 7am–2am. Metro: San Martín.

SAN TELMO
Expensive
La Brigada 🖈🖈🖈 ARGENTINE   The best parrilla in San Telmo is reminiscent of the pampas, with memorabilia of gauchos filling the restaurant. White linen tablecloths and tango music complement the atmosphere, with an upstairs dining room that faces an excellent walled wine rack. The professional staff makes sure diners are never disappointed. Chef-owner Hugo Echevarrieta, known as *el maestro parrillero,* carefully selects meats. The best choices include the *asado* (short rib roast), lomo (sirloin steak, prepared with a mushroom or pepper sauce), baby beef (an enormous 850g/30 oz., served for two), and the *mollejas de chivito al verdero* (young goat sweetbreads in a scallion sauce). Less glamorous—but equally recommended—selections include young kid tripe and blood sausage. The Felipe Rutini merlot goes perfectly with baby beef and chorizo. Service is outstanding.

Estados Unidos 465. (℃) 11/4361-5557. Reservations recommended. Main courses $4–$8. AE, DC, MC, V. Daily noon–3pm and 8pm–midnight. Metro: Constitución.

Moderate
La Casa de Esteban de Luca 🖈 ARGENTINE   This historic house, once inhabited by Argentina's beloved poet and soldier Esteban de Luca (who wrote the country's 1st national anthem, "Marcha Patriótica"), was built in 1786 and declared a National Historic Monument in 1941. Today, it's a popular restaurant serving pasta and meat dishes. Come on Thursday, Friday, or Saturday night after 9pm for the spirited piano show.

Calle Defensa 1000. (℃) 11/4361-4338. Main courses $4–$6. AE, DC, MC, V. Tues–Sun noon–4pm and 8pm–1am. Metro: Constitución.

BUENOS AIRES AFTER DARK
From the Teatro Colón to dimly lit tango salons, Buenos Aires offers an exceptional variety of nightlife. *Porteños* eat late and play later, with theater performances starting around 9pm, bars and nightclubs opening around midnight, and no one showing up until after 1am. Thursday, Friday, and Saturday are the big going-out nights, with the bulk of activity in Recoleta, Palermo, and Costanera. Summer is quieter because most of the town flees to the coast.

Performing arts in Buenos Aires are centered on the highly regarded Teatro Colón, home to the National Opera, National Symphony, and National Ballet. In addition, there are nearly 40 professional theaters around town showing Broadway- and off-Broadway-style hits, Argentine plays, and music reviews. Buy tickets for most productions at the box office or through **Ticketron** (℃ 011/ 4321-9700) or **Ticketmaster** (℃ 011/4326-9903).

For current information on after-dark entertainment, consult the *Buenos Aires Herald* (in English) or any of the major local publications. The "QuickGuide Buenos Aires" also has information on shows, theaters, and nightclubs.

THE PERFORMING ARTS
Opera, Ballet & Classical Music
Luna Park   Once the home of international boxing matches, the Luna is the largest indoor stadium in Argentina and hosts the biggest shows and concerts

Moments Tango: Lessons in the Dance of Seduction & Despair

It seems impossible to imagine Argentina without thinking of tango, its greatest export to the world. What is this sad, soulful melody that captures the hearts of musicians and poets and makes dancing such a seductive art form? Tango originated with a guitar and violin toward the end of the 19th century and was first danced by working-class men in La Boca, San Telmo, and the port area. Combining African rhythms with the *habanera* and *candombe*, it was not the sophisticated dance you know today—rather, the tango originated in brothels and was accompanied by obscene lyrics, not unlike the origins of early American jazz.

Increasing waves of immigrants meant the tango soon made its way to Europe, however, and the dance was internationalized in Paris. With a sense of European approval, Argentine middle and upper classes began to accept the newly refined dance as part of their cultural identity, and the form blossomed under the extraordinary voice of Carlos Gardel. Gardel, who brought tango to Broadway and Hollywood, is nothing short of legendary among Argentines. Astor Piazzola further internationalized the tango, elevating it to a more complex form incorporating classical elements. Tango involves not one but three forms of expression: music, poetry, and dance. While tango may be played by two musicians or a complete orchestra, a piano and *bandoneón*—a German instrument akin to an accordion—are usually included. If there is a singer, the lyrics might come from one of Argentina's great poets, such as Jorge Luis Borges, Homero Manzi, or Horacio Ferrer. The words often concern the connectedness and separateness of man and woman. The dance itself is improvised rather than standardized, although it consists of a series of long walks and intertwined movements, usually in eight-step. In the tango, the man

in Buenos Aires. Many of these are classical music concerts, and the National Symphonic Orchestra often plays here. Av. Corrientes and Bouchard. ℂ 11/4311-1990. Metro: L. N. Alem.

Teatro Colón Known across the world for its impeccable acoustics, the Colón has attracted the world's finest opera performers—Luciano Pavarotti, Julio Bocca, Maria Callas, Plácido Domingo, and Arturo Toscanini among them. Opera season runs from April to November, and the Colón has its own philharmonic orchestra, ballet, and choir companies. The main theater seats 2,500. Calle Libertad 621. ℂ 11/4378-7100. Metro: Tribunales.

Theaters & Exhibitions

The city's best theater takes place at the **Teatro Nacional Cervantes,** Calle Libertad 815 (℗ **11/4816-4224**). **Teatro Opera,** Av. Corrientes 860 (℗ **11/4326-1335**), has been adapted for Broadway-style shows. The **Teatro Municipal General San Martín,** Av. Corrientes 1530 (℗ **0800/333-5254**), has three theaters offering drama, comedy, ballet, music, and children's plays. In Recoleta, **Teatro Coliseo,** Marcelo T. de Alvear 1125 (℗ **11/4816-5943**), puts on classical music

Travel Tip: He who finds the best hotel deal has more to spend on facials involving knobbly vegetables.

Hello, the Roaming Gnome here. I've been nabbed from the garden and taken round the world. The people who took me are so terribly clever. They find the best offerings on Travelocity. For very little cha-ching. And that means I get to be pampered and exfoliated till I'm pink as a bunny's doodah.

travelocity®

1-888-TRAVELOCITY / travelocity.com / America Online Keyword: Travel

and woman glide across the floor as an exquisitely orchestrated duo with early flirtatious movements giving way to dramatic leads and heartfelt turns. Depending on the music, the dance might proceed slowly and sensually or with furious splendor.

Learning to dance the tango is an excellent way for a visitor to get a sense of what makes the music—and the dance—so alluring. Entering a tango salon—called a *salón de baile*—can be intimidating for the novice. The style of tango danced in salons is considerably different from, and more subdued than, "show tango." Most respectable dancers would not show up before midnight, giving you the perfect opportunity to sneak in for a group lesson, offered at most of the salons starting around 8 or 9pm. They usually cost between $1 and $3 for an hour; you can request private instruction for between $10 and $20 per hour, depending on the instructor's skill level.

For additional advice on places to dance and learn tango, get a copy of *B.A. Tango* or *El Tangauta*, the city's dedicated tango magazines. One of the best spots to learn is **Gricel,** La Rioja 1180 (© 11/4957-7157) which offers lessons Monday through Friday at 8pm and opens its doors to the city's best dancers on Saturday and Sunday nights. **La Galería,** Boedo 722 (© 11/4957-1829), is open Thursday, Saturday, and Sunday and attracts excellent dancers, many of whom compete professionally. **Ideal,** Suipacha 384 (© 155/006-4102), is open Monday, Wednesday, and Friday. The dancers here come in all ages and have varied abilities. Ongoing evening lessons are also offered at the **Academia Nacional de Tango,** Av. de Mayo 833 (© 11/4345-6968), which is an institute rather than a tango salon.

productions. **Teatro Presidente Alvear,** Av. Corrientes 1659 (© 11/4374-6076), features tango and other music shows. The majority of foreign and national music concerts are held at the **Teatro Gran Rex,** Av. Corrientes 857 (© 11/4322-8000).

Centro Cultural Recoleta   The distinctive building—originally designed as a Franciscan convent—hosts Argentine and international art exhibits, experimental theater works, occasional music concerts, and an interactive science museum for children. The Hard Rock Cafe is located behind the cultural center. Junín 1930. © 11/4803-1041.

THE CLUB & MUSIC SCENE
Tango Clubs

In Buenos Aires, you can *watch* the tango or *dance* the tango. (Perhaps the former will lend inspiration to the latter.) You'll have many opportunities to see the dance during your visit: Tango and *milonga* dancers frequent the streets of La Boca and San Telmo, many high-end hotels offer tango shows in their lobbies and bars, and tango salons blanket the city. The most famous (besides Café Tortoni) are in San Telmo and combine dinner and show. Have a hotel driver or *remise* take you to San Telmo, La Boca, or Barracas at night, rather than taking the metro or trying to walk.

Café Tortoni   High-quality yet inexpensive tango shows are held in the back room of the Café Tortoni and do not include dinner. There is a show every day at 9pm except Tuesday. Av. de Mayo 825. ℂ 11/4342-4328. Metro: Plaza de Mayo.

El Querandí   Some people swear that El Querandí offers the best package in the city—a good meal of Argentine beef and wine with an excellent tango show. Open Monday through Saturday, dinner begins at 8:30pm followed by show at 10:15pm. Perú 302. ℂ 11/4345-0331.

El Viejo Almacén   The most famous of the city's tango salons, the Almacén offers what some consider the city's most authentic performance. Shows involve traditional Argentine-style (rather than international-style) tango. Performances take place Sunday through Friday with dinner at 8:30pm, show at 9:30pm; Saturday shows are at 9:30 and 11:30pm. Transportation is offered from some downtown hotels. Independencia and Balcarce. ℂ 11/4307-6689.

Esquina Carlos Gardel   One of the city's newest tango spots, Esquina Carlos Gardel lies in the same location where "Chanta Cuatro"—a restaurant where Carlos Gardel used to dine with his friends—was located. The luxurious old-time dining room features high-tech acoustics and superb dancers, creating a wonderful tango environment. Doors open at 8pm. Carlos Gardel 3200. ℂ 11/4876-6363.

Recoleta Tango   Opened in December 2002, this small, intimate tango bar next to the Alvear Palace Hotel is reminiscent of a tango salon of the 1940s. Destined to become one of the city's sleekest shows, dancers interact with members of the audience in a number of the sets. Dinner shows begin at 8pm. Bring your dancing shoes! Av. Alvear 1885. ℂ 11/4808-0600.

Señor Tango   This enormous theater is more akin to a Broadway production hall than a traditional tango salon, but the dancers are fantastic and the owner, who clearly loves to perform, is a good singer. The walls are decorated with photos of what appear to be every celebrity who's ever visited Buenos Aires—and all seem to have made it to Señor Tango! Diners choose between steak, chicken, or fish for dinner and, despite the huge crowd, the food quality is commendable. Have dinner or come only for the show. Vieytes 1653. ℂ 11/4303-0212.

Other Dance Clubs

Dancing in Buenos Aires is not just about tango. A small number of residents can actually dance tango, with the majority of the younger population preferring salsa and European beats. Of course, nothing in life changes quite so fast as the "in" discos, so ask around for the latest hot spots. The biggest nights out are Thursday, Friday, and Saturday. Here are some of the hottest clubs as this book went to press: **Opera Bay,** Cecilia Grierson 225 in Puerto Madero, boasts the top spot among the city's clubs, attracting an affluent and fashionable crowd. Built along the waterfront and resembling the Sydney opera house, Opera Bay features an international restaurant, tango show, and disco. The city's best salsa dancers head to **Salsón,** Av. Alvarez Thomas 1166 (ℂ 11/4637-6970), which offers lessons on Wednesday and Friday at 9pm. In Palermo, **Buenos Aires News,** Av. del Libertador 3883 (ℂ 11/4778-1500), is a rocking late-night club with Latin and European mixes. **Tequila,** Costanera Norte and La Pampa (ℂ 11/4788-0438), is packed every night. There are a number of popular discos nearby, as well. The most popular gay and lesbian club is **Amerika,** Gascón 1040 (ℂ 11/4865-4416), which has three floors of dance music and all-you can drink specials on Friday and Saturday.

THE BAR SCENE

There is no shortage of popular bars in Buenos Aires, and *Porteños* need little excuse to party. The following are only a few of many bars and pubs worthy of recommendation.

Chandon Bar This intimate champagne lounge serves bottles and flutes of Chandon, produced in both France and Argentina. Located in Puerto Madero adjacent to some of the city's best restaurants, Chandon is perfect for a before- or after-dinner drink. Light fare is offered as well. Av. Alicia Moreau de Justo 152. (C) 11/4315-3533. Metro: L. N. Alem.

Danzon A small intimate bar, Danzon attracts a fashionable crowd. An excellent barman serves exquisite cocktails, and a small selection of international food is offered, as well. Smart, relaxing lounge music is played at night. Libertad 1161. (C) 11/4811-1108.

Henry J. Beans A favorite of the expat American community and visiting foreigners, this casual Recoleta bar serves burgers, sandwiches, and nachos, along with cocktails and beer. Old Coca-Cola ads, Miller and Budweiser neon signs, and model airplanes hang from the ceilings. The waiters do occasional impromptu dances, and the place is packed after midnight. There are a number of other popular restaurants, bars, and discos along Junín. Junín 1749. (C) 11/4801-8477.

The Kilkenny This trendy cafe-bar is more like a rock house than an Irish pub, although you will still be able to order Guinness, Kilkenny, and Harp Irish draft beers. Packed with both locals and foreigners, you are as likely to find people in suits and ties as in jeans and T-shirts. The Kilkenny offers happy hour from 6 to 8pm and live bands every night after midnight; it stays open until 5am. A new whisky bar has opened on the first floor. Marcelo T. de Alvear 399. (C) 11/4312-9179 or 4312-7291. Metro: San Martín.

Plaza Bar Nearly every Argentine president and his cabinet have come here, as well as visiting celebs such as the queen of Spain, the emperor of Japan, Luciano Pavarotti, and David Copperfield. The English-style bar features mahogany furniture and velvet upholstery, where guests can sip martinis and smoke Cuban cigars. Tuxedo-clad waiters recommend a fine selection of whiskies and brandies. Marriott Plaza Hotel, Calle Florida 1005. (C) 11/4318-3000. Metro: San Martín.

Plaza Dorrego Bar (*) Representative of a typical *Porteño* bar from the 19th century, Plaza Dorrego displays portraits of Carlos Gardel, antique liquor bottles in cases along the walls, and anonymous writings engraved in the wood. Stop by on Sunday, when you can catch the San Telmo antiques market on the plaza in front. Calle Defensa 1098. (C) 11/4361-0141. Metro: Constitución.

The Shamrock The city's best-known Irish pub is somewhat lacking in authenticity, betrayed by the hot Latin rhythms rather than soft Gaelic music. That said, it remains hugely popular with both Argentines and foreign visitors, and is a great spot to begin the night. Rodríguez Peña 1220. (C) 11/4812-3584. Metro: Callao.

4 Puerto Iguazú & Iguazú Falls (★(★(★

1,330km (825 miles) NE of Buenos Aires

A dazzling panorama of cascades whose power overwhelms the sounds of the surrounding jungle, *Las Cataratas del Iguazú* (Iguazú Falls) refers to the spectacular canyon of waterfalls fed by the Río Iguazú. Declared a World Heritage Area by UNESCO in 1984, these 275 waterfalls were shaped by 120 million years of geological history and form one of earth's most unforgettable sights. Iguazú falls are shared by Argentina and Brazil and are easily accessible from nearby Paraguay. Excellent walking circuits on both the Argentine and Brazilian sides allow visitors to peak over the tops of or stare at the faces of raging sheets of water, some with sprays so intense it seems as though geysers have erupted from below. Although a luxury hotel overlooking the falls exists in both the Argentine and Brazilian national parks, many visitors looking for less expensive accommodations stay in Puerto Iguazú in Argentina or in Foz do Iguaçu in Brazil.

While Iguazú is best known for its waterfalls, the surrounding subtropical jungle is well worth including in your itinerary. Here, *cupay* (a South American hardwood) trees tower over the various layers of life that compete for light, and the national park is known to contain 200 species of trees, 448 species of birds, 71 kinds of mammals, 36 species of reptiles, 20 species of amphibians, and more than 250 kinds of butterflies. Spray from the waterfall keeps the humidity levels over 75%, leading to a tremendous growth of epiphytes (plants that grow on other plants without taking nutrients from their hosts). Iguazú's climate also provides for the flowering of plants year-round, lending brilliant color to the forest.

You can visit the waterfalls on your own, but you will most certainly need a tour operator to explore the jungle. Allow at least 1 full day to explore the waterfalls on the Argentine side, another to visit the Brazilian side, and perhaps half a day for a jungle tour (see chapter 6 for more details).

The sedate town of **Puerto Iguazú** is a good base from which to explore Iguazú National Park, 18km (11 miles) away. It is smaller and safer than its Brazilian counterpart, Foz do Iguaçu, and the hotels and restaurants are inexpensive and commendable. Nights are generally very quiet.

ESSENTIALS
GETTING THERE
BY PLANE Aerolíneas Argentinas (✆ 3757/420-194) flies daily from Buenos Aires to **Aeropuerto Internacional Cataratas del Iguazú;** the trip takes 1½ hours. Round-trip fares range between $100 and $300, depending on whether any specials are offered. Catch a taxi or one of the shuttle buses from the airport to town, a 20-minute drive.

BY BUS The fastest bus service from Buenos Aires is with **Vía Bariloche** (✆ 011/4315-4456 in Buenos Aires), which takes 16 hours for $75 one-way. Less expensive but longer (21 hr.) are **Expreso Singer** (✆ 011/4313-3927 in Buenos Aires) and **Expreso Tigre Iguazú** (✆ 011/4313-3915 in Buenos Aires).

GETTING AROUND
El Práctico local buses run every 45 minutes from 7am to 8pm between Puerto Iguazú and the national park, and cost less than $1. **Parada 10** (✆ 3757/421-527) provides 24-hour taxi service. You can rent a car at the airport, although this is much more a luxury than a necessity. Within both Puerto Iguazú and the national park, you can easily walk.

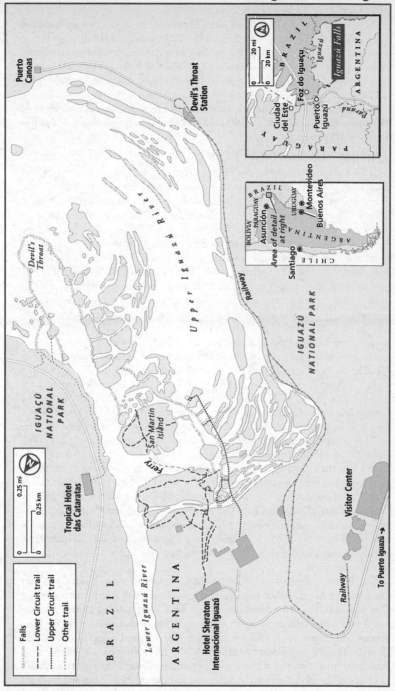

Puerto Canoas

Devil's Throat Station

Devil's Throat

Upper Iguazú River

Railway

San Martin Island

Ferry

IGUAZÚ NATIONAL PARK

Tropical Hotel das Cataratas

0.25 mi
0.25 km
0

Falls
Lower Circuit trail
Upper Circuit trail
Other trail

BRAZIL

Lower Iguazú River

ARGENTINA

Hotel Sheraton Internacional Iguazú

IGUAZÚ NATIONAL PARK

Visitor Center

Railway

To Puerto Iguazú →

20 mi
20 km
0

BRAZIL

Iguazú Falls

Iguazú

ARGENTINA

Foz do Iguaçu

Ciudad del Este

Puerto Iguazú

Paraná

P A R A G U A Y

BRAZIL

PARAGUAY

Asunción

URUGUAY

Montevideo

Buenos Aires

A R G E N T I N A

Area of detail at right

Santiago

C H I L E

BOLIVIA

VISITOR INFORMATION

In Puerto Iguazú, obtain maps and park information from the **Parque National** office at Victoria Aguirre 66 (℗ **3757/420-722**), open Monday through Friday from 8am to 2pm. For information on the town, contact the **municipal tourist office,** at Victoria Aguirre and Brañas (℗ **3757/420-800**). It's open daily from 8am to 8pm. Visitor information is also available near the national park entrance (see below).

In Buenos Aires, get information about Iguazú from **Casa de la Provincia de Misiones,** Av. Santa Fe 989 (℗ **011/4322-0686**), open Monday through Friday from 10am to 5pm.

VISITING THE NATIONAL PARK

Your first stop will likely be the **visitor center,** where you can get maps and information about the area's flora and fauna. A new, environmentally friendly visitor center located 1km (½ mile) from the park entrance has been opened (next to the parking), along with new footbridges for the waterfall circuits. Next to the visitor center, you will find a restaurant, snack shops, and souvenir stores. A natural gas train takes visitors to the path entrance for the Upper and Lower circuits and to the footbridge leading to the Devil's Throat (footpaths remain open for walkers, but the walk to Devil's Throat is about 3km/2 miles). The visitor center is staffed with a number of English-speaking guides, available for individual and private tours, so you may opt to see the falls on your own or with an experienced local guide. There is a 30-peso ($8) entrance fee for non-Argentines to enter the national park, which includes the train ride. The national park is open from 8am to 7pm in summer, and until 6pm in winter.

The two main paths to view the waterfalls are the **Circuito Superior (Upper Circuit)** 𝕲 and **Circuito Inferior (Lower Circuit)** 𝕲, both of which begin within walking distance of the visitor center. There's a small snack shop near the beginning of the trails. The Upper Circuit winds its way along the top of the canyon, allowing you to look down the falls and see the area's rich flora, including cacti, ferns, and orchids. The Lower Circuit offers the best views, as magnificent waterfalls come hurtling down before you in walls of silvery spray. The waterfalls are clearly marked by signs along the way.

The best time to walk the Upper Circuit is early in the morning or late in the afternoon, and rainbows often appear near sunset. This 1km (½-mile) path takes 1 to 2 hours, starting at the viewing tower and leading past **Dos Hermanos (Two Brothers), Bossetti, Chico (Small), Ramírez,** and **San Martín** (the park's widest) falls. You can come right to the edges of these falls and look over them as they fall up to 60m (200 ft.) below. Along your walk, you can also look across to San Martín Island and the Brazilian side, and you'll pass a number of small streams and creeks.

The 1.8km (1-mile) Lower Circuit takes 2 hours to walk, leading you past **Lanusse** and **Alvar Núñez** falls, along the Lower Iguazú River past the raging **Dos Mosqueteros (Two Musketeers)** and **Tres Mosqueteros (Three Musketeers)** falls. The trail then winds its way toward **Ramírez, Chico,** and **Dos Hermanos** falls. Here, you'll find an inspiring view of the **Garganta del Diablo (Devil's Throat)** and **Bossetti** falls. From the Salto Bossetti, a small pathway leads down to a small pier where you can catch a free boat to **San Martín Island.**

Once on the island, climb the stairs and walk along clearly marked trails for remarkable views of the surrounding *cataratas*—to the left, you see Garganta del Diablo, **Saltos Brasileros (Brazilian Falls),** and **Ventana;** to the right, you overlook the mighty **Salto San Martín,** which sprays 30m (100 ft.) high after

Behind the Falls & into the Iguazú Jungle

Dawn in Iguazú brings the first rays of light through the forest canopy, as orchids, butterflies, frogs, lizards, parrots, and monkeys wake and spread color and life through the forest. Binoculars in hand, step softly into this wonderland, where most sounds are masked by the roar from the falls.

You see parakeets long before entering the jungle. Their green bodies and loud song make them easy to spot; macaws, parrots, and toucans are other feathered residents. Look and listen carefully for the great dusky swift, which nests near the waterfalls, and the great kiskadee, whose family name—*Tyrannidae*—tells much about this yellow-breasted bird's hunting prowess. Look below the canopy to observe other flying wonders of the park—an enormous population of butterflies. Brilliant blue flyers known as morpho butterflies flit between deciduous trees and above lines of leaf-cutter ants, along with beautiful red, black, and yellow species of butterflies.

It's close to impossible to walk through the park without running across some of the area's indigenous reptiles. The ubiquitous tropidurus lizards, which feed on bird eggs, scamper everywhere, while colorful tree frogs hop and croak the nights away. Larger and rarer creatures, such as the 1.5m-long (5-ft.) tegu lizard and the caiman, a crocodile-like reptile, are discovered only by the patient and persistent visitor.

Warm-blooded creatures share the forest as well. Coatis—aardvarkesque mammals that travel in groups searching for insects and fruit—are frequent and fearless visitors to the trails. Swinging above the footpaths are brown capuchin monkeys, whose chatter and gestures make them seem more human than most primates. The predators of this warm-blooded group range from vampire bats to endangered jaguars and pumas. Stay on the walking paths and, when in the jungle, with your tour operator.

An array of subtropical flora surrounds Iguazú's resident animals and insects. Bamboo, ficus, fig, and ancient rosewood trees—up to 1,000 years old—are but a few of the trees that grow near the river and compete for light, and there is a proliferation of epiphytes (plants growing on others) such as bromeliads, güembés, and orchids. In fact, 85 species of orchid thrive in the park, mostly close to the damp and well-lit waterfalls.

hitting the river below. This panoramic view looks out at dozens of falls forming an arch before you. San Martín Island also has a small, idyllic beach perfect for sunbathing and swimming.

Garganta del Diablo is the mother of all waterfalls in Iguazú, visible from vantage points in both the Brazilian and Argentine parks. Cross the walking bridge to the observation point, at the top of Diablo: The water is calm as it makes its way down the Iguazú River, although it begins to speed up as it approaches the gorge ahead. In front of you, Mother Nature has created a furious avalanche of water and spray that is the highest waterfall in Iguazú and one of the world's greatest natural spectacles. You might want to bring a raincoat—you *will* get wet.

TOUR OPERATORS

The main tour operator is **Iguazú Jungle Explorer** (© 3757/421-696), located both inside the national park and in the Sheraton International Iguazú. This company offers a "Nautical Adventure" ($11) that visits the falls by inflatable raft, an "Ecological Tour" ($5) that takes you to Devil's Throat and lets you paddle rubber boats along the Upper Iguazú Delta, and the *Gran Aventura* (Great Adventure) tour ($25). This last tour begins with an 8km (5-mile) safari ride along the Yacoratia Path, the original dirt road that led through the forest and on to Buenos Aires. During the ride, you'll view the jungle's extensive flora and might glimpse some of the region's indigenous wildlife (see "Behind the Falls & into the Iguazú Jungle," below). You will be let off at Puerto Macuco, where you then hop in an inflatable boat with your tour group and navigate 6.5km (4 miles) along the lower Iguazú River, braving 1.6km (1 mile) of rapids as you approach the falls in Devil's Throat Canyon. After a thrilling and wet ride, the raft lets you off across from San Martín Island—you can then catch a free boat to the island, where there's a small beach for swimming and sunbathing as well as excellent hiking trails. You can combine the Ecological Tour and Great Adventure by buying a full-day Pasaporte Verde ($28).

If you want to arrange a private tour for your specific interests, the best outfit is **Explorador Expediciones,** with offices in the Sheraton International Iguazú and in Puerto Iguazú at Puerto Moreno 217 (© 3757/421-632). The guides are experts on life in the Iguazú jungle.

WHERE TO STAY

Peak season for hotels in Iguazú is January and February (summer holiday), July (winter break), Semana Santa (Holy Week, the week before Easter), and long weekends. On the Argentine side, the Sheraton International Iguazú is the only hotel inside the national park; the rest are in Puerto Iguazú, 18km (11 miles) away. Rates are often substantially discounted in the off season.

EXPENSIVE

Hotel Cataratas 🐾🐾   While not located next to the falls, Hotel Cataratas deserves consideration for its excellent service. Staff members go out of their way to make you feel at home, from the helpful receptionists to the meticulous housekeepers. None of the stuffiness you sometimes feel at luxury hotels is evident. Despite the hotel's unimpressive exterior, rooms are among the most modern and spacious in the area—especially the 30 "master rooms" that feature two double beds, handsome wood furniture, colorful artwork, large bathrooms with separate toilet rooms, in-room safes, and views of the pool or gardens (these rooms are only slightly more than the standard rooms—called "superior"—and the staff is often willing to offer promotional rates). The hotel's many facilities, including outdoor pool, volleyball courts, a playroom, and a gymnasium make this a great choice for families. Restaurant Cataratas offers a fine selection of regional and international dishes, and you can dine inside or out. The hotel lies 4km (2½ miles) from the center of Puerto Iguazú and 17km (11 miles) from the national park entrance. Bus service is available.

Ruta 12, Km 4, 3370 Misiones. © 3757/421100. Fax 3757/421090. www.hotelcataratas.com.ar. 111 units. $100 double; from $150 suite. Rates include buffet breakfast. AE, DC, MC, V. **Amenities:** Restaurant; outdoor pool; Jacuzzi; sauna; tennis court; game room; concierge; room service; laundry service; massage; secretarial services. *In room:* A/C, TV, minibar, hair dryer, safe.

Sheraton Internacional Iguazú Resort 🐸🐸 Once the famous Internacional Cataratas de Iguazú, the Sheraton enjoys a magnificent location inside the national park. Guests have little need to leave the resort, a self-contained paradise overlooking the falls. The hotel lies only steps from the Upper and Lower Circuit trails, and half of the guest rooms have direct views of the water (the others have splendid views of the jungle). The only drawback to the rooms is that they are fairly standard Sheraton decor. The hotel's restaurants include the stunning Garganta del Diablo, which peers over the Devil's Throat and serves outstanding, if pricey, international dishes. The hotel also offers numerous daytime activities, including swimming, golf, tennis, shopping, and access to national park tour operators. If you're making the trip all the way to Iguazú, you should seriously consider staying inside the national park at this hotel.

Parque Nacional Iguazú, 3370 Misiones. ℭ 0800/888-9180 local toll free, or 3757/491-800. Fax 3757/491-848. www.sheraton.com. 180 units. $170 double with jungle view; $210 with view of waterfalls; from $350 suite. Rates include buffet breakfast. AE, DC, MC, V. **Amenities:** 2 restaurants; outdoor pool; 2 tennis courts; fitness center; car-rental desk; concierge; room service; laundry service; babysitting. In room: A/C, TV, minibar, hair dryer, safe.

MODERATE
Hotel Saint George 🐸 *Finds* A modest hotel in the heart of Puerto Iguazú, the Saint George features colorful rooms with single beds, an inviting pool surrounded by lush vegetation, and a commendable international restaurant that serves tasty fish from the local river. The friendly and enthusiastic staff will answer questions about the national park and help arrange tours if requested.

Av. Córdoba 148, 3370 Puerto Iguazú. ℭ 3757/420-633. Fax 3757/420-651. www.hotelsaintgeorge.com. 56 units. $30 double. Rates include buffet breakfast. AE, DC, MC, V. **Amenities:** Restaurant; bar; 2 pools (1 for children). In room: A/C, TV, hair dryer, minibar.

INEXPENSIVE
Los Helechos *Value* Los Helechos is a great bargain for those seeking comfortable, inexpensive accommodations in Puerto Iguazú. Located in the city center, this intimate hotel offers simple rooms, many of which surround a plant-filled courtyard, and a sense of sleeping near the jungle.

Paulino Amarante 76, 3370 Puerto Iguazú. ℭ/fax 3757/420-338. 54 units. $10 double. AE, DC, MC, V. **Amenities:** Restaurant; bar; pool. In room: A/C, TV in some rooms.

WHERE TO DINE
Dining in Puerto Iguazú is casual and inexpensive, provided you're looking for a meal outside your hotel. Argentine steaks, seafood, and pasta are common on most menus. The Sheraton, inside the national park, has the area's best restaurant.

EXPENSIVE
Garganta del Diablo 🐸🐸 INTERNATIONAL Located inside the national park at the Sheraton Internacional Iguazú Resort, this inspiring restaurant serves excellent, though pricey, international and regional dishes. Opened for nearly 25 years, the restaurant is best known for its magnificent view of the Devil's Throat. Enjoy a romantic table for two overlooking the falls, and consider the grilled *suribí* (a mild fish from the river in front of you) or bife de chorizo (a New York strip steak).

Parque Nacional Iguazú. ℭ 3757/491-800. Main courses $8–$12. AE, DC, MC, V. Daily noon–3pm and 7–11pm.

INEXPENSIVE

El Charo *Finds* ARGENTINE   El Charo is a shambles of a restaurant: Its sagging roof is missing a number of wood beams, pictures hang crooked on the walls, and the bindings on the menus are falling apart. Consider it part of the charm. The casual, cozy restaurant offers cheap, delicious food and is tremendously popular with both tourists and locals. Among the main dishes, you'll find breaded veal, sirloin steaks, pork chops, catfish, and items from the parrilla. There is also a healthy selection of salads and pastas such as ravioli and cannelloni.

Av. Córdoba 106. *C* 3757/421529. Main courses $2–$3. No credit cards. Daily 11am–1am.

La Rueda *Finds* ARGENTINE   Nothing more than a small A-frame house with an outdoor patio, La Rueda is a delightful place to eat. Despite the casual atmosphere, tables have carefully prepared place settings, waiters are attentive and friendly, and the food—served in large portions—is very good. The diverse menu features pasta, steaks, and fish dishes. Try the *suribí brochette,* a local whitefish served with bacon, tomatoes, onions, and peppers, served with green rice and potatoes.

Av. Córdoba 28. *C* 3757/422531. Main courses $2–$4. No credit cards. Daily noon–4pm and 7pm–1am.

PUERTO IGUAZU AFTER DARK

Puerto Iguazú offers little in the way of nightlife, although the major hotels often have live music and other entertainment during peak seasons. Try **La Reserva,** a popular bar-restaurant, or **La Baranca** (*C* 3757/423-295), a pub with nightly live music. Both are located next to each other at Av. Tres Fronteras and Costanera. **Casino Iguazú,** Ruta 12, Km 1640 (*C* 3757/498-000), attracts a well-dressed Argentine and Brazilian crowd and is open weekdays from 2pm to 5am and 24 hours on weekends. Foz do Iguaçu, on the Brazilian side (see chapter 6), offers more evening entertainment than Puerto Iguazú.

5 Mendoza

710km (440 miles) NW of Buenos Aires; 721km (447 miles) SW of Córdoba

"And so you are traveling to the land of *sol y vino,*" my taxi driver says with a smile, capturing the two great temptations of a region showered with sun and flowing with wine. Boasting nearly 300 annual days of sun and three-fourths of the nation's wine production, Mendoza seems destined for the distinction of Napa South. Few might imagine, however, that the sweet, voluptuous grapes coloring the province grow on inhospitable desert land brought to life only through a vast network of irrigation canals dating from the Incas. The canals extend not just through the diverse vineyards but also into the streets of Mendoza itself. This picturesque city lies at the heart of the Cuyo, the name of the region that comprises the provinces of Mendoza, San Juan, and San Luis. It was founded in 1561 by Spanish colonialists, and retains an idyllic serenity that has carried over from centuries past.

Ask a local what she likes best about Mendoza, and she is likely to tell you *"la tranquilidad,"* the tranquillity of what must be Argentina's loveliest city. You'll want to linger about these streets and parks for at least a day or two before rushing to the countryside, where a seductive journey along Los Caminos de Vino (see "Touring the Wineries," below) awaits. Choose your own pace when touring the bodegas (wineries); two or three visits are possible in half a day. Keep in mind that the bodegas, which offer free tours with tastings, are open only on weekdays.

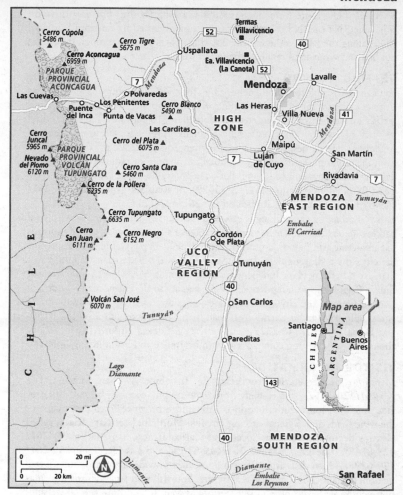

ESSENTIALS
GETTING THERE

BY PLANE Mendoza's international airport, **Francisco Gabrielli** (© 261/520-6000), lies 8km (5 miles) north of town on R40. **Aerolíneas Argentinas** (© 0810/222-86527), **Southern Winds** (© 0810/777-7979), and **LanChile** (© 261/425-7900) operate here, with flights to Buenos Aires, Córdoba, and Santiago de Chile. LAPA offers sporadic service, but the company's future is uncertain.

BY BUS The **Terminal del Sol** (© 261/431-3001), or central bus station, lies in the department of Guaymallén, just east of central Mendoza. Buses travel to Buenos Aires (12–14 hr., $18), Córdoba (12 hr., $9), Santiago de Chile (6 hr., $9), Las Leñas (7 hr., $5), and other cities throughout the region. **Chevallier** (© 261/431-0235), **Expreso Uspallata** (© 261/438-1092), and **Andesmar** (© 261/431-0585) are the main bus companies.

BY CAR   The route from Buenos Aires is a long (10 hr.) but easy drive on either the RN7 or RN8. Mendoza is more easily reached by car from Santiago, Chile, along the RN7, although the 250km (155-mile) trek through the Andes can be treacherous (and requires chains) in winter.

GETTING AROUND

You can easily explore central Mendoza by foot, although you will want to hire a driver or rent a car to visit the wine roads and tour the mountains. Taxis and *remises* are inexpensive: drivers cost no more than $10 per hour. Travelers should be wary of walking alone, especially at night. Although traditionally one of Argentina's safest cities, Mendoza has experienced an increase in crime resulting from the economic crisis. Have your hotel call a *remise* or radio-taxi, rather than flagging a taxi down on your own. For a *remise,* try **La Veloz Del Este** (℗ 261/ 423-9090), **Mendozar** (℗ 261/431-3689), or **Remises-Transporte** (℗ 261/ 429-8734). For a taxi, call **Radiotaxi** (℗ 261/437-1111).

If you do rent a car, parking is easy and inexpensive inside the city, with paid parking meters and private lots clearly marked. Easy to navigate, the city spreads out in a clear grid pattern around Plaza Independencia. Avenida San Martín is the city's main thoroughfare, Paseo Sarmiento is the pedestrian walking street that extends from Plaza Independencia to Avenida San Martín, and Avenida Emilio Civit is the posh residential avenue leading to the entrance of Parque San Martín. Outside the city, road signs are sometimes missing or misleading and you should pay careful attention to road maps. Both **Avis** (℗ 261/447-0150) and **Hertz** (℗ 261/448-2327) rent cars at Mendoza's airport. Expect to pay about $40 per day for a compact car with insurance and unlimited mileage.

VISITOR INFORMATION

Mendoza's **Subsecretaría Provincial de Turismo,** Av. San Martín 1143 (℗ 261/420-2357), is open daily from 9am to 9pm. The helpful staff will provide you with tourist information on the entire province, including maps of the wine roads and regional driving circuits. **Municipal tourist offices,** called Centros de Información, are located at Garibaldi near San Martín (℗ 261/ 423-8745), 9 de Julio 500 (℗ 261/449-5185), and Las Heras 340 (℗ 261/ 429-6298). Open daily from 9am to 9pm, they provide city maps, hotel information, and brochures of tourist activities. You will find small visitor information booths at the airport and bus station, as well. In addition, several websites offer useful tourist information: www.turismo.mendoza.gov.ar, www.aconcagua. mendoza.gov.ar, www.culturamendoza.com.ar, and www.mendoza.com.ar.

FAST FACTS   ATMs and currency exchange houses have been plagued by long lines and limited cash since the beginning of the economic crisis. Two reliable exchange houses, both at the corner of San Martín and Catamarca, are **Maguitur** (℗ 261/425-3405) and **Cambio Santiago** (℗ 261/420-0277). They are open Monday through Friday from 8:30am to 1pm and 5 to 8:30pm and Saturday from 9:30am to 1pm. **Citibank,** Av. Sarmiento 20 (℗ 261/49-6519) has an ATM with Cirrus and PLUS access.

In case of **emergency,** dial ℗ 107 or 261/428-0000 for an ambulance, ℗ 101 or 261/423-8710 for the police, or ℗ 100 for fire assistance. **Hospital Central** (℗ 261/428-0600) is near the bus station at Salta and Alem.

Internet access in most places costs a meager 1 or 2 pesos (35¢–65¢) per hour. There are a number of cybercafes along Avenida Sarmiento; try **Mundo Internet,** Sarmiento 107 (℗ 261/420-3795), open daily from 8:30am to 1am.

Official Telefónica and Telecentro offices, located all over town, also offer Internet use. The main post office, Correo Argentino (© 261/429-0848), located at the corner of Avenida San Martín and Colón, is open weekdays from 8am to 8pm.

WHAT TO SEE & DO
IN TOWN

Plaza Independencia ✸✸ marks the city center, a beautiful square with pergolas, fountains, frequent artesian fairs, and cultural events. Following the 1861 earthquake, the new city was rebuilt around this area. Four additional plazas, San Martín, Chile, Italia, and España, are located 2 blocks off each corner of Independence Square. Surrounding the square you will find the Julio Quintanilla Theater, the National School, the Independencia Theater, the Provincial Legislature, and the small Modern Art Museum (© 261/425-7279; admission $1).

Adjacent to the "Alameda," a beautiful promenade under white poplars, Museo Histórico General San Martín ✸, Remedios Escalada de San Martín 1843 (© 261/425-7947), stands in the spot where General San Martín had hoped to make his home. The museum's small collection of artifacts pays homage to Argentina's beloved hero, who prepared his liberation campaigns from Mendoza. It's open weekdays from 9am to 1pm; admission costs $1. Another museum worth visiting is Museo Fundacional ✸✸, Videla Castillo between Beltrán and Alberdi (© 261/425-6927), located 3km (2 miles) from downtown. Chronicling the early history of Mendoza, the museum begins by looking at the culture of the indigenous Huarpes and continues with an examination of the city's development through Spanish colonization to independence. It's open Tuesday through Saturday from 8am to 8pm, Sunday from 3 to 8pm; admission is $1.

Almost as big as the city itself, the wonderful Parque General San Martín ✸✸✸ has 17km (11 miles) of idyllic pathways and 300 species of plants and trees. A tourist office, located near the park's main entrance at avenidas Emilio Civit and Bologne sur Mer, provides information on all park activities, which include boating, horseback riding (outside the park's perimeters), and hang-gliding. A national science museum and zoo (daily 9am–6pm) are located inside the park, and you can also camp here. The best hike leads to the top of Cerro de la Gloria, which offers a panoramic view of the city and surrounding valley.

TOURING THE WINERIES

Less commercialized than their European and American counterparts, Mendoza's wineries are free to visit and easily accessible along wine roads known locally as Los Caminos del Vino. These roads are as enticing as the wine itself, weaving and winding through tunnels of trees to vast dry valleys dominated by breathtaking views of the snowcapped Andes. Some roads climb as high as 1,524m (5,000 ft.) in the High Zone surrounding the Mendoza River, while others lead to lower-level vineyards in the south. Mendoza's wine region is divided into four zones: the High Zone, Mendoza East, Uco Valley, and Mendoza South. Different wine roads branch out through these zones and can be driven in part or total, allowing you to tour as many of Mendoza's bodegas as you like. There are presently 552 functioning wineries, 80 of which formally offer tours.

The **High Zone** that surrounds the Mendoza River includes Luján de Cuyo and parts of Las Heras, Guaymallén, Luján, and Maipú. This first zone is best regarded for its production of Malbec, although cabernet sauvignon, Chenin, merlot, chardonnay, and sirah are all bottled as well. Many of the bodegas in this zone lie within one hour's drive of Mendoza. The **Mendoza East Region** is the second zone, comprised of Junín, Rivadavia, San Martín, Santa Rosa, and La Paz. This is the province's largest wine-producing area, where vineyards irrigated by the Tumuyán and Mendoza rivers harvest Malbec, merlot, Sangiovese, and Syrah, among others. South of Mendoza, the **Uco Valley Region,** including Tunuyán, Tupungato, and San Carlos, produces excellent Malbec, Semillon (a white), and Torrontés (another white, more common in Salta). Allow at least two hours to reach here. The final zone is the **Mendoza South Region,** between San Rafael and General Alvear. Fed by the Atuel and Diamante rivers, its best varieties are Malbec, Bonarda, and cabernet sauvignon. You will need at least a day to visit this region.

Throughout your drive you will stumble upon wineries old and new, some producing on a large scale and exporting internationally, others small and focused on the local market. It is difficult to say which bodegas excel over others, as each has its own focus and success. Among some of the best-known are Bodega Catena Zapata (Luján), which is a boutique winery of the larger Bodegas Esmeralda; Chandon (Luján), a subsidiary of France's Moet & Chandon; Salentein (Tunuyán); Norton (Luján); López (Maipú); Nieto Senetiner (Luján); Bodega Jacques et Françoise Lurton (Tunuyán); Etchart (Luján); Finca La Cilia (San Carlos); and Cavas de Weinert (Luján). Close to Mendoza in neighboring Maipú, Bodega La Rural has a small winery museum that exhibits Mendoza's earliest wine production methods. Another excellent winery close to town is Dolium, one of the only bodegas producing underground to allow for natural cooling. As at most bodegas, a tasting follows a tour of the laboratory and winery, and there is little pressure to buy. As Italian owner Mario Giadorou proudly states, "We offer an institutional show, not a sales show."

You can pick up a map of the wine routes, as well as information on individual bodegas, from any of the tourist offices. Each February, the wine season culminates with the **Fiesta Nacional de la Venimia (National Wine Harvest Festival),** which includes a parade, folk dancing, and coronation of the festival's queen.

OUTDOOR ACTIVITIES

Mendoza offers a wealth of outdoor activities. Tour operators in Mendoza will arrange an itinerary according to your choice, from part-day outings to multiple-day excursions. For hiking, contact **Huentata,** Las Heras 680, Mendoza (© 261/425-3108), or **Argentina Rafting Expediciones,** Ruta 7 s/n, 5549 Potrerillos (© 262/448-2037). Argentina Rafting Expediciones (in coordination with **Juan Jardel;** © 262/448-3030) and **Ríos Andinos,** Ruta 7 Km 64, 5549 Potrerillos (© 261/431-6074), also offer horseback riding trips and mountain biking adventures.

Mendoza offers the best white-water rafting in Argentina, and during the summer months when the snow melts in the Andes and fills the Mendoza River, rafters enjoy up to class IV and V rapids. Rafting is possible year-round, but the river is colder and calmer in winter months. **Argentina Rafting Expediciones** and **Ríos Andinos** (see above) offer half-, whole-, and 2-day trips on the Mendoza River. Be sure to bring an extra pair of clothes and a towel, because you are guaranteed to get soaked. Children under 12 are not allowed to raft.

SHOPPING

On Friday, Saturday, and Sunday, an outdoor **handicrafts market** takes place during the day on Plaza Independencia. Regional shops selling handicrafts, leather goods, gaucho paraphernalia, and *mate* are located along Avenida Las Heras, two of which are **Las Veñas,** Av. Las Heras 399 (© 261/425-0498) and **Los Andes,** Av. Las Heras 445 (© 261/425-6688). More mainstream stores line Avenida San Martín. The city's best shopping mall is **Palmares Open Mall,** located on Ruta Panamericana 2650 in Godoy Cruz (© 261/413-9100). Most shops close from 1 to 4pm each day for siesta. You can also buy Mendocine wines at many shops, the least expensive costing no more than a few dollars a bottle and premiums going for $25 to $80. The Park Hyatt, Chile 1124 (© 261/441-1234), has an excellent wine shop, with a knowledgeable sommelier.

WHERE TO STAY

Mendoza has recently opened a few new hotels, which have substantially boosted the city's lodging quality. However, after the Park Hyatt, the level of hotel service quickly drops and the star classification posted at local accommodations is not reliable. In addition to the hotels listed below, a couple of up-and-coming, modestly priced accommodations worth looking into are the **Microtel,** outside the city center at Acc. Sur and Lamadrid (© 261/432-0503), and a new bed-and-breakfast called **Quinta Rufino,** Rufino Ortega 142 (© 261/420-4696). Prices quoted are for high season, which in Mendoza is February through March, July, and September through November. Hotel rates are often discounted 15% to 20% in the off season. Prices listed below do not include the 21% tax.

EXPENSIVE

Park Hyatt Mendoza ⭐⭐⭐   Peering majestically over the Plaza de la Independencia, the Park Hyatt opened in 2001 after restoring the original facade of the 19th-century Plaza Hotel and building a seven-floor tower for guest rooms. Sweeping columns of granite and stone showcase the lobby, and an impressive collection of Mendocino art pays tribute to local culture. A landscaped courtyard separates different sections of the hotel, leading past water fountains and an outdoor dining area to a warm, inviting pool. Guest rooms could stand to lose a bit of the wood paneling, but are nevertheless spacious and contemporary. Fluffy duvets and feather pillows blanket the beds, and white marble bathrooms have separate bathtubs and showers with crystal washbasins. Kaua Spa deserves special mention because of its uniqueness: A professional team of masseurs from Bangkok gives wonderful Thai massages, and the spa incorporates Mendocino wines in a variety of its body treatments (for example, shampoo based on wine acids or grape-seed oil body lotion). A well-equipped fitness room, Jacuzzi, sauna, and steam bath are here too. Hotel guests benefit from frequent cultural events, ranging from jazz and music shows to Spanish festivals and flamenco dances. Some events take place in **Bistro M** ⭐⭐, an excellent international restaurant boasting South America's first open kitchen. Bar Uvas is the city's premier wine bar, and the Regency Casino is Mendoza's try at Las Vegas. Many guests are from Buenos Aires and Chile, the latter taking advantage of favorable exchange rates across the border.

Chile 1124, 5500 Mendoza. © 261/441-1234. Fax 261/441-1235. www.mendoza.park.hyatt.com. 186 units. $145 double; from $175 suite. Rates include a beautiful buffet breakfast. AE, DC, MC, V. **Amenities:** Restaurant; wine bar; sports bar; heated outdoor pool; nearby golf; excellent health club and spa; concierge; business center; room service; babysitting; dry cleaning; laundry service. *In room:* A/C, TV, minibar, hair dryer, safe.

MODERATE

A centrally located option in this price range is **Hotel NH Cordillera** $\mathcal{R}$, Av. España 1324 (© **261/441-6464;** www.nh-hotels.com). Part of a Spanish chain that caters to business travelers, the NH has four floors of crisp, compact rooms, half of which face Plaza San Martín.

Park Suites Apart Hotel $\mathcal{R}$ A stylish new hotel 2 blocks from Plaza Independencia, the Park Suites attracts business people during the week and tourists on weekends. Single rooms are called "suites," ranging in size from junior to grand, while those with more than one room are called "apartments," accommodating up to six people. All have hardwood floors, kitchenettes, firm mattresses, stereo systems, and light, modern decor, although bathrooms are on the small size. Ask for a room with a mountain view. The staff is small, but friendly.

Mitre 753, 5500 Mendoza. © 261/413-1000. Fax 261/413-1019. www.parksuitesmza.com.ar. 56 units. From $50 double. Rates do not include breakfast. AE, DC, MC, V. **Amenities:** Restaurant; bar; pool; sauna; fitness room. *In room:* A/C, TV, minibar, fridge, hair dryer, safe.

WHERE TO DINE
EXPENSIVE

1884 $\mathcal{RRR}$ INTERNATIONAL   Francis Mallman has created Mendoza's top restaurant inside Bodega Escorihuela, known among other things for housing the biggest wine barrel in the province. Using fine Argentine meats and fresh local produce, his carefully presented cuisine combines his Patagonian roots with his French culinary training. Dishes are prepared with matching wine selections, with Malbec and sirah topping the list. You can easily combine a tour of the bodega, which also has an art gallery, in the same visit. Tours are offered weekdays, every hour from 9:30am to 3:30pm.

Belgrano 1188, Godoy Cruz. © 261/424-2698. Reservations recommended. Main courses $9–$15. AE, DC, MC, V. Daily 6:30–11am, 12:30–3:30pm, and 8pm–midnight.

MODERATE

If you're in the mood for Italian food, go straight to **La Marchigiana** $\mathcal{RR}$, at the Palmares Open Mall (© **261/439-1961**).

Don Mario $\mathcal{RR}$ ARGENTINE   Don Mario serves the best Argentine steaks in town. Don't let the soothing country house atmosphere fool you—this is a serious Argentine parrilla. The *bife de chorizo* (strip steak) served *a punto* (medium rare) is the top selection, but any of the meats are outstanding. The "Don Mario brochette" includes sirloin, chicken, tomatoes, onions, and peppers on one delicious skewer. Non–meat eaters can choose from pizza, pasta, or one of the fish dishes. Two shelves of Mendoza wines beg to be disturbed, and the expert waitstaff will help guide you to a selection.

Palmares Open Mall. © 261/439-4838. Main courses $4–$6. AE, DC, MC, V. Daily noon–3pm and 8pm–midnight.

INEXPENSIVE

Estancia La Florencia $\mathcal{(Value)}$ ARGENTINE   This casual eatery pays homage to the legendary gaucho, and its two levels mimic a traditional *estancia*. Ask one of the waiters, none of whom is under 50, for a recommended plate and he is likely to tell you, *"Una comida sin carne no es comida"* (a meal without meat isn't a meal). So choose one of the many varieties of steaks, the lomo being the most tender, or order a half grilled chicken served with a lemon slice. Just remember that a plate of meat is a plate of meat, uncorrupted by green vegetables or anything but potatoes (usually fries). Other accouterments must be ordered separately. Food is served promptly and without fanfare, and the bill may be one of the lowest you will ever find.

Sarmiento and Perú. © 261/429-9117. Main courses $2–$4. AE, DC, MC, V. Mon–Wed noon–5pm and 8pm–2am; Thurs–Sun noon–2am.

MENDOZA AFTER DARK

Mendoza nightlife is substantially more subdued than in Buenos Aires or Córdoba, but there is still a fair selection of bars and nightclubs that capture a night owl's attention. Thursday through Sunday are the biggest nights, with people getting started around midnight. The Park Hyatt Mendoza **Bar Uvas,** Chile 1124 (© 261/441-1234), begins a bit earlier and offers a complete selection of Mendocine wines, with jazz and bossa nova groups playing most nights. Wine tastings are offered every Thursday at 9pm. **Apeteco,** at San Juan and Barraquero, has live music and dancing most nights. The city's best bars line Call Aristides Villanueva in the center of town, and many people begin here with a drink before heading to a disco along Ruta Panamericana, located roughly 10km (6 miles) from the town center. **Runner** and **El Diablo** are the top discos in this area. There are a few tango bars in Mendoza, two of which are **C'Gastón,** at Lavalle 35 (© 261/423-0986) and **Abril Café,** at Las Heras 346 (© 261/420-4224). For you gamblers, the **Regency Casino,** Chile 1124 (© 261/441-1234), is substantially better than the Casino Provincial, offering blackjack, roulette, poker, and slots. Table bets are $1 to $50.

6 The Argentine Lake District ★★★

The Lake District is Argentina's premier vacation destination, a ruggedly beautiful jewel characterized by snowcapped mountains, waterfalls, lush forest, the area's namesake lakes, and trout-filled crystalline rivers. The region stretches from north of Junín de los Andes to the south of Esquel, incorporating small villages, ranches, several spectacular national parks, and the thriving city of Bariloche. Visitors often liken the Lake District to Alpine Europe, as much for the landscape as for the clapboard architecture influenced by Swiss and German immigration. Although it is considered part of Patagonia, the Lake District has little in common with its southern neighbors, especially now that increased migration from cities such as Buenos Aires continues to urbanize the region.

The allure of the Lake District is that it offers year-round activities, from hiking to biking, fishing to hunting, sightseeing to sunbathing, summer boating to winter skiing. The region is also well known for its food—venison, wild boar, trout, smoked cheeses, wild mushrooms, sweet marmalades, chocolates, and more. Tourism is the principal economic force here, which means that prices soar as the swarming masses pour into this region from December to March and during the month of July. We highly recommend that you plan a trip during the off season, especially in November or April, when the weather is still pleasant, although it is possible to escape the crowds even during the middle of summer.

Considering the enormous, flat pampa that separates Buenos Aires from the Lake District, and the region's proximity to the border with Chile, many visitors include a trip to Chile's Lake District. (For more information, see chapter 7.) This can be done by boat aboard the popular "Lake Crossing" through Puerto Blest to Lago Todos los Santos near Ensenada, or by vehicle.

EXPLORING THE REGION

Although the Lake District extends from Esquel north to Junín de los Andes, we have focused in this section on the most scenic and accessible destinations in the region: San Carlos de Bariloche (usually called simply Bariloche) and San Martín de los Andes. This coverage includes the area's many national parks as well as driving tours and boat trips that take in the best of that stunning lakeside scenery. The best way to view this region is to base yourself in one of these towns and explore the surrounding wilderness. All of the towns described in this section offer enough outdoor and sightseeing excursions to fill 1 or even 2 weeks, but 4 to 5 days in one location is ample time for a visit. An interesting option for travelers is to make a detour into Chile via the lake crossing from Bariloche, or to organize a boat/bus combination that loops from Bariloche and Villa La Angostura in Argentina, then crosses the border into Chile and stops in Puyehue, continuing on south to Puerto Varas or Puerto Montt, then crossing back into Argentina and Bariloche via the Lake Crossing. This takes some planning; see chapter 7 for more information.

SAN CARLOS DE BARILOCHE ☆☆

1,621km (1,005 miles) SW of Buenos Aires, 180km (112 miles) S of San Martín de los Andes

San Carlos de Bariloche, or simply Bariloche, is the winter and summer playground for vacationing Argentines and the second-most visited destination in the country. The city sits in the center of Nahuel Huapi National Park and is fronted by an enormous lake of the same name. Bariloche offers many outdoor activities, sightseeing drives, boat trips, great restaurants, and shopping opportunities. Visitors could occupy themselves for a week in any season.

Bariloche began as an ill-fated mission in 1670, founded by Jesuits from Chiloé, Chile. In the late 1800s, immigrants from Europe and migrants settled in the region and based their economy primarily on sheep and cattle ranching. The city was incorporated in 1902, and at that time, tourism was already showing signs of becoming an economic force. As the city grew, it replaced Europe as the top vacation destination for wealthy families from Buenos Aires, who built grand houses along the Avenida Bustillo out toward the Llao Llao Peninsula—a crowd eventually replaced by middle-class and student travelers during the 1950s.

The city itself embodies a strange juxtaposition: an urban city in the middle of beautiful wilderness. Unfortunately, Argentine migrants fleeing Buenos Aires, an ever-growing tourism industry, and 2 decades of unchecked development have left a cluttered mess in what once was an idyllic mountain town. Bits and pieces of the charming architecture influenced by German, Swiss, and English immigration are still in evidence, but visitors can be overwhelmed by the hodgepodge of ugly apartment buildings, discos, and crowds that descend on this area, especially from mid-December until the end of February and during ski season in July. Yet drive 15 minutes outside town, and thick forests of pine, beech, and cypress will surround you, along with rippling lakes and snowcapped peaks that rival those found in Alpine Europe. If you're looking for a quiet destination, you'd be better off lodging in the town of Villa La Angostura or along the road to the Llao Llao Peninsula (see below). On the flip side, Bariloche offers a wealth of services.

ESSENTIALS
Getting There
BY PLANE   The **Aeropuerto Bariloche** (© 02944/426162) is 13km (8 miles) from downtown. Buses to the city center are timed with the arrival of flights, and can be found outside at the arrivals area; some are run by the airlines themselves. A taxi costs about $10. **Aerolíneas Argentinas,** Quaglia 238 (© 02944/422425; www.aerolineasargentinas.com.ar), has about three daily flights from Buenos Aires (schedules change with the seasons), and a weekly flight from Santiago, El Calafate, Trelew, Neuquén, Esquel, and Cordoba. Aerolíneas also operates flights from Sao Paolo, Brazil, during the ski season only. **Southern Winds,** Villegas 147 (© 02944/423704; www.sw.com.ar), and **American Falcon Air,** Mitre 159 (© 02944/42-5200; www.americanfalcon.com.ar), both offer one daily flight from Buenos Aires.

BY BUS   The **Terminal de Omnibus** (© 02944/432860) is at Av. 12 de Octubre 2400; there are a dozen companies that serve most major destinations in Argentina and Chile. **TAC** (© 02944/431521) has three daily arrivals from Buenos Aires and daily service from El Bolsón, Esquel, Mendoza, and Córdoba. **Vía Bariloche** (© 02944/435770) has three daily arrivals from Buenos Aires and one daily trip from Mar del Plata. **Andesmar** (© 02944/422140) has service from Mendoza, Río Gallegos, and Neuquén, and service from Osorno, Valdivia, and Puerto Montt in Chile. For service from San Martín de los Andes via the scenic Siete Lagos (Seven Lakes) route (during the summer only) or any other route from that city or from Villa La Angostura, try **Ko-Ko** (© 02944/423090).

BY CAR   Bariloche can be reached from San Martín via several picturesque routes. The 200km (124-mile) scenic Siete Lagos route from San Martín de los Andes follows routes 234-231-237; the 160km (99-mile) Paso Córdoba takes routes 234-63-237; the longest, yet entirely paved, 260km (161-mile) Collón Curá route follows routes 234-40-237 and is recommended for night driving or when the weather is crummy. To get to El Bolsón, follow Route 258 south; continue down Route 40 to get to Esquel. During periods of heavy snowfall, chains are required.

Getting Around
When navigating the streets of Bariloche, do not confuse two streets with similar names: V. A. O'Connor runs parallel to the Costanera, and J. O'Connor bisects it.

BY FOOT   The city is compact enough to explore by foot. However, most visitors spend just a few hours touring the city, and instead use Bariloche as a base to explore surrounding areas.

Tips Taking a Car into Chile

If you're hoping to do a Lake District circuit combining both the Argentine and Chilean lake districts, be warned that you'll need additional insurance and written permission from the car-rental agency to take the vehicle across the border. We suggest using **Avis** (www.avis.com) for these trips, as it's the only company that has offices in numerous towns in both countries and can offer roadside assistance and get a replacement car to you quickly if you run into any problems.

BY CAR A rental car is how most savvy travelers visit this area; you'll want one here if you're staying outside the city center and also to drive through the region's sinuous roads that pass through exceptionally scenic landscapes, such as the Circuito Chico. All travel agencies offer excursions to these areas, which is another option. Rental agencies, including Budget, Dollar, Hertz, and Avis, have kiosks at the airport, and many downtown offices: **Avis** at San Martín 162 (© 02944/431648), **Budget** at Mitre 106 (© 02944/422482), **AI Rent a Car** at Av. San Martín 235 (© 02944/422582), **Dollar** at Villegas 285 (© 02944/430333), **Hertz** at Quaglia 165 (© 02944/434543), **Baricoche Rent A Car** at Moreno 115 (© 02944/427638), **Localiza** at Av. San Martín 463 (© 02944/424767), and **A Open Rent a Car** at Mitre 171 #15 (© 02944/426325).

Visitor Information

The **Secretaría de Turismo,** in the stone-and-wood Civic Center complex between calles Urquiza and Panzoni (© **02944/426784;** securismo@bariloche. com.ar), has general information about Bariloche, and it is an indispensable source for accommodations listings, especially during the high season. It also operates an information stand in the bus terminal. It's open Monday through Friday from 8am to 9pm, Saturday and Sunday from 9am to 9pm. For information about lodging and attractions surrounding Bariloche, try the **Secretaría de Turismo de Río Negro,** Av. 12 de Octubre 605, at the waterfront (© **02944/426644**); it's open Monday through Friday from 9am to 2pm.

The **Club Andino Bariloche,** Av. 20 de Febrero 30 (© **02944/422266;** fax 02944/424579; transitando@bariloche.com.ar), provides excellent information about hiking, backpacking, and mountaineering. They sell maps and provide treks, mountain ascents, and guided ice walks, as well as rafting, photo safaris, and horseback rides; open daily from 9am to 1pm and 6 to 9pm during winter, daily from 8:30am to 3pm and 5 to 9pm during summer. For general info about Nahuel Huapi National Park, head to the park's headquarters in the Civic Center (© **02944/424111**), open Monday through Friday from 8:30am to 12:30pm.

Two good new websites for all sorts of up-to-date travel information is www.bariloche.org and www.bariloche.com.

FAST FACTS   Most banks exchange currency, including **Citibank,** Mitre 694 (© **02944/436301**). Try also **Cambio Sudamérica,** Mitre 63 (© **02944/434555**).

For **emergencies,** dial © 101; for **general assistance,** call © 02944/423434. For **medical attention,** go to **Hospital Privado Regional,** 20 de Febrero 594 (© 02944/423074).

The central **post office** is in the Civic Center, next to the tourist office. For Internet access, try **Cybermac Café,** Rolando 217 no. 12 (no phone); or **Net & Cappuccino,** Quaglia 220 (© **02944/426128**).

WHAT TO SEE & DO IN & AROUND BARILOCHE

Bariloche's **Civic Center,** Avenida Juan Manuel de Rosas and Panzoni, is a charming stone-and-wood complex that houses most municipal offices and tourism services, such as the information center and national park headquarters. The complex, built in 1940, was inspired by the architecture of Bern, Switzerland. Here you'll find the **Museo de la Patagonia Perito Moreno** (© **02944/422309**), open Tuesday through Friday from 10am to 12:30pm and 2 to 7pm, Monday from 10am to 1pm; closed Sunday. Admission is $1. The museum has five salons dedicated to the natural science, history, and ethnography of the Bariloche region. It's somewhat interesting, but not worth a special trip; it'll take you about 45 minutes to breeze through it.

Tour Operators

A plethora of travel agencies offer everything under the sun along the streets of Bariloche. Most tours do not include lunch, and some charge extra for a bilingual guide. The best of the lot include **Catedral Turismo** at Moreno 238 (© **02944/425443**), with a wide variety of land excursions to El Bolsón, Cerro Tronador, and circuit sightseeing routes. **Tom Wesley Viajes de Aventura** at Mitre 385 (© **02944/435040**) specializes in horseback riding, but offers everything else, too, even sightseeing tours and an adventure camp. **Cumbres Patagonia,** Villegas 222 (© **02944/423283;** cumbres@bariloche.com.ar), has easy sightseeing trips and more adventurous excursions, including trekking, fishing, and 4×4 trips. Also try **Ati Viajes** at V. A. O'Connor 335 (© **02944/426782**), **Barlan Travel** at Mitre 340 no. 68 (© **02944/426782**), or **Viajes Danneman** at Mitre 86 (© **02944/428793**).

Outdoor Activities

BIKING   Mountain-bike rental for paved roads and information about bike trails and guided trips in Nahuel Huapi is available from **Bike Way** at V. A. O'Connor 867 (© **02944/424202**), **Bariloche Mountain Bike** at Gallardo 375 (© **02944/462397**), and **Dirty Bikes** at V. A. O'Connor 681 (© **02944/425616**).

FISHING   This region provides anglers with excellent fly-fishing on the Manso, Traful, and Machico rivers, and trolling on Lake Nahuel Huapi for introduced species such as brown and rainbow trout and landlocked salmon. You can pick up information and fishing licenses at the **Club Caza y Pesca** on the coast at Onelli and Avenida 12 de Octubre (© **02944/421515**), open Monday through Friday from 9am to 1pm, or at the office of the Parque Nacional Nahuel Huapi in the Civic Center. The **Patagonia Fly-Shop** and its owner-guide Ricardo Ameijeiras offer great fly-fishing expeditions, multiday programs in lodges, and day tours with bilingual guides. They can be found at Quichahuala 200 (© **02944/441944;** flyshop@bariloche.com.ar). Tour agencies such as **Cumbres Patagonia,** at Villegas 222 (© **02944/423283**), offer half- and full-day fly-casting and trolling fishing excursions.

HIKING   The Nahuel Huapi National Park has a well-developed trail system that offers day hikes, multiday hikes, and loops that connect several backcountry *refugios,* some of which offer rustic lodging. The national park office in the Civic Center provides detailed maps and guides that include the difficulty levels of trails. Another great source for information is the **Club Andino,** Av. 20 de Febrero 30 (© **02944/422266;** transitando@bariloche.com.ar), which also has trails, guided trekking, ice walks, and climbing trips on Cerro Tronador.

HORSEBACK RIDING   Horseback rides in the park are offered by **Tom Wesley Viajes de Aventura,** Mitre 385 (© **02944/435040**), which also has a kid-friendly adventure camp. Rides cost an average of $8 for 2 hours and $12 for 3 hours. **Cumbres Patagonia,** Villegas 222 (© **02944/423283**), has trips to Fortín Chacabuco for $15 per half-day and $22 per full day, including lunch.

RAFTING   Various companies offer river rafting on the Río Manso in both class III and class IV sections, either half- or full-day trips. The average cost for a half-day is $22 to $25, a full day, $30 to $38. Easier floats down the class I Río Limay are also available, for about $12 for a half-day. Excursions include all equipment, transportation, and a snack or lunch (full-day trips). Try **Cumbres Patagonia** at Villegas 222 (© **02944/423283**), **Transitando lo Natural** at Mandisoví 72 (© **02944/423918**), or **Rafting Adventure** at Mitre 161 (© **02944/432928**).

SKIING & SNOWBOARDING   Bariloche's main winter draw is the ski resorts at Cerro Catedral. The resort is divided in two, with separate tickets (it's possible to buy a more expensive ticket for both resorts) for Robles and Catedral. Robles's bonus is that it is typically less crowded, with excellent open-bowl skiing. Catedral offers more advanced lift services, but its runs are usually packed. Lift tickets cost between $10 and $15 for adults and $6 and $10 for kids, depending on high and low seasons. Both resorts are well liked by families and beginners for their abundance of intermediate terrain, but there's plenty of advanced terrain, too.

Shopping

You'll find anything and everything along Bariloche's main street, Mitre, including shops selling souvenirs and Argentine products such as *mate* gourds and leather goods. For the region's famous smoked meats and cheese, and for other regional specialties such as trout pâté, try the renowned **Familia Weiss** at Mitre 360 (© **02944/424829**) or **Del Turista** at Av. San Martín 252 or Mitre 239 (no phone). Del Turista also has an enormous array of chocolates and candy, as do other confectioneries on Calle Mitre, such as **Abuela Goye** at Mitre 258 (© **02944/423311**) and Quaglia 221 (© **02944/422276**), **Bari** at Mitre 339

(© **02944/422305**), **Mexicana** at Mitre 288 (© **02944/422505**), and **Mamuschka** at Mitre 216 (© **02944/423294**). Stop by the visitor center for a map of Avenida Bustillo and the Llao Llao Peninsula, along which are dozens of shops selling regional specialties.

WHERE TO STAY

If you're looking for luxury, you'll find the most options along the main road outside town that runs parallel to the lake and leads to the Llao Llao Peninsula. The larger hotels in the city (such as the Panamericano) tend to cater to tour groups and aren't especially luxurious or service oriented, but their advantage is location; staying in town puts you steps from the many excellent restaurants and shops in this tiny metropolis in the mountains. If you're planning to rent a car, then by all means stay outside the city and drive in at your convenience.

Note that during the high season (Dec 15–Feb 28, July 1–Aug 30, and Easter week), prices may be higher than listed below, as hotels adjust their rates according to demand and the ever-precarious financial situation in Argentina.

City Center
Expensive

Hotel Edelweiss (*Kids*)   This full-service hotel offers reliable service and huge double bedrooms, and is a solid choice in downtown Bariloche in this price category (but don't expect much luxury). Double superiors come with two full-size beds, bay windows, and lake views, as do the suites. The double standards are smaller, with a single full-size bed or two twins and a view of a building in the back, but they are just as comfortable and $10 cheaper. All rooms and bathrooms have recently been updated. The design is pleasant but very run-of-the-mill. There is an aging penthouse pool with glass walls affording views of Lake Nahuel Huapi. The lounge area has polished floors, leather couches, and fresh flowers; there's also a computer with Internet access available for a nominal fee. The hotel offers several attractive packages and promotional rates, so be sure to ask when making your reservations.

Av. San Martín 202, San Carlos de Bariloche. © **800/207-6900** in the U.S., or 02944/426165; 08705/300-200 in the U.K.; or 800/221-176 in Australia. Fax 02944/425655. www.edelweiss.com.ar. 100 units. $95–$160 double superior; from $170 suite. Rates include buffet breakfast. AE, DC, MC, V. Valet parking. **Amenities:** 2 restaurants; bar; small indoor pool; sauna; game room; room service. *In room:* TV, minibar, hair dryer, safe.

Hotel Panamericano (*Overrated*)   The Hotel Panamericano has long coasted on its reputation as one of Bariloche's premier accommodations, boasting a casino, a lake view, a range of amenities, and an in-town branch of the excellent El Patacón restaurant. Its deluxe rating is exaggerated, however, especially when compared to rivals such as the Llao Llao Hotel & Resort (see below). The rooms are spacious and comfortable, but the design needs a face-lift and everything seems rather aging and tired. The lake views are available only above the fifth floor; in fact, the hotel rarely books rooms on the bottom floors unless they're hosting a convention, although they have plenty of tour groups that fill the hotel year-round. The back rooms face an ugly building, but are cheaper. Inside the lobby, a faux waterfall trickles in the background, and a bar/lounge regularly has live piano music. The hotel has another 100 or so rooms and a casino on the other side of the street, connected by an aerial walkway.

Av. San Martín 536, San Carlos de Bariloche. ©/fax **02944/425846**. www.panamericanobariloche.com. 306 units. $110 double; from $185 suite. Rates include buffet breakfast. AE, DC, MC, V. Valet parking. **Amenities:** 2 restaurants; lounge; bar; indoor pool; exercise room; sauna; room service; massage; laundry service; dry cleaning. *In room:* TV, minibar, coffeemaker.

Inexpensive

Hotel Aconcagua *(Value*   This small, well-kept but older hotel is one of the best values in Bariloche. The establishment runs like clockwork, a carry-over from the German immigrant who built the hotel and whose design influence can be found throughout the lobby and lounge area. The rooms are nothing to go wild over, with average beds and a late 1960s design, but a few have lake views, and doubles with a full-size bed are spacious (doubles with two twins are not, however). The bathrooms are old but impeccable; the showers do not have stalls, just a curtain. The included American breakfast is quite good, and the dining area is pleasant and sunny. The receptionists are friendly and try hard to help with directions, but be patient, as they don't speak much English.

Av. San Martín 289, San Carlos de Bariloche. ℂ **02944/424718.** Fax 02944/424719. aconcagua@ infovia.com.ar. 32 units. $18–$30 double. Rates include continental breakfast. AE, MC, V. **Amenities:** Lounge; room service. *In room:* TV.

On the Road to the Llao Llao Peninsula
Very Expensive

Llao Llao Hotel & Resort ⭐⭐⭐ *(Kids*   The internationally renowned Llao Llao Hotel & Resort is one of the finest hotels in Latin America, as much for its magnificent location as its sumptuous, elegant interiors and refined service. Situated on a grassy crest of the Llao Llao Peninsula and framed by rugged peaks, this luxurious hotel was modeled after the style of Canadian mountain lodges, taking cues such as cypress and pine-log walls, stone fireplaces, antler chandeliers, and barn-size salons. The hotel was first built in 1938, but burned to the ground and was rebuilt again in 1939; since its inception it has been scrupulously maintained. A driveway winds up to the hotel where a discreet security guard monitors traffic: The hotel tries to keep gawkers at a distance, although visitors may come for a drink, afternoon tea, or a meal. The nearby Club House has a daily tea from 4 to 7pm.

A monumental hallway adorned with paintings from local artists leads to the rooms, all of which have been decorated in a rustic country design and come with gleaming white bathrooms—nice, but the style is not as exceptional as one would expect from a hotel of this caliber. Standard rooms are comfortable but quite small; superior suites are split into bedroom and living areas and come with a wraparound deck and fireplace. The hotel has a handful of unadvertised inside standard double rooms that come without a view. Those are reserved for drop-ins who inquire at reception for the cheapest accommodations (no prior reservations accepted for these rooms). There's a new spa with treatment rooms affording breathtaking lake and mountain views. Included in the price of the rooms is a myriad of daily activities from watercolor painting classes for adults to games and events for kids.

The hotel's fine-dining restaurant, Los Césares, is the best in the Bariloche area (see "Where to Dine," below), and the business center has free Internet access available for registered guests.

Av. Bustillo, Km 25. ℂ **02944/448530.** Fax 02944/445789. Reservations (in Buenos Aires): ℂ 11/4311-3434; fax 11/4314-4646. www.llaollao.com. 159 units. $160–$402 double; $318–$1,365 suite; $378–$531 cottage. Rates include buffet breakfast. AE, DC, MC, V. **Amenities:** 2 restaurants; bar; lounge; small indoor heated pool; golf course; tennis courts; exercise room; fabulous spa; Jacuzzi; extensive watersports equipment; children's center; video arcade; tour and car-rental desk; business center; shopping arcade; salon; room service; massage; babysitting; laundry service; dry cleaning. *In room:* TV, safe.

Expensive

Villa Huinid 🐫🐫 *Finds*   The country-style, luxurious cabins and suites that make up the brand-new Villa Huinid are top-notch choices for travelers looking for independent accommodations outside town. The complex faces the lake, where it has a private beach, and is backed by a thick forest with a walking trail. Each room is handcrafted of knotty cypress, with stone fireplaces, decks with a full-size barbecue, and a handsome decor of floral wallpaper, plaid bedspreads, craftsy furniture, and other accents, such as dried flowers and iron lamps. The rooms come as four-, six-, and eight-person cabañas with fully stocked kitchens and living areas; the bathrooms are sumptuous, with wooden sinks and hydro-massage bathtubs. Service provided by the gracious owners of the Villa Huinid is one of this hotel's highlights, as are the property's well-manicured grounds with a trickling stream meandering through the property.

Av. Bustillo, Km 2.5. ℂ/fax 02944/5235234. www.villahuinid.com.ar. 16 units. $72–$120 suite; $120–$200 4-person cabaña. AE, DC, MC, V. Private parking. **Amenities:** Shuttles to downtown and ski resorts. *In room:* TV.

WHERE TO DINE

Bariloche is full of eateries and cafes, especially on Avenida San Martín and the side streets leading to it. Below is the best of the best. Just like accommodations, Bariloche's best restaurants are outside the city center. In addition to the restaurants listed below, **The Familia Weiss,** at the corner of Palacios and V. A. O'Connor (ℂ **02944/435789;** daily 11:30am–1am) and the **Casita Suiza,** Quaglia 342 (ℂ **02944/435963;** daily 8pm–midnight) are solid choices for both lunch and dinner.

City Center
Moderate

Jauja 🐫🐫 REGIONAL   Jauja is one of the best restaurants in the center of town, both for its extensive menu and woodsy atmosphere. You'll find just about everything on offer here, from regional to German-influenced dishes, including grilled or stewed venison, goulash with spaetzle, stuffed crepes, homemade pastas, barbecued meats, and trout served 15 different ways. The semicasual dining area is made entirely of wood, with wooden tables and lots of glass, plants, basket lamps, and candles. A glass-and-wood wall divides smoking and non-smoking sections. The Jauja's fresh salads and desserts are quite good, especially the poached pears and apple mousse. Food is available to go.

Quaglia 366. ℂ 02944/422952. Main courses $6–$12. AE, MC, V. Daily 11:30am–3pm and 7:30pm–midnight.

Inexpensive

El Boliche de Alberto 🐫 *Value* STEAKHOUSE   If you're in the mood for steak, this is your place. El Boliche de Alberto is our favorite parrilla in Bariloche, and everyone else's too, it seems. Some regulars have been coming back for 20 years and some make the crossing from Chile to have an inexpensive delicious meal here. The quality of meat is outstanding, and the prices are extremely reasonable. The menu is brief: several cuts of beef, chicken, and sausages, with salads and side dishes such as french fries. The dining area is unpretentious and brightly lit, with wooden tables. The charismatic owner, Alberto, has plastered an entire wall with photos of regulars and luminaries who have paid a visit, along with notes thanking him for a wonderful meal. Alberto will usually take your order. A typical *bife de chorizo* steak is so thick you'll need to split it with your dining partner; if you're alone, they can do a half order for $3. The Boliche de Alberto has a very good pasta restaurant at Elflein 163 (ℂ **02944/431084**).

Villegas 347. ℂ 02944/431433. Main courses $4–$7. AE, MC, V. Daily noon–3:30pm and 8pm–midnight.

Outside the City Center
Expensive

El Patacón ★★ *Finds* ARGENTINE/REGIONAL   This superb restaurant is a 7km (4-mile) drive from the city center. El Patacón's unique architecture and mouth-watering cuisine are so appealing that it was chosen as the dining spot for Bill Clinton and Argentina's Carlos Ménem during a presidential meeting several years back, a fact the restaurant is more than happy to advertise. The building is made of chipped stone inlaid with polished, knotty tree trunks and branches left in their natural shape, which form zany crooked beams and pillars.

Start your meal with a platter of five provolone cheeses served crispy warm off the grill, and follow it with venison ravioli or goulash, trout in a creamy leek sauce with puffy potatoes, wild boar in wine, or mustard chicken. There is also a parrilla with grilled meats and daily specials, and a bodega with an excellent selection of wines. If you're staying in the city center you can opt to dine at the downtown branch of this restaurant, located at the Hotel Panamericano (see "Where to Stay," above) where the menu is identical but the decor is not nearly as enticing as this location's.

Av. Bustillo, Km 7. © 02944/442898. Reservations recommended on weekends. Main courses $6–$14. AE, DC, MC, V. Daily noon–3pm and 8pm–midnight.

Los Césares ★★★ *Moments* PATAGONIAN   This enchantingly romantic restaurant offers the only fine dining experience in the Bariloche area. Located in the luxurious Llao Llao Hotel & Resort (see "Where to Stay," above), the refined and slightly formal setting comes complete with fireplace, antiques, white tablecloths, and ultracomfortable chairs with armrests. The restaurant prides itself on using the highest quality ingredients grown locally—from wild game for the main courses to the wild berries for dessert. Specialties include grilled venison with blackberry sauce, almond-crusted local trout (from the nearby lake), and a good selection of Argentine steaks. The excellent wine list features many regional wines for under $18. Service is superb, and when you finally get the bill, you'll be pleasantly surprised at how affordable it really is for such an exquisite place.

Av. Bustillo, Km 25. In the Llao Llao Hotel & Resort. © 02944/448530. Reservations required. Main courses $12–$22. AE, DC, MC, V. Daily 7:30–11:30pm.

BARILOCHE AFTER DARK

Bariloche is home to a handful of discos catering to the 20- to 30-something crowd. These discos adhere to Buenos Aires nightlife hours, beginning about midnight, with the peak of the evening at about 3 or 4am. The cover charge is usually $10 per person, and often women enter for free. Try **Roket** at J. M. de Rosas 424 (© 02944/431940) or **Cerebro** at J. M. de Rosas 405 (© 02944/424965). The Hotel Panamericano runs Bariloche's **Casino**, Av. San Martín 570 (© 02944/425846); call for opening hours. The Casino hosts live shows every evening. Guests must be over 18; entrance is free. The local cinema can be found at Moreno 39 (© 02944/422860).

SAN MARTÍN DE LOS ANDES ★★
1,640km (1,017 miles) SW of Buenos Aires, 200km (124 miles) N of San Carlos de Bariloche

San Martín de los Andes is a charming mountain town of 15,000 nestled on the tip of Lago Lácar between high peaks. The town is considered the tourism capital of the Neuquén region, a claim that's hard to negate considering the copious arts-and-crafts shops, gear rental shops, restaurants, and hotels that constitute much of downtown. San Martín has grown considerably in the past 10 years, but thankfully hasn't succumbed to the whims of developers as Bariloche has, owing to city laws that limit building height and regulate architectural styles. The town is quieter than Bariloche, and decidedly more picturesque, thanks to its timber-heavy architecture and Alpine Swiss influence. San Martín overflows with activities, from biking to hiking to boating to skiing, but it is also very popular for hunting and fishing, and some do come just to relax. The tourism infrastructure here is excellent, with every lodging option imaginable and plenty of great restaurants.

ESSENTIALS
Getting There
BY PLANE   **Aeropuerto Internacional Chapelco** (✆ **02972/428388**) sits halfway between San Martín and Junín de los Andes (see below), and serves both. **Aerolíneas Argentinas,** Capitán Drury 876 (✆ **02972/427003**), has at least one daily flight from Buenos Aires and one daily flight from Bariloche. Note that at press time, Aerolíneas did not operate a flight *to* Bariloche, just *from* that city. A taxi to San Martín costs about $6; there are also transfer services at the airport for $2 per person. **By Mich Rent A Car** and **Avis** both have car-rental kiosks at the airport.

BY BUS   The **Terminal de Omnibus** is at Villegas and Juez del Valle (✆ **02972/427044**). **El Valle** (✆ **02972/422800**) offers daily bus service to San Martín de los Andes from Buenos Aires. **Ko-Ko Chevalier** (✆ **02972/427422**) also offers service to and from Buenos Aires, and serves Villa La Angostura and Bariloche by the paved Collón Curá route or by the scenic Siete Lagos route. **Centenario** (✆ **02972/427294**) has service to Chile, and offers daily service to Buenos Aires; Villarrica- and Pucón-bound buses leave Monday through Saturday, and those for Puerto Montt leave Tuesday through Thursday. **Albus** (✆ **02972/428100**) has trips to Bariloche via the Siete Lagos route (about 3 hr). Bus service can vary seasonally, and it's best to evaluate a coach's condition and services before buying a ticket, especially for trips to and from Buenos Aires. Buses from Buenos Aires to San Martín de los Andes take 23 hours.

BY CAR   San Martín de los Andes can be reached from San Carlos de Bariloche following one of three routes. The popular 200km (124-mile) Siete Lagos route takes routes 234-231-237, and sometimes closes during the winter. The 160km (99-mile) Paso Córdoba route takes routes 234-63-237. The longest, yet entirely paved, 260km (161-mile) Collón Curá route follows routes 234-40-237. If driving at night, take the paved route. To get to Neuquén (420km/260 miles), take routes 234-40-22.

Getting Around
San Martín is compact enough to explore by foot. For outlying excursions, tour companies can arrange transportation. **Avis** car rental has an office at Av. San Martín 998 (✆ 02972/427704; fax 02972/428500) as well as a kiosk at the airport; **ICI Rent-A-Car** is at Villegas 590 (✆ 02972/427800); **Nieves Rent-A-Car** is at Villegas 725 (✆ 02972/428684); **Localiza/El Claro** is at Villegas 977 (✆ 02972/428876); and **By Mich Rent A Car** is at Av. San Martín 960 (✆ 02972/427997) and at the airport.

Note that two main streets have similar names and can be confusing: Perito Moreno and Mariano Moreno.

Visitor Information

San Martín's **Oficina de Turismo** offers comprehensive accommodations listings with prices and other info, and the staff is friendly and helpful. They can be found at Rosas and Avenida San Martín at the main plaza and are open Monday through Sunday from 8 to 11pm (©/fax **02972/427347** and 02972/427695). The **Asociación Hotelera y Gastronomía** (© **02972/427166**) also offers lodging information, including photographs of each establishment. It's open Monday through Sunday from 9am to 1pm and 3 to 7pm, and during high season Monday through Sunday from 9am to 10pm, but they are not as efficient as the Oficina de Turismo.

A new website that's chock-full of valuable information is www.sanmartin delosandes.com.

FAST FACTS Andina International at Capitán Drury 876 exchanges money; banks such as **Banco de la Nación** at Av. San Martín 687, **Banco de la Provincia Neuquén** at Belgrano and Obeid, and **Banco Río Negro** at Perito Moreno and Elordi have ATMs and money exchange. All banks are open Monday through Friday from 10am to 3pm.

In an **emergency,** dial © 107. For **police** emergencies, dial © 101. The **federal police station** is at Av. San Martín 915 (© 02972/428249); the **provincial police station** is at Belgrano 635 (© 02972/427300). For medical attention, go to **Hospital Regional Ramón Carrillo** at Avenida San Martín and Coronel Rodhe (© 02972/427211).

The post office, **Correo Argentino,** is at the corner of General Roca and Coronel Pérez (© **02972/427201**). For Internet access, try logging on at **Cooperativa Telefónica** at Capitán Drury 761; it's open daily from 9am to 11pm. Half an hour of Internet use costs $1.10.

WHAT TO SEE & DO

San Martín de los Andes is heavily geared toward tourism, and its streets are lined with shops selling arts and crafts, regional specialties such as smoked meats and cheeses, outdoor gear, books, and more. Visitors will find most of these shops on **Avenida San Martín** and **General Villegas,** but you could lose an afternoon wandering the downtown area and poking your head into these well-stocked shops. For regional specialties and/or chocolates, try **Ahumadero El Ciervo,** General Villegas 724 (© **02972/427450**); **El Turista,** Belgrano 845 (© **02972/428524**); or **Su Chocolate Casero,** Villegas 453 (© **02972/427924**). For arts and crafts, try **Artesanías Neuquinas,** J. M. de Rosas 790 (© **02972/428396**).

San Martín is a mountain town geared toward outdoor activities. If you're not up to a lot of physical activity, take a stroll down to the lake and kick back on the beach. Alternatively, rent a bike and take a slow pedal around town. Pack a picnic lunch and head to Hua Hum (see below).

Tour Operators & Travel Agencies

Both **Tiempo,** Av. San Martín 950 (©/fax **02972/427113;** tiempopatagonico@ usa.net), and **Pucará,** Av. San Martín 943 (© **02972/427218;** pucara@smandes. com.ar), offer similar tours and prices, and also operate as travel agencies for booking plane tickets. Excursions to the village Quila Quina, via a sinuous road that offers dramatic views of Lago Lácar, cost $6; a longer excursion including Chapelco and Arrayán is $8. Excursions to the hot springs Termas de Lahuenco are $10; scenic drives through the Siete Lagos route are $10 (to Villa La Angostura) and $12 (to Bariloche). A gorgeous circuit trip to Volcán Lanín and Lago

Huechulafquén goes for $10. Tours do not include lunch, which must be brought along or arranged ahead of time.

Outdoor Activities

BIKING   San Martín is well suited for biking, and shops offer directions and maps. Bike rentals are available at **Enduro Kawa & Bikes** at Belgrano 845 (© 02972/427093), **HD Rodados** at Av. San Martín 1061 (© 02972/427345), and **Mountain Snow Shop** at Av. San Martín 861 (© 02972/427728).

BOATING   Naviera Lácar & Nonthué (© 02972/428427) at the Costanera and main pier offers year-round boat trips on Lago Lácar. A full-day excursion to Hua Hum includes a short navigation through Lago Nonthué. The cost is $12 adults, $6 children 6 to 12 and seniors, free for children under 6, plus park entrance fees; there's a restaurant in Hua Hum, or you can bring a lunch. Naviera also operates a ferry service to the beautiful, but packed during the summer, beaches of Quila Quina for $4 adults, $3 children 6 to 12 and seniors, and free for children under 6. Naviera rents kayaks for $2 per hour.

To raft the Río Hua Hum, get in touch with **Tiempo** or **Pucará** (see "Tour Operators & Travel Agencies," above).

FISHING INFORMATION & LICENSES   Jorge Cardillo Pesca at General Roca 636 (© 02972/428372; cardillo@smandes.com.ar) is a well-stocked fly-fishing shop that organizes day and overnight fishing expeditions to the Meliquina, Chimehuín, and Malleo rivers, among other areas. The other local fishing expert is **Alberto Cordero** (© 02972/421453; acordero@smandes.neuquen.com.ar), who will arrange fishing expeditions around the area.

You can pick up a fishing guide at the **Oficina Guardafauna** at General Roca 849 (© 02972/427091).

MOUNTAINEERING   Victor Gutiérrez and his son Jano Gutiérrez are the top climbing and mountaineering guides in the region (Victor has more than 40 years' experience in the region) and offer climbing and orientation courses, ascents of Lanín and Domuyo volcanoes, and treks, climbs and overnight trips in Lanín and Nahuel Huapi national parks. Both have cellphones; Victor can be reached at © 02944/15-61-0440 or victorg11@latinmail.com, Jano at © 02944/15-63-3260 or janoclif@latinmail.com.

SKIING   The principal winter draw for San Martín de los Andes is **Cerro Chapelco,** one of the premier ski resorts in South America. Just 20km (12 miles) outside town, Cerro Chapelco is known for its plentiful, varying terrain and great amenities. Although popular, the resort isn't as swamped as Bariloche is. The resort sports one gondola (which takes skiers and visitors to the main lodge), five chairlifts, and five T-bars. The terrain is 40% beginner, 30% intermediate, and 30% advanced/expert. Chapelco offers excellent, bilingual ski instruction; ski and snowboard rental; and special activities such as dog sledding. The resort has open-bowl skiing and tree skiing, and numerous restaurants. To get here without renting a car, ask your hotel to arrange transportation or hire a *remise.*

To drive to the resort from town, follow Ruta 234 south along Lago Lácar; it's paved except for the last 5km (3 miles). Lift tickets are quite reasonable and vary from low to high season. A 3-day ticket runs $19 to $45 for adults, and $16 to $29 for children under 18. During the summer, the resort is open for hiking and sightseeing, with lift access. For more information, call © 02972/427460 or visit www.sanmartindelosandes.com. The road is usually passable, but you may need chains during heavy snowfall; check road conditions before heading up.

WHERE TO STAY

What is lacking in San Martín is a luxury hotel. Although there are plenty of excellent hosterías and cabañas, if it's luxury you're looking for, you'd be better off spending the bulk of your time in the Bariloche or Villa la Angostura areas. This is a very laid-back, slightly rugged, outdoorsy town and its hotels reflect that.

Moderate

La Cheminée ⍟ Warm, attentive service and snug accommodations make La Cheminée a top choice, which is why so many foreign travel groups book a few nights here. The Alpine Swiss design popular in San Martín is in full swing here, with carved and stenciled woodwork and other touches that have been meticulously well maintained since the hotel opened 15 years ago. Spacious rooms are carpeted and feature wood ceilings and a pastel country design with thick cotton floral bedspreads and striped wallpaper. Book the room they call a double *hogar*—for $8 more, it includes a fireplace.

General Roca and Mariano Moreno, San Martín de los Andes. ℂ 02972/427617. Fax 02972/427762. www.hosterialacheminee.com.ar. 19 units. $43–$64 double. Rates include breakfast. AE, DC, MC, V. **Amenities:** Restaurant; bar; lounge; small outdoor pool; Jacuzzi; sauna; room service; laundry service. *In room:* TV, minibar.

Patagonia Plaza Hotel *Overrated* San Martín's only large, full service hotel feels like a bland, generic motel. Although the public areas are expansive with lots of windows overlooking the street, there's a feeling that everything is fading already. Rooms are comfortable and fairly modern with colorful bedspreads and large windows overlooking the street. Bathrooms are sparkling clean and adequate. There's a small indoor heated pool and sauna and an ample breakfast buffet every morning. This is a good place for a hassle-free overnight stay located just steps from all the shops and restaurants, but don't expect much luxury or charm.

Av. San Martín and Rivadavia. ℂ 02972/422280. Fax 02972/422284. www.patagoniaplazahotel.com.ar. 78 units. $65–$110 double. Rates include buffet breakfast. AE, DC, MC, V. **Amenities:** Restaurant; bar; lounge; indoor heated pool; sauna; tour desk; room service; massage; laundry service; dry cleaning. *In room:* TV, minibar in some units.

Rincón de los Andes *Kids* The sizable resort abuts a steep, forested mountain slope and is recommended both for the smartly decorated apartments and the wealth of activities offered—especially for families. Set up like a town-house complex and centered on a large, airy restaurant with outdoor deck, the 100 apartments range in size to accommodate two to eight guests. All have fully stocked kitchens and spacious bedrooms. The grassy grounds include a golf driving range and paddle court, and there's a heated pool in a steamy, glass-enclosed building. One of the prize amenities is a travel office that rents bicycles and plans excursions for individual guests and for kids.

Juez de Valle 611, San Martín de los Andes. ℂ 02972/428583. www.rinconclub.com.ar. 100 units. $59–$93 double. AE, MC, V. **Amenities:** Restaurant; lounge; indoor pool; sauna; bike rental; game room; tour desk; room service; massage; laundry service. *In room:* TV, kitchen.

Inexpensive

Hostería del Chapelco *Value* Just about every kind of unit is available at this hostería, including new hotel rooms and cabañas, and cheaper, older duplex and A-frame units. Although it sits on the lakeshore, the rooms do not benefit from the view, but a bright lobby takes advantage of the location with giant picture windows. The hotel rooms and the six attached cabañas are new, with stark, modern furnishings and tile floors; the cabañas have open living/kitchen areas. The duplex units are more economical, but they feel like family rumpus rooms, and the interiors could use new carpet and fresh paint. Las Alpinas houses the oldest units, six small but decent A-frame detached cabañas. The lobby's fireside chairs and wraparound banquette are a nice place to watch the rippling lake.

Almirante Brown 297, San Martín de los Andes. © 02972/427610. Fax 02972/427097. 14 units, 22 cabañas. $16–$19 double. AE, MC, DC, V. **Amenities:** Bar; room service. *In room:* TV.

Hostería La Casa de Eugenia 🔍 *(Finds* Built in 1927, this lovely old building with bright blue trim used to house the local Historical Society; now it's a bed-and-breakfast. The charming living room with its large fireplace, piano, and colorful sofas leads to five bedrooms, named by color. The *verde* (green) has a skylight keeping it bright throughout the day; all the rooms come with comfortable beds with down comforters, gleaming white bathrooms, and little else. Breakfast is served in the bright dining room overlooking a small park, and the friendly managers can help you plan excursions in and around San Martín.

Colonel Díaz 1186. © 02792/427206. www.lacasadeeugenia.com.ar. 5 units. $20–$34 double. Rates include continental breakfast. No credit cards. **Amenities:** Lounge; room service. *In room:* No phone.

WHERE TO DINE

San Martín has several excellent restaurants. For sandwiches and quick meals, try **Peuma Café,** Av. San Martín 851 (© **02972/428289**); for afternoon tea and delicious cakes and pastries, try **La Casa de Alicia,** Capitán Drury 814, #3 (© **02944/616215**).

Expensive

Avataras 🔍 *(Finds* INTERNATIONAL   Exceptionally warm, friendly service and a marvelous variety of international dishes from Hungarian to Chinese to Egyptian make Avataras shine. The chefs, transplants from Buenos Aires, whip up exquisite items such as Indian lamb curry, wild boar with juniper-berry sauce, Malaysian shrimp sambal, and filet mignon with four-pepper sauce. The appetizer menu features Scandinavian gravlax and Caribbean citrus shrimp, and the herbs and specialty items used to flavor such dishes are imported from Buenos Aires and abroad.

Teniente Ramayón 765. © 02972/427104. Reservations recommended. Main courses $10–$18. AE, DC, MC, V. Daily 8:30am–midnight.

Moderate

La Pierrade 🔍🔍 *(Finds* INTERNATIONAL   San Martín's newest restaurant opened in late 2002 and is the town's most modern and sleek eatery. A giant stone fireplace and a long bar can be found on the ground floor and there are two cozy dining areas on the floor above. Soothing and romantic lighting gives the place a very relaxing atmosphere. Fluffy red pillows are strewn around the fireplace so you can unwind with your predinner drink. Begin with the very unusual rabbit pudding with green salad and dried tomatoes, a delicate deer carpaccio, or a tasting of Patagonian pâtés; then move on to the exquisite pumpkin cannelloni with a mushroom ragout or the grilled steak encrusted in sesame seeds and served with tomato and basil risotto. There's usually also a fish or shrimp specialty, along with a choice of wild game. For dessert, the tiramisu is divine, and so is the homemade ice cream.

Mariano Moreno and Villegas. © 02972/421421. Reservations recommended. Main courses $6–$14. No credit cards. Daily 8pm–1am.

La Reserva ★★ *(Moments* ARGENTINE   This lovely stone and wood house has recently been transformed into one of the most romantic restaurants in Patagonia with a stone fireplace, elegant cloth-covered tables, soothing music, and superb service. La Reserva is run by the talented chef Rodrigo Toso, who is influenced by many ethnic cuisines while using mostly Patagonian ingredients. Begin with a cold glass of Argentine champagne to go with an order of tapas— a tasting of cheeses and dried meats. Then move on to grilled trout fresh from the nearby lake, tender venison with fresh berry sauce, or chicken breast stuffed with feta cheese and herbs. There are excellent regional wines for under $10 a bottle, and the desserts, a selection of homemade fruit tarts and ice creams, are divine.

Belgrano 940. © 02972/428734. Reservations recommended. Main courses $6–$12. AE, DC, MC, V. Daily noon–3pm and 8pm–midnight.

INEXPENSIVE

La Costa del Pueblo ★ *(Kids* INTERNATIONAL   A lake view and an extensive menu with everything from pasta to parrilla make this restaurant a good bet. The establishment operated as a cafe for 20 years until new owners expanded to include a dozen more tables, a cozy fireside nook, and a children's eating area separate from the main dining room, complete with miniature tables and chairs. It's a great spot for a cold beer and an appetizer platter of smoked cheeses and venison while watching the lake lap the shore. Service can sometimes be horrendously slow. That said, La Costa offers good, homemade pasta dishes such as cannelloni stuffed with ricotta and walnuts, grilled meats, and pizza. There are vegetarian sandwiches and a children's menu.

Av. Costanera and Obeid. © 02972/429289. Main courses $3–$7. No credit cards. Daily 11am–1am.

7 Patagonia & Tierra del Fuego ★★★

Few places in the world have captivated the imagination of explorers and travelers like Patagonia and Tierra del Fuego. It has been 4 centuries since the first Europeans sailed through on a boat captained by Ferdinand Magellan, and this vast, remote region is still for the most part unexplored.

A traveler can drive for days without seeing another soul on the vast Patagonian pampa. What seduces people to travel to Patagonia is the idea of the "remote" indeed, the very notion of traveling to the end of the world. The people who live here (both Chileans and Argentines) are hardy survivors.

A harsh climate and Patagonia's geological curiosities have produced some of the most beautiful natural attractions in the world: the granite towers of Torres del Paine and Los Glaciares national parks (though the former is found across the Chilean border), the Southern and Northern ice fields with their colossal glaciers, and the flat pampa broken by multicolored sedentary bluffs.

EL CALAFATE ★★

222km (138 miles) S of El Chaltén; 2,727km (1,691 miles) SW of Buenos Aires

El Calafate is a tourist-oriented village that hugs the shore of turquoise Lago Argentino, a location that, combined with the town's leafy streets, gives it the

It's "Chile" in Patagonia

For information on traveling on the Chilean side of Patagonia, see chapter 7.

Tips Recommended Reading

Bruce Chatwin (1940–89) created "a modern masterpiece of travel writing" *(Reader's Catalog)* with *In Patagonia* (Penguin, 1988), in which he recorded his journey through the physical and cultural landscape of the ends of the earth.

---

feel of an oasis in the desert pampa of this region. The town depends almost entirely on its neighboring natural wonder, the Perito Moreno Glacier, for tourism. Thousands of visitors come for the chance to stand face-to-face with this tremendous wall of ice, one of the few glaciers in the ice field that isn't retreating.

The town was named for the calafate bush found throughout Patagonia that produces a sweet berry commonly used in syrups and jams. As the economy in Buenos Aires deteriorated, many Argentines fled to the countryside and some came here, to El Calafate, which had suffered from a tourist trap mentality for years. Thankfully this tendency is waning as more migrants head south to set up businesses that are meant to really serve visitors. The town itself is quite a pleasant little place, but you won't find many attractions here—they are all within the confines of Los Glaciares National Park. What you will find are several good restaurants and a charming main street lined with boutiques boasting fine leather goods, and shops selling locally manufactured chocolates, jams, and delicious caramel cookies called *alfajores*.

ESSENTIALS
Getting There
BY PLANE El Calafate's brand-new **Aeropuerto Lago Argentino** (no phone) has dramatically changed transportation options here; before you would have to fly into Río Gallegos and then take a long bus ride across the flat pampa. Service is from Argentine destinations only: **Aerolíneas Argentinas** (© 11/4340-3777 in Buenos Aires; www.aerolineas.com.ar) has two daily flights from Buenos Aires. During high season (Dec–Mar), there may be up to three daily flights; there's also a daily flight from Ushuaia and three flights a week from Bariloche. There are now flights arriving directly from Ezeiza International Airport in Buenos Aires (before, all flights left from Aeroparque, downtown). Be sure to specify which airport you'd like to fly from.

Aerovías Dap (no phone; www.aeroviasdap.cl) has a daily morning flight to Puerto Natales aboard a nine-seater propeller; but that service is frequently canceled due to high winds. Neither company has an office in El Calafate, but any travel agency can book tickets for you. From the airport, **Aerobús** (© 02901/492492) operates a bus to all the hotels in town for $2.25; they can also pick you up for your return trip if you call 24 hours ahead. A **taxi** into town should cost no more than $6.50 for up to four people. There's a brand-new **Hertz** desk (no phone; www.hertz.com) at the airport, as well.

BY BUS El Calafate has a bus terminal located on Julio A. Roca, reached by taking the stairs up from the main street Avenida del Libertador. To and from Puerto Natales, Chile: **Buses Sur** (© 02901/491631) and **Turismo Zaahj** (© 02902/411325) have five weekly trips leaving at 8am, as does **Cootra** (© 02902/491444). The trip takes 5 to 6 hours, depending on how long you get held up at the border. To get to El Chaltén, take **Chaltén Travel,** which

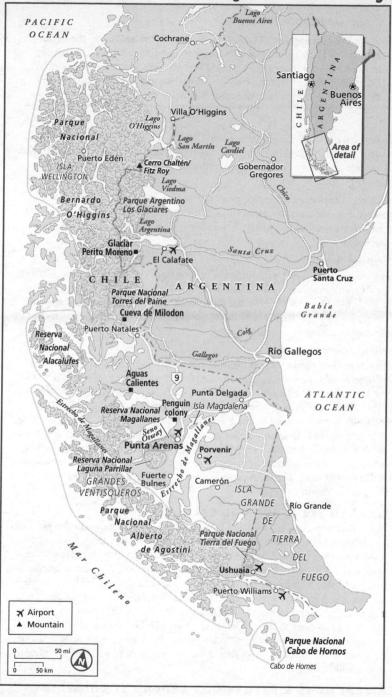

PACIFIC
OCEAN

Lago
Buenos Aires

Cochrane

Santiago

CHILE

ARGENTINA

Buenos
Aires

Area of
detail

Parque
Nacional

Villa O'Higgins

Lago
O'Higgins

Lago
San Martín

Lago
Cardiel

Puerto Edén

Cerro Chaltén/
Fitz Roy

Gobernador
Gregores

ISLA
WELLINGTON

Lago
Viedma

Chico

Bernardo
O'Higgins

Parque Argentino
Los Glaciares

Lago
Argentina

Glaciar
Perito Moreno

El Calafate

Santa Cruz

Puerto
Santa Cruz

CHILE

ARGENTINA

Parque Nacional
Torres del Paine

Cueva de Milodon

Bahía
Grande

Puerto Natales

Coig

Reserva
Nacional
Alacalufes

Gallegos

Río Gallegos

Aguas
Calientes

9

Punta Delgada

ATLANTIC
OCEAN

Penguin
colony

Isla Magdalena

Reserva Nacional
Magallanes

Seno
Otway

Porvenir

Estrecho de Magallanes

Punta Arenas

Reserva Nacional
Laguna Parrillar

Estrecho de Magallanes

Camerón

ISLA
GRANDE

Fuerte
Bulnes

GRANDES
VENTISQUEROS

Río Grande

Parque
Nacional

DE

Alberto
de Agostini

Parque Nacional
Tierra del Fuego

TIERRA

Mar
Chileno

DEL

FUEGO

Ushuaia

Puerto Williams

✈ Airport
▲ Mountain

Parque Nacional
Cabo de Hornos

Cabo de Hornes

0   50 mi
0   50 km

Tips **Departure Taxes**

If you're departing from El Calafate airport, remember to pay the departure tax of $5.50 before going through security. They'll take your money and stamp your boarding pass. Otherwise, you won't be allowed to board the flight. There are no signs posted saying you must do this, nor do the airline agents remind you of this when checking in.

---

leaves daily at 8am and returns from Chaltén at 6pm (© **02902/492212**); **Caltur** (© **02902/491842**); or **Interlagos Turismo** (© **02902/491179**); the latter two leave daily at 7:30am and return from El Chaltén at 5pm.

BY CAR Ruta 5, followed by Ruta 11, is paved from Río Gallegos to El Calafate. From Puerto Natales, cross the border at Cerro Castillo, which will lead you to the Ruta Nacional 40 and up to the paved portion of Ruta 11. The drive from Puerto Natales is roughly 5 hours, not including the border checkpoint.

Getting Around

For information about transportation to and from the Perito Moreno Glacier, see "Parque Nacional Los Glaciares & the Perito Moreno Glacier," below. If you'd like to rent a car, you can do so at the new **Europcar** office at Av. del Libertador 1741 (© **02902/493606;** www.europcar.com.ar). Rates begin at $21 per day, including insurance and taxes.

Visitor Information

The city's **visitor information kiosk** can be found inside the bus terminal. They offer an ample amount of printed material and can assist in planning a trip to the Perito Moreno Glacier; it's open October through April daily from 8am to 11pm and May through September daily from 8am to 8pm (© **02902/491090**). A good website to check is www.elcalafate.com.ar.

If you require help arranging any aspect of your trip, a very helpful agency to contact is **SurTurismo,** 25 de Mayo 23 (© **02902/491266;** suring@cotecal.com.ar). They can secure everything from airport transfers to hotel reservations at discounted rates. They also provide private and licensed guides for treks and tours of the region

WHAT TO SEE & DO IN EL CALAFATE

El Calafate is really a service town for visitors on their way to visit the glaciers (see "Parque Nacional Los Glaciares & the Perito Moreno Glacier," below), but it does present a pleasant main avenue and there are lots of bookstores and souvenir and crafts shops. Heading out of town on Avenida del Libertador, you'll pass the **Museo Municipal** (no phone), open Monday through Friday from 8am to 1pm and 3 to 9pm, with a collection of farming and ranching implements, Indian artifacts, and historical and ethnographical displays. It's worth a stop if you have a half-hour to spare. And that's about it in El Calafate, although if you are interested in bird-watching, you could take a short walk to the Bahía Redonda at the shore of Lago Argentino to view upland geese, black-necked swans, and flamingos.

ATTRACTIONS & EXCURSIONS AROUND EL CALAFATE

For information about visiting the glaciers and the national park, see "Parque Nacional Los Glaciares & the Perito Moreno Glacier," below.

HORSEBACK RIDING **Cabalgata en Patagonia,** Julio A. Roca 2063 (© **02902/493203;** cabalgataenpatagonia@cotecal.com.ar), offers two horse-back riding options: a 2-hour ride to Bahía Redonda for a panoramic view of El Calafate ($12), and a full-day trip bordering Lago Argentino, with an optional stop at the Walicho Caves where you can view supposedly Indian "paintings," which are billed as real but are really reproductions. This tour costs $18 per person and includes lunch. Book directly or with a travel agency.

VISITING AN *ESTANCIA*   An option worth looking into is a trip to an *estancia,* or ranch, that is open to the public and offers day activities, restaurant service, and lodging. Perhaps the best known is the **Estancia Helsingfors,** open October to March on the shore of Lago Viedma about 150km (93 miles) from El Calafate. Helsingfors offers lodging, horseback riding, overflights, bird-watching, boat trips, and high gastronomy. For more information, contact their offices in Río Gallegos at Av. del Libertador 516 (©/fax **02966/420719**).

WHERE TO STAY

There are several excellent hotels in El Calafate and the breathtakingly luxurious Los Nostros faces the Perito Merino Glacier (see below). For all hotels, parking is free or street parking is plentiful.

Expensive

Hotel Kosten Aike 🏵🏵 *Value*   This charming newer hotel offers modern and attractive accommodations paired with high-quality service. The Kosten Aike is priced lower than its competitor, the Posada los Alamos (see below); but the only difference here is that the Posada's design is buttoned-up conservative and the Kosten Aike is fresh and stylish. Both the architect's and the designer's good taste saved the Kosten Aike from the cookie-cutter style usually seen in new hotels. Furnishings and artwork imported from Buenos Aires include matching drapes and bedspreads in rust and beige accented with black geometric squiggles, papier-mâché lamps, iron and rosewood tables and chairs, and petal-soft carpets, and all rooms feature sumptuous bathrooms. Some rooms have bay windows and are very large; they aren't any more expensive, so ask for one when booking. The airy lobby is inlaid completely with gray stone. The Kosten Aike has a chic restaurant off the lobby that serves contemporary regional and Argentine fare.

Gobernador Moyano 1243, El Calafate. © 02902/492424, or 11/4811-1314 (reservations). Fax 02902/491538. www.kostenaike.com.ar. 60 units. $63–$97 double. AE, DC, MC, V. **Amenities:** Restaurant; wine bar; fireside lounge; exercise room; spa; game room; concierge; room service; massage; laundry service. *In room:* TV, dataport, minibar, hair dryer, safe.

Hotel Posada Los Alamos 🏵🏵 *Finds*   The Posada Los Alamos is as conserva-tive as a Brooks Brothers suit. Because of the low-key design of the "complex" and the slightly aloof service, you can't help shake the feeling that you're in a pri-vate country club. The style is classic: a red-brick exterior fringed with the hotel's namesake alamo trees, plaid carpet, old English furniture, and windows with wooden, triangular eaves. Downstairs is a comfortable lounge, and the lobby's large windows look out onto an expansive lawn. Rooms have ample space and each has a slightly different color and style. Ask for one that looks out onto the quiet, grassy backyard instead of the dusty dirt road.

Gobernador Moyano and Bustillo, El Calafate. © 02902/491144. Fax 02902/491186. www.posadalos alamos.com. 144 units. $92–$163 double; from $240 suite. AE, MC, V. **Amenities:** Restaurant; bar; lounge; golf course; tennis court; tour desk; room service; massage; babysitting; laundry service; dry cleaning. *In room:* TV, minibar, safe.

Moderate

Hostería Sierra Nevada ♠ *Finds*   This charming hostería is a 15-minute walk from all the shops and restaurants. It's the only recommended property right on the lake (not across the street like the Mirador del Lago, above), and every room comes with a water view. Built in 2000, the two-story building has a pleasant expansiveness to it and the rooms are fresh and modern with wrought-iron furniture, firm mattresses, and beautiful granite tiled bathrooms and showers. Large French doors in each room slide open to reveal the garden and the lake just beyond. Most of the guests here are South American, so the staff members don't speak much English, but they're friendly and pleasant and will try their best.

Libertador 1888, El Calafate. © 02902/493129. sierranevada@cotecal.com.ar. 18 units. $52–$70 double. Rates include buffet breakfast. MC, V. **Amenities:** Restaurant; bar. *In room:* TV, safe.

WHERE TO DINE
Moderate

Casimiro ♠ *Finds* REGIONAL   This new wine bar and restaurant opened in the fall of 2002 and has quickly become the number-one hot spot in El Calafate. The sleek and modern black-and-white decor, thick tablecloths and flickering candles on every table, and the young and energetic waitstaff make this place a winner. You can sample one of the many wines while enjoying an appetizer platter of regional Patagonian specialties such as smoked trout, smoked wild boar, and a variety of cheeses. Main courses change frequently but usually range from a simple steak to an elaborate pasta with salmon, cream, and capers in white-wine sauce; there's always a chicken and seafood offering, as well. If you're celebrating a special occasion, this would be an excellent place to try a glass of dry Argentine sparkling wine.

Av. del Libertador 963. © 02902/492590. Main courses $7–$12. MC, V. Daily 10am–1am.

La Posta ♠♠♠ ARGENTINE   Although it's in a building separate from the Posada Los Alamos, the La Posta is considered to be part of that hotel. This is El Calafate's most upscale restaurant, serving great cuisine and choice wines in a cozy, candlelit environment. The menu, printed in four languages, offers well-prepared dishes that effectively blend Argentine and international-flavored fare, like filet mignon in a puff pastry with rosemary-roasted potatoes, king crab ravioli, almond trout, or curried crayfish. Desserts are superb. If you're staying at the hotel, a lovely breakfast buffet is served here every morning, and the service both morning and night is exquisite.

Gobernador Moyano and Bustillo. © 02902/491144. Reservations recommended in high season. Main courses $8–$17. AE, DC, MC, V. Daily 7pm–midnight.

Inexpensive

La Tablita ♠♠ *Value* STEAKHOUSE   Carnivores need not look any further. La Tablita is all about meat, and it's one of the local favorites in town for its heaping platters and giant parrilladas (mixed grills) that come sizzling to your table on their own mini-barbecues. The parrilladas for two cost $9, but they really serve three diners given the size and assortment of chicken, sausage, beef, lamb, and a few innards you may or may not recognize. The filet mignon is incredibly tender here, and at $6 is one of the least expensive filets that I've ever had. The sunny, airy restaurant can be found on the other side of the bridge that spans the Arroyo Calafate, about a 2-minute walk from downtown.

Coronel Rosales 24. © 02902/491065. Main courses $4–$7. AE, MC, V. Daily 11am–3pm and 7pm–midnight (Wed closed for lunch).

PARQUE NACIONAL LOS GLACIARES & THE PERITO MORENO GLACIER ⟨★★★⟩

The Los Glaciares National Park covers 600,000 hectares (1,482,000 acres) of rugged land that stretches vertically along the crest of the Andes and spills east into flat pampa. Most of Los Glaciares is inaccessible to visitors except for the park's two dramatic highlights: the granite needles, such as Fitz Roy near El Chaltén (see "El Chaltén & the Fitz Roy Area," below), and this region's magnificent Perito Moreno Glacier. The park is also home to thundering rivers, blue lakes, and thick beech forest. Los Glaciares National Park was formed in 1937 as a means of protecting this unique wilderness, notable for its landscape carved and sculpted by Ice Age and present-day glaciation.

If you don't get a chance to visit Glacier Grey in Torres del Paine, the Perito Moreno is a must-see. Few natural wonders in South America are as spectacular or as easily accessed as this glacier, and unlike the hundreds of glaciers that drain from the Southern Ice Field, the Perito Moreno is one of the few that are not receding. At the turn of the last century, the Perito Moreno was measured at 750m (2,460 ft.) from the Península Magallanes; by 1920, it had advanced so far that it finally made contact with the peninsula. Each time the glacier reached the peninsula, which would occur every 3 to 4 years, the Perito Moreno created a dam in the channel and the built-up pressure would set off a calving explosion for 48 to 72 hours, breaking the face of the glacier in a crashing fury. This phenomenon has not occurred in many years, but the Perito Moreno is usually reliable for sending a few huge chunks hurling into the channel throughout the day.

What impresses visitors most is the sheer size of the Perito Moreno Glacier; it's a wall of jagged blue ice measuring 4,500m (14,760 ft.) across and soaring 60m (197 ft.) above the channel. From the parking lot on the Península Magallanes, a series of vista-point walkways descends, which take visitors to the glacier's face. It's truly an unforgettable, spellbinding experience. There are opportunities to join an organized group for a walk on the glacier as well as boat journeys that leave from Puerto Banderas for visits to the neighboring glaciers Upsala and Spegazzini.

GETTING THERE & ESSENTIALS

At Km 49 (30 miles) from El Calafate, you'll pass through the park's entrance, where there's an information booth with erratic hours (no phone; www.calafate.com). Entrance fee is $5.75 per person. If you're looking for information about the park and the glacier, pick up an interpretive guide or book from one of the bookstores or tourist shops along Avenida del Libertador in El Calafate. There is a restaurant near the principal lookout platform near the glacier, and a good, though expensive, restaurant inside the Los Notros hotel (see "Lodging Near the Glacier," below).

To get to the park:

BY CAR   Following Avenida del Libertador west out of town, the route turns into a well-maintained dirt road. From here, it's 80km (50 miles) to the glacier.

BY TAXI OR *REMISE*   If you want to see the glacier at your own pace, hire a taxi or *remise*. The cost averages $40 for two passengers, $65 for three, and $90 for four, although many taxi companies will negotiate a price. Be sure to agree on an estimated amount of time to spend at the glacier.

BY ORGANIZED TOUR   Several companies offer transportation to and from the glacier, such as **Interlagos,** Av. del Libertador 1175 (**© 02902/ 491175;** interlagos@cotecal.com.ar); **City Tour,** Av. del Libertador 1341

(© **02902/492276;** morresi@cotecal.com.ar); **Caltur,** Av. del Libertador 1177 (© **02902/491368;** caltur@cotecal.com.ar); and **TAQSA** in the bus terminal (© **02902/491843**). These minivan and bus services provide bilingual guides and leave around 9am, spending an average of 4 hours at the peninsula; the cost is $25 to $30 per person, not including lunch. For a more personalized tour (a private car with driver and a bilingual, licensed guide), contact **SurTur-ismo,** 25 de Mayo 23 (© **02902/491266;** suring@cotecal.com.ar); they can arrange for a half-day trip costing $60 to $75 for two people; prices vary with the seasons.

OUTDOOR ACTIVITIES

There are several activities in this region, including a "minitrek" that takes guests for a walk upon the glacier. The trip begins with a 20-minute boat ride across the Brazo Rico, followed by a 30-minute walk to the glacier. From here, guests are outfitted with crampons and other safety gear, then spend about 1½ hours atop the ice, complete with a stop for a whisky on the thousand-year-old "rocks." This trip gives visitors the chance to peer into the electric-blue crevasses of the glacier and truly appreciate its size. You can book it through any travel agency.

   Solo Patagonia, Av. del Libertador 963 (© **02902/491298;** www.solo patagonia.com.ar), offers visitors navigation through the Brazo Rico to the face of the Perito Moreno Glacier, including treks to the base of the Cerro Negro with a view of the Glacier Negro. Both Solo Patagonia and **Upsala Explorer** ⊛, Av. 9 de Julio 69 (© **02902/491034;** www.upsalaexplorer.com.ar), offer a variety of combinations from Puerto Banderas to Los Glaciares National Park's largest and tallest glaciers, respectively the Upsala and Spegazzini. Upsala Explorer makes a stop at the Estancia Cristina for lunch and optional trekking and 4×4 trips to the Upsala Lookout. Solo Patagonia offers similar journeys, including a stop at the Onelli area for trekking, as well as navigation-only journeys. Both companies charge $90 to $105 for this all-day excursion.

LODGING NEAR THE GLACIER

Los Notros ⊛⊛⊛ _(Moments_   Few hotels in Argentina boast as spectacular and breathtaking a view as Los Notros—but it doesn't come cheap. This luxury lodge sits high on a slope looking out at the Perito Moreno Glacier, and all common areas and rooms have been fitted with picture windows to really soak up the marvelous sight. Although the wood-hewn exteriors give the hotel the feel of a mountain lodge, the interior decor is contemporary. Each room is slightly different, with personal touches like antique lamps and regional photos; crocheted or gingham bedspreads; lilac, peach, or lemon-yellow walls; padded floral headboards or iron bed frames; and tweedy brown or raspberry corduroy chairs. Bathrooms are gleaming white, and premium rooms in the newer wing have whirlpool baths. The older "Cascada bungalow" rooms have very thin walls; if you're a light sleeper, be sure to request a top floor room or a room in the newer "Premium" (and more expensive) wing.

   Inside the main building is a large, chic, expensive restaurant renowned for serving creative regional cuisine; guests can expect to pay $38 for a fixed-price dinner, $20 at lunch. Upstairs is an airy lounge area with chaise longues positioned in front of panoramic windows; here you'll find a TV room with a selection of nature videos. Guests at the Los Notros frequently opt for one of the multiple-day packages that includes airport transfers, meals, box lunches for expeditions, nightly discussions, guided trekking, boat excursions, and ice walks. Even if you're not staying here, you should stop by to take in the view.

Main office in Buenos Aires: Arenales 1457, 7th floor. © 11/4814-3934. Fax 11/4815-7645. www.
losnotros.com. 32 units. $330 double Cascada bungalow; $390 double superior; $480 double premium. Rates
include buffet breakfast. All-inclusive, 2-night packages average $843 in a premium room, per person. AE, DC,
MC, V. **Amenities:** Restaurant; bar; lounge; tour desk; room service; laundry service. *In room:* Minibar.

EL CHALTEN & THE FITZ ROY AREA ⚑
222km (138 miles) N of El Calafate

El Chaltén is a tiny village of about 200 whose lifeblood, like El Calafate's,
depends entirely on the throng of visitors who come each summer to marvel
over the towers of mounts Fitz Roy, Cerro Torre, and Puntiagudo. This is the
second most-visited region of Argentina's Los Glaciares National Park and quite
possibly its most exquisite, for the singular nature of the granite spires here that
shoot up, torpedo-like, above massive tongues of ice that descend from the
Southern Ice Field. In the world of mountaineering, these sheer and ice-
encrusted peaks are considered to present one of the most formidable challenges
in the world. Because of the capricious nature of Patagonian weather, climbers
can be seen camping out for weeks, even a month, until they are presented with
an opportunity to ascend.

Little more than 5 years ago, El Chaltén counted just a dozen houses and a
hostel or two, but the Fitz Roy's rugged beauty and great hiking opportunities
have created somewhat of a boomtown here. The town sits nestled in a circular
rock outcrop at the base of the Fitz Roy and is fronted by the vast, dry pampa.
Visitors use El Chaltén either as a base from which to take day hikes or as an
overnighter before setting off for a multiday backpacking trip.

ESSENTIALS
Getting There
BY PLANE   All transportation to El Chaltén comes from El Calafate, which
has daily plane service from Ushuaia, Buenos Aires, and Bariloche. From El
Calafate, you need to take a bus or rent a car; the trip takes up to 3½ hours.

BY CAR   Take the Ruta Nacional 11 west for 30km (19 miles) and turn left
on Ruta Nacional 40 north. Turn again, heading northwest, on Ruta Provincial
23 to El Chaltén. The road is unpaved.

BY BUS   Buses from El Calafate leave from the terminal, and all cost about
$30 round-trip. **Chaltén Travel,** with offices in El Chaltén in the Albergue Ran-
cho Grande on Avenida del Libertador (© **02962/493005;** chaltentravel@
cotecal.com.ar), leaves El Calafate daily at 8am and El Chaltén at 6pm. Chaltén
Travel can arrange private tours and day trips to outlying destinations such as
Patagonian ranches, as well as summer-only transportation up Ruta Nacional 40
for those crossing into Chile. **Caltur,** which leaves from El Chaltén's Hostería
Fitz Roy at Av. San Martín 520 (© **02962/493062;** caltur@cotecal.com.ar),
leaves El Calafate daily at 7:30am and leaves El Chaltén at 6pm. **Los Glaciares,**
San Martín 100 (© **02962/493063;** www.losglaciaresturismo.com), leaves El
Calafate daily at 8am and returns at 5:30pm.

Visitor Information
There is a $5.75 fee to enter the park. The Park Service has an **information cen-
ter** located at the entrance to town; here you'll find maps, pamphlets, and brief
interpretive displays about the region's flora and fauna. It's open daily from 8am
to 8pm. El Chaltén also has a well-organized visitor center at the town's
entrance—the **Comisión de Fomento,** Perito Moreno and Avenida Güemes
(© **02962/493011**), open daily from 8am to 8pm. In El Calafate, the **APN**

Intendencia (park service) has its offices at Av. del Libertador 1302, with a visitor center that is open daily from 9am to 3pm (© **02902/491005**).

OUTDOOR ACTIVITIES

TOUR OPERATORS   **Fitz Roy Expediciones** ⚐, Lionel Terray 212 (©/fax **02962/493017**; fitzroyexpediciones@videodata.com.ar), offers a full-day excursion trekking through the Valle de Río Fitz Roy combined with ice climbing at the Glacier Torre. No experience is necessary, but they do ask that you be in fit condition. They can also arrange for you to make the descent back to the base on horseback. Fitz Roy Expediciones offers a variety of trekking excursions, including a complete 10-day circuit around the backside of the Fitz Roy and Cerro Torre peaks, for $1,083 per person, all equipment and meals included, as well as 2 nights' lodging in an *albergue*. **Alta Montaña** at Lionel Terray 501 (© **02962/493018**; altamont@infovia.com.ar) also offers summer-only, day-trekking excursions. There are several resident mountaineering and trekking guides who speak English and can be hired on a freelance basis including Alberto del Castillo (© **02962/493017**), Jorge Tarditti (© **02962/4993013**), and Oscar Pandolfi (© **02962/493016**).

HIKING & CAMPING   If you're planning on doing any hiking in the park, you'll want to pick up a copy of Zagier & Urruty's trekking map, "Monte Fitz Roy & Cerro Torre," available at most bookstores and tourist shops in El Calafate and El Chaltén. You'll also need to register at the park service office at the entrance to El Chaltén. You won't find a well-defined circuit here as you do in Torres del Paine, but there is a loop of sorts, and all stretches of this 3- to 4-day loop can be done one leg at a time on day hikes. Trails here run from easy to difficult and take anywhere from 4 to 10 hours to complete.

One of the most spectacular day hikes, which can also be done as an overnight, 2-day hike, is the 19km (12-mile) trail to the **Mirador D'Agostini,** also known as Maestri, that affords exhilarating views of the spire Cerro Torre. The hike takes 5½ to 6 hours to complete and is classified as easy, except for the last steep climb to the lookout point. It's possible to camp nearby at the D'Agostini campground (formerly Bridwell). Leaving from the Madsen campground, a more demanding, though beautiful, trail heads to several campsites and eventually the Laguna de los Tres, where there is a lookout point for views of Mount Fitz Roy. This walk is best done as an overnight trip; it's too much to undertake in 1 day. Campgrounds inside the park's boundaries are free, but do not have services; paid campgrounds (outside the park) have water and some have showers.

HORSEBACK RIDING   There's nothing like horseback riding in Patagonia, and two outfitters offer several day excursions: **Rodolfo Guerra** at Las Loicas 773 (© **02962/493020**) has horseback rides and a horse-pack service for carrying gear to campsites. Also try the **El Relincho** at Av. del Libertador s/n (© **02962/493007**).

WHERE TO STAY

For these hotels, parking is either free, or street parking is plentiful.

Hostería El Pilar ⚐*Finds*   The Hostería El Pilar is undoubtedly the choice lodging option in the area. True, the hotel's location 15km (9 miles) from El Chaltén toward Lago del Desierto does put guests far from restaurants and shops, but then lovely, peaceful surroundings are what many guests look for when they come to visit the national park. The yellow-walled and red-roofed El Pilar was once an *estancia;* now it's tastefully and artistically decorated with just enough detail not to distract you from the outdoors. The lounge offers a few couches and a fireplace and is a comfy spot to lounge and read a book. Rooms are simple but attractive, with peach walls, comfortable beds, and sunlight that streams through half-curtained windows. Guests normally take their meals at the hotel's restaurant, which serves great cuisine. The hotel offers guided excursions and is located next to several trail heads. If you're driving here, really keep an eye open for the sign to this hotel because it's easy to miss.

Ruta Provincial 23, 15km (9 miles) from El Chaltén. ⓒ/fax 02962/493002. 16 units. $80 double. MC, V. Open Oct–Apr; May–Sept by reservation. **Amenities:** Restaurant; bar; lounge.

Hostería El Puma ⓖ   El Puma offers the most stylish and comfortable accommodations in El Chaltén. The owners of this hotel work with the outfitter Fitz Roy Expediciones, who have an office next door. The hotel sits back from the main road, and faces out toward snowy peaks, although without a view of Fitz Roy. Inside, warm beige walls and wooden beams interplay with brick, and are offset with soft cotton curtains and ironwork. Although the common areas have terra-cotta ceramic floors, all rooms are carpeted. The rooms are well designed and bright; the lounge has a few chairs that face a roaring fire. There's also an eating area with wooden tables and a small bar. Very friendly service.

Lionel Terray 512, El Chaltén. ⓒ 02962/493095. Fax 02962/493017. elpuma@videodata.com.ar. 8 units. $83 double. Rates include buffet breakfast. No credit cards. Closed Apr–Oct. **Amenities:** Restaurant; bar.

WHERE TO DINE

During the winter only one restaurant valiantly stays open: **La Casita,** Avenida del Libertador at Lionel Terray, in the pink building (ⓒ **02966/493042**). La Casita offers average, home-style fare, including sandwiches, meats, pastas, and stuffed crepes, and absent-minded service. At other times of the year, the best restaurant in town for food and ambience is **Patagonicus,** Güemes at Andreas Madsen (ⓒ **02966/493025**). Patagonicus serves mostly pizza and enormous salads in a woodsy dining area. Another good restaurant can be found inside the **Hostería Fitz Roy,** Av. San Martín 520 (ⓒ **02966/493062**), which serves Argentine and international fare such as grilled meats and seafood, pastas, and more in a pleasant dining area with white linen-draped tables. For sandwiches, snacks, coffee, and cakes, try the **Albergue Rancho Grande,** Av. del Libertador s/n (ⓒ **02966/493005**).

USHUAIA ⓖⓖ
461km (286 miles) SW of Punta Arenas; 594km (368 miles) S of Río Gallegos

The name *Ushuaia* comes from the Yamana Indian language; it means "bay penetrating westward," a simple name for a city in such a spectacular location. It's the southernmost city in the world (although the naval base and town Puerto Williams is farther south across the channel), a fact Ushuaia sells as a tourist attraction. It is encircled by a range of rugged peaks and fronted by the Beagle Channel. The Yamana Indians inhabited it until the late 1800s, when it became a penal colony for criminals who toiled here until 1947. The region grew as a result of immigration from Croatia, Italy, and Spain and migration from the Argentine mainland; government incentives such as tax-free duty on many goods were part of the draw. Today, the city has about 40,000 residents. Ushuaia is a great destination with plenty of activities, and many use the city as a jumping-off point for trips to Antarctica or sailing trips around Cape Horn.

ESSENTIALS
Getting There
BY PLANE   There is no bus service to town from the Ushuaia Airport, but cab fares are only about $1.50; always ask for a quote before accepting a ride. **Aerolíneas Argentinas,** Roca 116 (© **02901/421218;** www.aerolineas.com.ar), has a daily flight from both Buenos Aires airports; air service frequency increases from November to March when there's also a daily flight from El Calafate, a weekly flight from Trelew, and three weekly flights from Rio Gallegos. **Aerovías DAP** now has air service to and from Punta Arenas for $120 one-way (plus $5 airport tax), leaving Wednesday only at 9am from Punta Arenas and 10:30am from Ushuaia; its offices are at Av. 25 de Mayo 62 (© **02901/431110;** www. aeroviasdap.cl). During high season, DAP increases flights from Punta Arenas to five weekly in addition to a daily flight from Cape Horn.

BY BUS   Service from Punta Arenas, Chile, costs $19 and takes about 12 hours. **Tecni Austral** (© **02901/431407** in Ushuaia, or 61/222078 in Punta Arenas) leaves Monday, Wednesday, and Friday at 7am; tickets are sold in Ushuaia from the Tolkar office at Roca 157, and in Punta Arenas at Lautaro Navarro 975. **Tolkeyen,** Maipú 237 (© **02901/437073;** tolkeyenventas@ arnet.com.ar), works in combination with the Chilean company Pacheco for trips to Punta Arenas, leaving Tuesday, Thursday, and Saturday at 8am; it also goes to Río Grande, with three daily trips. Both companies take the route to Punta Arenas via Bahía Azul. Techni Austral offers service to Punta Arenas via Porvenir for the same price, leaving Saturday at 6am. **Lidded LTD,** Gobernador Paz 921 (© **02901/436421**), Techni Austral, and Tolkeyen all have multiple day trips to Río Grande.

BY BOAT   The company **Crucero Australis** operates a cruise to Ushuaia from Punta Arenas, and vice versa, aboard its ship the M/V *Mare Australis.* If you have the time, this is a recommended journey for any age.

Getting Around
BY CAR   Everything in and around Ushuaia is easily accessible via bus or taxi or by using an inexpensive shuttle or tour service, so renting a car is really not necessary. Rentals, however, are very reasonable, from $20 to $45 per day. **Avis** at Avenida del Libertador and Belgrano drops its prices for multiple-day rentals (© **02901/422744**); **Cardos Rent A Car** is at Av. del Libertador 845 (© **02901/436388**); **Dollar Rent A Car** is at Maipú and Sarmiento (© **02901/432134**).

Visitor Information
The **Subsecretaría de Turismo** has a helpful, well-stocked office at Maipu 505 (© **02901/423340;** fax 02901/430694; www.tierradelfuego.org.ar). They also have a counter at the airport that is open to assist passengers on all arriving flights. From November to March, the office is open daily from 8am to 10pm; the rest of the year it's open Monday through Friday from 8am to 9pm, weekends and holidays from 9am to 8pm. The national park administration office can be found at Av. del Libertador 1395 (© **02901/421395;** Mon–Fri 9am–3pm).

FAST FACTS   To exchange money, go to **Banco Sud** at Avenida del Libertador and Godoy (© **02901/432080**), or **Banco Nación** at Av. del Libertador 190 (© **02901/422086**). Both have 24-hour ATMs. **American Express** travel and credit card services are provided by All Patagonia, Juana Fadul 26 (© **02901/433622**).

If you need a pharmacy, visit **Andina** at Av. del Libertador 638 (© **02901/ 423431**); it's open 24 hours a day.

The **post office** is at Avenida del Libertador and Godoy (© **02901/421347**), open Monday through Friday from 9am to 7pm, Saturday from 9am to 1pm; the private postal company **OCA** is at Maipú and Avenida 9 de Julio (© **02901/ 424729**), open Monday through Saturday from 9am to 6pm.

WHAT TO SEE & DO IN & AROUND TOWN

An in-town walk can be taken to the city park and **Punto Panorámico,** which takes visitors up to a lookout point with good views of the city and the channel. It can be reached at the southwest terminus of Avenida del Libertador and is free.

Museo del Fin de Mundo ⟨✿⟩
The museum's main room has an assortment of Indian hunting tools and colonial maritime instruments. There's also a natural history display of stuffed birds and a "grandfather's room" set up to resemble an old general store, packed with antique products. But the strength of this museum is its 60 history and nature videos and its reference library with more than 3,650 volumes, including a fascinating birth record. It's worth a visit and it won't take you more than an hour to inspect everything.

Maipú 175. © 02901/421863. Admission $1.50 adults, 60¢ students, free for children under 14. Daily 10am–1pm and 3–7:30pm.

Museo Marítimo y Presidio de Ushuaia ⟨Finds⟩
Ushuaia was founded in the late 1800s as a penal colony for Argentina's most dangerous criminals. The museum is sort of Ushuaia's Alcatraz, offering a fascinating look into prisoners and prison workers' lives during that time through interpretive displays and artifacts, including the wool, striped prison uniforms the prisoners were forced to wear. There's a restaurant here, with "prison" meals and other theme items. Great for a rainy day; plan on spending at least an hour here, longer if you plan to have a meal or snack.

Yaganes and Gobernador Paz. © 02901/437481. Admission $2 adults, $1.50 seniors, $1 children 5–12, free for children under 5. Daily 10am–1pm and 3–8pm.

Glacier Martial/Aerosilla ⟨✿⟩
The Glacier Martial excursion sits in the backyard of Ushuaia. Avenida Luis Fernando Martial winds 7km (4 miles) up from town to the base of a beautiful mountain amphitheater, where you'll find a chairlift that takes visitors to the small Glacier Martial. It's a long walk up the road, and there are no buses to take you there. Visitors usually hire a taxi for $5 and walk all the way back down, or arrange for the driver to pick them up later.

Av. Luis Fernando Martial, 7km (4 miles) from town. No phone. Admission $2 adults, $1 children under 9. Daily 10:30am–5:30pm.

Outdoor Activities

BOATING   Navigation excursions are very popular, with several companies offering a variety of trips. The most popular is a half-day trip cruising the Beagle Channel to view sea lions, penguins, and more. You'll find a cluster of kiosks near the pier offering a variety of trips. **Motonave Barracuda** leaves twice daily for its 3-hour trip around the channel for $25 per person, visiting Isla de Lobos, Isla de Pájaros, and a lighthouse (© **02901/436453**). **Motovelero Tres Marías** also leaves twice daily and sails to the same locations; it has a maximum of nine guests and adds an hour's walk, crab fishing, cognac, and an underwater camera to the menu (© **02901/421897**). **Motovelero Patagonia Adventure** has an 18-passenger maximum and leaves daily; it visits the sea lion colony and includes a walk on the Isla Bridges for $20. This company also works with the Aventuras Isla Verde in the park for a full-day sail; inquire at their kiosk (© 1560-3181).

FISHING For a fishing license and information, go the **Club de Pesca y Caza** at Av. del Libertador 818 (no phone). The cost is about $12 per day for foreigners.

SKIING Ushuaia's new ski resort, **Cerro Castor** (© 1560-5706; www.cerro castor.com), is surprisingly good, with more than 400 skiable hectares (988 acres), 15 runs, three quad chairs and one double, a lodge/restaurant, and a slope-side bar. Day tickets cost $17 to $24, depending on low or high season, and the resort is open from June 15 to October 15. To get there, take the shuttle buses **Pasarela** (© 02901/433712) or **Bella Vista** (© 02901/443161); the fare is $4.

Tour Operators

All Patagonia Viajes y Turismo, Juana Fadul 26 (© 02901/433622; allpat@tierradelfuego.org.ar), is the local American Express travel representative, and acts as a clearinghouse for everything—if they don't offer it themselves, they'll arrange an excursion with other outfitters, and they can reserve excursions in other destinations in Argentina and Chile. All Patagonia offers three glacier walks for those in physically good shape, scenic flights over Tierra del Fuego ($35 per person for 30 min.), and treks and drives in its Land Rover with nature guides. If you're not sure what you want, start here. **Canal Fun & Nature,** Rivadavia 82 (© 02901/437395; www.canalfun.com), is a great company with excellent guides who provide 4×4 trips and walks culminating with a barbecue, as well as kayaking and nighttime beaver watching, and they'll custom-build a trip for you. **Rumbo Sur,** Av. del Libertador 350 (© 02901/430699; www.rumbosur.com.ar), and **Tolkeyen/PreTour,** Maipú 237 (© 02901/437073; tolekeyenventas@arnet.com.ar), are two operators that deal with larger groups and arrange more classic excursions, such as a city tour and guided visits to the national park and Lagos Escondido and Fagnano.

PARQUE NACIONAL TIERRA DEL FUEGO ⊛

Parque Nacional Tierra del Fuego was created in 1960 to protect a 63,000-hectare (155,610-acre) chunk of wilderness that includes mighty peaks, crystalline rivers, black-water swamps, and forests of *lenga,* or deciduous beech. Only 2,000 hectares (4,940 acres) are designated as recreation areas, part of which offer a chance to view the prolific dam-building carried out by beavers introduced to Tierra del Fuego in the 1950s.

This is the only Argentine national park with a maritime coast. If you've been traveling around southern Argentina or Chile, chances are this park won't blow you away. Much of the landscape is identical to the thousands of kilometers of mountainous terrain in Patagonia, and there really isn't any special "thing" to see. Instead, it offers easy and medium day hikes, fresh air, boat rides, and birdwatching. Also, there are areas where the road runs through thick beech forest and then abruptly opens into wide views of mountains whose dramatic height can be viewed from sea level to more than 2,000m (6,560 ft.). Anglers can fish for trout in the park, but must first pick up a license at the **National Park Administration** office at Av. del Libertador 1395 (© 02901/421395; Mon–Fri 9am–3pm), in Ushuaia. The Park Service issues maps at the park entrance showing the walking trails here, ranging from 300m (980 ft.) to 8km (5 miles); admission into the park is $3.50. Parque Nacional Tierra del Fuego is located

11km (7 miles) west of Ushuaia on Ruta Nacional 3. Camping in the park is free, and although there are no services, potable water is available. At the end of the road to Lago Roca, there is a snack bar/restaurant. At Bahía Ensenada, you'll find boats that take visitors to the Isla Redonda, where there are several walking trails. The cost is about $8, or $16 with a guide. All tour companies offer guided trips to the park, but if you just need transportation there, call these shuttle bus companies: **Pasarela** (© 02901/433712) or **Bella Vista** (© 02901/443161).

WHERE TO STAY

Accommodations are not cheap in Ushuaia, and quality is often not on a par with price. For all hotels, parking is either free, or street parking is plentiful.

Expensive

Las Hayas Resort Hotel ☆☆☆ *Finds* The city's only luxury property is a member of The Leading Hotels of the World and sits nestled in a forest of beech, a location that gives sweeping views of the town and the Beagle Channel. It's at least 3km (2 miles) from downtown, however, so you'll need to take a cab, hike, or use one of the hotel's summer-only transfer shuttles. The rooms are lavishly decorated with rich tapestries, upholstered walls, and bathrooms that are big and bright. The ultra-comfortable beds with thick linens are dreamy. A glass-enclosed walkway leads to one of Ushuaia's few swimming pools and an indoor squash court; the hotel also offers automatic membership at the region's golf club. The owner of Las Hayas promotes an air of genteel exclusivity, making the hotel not entirely suitable for children. The hotel's gourmet restaurant changes its menu weekly, but specializes in black hake and king crab dishes.

Av. Luis Fernando Martial 1650, Ushuaia. © 02901/430710. Fax 02901/430719. www.lashayas.com.ar. 93 units. $170–$195 double; $220–$252 junior suite superior; $238–$285 deluxe junior suite; $355 gala suite. Rates include buffet breakfast. AE, DC, MC, V. **Amenities:** 2 restaurants; bar; lounge; indoor pool; exercise room; Jacuzzi; sauna; concierge; room service; massage; laundry service; dry cleaning. *In room:* TV, hair dryer, safe.

Moderate

Hostal del Bosque Apart Hotel *Value* The Hostal del Bosque gives guests a huge amount of space, including a separate living/dining area and a kitchenette. However, the kitchenette is intended more than anything for heating water, not cooking—for that reason they include breakfast, which is not common with apartment-hotels. The 40 guest rooms are spread out much like a condominium complex, each with a separate entrance and maid service. The exteriors and the decor are pretty bland, but very clean. Inside the main building there's a cozy restaurant with wooden tables where they serve fixed-price meals. The hotel is located in a residential area about a 3-minute walk from downtown.

Magallanes 709, Ushuaia. ©/fax 02901/430777. www.hostaldelbosque.com.ar. 40 units. $35 double Apr–Sept; $60 double Oct–Mar. Rates include continental breakfast. AE, DC, MC, V. **Amenities:** Restaurant; room service; laundry service. *In room:* TV, kitchenette, minibar, hair dryer.

Posada Fueguina ☆☆ *Finds* This is one of my favorite hotels in the center of town, full of flavor and cozier than anything else. The Fueguina has hotel rooms and a row of inviting, wooden cabañas (no kitchen) on a well-manicured lot, and their freshly painted cream and mauve exteriors stand out among the clapboard homes that surround them. Inside, Oriental floor-runners, dark glossy wood, and tartan curtains set the tone. Everything is meticulously maintained. Most rooms are spacious; the second and third floors have good views, and the three rooms on the bottom floor are brand-new. Bathrooms are sparkling clean;

many received new fixtures in 2002. The cabins do not have interesting views, but they're so comfy you probably won't mind. The hotel is a short 3-block walk to downtown.

Lasserre 438, Ushuaia. ✆ 02901/423467. Fax 02901/424758. www.posadafueguina.com.ar. 23 units, 5 cabañas. $112 double Apr–Dec; $80 double Jan–Mar. Rates include buffet breakfast. AE, MC, V. **Amenities:** Restaurant; bar; lounge; laundry service. *In room:* TV, minibar, hair dryer.

WHERE TO DINE

A dozen *confiterías* and cafes can be found on Avenida del Libertador between Godoy and Rosas, all of which offer inexpensive sandwiches and quick meals.

Chez Manu 🄰 *(Finds* SEAFOOD/FRENCH The Chez Manu offers great food and even better views seen through a generous supply of windows. The two transplants from France who run this restaurant, one of whom was once the chef at the luxury resort Las Hayas, stay true to their roots with a menu that offers French-style cooking using fresh local ingredients. Dishes include black hake cooked with anise and herbs, or Fueguian lamb. Before taking your order, the owner/chef will describe the catch of the day, usually a cold-water fish from the bay such as Abejado or a Merlooza from Chile. The side dishes include a delicious eggplant ratatouille, made with extra-virgin olive oil and herbes de Provence. The wine list includes several excellent regional dry whites.

Av. Luis Fernando Martial 2135. ✆ 02970/432253. Main courses $6–$12. AE, MC, V. Mon–Sun noon–3pm and 8pm–midnight.

Kapué Restaurant 🄰🄰🄰 ARGENTINE This is undoubtedly the best restaurant in Ushuaia, for its superb cuisine, lovely view, and warm, attentive service. Kapué, which means "at home" in Selk'nam, is owned and operated by the friendly, gracious Vivian family—the husband, Ernesto, is chef and his wife runs the dining area and waits tables, and often one of their kids can be found behind the bar. The menu is brief, but the offerings are delicious. Don't start your meal without ordering a sumptuous appetizer of king crab wrapped in a crepe and bathed in saffron sauce. Main courses include seafood, beef, and chicken; sample items include tenderloin beef in a plum sauce or a subtly flavored sea bass steamed in parchment paper. Kapué offers a special "sampler" with appetizers, a main dish, wine, dessert, and coffee for $26 per person.

Roca 470. ✆ 02901/422704. Reservations recommended on weekends. Main courses $7–$14. AE, MC, V. Nov 15–Apr 15 daily noon–2pm and 6–11pm; rest of the year dinner only 7–11pm.

Punto Final 🄰🄰 *(Moments* INTERNATIONAL Open since fall 2002, Punto Final has quickly become the most hip and happening place in Ushuaia. The location couldn't be better: right on the waterfront with fabulous bay and mountain views from the large windows that wrap around the entire building. The atmosphere is much like a big-city club, with leopard-print fabric upholstery on the booths and bar stools. Techno music plays in the background during the early evening when full meals are served. You'll find dishes such as sliced melon with ham, grilled steaks, chicken breast with white wine and cream sauce, and a simple trout with butter sauce. Most of the trendy people who come here come for drinks, and after midnight, to dance. This place is a zoo from midnight to 3am, and even later on the weekends. If you're looking to live it up with young Argentines, then this is your place for the night.

Maipú 822. ✆ 02901/422423. Main courses $6–$10. AE, MC, V. Daily 11am–4am (till 5am Fri–Sat).

Bolivia

by Haas Mroue

Few people seem to know much about Bolivia, a vast, isolated country tucked into the middle of South America. It's surrounded by the Andes to the south, north, and west, and by the jungle to the east. To get to the nearest ocean, you have to cross Chile's desert. Bolivia is hardly the type of place where you happen to stop in by accident. There are no direct flights here from Europe and only two a day from North America. To make matters worse, because the air is so thin at La Paz's 3,900m-high (13,000-ft.) El Alto Airport, only small planes can make the landing at Bolivia's most important city. It's not surprising that Bolivia, a country that's twice the size of France, receives less than 300,000 visitors a year.

Because so few visitors come here, you can expect to find a country still in its natural state. Nothing has been changed for the sake of tourists. In fact, it almost feels as though nothing has changed here at all in the past few hundred years—and that's what I love most about this place. Bolivia's isolation has allowed it to keep its traditions alive. This is a country where indigenous women still wear multilayered petticoats, where you can buy good-luck llama fetuses on a city street, and where locals in the rural mountainside weave ponchos and textiles just as their ancestors did hundreds of years ago. Lake Titicaca, which was one of the most sacred places in the Inca empire, still attracts thousands of religious pilgrims a year, all of them paying homage to the beloved Virgin of Copacabana, who in reality is the ultimate symbol of the mixture of Catholicism and ancient traditional beliefs.

If you brave Bolivia's bumpy unpaved roads and travel by bus, you can see the landscape change minute by minute before your eyes. In just 3 hours, you can leave the barren high-plateau terrain of La Paz and arrive in the lush, tropical land of Los Yungas in the foothills of the Andes. You can also visit the remains of Bolivia's days of grandeur in Potosí, once the world's silver mining capital and thus one of its wealthiest cities. Potosí and its administrative center in Sucre were bastions of art and high culture, with some of the finest architecture on the continent.

A trip to Bolivia will certainly never be boring. From its colorful people to its rich landscapes to its sordid past, Bolivia offers visitors some of the most unique experiences anywhere. And, most importantly, it's a place where you'll feel like the only traveler for miles around.

1 The Regions in Brief

Bolivia sits practically in the middle of South America, sharing its borders with Peru, Chile, Argentina, Paraguay, and Brazil. Landlocked since losing access to a seacoast during the Pacific War (1879–84), Bolivia still maintains a navy to protect the sacred Lake Titicaca, which it shares with Peru. Much of Bolivia is defined by the Andes Mountains. The range is at its widest in Bolivia and consists of two parallel chains here, separated by the *altiplano* (high plain), the most densely populated area of the country. As you move farther east, the Andes give way to the jungle and tropical landscapes.

Because Bolivia is so vast, it's difficult to get a good feeling for the country if you have only 1 week to spend here. But you will have enough time to see all the highlights of La Paz, take a day trip to Tiwanaku, visit Lake Titicaca, and view Inca ruins on Isla del Sol (Island of the Sun) and in Copacabana. If you have 2 weeks, you can also explore Sucre, tour the mines at Potosí, and relax in Santa Cruz. The more physically adventurous traveler might consider sea kayaking on Lake Titicaca, climbing Huayna Potosí, trekking around the Illampu circuit, or taking a 4-day journey through the salt flats and desert near Salar de Uyuni.

LA PAZ   La Paz is the administrative capital of Bolivia. From here, you can easily travel to **Lake Titicaca,** which is considered to be the birthplace of the Incas. The impressive pre-Inca archaeological site, **Tiwanaku,** is also only 2 hours away. Drive 3 hours to the east, and you will descend into the tropical area known as **Los Yungas.**

SOUTHERN *ALTIPLANO*   This area made its mark on the world in the 16th, 17th, and 18th centuries, when **Potosí** was one of the great silver mining centers and consequently one of the wealthiest cities in the world. Today, highlights of the region include Potosí and **Sucre,** both of which are historical gems.

CENTRAL BOLIVIA   The area of central Bolivia extends from the pleasant town of **Cochabamba** at the foothills of the Andes all the way east to **Santa Cruz.** Cochabamba is one of the commercial centers of Bolivia, with several major industry headquarters here, including chicken farms, airlines, and shoe companies. Some of the most colorful markets in Bolivia take place in the rural areas outside of the city. There's not much to see in the tropical city of Santa Cruz, but Amboró National Park, the Inca Ruins of Samaipata, and the Jesuit Mission are within easy reach.

2 Planning Your Trip to Bolivia

VISITOR INFORMATION

The Bolivian Ministry of Tourism has very limited resources. There are virtually no government-sponsored tourist offices outside of Bolivia. The U.S.-based Embassy of Bolivia has a moderately useful website at **www.bolivia-usa.org**. For general travel information, you can also log onto **www.boliviaweb.com** or **www.boliviabiz.com**.

For more specific travel-related information, your best bet is to contact travel agencies that specialize in trips to Bolivia. Some of the best include:

- **Andean Summits,** 710 Calle Prolongación Armaza, P.O. Box 6976, La Paz (©/fax **0102/2422-106;** www.andeansummits.com). This Bolivia-based company specializes in active vacation packages, including sea-kayaking trips in Lake Titicaca and treks up Huayna Potosí. All of the guides are certified by the German Alpine Club.
- **Bahia Travel Agency,** 81-31 Baxter Ave., Elmhurst, NY 11373 (© **800/ 833-3138** or 718/639-3310; www.bahiatravelagency.com). Based in New York and La Paz, Bahia offers great air deals to Bolivia.

- **Crillon Tours** ⭐⭐, 1450 S. Bayshore Dr., Suite 815, Miami, FL 33131 (© **888/TITICACA** or 305/358-5353; www.titicaca.com). This is by far the best travel agency offering organized tours to Bolivia. The Bolivian owner is based in Miami, but the company has a huge infrastructure in Bolivia. Crillon Tours is the owner of several fantastic hotels in the Lake Titicaca area, and the company arranges high-end package tours throughout Bolivia.
- **Explore Bolivia, Inc.,** 2510 N. 47th St., Suite 207, Boulder, CO 80301 (© **877/708-8810** or 303/545-5728; www.explorebolivia.com). This company is your best bet if you're looking for adventure tours in Bolivia— they specialize in kayaking, trekking, and mountain-climbing packages.
- **Journey Latin America,** 12 & 13 Heathfield Terrace, Chiswick, London W4 4JE (© **020/8747-3108**; www.journeylatinamerica.co.uk). This is one of the premier British travel agencies that can arrange airfare and tour packages throughout South America.

IN BOLIVIA

Although the **Viceministerio de Turismo** has an office in La Paz (© **02/2358-213**), the staff doesn't speak English, and the only resources on hand are some promotional brochures. You're much better off heading to the visitor information office on Plaza del Estudiante, where you can buy regional maps; see "Visitor Information" in "La Paz," later in this chapter.

Telephone Dialing Info at a Glance

- **To place a call from your home country to Bolivia,** dial the international access code (011 in the U.S. and Canada, 0011 in Australia, 0170 in New Zealand, 00 in the U.K.) plus the country code (591), plus the Bolivian area code minus the 010 (for example, La Paz 2, Santa Cruz 3, Cochabamba 4, Sucre 464, Potosí 262, Copacabana 2862), followed by the number. For example, a call from the United States to La Paz would be 011+591+2+0000+000.
- **To place a call within Bolivia,** you must use area codes if you're calling from one department (administrative district) to another. Note that for all calls within the country, area codes are preceded by 010 (for example, La Paz 0102, Santa Cruz 0103, Cochabamba 0104, Sucre 010464, Potosí 010262, Copacabana 0102862).
- **To place a direct international call from Bolivia,** dial the international access code (00), plus the country code of the place you are dialing, plus the area code and the local number.
- **To reach an international operator,** dial ℂ 35-67-00. Major long distance company access codes are as follows: **AT&T** ℂ 0800-1111; **Bell Canada** ℂ 0800-0101; **British Telecom** ℂ 0800-0044; **MCI** ℂ 0800-2222; **Sprint** ℂ 0800-3333.

ENTRY REQUIREMENTS

A valid passport is required to enter and depart Bolivia. Visas are not required for stays of up to 30 days if you're a citizen of one of 45 designated countries, which include the United States, the United Kingdom, Canada, Australia, New Zealand, South Africa, France, Germany, and Switzerland. (Visit www.bolivia-usa.org or check with your local embassy to determine whether you'll need a visa.) It's very easy to extend the tourist card for an additional 60 days by requesting one at an Oficina de Migración (immigration office). In La Paz, the office is located at Camacho 1433. It's open Monday through Friday from 9am to 12:30pm and 3 to 6pm; it's best to go late in the afternoon. For more information, call ℂ **0800/10-3007.**

BOLIVIAN EMBASSY LOCATIONS

In the U.S.: 3014 Massachusetts Ave. NW, Washington, DC 20008 (ℂ **202/483-4410;** www.bolivia-usa.org)

In Canada: 130 Albert St., Suite 416, Ottawa, ON K1P 5G4 (ℂ **613/236-5730;** fax 613/236-8237)

In the U.K.: 106 Eaton Sq., London SW1W 9AD (ℂ **020/7235-4248** or 020/7235-2257; fax 020/7235-1286; embolivia-londres@rree.gov.bo)

In Australia: The Consulate of the Republic of Bolivia is located at 4 Bridge St., Suite 305, Sydney NSW 2000 (ℂ **02/9247-4235;** fax 02/9251-7741).

CUSTOMS

Visitors to Bolivia are legally permitted to bring in up to $2,000 worth of items for personal use, including cameras, portable typewriters, tape recorders, sports equipment, 5 liters of alcoholic beverages, and 400 cigarettes (two cartons),

50 cigars, or 500 grams of tobacco. If you bring in any new consumer goods with a value of more than $1,000, you must declare it at Customs.

There are very strict laws regarding removing national treasures (for example, pre-Columbian artifacts, historical paintings, items of Spanish colonial architecture and history, fossils, and some native textiles). *Beware:* The Customs officials at the airports do search every person (for both drugs and national treasures) leaving the country.

MONEY

The Bolivian unit of currency is the **boliviano (Bs).** Besides coins with values of 1 and 2 bolivianos, all the currency is paper, in denominations of 2, 5, 10, 20, 50, and 100. It's very hard to make change, especially for a 100Bs note. If you are retrieving money from an ATM, be sure to request a denomination ending in 50. Restaurants seem to be the only places in the country capable of changing large bills.

Here's a general idea of what things cost in La Paz: A taxi within the center of town, $1; a double room at a budget hotel with private bathroom, $15 to $30; a double room at a moderate hotel with private bathroom, $40 to $65; a double room at an expensive hotel, $100 to $200; fresh juice on the street, 35¢; a 36-exposure roll of film, $4; a three-course lunch for one at a cafe, $2; a three-course dinner for one, $6 to $9.

CURRENCY EXCHANGE & RATES   At press time, the boliviano was trading at a rate of 7.70Bs to US$1. The boliviano has been relatively stable for the past few years. You should note, however, that Bolivia is the poorest country in South America, and with the worldwide economic slump, it's hard to predict what will happen in the future.

When exchanging foreign currency in Bolivia, it's best to head to a *casa de cambio* (money-exchange house). Some banks will exchange American dollars and British pounds, but the lines are often long and the process can be chaotic. U.S. dollars are widely accepted throughout Bolivia, especially at hotels and restaurants. All hotel rates are quoted in U.S. dollars.

ATMs   ATMs are ubiquitous in Bolivia, except in small towns such as Coroico, Sorata, and Copacabana. Major banks include **Banco Santa Cruz** and **Banco de Crédito;** there are **Citibank** branches in both La Paz and Santa Cruz. Most ATMs accept cards on the **Cirrus** (© 800/424-7787) and **PLUS** (© 800/843-7587) networks; however, they can't deal with PINs that are more than four digits. Before you go to Bolivia, make sure that your PIN fits the bill.

TRAVELER'S CHECKS   Citibank will exchange its own traveler's checks. But you can't change American Express traveler's checks at the American Express offices in Bolivia (sounds strange, but it's true). If you're traveling with traveler's checks, your best bet is to cash them at a *casa de cambio.* Most upscale hotels and restaurants in Bolivia will accept traveler's checks. For lost American Express traveler's checks, you must call collect to the United States at © **801/964-6665.**

CREDIT CARDS   MasterCard and Visa are accepted most everywhere in Bolivia. American Express is less common, but it's still widely accepted. To report a lost or stolen **MasterCard,** call © 0800-0172; for **Visa,** © 0800-0188; for **American Express,** call © 800/327-1267 (via an AT&T operator).

WHEN TO GO

PEAK SEASON & CLIMATE   The peak season for travelers in Bolivia is mid-June through early September. But this is only because most travelers come here when it's summer in the northern hemisphere. Ironically, this is the coldest time of year in Bolivia. Fortunately, it's also the dry season.

In the high plateau areas of Bolivia—La Paz, Lake Titicaca, and Potosí—it's generally always cold. The weather is only mildly more pleasant in the off season. La Paz has an average daytime high of 57°F (14°C) and an average nighttime low of 34°F (1°C). Santa Cruz has a tropical climate, although it can get chilly from June through September. Cochabamba has a pleasant springlike climate year-round.

PUBLIC HOLIDAYS   Each city in Bolivia celebrates its own independence day, which always seems to correspond with a local festival. La Paz's independence day is July 16. The whole world seems to converge on Sucre on August 6, Bolivia's official independence day. In small towns throughout the country, you'll find colorful indigenous festivals on or near the summer solstice (June 21). National holidays include: New Year's Day (Jan 1); Carnaval (dates vary); Good Friday; Labor Day (May 1); Corpus Christi (dates vary; usually in mid-June); Independence Day (Aug 6); All Saints' Day (Nov 1); and Christmas (Dec 25).

HEALTH CONCERNS
COMMON AILMENTS   Travelers to Bolivia should be very careful about contracting **food-borne illnesses.** Always drink bottled water. Never drink beverages with ice, unless you are sure that the water for the ice has been previously boiled. Be very careful about eating food purchased from street vendors. I recommend taking a vitamin such as super bromelain, which helps aid in the digestion of parasites.

Because most of the popular tourist attractions in Bolivia are at an altitude of more than 2,500m (8,200 ft.), **altitude sickness** can be a serious problem. Common symptoms include headaches, nausea, sleeplessness, and a tendency to tire easily. The most common remedies include rest, abstaining from alcohol, drinking lots of bottled water, chewing coca leaves, or drinking coca tea. Coca leaves are readily available at street markets, and most restaurants offer some form of coca tea. To help alleviate the symptoms, you can also take the drug acetazolamide (Diamox); it's available by prescription only in the United States.

The **sun** can also be very dangerous in Bolivia, especially at high altitudes. Bring plenty of high-powered sunblock and a wide-brimmed hat. It gets very cold in cities such as La Paz and Potosí, but don't let this fool you into complacency—even when it's cold, the sun can inflict serious damage on your skin.

In general, the healthcare system in Bolivia is good enough to take care of mild illnesses. For a list of hospitals in La Paz, see "Hospitals" in "Fast Facts: Bolivia," below.

VACCINATIONS   No vaccines are required, unless you're planning to visit the difficult-to-reach Pantanal in the far eastern end of Bolivia, in which case you'll need a yellow fever vaccination certificate. Additionally, the Centers for Disease Control and Prevention (CDC) recommend that visitors to Bolivia vaccinate themselves against hepatitis A. Fortunately, since mosquitoes can't live in high altitudes, malaria is not a risk in the high plateau region of Bolivia, but there have been cases reported in rural parts of the Beni area and Santa Cruz.

GETTING THERE
BY PLANE
At 3,900m (more than 13,000 ft.), La Paz's **El Alto Airport** (© 0102/2810-122) is one of the highest commercial airports in the world. Large planes, such

as 747s, cannot land at such a high altitude; even smaller planes have to make sure that they have a light load before touching down. For this reason, very few international flights fly directly into La Paz. All international passengers leaving by air from Bolivia must pay a $20 departure tax.

FROM NORTH AMERICA **American Airlines** (© 800/433-7300; www. aa.com) is the only airline that offers nonstop flights from the United States (via Miami) to La Paz. **LAB** (© 800/337-0918; www.labairlines.com) also offers flights from Miami, with a change of planes in Santa Cruz. **Grupo Taca** (© 800/535-8780; www.grupotaca.com), which is a consortium of several different South American carriers, offers flights from New York to La Paz, but you have to change planes both in San José, Costa Rica, and Lima, Peru. Currently, there are no direct flights from Canada to Bolivia. Canadian travelers must catch a connecting flight in Miami.

For the lowest airfares from the United States to Bolivia, I highly recommend contacting **Bahia Travel Agency** (© 800/833-3138 or 718/639-3310; www. bahiatravelagency.com).

FROM THE U.K. There are no direct flights from the United Kingdom to Bolivia. British travelers have several options, none of which are quick. You can fly **American Airlines** (© 020/8572-5555 in London, or 08457/789-789; www.aa.com) direct from London to Miami, and then from Miami nonstop to La Paz. Alternatively, **Varig Airlines** (© 0845/603-7601; www.varig.com.br) offers direct flights from London to São Paulo, Brazil; from there, Varig offers a daily flight to Santa Cruz, continuing on to La Paz.

FROM AUSTRALIA Get ready for a long, long flight. The easiest way to get to Bolivia from Australia is to hop on an **Aerolíneas Argentinas** (© 800/ 222-215; www.aerolineas.com.ar) flight from Sydney to Buenos Aires. From there, Aerolíneas Argentinas offers daily flights to Santa Cruz. Another route includes flying from Australia to Los Angeles to Miami and then on to La Paz. **Qantas** (© 13-13-13; www.qantas.com.au) offers flights from Australia to Los Angeles—but from there, you must switch to American Airlines to Miami and then Bolivia.

BY BUS

It is possible to travel by bus to Bolivia from Peru, Argentina, and Brazil. Usually, the bus routes end at the border, and you'll have to cross on your own and pick up another bus once you arrive in Bolivia. The most popular international route is from Puno, Peru, to Copacabana or La Paz. **Nuevo Continente,** Calle Sagárnaga 340 (between Illampu and Linares), La Paz (© 0102/2373-423), can arrange trips from both La Paz and Copacabana to Puno and beyond.

GETTING AROUND

Getting around Bolivia is often unpleasant. Only about 5% of the all the roads in the country are paved. Flying is a much better option, but flights are often canceled and schedules change with little warning.

BY PLANE

Traveling by plane is my preferred method of travel in Bolivia. Flights aren't too expensive ($55–$100), and because the roads are so bad in Bolivia, it's really worthwhile to spend the extra money to fly. Additionally, if you take a plane instead of a bus, you will save at least 12 hours in travel time. On the minus side, air travel in Bolivia is not terribly reliable—schedules change all the time. It is imperative that you reconfirm your flight, or you might miss it (and the next departing flight might not leave for another 27 hr.!).

Lloyd Aéreo Boliviano (LAB), Camacho 1460, La Paz (© **0800-4321;** www.labairlines.com), is the major air carrier in Bolivia. Lloyd, as it is informally known, offers flights throughout the country. You can buy a LABPASS, which allows you to fly to four different destinations anywhere in Bolivia. You can only purchase the pass outside of Bolivia; it costs $220 if you fly to Bolivia on LAB, $260 if you arrive on a different carrier. However, because internal flights are relatively inexpensive ($55–$100 each way), you may find that it's not worth it to buy the LABPASS.

Aero Sur, Av. 16 de Julio 1616, La Paz (© **0102/2430-430;** www.aerosur. com), is the second-largest airline in Bolivia. Its schedules are more limited, but prices are similar to LAB.

Both LAB and Aero Sur fly a fleet of aging Boeing 727s (some built in the early 1960s), and I must warn you that these flights are not for the faint of heart. You must be an adventurer and love to fly to bear the trip! Delays abound and landings are harrowing as the thin air and short runways usually dictate a fast approach.

BY BUS

Traveling by bus in Bolivia has its charms, including economical bus fares and riding with the real people of Bolivia. (You may even have the opportunity to sit next to live chickens.) But overall, buses are horribly slow and uncomfortable. Most buses don't have bathrooms, and bus drivers don't like to stop along their route—some 12-hour bus rides will only make two (!) bathroom stops during the entire journey. Buses are often terribly crowded because most drivers will pick up anyone who needs a ride, regardless of how much space is left on the bus. Passengers sit on the floor, and then more passengers sit on their laps. Also, beware of strapping your bags to the top of buses: I have seen bags fall off, while the driver continued on his merry way. One other thought: 95% of the roads in Bolivia are unpaved, which means that 100-mile journeys can take more than 12 hours.

Overall, if you have a lot of time and not much money, the buses in Bolivia are perfectly adequate. If you're traveling on an overnight bus, I highly recommend splurging for the *bus cama* (buses where the seats recline enough to almost resemble a bed). *Bus camas* usually only cost $2 to $3 more than the regular bus. Most bus companies offer very similar services. One of the most reputable companies is **Flota Copacabana** (© **0102/2281-596**). Note that in the rainy season from October through April, some roads may become impassable.

BY CAR

In Bolivia, there are 49,311km (30,628 miles) of highway. Guess how many of those are paved? About 2,496km (1,550 miles). That's it. For the other 46,816km (29,078 miles), you're stuck on some of the bumpiest and most poorly maintained roads in the world. Additionally, there are no signs anywhere, so it's quite easy to get lost. If you decide to be adventurous and explore Bolivia by car, be sure to rent a 4×4. You'll definitely need it, especially in the rainy season (Oct–Apr), when most of the roads turn to mud.

There are no car-rental agencies at the La Paz airport. Instead, when you reserve a car, you can request it to be delivered right to your door or to the airport. **Localiza Rent A Car** (© **0800/2050;** www.localiza.com.bo) is one of the largest car-rental companies in the country. **International Rent A Car** has offices in La Paz (℗ 0107/1530-432) on Calle Federico Zuazo 1942, Cochabamba (℗ 0107/1720-091), and in Santa Cruz (℗ 0103/3344-425). **Hertz** also has offices in La Paz (℗ 0102/2772-929), Santa Cruz (℗ 0103/3336-010), and Cochabamba (℗ 0104/4450-081). The rate for 4×4 vehicles ranges from $45 to $82 per day, including insurance. To rent a car in Bolivia, you must be at least 21 and have a valid driver's license and a passport.

TIPS ON ACCOMMODATIONS

Accommodations in Bolivia run the gamut in quality and expense. There are no world-renowned luxury hotels in Bolivia, but in both Santa Cruz and La Paz you will find some high-quality accommodations. Bolivia's specialty is historic hotels; in Sucre, you can stay in a 300-year-old mansion. Moderately priced hotels are usually spotless, with decent towels in the bathrooms. It's not uncommon to find hotels that charge $5 a night—just don't expect anything other than a bed.

Most hotels, except for the very best ones, don't have heat. Some hotels have a limited number of space heaters *(estufas)*, but you must specifically request one. Otherwise, be sure to bring warm pajamas! Also note that most showers are heated by electric power. All hotel prices are quoted in U.S. dollars. Room availability is rarely an issue in Bolivia, except in Sucre on August 6, when rooms fill for Bolivia's independence day celebrations.

TIPS ON DINING

The food is good in Bolivia—it's just not terribly varied. The diet here is rich in meat, corn, and potatoes. For breakfast, it's common to eat *salteñas* (either chicken or beef, spiced with onions and raisins, and wrapped up in a doughy pastry shell). In most towns, you'll find vendors selling them on almost every street corner. It's also very easy to buy freshly squeezed orange juice on the street. Most typical Bolivian restaurants offer similar menus with local specialties such as *ají de lengua* (cow's tongue in a chile sauce); *picante surtido,* which consists of *sajta* (chicken in a chile sauce) and *saice* (chopped meat in a chile sauce); and *silpancho* (a very thin breaded piece of veal with two fried eggs, onions, and tomatoes). *Chuño putti* (dehydrated potatoes mixed together with milk and cheese) is a popular side dish. Usually, these restaurants also offer more international fare such as filet mignon, pineapple chicken, pasta, and omelets. In La Paz, there are a good variety of ethnic restaurants including Japanese, Korean, French, German, and Italian. Outside of La Paz, pizza and pasta are as international as it gets. To combat altitude sickness, many people drink *mate de coca,* which is tea made from coca leaves. *Tri-mate* tea, which is a combination of three herbal teas, is also a popular after-dinner drink. Fresh fruit is the most popular dessert. Flan (egg custard) is also available at many local restaurants.

TIPS ON SHOPPING

Handicrafts are the name of the game in Bolivia. The indigenous people have been creating beautiful hand-woven goods for thousands of years. In La Paz, Calle Sagárnaga is shopper's central. Here you'll have the opportunity to browse in thousands of stores selling handmade goods, including alpaca sweaters, hats, gloves, leather bags, and textile products. Besides handicrafts, you can also buy folksy good luck charms, from llama fetuses to miniature homes (supposedly, if you buy something in miniature, you'll soon have the *real* thing). Local markets are also a great place to find unique gifts. The Sunday market in Tarabuco, about an hour outside of Sucre, is considered one of the best in Bolivia.

Bargaining is not part of Bolivian culture—for the most part, prices are fixed. If you play your cards right, you may be able to shave a few dollars off the asking price, but in general, most salespeople won't drop their prices significantly. Fortunately, prices are already rock bottom.

FAST FACTS: Bolivia

American Express There are two American Express travel offices in Bolivia, both run by Magri Turismo. Unfortunately, these are more travel agencies than American Express offices. Note that you can't exchange traveler's checks at either office. In La Paz, the office is located on Calle Capitán Ravelo 2101 (© **0102/2442-727**). In Santa Cruz, the office is located at the intersection of Calle Warnes and Calle Potosí.

Business Hours In general, business hours are Monday through Friday from 9am to 12:30pm and from 2:30 to 6:30pm. In smaller towns such as Sucre and Potosí, *everything* closes down from noon until 3pm. In La Paz and Santa Cruz, most banks are open from about 9am to 4pm. Some banks do close in the middle of the day, so it's best to take care of your banking needs early in the morning. Most banks, museums, and stores are open on Saturday from 10am to noon. Everything is closed on Sunday.

Drug Laws In Bolivia, it is legal to chew coca leaves and drink tea made from coca. (But note that it is illegal to bring these products into the U.S.) Cocaine, marijuana, and heroin are all highly illegal. Penalties are strongest for people caught selling drugs, but if you're caught buying or in possession, you're in for a lot of trouble.

Electricity The majority of outlets in Bolivia are 220 volts at 50 cycles. But in places such as La Paz and Potosí, it's common to see 110 volts at 50 cycles. To be on the safe side, always ask before plugging anything in.

Embassies & Consulates In La Paz: **United States,** Av. Arce 2780 (© 0102/2430-120); **Australia,** Av. Arce 2081, Edificio Montevideo (© 0102/2440-459); **Canada,** Calle Victor Sanjínez 2678, Edificio Barcelona 2nd Floor (© 0102/2415-021); and the **United Kingdom,** Av. Arce 2732 (© 0102/433-424).

Emergencies In case of an emergency, call © **110** for the police or © **118** for an ambulance.

Hospitals **Clínica Cemes,** Av. 6 De Agosto 2881 (© **0102/2430-360**), and **Clínica del Sur** (© **0102/278-4001** or 0102/278-4002) on Avenida Hernando Siles and the corner of Calle 7 in the Obrajes neighborhood, are the best hospitals in La Paz. These hospitals are also where you'll most likely find English-speaking doctors. For hospitals in other cities, see the "Fast Facts" for each individual city.

Internet Access Internet service is available almost everywhere in Bolivia, with the possible exception of Isla del Sol on Lake Titicaca. Connections in major cities cost 7Bs (90¢) per hour. In more faraway places, such as Sorata and Copacabana, connections can cost up to 20Bs ($2.60) an hour.

Language Spanish is the language most commonly used in business transactions. But indigenous languages such as Quechua and Aymara are also widely spoken throughout the country. It's best to come to Bolivia with a basic knowledge of Spanish. Outside of the most major tourist sights, it's hard to find someone who speaks English.

Liquor Laws The official drinking age in Bolivia is 18. At discos, you often need to show a picture ID for admittance.

Newspapers & Magazines La Razón (published in La Paz) is one of the most popular Spanish-language newspapers in Bolivia. El Nuevo Día (in Santa Cruz) and Los Tiempos (in Cochabamba) also provide local news for their respective regions. The Bolivian Times is a weekly English-language newspaper, available at newsstands throughout the country. If you're lucky, you may also find English copies of Time or Newsweek.

Police Throughout Bolivia, you can reach the police by dialing ✆ **110**. The tourist police can also help sort out your problems in non-emergency situations. In La Paz, call ✆ **0102/2225-016**; in Cochabamba, ✆ **0104/423364** or 0104/504102; in Santa Cruz, ✆ **0103/3368-900**; in Sucre, ✆ **0104/6423-107**; in Potosí, ✆ **0102/6227-477**.

Post Offices/Mail Most post offices in Bolivia are open Monday through Friday from 8:30am to 8pm, Saturday from 8:30am to 6pm, and Sunday from 9am to noon. It costs 5Bs (65¢) to mail a letter to the United States, 7Bs (90¢) to Australia, and 6Bs (80¢) to Europe. From time to time, you can buy stamps at kiosks and newspaper stands. There are no public mailboxes, so you'll have to mail your letter from the post office.

Restrooms The condition of public facilities is surprisingly good in Bolivia. In museums, the toilets are relatively clean, but they never have toilet paper. If you have an emergency, you can also use the restrooms in hotel lobbies without much problem. Note that most buses don't have toilet facilities, and on long-distance bus rides, the driver may only stop once or twice in a 12-hour stretch. And when they do stop, the facilities are often horrendous—usually smelly squat toilets. It's always useful to have a roll of toilet paper handy.

Safety La Paz and Santa Cruz are the most dangerous cities in Bolivia. I know people who have had cameras ripped off their bodies. Be careful in crowded areas and hold on tightly to your personal belongings. Watch out for thieves who try to stain your bags (usually with mustard or peanut butter); they offer to help clean you off while cleaning you out. Taxis in La Paz can also be dangerous. Never get in an unmarked taxi. Legitimate cabs have bright signs on top that illuminate their telephone numbers. Before you get in, be sure to write down the cab's number. If ever in doubt, ask a restaurant or hotel to call you a taxi. Report all problems to the tourist police (see "Police," above.)

Telephone & Fax Most high-end hotels in La Paz, Santa Cruz, and Cochabamba offer international direct dial and long-distance service and in-house fax transmission. But these calls tend to be quite expensive, as hotels often levy a surcharge, even if you're calling a toll-free access number.

Practically every single town in Bolivia has an **Entel** office (almost always located in the main plaza). From here, you can make local, long-distance, and international calls. It's actually much more economical to make your international calls from an Entel office than to use an international calling card. For example, for calls to the United States, AT&T, MCI, and Sprint all charge about $9 for the first minute and $2 for each additional minute, plus a 10% surcharge. Entel charges 5Bs (65¢) to 10Bs ($1.30) per minute.

To make local calls from a public phone, you need a phone card. You can buy them at any Entel office or any kiosk on the street. The average local call costs about 2Bs (25¢) for 3 minutes.

For tips on dialing, see "Telephone Dialing Info at a Glance" on p. 170.

Time Zone Bolivia is 4 hours behind GMT (Greenwich mean time), except during daylight savings time, when it is 5 hours behind.

Tipping Restaurants in Bolivia never add a service charge. It's expected that you will add a 10% to 15% gratuity to the total bill. Taxi drivers don't expect tips. It's common to tip hotel porters about 50¢ to $1 per bag.

Water Always drink bottled water in Bolivia. Most hotels provide bottled water in the bathrooms, and you can buy bottles of water on practically any street corner. Small bottles cost about 1Bs to 2Bs (15¢–25¢); large bottles cost just 3Bs (40¢). Most restaurants use ice made from boiled water, but always ask to be sure.

3 La Paz ★★

The city of La Paz is nestled in a valley atop the Bolivian plateau, surrounded by snowy peaks and dominated by the white head of Illimani, the sacred mountain. The setting is sure to take your breath away (and if the setting doesn't, the 3,739m/12,464-ft. altitude will), but that's not what I love best about La Paz. The *Paceños* themselves, the city's inhabitants, are what make this place unforgettable. No other major South American city holds on to its past so firmly. Many of the women wear traditional clothing every day: colorful multilayered petticoats, fringed shawls, lace aprons, and (oddest of all) bowler hats, which look like they came straight from a prewar London haberdashery. You'll see these women throughout the city—on the buses, in the churches, shopping, or perhaps setting up their own shops.

They probably won't be setting up shop inside, though—hardly anyone does in La Paz. The city is one giant street market. In stalls on the sidewalks or at street corners you can buy not only batteries and chewing gum, but also dice and leather dice-cups, socks, hats, sneakers, cameras, and telephones. In the Mercado Negro (Black Market) area of the city, computers, electric drills, bookcases, office supplies, and everything else you could think of are all displayed on the sidewalk. At the Mercado de los Brujos (Witch Doctors' Market), the discerning shopper can find the finest in good-luck statuettes and all the materials required for a proper offering to Pachamama, including baskets of dried llama fetuses. Perhaps *you* aren't in the market for such things, but just being in a place where people are is half the fun of La Paz.

ESSENTIALS
GETTING THERE
Getting to La Paz is not an easy feat. For information on arriving by plane or bus, see "Getting There" in "Planning Your Trip to Bolivia," earlier in this chapter.

El Alto Airport is 25 minutes from the center of La Paz. A **taxi** ride to the city center should cost about 50Bs ($6.50). Most hotels will send a taxi to pick you up at the airport (when you arrive, a driver will be waiting for you with a welcome sign), but the taxi still costs about $7. Alternatively, you can take a minibus into the center of town. **GoTransTur buses** wait outside the airport (behind the taxis) and leave every 4 minutes daily from 6:15am to 9pm. The minibuses go past Plaza San Francisco and up Avenida 16 de Julio (La Paz's main street) to Plaza Isabel La Católica. The ride costs only 5Bs (65¢), but the buses usually fill up, and it's hard to squeeze into the tight seats if you have luggage with you.

If you're arriving by bus, the main bus terminal is located on Plaza Antofagasta at the intersection of Avenida Uruguay, a short taxi ride (about 4 min. and $1) from the heart of town. You'll easily find a taxi outside the terminal.

ORIENTATION

Historically, La Paz's main street—known interchangeably as El Prado, Avenida 16 de Julio, and Avenida Mariscal Santa Cruz—divided the city into two parts. The indigenous people lived to the south of this main area, the Spanish to the north. Before the age of cement, this main street was actually a river. Water still runs along this path, but you'd have to dig pretty deep to find it. Nevertheless, this is still the lowest point of La Paz. So, if you're lost, just walk downhill and eventually you will arrive at El Prado. The old colonial divisions still linger: The Witch Doctors' Market, the Black Market, and most of the indigenous-run street stands are all still on the south side of El Prado, while the colonial buildings, main plaza, and government offices are all to the north. The area of town from Plaza San Francisco to Plaza del Estudiante is considered the heart of La Paz. Still considered quite central, the **Sopocachi** neighborhood extends south and east of Plaza del Estudiante. Along 20 de Octubre and Avenida 6 de Agosto, you'll find some of the trendier restaurants and bars in town. **Miraflores** borders Sopocachi to the north. This is mainly a residential area, but visitors do sometimes venture here to catch a soccer game at Estadio Hernando Siles, or to admire the views of La Paz from the Mirador Laikakota.

GETTING AROUND

BY TAXI   You will never be at a loss for a taxi in La Paz. Because unemployment is so high in Bolivia, many people have converted their cars into taxis. *But beware:* I have heard sketchy stories about these rogue taxi drivers. The most reliable taxi companies display brightly lit signs with their telephone numbers on top of their taxis. Drivers don't use meters, but fares are generally fixed. Rides within the center of town or to the Sopocachi neighborhood should only cost 7Bs (90¢).

BY *TRUFI*   The streets of La Paz are clogged with *trufis* (minibuses), which are always packed with locals. The routes are convoluted and confusing, except in the center of town (from Plaza San Francisco to Plaza del Estudiante) where *trufis* travel down one street without making any turns. So, if you're in the center of town, and you're planning on going straight, flag down a *trufi*. There are no designated stops; drivers stop when they see prospective passengers. The fare is 2Bs (25¢), payable to the driver at the end of your ride. To signal that you want to get off, simply shout, *"Bajo"* or *"Me quedo aquí."*

BY FOOT   It's hard to walk anywhere at an altitude of 3,739m (12,464 ft.) without feeling winded. But it's especially hard to walk around La Paz, where it

La Paz

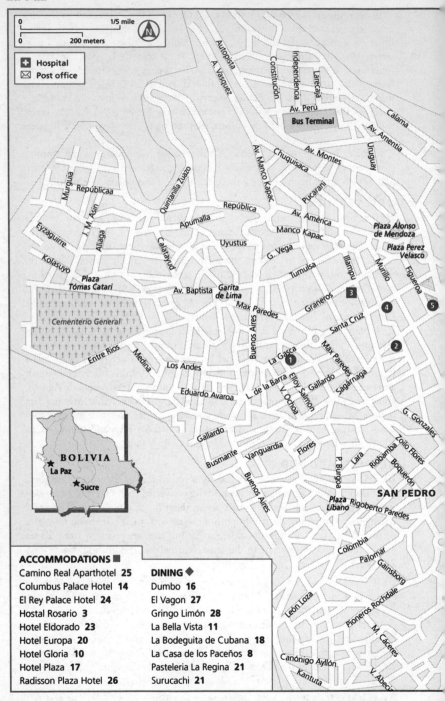

Hospital
Post office

BOLIVIA
La Paz
Sucre

ACCOMMODATIONS ■
Camino Real Aparthotel **25**
Columbus Palace Hotel **14**
El Rey Palace Hotel **24**
Hostal Rosario **3**
Hotel Eldorado **23**
Hotel Europa **20**
Hotel Gloria **10**
Hotel Plaza **17**
Radisson Plaza Hotel **26**

DINING ◆
Dumbo **16**
El Vagon **27**
Gringo Limón **28**
La Bella Vista **11**
La Bodeguita de Cubana **18**
La Casa de los Paceños **8**
Pasteleria La Regina **21**
Surucachi **21**

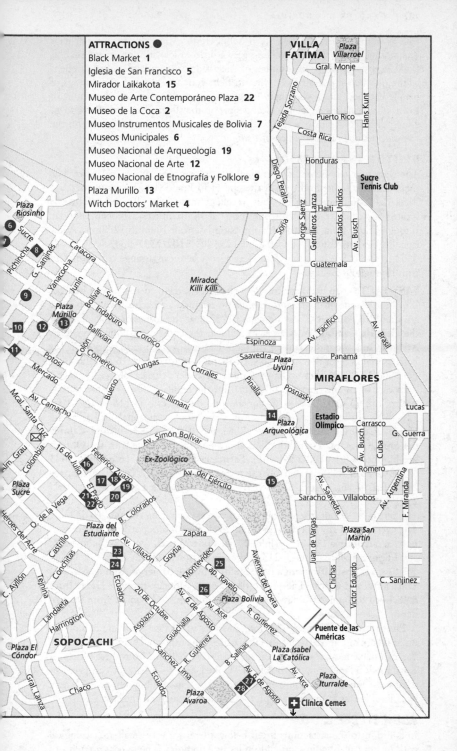

ATTRACTIONS ●
Black Market **1**
Iglesia de San Francisco **5**
Mirador Laikakota **15**
Museo de Arte Contemporáneo Plaza **22**
Museo de la Coca **2**
Museo Instrumentos Musicales de Bolivia **7**
Museos Municipales **6**
Museo Nacional de Arqueología **19**
Museo Nacional de Arte **12**
Museo Nacional de Etnografía y Folklore **9**
Plaza Murillo **13**
Witch Doctors' Market **4**

feels as if all the streets have a steep uphill climb. After you spend a few days acclimating to the altitude, walking gets a little easier. Still, on streets such as Calle Sagárnaga, where the number of street-side vendors is roughly equivalent to the number of pedestrians, trying to fight your way through the throngs of people can be quite a challenge. I recommend walking around the center of town; it's fascinating to see the local people on the streets. But if you have to go a long distance—from one side of the city to another—it's much easier on the feet and the body to take a taxi or *trufi*.

VISITOR INFORMATION

There are two very helpful government-run information offices in La Paz. The most centrally located office is at the end of El Prado (La Paz's main street) at Plaza del Estudiante; you can buy excellent maps here. The other office is located just outside the main bus terminal. Both offices are open Monday through Friday from 9am to 6pm and Saturday from 10am to 12:30pm. Additionally, **Crillon Tours,** Av. Camacho 1233 (© **0102/2337-533,** or 305/358-5353 in the U.S.), is very helpful. The agents here can arrange city tours and trips throughout Bolivia.

FAST FACTS   To exchange traveler's checks or foreign currency, your best bet is to head to one of the *casas de cambio* on Avenida Camacho. Two of the best are **Cambios "America,"** Av. Camacho 1233 near the corner of Ayacucho, and the **Casa de Cambio,** Av. Camacho 1311 at the corner of Colón. In general, Avenida Camacho is the banking center of La Paz—you'll find all types of ATMs here, as well as most Bolivian banks. **Citibank** is nearby at Av. 16 de Julio 1434 (© 0800/10-2000); they exchange Citibank traveler's checks for free.

In case of an **emergency,** call © 110 for the regular police. For the **tourist police,** call © 0102/2225-016. For an **ambulance,** call © 118 or © 0107/1268-502. If you need medical attention, the two best hospitals in La Paz are **Clínica Cemes,** Av. 6 De Agosto 2881 (© 0102/2430-360), and **Clínica del Sur,** at Avenida Hernando Siles and the corner of Calle 7 in the Obrajes neighborhood (© 0102/2784-001). **Farmacia Red Bolivia,** 16 de Julio 1473 (© 0102/2331-838), is probably the most centrally located 24-hour pharmacy in La Paz. If you need a delivery, try calling **Farmacia La Paz** at © 0102/2371-828.

There is no lack of Internet cafes in La Paz, especially on Avenida 16 de Julio. The average cost is 7Bs (90¢) an hour. You'll find the fastest Internet connections at **WeBolivia,** Av. 16 de Julio 1764; **Punto Entel,** Av. 16 de Julio 1473; and **Pl@net,** Calle Sagárnaga 213 at the corner of Murillo.

The main **post office** is in a large building on the corner of Avenida Mariscal Santa Cruz and Oruro. The post office is open Monday through Friday from 8:30am to 8:30pm, Saturday from 8:30am to 6pm, and Sunday from 9am to noon.

Punto Entel is the main telephone provider in La Paz. There are two offices on El Prado: one at Mariscal Santa Cruz 1287, the other at Av. 15 de Julio 1473. You can make local, long-distance, and international calls from these offices. It costs about $1 per minute to call the United States—a bargain compared to what most international companies charge. You can also buy phone cards here or at local kiosks to use the pay phones located throughout the city.

WHAT TO SEE & DO

In addition to the attractions listed below, there is a very small archaeological park in front of Estadio Hernando Siles in Miraflores. The park is a replica of the Semi-Underground Temple found at the actual Tiwanaku archaeological site. The monolith here is one of the only authentic artifacts; unfortunately, it's in bad shape. Instead of going to this archaeological park, I recommend traveling to the real thing in Tiwanaku (see "Side Trips from La Paz," later in this chapter).

Mirador Laikakota   From the lower points of La Paz, you may have noticed that, in the near distance, there is a large hill with a funky blue tower on top of it. This is the Mirador Laikakota, a good lookout point, offering a 360-degree view of La Paz. The Mirador isn't simply a *mirador* (view point)—it's also a very large children's park with rides, playgrounds, and food stands. To enjoy the best views, walk past all the playgrounds to the far end of the park. This is a good spot for a photo of the mighty snow-covered Illimani.

Av. del Ejército near the corner of Díaz Romero, Miraflores. Admission 7Bs (90¢). Daily 8:30am–7pm.

Museo de Arte Contemporáneo Plaza ★★   The powerful art in this museum does an excellent job of conveying the issues that affect modern-day Bolivians. Notable permanent pieces include a collection of plaster sculptures by the museum's owner, Herman Plaza, called *Cuando los Hijos se Van* ("When the Kids Leave"), a very real depiction of young people who are leaving Bolivia for the United States; and paintings by José Rodríguez-Sánchez who comes from Cochabamba, where the U.S.-directed program to eradicate coca growing in the region has wreaked havoc on the local people. The museum also houses the work of some well-known international artists, including portraits by Choi-Sung Man, considered one of the best portrait artists in the world. (His subjects have included George H. W. Bush, Mikhail Gorbachev, and Princess Diana.) Occasionally, there is a Spanish-speaking guide who can take you on a 30-minute tour of the museum. If you can't find the guide, stop in the gift shop and ask Luis for help—he's very knowledgeable.

Even if there were no art here, it still would be worth a visit to see the interior of the 126-year-old mansion that houses the museum. This building and the bus station are the only structures in Bolivia that were designed by Señor Eiffel of Eiffel Tower fame.

Av. 16 de Julio 1698 (near Plaza del Estudiante). ℂ 0102/2335-905. Admission 10Bs ($1.30). Daily 9am–9pm.

Museo de la Coca *(Moments*   This museum provides visitors with a true "only in Bolivia" experience. Coca leaves have been an important part of Bolivian culture for thousands of years, and this tiny museum is dedicated solely to the coca leaf and its history. You'll learn tons of interesting facts about the coca leaf's healing properties, its nutritional value, and how it's transformed into cocaine. However, the real highlight is learning the proper way to chew coca leaves. Apparently, you must chew the bitter leaves for several minutes on one side of your mouth; once you've mashed up the leaves, the museum's owner will give you a pasty but sweet coca substance to add to the mix. Goodbye, altitude sickness! Set aside about an hour for your visit here.

Linares 906 (near Calle Sagárnaga). Admission 10Bs ($1.30). Daily 10am–1pm and 2:30–7pm.

Museo Instrumentos Musicales de Bolivia *(Kids*   This small museum, housed in a colonial mansion on a beautiful street, does a good job of explaining how Bolivians have historically depended on nature to make music. On display are prehistoric instruments made of bone, wood, stone, and reeds; guitars made from turtle shells; harps made from armadillo shells; and an instrument consisting solely of toucan beaks. The museum is great for children because visitors are encouraged to experiment with the unusual instruments. However, if you don't have kids or your time is limited in La Paz, you won't miss much if you don't make it here. If you do, it'll take you all of half an hour to see everything; if you have kids, it might take longer.

Calle Jaén 711. *C* **0102/2408-177.** Admission 7Bs (90¢). Daily 9:30am–12:30pm and 2:30–6:30pm.

Museo Nacional de Arqueología

The exhibits here focus on findings from the Tiwanaku and Inca cultures; however, the displays vary widely in quality and, compared to other archaeology museums in South America, the quality of the pieces is quite poor. The back room is the best part of the museum: On display are some fascinating and very descriptive figures from the Tiwanaku culture, including a monolith, and bronze Inca figures. Also of note are eerie mummies from the Inca period (1200–1400). You can visit this museum in less than an hour.

Tiwanaku 93 (at the corner of Federico Zuazo). *C* **0102/2311-621.** Admission 10Bs ($1.30). Mon–Sat 9am–noon and 3–7pm; Sun 10am–1pm.

Museo Nacional de Arte

In the 17th and 18th centuries, Potosí may have been the mining center of the world. However, it was also a thriving cultural center and the home of some of the most famous colonial artists in the Americas. This museum is a treasure trove of colonial art, and it displays some of the most famous works of these artists. One of the most impressive is Gaspar Miguel de Berrio's two-paneled *Adoración de los Reyes y Adoración de los Pastores,* which is one of the few Bolivian colonial paintings with an African figure in it. There is a whole room dedicated to Melchor Pérez Holguín, who was actually a mestizo; if you look carefully at his work, you can see some indigenous influences. There are also several galleries dedicated to contemporary Bolivian art.

In addition to seeing some fine art, you will find yourself in one of the most important colonial structures of the Americas: The building dates from 1775. The interior courtyard has some marvelous stonework. Plan on spending about an hour and a half here.

On the corner of Comercio and Socabaya (off Plaza Murillo). Admission 7Bs (90¢). Mon–Fri 9am–12:30pm and 3–7pm; Sat 9am–1pm; Sun 10am–1pm.

Museo Nacional de Etnografía y Folklore

This museum is dedicated to the rich local culture in Bolivia. There are exhibits dedicated to specific tribes, including the URKU, who live near Lake Titicaca, as well as art that relates to the Casa de la Moneda (the Royal Mint) in Potosí. The real star here, however, is the *Tres Milenios de Tejidos* ("3,000 Years of Textiles") exhibit, a varied collection of richly colored ponchos, skirts, and blankets that women use to carry their children. When you see all of them together, you really begin to understand that these aren't simply ponchos, skirts, or blankets—rather, these are works of art and self-expression. Plan on spending about 45 minutes here.

Ingavi 916 (at the corner of Genaro Sanjinés). Free admission. Tues–Fri 9am–12:30pm and 3–7pm; Sat–Sun 9am–1pm.

Museos Municipales

The Museos Municipales is actually a collection of four museums all located on the beautiful Spanish-style Calle Jaén. One ticket—purchased from the Museo Costumbrista Juan de Vargas (see below)—will gain you access to all of them. Visiting four museums sounds like a lot, but they are all small, and it only takes about an hour to see everything. Personally, I thought the museums were a little weak, especially since there are very few explanations in English, and the ones in Spanish aren't especially descriptive.

If you only have time (or patience) for one museum, I recommend visiting the **Museo de Metales Preciosos** ⚐, Calle Jaén 777, where you'll see interesting gold and silver belts, necklaces, bowls, crowns, and bracelets from both the Inca and Tiwanaku cultures, as well as a Tiwanaku monolith. The courtyard here is also quite interesting: If you look closely at the ground, you can see the remains of sheep bones, which the Spanish used as home decorations during the colonial era.

The **Museo Costumbrista Juan de Vargas,** Calle Jaén on the corner of Calle Sucre, specializes in the early-20th-century history of La Paz. Some amazing photographs are on display, as well as old pianos and phonographs and many modern figurines depicting all styles of life and clothing in La Paz.

The **Museo del Litoral Boliviano,** Calle Jaén 789, is the least interesting of the bunch. It's tiny, and it houses relics from the Pacific War (1879–84) when Bolivia lost its access to the sea. On display are portraits of Bolivian generals, uniforms, guns, gun cases, and information about Ignacia Zeballos (one of the founders of the Red Cross, who was from Santa Cruz, Bolivia).

The **Museo Casa de Murillo,** Calle Jaén 790, is a beautiful old mansion dating from the 18th century. Inside, you will find baroque-style carved-wood furniture, including intricate picture frames. The house itself is also historically significant—the home of General Murillo, a prominent player in Bolivia's independence movement, is where the revolutionary leaders drew up Bolivia's declaration of independence.

Calle Jaén (near Calle Sucre). Admission 5Bs (65¢) adults, free for students and seniors over 65. Mon–Fri 9:30am–12:30pm and 3–7pm; Sat–Sun 10am–1pm.

Plaza Murillo   Plaza Murillo is the historical center of La Paz. During colonial times, Plaza Murillo was on the Spanish side of the Prado, and it became the center of the action because it was the main water source in town. In its glory days, the plaza was surrounded by eucalyptus trees and a statue of Neptune. In 1900, the plaza was officially named Plaza Murillo after General Murillo, one of the heroes of the Bolivian independence movement.

On one side of the plaza, you'll find the neoclassical **cathedral,** which took 152 years to build (1835–1987). The towers are the newest part—they were constructed for the arrival of the Pope. If you want to visit the inside of the cathedral, it's open weekdays from 3:30 to 7pm and in the mornings on weekends.

Next to the cathedral is the colonial **Government Palace,** or the Palacio Quemado (burned palace). Originally, La Paz's City Hall and now the office of Bolivia's president, the building has been burned eight times. Every Thursday at 9am, you can take 15-minute guided tours in Spanish. Outside the Government Palace, you will probably notice guards in red uniforms. During the Pacific War (1879–84), when Bolivia lost its seacoast to Chile, the soldiers wore red uniforms. Today, these uniforms send the message that Chile must return that land to Bolivia.

Across from the palace is the **Congress** building, which has a long history: It was a convent, a jail, and a university before a 1904 renovation to house Bolivia's congress. Standing opposite the cathedral and the Government Palace is the 1911 **Grand Hotel París,** the first movie house in Bolivia.

To get here from El Prado, walk 3 blocks on Calle Ayacucho or Calle Socabaya.

Iglesia de San Francisco The intricately stone-carved facade of the San Francisco church is one the finest examples of baroque-mestizo architecture in the Americas. Look closely and you'll see a wealth of indigenous symbols—from masked figures to snakes, dragons, and tropical birds. The cornerstone for the original San Francisco church was placed in this spot in 1548, 1 year before the founding of La Paz. The church standing here today is not the original; it was completed in 1784. Once inside, the baroque influence seems to disappear. The small cedar altars with gold-leaf designs are much more typical of the neo-classical era.

Plaza San Francisco, at the north end of Av. Mariscal Santa Cruz. Free admission. Mon–Sat 4–6pm.

SPORTS & OUTDOOR ACTIVITIES

Bolivia is a haven for outdoor enthusiasts. It's nice to spend a few days in La Paz, but the surrounding mountains are truly spectacular and mighty enticing. If you travel a couple of hours outside of La Paz, you will have the opportunity to climb some of the highest peaks in the world, bike down one of the most dangerous roads in the world, golf in one of the highest courses in the world, or ski down one of the highest slopes in the world.

CLIMBING, HIKING & TREKKING If you're serious about climbing, you should check out **Club Andino** on Calle México 1638 (② **0102/2312-875;** Mon–Fri 9:30am–12:30pm and 3–7pm). This nonprofit climbing club knows all the secrets of the Andes; the staff here can help arrange treks and climbs as well as recommend the best outfitters and guides. It can also help organize a trip to an acclimatizing center or a ski outing to **Chacaltaya** (see "Skiing," below). But you don't have to be a skier to enjoy Chacaltaya: You can hike from the ski lift to the glacier. At 5,240m (17,187 ft.), the air is thin, but the views are what's really breathtaking. Hiking trips to Chacaltaya cost $10, including transportation and admission.

Bolivian Journeys ⊛, Sagárnaga 363 between Linares and Illampu (② **0102/ 2357-848;** www.bolivianjourneys.com), is one of the most experienced climbing and hiking outfitters. For the brave and experienced, the company organizes climbs up the 5,990m (19,968-ft.) **Huayna Potosí.**

FUTBOL (SOCCER) Four teams play year-round at **Estadio Hernando Siles** in Miraflores. There are games most every week on Tuesday, Wednesday, and Sunday. You can buy tickets on game day at the stadium. Prices range from 10Bs to 25Bs ($1.30–$3.25). To get here, just hop on any *trufi* with a sign marked ESTADIO in the front window, or take a taxi.

GOLF The 18-hole, 6,900-yard **Mallasilla La Paz Golf Club** (② **0102/ 2745-462**), located about 15 minutes outside of La Paz, is considered to be one of the highest golf clubs in the worlds. Greens fees are $70 per person plus $10 for equipment and $10 for a caddie. **Crillon Tours,** Av. Camacho 1233 (② **0102/2337-533,** or 305/358-5353 in the U.S.), can arrange golf packages.

MOUNTAIN BIKING **Gravity Assisted Mountain Biking** ⊛⊛, Av. 16 de Julio 1490 (② **0102/2374-204;** www.gravitybolivia.com), is by far the best biking outfitter in Bolivia. From La Paz, you can choose from more than nine different 1-day biking trips. The most popular is the 64km (40-mile) descent from La Paz to Coroico along the most dangerous road in the world. The road is narrow, unpaved, crowded with trucks, and carved out of a cliff. *Be careful:* In 2001, a woman died when her brakes snapped. Make sure your bike is in good condition. Gravity Assisted Mountain Biking also arranges rides to Sorata and the Zongo Valley.

SKIING   From January through May, you can ski on the glacier at Chacaltaya, one of the highest ski slopes in the world. **Club Andino,** Calle México 1638 (© **0102/2312-875**), is in charge of arranging ski outings; they're open Monday through Friday from 9:30am to 12:30pm and 3 to 7pm. Trips leave only on Wednesdays and Saturdays, but if you have a group of four or more people, you can swish down the slope any day you want. Transportation costs $10 per person, equipment rental is $10, and you have to pay $7 for the lift ticket. Dress warmly (although at this altitude the sun is brutal) and make sure that you have acclimated to the altitude—there's not much air at 5,156m (17,187 ft.).

SHOPPING

At times, it feels as though La Paz is one big shopping center. The streets teem with vendors peddling everything you can imagine. You never have to walk far to find what you need. The city is a mecca for handmade arts-and-crafts products. **Calle Sagárnaga** is shopper's central, with thousands of stores all packed to the gills with local handicrafts. In general, most of the quality is mediocre, but the variety and uniqueness of the goods sold here is mighty impressive. Some of the more popular items include alpaca sweaters (usually about $8–$10 each), hand-woven shoulder bags, leather bags, wool hats, textiles, gloves, and all sorts of things that you will never find in your hometown. **ComArt,** Calle Linares 958 (about 1 block down from Sagárnaga), is the only association of organized workers in La Paz. When you buy something here, your money goes directly to the workers, not the shopkeepers. If you're trying to find some differences between all the stores in the area, here's a tip: Both **Millma,** Calle Sagárnaga 225, and **Artesanía Sorata,** Calle Sagárnaga 311 and Calle Linares 862, sell some of the best quality alpaca sweaters in town. On the other side of town, you'll find beautiful silver jewelry at **Kuka Pradel,** Av. 6 de Agosto 2190.

Note that Bolivian vendors are not seasoned negotiators—they may drop the price by a dollar or two, but for the most part, prices are firm. Once you walk away, say goodbye forever to that gorgeous $4 hand-woven bag. The shopkeepers know that someone else will fork over the dough.

THE WITCH DOCTORS' MARKET ☞☞   Venture off of Calle Sagárnaga onto Calle Linares and you'll find yourself in the appropriately named Witch Doctors' Market. Here, you can buy a ghoulish variety of charms, spices, and magic potions to help cast a positive spell on your future. Llama fetuses are one of the most popular items for sale here. If you're looking for luck, here's a list to help you decode the meaning of all the amulets on display: Frogs are said to bring good fortune; turtles are the symbol of long life; owls bring knowledge; snakes are a sign of progression (or moving in the right direction); koa—a dried plant made with molasses—is supposed to help your harvest; and pumas will help you achieve victory over your enemy.

THE BLACK MARKET   Need a computer, a toilet bowl, tools, or a stereo? You'll find them all at the Black Market. Apparently, everything here is smuggled in from Chile. It's widely known that the merchandise is not always totally legit, but these days, even police officers do their shopping here. You'll find some incredible bargains. Even if you can't fit a toilet bowl in your suitcase, it's still a hoot to wander the crowded streets and watch as the locals wheel and deal. The Black Market is a few blocks uphill from the heart of Sagárnaga, past Max Paredes; you'll find a lot of action around Calle La Gasca and Eloy Salmón.

WHERE TO STAY
Expensive

Hotel Europa 😊😊😊   Tucked away a few steps from the Prado, this is the best hotel in La Paz. But don't let the name fool you—Hotel Europa doesn't have an ounce of European flavor to it. It's pure nouveau Bolivian. From the free cellphones to the local art displayed in the lobby, it's clear that this hotel caters to high-class Bolivians who have developed a fondness for modern Florida-style high-rises. Because the hotel is only 6 years old, it knocks its competition (the 28-year-old Radisson Plaza Hotel) out of the water. The large, cream-colored rooms have fancy green and white carpets, built-in desks, and fresh plants. Mattresses are firm and all beds come with luxurious down comforters. The spacious bathrooms have white tiles and marble sinks. The Hotel Europa is the only hotel in Bolivia to have "floor heating" and a state-of-the-art air-circulation system. The suites are all full apartments with kitchenettes; some even have Jacuzzis. The Matisse and Picasso suites are perfect for executives who might want to host parties in their rooms. The informal cafeteria serves good local specialties, and there's live music at the cozy bar on weekend evenings. Internet access is free for guests in the business center, but the connection can be painfully slow.

Calle Tiwanaku 64 (between El Prado and F. Zuazo), La Paz. ✆ 0102/2315-656. Fax 0102/2315-656. www.summithotels.com. 110 units. $170–$200 double; $235–$380 suite. AE, MC, V. **Amenities:** 2 restaurants; bar; largest indoor pool in La Paz; really tiny exercise room; sauna; concierge; small business center; salon; room service; massage; babysitting; same-day laundry service; dry cleaning; nonsmoking rooms; executive floor. *In room:* A/C, TV, dataport, minibar, hair dryer, safe; fax and kitchenette in suites.

Hotel Plaza 😊   This would be my second choice for a centrally located hotel, after the Europa (above). Managed by Radisson, this 22-year-old property is showing its age slightly, but it boasts a fantastic location directly on the Prado, just steps away from everything. The airy, expansive lobby with its colorful modern art leads to not-so-bright rooms with dark carpets and aging satiny bedspreads. They are very spacious, however, and those on the 7th floor and above come with wonderful views of the city. You can open the windows here, a rarity in high-rise hotels. The marble bathrooms are small but clean with big mirrors. There's a formal restaurant on the top floor with amazing views, and an informal coffee shop (adjacent to the lobby) that serves an excellent buffet lunch. The Plaza has the best hotel gym in La Paz, but the pool area is not very attractive. Guests get complimentary use of the Internet at the business center. All in all, this is a good value if you score a good rate, but if you're paying full price, choose Hotel Europa instead.

Paseo del Prado, La Paz. ✆ 0102/2378-311. Fax 0102/2378-318. www.plazabolivia.com.bo. 147 units. $119–$150 double; $220 suite. Rates include breakfast. AE, MC, V. **Amenities:** 2 restaurants; bar; small indoor pool; large exercise room; Jacuzzi; sauna; concierge; business center; room service; laundry service; dry cleaning; nonsmoking rooms; executive floor. *In room:* A/C, TV, minibar, hair dryer.

Radisson Plaza Hotel 😊😊   Radisson Plaza is the only hotel in all of Bolivia that is part of a North American hotel chain. You can expect all the amenities of an exclusive business hotel here, but compared to modern, sexy Hotel Europa (above), it feels more like a comfortable old shoe. So, if you're simply looking for a familiar place to flop for the night, the Radisson is a perfect choice. The rooms are usually spacious enough for two double beds, a large dresser, and two chairs. They also have huge picture windows, but only some have views of the city or snow-covered Illimani; unfortunately, a few years ago, a high-rise went up right in front of the rooms with the best views. The suites have fancy inlaid night tables, mahogany headboards, and a spacious sitting area. The presidential suite, with its three fashionably designed bedrooms, elegant living room, and formal dining room, is fit for, well, a president. The sleek Aransaya Restaurant, which has outstanding views, looks like it was airlifted here from New York City. This is also one of the only hotels in La Paz that offers a free airport shuttle. Be sure to ask for the "Super Saver" rates that sometimes shave almost 30% off the regular prices. You can also score a really low Internet-only rate by making your reservation through the hotel's website.

Av. Arce 2177 (corner of F. Guachalla), La Paz. ⓒ **800/333-3333** in the U.S., or 0102/2441-111. Fax 0102/2440-402. www.radisson.com/lapazbo. 246 units. $120–$210 double; $230–$385 suite. Rates include breakfast. AE, MC, V. **Amenities:** 2 restaurants; bar; small indoor pool; exercise room; Jacuzzi; sauna; activities desk; large business center; room service; massage; babysitting; laundry service; dry cleaning; nonsmoking rooms; executive floor. *In room:* A/C, TV, minibar, hair dryer, safe.

Moderate

Camino Real Aparthotel ⍟ *Kids*   This modern hotel offers one of the best values in La Paz. Each hotel room is its own apartment with wonderfully soft beds, a separate living room, a sleeper sofa, and an enormous and fully stocked kitchen. It truly feels like a home away from home. Plus, the location is excellent—the hotel is on a quiet street only a few blocks from the Prado. Try to request an apartment on the 11th or 12th floor—these units come with the best views and balconies.

Capitán Ravelo 2123 (between Montevideo and F. Guachalla), La Paz. ⓒ **0102/2441-515.** Fax 0102/2440-055. www.caminoreal.com.bo. 52 units. $98 double, triple, or quad. Rates include American breakfast. AE, MC, V. **Amenities:** Restaurant; small exercise room; Jacuzzi; sauna; tour desk; small business center; room service; massage; babysitting; laundry service; dry cleaning. *In room:* TV, kitchen, minibar, hair dryer, safe.

El Rey Palace Hotel ⍟ *Value*   The name translates to King's Palace, but in reality this hotel, which is housed in a 1940s former apartment building, feels more like a small, midrange European hotel. All the rooms have bright red carpeting and dark wood furniture. The doubles have two king-size beds, a large dressing table, a small table with two chairs, and enough open space to throw all your dirty clothes on the floor. The suites have separate sitting areas with velvety armchairs; some also have Jacuzzis. For the most part, the bathrooms are spacious. The higher floors have good views of the city, but the lower floors are quite dark because nearby buildings prevent any light from entering the rooms. Note that the elevator stops at the seventh floor, so guests with rooms on the eighth floor have to walk up a flight of stairs. I have to give the hotel points for its location—it's only about 2 blocks from the action of the Prado, but it's on a quiet street that feels millions of miles away. If you're staying longer than a month, the daily rate goes down to $45 for a room for two people.

Av. 20 de Octubre 1947, La Paz. ⓒ **0102/2393-016.** Fax 0102/2367-759. www.hotel-rey-palace-bolivia.com. 60 units. $80 double; $85 junior suite; $95–$105 suite. Rates include buffet breakfast. AE, MC, V. **Amenities:** Restaurant; bar; small business center; room service; laundry service; dry cleaning. *In room:* TV, dataport, minibar, hair dryer, safe.

Hotel Gloria   You can't beat Hotel Gloria's location. You can fall out of bed onto both Plaza San Francisco and Plaza Murillo . . . or onto an orange shag carpet straight from the 1970s. That's the problem with the Hotel Gloria—the rooms feel quite dated. But that's only a minor complaint. The shag carpets are clean and they do add some character. The rooms aren't huge, but there is enough space for both a comfortable bed and a desk. The bathrooms are small but spotless, and they have tubs. Rooms on the higher floors (5–10) offer the best views. If you're looking to be in the center of the action, Hotel Gloria is a perfectly good choice.

Potosí 909 (corner of Genaro Sanjinés), La Paz. © 0102/2407-070. Fax 0102/2406-622. www.gloria-tours-bolivia.com. 90 units. $60 double; $75 triple; $78 quad. Rates include breakfast. AE, MC, V. **Amenities:** Restaurants; activities desk; small business center; room service; laundry service. *In room:* TV.

Inexpensive

Columbus Palace Hotel *Finds* This 4-year-old hotel is one of the newest less expensive hotels in town. It's close to the soccer stadium and the archaeological park but about a 15-minute walk away from Plaza Murillo in the center of La Paz, so compared to its more centrally located counterparts (Hotel Eldorado, for example), it loses points. (A taxi to the center, however, only costs about $1, and rooms here are much less expensive.) On the plus side, because this hotel is so new, its amenities are comparatively high-tech, including a choice of 10 different pillow styles. The rooms are small but the beds are comfortable, and the cheery bedspreads somehow make the rooms feel less cramped. The shiny, tiled bathrooms are also small but very clean. All the rooms have large, double-paned windows, which offer nice views; some of the rooms even have views of the snow-covered Illimani. Service here can be unfortunately nonexistent, so if you stay here, be sure to bring your good cheer (and your patience) with you.

Av. Illimani 1990 (at the corner of Plaza del Estadio), La Paz. © 0102/2227-460. Fax 0102/2245-367. www.hotel-columbus.com. 33 units (shower only). $36 double; $45 triple; $45 suite. Rates include buffet breakfast. AE, MC, V. **Amenities:** Restaurant and disco; room service; in-room massage; babysitting; laundry service; dry cleaning. *In room:* TV, minibar.

Hostal Rosario *Finds* Hostal Rosario has good karma. The hotel is housed in a converted colonial mansion, and there's something in the air that makes you feel comfortable. The 27-year-old hotel has grown and expanded into more modern buildings in the back, but it's an expansion done right. There are two peaceful colonial-style courtyards, and you can't tell where the old part ends and the new part begins. The rooms are small, but they are cozy in a charming way, with parquet floors and bright Andean-style bedspreads. The bathrooms aren't big either, but they do have bright, spotless tiles. The owners are constantly making improvements, so although the hotel is old, it feels new. If you're traveling in a group, request the suite, which has great views and sleeps up to six people. The rooms with the best views are on the third floor in the original building (nos. 304, 305, and 306). The hotel is conveniently close to the Witch Doctors' Market and all the handicrafts stores on Calle Sagárnaga. Most of the guests here tend to be backpackers on long journeys through South America.

Av. Illampu 704 (between Graneros and Santa Cruz), La Paz. © 0102/2451-341. Fax 0102/2451-658. www. hotelrosario.com. 45 units (3 w/shared bathroom, most w/shower only). $37–$41 double; $54 triple; $74 suite. Rates include continental breakfast. AE, MC, V. **Amenities:** Restaurant; bar; tour desk; room service; laundry service. *In room:* TV, dataport, safe.

Hotel Eldorado *Value* This simple hotel boasts a great location just a 2-minute walk from the Prado. Rooms are very simple with faux wood furniture and clean carpets; bathrooms are tiny but have yellow or green tile and are sparkling. Rooms overlooking the main road can get quite noisy; ask for a room on the upper floors and facing the back. Room no. 507 has a nice view out towards El Alto and is one of the quietest rooms in the hotel. There are so many cafes and restaurants nearby that there's no need to stay at the hotel for a meal or a drink. The Eldorado is a good choice for the price and location, but don't expect much luxury or service from the sometimes harried staff.

Av. Villazón, La Paz. © 0102/2363-320. Fax 0102/2391-438. www.hoteleldorado.net. 74 units. $40 double; $50 suite. Rates include continental breakfast. AE, MC, V. **Amenities:** Restaurant; bar; room service; laundry service. *In room:* TV.

WHERE TO DINE
MODERATE

El Vagón/El Vagón del Sur ⭐⭐ BOLIVIAN   If you're looking for typical, high-quality Bolivian food that's not simply grilled meat, El Vagón should be your first choice. These two restaurants are a father/son team. The father runs the restaurant in the downtown area of La Paz; the son is the manager of El Vagón del Sur in the ritzy Zona Sur (a 15-min., $4 taxi ride from the center of La Paz). El Vagón feels a bit older and dowdier than El Vagón del Sur. For some atmosphere, try to sit in the back room near the fireplace. In contrast, the Zona Sur location looks as if it could be in California, with nice wood floors, stone walls, folksy art, hand-painted chairs, and colorful tablecloths. In the warmer months (Nov–Mar), there's a huge garden for outdoor dining. Basically, the two restaurants offer the same excellent menu. For a sampling of typical Bolivian food, order the *picante surtido* (tongue, chicken, and chopped meat all in a spicy red chile sauce), served with chuño putti (dehydrated potatoes mixed with milk and cheese) and a spicy onion ring. If tongue isn't your thing, try the *silpancho* (a very thin breaded piece of veal with two fried eggs, onions, and tomatoes). You can also order more conventional dishes such as filet mignon, chateaubriand, pasta, and trout and *pejerrey* (fresh kingfish from Lake Titicaca). All dishes come with a complimentary chicken *empanada* (nice touch!).

El Vagón: Pedro Salazar 384 (near Plaza Avaroa and 20 de Octubre). ✆ 0102/2432-477. Main courses 39Bs–70Bs ($5–$9). MC, V. Mon–Fri noon–3pm and 7–10pm; Sun noon–3pm. El Vagón del Sur: Av. Julio C. Patiño 1295 (corner of Calle 19; Calacoto, Zona Sur). ✆ 0102/2793-700. Main courses 39Bs–70Bs ($5–$9). MC, V. Tues–Sat noon–3pm and 7–11pm; Sun noon–3pm.

La Bella Vista ⭐⭐⭐ (Moments) BOLIVIAN/INTERNATIONAL   The aliens have landed! Right here in La Paz on top of the Hotel Presidente. No one knows what happened to the aliens themselves, but they left behind their spaceship, which has been converted into an excellent restaurant with spectacular views of the city. This restaurant really feels like something from outer space, with an unbeatable 360-degree view of La Paz at night. The food is out of this world as well. If you like fish, you must order the grilled trout—I have never eaten a more succulent piece of fish. The *parrilla mixta* (assorted cuts of grilled meat for two people) is also excellent. The menu also includes homemade pasta, lamb kabobs, grilled chicken, and seafood. While you're in La Paz, you must dine here; it is, hands down, the best restaurant in the city.

In the Hotel Presidente, Calle Potosí 920 (at the corner of Genaro Sanjinés). ✆ 0102/2367-193. Reservations recommended Thurs–Fri. Main courses 45Bs–117Bs ($5.85–$15). AE, MC, V. Daily 11am–3pm and 7–11pm.

INEXPENSIVE

Dumbo (Kids) BOLIVIAN/ICE CREAM   Located right in the middle of the Prado, Dumbo is one of the most popular places in La Paz for a light snack. The specialties here are ice cream and pastries. Some of my favorites are the Milk Shake Hawaii (pineapple, strawberries, strawberry ice cream, and milk) and the California (orange juice, vanilla ice cream, crema chantilly, and orange slices). But Dumbo is also great for full meals: There's a whole selection of sandwiches, and you can also sample Bolivian specialties here, such as *empanadas, pacumuto Dumbo* (a kabob of grilled pork, chicken breast, bacon, peppers, and onions), or *lomito a la paila* (filet served in a bowl of soup with potatoes and an egg). The restaurant is very cheerful, with colorful walls, waterfalls, fresh plants, and an enclosed patio in the back. From 8 to 10pm nightly, there is a live piano player and it seems half of La Paz (and their kids) is here.

Prado 1523 (between Bueno and Campero) © 0102/2313-331. Ice cream dishes 17Bs–19Bs ($2.20–$2.45); sandwiches 7Bs–20Bs (90¢–$2.60); main courses 27Bs–30Bs ($3.50–$3.90). MC, V. Daily 7am–12:30am.

Gringo Limón ☜ GRILLED MEAT   If you're a meat eater and you have time for only one meal in La Paz, you must eat here. The specialty is grilled meat, but you can also order grilled chicken and fish or pasta, or stick to the very fresh salad bar. The star of the show is *brazuelo de cordero chismoso* (a huge leg of lamb), but the *brochetas* (kabobs with pork or chicken and onions), *tiras de costilla* (ribs), and the *churrasco Gringo Limón* (filet of beef with onions, peppers, and garlic) are also outstanding. All the entrees from the grill come with french fries, rice with cheese (similar to macaroni and cheese), and full access to the salad bar. The restaurant has a light, airy feeling, and each table has its own personal space heater (very comforting on cold nights).

Plaza Avaroa 2497 (corner of P. Salazar and 20 de Octubre). © 0102/2434-429. Main courses 30Bs–45Bs ($3.90–$5.85). AE, MC, V. Mon–Sat noon–3:30pm and 7–11:30pm; Sun noon–4pm.

La Bodeguita de Cubana CUBAN   It gets pretty darn cold in La Paz. But once you walk into the tiny and cozy La Bodeguita de Cubana, things sure do heat up. The Cuban music is loud, the drinks are strong, and the food is spicy. For a real taste of old Havana, order *ropa vieja* (shredded beef in a spicy tomato-based sauce with garlic, onions, and pepper) accompanied by a mojito. The *chilindrón de cordero* (lamb with tomatoes, onions, peppers, and beer) is another house specialty. All the dishes come with rice and beans, yuca with little bits of pork and onions, or fried bananas. Occasionally, you can hear live Cuban music on Friday nights. Now, if only they served Cuban cigars for dessert.

Federico Zuazo 1165 (between Campero and Tiwanaku). © 0102/2310-064. Main courses 26Bs–30Bs ($3.40–$3.90). No credit cards. Mon–Fri noon–3:30pm and 6:30pm–midnight; Sat 6:30pm–midnight; Sun noon–3:30pm.

La Casa de los Paceños BOLIVIAN   This charming restaurant is housed on the second floor of an old colonial building, and it doesn't look as if much has changed in this dining room since colonial times. Traditional Bolivian food is the specialty here. For example, you can order *ají de lengua* (cow's tongue in a chile sauce) or *charquekán* (llama meat in a chile sauce). If you're feeling adventurous, you should order the picante surtido, which consists of *sajta* (chicken in a chile sauce), saice (chopped meat in a chile sauce), *ranga* (cow's stomach),

---

(Tips Bolivian Breakfast

Most hotels in Bolivia serve eggs and toast for breakfast. But if you want to feel like a local, you really should be eating *salteñas* (either chicken or beef, spiced with onions and raisins and wrapped up in a doughy pastry shell). True *salteña* eaters buy their breakfast from vendors on the streets, but if you're a bit squeamish about eating food from street vendors, not to worry: **Al Pazzo Salteñas,** Capitán Revelo 2019 (at the corner of Calle Goytia), is a tiny little storefront that sells nothing but *salteñas.* Once you place your order, the owner picks up a phone and calls her kitchen. Her workers—who have perfected her grandmother's recipe—will make your *salteñas* to order. Remember, *salteñas* are served only for breakfast, so this place closes down around 1pm. The **Pastelería La Regina,** right below the Restaurant Surucachi at Av. 16 de Julio 1598, also serves a mean *salteña.*

---

fritanga (pork), and *charquekán.* More timid eaters should opt for the *pollo dorado* (chicken grilled in olive oil). Trout and grilled steaks are also available. If you're looking for Bolivian food in a livelier atmosphere, you should head to the newer La Casa de los Paceños in the Zona Sur (Av. Fuerza Naval 275, between 18th and 19th sts; © 0102/2794-629), where there is outdoor seating and live music on the weekends. A taxi from the center should cost no more than $4.

Av. Sucre 856 (between Genaro Sanjinés and Pichincha). © 0102/2280-955. Main courses 22Bs–33Bs ($2.85–$4.30). AE, MC, V. Tues–Fri 11:30am–4pm and 6–10pm; Sat–Sun 11:30am–4pm.

Surucachi *(Finds* BOLIVIAN You may have noticed that between 12:30 and 2:30pm, the streets of La Paz become mighty quiet. That's probably because everyone and his mother is eating lunch here at Surucachi. The food is pure Bolivian—*milanesas* (fried chicken or veal cutlets), *pejerrey* (kingfish from Lake Titicaca), and picante mixto (tongue, chicken, and chopped meat all in a spicy chile sauce). The *almuerzo del día* (lunch special), which includes a salad, soup, a main course, and dessert, is only 20Bs ($2.60). Add a colonial building with fancy gold leaf moldings and huge picture windows to the mix, and you've got yourself the most popular lunch spot in town.

Av. 16 de Julio 1598. No phone. Lunch special 20Bs ($2.60); a la carte main courses 25Bs–40Bs ($3.25–$5.20). No credit cards. Daily 9am–10pm.

LA PAZ AFTER DARK

Once the sun sets in La Paz, the temperature drops dramatically. Instead of going home (often to unheated apartments), many locals seek the warmth of bars and pubs. The nightlife scene in La Paz can hardly compare to New York or even Buenos Aires, but there are some funky places in the heart of the city where you can relax and kick back a few drinks. **Peñas** provide a place for visitors to experience traditional folk music and dance, although they tend to be very touristy. *Note:* Most bars (except in hotels) are open only Wednesday through Saturday.

BARS & PUBS The best hotel bar in La Paz is at the **Radisson** (p. 188); they have a very popular happy hour nightly from 6:30 to 8:30pm offering two-for-one drinks, and it's popular with expatriates and tourists alike. One of the most popular British-style watering holes in the city is **Mongo's** *(Finds,* Hermanos Manchego 2444 (near the corner of Pedro Salazar, half a block up from Av. 6 de Agosto). It has a cozy feel and a wood-burning fireplace. Get here early, as the place fills up late at night; the food here is also surprisingly good. **Coyote Bar,** Av. 20 de Octubre 2228 (corner of Pasaje Medinacelli), is smaller and less popular than Mongo's. **Malegría,** Calle Goitia 155 (a few steps from the Plaza del Estudiante), is very popular on Thursday nights for its Afro-Bolivian band; the lively music sometimes gets people dancing on the bar. One of the trendiest bars in town is **Sol y Luna,** Calle Murillo 999. Metal revolving doors lead into an industrial-looking space with a very in-crowd sipping on rather expensive cocktails. Nearby on Illampu between Santa Cruz and Sagárnaga is **Ojo de Agua,** where you can drink wine and chew coca leaves while you listen to a mix of classic rock and native music.

DISCOS & DANCE CLUBS El Loro en Su Salsa (© 0102/2342-787), down from 6 de Agosto on Rosendo Gutiérrez, is one of the best dance clubs in La Paz; salsa is the specialty here. **Boccaccio,** J. M. Reyes 28 in the Calacoto neighborhood (© 0102/2771-112), is also happening on Friday and Saturday nights. Also popular are **Coco Loco** in Miraflores in the Edificio Providencia, which is on the curve right south of the stadium, and **Noa Noa** on Calle

Conchitas between 20 de Octubre and Heroes del Arce. In general, the cover charge for clubs in La Paz is about 10Bs ($1.30).

PEÑAS & LIVE MUSIC   These days, it's hard to find an authentic peña that caters to locals. Fortunately, for the most part, you'll hear authentic Andean music and watch folk dancers wearing unique but traditional costumes. **Restaurant Peña Marka Tambo,** Calle Jaén 710 near the corner of Indaburo, puts on a good show Thursday through Saturday nights. The cover is 25Bs ($3.25). The traditional Bolivian dishes are good, so I recommend that you eat dinner here as well. The show starts at 9:30pm. **Casa de Corregidor,** Calle Murillo 1040, is a similar venue—typical Bolivian food and music. There is a show here every night during the week; this place feels a bit more laid-back than Marka Tambo. **Boca y Sapo,** Indaburo 654 (corner of Jaén), attracts locals as well as tourists; there's no dinner here, only live music, which makes it feel a bit more authentic.

   Equinoccio, Sánchez Lima 2191 between Aspiazu and Guachalla, is one of the best venues for live music; the club manages to book some great local bands. For live jazz, try **Thelonious Jazz Bar,** Av. 20 de Octubre 2172. A lot of the bands that play here are from the United States.

SIDE TRIPS FROM LA PAZ
TIWANAKU (*)

A visit to Tiwanaku will take you back in time to an impressive city built by an extremely technologically advanced pre-Inca society. The Tiwanaku culture is believed to have lasted for 28 centuries from 1600 B.C. to A.D. 1200. In this time, they created some of the most impressive stone monoliths in the world, developed a sophisticated irrigation system, and gained an advanced understanding of astronomy and the workings of the sun. Their territory spread from northern Argentina and Chile through Bolivia to the south of Peru. These people never came into contact with the Incas. By the time the Incas made it to Peru, a 100-year drought had ravaged the Titicaca area. The Tiwanaku people had long ago left the region in small groups and moved to different areas in the *altiplano* or valleys.

   When you visit Tiwanaku, you will first stop in at the museum, where you can observe firsthand the magnificence of the ceramics, monoliths, and figurines found at the site. The exhibits will help you understand a bit of the history of this culture. Armed with your new Tiwanaku knowledge, you can then head out to the site itself, where you'll often have to use your imagination. The Incas and the Spaniards destroyed the site while searching for gold and silver. Even the most respected archaeologists disagree on the meanings of the monoliths and the sun gate. But when you actually see these impressive structures firsthand, you can't help but stand in awe and wonderment of the amazing achievements of this pre-Columbian society. Unlike Machu Picchu, which feels more temporary and modern, here you gain a much deeper insight into the daily life and rituals of the people who inhabited this area for thousands of years. Highlights of the site include the **Semi-Underground Temple** (*), which is decorated with stones carved in the shape of different heads from around the world; the **Kalassaya** (*), the main temple area of the site and believed to be dedicated to the sun; and the **Akapana (pyramid),** believed to be an observatory and a temple to worship the sky. The museum and the archaeological site are open daily from 9am to 4:30pm. Admission is 15Bs ($1.95).

GETTING THERE   Tiwanaku is located 1½ hours outside of La Paz. I strongly recommend coming here on a guided tour. **Diana Tours,** Sagárnaga

326 (© **0102/2350-252**), organizes English-speaking tours to Tiwanaku for only 70Bs ($9), not including the 15Bs ($1.95) site admission fee. **Crillon Tours,** Av. Camacho 1233 (© **0102/2337-533**), also arranges tours to the area. If you prefer to visit on your own, **Trans Tours Tiwanaku,** Calle José Aliaga, operates buses that stop at Tiwanaku. The buses leave from the Cementerio District every half-hour from 8am to 4:30pm. The ride costs 7Bs (90¢).

THE BEST OF LOS YUNGAS: COROICO

Coroico makes a popular side trip for visitors to La Paz, but you'll probably remember the journey better than the destination. The road to Coroico narrows to one unpaved lane twisting down through the mountains. To one side is the mountain, to the other, a sheer drop of often hundreds of feet to the lush valley below. There will be times when the passage is tight and your vehicle is only an inch or two from the edge; there will be other times when you round a blind curve and your driver, confronted by oncoming traffic, has to slam on the brakes.

When the ride is over and your heart rate has returned to normal, you may be surprised at the tranquillity of Coroico. The views of the surrounding hills are lovely, the nearby hiking trails are picturesque, the bars and restaurants in town are pleasant, and there are some worthwhile excursions; but there's really nothing here to take your breath away. Nonetheless, Coroico makes a wonderful contrast to La Paz. Here in this tropical town, you'll find fruit orchards, twittering birds, coca fields, endless greenery, oxygen-rich air, warm weather, and friendly locals. The climate here seems to put everyone in a better mood.

The town of Coroico itself isn't anything special, but it's a lot of fun to explore the lush, colorful surrounding area. You can take a half-day tour of **Tocaña** ★, a small Afro-Bolivian community located about 7km (4 miles) downhill from Coroico. It feels as if not much has changed over the past few hundred years in this farming village, where the locals survive mainly by growing coca. Also nearby are the **Vagante River Springs.** Here you can swim under a waterfall and in beautiful pools of water. **Vagantes Ecoaventuras,** located at the kiosk in the Coroico main plaza, provides guides (not always English-speaking) and jeeps to Tocaña and Vagante River Springs. Note that the jeeps are open and the roads aren't paved, so you will get extremely dirty.

It's surprising that in a town like Coroico, which is set high up in the mountains, there aren't many **hiking trails.** Perhaps this is because most of the land in the area is farmland. The most popular hike is the 6km (4-mile) trek to the waterfalls *(las cascadas).* It's not really a hike, but more of a long walk on a dusty road. The waterfalls are pleasant, but you can't swim in them, and to be honest, I'm not sure they are worth the long walk. However, the mountains and the valleys on the road are breathtaking. For more information about this and other walks in the area, contact the tourist information office on Coroico's main plaza.

In the dry season, the rivers in the Coroico area become low and unsuitable for **rafting.** However, in January through March, the Coroico River runs wild. River levels range from Class III to Class V. **Liquid Madness,** Sagárnaga no. 339, La Paz (© **0102/2391-810;** www.andes-amazon.com), and **Vagantes Ecoaventuras** (at the kiosk in Coroico's main plaza, on the corner of Heroes del Chaco) organize rafting and kayaking tours in the area.

GETTING THERE   Buses for Coroico leave La Paz on a frequent schedule from the Villa Fátima neighborhood, which is about 15 minutes by taxi from the center of La Paz. (It costs about 9Bs/$1.15.) Most of the bus companies are located on Calle Yanacachi. One of the best is **Yungueña** (© **0102/2213-513;**

call ahead for the schedule); the ride costs 15Bs ($1.95) each way. I recommend leaving around 10am—this way, you'll arrive in Coroico for lunch and then have the rest of the afternoon to walk around town or hang out by a pool. Buses depart less frequently in the afternoon (the last one leaves at about 4pm), but it's much nicer to travel during daylight and enjoy the view. Try to get a seat on the left side of the bus for the best views.

For information about **trekking** or **biking** to Coroico, see "Sports & Outdoor Activities," earlier in this section.

4 Lake Titicaca ⟨★⟨★⟨★

Copacabana: 151km (94 miles) NW of La Paz; 8km (5 miles) N of Kasani (the border of Peru)

Lake Titicaca is much more than a phrase you found hilarious in third grade. This serene expanse of chilly water is not only the highest navigable lake in the world, but it's also, according to legend, the birthplace of one of the greatest empires in history. Here, in the midst of the lake, the children of the Sun, Manco Capac and Mama Ocllo, stepped forth from the sacred rock that still stands near the northwest tip of the Isla del Sol (the Sun Island).

The rugged, snow-covered peaks of the Cordillera Real loom over the shores of the lake, but its waters are calm and relaxing to the eye. They're disturbed only by the operators of a few tour boats, launches, and hydrofoils and by local fishermen searching for trout, often in wooden sailboats or rowboats. Even the most primitive of these vessels are relative newcomers. The swaying reeds on the water's shore provided the material for the first boats on Lake Titicaca, and today there are still a few craftsmen who remember how to make boats from reeds, as their ancestors did.

Besides the lake itself, and the Isla del Sol within it, the highlight of the region is the picturesque lakeshore town of Copacabana, allegedly established by the Inca Tupac Yupanqui. Copacabana has a number of small but important Inca ruins, but all of them are overshadowed by the town's main attraction, the Virgin of Copacabana. Pilgrims travel from all over South America for the Virgin's blessing. If you're here on a Sunday, you'll notice above all the car and truck drivers, who come to have their vehicles blessed by one of the local priests in a ceremony that involves lots of garlands, the shaking and spraying of fizzy drinks, and of course, a small donation to the church. Nobody seems to mind paying.

ESSENTIALS
GETTING THERE
BY BUS   Buses from La Paz to Copacabana leave from the Cementerio District, not from the main terminal; it costs about $2 to get here by taxi from the center of La Paz. **Trans "6 de Junio,"** Plaza Tupac Katari no. 55 (© **0102/ 2455-258**), is one of the most reliable bus companies. A one-way ticket costs 15Bs ($1.95); buses depart at 9:30, 10:30am, noon, 2:30, 5, 6, 7:30, and 8:30pm. The ride takes 3 hours, including a 3-minute ferry ride (2Bs/25¢) across the Straits of Tiquina. Here, you must disembark from the bus and take a ferry across to the other side. The bus is carried over on a separate boat.

BY GUIDED TOUR   Crillon Tours, Av. Camacho 1233 (© **0102/2337- 533,** or 305/358-5353 in the U.S.; www.titicaca.com), specializes in tours to the Lake Titicaca area. The company owns two of the best hotels in the area—Inca Utama Hotel & Spa in Huatajata and La Posada del Inca hotel on the Sun Island—and is the only company that operates hydrofoils on the lake. Because

ACCOMMODATIONS ■
Hostal La Cúpula **3**
Hotel Rosario del Lago **5**

DINING ◆
La Orilla **4**

ATTRACTIONS ●
Asiento del Inca **7**
Baño del Inca **1**
The Calvario **2**
Cathedral of
  Copacabana **6**
Horca del Inca **8**

✝ Church
🚢 Boat launches
✚ Hospital
$ Money changers
✉ Post office
🗺 Ruins

of a business deal meant to protect local businesses, you can't stay at these hotels
or use the hydrofoil if you're traveling independently. Crillon's tours are really
the best way to see the area; they include excellent English-speaking guides and
all transportation.

GETTING AROUND

Copacabana, the largest city in the Lake Titicaca area, is where you'll find the
best hotels and travel agencies, as well as some Inca ruins and the famous statue
of the Virgen de Copacabana. From here, you can easily take a day trip to the
Isla del Sol. **Huatajata** isn't much of a town—its only attraction is Inca Utama
Hotel & Spa—but it's only 1½ hours by car from La Paz. So instead of traveling 3 hours to Copacabana, you can spend the night here, and then hop on the
hydrofoil for a quick jaunt over to the Sun Island. The hydrofoil also makes
stops in Copacabana.

  The only way to go from Copacabana or Huatajata to the Sun Island is by
boat. From Huatajata, you can also take a hydrofoil to Copacabana or the Sun
Island; contact **Crillon Tours** (*C* **0102/2337-533,** or 305/358-5353 in the
U.S.; www.titicaca.com) for more information. From Copacabana, non-hydro-
foil boats leave around 8:15am and arrive at the Sun Island at 10:30am. The
boat returns to pick you up at 4pm. If you want to walk from one side of the
island to the other, the ride costs 30Bs ($3.90); if you want the boat to take you
around the island, the whole trip will set you back 35Bs ($4.55). If you plan on

spending the night on the Isla del Sol, you can catch a boat back to Copacabana at 10:30am. Both **Grace Tours,** Av. 6 de Agosto 200 (© **0102/862-2160**), and **Titicaca Tours,** located at the dock at the end of Avenida 6 de Agosto (© **0102/862-2060**), are recommended tour agencies.

Transturin (© **0102/862-2284;** www.turismobolivia.com) on Avenida 6 de Agosto, about half a block up from the beach, organizes cruises to the Isla del Sol and to Puno on the Peruvian side of the lake. Day trips to both the Sun Island and Puno cost $60. You can also sleep on the boat; overnight trips to the Sun Island cost $75 per person.

VISITOR INFORMATION

The main tourist office is located on Plaza 2 de Febrero at the corner of Ballivián and La Paz in Copacabana. The office doesn't have a phone, the hours of operation are sporadic, there are no maps available, and in general, the staff is of limited help.

FAST FACTS: COPACABANA There are several **banks** on Avenida 6 de Agosto; note that none of them exchange traveler's checks. You'll find a **pharmacy** on Plaza Tito Yupanqui right across from the Entel office behind the basilica. The **post office** is located on La Paz near the corner of Ballivián. You can take care of all your **laundry** needs at Hostal Sucre, Murillo 228 near the corner of José P. Mejía. **ALF@Net,** Av. 6 de Agosto 100 at the corner of Avenida 10 de Julio, is the only Internet cafe in Copacabana. Rates are about 20Bs ($2.60) per hour.

WHAT TO SEE & DO
IN COPACABANA

Copacabana was an important religious site way before the Spanish realized that the world was round. Lake Titicaca is believed to be the birthplace of the Incas, and for many years, this city was one of the holiest of the Inca Empire. These days, pilgrims come from far and wide to visit the Cathedral of Copacabana to pay homage to the Virgin of Copacabana (also known as the Queen of Bolivia and the Virgin of Candelaria), who has supposedly bestowed many miracles upon her true believers. She is the most venerated virgin in all of Bolivia. In addition to visiting the most important Catholic icon in Bolivia, you can also explore some important Inca ruins.

THE CATHEDRAL OF COPACABANA In 1580, the Virgin of Copacabana appeared in a dream to Tito Yupanqui. He was so taken by this vision that he set out to Potosí (then one of the most important art centers in the world) to learn to sculpt. With his new skill, he hand-carved the Virgin from the wood of a maguey cactus. He then carried her by foot from Potosí to Copacabana (a journey of more than 400 miles), where she was placed in an adobe chapel in 1583. Immediately afterwards, the crops of those who doubted her power were mysteriously destroyed. The Spanish, smitten with the Virgin, completed this Moorish-style cathedral for her in 1617. The Virgin stands in a majestic mechanical altar. On weekends, the priests rotate the Virgin so that she faces the main chapel; on weekdays, when there are fewer pilgrims here, they spin her around so that she looks over a smaller chapel on the other side. The silver ship at the bottom of the altar represents the moon, while the gold statue above the Virgin's head is believed to symbolize the power of the sun. Believers have bestowed millions of dollars worth of gifts upon the Virgin. In 1879, the government of Bolivia sold some of her jewelry to finance the War of the Pacific against Chile.

The cathedral is open daily from 11am to noon and from 2 to 6pm; admission is free.

THE CALVARIO   For the past few hundred years, Copacabana has been inundated with pilgrims. In the 1950s, the government decided that their city should have more to offer these people than just the Virgin of Copacabana, so the Stations of the Cross were built on a hill overlooking the lake. The strenuous uphill walk takes more than 30 minutes, but the views of the lake are worth the effort. At the very bottom of the stairs, there is a man who can divine your future by dropping lead into a boiling pot of water. About halfway up, you will find native priests burning candles and working with coca leaves. If you're so inclined, this is a good place to stop and learn about the ancient rituals of fortunetelling. For the trip down, there are two options: You can return the way you came up, or you can take a rocky path that will lead you to the shores of the lake. Note that the winding path can get steep and narrow—it's best to descend it only if you're wearing a good pair of hiking shoes.

INCA RUINS   Within Copacabana, there are three interesting archaeological sites. They are open Tuesday through Sunday from 9am to noon and from 2 to 5pm; admission to all three costs 10Bs ($1.30).

The **Asiento del Inca (Seat of the Inca)** ★★ is my favorite of the three sites. No one knows the actual purpose of the stone carvings here, but some archaeologists speculate that this may have been a meeting point for Inca priests. The carvings are called Asiento del Inca because the huge indentations in the rocks resemble thrones. The rock carvings span different levels and what appear to be different rooms, and the "seats" don't all face the same direction. It's fun to sit on one of the thronelike rocks and dream about what may have happened here. To get here, walk from Plaza 2 de Febrero along Calle Murillo for 4 blocks until you reach the road to La Paz, where you should take a left. Walk 3 blocks uphill to the cemetery. The Asiento del Inca is about 90m (300 ft.) from the cemetery, in what looks to be a small farm.

A bit farther outside of town is the **Horca del Inca,** a three-rock structure that resembles a gallows (hence the name). In actuality, it's believed that the Incas used these rocks as a tool to observe the sun and stars. If you happen to be here during one of the equinoxes, you can actually observe the sun as it reflects off the boulders. Unfortunately, the Spanish destroyed much of the site because they thought gold might be hidden inside some of the rocks. Of course, they found nothing. To get here, walk straight on Calle Murillo from the plaza until the road ends; here, you will see a rocky hill. About halfway up the hill, you'll find the Horca del Inca. The walk up to the actual site is steep and the terrain is rough. You should only head up here if you have good walking shoes and lots of energy. Young boys hanging around the area will offer to show you the way to the site for about $1. I recommend taking them up on their offer, because the climb is tricky.

At the **Baño del Inca,** about 30 minutes outside of town, you'll find a small museum dedicated to some archaeological finds in the area. Behind the museum, there's a pretty little spring, which is said to have mystical powers. Baño del Inca is a nice peaceful spot outside of the city—great for a romantic picnic. To get here, start at Plaza 2 de Febrero and walk straight down Ballivián to Plaza de Toros. From Plaza de Toros, walk straight for about 20 minutes, until you see a green house. Take a right here and walk uphill for about 10 minutes. The Baño del Inca is on the right-hand side across from a church. There is no sign, but it's right behind a small farm.

ISLA DEL SOL 𝕽𝕽𝕽 & ISLA DE LA LUNA

Welcome to the birthplace of the Incas. The **Isla del Sol,** measuring only 9km (5½ miles) long by 6km (3¾ miles) wide, is one of the most spectacular places in all of Bolivia. On the north end are Challapampa and some fascinating Inca ruins. Yumani, on the south end, is the largest town on the island and also the site of the Inca steps.

Most tour operators run a day trip from Copacabana to the Sun Island, with a quick stop at the Isla de la Luna (Moon Island). You'll leave Copacabana at 8:15am and arrive at Challapampa around 10:30am. Here you pay a 15Bs ($1.95) entry fee, and a Spanish-speaking guide will show you around Chinkana (see "Challapamba," below, for more information). If you're feeling ambitious, you can walk from here all the way to the Fuente del Inca on the southern end of the island. I highly recommend this long and hilly hike. Along the way, you'll come across wild llamas, herds of sheep, and some of the most breathtaking vistas in the world. But you should keep in mind that the hike is difficult and more than 4 hours long, so you won't have time to sit and eat a proper lunch. If you have a hard time walking, you might not make it to the other side in time for the last boat to Copacabana at 4pm.

If you don't want to walk, the boat will then drop you off for a quick stop at the **Isla de la Luna.** During the time of the Incas, this island was used to house "chosen" women. The island was similar to a convent. The women here wove garments by hand with alpaca wool and performed special ceremonies dedicated to the sun. Unfortunately, most of the structures here have been destroyed. From the 1930s to the 1960s, this island became a political prison. In the 1960s, when some archaeologists got wind of what had become of the island, the prisoners were ordered to rebuild the main palace, which has 35 rooms around a courtyard. This is historically significant because the Aymara culture—not the Incas—used constructions with courtyards, thus proving that the Moon Island was used by pre-Inca cultures. However, most of the remaining doors are trapezoidal shaped, which is very typical of the Incas. As you first walk onto the island, keep an eye out for the polished stones. These stones are similar to what you'd find in Machu Picchu, and they allow you to understand how the Incas used hinges to hold rocks together.

Note: When your boat driver forces you to choose between visiting the Moon Island and walking across the Sun Island, I recommend opting for the walk on the Sun Island. You won't miss much if you don't stop off at the Moon Island, and the setting of the sun on Sun Island is much more spectacular.

CHALLAPAMPA 𝕽𝕽   A visit to Challapampa will be the highlight of your visit to the Sun Island. Here, you will find the ruins of **Chinkana (labyrinth).**

⸨Moments Sunset on the Isla del Sol

There is something intrinsically romantic about the Sun Island. Perhaps it's the slow pace of life, the sparkle of the sun reflecting off the deep blue waters, or the snow-covered peaks standing proudly in the distance. To really capture the vibe of the island, I recommend spending the night here. If you do, you must hike up to the lighthouse, which at 4,032m (13,441 ft.) is the highest point on the island. Come here at sunset, and your heart may melt as the sun dips into the distance, bathing the mountains in a glow of bright fuchsia before they disappear in the darkness.

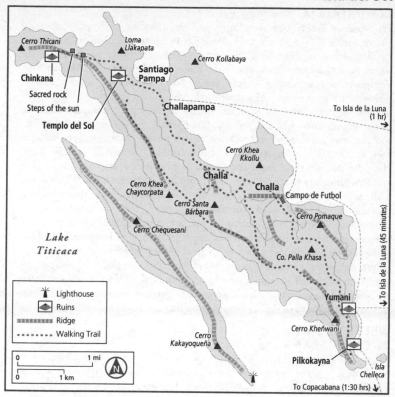

It's a huge stone complex full of mazes, believed to be a seminary for Inca priests. The construction is actually a bit sloppy, which is very uncharacteristic of the Incas; some archaeologists theorize that the Incas must have been in a rush when they built it. A natural spring here runs under the island and appears again in a sacred stone fountain in Yumani (see below). On the path back to the town of Challapampa, about 100m (270 ft.) from Chinkana, you will pass by the **sacred rock,** carved in the shape of a puma. As you continue along this path toward Challapampa, look down: You will soon see two very large footprints, said to have been created when the sun dropped down to earth to give birth to Manco Capac and Mama Ocllo, the Adam and Eve of the Incas.

YUMANI/INCA STEPS   If you arrive by boat to Yumani, you will have to walk up 206 steps to reach the main part of the town here. These steps are original Inca constructions, and they lead up to a sacred stone fountain with three separate springs, which are said to be a fountain of youth.

PILKOKAYNA   There is a half-mile path from the top of the Inca Steps down to Pilkokayna (which literally means "where birds sleep"). This 14-room structure may have been used as a fortress to guard the Virgins of the Sun who were living nearby on the Moon Island. From here, you have a very clear view of the Moon Island. The structure does have trapezoidal doors, which means that it was used by the Incas. However, some archaeologists speculate that the buildings here date back to the Classic Age of the Tiwanaku period (A.D.100–900). One of the most impressive features is the remains of the original stone roof.

IN HUATAJATA

The **Andean Roots Cultural Complex,** connected to Crillon Tours's Inca Utama Hotel & Spa, is the only attraction in Huatajata. Essentially, it's the "Williamsburg" of Lake Titicaca. The complex consists of an Andean Eco Village, the Altiplano Museum, and the Kallawaya Museum. The **Andean Eco Village** recreates an historic Andean village, with buildings and farms typical of this area. It's an attempt to preserve local cultures and traditions. The people working here are working in exactly the same way their ancestors used to work—taking care of llamas and vicuñas, growing guinea pigs, storing corn, cooking traditional food, and weaving alpaca shawls. In the Andean Village, there is also a full-size reproduction of the reed boat, the *RA II,* used by Thor Heyerdahl to cross the Atlantic and designed by the local Limachi brothers, who work here building new reed boats. The **Altiplano Museum** is a small museum with exhibits about the history of Bolivia, with emphasis on the Tiwanaku and Inca cultures. The **Kallawaya Museum** *@@* is one of the most interesting museums in Bolivia. At the beginning of the museum, you will learn about the healing powers of local herbs, plants, fruits, and vegetables. When you reach the end, you will enter a small brick room, brightened only by the warm glow of candles. Here a Kallawaya (natural medicine doctor) will bless you and, with the help of some coca leaves, tell you about your future. Finally, there is an observatory here (with the second-most powerful telescope in Bolivia), where you can learn about all the constellations in the Southern Hemisphere.

WHERE TO STAY
IN COPACABANA

Hostal La Cúpula *(Finds)*   There's something to be said for artists who open hotels. The owner of La Cúpula is a sculptor, and the beautiful garden areas here are filled with delightful pieces of his work. The guest room walls are covered with modern art, and some even have lofts, so you really feel as though you're staying in an artist's studio. Some of the rooms have views of the lake, while others look out onto the surrounding mountainside. They are all bright with big windows and funky bamboo furniture. And, true to the hotel's name, there are cupolas: Room no. 11, the Honeymoon Suite, has the ultimate in cupolas, plus views of the lake, a hammock, and its own personal veranda. Only seven of the rooms here have private shower-only bathrooms, but the public facilities are immaculate. The hotel is a 10-minute walk uphill from the heart of Copacabana, but it's not much of a problem. After eating at the excellent restaurant (or cooking your own meal in the public kitchen), you can relax in the cozy library or play one of many board games here.

Calle Michel Pérez 1–3, Copacabana. © **0102/862-2029.** www.hotelcupula.com. 17 units (7 w/private bathroom, shower only). $14–$32 double; $20–$28 triple. MC, V. **Amenities:** Restaurant. *In room:* No phone.

Hotel Rosario del Lago *@*   The design of this hotel blends in perfectly with its surroundings. From the outside, the bright yellow stucco building looks like an old Spanish colonial–style castle. Inside, the brick tiles and earthy tones envelop you in a soothing way. In every room, there is a cozy sitting area with large bay windows, where you can curl up with a good book and gaze out over the shores of Lake Titicaca. The rooms aren't fancy, but with their shiny hardwood floors and dark red bedspreads, they certainly have tons of charm. The bathrooms are small, but the rooms are so cute, it doesn't really matter. Families should try to request the suite—it feels like a small apartment, complete with two bedrooms, a refrigerator, and a separate living room and dining area. If you're sensitive to noise, make sure that your room is toward the back of the hotel; the rooms close to the reception area tend to be quite loud.

Rigoberto Paredes and Av. Costanera, Copacabana. © **0102/862-2141.** Fax 0102/862-2140. www.travel perubolivia.com/rosariohotels/index.htm. 32 units (shower only). $47–$53 double; $63–$69 triple. Rates include breakfast. AE, MC, V. **Amenities:** Restaurant; game room; travel agency; room service; laundry service. *In room:* TV, safe.

ON THE ISLA DEL SOL

Most of the accommodations on the Sun Island are, to put it kindly, rustic. Very few rooms have private bathrooms, and it's almost impossible to find a hot shower here. But once all the day-trippers leave, you will have the island to yourself. I think it's worth it to stay here just to feel the magic of the island.

There is one exception to the rule, however: Crillon Tours's **La Posada del Inca** ᴳᴳ is probably one of the best hotels in all of Bolivia. By Sun Island standards, it's luxurious—all rooms come with private bathrooms, hot showers, and electric blankets (a nice touch on those freezing nights). The Spanish-style adobe hotel feels like an old farm. The rooms are cute, with handmade bamboo beds and Andean area rugs. Overall, the hotel is unbelievably charming. To book a room, you must reserve in advance with **Crillon Tours,** Av. Camacho 1233, La Paz (© **0102/2337-533,** or 305/358-5353 in the U.S.; www.titicaca.com).

IN HUATAJATA

If you've decided to stay in Huatajata, your best bet is Crillon Tours's **Inca Utama Hotel & Spa.** The rooms here aren't anything special; they are modern, typical motel-style rooms, all with comfortable twin beds, good hot showers, electric blankets, and hair dryers. But no one stays here because of the rooms. Stay here to enjoy the Andean Roots Cultural Complex, where a traditional medicine doctor will send good blessings your way. Another attraction is the spa, where you can relax in the Jacuzzi or enjoy treatments based on ancient traditions. Finally, this is where you can pick up the Titicaca hydrofoils. These boats move twice as fast as any other on the lake, so when you stay here, you can spend more time on the Sun Island or in Copacabana and less time riding on the lake. To stay here, you must make a reservation in advance with **Crillon Tours,** Av. Camacho 1233, La Paz (© **0102/2337-533,** or © 305/358-5353 in the U.S.; www.titicaca.com).

WHERE TO DINE

Copacabana is the culinary capital of Lake Titicaca. Almost every restaurant here specializes in preparing trout fresh from the lake. The best restaurants are on Avenida 6 de Agosto. They all have pretty much the same menu, which consists of trout, pasta, and pizza. But **La Orilla** (on Av. 6 de Agosto, about 20m/54 ft. from the beach) stands head and shoulders above the rest. If you come here for lunch, you can sit on the terrace, which overlooks the lake. In the evening, the lights go dim, and the dining room feels like a romantic hideaway. I highly recommend the trout curry. Other excellent options include a vegetable stir-fry, fajitas, and the spring roll. On the weekends, live bands sometimes perform here.

On the Sun Island, there are a few small restaurants. None have names or addresses, but they all have similar menus, including fresh trout and grilled chicken. Your best bet is to ask your hotel for a recommendation.

LAKE TITICACA AFTER DARK

Don't expect to find a wild nightlife scene anywhere near Lake Titicaca. In Copacabana, **Sol y Luna,** Av. 16 de Julio 3, is one of the hippest places in town. Live bands sometimes play here, but it's more of a laid-back place, where you can kick back a few drinks while playing some of their board games.

If you stay at **Inca Utama Hotel & Spa** in Huatajata, you can enjoy a live folk music show after dinner in the main restaurant. Or, since the hotel is in possession of the second-most powerful telescope in Bolivia (a gift from NASA), this is a great place for stargazing.

5 Sucre ⟨★⟨★

701km (435 miles) SE of La Paz; 366km (227 miles) SE of Cochabamba; 612km (379 miles) SW of Santa Cruz; 162km (100 miles) NE of Potosí

During Bolivia's glory days, when Sucre existed solely for the purpose of administering the silver mines in nearby Potosí, the wealthy locals here would often brag, "My mines are in Potosí, but I live in Chuquisaca [the former name of Sucre]." For those who could afford it, it made sense to live 161km (100 miles) down the road from Potosí in the relative lowlands (2,706m/9,020 ft.) of Sucre, which is blessed with a mild climate and a much cheerier disposition. Gradually, Sucre became a city of understated prestige. It's been called the Paris of South America because the wealth here attracted some of the finest arts and culture from all over the world. It's also been known as the Athens of South America because it's home to the continent's second-oldest and most prestigious university, San Francisco Xavier University, which dates to 1624 and has educated presidents of Argentina, Paraguay, Chile, Uruguay, and of course, Bolivia. (Today, out of a total pop. of 200,000, over 30,000 are students, many of them studying medicine or law.)

For a city like Sucre, money, prestige, and knowledge weren't enough. It also had to have a place in the history books. In 1825, some of the most important South American revolutionaries converged upon the city and signed the country's declaration of independence. Sucre then became the capital of the new republic.

These days, Sucre is the capital of Bolivia in name only—both the executive and legislative branches of the government left long ago for La Paz. The silver in nearby Potosí has pretty much run out, and the high culture has returned to Paris. Nevertheless, the city remains one of the most colorful and interesting places in Bolivia. Visitors can sit in the room where the Bolivian declaration of independence was signed, tour churches and museums that still have impressive collections of colonial art, and view the dinosaur tracks that archaeologists recently discovered right in Sucre's backyard.

ESSENTIALS
GETTING THERE

BY PLANE   LAB (℃ **0800-3001**) and **Aero Sur** (℃ **0102/22430-430** in La Paz, or 0104/6423-838 in Sucre) offer daily flights to Sucre from La Paz, Cochabamba, and Santa Cruz. One-way tickets cost about $70 each. All planes arrive at the Juana Azurduy de Padilla Airport, which is only a few miles outside of town. Taxis from the airport to the center of town cost 25Bs ($3.25).

BY BUS   The Sucre bus terminal is about 1.5km (1 mile) northeast of the center of town at the corner of Alfredo Ostria Gutiérrez and Bustillos. See "Getting Around: By Bus" in "Planning Your Trip to Bolivia," earlier in this chapter, for

Sucre

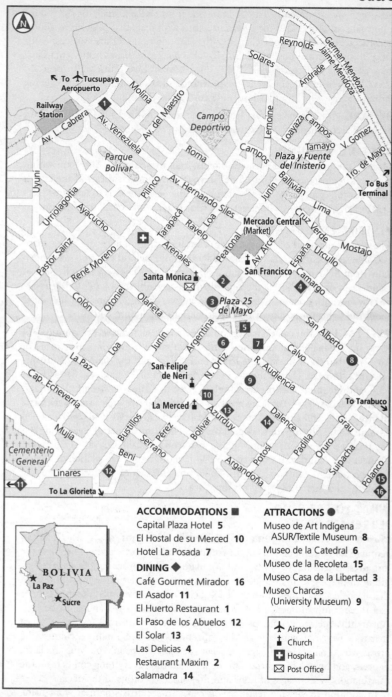

ACCOMMODATIONS ■
Capital Plaza Hotel **5**
El Hostal de su Merced **10**
Hotel La Posada **7**

DINING ◆
Café Gourmet Mirador **16**
El Asador **11**
El Huerto Restaurant **1**
El Paso de los Abuelos **12**
El Solar **13**
Las Delicias **4**
Restaurant Maxim **2**
Salamadra **14**

ATTRACTIONS ●
Museo de Art Indígena
  ASUR/Textile Museum **8**
Museo de la Catedral **6**
Museo de la Recoleta **15**
Museo Casa de la Libertad **3**
Museo Charcas
  (University Museum) **9**

✈ Airport
🛉 Church
✚ Hospital
✉ Post Office

bus company information. The 14-hour ride from La Paz costs 70Bs ($7.80) for a normal bus, 90Bs ($12) for a *bus cama* (bus with seats that fold out to almost become a bed). Buses from Cochabamba take about 12 hours and cost 30Bs ($3.90) for a normal bus, 50Bs ($6.50) for a *bus cama*. Buses from Santa Cruz take 12 hours and cost 60Bs ($7.80) for a normal bus, 80Bs ($10) for a *bus cama*. Buses from Potosí leave in the morning, midafternoon, and early evening (around 5pm). The 2½- to 3-hour ride costs 20Bs ($2.60).

BY TAXI   You can take a taxi from Potosí to Sucre for 150Bs ($19) for four people. I recommend using **Expreso Infinito** (© 0104/6422-277).

GETTING AROUND

Most of the banks, travel agencies, hotels, and attractions in Sucre are within easy walking distance of Plaza 25 de Mayo, the commercial heart of the city. If you want to get a bit off of the beaten path, the best option is to take a taxi. It's easy to hail one right off the street, but your hotel can also call one for you.

VISITOR INFORMATION

The main tourist office is located on Estudiantes 35. There aren't any maps available here, but the staff is knowledgeable and helpful. The office is open daily from 8:30am to 12:30pm and 2:30 to 6:30pm. The very friendly staff at **Candelaria Tours** 禾禾, off the central square at Audiencia 1 (© 0104/6461-661; www.candelariatours.com), can also answer any questions you may have about the sights in the city or nearby attractions (including Potosí).

FAST FACTS   You can exchange money and traveler's checks at **Cambios "El Arca"** on España 134 or **Casa de Cambio Ambar** on Ravelo 7 at the corner of Arce. You'll find ATMs on Calle España and all around the main Plaza. **Hospital Santa Bárbara,** Destacamento 111 at the corner of Arenales (© 0104/6460-133), and **Hospital Gastroenterológico,** Avenida Colón between El Villar and Japón (© 0104/6454-700), are the two best hospitals in Sucre. **Farmacia Cruz Blanca,** Junín 558 between Arenales and Ravelo (© 0104/6444-288), is open 24 hours. The **post office** is located on Junín and the corner of Ayacucho. You can take care of all your laundry needs at **LaveRap,** Calle Bolívar 617 between Olañeta and Azurday. It's one of the few laundromats in all of Bolivia that is open on Sundays (only until 1pm). You'll find Internet cafes of varying quality on all the side streets that lead off the plaza.

WHAT TO SEE & DO
MUSEUMS

Museo de Arte Indígena ASUR/Textile Museum 禾禾   ASUR is an acronym for Anthropologists of the Andean South, who are trying to recover the lost artesian techniques of the local population. This museum does an excellent job of displaying some magnificent pieces of art, mainly in the form of textiles that provide a real insight into these local cultures. For example, the Inca culture had three commandments: Don't be a thief, don't be a liar, and don't be lazy. Apparently, the indigenous people would create big intricate textiles as proof that they weren't being lazy. In the collection from the Tarabuco culture, the artists would only weave images of what they knew—people plowing the land, dancers, and horses. By contrast, in the Jalq'a culture, everything comes from the imagination, with images of lions and dragons and visions of the devil.

In addition to viewing textiles, you can also see artists hard at work using ancient techniques of weaving, washing, and spinning the wool. It's amazing to

> ## ╭Moments Take a Walk
>
> Be sure to set aside some time to stroll around Sucre's main Plaza 25 de
> Mayo. This is the largest and most beautiful square in all of Bolivia, ringed
> with Palm and Jacaranda trees.

witness the intense work that goes into creating these unique forms of art. There
is also a wonderful gift shop here that supports local communities. Plan on
spending at least 2 hours here.

San Alberto 413 (near the corner of Potosí). ℭ 0104/6453-841. Admission 15Bs ($1.95). Mon–Fri
8am–noon and 2:30–6pm; Sat 9:30am–noon. Closed Sat Oct–May.

Museo de la Recoleta ⋆⋆ *Moments*   This museum is housed in a convent
that dates from the year 1600. Inside, you will find an excellent collection of
colonial art and a courtyard that offers an incredible bird's-eye view of Sucre.
Plus, you'll get a glimpse of what it must have been like to live and work here in
the 17th century. For example, you can visit a re-created priest's room, very basic
accommodations with only one blanket and a whip (used for self-flagellation).
The **Courtyard of the Orange Trees** ⋆⋆ is the most impressive part of the
museum, featuring an orange tree that is said to be more than 1,000 years old.
Before the Spanish arrived, the indigenous people used this tree as a totem pole.
Once the Catholic priests settled in here, however, the three big branches of the
tree took on new meaning, representing the Father, the Son, and the Holy Spirit.
Nowadays, the tree is also a modern-day Cupid: It is said that if you walk around
it three times in a clockwise direction, you will marry in the next year. The
museum also houses works by colonial painter Melchor Pérez de Holguín, pieces
from the Cusqueña school, and an interesting painting of Jesus with an exaggerated flagellation scene, said to justify all the abuse being committed at that
time. As you walk around the museum, you may notice that the walls are
crooked. This is intentional—it protects the building from the destructive powers of earthquakes. It'll take you an hour to visit the museum and spend a little
time enjoying the beautiful courtyard.

Polano 162 (right in front of Plaza Anzures). Admission 10Bs ($1.30). Mon–Fri 9:30–11:30am and
2:30–4:30pm; Sat 3–4:30pm.

Museo Charcas (University Museum Colonial & Anthropological)
This museum, which is housed in a 17th-century mansion, consists of three different mini-museums: colonial art, an ethnography and folk collection, and
modern art. Overall, the museum provides a comprehensive look at the wide
breadth of art forms—both indigenous and European—in Bolivia.

In the Colonial Museum, most of the art dates from the 16th and 17th centuries. The museum houses paintings by the half-indigenous Melchor Pérez
Holguín, including his most famous work, *San Juan de Dios*, which has an
almost perfect depiction of human hands. You'll also find a collection of beautiful antique furniture on display. In the Ethnographic and Folkloric Museum,
you can learn about local rituals and view a collection of mummified bodies that
provide insight on local death rituals. Also on display is a good collection of pottery from the Yampara culture. Its pottery is some of the most beautiful and
technically advanced of all pre-Columbian cultures—you can see tears on the
faces and evidence of ponchos. The pieces in the Modern Art Gallery reflect

contemporary Bolivian artists' focus on poverty and the back-breaking labor involved in working in the mines. Set aside at least 1½ hours to visit the entire collection.

Bolívar 698 (near the corner of Olañeta). © 0104/6453-285. Admission 10Bs ($1.30). Mon–Sat 8:30am–noon and 2:30–6pm.

Museo Casa de la Libertad The United States has Liberty Hall in Philadelphia; Bolivia has the equivalent in Museo Casa de la Libertad. On August 6, 1825, the freedom fighters of Bolivia assembled here to declare independence from Spain. You can visit the exact room where the liberators met. Now known as the "Salón de la Independencia," it's filled with portraits of the great liberators and baroque-style wood chairs painted in gold leaf. The portrait here of Simón Bolívar is believed to be the most lifelike reproduction of the great independence hero.

The museum complex was originally part of a Jesuit university that dates from 1624 (one of the oldest in Bolivia). In addition to the Salón de la Independencia, there are several galleries here dedicated to the history of Bolivia. Items on display include the first Argentine flag (the Bolivians refuse to return it to Argentina, saying "we are all the same"), a copy of the Bolivian declaration of independence, and paintings of the city of Sucre in the independence era. There's also a room dedicated to Mariscal Sucre, the first president of Bolivia. Plan on spending about 45 minutes here.

Plaza 25 de Mayo 25. © 0104/6454-200. Admission 10Bs ($1.30). Tues–Sat 9–11:15am; Sun 9am–2pm.

Museo de la Catedral The Museo de la Catedral houses an excellent collection of colonial art and silver religious relics, but the **Chapel of the Virgin of Guadalupe** is the star of the show here (and will probably be the highlight of your visit to Sucre). Fray Diego de Ocaña painted the original *Virgen de Guadalupe* in 1601. Today, you can see some remains of this oil painting and the canvas, but mostly it has been destroyed by the thousands of pounds of jewelry that the faithful have offered the Virgin over the past 400 years. The weight of the jewels (and 40,000 emeralds can certainly do a lot of damage) have torn the canvas to bits. All that survive are her face, her hands, and the face of the baby—the rest is pure gemstones. In addition to the Chapel of the Virgin, you can also visit the cathedral, which dates from 1559 but is purely neoclassical. After the independence from Spain in 1825, the liberators tried to erase all colonial influences from the churches in the area. Instead of seeing the elaborate baroque designs from the colonial period, you'll find that this cathedral is very simple and understated.

Calle Nicolás Ortiz 61 (around the corner from Plaza 25 de Mayo). © 0104/6452-257. Admission 15Bs ($1.95). Mon–Fri 10am–noon and 3–5pm; Sat 10am–noon.

AN ATTRACTION OUTSIDE OF TOWN

Cal Orck'o (Dinosaur Tracks) *(Moments)* This is definitely one of the most unique attractions in Bolivia. At first glance, the dinosaur tracks look like simple holes in rocks. But after your eyes adjust, you'll start to see distinct patterns of movement. All of sudden, it's very easy to envision dinosaurs slopping through the mud, trying to escape from their enemies, and searching for water. It is believed that the rocks in the area date back some 68 million years—well before the Andes were formed. Supposedly, there was a lake here surrounded by a forest. Dinosaurs trudged through the mud in the forest toward the lake in search of water. Before the footprints had a chance to disappear (about a 2-week time period), they would be covered by sediment, which settled over the mud and preserved the prints. The bilingual guides will be able to tell you their theories about which dinosaurs were doing what when they walked through this area 68 million years ago. I recommend taking the Dino-Truck to get here— you'll ride in the back of a pickup through the outskirts of Sucre and along roads with beautiful vistas. If you choose to take a taxi, it will cost you about $3. The tour lasts about 1½ hours.

About 20 min. outside of Sucre. © 0104/6451-863. Take the Dino-Truck, which leaves daily from the Cathedral on Plaza 25 de Mayo at 9:30am, noon, and 2:30pm. Dino-Truck and admission is 25Bs ($3.25). Admission w/o transportation is 20Bs ($2.60). Guided tours daily 10, 11:30am, 12:30, 2, and 3pm.

SHOPPING

Sucre and the surrounding area are famous for handicrafts. If you happen to be in town on a Sunday and you're looking for handicrafts, you should head to the market in **Tarabuco** 🎯 (about 56km/35 miles from Sucre). Here, you will find thousands of different textiles, hats, gloves, bags, and other hand-woven goodies. The market is one of the best in Bolivia. On Sunday mornings, buses leave from Sucre for Tarabuco from 7 to 9am at the corner of Avenida de la Américas and Manco Capac. The 1½-hour ride costs 15Bs ($1.95) each way. **Candelaria Tours** 🎯🎯, right off the central square at Audiencia 1 (© **0104/6461-661;** www.candelariatours.com), also organizes day trips to the market and the surrounding area.

The gift shop at the **Museo de Arte Indígena ASUR/Textile Museum** on San Alberto 413 (near the corner of Potosí) offers the best selection of textiles and handmade crafts in Sucre. **Artesanías Sucre,** Calle Olañeta 42 at Plazuela Zudáñez, and **Artesanías Tesoros del Inca,** Calle Camargo 514, also sell local handicrafts. You will find everything under the sun at the unique **Central Market** on the corner of Junín and Ravelo. I recommend heading up to the second floor to try the local *Tojorí* drink for breakfast. The drink consists of boiled corn, cinnamon, and sugar. Because of its high protein content, it's called "the cornflakes of the Andes."

Para Ti 🎯🎯 on Arenales (about ⅓ block in from the plaza) sells the most divine handmade chocolate that I've ever tasted.

WHERE TO STAY

Capital Plaza Hotel If you stay at Capital Plaza Hotel, you'll get a generous dose of both modern amenities and colonial charm. The hotel is located in a colonial-style house (although it was built in the early 20th c.). The comfortable rooms have gleaming parquet floors; pretty, flowery wallpaper; and good-size bathrooms. In the old part of the hotel, the rooms overlook a charming pink courtyard, complete with an old-fashioned stone fountain. The real winner here is the Presidential Suite: It has a separate sitting area, a dressing room, beautiful old French doors, and wonderful antique furniture. The bathroom is equally sumptuous—it comes with a huge Jacuzzi. One complaint: Because it's right on the main plaza, the rooms tend to be quite noisy. If you're a light sleeper, be sure to ask for a room away from the road, preferably in the back overlooking the courtyard.

Plaza 25 de Mayo 28–29, Sucre. © 0104/6422-999. Fax 0104/6453-588. www.capitalplazahotel.com. 40 units. $55 double; $70 triple; $80 presidential suite. Rates include breakfast. MC, V. **Amenities:** 2 restaurants; piano bar; small indoor pool; steam room; game room; small business center; room service; laundry service; dry cleaning. *In room:* TV, minibar, hair dryer.

El Hostal de Su Merced 🏨🏨🏨 *Finds*   Once you have stayed at this hotel, you can rest assured that you have slept in the best small hotel in Bolivia. The hotel is housed in a magnificent converted mansion from the 18th century. It's not luxurious, but what it lacks in luxury, it makes up for in charm and character. All the rooms are unique, with thick white adobe walls and antique furniture (some is original to this house). The president of Bolivia prefers room no. 7, and I can certainly understand why: This junior suite has a separate sitting area with large antique chairs and a hand-embroidered ottoman, hand-carved wooden doors, lace curtains, a brass bed, and the aura of true elegance. All the rooms have similar personal touches—including crystal chandeliers, brick floors, adorable basket-weave garbage bins, sloped ceilings, and antiques galore. If you plan on staying here for a while, I recommend room no. 16. It's very private, and it has its own quiet patio. The beautiful rooftop terrace has awesome views of the Cathedral; it's a lovely place to lounge in the sun. Another bonus: The owners here couldn't be nicer. Guests get 15 minutes free daily use of the Internet.

Calle Azurduy 16 (between N. Ortiz and Bolívar), Sucre. ℂ **0104/6442-706.** Fax 0104/6912-078. www.boliviaweb.com/companies/sumerced. 16 units. $45 double; $60 triple; $60 junior suite. Rates include breakfast. AE, MC, V. **Amenities:** Restaurant; room service; laundry service; dry cleaning. *In room:* TV, minibar in junior suites.

Hotel La Posada 🏨🏨 *Value*   If you can't stay at the Hostal de su Merced, this hotel is an excellent second choice, especially if you're looking for the best bargain in Sucre. Opened in 2003 in a renovated old house, La Posada's rooms overlook a lovely courtyard with mature trees and colorful plants; they all have tile floors, colorful blue and yellow bedspreads and wrought-iron lamps. Rooms on the second floor have wood-beamed ceilings and are slightly more spacious than those on the ground floor. Bathrooms are nicely tiled and sparkling, if a bit small. The Posada's restaurant is excellent, serving a daily three-course menu for lunch and dinner priced at 20Bs ($2.60); in warm weather, you can dine outside under elegant parasols. If you're looking for the best deal in town with a healthy dose of charm and elegance, then this is it.

Calle Audiencia 92, Sucre. ℂ **0104/6913-427.** Fax 0104/6913-427. laposadahostal@entel.bo. 9 units. $35 double; $60 suite. Rates include breakfast. MC, V. **Amenities:** Charming restaurant; room service. *In room:* TV.

WHERE TO DINE

You will dine really well in Sucre; this city has tons of interesting and delicious eateries. In addition to the restaurants listed below, here are some other good choices: The most delicious *salteñas* in town can be found at **El Paso de los Abuelos**, Bustillo 216 (ℂ **0104/6455-173**); they're open daily from 8am to 1pm. The newest and hippest cafe/restaurant is **Salamadra,** Calle Avaroa 510 (ℂ **0104/6913-433**), where the crème de la crème of Sucre's residents gather for lunch, dinner, and coffee and snacks. For a much simpler but exquisite local experience, visit **Las Delicias** 🍴, Estudiantes 50 (ℂ **0104/6442-502**). Here, owner (and baker) Dorly Fernández de Toro serves her amazing pastries; some are very unusual but delicious, like the *sonso,* made from mashed yucas. There's also a good selection of yummy *empanadas* and *humitas.* Las Delicias is open only Tuesday through Saturday from 4 to 8pm—come early as this place fills up fast.

The best place for lunch with a terrific view is the **Café Gourmet Mirador,** Plaza Anzures, across from the Recoleta (ℂ **0104/6440-299**). You'll dine outside under lovely bamboo umbrellas with Sucre stretched at your feet; the speciality here is crepes. They're open daily until 6pm.

El Asador *Finds* GRILLED MEAT   This may very well be the best place in Bolivia for grilled meats. It's worth the 10-minute taxi ride to this nice residential area. The restaurant is located in a nondescript house, but it has a beautiful backyard. If it's warm, you can dine al fresco under the trees. On the weekends the place fills with locals—families mostly—and the atmosphere is delightfully festive; weekday evenings are quiet. They are very serious about serving your steak correctly here—they will ask for a detailed description of how you like it. Beef is the most popular choice, although there's pork, too; occasionally they have fresh fish, but don't count on it. Most diners order a steak and a couple of sides, such as cheese rice, french fries, green salad, and a variety of sauces (both mild and hot). There's a good selection of sausages, too, if you're feeling adventurous. Bottles of Bolivian wines start at 35Bs ($4.55), although I recommend splurging here on a bottle of Campos de Solana Cabernet for 65Bs ($8.50). For dessert, there's fresh fruit and homemade ice creams. The owners will happily call a taxi for your return trip to your hotel.

Plazuela Cumana, on the outskirts of town (a taxi here should cost no more than $1). ✆ 0104/6445-929. Main courses 31Bs ($4). No credit cards. Tues–Fri 6–11pm; Sat–Sun 11:30am–11pm.

El Huerto Restaurant *Moments* BOLIVIAN   In Spanish, *el huerto* means "the orchard," and that's exactly where you'll feel like you are when you dine outside in the lovely garden area of this popular lunch spot. Your fellow diners will probably be some of Sucre's biggest bigwigs, who come here for the relaxed atmosphere and excellent food. This is a great place to try some of Sucre's local specialties such as *chorizos chuquisaqueños especiales* (a spicy pork sausage) and *cjoko de pollo* (chicken seasoned with a yellow chile paste in a broth with wine, stewed prunes, and linguine). You can also order more international fare, including filet mignon, pineapple chicken, and omelets. For dessert, I highly recommend the homemade ice cream.

Ladislao Cabrera 86 (it's a bit outside of town, so take a taxi). ✆ 0104/6451-538. Main courses 35Bs ($4.55). V. Daily 11:30am–2:30pm; Thurs–Sat 6–9pm.

Restaurant Maxim BOLIVIAN/FRENCH   This restaurant feels very formal in a European way. The walls are covered with fancy lace French-style wallpaper, crystal chandeliers hang from the ceiling, and the tablecloths have hand-embroidered paisley designs. The waiters wear white tuxes and cater to your every need. Although the ambience is unique, the food here has its own special flair. For an appetizer, you can order the tasty *ceviche de pejerrey* (raw kingfish marinated in a tangy lemon juice and served in an oyster shell). The *pollo Maxim* (chicken filled with ham and cheese) is one of the house specialties. You can also order local dishes such as *chorizos chuquisaqueños* (pork sausage) and picante mixto. In a nod to French cooking, almost all of the dishes come bathed in a cream sauce, except for the *chuletas de cerdo glaseados* (pork chops in a red-wine sauce with a touch of sugar).

Arenales 19 (½ block from the main plaza; on the 2nd floor). ✆ 0104/6451-798. Reservations recommended on weekends. Main courses 30Bs–35Bs ($3.90–$4.55). MC, V. Mon–Sat 7–11pm.

SUCRE AFTER DARK

Because Sucre is crawling with young university students, there are tons of charming bars near Plaza 25 de Mayo, especially on Calle N. Ortiz leading away from the square. I recommend the **Joy Ride Café & Bar,** Calle N. Ortiz 14 (✆ 0104/6425-544), owned by a Dutch guy and serving good beer and excellent light meals. This is where many gringos spend the evening. Next door, **Picadilly** (no phone) is another popular bar. If you're looking to boogie, there are some great dance clubs here, too. Some of the best are **Coyote Rodeo,** Avenida Venezuela at the corner of Avenida Del Maestro; **Mitos,** Calle Francisco Cerro at the corner of Calle Loyaza; and **Tío Lalo,** Calle San Alberto 680. **Up/Down,** Calle Gregorio Mendizábal and F. Ruck (© **0104/6453-587**), is a popular spot for karaoke; the cover charge is usually 10Bs ($1.30). Note that most everything is eerily quiet during the week; the above bars and clubs, with the exception of Joy Ride, are open only Wednesday through Saturday.

6 Potosí ★★

539km (334 miles) SE of La Paz; 162km (100 miles) SW of Sucre; 219km (136 miles) NE of Uyuni

In the 17th century, Potosí was one of the richest cities in the world, thanks to Cerro Rico (the Rich Hill). It's been said that enough silver was pulled from the bowels of Cerro Rico to build a bridge from Potosí all the way to Madrid—and enough people died inside the mines to build a bridge of bones all the way back.

Nowadays, visitors can still see the two disparate sides of the city. The silver supply has been depleted, but 7,000 workers still spend their days inside Cerro Rico searching for tin, lead, and new silver deposits. On average, they make about $100 a month. You can take tours that will bring you face to face with these miners and the dreary conditions in which they work. But after you leave the mines and take a nice hot shower, you can then tour the sights that evoke the city's former glory.

Potosí is not a heartwarming place. At more than 3,900m (13,000 ft.), it's one of the highest cities in the world. Even when the sun is shining bright, there is always a bitter chill in the air. When you're here, it really feels as if you're in the middle of nowhere. It's painful to visit the mines and learn about the past exploitation of these workers, but it's also fascinating to see the remains of a place that was once the home of some of the wealthiest people in the world.

ESSENTIALS
GETTING THERE
BY PLANE   There is a small airport in Potosí but only small charter planes from Cochabamba land there. The nearest airport with scheduled flights is in Sucre—see "Getting There: By Plane" in "Sucre," earlier in this chapter, for more information. From there, you can take a taxi or bus for the 161km (100-mile) ride to Potosí.

BY BUS   The Potosí bus station is on the edge of town at the end of Avenida Universitaria (near the intersection of Av. Sevilla). See "Getting Around: By Bus" in "Planning Your Trip to Bolivia," earlier in this chapter, for bus company information. The 12-hour ride from La Paz costs 50Bs ($6.50) for a normal bus, 80Bs ($10) for a *bus cama*. Buses from Santa Cruz go through Cochabamba or

---

Tips Jetting to Potosí

If you're pressed for time and don't want to spend hours in a car getting to Potosí, then do what the adventurous do and charter a small plane for the day. Departures are available from Cochabamba or Sucre and cost $600 round-trip. Contact **Todo Turismo** ★★, Av. America E-786, Cochabamaba (© **0104/4485-246;** cbbturismo@hotmail.com), to arrange for your charter.

Potosí

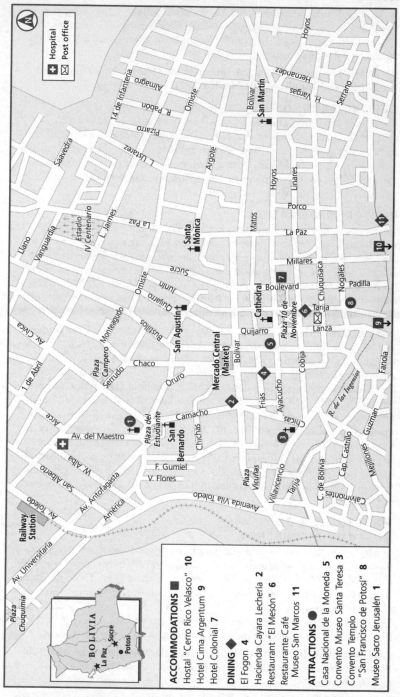

ACCOMMODATIONS ■
Hostal "Cerro Rico Velasco" **10**
Hotel Cima Argentum **9**
Hotel Colonial **7**

DINING ◆
El Fogon **4**
Hacienda Cayara Lechería **2**
Restaurant "El Mesón" **6**
Restaurante Café
Museo San Marcos **11**

ATTRACTIONS ●
Casa Nacional de la Moneda **5**
Convento Museo Santa Teresa **3**
Convento Templo
"San Francisco de Potosí" **8**
Museo Sacro Jerusalén **1**

Sucre. The 2-hour ride from Cochabamba costs 30Bs ($3.90). Buses depart from Sucre in the morning, midafternoon, and early evening (around 5pm). The 2½- to 3-hour ride costs 15Bs ($1.95). Buses depart from Uyuni at 10am and 7pm. The 5-hour ride costs 25Bs ($3.25).

BY TAXI   You can also take a taxi from Sucre for 150Bs ($20) for four people. Contact **Expreso Infinito** (© 0104/6422-277).

GETTING AROUND
Plaza 10 de Noviembre and Plaza 6 de Agosto (they are adjacent to each other) are in the commercial heart of Potosí. From here, you can easily walk to all the banks, travel agencies, hotels, and major attractions in town. If you get tired of walking, it's easy to find a taxi; rides to most points in the city don't cost more than 5Bs (65¢). To visit the mines on Cerro Rico, I recommend taking a guided tour (see "Visiting the Mines" on p. 216).

VISITOR INFORMATION
The main tourist office is located in a kiosk on Plaza 6 de Agosto. It's open Monday through Saturday from 9am to noon, and Monday through Friday from 2 to 5pm. No maps are available here, but the staff is knowledgeable and helpful. For more specific information about Potosí and the mines, contact **Koala Tours,** Calle Ayacucho 5, right in front of Casa de la Moneda (© 0102/6224-708). The office is open daily from 8am to 7pm. The owner speaks excellent English and knows Potosí like the back of his hand.

FAST FACTS   You can exchange money and traveler's checks at **Casa Fernández** on Pasaje Boulevard 10. (It's on the pedestrian street that passes by Plaza 6 de Agosto.) Casa Fernández is an all-purpose store, not a bank, but it will indeed change traveler's checks. The city's most reliable ATM is connected to the **Banco de Crédito** on the corner of Bolívar and Sucre. **Hospital Daniel Bracamonte,** Avenida Japón (© 0102/6243-928), is the best hospital in Potosí. If you need a pharmacy, try **Farmacia Nazareth,** Bolívar 900 (© 0102/6225-854), or **Farmacia Copacabana,** Bolívar 712 (© 0102/6222-347). The **post office** is located at Calle Lanza 3 between Cobija and Chuquisaca. You can take care of all your laundry needs at **Limpieza La Veloz** on Calle Quijarro at the corner of Matos. You'll find Internet cafes on all the side streets that lead off the plaza; my favorite is **Ciberblue** on Pasaje Boulevard (the pedestrian street) and the corner of Linares.

WHAT TO SEE & DO
MUSEUMS & CHURCHES
In addition to the churches and museums listed below, I also recommend making a quick stop at the **Museo Sacro Jerusalén** on Avenida Camacho at the corner of Avenida del Maestro. The church here dates from 1708; the four laminated pictures on the pulpit are by the great master Melchor Pérez de Holguín. The museum is open Monday through Friday from 3 to 7pm and on Saturday from 9am to noon. *Note:* Occasionally this museum closes earlier than it should; I suggest coming in the early afternoon to avoid disappointment.

Casa Nacional de la Moneda 🟊🟊   To really understand the history of Potosí, you have to visit this museum. Most of the silver mined in Cerro Rico came here to the Casa Nacional de la Moneda to be transformed into coins. This mint, which dates back to 1759, was the second mint in Potosí. When it was completed, it was the biggest building in the Americas. The building also housed Spanish families who worked for the government, while the third floor was used as a prison for African slaves. The whole complex is now a museum with 20 different galleries that all speak of the wealth and rich history of this city. For example, during Potosí's glory days, there were 32 churches in the city. And because Potosí was a center for the arts, the local churches managed to accumulate some of the finest collections of religious art in the Americas. Several galleries here display the highlights of these collections, including *La Virgen del Cerro,* which tells the whole history of Cerro Rico, and works by Gaspar Miguel Berrio, Diego Quispe Tito, and Melchor Pérez de Holguín. Other galleries are dedicated to Bolivian weapons, modern art, minerals, and archaeology. Also on view are the original metal pressing machines, which were powered by mules, and exhibits about the minting process.

Note that you can only visit the museum on a 2-hour guided tour. The English-speaking tours are supposed to depart at 9, 11am, 2, and 4pm, but it seems as though the 9am tour is the only one that actually leaves on time—some leave earlier, others later.

Calle Ayacucho (between Quijarro and Bustillos). © 0102/6223-986. Admission 20Bs ($2.60). Tues–Sat 9am–noon and 2:30–6:30pm; Sun 9am–1pm. English tours available at 9, 11am, 2, and 4pm; only the 9am tour leaves on time.

Convento y Templo "San Francisco" de Potosí ⊛

Although the church here only dates back to 1708, the convent is an excellent example of 16th-century religious architecture. Yet the church is one of the most impressive in Bolivia. It has 11 cupolas, four each on the two far sides of the temple. Each group of four represents the 40 days that Jesus spent in the desert. The three in the center are said to represent the Holy Trinity. The dramatic and bloody figure of the Imágen del Señor de la Cruz is also on display here. It dates from 1550 and is one of the oldest religious figures in Bolivia. Its crown is pure silver; it is also believed to have miraculous powers. As you walk around the grounds, you can see an excellent collection of colonial art and some of the most beautifully constructed **catacombs** ⊛⊛ in Bolivia. (It's one of the few structures in the country that is pure stone.) Plus, you can climb to the top for panoramic views of Potosí or walk around the peaceful convent and admire the beautiful stonework and perfectly balanced archways.

Calle Tarija 47 (corner of Nogales). © 0102/6222-539. Admission 10Bs ($1.30). Mon–Fri 9am–noon and 2:30–5pm; Sat 9am–noon.

Convento Museo Santa Teresa ⊛

Ever wondered what it would have been like to live as a nun in Bolivia? Once you visit this renovated church and convent, you will have an excellent picture of the day-to-day routine of the Sisters of the Carmelita order. This was a working convent from 1691 through 1976 (nowadays, the sisters live next door), and it seems as if for those 300 years, the daily rituals changed very little. On the 3-hour guided tour, you will see the nun's simple bedrooms, their recreation room, the room and the tools that the nuns used to prepare the wafers for Mass (this is the only convent in Bolivia that continues to make these wafers by hand), and the place where the nuns received their visitors. Here, the nuns were separated from their callers by a dark screened wall. They weren't allowed to touch or see their guests; they could only exchange words. It wasn't until 1967 that the pope revoked this order. You will also visit the impressive church, with an elegant gold-leaf altarpiece, where the aristocrats of Potosí would pray. There is also a gallery here filled with opulent gold, silver, and hand-carved wood mirrors given to the convent by wealthy parishioners, and countless other galleries full of colonial art, antiques, Murano glass, and hand-painted porcelain dishes.

You can only tour the convent on guided tours, which leave only when there are three or more people. It's best to arrive when the museum opens in the morning or the afternoon to make sure that you will have enough time for the 3-hour tour.

Calle Santa Teresa 15 (at the end of Calle Ayacucho). © 0102/6223-847. Admission 21Bs ($2.70). Daily 9–11am and 3–5pm by guided tour only (try to arrive at 9am to be assured of a tour).

VISITING THE MINES

The history of Potosí is inextricably linked to Cerro Rico. For the past 400 years, miners have been crawling into the bowels of this hill, risking their lives to extract valuable minerals mainly for the benefit of the Spanish empire. When you visit the main attractions in the center of Potosí, you can see the remnants of the great wealth that this mine has created—extravagant churches, magnificent pieces of art—but you don't learn much about the actual labor involved in this whole process. Taking a tour of the mines will open your eyes to a different side of Potosí, to the world of the people who actually work here. Let me warn you beforehand that it's not a pretty picture. Currently, there are about 7,000 workers in the 455 mines of Cerro Rico. (Only 120 mines are in working operation.) Not much has changed here over the past few hundred years. Here's an idea of one of the most recent technological advances: A few years ago, pulleys were introduced. Now, instead of carrying rocks up five or more levels on their backs, the miners can use a pulley to lift their loads. Fortunately, the miners now work in cooperatives, and they do earn a percentage of what they find. The average salary here is about $100 a month.

The tours take you to the working mines, where you will see workers igniting dynamite to open new areas, shoveling rocks, and carrying heavy loads, all in one of the most abysmal work environments that you could ever imagine. These miners often spend 24-hour stretches in utter darkness, with cigarettes, soda, and coca leaves as their only form of sustenance. These tours are not for wimps—it's extremely difficult to maneuver inside the mines. There are no proper stairways with handrails (rather, you have to descend using footholds that have been perfunctorily carved into the walls); the paths are narrow and very steep; and there is mud everywhere, which makes walking treacherous. Expect to get dirty. Although none of the tour companies have a fitness requirement for touring the mines, I would recommend that anyone with heart or breathing problems or claustrophobia skip the trip to the mines.

There are several companies in Potosí that offer mine tours. The best ones use guides who are former miners. Overall, however, the quality of the tours is horrendous: The equipment (hard hats, waterproof clothing, gloves, boots, lamps, surgical masks) is often in poor condition, and the guides can be unreliable. **Koala Tours,** Ayacucho 5 in front of Casa de la Moneda (© **0102/6222-092**), is one of the more reputable companies. Koala Tours also takes you to a museum in the mine, which provides an excellent history. Tours leave Monday through Saturday, but it's best to go on a weekday because the mines are quiet on the weekends. The 5-hour tour costs $10 per person; a percentage of the profits is donated to the cooperatives working in the mines.

WHERE TO STAY

Most visitors come to Potosí on a day trip; accommodations here are nothing special and many don't have heat (it gets real cold at night). In addition to the hotels below, the third-best place in town (with decent rooms and heat) is the **Hostal Cerro Rico Velasco,** Calle Ramos 123 (© **0102/6223-539;** www.

cerrorico.place.cc). It offers modern and clean rooms, though the staff is surly and not very helpful. Doubles are $28.

Hostal Colonial   This is the second-best hotel in Potosí. But because the level of accommodations in Potosí is, on the whole, quite low, don't expect anything extraordinary. It's one of the few places in town with heat—a huge plus, as Potosí can get unbearably cold at night. The rooms have musty carpets and the furniture is way out-of-date, but they are clean and comfortable. The large bathrooms are the best part, with strong showers. (Half the bathrooms also have tubs.) Fortunately, the hotel has a nice setting; all the rooms are centered around a charming brick courtyard. Another plus is the perfect location—the hotel is only about a block from the main square.

Calle Hoyos 8, Potosí. ⓒ **0102/6224-809.** Fax 0102/6227-146. colonial@mara.scr.entelnet.bo. 20 units (about half w/tub). $43 double; $45 triple; $65 suite. AE, MC, V. **Amenities:** Breakfast room; room service; laundry service; dry cleaning. In room: TV, fridge.

Hotel Cima Argentum ⓐ   Finally a modern—even attractive—hotel in Potosí. Opened in 2002, the Cima Argentum is situated about 6 blocks from the center of town, but it's worth the walk (or a short taxi ride) here. Service is gracious and the staff surprisingly friendly and efficient. Rooms are not especially bright but are modern with colorful bedspreads, dark clean carpets, and wood furniture. Bathrooms have marble-topped vanities and decent showers. There are also nine spacious apartments (with kitchenettes) that can sleep up to four people. The restaurant here is excellent and is itself enough reason to stay at this hotel.

Av. Villazon 239, Potosí. ⓒ **0102/6229-538.** Fax 0102/6122-603. www.hca-potosi.com. 20 units. $48 double; $54 apt for 2; $66 apt for 3; $74 apt for 4. Rates include breakfast. MC, V. **Amenities:** Restaurant; concierge; room service. In room: TV, kitchenette in apts.

WHERE TO DINE

If you're looking for a place to refuel and take a break, you must stop in at the heavenly **Hacienda Cayara Lechería** ⓐ on Calle Cochabamba 532. (It's located about 1½ blocks down from Plaza Arce—the plaza with the Entel Building, which is the tallest building in the city.) Hacienda Cayara is a dairy farm located about 24km (15 miles) outside of Potosí. Every day, fresh dairy products are delivered here to this small cafeteria. I recommend ordering the fruit shakes made with yogurt and the fresh pastries, but everything here is absolutely divine.

The restaurant at the **Hotel Cima Argentum** (see above) is one of the best in town; it offers both Bolivian and international cuisine in a gracious setting with superb service.

Restaurant Café Museo San Marcos ⓐ (finds) BOLIVIAN   This is one of the more unique restaurants in Bolivia and it's the best restaurant in Potosí. It's housed in a former mineral refinery, but it has been superbly renovated, and it feels hip. The restaurant has huge windows and high ceilings, which give it a bright and airy feeling. The charming stone walls are original, and refurbished refinery machines are placed throughout the large restaurant. The menu also has its quirks. For example, the house specialty is tender llama meat served in a light butter sauce flavored with lemon and mint—it's quite tasty. Overall, the menu is actually quite varied. You can also order pasta, omelets, trout, kingfish, grilled pork chops, or chicken dishes.

Calle La Paz (near the corner of Betanzos). ⓒ **0102/6222-781.** Main courses 20Bs–31Bs ($2.60–$4). No credit cards. Daily noon–4pm and 6–10pm.

Restaurant "El Mesón" *Finds* BOLIVIAN/INTERNATIONAL When you're in a historic city such as Potosí, it makes sense to eat in a historic restaurant. El Mesón fits the bill perfectly. The restaurant is housed in an old bookstore in a colonial-style building. The majestic bricks walls, old-fashioned iron chandeliers, and grand archways all add to the restaurant's character. The menu caters mostly to the palates of foreign travelers—you can order omelets, pasta, filet mignon, or pineapple chicken. But I recommend trying the local dishes such as the *cjoko de pollo* (chicken in red wine and chile sauce served with noodles) and the *asado borracho* (steak with tomatoes and onions in a red-wine sauce). When you eat here, you will feel as if you are taking a trip back in time.

Plaza 10 de Noviembre (on Tarija at the corner of Linares). ℂ 0102/6223-807. Main courses 20Bs–35Bs ($2.60–$4.55). No credit cards. Daily noon–2:30pm and 5:30–10pm.

A SIDE TRIP TO SALAR DE UYUNI

Hearty souls who have extra time on their hands should seriously consider making a trip to the Salar de Uyuni. The town of Uyuni is located on the eastern edge of the Salar de Uyuni, which is the largest salt lake in the world. To see the area, you have to travel on a guided tour that usually lasts for 4 days and 3 nights. There are no roads in these parts, so all the agencies use almost-antique Toyota Land Cruisers to transport you through the desert. The trip can be rough, especially on your bottom. But the desert landscape, with its volcanoes in the background and bizarre rock formations, is truly surreal. Some of the highlights of the trip include a stop at the salt lake itself; the oddly shaped **Isla del Pescado,** which is covered with cactuses; and the **Laguna Colorado,** with its red algae that attracts flamingoes. My favorite stop on the tour is the **Sol de la Mañana,** where you can see geysers, fumaroles, and mud boiling in the earth. It's called Sol de la Mañana because it's best seen early in the morning. At the **Laguna Verde** (in the farthest southwest corner of Bolivia), be sure to hold on tightly to your hat, because the wind here is vicious. The emerald green Laguna Verde sits right below the Lincancabur Volcano (5,835m/19,450 ft.) and makes for a fantastic photograph.

I only recommend this trip for people who are ready to rough it. The accommodations along the way are very basic (simple dorm-style rooms and rustic outhouses). Bring tons of warm clothing and a thick sleeping bag, because the temperature can drop below zero, and there's no heat where you're going.

If you have to spend the night in Uyuni, two hotels to try are **Avenida** (ℂ **0102/6932-078**) and **Magia de Uyuni** (ℂ **0102/6932-541**). Avenida, located on Avenida Ferroviaria across from the train station, offers a double with private bathroom for 50Bs ($6.50) per person; note that rooms are not heated. At Magia de Uyuni, located on Avenida Colón between Sucre and Camacho, you'll pay $22 per night for a double with bathroom, including breakfast and electric heat.

GETTING THERE   The easiest way to get to Uyuni is to take a **bus** from Potosí. Buses leave daily at 11:30, 11:45am, and 6:30pm from the small bus terminal on Avenida Universitaria at the intersection of Sevilla. (They leave Uyuni for Potosí at 10am and 7pm.) The 5-hour ride costs 25Bs ($3.25).

If you want a **guided tour,** it's not easy to find a reputable company. I suggest contacting **Mariana Tours** (Olaneta 105 A, Sucre; ℂ **0104/6429-329; mtours@cotes.net.bo**); ask to speak to the manager, Rodrigo Garron, and he'll arrange the highest quality trip for you. Their tours are tailor-made to fit your needs and leave from either Sucre or Potosí.

7 Cochabamba

385km (239 miles) SE of La Paz; 473km (293 miles) W of Santa Cruz; 366km (227 miles) NW of Sucre

Okay, so La Paz is the highest capital city in the world and it has the highest airport and the highest golf course. Big deal. If you're looking for a spiritual high, you need to head to Cochabamba, whose 33m (108-ft.) Cristo de la Concordia is the largest statue of Christ in the world. In Spanish, *concordia* means harmony. Because Cochabamba is located in the middle of Bolivia, the local people wanted to build this harmonious statue as a symbol of the country's unity. It's hard to know whether the country has come closer together because of this. No one can deny, however, that there's something very welcoming about Cochabamba: The quiet plazas invite you to linger, the year-round springlike climate encourages you to stroll along the quaint streets, and the locals are friendly. There may not be much to see and do in the city itself, but Cochabamba is a great place to relax and get to know the people of Bolivia. Or you can travel to the small towns in the nearby valleys and visit some of the most colorful local markets in the country.

ESSENTIALS
GETTING THERE
BY PLANE LAB (© 0800-3001) and **Aero Sur** (© 0102/2430-430 in La Paz, or 0104/4400-910 in Cochabamba) offer daily flights to Cochabamba from La Paz, Santa Cruz, and Sucre. One-way tickets cost about $50 each. All planes arrive at the Aeropuerto Internacional Jorge Wilstermann. Taxis from the airport to the center of town cost about $3.

BY BUS The Cochabamba bus terminal, Avenida Ayacucho and Avenida Aroma, is probably the nicest bus station in all of Bolivia. Buses from La Paz arrive almost every half-hour. The 8-hour journey costs 35Bs ($4.55) for a regular bus, 50Bs ($6.50) for a *bus cama.* Buses from Santa Cruz take 11 hours and cost 35Bs ($4.55) for a normal bus, 60Bs ($7.80) for a *bus cama.* Buses from Sucre take 11 hours and cost 30Bs ($3.90) for a normal bus, 50Bs ($6.50) for a *bus cama.* See "Getting Around: By Bus" in "Planning Your Trip to Bolivia," earlier in this chapter, for bus company information.

GETTING AROUND
Cochabamba is an extremely walkable city. For the most part, the city is compact. The streets Ayacucho and Las Heroínas are the center of Cochabamba. From Ayacucho the streets are labeled north and south. From Las Heroínas, the streets are numbered east to west. The best restaurants and hotels are located in the upscale residential neighborhood known as Recoleta; it's best to take a taxi, which only costs about $1 from the center of town. To reach the statue of Christ, you can walk east 15 minutes from the center of town, or take a taxi for about 20Bs ($2.60) round-trip. *Trufis* are available throughout the city for 1.50Bs (20¢); numbers are clearly marked on the front of the vans.

VISITOR INFORMATION
The tourist information office is on General Acha and Calle Bautista; it's open Monday through Friday from 8:30am to 4:30pm. But unless you speak Spanish and have a very specific question, the tourist office is virtually useless.

   Todo Turismo *&&*, Av. América E-786 (© 0104/4485-246; cbbturismo@ hotmail.com), can help you find your bearings and organize city tours and trips to the valley, Tunari, and the Chapare area. They have trips ranging from 1 to

7 days with experienced guides, camping equipment, and sleeping bags. If you're looking for an English-speaking tour guide, I highly recommend **Tim Johnson;** contact him at tim@bolivia.com.

FAST FACTS   To change traveler's checks or exchange money, you should head to the travel agency **Exprintbol S.R.L,** Plaza 14 de Septiembre 242 (© 0104/4255-834). **Hospital Belga** (© 0104/4251-579), on Antezana between Paxxieri and Venezuela, is the best hospital in town. Pharmacies abound in Cochabamba. **Farmacia Boliviana** on 14 de Septiembre E-0202 was the first pharmacy in Cochabamba; **Farmacia San Mateo** on Las Heroínas E-0323 (between España and 25 de Mayo) is a bit more modern. The **post office** is on the corner of Las Heroínas and Ayacucho; the entrance is on Ayacucho. The best **Internet** cafe is **Black Cat Internet,** which is located on General Acha, just half a block off the Plaza de 14 Septiembre. **Entelnet** on the Prado, Av. Ballivián 539 adjacent to Plaza Colón, is also reliable for Internet use.

WHAT TO SEE & DO

In addition to the sights listed below, you can also visit the **Capilla Cristo de las Lágrimas de San Pedro,** a chapel where there is a sculpture of Christ that allegedly cries tears of human blood every Good Friday. The tears have been tested in an Australian lab, and they are indeed of human blood. The chapel is only 4 years old and you can see pictures of what this particular sculpture looked like when it was new (much less blood). The chapel, located on the corner of Belzu and Las Heroínas, is open Monday and Wednesday through Saturday from 3 to 6pm.

The new **Casona Santiváñez,** at 158 Calle Santiváñez, is also worth a stop if you're downtown. An old house, restored in 2001 by the municipality of Cochabamba, it is now a cultural center. It's home to the **Museo de Fotografía Antigua,** which has some interesting old photographs of the city. There's also a room devoted to writers, the **Museo de Escritores,** with letters and photos from Latin American writers. The salons upstairs are worth a peek if they're open (official city functions are held here); they are grand with old colonial furniture. Admission is free and the center is open Monday through from Friday 9am to noon and 2:30 to 6pm.

Centro Simón I Patiño/Palacio Portales

A visit to the Palacio Portales is a must for anyone interested in seeing how the upper, upper crust of Bolivia lived in the early 20th century. Ironically, the tin baron Simón Patiño never lived here—he suffered a heart attack during its construction, and his heart condition prevented his return to his native country. In fact, Charles de Gaulle is the only person who has ever spent the night in the house. What a pity, because this mansion is a real beaut.

Patiño was originally from the Cochabamba area, but he discovered an enormous tin deposit near the mining town of Oruro. By the turn of the 20th century, he controlled 10% of the world's tin. He commissioned a French architect to design and build the house from 1915 to 1927 while he was living in Europe. You'll enter the house through a round, neoclassical entrance. Inside, your guide will take you to several different rooms, which speak of the opulence of that time period. The walls are covered with silk wallpaper; crystal chandeliers from Venice hang from the rafters; and green and white marble fireplaces were built to keep the house warm. Each room has its own unique floor design. Thanks to the dry climate of Cochabamba, everything here has been impeccably preserved. Today, the house is used as a cultural center. After the tour, you can walk through the beautiful Japanese gardens or visit the Contemporary Art Center (Mon–Fri 3–9pm; admission is 3Bs/40¢). Plan on spending about an hour here.

Av. Potosí 1450 (near the intersection of Av. Portales). Admission 10Bs ($1.30). Tours in English Mon–Fri at 5:30pm and Sat at 11am. Take *trufi* no. 10 north from the corner of San Martín and Bolívar.

Cristo de la Concordia *(Moments* This steel-and-cement sculpture is believed to be the largest statue of Christ in the world. It measures 33m (108 ft.) because Christ died when he was 33 years old. I recommend riding the cable car to the top, but if you're feeling energetic, you can climb the 2,000 stairs. However you reach the summit, you will be rewarded with lovely views of the area. Christ is facing the lower valley area of Cochabamba. From here, you can see Tunari—at 4,800m (16,000 ft.), these are the highest twin peaks in the area. The Cristo Redentor (Christ the Redeemer) statue in Rio de Janeiro is the model for Cristo de la Concordia, but the locals like to think that this one is more loving—the face has more human features and unlike its counterpart in Rio, its hands seem to be in a welcoming embrace. There is an outdoor Mass here every Sunday morning. Set aside at least two hours for your visit here.

Located at the far eastern end of Av. Las Heroínas. Cable car fare 3Bs (40¢) each way. Tues–Sat 10am–7pm; Sun 9am–8pm.

Museo Arqueológico de la Universidad *(R* This small museum is quite interesting. Unfortunately, there isn't much information available in English, but the museum nevertheless does a good job of displaying artifacts that create a clear picture of the history of Bolivia. Several exhibits focus on the indigenous people of Bolivia, with a map showing where different indigenous groups have traditionally lived and relics that they have historically used. You will see straw baskets, sewing tools, hammocks, and spears used by the Yuracare people; pipes from the Agro-Alfares culture (who thrived 2000 B.C.–A.D. 300); pre-Inca mummies, with teeth and facial expressions still intact; and Inca artifacts. There's also a fantastic collection of pre-Columbian textiles, and an impressive collection of fossils—including fossilized horse teeth from horses that became extinct more than 6,000 years ago—and trilobites. You will also see mastodon bones that were found in the Andean valleys. It'll take you an hour to visit this museum.

On the corner of calles Jordan and Aguirre. Admission 15Bs ($1.95). Mon–Fri 8:30am–6:30pm; Sat–Sun 9am–noon.

HISTORIC CHURCHES & PLAZAS

Cochabamba was founded in 1574. By walking around the city's plazas and visiting the historic churches, you can travel back in time and feel what it must have been like to live here hundreds of years ago. In **Plaza San Sebastián,** you can see one of the first houses ever built in Cochabamba. Nearby is the first railroad station built in Bolivia. **Plaza 14 de Septiembre** is the historic heart of Cochabamba. September 14 is known as Cochabamba Day, the day when Cochabamba formally became a city. The plaza dates from 1571, and it is most remarkable because it has preserved its colonial archways on all four sides. (Very few plazas in South America can boast that the buildings on all four sides are original.) On this plaza, you can visit the **cathedral,** which was the first church of Cochabamba. It still has its original baroque facade, and there's a good collection of colonial art inside. Nearby on Ayacucho and Santiváñez is **Santo Domingo,** which is one of my favorite churches. It's very simple inside (unlike the cathedral), which gives it a majestic air. The wooden doors are from 1612.

SHOPPING

MARKETS   Cochabamba and the surrounding area are famous for their colorful markets. If you happen to be in town on a Wednesday or Saturday, you must stop in at **La Cancha,** Avenida San Martín between Tarata and Pulacayo, a huge market where you can find handicrafts, fresh produce, herbs, and just about anything else you could ever want.

In the valleys outside of Cochabamba, there are also several towns that have authentic markets. **Caixa Tours,** Esteban Arze S-0563 (© **0104/4250-937**), organizes day trips to these market towns. **Tarata** in the Upper Valley is a lovely historic village about 1 hour from Cochabamba; market day is Thursday. The market in **Punata** (about 1½ hr. from Cochabamba) is considered to be one of the best and biggest in Bolivia. It's also one of the least touristy. On Sunday, you should head to **Cliza** for a taste of real Bolivian cooking. One of the specialties here is baked pigeon. Minibuses to these towns leave from the corner of Avenida Barrientos and Avenida 6 de Agosto; the trip costs 5Bs (65¢).

HANDICRAFTS   Shopping at the local markets can be a chaotic experience. If you're looking for something more tranquil, you should stop by **Vicuñita Handicrafts** on Av. Rafael Pabón 777 (© **0104/4255-615**). Here you can shop for leather goods, tapestries, bags, and ceramic figurines (all handmade!) in the comfort of a private, uncrowded warehouse. For alpaca sweaters, I recommend **Amerindia** on Calle España 264.

WHERE TO STAY

Anteus Apart Hotel *(Value)*   This is Cochabamba's best value: An attractive budget hotel located in the upscale Recoleta residential neighborhood. Opened 4 years ago, the three-story building overlooks a nice garden in the back and the eastern range of the Andes in the distance. Rooms are bright and cheerful with large windows and simple, modern furnishings. The smallish bathrooms are nicely tiled and come with shower only. The 10 apartments come with a fully equipped kitchen and separate living area, and at $35 they are a great bargain. Also, free transportation is offered from/to the airport. You can walk from here to several good cafes, restaurants, bars and a huge grocery store.

Av. Potosí 1365, Cochabamba. © 0104/4245-067. Fax 0104/4320-166. hotelanteus@hotmail.com. 24 units (shower only). $30 double; $40 triple; $50 quad; $35 apt for 2; $50 apt for 3. Additional person $10. MC, V. **Amenities:** Restaurant; laundry service. *In room:* TV.

Hotel Diplomat   Hotel Diplomat is a cement-and-glass high-rise that looks a lot nicer on the outside than it actually is on the inside. The hotel's forte is its location: Right on the Prado in the heart of downtown Cochabamba. In general, the rooms look like they belong in a middle-of-the-road hotel—pink carpeting, a light-colored wood dresser and headboard, and typical flowery bedspreads. Don't expect gigantic rooms, but on the plus side, they do have nice views of the mountains and the surrounding area. The bathrooms are of a decent size with marble-style counters. If you call ahead, the hotel will pick you up from the airport for free. This hotel caters mainly to businesspeople, so you won't find much charm or personal attention here. However, the business center has the fastest Internet connection in town.

Av. Ballivián 0611 (Paseo el Prado), Cochabamba. © 0104/4250-687. Fax 0104/4250-897. www.hdiplomat. com. 86 units. $73 double; $83 junior suite. Rates include buffet breakfast. AE, MC, V. **Amenities:** Rooftop restaurant; bar; small business center; room service; laundry service; dry cleaning; executive floor. *In room:* A/C, TV, minibar, hair dryer.

Portales Hotel 🟊 Portales Hotel is one of the more gracious hotels in Bolivia. It's located in Cochabamba's ritziest residential neighborhood, Recoleta, surrounded by the city's most popular restaurants and bars. Almost all of the rooms look out onto the sunny and lush pool area. They are all comfortable and spacious with dark-wood tones and very clean carpets. The sparkling, tiled bathrooms are large with their own bidets. Don't expect much luxury here, though: The rooms are more like what you'd find in a roadside motel in the U.S, functional but not elegant. The suites have separate sitting areas with a table and two chairs. The bathrooms in the suites are enormous and wood-paneled—they feel like locker rooms in an exclusive club. One complaint: The exercise room, sauna, and Jacuzzi are pretty run down and in desperate need of renovation; I suggest paying the 20Bs ($2.60) admission to enjoy the facilities of a nearby health club. The friendly staff will happily give you directions.

Av. Pando 1271, Cochabamba. © **0800-6868** or 0104/4285-444. Fax 0104/4242-071. www.portales hotel.com. 106 units. $95 double; $170 suite. Rates include buffet breakfast. AE, MC, V. **Amenities:** 2 restaurants; bar; outdoor pool w/beautiful landscaping; squash court; really tiny exercise room; Jacuzzi; sauna; small business center; salon; room service; massage; same-day laundry service; dry cleaning. *In room:* A/C, TV, minibar, hair dryer, safe.

A HOTEL OUTSIDE OF TOWN

Hacienda De Kaluyo Resort 🟊🟊🟊 *(Finds* For the ultimate escape, stay 30 minutes outside of town at the newest and most interesting resort in all of Bolivia. Under construction for 12 years, the Hacienda De Kaluyo finally opened in 2003 and provides a restful getaway. The place feels more like the South of France than Bolivia; a grand private driveway leads to a beautiful hacienda built next to a 19th-century chapel (where weddings are frequently held). The vistas are beautiful, the swimming pool is incredibly serene, and the outdoor restaurant overlooks the endless fields leading down to a large lake. Rooms are in a two-story building, separate from the pool and restaurant area so guests won't be disturbed when events are in progress. Every piece of furniture in the rooms was designed and built in Bolivia—from the lovely wooden beds to the delicate wrought-iron lamps and ceramic sconces. The bathrooms are spacious and sparkling. There are also two large cabins with their own private garages and kitchenettes; these cabins are very cozy and rustic with wood-beamed ceilings and exposed brick. There are hiking trails all around the property, a lovely open-air gym, a soccer field, and a basketball court. If you ask the friendly owners, they will arrange a water-skiing excursion for you; mountain bikes are also available. This is an incredibly romantic place, perfect for a wedding or anniversary reunion, but as yet is almost totally undiscovered.

Camino La Angostura (at the intersection of the old highway to Santa Cruz), Tarata. © **0104/4576-594.** Fax 0104/4451-662. www.kaluyo.com. 17 units. $60 double; $120 cabin for 4 people. Rates include breakfast. AE, MC, V. **Amenities:** 2 restaurants; bar; lounge; beautiful outdoor pool w/magnificent vistas; tennis court; outdoor exercise room; game room; limited watersports equipment rental; laundry service. *In room:* TV, kitchenette in cabins.

WHERE TO DINE

Saltenería "Los Castores" 🟊 on Av. Ballivián 790 at the corner of Oruro (© **0104/4259-585**) specializes in *salteñas*. There's no menu here; you can only order *salteñas de pollo* (chicken) or *de carne* (meat). They cost 3.50Bs (45¢) each, and they are out of this world. You can do as the Bolivians do and eat breakfast here, but the place is open until 2pm.

Casa de Campo *Finds* BOLIVIAN   Cochabamba's best Bolivian restaurant is enormous. On weekends the place is filled to the brim with locals enjoying traditional cuisine. It's an unassuming place but the food is divine. Come here to sample real Cochabamban dishes such as the *chanka de pollo* (chicken soup with beans) or the spicy *pique lobo* soup. If you're feeling adventurous, try one of the local sausages—chorizo or *chuleta*. For the main course, there are several stews; the most popular is the *picante de pollo* (a bit spicy with a locally grown green pepper). If you're in the mood for meat, the "Lapping" is excellent. It's a very thin (although sometimes not very tender) steak, grilled and served with broad beans, tomatoes, and sliced onion. (It seems to be a big mystery to everyone why it's called "Lapping.") This place really gets busy after 9pm on Friday and Saturday when there's a long wait for tables, so arrive early.

Av. Uyuni 618. © 0104/4243-937. Main courses 24Bs–35Bs ($3.10–$4.55). MC, V. Daily noon–midnight (till 1am Fri–Sat).

La Cantonata ITALIAN   This is one of the most romantic restaurants in town, with fancy tablecloths, formal place settings, and flickering candles. You can also relax by the cozy fireplace and gaze out through the huge picture windows. For a few hours, you might forget that you're in Bolivia; it's easy to imagine that you're in your local Italian restaurant. All the pasta except the spaghetti is homemade. Choices include ravioli Bolognese, *spaghetti pescatore* (spaghetti with a garlic tomato sauce and shellfish), and *pasta al pesto*. Besides pasta, there is a good selection of meat and fish, including several different types of steak. I recommend the *surubí alla Cantonata* (an Amazonian fish with oysters, white wine, and lemon sauce). The pizza here is also quite good.

Calle Mayor Rocha 409 (corner of España). © 0104/4259-222. Main courses 31Bs–84Bs ($4–$11). AE, MC, V. Daily noon–2:30pm and 6:30–11:30pm.

La Estancia PARRILLADA/GRILLED MEAT   At more than 25 years old, La Estancia is one of the oldest restaurants in Cochabamba, and it's still going strong. The chefs must be doing something right. All the meat is juicy, accented with a fresh charcoal taste. However, red meat isn't the only thing cooking on the grill—grilled fish is another specialty of the house. The *surubí* (an Amazonian fish) is done just right. You can also order chicken and all the intestines that you could ever want. For a sampling of several different cuts of meat, try the *carne argentina*. Also tasty is the *filete de lomo* (filet of beef). The restaurant is located in the residential area of Recolata, on a pleasant pedestrian-only street, a cheap, 5-minute cab ride from downtown. The Portales Hotel (p. 223) is a short 10-minute walk away.

Av. Uyuni 786. © 0104/4249-262. Main courses 30Bs–35Bs ($3.90–$4.55). AE, MC, V. Daily noon–4pm and 7pm–12:30am.

COCHABAMBA AFTER DARK

Cochabamba is a university town with more than 27,000 students. On Friday and Saturday nights, this town is hopping. Most of the trendy bars and cafes are clustered around Avenida España between Colombia and Ecuador. One of the most happening is newly reopened **Metrópolis** on the corner of España and Ecuador. In Recoleta, there are several bars and nightclubs on Av. Uyuni, close to La Estancia restaurant (see above). Also, locals come out in droves on the weekends to sip beer and watch the action on the Prado—there are tons of cafes and places on Avenida Ballivián (Paseo el Prado). They're all within a block or two of the Hotel Diplomat (p. 222).

8 Santa Cruz de la Sierra

858km (532 miles) SE of La Paz; 473km (293 miles) E of Cochabamba; 612km (379 miles) NE of Sucre

Santa Cruz (also known as Santa Cruz de la Sierra) is the least Bolivian of all Bolivian cities. In a country defined by the peaks and valleys of the Andes, the flat roads here seem terribly out of place. If you come here after you have acclimated yourself to the cold nights and thin air so characteristic of the high plateau area, the tropical heat and humidity might feel a bit oppressive. Unlike Potosí or La Paz, Santa Cruz—Bolivia's largest city—doesn't have much history or a charming historic area. It's a major railroad hub, and oil refining is a major industry here, so people come to Santa Cruz to make money and to escape their past. In this brash and flashy city, SUVs outnumber *trufis*. But visitors should make Santa Cruz their base for exploring the wealth of attractions—Inca ruins, historic Jesuit missions, and a unique national park—only a few hours away from this booming metropolis.

ESSENTIALS
GETTING THERE
BY PLANE   **LAB** (© 0800-3001) and **Aero Sur** (© 0102/22430-430 in La Paz, or 0103/367-400 in Santa Cruz) offer daily flights to Santa Cruz from La Paz, Cochabamba, and Sucre. One-way tickets cost between $60 and $110 each. Additionally, both LAB and **American Airlines** (© 800/433-7300) offer service from Miami to Santa Cruz (LAB flies nonstop while American's flights touch down in La Paz first).

All planes arrive at the very modern Viru Viru Airport, which is about 16km (10 miles) outside of town. Taxis from the airport to the center of town cost between 50Bs and 60Bs ($6.50–$8). There's also an airport bus, which leaves the airport about every 20 minutes and drops passengers off at the bus terminal and in the nearby neighborhoods. The ride costs 8Bs ($1).

BY BUS   The Santa Cruz bus terminal on Avenida Cañoto and Avenida Irala is a truly mad scene. Thousands of people crowd the station at all times of the day, and there's no central information office, so you have to figure out on your own where the bus you want is leaving from. Plus, not all the buses leave from the terminal—many buses depart from offices across the street from the terminal. Many bus companies have offices outside the terminal on Avenida Irala. Buses from La Paz usually arrive in the morning. The 14-hour journey costs 120Bs ($16). Buses from Cochabamba take 10 hours and cost 50Bs ($6.50) for a normal bus, 80Bs ($10) for a *bus cama*. Buses from Sucre take a grueling 12 hours and cost 60Bs ($8) for a normal bus, 80Bs ($10) for a *bus cama*. See "Getting Around: By Bus" in "Planning Your Trip to Bolivia," earlier in this chapter, for bus company information.

GETTING AROUND
Santa Cruz is a circular city, with each neighborhood known as a "ring" *(anillo)*. The first ring is the first circle around the city; as you move further from the center, you reach the second and third anillos. Santa Cruz is quickly becoming a prime example of urban sprawl. The center of the city is getting smaller, while the outskirts of town keep moving farther and farther away from the center of town. Taxis are by far the easiest way to get around. From the center of town to the hotels and restaurants in the nearby suburbs, a taxi should cost $2 to $3. Plaza 24 de Septiembre is the commercial heart of Santa Cruz; from here, you can walk to all the banks, travel agencies, and centrally located hotels.

VISITOR INFORMATION

For information about Santa Cruz and nearby attractions (the Jesuit missions, the Inca ruins of Samaipata, and Amboró National Park), your best bet is to contact **Rosario Tours** ✆ (ℂ **0103/369-656;** www.rosario-tours.com), Arenales 193 between Beni and Murillo.

FAST FACTS   Magri Turismo (ℂ 0103/345-663), Calle Warnes and the corner of Potosí, is the American Express representative in Santa Cruz. Unfortunately, you can't change traveler's checks here. If you need to change traveler's checks or exchange money, you should head to **Cambio Alemán Transatlántico** on Calle 24 de Septiembre in the main plaza. There is also a **Citibank** on Avenida Mons Rivero at the corner of Asunción. **Hospital Universitario Japonés** (ℂ 0103/462-032) on Avenida Japón in the *tercer anillo* (3rd ring) is the best hospital in town. In an emergency, call ℂ 0103/462-031. If you need a pharmacy, try **Farmacia Gutiérrez** at 21 de Mayo 26; for deliveries, call ℂ 0103/361-777. Also nearby is **Farmacia Santa María** on the corner of 21 de Mayo and Junín. The **post office** is located at Junín 150 between Plaza 24 de Septiembre and 21 de Mayo. You can take care of all your laundry needs at **Lavandería España** on Calle España 160. The best Internet cafe is **Full Internet,** Ayacucho 208, on the corner of Velasco. The entrance is on the second floor, so look for the stairs on Ayacucho.

WHAT TO SEE & DO

There is not much to see and do in Santa Cruz itself—most travelers use Santa Cruz as a base for trips to the surrounding area. If you're determined to do something while you're in Santa Cruz, here are a few suggestions: The **Museo Etno-folklórico Municipal,** located in Parque Arenal, has an interesting display of tools, baskets, and musical instruments used by indigenous groups of Bolivia. The museum is open Monday through Friday from 8:30am to noon and 2:30 to 6:30pm; admission is 5Bs (65¢). Right next door, you can explore **Parque Arenal,** where you can rent paddleboats for 8Bs ($1) per half-hour. The **cathedral** on Plaza 24 de Septiembre houses a small religious museum that is open on Tuesday and Thursday from 10am to noon and 4 to 6pm and on Sunday from 10am to noon and 6 to 8pm. The **Museo de Historia y Archivo Regional de Santa Cruz de la Sierra,** Junín 151, offers a host of exhibits ranging from ceramics to photography.

For something outdoorsy just 15 minutes from the city, check out the new **Ecological Park Yuaga Guazu** ("Grand Paradise"). It's a private botanical garden that used to be a nursery. You must prearrange a visit with a guide. The walking tour takes about an hour and a half and will give you a great glimpse of the flora and fauna of the Amazon (though it's not worth coming here if you're actually heading to the Amazon). You'll see a dizzying variety of native plants from mango trees to 15 different kinds of palm trees, including the Mara hardwood tree (a kind of mahogany). There are 200 native plants for a total of 750 different species. This is definitely a paradise for garden-lovers. To arrange your visit here, contact **Rosario Tours** ✆ (ℂ **0103/369-656;** www.rosario-tours. com), Arenales 193 between Beni and Murillo; they arrange transportation and a guide, and it usually costs no more than $18 per person.

SAMAIPATA

Samaipata is a charming mountain town located about 2 hours southwest of Santa Cruz. The main attraction here are the Inca ruins known as **El Fuerte.** The ruins are a huge mysterious complex, much of it unexcavated. From what remains, it's hard to envision the site's former glory. The most impressive structure here is the **Chinkana** ⚑, also known as the labyrinth. It consists mainly of a hole that was originally 30m (9 ft.) deep. The actual function of this hole is unknown, but some scientists believe that it may have been used as a cemetery; other scientists have found nearby tunnels and surmise that this may have been an underground tunnel used to connect other Inca villages. From the top of El Fuerte, you have great views of the surrounding mountains and perfect sight-lines of other Inca sites. Most scientists believe that the Incas built these villages in a pattern. At this site, you will also see what are believed to be amphitheaters and temples for religious ceremonies. The site is open daily from 9am to 5pm, and admission is 20Bs ($2.60).

GETTING THERE   To understand Samaipata and the ruins of El Fuerte, you really need an experienced guide. **Rosario Tours** ⚑, Arenales 193 between Beni and Murillo (© **0103/369-656;** www.rosario-tours.com), organizes day trips here with English-speaking guides. **Michael Blendinger** (© **0103/9446-816;** mblendinger@cotas.com.bo) also arranges trips to El Fuerte and nature hikes through the area. His office is in Samaipata, but he can arrange transportation from Santa Cruz. You can also arrange your own private taxi to Samaipata by contacting **Expreso Samaipata** (© **0102/2335-067**). In Santa Cruz, the taxis leave from the Residencial Señor de Los Milagros on Avenida Omar Chávez Ortiz.

AMBORO NATIONAL PARK

Amboró is only 3 hours west of Santa Cruz, and it is one of the most pristine national parks in all of Bolivia. The park covers more than 1.5 million acres and encompasses four different biodiversity zones, including a part of the Amazon basin, subtropical forests, temperate woodlands, and the cool mountainous terrain of the Andes. More than 700 species of birds have been seen in the area. Some of the rarer species include the red-fronted macaw, Bolivian recurve-bill, and rufous-faced antpitta. Plus, you'll have the opportunity to see monkeys here. There are also some fantastic hiking trails that will take you to caves and waterfalls.

GETTING THERE   The roads to Amboró can be rough. I highly recommend taking a trip here with a guided tour. **Rosario Tours** ⚑ (© **0103/3369-656;** www.rosario-tours.com) organizes overnight bird-watching trips. **Michael Blendinger** (© **0103/9446-816;** mblendinger@cotas.com.bo) also arranges excursions into the park.

THE JESUIT MISSIONS ⚑

In the late 16th century, the Jesuits set out to the hinterlands of Bolivia to save the souls of the indigenous people. These missionaries set up settlements *(reducciones)* headed by two to three Jesuit priests who helped develop thriving cultural and religious centers for the local people. For mainly political reasons, the Jesuits were expelled from South America in 1773 and suppressed by Pope Clement XIV. Today, you can visit some of these missions, which have been amazingly preserved and restored. **San Javier** and **Concepción** are the two closest and most accessible missions from Santa Cruz. The 5-hour drive to San Javier is a sight itself: Along the way, you'll pass through Mennonite communities and see the landscape change from lush green farmland to tropical shrubbery. The road is paved, but it can be a bit rough.

San Javier was founded in 1691; it was the first Jesuit mission in Bolivia. At its height, the community included about 3,000 people. The church of San Javier is the centerpiece of the town's original central plaza. The remarkable church was constructed entirely of local wood. The ornate woodcarvings painted with local dyes are quite spectacular; the gold-colored interior is just as impressive. The carvings on the altars illustrate the story of the Jesuits.

The road to Concepción from San Javier is mostly unpaved. Once you arrive, you will find a similarly ornate wood church (with a silver altar), cloisters, and a historic main plaza. Unlike San Javier, much of Concepción has been restored. In the workshops adjacent to the church, you can observe local artisans restoring statues and creating new ones. In my opinion, these two missions are the most impressive of the six Jesuit missions in the Santa Cruz area. If you don't feel like spending a few extra days traveling along some rough roads to the Santa Ana, San Miguel, San Rafael, and San José missions, don't worry—you won't be missing out.

GETTING THERE   It's extremely difficult to arrange public transportation to the Jesuit missions. Your best bet is to arrange a trip through a travel agency. I recommend using **Rosario Tours** ⟨⟨, Arenales 193 between Beni and Murillo (© **0103/369-656;** www.rosario-tours.com). The trip includes an English-speaking guide, transportation, and all meals. The price varies depending on how many people are on the trip. **Magri Turismo,** Calle Warnes and the corner of Potosí (© **0103/345-663**), also organizes excursions to the missions.

SHOPPING IN SANTA CRUZ

Because Santa Cruz is one of the largest and wealthiest cities in Bolivia, you'll find many trendy boutiques and international retailers here. If you're looking for unique gifts typical of the area, you should buy jewelry or handicrafts. For jewelry, I recommend **Joyería Andrea** at Junín 177. This store specializes in a stone called the Bolivian, a mix of amethyst and citrine. For high-quality handicrafts, your best option is **ARTECAMPO** at Mons Salvatierra 407 (near the corner of Vallegrande). This beautiful store is an association of artists from the countryside. All the money you spend here will go directly to the artisans.

WHERE TO STAY

If you're in town for the International Trade Fair (held annually in late Sept), you won't find a better place than **Buganvillas** ⟨⟨, Avenida Roca Coronado (© **0103/551-212;** www.buganvillasbolivia.com). The hotel complex is located right next to the convention center (although it is about a 15-min. ride from the center of the city). The beautiful rooms are all actually fully equipped apartments. The complex has three pools, a spa, several restaurants, and a minimart. Rates range from $60 for a one-bedroom apartment to $130 for a five-bedroom apartment.

If you're looking for budget accommodations, I recommend **La Siesta Hotel,** Calle Vallegrande 17, near the corner of Ayacucho (© **0103/330-146;** lasiesta@ infonet.com.bo). The rooms aren't fancy (they all have ugly linoleum floors), but they are comfortable with private bathrooms. The more expensive rooms ($35 for a double) have cable TV and air-conditioning. Plus, when it gets hot here, you can relax by the pool. Rates include breakfast, and there's a computer with free Internet access for guests.

Gran Hotel Santa Cruz ⟨⟨   This is the best hotel downtown, close to the main plaza, about a block away. The building has a faux-colonial touch with pillars and grand archways, but once you walk inside, it's clear that you're in a modern-day first-class hotel. The management seems to have the knack for putting everything together perfectly. The rooms have classic moldings and are spacious with bright tiles and large comfy chairs, perfect for sitting back and relaxing. The bathrooms are medium-sized with marble sinks and tiles. The spacious junior suites come with in-room Jacuzzis.

Calle René Moreno, Santa Cruz. © **0103/348-811.** Fax 0103/324-194. hsancruz@bibosi.sca.entelnet.bo. 80 units. $139–$159 double; $169–$189 suite. AE, MC, V. **Amenities:** Restaurant; bar; large outdoor pool; small exercise room; Jacuzzi; sauna; small business center; room service; massage; laundry service; dry cleaning, nonsmoking rooms. *In room:* A/C, TV, minibar, hair dryer, safe.

Hotel Los Tajibos ✿✿ The best hotel in Santa Cruz is a 10-minute taxi ride from the center of town, but if you stay here you can walk to the many bars and restaurants on Avenida San Martín. The hotel's centerpiece is the lush pool area, and the whole place feels more like a resort than a business hotel. Many of the guests here are, in fact, business travelers—including a continuous influx of flight crews and visiting sports teams. Rooms are scattered in several low-rise buildings and have a tropical theme. They are extremely comfortable with small sitting areas, large balconies, and large marble bathrooms. The two airy restaurants open up onto the pool area; there is live entertainment in the evening. Free Internet service is available for guests in the tiny business center (the connection is awfully slow, though). This hotel has one of the most lavish breakfast buffets in Bolivia—it's more like a brunch with made-to-order omelettes and all kinds of local sausages and pastries—so bring your appetite!

Av. San Martín 455, Santa Cruz. © **0103/3421-000.** Fax 0103/3426-994. www.lostajiboshotel.com. 185 units. $140–$185 double; $220 suite. Rates include breakfast buffet. AE, DC, MC, V. **Amenities:** 2 restaurants; bar; lounge; large outdoor pool; small exercise room; Jacuzzi; sauna; small business center; room service; massage; same-day laundry service; dry cleaning; nonsmoking room. *In room:* A/C, TV, minibar, hair dryer.

Yotaú ✿ *(finds)* From the outside, this all-suite hotel resembles a Swiss chalet. On the inside, it feels more like a high-rise apartment building. The hotel has the aura of a resort, although it is only 10 minutes outside of the city center. The large rooms have heavy wood furniture, big beds, and dark carpeting with separate sitting areas and their own plant-covered terraces. The bathrooms are huge. The large family apartment comes with three bedrooms and sleeps six. This hotel is a great choice if you want to escape from the city and spend your time in Santa Cruz relaxing by a nice pool. If you want to be closer to the action, stay at the Gran Hotel Santa Cruz.

Av. San Martín 7, Barrio Equipetrol, Santa Cruz. © **0103/367-799.** Fax 0103/363-952. www.yotau.com.bo. 95 units. $179 double; $205 apt for 2; $252 apt for 4; $300 3-bedroom apt for 6. Rates include breakfast. MC, V. **Amenities:** Restaurant; bar; outdoor pool; exercise room; Jacuzzi; sauna; small business center; room service; massage; laundry service; dry cleaning. *In room:* A/C, TV, minibar, fridge, hair dryer, safe.

WHERE TO DINE

If you need a break while wandering downtown, stop in at the **Victory Café,** in the Galería Pasco Viejo at Junín and 21 de Mayo (© **0103/3322-935**). There's a great big terrace on the second floor where locals gather for coffee, drinks, and light meals. It's the most happening place near the main plaza; it's open Monday through Saturday from 9am to 2am.

Casa del Camba ✿✿✿ *(Moments)* BOLIVIAN The food here is excellent, but I also recommend coming for the lively atmosphere. Every night, local singers and dancers dress up in traditional costumes and really ham it up, while the fast-moving waiters scurry about wearing white gaucho (cowboy) uniforms and straw hats. Plus, because Santa Cruz has such pleasant weather, it's great to find a restaurant where you can dine alfresco. The huge outdoor dining area is filled with trees and even a waterfall. The whole place has a *Fantasy Island* atmosphere. Even if there were no show here, the food could keep the place going. Some of the dishes, such as *keperi* (corned beef with salad, yuca, and rice and cheese) and *majao de charque* (beef jerky), are specialties from the Santa Cruz area. There are also dishes here that I have never seen before anywhere in Bolivia. I especially recommend the tasty *majao de pato* (rice and duck, with a fried egg and a fried banana). Overall, dining at this restaurant is a very unique Bolivian experience, one that you won't soon forget.

Av. Cristóbal de Mendoza 539. ℂ 0103/427-864. Main courses 28Bs–38Bs ($3.65–$4.95). MC, V. Daily noon–4pm and 6pm–2am.

Parrilla Don Miguel ☆ *Finds* GRILLED MEAT   If you like steak, you must dine here. Don Miguel is an unassuming restaurant located on a main thoroughfare leading away from downtown, but it's the best place in town for anything grilled. You'll find succulent Argentine and Bolivian beef grilled to perfection, all kinds of sausages, chicken, and *surubí* (an Amazonian whitefish). A popular family option is a parrilla that feeds four to five people for 110Bs ($14) and a variety of sides including the yummy fried yuca and *arroz con queso* (rice pilaf with cheese), the quintessential dish from Santa Cruz. There's also a good selection of Bolivian wines and interesting deserts such as the *dulce de batata* (sweet potato jam). To get here from either downtown or one of the outlying hotels, a taxi should cost no more than $2. The friendly staff will call a taxi for your return trip.

Av. Viedma 586. ℂ 0103/3321-823. Main courses 35Bs ($4.55); parrilla for 2–3 people 60Bs ($8), parrilla for 4–5 people 110Bs ($14). AE, DC, MC, V. Daily 11:30am–3pm and 6:30pm–1am.

SANTA CRUZ AFTER DARK

The **Irish Pub** on Calle 24 de Septiembre right on the main plaza is a popular watering hole for foreigners. **Avenida San Martín** in the second ring is lined with outdoor cafes, bars, and pubs. **Automanía** on Calle Comercial El Chuubi and **La Ronería** (right next door) are two of the most happening places in town. Salsa dancers should seek out **El Loro en Su Salsa** at Warnes 280.

6

Brazil

by Shawn Blore & Alexandra de Vries

There's a joke Brazilians like to tell: During the creation of the world, one of the archangels peering over God's shoulder at the work in progress couldn't help noticing that one country had been especially favored. "You've given everything to Brazil," he said. "It has the longest beaches, the largest river, the biggest forest, the best soil. The weather's always warm and sunny. There are no floods or hurricanes, no natural disasters at all. Don't you think that's a little unfair?" "Ah," God replied, "but just wait until you see the people I'm putting there."

One hundred percent accuracy rarely comes with a punch line, but there is a large grain of truth in that joke. Brazil as a nation is unusually blessed, especially if you're a visitor. There are 8,050km (5,000 miles) of coastline, some of it packed with cafes and partygoers, some of it blissfully empty. For adventurers and wildlife-watchers, there are rainforests and wetlands teeming with all manner of exotic critters. For those who thrive on cities and civic architecture, Brazil has some of the oldest in the New World—and some of the newest in the whole world. For foodies, there are restaurants to match the loftiest standards, and regional cuisine that's as yet unavailable in New York. For those who like music, Brazil could be a lifetime study. And for those who like their music loud and outdoors, preferably with cold beer to boot, there's Carnaval (and New Year's Eve, not to mention almost any night of the week in Salvador).

In recent years, Brazil has been devoting extra time and resources to its tourism infrastructure. New hotels and inns have gone up throughout the country. Many cities have brand-new airports. Yet despite the modern Western appearance of the place, no one could ever accuse Brazilians of making a religion of efficiency. When it comes to getting things done, Brazilians much prefer to get along.

Harmony can mean literally staying in key when you sing along at a street party, or it can mean spending all of Sunday watching soccer, or taking off weekends and some afternoons for quality time with your buddies at the beach. It can mean devoting countless hours of effort to a single night's party. Mostly, harmony seems to require never taking anything all that seriously. At this, Brazilians excel.

1 The Regions in Brief

Brazil is huge. Its 160 million citizens inhabit the fifth-largest country in the world. In a country this size, geographic variation is only to be expected. The northern third of the county is dominated by the Amazon, the vast tropical rainforest with the river at its heart. The central interior of the country is dominated by the *planalto,* a high dry plateau covered in *cerrado,* a type of dry scrub forest reminiscent of California chaparral. West of the planalto but south of the

Brazil

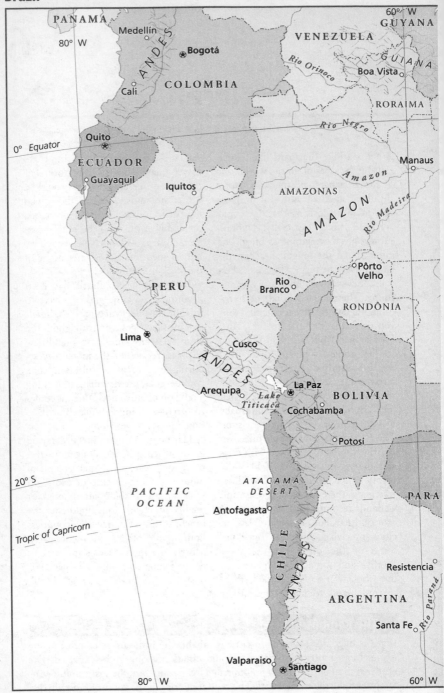

Georgetown

Paramaribo

Cayenne

SURINAME

FRENCH
GUIANA
(FRANCE)

HIGHLANDS

AMAPÁ

Macapá

40° W

ATLANTIC
OCEAN

Equator 0°

BASIN

Belém

São Luís

Santarém

Rio Tapajós

Rio Xingu

Rio Tocantins

Fortaleza

Fernando
de Noronha

PARÁ

MARANHÃO

CEARÁ

Teresina

RIO GRANDE
DO NORTE

Natal

B R A Z I L

PIAUÍ

PARAÍBA

João
Pessoa

PERNAMBUCO

Recife

TOCANTINS

Rio São Francisco

Maceió

ALAGOAS

SERGIPE

MATO
GROSSO

BAHIA

Aracaju

Salvador

R. Paraguai

Cuiabá

Cáceres

BRAZILIAN

Brasília

GOIÁS

HIGHLANDS

PANTANAL

Goiânia

Corumbá

Campo
Grande

Uberlândia

MINAS
GERAIS

Belo
Horizonte

ESPÍRITO
SANTO

MATO GROSSO
DO SUL

Rio Paraná

SÃO
PAULO

São
Paulo

RIO DE
JANEIRO

Vitória

20° S

GUAY

Asunción

PARANÁ

Santos

Rio de Janeiro

Tropic of Capricorn

Foz do Iguaçu

Curitiba

SANTA
CATARINA

Florianópolis

ATLANTIC
OCEAN

RIO GRANDE
DO SUL

Pôrto Alegre

URUGUAY

Rio Grande

Buenos
Aires

Montevideo

40° W

0   400 mi

0   400 km

233

Amazon rainforest, you find the Pantanal, a wetland the size of Florida. Brazil's northeast is a land apart: Running roughly from São Luis to Salvador, the coast is still dominated by small cities and sugar cane, and the culture is strongly Afro-Brazilian, while on the very dry interior plateau those *Nordestinos* (northeasterners) who haven't yet fled to the cities still eke out a living on the land. Brazil's two chief cities, Rio de Janeiro and São Paulo, stand within a few hundred kilometers of each other close to the country's south coast. São Paulo is the larger and more important of the two, but Rio is by far the more interesting. Brazil's small south is inhabited largely by descendants of European immigrants. It's the most densely settled and best-organized part of Brazil. It has small, livable cites and quiet beaches, but its interest to visitors is limited.

Politically, Brazil is a federal republic—much like the United States or Germany—that's divided into 26 states and one federal territory. Periodically, as the Brazilian population continues its slow shift inland, parts of existing states are hived off to create whole new ones. The youngest state, Tocantins, was created in 1988.

If you have just 1 week to spend in Brazil, make the most of two or three destinations. Rio de Janeiro is a must-see—plan to spend 3 days visiting its sights. With 4 days left, you must make a choice. If historic architecture and vibrant Brazilian music are your thing, Salvador is your destination. Beach buffs may want to spend a day at Praia do Forte near Salvador or Porto de Galinhas near Recife. Nature lovers should head for the Pantanal or Iguaçu Falls; the Amazon is out of reach (you'll waste almost 2 days getting there and back), and the wildlife viewing in the Pantanal is more impressive. Architecture buffs should travel to Brasília to see the incredible modernist architecture.

If you have 2 weeks to travel, and your heart is set on seeing the Amazon, spend your first week as detailed above and then fly to Manaus. If comfort is high on your list, by all means book a lodge on the Rio Negro, but if you can handle just a little discomfort, you'll get a far better jungle experience by booking a guided boat or kayak trip. Next, head to Iguaçu Falls and/or Brasília (a day in each is enough). It's worth ending your trip in São Paulo to spend a day or so in one of the world's largest cities.

RIO DE JANEIRO   Few cities are as striking as Rio de Janeiro. From tropical beach, the mountains leap up to 800m (2,600-ft.) heights; one of the mountains, Corcovado, is crowned by the city's landmark statue of Christ. The city folds itself into the narrow bits of land between beach and mountain and offers a great variety of sightseeing. As striking as the geography is the culture, perhaps best expressed in music and nightlife. Samba is alive and well, augmented by many vibrant newer forms of distinctly Brazilian music. It's a great way to explore the local culture. The event of the year is Carnaval, truly the biggest party in the world.

SÃO PAULO   Some 30 million people live in and around São Paulo. It's the largest city not only in Brazil but also in all of South America. In many ways, São Paulo is Brazil's New York: It's the economic and financial heart of the country. It's also the melting pot, attracting the best and brightest to come and make their fortune. The range of ethnicities in São Paulo is astounding—Italian, Middle Eastern, Japanese, Jewish, Nordestino, and countless others. The city overflows with restaurants, including the best fine dining in Brazil. Much to the annoyance of Rio, São Paulo has also emerged as the cultural capital of Brazil, particularly strong in new Brazilian theater. And it's the best place in Brazil to shop.

Shameless Plug
For more in-depth coverage of Brazil, pick up a copy of *Frommer's Brazil*.

THE NORTHEAST   Even in a country with such strong regional differences, Brazil's northeast stands apart. Everything *Nordeste* is different: Its food is richer, its cities more historic, its music more vibrant, and its people more African. (Nordeste politics, a Brazilian would likely add, are also more Byzantine and more corrupt.) This was the first part of Brazil to be settled, the area where sugar cane and slavery dominated the economy and society for more than 3 centuries. The downturn in the sugar economy left the area a backwater for decades, and only with the recent advent of tourism have Nordeste fortunes really begun to pick up. For visitors, the northeast (which roughly encompasses the area from Salvador to Recife and Natal) offers a year-round tropical climate with long white-sand beaches, historic cities, and a vibrant Afro-Brazilian culture, which is reflected in the cuisine, the festivals, and especially the music and dance. **Olinda** is a quiet colonial gem of a city, while **Salvador**'s 16th-century colonial core has been transformed into a kind of permanent musical main stage.

THE AMAZON   The largest rainforest in the world is so vast that it defies easy description. All of western Europe would fit comfortably with space to spare beneath its leafy canopy. Thanks in large part to media coverage of the many threats to this region, interest in ecotourism and visits to the Amazon have exploded. The jumping-off point for most trips to the Brazilian Amazon is the city of **Manaus,** located where the Rio Negro joins the Rio Solimões to form the Amazon River. Manaus itself is surprisingly modern and moderately interesting.

THE PLANALTO   The central interior of Brazil is a high, hot plateau, originally covered in a *cerrado,* a type of dry scrub forest reminiscent of California chaparral. The chief city of this region is **Brasília,** created from scratch to serve as the federal capital in 1960. As people moved to the interior and irrigation schemes came on line, the cerrado was cleared for agriculture. Much of Goânia (the state surrounding Brasília) now consists of large-scale farms, while the cerrado has become the most threatened ecosystem in Brazil.

THE SOUTHWEST   Brazil's southwest is a broad flat plain, dotted with craggy highlands and populated chiefly by ranchers, cowhands, and commercial farms. Within this vast and not especially intriguing region, the two highlights are the **Pantanal** and **Iguaçu Falls.** A wetland the size of France, the Pantanal has traditionally been overlooked in favor of the Amazon, but that's changing as people become increasingly aware of the incredible wildlife-viewing opportunities the area offers. The Iguaçu Falls, a UNESCO World Heritage site, are located where the borders of Brazil, Argentina, and Paraguay meet. These truly spectacular falls are made up of 275 falls that cascade from 72m (240 ft.) down a 2km (1½-mile) wide precipice in a fabulous jungle setting.

The region's gateways, Cuiabá and Campo Grande, are small and modern cities; each contains a university and distribution networks for its surrounding agricultural industries.

THE SOUTHEAST   Settled largely by immigrants from Europe, Brazil's southeast is the wealthiest and best organized part of the country. The main tourist destination is the **Ilha de Santa Catarina** (aka **Florianópolis**) best known for its miles and miles of gorgeous beaches, excellent seafood, and quaint Azorean fishing villages. The area is particularly popular with Brazilians from other parts of the country, who rave about Floripa's fair-skinned, green-eyed residents, affluent communities, quaint Portuguese fishing villages, pristine and unpolluted beaches, and calm traffic. It can be a restorative change of pace from the rest of South America

2 Planning Your Trip to Brazil

VISITOR INFORMATION

Travelers planning their trip to Brazil can browse the site of the Brazilian national tourism agency Embratur at **www.embratur.gov.bv**. The Brazilian Embassy in the United Kingdom has an outstanding website with links to all the state and many city tourism websites at **www.brazil.org.uk**. Visitors to Rio de Janeiro can get in touch with the city's tourist agency **Riotur** at © **212/375-0801** or www.riodejaneiro-turismo.com.br. Other useful websites include:

- **www.brazilnuts.com**: For information on packages and tours of Brazil.
- **www.naturesafaris.com.br**: A commercial site with a good, basic natural history of the Amazon.
- **www.emtursa.ba.gov.br**: Salvador's good official tourism agency.
- **www.infoBrasilia.com.br**: For great info on Brasília's architecture and design.
- **www.turismo.mt.gov.br**: The Pantanal is covered by the official site of the state of Mato Grosso.
- **www.iguassu.com.br**: Iguaçu's very good official site.

IN BRAZIL

Within Brazil, you'll have to rely on each city's tourist office, varying in quality from the extremely helpful in Rio, Salvador, Recife, and Manaus to the more indifferent ones in São Paulo or Natal. There is no helpful **Embratur** office in Brazil to provide assistance to the traveler in need of Brazil-wide information; its website (**www.embratur.gov.bv**) is your best bet. For more detailed planning information, contact **Brazil Nuts** (© **800/553-9959;** www.brazilnuts.com). The staff possesses a vast amount of knowledge about the country and its attractions. Its website is a fount of information; it can answer any questions you may have about Brazil.

Tip: Good countrywide or regional maps are almost nonexistent in Brazil. It's best to bring a good map with you.

ENTRY REQUIREMENTS

Nationals of the United States, Canada, Australia, and New Zealand require a visa to visit Brazil. British nationals and holders of an E.U. passport do not require a visa, but do need a passport valid for at least 6 months and a return ticket. A number of visa types are available; cost, processing time, and documentation requirements vary. American citizens pay $100 for a standard single-entry tourist visa that is valid for 90 days; count on at least 2 weeks of processing time. For Canadians, a similar visa costs C$72 and takes about the same processing time. Visas for Australians and New Zealanders cost A$88 and NZ$55, respectively, plus local handling fees; visas in both countries take about 2 weeks to process.

Upon arrival in Brazil, visitors will receive a 90-day entry stamp in their passport and a stamped entry card. Hang on to the card for dear life, as losing it will result in a major hassle and a possible fine when you leave. If necessary, the visa can be renewed once for another 90 days. Visa renewals are obtained through

Telephone Dialing Info at a Glance

Brazilian phone companies are going from seven-digit dialing to eight-digit dialing. In São Paulo both seven- and eight-digit numbers are used and many cities haven't started the switchover yet. Telephone numbers are up-to-date as of press time, but if you encounter difficulty getting through to a number, check with the hotel staff for any recent changes. In some cities, new numbers just require adding one digit; in other cities, entire prefixes are being changed.

- **To place a call from your home country to Brazil,** dial the international access code (011 in the U.S. and Canada, 0011 in Australia, 0170 in New Zealand, 00 in the U.K.), plus the country code (55), plus the Brazilian area code minus the first 0, followed by the number. For example, a call from the United States to Rio would be 011+55+21+0000+0000.

- **To place a long-distance call within Brazil,** you must use the access code of a *prestadora* (service provider). Any phone can be used to access any provider; however, the only code that works in all of Brazil—and as a visitor, the only one you need to remember—is the one for Embratel, 21. For example, to call Salvador from Rio, dial 021+071+000+0000. Note that for all calls within the country, area codes are preceded by 0.

- **To place a direct international call from Brazil,** dial the access code (021), plus the country code of the place you're calling, plus the area code and the local number.

- **To reach an international operator,** dial ✆ 000-111. Major long distance company access codes are as follows: **AT&T** ✆ 0800-890-0288; **Canada Direct** ✆ 0800-890-0014; **MCI** ✆ 0800-890-0012; **Sprint** ✆ 0800-888-8000.

the local Polícia Federal. In Rio de Janeiro, the office is located at Av. Venezuela 2, Centro, just behind Praça Mauá (✆ 021/2291-2142). In São Paulo, the office is located at Av. Prestes Maia 700, Centro (✆ 011/223-7177, ext. 231). Hours for both offices are daily from 10am to 4pm. This is best done in large cities where the staff has experience with tourists.

Brazil requires children under 18 traveling alone, with one parent, or with a third party to present written, notarized authorization by the absent parent(s) or legal guardian granting permission to travel alone, with one parent, or with a third party. Additionally, the authorization must be authenticated by the Brazilian embassy or consulate and translated into Portuguese. For more details, contact your embassy or consulate.

BRAZILIAN EMBASSY LOCATIONS

In the U.S.: 3006 Massachusetts Ave. NW, Washington, DC 20008 (✆ **202/238-2700;** fax 202/238-2827; www.brasilemb.org)

In Canada: 450 Wilbroad St., Ottawa, ON K1N 6M8 (✆ **613/237-1090;** fax 613/237-6144; www.brasembottawa.org)

In the U.K.: 32 Green St., London W1K 7AT (© **020/7399-9000;** fax 020/ 7399-9100; www.brazil.org.uk)

In Australia: 19 Forster Crescent, Yarralumla, ACT 2600 (© **02/6273-2372;** fax 02/6273-2375; www.brazil.org.au)

In New Zealand: 10 Brandon St., Level 9, Wellington 6001 (© **04/473-3516;** fax 04/473-3517)

CUSTOMS

As a visitor, you are unlikely to be scrutinized very closely upon arrival; Customs officers are too busy nabbing returning Brazilians loaded down with consumer goods far in excess of their duty-free limit. However, there are random checks, and your luggage may be thoroughly inspected. Visitors are allowed to bring a reasonable amount of personal belongings, including electronics such as a camera and a laptop.

Other countries normally force you to do your duty-free shopping before arrival, and they only allow you to bring in a single measly bottle of liquor, a box of cigarettes, and a few bottles of perfume. In Brazil, you're allowed to spend up to $500 in the duty-free shop *upon arrival,* and it's completely up to you whether you blow the money on cases of Johnny Walker or gallons of aftershave. In the airport, just follow the signs after immigration but before going through Customs. Prices in these duty-free shops are much cheaper than you'll find in Brazil itself. Note that the generous import allowance counts *only* for goods purchased in the Brazilian duty-free shop upon arrival.

MONEY

The Brazilian unit of currency is the **real** (R$), pronounced "hey-*al*" (plural reais, pronounced "hey-*eyes*"), which is made up of 100 centavos. The real comes in bills of 1, 5, 10, 50, and 100, and coins of R$1 and 1, 5, 10, 25, and 50 centavos. There seems to be a chronic lack of small bills in Brazil, particularly in the northeast. Try paying for a R$4 item with a R$10 bill, and you may have to wait a half-hour while the vendor moans about the horror of making change then runs around begging other shopkeepers to help him break a R$10 bill. Buses, street vendors, and taxi drivers also usually carry little or no change, so hoard those ones and fives!

Here's a general idea of what things cost in Rio: a taxi ride from downtown Rio to Copacabana, R$20 (US$7); a ride from Rio's airport to an Ipanema hotel, R$60 (US$20); a double room at a budget hotel in high season, R$150 (US$50); a double room in a moderate hotel, R$150 to R$200 (US$50–US$70); a double room in an expensive hotel, R$300 to R$600 (US$100–US$200); a Coca-Cola, mineral water, or can of beer from a street vendor, R$1.50 to R$2.50 (50¢–85¢); lunch for one at a moderate restaurant, R$8 to R$12 (US$2.65–US$4); dinner for one in a moderate restaurant, R$12 to R$20 (US$4–US$7); a roll of film, R$10 to R$15 (US$3.35–US$5).

Tips **Photo ID**

You are required to carry ID in Brazil, and it is sometimes requested when entering office buildings or even tourist sites. We recommend bringing an alternative picture ID, such as a driver's license or student ID, to use instead of carrying your passport with you at all times.

> **Tips Currency Exchange Receipts**
>
> When exchanging money, whether it is cash or traveler's checks, always keep the receipt. You will need it in case you want to change back any unused reais at the end of your trip.

CURRENCY EXCHANGE & RATES   In an attempt to rein in inflation, the Brazilian government introduced the real in 1994. It was stable for a number of years, then devalued by almost 50% in 1999, after which it remained stable for most of 2000 before embarking yet again on a slower but steady decline, losing more than 20% in value against the U.S. dollar over the course of 2001. Throughout this chapter, we give the prices in reais and U.S. dollars; as of press time, the exchange rate was R$3 to US$1.

Banks usually provide a slightly better exchange rate but have limited hours of operation for currency exchange (usually 11am–2pm), and the wait can be long. *Casas de cambio* (money-exchange houses) are often more efficient and have better hours of operation, but the rates may be less favorable. The best rates are available through ATMs and credit cards.

After years of experience with unstable local currencies, Brazilians learned to use the U.S. dollar as the unofficial yardstick for their economy and are consequently accustomed to keeping track of prices in dollars. Many tourism companies will quote prices directly in dollars. Sometimes, websites or brochures list prices in U.S. dollars only. When in doubt, ask. And though it's a bad idea to carry large wads of cash, it can be helpful to bring a small amount of U.S. cash (10s or 20s only) as an emergency supply in case an ATM is broken or your credit card isn't working. Even in the smallest towns, people will know the exchange rate, and someone will be happy to take those U.S. dollars off your hands.

ATMs   Brazil's financial infrastructure is very sophisticated and ATMs are everywhere in Brazil, even in the smallest towns. The only trick is finding one that works with your card. **Cirrus** (© **800/424-7787;** www.mastercard.com) and **PLUS** (© **800/842-7587;** www.visa.com) are the two most popular networks; call or check online for ATM locations. Be sure your PIN is four digits, and find out your daily withdrawal limit before you depart.

The vast majority of travelers find they are able to use the Banco do Brasil ATMs bearing a PLUS/Visa logo. However, it's not a bad idea to bring two different cards to increase your access options. (Small towns normally have only one ATM, accepting PLUS/Visa or Cirrus/MasterCard, but not both.) When in doubt, check with your bank to find out which Brazilian bank networks are compatible with your card. Finally, make sure that during New Year's and Carnaval you get enough cash ahead of time, as machines often run out of money by the end of the holidays.

TRAVELER'S CHECKS   Traveler's checks don't work well in Brazil. Most shops won't accept them, hotels give a miserable exchange rate, and many banks won't cash your traveler's checks unless you have an account at that branch of that bank. Others, such as Bank Boston, will only cash a minimum of $500. The Banco do Brasil is the only bank that will cash them with minimum hassle (expect to spend at least 20–30 min.) but charges a flat rate of $20 for the pleasure. Only American Express will cash their own checks for free, but they have only a few offices in major centers such as Rio, Salvador, and São Paulo.

CREDIT CARDS   The best exchange rates can be obtained through credit cards, which are accepted at most shops, hotels, and restaurants. Just keep in mind that you are sometimes able to negotiate a better discount on a room or in a store if you pay cash. The most commonly accepted cards are Visa and MasterCard. American Express and Diners Club are also frequently accepted. It's a good idea to have at least two cards as some stores and restaurants accept only one card (usually Visa). Discover is rarely (if ever) accepted in Brazil.

If you need to report a lost or stolen credit card or have any questions, you can contact the agencies anywhere in Brazil at the following numbers: **American Express,** 🕾 0800/785-050; **MasterCard** and **Visa,** 🕾 0800/784-456; and **Diners Club** 🕾 0800/784-444.

WHEN TO GO

PEAK SEASON   High season in Brazil is from the week before Christmas until Carnaval (which falls sometime in Feb or early Mar). Flights and accommodations are both more expensive and more likely to be full during this period. For accommodations during New Year's and Carnaval, you need to book at least 4 to 6 months in advance for hotel packages, and at least 2 months in advance for international air travel and air passes. That said, high season is also the most fun time to travel—towns and resorts are bustling as many Brazilians take their summer vacations, the weather is warm, and New Year's and Carnaval are fabulous events.

Other busy times of the year include Easter week and the month of July, when schools and universities take their winter break. This is probably the worst time of year to travel; prices go up significantly, and the weather can be iffy. (One year in Rio, we suffered through 4 straight weeks of rain.) If you want to take advantage of the best deals and still have good weather, consider visiting Brazil in September or October. The spring weather means warm days in São Paulo, Iguaçu, and Rio, and tropical heat everywhere else; in the Amazon and the Pantanal, you'll be there just before the wet season starts. As an added bonus, in Rio, you'll be able to attend some of the samba school rehearsals as they prepare for Carnaval. Another good period for a visit is after Carnaval through May, when you can take advantage of low-season prices, particularly in hotels, while enjoying good weather.

CLIMATE   Brazil lies in the Southern Hemisphere, so its seasons are the exact opposite of what residents of the Northern Hemisphere are used to: Summer is from December through March, and winter is from June through September. Within the country, the climate varies considerably from region to region. In most of Brazil, the summers are very hot—temperatures can rise to 110°F (44°C) with high humidity. The **northeast** is warm year-round, often with a pleasant breeze from the ocean. Temperatures hover between the low 80s and the mid-90s (26°C–34°C). The winter months are slightly wetter, but even then, the amount of rain is limited. As befits a rainforest, the **Amazon** is hot and humid year-round, with summer temperatures hovering around the mid-90s (35°C), and winter temperatures coming in around 5° cooler. The humidity is higher in the summer rainy season, building up over the course of the day to produce a heavy downpour most every afternoon. Even then, however, mornings and early afternoons are generally clear and sunny. The **Pantanal** is very hot in the summer, with temperatures climbing to 104°F (40°C). Most of the rain falls from December through March; the driest time of the year is May through October. In the winter, it cools down considerably, though nighttime temperatures will seldom drop below 68°F (16°C).

Heads Up: Beware of Dengue Fever in Brazil

Brazil occasionally experiences outbreaks of dengue fever, a malaria-like illness transmitted by mosquitoes. Most of the cases were reported in the state of Rio de Janeiro, with additional outbreaks in São Paulo as well.

There is no vaccine for dengue fever; symptoms can be treated with bed rest, fluids, and medications, such as acetaminophen (Tylenol), to reduce fever; aspirin should be avoided. The most important precaution a traveler can take is to avoid mosquito bites when visiting a dengue-prone area. Try to remain in well-screened or air-conditioned areas; use mosquito repellents (preferably those containing DEET) on skin and clothing; use aerosol insecticides indoors; and sleep with bed nets. For the most up-to-date information on the status of dengue fever in Brazil, consult the Centers for Disease Control and Prevention website (www.cdc.gov) before departing.

Rio has very hot and humid summers—100°F (38°C) temperatures and 98% humidity are not uncommon. Rio winters are quite mild, with nighttime temperatures dropping as low as 66°F (15°C), and daytime temperatures climbing to a pleasant and sunny 82°F (28°C). **São Paulo** has a similar climate to Rio's; however, as São Paulo sits atop a plateau at nearly 700m (2,100 ft.), it can sometimes get downright chilly, with daytime lows reaching 54°F (12°C) June through September. South of São Paulo, things get even colder in the winter. In the mountain resort of **Petrópolis,** the historic towns of **Minas Gerais** (Ouro Prêto, Tiradentes), and further south to **Iguaçu** and **Florianópolis,** it often gets cold enough to see your breath in the fall and winter.

PUBLIC HOLIDAYS   The following holidays are observed in Brazil: New Year's Day (Jan 1); Carnaval (Feb 22–25, 2004, and Feb 6–9, 2005); Good Friday; Tiradentes Day (Apr 21); Labor Day (May 1); Corpus Christi (June 10, 2004, and May 26, 2005); Independence Day (Sept 7); Our Lady of Apparition (Oct 12); All Souls' Day (Nov 2); Proclamation of the Republic (Nov 15); and Christmas (Dec 25).

HEALTH CONCERNS

COMMON AILMENTS   The main concerns for visitors are yellow fever, malaria, and dengue fever. **Yellow fever,** which is transmitted by mosquitoes, is endemic in most of Brazil's interior and occasionally makes forays into the hinterland of São Paulo and Minas Gerais. Also transmitted by mosquitoes is **malaria.** Mostly travelers to the Amazon are at risk; however, lodges around Manaus have not experienced any problems with malaria. Ask for your doctor's specific recommendations on malaria prophylaxes, as the guidelines change regularly.

Another mosquito-borne disease that is widespread in Brazil, particularly on the coast around Rio and São Paulo, is **dengue fever.** First-time sufferers will experience severe flulike symptoms (fever, joint pain, and headache) that can last up to 10 days. Unlike yellow fever and malaria, dengue has no vaccine or prophylaxis—the best prevention is to avoid mosquito bites.

Other tropical diseases, such as cholera or Chagas' disease, are only found in very remote areas. For those planning to explore beyond the beaten track, please obtain more detailed advice from a travel clinic before heading out.

VACCINATIONS   It's always a good idea before going on a trip to check your vaccinations and get booster shots for tetanus and polio, if necessary. Children 3 months to 6 years may be required to show proof of polio vaccination. The one vaccination that is definitely required for Brazil is **yellow fever.** If you're traveling to the Amazon, the Pantanal, Brasília, or even Minas Gerais, you may come in contact with it. Get an international certificate of vaccination, as Brazilian authorities sometimes require proof of vaccination for people going to or coming from an affected area. Travelers who have been to Colombia, Bolivia, Ecuador, French Guyana, Peru, or Venezuela within 90 days before arriving in Brazil are also required to show proof of yellow fever vaccination. Please keep in mind that the vaccine takes 10 days to take effect. If you're traveling to the Amazon or the Pantanal, a **malaria** prophylaxis (usually pills that you take daily) may be recommended as well. Consult your doctor and the Centers for Disease Control and Prevention (CDC) website (www.cdc.gov/travel/tropsam.htm) prior to traveling, as advisories change regularly.

HEALTH PRECAUTIONS   Brazil's standards for hygiene and public health are generally high. If you do wind up with traveler's tummy or some other ailment, Brazilian pharmacies are a wonder. Each has a licensed pharmacist who is trained to deal with small medical emergencies and—better yet—fully authorized to give prescriptions. The service is free, and medication is fairly inexpensive. If you're taking medication that may need replacement while in Brazil, ask your doctor to write out the generic name, as many drugs are sold under different brand names in Brazil. Many drugs available by prescription only in the United States and Canada are available over the counter in Brazil.

According to recent U.N. statistics, Brazil ranks third in the world for the total number of people with HIV infections. Be careful and be safe—always insist on using a condom. Though condoms are readily available in Brazilian pharmacies, it's best to bring your own, as North American and European brands are more reliable. To purchase condoms in Brazil ask for *camisinha* (literally "small shirt").

GETTING THERE
BY PLANE
Rio de Janeiro's **Antonio Carlos Jobim Airport** (© 0800/999-099 or 021/ 3398-5050) and São Paulo's **Guarulhos Airport** (© 011/6445-2945) are the two major gateways to Brazil and are served by most international airlines. International departure taxes are a hefty $36, payable in cash only (in U.S. dollars or in reais).

The two big Brazilian airlines—**Varig** and **TAM**—also operate a number of international flights. Varig (© 800/468-2744; www.varig.com.br) is by far the largest Brazilian airline with international connections from North America, Europe, Asia, and the rest of South America. **TAM** (© 888/2FLY-TAM; www.tam.com.br) has a limited number of flights from Europe and the United States, including a nonstop flight from Miami to Manaus.

From North America   U.S. airlines that fly to Brazil include **United** (© 800/241-6522; www.ual.com), with nonstop flights from Miami to Rio and São Paulo; **American** (© 800/433-7300; www.aa.com), which serves Rio and São Paulo from New York and Miami; and **Continental** (© 800/231-0856; www.continental.com), which offers nonstop flights from Houston and New York. **Delta** (© 800/241-4141; www.delta.com) offers direct flights from its

Atlanta hub to Rio and São Paulo. Canadian travelers can book with **Air Canada,** which partners with Varig for flights to Brazil, offering nonstop Toronto–São Paulo service (© **888/247-2262;** www.aircanada.ca).

From the U.K.   British Airways (© **0845/702-0212;** www.british-airways. com) offers several nonstop flights to Rio and São Paulo. Travelers from Europe can also choose from an array of nonstop flights to Rio and/or São Paulo; **Alitalia, Lufthansa, Air France,** and **KLM** offer daily (or almost daily) service.

From Australia & New Zealand   Travelers from Australia can fly **Qantas** (© **13-13-13** in Australia, or 0800/0014-0014 in New Zealand; www.qantas. com) and connect with its partner **British Airways** in London or fly to Los Angeles and transfer to a **Varig** flight.

BY PACKAGE TOUR

Many travel agencies offer package tours to Brazil, but few have the knowledge to effectively customize your trip or make interesting recommendations. To book a package with Brazil travel experts, contact **Brazil Nuts** (© **800/553-9959** or 914/593-0266; www.brazilnuts.com). The owners and staff are indeed nuts about Brazil and possess a vast amount of knowledge about the country and its attractions. Depending on your needs, you can book just a flight and hotels or you can add one or more group excursions to more inaccessible places such as the Amazon. Its website is a fount of information, and its staff can answer any questions you may have about Brazil.

Another excellent Internet-based company is **4StarBrazil** (© **866/464-7827;** http://4starbrazil.com). Similar to Brazil Nuts, 4StarBrazil offers packages customizable to whatever level you're comfortable with. The company has recently added on a number of other South American travel destinations, making it easy to put together your own customized package. A good travel agency to book your ticket through is **Santini Tours,** 6575 Shattuck Ave., Oakland, CA 94609 (© **800/769-9669** or 510/652-8600; www.santours.com). The owner and many of the travel agents are Brazilian and can give you many useful suggestions on air-pass routings and answer any questions you have about your itinerary.

GETTING AROUND
BY PLANE

Though there are highways and buses, the sheer vastness of Brazil (and the absence of rail travel) makes flying the only viable option for those who want to visit a variety of cities and regions. Regular fares on the main domestic carriers are outrageously expensive, but affordable air travel is available to foreigners through the purchase of an air pass (much to the envy of Brazilians). Each of the Brazilian airlines offers one; prices, the number of flights, and destinations vary, but all air passes provide a number of flights over a set time period. Air passes must be purchased and booked outside of Brazil through a travel agent. Only limited changes are allowed once you arrive in the country. Also, it's a good idea to scrutinize the fine print before choosing your pass. Usually, flights between Rio and São Paulo are excluded, and the pass does not allow returns on the same stretch.

VASP (© **0300/789-1010;** www.vasp.com.br) offers five flights for US$440; extra flights can be purchased for US$100 each up to a total of nine flights. The pass is valid for 21 days. **Varig** (© **0800/997-000** in Brazil; www.varig.com.br) and **TAM** (© **0800/123-100** in Brazil; www.tam.com.br) both offer five segments for US$540. Extra segments can be purchased for US$100 each. The pass is valid for 21 days and is the only one that includes flights to Fernando de Noronha.

If you're traveling to only one or two destinations within Brazil, it can be cheaper to skip the air pass and fly instead with one of the new discount airlines. **Gol** (② **0300/789-2121;** www.voegol.com.br) has modeled itself after American discount carriers such as Southwest and jetBlue, offering no-frills flights to popular destinations such as Rio, São Paulo, Salvador, Fortaleza, Recife, Belém, Cuiabá, Natal, Florianópolis and Brasília. You are not able to purchase online tickets (yet) with a foreign credit card but Gol has offices at most Brazilian airports.

BY BUS

Bus travel in Brazil is very efficient and affordable—the only problem is that it's a long way between destinations. To see the country by bus, you will need a lot of time, especially in the west and northwest, where roads are precarious. The 644km (400-mile) journey from Campo Grande to Cuiabá, the two gateway cities into the Pantanal, takes about 11 hours on the bus. Still, for shorter distances and for the occasional long haul, Brazilian buses are excellent; all buses are nonsmoking, and on many popular routes, travelers can opt for a deluxe coach with air-conditioning and *leito,* reclinable seats. See individual city sections in this chapter for more information about bus travel. Many local travel agencies will have schedule information and may sell tickets. You can also contact the bus station *(rodoviária)* directly.

BY CAR

Car rentals are expensive in Brazil, and the distances are huge. For example, from Recife to Brasília is a distance of 2,121km (1,400 miles), while from Salvador to Rio, it's a 1,800km (1,100-mile) drive. Within Brazilian cities, renting a car is only for the bold and the foolish: Drivers are aggressive, rules are loosely observed, and parking is a competitive sport. Still, there are occasions—a side trip to the mountain resorts of Rio, for example, or a drive to the Chapada dos Guimarães outside of Cuiabá—when renting a car does make sense. The following companies have offices across Brazil: **Avis,** ② 0800/118-066; **Budget,** ② 0800/142-499; **Hertz,** ② 0800/147-300; **Localiza,** ② 0800/312-121; and **Unidas,** ② 0800/121-121. To drive in Brazil, you need to have an international driver's license; contact your local automobile association for details.

Each company normally has a national rate, and only rarely are there local discounts or special offers. For a tiny car (a Fiat Palio or Gol) with air-conditioning you can typically expect to pay around R$90 (US$30) per day plus 60 centavos (20¢) per kilometer or R$110 to R$130 (US$37–US$435) per day with unlimited mileage. Add to that another R$30 (US$10) per day for comprehensive insurance. While expensive, the comprehensive insurance is probably a good idea, as Brazilian drivers are not as gentle with their cars as the folks in North America are. Gasoline costs R$2.50 (85¢) per liter (about US$4.60 per gal.).

TIPS ON ACCOMMODATIONS

Brazil offers a wide range of accommodations. In the large cities, there are modern high-rise hotels as well as apartment hotels (known in Brazil as apart-hotels). The apart-hotels are often a better deal than regular hotel rooms, offering both cheaper rates and more space; the drawback is that you often don't get the pool and restaurants and other amenities of a hotel. Outside of the large cities, you will often find *pousadas*, essentially the equivalent of a bed-and-breakfast or small inn.

Accommodations prices fluctuate widely. The rates posted at the front desk—the rack rate or *tarifa balcão*—are just a guideline. Outside of the high season and weekends, you can almost always negotiate significant (20%–30%) discounts. Notable exceptions are Brasília and São Paulo, where business dies during high season and weekends, and rooms are heavily discounted. Hotel charges for children are all over the map. Most hotels allow children under 6 to stay for free in their parent's room, but for children over 6, the rates can vary from a 10% surcharge to a full adult supplement rate. Please note that these rates and policies are always negotiable.

Unlike North American hotel rooms, Brazilian hotel rooms have neither coffeemakers nor iron and ironing board as standard features. On the other hand, except for some five-star hotels, a very generous breakfast is always included.

Accommodations taxes range from nothing to 15%, varying from city to city and hotel to hotel. Always check in advance what taxes will be added to your final bill.

TIPS ON DINING

Brazilians love to eat out. There is no shortage of eateries, from beach vendors selling grilled cheese and sweets, to lunch-bars serving pastries and cold beers, to fine French cuisine complete with the elegance and pretensions of Paris. Lunch is traditionally a full hot meal, but these days you can also find North American–style sandwiches and salads as a lighter alternative. Dinner is eaten late; most restaurants don't get busy until 9 or 10pm and will often serve dinner until 1 or 2am. In Rio and São Paulo, the restaurant scene is very cosmopolitan: excellent Japanese restaurants, fabulous Italian eateries, traditional Portuguese and Spanish food, as well as popular restaurants that serve Brazilian food—rice, black beans, *farofa* (manioc flour), and steak.

Brazilian cuisine comes in many regional varieties, but the one truly national dish is *feijoada*, a black bean stew that originated with African slaves who used leftovers to make a tasty meal. Traditionally served on Saturday, the beans are spiced with garlic, onions, and bay leaves and left to stew for hours with a hodgepodge of meats that may include sausage, beef, dried meat, and bits of pork. Accompanied by rice, *farofa*, slices of orange, and stir-fried cabbage, it's a meal in itself.

Brazil's most distinguished regional cuisine is found in coastal Bahia, a region with very strong African influences. Bahia's most famous dish is the *moqueca*, a rich stew made with fresh fish or seafood, coconut milk, lime juice, cilantro, and spicy *malagueta* peppers and flavored with the red oil from a *dendê* palm. In the Amazon and the Pantanal, local cuisine makes the best of the large variety of freshwater fish and local fruits and vegetables. The fish is delicious—firm white meat that tastes best plainly grilled with salt and herbs or sometimes served in a spicy stew. In the south and southwest of Brazil, the cuisine is more European, and meat is always present on the menu. *Churrascarias*, or Brazilian steakhouses, are everywhere. Often, *churrascarias* operate on a *rodízio* (all-you-can-eat) system. Waiters scurry from grill to tables bearing giant skewers of beautifully roasted beef or chicken or pork or sausage, from which they slice off a few succulent slices onto your plate. The parade of meat continues until you throw your hands up and cry, "Enough!"

Almost everyone has heard of Brazil's most famous cocktail, the *caipirinha* (made with limes, sugar, and *cachaça*), but even Brazilians can't live on booze alone. It makes sense in a tropical country to have lots of cold drinks, often made with tropical fruits. Freshly made juices *(suco)* or milkshakes *(vitaminas)* can be ordered at snack bars and restaurants. Tastier than regular cola drinks is Brazil's very own Guaraná, a sparkling ginger ale–like drink made with Amazonian guaraná berries. Wine lovers may want to experiment with some Brazilian wines but will probably be better off choosing a more reliable Argentine or Chilean varietal; Brazil's wine industry is small and still developing. Beer is drunk the way it is meant to be in a hot country: ice cold and light. Remember that *cerveja* refers to beer served in a can or bottle and *chopp* means draft beer.

Saying that Brazilians have a sweet tooth is like saying that Italians have been known to eat pasta. Most Brazilian desserts are just a few ingredients shy of pure sugar. Most traditional sweets are just variations on the combination of sugar, egg yolks, and coconut. *Cocada,* the little clusters of coconut you see everywhere, are nothing more than grated coconut with white or burnt sugar; *quindim,* something between a pudding and a pie, is made with coconut, an incredible number of egg yolks (at least 10 per tiny serving!), and sugar; and *manjar,* a soft pudding often served with plum sauce, combines sugar, coconut milk, and milk. My personal favorite is *babá de moça,* made of coconut milk, egg yolks, and sugar syrup. The name translates as "girl drool."

TIPS ON SHOPPING

Brazil offers excellent shopping opportunities, particularly for precious stones; leather goods such as shoes, belts, purses, and wallets; and Brazilian music and musical instruments. Clothing is also very affordable and often of good quality. Rio and São Paulo are the best cities for buying fashionable clothes and shoes. If you plan on visiting Petrópolis, do so early in your trip and stock up on inexpensive clothes. Styles follow the opposite seasonal calendar, so those visiting Brazil during the Northern Hemisphere winter can stock up on an excellent summer wardrobe. Sizes follow the European numbering system (36, 38, 40, and so on) or are marked P (*pequeno,* small), M (*medio,* medium), and G (*grande,* large).

Expect to haggle with street vendors. Even in stores, you can ask for a discount when buying more than one item or when paying cash. Shops will often advertise prices *"a vista"*—this means cash purchases only, and they can be 10% to 20% cheaper than paying by credit card.

Each region has its own crafts traditions. In the Amazon and Pantanal, good buys include Indian carvings and hammocks. The northeast is particularly well known for its lovely linen and woodcarvings. Throughout Brazil, there are plenty of opportunities to shop for semiprecious stones, although the largest collections can be found in Rio and São Paulo jewelry stores.

FAST FACTS: Brazil

Addresses Large buildings or attractions such as museums, palaces, or churches often don't have a street number and are listed as s/n (*sem numero*—"without a number"). This is also often the case in small towns with just a few streets. In most cases, what you are looking for is pretty obvious and hard to miss. Other address notes to pay attention to: *sala* (room or office), *loja* (shop), *sobre loja* (1st floor), and *subsolo* (basement).

American Express In Rio de Janeiro, there's an office on Av. Atlântica 1702, Loja 1, Copacabana (© 021/2548-2148); it's open Monday through Friday from 9am to 4pm. In São Paulo, there's an office at the Hotel Sheraton Mofarrej, Av. Al. Santos 1437, Cerqueira César (© 011/251-3383). The office is open Monday through Friday from 9:30am to 5:30pm.

Business Hours Stores are usually open weekdays from 9am to 7pm, Saturday from 9am to 2pm, and not at all on Sunday. Small stores may close for lunch. Shopping centers are usually open Monday through Saturday from 10am to 10pm; on Sunday, only the food court and entertainment section are open. Banks are open Monday through Friday either from 10am to 4pm or from 9am to 3pm. Hours for changing money are often limited to 11am to 2pm.

Doctors For small medical problems, pharmacies are good resources. Many large hotels also have a nurse on staff or can refer you to the nearest 24-hour clinic. Brazil's healthcare is modern and up-to-date, especially in private hospitals. In Rio de Janeiro, contact **Hospital Miguel Couto,** Rua Bartolomeu Mitre 1108, Leblon (© 021/2274-6050). In São Paulo, contact **Albert Einstein Hospital,** Av. Albert Einstein 627, Morumbi (© 011/3747-1233).

Drug Laws Simple possession of soft drugs such as marijuana remains illegal, though Brazilians are quite tolerant about casual use. The use of harder drugs, and anything that could be construed as trafficking, carries heavy penalties that police and courts enforce. Putting yourself at the mercy of the Brazilian police and judicial system is not recommended.

Electricity Brazil's electric current varies from 100 to 240 volts, and from 50 to 60Hz; even within one city, there can be variations, and power surges are not uncommon. Brazilians protect their equipment with current stabilizers, but these heavy appliances are far from portable. For laptops or battery chargers, bring an adapter that can handle the full range of voltage so you never have to worry. Most hotels do a good job of labeling their outlets, but check before plugging in! Brazilian plugs usually have three prongs: two round and one flat. Adapters for converting North American plugs are widely available in Brazil and are very reasonably priced at R$3 to R$5 (US$1–US$1.65)

Embassies & Consulates In Rio de Janeiro: **United States,** Av. Presidente Wilson 147, Centro (© 021/2292-7117); **Canada,** Rua Lauro Muller 116, Suite 2707, Centro (© 021/2543-3004); **United Kingdom,** Praia do Flamengo 284, Flamengo (© 021/2553-3223); **Australia,** Av. Presidente Wilson 231, Suite 23, Centro (© 021/3824-4624).

In São Paulo: **United States,** Rua Padre João Manoel 933, Cerqueira César (© 011/3081-6511); **Canada,** Ave. das Nações Unidas 12901, 16th floor (© 11/5509-4343); **United Kingdom,** Rua Ferreira de Araujo 741 (© 011/3816-2303); **Australia,** Alameda Rocha Azevedo 456, Jardim Paulista (© 011/3085-6247).

In Brasília: **United States,** Setor de Embaixadas Sul (SES), Av. das Nações Quadra 807, Lote 27 (© 061/443-3315); **Canada,** SES, Av. das Nações Quadra 803, Lote 16 (© 061/321-4529); **United Kingdom,** SES, Av. das Nações Quadra 801, Lote 8 (© 061/225-1777); **Australia,** Setor de

Habitações Individuais Sul (SHIS), Q1 09, Conjunto 16, Casa 1 (℃ 061/248-1066).

Emergencies In an emergency, call the police at ℃ **190**, an ambulance at ℃ **193**, or firefighters at ℃ **193**.

Internet Access Even in the smallest towns, Internet access is readily available most of the time. Rates are usually $2 to $4 per hour.

Language The official language of Brazil is Portuguese. In the large cities, you will find people in the tourism industry who speak good English, but in smaller towns and resorts, English is very limited. If you are picking up language books or tapes, make sure they are Brazilian Portuguese and not Portuguese from Portugal—there's a big difference! If you know a bit of Spanish it can certainly help in learning Portuguese words more quickly but don't assume that most Brazilians will be able to understand you.

Liquor Laws Officially, Brazil's drinking laws allow only those over 18 to drink. Beer, wine, and liquor can be bought any day of the week from supermarkets, grocery stores, and delis.

Maps Good maps aren't Brazil's strong suit. Your best bet for city maps is the *Guia Quatro Rodas Mapas das Capitais,* on sale at all newsstands ($4) and full of indexed maps of all state capitals, including São Paulo, Rio, Salvador, Manaus, Brasília, and Recife. Unfortunately, it does not include any highways. The best highway map is sold with the *Guia Quatro Rodas Brasil* (available at newsstands for $8), a Brazilian guidebook with very brief accommodations and restaurant information for the entire country.

Newspapers & Magazines There are no English-language newspapers or magazines made in Brazil. Foreign papers and magazines are easily found only in Rio and São Paulo, usually at large hotels or in the business district of each city. The most popular Brazilian newspapers are *O Globo, Jornal do Brasil,* and *Folha de São Paulo.* The most popular current affairs magazine (the equivalent of *Newsweek*) is *Veja,* which is published weekly. In Rio and São Paulo, *Veja* magazine always includes an entertainment insert that provides detailed listings of nightlife, restaurants, and events.

Police Both Rio and São Paulo have a tourist police office with trained staff members who are used to dealing with foreign visitors. In São Paulo, the tourist police office is located at Rua São Bento 380, Fifth Floor (℃ 011/3107-5642). In Rio, the office is at Av. Afranio de Melo Franco 159, Leblon (℃ 021/3399-7170).

Post Offices/Mail Mail from Brazil is quick and efficient. Post offices *(correios)* can be found everywhere, readily identifiable by the blue and yellow sign. A postcard or letter to Europe or North America costs R$1.20 (60¢). Parcels can be sent through FedEx or regular mail (express or common); a small parcel weighing up to 2.5 kilograms (5½ lb.) costs about $15 by common mail and takes about a week.

Restrooms Bathrooms are often marked *homens* (men) or *mulheres* (women) or just a simple *H* or *M.* Also used is the more old-fashioned *damas* (ladies) or *cavalheiros* (gentlemen). Occasionally, you may come across the sign LAVABO for washroom. In public washrooms (parks, bus stations), you'll pay 25¢ to 50¢ to use the facilities.

Safety In the 1980s, Brazil developed a reputation for violence and crime. Rio, especially, was seen as the sort of place where walking down the street was openly asking for a mugging. Some of this was pure sensationalism, but there was a good measure of truth in it as well. At the time, Brazil was massively in debt to first-world banks, and the combination of crippling interest payments and International Monetary Fund (IMF) austerity measures left governments at all levels with no money for basics such as street lighting and police, much less schools and hospitals.

Fortunately, in the early 1990s, things began to turn around. Governments began pouring money back into basic services, starting with policing. Cops were stationed on city streets, on public beaches, and anywhere else there seemed to be a problem. Nowadays, though still not perfect by any means, Rio, São Paulo, and Brazil's other big cities have bounced back to the point where they're as safe as most large international cities. Statistically, of course, Rio and other Brazilian cities still have unfortunately high crime rates; most of that crime, however, takes place in the *favelas* (shantytowns) in the far-off industrial outskirts. Take the usual commonsense precautions you would in any major city to protect yourself. Muggings are not as common as they used to be, and many heavily touristed areas are also heavily patrolled, but you should be vigilant at all times.

Taxes There is no tax added to goods purchased in Brazil. Restaurants and hotels normally add a general 10% service tax. In Rio, the city also levies a 5% tax on hotels. All airports in Brazil charge departure taxes; sometimes it's included in your ticket price, sometimes it's not. It's wise to check. Domestic departures cost around R$14 (US$5) at most airports, and international departure taxes are a hefty $36.

Telephone & Fax Public phones can be found everywhere and are called *orelhões* (big ears), as the cover has traditionally been shaped like a giant ear. To use these phones, you need a *cartão telefonico* (phone card), available at all newsstands. Cards come in 30 or 60 units. A local call costs one unit, approximately 10 centavos (3¢). In hotels, it is usually much cheaper to use your international calling card than to pay the local rates. International cellphones usually don't work in Brazil—check with your provider. For local directory assistance, dial ⓒ 102.

Time Zones Brazil has three time zones in the winter (Mar–Sept) and three to four time zones in the summer (Oct–Feb). The coast, including São Paulo, Rio de Janeiro, Salvador, and as far inland as Brasília, is 3 hours behind Greenwich mean time (GMT). The ranching states of Mato Grosso and Mato Grosso do Sul and the Amazon around Manaus are on Atlantic Standard Time (AST), 1 hour behind Rio. The third time zone includes the state of Acre and the western part of the Amazon; it's on Eastern Standard Time (EST), 2 hours behind Rio. The fourth time zone results from a bizarre expression of local politics, in which certain cities (this varies from year to year depending on who gets into office) refuse to follow daylight savings time, therefore creating a de facto fourth time zone. On occasion, the time zone for a city has been 1 hour off that of its surrounding state.

Tipping A 10% service charge is automatically included on most restaurant and hotel bills, and you are not expected to tip on top of this amount. If service has been particularly bad, you can request to have the

10% removed from your bill. Conversely, if service has been wonderful, you can leave a little extra. Taxi drivers do not get tipped; just round up the amount to facilitate change. Hairdressers usually receive a 10% tip. Bellhops get tipped R$1 (50¢) per bag.

Water The tap water in Brazil is becoming increasingly safe to drink. However, as a result of the treatment process, it still doesn't taste that great and may leave your stomach upset. To be on the safe side, drink bottled or filtered water. However, you can certainly shower, brush your teeth, or rinse an apple with the water.

3 Rio de Janeiro

Rio is a city whose reputation precedes it. Ask someone to picture "Albuquerque" or "Tampa," and odds are nothing much will come to mind. Say "Rio de Janeiro," and mental images explode: the statue of Christ, arms outspread on the mountaintop; the beach at Ipanema or Copacabana, crowded with women in the most minuscule of bikinis; the rocky height of the Sugar Loaf; the persistent rhythm of samba; the glittering skimpy costumes of Carnaval. With some cities, the image is all there is. Fortunately, in Rio, there's much more beyond the glittering mental images: historic neighborhoods; compelling architecture and nature; nightspots, cafes, and museums; and enclaves of rich and poor. In Rio, the more you explore, the more there is.

The city's famous name is a result of a geographical mistake: The Portuguese explorers who sailed into Guanabara Bay on January 1, 1502, thought they had discovered the mouth of a very large river *(rio)*. Though a small city was established shortly afterwards, the capital of Portuguese Brazil wasn't moved to Rio until 1763, and the city didn't really hit the big time until 1808, when the Portuguese emperor—fleeing advancing Napoleonic armies—moved his court and capital to Rio. The city grew quickly; by the late 1800s, it was one of the largest cities in the world, and it remained the dominant Brazilian city, politically and economically, until the advent of World War II.

In the years since, Saõ Paulo has taken over the lead industrial role, while the federal capital was moved inland to Brasília in 1960. For a time, Cariocas—as natives of Rio are called—feared for the future of their city. Now a city of some seven million and growing, Rio remains the country's media capital, an important financial center, and Brazil's key tourist destination.

Most visitors to Brazil start or end their visit in Rio de Janeiro. A wise choice. There may be wider beaches in the north and higher mountains in the south, but nowhere else on earth is there a comparable combination of white-hot sand and tall green peaks, with a blaze of urban humanity filling all the spaces in between. Most people stay in the beachfront neighborhoods of Copacabana and Ipanema, but even if your time is limited, it's worth making the effort to explore further. In the historic downtown neighborhoods of Centro and Lapa and Santa Teresa, there are narrow cobblestone streets and grand plazas, gold-covered churches, and buildings in the baroque, beaux arts, and Art Deco styles. If you have the energy, Rio's stunning setting offers numerous recreational activities, including hiking, hang gliding, surfing, and kayaking. The city's vibrant cultural scene comes to life in the evening and never disappoints: See some of the local samba bands or emerging talents or splurge to see a big national star such as Caetano Veloso.

ESSENTIALS
GETTING THERE
BY PLANE   Antonio Carlos Jobim Airport, often called Galeão (© **0800/ 999-099**), is where all international flights and most domestic flights arrive. Regular taxis can be hailed outside the airport; a ride to Copacabana should cost about R$45 (US$15) in average traffic. The most comfortable ones are the radio taxis, usually with air-conditioning, that allow you to prepay the fee to your destination. They are usually a little bit more expensive but give you peace of mind. Buy prepaid vouchers at the **Transcoopass** desk in the arrivals hall (© **021/ 2560-4888;** all major credit cards accepted). Rates vary from R$40 to R$55 (US$13–US$18) to Centro and Flamengo, and R$58 to R$65 (US$19–US$21) to the beach hotels of Copacabana and Ipanema. **Realtur/Reitur Turismo** (© **0800/240-850** or 021/2560-7041) runs an airport bus to the tourist areas along the beaches. From 5:30am to 11pm, a bus departs every 30 minutes and takes about 1 hour to make the full trip; the ride costs R$6 (US$2) per person.

Rio's second airport, **Santos Dumont** (© **0800/244-646**), is located downtown and is used by Gol, Varig, Vaso, and Tam for the Rio–São Paulo shuttles and a number of other domestic destinations. The Realtur bus from Galeão stops here on its way to and from the Zona Sul. A taxi ride to Ipanema will cost about R$30 (US$10) or a prepaid voucher can be purchased in the arrivals hall at the **Transcoopass.**

BY BUS   All long-distance buses arrive at the **Rodoviária Novo Rio,** Av. Francisco Bicalho 1, Santo Cristo (© **021/2291-5151;** www.novorio.com.br), 5 minutes from downtown in the old port section of the city. It's not a good idea to walk from the station with all your belongings. Prepaid taxi vouchers are available at the booth next to the taxi stand; a ride from the bus station to Ipanema costs about R$28 (US$9) prepaid.

ORIENTATION
Rio is normally divided into three zones: north *(Zona Norte),* center *(Centro),* and south *(Zona Sul).* The largest and least interesting area of the city, the Zona Norte stretches from a few blocks north of Avenida Presidente Vargas all the way to the city limits. This region is a dull swath of port, industrial suburb, and *favela.* It is not the sort of place you should wander around unaccompanied.

Rio's Centro neighborhood contains most of the city's notable churches, squares, monuments, and museums, as well as the modern office towers where Rio's white-collar elite earn their daily bread. Roughly speaking, Centro stretches from the **São Bento Monastery** in the north to the seaside **Monument to the Dead of World War II** in the south, and from **Praça XV** on the waterfront east to the **Sambódromo** (near Praça XI). Just to the south of Centro lies the fun and slightly bohemian hilltop neighborhood of **Santa Teresa,** as well as the neighborhoods of **Glória, Catete,** and **Flamengo.** Other neighborhoods in this section of the city include **Botafogo** and **Urca** (nestled beneath the Sugar Loaf). They're all pleasant and walkable.

The Zona Sul neighborhoods of **Copacabana, Ipanema, São Conrado,** and **Barra de Tijuca** face the open Atlantic. The first to be developed, Copacabana's wide expanse of beach still impresses locals and visitors alike. Like Copacabana, Ipanema is a very modern neighborhood, consisting almost exclusively of

Rio de Janeiro at a Glance

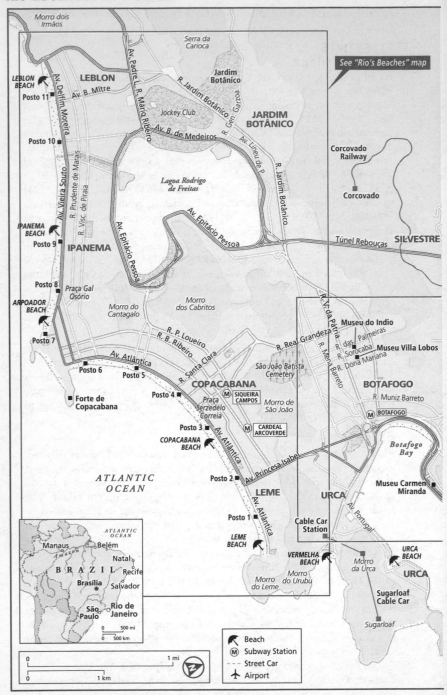

See "Rio's Beaches" map

Morro dois Irmãos

Serra da Carioca

LEBLON BEACH
Posto 11

LEBLON

Av. Delfim Moreira
Av. B. Mitre

Av. Padre L. R. Maria Ribeiro

Jardim Botânico

R. Jardim Botânico

R. Gen. Garzon

JARDIM BOTÂNICO

Corcovado Railway

Corcovado

Jockey Club

Posto 10

Av. B. de Medeiros

Av. Lineu de P.

R. Jardim Botânico

Av. Vieira Souto

R. Prudente de Marais

R. Visc. de Piraja

Lagoa Rodrigo de Freitas

Av. Epitácio Pessoa

SILVESTRE

Túnel Rebouças

IPANEMA BEACH
Posto 9

IPANEMA

Av. Epitácio Pessoa

Posto 8

Praça Gal Osório

Morro do Cantagalo

Morro dos Cabritos

R. Vz. da Pátria

Museu do Indio

R. das Palmeiras

ARPOADOR BEACH
Posto 7

R. P. Loureiro
R. B. Ribeiro

R. Real Grandeza

R. Mena Barreto

R. Sorocaba

R. Dona Mariana

Museu Villa Lobos

BOTAFOGO

Av. Atlântica

R. Santa Clara

São João Batista Cemetery

R. Muniz Barreto

Posto 6

Posto 5

COPACABANA

BOTAFOGO

Forte de Copacabana

Posto 4

Praça Serzedelo Correia

M SIQUEIRA CAMPOS

Morro de São João

Botafogo Bay

Posto 3

CARDEAL ARCOVERDE

COPACABANA BEACH

Av. Atlântica

Museu Carmen Miranda

ATLANTIC OCEAN

Posto 2

Av. Princesa Isabel

LEME

URCA

Av. Atlântica

Posto 1

Cable Car Station

Av. Portugal

LEME BEACH

VERMELHA BEACH

URCA BEACH

ATLANTIC OCEAN

Manaus
Belém

Natal

BRAZIL
Brasília
Recife
Salvador

Morro do Leme

Morro do Urubu

Morro da Urca

URCA

São Paulo
Rio de Janeiro

0   500 mi
0   500 km

Sugarloaf Cable Car

Sugarloaf

0   1 mi
0   1 km

Beach
M Subway Station
- - - Street Car
✈ Airport

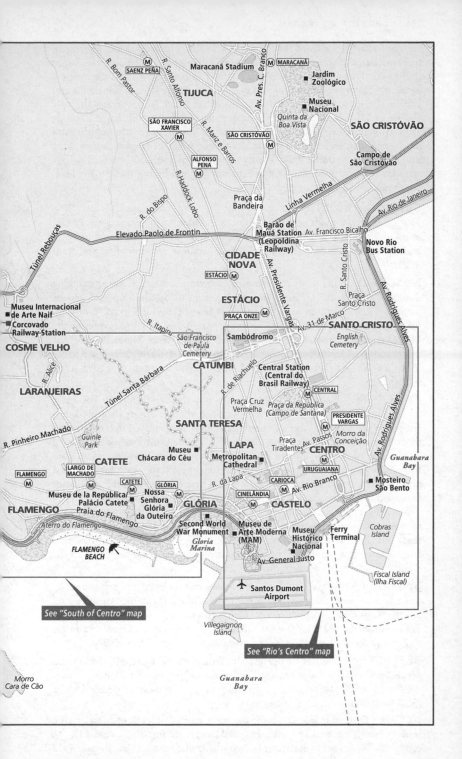

Maracanã Stadium
TIJUCA
SAENZ PEÑA
R. Bom Pastor
R. Santo Afonso
Av. Pres. C. Branco
MARACANÃ
Jardim
Zoológico
Museu
Nacional
SÃO CRISTÓVÃO
Quinta da
Boa Vista
SÃO FRANCISCO
XAVIER
R. Mariz e Barros
SÃO CRISTÓVÃO
ALFONSO
PENA
R. Haddock Lobo
Campo de
São Cristóvão
Praça da
Bandeira
Linha Vermelha
Av. Rio de Janeiro
R. do Bispo
Elevado Paolo de Frontin
Barão de
Mauá Station
(Leopoldina
Railway)
Av. Francisco Bicalho
Novo Rio
Bus Station
Túnel Rebouças
**CIDADE
NOVA**
ESTÁCIO
Av. Presidente Vargas
R. Santo Cristo
Praça
Santo Cristo
Av. Rodrigues Alves
**Museu Internacional
de Arte Naif
Corcovado
Railway Station**
COSME VELHO
R. Itapiru
ESTÁCIO
PRAÇA ONZE
Av. 31 de Março
SANTO CRISTO
São Francisco
de Paula
Cemetery
Sambódromo
English
Cemetery
R. Alice
CATUMBI
Central Station
(Central do
Brasil Railway)
CENTRAL
LARANJEIRAS
Túnel Santa Bárbara
R. de Riachuelo
Praça Cruz
Vermelha
Praça da República
(Campo de Santana)
PRESIDENTE
VARGAS
Morro da
Conceição
R. Pinheiro Machado
Guinle
Park
SANTA TERESA
LAPA
Praça
Tiradentes
Av. Passos
CENTRO
Guanabara
Bay
CATETE
Museu
Chácara do Céu
Metropolitan
Cathedral
CARIOCA
URUGUAIANA
Mosteiro
São Bento
FLAMENGO
LARGO DE
MACHADO
CATETE
GLÓRIA
R. da Lapa
Av. Rio Branco
CINELÂNDIA
CASTELO
Museu de la República/
Palácio Catete
Praia do Flamengo
Nossa
Senhora
Glória
da Outeiro
GLÓRIA
Second World
War Monument
Museu de
Arte Moderna
(MAM)
Museu
Histórico
Nacional
Ferry
Terminal
Cobras
Island
FLAMENGO
Aterro do Flamengo
Gloria
Marina
Av. General Justo
Fiscal Island
(Ilha Fiscal)
*FLAMENGO
BEACH*
See "South of Centro" map
Santos Dumont
Airport
See "Rio's Centro" map
Villegaignon
Island
*Morro
Cara de Cão*
*Guanabara
Bay*

high-rise apartments from the 1960s and 1970s. The area at the far end of Ipanema beach is known as Leblon. Behind Ipanema is a lagoon, the Lagoa Rodrigo de Freitas; known simply as Lagoa, this body of water is circled by a pleasant 8.5km (5-mile) walking and cycling trail. At the far end of Ipanema and Leblon the road carries on, winding around the cliff face to reach the tiny enclave of São Conrado, where the hang gliders land. Beyond that is Barra de Tijuca (usually called just Barra), an area of big streets, big malls, big cars, and little intrinsic interest. Backstopping all of these Zona Sul neighborhoods is the massive **Tijuca National Park.** Mostly mountainous, the 3,300-hectare (8,151-acre) forest is cut through with excellent walking and hiking trails, many leading to peaks with fabulous views.

GETTING AROUND

The Rio neighborhoods in which visitors spend most of their time are very easy to get around. You can almost always see the mountains or the ocean or both; with landmarks like that, it's pretty hard to stray too far from where you want to go.

BY SUBWAY   Line 1 goes downtown, covering most of Centro, swinging through Glória, Catete, Flamengo, and Botafogo before ducking through the mountain to its terminus in Copacabana. It takes 20 minutes to go from Centro to Copacabana. Line 2 starts in downtown and is useful for going to the Maracanã stadium and the Quinta da Boa Vista (National Museum). The system is very safe, and it operates daily 6am to 11pm. A single ride costs R$1.90 (65¢), a two-ride ticket costs R$3.75 (US$1.25), and a 10-ride card costs R$19 (US$6.25).

BY BUS   Rio's buses follow direct pathways, always sticking to the main streets. On the Centro-Copacabana route alone, there are more than 30 different buses. The route number and final destination are displayed in big letters on the front of the bus. Smaller signs displayed inside the front window and posted on the side of the bus list the intermediate stops. *Tip:* If you're going from Ipanema or Copacabana all the way to Centro (or vice versa), look for a bus that says VIA ATERRO in its smaller window sign. These buses get on the waterfront boulevard in Botafogo and don't stop again until they reach downtown.

Many buses are boarded from the rear and exited from the front (although increasingly more buses board from the front now). Have your bus money ready—R$1.50 to R$2 (50¢–65¢)—as you will go through a turnstile right away. There are no transfers. Buses are quite safe during the day; later in the evening (after 10pm), it's better to take a taxi.

BY TAXI   Regular taxis can be hailed anywhere on the street or at the many taxi stands around the city. Radio taxis are about 20% more expensive and can be contacted by phone; try **Coopertramo** (© **021/2560-2022**) or **Transcoopass** (© **021/2560-4888**). Radio taxis have air-conditioning and are supposedly more reliable, but we've never had a problem with regular taxis.

BY FERRY   Rio's ferries are operated by **Barcas SA** (© **021/2533-6661**) and depart from Praça XV downtown. The service to Niterói runs 24 hours a day, with hourly service between midnight and 5am. The cheapest ferry costs R$1.50 (50¢) and takes about 25 minutes to cross.

BY CAR   Driving in Rio is not for the meek of soul or weak of heart. Traffic is hectic, street patterns are confusing, and drivers are just a few shades shy of courteous. Things get even trickier later at night, when drivers start to regard red lights as optional. Be careful when approaching intersections.

Major car-rental companies include **Hertz,** Av. Princesa Isabel 334, Copacabana (© 021/2275-7440); **Interlocadora,** at Galeão airport (© 021/3398-3181) and Santos Dumont airport (© 021/2240-0754); **Localiza Rent A Car,** Av. Princesa Isabel 214, Copacabana (© 021/2275-3340); and **Unidas,** at Galeão airport (© 021/3398-3452) and Santos Dumont airport (© 021/2240-6715). Rates start at R$100 (US$33) per day for a small car with air-conditioning. Insurance adds another R$30 (US$10) per day.

VISITOR INFORMATION

Riotur (© 021/2217-7575; www.riodejaneiro-turismo.com.br) operates a number of offices and kiosks around town. There's an information booth at Galeão airport (© **021/3398-2245**), located in the international arrivals hall of Terminal 1 (daily 6am–noon) and Terminal 2 (daily 6am–noon and 5–11pm). There's also a booth in the domestic arrivals hall, open from 6am to noon and 5 to 11pm. There's another Riotur kiosk in the arrivals area of the Novo Rio Rodoviária bus station, open from 8am to 8pm (© **021/2263-4857**). The main Riotur information center is located at Av. Princesa Isabel 183, Copacabana (© **021/2541-7522**). Open Monday through Friday from 9am to 6pm, this office has the largest selection of brochures and information. This office also operates an information phone line, **Alô Rio,** at © **021/2542-8080** with an English-speaking staff; it's available Monday through Friday from 9am to 6pm.

FAST FACTS   To exchange traveler's checks or currency, try **Banco do Brasil;** branches are located at Av. N. S. de Copacabana 594, Copacabana (© 021/2548-8992); and Galeão airport, Terminal 1, Third Floor (© 021/3398-3652). There's also a **Citibank** at Rua da Assembleia 100, Centro (© 021/2291-1232). The exchange house **Imatur,** Rua Visconde de Pirajá 281, Loja A, Ipanema (© 021/2219-4205), is open Monday through Friday from 9am to 6pm and Saturday from 9am to1pm.

In an emergency, call the **police** at © 190; for the **fire brigade** or an **ambulance,** call © 193. You can also try the **tourist police** at Av. Afranio de Melo Franco 159, Leblon (© 021/3399-7170). If you need a doctor, call **Medtur,** Av. N. S. de Copacabana, Copacabana (© 021/2235-3339). The best hospitals are **Miguel Couto,** Rua Bartolomeu Mitre 1108, Leblon (© 021/2274-6050), or **Rocha Maia,** Rua General Severiano 91, Botafogo (© 021/2295-2121). Should you require any further vaccinations, contact the **Health Office,** Rua Mexico 128, Centro (© 021/2240-3568); vaccinations are given Monday through Friday from 10 to 11am and 2 to 3pm.

Telerede Internet Café, Rua N. S. de Copacabana 209, Copacabana (© 021/2275-3148), has one of the fastest Internet connections in town; each 15 minutes in cyberspace will set you back R$2 (65¢). For other Internet locations try the large bookstores such as Saraiva or Letras e Expressões around town.

You will find **post offices** all over town; look for the yellow-and-blue signs that read CORREIOS. Three main locations are Rua Primeiro de Março 64, Centro (© 021/2503-8331); Av. N. S. de Copacabana 540, Copacabana (© 021/2503-8398); and Rua Visconde de Pirajá 452, Ipanema (© 021/2563-8568). These branches are open Monday through Friday from 10am to 4pm.

WHAT TO SEE & DO

If you're interested in taking a guided tour, try **Blumar** ⋆ (© 021/2511-3636). Tours can be organized for one to three people and a guide, and include all of Rio's landmarks and a variety of cultural evening programs as well. Prices range from $36 for a tour of the Tijuca forest to $93 for a "Rio by Night" tour that includes dinner and a show (prices are per person based on two people). For the basic city tour contact **Gray Line** (Ⓢ **021/2512-9919**): The $29 afternoon tour of the Sugar Loaf and Rio's historic downtown is a reasonable value. The $29 half-day tour (morning or afternoon) of the Corcovado is really a bit of a racket; all they're providing is transfer to and from the train station at a markup. If your time is very limited you can also combine these two tours and see the Corcovado, Sugar Loaf Mountain, and historic Rio in one full-day trip for $72, lunch included.

Tip: When booking a tour, it's best to make the call yourself. If the concierge or front desk makes the booking, it will cost you 10% to 50% more, and you won't necessarily get the tour you want. Rio concierges are notorious for claiming a tour is "full," then putting guests on a tour with another company that offers the concierge a bigger commission.

THE TOP ATTRACTIONS
Centro

Ilha Fiscal ☖☖   This blue-green ceramic castle in the bay off Praça XV looks like the dwelling place of a princess, but in fact, it was built as the headquarters of the Customs service. When construction was finished in 1889, the normally reclusive Emperor Dom Pedro II decided to have a grand ball on Ilha Fiscal. Arriving by boat, Dom Pedro stumbled on the stone steps of the quay but recovered and quipped, "The monarch may have slipped, but the monarchy remains in place." Six days later, the empire collapsed. Visitors to the island get to see some of this history, notably a large oil painting entitled *The Last Ball of the Monarchy,* and you can see the building itself, which is a gorgeous piece of work. The tour lasts about 2½ hours.

Tip: The navy also offers a 90-minute boat tour of four small islands in the Bahia Guanabara bristling with destroyers, aircraft carriers, and lots more military hardware. The voyage to Ilha Fiscal, Ilha das Cobras, Ilha dos Enxadas, and Ilha Villagagnon takes place aboard a World War I–era tugboat. Departures are Thursday through Sunday at 1:15 and 3:15pm; the tour costs R$6 (US$2) for adults, R$3 (US$1) for children and students. Call ahead to confirm at Ⓢ 021/2233-9165 or 021/3870-6992.

Av. Alfredo Agache s/n. Centro. Ⓢ **021/3870-6025**. Admission by guided tour only, R$6 (US$2) adults, R$3 (US$1) children under 13. Tours depart Thurs–Sun at 1 and 4pm; Sat–Sun additional 2:30pm departure. Bus: 119 or 415 (Praça XV).

Museu de Arte Moderna (MAM) ☖☖   Located in the waterfront Flamengo Park, the MAM is a long rectangular building lofted off the ground by an arcade of concrete struts. Like the arches of a Gothic cathedral, the concrete struts do all the load-bearing work, allowing for walls of solid plate glass that welcome in city and sea and provide a vast display area free of obstructions. The MAM presents the best of what's happening in Brazil and Latin America and hosts traveling international exhibits. As with all modern art museums, some stuff is obscure to the point of utter boredom, while some is quite remarkably clever. Signage is in both English and Portuguese. Allow an hour to 90 minutes to view the entire museum.

Av. Infante Dom Henrique 85, Parque do Flamengo (Aterro), Centro. Ⓢ **021/2240-4944**. www.mamrio. com.br. Admission R$8 (US$2.65) adults, R$6 (US$2) students and seniors, free for children under 13. Tues–Fri noon–6pm; Sat–Sun noon–7pm. Metrô: Cinelândia. Bus: 472 or 438 (get off at Av. Beira Mar by the museum's footbridge).

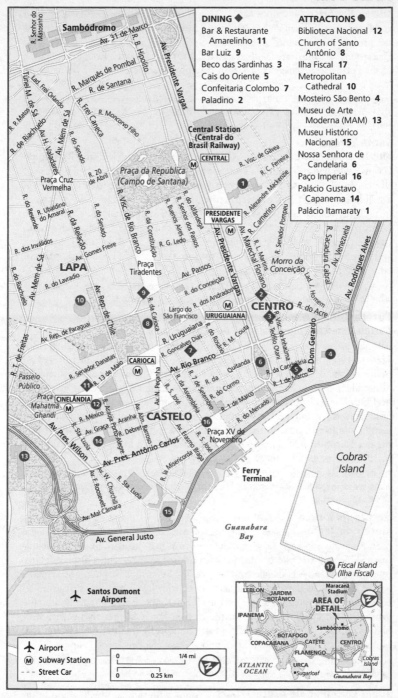

Rio's Centro

DINING ◆
Bar & Restaurante
  Amarelinho **11**
Bar Luiz **9**
Beco das Sardinhas **3**
Cais do Oriente **5**
Confeitaria Colombo **7**
Paladino **2**

ATTRACTIONS ●
Biblioteca Nacional **12**
Church of Santo
  Antônio **8**
Ilha Fiscal **17**
Metropolitan
  Cathedral **10**
Mosteiro São Bento **4**
Museu de Arte
  Moderna (MAM) **13**
Museu Histórico
  Nacional **15**
Nossa Senhora de
  Candelaria **6**
Paço Imperial **16**
Palácio Gustavo
  Capanema **14**
Palácio Itamaraty **1**

Sambódromo

Central Station
(Central do
Brasil Railway)
CENTRAL

PRESIDENTE
VARGAS

Praça da República
(Campo de Santana)

Praça Cruz
Vermelha

LAPA

Praça
Tiradentes

Largo do
São Francisco

URUGUAIANA

CENTRO

Morro da
Conceição

Passeio
Público

Praça
Mahatma
Ghandi

CINELÂNDIA

CARIOCA

CASTELO

Praça XV de
Novembro

Ferry
Terminal

Cobras
Island

Guanabara
Bay

Fiscal Island
(Ilha Fiscal)

Santos Dumont
Airport

✈ Airport
Ⓜ Subway Station
--- Street Car

0   1/4 mi
0   0.25 km

**AREA OF
DETAIL**

LEBLON
JARDIM
BOTÂNICO
IPANEMA
BOTAFOGO
COPACABANA
CATETE
FLAMENGO
URCA
Sugarloaf
Sambódromo
CENTRO
Cobras
Island
ATLANTIC
OCEAN
Maracanã
Stadium
Guanabara Bay

Museu Histórico Nacional ✮✮   This is the place for anyone looking for a good overview of Brazilian history, from Cabral's arrival in 1500 to the events of the present day. Exhibits on themes such as "Early Exploration" and "Coffee Plantations" are illustrated with abundant maps and artifacts. Even better, much of the Portuguese signage comes with English translation. Allow 2 hours to see it all.

Praça Marechal Âncora s/n. © 021/2550-9224. www.museuhistoriconacional.com.br. Admission R$5 (US$1.65) adults, R$3 (US$1) seniors and children under 13. Tues–Fri 10am–5:30pm; Sat–Sun 10am–6pm. Bus: 119 or 415 (10-min. walk from Praça XV).

Santa Teresa

Museu Chácara do Céu ✮✮   A wealthy man with eclectic tastes, Raymundo Castro Maya had this mansion built in the hills of Santa Teresa, then filled with all manner of paintings and pottery and sculpture. The house itself is a charmer, a stylish melding of hillside and structure that evokes Frank Lloyd Wright's work in the American West. The views from the garden are fabulous. Castro Mayo seems to have had three main interests: European painters, including Monet, Matisse, Picasso, and Dalí; Brazilian art, particularly 19th-century landscapes; and Chinese pottery. Also worth perusing are the maps and paintings, particularly those of Rio in its early years.

Rua Murtinho Nobre 93, Santa Teresa. © 021/2507-1932. Admission R$2 (65¢) adults, free for children under 12; free for all on Wed. Wed–Mon noon–5pm. Tram: Curvelo (Chácara do Céu).

Catete, Glória & Flamengo

Museu da República/Palácio do Catete ✮✮   Located in a gorgeous baroque palace that served as the official residence of Brazilian presidents from 1897 to 1960, this museum tries very hard to engage visitors in the history and politics of the Brazilian republic. The best exhibit is the three-room hagiography of President Getúlio Vargas. It's a curious treatment for this museum, given that in 1930, Vargas launched the coup that brought the first republic to an end. Still, they do a fabulous job, creating a multimedia sensory experience of Getúlio's life and times. In the final room, in a softly backlit glass case, there's the pearl-handled 32-caliber Colt that Getúlio used to blast a hole in his heart in 1954. Allow an hour to 90 minutes.

Rua do Catete 153, Catete. © 021/2558-6350. www.museudarepublica.org.br. Admission R$5 (US$1.65) adults, free for seniors and children under 12; free for all Wed. Tues–Fri noon–5pm; Sat–Sun 2–6pm. Metrô: Catete.

Botafogo & Urca

Museu do Indio ✮✮ *(Kids)*   The Indian Museum's exhibits are some of the most innovative and artistic we have come across in a Brazilian museum, including striking wall-size photos adorned with colored feathers, and a display of kids' toys where the objects dangle from the ceiling at various heights. The symbolism of the hunt is portrayed in a dark room with just a ray of light casting an eerie glow on spears and animal skulls. There is no English signage, but the exhibits are so vivid, they speak for themselves. For kids, there is a gallery with body paint and stamps so they can practice adorning themselves as warriors or hunters. It's a great spot for children and an easy place to spend 2 hours.

Rua das Palmeiras 55, Botafogo. © 021/2286-8899. www.museudoindio.org.br. Admission R$3 (US$1), free for children in strollers. Tues–Sun 9am–5:30pm; Sat–Sun 1–5pm. Metrô: Botafogo.

Sugar Loaf (Pão de Açúcar) ✮✮✮   Along with samba, beaches, and beautiful people, the Sugar Loaf remains one of the original and enduring Rio attractions. When you stand on its peak, the entire *cidade maravilhosa* (marvelous

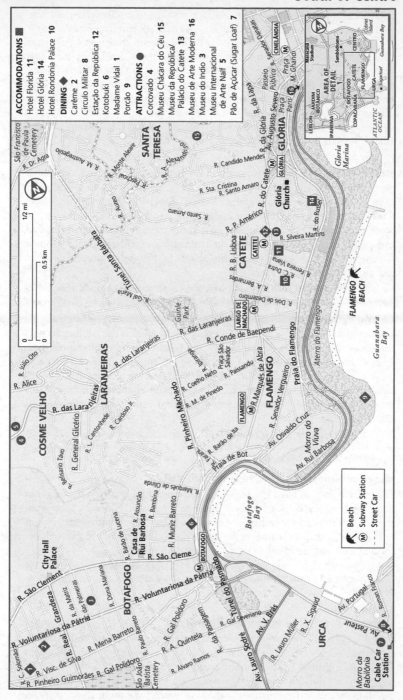

South of Centro

ACCOMMODATIONS ■
Hotel Florida 11
Hotel Glória 14
Hotel Rondonia Palace 10

DINING ◆
Carême 2
Circulo Militar 8
Estação da República 12
Kotobuki 6
Madame Vidal 1
Porção 9

ATTRACTIONS ●
Corcovado 4
Museu Chácara do Céu 15
Museu da República/
Palácio do Catete 13
Museu de Arte Moderna 16
Museu do Indio 3
Museu Internacional
de Arte Naïf 5
Pão de Açúcar (Sugar Loaf) 7

Beach
ⓂSubway Station
- - - Street Car

259

city) lays at your feet—it's a truly beautiful sight. The cable car leaves every half-hour from 8am to 10pm, more frequently if there are enough people waiting. The ascent takes two phases: the first from the ground station in Urca to the 220m (722-ft.) Morro de Urca, the second up to the 396m (1,300-ft.) Sugar Loaf itself. Trams are timed, so it's next to impossible to make both trips without spending transition time on the halfway stop. The Morro offers excellent views, as well as a cafe, a snack bar, a restaurant, souvenir stands, and a children's play area.

Av. Pasteur 520, Urca. ✆ 021/2546-8400. www.bondinho.com.br. Admission R$30 (US$10) adults, R$15 (US$5) children 6–12, free for children under 6. Daily 8am–10pm. Bus: 107.

Lagoa
Jardim Botânico ⚘   A photograph of the botanical gardens' stately imperial palms graces nearly every tour brochure of Rio. The reality is a pretty and calm refuge with lots of interesting plants. The 141-hectare (348-acre) gardens have 6,000 species of tropical plants and trees in their collection. The gardens make no effort to explain the collection so you're pretty much on your own. Bromeliad and orchid lovers will love the bromeliad and orchid greenhouses. Our personal favorite was a greenhouse full of pitcher plants and Venus flytraps. There's a cafe and a small bookshop on site.

Rua Jardim Botânico 1008. ✆ 021/2294-9349. www.jbrj.gov.br. Admission R$4 (US$1.35) adults, free for children under 8. Daily 8am–5pm. Bus: 170 (from Centro), 571 (from Glória/Botafogo), 572 (from Zona Sul).

Cosme Velho
Corcovado ⚘⚘⚘   The price is a bit steep but then so is the rail line, its narrow gauge winding upwards past hillside shacks and tangled rainforest creepers, up to the very feet of Christ. The *Cristo Redentor* (Christ the Redeemer) is a stylish Art Deco statue, standing 30m (98 ft.) tall on the top of Corcovado Mountain, 710m (2,330 ft.) above sea level. The view from his toes is definitely worth the money—it's enough to give you feelings of omniscience. Allow about 2 hours round-trip.

Rua Cosme Velho 512, Cosme Velho. ✆ 021/2558-1329. www.corcovado.com.br. Admission R$25 (US$8) adults, R$12 (US$4) children 6–12, free for children under 6. Trains going up depart every 30 min. Daily 9am–6pm; last train down 7:30pm. Bus: 422, 583, or 584 to Cosme Velho.

Museu Internacional de Arte Naif do Brasil ⚘⚘   Don't miss the Museu de Arte Naif, located just a few hundred yards from the Corcovado train station. Sometimes known as "primitive" or "ingénue" art, its practitioners paint from the heart, portraying the daily life of common folks. Whatever they may lack in technical skill, they more than make up for with cheerful and expressive drawing and a vibrant use of color. Expect to spend 45 minutes.

Rua do Cosme Velho 561, Cosme Velho. ✆ 021/2205-8612. www.museunaif.com.br. Admission R$5 (US$1.65) adults, R$3 (US$1) children. Tues–Fri 10am–6pm; Sat–Sun noon–6pm. Bus: 422, 583, or 584 to Cosme Velho.

Farther Afield
Museu de Arte Contemporânea–Niterói ⚘⚘   Oscar Niemeyer's spaceship design for Niterói's new contemporary art museum has done for this bedroom city what Gehry's Guggenheim did for Bilbao: put it on the map (at least in Brazil). As a gallery, however, the museum has drawbacks. Circular buildings are inherently difficult to make functional, on top of which the finishing on the inside seems extraordinarily cheap, as if most of the budget was spent on architectural fees. The curators do their best, bringing in a constantly changing

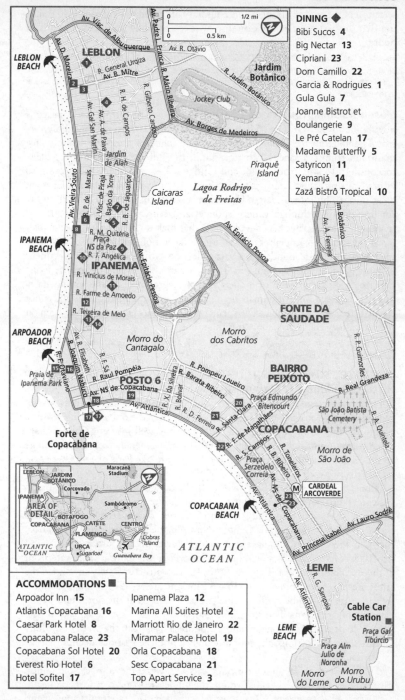

Rio's Beaches

DINING ◆
Bibi Sucos **4**
Big Nectar **13**
Cipriani **23**
Dom Camillo **22**
Garcia & Rodrigues **1**
Gula Gula **7**
Joanne Bistrot et
Boulangerie **9**
Le Pré Catelan **17**
Madame Butterfly **5**
Satyricon **11**
Yemanjá **14**
Zazá Bistrô Tropical **10**

LEBLON
BEACH
LEBLON
Av. Visc. de Albuquerque
Av. Padre Praça Franca
Av. R. Otávio
R. General Urqiza
Av. B. Mítre
R. H. de Campos
Av. D. Moreira
Av. Gal San Martin
Av. A. de Campos
Av. de Paiva
R. Gilberto Cardoso
R. Jardim Botânico
Jardim Botânico
Jockey Club
Av. Borges de Medeiros
Jardim de Alah
Piraquê Island
Lagoa Rodrigo de Freitas
Caicaras Island
Av. Vieira Souto
R. P. de Marais
R. Visc. de Piraja
R. Barão da Torre
R. B. de Jaguaripe
IPANEMA BEACH
R. M. Quitéria
Praça NS da Paz
R. J. Angélica
IPANEMA
R. Vinícius de Morais
R. Farme de Amoedo
R. Teixeira de Melo
ARPOADOR BEACH
Av. R. Elisabeth
R. F. S.
R. Raul Pompéia
R. F. Otaviano
Av. Joaquim Nabuco
Praia de Ipanema Park
POSTO 6
Av. NS de Copacabana
Av. Atlântica
R. X. da Silveira
R. Bolivar
R. R. D. Ferreira
R. Barata Ribeiro
R. Pompeu Loureiro
R. Santa Clara
Praça Edmundo Bitencourt
FONTE DA SAUDADE
Morro dos Cabritos
Av. Epitácio Pessoa
Av. A. Ferreira
Jardim Botânico
Morro do Cantagalo
BAIRRO PEIXOTO
R. Real Grandeza
R. P. Guimarães
São João Batista Cemetery
R. A. Quintela
Forte de Copacabana
R. F. de Magalhães
R. S. Campos
COPACABANA
Praça Serzedelo Correia
Av. N.S. de Copacabana
Av. Atlântica
Av. R. Tomeiro
R. B. Ribeiro
Morro de São João
CARDEAL ARCOVERDE
Av. Princesa Isabel
Av. Lauro Sodré
LEME
COPACABANA BEACH
ATLANTIC OCEAN
LEME BEACH
Av. Atlântica
R. G. Sampaio
Cable Car Station
Praça Gal Tibúrcio
Praça Alm Julio de Noronha
Morro do Leme
Morro do Urubu

LEBLON
JARDIM BOTÂNICO
Maracanã Stadium
Corcovado
IPANEMA
AREA OF DETAIL
COPACABANA
BOTAFOGO
CATETE
CENTRO
FLAMENGO
Sambódromo
Cobras Island
ATLANTIC OCEAN
URCA
Sugarloaf
Guanabara Bay

0   1/2 mi
0   0.5 km

ACCOMMODATIONS ■
Arpoador Inn **15**
Atlantis Copacabana **16**
Caesar Park Hotel **8**
Copacabana Palace **23**
Copacabana Sol Hotel **20**
Everest Rio Hotel **6**
Hotel Sofitel **17**
Ipanema Plaza **12**
Marina All Suites Hotel **2**
Marriott Rio de Janeiro **22**
Miramar Palace Hotel **19**
Orla Copacabana **18**
Sesc Copacabana **21**
Top Apart Service **3**

selection of the best of Brazilian contemporary art. Even so, you can't help thinking that the best piece of work on display is the building itself. Allow about an hour.

Mirante de Boa Viagem s/n, Niterói. © 021/2620-2481. www.macniteroi.com.br. Admission R$5 (US$1.65) adults, R$3 (US$1) students and seniors, free for children under 8. Tues–Fri and Sun 11am–6pm; Sat 1–9pm. From Praça XV take the ferry to Niterói, then take a short taxi ride along Niterói's waterfront and up the hill to the museum.

Museu Nacional (Quinta da Boa Vista) 🕿🕿   The former royal palace is now home to the National Museum. The collection is vast and incredibly varied. Assembled in the grand entrance hall are many of the more exotic items: mastodon trunks, a saber-tooth tiger skull, the full skeleton of a giant Pleistocene sloth (4.8m/16 ft. long!), and a huge meteorite cut in cross section so visitors can run their hands across its polished iron-nickel surface. The main collection is a bit more ordered. One wing presents the whole of life—from the smallest protozoa through various sponges and crustaceans to arthropods and mammals. The displays here are old, but what makes it worthwhile is the quality of the specimens: a giant crab that looks like a monster from a 1950s horror movie, tarantulas in abundance, a vast collection of fish, and stuffed specimens of most of the mammals found in Brazil. A particular gross-out favorite is the protozoa room, chock-full of models and photographs of all the various nasty buggies that feed on live human flesh. Signage is all in Portuguese, but is not essential to enjoy the exhibits. We spent a good 2 hours here; others less keen on natural history could probably do it in an hour.

Quinta da Boa Vista s/n, São Cristóvão. © 021/2568-1149. Admission R$3 (US$1) adults, free for seniors and children under 11. Tues–Sun 10am–4pm. Metrô: São Cristóvão.

ARCHITECTURAL HIGHLIGHTS
Historic Buildings & Monuments
For a city so blessed with mountains and ocean and historical roots several centuries deep, Rio's movers and shakers have suffered from a striking sense of inferiority. As a result, since the early 1900s, various well-meaning Cariocas have taken turns ripping out, blowing up, filling in, and generally reconfiguring huge swaths of their city in order to make Rio look more like Paris or Los Angeles or, lately, Miami Beach.

Armed with the slogan "Rio Civilizes Itself!" and a deep envy of what Baron Haussman had done in Paris, engineer-mayor Pereiro Passos set to work in 1903 ripping a large swath through Rio's Centro district to create the first of the city's grand boulevards, the Avenida Central. Now renamed the **Avenida Rio Branco,** the 32m-wide (108-ft.) boulevard runs from Praça Mauá south past the grand neoclassical Igreja de Nossa Senhora da Candelária to what was then waterfront at the Avenida Beira Mar. The four-story Parisian structures that once lined the street are now found only on the **Praça Floriano,** referred to by most Cariocas by the name of its subway stop, Cinelândia. Anchored at the north end by the extravagant beaux arts Theatro Municipal, and flanked by the equally ornate Museu de Belas Artes and neoclassical Biblioteca Nacional, the praça beautifully emulates the proportions, the monumentality, and the glorious detail of a classic Parisian square.

The next stage in urban reform came in 1922, when the 400-year-old hilltop castle south of Praça XV was blown up, the hill leveled, and construction begun on a series of government office towers inspired by the modernist movement. The first of these—now known as the **Palácio Gustavo Capanema** (Rua da Imprensa 16)—listed among its architects nearly all the greats of Brazilian architecture, including Lucio Costa, Oscar Niemeyer, and Roberto Burle Marx, with painter Candido Portinari. International architects sat up and took note; other less avant-garde government departments commissioned architects with different ideologies, resulting in the War of the Styles that raged through the remainder of the 1930s. The resulting enclave of office towers, known as **Castelo,** lies on a patch centered on the Avenida Presidente Antonio Carlos. Chiefly of interest to architectural buffs, it should be toured only during office hours.

When it came to razing the city, Passos had nothing on Brazilian dictator Getúlio Vargas. In 1940, on Vargas's personal order, a monster 12-lane boulevard, the Avenida Presidente Vargas, was cut through the city fabric from the beautiful Nossa Senhora da Candelária church through the Campo de Santana Park to the northern edges of downtown. Anchoring this new mega-boulevard was the **Central Station,** a graceful modern building with a 132m (440-ft.) clock tower that still stands overlooking the city. Vargas's plan called for the entire 4km (2½-mile) street to be lined with identical 22-story office blocks. Only a few were ever built; they can be seen on the block crossed by Rua Uruguaiana.

The next great reconfiguration of Rio came 2 years after the federal capital fled inland to Brasília. City designers scooped away the huge high hill—Morro Santo Antônio—that once dominated the Largo Carioca, and dumped the earth on the beach from Lapa to Flamengo to create a vast new waterfront park. On the raw spot where the hill once stood arose the innovative cone-shaped **Metropolitan Cathedral,** and at the intersection of the new avenidas República do Chile and República do Paraguai, a trio of towering skyscrapers were built, the most interesting of which is the "hanging gardens" headquarters of Brazil's state oil company **Petrobras.** On the waterfront park—officially called **Parque do Flamengo** but most often referred to as *Aterro,* the Portuguese word for landfill—designers created new gardens and pathways, a new beach, and a pair of modernist monuments: the **Modern Art Museum** and the impressive **Monument to the Dead of World War II.** Not incidentally, the park also bears two wide and fast roadways connecting Centro with the fashionable neighborhoods in the Zona Sul.

Churches & Temples

Rio is awash with churches, with about 20 in Centro alone. The most impressive traditional church in Rio is **Nossa Senhora da Candelária** ⚐, set on a traffic island of its own at the head of Avenida Presidente Vargas (**②** **021/2233-2324**). It's open Monday through Friday from 7:30am to 4pm, Saturday and Sunday from 7:30am to noon. Also impressive, if not quite worth the hype or the long trek, is the **Mosteiro São Bento,** located on a hill on the far north corner of downtown (access is via an elevator located in Rua Dom Gerardo 40; **②** **021/2291-7122**). The main church itself is a shining example of the Golden Church, the high baroque practice of plastering every inch of a church's richly carved interior in gold leaf. It's open daily from 8 to 11am and 2:30 to 6pm. Newly re-opened, the **Igreja da Ordem Terceira de São Francisco da Penitência** ⚐, Largo da Carioca 5 (**②** **021/2262-0197**), is set on a hilltop overlooking Largo Carioca. It and the next-door **Church of Santo Antônio** (**②** **021/2262-0129**) form part of the large Franciscan complex in the city center. The São Francisco church is simply outstanding: Interior surfaces are filled with golden carvings and hung with censers of heavy ornate silver. You can pay a visit Wednesday through Friday from 11am to 4pm. Last and most innovative of Rio's significant churches is the **Catedral Metropolitana** ★★, Av. República de Chile 245 (℡ 021/2240-2869). The form is ultimately modern, and the feeling is soaring High Gothic. It's open daily from 7am to 6pm.

BEACHES, PARKS & PLAZAS
Beaches
The older bay beaches such as **Botafogo** and **Flamengo** are now unfortunately quite polluted. They're fine and picturesque places for an afternoon stroll, but a poor spot if your heart is set on swimming. The first of the ocean beaches to see development back in the 1920s, **Copacabana** ★★ remains one of the favorites. The wide and beautifully landscaped Avenida Atlântica is a great place for a stroll. **Ipanema beach** ★★ was famous among Brazilians even before Tom Jobim wrote his famous song about the tall and tan and lovely girl he saw and sighed over. Stretching nearly 3km (2 miles) from the foot of the Pedra Dois Irmãos to the Ponta Arpoador, Ipanema is a carnival. Watch volleyball or footvollei (like volleyball but no hands allowed), beach soccer, hand shuttle, surfing, and wake boarding. Forgot your bikini? Wait but a moment, and one will come by for sale, along with towels, hats, shades, peanuts, beer, cookies, suntan lotion, styrofoam airplanes, sticks of grilled shrimp, and coconuts. Off on its own, surrounded by mountains, **São Conrado** beach offers some fine scenery and a (relative) sense of isolation. Its other main claim to fame is as a landing strip for all the hang gliders who leap from nearby peaks.

Squares & Plazas
Tucked away just a few hundred meters uphill along Rua Cosme Velho from the Corcovado train station is one of Rio's prettiest squares, the **Largo de Boticario** ★★, named for the druggist Luis da Silva Souto who settled there in 1831. It's a gem of a spot, with five gaily painted colonial houses encircling a fountain in the middle of a flagstone square. If you're going to the Corcovado anyway, it's well worth the 5-minute detour.

Perhaps the city's prettiest square (next to Cinelândia) is the **Largo do Machado** in the Catete neighborhood. Perfectly proportioned, the square is dominated by the **Igreja Matriz de Nossa Senhora da Glória,** a strange but rather elegant combination of traditional Greek temple and a three-story bell tower. As an added bonus, there are a number of Parisian-style sidewalk cafes on the square's northern flank.

Parks & Gardens
On the waterfront near Centro is **Flamengo Park,** a good place to stroll in the late afternoon if you're looking for a nice view of the Sugar Loaf. In the other direction, just past the northern edge of downtown, lies the **Quinta da Boa Vista,** the royal family's former country residence (p. 262). Though it's been a century or more since the exiled royals departed, their former country residence is as delightful now as it was when the royal princesses scampered round the villa gardens. The best of the bunch, the **Parque Nacional Da Tijuca (Tijuca National Park)** is a wonder. At 3,300 hectares (8,151 acres), it's the biggest urban forest in the world, and one of the last remnants of Atlantic rainforest on Brazil's southern coast. It's a great place to go for a hike (see "Sports & Outdoor Activities," below), splash in a waterfall, or admire the view.

SPECTACULAR VIEWS
The two best views in Rio—from the **Sugar Loaf** and the **Corcovado**—are both admission-charging attractions. But in a city with so much wonderful geography, it's impossible to fence off everything.

One of the best views is from the **Ruin Park** 🕊🕊 in Santa Teresa. Located right next to the Museu Chácara de Céu (Rua Murtinho Nobre 93), the park was once a sizable mansion belonging to one of Rio's leading socialites. When the house burned down, the city cleverly reinforced the gutted shell and then installed all manner of ramps and catwalks. One lookout at the top of the building provides a 270-degree view of Rio.

Walk to the end of Leblon beach and keep going along Rua Aperana— eventually (after gaining 70m/230 ft. in altitude), you'll get to **Seventh Heaven Lookout (Mirante de Setimo Céu).** Part of the Parque Penhasco Dois Irmãos, the lookout provides an excellent view of the beach, the Sugar Loaf, and the Corcovado high above.

Just a short 3km (1¾-mile) drive uphill along Estrada da Canoa from the beach at São Conrado, the **Canoas Lookout (Mirante de Canoas)** provides a view of São Conrado, Rocinha, the Pedra Dois Irmaos near Leblon, and, looking back uphill, the Pedra Bonita from where the hang gliders launch. Carry on up the road for 2km (1¾ miles) then turn left on Caminho da Pedra Bonita, and you can stand by the hang gliders as they launch.

SPORTS & OUTDOOR ACTIVITIES

GOLF The **Gávea Golf Club,** Estrada da Gávea 800, São Conrado (© 021/ 3332-4141), is private. However, the Copacabana Palace hotel (p. 273) has an arrangement allowing their guests to tee off.

HANG GLIDING If you want to do some hang gliding, contact **Just Fly Rio** 🕊🕊 (© 021/2268-0565; www.justfly.lookscool.com). Flight instructor Paulo Celani has soared in tandem with hundreds of people ages 5 to 85. There are no special skills necessary, aside from a willingness to run off a ramp into the open sky. It's well worth the US$80 per flight, with pickup and drop-off included.

HIKING **Tijuca National Park** offers some fabulous hiking opportunities within the city limits. Pico de Tijuca (1,022m/3,352 ft.) makes an excellent 2-hour hike; the trail head is at the end of Caminho do Pico da Tijuca. Pedra da Gávea (828m/2,715 ft.) usually takes a full 6 hours; there are numerous trail heads, one from the top of Estrada Sorimã in Barra de Tijuca. Also within Tijuca Park, and more easily accessible, is the 704m (2,310-ft.) hike up to the Corcovado. The trail head is in the Parque Lage, Rua Jardim Botânico 414, in Lagoa. Note that while trails in Tijuca Forest are usually in good condition, they're generally very poorly marked.

Rio Hiking 🕊🕊 (© 021/9721-0594; www.riohiking.com.br) offers guided hiking trips to most of these peaks. The 4-hour Sugar Loaf trip costs $40. The 6-hour Pedra da Gávea hike offers terrific views, a waterfall in the middle, and an ocean dip at the end; it costs $45. Less strenuous is the Tijuca Forest tour, which involves a jeep tour of the forest, stops at a waterfall and a couple of lookouts, and a 2-hour hike to Pico de Tijuca. The trip costs $55, with the option of returning via the fascinating hilltop neighborhood of Santa Teresa. Guides Denise Werneck and Gabriel Barrouin know Rio well, speak excellent English, and are a delight to be with.

SEA KAYAKING **Simone Miranda Duarte** (© 021/9954-9632) runs guided sea-kayak trips from Praia Vermelha in Urca out and around some of the small islands. The fiberglass kayaks aren't quite up to North American quality, but it's nice to be on the water. The cost is R$20 (US$7) per hour.

Moments   *Futebol* at the Maracanã

What an experience! Fans arrive hours beforehand (literally—for a 4pm game, show up at 1pm at the latest) and the world's biggest party begins. *Torcedores* (fan club members) bring out the samba drums and pound away while parading with huge flags in team colors, to the wild applause of their fellow fans. When the other team parades their flags, your team boos. Insulting songs fly back and forth. After several hours of this silliness, a soccer game breaks out. The Brazilian game has utter contempt for defense—it's attack, attack, attack for the full 90 minutes. The four best teams in Rio are Flamengo, Fluminense, Botafogo, and Vasco de Gama. Any game pitting one of these teams against the other is worth seeing. Scheduling is incredibly complex, but your hotel clerk will definitely know about the next big game. Tickets are quite affordable, ranging from R$15 to R$45 (US$5–US$15). Although you can sit in the neutral stands in the middle, it's more fun if you choose sides. Violence at Brazilian football matches has never come anywhere close to the problems seen in Europe; since they prohibited beer inside and reduced the stadium seating capacity, it's nearly vanished altogether. Maracanã Stadium is located at Rua Profesor Eurico Rabelo s/n, São Cristovão (© 021/2569-4916). Metrô: Maracanã.

SURFING   Rio has a number of good spots to catch the waves. The surfing beach closest to the main part of Rio is **Arpoador beach** in Ipanema. Waves are between 1m and 3m (3–10 ft.). **São Conrado beach** is off and on—sometimes there are good 1.8m (6-ft.) waves, sometimes it's dead. Out in Barra de Tijuca, the main surf beach is **Barra-Meio,** a half-mile stretch in the middle of the beach (around Av. Sernambetiba 3100). Waves average around 1.8m (6 ft.). Continue down that same beach another 8km (5 miles) and you come to **Macumba-Pontal,** a beach with waves of up to 3m (10 ft.).

If you've brought your board and just need transportation, there's a **Surf Bus** that departs the Largo do Machado (the square by the metrô stop of the same name) daily at 6am and 2pm, going along Copacabana, Arpoador, São Conrado, and Barra de Tijuca before returning. **Spirit,** Galeria River, Rua Francisco Otaviano 67, Loja 4, Ipanema (© 021/2267-9943), rents short boards, fun boards, and long boards for R$20 to R$30 (US$7–US$10) a day. You'll need to book ahead if you want a board on the weekend. If you're looking for lessons, there are a couple of instructors in Rio. However, like true surf dudes, they will neither have nor answer phones; you have to go find them. In Barra, go to Pepê's shack *(Barraca do Pepê)* and look for **Pedro Muller** or **Gagu.** The price of a private lesson is around R$30 (US$10) an hour.

SHOPPING

Shoppers will be in heaven in Rio. Browse the crafts markets in Ipanema or Copacabana for souvenirs or check out the small shops in downtown's pedestrian streets. Upscale shoppers will love the Rio Sul mall and the fancy boutiques in Rio's tony Ipanema.

ARTS & CRAFTS   **Brumado,** Rua das Laranjeiras 486, Loja 924, Laranjeiras (© 021/2558-2271; bus: 584), sells beautiful handicrafts as well as a variety of colonial furniture and some antiques. **Pé de Boi,** Rua Ipiranga 55, Laranjeiras

(② 021/2285-4395; bus: 584), goes beyond Brazilian handicrafts and sells works from popular Peruvian, Ecuadorian, and Guatemalan artists. **Jeito Brasileiro,** Rua Ererê 11A next to the Corcovado station, Cosme Velho (no phone), includes some above-average souvenirs, such as ceramics, leather, and wooden crafts.

BEACHWEAR & SURF SHOPS   Bum Bum, Rua Vinicius de Morais 130, Ipanema (② 021/2521-1229), is the best store to shop for the infamous Rio bikini. Collections vary constantly, but one thing never changes—the smaller, the better. Known for its original designs and prints, **Blue Man,** Visconde de Pirajá 351, Loja 108, Ipanema (② 021/2247-4905), is one of the beachwear trendsetters.

   Atol das Rocas, Rua Ouvidor 161, Centro (② 021/2232-4965), has every-thing you need to catch those waves—surfboards, body boards, and wet suits as well as shorts and T-shirts. To rent a board check out **Spirit,** Galeria River, Rua Francisco Otaviano 67, Loja 4, Ipanema (② 021/2267-9943). Open Monday through Saturday only, you will have to book ahead if you want to surf over the weekend. Rentals range from R$20 to R$30 (US$7–US$10) for a short board, fun board, or long board.

BOOKS   Livraria da Travessa invites browsing sessions of several hours or more with its great collection of English-language books, including all the usual pocket books plus children's books and guidebooks. There are two locations: one at Av. Rio Branco 44, Centro (② 021/2242-9294), and another at Rua Visconde de Pirajá 462A, Ipanema (② 021/2521-7734). For an excellent selec-tion of foreign magazines and newspapers, check out **Letras e Expressões,** Rua Visconde de Pirajá 276, Ipanema (② 021/2521-6110).

CLOTHING FOR MEN   Rio's the perfect place to add to your summer wardrobe, especially if you like a bit of color. **Toulon, Rua Visconde de Pirajá 135, Ipanema (② 021/2247-8716), is an excellent spot to pick up some smart casual wear: good quality jeans, khakis, colorful long-sleeved cotton dress shirts, and T-shirts at reasonable prices. If you're shopping for some shirts or informal jackets check out **Sandpiper,** Rua Santa Clara 75, Copacabana (② 021/2236-7652).

CLOTHING FOR WOMEN   Carioca women like to dress up, and even though most of their ensembles may seem a tad too colorful for North Ameri-can tastes, adding a few pieces to your wardrobe is bound to spice things up. **Rabo de Saia, Santa Clara 75, Copacabana (② 021/2255-7332), sells elegant women's clothing for those who like simple and clean styles with just a dash of color. For young and trendy pieces, check out the **Dimpus** collection, Rua Maria Quiteria 85, Ipanema (② 021/2523-1544), a popular store with Rio's 18- to 35-year-olds. One of the more elegant and upscale shops in Ipanema's tony shopping district, **Lelé da Cuca,** Rua Visconde de Pirajá 430B, Ipanema (② 021/2287-5295), caters to many of Rio's society women.

JEWELRY   The best-known name in Brazil for gems, jewelry, and souvenirs made with semiprecious and precious stones is **Amsterdam Sauer, Rua Visconde de Pirajá 484, Ipanema (② 0800/266-092 or 021/2512-9878). The store offers a wide range of jewelry and loose gemstones such as emeralds, aquamarines, imperial topaz (mined only in Brazil), tourmalines, citrines, and Brazilian opal.

MALLS & SHOPPING CENTERS   One of the most popular malls in the city, **Rio Sul, Rua Lauro Muller 116, Botafogo (② 021/2545-7200), has more than 450 stores, a movie theater, and an excellent food court. For serious shoppers, **Barra Shopping** will have everything you need. The largest mall in Latin America, with close to 600 stores, the disadvantage is its distance from the rest of Rio; it's located at Av. das Americas 4666, Barra da Tijuca (© 021/2431-9922). **Botafogo Praia Shopping,** Praia de Botafogo 400, Botafogo (© 021/2559-9559), has an excellent selection of clothing stores such as Dimpus, Folic, Corpo and Alma, Exchange, Old Factory, and Madame MS.

MUSIC   In the heart of Ipanema stands **Toca de Vinicius** ☆☆, Rua Vinicius de Moraes 129 (© 021/2247-5227), a small temple dedicated to the god of bossa nova, the poet and composer Vinicius de Moraes. Anything related to bossa nova can be found in this tiny store: an impressive collection of bossa nova CDs and vinyl, songbooks, and (mostly Portuguese) books and magazines on the smooth and mellow sounds of Brazil.

CARNAVAL

Carnaval—what a party! Thousands of people—many of them of limited means or just plain poor—spend hundreds of hours preparing for the Samba School Parade that culminates this 4-day celebration. Originally, Carnaval marked the last few days of fun before Lent, the 40-day period of fasting and penitence preceding Holy Saturday and Easter. The religious aspect of the celebration faded some time ago, but Carnaval's date is still determined by the ecclesiastical calendar. If you're not able to attend Carnaval itself, the **rehearsals**—which usually start in mid-September or early October—are an absolute must, the closest thing you'll experience to the event itself. In the 2 weeks leading up to the big event, you'll begin to see the **blocos.** These are community groups—usually associated with a particular neighborhood or sometimes with a bar—who go around the neighborhood, playing music and singing and dancing through the streets. Carnaval finally kicks off the Friday before Ash Wednesday with an explosion of lavish *bailes* **(balls.)** Then there is the pièce de résistance, the **Samba School Parade,** an event that the samba schools plan and sweat over for an entire year. Starting Sunday and continuing Monday night, the 14 top-ranked samba schools show their stuff in the Sambódromo, a mile-long concrete parade ground built in the center of Rio especially for this annual event.

WATCHING THE SAMBA PARADE

One of Carnaval's unique events, the Samba School Parade is an all-night feast of color and sound. Tens of thousands of costumed dancers, thousands of percussionists, and hundreds of gorgeous performers atop dozens of floats all move

---

Tips **Participating in the Parade**

If you think watching the parade from up close sounds pretty amazing, imagine being in it. To parade (*desfilar* in Portuguese), you need to commit to a school and buy a costume. Many schools now have websites with pictures of their costumes (look under *"fantasia"*). To contact a school directly, see the websites and phone numbers below under "Rehearsals." Prices range from R$150 to R$600 (US$50–US$200). A number of agencies in Rio will organize it all for you, at a markup of 25% to 50%. **Blumar** (© 021/2511-3636) can organize the whole event for you for $300. For other organizations, contact **Alô Rio** at © 021/2542-8080.

in choreographed harmony to the nonstop rhythm of samba. Over the course of 2 nights, 14 teams compete for the honor of putting on the best show ever.

Well before the parade starts, the grounds surrounding the Sambódromo are transformed into Carnaval central. A main stage hosts a variety of acts and performances and hundreds of vendors set up shop with food and drinks. This *terreirão do samba* (samba land) is open the weekend before Carnaval, Friday through Tuesday during Carnaval, and again the Saturday after for the Parade of Champions. Contact **Riotur** (© **021/2217-7575**) for more detailed programming information. For information on tickets, contact the **Liga das Escolas de Samba** (© **021/2253-7676;** www.liesa.com.br). You can also purchase tickets through a designated travel agency such as **Blumar** (© **021/2511-3636**). Tickets for the best bleacher sections cost $85; chairs start at $193 in sectors 9 and 11. As a last resort, try your hotel, but expect to pay a fair premium for this service. Unless you snag some fancy front row seats or box seats (very pricey, starting at $290!), you will be sitting on concrete bleachers.

The parade starts at 9pm, but unless you want to stake out a particular spot, you may as well take your time arriving, as the event will continue nonstop until about 6am.

REHEARSALS

Every Saturday from September until Carnaval, each samba school holds a general samba rehearsal *(ensaio)* at their home base. The band and key people come out and practice their theme song over and over to perfection. People dance for hours, taking a break now and then for snacks and beer. Both Mangueira and Salgueiro are located no more than a R$25 (US$13) cab ride from Copacabana. Plan to arrive anytime after 11pm. When you are ready to leave, there'll be lots of taxis around. The events are well attended and very safe; just don't go wandering off into an unfamiliar neighborhood. To find out more about rehearsals or participating in the parade, contact the **Liga das Escolas de Samba** at © **021/2253-7676,** or check out www.liesa.com.br. You can also contact the schools directly: **Imperatriz,** Professor Lacê 235, Ramos (© 021/2270-8037; www.imperatrizleopoldinense.com.br); **Império,** Av. M. Edgard Romero 114, Madureira (© 021/3359-4944; www.imperioserrano.art.br); **Mangueira** (Rio's favorite school and close to downtown), Rua Visconde de Niterói 1072, Mangueira (© 021/3872-6786; www.mangueira.com.br); and **Salgueiro,** Rua Silva Telles 104, Andaraí (© 021/2238-5564; www.salgueiro.com.br). If you can't find anyone who speaks English, contact **Alô Rio** for assistance at © **021/2542-8080.**

BLOCOS

Don't miss the blocos, neighborhood groups of musicians and merrymakers who parade through the streets in the days and nights before and during Carnaval. Everyone is welcome, and you don't need a costume, just comfortable clothes and shoes. Riotur publishes an excellent brochure called *Bandas, Blocos and Ensaios,* available through **Alô Rio** (© 021/2542-8080), or pick one up at Av. Princesa Isabel 183, Copacabana. In the list of blocos below, the days of the week refer specifically to the days of Carnaval unless otherwise stated.

The Saturday morning **Cordão do Bola Preta** meets in front of the Bola Preta Club, on the corner of Rua Treze de Maio and Rua Evaristo da Veiga just across from the Theatro Municipal in Cinelândia. Though this is not a gay group, men often dress in drag. Lots of musicians join in the **Bloco do Bip Bip,** the first and last bloco to parade. The first time begins at the stroke of midnight

New Year's Eve in Rio

The New Year's Eve extravaganza put on every single year in Rio puts any of the special millennium celebrations to shame. Millions of people pack Copacabana beach for an all-night festival of music, food, and fun, punctuated by the greatest fireworks show on earth. Trust the Brazilians to put on a great party where everyone is welcome and admission is absolutely free.

on Friday and the last time at 9:30pm on Tuesday evening, with Ash Wednesday looming just a few hours away. They meet at Bar Bip Bip, Rua Almirante Gonçalves 50 (close to the Luxor Regente Hotel). The biggest bloco of all is the **Banda de Ipanema,** counting up to 10,000 followers in its throng. The group meets on the two Saturdays preceding Carnaval as well as on Saturday during Carnaval at 3pm, starting at the Praça General Osorio. You'll see quite a few costumes at this parade, although not as many as at the **Banda da Carmen Miranda,** the prime gay parade. This bloco is an absolute blast, with outlandish costumes, extravagant drag queens, great music, and even some floats. It takes place on the Sunday before Carnaval, gathering at 4pm on the corner of Avenida Visconde de Pirajá and Rua Joana Angelica. The only bloco so far with a website, **Simpatia é Quase Amor** has close to 10,000 followers who all dress in the group's lilac-and-yellow shirts. The shirt is for sale at the meeting place, Praça General Osorio, starting at 3pm on the Saturday before Carnaval and the Sunday during Carnaval. Check out www.sitesbrasil.com/simpatia to see some wonderful pictures of the crowds.

BAILES

More formal than the blocos, the samba *bailes* are where you go to see and be seen. The notorious *Baile Vermelho e Preto* (**Red and Black Costume Ball**) is held every year on Carnaval Friday in honor of Rio's most popular soccer club, Flamengo. A great spot to rub shoulders with soccer players and their groupies, the event recently moved to the ATL Hall in Barra da Tijuca. Contact **Âlo Rio** (© **021/2542-8080**) for details and ticket information. The popular Copacabana nightclub **Le Boy** in Copacabana (p. 285) organizes a differently themed ball every night during Carnaval, Friday through Tuesday. These balls are gay-friendly but by no means gay-only. Call © **021/2240-3338** for details and ticket information. The prime gay event—and one of Rio's most famous balls— is the Tuesday night **Gala Gay** at the Scala nightclub, Av. Afranio de Melo Franco 296, Leblon (© **021/2239-4448**). TV stations vie for position by the red carpet to interview illustrious or notorious arrivals; wild and colorful costumes are a must. The grand slam of all Carnaval balls is the Saturday night extravaganza at the Copacabana Palace Hotel, the *Baile do Copa.* The hotel plays host to the crème de la crème of Rio's (and Brazil's) high society dressed in tuxedos and elegant costumes. Tickets start at $250 per person and sell out quickly. Call © **021/2548-7070** for more details.

WHERE TO STAY

The only neighborhood to avoid staying in is downtown Rio. Hotels always list the rack rates on a sign behind the desk, but you can usually expect to pay 50% to 80% of this amount, depending on the season, the staff person, and your bargaining skills. Always negotiate. Be sure to ask about taxes that will be added to your bill. Most hotels charge a 10% service tax, a 5% city tax, and if they are a member of the Rio Convention and Visitor's bureau, a tourist tax of $1 to $3 per day.

A substantial breakfast (*café de manha*) is included at most Brazilian hotels. In recent years, a few of the more expensive hotels have taken to charging for *café de manha*; if this is the case, it's noted in the rate information below.

IPANEMA/LEBLON
Very Expensive
Caesar Park Hotel ★★★ One of Rio's most luxurious hotels, the Caesar Park is very popular with visiting Americans. The hotel has recently undergone major renovations and is in tip-top shape. All 220 rooms received new furniture, mattresses, carpets, and soundproof windows, and the bathrooms were completely redone with granite counters and tile. Even the standard rooms are quite spacious. The usual "view hierarchy" applies: The standard rooms are those from the 5th to 10th floors, overlooking a side street; superior rooms face the same direction as standard rooms but are located from the 11th floor up; and the deluxe rooms provide an ocean view. Unfortunately, the building has alcoves around the windows that restrict views to the side. Amenities are all outstanding, and the view from the rooftop pool deck and fitness center is amazing.

Av. Vieira Souto 460, Ipanema, Rio de Janeiro, 22420-000 RJ. © 021/2525-2525. Fax 021/2521-6000. www. caesar-park.com. 222 units. R$600–R$780 (US$200–US$260) double; R$1,245 (US$415) junior suite double. Higher rates during New Year's and Carnaval. Extra person R$60 (US$30). Children under 13 stay free in parent's room. AE, DC, MC, V. Free valet parking. Bus: 415. **Amenities:** Restaurant; bar; rooftop pool; excellent health club; sauna; concierge; tour desk; car rental; business center; shopping arcade; 24-hr. room service; massage; babysitting; laundry; dry cleaning; nonsmoking rooms; executive level rooms. *In room:* A/C, TV, dataport, minibar, fridge, hair dryer, safe.

Hotel Marina All Suites ★★★ *(Finds)* Rio's first "design hotel," the Marina All Suites is the brainchild of a consortium of local architects and decorators who bought, gutted, replanned, and redecorated all the rooms, in the process reducing the original layout of six rooms per floor to a very spacious three. What must be the most beautiful suite in Rio is the two-bedroom suite diamante. Looking out of its large windows, it seems as though the room adjoins the ocean, the white tones of the room merging with Ipanema's white sands and the blue ocean beyond. All suites feature a kitchen with a microwave, fridge, and wet bar; ample desk space and sitting areas; spacious bathrooms; and large bedrooms, making this truly one of Rio's most outstanding hotels.

Av. Delfim Moreira 696, Leblon, Rio de Janeiro, 22441-000 RJ. © 021/2540-4990 or 021/2540-5212. Fax 021/2294-1644. www.marinaallsuites.com.br. 38 units (some w/shower only). R$690–R$1,080 (US$230–US$360) deluxe suite; R$1,485 (US$495) suite diamante. AE, DC, MC, V. Free parking. Bus: 474. **Amenities:** Restaurant; pool; excellent gym; sauna; game room; concierge; business center; 24-hr. room service; massage; babysitting; laundry service. *In room:* A/C, TV, dataport, kitchen w/fridge, microwave, toaster and coffeemaker, minibar, hair dryer, electronic safe.

Expensive
Everest Rio Hotel ★★ Unassuming from the outside, this elegant hotel provides surprisingly luxurious accommodations on the inside. All rooms are very bright and beautifully appointed. Large closets, a good-size desk, and a separate

---

Tips **No-Tell Motel**

A motel in Brazil is a very different thing from a motel in America. Brazilian motel rentals are strictly short-term, and strictly for sex.

table add to the spacious feel. And though the hotel is a block from the beach, views from the higher floors are none too shabby, looking toward either the mountains or the ocean. Unlike at other hotels, there are no extra charges for a room with a view. Well worth the splurge are the junior and executive suites, which feature sitting rooms and wonderfully large bedrooms elegantly decorated in pale colors. Breakfast on the 23rd floor features outstanding views.

Rua Prudente de Morais 1117, Ipanema Rio de Janeiro, 22420-041 RJ. ℂ 021/2523-2282. www.everest. com.br. 156 units. R$300 (US$100) standard double; R$360 (US$120) deluxe double; R$600 (US$200) suite. Children under 8 stay free in parent's room. Over 8, 25% extra. Parking R$15 (US$5) per day. AE, MC, V. Bus: 474. **Amenities:** 2 restaurants; bar; rooftop pool; business center; 24-hr. room service; babysitting; laundry service. *In room:* A/C, TV, dataport, minibar, fridge, safe.

Ipanema Plaza ⟨✰✰✰⟩   A member of the Holland based Golden Tulip hotel chain, the Ipanema Plaza opened in 2000, just 1 block from Ipanema beach. The hotel's modern and sleek design looks fabulous and the attention to detail carries over into the rooms. Furnished in beige tones and cherrywood, the rooms are quite spacious, particularly the deluxe rooms. A number of them come with a large balcony, and all double beds are king size; twin beds are much larger than the average Brazilian single bed. Now if you are splurging, the master suites are just gorgeous and have a separate sitting room adjacent to the bedroom.

Rua Farme de Amoedo 34, Ipanema, Rio de Janeiro, 22420-020 RJ. ℂ 021/3687-2000. Fax 021/3687-2001. www.ipanemaplazahotel.com. 135 units. R$315 (US$105) standard double, R$345 (US$115) deluxe double. Extra person 25%. Children under 10 stay free in parent's room. AE, DC, MC, V. Bus: 474 or 404. **Amenities:** Restaurant; bar; rooftop outdoor pool; small gym; tour desk; business center; 24-hr. room service; laundry service and dry cleaning; beach service. *In room:* A/C, TV/VCR, dataport, minibar, hair dryer, safe.

Moderate

Arpoador Inn ⟨✰⟩ ⟨Value⟩   The only budget-priced oceanfront hotel in Ipanema, the Arpoador Inn is located on a quiet stretch of beach popular with the surfing crowd, just off the Garota de Ipanema park. Deluxe rooms all face the ocean and are bright and spacious (those ending in "04" have recently been renovated)— book ahead for these. The superior rooms, overlooking the street behind the beach, make a fine alternative. The only rooms to avoid are the standard ones, which are very small, dark, and a tad beat-up, and look onto an interior wall.

Rua Francisco Otaviano 177, Ipanema, Rio de Janeiro, 22080-040 RJ. ℂ 021/2523-0060. Fax 021/2511-5094. http://ipanema.com/hotel/arpoador_inn.htm. 50 units (showers only). R$144 (US$48) standard double; R$192 (US$64) street-view superior double; R$288 (US$96) deluxe ocean view. Extra person R$25–R$40 (US$8–US$13). Children under 7 stay free in parent's room. AE, DC, MC, V. No parking. Bus: 474. **Amenities:** Restaurant; limited room service; laundry. *In room:* A/C, TV, fridge, safe

Top Apart Service ⟨✰✰⟩ ⟨Kids⟩   The advantage of an apart-hotel is the space; you get a furnished suite with a completely equipped kitchen. The most recently renovated suites have tile floors, modern furniture, and granite countertops in the kitchen and bathroom. All suites have a small balcony and a sofa bed in the living room. Unlike some apart-hotels, Top Apart Service doesn't skimp on amenities, providing free parking, an outdoor pool, sauna, and gym—all only 2 blocks from the beach.

Rua João Lira 95, Leblon, Rio de Janeiro, 22430-210 RJ. ℂ 021/2511-2442. www.accorhotels.com.br. 120 units (showers only). R$200 (US$67) 1-bedroom suite; R$275 (US$92) 2-bedroom suite. All rates are based on double. Extra person 25%. Up to 20% discount during low season. AE, DC, MC, V. Free parking. Bus: 474. **Amenities:** Restaurant; outdoor rooftop pool; small gym; sauna; limited room service; laundry; dry cleaning. *In room:* A/C, TV, kitchen, minibar, fridge, hair dryer.

COPACABANA
Very Expensive
The Copacabana Palace ★★ The Copacabana Palace is the place to splurge. The surrounding neighborhood may have lost some of its appeal in the 8 decades since this opulent hotel first appeared, but the hotel itself maintains all of its Jazz Age charm. But if you're going to get value for the money, it's really a case of go big or go home, and there's nothing bigger than the penthouse suites. Elegant and tastefully decorated, these spacious one-bedroom suites have their own private veranda overlooking Copacabana beach. Just as stylish and almost as spacious are the poolside suites, which also feature a partial ocean view. Of course, this kind of lifestyle comes with a hefty price tag, but how often do you fly down to Rio? Breakfast not included.

Av. Atlântica 1702, Copacabana, Rio de Janeiro, 22021-001 RJ. © 0800/211-533 or 021/2548-7070. Fax 021/2235-7330. www.copacabanapalace.orient-express.com. 226 units. R$780 (US$260) superior double; R$900 (US$300) deluxe double; R$990 (US$495) junior suite double; R$2,550–R$3,750 (US$850–US$1,250) penthouse suite. Seasonal discounts may be available, particularly June–Aug; discounts available for 4-night stays. Extra person about 25%. Children under 11 stay free in parent's room. AE, DC, MC, V. Free parking. Metrô: Arcoverde. **Amenities:** 2 restaurants (see "Cipriani" on p. 279); bar; large outdoor pool; rooftop tennis courts; health club; Jacuzzi; sauna; concierge; tour desk; car rental; business center; salon; 24-hr. room service; massage; babysitting; laundry; dry cleaning; executive level rooms. In room: A/C, TV, dataport, kitchen, minibar, hair dryer, safe.

Hotel Sofitel ★★★ One of Rio's most elegant hotels, the Sofitel is also one of the most cleverly designed: The U-shaped structure guarantees all rooms either a full or partial view of the shimmering ocean. The hotel also offers superb service and—thanks to a $25 million renovation—a clean modern look to match. Superior rooms are elegantly decorated with new furnishings and fixtures. All rooms have balconies, soundproof windows, and electronic safes big enough to hold a laptop. The deluxe rooms differ only in offering a guaranteed full ocean view. For sunbathing, there is Copacabana beach with complimentary hotel beach service or a choice of two swimming pools. Breakfast not included.

Av. Atlântica 4240, Copacabana, Rio de Janeiro, 22070-002 RJ. © 0800/241-232 or 021/2525-1232. Fax 021/2525-1200. www.sofitel-brasil.com.br. 388 units. R$450 (US$150) superior double; R$675 (US$225) superior Imperial Club double; R$500 (US$167) deluxe double; R$800 (US$267) deluxe Imperial Club double; R$850–R$1,275 (US$283–US$425) junior or executive suite double. Children under 13 stay free in parent's room. AE, DC, MC, V. Free parking. Bus: 474. **Amenities:** 2 restaurants (see "Le Pré-Catelan" on p. 279); bar; 2 pools; health club; sauna; concierge; tour desk; car rental; business center; shopping arcade; 24-hr. room service; massage; babysitting; laundry; dry cleaning; nonsmoking rooms or floors; executive level rooms. In room: A/C, TV, dataport, minibar, fridge, hair dryer, safe.

Marriott Rio de Janeiro ★★★ The Marriott's modern glass design stands out among Copa's older apartment buildings. Inside, a soaring multistory atrium gives the hotel an incredibly light and airy feel. The price for using so much space on empty atrium, unfortunately, is that the rooms themselves are a bit on the small side, though they're well laid out to maximize the space. The prime rooms offer sweeping views of Copacabana; book early, pay the $50 premium, and you won't regret it. The Marriott also offers outstanding service and excellent amenities that American travelers take for granted. The Marriott is the only hotel we've found in Brazil that provides every room with a free newspaper, complimentary mineral water, coffeemaker, iron and ironing board, and CD player. Breakfast not included.

Av. Atlântica 2600, Copacabana, Rio de Janeiro, 22041-001 RJ. © **800/228-9290** in the U.S. and Canada, 021/2545-6500, or 011/3069-2807. Fax 011/2545-6589. www.marriott.com. 245 units. R$596 (US$199) double, interior view; R$700 (US$233) ocean view. Children under 12 stay free in parent's room. AE, DC, MC, V. Parking R$25 (US$8) per day. Metrô: Arcoverde. **Amenities:** Restaurant; bar; rooftop pool; state-of-the-art health club; concierge; tour desk; car rental; business center; 24-hr. room service; massage; babysitting; laundry; dry cleaning; nonsmoking rooms; executive level rooms. *In room:* A/C, TV, dataport, high-speed Internet access, fridge, coffeemaker, hair dryer, iron, safe.

Expensive

Miramar Palace Hotel 🔍🔍 A member of the excellent Windsor chain (see the listing for Hotel Florida under "Catete," below), the Miramar offers luxury beachfront accommodations at a reasonable rate. The hotel is undergoing major renovations to bring it up to 21st-century standards. When making your reservation request a room on a renovated floor; modern blond wood furniture and splashes of cheerful tropical colors give these rooms a fresh feel. Standard rooms are spacious and located on the lower floors (4th–13th); you can still see the ocean albeit from the side. Superior rooms on the 14th and 15th floors have better views but give up some space in exchange for a veranda. The deluxe ocean view rooms have gorgeous views of Copacabana but the best rooms in the house are the suites. All are bright corner units with spacious bedrooms and a separate workspace.

Av. Atlântica 3668, Copacabana, Rio de Janeiro, 22070-001 RJ. © **0800/232-211** or 021/2521-1122. Fax 021/2521-3294. www.windsorhoteis.com. 156 units (many units have tubs). R$445 (US$115) standard double; R$390 (US$130) superior double; R$540 (US$180) deluxe double; R$735 (US$245) suite double. Children under 11 stay free in parent's room. Parking free. AE, DC, MC, V. Bus: 128 or 474. **Amenities:** Restaurant; bar; rooftop pool; exercise room; Jacuzzi; sauna; concierge; tour desk; business center; 24-hr. room service; laundry; nonsmoking floors. *In room:* A/C, TV, dataport, minibar, fridge, hair dryer, safe.

Orla Copacabana Hotel 🔍 *(Finds* Located just a block down from the Sofitel, the Orla shares the same fabulous location across from Copacabana beach and is only a short walk from Ipanema. Thanks to major renovations, the hotel has an updated trendy and clean look. The 115 rooms are very pleasantly decorated with modern furniture, and the bathrooms have been completely redone in gray and white granite. The best rooms in the house are the deluxe oceanview rooms. Alas no balconies but the views are prime, looking out over the Copacabana Fort. The superior rooms look out over the street behind the hotel and the standard rooms look into an interior wall; soundproofed windows keep a lot of the noise out. Note that the rates listed are the rack rates; inquire about discounts or seasonal rates.

Av. Atlântica 4122, Copacabana, Rio de Janeiro, 22070-002 RJ. © **021/2525-2425.** Fax 021/22879134. www.orlahotel.com.br. 115 units (showers only). R$345 (US$115) double standard; R$405 (US$135) double superior; R$525 (US$175) double deluxe. Extra person R$60 (US$20). Children under 11 stay free in parent's room. AE, DC, MC, V. Bus: 415 **Amenities:** Restaurant, bar; pool; sauna; small exercise room; limited room service; laundry. *In room:* A/C, TV, minibar, safe.

Moderate

Atlantis Copacabana Hotel 🔍 Located just between Ipanema and Copacabana on a quiet residential street, the Atlantis Copacabana Hotel is perfect for those who can't decide which neighborhood to stay in. Either beach is within minutes from your hotel, and shopping and restaurants are easily accessible as well. The hotel offers basic accommodations; all 87 rooms are standard with only a small variation in size and layout; rooms ending in 07 and 08 (such as 107 and 108) are slightly larger than the rest. From the eighth floor up the rooms that look out the back offer a view of Ipanema beach. Recently renovated, the property is in great shape.

Rua Bulhões de Carvalho 61, Copacabana, Rio de Janeiro, RJ 22081-000. © 021/2521-1142. Fax 021/2287-8896. atlantisreservas@uol.com.br. 87 units (shower only). R$160–R$220 (US$53–US$73) double. Extra person R$50 (US$17). Children under 6 stay free in parent's room. AE, DC, MC, V. Limited street parking. Bus: 128 or 474. **Amenities:** Rooftop pool; sauna; concierge; 24-hr. room service; laundry; tour desk. In room: A/C, TV, minibar, fridge, safe.

Copacabana Sol Hotel ★★ Finds   The Sol has recently undergone some renovations and offers good value only 4 blocks from Copacabana beach. The suites in particular are a great deal: Spacious and cool with granite floors, they have comfortable sitting rooms and gorgeous bathrooms with Jacuzzi tubs and separate showers. The superior and standard rooms have very small bathrooms with showers only, but are spotless and well maintained. Superior rooms overlook the street and have balconies and a small sitting area. As the Rua Santa Clara is not too noisy—especially at night—the superior rooms are preferable to the standard rooms that look out the back of the building and lack balconies.

Rua Santa Clara 141, Copacabana, Rio de Janeiro 22041-010, RJ. © **0800/254-477** or 021/2549-4577. Fax 021/2255-0744. www.copacabanasolhotel.com.br. 70 units. R$130–R$175 (US$65–US$88) standard and superior; R$200–R$265 (US$100–US$133) suite. Extra person R$40 (US$20). Children under 6 stay free in parent's room. AE, DC, MC, V. Free parking. Bus: 128 or 474. **Amenities:** Restaurant; concierge; tour desk; business center; 24-hr. room service; laundry service. In room: A/C, TV, dataport, minibar, fridge, safe.

Inexpensive

Sesc Copacabana ★ Finds   A well-known Brazilian institution, the Sesc offers a range of leisure and cultural activities to its members; however, all of their facilities (including hotels and theaters) are open to the community at a slightly higher rate. The Sesc Copacabana hotel happens to be particularly well situated, just a block from the beach, on a quiet street, and offers simple and pleasant accommodations, The hallways have a slight institutional feel and the furnishings are very basic, but the rooms look bright and new and are absolutely spotless. Standard rooms come only with two twin beds; the suites have a double bed as well as a sofa bed. The Sesc also offers rooms for travelers with disabilities, with a shower chair, handlebars in the bathroom, lower closets, and even air-conditioning controls at a lower level.

Rua Domingos Ferreira 160, Copacabana, Rio de Janeiro, 22070-002 RJ. © **021/2548-1088.** Fax 021/2255-1262. copacabana.hotel@sescrj.com.br. 120 units. Mar–June and Aug–Nov R$96 (US$32) double, R$110 (US$37) suite; Dec–Feb, July, and holidays R$140 (US$47) double, R$155 (US$52) suite. Extra person R$35 (US$12). Children under 3 stay free in parent's room. MC, V. Bus: 415. **Amenities:** Restaurant; laundry. In room: A/C, TV, fridge.

FLAMENGO/CATETE/GLORIA
Expensive

Hotel Florida ★★ Finds   Built in the 1940s, this gem of a hotel doesn't suffer from the modern "small room" syndrome, and thanks to a recent renovation, the rooms don't feel old either. The standard rooms overlook the rear or the side of the building and come with showers only. Both the superior and deluxe rooms offer views and have bathrooms with jetted tubs. The nicest rooms are those overlooking the lush gardens of the Palácio do Catete, Brazil's former presidential palace. The deluxe rooms are the most spacious with a large entrance hall, king-size bed (very unusual in Brazil), sitting area, and desk. The hotel offers excellent discounts on weekends.

Rua Ferreira Viana 81, Flamengo, Rio de Janeiro, 22210-040 RJ. ℭ **021/2556-5242.** Fax 021/2285-5777. www.windsorhoteis.com. 225 units. R$214–R$360 (US$72–US$120) standard double; R$268–R$372 (US$89–US$124) superior double; R$280–US$420 (US$93–US$140) deluxe double. Extra person 25%. Children under 11 stay free in parent's room. AE, DC, MC, V. Free parking. Metrô: Catete. **Amenities:** Restaurant; bar; outdoor rooftop pool; weight room; sauna; concierge; tour desk; business center; 24-hr. room service; laundry; dry cleaning; nonsmoking floors. *In room:* A/C, TV, dataport, minibar, fridge, hair dryer, safe.

Hotel Glória 𝕏𝕏   Truly the grande dame of Rio hotels, the Hotel Glória was built in 1922 to provide luxury accommodations for Brazil's centennial celebrations. The cheapest rooms are in the 1970s-era annex. All standard, these rooms are small with garden views and dated furnishings. Rooms in the original building reflect the higher standards of that bygone era: Ceilings are high, bathrooms are spacious, and furnishings are truly elegant. Standard and superior rooms in this section are not to be scoffed at, but if you can afford it, you should splurge on one of the spacious deluxe rooms—the views of the marina and the Sugar Loaf are worth it. For those rolling in cash, the lovely junior suites feature a large living room and a spacious master bedroom with big windows overlooking some of Rio's finest scenery.

Rua do Russel 632, Glória, Rio de Janeiro, 22210 RJ. ℭ **0800/213-077** or 021/2555-7272. Fax 021/2555-7283. www.hotelgloriario.com.br. 630 units (standard rooms in annex have showers only). R$180–R$280 (US$60–US$93) standard double; R$260–R$360 (US$87–US$120) superior and deluxe double; R$660–R$780 (US$229–US$260) junior suite. Extra person R$60 (US$25). Parking R$10 (US$3.35). Children under 11 stay free in parent's room. AE, DC, MC, V. No parking. Metrô: Glória. **Amenities:** 4 restaurants; bar; 2 outdoor heated pools; health club; sauna; concierge; tour desk; car rental; business center; salon; 24-hr. room service; massage; babysitting; laundry; dry cleaning; nonsmoking rooms or floors. *In room:* A/C, TV, dataport, minibar, fridge, hair dryer, safe.

Moderate

Hotel Rondonia Palace 𝕏   This hotel offers a little bit of luxury at a budget price. It's located on a quiet side street within easy walking distance of Flamengo Park and the cafes of the Largo do Machado. All the deluxe rooms come with a tiny sauna in the bathroom, as well as a large Jacuzzi tub. There are no views to speak of, as the rooms look out over either the buildings behind the hotel or the narrow street in front, but the rooms themselves are comfortably furnished and very clean. Rooms ending in 07 and 08 are a bit smaller than the others.

Rua Buarque de Macedo 60, Flamengo, Rio de Janeiro, 22220-030 RJ. ℭ **021/2556-0616.** Fax 021/2558-4133. www.hotelrondonia.com.br. 62 units (standard rooms w/showers only). R$110 (US$55) standard double; R$120 (US$60) deluxe double w/sauna and Jacuzzi. Small seasonal discount. Children under 5 stay free in parent's room. Over 5, extra bed R$30–R$40 (US$15–US$20). AE, DC, MC, V. Free parking. Bus: 119. **Amenities:** Restaurant; bar; limited room service; laundry service. *In room:* A/C, TV, minibar, fridge, safe.

WHERE TO DINE
CENTRO
Expensive
Cais do Oriente 𝕏𝕏𝕏 ASIAN/MEDITERRANEAN   A former warehouse, Cais do Oriente has undergone major renovations and emerged as a stunning venue for a restaurant and bar, complete with opulent antique furniture, large mirrors and elegant furnishings. The menu is all over the map, literally, covering the Orient as well as the Mediterranean. You'll find a number of Asian dishes such as Thai noodles, grilled tuna with sesame seeds, or sweet-and-sour duck. The Mediterranean dishes include grilled salmon served with a Gorgonzola-and-ricotta-stuffed pancake and the beautiful fresh figs with goat cheese and Parma ham.

Rua Viscone de Itaboraí 8, Centro. ℭ 021/2233-2531. www.caisdooriente.com.br. Main courses R$25–R$40 (US$8–US$13). AE, DC, MC, V. Mon noon–5pm; Tues–Sat noon–midnight; Sun noon–4pm. Metrô: Uruguaiana.

Confeitaria Colombo ✮✮✮ BRAZILIAN/DESSERTS This stunning ornate tearoom hasn't changed much since it opened in 1894. Two large deli counters flanking both sides of the entrance serve up sweet and savory snacks with coffee. The remainder of the ground floor is taken up by the elegant tearoom, where a variety of teas, sandwiches, salads, and sweets are served on fine china beneath a 1920s stained-glass window. The upstairs room is reserved for full lunches—on Saturday, the *feijoada* is worth the trip downtown.

Rua Gonçalves Dias 32, Centro. ℭ 021/2232-2300. www.confeitariacolombo.com.br. Main courses R$27–R$39 (US$9–US$13), *feijoada* buffet R$36 (US$12), includes dessert. Tea service R$5–R$20 (US$1.65–US$7). AE, DC, MC, V. Mon–Fri 8:30am–7pm; Sat 9am–5pm. Metrô: Carioca.

Moderate

Bar & Restaurante Amarelinho ✮ BRAZILIAN The prime patio on the prettiest square in Rio, the Amarelinho is the place to come to have a cold *chopp* (a pale draft beer) and gaze on the Parisian beauty that is the Praça Floriano. The menu offers a selection of standard Brazilian dishes, but nothing too special; most people are here for a drink and a chat with friends.

Praça Floriano 55B. ℭ 021/2240-8434. Main courses R$10–R$22 (US$3.35–US$7). AE, DC, MC, V. Daily 8am–midnight. Metrô: Cinelândia.

Bar Luiz *Finds* GERMAN One of Rio's most beloved little restaurants, Bar Luiz has been around since 1887. The long room is simply furnished with wooden tables, chairs, and a lovely tile floor. The walls are plainly adorned with old photographs of Rio, while overhead big Casablanca fans whirl to keep the heat down. Cariocas flock here to gorge themselves on generous portions of sausage and sauerkraut, Wiener schnitzel, Kassler ham, and potato salad. (Health craze, what health craze?) The draft beer—lager and dark—is pumped through a 720m-long (2,400-ft.) refrigerated hose before finding its way into your glass. *Prost!*

Rua da Carioca 39, Centro. ℭ 021/2262-6900. Main courses R$7.50–R$23 (US$2.50–US$8). AE, DC, V. Mon–Sat 11am–11pm. Metrô: Carioca.

Inexpensive

Beco das Sardinhas (Rei dos Frangos Maritimos) ✮ *Finds* BRAZILIAN On Friday afternoon, locals gather in this corner of historic Rio, known as "sardine alley," to unwind from the work week. It started in the 1960s, and these days, the original three-restaurant triangle has expanded to include six restaurants in a pedestrian area between Rua do Acre and Rua Mayrink Veiga. Every Friday after 6pm, it transforms into a giant TGIF party as people grab some fried sardines and wash 'em down with a cold beer. The restaurants have other snacks (Brazilian pub food such as grilled beef, sausage, and french fries), but the main attractions are definitely the sardines and the atmosphere.

Rua Miguel Couto 139, Centro. ℭ 021/2233-6119. Everything under R$12 (US$4). No credit cards. Mon–Fri 11am–10pm. Metrô: Uruguaiana.

Paladino BRAZILIAN Is it a liquor store? Is it a deli? Or is it, as the crowds seem to indicate, a bustling lunch bar with some of the best draft beer in town? Does it matter? Probably not. What matters is that the beer is clear and cold, the atmosphere is that of Rio in the Belle Epoque, and the sandwiches and snack plates are delicious. *Pratinhos,* as the latter are known in Portuguese, cost next to nothing—R$3 to R$6 (US$1–US$2)—and come loaded with sardines (whatever you do, order the sardines!), olives, or heaping stacks of smoked sausage.

Rua Uruguaiana 226, Centro. © 021/2263-2094. Reservations not accepted. Main courses R$3–R$13 (US$1–US$4.35). Cash only. Mon–Fri 8am–8:30pm; Sat 7am–noon. Metrô: Uruguaiana

URCA
Moderate
Circulo Militar *Finds* BRAZILIAN   The best view of the Sugar Loaf is from the tree-shaded patio of this military club in Urca. Civilians are completely welcome at the club (although some of the prime tables are sometimes reserved for officers). The view certainly outshines the food, but the menu provides enough K rations to accompany a drink or two. There's Bella Praia pizza with shrimp, squid, and octopus, or for a more substantial meal try the mixed *churrasco* (grilled meat) for two with beef, sausage, chicken, and pork served with french fries and rice (R$29/US$9). Live music Tuesday to Saturday after 8pm.

Praça General Tiburcio s/n, Praia Vermelha (on the far right, inside the military complex). © 021/2295-6079. Main courses R$12–R$32 (US$4–US$11). No credit cards. Tues–Sun 10am–midnight. Bus: 107 (from downtown) or 512 (from Ipanema and Copacabana).

FLAMENGO/GLORIA/CATETE
Expensive
Porcão *Finds* BRAZILIAN/STEAK   A mass carnivorous orgy. Porcão is where you go to gorge yourself on some of the best beef in the world, in this case served up with some of the best views in the world. Porcão operates on the *rodízio* system: It's one all-you-can-eat price (dessert and drinks are extra), and once you sit down, waiters come bearing all manner of meats (steak cuts, roast cuts, filet mignon, chicken breast, chicken hearts, sausages, and much more), which they slice to perfection on your plate. Also included is a buffet with dozens of antipasto items, hot and cold seafood dishes, and at least 15 different kinds of salad and cheese. No doggie bags allowed.

Av. Infante Dom Henrique s/n, Parque do Flamengo. © 021/2554-8535. R$39 (US$13) per person. 50% discount for children under 10. AE, DC, MC, V. Daily 11:30am–1am. Bus: Any bus to Praia do Flamengo.

Moderate
Estação da República *Kids* KILO/BUFFET   The Estação is top of the heap in the kilo category (excellent buffets where you pay by the weight of the food on your plate). It offers a daily selection of at least 20 salads, a range of pastas, and many favorite Brazilian dishes such as *feijoada, vatapá* (seafood stew), and *bobó* (shrimp stew). The *pièce de résistance* is the grill, where skilled chefs fire up the barbecue and serve your choice of beef, chicken, and a wide assortment of fish.

Rua do Catete 104, Catete. © 021/2225-2650. Reservations not accepted. R$22 (US$7) per kilo (2¼ lb.). AE, DC, MC, V. Daily 11am–midnight. Metrô: Catete.

BOTAFOGO
Very Expensive
Carême *Finds* BRAZILIAN   The hottest chef in town, Flavia Caresma has Rio's foodies flocking to her establishment en masse. Her cuisine is classically inspired, her ingredients always top quality and fresh. The menu changes monthly. For main courses, we like the chicken breast stuffed with duck pâté, sage, and dried mushroom sauce, and a grilled entrecôte with mashed potatoes in a juniper-and-thyme sauce. Desserts are the creations of the patisserie chef

who does an amazing job with fresh fruits and chocolate. The wine list is conservative with a small selection of well-chosen merlots, cabernet sauvignons, and Chilean chardonnays.

Rua Visconde de Caravelas 113, Botafogo. ✆ 021/2537-2374. Reservations required. Tasting menu (includes appetizer, main course, and dessert) R$120 (US$40). AE, DC, MC, V. Tues–Sat 8pm–close. Dinner is usually served in 2 seatings, 8:30 and 11pm. Bus: 176 or 178.

Madame Vidal ★★ BRAZILIAN/ITALIAN In a calculated attempt to attract the artistic, the trendy, and the well-heeled who tag along after them, Madame Vidal has a tarted exterior of blue-and-gold colonial kitsch and a clashing interior of New York SoHo minimal. The menu offers an amazing selection of risotto, pasta, and meat dishes, including a signature veal. It's all simply prepared with quality ingredients. As you'd expect, Madame Vidal's is open late, daily until at least 2am, until 3am on weekends.

Rua Capitão Salomão 69 (corner of Visconde da Silva), Humaitá. ✆ 021/2539-2058. Main courses R$18–R$42 (US$6–US$14). AE, MC, V. Mon–Fri noon–3pm and 7pm–2am; Sat–Sun 7pm–3am. Bus: 178.

Expensive

Kotobuki ★ JAPANESE The food at Kotobuki is good, but it's the view that's truly outstanding. Kotobuki offers a sweeping view of Botafogo beach and bay and the soaring Pão de Açúcar. Located in the seventh-floor food court of the Botafogo Praia Shopping, Kotobuki offers lunchtime specials including the *prato executivo:* 15 pieces of sushi and sashimi with a miso soup for R$17 (US$5.65). A favorite lunch special on the weekends is the Japanese buffet: a variety of sushi, sashimi, appetizers, tempura, and yakisoba for R$34 (US$11).

Praia de Botafogo 400, 7th floor, Botafogo. ✆ 021/2559-9595. Reservations accepted, but window tables are on a 1st-come, 1st-served basis. R$15–R$49 (US$5–US$16). AE, DC, MC, V. Daily noon–midnight. Metrô: Botafogo.

COPACABANA/LEME
Very Expensive

Cipriani ★★★ ITALIAN The dining in the elegant Copacabana Palace overlooks the hotel's swimming pool and courtyard, both magically illuminated at night. Reserve early to book a window table. The menu is mostly classic Italian with a few contemporary twists. A signature dish is the potato ravioli with black truffle—simple yet so satisfying. Our favorite, however, was the duck breast in a balsamic sauce with blueberries, the perfect balance between sweet and savory.

Copacabana Palace Hotel, Av. Atlântica 1702, Copacabana. ✆ 021/2548-7070. Reservations required. Semiformal. Main courses R$38–R$58 (US$13–US$19). AE, DC, MC, V. Daily 12:30–3pm and 8pm–1am. Metrô: Arco Verde.

Le Pré-Catelan ★★★ FRENCH Ever since French chef Roland Villard took over the kitchen in 1998, it's been raining awards at Le Pré-Catelan. Updated every 2 weeks, the menu offers a selection of appetizers, main courses, and a dessert for R$125 (US$42), a steal considering the quality of the ingredients, the preparation, and the service. Some of the best dishes we've tried so far include the langoustines soup with coconut milk and tomato confit, the terrine of foie gras with fresh truffles and a side of chutney, and the tournedos with wild mushrooms and a vegetable sautéed with sweet potato. All dishes are beautifully presented.

Hotel Sofitel. Av. Atlântica 4240, Copacabana. ✆ 021/2525-1232. Reservations required. Business casual. Main courses R$39–R$65 (US$13–US$22). AE, DC, MC, V. Mon–Wed 7:30–11:30pm; Thurs–Sat 7:30pm–midnight. Bus: 415.

Expensive

Dom Camillo ☆ ITALIAN   Dom Camillo offers beachfront fine dining in the open-air heart of Copa. A large pasta selection includes the Dom Camillo spaghetti, served with prawns, garlic, and green and red peppers. Vegetarians will like the ravioli with spinach, ricotta, and fresh Parmesan. One of the house specialties is the fresh fish, roasted in a thick salt crust or served with a tomato, olive, and herb dressing. Meat lovers will enjoy a scaloppini with porcini mushrooms and roasted potatoes. Traditional Italian music is served up live daily from 9pm to midnight.

Av. Atlântica 3056, Copacabana. ✆ 021/2549-9958. Main courses R$16–R$34 (US$5–US$11). AE, DC, MC, V. Daily noon–2am. Bus: 415.

IPANEMA
Very Expensive

Madame Butterfly ☆☆ JAPANESE   Now that Japanese cuisine has arrived in Rio, the two sisters who have guided Rio's favorite Japanese restaurant for the past 12 years have decided to spread their wings and develop new Brazilian-Japanese hybrids such as gyoza with Brazilian *abóbora* pumpkin or ginger-flavored lobster served on a cheese risotto. All these new taste combinations seem to be paying off; *Veja* magazine just awarded the restaurant top honors for best Japanese restaurant. We certainly look forward to seeing what comes out of the kitchen; it's always worth a visit.

Rua Barão de Torre 472, Ipanema. ✆ 021/2267-4347. Reservations recommended on weekends. R$28–R$55 (US$9–US$18). AE, DC, MC. Daily noon–2am. Bus: 415.

Satyricon ☆☆☆ SEAFOOD   This is one of Rio's most select celebrity hangouts, so society columnists and snap-happy photogs are never far away. Start your dinner with the three-fish carpaccio, made fresh every day with an ever-changing variety of fish. If you're feeling hungry, you could opt for the seafood platter—not only is it outstanding, but it's also humongous. One of the restaurant's trademark dishes is the *pargo,* a firm white fish that comes with filets crusted in a layer of kosher sea salt. For a heartier dish, try the codfish stew in red wine, olives, tomatoes, and peppers.

Rua Barão da Torre 192, Ipanema. ✆ 021/2521-0627. www.satyricon.com.br. Reservations required. Main courses R$34–R$65 (US$11–US$22). AE, DC, MC, V. Mon 6pm–2am; Tues–Sat noon–2am; Sun noon–midnight. Bus: 415.

Expensive

Yemanjá ☆☆ BAHIAN   You may want to go easy on the appetizers, as the dishes are hearty and the portions large. Prominent on the list of main courses are the *moquecas,* a traditional Bahian stew made with coconut milk, red palm oil, peppers, cilantro, and a generous amount of lime juice. Other Bahian favorites include *bobó* and *vatapá.* All main courses serve two with plenty of food left over.

Rua Visconde de Pirajá 128, Ipanema. ✆ 021/2247-7004. Main courses R$22–R$39 (US$7–US$13). AE, DC, MC, V. Mon–Thurs 6pm–midnight; Fri–Sat and holidays noon–midnight; Sun noon–10pm. Bus: 415.

Zazá Bistrô Tropical ☆☆ BRAZILIAN/FUSION   Dishes at Zazá blend South American cuisine with Asian flavors. Appetizers include sautéed shrimp with palm hearts in a sweet-and-sour sauce. Main courses don't disappoint when it comes to mixing up the flavors; for example, the tuna steak comes grilled in a soy-and-passion-fruit sauce on a bed of cardamom rice. Vegetarians always have a daily special to choose from, made with seasonal produce and interesting spices. *Tip:* The folks lined up at the door are waiting for an upstairs spot, where everyone sits on the floor leaning back on masses of silk pillows. Surrounded by candlelight and lanterns, the room feels like a palace from *1,001 Arabian Nights.*

Rua Joana Angelica 40, Ipanema. ℂ 021/2247-9101. R$28–R$42 (US$9–US$14). AE, DC, MC, V. Sun–Thurs 7:30pm–1am; Fri–Sat 7:30pm–2am. Bus: 415.

Moderate

Gula Gula ⭐ BRAZILIAN   For a lighter and healthier meal or snack, stop in at Gula Gula. The menu includes delicious fresh salads such as the caprese—a layered tower of sliced tomatoes, basil, and mozzarella—the salad da Casa with mixed greens, pumpkin, goat cheese, and crisp bits of Parma ham, or the more Brazilian palm heart salad with turkey and pineapple. Gula also serves a variety of grilled meats, chicken, and fish as well as pasta, quiches, and sandwiches. The Ipanema location has a lovely sidewalk patio. For dessert, you can try some of the low-cal options but to live up to the name (*gula* means "gluttony") it behooves you to try a banana crème brûlée or fruit strudel.

Rua Anibal de Mendonça 132, Ipanema. ℂ 021/2259-3084. Main courses R$15–R$26 (US$5–US$8.50). AE, MC, V. Daily noon–midnight. Bus: 415.

Joanne Bistrot e Boulangerie *Value* BAKERY   Joanne Bistrot is that perfect spot to take a break from your busy sightseeing schedule. Grab a table on the pleasantly shaded patio and start with a perfectly made cappuccino. Breakfast options include flaky brioches with jam, baked goods, or a continental breakfast with breads, juices, cold cuts, and cheese. The bistro menu offers a variety of elaborate sandwiches and Joanne also has a full lunch and dinner menu with dishes such as lamb chops in an herb crust or entrecôte with french fries and green salad, but the atmosphere is best enjoyed in the morning as the streets slowly come to life and Cariocas get on with their day.

Rua Joana Angelica 159, Ipanema. ℂ 021/2513-3380. Breakfast items R$6–R$20 (US$2–US$6.65), lunch and dinner menu R$15–R$32 (US$5–US$11). DC, MC, V. Daily 7am–midnight. Bus: 415.

Inexpensive

Big Nectar *Value* QUICK BITES   The menu in this standing-room-only spot lists just over 25 different kinds of fruit juice. In addition to the standards such as passion fruit (*maracujá*), pineapple (*abacaxi*), and cashew fruit (*caju*), there's *carambola* (star fruit), *goiaba* (guava), *jáca* (jack fruit), and *açerola* (red juice from the tiny *açerola* fruit). You can mix flavors—try *laranja com açerola* (orange juice with *açerola*), *maracujá* with mango, pineapple with guava, or cashew with *açerola.*

Teixeira de Melo 34A, Ipanema. No phone. All items under R$12 (US$4). No credit cards. Daily 7am–midnight. Bus: 404 or 474.

LEBLON
Very Expensive

Garcia & Rodrigues ⭐⭐ BRAZILIAN/FRENCH   This veritable food megacomplex encompasses a delicatessen, bakery, cafe, patisserie, ice cream parlor, wine bar, and restaurant with fine dining. The menu changes frequently, adjusting to the ingredients available seasonally. One recurring favorite is the *galinha d'angola,* a roasted chicken stuffed with a compote of pears and spices. We wouldn't mind seeing the garlic-roasted swordfish again someday, and we have equally fond memories of the duck breast with figs. For dessert, try the chocolate cake with pineapple mousse or one of the many delicious tropically flavored ice creams.

Rio's Avenida Gourmet

We could probably fill half the Rio section with reviews of restaurants on the **Rua Dias Ferreira,** as this windy street on the far edge of Leblon is quickly emerging as Rio's main *avenida gourmet.* One could live on salad alone at **O Celeiro** (Rua Dias Ferreira 199; Ⓒ 021/2274-7843). You pay by the weight so help yourself to the delicious buffet to try a variety of salads and grab a spot on the large patio. New kid on the block **Zuka** (Rua Dias Ferreira 233; Ⓒ 021/3205-7154) may look like just another funky lounge but actually packs quite a punch with inventive dishes including a delicious grilled lamb with cardamom. Across the street you'll find **Carlota** (Rua Dias Ferreira 64; Ⓒ 021/2540-6821), chosen by *Condé Nast Traveller* as one of the 50 most exciting restaurants in the world. Chef Carlota opened this Rio restaurant after her original São Paulo digs became the toast of the town. Farther down on the corner of Rua Rainha Guilermina is the sushi hot spot of the city, **Sushi Leblon** (Rua Dias Ferreira 256; Ⓒ 021/2512-7830). On Thursday to Saturday evenings the lines can be long, but most people don't seem to mind the wait. If you're up on who's who in the Brazilian entertainment world you can pass the time spotting artists, models, and actresses.

Av. Ataulfo de Paiva 1251, Leblon. Ⓒ 021/2512-8188. Reservations recommended. Main courses R$30–R$68 (US$10–US$23). AE, DC, MC, V. Mon 8pm–midnight; Tues–Sun 1–4pm. *Note:* Deli and bakery open daily 8am–midnight. Bus: 415.

Inexpensive

Bibi Sucos 🅡 🅥ᵃˡᵘᵉ QUICK BITES   The menu at this popular juice bar is refreshingly straightforward: juice, juice, and juice. You pick one or more fruit combinations and into the blender they go. It's trendy in newly health conscious Rio to add on a scoop of protein powder for strength, guaraná for energy, or pollen for general health. Bibi also sells hamburgers, sandwiches, and a variety of savory pastries.

Av. Ataulfo de Paiva 591, Leblon. Ⓒ 021/2259-4298. All items under R$10 (US$5). No credit cards. Daily 8am–2am, later on weekends if busy. Bus: 415.

JARDIM BOTÂNICO
EXPENSIVE

Bistrô Madeleine 🅡🅡 MEDITERRANEAN   This charming bistro is the labor of love of chef and owner Madeleine, who blends the flavors of the Mediterranean and her own native Lebanon in fabulous salads, pastas, and other inventive dishes made with fresh vegetables and herbs. The pastas deserve a special note; made in house, they are light as a feather and full of flavor. The lemon butter linguini is simply amazing. A comprehensive wine list offers plenty of affordable bottles (under US$30) mostly from Italy and France. Desserts tend to tropical flavors such as the delicious grilled pineapple and ice cream or the St. Tropez, a light chocolate cake (almost a mousse) served with mango sauce. On Sundays, Madeleine cooks up a full all-you-can-eat Lebanese lunch buffet for R$39 (US$13).

Rua Frei Leandro 20, Jardim Botânico, ℂ 021/2527-9003. Main courses R$28–R$45 (US$9–US$15). AE, DC, MC V. Mon–Sat 7pm–1am; Sun noon–6pm. Bus: 572 (from Leblon or Copacabana) or 170 (from downtown).

Capricciosa ℛ PIZZA With its high ceiling, brick walls, and suspended light panels, Capricciosa feels like a modern dining hall, albeit one that comes with great food and excellent service. A large wood-burning oven dominates the back of the room and turns out great tasting pizzas and calzones, from the plain Pizza Margarita with mozzarella, Parmesan, and fresh basil and tomato to the signature Capricciosa with tomato, ham, artichoke, mushrooms, bacon, and egg. The restaurant also has a delicious cold cut and antipasto buffet, all served with slices of homemade crusty bread.

Rua Maria Angelica 37, Jardim Botânico, ℂ 021/2527-2656. Main courses R$22–R$33 (US$7–US$11). AE, DC, MC, V. Mon–Sat 7pm–1am (later if it's busy); Sun noon–6pm. Bus: Bus: 572 (from Leblon or Copabana) or 170 (from downtown).

RIO AFTER DARK

There's a lot to do in Rio, whether you want live music, samba school rehearsals, modern clubs, or seaside patios. Everything starts early and continues very late. For updated listings, check the Friday edition of *O Globo* or *Jornal do Brasil* newspapers. Under *musica* or *show,* you will find the listings for live music; listings under *pista* refer to events at nightclubs or discos. *Couvert* is the cover charge and *consumação* states the drink minimum; it's quite common to see two rates, one for women *(mulher)* and one for men *(homem)*. The days of the week are given in abbreviations: *seg* or *2a* (Mon), *ter* or *3a* (Tues), *qua* or *4a* (Wed), *qui* or *5a* (Thurs), *sex* or *6a* (Fri), *sab* (Sat), and *dom* (Sun).

In most clubs and discos, you can expect to pay a cover charge or drink minimum. In most venues, you are handed a card upon entry to record all of your purchases. The bill is then settled when you leave. A 10% service charge will be included, and a tip beyond that is not required. Hang on to your card for dear life—if you lose it you'll be charged an astronomical fee.

PERFORMING ARTS

The elegant Parisian-style **Theatro Municipal,** Praça Marechal Floriano s/n, Centro (ℂ **021/2299-1717;** www.theatromunicipal.rj.gov.br), stages everything from opera to ballet to symphony concerts. Ticket prices range from R$15 to R$60 (US$5–US$20) for most performances.

Located in downtown Rio, the small **Teatro Rival,** Rua Alvaro Alvim 33, Centro (ℂ **021/2240-4469**), does an outstanding job of booking local and popular national acts, mostly of MPB *(musica popular brasileira)*. Ticket prices are quite reasonable—usually R$10 to R$40 (US$3.35–US$13)—so give it a shot. You may be looking at the next Marisa Monte or one of Brazil's many talented performers who haven't made it big internationally.

CLUBS & LIVE MUSIC

GAFIEIRAS The traditional ballroom dance halls known as *gafieiras* are a legacy of the elegant days of old, when couples would dress for the occasion and everyone knew the steps. Most folks don't show up in suits or ball gowns anymore, but couples still dance with elegance, and the tunes are unmistakably Brazilian: samba and *pagode,* a bit of rumba or fox-trot, and nowadays, lots of *forró.* One popular *gafieira* is the **Elite,** Rua Frei Caneca 4, Centro (ℂ **021/ 2232-3217**). Even if you can't dance, it's worth having a drink and watching in awe and admiration as some of the older folks strut their stuff; it's open Friday after 7pm, Saturday after 10pm, and Sunday after 6pm. **Gafieira Estudantina,**

Praça Tiradentes 79, Centro (℃ 021/2507-8067), is another mainstay on the Carioca ballroom scene. Many students of the dance school come and show off, but novices are made to feel equally welcome. A 10-piece band plays every weekend. It's open on Friday and Saturday from 11pm.

LIVE MUSIC It's old and tattered and the sightlines aren't terrific, but the **Canecão,** Av. Venceslau Brás 215, Botafogo (℃ 021/2543-1241), has tradition. Everyone who's anyone in Brazilian music has played this aging 3,000-person auditorium. A newcomer on the music scene, the **Centro Cultural Carioca,** Rua do Teatro, Centro (℃ 021/2242-9642; www.centroculturalcarioca.com; Metrô: Cinelândia), is housed in a restored 1920s historic building and provides a fabulous venue for local musicians and big names who specialize in samba, MPB, *choro,* and *gafieira.* No shows on Sundays usually. **Carioca da Gema,** Rua Mem de Sá 79, Lapa (℃ 021/2221-0043), is a fine little restaurant, but music is really the chief thing on order. On Friday and Saturday nights, the place is packed. The show normally kicks off about 8pm, but space is very limited, so come early.

DANCE CLUBS A restaurant by day, **Ballroom,** Rua Humaitá 10, Botafogo (℃ 021/2537-7600), transforms itself into a packed and hopping dance club after 10pm, complete with lots of live music; Thursdays are *forró* nights. In Ipanema, **Baronetti,** Rua Barão da Torre 354 (℃ 021/25222-1460), attracts an attractive upscale crowd. The deejays pack the dance floor by playing mostly dance music. A more casual venue is **Melt,** Rua Rita Ludolf 47, Leblon (℃ 021/2249-9309). In addition to excellent deejays, Melt also frequently invites local bands to play it up for the crowds. **Melí-Meló,** Av. Borges de Medeiros 1426, Lagoa (℃ 021/2219-3132), has two dance floors with excellent deejays, a cybercafe, and a sushi bar. Sightings of models, starlets, socialites, soccer players, and other assorted celebs are a dime a dozen.

BARS & PUBS

BOTEQUINS *Botequins* are to Rio what pubs are to London and cafes are to Paris: the spot where locals traditionally gather, whether it be for end of day drinks or impassioned late-night philosophizing. Tucked away in an alley just off the Praça XV, the **Arco do Teles** looks like a movie set of old Rio with colonial two-story walk-ups set on narrow cobblestone streets lined with restaurants and cafes. (From the Praça XV, facing the bay, you will see the arch that marks the entrance to the alley on your left.) Prime time is after work hours, especially on Thursday and Friday nights, when office workers flock here to grab a few cold beers and catch some music.

Unanimously voted the best *botequim* in town, **Bracarense,** Rua Jose Linhares 85, Leblon (℃ 021/2294-3549), serves up a perfectly chilled beer and delicious munchies. Another acclaimed *botequim,* **Bip Bip,** Rua Almirante Gonçalves 50, Copacabana (℃ 021/2267-9696), owes its fame to an outstanding musical program. Tuesday and Sunday nights are the best evenings to catch some great samba or *pagode.* One of the trendier *botequins,* **Jobi,** Av. Ataulfo de Paiva 1166, Leblon (℃ 021/2274-0547), is busy every day of the week, but on Friday and Saturday, a lineup is guaranteed.

OTHER BARS & PUBS A field trip to the **Academia da Cachaça,** Rua Conde de Bernadote 26, Loja G, Leblon (℃ 021/2239-1542), puts the concept of advanced education in a whole new light. It is here that 40 members of the Cachaça Academy meet to dispute, discuss, and sample the finer points of the fiery white-cane liquor that is Brazil's national drink. **Lord Jim,** Rua Paulo

Redfern 63, Ipanema (© **021/2259-3047**), is a more or less authentic British pub where you'll find expats crying in their Guinness. By day a mild-mannered (and quite fun) fruit and vegetable market, the **Mercado Cobal,** Cobal de Humaitá, Rua Voluntarios da Patria 446, Botafogo, transforms itself at night into a huge outdoor bar scene with seven or eight different restaurants and *chopperias* melding into one large bustling patio. On a hot summer night there is nothing better than spending an evening with a blonde *(loura),* redhead *(ruiva),* or brunette *(morena)*—home-brews that is. **Devassa,** Rua General San Martin 1241, Leblon (© **021/2540-6087**), a casual bistro, is the perfect neighborhood cafe serving draft beer from its own microbrewery.

GAY & LESBIAN NIGHTLIFE

Rio's gay community is fairly small and, despite Rio's reputation for sexual hedonism, fairly restrained. As lasciviously as heterosexual couples may behave in public, open displays of affection between same-sex couples are still not accepted in Brazil. To find out what's hot and happening, pick up the latest edition of the *Gay Guide Brazil,* a small booklet available at some of the clubs and bookstores in Ipanema, or check out http://riogayguide.com and www.gay-rio.com. The Brazilian term for gay-friendly is *GLS,* which stands for gay, lesbian, and sympathizers.

The largest gay club in Rio, **Le Boy,** Rua Raul Pompeia 102, Copacabana (© **021/2513-4993**), is modeled on the high-end clubs of New York and London and is the place to be seen. All for equal opportunity, Le Boy's owner recently inaugurated **La Girl** next door at Rua Raul Pompeia 102 (© **021/ 2247-8342**). Rio's first truly upscale nightclub for gay women, La Girl opens Thursday through Sundays. Venture round the corner from Le Boy and La Girl and lo, there appeareth the **Blue Angel,** Rua Julio de Castilhos 15, Copacabana (© **021/2513-2501**), a mixed gay and lesbian bar with a small gallery of avant-garde art. **Dama de Ferro,** Rua Vinicius de Moraes 288, Ipanema (© **021/ 2247-2330**), is the it-spot at the moment, popular with gay and straight (although definitely gay); high tolerance for electronic music is a must. Not for the claustrophobic, the **Galeria Café,** Rua Teixeira de Melo 31, Ipanema (© **021/2523-8250**), packs them into its combo art space, dance club, and bar; people stand shoulder-to-shoulder, bicep to bicep. Those who can't squeeze in just hang out in front chatting and drinking. **The Copa,** Rua Aires Saldanha 13A, Copacabana (© **021/2256-7412**), is a bar, restaurant, club, and tea salon all in one. Certainly not the most typical gay bar, the Copa's ultrakitsch 1950s and 1960s decor has quickly established a great following among Rio's GLS crowd since it opened in late 2000.

SIDE TRIPS FROM RIO

On weekends and holidays, many Cariocas direct their tires northward to the beach resorts dotting the warm Atlantic coast. First and most famous of these is the town of **Búzios,** set on the tip of a long peninsula jutting out into the clear blue Atlantic. Heading up and inland, you find the summer refuge of an earlier generation, the mountain resort **Petrôpolis,** the former summer capital of Emperor Pedro II. Just an hour or so from Rio, this green and graceful refuge offers good strolling and some great museums.

BÚZIOS

It's anyone's guess how small or sleepy the fishing town of Búzios truly was when French starlet Brigitte Bardot stumbled onto its sandy beaches in 1964, but it's certain that in the years since, the little town used the publicity to turn itself into

Rio's premier beach resort. Much of that charm is due to the sheer beauty of the surroundings; the number of beaches close to town makes it easy to experience all the wonderful permutations of Brazilian beach culture.

Essentials

GETTING THERE   **Búzios Rádio Táxi** (© 022/2623-1911) offers transfer from and to Rio by van and taxi. The fare for a 15-person air-conditioned minibus is R$70 (US$23) per person. A four-person private taxi costs R$120 (US$40) per person.

The bus company **Auto Viação 1001** (© 0800/251-001; www.autoviacao 1001.com.br) departs for Búzios seven times a day from Rio's main bus station (© 021/2291-5151). The 2½-hour trip costs approximately R$18 (US$6). In Búzios, buses arrive at the Búzios bus station on Estrada da Usina at the corner of Rua Manoel de Carvalho (© 022/2623-2050), a 10-minute walk from the center of town.

VISITOR INFORMATION   The **Búzios Tourism Secretariat** (© 022/2623-2099) has an information kiosk on the downtown Praça Santos Dumont 111, open daily from 9am to 10pm. Two good websites for information about Búzios are **www.buziosonline.com.br** and **www.buziosturismo.com**.

What to See & Do in Búzios

The charm of Búzios lies largely in its beaches, the 20 stretches of sand large and small within a few miles of the old town. Thanks to the irregular topography of this rugged little peninsula, each beach is set off from the other and has developed its own beach personality. Furthest from the old town is **Manguinhos** beach. Sheltered from the heavy surf, this gentle beach is where many learn to sail and windsurf. Closer to town is **Ferradura,** or Horseshoe, beach; this beach offers calm crystal-clear waters, making it the perfect place for a long, lazy afternoon's snorkel. Back on the calm inland side of the peninsula, **João Fernandes** and the pocket-size **João Fernandinho** beaches are happening places lined with beachside cafes.

On Ferradura beach, **Happy Surf** (© 022/2623-2016) rents sailboards, lasers, Hobie Cats, and kayaks. Lasers and Hobie Cats rent for R$35 (US$12) per half-hour, R$45 (US$15) with instructor. Kayaks rent for R$5 (US$1.65) per half-hour, R$8 (US$2.65) per hour. Paddleboats can be rented for R$22 (US$7) per hour. The following equipment is available at João Fernandes beach: kayaks, R$5 (US$1.65) per half-hour; mask and snorkel package, R$12 (US$4) per hour; sailboard, R$30 (US$10) per hour.

Schooner trips are a great way to spend a day in Búzios. Onboard, you trundle along in the sunshine eating complimentary fresh fruit and drinking free *caipirinhas* (or mineral water). At any of the beaches, you're free to get off, hang out, and swim for a bit. One company is **Escuna Buziana** (© 022/9972-7030), but just walk along Rua das Pedras anywhere near the pier and you're guaranteed to be approached by a schooner tout. Depending on the season and time of day expect to pay from R$12 to R$35 (US$4–US$12) for a half-day cruise.

The islands just off Búzios are—along with Angra dos Reis and Arraial do Cabo—some of the best diving spots within a 1-day drive of Rio. Coral formations are fairly basic, but there are lots of parrotfish and, often, sea turtles (green and hawksbill) and stingrays of considerable size. Visibility ranges from 10m to 15m (32–50 ft.). The two dive shops in town are **True Blue,** Av. Bento Ribeiro Dantas 21, Loja 13, at the beginning of Rua das Pedras (© 022/2623-2357), and **Ponto Mar,** Rua das Pedras 212 (© 022/2623-2173). The companies' equipment, dive boats, and prices are nearly identical. For a certified diver, a two-dive excursion including all your gear costs R$120 (US$40).

Where to Stay in Búzios

Búzios is well known for its *pousadas,* similar to a North American bed-and-breakfast. However, you will not find too many at bargain prices. By avoiding high season (Dec–Mar and July) and weekends throughout the year, you should be able to get a discount.

Colonna Park Hotel ✿✿, Praia de João Fernandes, Armação dos Búzios (© 022/2623-2245; www.colonna.com.br), offers a superb setting, straddling the hill between the beaches of João Fernandes and João Fernandinho. Rooms in this sprawling Mediterranean-style mansion are spacious and simply yet elegantly furnished in cool tones of white and blue. If you're in the mood for a splurge, try suite 20; it comes with Jacuzzi tub and a large deck with a view of both beaches. In high season, a double without a view costs R$410 (US$137), a double with a view costs R$450 (US$150), and a suite will run you R$495 (US$165).

Tucked away on Orla Bardot, **Pousada Byblos** ✿✿, Morro do Humaitá 8, Praia da Armação (© 022/2623-1162), is just a 5-minute walk from busy Rua das Pedras. The best rooms are the oceanview rooms with a balcony (the top two floors). The top floor of the Pousada Byblos boasts a fabulous rooftop deck with a small swimming pool and a lounge. Rooms cost R$300 to R$450 (US$100–US$150).

One of the few relatively inexpensive options in town, **Búzios Internacional Apart Hotel,** Estrada da Usina Velha 99 (©/fax 022/2537-3876; www.buzios beach.com.br), is located just a few blocks from Rua das Pedras. Units are all self-contained flats equipped with a living room with foldout couch, a kitchen, and either one or two bedrooms. All units come with a balcony and hammock looking out over a central garden. The price is the same whether you're one person or four (or six in the two-bedroom units). In high season, rates range from R2,000 to R$3,000 (US$667–US$1,000) per week. In the low season, the flats cost R$1,000 (US$333) per week or R$140 (US$47) per day.

Authentic is the operative word at **Pousada do Sol,** Rua das Pedras s/n, near the pier (© 022/2623-1249; pousadadosol@mar.com.br). When French film star Brigitte Bardot spent a summer in Búzios in the early 1960s, this is where she stayed. (It was then the house of a friend of hers.) Now reincarnated as a *pousada,* the Sol offers inexpensive rooms with an ocean view. In high season, rooms cost R$140 to R$180 (US$47–US$60) double. During the rest of the year, the rate is R$100 to R$140 (US$33–US$47).

Where to Dine in Búzios

You couldn't be any closer to the beach than at **Recanto do Sol** ✿, Praia João Fernandes s/n (© 022/2623-2293). The menu offers seafood and seafood: grilled fish, moqueca stews, shrimp, or squid. The portions are generous—plenty for two very hungry people.

Guapo Loco, Rua das Pedras 233 (© 022/2623-2657), lives in a kind of topsy-turvy Frank Gehry hacienda, and it's one of the few Mexican restaurants in all Brazil. The menu includes tacos, quesadillas, and burritos, as well as house specialties such as the Drunken Chicken—chicken breast sautéed in tequila, peppers, oregano, onions, and lemon juice.

Boom, Rua Manoel Turibe de Farias 110 (© 022/2623-6254), has one of the nicest interiors of any kilo (buffet) restaurant we've ever seen. The room is spacious and rustic looking, with old wood beams, iron window frames, and dark red tile. The price is R$29 (US$10) per kilo (2¼ lb.), which puts it at the upper end of kilo fare, but the quality is very high and the selection is good: salads, stewed meats, bean dishes, and chicken, sausage, and fresh picanha right off the grill.

At **Estancia Don Juan,** Rua das Pedras 178 (© **022/2623-2169**), the menu includes only meat: linguiça (smoked sausage) and numerous exquisite beef cuts such as picanha, entrecôte, and *olho de bife* (rib-eye). Dine on a lovely flowered patio or in a multilevel hacienda dripping with atmosphere. Wines include a number of South American reds ranging from R$33 to R$120 (US$11–US$40) per bottle.

Búzios After Dark

If you're on a mission for a night out, Rua das Pedras is the place to crawl. This 1.2km (¾-mile) street boasts pubs, bars, discos, and restaurants open on weekends until 3 or 4am. One of the most popular spots is the Mexican bar and disco **Zapata,** which is very busy during vacations and weekends. Next door, **Skipper** serves pizza and has a nightclub, which is normally open on Friday and Saturday. To simply sit, sip a drink, and check out the action, the place to be is **Ponto Bar,** which serves Japanese food with a musical background of The Rolling Stones, Eric Clapton, and others. If you'd prefer your entertainment live, there's **Pátio Havana,** which features a nightly selection of jazz, blues, and MPB served up on an ocean-side patio.

PETRÓPOLIS

Petrópolis is one of Rio de Janeiro's premier mountain resorts, located 850m (2,400 ft.) above sea level. Only an hour from Rio, it seems light years away from the traffic-jammed streets, concrete high-rises, and beaches. Emperor Dom Pedro II founded the city of Petrópolis in 1843 and built the summer palace (now the Imperial Museum) on a piece of land acquired by his father.

Nowadays, Petrópolis is a favorite weekend getaway for Cariocas—in the summer to escape from the hot and humid climate in Rio, in the fall and winter for a chance to experience "really cold" weather, wear winter clothes, eat fondue, and sit by the fireplace. Exploring Petrópolis can easily be done as a day trip from Rio using public transit. The historic part of the city, centered around the Museu Imperial and the cathedral and more or less bounded by Avenida Barão Rio Branco and Rua Imperador, contains the majority of the monuments and museums.

Essentials

GETTING THERE   Unica/Facil (© **021/2263-8792**) offers daily service from Rio to Petrópolis. The trip takes a little more than an hour. Buses leave Monday through Friday every 15 minutes from 5:15am to midnight; on Saturday and Sunday, buses depart until approximately 10pm. Tickets cost R$10 (US$3.35). Buses depart from the main bus station in Rio, **Rodoviária Novo Rio** (© **021/2291-5151**). Buses arrive at the main bus station in Petrópolis, within walking distance of all the attractions.

VISITOR INFORMATION   Petrotur's main office is at Av. Koeler 245 Centro (© **024/2243-9300;** www.petrotur.gov.rj.br). Kiosks are located at Rua do Imperador (by the Obelisk) and Casa do Barão de Mauá; both are open Monday through Sunday from 9am to 5pm. The English version of the excellent "Petrópolis Imperial Sightseeing" brochure comes with a map, visitor information, and opening hours for each of the attractions.

What to See & Do in Petrôpolis

The historic heart of Petrôpolis can easily be explored on foot. Following the directions below will take you to most points of interest.

Starting on the corners of Avenida Ipiranga and Tiradentes, the first thing you see is the **Catedral São Pedro de Alcantara,** a neo-Gothic church named for both the patron saint of the empire and Emperor Dom Pedro II himself. Construction began in 1876, but the celebratory first Mass wasn't held until 1925. Just inside the main doors to the right is the Imperial Chapel containing the remains of the emperor Dom Pedro II, the empress Dona Teresa, and their daughter Princesa Isabel and her husband, whose name no one remembers. Continuing along the Avenida Koeler as it follows the tree-lined canal, it's a 5-minute walk to the beautiful **Praça da Liberdade.** The bridge in front of this square offers the best view of the cathedral and the canal. Just behind the Praça da Liberdade is the **Casa de Santos Dumont,** Rua do Encanto 22, Petrôpolis (© 024/2231-3011). Dumont was Brazil's most famous aviator and, in 1906, the first in the world to take off and land under his own power (unlike the Wright brothers, who were catapulted on their 1st flight at Kitty Hawk). From here, follow Avenida Roberto Silveira, then turn right on Rua Alfredo Pachá to the **Palácio de Cristal,** Rua Alfredo Pachá s/n (© 024/2237-7953). Ordered by Princesa Isabel and built in France, the structure was inaugurated in 1894 as an agricultural exhibition hall. Nowadays, the palace is used for cultural events and exhibits. Crossing the bridge to Avenida Piabanha, you come to the **Casa Barão de Mauá,** Praça da Confluencia s/n (© 024/2231-2121), which was built in 1854 in neoclassic style by the industrial baron who constructed Brazil's first railway.

Continue by taking Rua 13 de Maio—right across the street from the Casa Barão de Mauá—toward the cathedral and then turning left on Avenida Ipiranga at the intersection just before the cathedral. Along this street are a number of interesting buildings as well as some gorgeous mansions and villas. Standing on the right side of the street, at no. 346, is the 1816 **Igreja Luterana,** the oldest church in Petrôpolis (open for visitation only during Sun morning service at 10am). A bit farther along the Avenida Ipiranga, at no. 716, is the lovely **Casa de Petrôpolis** (© 024/2246-0996), a museum, cultural center, restaurant, and garden. Guided tours of this beautifully preserved house will take you through numerous salons lavishly decorated with satin curtains and wallpaper, gold-leaf chandeliers, and ornate and beautiful furniture. Weekly concerts take place on Saturday night at 8pm; tickets cost R$10 (US$5). From here, it's a simple matter to retrace your steps to the cathedral and the **Museu Imperial,** Rua da Imperatriz 220 (© 024/2237-8000). Built by Dom Pedro II in 1845 as his summer palace, the much-loved Museu Imperial is now Petrôpolis's premier museum. The self-guided visits take you through numerous ground-floor salons decorated with period furniture, household items, and lovely paintings and drawings depicting the life and landscapes of 19th-century Rio. Best of all is Brazil's equivalent of the crown jewels: Dom Pedro II's crown, weighing almost 4 pounds, is encrusted with 639 diamonds and 77 pearls.

Where to Dine in Petrôpolis

Petrôpolis offers a range of dining opportunities, from schnitzel to sushi to *churrasco*. Check opening times carefully, as a number of restaurants are closed Monday through Wednesday or Monday through Thursday.

Hidden in the former coach house of the Casa de Petrôpolis is the lovely **Arte Temperada,** Rua Ipiranga 716 (© 024/2246-0996). Rustic decorations, a wood-burning stove, and long tables give the place a barnlike feel, but the food is far from unsophisticated. The main courses include a number of excellent trout dishes including *truta com molho de limão* (trout with lemon sauce) and the smoked trout with honey-and-mustard sauce. For lighter meals, the menu includes soufflés, sandwiches, and afternoon tea. Tucked away in the left corner of the gardens surrounding the museum, the **Museu Imperial Tearoom,** Rua da Imperatriz 220 (© **024/2237-8000**), is the perfect place for tea or lunch. Full tea service is available, including cakes, pies, croissants, madeleines, toast, jam, cold cuts, and pâté. For a smaller lunch or snack, the restaurant also serves a variety of quiches and sandwiches. A traditional-looking *churrascaria* with wood panels and booths, **Majoricá,** Rua do Imperador 754 (© **024/2242-2498**), is a local favorite when it comes to a good steak. Most dishes serve two people.

4 São Paulo

429km (268 miles) SW of Rio de Janeiro

The largest metropolis in South America and, with 17 million people, the third largest city in the world, São Paulo was but an obscure market town until the 1850s, when it became one of the largest coffee exporters in the world. When slavery was abolished in Brazil in 1888, coffee growers began encouraging immigration. Italians, Japanese, Eastern Europeans, Spanish, Portuguese, and Germans all made their way to São Paulo; to this day, São Paulo is the most culturally diverse city in Brazil.

Paulistas like to say that they earn the money not just for themselves but also for all of Brazil, and in a way they do. In 1996, 38% of the country's GDP was generated in São Paulo, and the state of São Paulo is responsible for 65% of Brazil's industrial production. Paulistas are proud of their work ethic and their "un-Brazilian" efficiency. Lacking beaches and mountains, Paulistas devote themselves entirely to urban pursuits. Shopping is a contact sport, while dining out is an almost religious observance. Though most travelers come to São Paulo for business, it's worth spending a day or two here for the shopping, the dining, and the sheer frenetic pace of the place—particularly if you're flying in or out Brazil through the city. However, if your time is truly limited, Iguaçu Falls, Salvador, or even Brasília will provide a more uniquely Brazilian travel experience.

ESSENTIALS
GETTING THERE
BY PLANE   All international flights arrive at **Guarulhos International Airport** (© **011/6445-2945**), a 45-minute drive northeast of the city. Prepaid taxi fares from Guarulhos to anywhere in São Paulo are available with **Taxi Guarucoop** (© **011/6440-7070**). Sample fares: São Paulo Centro and Tietê, R$52 (US$17), Cerqueira César and Jardins, R$62 (US$20). São Paulo's domestic airport, **Congonhas** (© **011/5090-9000**), is only a 15- to 20-minute taxi ride from Jardins or Avenida Paulista. Prepaid taxis to Centro or Jardins cost R$26 to R$36 (US$8.50–US$12). The **Airport Service** (© **011/6445-2505**) also operates shuttle buses between Congonhas Airport, Praça da República, Avenida Paulista (stopping at major hotels along the street), and the Rodoviária Tietê (bus station). The fare is R$17 (US$5.50), and each route takes approximately 50 minutes. Buses depart about every half-hour from 6am to 11pm, and then hourly overnight.

BY BUS   There are four bus terminals *(rodoviária).* All are connected to the metrô system. The easiest way to get to or from any bus station is by metrô—all are connected to the metrô system, and the metrô stations have the same name as the terminals. **Barra Funda** (© **011/3235-0322**) serves the interior of São Paulo, Northern Paraná, and Mato Grosso. **Bresser** (© **011/ 6692-5191**) provides buses to and from Minas Gerais. **Jabaquara** (© **011/ 5581-0856** or 011/5011-9345) serves Santos and the south coast. **Rodoviária Tietê** is by far the largest and most important bus station. Buses depart from here to Rio, most major Brazilian cities, and international destinations. Call © **011/3235-0322** for buses to Rio and © **011/3235-0322** for connections to Argentina, Uruguay, and Paraguay.

ORIENTATION

The old heart of the city stands around **Praça da Sé.** São Paulo's original main street, **Rua Direita,** leads through a maze of downtown streets to a viaduct crossing over a busy freeway into the "newer" section of the old town, centered on leafy green **Praça República.** Together, the newer and older halves of the inner city are known as **Centro.**

Immediately west of Centro is one of São Paulo's original upscale suburbs, **Higienópolis.** Though long since swallowed up in the city, Higienópolis remains a green and leafy enclave with some good restaurants and the city's Museu Arte Brasileira (Museum of Brazilian Art).

Due south of Centro is **Liberdade,** said to have the largest Japanese population of any city outside Japan. Southwest of Centro lies **Bela Vista,** more often referred to as **Bixiga,** São Paulo's Little Italy. Bela Vista butts up against São Paulo's proudest street, the **Avenida Paulista.** Set on a ridge above surrounding neighborhoods, the Avenida Paulista was long ago given up to rank upon rank of skyscrapers, the headquarters of the city's powerful banking and financial interests. On the adjacent side streets, there are numerous hotels catering to business travelers. Halfway along the street is São Paulo's top-notch Museum of Art, the MASP.

Extending southwest from Avenida Paulista are series of upscale neighborhoods named *jardins,* or gardens. Though each area has a particular name—Jardim Paulista, Jardim America, Cerqueira César, Jardim Europa—Paulistas tend to refer to them simply as **Jardins.** There are few attractions per se in the Jardins, but they do offer some terrific restaurants and the best shopping in São Paulo, notably where Rua Augusta is intersected by Alameda Lorena and Rua Oscar Freire.

From here, Rua Augusta continues its run straight through the Jardins, changing names as it goes to Avenida Europa and finally Avenida Cidade Jardim. At this point, it intersects with another broad and important street, Avenida Brigadeiro Faria Lima. Less fashionable than Rua Augusta, Avenida Brigadeiro Faria Lima is home to a number of big, American-style shopping malls. Continuing northwest, it leads to another Jardim-like area called **Pinheiros,** while going the opposite direction leads first to **Itaim Bibi** and then to a fun and slightly funky area of restaurants and clubs called **Vila Olimpia.**

The last key element to São Paulo is not a neighborhood but a green space—Ibirapuera Park. Located immediately south of the Jardins, Ibirapuera is to São Paulo what Central Park is to New York. It's a place for strolling, lazy suntanning, and outdoor concerts, and it's home to a couple of the city's top cultural facilities, including the Modern Art Museum.

São Paulo

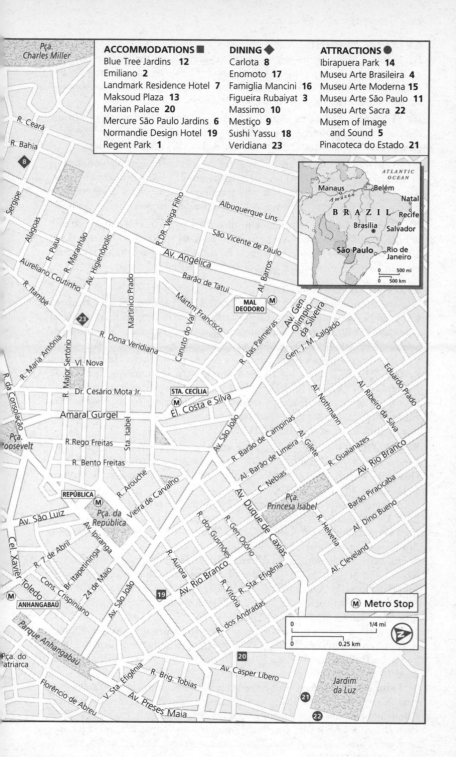

ACCOMMODATIONS ■
Blue Tree Jardins **12**
Emiliano **2**
Landmark Residence Hotel **7**
Maksoud Plaza **13**
Marian Palace **20**
Mercure São Paulo Jardins **6**
Normandie Design Hotel **19**
Regent Park **1**

DINING ◆
Carlota **8**
Enomoto **17**
Famiglia Mancini **16**
Figueira Rubaiyat **3**
Massimo **10**
Mestiço **9**
Sushi Yassu **18**
Veridiana **23**

ATTRACTIONS ●
Ibirapuera Park **14**
Museu Arte Brasileira **4**
Museu Arte Moderna **15**
Museu Arte São Paulo **11**
Museu Arte Sacra **22**
Musem of Image
and Sound **5**
Pinacoteca do Estado **21**

ⓜ Metro Stop

Ⓜ **Metro Stop**

GETTING AROUND

BY FOOT   Many of the neighborhoods that make up the city are compact enough to be easily explored on foot. During the day, the city is very safe; the only areas to avoid at night are the quiet side streets of Centro, particularly the streets around Praça da Sé, Bixiga, and Luz station.

BY SUBWAY   The north-south line and the east-west line run from 5am to midnight. The line under Avenida Paulista runs from 6am to 10pm. Metrô tickets cost R$1.90 (65¢) for a single ride and R$17 (US$5.65) for 10 rides.

BY BUS   São Paulo buses are plentiful and frequent. The large sign on the top of the bus mentions the final stop or neighborhood, while a smaller sign in the window and on the side of the bus will mention a few key stops along the way. Buses cost R$1.70 (55¢), and you pay as you board from the front of the bus.

BY TAXI   **Rádio Táxi Vermelho e Branco** (Red and White) is one of the most reliable taxi companies and can be reached at © **011/251-1733** or 011/3146-4000. Taxis can also be hailed anywhere on the street, and taxi stands (*pontos de taxi*) are found at many major squares and main streets.

VISITOR INFORMATION

The city tourism information booths (**Central de Informações Turísticas,** or **CIT**) can be found downtown at Praça da República in front of Rua 7 de Abril (© **011/3231-2922;** daily 9am–6pm), and at Avenida Paulista in front of Trianon Park (© **011/251-0970;** Mon–Fri 9am–6pm and weekends 10am–4pm). CIT booths in Terminals 1 and 2 of Guarulhos Airport are open daily from 7am to 7pm. The **SET** (State Information Booths) can be found at **Rua XV de Novembro** 347, Centro (© **011/323-1445**), open daily from 9am to 6pm.

For sale on the newsstands is a publication called *Este Mês São Paulo* (or *São Paulo This Month*), a bilingual tourist guide. It has some maps, listings, and contact information, and it costs R$5 (US$1.65).

FAST FACTS   To exchange currency, go to **Banco do Brasil** at Av. Paulista 2163, Centro (© 011/3066-9322); Rua São João 32, Centro (© 011/3234-1646); or Guarulhos Airport (© 011/6445-2223). There's also a **Citibank** at Av. Paulista 1111, Centro (© 011/5576-1000).

In an **emergency,** call the police at © **190** or the fire brigade or an ambulance at © **193.** You can also contact the tourist police at Avenida São Luis (1 block from Praça da República), Centro (© **011/3214-0209**), or Rua São Bento 380, 5th floor, Centro (© **011/3107-5642**).

For medical attention, go to **Albert Einstein Hospital,** Av. Albert Einstein 627, Morumbi (© 011/3747-1233), or **Hospital das Clínicas,** 255 Av. Doutor Eneias de Carvalho Aguiar s/n (© 011/3069-6000). If you need a dentist, contact **Dr. Marcelo Erlich,** open 24 hours, English spoken, Rua Sergipe 401, Suite 403, Higienópolis (© 011/3214-1332/9935-8666).

Two good places for Internet access are **Centro Cultural FNAC,** Av. Pedroso de Moraes 858, Pinheiros (© 011/3976-0022), open daily from 10am to 10pm; and **Sebo Paulista,** Av. Paulista 1919, Centro (© 011/3285-2443), open daily from 10am to 10pm.

A note about telephone numbers: Many phone numbers in São Paulo either have changed in the past 3 years or will change soon. If you are not able to get through to a number, especially if it's a seven-digit number, it has likely recently been changed. Check with your hotel front desk to verify the number for you, or if your Portuguese is up to snuff, call the automated directory assistance service at © **800/771-5104.**

WHAT TO SEE & DO
THE TOP ATTRACTIONS

Ibirapuera Park ★★   Often called São Paulo's beach, Ibirapuera Park attracts more than 200,000 visitors on an average weekend. You can wander the paths beside pleasant lagoons or in the Japanese garden; or you can jog the exercise track or rent a bicycle (R$5/US$1.65 per hour). On Sunday morning, there's always a free outdoor concert in the park's Praça da Paz. Sunday from 10am to 4pm, you can also take advantage of the Bosque de Leitura, a free outdoor lending library that lets you borrow a magazine or book (including many in English) to read in the park for the day. In the corner near Gate 3, there's the Modern Art Museum (see below). There's fruit and juice and ice cream vendors everywhere in the park, but if you want more substantial fare, the Green Restaurant (✆ 011/557-9770) offers a good kilo selection at R$18 (US$6) per kilogram.

Administration ✆ 011/5174-5177. Free admission. Daily 6am–8pm. Bus: 675C from metrô Ana Rosa; 775 to Santa Cruz metrô station.

Monument to Latin America ★★   Designed by famed Brazilian architect Oscar Niemeyer, the monument is, well, *so* Niemeyer—shy of a visit to Brasília, it's the best place to see Brazilian modernism in all its pure concrete austerity. The South American Parliament and Art gallery are likely of the most interest to visitors unimpressed by architecture. The art gallery hosts changing fine art exhibits, while the hall is permanent home to a fun and fascinating display of folk art from across Latin America.

Av. Auro Soares de Moura Andrade 664, Barra Funda. ✆ 011/3823-9611. www.memorial.org.br. Free admission. Tues–Sun 9am–6pm. Metrô: Barra Funda.

Museu Arte Brasileira/FAAP ★★   Don't let the name fool you. What this majestic and slightly pompous building (think Mussolini monumental) in quiet Higienópolis plays host to is not Brazilian art, but an ever-changing parade of grand international exhibits—2 years ago it was Egypt, currently it's Napoléon. The museum also claims to house a number of the Brazilian greats—Portinari, Di Cavalcanti, and others—but they're never actually on display. (You may also see the museum referred to as FAAP, which is the acronym for the cultural institute where it's located.)

Rua Alagoas 903, Higienópolis. ✆ 011/3662-1662. www.faap.br/museu. Admission depends on exhibit. Typically R$10 (US$3.35) adults. Tues–Fri 10am–9pm; Sat–Sun 1–6pm. Bus: 137T.

Museu Arte Moderna (MAM) ★   Small but quite intriguing, the Modern Art Museum's main building in Ibirapuera Park has two galleries devoted to ever-changing exhibits of modern work, be it in the form of painting, sculpture, video, textiles, or some other medium. The museum's own permanent collection is now displayed at a pair of peripheral shopping-mall sites, the MAM-Higienópolis and the MAM-Villa-Lobos. About 45 minutes are plenty to enjoy it all, then head to the museum cafe for a snack.

Parque do Ibirapuera Gate 3. ✆ 011/5549-9688. www.mam.org.br. Admission R$5 (US$1.65) adults, R$2.50 (85¢) students and seniors, free for children under 11. Free Tues; free Thurs after 5pm. Tues–Wed and Fri noon–6pm; Thurs noon–10pm; Sat–Sun 10am–6pm. Bus: 5100, 5131 from metrô Brigadeiro.

Museu Arte São Paulo (MASP) ★★   Part of the MASP experience is the building itself. The main display space is a single long box raised two stories off the ground on bright red concrete piers. The idea was to create a broad courtyard with a view of the Anhangabaú Valley. Inside, the museum is somewhat of a disappointment. It does contain an excellent selection of Western art, from

14th-century Italian religious imagery to Picasso's early-20th-century works, but with the exception of one room dedicated to Candido Portinari, Brazilian art is entirely absent. The effect is somewhat like taking a first-year survey course in college. If you've missed out seeing these artists elsewhere in Europe or North America, the MASP is well worth a visit. But if Brazilian art is what you want, go to the Pinacoteca instead (p. 297).

Av. Paulista 1578, Cerqueira César. ⓒ 011/251-5644. Admission R$10 (US$3.35) adults, free for seniors and children under 11. Tues–Sun 11am–6pm. Metrô: Trianon-MASP.

Museu de Arte Sacra 🌟🌟   "Sacred Art" refers to objects—chalices, crosses, statues, paintings, sculptures—created to adorn churches or for use in Catholic service. The Mosteiro da Luz provides the perfect solemn and serene setting to view these works; choral music echoes through the stone corridors and light from the cloister casts a warm glow on the collection. The collection also displays beautifully carved and hand-painted oratories. Portuguese and English texts explain the origins and name of each piece. Expect to spend about an hour here. Outside in the garden is the Presepio, a miniature village composed of more than 1,600 pieces depicting life in an 18th-century Neapolitan village; admission is included with the ticket to the Museu de Arte Sacra.

Av. Tiradentes 676, Luz. ⓒ 011/227-7694. Admission R$5 (US$1.65) adults, free for children under 6. Tues–Fri 11am–6pm; Sat–Sun 10am–7pm. Metrô: Luz.

Museu do Imigrante 🌟🌟 Kids   São Paulo's Ellis Island: Three million immigrants have passed through the gates of this building to start a new life in Brazil. Today's visitors get an excellent idea of what it must have felt like to arrive here and get ready for a new life. The admission hall, office, hospital, and dormitories are shown in their original condition, and objects are on full display. Upstairs, the former dormitory has been converted into a replica of a typical early-20th-century Main Street in São Paulo, with a drugstore and street stalls. Don't forget to visit the old immigrant railway siding. The station building houses beautiful photo exhibits of immigrant families. Allow at least 2 hours.

Rua Visconde de Parnaiba 1316, Bras. ⓒ 011/6693-0917. www.memorialdoimigrante.sp.gov.br. R$4 (US$1.30). Train and tram ride R$3.50 (US$1.15). Tues–Sun 10am–5pm. Metrô: Estação Bresser. Take the Av. Alcantara Machado exit down the ramp and take the street to the right along the metrô tracks (Rua Visconde de Parnaiba) for about 3 blocks.

Museu do Ipiranga or Museu Paulista 🌟   Located at the birthplace of Brazilian independence—it was here in 1822 that Dom Pedro I declared Brazil's independence from Portugal—the museum is a grand neoclassical building with perfectly manicured Versailles-like gardens out front and a "wilder" botanical garden out back. The collection houses some real gems of Brazilian art. There are also a number of photo exhibits showing the development of 19th-century São Paulo. The remainder of the exhibit consists of period furniture, a collection of 19th-century horse-drawn fire trucks, household objects, and clothing. Unfortunately, there are no English signs. The park and gardens behind the museum are very pleasant and packed with Paulistas on weekends. Expect to spend an hour in the museum.

Praça da Independencia s/n, Ipiranga. ⓒ 011/215-4588. Admission R$3 (US$1) adults, free for children under 7. Tues–Sun 9am–5pm. Bus: 4506 Jardim Celeste.

Museum of Image and Sound 🌟🌟 Finds   The Museum of Image and Sound showcases the best Brazilian contemporary image makers. Photographs in the changing exhibits are always compelling, beautifully displayed, and deeply

engaged with contemporary themes such as sex, media manipulation, or marginalization. At all times they made you think. Also on-site is an archive of several hundred thousand stills and some 15,000 films and videos that may be consulted free of charge. Expect to spend an hour. Call ahead to verify hours. Due to funding shortfalls, the museum often closes between exhibits, sometimes for extended periods.

Av. Europa 158, Jardim Europa. (C) 011/3062-1917. www.mis.sp.gov.br. Free admission. Tues–Sun 2–10pm. Bus: 373T.

Pinacoteca do Estado ⭐⭐⭐   The Pinacoteca is a sun-lit joy to be in, and one of the best-curated Brazilian art collections in the city. Though unfortunately none of the signs are in English, the Pinacoteca does an excellent job of displaying some of the best Brazilian artists from the 19th and 20th centuries, from the landscapes of Antonio Parreiras and João da Costa to still-life painters such as Georgina de Albuquerque and João Batista Pagini. The 20th-century work starts to break free of European influence and includes some interesting examples of expressive Brazilian pieces, colorful and bursting with energy. In addition to paintings, the Pinacoteca collection contains sculpture including a lovely statue by Raphael Galvez entitled *O Brasileiro,* as well as works by Alfredo Ceschiatti, the artist who designed many of the sculptures in Brasília. Allow 2 hours.

Praça da Luz 2, Luz. (C) 011/229-9844. www.uol.com.br/pinasp. Admission R$4 (US$1.35) adults, R$2 (65¢) students, free for children under 11. Tues–Sun 10am–6pm. Guided tours leave at 10, 11:30am, 1, and 2:30pm. Metrô: Luz.

SHOPPING

Paulistas say that if you can't buy it in São Paulo, you can't buy it in Brazil. They're probably right. Even city-proud Cariocas begrudgingly admit that São Paulo's shopping scene is superior to theirs.

The city has a number of shopping areas, all unique and interesting to explore. **Jardins,** the upscale neighborhood just southwest of downtown, is well known for its high-end fashion boutiques. The main shopping streets in this neighborhood are Rua Augusta, the parallel Rua Haddock Lobo, and their cross streets Rua Oscar Freire and Alameda Lorena. On any given weekday during office hours, the many pedestrian streets of Centro—in particular **Rua Direita, Rua São Bento, Rua 25 de Março,** and **Rua 24 de Maio**—are one long outdoor fair, featuring every item you'd care to name, all of it very cheap.

Then there are the malls: In São Paulo, the mall has been elevated to an elegant, upscale, and refined shopping experience. The best-known malls are **Morumbi Shopping,** Av. Roque Petroni Junior 1089, Brooklin; **Iguatemi Shopping,** Av. Brigadeiro Faria Lima 2232, Jardim Paulistano; and **Patio Higienópolis,** Av. Higienópolis 615. All are located in upscale neighborhoods close to the city center. More downscale is the **Shopping Paulista,** Rua Treze de Maio 1947, Paraiso, close to the city center.

ART GALLERIES   This small gallery-cum-store, Artevial, Rua Haddock Lobo 1398, Jardins ((C) **011/3082-6715**), is a showcase for architect and decorator Flavio Miranda's work, mostly furniture made out of glass and wood. The gallery also displays paintings, ceramics, lamps, and other smaller art objects made by local artists such as Gustavo Rosa and Flavia Bruneti. **Monica Filgueiras de Almeida,** Alameda Ministro Rocha Azevedo 927, Cerqueira César ((C) **011/3082-5292**), usually has interesting exhibits of artwork in various media: paintings, bronze pieces, glass, or photo art.

BOOKS   The **Centro Cultural FNAC,** Av. Pedroso de Moraes 858 (℃ **011/ 3097-0022**), boasts many floors of books, but it also has a coffee shop, cybercafe, and large music and video department. The foreign language section is extensive, and the guidebook and map section offers a good selection for travelers. **Haddock Lobo Books and Magazines,** Rua Haddock 1503 (℃ **011/3082-9449**), open daily until midnight, has an excellent selection of international magazines.

GIFTS & SOUVENIRS   **Galeria Arte Brasileira,** Alameda Lorena 2163, Jardins (℃ **011/3062-9452**), specializes in Brazilian arts and crafts such as woodcarvings, hammocks, lace, and folk art. **Art India,** Rua Augusta 1371, Loja 119, Cerqueira César (℃ **011/283-2102**), sells indigenous crafts from tribes from across Brazil. **Petra Brazilis,** Alameda Itú 215, Jardins (℃ **011/251-3805**), specializes in Brazilian gemstones, including souvenirs, fine jewelry, and loose stones.

MARKETS   Located to the north of Praça da Sé, the fruit and vegetable market **Mercado Central,** Rua da Cantareira 306, is an imposing neo-Gothic hall built in 1933, with huge stained-glass windows. It's open Monday through Saturday from 5am to 4pm. Every Sunday from 10am to 5pm, there's an **antiques fair** in the open space beneath the MASP building on Avenida Paulista. Dealers are registered, and the quality of the wares is often good. On Sunday on the **Praça da Liberdade** (next to the Liberdade metrô stop), São Paulo's Japanese residents celebrate their heritage with an outdoor market featuring an excellent and inexpensive selection of Japanese cuisine.

MUSIC   **Casa Amadeus,** Av. Ipiranga 1129, Centro (℃ **011/228-0098**), sells a great selection of Brazilian sheet music and a variety of Brazilian musical instruments. **Saraiva,** Shopping Morumbi, Av. Roque Petroni Junior 1089, Brooklin (℃ **0800/177-600**), sells books and magazines as well as CDs. The CD collection is quite large, though limited to commercially successful artists.

WHERE TO STAY

São Paulo attracts business travelers Monday through Friday, then sits empty from Friday afternoon to Monday morning. Prices drop by as much as 50% if you can time your visit to this city on a weekend.

CENTRO
Very Expensive
Normandie Design Hotel 🟎 *(Finds)*   Sleek, stylish, and cool. From the moment you walk through the large metal doors, you know this place is different. The lobby is completely white; in contrast, the rooms are done entirely in black (although the staff will put on a white duvet cover if it's too much black for you). The bathrooms are spacious, with modern counters in elegant marble. In addition to the standard rooms, the hotel has a number of suites. The master suite, with its king-size bed and sitting room, is worth the extra money; however, the executive suites are a bit overpriced for their size.

Av. Ipiranga 1187, Centro, São Paulo 01039-000 SP. ℃ 011/3311-9855. Fax 011/228-3157. www.normandie designhotel.com.br. 171 units (shower only). R$280 (US$94) standard double; R$350 (US$117) suite. Up to 50% off on weekends. Extra person R$70 (US$23). Children under 7 stay free in parent's room. Over 6 R$35 (US$12) for extra bed. AE, DC, MC, V. Parking R$18 (US$6) per day. Metrô: República. **Amenities:** Restaurant; bar; concierge; tour desk; car rental; business center; 24-hr. room service; laundry; nonsmoking rooms. *In room:* A/C, TV, dataport, minibar, fridge, hair dryer, safe.

Moderate
Marian Palace 🟎🟎 *(Finds)*   The Marian Palace was converted into a hotel in 1950, preserving the original Art Deco character. All rooms are very spacious with

large closets; the superior ones have a small terrace or large curved windows. Nicely furnished, the rooms retain many original Art Deco features such as the lamps, the chairs, and even the color schemes. The bathrooms are done in colorful blue and yellow tiles; a few have bathtubs. Due to the curved shape of the building, there are a number of room configurations, so have a look at a few to choose one that suits you best. The hotel's swimming pool has a great sun deck.

Av. Casper Libero 65, Centro, São Paulo, 01033-001 SP. ✆ 0800/558-433 or 011/228-8433. Fax 011/228-8013. www.marian.com.br. 97 units (shower only). R$160 (US$53) standard double; R$185 (US$62) superior double. 20%–50% discount on weekends. Extra person R$65 (US$33). Children under 6 stay free in parent's room. AE, DC, MC, V. Parking R$25 (US$8.35) per day. Metrô: São Bento. **Amenities:** Restaurant; bar; outdoor pool; small weight room; concierge; tour desk; business center; limited room service; laundry; nonsmoking rooms. *In room:* A/C, TV, dataport, minibar, fridge.

AVENIDA PAULISTA
Expensive

Maksoud Plaza ✪✪✪   One of São Paulo's top luxury hotels, the Maksoud is over-the-top 1980s opulence at its oh-so-shameless finest. The more than 400 rooms are well appointed and updated with the latest technological features. There's an overwhelming number of room types to choose from: standard, superior, deluxe, deluxe studio, deluxe demisuite, deluxe demisuite corner room, and more. Just keep in mind that you get what you pay for. The standard and superior rooms are nothing more than basic, albeit spacious and of a high quality, hotel rooms; the deluxe and executive level rooms are where the extra dollars start to make a noticeable difference. Breakfast is not included. The Maksoud frequently advertises specials on its website well below the rates listed here.

Alameda Campinas 150, São Paulo, 01404-900 SP. ✆ 0800/134-411 or 011/3145-8000. Fax 011/3145-8001. www.maksoud.com.br. 415 units. R$417–R$567 (US$139–US$189) standard or superior double; R$540–R$930 (US$180–US$310) executive or deluxe. Extra person R$120 (US$40). Children under 13 stay free in parent's room. AE, DC, MC, V. Parking R$18 (US$9) per day. Metrô: Trianon-MASP. **Amenities:** 4 restaurants; 5 bars; heated indoor pool; health club; sauna; concierge; tour desk; car rental; business center; shopping arcade; salon; 24-hr. room service; massage; babysitting; laundry; dry cleaning; nonsmoking rooms and floors; executive level rooms. *In room:* A/C, TV, dataport, minibar, hair dryer, safe (not in standard rooms).

Mercure São Paulo Jardins ✪   This Mercure has that new hotel feel; everything's crisp and clean, and the decoration is Scandinavian modern with blond wood, simple design, and lots of light shining in everywhere. Rooms are of a good size with king-size beds (a rarity in Brazil), a couple of small sitting chairs, and a maplewood desk with desk lamp and phone and power jacks for laptops. Bathrooms have nice fixtures but are shower-only and functionally compact. The laptop focus is continued in the downstairs bar—all the little bar tables are wired with power and phone connections. Breakfast costs R$15 (US$5)

Alameda Itu 1151, Cerqueira César, 01421-001 SP. ✆ 0800/703-7000 or 011/3089-7555. Fax 011/3089-7550. www.accorhotels.com.br. 126 units (shower only). R$190–R$230 (US$63–US$77) double. Discounts available on weekends. No triples. Children under 11 stay free in parent's room. AE, DC, MC, V. Free parking. Metrô: Consolação. **Amenities:** Restaurant; laptop-friendly bar; small pool; 2 bike machines, treadmill; sauna; business center; 24-hr. room service; laundry; dry cleaning; floors 1–7 nonsmoking. *In room:* A/C, TV, dataport, minibar, fridge, hair dryer, safe.

Moderate

The Landmark Residence Hotel ✪ *Value*   This apart-hotel offers pretty good value for money, particularly on weekends. Rooms are like small suites; the bedroom is separated from the good-size sitting room by a sliding partition. Sitting rooms feature a pullout couch, chair, and breakfast table, and all rooms have a small kitchenette. Unfortunately, the only rooms with balconies come with single beds only. All units have a good-size bathroom with tub and shower. The only real drawback is the tacky pseudo-rustic decorating scheme.

Alameda Jaú 1607, Cerqueira César, 01420-002 SP. © 011/3082-8677. Fax 011/3082-0167. www.residence. com.br. 86 units. R$205 (US$68) double; weekend R$150 (US$50) double. Extra person 20%. Children under 8 stay free in parent's room. AE, DC, MC, V. Free parking. Metrô: Consolação. **Amenities:** Restaurant; bar; small pool; weight room w/free weights; sauna; children's play area; room service until midnight; laundry; dry cleaning; nonsmoking floors. *In room:* A/C, TV, kitchenette (but no oven), minibar, fridge, hair dryer, safe.

JARDINS
Very Expensive

Emiliano ✩✩✩ The exclusive Emiliano is five star treatment all the way from the welcome massage to the minibar stocked according to your preference and a personalized selection of pillows, carefully fluffed and placed on your Egyptian cotton sheets. There are two types of rooms: deluxe studios and suites. The studios (really just a large room) are marginally cheaper, but this is not the time to skimp. The spacious suites are fabulous: decorated with designer furniture, the latest in home entertainment electronics, and unique artwork. The bed is king-size (of course) and the bathroom is a minispa in itself; all toiletries are customized for your skin type and you can sit back and relax in the claw-foot tub, maybe watch a little TV or contemplate life on your heated toilet seat.

Rua Oscar Freire 384, Cerqueira César, 01426-000 SP. © 011/3069-4369. Fax 011/3068-4398. www.emiliano. com.br. 57 units. R$641–R$865 (US$214–US$288) double; R$1,166–R$1,555 (US$389–US$518) suite. Extra person 30%. Children under 11 stay free in parent's room. AE, DC, MC, V. Free parking. **Amenities:** French restaurant; upscale lobby bar; small exercise room; outstanding spa; concierge; business center; salon; 24-hr. room service; massage; babysitting service; laundry; dry-cleaning; nonsmoking floors. *In room:* A/C, TV, dataport, minibar, hair dryer, safe.

Unique ✩✩✩ This latest São Paulo design hotel is a teetering verdigris-colored disk, chopped off at the top to make a roof-deck, and propped up at either extremity by a pair of concrete pillars hanging down at tangents like unfurled banners. Large round portholes gazing out the side of this slice give Unique something of the air of a boat, though an abandoned *Martian Chronicles* kind of craft. Inside it's all high design, from the lobby bar to the rooms and suites which feature white-on-white decor, queen beds with luscious bedding, sparkling bathrooms with Jacuzzi tubs, clever desk space, and a plethora of room gadgets including electric blinds, flat-screen TV/DVD, lots of light options, and a console to control it all. Suites are all located on the rim of the disk so their outer walls all rise in one seamless curve from floor to ceiling.

Av. Brigadeiro Luis Antônio 4700, Jd. Paulista, 01402-002 SP. © 011/3055-4700. Fax 011/3889-8100. www. hotelunique.com.br. 95 units. R$725–R$770 (US$242–US$257) double; R$1,500–R$6,500 (US$500–US$2,167) suite. AE, DC, MC, V. Parking R$15 (US$5) daily. Metrô: Brigadeiro. **Amenities:** Rooftop restaurant; rooftop pool; concierge; room service. *In room:* A/C, 48-in. flat-screen TV, DVD, CD, cordless phone, high-speed Internet, minibar, fridge, laptop-size safe w/electrical outlet.

Expensive

Blue Tree Towers Jardins ✩✩ This excellent new hotel is built with the business traveler in mind. The spacious rooms are a cross between a studio and a regular hotel room; a desk and TV on a swivel separate the sitting area somewhat from the sleeping area. The rooms come with modern furnishings that are easy on the eyes: light colors, blond wood, and comfortable lighting. A number of units are fully wheelchair accessible, nonsmoking floors are available, and all rooms have fast Internet access.

Alameda Campinas 540, São Paulo, 01404-000 SP. © 0800/15-0500 or 011/3147-0400. Fax 011/3147-0401. www.bluetree.com.br. 228 units (shower only). R$180–R$250 (US$60–US$83) double. Extra person 25%.

Children under 7 stay free in parent's room. AE, DC, MC, V. Free parking. Metrô: Trianon-MASP. **Amenities:** Restaurant; indoor pool; health club; sauna; concierge; business center; limited room service; laundry; non-smoking floors. *In room:* A/C, TV, dataport, minibar, fridge, safe.

Moderate
Regent Park Hotel ⚘ This small apart-hotel is well situated, on one of the best-known streets in Jardins. The majority of units in this hotel are one-bedroom suites, but two- and three-bedroom suites are available as well. The furnishings are a little dated, 1980s rustic wood, but everything is very well maintained and clean, and all the suites have a full kitchen. The staff is exceptionally friendly and helpful, and business travelers will appreciate the small and efficient business center.

Rua Oscar Freire 533, Jardins. ℂ 011/3064-3666. www.regent.com.br. 70 units. 1-bedroom R$195 (US$65); 2-bedroom R$300 (US$100); 3-bedroom R$390 (US$130). Weekend discounts are available. Extra person R$30 (US$10). Children under 5 stay free in parent's room. Free parking. Bus: 702P. **Amenities:** Restaurant; outdoor rooftop pool; small weight room; sauna; concierge; tour desk; business center; limited room service; laundry; nonsmoking rooms. *In room:* A/C, TV, dataport, kitchen, minibar, fridge, safe.

WHERE TO DINE
São Paulo is the gourmet capital of Brazil. It's the city with the money to attract the country's best chefs. Plus, with no beaches or mountains to play on, Paulistas like to eat out for amusement. People go out around 9 or 10pm at the earliest. Most restaurants don't accept reservations; if you don't want to wait for a table, it's better to arrive unfashionably early at 8pm.

CENTRO
Moderate
Famiglia Mancini ⚘⚘ ITALIAN Though the restaurant seats 180 people, you always feel like you're dining in a typical old-style Italian cantina. Start your meal off at the antipasto buffet, where you can choose from a sizable spread of olives, cold cuts, marinated vegetables, cheese, quail eggs, and salad. For the main course, there's every kind of pasta you could dream of, and more than 30 different sauces to match it up with. There is also stuffed pasta, such as cannelloni, ravioli, and lasagna. Portions are huge; they serve at least two people, often three.

Rua Avanhandava 81, Centro. ℂ 011/3256-4320. Reservations not accepted. Main courses R$28–R$68 (US$9–US$23) for 2. AE, DC, MC, V. Tues–Sat 11:30am–3:30am; Sun–Mon 11:30am–1am. Metrô: Anhagabau.

AVENIDA PAULISTA
Very Expensive
Massimo ⚘⚘ ITALIAN Paulistas love the casual atmosphere, created by owners Massimo and little brother Venanzio, and of course, the food. Pasta is just a (very pleasant) side trip here. Some of the dishes that we definitely approve of include the fungi mushrooms with sausage and polenta, and the oven-roasted lamb with vegetables, tomato, and white-wine sauce, accompanied by potatoes and caramelized onions. The wine list travels to Italy with the food; Venanzio provides expert direction toward the perfect pairing.

Alameda Santos 1826, Cerqueira César. ℂ 011/3284-0311. Main courses R$24–R$75 (US$8–US$25). No credit cards. Mon–Fri noon–3pm and 7:30pm–midnight; Sat noon–4:30pm and 7:30pm–1am; Sun noon–4:30pm and 7:30pm–11:30pm. Metrô: Trianon-MASP.

Expensive
Jun Sakamoto ⚘⚘ JAPANESE The setting in this restaurant is modern, with wood and metal decorations; the large sushi bar dominates the room. Chef and owner Jun Sakamoto's creations include an amazing duck breast teppanyaki; the stronger flavor of the duck meat doesn't get lost in the sauce like chicken or beef do. The ultralight tempura batter includes sesame seeds, adding another

layer of delicate flavor to this classic dish. On weekends, reservations are highly recommended.

Rua Jose Maria Lisboa 55, Pinheiros. ℂ 011/3088-6019. Reservations recommended. Main courses R$18– R$52 (US$6–US$17). AE, DC, MC, V. Mon–Fri 6:30pm–12:30am; Fri–Sat 7pm–1am. Metrô: Trianon-MASP.

Moderate

Mestiço 🟊🟊 *Value* THAI/BAHIAN   This little restaurant is run by a woman from Bahia and her partner from Thailand; this must be the only restaurant in all creation where traditional Thai noodle salad (pad Thai) sits side by side on the menu with Acarajé, a Bahian fast food made with beans and shrimp and served with hot sauce. The salads are outstanding; the *Atlântica* comes stuffed with smoked turkey, lettuce, red cabbage, apple, cashews, and Swiss cheese while the *Cubana* boasts squid, palm hearts, grilled banana, and an intriguing variety of lettuces. For more substantial meals there's Thai dishes like chicken with shiitake mushrooms in ginger sauce, and grilled prawns with roasted peanuts in a sweet and sour sauce. The room is very pleasant, lots of light wood with high ceilings, dimmed lights, and soft yellow walls decorated with exotic photos and masks.

Rua Fernando de Albuquerque 277, Consolação. ℂ 011/3256-3165. Reservations accepted. R$18–R$42 (US$6–US$14). AE, MC, V. Sun–Mon 11:45am–midnight; Tues–Thurs 11:45am–1am; Fri–Sat 11:45am–2am. Metrô: Consolação.

LIBERDADE
Expensive

Sushi Yassu 🟊🟊 JAPANESE   Long a standard bearer in Liberdade, Sushi Yassu's second-generation owners are now trying to introduce some new dishes to the Paulista palette. Case in point: the wide variety of eels. Brazilians (and many gringos) are still figuring out what this "enguia" fish is all about. Sushi Yassu serves a delicious introduction, with the eel sautéed with soy sauce and sake. More adventurous travelers can try the braised sea urchins or the Japanese green onions with chicken livers. For the traditional and squeamish, there are the standard sushi and sashimi dishes, as well as noodles and teppanyakis, but if you've come this far, you shouldn't let yourself squirm out of trying at least one little eel. Chances are you'll like it.

Rua Tomas Gonzaga 98, Liberdade. ℂ 011/3209-6622. Main courses R$14–R$36 (US$5–US$12). AE, DC, MC, V. Tues–Fri 11:30am–2:30pm and 6–11:30pm; Sat noon–3:30pm and 6pm–midnight; Sun noon–4pm and 6–10pm. Metrô: Liberdade.

Moderate

Enomoto JAPANESE   Just half a block off the Praça da Liberdade, Enomoto is one of the many Japanese restaurants in this ethnic enclave. Located on the ground floor of an old house, it has a lovely garden out front while inside the menu serves up all the usual Japanese faves—sushi, sashimi, donburi, and tempura—all at a reasonable price. The food is fresh, and the portions are very generous. Sushi comes in portions of 18 pieces but you can order half portions if you ask. All the teppanyaki dishes can easily be shared by two people. For meat lovers, the beef teppanyaki comes with a huge piece of tender grilled steak (R$28/US$9).

Rua Galvão Bueno 54, Liberdade, Sao Paulo. ℂ 011/279-0198. Reservations accepted. R$12–R$35 (US$4– US$12). No credit cards. Mon–Sat 11:30am–3pm and 6–11pm; Sun 11:30am–10pm. Metrô: Liberdade.

JARDINS/ITAIM BIBI
Very Expensive

Fasano 🟊🟊🟊 ITALIAN   Fasano shows that good food doesn't have to be complicated, or at least it shouldn't look like it is. The pasta is made fresh on the spot on a large marble table in full view of customers. Two ravioli dishes that stand out are the pumpkin ravioli with almonds and the smoked fish ravioli in a white-wine sauce. Very rich but delicious is the lamb roast stuffed with fresh goose liver. The knowledgeable sommelier will happily match wines with your food selection, but with a limited choice of wines by the glass, you should team up with your partner and agree on a bottle.

Rua Vítorio Fasano 88, Jardim Paulista. © 011/3062-4000. R$36–R$78 (US$12–US$26). AE, DC, MC, V. Mon–Sat 7pm–1am. Bus: 206E.

Expensive

Figueira Rubaiyat ✸✸✸ BRAZILIAN/STEAK   Surely the most beautiful restaurant in the city, Figueira (fig tree) Rubaiyat is built around a magnificent centenary fig tree. Seating can be either "outside" in a gazebo that wraps around the tree or inside the beautiful restaurant. The menu specializes in a la carte meats; most of the beef, chicken, and other meats served at Rubaiyat is home-grown at the owners' *fazenda* (cattle ranch), ensuring that the quality is always top-notch.

Rua Haddock Lobo 1738, Jardins. © 011/3063-3888. Main courses R$24–R$69 (US$8–US$23). V. Mon–Thurs noon–3:30pm and 7pm–midnight; Fri noon–3:30pm and 7pm–1am; Sat noon–1am; Sun noon–midnight. Bus 206E.

Moderate

Bolinha ✸✸ BRAZILIAN   People come to Bolinha for the *feijoada,* served rich and steaming every day of the week. You pay one set price, like a *rodízio,* and your *feijoada* comes with all the trimmings: as much rice, baked bananas, *farofa,* sliced orange, and sautéed green cabbage as you can stomach. Steaming pots of the black bean stew are brought to your table, offering you a choice between the traditional heavy-hitting recipe with bacon, sausage, ear, nose, foot, and other obscure pork bits, or a lighter version with leaner cuts. But really, if you're going to do it, why not go whole hog?

Av. Cidade Jardim 53, Jardim Europa. © 011/3061-2010. R$28–R$32 (US$14–US$16). AE, DC, MC, V. Mon–Sat 11am–1am; Sun 11am–midnight. Bus: 7181.

VILA MADALENA

Capim Santo ✸✸ BRAZILIAN   Modeled after the Capim Santo restaurant located in the south of Bahia, the São Paulo version is set in a lovely garden with lush mango trees and plenty of outside tables. Like its sister restaurant, Capim Santo specializes in seafood dishes. Try the robalo fish stuffed with a prawn *farofa* and grilled plantains, or the delicious grilled tuna. Another delicious seafood dish is the stew of prawns in coconut milk, served in a hollowed-out pumpkin. There's homemade pastas in a variety of seafood combinations, or for a vegetarian option try the mini-cannelloni stuffed with asparagus, ricotta, and tomato confit.

Rua Arapiraca 152, Vila Madalena. © 011/3813-9103. www.restaurantecapimsanto.com.br. Main courses R$24–R$46 (US$8–US$15). AE. Tues–Fri noon–3pm; Sat–Sun 12:30–6pm; Tues–Thurs 6pm–12:30am; Fri–Sat 6pm–2am. Metrô: Vila Madalena.

Santa Gula ✸✸ *Finds* ITALIAN   You enter Santa Gula through a fairy-tale lane lush with tropical plants, banana trees, and flickering candlelight. Inside, the handmade furniture and decorations give the feel of a simple Tuscan villa. The kitchen serves up a mix of Italian and Brazilian flavors. Think pasta stuffed with Brie and sun-dried tomatoes or with *carne seca* (a flavorful dried meat) and pumpkin purée. Equally intriguing is the trout filet with a blue cheese risotto. For dessert, don't pass up the *charlotte de cupuaçu*—ladyfingers soaked in cupuaçu-fruit mousse and slathered in chocolate sauce.

Rua Fidalga, 340, Vila Madalena, Sao Paulo. (℃) 011/3812-7815. Reservations accepted. Dinner R$21–R$36 (US$7–US$12). AE, DC, MC, V. Mon 8pm–midnight; Tues–Thurs noon–3pm and 8pm–1am; Fri–Sat noon–4pm and 8pm–2am; Sun noon–5pm. Metrô: Vila Madalena.

HIGIENOPOLIS
Expensive
Carlota 🌟🌟 *Finds* BRAZILIAN   Carla Pernambuco's cuisine is garnering rave reviews. She earned her stripes in New York kitchens before coming home to Brazil and blends the ethnic flavors of cosmopolitan New York and her own Italian heritage with fresh Brazilian ingredients to create dishes such as the *camarão pacifico,* shrimp grilled with sesame seeds and Thai chile sauce on a bed of vegetable fried rice. She pulls off a great duck confit with honey and mustard served with a pear rice, and even though there is only one pasta dish on the menu, it is a keeper—large ravioli stuffed with Brie and asparagus. Expect a long wait for a table on most nights after 9pm.

Rua Sergipe 753, Higienópolis. (℃) 011/3661-8670. Main courses R$22–R$50 (US$7–US$17). AE, V. Mon 7:30pm–midnight; Tues–Fri noon–3pm and 7:30pm–12:30am; Sat 12:30–4:30pm and 7:30pm–12:30am; Sun 12:30–4:30pm. Bus: 8107.

Veridiana 🌟🌟 *Finds* PIZZA   In São Paulo even the pizzerias go upscale; trendy Veridiana doesn't even have a sign, but you can't miss the beautiful rust-colored heritage building on the corner of Av. Higienópolis and Rua da Veridiana (the valet parking guys give it away). The menu offers pizza at its most traditional—thin crusts and just a few quality ingredients per pizza. The grande (R$25–35/US$8–US$12) serves two people and you can order different combos on each half of the pizza.

Rua da Veridiana 661, Higienópolis. (℃) 011/3120-5050. Main courses R$22–R$35 (US$7–US$12). AE, DC, MC, V. Sun–Thurs 6pm–12:30am; Fri–Sat 8pm–1:30am. Metrô: Santa Cecilia.

SÃO PAULO AFTER DARK
Most Paulistas won't even set foot in a club until midnight. Most places will stay open until at least 4am, and on weekends as late (or early) as 6am. For those looking to catch the big names in popular Brazilian music, São Paulo gets more of the stars, performing more often, than any other city in Brazil.

THE PERFORMING ARTS
São Paulo's classical music scene is excellent, and the theater scene is positively thriving. The vast majority of high culture takes place at just two halls: the **Theatro Municipal,** Praça Ramos de Azevedo s/n (℃ **011/222-8698**), and the **Sala São Paulo,** Praça Julio Prestes s/n (℃ **011/3337-5414**).

MUSIC & DANCE CLUBS
Many bars and clubs charge a drink minimum instead of, or sometimes in addition to, a cover charge. Patrons receive a little card or slip of paper upon arrival. All your expenses are recorded on the card and tallied up when you leave. Lose the card and you get charged a ridiculously steep fee.

LIVE MUSIC   **Piu Piu,** Rua Treze de Maio 134, Bela Vista (℃ **011/3258-8066**), hosts a good range of Brazilian contemporary artists, from rock to samba to jazz. **Olympia,** Rua Clelia 1517, Lapa (℃ **011/3866-3000**), is the venue of choice for top-ranked Brazilian artists and well known foreign acts. Exclusively dedicated to Brazilian music, **Tom Brasil,** Rua Olimpiadas 66, Vila Olimpia (℃ **011/3044-5665**), was recently voted as best MPB venue in São Paulo. In the land of samba, *forró,* and *axé,* **Bourbon Street,** Rua dos Chanes 127, Moema (℃ **011/5561-1643**), also puts some blues and jazz on the menu.

DANCE CLUBS   Even in the land of Samba, Latin rhythms are stealing the show. **Azucar,** Rua Mario Feraz 423, Itaim Bibi (© 011/3078-3130), the latest hit on São Paulo's club scene plays lots of salsa, merengue, and other Latin beats to get the crowd going. Palm Beach chic comes south to São Paulo in **Cheers,** Alameda Vicente Pinzon 153, Vila Olimpia (© 011/3044-1427), a trendy Art Deco club. A popular dance venue, **Terra Brasil,** Av. Guilherme Cotching 580, Vila Maria (© 011/6954-9800), lays the Brazilian rhythms on thick. More than just a dance club, **Fabbrica 5,** Av. Alcantara Machado 770, Mooca (© 011/3399-3331), encompasses two dance floors, a bar, a cybercafe, a karaoke hall, a pizzeria, and a sushi bar; for fashion emergencies, there's also a salon.

BARS & PUBS
LOUNGES   Located in the Renaissance Hotel, the elegant **Havana Club,** Alameda Santos 2233, Cerquiera César (© 011/3069-2626), is a lovely place to come for a drink on your own or to meet friends before going out. Mellow live music warms up the evening from 7 to 10pm, when a deejay takes over. Located on the 41st and 42nd floors of the Edificio Italia, **Terraço Italia,** Av. Ipiranga 344, Centro (© 011/257-6566), provides the prime view of São Paulo. Time your arrival just before sunset so you can see the city lights come on over the rim of your evening cocktail.

BARS   Despite its rather plummy name, **Bar Charles Edward,** Av. Juscelino Kubitschek 1426, Itaim Bibi (© 011/3078-5022), throws a heckuva party; this loud and fun former antiques store is the prime spot for the 30-somethings looking to make a pickup. Voted best singles bar in the city, **Tipuana,** Rua Fiandeiras 555, Vila Olimpia (© 011/3848-9067), is the place for a close encounter with those Paulistas. In the evening, deejays spice up the beat. Also in Vila Olimpia, **MonteCristo** (Rua Jesuino Cardoso 194, corner of Atilio Innocenti (© 011/3846-7483), doesn't charge a cover, and as a result is often packed with patrons spilling out onto the sidewalks. Further down at Atilio Innocenti 780 is the **Buena Vista Club** (© 012/3045-5245). Despite the Cuban-sounding name, the music is mostly Brazilian from Wednesday to Saturday. **Bar Favela,** Prof. Atilio Innocenti 419 (© 011/3848-6988), is anything but downscale. This hip bar attracts a happening crowd that come to see and be seen.

GAY & LESBIAN NIGHTLIFE
The best-known gay dance club in São Paulo, **Massivo,** Rua Alameda Itu 1548, Jardins (© 011/3085-5830), packs them in on almost any night of the week. If **Salvation,** Largo do Arouche 301, Centro (© 011/223-0705), means dancing till you drop, this is the spot to find it. A happening club and live music venue in Vila Madalena is **Farol Madalena,** Rua Jericó 179, Vila Madalena (© 011/3032-6470). Although GLS, the emphasis here is definitely on the L for lesbian. The bar usually has live Brazilian music on most evenings Wednesday to Sunday.

A SIDE TRIP FROM SÃO PAULO
ILHABELA
The island of Ilhabela offers a perfect mix for visitors. On the "civilized" side of the island, there's great dining, some fun nightlife, and excellent upscale accommodations. In the middle, there's a rocky mountain spine, covered with virgin rainforest and cut through with small rivers and waterfalls. On the far side, there are wild and empty beaches.

Essentials
GETTING THERE   Ilhabela is located 209km (130 miles) from São Paulo. Leaving town, take in sequence the Rodovia (freeway) Presidente Dutra,

Rodovia Ayrton Senna, and Rodovia Carvalho Pinto, always following signs that read RIO DE JANEIRO. At the town of São Jose dos Campos, follow the signs to SÃO SEBASTIÃO or LITORAL (coast). The ferry to Ilhabela leaves from São Sebastião; the roads are well marked.

The bus company **Litoranea** (© 012/3892-1072) provides daily bus service from São Paulo, leaving from Jabaquara station at 5, 7, 9am, noon, 3, and 6pm. The trip takes about 3½ hours and costs R$29 (US$10). The bus will leave you at the ferry terminal in São Sebastião. Ferries to Ilhabela depart every 10 to 15 minutes.

VISITOR INFORMATION   An information office (© 012/3896-1091; http://ilhabela.terra.com.br) is located on the road just past the ferry terminal. From December through February, the office is open daily from 9am to 6pm; from March through November, hours are Monday through Friday from 9am to 6pm, Saturday from 9am to 3pm.

What to See & Do in Ilhabela

The more civilized west side of the island has a string of easily accessible beaches. One of the liveliest is **Praia do Curral,** located about 11km (7 miles) south of the ferry terminal. Here, you'll find great restaurants and bars with live music and a beach scene that keeps hopping until the early hours. In town, **Saco da Capela** beach is bustling with boat traffic and tourists; it even has a sushi bar! The wild east side of the island is where the most beautiful beaches are to be found. **Praia dos Castelhanos** is long and wild and completely undeveloped. Rising up from the beach, the mountains covered in untouched Atlantic rainforest provide a stunning backdrop. Access is by boat or over a bumpy 4WD track.

Maremar Turismo, Av. Princesa Isabel 90, Perequê Ilhabela (© 012/3896-1418; www.maremar.tur.br), is the outdoors specialist on Ilhabela, offering a variety of activities under its *Adventure Team Ilhabela* label.

Certified divers can enjoy some spectacular **scuba diving,** especially if you like wreck diving. Eleven diveable wrecks are found between 5m and 20m (16 ft.–66 ft.). A 1-day dive trip, including all equipment for two dives on two different wrecks, will cost R$180 (US$60) per person. **Fishing** is another popular sport on the island; deep-sea fishing for marlin, tuna, or albacore will set you back R$200 (US$67) per person, for up to three people, including all equipment, bait, and refreshments. A relaxing **boat trip** on a schooner is a great way to soak up some rays, see a number of beaches, and if you are lucky pods of dolphins, R$45 (US$15) per person. More extreme sports are starting to become more popular, and the Adventure team has some great packages, including a day of hiking and a day of **rappelling** down a 70m-tall (230-ft.) waterfall, instruction and equipment included. These packages with 2 nights of accommodations start at R$225 (US$75).

Serious hikers will be very pleased with this new outdoor company **Espaço Ecologico** (© 012/3896-2899). This outfit specializes in hiking and nature tours and offers a variety of 2-day hikes on the rugged side of the island combined with a 1-night stay at a remote beach; prices start at R$100 (US$33) per person.

Where to Stay in Ilhabela

Porto Pacuiaba, Av. Leonardo Reale 1578 (© 012/3896-2466; www.porto pacuiba.com.br), offers the perfect base for exploring Ilhabela. Close to town but on the beach, the sprawling wooden mansion is set around little courtyards lush with cool green foliage. Rooms are comfortably furnished; all have air-conditioning and most have verandas. In the high season, rooms cost R$175 to R$195 (US$58–US$65).

Pousada do Capitão, Av. Almirante Tamandaré 272 (© **012/3896-1037;** www.pousadadocapitao.com.br), fits into the sailing capital of Brazil with its nautical theme. All 21 rooms are decorated like cabins with lovely wood paneling, brass touches, and boating memorabilia. The *pousada* has a large deck swimming pool and a lovely garden. A sitting room and library as well as a game room ensure that nobody will feel cabin fever. In high season rooms cost R$175 to R$280 (US$58–US$93). Blending in perfectly with the hillside is the *pousada* **Saco da Capela,** Rua Itamepa 167, Saco da Capela (© **012/3896-2255;** www.sacodacapela.com.br), offering a rustic yet elegant experience. Spread out on a variety of levels, the buildings are set among the rocks and trees heavy with bromeliads and connected with many steep stairways. Some rooms have lofts, and all are comfortably furnished. In the high season, rooms cost R$150 to R$240 (US$5–US$80).

Where to Dine in Ilhabela

The seafood on Ilhabela is some of the best there is in Brazil. Ilhabela's prawns are famous nationwide. In high season, reservations are recommended.

For the prime patio in town head to **Aeroilha** ★★, Praça da Bandeira 1, Centro (© **012/3896-1178**), at the main dock overlooking the ocean and the mainland. The prawns here are among the best we have had in Brazil, thick, juicy, and succulent, whether grilled, breaded, or sautéed. A 15-minute drive south from Centro is **Ilha Sul,** Av. Riachuelo 287 (© **012/3894-9426**), a casual restaurant that serves some of the best seafood on the island. The breaded squid (calamari) is outstanding, tender and perfectly grilled. Main courses include everything maritime, from lobster to prawns to fish, all fresh, all excellently prepared. Reservations required on weekends and holidays. The same architect who designed the Porto Pacuiba Hotel also was responsible for the **Shopping Vila Pequeá,** Ave. Pedro de Morais s/n. The complex houses an excellent Italian restaurant **Pasta del Capitano** (© **012/3896-6861**). The menu changes regularly but always has a delicious variety of homemade pastas. The tagliatelle with shiitake and button mushrooms is outstanding. In Praia da Capela beach you'll find **Capela,** Av. Pedro de Morais 251 (© **012/3896-3156**). This lovely bar/restaurant is set completely among the large trees across from the beach and even though the patio is covered for rainy days it really is an outdoor space. On Fridays and Saturdays there's live music after 7:30pm and the bar serves up a great variety of cocktails and *caipirinhas*. More than just a bookstore, **Ponta das Letras,** Rua dr. Carvalho 146 (© **012/3896-2104**), serves as the meeting place for islanders and makes the best espresso for hundreds of miles around! The store has a great selection of English-language magazines, as well as CDs and souvenirs. Open daily from 9am to 8pm.

5 Brasília

1,140km (707 miles) NW of Rio de Janeiro, 1,015km (629 miles) N of Sao Pãulo, 1,415km (877 miles) SW of Salvador

Fifty years ago, had you flown over the spot where Brasília now stands, you would have seen nothing but short scrubby forest, stretching thousands of miles in any direction. The entire city was brought into being over the span of 4 years at the will of Juscelino Kubitschek, who'd been elected president in 1956 on the promise that he'd move the capital inland from Rio de Janeiro. A competition was held for city designs. The winning master plan was submitted by a Rio planner and architect named Lucio Costa. Groundbreaking began in 1957. Thousands of workers poured in, and by April 21, 1960, there was something so closely approximating a city that a grand inauguration could be held.

For visitors, the attractions of Brasília are purely architectural. Brazil's best designers, architects, and artists were commissioned to create the buildings and make them beautiful. Many buildings are indeed stunning, notably the Palácio do Itamaraty and the Metropolitan Cathedral. Equally interesting are the uncanny order and harmony of the place. There's nothing quite like it anywhere on earth, which makes it well worth a visit. That said, it takes only a little time to appreciate the architecture and city design, and beyond that, there's little of interest in Brasília. One day is enough to see it all.

ESSENTIALS
GETTING THERE
Brasília's **Aeroporto Internacional** (© **061/364-9000**) is located about 10km (6 miles) west of the Eixo Monumental. **TAM, Varig, Gol,** and **VASP** all fly here from Rio and São Paulo. Taxis from the airport to the hotel zones cost about R$30 (US$10).

Long-distance buses arrive at Brasília's bus station at the far western point of the Eixo Monumental (© **061/233-7200**). A taxi ride from the station costs approximately R$20 (US$7) to the main hotel section.

ORIENTATION
What makes Brasília unique besides its architecture is its layout. The city consists of two main axes: The Eixo Monumental runs dead straight from east to west, and the Eixo Rodoviário runs from north to south, curving as it goes. Seen from above, the city resembles an airplane or an arrow notched into a partially bent bow. Where the two axes intersect is the city's central bus station, the Rodoviária.

All the city's residential areas are in one of the two perfectly symmetrical wings, the *Asa Norte* or *N* (north wing) and the *Asa Sul* or *S* (south wing), on the Eixo Rodoviária. All of the city's important government buildings are located on the eastern end of the Eixo Monumental. All of the city's hotels are located in two hotel districts near the Rodoviária. All the city's offices, shopping malls, theaters, and hospitals are all located in their own little designated clusters.

GETTING AROUND
All city buses go through the Rodoviária, where the Eixo Monumental and Eixo Rodoviário intersect. It's also where you transfer from an east-west bus to a north-south one. Most of the city's attractions, malls, and hotels are within walking distance of the Rodoviária.

BY BUS Buses run from the tip of the south wing to the tip of the north wing, along roads W1 and W3 on the west side of the Eixo Rodoviário and on roads L1 and L3 on the east side of the Eixo Rodoviário. To travel across town, all you need to do is catch a bus traveling to the opposite part of the city; for example, from Asa Sul, catch a bus that says Asa Norte, or vice versa.

On the Eixo Monumental, you can catch buses labeled PLANO PILOTO CIRCULAR, which circle up and down this main boulevard. Many buses will go via the Rodoviária, which is right in the center of town. These will get you pretty close to the main monuments, hotels, and malls along the Eixo Monumental. Bus tickets are R$1.50 (50¢).

Brasília

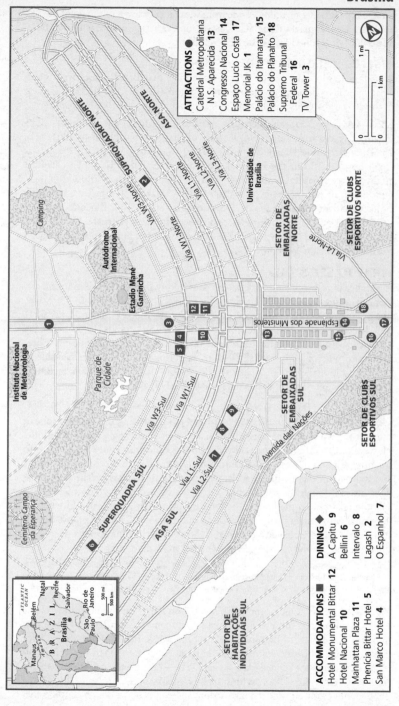

ATTRACTIONS ●
Catedral Metropolitana
N.S. Aparecida **13**
Congresso Nacional **14**
Espaço Lucio Costa **17**
Memorial JK **1**
Palácio do Itamaraty **15**
Palácio do Planalto **18**
Supremo Tribunal
Federal **16**
TV Tower **3**

ACCOMMODATIONS ■
Hotel Monumental Bittar **12**
Hotel Nacional **10**
Manhattan Plaza **11**
Phenicia Bittar Hotel **5**
San Marco Hotel **4**

DINING ◆
A Capitu **9**
Bellini **6**
Intervalo **8**
Lagash **2**
O Espanhol **7**

BY TAXI   Taxis are plentiful. A ride from the center of town to the tip of the Asa Sul costs approximately R$21 (US$7). To contact a taxi, call **Brasília** (*©* 061/ 344-1000) or **Rádio Táxi** (*©* 061/325-3030).

VISITOR INFORMATION

Providing tourist information is not something that Brasília does well. Grab what you can at the airport; the information desk (*©* 061/364-9135) is located in the arrivals hall close to the exit, and it's open daily from 7am to 11pm.

FAST FACTS   You can exchange currency at **Air Brazil Turismo,** SHS Quadra 01, Bloco A, Loja 33/4, Gallery of the National Hotel (*©* 061/321- 2304), or **Banco do Brasil** at Brasília Airport (*©* 061/365-1564).

All hospitals are in the Hospital section (SHLS and SHLN). For medical attention, try **Hospital Santa Lucia,** SHLS, Quadra 76, conjunto C (*©* 061/ 445-0000), or its emergency room (*©* 061/345-9260). If you need a dentist, contact **Instituto Brasiliense de Odontologia,** SQLS 406, Bloco A, Loja 35 (*©* 061/244-5095). For Internet access check **Albinet Cybercafé,** CLSW 104, Bloco C, Loja 44 (*©* 061/341-2092); R$6 (US$2) per hour; open Monday to Saturday from 8am to 10pm.

WHAT TO SEE & DO

A number of tour operators offer a city tour taking in most of the monuments. Contact **Bluepoint,** SEPN Q 509, Third Floor (*©* **061/274-0033;** www. bluepoint.com.br), or **Capri Turismo,** SCLN 110, Bloco C, Loja 34 (*©* **061/ 349-1228**); 3-hour tours range from R$60 to R$75 (US$20–US$25). To take a specialized 4-hour **architectural tour** of the city, contact **Bluepoint. Bluepoint** also offers a 3-hour **mystical tour,** exploring the hidden spiritual side of this most rational of cities. A visit to the Templo da Boa Vontade is included. Daily departures. Cost of either tour is R$142 (US$47).

THE TOP ATTRACTIONS

Catedral Metropolitana Nossa Senhora Aparecida ★★   Probably one of the best-known images of Brasília, the Catedral is surprisingly small in real life. However, as you descend the walkway into the cathedral, you will emerge into the brightest and most spacious church building you have ever seen. The floors and walls are made of white marble, with an expanse of glass overhead. Natural light filters through the white, blue, and green stained-glass windows, casting a sparkling pattern on the floors. The altar is surprisingly sparse, all white marble decorated with a plain image of Christ on the cross. One of Brazil's most famous sculptors, Alfredo Ceschiatti, designed the statues of the four apostles in front of the cathedral, as well as the angels suspended from the ceiling inside.

Esplanada dos Ministerios. *©* 061/224-4073. Daily 8am–6pm. Mass Mon–Fri 6:15pm; Tues–Fri 12:15pm; Sat 5pm; Sun 8:30, 10:30am, and 6pm. No touring of the cathedral during Mass. No shorts or Bermudas. Bus: Any bus to the Rodoviária, short walk to the Cathedral or the Plano Piloto circular.

Memorial JK ★   One of the more notable buildings on the north side of the Eixo Monumental is this pyramid-shaped monument built in 1980 by Niemeyer to honor the founder of Brasília, Juscelino Kubitschek. Inside on the second floor is J. K.'s tomb, which sits immersed in darkness except for the red-tinted light filtering in through the stained-glass skylight. The words on the coffin read O FUN-DADOR. On the same floor as this slightly spooky scene are some interesting photographs of the city under construction, and copies of the design concepts that didn't get chosen. (Check out the one with the kilometer-long 200-story towers.)

Eixo Monumental oeste. (© 061/225-9451. Admission R$3 (US$1). Tues–Sun 9am–5:45pm. Bus: Plano Piloto Circular.

Palácio do Itamaraty ★★   A gem of a building by Niemeyer with landscaping by Roberto Burle Marx and detailing by Milton Ramos, the Palácio do Itamaraty serves mainly as a ceremonial hall for the government's Department of Foreign Affairs. The two floors are mostly open space with white walls and floors, providing a beautiful backdrop for the rich antique furnishings of Persian carpets, hand-carved jacaranda wood furniture, and 18th- and 19th-century paintings. Up the grand staircase on the second floor, there's a small room where international treaties are signed. Visits are by guided tours.

Esplanada dos Ministerios. (© 061/411-6161. Free admission. Mon–Fri 3–5pm; Sat–Sun 10am–2pm. Guided tours only; no shorts or tank tops allowed. Bus: Circular Plano piloto.

TV Tower ★★ *Value*   The best view in town is from the TV tower—and it's free! Just take the elevator up to the 72m-high (240-ft.) lookout. It's a terrific place to see the Eixo Monumental; the ministry buildings look like dominos waiting to be knocked over. If you get one of Brasília's amazing colorful sunsets, it's worth heading back to the tower to take in the view. On the way down, you'll be routed through the gem museum, which is housed on the lower level of the tower. Mostly a lame excuse for a gift shop, it's not really worth lingering in.

Eixo Monumental (close to the bus station and malls). (© 061/325-5735. Free admission. Tues–Sun 9am–6pm; Mon 2–8pm. Bus: Rodoviária.

ARCHITECTURAL HIGHLIGHTS

The important buildings in Brasília were all designed by architect Oscar Niemeyer. The strength of this Brazilian ubermodernist has always been form; his structures are often brilliant. His weaknesses have always been detailing, materials, and landscaping. Fortunately, Niemeyer was teamed up with Brazil's best landscape designer, Roberto Burle Marx; detailing and materials-focused architects such as Milton Ramos; and talented sculptors and artists such as Alfredo Ceschiatti. Every building also had to conform to the overall plan of Lucio Costa. The result is a collection of buildings that has rightly been called the highest expression of architectural modernism on earth. Niemeyer's work is scattered far and wide throughout the city, but the best of the best are on the eastern portion of the Eixo Monumental, from the Rodoviário to the Praça dos Tres Poderes on the far side of the Congresso Nacional. To take a specialized architectural tour of the city contact **Bluepoint,** SEPN Q 509, Third Floor (© 061/274-0033; www.bluepoint.com.br).

PRAÇA DOS TRES PODERES

Behind the Congress building, the Praça dos Tres Poderes is immediately identifiable by the huge Brazilian flag flapping 99m (330 ft.) above the wide, hot, open space below. The plaza is named for the three branches of government that surround it: the judiciary branch in the **Supremo Tribunal Federal,** the executive branch in the presidential **Palácio do Planalto,** and the legislative branch in the **Congresso Nacional.** The last one is Brasília's best-known photo image: the shot of the two towers on the Planalto, flanked by the two "bowls," one face up and one face down. It is quite beautiful in an abstract way, contrasting with the red dirt and blue sky. A must for Brazilian visitors, but of marginal interest to foreigners, the Congresso Nacional is open to the public for guided tours or a short visit; no shorts or tank tops allowed. The praça itself is pure Niemeyer, a vast expanse of pure white stone, with nowhere to hide from the blazing Brasília sun. Don't visit on a hot afternoon—you'll fry. Near the front of the square there's a long, white marble box about the size and shape of a semitrailer, but cantilevered one floor off the ground. This is the **Museu de Cidade,** open Tuesday through Sunday from 9am to 6pm. Inside, it's a bare marble room with eight inscriptions on each long wall telling the story of Brasília. No maps, no photos, just words. However, it is cool, and they provide a pamphlet with English translations. Next to it, sunk below the square, is the **Espaço Lucio Costa.** Brasília owes its shape and design to Lucio Costa, an urban planner and architect. This space contains a full-scale model of the city, but it has very little on Costa's life and career. On the back wall, there are some photos of the city under construction and, best of all, reproduced and enlarged photostats of Costa's original submission.

SHOPPING

There are two big shopping areas on either side of the bus station, one in the Setor Commercial Norte (SCN), and the other in the Setor Commercial Sul (SCS). In the residential parts of town, the main streets inside the Super Quadras also have some shops, but these are geared more to the daily needs of neighborhood residents and are not very interesting for browsing. Built in 1971, the **Conjunto Nacional,** Asa Norte, SCN (℃ **061/316-9733**), was the first mall in Brasília. Stores include two large drugstores, the Pão de Açúcar supermarket and a post office (Mon–Sat 9am–10pm). The large Siciliano bookstore has a CD department, Internet access, and a good variety of English magazines. Just past the Setor Hoteleiro Norte (North Hotel Sector), **Brasília Shopping,** Asa Norte, SCN QD 5, Lote 2 (℃ **061/328-5259**), has a number of movie theaters and trendy clothing boutiques as well as a very popular bar, Frei Caneca (p. 315). **Feira de Artesanato da Torre de Televisão,** a large crafts fair, takes place every weekend underneath the TV Tower. Many of the stalls sell crafts from the northeast and the interior made from leather, semiprecious stones, dried flowers, and ceramics. It's open Saturday and Sunday from 8am to 6pm.

WHERE TO STAY

All hotels are located in the two hotel sections: the SHN *(Setor Hoteleiro Norte)* or the SHS *(Setor Hoteleiro Sul).* Both areas are within a 5-minute walk of each other and of the city's two shopping sectors. The only real variety is the level of luxury and the size of the building. Most hotel guests in Brasília are politicians and businesspeople in town for meetings and government business on weekdays; on weekends, beds are mostly empty, allowing visitors to get great deals. *Note:* Many monuments are open Saturday and Sunday and closed on Monday.

SETOR HOTELEIRO SUL
Expensive

Hotel Nacional 🐸🐸🐸   The Nacional was the first quality hotel built in the fledgling capital and has now been designated a heritage building. During the week, it can be tough to find a room, as a number of politicians and judges make their home in the hotel Monday through Friday. Rooms in the hotel are extremely spacious, with large bathrooms and modern fixtures. The amenities are all top-of-the-line, but the spa is truly outstanding, resembling a European bathhouse with a large Finnish sauna, a Turkish steam bath, Jacuzzis, massage services, and a cafe.

SHS, Q. 1, Bloco A, Brasília, 70322-900 DF. ℃ **0800/644-7070** or 061/321-7575. Fax 061/223-9213. www.hotel nacional.com.br. 346 units. R$240 (US$80) standard double; R$300 (US$100) superior double; R$450 (US$150) executive suite. Weekends and off season 20%–40% discount. AE, DC, MC, V. Free parking. **Amenities:** 3 restaurants; bar; disco; outdoor pool; large gym w/personal trainer; spa; sauna; concierge; car rental; tour desk; business center; salon; 24-hr. room service; massage; laundry service; dry cleaning; nonsmoking rooms. *In room:* A/C, TV, dataport, minibar, fridge, hair dryer.

Phenícia Bittar Hotel ✿   One of the smaller hotels in the Setor Sul, the Phenícia's recently renovated rooms are bright with lovely hardwood floors, double or twin beds, light wood furniture, a sitting area, and new beds. Suites on the renovated floors are particularly nice. They feature a living room with a dining table and a large desk, and a spacious bedroom with a second desk and furnished with stylish, sleek furniture in blond wood.

SHS, Q. 5, Bloco J, Brasília DF. *©* 061/321-4342. Fax 061/225-1406. www.hoteisbittar.com.br. 130 units (shower only). R$140–R$216 (US$47–US$72) double; R$380 (US$126) suite. Discount 30%–40% on weekends and low season. AE, DC, MC, V. Free parking. **Amenities:** Restaurant; car rental; tour desk; business center; salon; 24-hr. room service; laundry service. *In room:* A/C, TV, dataport, minibar, fridge.

San Marco Hotel ✿✿   The 15-year-old San Marco is a pleasant medium-size hotel, just across the street from the Patio Brasil Shopping Center. The rooms are standard, superior, or deluxe, facing either east or west. The standard and superior rooms are quite small but have a balcony. The more spacious deluxe rooms sacrifice the balcony for extra room space. The San Marco is one of the few smaller hotels to have an outdoor pool.

SHS, Q. 5, Bloco C, Brasília DF. *©* 0800/618-484 or 061/321-8484. Fax 061/226-3055. www.sanmarco.com.br. 256 units (shower only). R$220 (US$73) standard double; R$272 (US$91) superior double; R$350 (US$117) deluxe double on weekdays. 40% discount on weekends and low season. Children under 9 stay free in parent's room. AE, DC, MC, V. Free parking. **Amenities:** Restaurant; bar; rooftop outdoor pool; gym; sauna; concierge; business center; salon; 24-hr. room service; laundry service. *In room:* A/C, TV, minibar, fridge, hair dryer.

SETOR HOTELEIRO NORTE
Expensive
Manhattan Plaza ✿✿✿   The all-suites Manhattan is the only hotel with unobstructed views of the Esplanada dos Ministerios, the cathedral, and the congress building from the west-facing rooms (odd-numbered rooms only). The best suites are the ones on the ninth floor and up; recently renovated and redecorated, they come with beautiful, modern, blond wood furniture. All have a veranda, a sitting room with a bar, a large desk, and a spacious bedroom with a second TV.

SHN, Q. 2, Bloco A, Brasília, 70710-907 DF. *©* **0800/614-002** or 061/319-3060. Fax 061/328-5685. www.manhattan.com.br. 314 units (shower only). R$290 (US$97) double. Weekends 20% discount. Children under 8 stay free in parent's room. AE, DC, MC, V. Free parking. **Amenities:** 2 restaurants; bar; outdoor pool; gym; sauna; concierge; car rental; tour desk; business center; salon; 24-hr. room service; laundry service; dry cleaning; nonsmoking rooms. *In room:* A/C, TV (2 in each room), dataport, minibar, fridge, safe.

Moderate
Hotel Monumental Bittar ✿   The low-rise Monumental looks unassuming from the outside but is nonetheless a very pleasant hotel with reasonable rates. A recent purchase and spruce-up by the Bittar chain has meant new bedding and drapery. Rooms have either wall-to-wall carpeting or wood floors; the latter are far more comfortable. Rooms with double beds are better than those with two twins; they have larger desks and closets and are larger overall. The only rooms to avoid are the east-facing ones, which face the main cross street. A few rooms are adapted for travelers with disabilities.

SHN, Q. 3, Bloco B, Brasília, 70710-300 DF. *©* 061/328-4144. www.hoteisbittar.com.br. 111 units (shower only). R$140–R$175 (US$47–US$58) double. Extra person R$33 (US$11). Up to 40% off on weekends and low season. AE, DC, MC, V. Free parking. **Amenities:** Restaurant; bar; car rental; tour desk; business center; salon; 24-hr. room service; laundry service; dry cleaning; nonsmoking rooms. *In room:* A/C, TV, dataport, minibar, fridge.

WHERE TO DINE

Brasília has some outstanding restaurants; politicians and businesspeople like to eat well. The restaurants are more sophisticated than they are elsewhere in Brazil.

EXPENSIVE

Intervalo ⑆ BRAZILIAN   Customers who are familiar with the weekly specials at Intervalo return week after week to savor their favorite dish. On Sunday, try the *lombo Vila Rica,* a hearty dish with grilled pork tenderloin, accompanied by the traditional feijão tropeiro bean dish from Minas Gerais, served with sausage. The Tuesday special is the very popular *assado d'el rey,* a delicious roast beef marinated in red wine and garlic for up to 40 hours before it is slowly cooked. However, any day of the week the kitchen serves up hearty Brazilian meat-laden fare.

SCLS 404, Bloco A, Loja 27, Brasília. ✆ **061/223-5274.** R$21–R$45 (US$7–US$15). AE, V. Mon–Sat 11:30am–midnight; Sun 11:30am–5pm. Bus: L1 Asa Sul.

Lagash ⑆⑆ MIDDLE EASTERN   For the best Middle Eastern food in Brasília, visit Lagash. The most popular entree on the menu is the Moroccan lamb; tender pieces of boneless lamb are cooked with nuts, green onions, onions, and rice. Those wanting to splurge in style can order Lebanese wine (R$225/US$75 a bottle).

SCLN 308, Bloco B, Loja 11, Asa Norte, Brasília. ✆ **061/273-0098.** R$20–R$60 (US$6.50–US$20). AE, DC, MC, V. Mon–Sat noon–4pm and 7pm–midnight; Sun noon–6pm. Bus: W3 Asa Norte.

O Espanhol ⑆ SPANISH   This is the place to come for a mean paella; the dish comes in two versions, with seafood only (fish, squid, shrimp, crab, and mussels) and the traditional Valenciana with chicken, pork tenderloin, sausage, shrimp, and mussels. Other Spanish dishes on the menu include *zarzuela catalana,* a fish stew; and *gambas a la valenciana,* large prawns cooked with tomatoes, onions, and peppers.

SQLS 404/405 Bloco C, Loja 7. ✆ **061/224-2002.** R$20–R$65 (US$7–US$22). AE, DC, MC, V. Mon–Sat noon–3pm; Mon–Wed 7pm–midnight; Thurs–Sat 7pm–1am; Sun noon–5pm. Bus: L1 Asa Sul.

MODERATE

A Capitu ⑆ ITALIAN   With its pale salmon-colored walls and 19th-century European art, A Capitu's elegant dining room contrasts sharply with the modern city block outside. The kitchen leans toward Italian; the seafood risotto is delicious, combining creamy arborio rice with bite-size morsels of mussels, clams, shrimp, and crab. One of the house's most popular dishes is the grilled duck breast with passion-fruit sauce. A small wine list offers a selection of Italian and Brazilian wines.

SCLS 403, Bloco D, Loja 20, Brasília. ✆ **061/223-0080.** R$18–R$36 (US$6–US$12). AE, V. Mon–Sat noon–3pm and 7pm–midnight; Sun noon–8pm. Bus: L1 Asa Sul.

Bellini *(finds* CAFE/ITALIAN   Open since May 2001, Bellini's gourmet complex encompasses a deli, food store, restaurant, cafe, and cooking school. It's a great place to grab an espresso and some sweets or to enjoy a sandwich on the patio. For a more formal occasion, the restaurant upstairs serves fine Italian dishes such as lamb filet with mint sauce and risotto, or large prawns in an apple-and-ginger sauce.

SCLS 113 Bloco D, Loja 35. ✆ **061/345-0777.** www.belini-gastronomia.com.br. Main courses R$6–R$35 (US$2–US$12). MC, V. Tues–Sun 10am–midnight (bakery closes 10pm). Bus: W3 Asa Sul.

BRASÍLIA AFTER DARK

Designed by Oscar Niemeyer, the **Teatro Nacional,** Setor Cultural Norte (© **061/325-6240**), resembles the dark base of a pyramid. However, the dark reflective glass conceals a bright interior lobby with landscaping by Burle Marx. Most classical concerts, dance, and theater performances in Brasília take place here. For program information, stop by the box office, which is open daily from noon to 8pm.

The **Armazém do Bras,** CLN 107, Bloco B, Loja 49, Asa Norte (© **061/ 340-7317**), has a great patio and gets quite hopping at night. The antipasto buffet (available Sat–Wed only) allows you to load up on your favorite selection of goodies (R$30/$10 per kilo). The beer list offers an unusual variety of imported beers. **Frei Caneca,** Brasília Shopping, SCN (© **061/327-9467**), is a popular hangout for the 28- to 40-year-old crowd. The club has a large spacious covered patio, dance floor, and bar. **Gate's Pub,** SCLS 403, Bloco B, Loja 34 (© **061/ 225-4576**), may look like a British pub on the outside, but that's where the authenticity stops: The beer is cold, the crowd is beautiful, and the music is hip. For a mellow night out away from the teenage crowds, check out **Othello Piano Bar,** CLN 107, Bloco D, Loja 25 (© **061/272-2066**). This is the place to come for some MPB, samba, or *choro.*

6 Salvador

1,726km (1,070 miles) NE of Rio de Janeiro, 2,052km (1,272 miles) NE of São Paulo

Salvador is an easy place to enjoy. The sun shines almost year-round, and beneath the surface beauty of beaches and the island-studded Baía de Todos os Santos (Bay of All Saints), there's a deep and powerful culture that bubbles up in things such as the rich cuisine and the infectious rhythms of Bahian music.

Salvador was the first capital of Brazil, founded by the Portuguese in 1549. Sugar cane thrived in the heat and the rich soil of the northeast. To find enough labor to carry out the backbreaking work, the planters resorted to slaves bought in the markets of West Africa. It's estimated that by the mid–19th century, nearly five million slaves had been taken from Africa to Brazil. The wealth earned by slave labor is on display in the grand mansions and golden churches in Pelourinho, the restored colonial core of Salvador. Its legacy is also evident in the people: Modern Salvador is a city of two million—the third largest in Brazil—and approximately 80% of the population is of Afro-Brazilian descent. This heritage has had an enormous influence on Salvador's culture, food, religion, and especially its music.

The jewel of the city is Pelourinho. Derelict until as recently as the 1980s, in the past 10 years, the 16th-century heart of what was once the richest city in the Americas has been painstakingly brought back to very close to its former glory.

ESSENTIALS
GETTING THERE

BY PLANE   Salvador's international airport, **Aeroporto Deputado Luis Eduardo Magalhães** (© **071/204-1010**), is 32km (20 miles) from downtown. The airport is serviced by **Varig, VASP, TAM, Gol,** and **Fly Airlines.** To get from the airport to your hotel by taxi, **Coometas** (© **071/244-4500** or 071/252-2190) offers prepaid fares. A ride to Pelourinho costs R$65 (US$22), to Ondina R$62 (US$21), and to the northern beaches R$27 (US$9). Regular taxis are cheaper; a nonprepaid taxi from the airport to Pelourinho will cost around R$50 (US$17).

If you do not have too much luggage, an inexpensive bus runs along the coast from the airport to Pelourinho; its final stop is Praça da Sé on the edge of Pelourinho. The bus runs daily from 7am to 8pm and costs R$6 (US$2)

BY BUS Buses arrive at the **Terminal Rodoviária de Salvador Armando Viana de Castro,** Av. Antonio Carlos Magalhães 4362, Pituba (© 071/460-8300). Regular city buses to Pelourinho are marked PRAÇA DA SE. For the coast, look for buses marked VIA ORLA or with the destinations of the specific neighborhoods such as Ondina. Ticket prices range from R$1.25 to R$4 (65¢–US$2) for a regular city bus or an air-conditioned express bus.

GETTING AROUND

Pelourinho, the historic old downtown, sits on a cliff overlooking the Bay of All Saints. This area is also sometimes called the Cidade Alta (the upper city). At the foot of the cliff lies **Comércio,** a modern area of commercial office towers. This area is also sometimes known as the Cidade Baixa (the lower city). The upper and lower cities are connected via a cliffside elevator, the Lacerda. Except to visit a large crafts market called the Mercado Modelo, there's little reason to visit Comércio.

The **Avenida Sete de Setembro** starts on the southern edge of Pelourinho. At its beginning, Avenida Sete de Setembro has many small shops. A little further south, as it enters **Vitória,** it becomes more residential. Below that, the street drops down to the coast and continues by the ocean until it reaches the area around the lighthouse, or Farol de Barra. Known as **Barra,** this neighborhood has a number of good restaurants and hotels.

As it rounds the point, Avenida Sete de Setembro becomes **Avenida Oceanica** (also called Av. Presidente Vargas) and continues past a number of good hotels in the oceanside neighborhood of **Ondina.** From here out, neighborhoods (and road name changes) come thick and fast: **Vermelho, Amaralina, Pituba, Pituaçu, Piatã, Itapuã,** all the way to **Stella Maris** adjacent to the airport. There are pleasant beaches all along this stretch.

BY FOOT Pelourinho is a stroller's dream; the narrow streets and cobblestone alleys open onto large squares with baroque churches. The lower part of the city, Cidade Baixa around the Mercado Modelo, is less safe at night.

BY BUS Buses are marked by name instead of number; the main buses for travelers going from any of the beach neighborhoods to downtown are marked PRAÇA DA SE for Pelourinho or COMERCIO for the lower city. To travel to the city's main bus station, take a bus marked IGUATEMI. When going from downtown to the beaches, take a bus marked VIA ORLA and make sure that the bus's final destination lies beyond the beach neighborhood you want to reach. Along the coast, you have the option of taking a regular bus for R$1.25 (60¢) or an air-conditioned bus, called a *frescão* (fresh one), for R$4 (US$2).

BY TAXI For a radio taxi, contact **Teletaxi** (© 071/341-9988) or **LigueTaxi** (© 071/357-7777). You usually pay a surcharge of R$3 to R$5 (US$1.50–US$2.50), but these taxis have air-conditioning.

VISITOR INFORMATION

Bahiatursa, the state's main tourist information service, has a number of booths and kiosks throughout the city, including at Salvador International Airport in the arrivals hall (© 071/204-1244), open daily from 8:30am to 10:30pm; **Rodoviária** (© 071/450-3871), open daily from 8am to 10pm; **Mercado Modelo,** Praça Cayru, Cidade Baixa (© 071/241-0242), open daily from 8am

Salvador

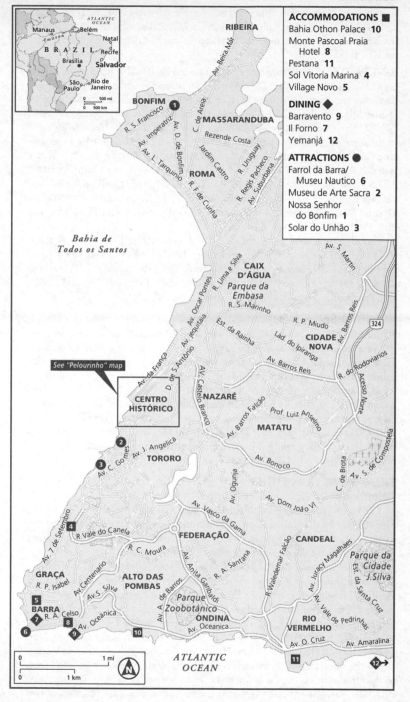

RIBEIRA

BONFIM ❶

MASSARANDUBA

Rezende Costa

ROMA

ATLANTIC OCEAN

Manaus Belém
Natal
B R A Z I L Recife
Brasília Salvador
São Rio de
Paulo Janeiro

Av. Beira Mar
C. de Areia
R. S. Francisco
Av. Imperatriz
Av. D. de Bonfim
Av. L. Tarquinio
R. F. de Cunha
Jardim Castro
R. Uruguay
R. Regis Pacheco
Av. Suburbana

Bahia de
Todos os Santos

CAIX
D'ÁGUA
Parque da
Embasa
R. S. Marinho
R. Lima e Silva
Av. Oscar Pontes
Av. Jequitaia
Est. da Rainha
R. P. Miudo
Lad. do Ipiranga
Av. Barros Reis
Av. S. Martin
Av. Barros Reis
R. do Rodoviarios
Acesso Norte

324

CIDADE
NOVA

Av. da França
D. de S. Antônio
Av. Castelo Branco

See "Pelourinho" map

CENTRO
HISTÓRICO

NAZARÉ

Av. Barros Falcão
Prof. Luiz Anselmo

MATATU

❷
Av. J. Angelica
Av. C. Gomes
❸
TORORO
Av. Bonoco
Av. Ogunja
C. de Brota
Av. S. de Compostela
Av. Dom João VI
Av. Vasco da Gama

Av. 7 de Setembro
❹
R. Vale do Canela
R. C. Moura

FEDERAÇÃO

CANDEAL

Av. Juracy Magalhaes
Parque da
Cidade
J.Silva
Est. da Santa Cruz

GRAÇA
R. P. Isabel
Av. Centenario
Av. S. Silva
ALTO DAS
POMBAS
Av. Anita Garibaldi
R. A. Santana
R. Waledemar Falcão
Av. Vale de Pedrinhas

❺
BARRA
❼ R. A. Celso
❽ Av. Oceanica
❻
❾
⑩
Parque
Zoobotánico
ÔNDINA
Av. Oceanica
Av. A. de Barros

RIO
VERMELHO
Av. O. Cruz
⑪
Av. Amaralina
⑫→

ATLANTIC
OCEAN

0 ———— 1 mi
0 ———— 1 km

to 9pm; and **Pelourinho,** Rua Francisco Muniz Barreto 12 (✆ **071/321-2463** or 071/321-2133), open daily from 8am to 10pm. The office at Pelourinho is the best one, offering the most information. It sells a very good map of Salvador for R$4 (US$2).

FAST FACTS To exchange money, go to **Banco do Brasil** at Praça Padre Anchieta 11, Pelourinho (✆ 071/321-9334); or Rua Miguel Bournier 4, Barra Avenida, parallel to the Avenida Oceanica (✆ 071/264-5099). There are **Citibank** branches at Rua Miguel Calmon 555, Comércio, close to the Mercado Modelo (✆ 071/ 241-4745); or at Av. Almirante Marques Leão 71, Barra (✆ 071/264-6728).

In an emergency, call the **police** at ✆ 190, or the **fire brigade** or an **ambulance** at ✆ 193. For medical attention, go to **Hospital Portugues,** Av. Princesa Isabel 2, Barra (✆ 071/203-5555, or 071/203-5159 emergency room), or **Hotel Aliança,** Av. Juracy Magalhães 2096, Rio Vermelho (✆ 071/350-5600). You can also ask your hotel for a referral to the nearest clinic. If you need a dentist, go to **Dentist Prontodonto,** a 24-hour dental clinic located at Rua Piauí 143, sala 202, Pituba (✆ 071/240-1784).

Most Internet cafes are open daily, and rates range from R$6 to R$10 (US$3–US$5) per hour. Ones to try include **Bahia Café,** Praça da Sé 20, Centro (✆ 071/322-1266); **Internet Café.com,** Arua João de Deus 2, Pelourinho (✆ 071/331-2147), and Avenida Sete de Setembro, Barra (✆ 071/264-3941); and **Pelourinho Virtual,** Largo do Pelourinho 2 (✆ 071/323-0427).

WHAT TO SEE & DO

Pelourinho boasts a wealth of richly decorated baroque churches, tiny squares, and fine old colonial mansions. By day, you could wander its cobblestone streets for hours. At night, Pelourinho's small squares and larger praças come alive with bands and singers and concerts. Many tourists attend, certainly, but so do an equal or even greater number of Salvadorans.

Salvador's attractions are so easily accessible that it's not really necessary to take an organized city tour, but if you want to do so, contact **Prive Tur** (✆ **071/ 336-7522**) or **GMG Turismo** (✆ **071/264-5811**). For Pelourinho, it is a much better deal to book a tour guide through **Singtur,** Praça Jose Anchieta 12, Second Floor, Pelourinho (✆ **071/322-1017**).

THE TOP ATTRACTIONS
Pelourinho ✮✮✮

In 1985, the historic core of colonial Salvador was rightly designated a World Heritage Site by the United Nations. You could spend years getting to know the history of the churches, squares, and colorful colonial mansions in this old part of the city. What follows is but a brief introduction.

The place to start a tour of Pelourinho is the main square, called the Terreiro de Jesus. Dominating the west end of the square is the 17th-century **Catedral Basilica.** Flanking the cathedral is the neoclassical Antiga Faculdade de Medicina, now home to the excellent Afro-Brazilian Museum. Facing the cathedral at the far end of the square is the **Igreja de Ordem Terceiro de São Domingos de Gusmão.** Built between 1713 and 1734, this baroque church suffered through an 1870s renovation that destroyed most of its fine interior painting and tile work.

On the south side of the church is a wide cobblestone street with a tall cross in the middle; this is the Praça Anchieta. The saint on the cross is São Francisco de Xavier, patron saint of Salvador. At the far end of this little praça stand two of the most impressive churches in the city. The large two-towered one on the right is the **Igreja de São Francisco,** the central element in the surrounding

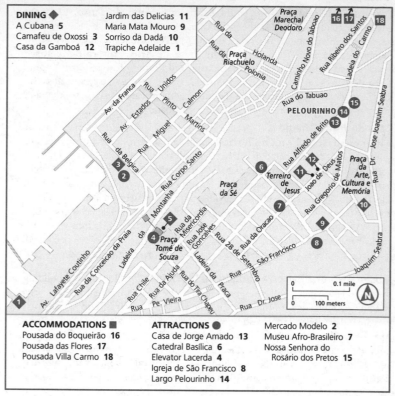

DINING ◆
A Cubana **5**
Camafeu de Oxossi **3**
Casa da Gamboá **12**

Jardim das Delicias **11**
Maria Mata Mouro **9**
Sorriso da Dadá **10**
Trapiche Adelaide **1**

ACCOMMODATIONS ■
Pousada do Boqueirão **16**
Pousada das Flores **17**
Pousada Villa Carmo **18**

ATTRACTIONS ●
Casa de Jorge Amado **13**
Catedral Basílica **6**
Elevator Lacerda **4**
Igreja de São Francisco **8**
Largo Pelourinho **14**

Mercado Modelo **2**
Museu Afro-Brasileiro **7**
Nossa Senhora do
Rosário dos Pretos **15**

Convento de São Francisco. The richest church in all of Brazil, it was built in 1708 by the sugar barons of Salvador to let folks know that their colony had *arrived.* More than 100 kilograms of gold are slathered over every available knob and curlicue in the richly carved interior of this high baroque church. The result could hardly be called beautiful, but it's impressive. Next to it is the **Igreja de Ordem Terceira de São Francisco,** immediately recognizable by its ornately carved sandstone facade.

Back at the Terreiro de Jesus, the two streets on either side of the Church of São Pedro, Rua João de Deus and Rua Alfredo de Brito, both run downhill to the **Largo Pelourinho.** This small, steeply sloping triangular square gets its name from the whipping post that used to stand at its top end. This was where slaves and criminals were flogged. The smaller building at the top of the square—now the **Casa de Jorge Amado**—used to serve as the city's slave market. Looking downhill, on the right-hand side of the largo, you'll find the blue–and–creamy yellow **Nossa Senhora do Rosário dos Pretos.** Literally translated as "Our Lady of the Rosary of the Blacks," this high baroque structure was erected over the course of the 18th century by slaves. Today, much of the congregation is still of African descent; new paintings inside show the Passion of Christ with an all-black Holy Family, and drums have largely taken the place of the organ in church services.

At the lowest point of the Largo Pelourinho, a narrow street leads steeply uphill to a trio of old baroque churches: the **Igreja de Carmo, Igreja de Ordem**

Terceiro de Carmo, and **Igreja do Santissimo Santo do Passo.** Only the Ordem Terceiro is open, and the views over the city are only OK. Retrace your steps and explore one of the other delights of Pelourinho, its hidden interior courtyards. There are four of them: the **Praça de Arte, Cultura e Memoria; Praça Tereza Batista; Praça Pedro Arcanjo;** and **Praça Quincas Berro d'Agua.** Their entrances branch off the little streets between the Largo Pelourinho and the Terreiro de Jesus. During the day, they contain cafes, artisan booths, and museums. At night, nearly every one features a band.

Casa de Jorge Amado 🐦 Brazil's most beloved writer, Jorge Amado's name is intrinsically linked with his home state of Bahia, so it's only fitting that this tribute to Amado be located in the heart of Salvador's old town. One of his most popular novels, *Dona Flor and Her Two Husbands,* was set in this very neighborhood. In all, his works span 6 decades and dozens of titles. The main exhibit tells the story of Amado's life. Unfortunately, the signage is in Portuguese only. Touring the two-floor exhibit takes only about half an hour. The book-cover collage in the ground-floor cafe shows the wide range of languages into which his works have been translated.

Largo do Pelourinho 51, Pelourinho. 🕐 071/321-0122. Mon–Sat 9am–6pm. R$3 (US$1.50). Bus: Praça da Sé.

Museu Afro-Brasileiro/Faculdade de Medicina 🐦 This fine old building (built in 1808) has three museums inside: the Memorial de Medicina, the Museu de Arqueologia e Etnologia, and the **Museu Afro-Brasileiro** 🐦. The first two are only marginally interesting; worth more than just a glance is the Museu Afro-Brasileiro. A large portion of the exhibit space is dedicated to the Candomblé religion, explaining the meaning and characteristics of each god (*orixá*) and the role they play in the community. Unfortunately, none of the information is in English, but large and beautiful photographs tell a good part of the story. In the back room are 27 huge carved wood panels—the work of noted Bahian artist Carybé—portraying the *orixás* and the animal and symbol that go with each. The museum staff can also provide information on Candomblé celebrations. Expect to spend 30 to 45 minutes.

Antiga Faculdade de Medicina, Terreiro de Jesus s/n, Pelourinho (just to the right of the Basilica). 🕐 071/321-0383. R$3 (US$1) for all 3 museums. Mon–Fri 9am–5pm. Bus: Praça da Sé.

Centro
Museu de Arte Sacra 🐦🐦🐦 When you walk into the first room of this small but splendid museum, what you hear is the soft sweet sound of Handel. It's a welcome touch, an indication of the care curators have taken in assembling and displaying one of Brazil's best collections of Catholic art. The collection includes oil paintings, oratorios (a cabinet containing a crucifix), metal work, and lots of wooden statues of saints. If you're pressed for time, head for the two rooms of silver at the back. Brazilian silversmiths had lots of material with which to work. Walk through the two rooms and you can see the smiths refining their technique, as the crude but massive works of the 18th century change and develop until, by the early 19th century, Brazilian artists were producing reliquaries and processional crosses of astonishing refinement. Allow 1½ hours.

Rua do Sodré 276 (just south of Pelourinho). 🕐 071/243-6310. Admission R$5 (US$1.65) adults, R$3 (US$1) students w/valid ID, free for children under 7. Mon–Fri 11:30am–5:30pm. From Praça de Sé, walk 10 min south on Av. Carlos Gomes, turn right, and walk downhill on Ladeira Santa Teresa for 45m (150 ft.). Bus: Praça de Sé.

Cidade Baixa
Mercado Modelo 🐦 There's no sense in pretending you're not a tourist in the Mercado Modelo. If you're here, you are. Still, it's a fun place to wander

around in. This former Customs building houses just about everything Bahia has to offer in terms of arts and crafts and souvenirs. There are musical instruments (drums, whistles, tambourines, and berimbaus), woodcarvings of all sorts of *orixás*, fine linen tablecloths, thick cotton hammocks, a wide collection of arte naif, jewelry, and much more.

Praça Cayru, Comércio (just across from the elevator). © 071/243-6543. Mon–Sat 8am–7pm; Sun 8am–noon. Bus: Comércio.

Solar do Unhão ☆☆   An old sugar mill, the Solar consists of a number of beautifully preserved heritage buildings centered around a lovely stone courtyard that dates back to the 18th century. Half the fun is just to wander around and explore the various buildings set on the waterfront (the views are fabulous). The main building houses a small modern art museum; you'll find some works of Portinari and Di Cavalcanti amongst the works on display. The restaurant, where a nightly folklore show is hosted, is located on the lower level of the main building. Taking the path to the right of the main building will take you out above the rocks to the sculpture garden with works by Caribé and Mario Cravo. The rest of the very small collection is housed in a side building behind the sculpture garden. Expect to spend 1 to 2 hours.

Ave do Contorno s/n, Cidade Baixa. © 071/329-0660. Tues–Sun 1–7pm. Free admission. It is best to take a taxi from the Mercado Modelo or Pelourinho.

Barra
Museu Nautico da Bahia, Farol da Barra & Forte de Santo Antônio ☆
This lighthouse, fort, and museum are mostly worth a visit for the views over the Bay of All Saints. Erected in 1534, the Forte de Santo Antônio was the first and most important Portuguese fortress protecting Salvador. The lighthouse was added in 1698 on the orders of the Portuguese king, who was rather annoyed by the sinking of one of his treasure galleons. The museum inside the lighthouse contains a small collection of maps and charts, navigational instruments, and a number of archaeological finds from shipwrecks that the lighthouse obviously didn't prevent. The cafe on the fort's upper ramparts is one of the prime sunset spots of the city.

Farol da Barra, Praia da Barra s/n, Barra. © 071/245-0539. Admission R$3 (US$1). Museum Tues–Sun 9am–7pm; cafe 9am–10pm. Bus: Barra or Via Orla.

Bonfim
Nosso Senhor do Bonfim ☆☆   This is not the prettiest church in Salvador by any means, but it's likely the one in which faith still beats the strongest. You'll be swamped on arrival by kids selling *fitas,* the colorful ribbons that people tie around their wrist for good luck. Step inside and you'll likely be distracted from the tall barrel vault and blue wall tiles by the fervor of the people offering up their prayers. To really see the extent of their devotion, go to the Room of Miracles at the back where people request or give thanks for miracles by donating valuable or important objects. Definitely eye-catching are the numerous hanging body parts—models made of wood and plastic and even gold.

Largo do Bonfim. © 071/316-2196. Tues–Sun 6:30am–noon. Located about 8km (5 miles)—or a R$15 (US$5) taxi ride—north of Pelourinho on the Bonfim Peninsula. Bus: Catch a Bonfim bus at Praça de Sé or at the bottom of the Elevator Lacerda in Comércio.

OUTDOOR ACTIVITIES
BEACHES & PARKS   With more than 48km (30 miles) of beaches within the city limits, finding a beach is much less trouble than deciding which one to go to. The beaches on the bay side of town (**Boa Viagem, Bonfim**) are not recommended

for bathing. **Barra** is the closest clean beach area to downtown, and its protected waters are great for swimming. Just around the bend is **Praia de Ondina,** the first of the true ocean beaches. It's popular with the many visitors who stay in the Ondina hotels. **Praia de Amarelina** is as much known for its food stalls as for the excellent surf and windsurf conditions; the strong seas make it less ideal for swimming. The **Jardim de Alah** is more park than beach, but its palm trees, grass, and small calm beach make for pleasant strolling. Some 5km (3 miles) up the road, **Praia dos Artistas** is highly recommended for swimmers and has waves gentle enough for children. **Praia de Piatã** has that tropical paradise look with lots of palm trees and kiosks offering cold drinks and perfect seafood snacks. One of the prettier beaches, **Itapuã** has inspired many a song. Fishermen still bring their rafts in at the end of the day. The most recently trendy beaches are the ones the furthest from downtown; **Praia de Stella Maris** and **Flamengo** are where the young and beautiful gather on the weekends. The buses from downtown that are marked VIA ORLA will follow the coastal road connecting all the beaches until their final destination. Sit on the right-hand side, check it out, and get off when you see the beach you like.

Parque Metropolitano do Abaeté, located just a short walk from Itapuã beach, is famous for the huge blackwater lagoon surrounded by dazzling-white

Candomblé

Candomblé is practiced throughout Brazil, but its roots are deepest in Salvador. In its original form, it was brought to Brazil by slaves from West Africa, who believed in a pantheon of gods and goddesses *(orixás)* who embodied various forces of nature, such as wind, ocean, and fire. A believer who is prepared and trained can become possessed by a certain *orixá.* In Catholic Brazil, the practice of Candomblé was prohibited; Brazilian slaves were converted to Catholicism. But by translating each of their gods into an equivalent saint, Candomblé followers found they could continue their native worship under the very noses of their priests and masters.

The actual ceremonies are both fun and fascinating; there's lots of chanting and drumming plus wonderful foods and perfumes, all used in order to please the *orixás* and encourage them to come and possess those present. Many *terreiros* (areas of worship) in Salvador accept visitors, provided they follow a few basic rules: no revealing clothing (white clothing is preferred) and no video- or picture-taking. Real *terreiros* will not quote an admission fee but would definitely appreciate a donation.

To attend a Candomblé session, check with **Federação Baiana de Culto Afro Brasileiro,** Rua Alfredo de Brito 39, Second Floor, Pelourinho (© 071/321-1444). Another good resource is the **Afro-Brazilian Museum,** Terreiro de Jesus s/n, Pelourinho (© 071/321-0383). Some *terreiros* that accept visitors are **Menininha do Gantois,** Alto do Gantois 23, Federação (© **071/331-9231;** service led by Mãe Carmen); **Abaça de Amazi,** Jose Ramos 165, Vila América (© 071/261-2354; service led by Mãe Aida); and **Casa Branca,** Av. Vasco da Gama 463, Vasco da Gama (close to Rio Vermelho) (© 071/334-2900; the oldest *terreiro* in the city, dating from 1836.

sand dunes. From Pituaçu beach, you can access **Parque Metropolitano de Pituaçu,** a 425-hectare (1,050-acre) reserve of Atlantic rainforest. This park has 18km (11 miles) of cycle trails (plus bikes for rent). A pleasant park close to downtown, the real attraction of **Dique do Tororó Park** is the set of 6m-tall (20-ft.) sculptures of eight *orixás* in the middle of the lake. In the evening, these are beautifully illuminated.

CAPOEIRA   There is no better place than Salvador to see capoeira. There are two good schools in Pelourinho where you can either watch or learn this most Bahian of sports. **Mestre Bimba's** academy, in the basement on Rua Gregorio de Matos 51, Pelourinho (℃ **071/322-5082**), is the best known. Visitors are welcome to have a look during lessons. For those interested in learning, the academy offers 1-hour lessons for R$10 (US$3.35) per person, no experience required.

Just across the street from Mestre Bimba is the **Associação Brasileira de Capoeira Angola,** Rua Gregorio de Matos 38, Pelourinho (℃ **071/321-3087**). This school also holds lessons and regular demonstrations in Pelourinho. Contact the office for details on the time and location of demonstrations.

DIVING   Dive sites on the coast and bay around Salvador include some interesting reefs and shipwrecks. Expect to pay around R$80 (US$27) for a dive trip excluding equipment, and R$140 (US$47) for a dive trip including full equipment rental. The trip includes two dives. Contact **Submariner,** Rua da Paciencia 223, Rio Vermelho (℃ **071/334-4747;** www.submariner.com.br), or **Dive Bahia,** Av. Sete de Setembro 3809, Barra (℃ **071/264-3820**).

GOLF   Golf's not a very popular sport in Salvador, but the **Sofitel Hotel** has a golf course that is open to the general public. The nine-hole 36-par course is located in Itapuã and subject to availability, as guests have preferred tee times. Greens fees are R$50 (US$17) per session. Contact the Sofitel at ℃ **071/374-8500** or the golf club directly at ℃ **071/374-8522.**

TENNIS   There are two clubs in Salvador that allow nonmembers access: **Clube Bahiano de Tênis,** Av. Princesa Leopoldina 398, Barra Avenida (℃ **071/336-9411**), has nine courts. **Costa Verde Tênis Clube,** Av. Orlando Gomes s/n, Piatã (℃ **071/367-9805**), has 13 courts. At both clubs, court time is R$20 (US$7) per hour, with no racket rental available.

SHOPPING

Salvador offers some of the best crafts in all of Brazil. The best buys include crafts made out of wood, ceramics, or leather; musical instruments; and CDs of *axé* music. Pelourinho's many gift shops sell wooden berimbaus, miniature terracotta figurines, woodcarvings of *orixás,* white lace tablecloths and blouses, colorful arte naif paintings, and much more. Remember to bargain.

ART   Pricey but unique pieces can be bought at some of the many galleries in Pelourinho. **Galeria 13,** Rua Santa Isabel 13 (℃ **071/242-7783**), has a large exhibit space with regular showings of work by local artists. **Galeria de Arte Bel Borba,** Rua Luis Viana 14 (℃ **071/243-9370**), specializes in sculptures and paintings by Bel Borba; his work is colorful and fresh. For top-of-the-line names, check out **Oxum Casa de Arte,** Rua Gregorio de Matos 18 (℃ **071/321-0617**). The large collection of art includes work by Mario Cravo and Carybé, who did the large wood panels of the *orixás* in the Afro-Brazilian museum.

Instituto de Artesanato Visconde de Mauá, Rua Gregorio de Matos s/n, Pelourinho (℃ **071/321-5638**), was founded by the government to promote and support regional artists and offers a huge collection of Bahian arts and crafts.

It's open Monday and Wednesday through Friday from 8am to 7pm, Tuesday from 8am to 6pm, and Saturday and Sunday from 10am to 4pm.

GIFTS & SOUVENIRS   For a different kind of souvenir, try **Lembranças da Fé,** Rua João de Deus 24, Pelourinho (✆ 071/321-0006), which specializes in religious articles. **Projeto Axé,** Rua das Laranjeiras 9 (✆ 071/321-7869), is a nonprofit organization that sells great skirts, shorts, kangas, and other clothing to raise funds to support projects for street children. The big problem with buying souvenirs at **Delicias Bahia,** Rua Inacio Accioli 9, Pelourinho (✆ 071/241-0775), is that they may not last until you get home. The shop has a large selection of coconut sweets, chocolates, jams, candied fruit, and more than 100 different kinds of liquors with fruit or spices.

MUSIC   To pick up the latest *axé* or reggae tunes, stop in at **Brazilian Sound,** Rua Francisco Muniz Barreto s/n (✆ 071/321-9522). Chances are that if you've heard it out on the streets, it will be in here for sale.

SHOPPING MALLS   Closest to the historic center is the **Shopping Barra,** Av. Centenario 2992, Barra (✆ 071/339-8222), just a few blocks from the Farol da Barra. Next to the bus station is one of the larger malls, **Shopping Iguatemi,** Av. Tancredo Neves 148, Pituba (✆ 071/350-5060); to get here, take a bus marked RODOVIARIA. The largest and newest mall in Salvador is the **Aeroclube Plaza Show,** Av. Otávio Mangabeira 6000 (✆ 071/462-8000), located on the outskirts of town, close to the airport. In addition to shopping, this open-air mall offers a large entertainment complex with mini-golf, bowling, a climbing wall, and a game center. In the evenings, the many bars, restaurants, and clubs attract people until the early hours. The shops are open on Sunday as well. To get here, take a bus to Praia de Flamengo or Itapuã.

CARNAVAL

Carnaval is Salvador's biggest party of the year. More than 1.5 million people join in. In contrast to Rio's more spectator-oriented celebration, in Salvador, the accent is on participation. The beat of choice is *axé;* the action is out on the streets with the blocos.

In Salvador, blocos started out as flatbed trucks with bands and sound systems leading people on an extended dance through the streets. As the number of participants has grown, Salvador blocos have evolved into more highly organized affairs. All now follow set routes, and many have corporate sponsorship. Your dancing-through-the-streets-of-Salvador experience now comes with a better sound system, security guards, and a support vehicle with washrooms and first-aid attendants. Unavoidably, it also now comes with a price tag.

The revelers that follow a bloco must buy a T-shirt *(abadá)* to identify themselves. In return, they get to sing and dance behind the music truck in a large cordoned-off area, staffed by security guards who keep troublemakers out. If you follow the entire route, you can expect to be on your feet for at least 6 hours. Most blocos parade 3 days in a row, and your *abadá* gives you the right to come on all 3 days. It is also possible to purchase an *abadá* for just 1 day.

Tip: Do not bring any valuables with you, and dress casually. For blocos, just wear your *abadá*, shorts, and running shoes; otherwise, shorts and a tank top will do just fine.

BLOCOS & REHEARSALS

The blocos parade Friday through Tuesday, some for 3 days, others for 4 days. Order and start times vary, so pick up an updated calendar just before Carnaval at one of the Bahiatursa offices. Another great resource available at newsstands is the *Guia do Ocio,* a monthly arts and entertainment magazine that publishes an amazingly detailed Carnaval edition for R$5 (US$1.65). See below to help you decide which blocos you want to see. To purchase an *abadá,* you can contact the bloco directly or contact **Central do Carnaval** (✆ **071/372-6000;** www.centraldocarnaval.com.br); they represent at least a dozen of the most popular blocos.

One of the most popular blocos, **Beijo** (✆ **071/336-6100**) parades on Sunday, Monday, and Tuesday. The lead singer Gil is a popular Bahian artist. *Abadás* cost R$350 (US$117). **Camaleão** (✆ **071/336-6100**) parades Sunday through Tuesday. Carlinhos Brown was the lead artist for a few years; now, Chiclete com Banana has taken on that role. *Abadás* cost R$650 (US$217). **Cerveja & Cia** (✆ **071/336-6100**) is owned by the producer of Salvador's new musical sensation Ivete Sangalo, so it only makes sense that she is the star attraction of this bloco that parades Thursday through Saturday. *Abadás* start at R$300 (US$100). One of the most traditional Afro blocos, **Ilê Aiyê** (✆ **071/388-4969**) only lets people of African descent parade, but everyone is welcome to watch and cheer. The drums are phenomenal. The group parades on Saturday, Sunday, and Tuesday. *Abadás* cost R$200 (US$70).

A small number of blocos meet regularly in the months leading up to Carnaval. The most popular group is **Olodum,** which meets on Tuesday night at the Praça Teresa Batista s/n, Pelourinho (✆ **071/321-3208**). Tickets are R$20 (US$7). On Sunday, Olodum holds a free rehearsal starting at 6pm at Largo do Pelô. **Araketu** was once simply a bloco but now performs all over Brazil. From September onwards, the group puts on rehearsals at the Aeroclube Plaza (✆ **071/461-0300**) on Thursday starting at 7pm. Tickets cost R$15 (US$5) or R$30 (US$10) for a box seat. **Ivete Sangalo,** the uncrowned queen of Bahian Carnaval, now has her own rehearsal space, **Pier Bahia.** She often gets big name Brazilian bands to join her for regular Sunday night rehearsals. The season kicks off at the end of September; Doors open at 7pm. Av. do Contorno s/n, Comercio (taxi recommended), ✆ **071/416-0402.** Tickets range from R$30 to R$50 (US$10–US$17).

WHERE TO STAY

Most visitors to Salvador have traditionally been either backpackers—who demand central and inexpensive digs—or Brazilians, who want modern luxury accommodations close to the beach. As a result, you must decide between staying in someplace old in Pelourinho or someplace new on the coast, at least 15 minutes outside of downtown.

Salvador's peak season ranges from mid-December to early March, and maxes out during Carnaval. Most Carnaval packages start at R$1,500 (US$750) and go up to R$4,000 (US$2,000). Even at these prices, rooms go fast. In the off season (Apr–June and Aug–Nov), hotels give as much as a 50% discount.

PELOURINHO

There are numerous advantages to staying in Pelourinho—you get to stay in restored 18th-century buildings, and you're minutes from the bustle and fun of the old city. The disadvantages? Rooms are small, and on weekends, things can get loud.

Expensive

Pousada das Flores ★ If we were staying at this *pousada,* we'd go for room no. 10 or 11. Located on the top floor, they have broad verandas with fabulous views of, respectively, the Bay of All Saints and the old city. Other rooms aren't a write-off, but they lack views. All rooms in this beautifully restored 18th-century structure come with high ceilings, gleaming hardwood floors, and period furniture, including a hammock slung in every room. Bathrooms are small and come equipped with a shower only.

Rua Direita de Santo Antonio 442, Centro Histórico, Salvador, 40030-080 BA. ©/fax **071/243-1836**. www. pflores.com.br. 9 units. R$132–R$187 (US$44–US$62) double standard; R$242 (US$80) double w/veranda. Extra person 30%. Children under 7 stay free in parent's room. No credit cards. Parking unavailable. Bus: Praça de Sé. **Amenities:** Laundry. *In room:* Ceiling fans only, minibar, safe.

Pousada do Boqueirão 🌟🌟 This may be the best place in Salvador to experience the look and feel of an old colonial home. The Boqueirão's accommodations stay largely true to the original, with soaring high ceilings and period furnishings. Built in the pre-air-conditioning era, vents and cross-drafts are designed to keep the rooms cool. (The only rooms with air-conditioning are the small ones that you don't want to stay in.) The best rooms—nos. 1, 2, and 5—come with little terraces and fabulous views. No. 5 covers two levels.

Rua Direita de Santa Antonio 48, Salvador, 40030 BA. © **071/241-2262**. Fax 071/241-8064. www.pousada boqueirao.com.br. 12 units. R$75–R$200 (US$25–US$67). Extra person 20%. Children under 6 stay free in parent's room. AE. Limited on-street parking. *Note:* Direita de Santa Antonio has both an old and a revised (official) numbering system. To cover all bets and add to the fun, many buildings post both. Bus: Praça de Sé. **Amenities:** Laundry. *In room:* Fridge, minibar.

MODERATE
Pousada Villa Carmo 🌟 Just past the classic Largo Pelourinho, Rua do Carmo tracks along the cliff top on the edge of the Cidade Alta, providing impressive views of the Bay of all Saints and the Lower Town. This well-kept old colonial *pousada* has three *quartos*—rooms without bathrooms, air-conditioning, or a view—and they are to be avoided. The seven *apartamentos*, on the other hand, come with a small, clean, functional bathroom, equipped with a shower only. The apartamentos at the back of this restored colonial structure—in addition to having lovely high ceilings—also come with air-conditioning and small terraces with truly fabulous views. These are the ones for which you should *pedir* (ask). The *pousada* also has a common TV room and lovely outside terrace.

Rua do Carmo 58, Centro Histórico, Salvador, 40030-130 BA. © **071/241-3924**. 10 units, 3 w/private bathroom outside of room. R$50–R$60 (US$25–US$30) bathroom outside; R$70–R$105 (US$23–US$35) bathroom inside. Extra person 30%. Each child under 12, add 25%. V. Limited on-street parking. Bus: Praça de Sé. **Amenities:** Common TV room. *In room:* A/C, minibar (rooms w/hall bathroom do not have A/C, minibar).

VITORIA
Vitória sits on a high clifftop between Pelourinho and Barra, the neighborhood on the point. It's the closest you can come to Pelourinho and yet still stay in a modern hotel.

EXPENSIVE
Sol Victoria Marina 🌟🌟 Perched on the edge of the cliffs along the Avenida Sete de Setembro, the Sol Victoria Marina offers spectacular views of the bay. The rooms come in standard with avenida view or deluxe with ocean view. The price is the same, so it's worth requesting an oceanview room when booking. If only avenida rooms are available request one on the higher floors as this will reduce the amount of street noise. The rooms are pleasantly furnished with a double bed, couch, and small table; all bathrooms come with bathtubs. Rooms for travelers with disabilities are available. The swimming pool is truly spectacular;

down at the bottom of the cliffs, the pool is accessed by a small cable car that zips down the side of the cliff. Breakfast is served on the terrace that overlooks the bay.

Av. Sete de Setembro 2068, Salvador, 40080-001 BA. ✆ **0800/703-3399** or 071/336-7736. Fax 071/336-0507. www.solbahia.com.br. 235 units. R$160–R$240 (US$53–US$80) standard double; R$750 (US$250) suite. Extra person 40%. Children under 7 stay free in parent's room. AE, DC, MC, V. Free parking. Bus: Campo Grande. **Amenities:** 2 restaurants; bar; large outdoor pool; tour desk; car rental; business center; 24-hr. room service; laundry. *In room:* A/C, TV, minibar, dataport, safe.

BARRA

If you opt not to stay downtown, Barra offers sea and sun and a good bit of fun in neighborhood restaurants and cafes, in easy striking distance of Pelourinho.

Expensive

Monte Pascoal Praia Hotel ★★ *Value*   Fabulously located across from Barra Beach and recently completely renovated, the Monte Pascoal Praia offers great value. All rooms come with a king-size bed or two double beds—great for families traveling with young children. Every room has a balcony and at least a partial view of the ocean. The 32 rooms with a full ocean view cost an additional 25%. This hotel is incredibly popular during Carnaval as its pool deck overlooks the main parade route and the beach is just 45m (150 ft.) across the street.

Av. Presidente Vargas 68 (aka Av. Oceanica), Barra, Salvador, 40170-010 BA. ✆ **071/203-4000.** Fax 071/245-4436. www.montepascoal.com.br. 80 units. R$250 (US$83) standard double; R$300 (US$100) oceanview double. Extra person R$60 (US$20). Seasonal discounts available. Children under 6 stay free in parent's room. AE, DC, MC, V. Parking R$12 (US$4) per day. **Amenities:** Restaurant; bar; outdoor pool; fitness room; sauna; game room; small business center (computer, Internet, fax, and printing) w/24-hr. access; salon; 24-hr. room service; laundry service. *In room:* A/C, TV, dataport (w/Internet provider), minibar, hair dryer, safe.

Moderate

Village Novo ★ *Value*   Housed in a 125-year-old heritage mansion just across from the beach, Village Novo has a number of beautiful rooms at very reasonable rates. The two best rooms are nos. 201 and 301. No. 201 (the only room without air-conditioning) is the biggest room in the house, with beautiful hardwood floors and a small veranda overlooking the beach. Just one floor up, no. 301 is the most comfortable room with a larger veranda and queen-size bed. The remaining rooms, located in the rear of the building, are still pleasant but quite a bit smaller. For families, no. 410 (located on the 4th-floor terrace) offers a kitchen and a sitting room with a pullout bed in addition to the queen-size bed.

Av. Sete de Setembro 3659, Porto da Barra, Salvador, 40170-010 BA. ✆ **071/267-4362.** www.villagenovo. com. 11 units. R$102 (US$34) beachfront double; R$90 (US$30) standard double; R$120 (US$40) rooftop double. Children under 6 free in parent's room. AE, MC, V. Street parking. **Amenities:** Laundry service. *In room:* A/C (in all but 1 room), TV.

ONDINA/RIO VERMELHO

Ondina and Rio Vermelho are oceanside neighborhoods that begin just around the bend from Barra on the open Atlantic coast. A number of good hotels are located right on the waterfront; some even have private beaches.

Very Expensive

Bahia Othon Palace ★★   The Othon Palace is 1970s fortress architecture at its glowering concrete best. However, once inside, it is remarkably pleasant. All the amenities are excellent, especially the large outdoor swimming pool on its own big deck. And despite the number of rooms, the staff is very personable and friendly. The rooms are spacious, modern, and comfortably decorated. For those who appreciate some extra space, the deluxe rooms provide a very spacious room with a large desk, a full sitting area, and a king-size bed. Rooms have either a partial ocean view over the pool or a full ocean view toward Barra.

Av. Presidente Vargas 2456 (aka Av. Oceanica), Ondina, Salvador 40170-010 BA. ✆ 0800/701-0098 or 071/203-2000. Fax 071/245-4877. www.othon.com.br. 278 units. R$270–R$350 (US$90–US$117) standard double; R$300–R$400 (US$100–US$133) deluxe double; R$350–R$560 (US$117–US$187) suite. Children under 6 stay free in parent's room. Extra person 30%. Free parking. Bus: Ondina or via Orla. **Amenities:** 2 restaurants; disco; bar; outdoor pool; gym (extra charge R$15/US$5); concierge; tour desk; car rental; business center; salon; 24-hr. room service; massage; dry cleaning/laundry; gold service rooms available. *In room:* A/C, TV, dataport, minibar, safe, hair dryer.

Pestana 🎟🎟🎟 Formerly the Meridien, the Pestana Bahia is positively buzzing after its extensive make-over. Set on an outcrop overlooking Rio Vermelho, its privileged location guarantees all 430 units an ocean view. All rooms are spacious with modern and funky decorations. Furnishings and artwork have splashes of green and orange making for very pleasant rooms. The outdoor pool and sun deck overlook the beach; the Pestana's beach service includes towels, chairs, umbrellas, and drink service. The hotel is about a R$20 (US$7) cab ride from Pelourinho.

Rua Fonte do Boi, Rio Vermelho, Salvador 41940-360 BA. ✆ 071/453-8005. Fax 071/453-8066. www.pestana hotels.com.br. 430 units. R$270 (US$110) superior double; R$330 (US$110) deluxe double. Extra person 30%. Children under 13 stay free in parent's room. AE, DC, MC, V. Free parking. Bus: Rio Vermelho. **Amenities:** 3 restaurants; bar; large outdoor pool; small health club; concierge; tour desk; car rental; business center; salon; massage; 24-hr. room service; laundry; nonsmoking floors. *In room:* A/C, TV, dataport, minibar, safe.

WHERE TO DINE
PELOURINHO
Expensive
Casa da Gamboá 🎟🎟 BAHIAN   The elegant Casa da Gamboá serves up a Bahian "nouvelle cuisine." The classic Bahian dishes such as *bobó de camarão* are still on the menu and very well done, but the kitchen has gone beyond to create some fabulous modern fare. The *camarão ao molho de manga* is a tropical explosion of flavor—big juicy prawns are flamed in cognac and served with large pieces of mango in a creamy mango sauce. Another elegant dish is the *peixe tropical*, the catch of the day grilled in a clove, cinnamon, and fruit sauce.

Rua João de Deus 31, Pelourinho. ✆ 071/321-3393. Main courses R$28–R$46 (US$9–US$15). AE, DC, MC, V. Mon–Sat noon–3pm and 7pm–midnight. Bus: Praça da Sé.

Maria Mata Mouro 🎟🎟 SEAFOOD   One of the more famous restaurants in Pelourinho, Maria Mata Mouro's menu is refreshingly light; the strong flavors of dendê oil and dried shrimp or coconut milk are used sparingly. A delicious appetizer is the salmon carpaccio; the thin layers of marinated fish are served with an anchovy-and-caper sauce. Recommended main courses include badejo fish in a ginger sauce, or the grilled bacalhau with broccoli and roasted garlic. Leave enough room for the signature dessert, banana in a puff pastry flambéed with *cachaça*.

Rua Inacio Acciole 8, Pelourinho. ✆ 071/321-3929. R$30–R$45 (US$10–US$15) for 2. AE, DC, MC, V. Daily noon–1am. Bus: Praça da Sé.

Sorriso da Dadá 🎟🎟 BAHIAN   Dadá has made quite a name for herself; journalists write articles about her, and gourmet magazines rave about her cozy restaurant but Dadá just does what she does best, making the meanest Bahian food in town. Even though the main courses are huge, don't pass up some of the appetizers. The octopus in a light vinaigrette is a good choice, or try the *casquinha de siri;* the crabmeat is mixed with dendê oil and cilantro and served

Bahian Food Glossary

Unique in its overwhelming African influences, Bahian cuisine comes with its own ingredients and terminology. Here's a list of the most common dishes and ingredients:

- **Acarajé:** The dough is made with mashed beans but the acarajé is deep-fried in *dendê* oil and stuffed with a shrimp sauce, hot peppers, and an onion-tomato vinaigrette.
- **Bobó de camarão:** A stew made with shrimp, cassava paste, onion, tomato, cilantro, coconut milk, and *dendê* oil.
- **Dendê oil:** A staple ingredient, this oil comes from the dendê palm tree and has a distinct red color. The oil has a strong nutlike flavor; it tastes much like a walnut or sesame oil.
- **Ensopado:** A lighter version of a *moqueca,* made without *dendê* oil.
- **Moqueca:** Bahia's most popular dish, the ingredients include any kind of seafood stewed with coconut milk, lime juice, cilantro, onion, and tomato.
- **Vatapá:** A stew made with fish, onion, tomato, cilantro, lime juice, dried shrimp, ground cashew nuts, peanuts, ginger, and coconut milk. The sauce is thickened with bread.

in a crab shell. For regulars there is only one main course, the *bobó de camarão.* Service can be temperamental, sometimes great, sometimes slow and sloppy, but the food is always worth a visit.

Rua Frei Vicente 5, Pelourinho. ℭ 071/321-9642. Main courses R$36–R$67 (US$12–US$22) for 2. AE, DC, MC, V. Daily 11am–midnight. Bus: Praça da Sé.

Moderate

Jardim das Delicias *Finds* BRAZILIAN/CAFE   The Jardim das Delicias (Garden of Delights) is appropriately named. Tucked away inside an antiques store on the ground floor of a colonial house in Pelourinho, this lovely courtyard restaurant is the perfect getaway from the bustle and crowding of Pelourinho. The restaurant serves a full Bahian menu, but we highly recommend coming here for a tea or coffee and some sweets. Just pick something from the display of delicious cakes and pies, or order some waffles with a generous scoop of ice cream. That should give you the boost you need for further exploring.

Rua João de Deus 12, Pelourinho. ℭ 071/321-1449. Main courses R$15–R$40 (US$5–US$13), the more expensive dishes serve 2. Sweets and desserts all under R$10 (US$3.35). No credit cards. Daily 10am–midnight. Bus: Praça da Sé.

Inexpensive

A Cubana *Finds* DESSERTS   It only makes sense that a city with an abundance of tropical fruits and a year-round warm climate would have great ice cream. One of the oldest *sorveterias* in town, A Cubana doesn't go for fads or trends. The menu features only 28 homemade flavors at any given time. Worth trying are the more unusual fruit flavors such as *jáca* (jack fruit) or *cupuaçu.*

Rua Alfredo de Brito 12, Pelourinho. ℭ 071/321-6162. All items under R$12 (US$4). No credit cards. Daily 8am–10pm. Bus: Praça da Sé.

COMERCIO

Located at the foot of a cliff directly below Pelourinho, the business and marina district of Comércio is fine for wandering in the daytime during office hours, but come evening, we recommend taking a taxi.

Very Expensive

Trapiche Adelaide 🏵🏵🏵 BRAZILIAN/ITALIAN   Salvador may not be a fine-dining kind of town, but there are a few exceptions and Trapiche ranks prominently among them. New chef Luciano Boseggia has given the menu a definite Italian twist with dishes such as risotto with quail and shimeji mushrooms (risotto de codorna). The wine list is outstanding with mainly Italian, Portuguese, Chilean, and Argentine selections; many are available by the glass. Oh, and if the fine food and wine weren't enough, the restaurant itself is stunningly beautiful. The stylish room feels like *Miami Vice* meets *Casablanca;* the stark all-white interior and floor-to-ceiling glass windows overlooking the bay contrast sharply with the marble tables, rattan chairs, and tall green plants.

Praça do Tupinambás 2, Av. Contorno, Comércio. © 071/326-2211. www.trapicheadelaide.com.br. Reservations required on weekends, recommended in high season. Main courses R$25–R$42 (US$8–US$14). AE, DC, MC, V. Mon–Thurs noon–4pm and 7pm–1am; Fri–Sat and holidays noon–1am; Sun noon–6pm. Taking a taxi is recommended; even though it is not too far from the Mercado Modelo, the street is dark and very quiet at night.

Moderate

Camafeu de Oxossi/Maria de São Pedro 🏵 BAHIAN   The two restaurants Camafeu de Oxossi and Maria de São Pedro share the lovely large patio upstairs in the Mercado Modelo. However, these restaurants have two very separate owners, which explains why, when you first walk in, two equally keen and friendly Baianos try to persuade you to sit in their restaurant. Does it really matter where you eat? We couldn't tell the difference; both menus serve up traditional Bahian food, including nine types of *moquecas*. Shunned by locals, these restaurants are very much geared to tourists wandering the Mercado, but the food is still fine, and the views over the bay and the São Marcelo Fort are worth the price of admission alone.

Praça Visc. De Cayru 250, Mercado Modelo, Comércio. © 071/242-9751. Main courses R$22–R$47 (US$7–US$16) for 2. AE, DC, MC, V. Mon and Wed 9:30am–7:30pm; Mon–Sat 11am–7pm, Sun 11am–4pm. Bus: Praça da Sé, then take the Elevator Lacerda.

BARRA

This beach neighborhood is a popular dining destination for locals getting together with friends; with the many hotels concentrated in this area, it's always a lively spot in the evening.

Moderate

Barravento 🏵🏵 BAHIAN   Offering one of the best views in Barra, Barravento's patio overlooks all of the beach as far as the Farol da Barra. The menu includes a large selection of typical Bahian dishes such as *moquecas,* marriscadas, and grilled fish. One dish that every Baiano will recommend, *moqueca de siri mole,* is a tasty concoction of coconut milk, fresh cilantro, peppers, red palm tree oil, and soft-shell crabs. If you're not in the mood for a full meal deal, Barravento serves a great variety of appetizers such as *casquinha de siri* (spiced crabmeat) and fish pastries.

Av. Getúlio Vargas 814 (aka Av. Oceanica), Barra. © 071/247-2577. Main courses R$19–R$38 (US$6–US$13), all dishes for 2. DC, MC, V. Daily noon–midnight. Bus: Barra or via Orla.

Il Forno 🏵 *Value* PIZZA   The best pizza in town. Located in a lovely old house 1 block from Barra beach, the restaurant's best spots are upstairs on the patio where small tables with oh-so-Italian red-and-white checked tablecloths pack the deck. The wood-oven has been baking thin-crust pizzas for nearly 20 years, and over time, the menu has grown to include more than 40 choices of toppings. Very popular is the house specialty Il Forno, made with bacon, palm heart, egg, tomato, mozzarella, olives, and oregano. For cheese lovers, the Mineira is a must, combining catupiry, Gorgonzola, mozzarella, and provolone.

Rua Almirante Marques de Leão 77, Barra (close to the lighthouse). © 071/264-7287. Main courses R$18–R$32 (US$6–US$11) for 2. AE, DC, MC, V. Mon–Sat noon–3pm and 6pm–1am; Sun noon–4pm and 6pm–1am. Bus: Barra or via Orla.

THE BEACHES

There are some excellent restaurants a bit further out in the beach neighborhoods along the Atlantic coast. Easily accessible by bus, they make a fine destination on their own or in combination with an afternoon on the beach.

Expensive

Yemanjá BAHIAN   One of the perennial contenders for best restaurant in Salvador, Yemanjá offers all the traditional Bahian choices. The *moqueca de pitu* is particularly worthy of recommendation; pitu is a sweet-tasting freshwater prawn not often found on menus. Those who can't stand the sight of another stew (it does happen after a few days) will be pleased to see some grilled fish and prawns on the menu. Dessert is a must here. The Bahian desserts laden with sugar, coconut, and egg yolks are superb, and the homemade ice cream is some of the best in town.

Av. Otavio Mangabeira 4655, Boca do Rio. © 071/231-3036. Main courses R$28–R$56 (US$9–US$19) for 2. AE, V. Mon–Thurs 11:30am–midnight; Fri–Sun 11:30am–1am. Bus: Orla or via Boca do Rio.

Moderate

Caranguejo da Dadá BRAZILIAN   Overlooking Patamares beach, this bar/restaurant is perfect for a casual afternoon drink or snack, and makes a fine dinner destination as well. The menu offers great seafood; very popular are the *moquecas, ensopados,* and *bobó de camarão* (these dishes serve two people). Crab lovers can choose from a variety of dishes such as crab with *dendê* oil or stewed with veggies and potatoes. One of the most popular appetizers is the *Casquinha da Dadá* (crabmeat with catupiry cheese and palm heart gratiné in the oven).

Av. Otavio Mangabeira 940, Patamares. © 071/363-5151. Main courses R$27–R$68 (US$9–US$23) for 2. AE, MC, V. Daily 11:30am–midnight; Fri–Sat open until at least 2am. Bus: Orla or Itapuã.

SALVADOR AFTER DARK

Salvador's nightlife is one of the most vibrant in all of Brazil. Pelourinho explodes at night with music and people and activity, what Brazilians call *movimento.*

THE PERFORMING ARTS

Home to the Bahian Symphony Orchestra and the Balé (ballet) de Castro Alves, **Teatro Castro Alves,** Praça Dois de Julho s/n, Campo Grande (© 071/339-8000), is your best bet for catching some fine arts performances. One of the best places to see contemporary bands is at the **Teatro Sesi Rio Vermelho,** Rua Borges dos Reis 9, Rio Vermelho (© 071/334-0668). Housed in a renovated heritage building, it specializes in local and Brazilian acts. Music varies from jazz to blues to MPB and even pop.

LIVE MUSIC & DANCE CLUBS

In the evenings, Pelourinho transforms itself into one big live music venue. We have given a few suggestions of bars and clubs, but the best tip we can give you is just to get out and explore. Two of the most popular venues for concerts are the **Praça Quincas Berro D'Agua** and the **Largo Pedro Archanjo.** Stop by the Pelourinho tourist office and pick up the free entertainment guide listing upcoming events.

LIVE MUSIC   Every Friday and Saturday the three bars ringing Pelourinho's **Praça do Reggae,** Ladeiro do Pelourinho, by the Nossa Senhora do Rosário dos Pretos church, bring in a band that plays on their common front yard. One of the best-known groups in Salvador, Olodum performs every Tuesday night at the Praça Teresa Batista (© **071/322-1396**), starting at 8pm. One of the city's newest venues is the Aeroclube Plaza Show, Av. Otávio Mangabeira 6000 (© **071/462-8000**), an open-air mall located right on the ocean up towards the airport. In addition to shops and restaurants, there's also a large nightlife area with bars, dance clubs, and concerts.

DANCE CLUBS   Salvador's most popular dance clubs are located at the Aeroclube Plaza. The 25- to 40-year-old crowd heads straight to **Café Cancun,** Otavio Mangabeira 6000, Aeroclube Plaza (© **071/461-0603**). Deejays keep people on their feet with salsa, merengue, mambo, *forró,* and "oldies" from the 1970s and 1980s up to the latest Brazilian hits. The younger crowd (18- to 30-year-olds) hangs out at the **Rock in Rio,** Av. Otávio Mangabeira 6000, Aeroclube Plaza Show (© **071/461-0300**). Loaded with the memorabilia of famous Brazilian pop and rock stars, the music here includes an enormous variety of music, including salsa, *pagode,* pop, dance, and *forró.* A small club in a renovated colonial house, **Quereres,** Rua Frei Vicente 7, Pelourinho (© **071/321-1616**), is popular with locals who flock in for the latest music trend, funk; every Friday night, the deejays spin the best of Brazilian funk.

BARS & PUBS

There are some excellent beach *barracas* (kiosks) to keep you hydrated while you frolic in the sun. A popular daytime kiosk, **Barraca Cabana do Sol,** Praia do Flamengo (© **071/374-5832**), is set underneath impressive coconut palms in a lovely garden setting; it's open daily from 8am to 6pm. For an upscale *barraca,* check out **Barraca do Loro,** Praia do Aleluia, just before Praia do Flamengo (© **071/374-7509**). Snacks include octopus and salmon carpaccio, grilled fish, and steamed crab; drinks include wine, cognac, and whisky. It's open Tuesday through Sunday from 9am to 9pm. A downsized former civil servant, Luciano used his severance package to start up **Barraca do Luciano,** Avenida Otávio Mangabeira in front of the Parque de Pituaçu (© **071/461-1761**), and has never looked back. It's open Tuesday through Sunday from 8am to 7pm.

A prime sunset spot, **Bar da Ponta,** Praça dos Tupinambas 2, Avenida Contorno (© **071/326-2211**), is tucked away on the waterfront next to the Trapiche Adelaide restaurant and offers sweeping views of the Bay of All Saints. So what if you and every other tourist in town are at **Cantina da Lua,** Praça Quinze de Novembro 2, Terreiro de Jesus, Pelourinho (© **071/322-4041**). It happens to be one of the loveliest and largest patios on the Praça Terreiro de Jesus. A great casual bar for after the sun has set, **Porto de Encontro,** Rua César Zama 41, Porto da Barra (© **071/267-2355**), is located in a narrow lane off the Ave. Sete de Setembro just before the Praça dos Tamarineros. Friday to Sunday starting at 8:30pm the bar features live music (MPB, Latin, Brazilian contemporary). Local artists exhibit their work in the cafe.

GAY & LESBIAN NIGHTLIFE

A great resource for gay travelers is the **Grupo Gay da Bahia,** Rua Frei Vicente 24, Pelourinho (© **071/321-1848;** www.ggb.org.br). The group has information on tourism and recreational opportunities in Salvador as well as on local social issues and community activism.

Queens Clube's bar, Rua Teodoro Sampaio 160, Barris (© **071/328-6220**), is open every day, but the club and dance floor are open only Friday and Saturday. One of the newer gay clubs, **Off Club**, Rua Dias D'Avilla 33, Barra (© **071/ 267-6215**), attracts a mixed crowd of both male and female clubbers. A large modern club, **Club Mix Ozone**, Rua Augusto França 55, Largo Dois de Julho (© **071/321-5373**), is popular for drag shows and go-go boys who all put in an appearance on the weekend.

A SIDE TRIP FROM SALVADOR
MORRO DE SÃO PAULO

To really get away from it all (as if the rest of Bahia wasn't relaxed enough) consider the ultimate beach holiday in Morro de São Paulo. Located on an island only accessible by boat or plane, this small beachside village is blissfully isolated—no cars, no motorcycles, no traffic lights or city noise and definitely no McDonald's. The island itself is lush and green and the beaches vary from busy and fun to quieter or almost deserted.

Essentials

GETTING THERE   By Catamaran   The most pleasant way to reach Morro de São Paulo is the catamaran departing from downtown Salvador; the Terminal Maritimo do Mercado Modelo is just across the street from the Mercado Modelo. There are at least three daily departures. Contact **Lancha Ilhabela** (© **071/9989-4282**), **Catamarã Farol do Morro** (© **071/483-1036**), or **Catamarã Gamboa do Morro** (© **071/641-2254**) for details. All cost R$45 (US$15) and take about 2 hours.

By Plane   The quickest way to get to Morro de São Paulo is to fly (20–25 min.). Two companies fly the route, **Adey** (© **071/377-1993**) and Aerostar (© **071/377-4406**). There are at least three flights a day, more on weekends and in high season; one-way fare is R$135 (US$45). Flights depart and arrive at Salvador's international airport, making it very convenient for connecting with onward flights.

VISITOR INFORMATION   The **CIT** (Central de Informações Turisticas), Praça Aureliano Lima s/n (© **075/483-1083**), can assist you with accommodations and transportation as well as book excursions. It also has a number of Internet terminals and doubles as the post office. An excellent website on the area is www.morrodesaopaulo.com.br.

What to See & Do in Morro de São Paulo

The main attraction of Morro de São Paulo is the beach, or better, the beaches. Each has a unique flavor. **First beach** is mostly residential; **Second beach** has lots of *pousadas* and people. This is where you'll find vendors, watersports, and restaurants. **Third beach** is quite narrow; at high tide it almost disappears. It is much more quiet, perfect for a stroll. **Fourth beach** is the (almost) deserted island tropical beach; wide, white sand, palm trees and a few small restaurants. The town itself consists of just a few streets and the main square. During the day it's pretty quiet, as most people hang out at the beach. Around dinner time a craft market starts up and the main square fills with restaurants packed with diners.

More active pursuits include boating, horseback riding, and hiking. There are a number of interesting local excursions. See below for more information.

Outdoor Activities

Marlins, Rua da Prainha s/n (© 075/483-1242), the island's main tour operator offers a number of trips. The most popular is the **8-hour boat trip** around the island with plenty of stops for swimming or snorkeling. Another great boat tour goes out to **Ilha de Boibepa** (a small island off the main island). Tours cost R$50 (US$17) per person, lunch not included. More active trips include a **hike** to waterfalls or a **walk** along the cliffs and beach to Gamboa (R$20–R$30/US$7–US$10 per person).

Along Third and Fourth beaches you will find a number of local **horseback-riding** tour operators; the common rate is R$15 (US$5) per person per hour.

For scuba diving contact **Morro Dive,** Terceira Praia (© 075/483-1333). Conditions are best season in the summer months. In the winter (June–Sept) when the rains are heavy visibility can be very poor. A single dive with all equipment included costs R$65 (US$22), a double dive costs R$100 (US$33), and night dives cost R$80 (US$27).

Snorkelers can rent equipment at **Zimbo Diving** (a booth in front of Villa Gagnon/Terceira Praia; © 075/8803-4749). A mask, fins, and snorkel costs (R$10/US$3.35 per day). A **kayak** costs (R$10/US$3.35 per hour).

Where to Stay in Morro de São Paulo

Morro de São Paulo is not a luxury destination; although there are many lovely *pousadas,* most tend to be small, simple, and casual, and amenities are minimal.

Located in the heart of the village overlooking the main square, **Pousada o Casarão** ♠♠, Praça Aureliano Lima s/n (© 075/483-1022; www.ocasarao.net), offers pleasant rooms in the main heritage building but what you can't see from the street is the lush back garden with nine bungalows set against the sloping hillside. Each is decorated in a different style—Indonesian, Japanese, Indian, African—with rich furnishings and artwork. Rooms in the main building cost R$170 (US$57) for a double; bungalows are R$190 (US$63) for a double (showers only).

Just steps from the ocean and the beachfront activities, **Pousada da Torre,** Segunda Praia 5 (© 075/483-1038; www.pousadadatorre.com.br), is a 10-minute walk from the village and just a few minutes from the nightlife area. The rooms with the best views are the four oceanfront rooms (R$160–R$200/US$53–US$67 in high season); these also overlook the pool and bar and are noisy during the day. Most of the other rooms are in two small buildings behind the main building and are quiet and comfortable (R$110–R$180/US$37–US$60 in high season).

For a little more peace and quiet try **Vila Guaiamú** ♠, Terceira Praia (© 075/483-1035; www.vilaguaiamu.com.br). This lovely *pousada* consists of 24 cabins set amongst the lush green gardens. All are simply furnished and come in standard or deluxe; the only difference being the air-conditioning and TV in the deluxe rooms. The *pousada* is located halfway down Terceira Praia, about a 20-minute walk from the village. Closed May and June. High-season rates are R$180 (US$60) double with air-conditioning and TV. Extra person, add R$50 (US$17).

Where to Dine in Morro de São Paulo

For a small village in the middle of nowhere, Morro de São Paulo has a surprising number of excellent restaurants. The main street in the village, Broadway, is literally lined with eateries. Although most are open for lunch it's in the evening that things really get hopping. **Restaurante e Pizzeria Bianco e Nero** (© 075/483-1097) sells some of the world's best pizza, hot out of the wood-burning oven. It also offers find a number of excellent seafood, grilled meat and chicken, and pasta dishes; closed on Monday. One of the prettiest patios is that of

O Casarão (© 075/483-1022), overlooking the main square. The menu offers a number of excellent fish and seafood dishes (portions serve two people) including *moquecas* and grilled fish. Closed on Sundays. **Quatro Estações** (© 075/483-1513) is known for its seafood. *Marriscada* is a stew made with fish, shrimp, octopus, and crab. Also popular are the *moquecas* and *bobó de camarão* (prawn stew). The tables on the veranda offer great views of the main street. All the restaurants mentioned above accept Visa.

7 Recife & Olinda

2,392km (1,483 miles) NE of Rio de Janeiro, 2,716km (1,684 miles) NE of São Paulo, 842km (522 miles) NE of Salvador

The second largest city in Brazil's northeast, Recife's main claim to fame is Olinda, a restored 17th-century colonial town that, in 1982, was declared a UNESCO World Heritage Site. Olinda was founded by the Portuguese in 1530 on a steep hill overlooking the harbor. The Dutch showed up in Pernambuco in 1630, took Olinda and, with the exception of a few churches, destroyed it utterly. In need of a capital of their own, the Dutch set to work draining and diking the islands at the mouth of the harbor.

The new city quickly turned into a bustling commercial center. When the Dutch were expelled in 1654, the Portuguese rebuilt Olinda as a matter of pride, but the center of the region had already started to move to the Dutch-built town. The city was renamed Recife, after the long coral reefs that guard the harbor. By the 1800s, Recife had far outgrown Olinda; thus, the older town has been left blissfully free of development pressures, still in its largely pristine 17th-century condition and now preserved for posterity.

ESSENTIALS
GETTING THERE
BY PLANE Recife's **Aeroporto Internacional dos Guararapes,** Praça Ministro Salgado Filho s/n, Boa Viagem (© **081/3464-4188**), is located 11km (7 miles) south of the city center and just a few miles from the beachside hotels in Boa Viagem. The airport is serviced by **VASP, Varig, TAM, Gol,** and **Fly Airlines.** A taxi to Boa Viagem costs R$12 to R$18 (US$4–US$6) and to Olinda R$45 to R$60 (US$15–US$20). You'll find a queue for Taxi Coopseta Aeroporto (© **081/3464-4153**) on the arrivals level.

BY BUS Buses arrive at Recife's **Terminal Integrado de Passageiros (TIP,** pronounced *tchee-pee*), Rodovia BR232, Km 15 Curado (© **081/3452-1999**), located 15km (9 miles) west of downtown. A metrô connects the bus station to downtown Recife's final station Estação Central. All interstate buses arrive at this terminal. *Note:* Buses to Olinda leave from downtown and Boa Viagem, not from this station.

GETTING AROUND
Downtown Recife consists of two main areas: **Bairro do Recife** (often called Recife Velho, or Old Recife) and **Santo Antônio.** Recife Velho is the oldest part of the city. Ongoing renovations are reviving and revitalizing this area. On the key street, **Rua da Bom Jesus,** the restored colonial warehouses are now home to bars and cafes, and at night, there's often free live music on the street. Three bridges connect Old Recife with **Santo Antônio.** This is the home of many of Recife's most interesting sights, as well as one of its main commercial areas. The principal street in Santo Antônio is **Avenida Dantas Barreto,** a wide boulevard that runs

down the spine of the island. Buses to and from downtown leave from this street, either from Praça da Independencia, where Dantas Barreto meets Rua Primeiro de Março, or from farther up opposite Nossa Senhora do Carmo Basilica.

The main beach and residential area of Recife starts just south of downtown. The first stretch, where Avenida Boa Viagem begins, is called **Pina.** The area around **Polo Pina** is a popular nightlife spot. Further along the beach, the neighborhood changes its name to **Boa Viagem,** the city's main hotel area.

Olinda lies 6km (4 miles) north of downtown, a hilltop redoubt now almost swallowed by Recife's suburban sprawl. Regular buses make the trip in about 30 minutes. Buses arrive at the Praça do Carmo bus station. The town is small enough that in a day's wandering you'll see everything.

BY BUS Most travelers stay either in Boa Viagem or Olinda. From Boa Viagem, regular buses run along Avenida Domingos Ferreira into downtown. The trip takes about 20 minutes. Those marked CONDE DA BOA VISTA will loop through Boa Vista and into Santo Antônio, stopping at Praça da Independencia. Once you're downtown, all sights are easily accessible by foot.

From Boa Viagem, two regular buses travel directly to and from Olinda's Praça do Carmo bus station: Setubal-Principe or Setubal-Conde da Boa Vista. The trip takes about 50 minutes.

From Olinda, all buses depart from the bus station on Praça do Carmo. Buses marked RIO DOCE go to Santo Antônio, stopping on Avenida N. S. do Carmo. Buses marked JARDIM ATLANTICO also go to Santo Antônio but stop in front of the post office on Rua Siqueira Campos. The trip takes about 30 minutes. All buses cost R$2 (65¢).

BY TAXI Coopseta Aeroporto (© **081/3464-4153**) specializes in airport service. Both Ligue-taxi (© **081/3428-6830**) and Tele-Taxi (© **081/3429-4242**) can be booked ahead of time.

BY METRÔ There's a metrô in Recife, but it's not very useful to tourists. The stations are too far from Boa Viagem to walk, and by the time you've taken a bus to the station to take the metrô downtown, you might as well just take the bus the whole way into town.

VISITOR INFORMATION

Recife's airport has a tourist information booth at the arrivals level (© **081/3462-4960**), open daily from 8am to 6pm. There's another information booth in Praça Boa Viagem (© **081/3463-3621**), open daily from 8am to 8pm. In Olinda, the tourist information office is located near the Largo do Amparo on Rua do Bonsucesso 183 (© **081/3439-9434**), open daily from 9am to 6pm. There is also a kiosk at the Praça do Carmo, where the buses from Recife arrive.

FAST FACTS To exchange currency, try **Banco do Brasil,** Rua Barão De Souza Leão 440, Boa Viagem (© **081/3462-3777**); in Olinda, Av. Getúlio Vargas 1470, Bairro Novo (© **081/3439-1344**). **Monaco Cambio,** Praça Joaquim Nabuco 19, Santo Antônio (© **081/3424-3727**); or **Colmeia Cambio,** Rua dos Navegantes 783, Boa Viagem (© **081/3465-3822**).

In an emergency, contact the **tourist police,** Praça Min. Salgado Filho s/n (© **081/3326-9603**). For medical attention, go to **Centro Hospitalar Albert Sabin,** Rua Senador Jose Henrique 141, Ilha do Leite (© **081/3421-5411**) For nonurgent cases, ask your hotel for a referral to the nearest walk-in clinic.

For Internet access, try **Olind@.com Cyber Café,** Praça João Pessoa 15, Carmo, Olinda (© **081/3429-4365**); it costs R$9 (US$3) per hour. There's also

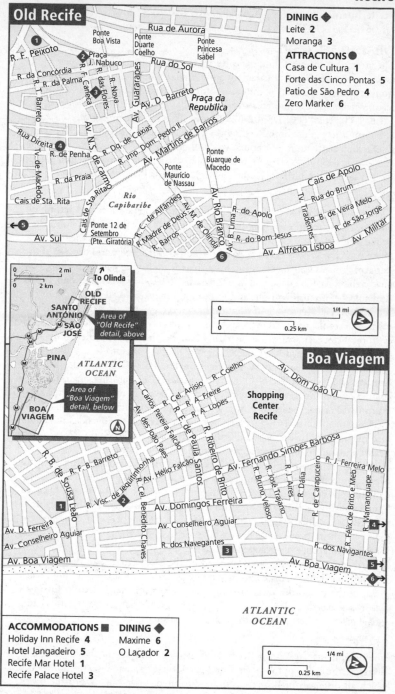

Recife

DINING ◆
Leite **2**
Moranga **3**

ATTRACTIONS ●
Casa de Cultura **1**
Forte das Cinco Pontas **5**
Patio de São Pedro **4**
Zero Marker **6**

Old Recife

Rua de Aurora
R. F. Peixoto
Ponte Boa Vista
Ponte Duarte Coelho
Ponte Princesa Isabel
Praça J. Nabuco
R. da Concórdia
R. da Palma
R. T. Barreto
R. das Flores
R. Nova
R. F. Carteca
Rua do Sol
Av. Guararapes
Av. D. Barreto
Praça da Republica
Rua Direita
R. de Penha
Av. N.S. de Carmo
R. Dq. de Caxias
R. Imp. Dom. Pedro II
Av. Martins de Barros
R. da Praia
Cais de Sta. Rita
Cais de Sta. Rita
Tv. de Macêdo
Rio Capibaribe
Ponte Maurício de Nassau
Ponte Buarque de Macedo
R. C. da Alfândeg
R. Madre de Deus
R. Barros
Av. M. de Olinda
Av. Rio Branco
R. B. Lima
R. do Apolo
R. do Bom Jesus
Cais de Apolo
Tv. Tiradentes
Rua do Brum
R. B. de Veira Melo
R. de São Jorge
Av. Militar
Av. Sul
Ponte 12 de Setembro (Pte. Giratória)
Av. Alfredo Lisboa

0 2 mi
0 2 km
↗ To Olinda
OLD RECIFE
SANTO ANTÓNIO
SÃO JOSÉ
Area of "Old Recife" detail, above
PINA
ATLANTIC OCEAN
Area of "Boa Viagem" detail, below
BOA VIAGEM

0 1/4 mi
0 0.25 km

Boa Viagem

Av. Dom João VI
R. Coelho
R. Cel. Anísio
R. A. Freire
R. A. Lopes
R. Carlos Pereira Falcão
R. des João Paés
R. E. de Paula Santos
Shopping Center Recife
R. Ribeiro de Brito
Av. Fernando Simões Barbosa
R. José Trajano
R. J. Aires
R. Dália
R. de Carapuceiro
R. J. Ferreira Melo
R. B. de Sousa Leão
R. R. F. B. Barreto
R. Visc. de Jequitinhonha
Av. Hélio Falcão
R. Cel. Benedito Chaves
Av. Domingos Ferreira
R. Bruno Veloso
R. Félix de Brito e Meb
R. Mamanguape
Av. D. Ferreira
Av. Conselheiro Aguiar
Av. Conselheiro Aguiar
R. dos Navegantes
R. dos Navegantes
Av. Boa Viagem
Av. Boa Viagem

ATLANTIC OCEAN

0 1/4 mi
0 0.25 km

ACCOMMODATIONS ■
Holiday Inn Recife **4**
Hotel Jangadeiro **5**
Recife Mar Hotel **1**
Recife Palace Hotel **3**

DINING ◆
Maxime **6**
O Laçador **2**

Recife Internet, Shopping Guararapes, Av. Barreto de Menezes 800, Piedade (© 081/3464-2107), which charges R$9 (US$3) per hour.

WHAT TO SEE & DO

The attraction of both Olinda and Recife lies not so much in particular sights as in the urban fabric. Particularly in Olinda, while any particular church wouldn't merit a special trip, the ensemble of all that 300- to 400-year-old architecture makes for a memorable stroll.

Luck Viagens (© 081/3302-6222; www.luckviagens.com.br) offers a range of bus tours to explore both Recife and Olinda. If your time is very limited, consider taking a city tour; in 4 hours, you will quickly see the highlights of Recife and Olinda (R$30/US$10). An interesting day trip is a visit to Itamaracá island, where the Dutch built Fort Orange in 1631; it costs R$75 (US$25).

OLINDA

The way to truly explore Olinda is by hitting the cobblestones and setting off on foot. Buses from Recife will drop you off at the Praça do Carmo, dominated by the lovely **N. S. do Carmo church** ⟨ᴿ⟩. The large leafy square on the front side of the church is known as **Praça da Abolição (Abolition Square)** because of the statue of Princess Isabel, who was responsible for abolishing slavery in 1888. Follow Avenida da Liberdade and you'll pass by the 1590 **Church of São Pedro Apostolo** before turning right and walking up the steep **Ladeira da Sé** to the **Igreja da Sé** ⟨ᴿ⟩. The square in front of the Igreja da Sé provides the best view in town. You see the red-tiled roofs and church towers of Olinda, and thick stands of tropical trees set against the sparkling blue ocean below. Further south, you get great views of Recife's skyline all the way to Boa Viagem.

The very steep **Ladeira da Misericordia** leads down towards the **Rua do Amparo** ⟨ᴿᴿ⟩. This is one of Olinda's prettiest streets, featuring small, brightly colored colonial houses packed with galleries, restaurants, and shops. The **Largo do Amparo** ⟨ᴿ⟩ has the feel of a little Mexican square. On the square itself, **N. S. do Amparo** (built in 1613) features two bell towers on the outside, and some nice tiles and gold work inside. Further up the hillside, **N. S. do Rosário dos Pretos** and **São João Batista** aren't worth hoofing it up the hill.

Leaving the square and following Rua Amparo until it becomes **Rua Treze de Maio,** you come to the **Mamulengo Puppet Museum** ⟨ᴿ⟩, which is open Tuesday through Friday from 9am to 5pm, Saturday through Monday from 11am to 5pm; admission is free. The small three-floor museum assembles puppets used in northeastern folk drama. The guide explains the puppets and then lets you play with them. Some have hidden levers that cause them to stick out their tongues—and other ruder appendages.

Further down, the Rua São Bento leads to the **Mosteiro de São Bento,** which is unfortunately now closed. From the monastery, Rua XV de Novembro leads down to the **Largo do Varadouro;** the large crafts market **Mercado Eufrasio Barbosa** is worth a visit. Those returning to Recife can take a bus from this square instead of returning to the Praça do Carmo.

RECIFE

The place to start a tour of Recife is at the **Zero Marker** in the heart of Old Recife. In the center of this open round plaza, there's a small disc, the point from which all distances in Pernambuco are measured. Gaze out toward the ocean from here, and about 98m (328 ft.) offshore, you'll see the long low reef from which the city draws its name.

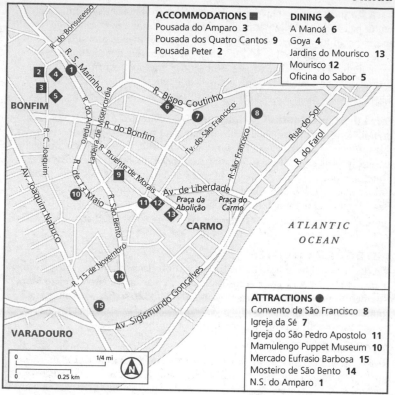

Olinda

ACCOMMODATIONS ■

Pousada do Amparo **3**
Pousada dos Quatro Cantos **9**
Pousada Peter **2**

DINING ◆

A Manoá **6**
Goya **4**
Jardins do Mourisco **13**
Mourisco **12**
Oficina do Sabor **5**

ATTRACTIONS ●

Convento de São Francisco **8**
Igreja da Sé **7**
Igreja do São Pedro Apostolo **11**
Mamulengo Puppet Museum **10**
Mercado Eufrasio Barbosa **15**
Mosteiro de São Bento **14**
N.S. do Amparo **1**

BONFIM

CARMO

ATLANTIC OCEAN

VARADOURO

0   1/4 mi
0   0.25 km

A block back from the Zero Marker is the **Rua do Bom Jesus.** The street and this whole island are the oldest part of Recife, founded not by the Portuguese but by the Dutch. Taking the Avenida Rio Branco across the bridge will lead you to **Santo Antônio,** called Mauritspolis under Dutch rule, after the founder Maurits van Nassau. The large green neoclassical square almost at the foot of the bridge was once van Nassau's private estate, but it is now the **Praça da República.** This pretty park, with a fountain circled by Imperial Palms and Roman statuary, is enclosed on three sides by grand beaux arts buildings: the **Palácio da Justiça,** the **Palácio do Campo das Princesas,** and the **Teatro Santa Isabel.**

Behind the Palácio da Justiça at Rua do Imperador Dom Pedro II 206, you pass by the **Capela Dourada (Golden Chapel).** Aptly named, its altar is a two-story arch of jacaranda and cedar, all covered in gold leaf. Christ hangs on a golden cross with gold and silver rays shining out behind his head.

Crossing Primeiro do Marco and sneaking south through the fun maze of narrow streets (parallel to but not on Av. Dantas Barreto), you will come—provided you find **Rua do Fogo** on the far side of Avenida N. S. do Carmo—to the **Pátio de São Pedro.** This broad cobblestone square is enclosed by dozens of small restored shops, all gaily painted in bright pinks and blues and greens.

Crossing Avenida Dantas Barreto from here, you come to the **N. S. de Carmo Basilica,** currently closed for repairs, and some blocks beyond that, the **Casa da Cultura** and the **Estação Geral,** Recife's former train station. In the other direction, a maze of fun and narrow streets leads to the **Mercado São Jose.**

Casa Da Cultura ⊛   This former jail was built in the shape of a cross, with a center hall and four hallways to allow the guards to stand in one spot and keep an eye on all four wings. The building has been modified hardly at all since its prison days; the cells, still with their original numbers, are now occupied by souvenir shops. The best time to visit is on Friday afternoon when there are concerts after 4pm. On Sunday, only a few stalls open.

Rua Floriano Peixoto, Santo Antônio. ℂ 081/3224-2850. Mon–Sat 9am–7pm; Sun 9am–1pm.

Forte das Cinco Pontas/City Museum ⊛⊛   This 1677 fort has been wonderfully restored; unfortunately, the city has crept out, leaving the once-seaside fort outflanked by a freeway. The city museum, which takes up two wings, is extremely well done. Two whole air-conditioned rooms are devoted to the Dutch period, and there's a wealth of maps and drawings of this early colony. Other rooms show the development of Recife over time; as late as the 1950s, Boa Viagem had nothing but a few lonely beach cottages.

Largo dos Cinco Pontas. ℂ 084/3224-8492. Admission R$3 (US$1) adults, R$1.50 (50¢) students and seniors, free for children 7 and under. Mon–Fri 9am–6pm; Sat–Sun 1–5pm. Bus: São Jose.

OUTDOOR ACTIVITIES

Wreck divers will be in heaven; the tricky coast off Recife's harbor is littered with shipwrecks, and at least 15 or so are diveable. For excursions, contact **Projeto Mar,** Rua Bernardino Pessoa 410, Boa Viagem (ℂ **081/3326-0162;** www.projetomar. com.br). Two dives including all the gear cost R$90 (US$30); a nondiving companion pays R$30 (US$10) to come along just for the boat ride.

SHOPPING

Recife's downtown neighborhood of **Santo Antônio** boasts a large number of small local shops. The streets around the Patio São Pedro, and in between Avenida N. S. do Carmo and Rua Primeiro de Março, are all jam-packed with little shops. Some of the alleys are so narrow that they resemble Asian street markets. The best time to explore these streets is weekdays during office hours, when it is busy and bustling.

Olinda's historic downtown also offers prime shopping. You will find many galleries and interesting shops once you start to explore the winding streets. Two markets sell a good variety of local handicrafts. **Mercado Eufrasio Barbosa** (or Mercado Varadouro) is located in the former customs house at Sigismundo Gonçalves s/n (ℂ **081/3439-1415**), and it's open Monday through Saturday from 9am to 6pm. Up the hill close to the Praça João Alfredo is another arts and crafts market, the **Mercado Ribeira,** Bernardo Vieira de Melo s/n (ℂ **081/3439-1660;** daily 9am–6pm). The merchants specialize in religious arts, paintings, woodcarvings, and regional crafts.

WHERE TO STAY
RECIFE
Recife's main hotel neighborhood is Boa Viagem beach, the closest you can get to downtown while still being in a safe neighborhood on a clean beach.

Very Expensive
Recife Palace Hotel ⊛⊛⊛   Size does matter. This hotel offers a prime location across the street from Boa Viagem beach, and the largest rooms in all of Recife. The amenities of a five-star hotel don't hurt. Recent renovations have left rooms looking fabulous: fresh and modern with pleasant lighting, blond wood, and soft-toned colors. All rooms have a bathtub and a partial view (superior

room) or full view (deluxe room) of the ocean. The suites are even bigger but considering how pleasant the superior and deluxe rooms are, it doesn't seem worth the extra money.

Av. Boa Viagem 4070, Recife, 51012-000 PE. © **0800-813161** or 081/3464-2500. Fax 081/3465-2525. www. lucsimhoteis.com.br. 295 units. High season R$350 (US$116) superior double; R$400 (US$133) deluxe double; R$550 (US$183) suite. 20% discount in low season. Children under 12 stay free in parent's room. Over 12, 25% extra bed. Wheelchair-accessible rooms available. **Amenities:** 2 restaurants; disco; bar; pool; gym; sauna; concierge; car rental; business center; salon; 24-hr. room service; babysitting; dry cleaning; laundry; tour desk. *In room:* A/C, TV, dataport, minibar, fridge, hair dryer, safe.

Expensive

Holiday Inn Recife ☆ *Kids*   Recently built to North American hotel standards, the rooms here are spacious and equipped with king-size beds, down pillows, and ample storage space. The two suites are especially spacious; the bedroom is very large, and the sitting room comes with a sofa bed, which allows a family of four to sleep comfortably.

Av. Domingos Fereira 3067, Boa Viagem, Recife, 51021-040 PE. © **0800/118-778** or 081/3465-7050. Fax 081/3326-2009. www.modesto.com.br. 130 units (shower only). R$240 (US$80) double; R$360 (US$120) suite. Extra person 25%. In low season doubles can be as low as R$99 (US$33). AE, DC, MC, V. Free parking. **Amenities:** Restaurant; bar; small pool; weight room; car rental; tour desk; 24-hr. room service; laundry; non-smoking rooms. *In room:* A/C, TV, dataport, minibar, fridge, hair dryer, safe.

Recife Mar Hotel ☆☆ *Kids*   The Mar is just 3 blocks from Boa Viagem beach and a short drive from the airport. Its guest rooms are comfortably furnished with nice firm beds, a breakfast table, and a desk. However, it's in the amenities that the hotel really shines. The large swimming pool has a beautiful waterfall and smaller children's pool; the breakfast buffet is one of the best we've ever seen in Brazil, with local dishes such as tapioca pancakes, corn cakes, scrambled eggs, fresh fruit, and a variety of excellent baked goods.

Rua Barão de Souza Leão 451, Boa Viagem, Recife, 51030-300 PE. © **081/3302-4444.** Fax 081/3302-4445. www.marhotel.com.br. 207 units. R$480–R$600 (US$160–US$200) double. Extra person about 25%. Children under 11 free in parent's room. AE, DC, MC, V. Free parking. Bus: Boa Viagem. **Amenities:** 2 restaurants; bar; large outdoor pool; health club; sauna; watersports rental; concierge; car rental; tour desk; business center; shopping arcade; salon; 24-hr. room service; massage; babysitting; laundry; dry cleaning; executive level rooms. *In room:* A/C, TV, dataport, minibar, fridge, hair dryer, safe.

Moderate

Hotel Jangadeiro ☆ *Value*   Overlooking Boa Viagem beach, Hotel Jangadeiro offers the best value in this upscale neighborhood. The hallways may look a little rough around the edges, but all of the rooms have recently been renovated and are spacious and bright. It's definitely worth paying a little bit extra for the oceanview rooms; all come with a balcony and offer stunning views of Boa Viagem beach. Bathrooms are spotless and modern.

Av. Boa Viagem 3114, Boa Viagem, Recife, 51020-001 PE. © **081/3465-3544.** Fax 081/3466-5786. www. jangadeirohotel.com.br. 93 units (shower only). R$140–R$160 (US$47–US$53) standard double; R$180–R$200 (US$60–US$67) oceanview double. Children under 8 stay free in parent's room. Over 8, 25% extra bed. AE, MC, V. Free parking. **Amenities:** Restaurant; small rooftop pool; 24-hr. room service; laundry service. *In room:* A/C, TV, dataport, minibar, fridge.

OLINDA

Olinda offers some of the nicest accommodations for those who appreciate small bed-and-breakfasts or inns at a fraction of the cost in Recife.

Expensive

Pousada do Amparo ☆☆☆   The most charming place to stay in all greater Recife is this concentration of two 200-year-old colonial buildings in the heart of historic Olinda. The building is perched on a hillside offering fabulous views. Inside, the owners have preserved the period feel with tile floors and lots of dark colonial furniture. At the same time, the addition of light wells and an internal courtyard space have given the building a wonderfully sunlit feel. All rooms are furnished with a combination of antiques and modern artwork, and some have verandas.

Rua do Amparo 199, Olinda, 53020-170 PE. ℂ 081/3439-1749. Fax 081/3419-6889. www.pousadadoamparo. com.br. 12 units (shower only). R$135–R$297 (US$45–US$99) double. Extra person about 25%. Children under 8 stay free in parent's room. V. Street parking. Bus: Rio Doce. **Amenities:** Restaurant; small pool; children's pool; sauna; car rental; laundry; garden; Internet (R$45/US$15 per hour). *In room:* A/C, TV, minibar, fridge, safe.

Moderate
Pousada dos Quatro Cantos ℛ   A lovely colonial building, the Pousada dos Quatro Cantos takes up the entire block, hence the name "four corners." The best rooms are the 13 units in the original heritage building. Rooms themselves are plainly but comfortably furnished with modern appliances and facilities. Standard rooms do not have bathrooms or air-conditioning. The best room in the house is the Veranda Suite, a spacious chamber overlooking the garden.

Rua Prudente de Morais 441, Carmo, Olinda PE. ℂ 081/3429-0220. www.pousada4cantos.com.br. 20 units (shower only). R$72 (US$24) annex double, no bathroom, no A/C, fan only; R$103 (US$34) standard double; R$121 (US$41) deluxe double; R$176 (US$59) veranda suite. Children under 6 stay free in parent's room. Extra bed, additional 25% of room rate. Seasonal discounts up to 30%. MC, V. Street parking. **Amenities:** Car rental; laundry. *In room:* A/C, TV, fridge.

Inexpensive
Pousada Peter ℛℛ ⟨Value⟩   Spread out over three levels on the hillside, the *pousada* offers magnificent views of Olinda and Recife from each floor. The eight rooms are small but spotless and simply furnished; six rooms come with private bathroom (showers only), and two rooms share a bathroom. Room no. 6 is the only one to avoid—the dull tile on the walls gives it all the coziness of an emergency room. The common spaces are all beautifully decorated.

Rua do Amparo 215, Olinda, 53020-170 PE. ℂ 081/3439-2171. www.pousadapeter.com.br. 12 units (2 w/shared bathroom). R$65 (US$22) double w/shared bathroom; R$75–R$130 (US$25–US$43) double w/private bathroom. Children under 5 stay free in parent's room. Extra bed 25%. No credit cards. Limited street parking. **Amenities:** Restaurant; bar; outdoor pool; laundry. *In room:* A/C, TV, fridge.

WHERE TO DINE
RECIFE
Leite ℛ   One of the oldest restaurants in all Brazil, Leite is an oasis of old-world elegance with fine linen and china. The menu includes a variety of meat dishes such as steak au poivre and, of course, seafood; the *sinfonia maritima* is a delicious sauté with lobster, fish, oysters, and prawns.

Praça Joaquim Nabuco 147, Santo Antonio. ℂ 081/3224-7977. www.recifecentro.com.br/moranga.htm. Main courses R$18–R$36 (US$6–US$12). AE, DC, MC, V. Mon–Fri lunch only, 11am–4pm.

Maxine's ℛ SEAFOOD   Located right across from the beach in Pina, Maxine's spacious wooden structure allows for big windows and big views. The menu offers a good selection of seafood dishes: rich seafood soups, juicy shrimp, and fresh lobster as well as a daily selection of grilled fish and seafood stews.

Av. Boa Viagem 21, Pina. ℂ 081/3326-5314. Main courses R$18–R$39 (US$6–US$13) for 2. AE, DC, MC, V. Daily 10am–2am. Bus: Boa Viagem.

Moranga ⟨Value⟩ KILO/BUFFET   To take a bit of a break from sightseeing, tuck into Moranga. The excellent self-service buffet offers at least 10 salads and

15 hot dishes, including *morangas* (seafood stew with pumpkin), palm-heart cream, and carne-de-sol, a tasty dried meat.

Rua das Flores 129, Centro. © 081/3224-1573. Buffet R$21 (US$7) per kilo (2¼ lb.). AE, V. Mon–Fri 11am–3pm.

O Laçador 🌟 GRILLED MEAT   Just a few blocks from the beach, O Laçador is a very popular *churrasco* restaurant. You have the option of the stuff-yourself-silly *rodízio* menu or the more civilized self-service pay-for-what-you-eat option. Both options include a selection of excellent side dishes as well as appetizers such as cold cuts, pastries *(bolinhos)*, and salads.

Av. Visconde de Jequitinhonha 138-A, Boa Viagem. © 081/3423-2521. R$27 (US$9) for 2; R$12 (US$4) per child. For kilo service R$18 (US$6) per kilo (2¼ lb.; 11am–1am). AE, MC, V. Daily 11am–1am. Bus: Boa Viagem.

OLINDA

Goya 🌟🌟 BRAZILIAN   Goya serves what's called *regional* in Brazil: local recipes and fresh local ingredients, served up, in Goya's case, with creativity and flair. Typically, creative dishes include lobster medallions flambéed in *cachaça*, cod grilled with pineapple and served with melon or mango, and—more traditionally—a rich seafood-and-coconut-milk *moqueca*.

Rua do Amparo 157. © 081/3439-4875. Reservations accepted. Main courses R$18–R$35 (US$6–US$12). AE, DC, MC, V. Daily noon–5pm and 6pm–midnight. Closed Tues. Bus: Rio Doce.

Jardins do Mourisco *Value* KILO   For a quick inexpensive lunch, try this restaurant set in a lovely garden with stone statues and outdoor seating. The kilo buffet offers hearty home-cooked food with a good variety of salads, beans, rice, *farofa,* and a selection of meat and fish.

Augustino Gonçalves 7, Carmo, Olinda. © 081/3429-1390. R$15 (US$5) per kilo (2¼ lb.). No credit cards. Daily noon–5pm.

Oficina do Sabor 🌟🌟 BRAZILIAN/REGIONAL   Oficina do Sabor's well deserved reputation has spread far beyond Olinda and Recife. The most popular dish is *Jerimum Frevo é,* shrimp and lobster with a passion-fruit sauce served in the shell of a jerimum, a kind of pumpkin. Another good choice is the jerimum filled with octopus stew in coconut sauce. The restaurant is in a lovely heritage building with a killer patio.

Rua do Amparo 335, Olinda. © 081/3429-3331. www.oficinadosabor.com. Reservations recommended for weekends. R$25–R$42 (US$8–US$14), except for the Jerimum Frevo é, all dishes serve 2. AE, DC, MC, V. Tues–Fri noon–4pm and 6pm–midnight; Sat noon–midnight; Sun noon–5pm.

RECIFE & OLINDA AFTER DARK

Recife's historic downtown has undergone a complete face-lift and has been revived as a cultural and entertainment district. The activities happen around the **Rua do Bom Jesus;** lined with at least 15 bars and restaurants, this is one of the best places in town almost any night of the week.

One of Old Recife's nicest bars is the **Arsenal do Chopp,** Praça Arthur Oscar 59 at the corner of Rua do Bom Jesus (© **081/3224-6259**), with tables spread out over the sidewalk, leaving you in the middle of the action. Very popular is **Pina de Copacabana,** Rua da Moeda 121 (© **081/9127-9435**), just a few blocks from the Rua de Bom Jesus. On Tuesday, there is usually a live band, and on Friday and Saturday, various deejays keep things moving.

In Boa Viagem, the favorite nightspot is the **Polo Pina,** an area around Pina beach and Avenida Herculano Bandeira de Melo. **Marinhos,** Av. Herculano Bandeira de Melo 77 (© 081/3465-4742), has live music and MPB such as samba and chorinho on Friday. Another favorite for lovers of MPB is **Baracho,**

Rua Carneiro Pessoa 208, Pina (© 081/3224-3518). Just a few blocks in from the beach, this bar has samba and *choro* on Thursday and more MPB on Saturday with house singer Dalva Torres.

Olinda is not known for its nightlife; most folks settle for wine and conversation over a late-night supper. However, there are a few other options. The **Uruguay Club,** Av. Prudente de Morais 281 (© 081/3439-8552), is a wine-bar and restaurant with live classical, jazz, and blues Monday through Saturday. The **Crazy Dance Club,** Rua do Amparo 27 (© 081/3429-3953), is a gay dance club with karaoke and go-go dancers; it's open Thursday through Sunday.

A SIDE TRIP TO PORTO DE GALINHAS

Porto de Galinhas is one of the nicest beach destinations in the northeast. There are no high-rise buildings, just small *pousadas* and a few low-rise hotels. The town of Porto de Galinhas boasts perhaps four streets, enough for a dozen restaurants, a bank, some surf shops, and a beachside bar or two. **Cupe beach** stretches 4km (2½ miles) north from town; it's wide and warm, punctuated at either end by small coral reefs full of fish. Around the point in the other direction, **Maracaípi beach** is the place for surfers; the beach regularly hosts national and international surfing competitions.

ESSENTIALS
GETTING THERE   Only 69km (43 miles) from Recife by car, you can take BR 101 south until it connects with the PE 60. Stay on the PE 60 until the turnoff for the PE 38 that leads to Porto de Galinhas; destinations and exits are well marked. You can also take a taxi from Recife airport to Porto de Galinhas; the ride will cost R$120 (US$40) for up to four people with luggage. Don't rely on the meter, though—agree on a price beforehand.

Buses for Porto de Galinhas leave daily from 6:30am to 6:30pm every hour on the half-hour from the Avenida Dantas Barreto bus terminal in downtown Recife (across from N. S. do Carmo). Tickets are R$6 (US$2), and the journey takes about 1½ hours.

VISITOR INFORMATION   The tourist office is located at Rua da Esperança 188 (© 081/3552-1480; www.portodegalinhas.com.br). It's open Monday through Friday from 9am to 5pm, Saturday and Sunday from 9am to 3pm.

WHAT TO SEE & DO IN PORTO DE GALINHAS
The main attraction at Porto de Galinhas is the beach, whether you swim, surf, snorkel, or snooze. If that gets dull, the options include nature hikes, trips to nearby islands, or dive trips to reefs offshore.

The best way to see the local beaches is to head out in a buggy. These tiny cars zoom effortlessly across the sand while you hang out the back. A 2-hour tour costs R$15 (US$5), leaving from Avenida Beira Mar at the main square (© 081/9192-0280).

The coast just off Porto de Galinhas is lined with coral reefs. Although they're not Great Barrier Reef quality, at low tide, these form natural pools that trap hundreds of tropical fishes. Most pools are close enough that you could swim out, but another fun way of getting close is by taking a *jangada,* the one-sail fishing raft used by local fishermen. For R$9 (US$3) per person, local sailors will take you out and provide you with a mask and snorkel.

The specialist in soft adventure in town is the firm **Pé no Mangue** ("Foot in the Mangroves"), Rua da Esperança 101, First Floor (© 081/9942-8715; www. penomangue.com), run by a congenial pair of young São Paulo refugees. They have a wide range of outings, all under R$45 (US$15) including guide and transfer. They include 2½-hour guided nature hikes through Atlantic rainforest or low-lying mangrove forest; a 2-hour kayaking tour down a wide mangrove-lined river to the sea; 2-hour horseback rides on very slow horses through Atlantic rainforest; snorkeling by starlight in the natural pools just offshore; and several boat trips, ranging from a 3-hour *jangada* trip to the less-visited coral reefs off Maracaípi to 4- and 6-hour trips to off-shore islands and local beaches.

Porto Point, Praça Principal s/n (© **081/3552-1111**), is an excellent resource for all kinds of watersports. They rent surfboards (long and short) and body boards for R$5 (US$1.65) per hour or R$15 (US$5) per day. Short fiberglass ocean kayaks (no spray skirts) rent at the same rate. Mask/snorkel combos rent for R$10 (US$3.35) per day. The shop also rents bicycles for R$5 (US$1.65) per hour. If you need surf lessons, contact **Luizinho** at © **081/3552-2095.** Lessons are given on Maracaípe beach.

WHERE TO STAY IN PORTO DE GALINHAS

Accommodations are mostly in small family-run *pousadas* and a few larger cabana-style hotels. Prices are low, and the quality of the accommodations is high.

Located 2km (1 mile) from the village, **Hotel Armação de Porto** ⍟, Praia de Porto de Galinhas (© **081/3471-1025;** www.hotelarmacao.com.br), attracts a young and active crowd. The beach has a volleyball court as well as a great bar that serves up fresh seafood and drinks while you wiggle your toes in the sand. Built as a sprawling low-rise hotel, the rooms are cleverly spaced to allow for a maximum of privacy. All rooms are spacious and well furnished with comfortable beds; in high season, they cost R$210 to R$264 (US$70–US$88).

Pousada Marahu ⍟, Praça 2, Lote 1 (© **081/3552-1700;** www.pousada marahu.com.br), provides a convenient option for those who want to stay in the village. The rooms are all a good size and very comfortably decorated; all have a veranda or a patio with a hammock for lazing about. Rooms cost R$120 (US$40) in the high season. The Swiss owners of **Pousada Beira Mar** ⍟⍟, Av. Beira Mar 12 (©/fax **081/3552-1052;** www.pousadabeiramar.com.br), have certainly capitalized on its prime beach location in the heart of Porto de Galinhas, putting a large patio with deck chairs and bar service seaside. The three upstairs deluxe rooms (nos. 10, 11, and 12) make the most of the location, with huge private terraces equipped with hammocks. The eight standard-size rooms lack terraces but are still roomier than the local norm and come with firm top-quality mattresses. Rooms cost R$174 to R$321 (US$58–US$107).

At the **Beira Mar Porto de Galinhas Hotel,** Av. Beira Mar s/n (© **081/3552-2088;** www.mvm.com.br/beiramarhotel), the rooms aren't spectacular, but the view's fantastic. With the exception of four (nos. 5, 16, 17, and 21), each of the rooms has a balcony facing one of the prettiest beaches in northern Brazil. Rooms cost R$100 (US$33). On the hotel grounds, there's a medium-size pool, but if it doesn't tickle your fancy, hop the small stone wall, take 10 long strides across the sand, and splash, you're in the ocean.

WHERE TO DINE IN PORTO DE GALINHAS

One of the best restaurants in the region, **Beijupirá,** Via Porto de Galinhas s/n (© **081/3552-2354**), is also one of the loveliest. Set in a garden aglow with hundreds of candles and lanterns, Beijupirá's cute and whimsical decorations offer plenty of eye candy. The menu offers seafood cooked up with interesting spice mixes and a blend of sweet and savory.

One of the best views of the Porto de Galinhas beach is from the patio of **Tropical Tempura House,** Av. Beira Mar s/n (© **081/3552-1590**). The menu lists traditional Japanese dishes as well as local favorites. On the Japanese side, you can order a variety of sashimi or sushi, teppanyaki, and yakisoba noodles. For the regional cuisine, expect all the local standards: *camarão a Bahiana* (spicy shrimp with coconut milk), grilled fish, and seafood stews.

Also on the waterfront, **Peixe na Telha,** Av. Beira Mar s/n (© **081/3552-1323**), is an excellent seafood restaurant that's open all day. It's a great spot to grab some appetizers and a beer.

8 Natal

2,680km (1,661 miles) NE of Rio de Janeiro, 2,981km (1,848 miles) NE of São Paulo, 1,111km (689 miles) NE of Salvador

Natal has been overlooked for much of its history, noticed only when someone else tried to take it away. The Portuguese founded a town on the banks of the Potengi River only to drive out the French, who tried to establish a base from which to raid Portuguese shipping. The laying of the fort's foundation was celebrated with a Mass on December 25, 1599, and so the city was named *Natal* (the Portuguese word for Christmas). Natal's real glory days wouldn't come until World War II, when Americans used Natal as an air and communications base. The closest point in the Americas to Africa, the city became known as the "Trampoline of Victory." These days, the big boom is in tourism. Natal today is a sprawling, modern place, a city of little history and less culture. What it does have is endless sunshine, lots of beaches for surfing and tanning, and dunes—glorious dunes, hundreds of feet high and spilling down to within inches of the seashore.

ESSENTIALS
GETTING THERE
BY PLANE   Natal is served by **TAM, VASP, Gol,** and **Varig.** Flights arrive and depart daily from all major cities in Brazil. All flights arrive at **Aeroporto Augusto Severino,** Rua Eduardo Gomes s/n (© **084/643-1811**), about 15km (9 miles) from downtown and just a few miles from Ponta Negra beach. Taxis from the airport are inexpensive, about R$15 to R$21 (US$5–US$7) to Ponta Negra and R$30 (US$10) to Praia dos Artistas, close to downtown.

BY BUS   Long-distance buses arrive at the **Rodoviária,** Av. Cap. Mor Gouveia 1237, Cidade Esperança (© **084/205-4377**), about 5km (3 miles) from downtown and Ponta Negra beach.

GETTING AROUND
Modern and sprawling and not especially pretty—that's Natal in a nutshell. The original city was founded on a peninsula between the Potengi River and the Atlantic Ocean. Just off the tip of the peninsula, where ocean and river meet, the original **Forte de Reis Magos** still stands, a forgotten bit of the 17th century. Where the fort's causeway touches the mainland, the 21st century begins—a modern ocean-side boulevard that, under various names and guises, runs from here south through the length of the city and out into the dunes beyond. About 3km (1¾ miles) south of the fort, the street is called **Avenida Presidente Café Filho,** and the surrounding neighborhood is **Praia dos Artistas.** This is one of the city's main nightlife areas. There are also some good hotels and a few restaurants.

The road continues, becoming Avenida Governo Silvio Pedroso, then **Via Costeira,** which runs for some 9km (5½ miles) between the ocean and a large

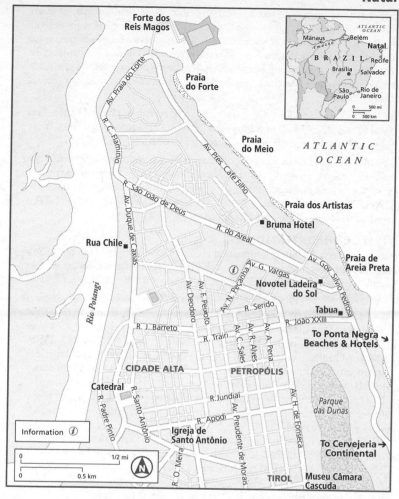

off-limits nature preserve called **Parque das Dunas.** Where the park ends, the road goes over a small headland and becomes **Estrada de Ponta Negra,** the backbone of the city's best beach neighborhood, **Ponta Negra.**

Going the other direction from the Forte dos Reis Magos, along the banks of the Rio Potengi, you come to the old dock area around the **Rua Chile,** a popular nightlife destination. A little further south and up the hill, you come to **Centro,** also called the **Cidade Alta,** the commercial heart of Natal.

North of Natal, the dunes and beaches begin as soon as you cross the river. This area is called the **Litoral Norte (north coast).** The first settlement in the Literal Norte is the small, quiet village of **Genipabu,** about 25km (15 miles) north of downtown Natal. Once a fishing village, Genipabu now caters to tourists who come to swim at the beach and buggy through the huge surrounding dunes.

BY BUS   Most visitors use the bus to get from Ponta Negra to Centro, and vice versa. In Ponta Negra, buses run along Estrada Ponta Negra. For downtown, look for buses marked CENTRO or CIDADE ALTA. Bear in mind that there are two routes. Buses with signs saying VIA COSTEIRA follow the coast as far as Praia dos Artistas and then cut across to Centro. Other CENTRO buses use the inland route along Avenida Prudente de Morais or Avenida Hermes da Fonseca. To return to Ponta Negra, any bus that says PONTA NEGRA or even VIA COSTEIRA will do. Unlike in some cities, you enter these buses through the front. Fare is R$1.50 (50¢).

BY TAXI   You can hail a taxi anywhere. To reserve one, phone **Disque Taxi Natal** (© 084/223-7388) or **Rádio Táxi** (© 084/221-5666). A taxi from Ponta Negra to Praia dos Artistas will cost about R$15 to R$21 (US$5–US$7)

BY CAR   Natal is an easy city for driving; streets are wide, traffic light, and the road along the coast will take you most places you want to go. Except in downtown, parking is never a problem. Among the companies to try: **Localiza** (© 084/206-5296 or 0800/992-000); **Avis** (© 0800/198-456); **Unidas** (© 0800/121-121); **Hertz** (© 084/207-3399); and **Interlocadora** (© 0800/138-000).

VISITOR INFORMATION

Natal's **airport** has a tourist information center (© 084/643-1811) in the arrivals hall; it's open daily from 9am to 5pm. The **main tourist information center** is in Natal's Centro de Turismo, Rua Aderbal de Figueiredo 980, Petrópolis (© **084/211-6149**). See "Shopping," below, for more details.

FAST FACTS   To exchange money, try **Banco do Brasil,** Banco do Brasil, Av. Rio Branco 510, Cidade Alta (© **084/216-4640**), which also has a 24-hour ATM; Sunset Cambio, Av. Hermes da Fonseca 628, Tirol (© **084/212-2552**); or Master Cambio, Rua Jundiaí 710, Tirol (© **084/221-4490**). The **American Express** office is at Av. Hermes da Fonseca 1542 (© **084/211-0880**); it's open Monday through Friday from 10am to 4pm.

For medical attention, to go **Monsenhor Walfredo Gurgel,** the largest hospital in the city and in Rio Grande do Norte state; it's located at Avenida Salgado Filho s/n, Tirol (© 084/221-4243).

For Internet access, visit **Sobre Ondas** restaurant, Rua Erivan Franca, Beiramar, Ponta Negra (© 084/219-4222), which has an Internet cafe with four terminals. Cost for 1 hour is R$9 (US$3.35). **Gitana Cyber Café,** Av. Gov. Silvio Pedrosa 18, in Praia dos Artistas (© 084/202-4394), has the best hours (Tues–Sun 11am–4am), but frequently there's a wait. Cost is R$6 (US$2) for 1 hour.

WHAT TO SEE & DO

Natal is a small city with a limited number of historical attractions. If you've already been or will go to Salvador or Olinda, the man-made bits of Natal will seem a little empty. That's fine; odds are you're here to see those famous dunes.

OUTDOOR FUN

AEROBUNDA JACUMÃ   The perfect antidote to the high-tech world of the American amusement park. At Lagoa Jacumã, Litoral Norte, Km 35, there's a dune about 60m (200 ft.) high. At its foot is a big lake. At the top of the dune someone has hammered in three telephone poles to make a scaffold, then attached a thick rope from there to another peg on the far side of the lake. To execute the *aerobunda,* you slide your butt into a sling hanging from a pulley attached to the line. The attendant then lets go. You scream down towards the lake, gathering speed and momentum. Splash! Huge fun. A couple of 12-year-olds stand by on a raft just in case you can't swim (a surprising number of Brazilians can't). Once on shore, you hop into a rickety iron cart, wave your arm at the guy on the donkey engine, and he hauls you up the dune so you can go again. If you tell the attendant you want your ride *com emoção* (translated roughly, in this case, as "with excitement"), he bounces you up and down before letting go. Cost is R$3 (US$1) per ride, and it's open daily from 8am to 5:30pm. For more information, call © 084/228-2402.

BUGGY EXPEDITIONS 🏵🏵🏵   The best and only way to see the dunes, beaches, and lagoons is to rent a buggy and driver. Buggies have the classic fiberglass body, roll bar, fat tires, and noisy air-cooled engine. Prices are slightly negotiable but average out around R$150 (US$50) for a full day for up to four people. A typical expedition goes up the coast to Maracajaú where, at low tide, you can snorkel in the natural pools in the offshore coral reef. The buggy then putters back along the shoreline, stopping for lunch and for a bit of *aerobunda*-ing. At one or two points on the trip back, you'll also have to float your buggy over estuaries on little balsa rafts. An hour or so before sunset, the driver will take you in to Genipabu for a wicked tour through the extreme dune park.

A shorter half-day trip south along the coast as far as Praia da Pipa should cost around R$60 (US$20). You don't have to seek out buggy drivers; if you're on the beach at Ponta Negra, Praia dos Artistas, or Genipabu, they will find you, but here are some contacts just in case: **SoBuggy** (© 084/236-2991; www.sobuggy. com.br); (in Genipabu) **Villa do Sol** (© 084/225-2132).

JANGADA **RIDING**   A *jangada* is a narrow raft made of balsa wood (nowadays augmented with Styrofoam) and equipped with just one triangular sail. Taking a *jangada* is a quiet, gentle way to get out to the small offshore reefs. These little boats are still used by local fishermen, many of whom will happily augment their income by taking you to the reefs or for a quick sail. You'll find them along Genipabu Beach. Cost is R$9 (US$3) per person for an hour or so.

SANDBOARDING   Sandboarding is worth doing as long as you believe that no sport is too stupid to be tried at least once. As snowboarders, we felt obligated. So we strapped our bare beet to a pair of heavy boards, hopped into a downhill crouch, and down we went . . . sort of. Turns out that sand doesn't glide nearly as well as snow; it takes effort to get down. Still, it was an experience worth remembering this winter as we put on three layers of clothing to rip down a snowcapped mountain. If you're interested, look for the entrepreneurs at the south end of Genipabu Beach; cost is R$5 (US$1.65) per trip (less, if you bargain).

SNORKELING AT MARACAJAÚ 🏵🏵   The entire coast north and south of Natal is hemmed with shallow coral reefs that make for perfect snorkeling. Nowhere are they more impressive than in Maracajaú, about 1 hour north of Natal. A stop here is often included in a full-day buggy tour; if not, ask your buggy driver. You need to time your arrival with low tide to get the most out of your snorkeling. From the beach, a boat takes you about 7km (4¼ miles) offshore to a permanently moored diving platform. At low tide, the honeycomb of reefs form natural pools rich in tropical fish and other marine life. As the maximum depth is about 4.8m (16 ft.), these pools can be easily explored with just a mask and snorkel. The water is crystal clear and warm. It's up to you how long you stay out here; boats go back and forth all the time. When the tide starts to come in, however, the water gets rougher and the pools too deep for easy snorkeling. Expect to spend at least 2 hours. Contact **Maracajaú Diver,** Praia de Maracajaú (© 084/261-6200, or 084/9983-4264 cellphone; www.maracajau diver.com.br). Snorkeling costs R$42 (US$14) adults, R$21 (US$7) for children 6 to 12, free for children under 5.

SURFING   The beach at Ponta Negra is a great place to learn to surf. Waves vary from small and manageable to large and exciting. Marcelo Alves of **Sem Limites** surf school is a great instructor (© 084/9418-4030). One-on-one instruction will get you up on the board in no time. Lessons cost R$15 (US$5) per hour. The school is in a tent about halfway along Ponta Negra beach.

ORGANIZED TOURS

ADVENTURE TOURS   If you can't get enough of the coast, consider the 4-day adventure trip from Natal 500km (310 miles) up the coast to Fortaleza. On the way you'll visit 85 beaches, countless dunes, pocket deserts, and salt mines. The trip is done in a comfortable air-conditioned Land Rover. Contact **Aventura Expedições** for more information, Rua Mipibu 758, Petrópolis, Natal (© 084/206-4949; www.aventuraturismo.com.br). The trip costs R$1,200 (US$400) per person including all meals, refreshments, and accommodations.

BOAT TOURS   Various companies offer 2-hour boat trips up the Potengi River. You will have time for a swim and the chance to see Natal and the surrounding area from the water. The trip costs R$25 (US$8). Contact **Marina Badaué** (© 084/238-2065; www.marinabadaue.com.br). The trip to **Barra de Cunhú** takes you to the mangroves south of Natal and includes time on the beach. Contact **Tropical Tur** (© 084/219-6377; www.tropicaltour.com.br). The 3-hour trip starts at R$50 (US$17) including pickup from your hotel.

ECOTOURS   **Manary Ecourismo** specializes in ecotourism but instead of focusing on the beaches, it takes people to the unexplored interior. Trips include visits to beautiful rock formations, some with petroglyphs made by Brazil's early inhabitants. Walk where the dinosaurs did and learn more about the natural history of the region. Packages include 2-, 3-, 4- and 5-day trips. For more information call © 084/219-2900, or check the website (www.manary.com.br) for information in English and photos of the tours.

SHOPPING

Just like Recife's Casa da Cultura, Natal transformed its former prison complex into a crafts market, **Centro de Turismo,** Rua Aderbal de Figueiredo 980, Petrópolis (© 084/211-6149). About 40 crafts shops, an art gallery, and a coffee shop are now housed in the cells and provide an easy one-stop shopping for local crafts. The best-known items are the handmade white-linen tablecloths and napkins. You will also find hammocks, T-shirts, woodwork, and lots of sweets made with sugar cane and coconut. Prices are negotiable, and shopkeepers let you browse freely, often welcoming you with the phrase *"Fica a vontade"* (roughly translated as "Take your time, be at home"). The market is a steep 15-minute walk uphill from Praia dos Artistas, and is open daily from 9am to 7pm.

In Praia dos Artistas, on Avenida Pres. Cafe Filho s/n, is the large **Centro Municipal de Artesanato** (© 084/202-4971). Dozens of booths are packed with tacky souvenir T-shirts and trinkets as well as nice locally made handicrafts of linen, leather, and lace. The colored-sand bottles are one of the most typical souvenirs from this area—intricate designs are made with layer upon layer of sand and poured into a tiny bottle. The market is open daily from 10am to 10pm.

WHERE TO STAY
PONTA NEGRA

Ponta Negra is the most popular beach within the city limits. It's wide, clean and busy, with good waves for surfing. A pleasant waterfront walkway runs along the beach past a number of beachside restaurants and *barracas*. Downtown Natal is a

15-minute cab ride or a 30- to 40-minute trip by city bus. The main road along the ridge above the hotels (known as either Estrada do Ponta Negra or Avenida Eng. Roberto Freire) is wide, barren, and unpleasant for walking—perhaps the reason Ponta Negra has never developed a nightlife scene.

Very Expensive

Manary Praia Hotel ★★★   Every town has one, the small hotel with not a hair out of place. In Ponta Negra, it's the Manary Praia. Done up like a Spanish hacienda, with old dark-beam, red-tile roofs, and large cool flagstones on the floor, this hotel is a member of the Roteiro de Charme association of select inns and *pousadas*. The location is premium, with a large deck—and two pools, including a children's pool—facing out over sea. In the rooms, the mattresses, linen, and furniture are all top-notch. All rooms come with a balcony and view of the ocean. The hotel also offers a variety of ecotours, several of which are not available from other tour operators in town.

Rua Francisco Gurgel 9067, Praia de Ponta Negra, Natal, 59090-050 RN. ⓒ/fax **84/219-2900**. www.manary. com.br. 26 units. R$300–R$375 (US$100–US$125) double; R$450 (US$150) suite. Extra person about 20%. Children under 7 stay free in parent's room. Off-season discounts (20%–30%) Mar–Aug. AE, DC, MC, V. Free parking. Bus: Ponta Negra. **Amenities:** Restaurant; bar; small outdoor pool, children's pool; game room; eco-tourism-focused tour desk; business center; 24-hr. room service; laundry. *In room:* A/C, TV, dataport, minibar, hair dryer, safe.

Expensive

Visual Praia Hotel ★★   It will be tough to find a nicer spot at this price with such a fabulous location. Right on the sea wall in Ponta Negra, the Visual Praia Hotel provides direct access to the lovely beach just below. Sought after by Scandinavian, Italian, and Portuguese tourists, this lovely hotel has recently been expanded to include another 32 apartments. Rooms are all very comfortable and beautifully furnished with blond wood and marble desktops. Breakfast is served on the patio overlooking the beach.

Rua Francisco Gurgel 9184, Praia Ponta Negra, Natal, 59090-050 RN. ⓒ **084/646-4646**. www.visualpraiahotel. com.br. 86 units (shower only). High season R$275–R$325 (US$92–US$108) double. Extra person R$45 (US$15). 30% discount in low season. Children under 6 stay free in parent's room. AE, DC, MC, V. Free parking. Bus: Ponta Negra. **Amenities:** Restaurant; bar; large pool; children's playground; laundry service. *In room:* A/C, TV, minibar, fridge, safe.

PRAIA DOS ARTISTAS

On the beach a little east of downtown, Praia dos Artistas is the nightlife and entertainment hub of Natal. The area has a range of hotels, from small and moderate to large and expensive. The beach is not as nice as Ponta Negra in the daytime, but there's more to do at night. And if you're going to be spending your days exploring the coast in a buggy, Praia dos Artistas is actually a more convenient jumping-off point.

Expensive

Novotel Ladeira do Sol ★   This 5-year-old hotel offers international level service at a quite reasonable price. Rooms are only moderate-size but come with good quality fixtures and furniture. Suites are the same as rooms, but have a sitting room attached. Both suites and rooms come with French doors leading to a small veranda. However, because the hotel is built into the hillside, the only rooms offering much of a view are nos. 351 through 360, the ones on the third floor of the north wing. Should these prove unavailable, the pool deck and patio bar offer outstanding views.

Rua Fabrício Pedrosa 915, Natal, 59014-030 RN. ⓒ **800/NOVOTEL** in the U.S. and Canada, or 84/202-1133. Fax 84/202-1168. www.novotelnatal.com.br. 100 units. R$221 (US$74) double; R$340 (US$113) suite. Extra person about 25%. Children under 13 stay free in parent's room. AE, DC, MC, V. Free parking. Bus: Via Costeira. **Amenities:** Restaurant; bar; outside pool; children's pool; business center; 24-hr. room service; laundry; nonsmoking rooms. *In room:* A/C, TV, dataport, minibar, hair dryer, safe.

Moderate

Bruma Hotel   This is a clean and unpretentious little hotel, with a small pool and sun deck looking out over the fun and *movimento* on the Praia dos Artistas. Though somewhat spartan, standard rooms come with all the requisite equipment: shower, (somewhat soft) bed, writing desk, and frigobar. Room nos. 101 and 102 have all this plus large windows looking out over the beach. Room nos. 201, 202, 301, and 302 (the suites) have all this plus verandas with a commanding view over the bay. Considering the price jump from room to suite is only $12, it's worth the effort, if only so you can lie back in your hammock (standard equipment with the suites) and contemplate the finer points of surfing.

Av. Presidente Café Filho 1176 (at Ladeira do Sol), Praia dos Artistas, Natal, 59090 RN. ℂ 084/202-4303 or 84/202-2847. www.hotelbruma.com.br. 29 units. R$65–R$98 (US$22–US$33) double; R$95–R$115 (US$32–US$38) suite. Extra person about 20%. Children under 6 stay free in parent's room. AE, DC, MC, V. Supervised street parking. Bus: Via Costeira. **Amenities:** Bar; small outdoor pool; laundry. *In room:* A/C, TV, minibar.

GENIPABU

Located on the beach 25km (15 miles) north of Natal, Genipabu is a quiet beach location for those with no need of nightlife.

Expensive

Hotel Genipabu 🌟🌟 *Finds*   Just a 30-minute drive from Natal, Hotel Genipabu's hilltop location offers spectacular views over Genipabu beach, the surrounding nature reserve, and Natal in the distance. All 24 rooms have balconies with ocean views and hammocks to relax in, and the rooms are very spacious and comfortably furnished. The beach of Genipabu is about 765m (2,250 ft.) away, but the hotel offers free transportation to and from the beach; pickup from the airport can be arranged for R$50 (US$17) per person. While you are here, you can frolic on the beach, check out the large sand dunes right on the beach (you are allowed to climb these, unlike in Ponta Negra), or head out for a day of dune-buggying or snorkeling.

Praia de Genipabu s/n, Caixa Postal 2740, Genipabu, Natal, RN. ℂ **084/225-2063.** Fax 084/225-2071. www.genipabu.com.br. 24 units (shower only). R$180 (US$60) double. Extra person about 25%. Children under 11 stay free in parent's room. AE, DC, MC, V. Free parking. **Amenities:** Restaurant; bar; large outdoor pool; game room; tour desk; courtesy car (free shuttle to the beach); limited room service; laundry. *In room:* A/C, TV, minibar, fridge, hair dryer.

Moderate

Hotel Aldeia 🌟   The best, less expensive place to stay in Genipabu, the Aldeia offers stand-alone Polynesian-style bungalows set in a large green garden a few hundred yards from the beach. The chalets are quite spacious with a good double bed set beneath mosquito netting and a fan. The two rooms in the back aren't quite as nice but may be a better bet for families, as they each feature three twin beds, a large bathroom, and a small sitting area. The beach is a short walk away.

Praia de Genipabu, Caixa Postal 274, Natal, 59001 RN. ℂ/fax **084/225-2011.** www.hotelaldeia.hpg.com.br. 7 units, including 5 chalets (shower only). R$90 (US$30) double. Extra person R$15 (US$5). Children under 11 free in parent's room. DC, MC. Free parking. No public transit. **Amenities:** Restaurant; small pool; children's swing and slides. *In room:* TV, minibar, fridge, no phone.

WHERE TO DINE

Good dining options in Praia dos Artistas include **Chaplin's,** Av. Café Filho 27 (ℂ **084/202-1188**), mostly for its location and atmosphere. Part of a large entertainment complex, the restaurant overlooks the beach and is the hangout of choice for locals and visitors alike. The food is standard seafood—think prawns and grilled fish. Arrive early to grab a window table. It's open daily from 6pm to 2am.

EXPENSIVE

Samô ☆ BRAZILIAN/SEAFOOD   Samô's specialty is seafood and, more specifically, prawns. The most-ordered dish and house favorite is *camarão Samô*—large prawns stuffed with the creamy Brazilian catupiry cheese and then lightly breaded and fried. The tasty morsels are served with a white sauce on *arroz maluco* (crazy rice) flavored with bacon bits, egg, garlic, onion, and tomato paste. Samô also serves a number of fish dishes using either *sirigado* or *garoupa,* always fresh and local. All dishes are for two, generously so, but if you can squeeze in an appetizer, try the coquille with squid, octopus, or shrimp; served on a small shell, the seafood is baked in the oven au gratin. With 30 minutes' notice, the restaurant provides free transport to and from any hotel in the Ponta Negra, Via Costeira, or Praia dos Artistas areas.

Av. Eng. Roberto Freire 9036, Ponta Negra. ⓒ 084/219-3669. Main courses R$18–R$45 (US$6–US$15). AE, DC, MC, V. Daily 11:30am–3:30pm and 6:30pm–midnight. Free parking. Bus: Ponta Negra.

MODERATE

Bar 21 ☆ *(Finds* SEAFOOD   For the postcard-perfect setting, check out Bar 21. Built on stilts, the small thatched-roof restaurant sits precariously over the ocean, and at high tide, the waves lap right at the stairs. Start with the *caldo de ostra;* this rich broth stuffed to the brim with little oysters is deliciously yummy (don't forget to squeeze on some lime juice). For the main course, there is fish and fish and fish. The catch of the day will arrive delicately grilled and coarsely salted with just some lime juice for flavoring. Generous helpings of salad and french fries accompany your meal, and two people will have plenty upon which to nosh. A single portion can easily serve two; if you are dining alone, the kitchen will happily cook up a smaller portion.

Avenida Beira Mar s/n, Praia Genipabu. ⓒ 084/224-2484. www.digi.com.br/bar21. Main courses R$9–R$25 (US$3–US$8). AE, DC, MC. Daily 9am–6:30pm.

Cervejeria Continental CAFE   The Continental is actually located on the Via Costeira just before Ponta Negra. Within this sprawling seaside establishment there lurks a restaurant, a general store, a beer and cold-cut buffet, a "Dance Beer" (dance floor with deejay and six beers on tap), and a brewpub. Plates of cold cuts make excellent appetizers, and the brews go really well with the grilled prawns or sautéed lobster. The crowd is mostly Brazilian, friendly and lots of fun.

Avenida Dinarte Matriz s/n, Via Costeira. ⓒ 084/202-1089. Main courses R$15–R$30 (US$5–US$10). AE, DC, MC, V. Fri–Sun noon–3am; Mon–Thurs 7pm–3am. Bus: Take any bus to Via Costeira and ask the driver to let you off at Continental.

Tabua ☆ *(Value* BRAZILIAN   Did we mention how much Brazilians like meat? Located across an old cobblestone road from a rocky beach where the waves crash in, Tabua offers indoor dining beside big windows looking out over ocean, and outdoor dining on a broad flagstone patio. The one thing it doesn't offer is non-carnivorous options. Instead, Tabua serves four different types of meat: carne de sol (salted sun-dried beef, a specialty of northeastern Brazil); good old Brazilian picanha; chicken; and, for those who are decision-shy, the tabua, a wood platter containing sausage, chicken, and carne de sol. Dishes here are made for two and can easily feed three. A minichain of sorts, Tabua has a second location in Ponta Negra, at Av. Eng. Roberto Freire 3241 (© 084/642-1236).

Av. Silvio Pedro 54 (just south of Praia dos Artistas). © **084/202-2920.** www.tabuadecarne.com.br. Main courses R$18–R$24 (US$6–US$8) for 2. AE, DC, MC, V. Daily 11:30am–9:30pm.

NATAL AFTER DARK

Natal has a few clusters of nightlife, but there's surprisingly little hard-core partying for a town whose main attraction is the beach. All three nightlife areas are widely separate, so it's either stick with one or resign yourself to long cab rides.

The most promising spot is **Rua do Chile.** Following Recife's success with its Bairro do Recife, Natal is renovating colonial buildings in the old port and converting the area into an entertainment complex. At the moment, about eight old buildings have been fully renovated and repainted in the typical colonial pastels. During the day, the place is deserted, even a bit spooky. Starting at 9pm, the bars open, and on weekends and warm summer nights, the square out front gets packed with vendors selling beer and with people chatting, drinking, and milling about until the wee hours. Inside, there's a mix of live and deejay music. Clubs to check out include **Anexo** (© 084/221-1282), **Blackout** (© 084/221-1282), and **Downtown** (© 084/611-1950).

Praia dos Artistas is a popular nightclub area; a few large discos are situated almost across the street from each other, but again, except during very peak season, there's a Saturday night in a small town feel. Check out the **Praia dos Artistas entertainment complex** on Avenida Presidente Café Filho 27 (© 084/220-1188) or **Nova Kapital,** which is just across the street (© 084/202-7111). Out in **Ponta Negra,** the scene is even mellower; people go for a beer on the beach or at beachside patios.

9 Fortaleza

2,808km (1,741 miles) NE of Rio de Janeiro, 3,144km (1,949 miles) NE of São Paulo, 1,317km (816 miles) N of Salvador

Though a city of over two million people, the capital of the state of Ceará is best known for its beaches: glorious long stretches of sand interrupted by impressive red cliffs, palm trees, dunes and lagoons that offer a true tropical playground.

The first Portuguese settlers arrived in the area in 1603, beginning what would become a shaky period of colonization. In 1637 the Dutch showed up and drove out the Portuguese, but were themselves driven out by the Tabajara Indians a few years later. The Dutch returned in force in 1649 and erected the substantial five-pointed Fort Schoonenborch, but only 5 years later the entire Dutch enterprise in Brazil came to an end. The Portuguese took over the fort and renamed it Fortaleza N. S. de Assunção.

Ceará remained a backwater until, with the opening of Brazilian ports to foreign ships in the 1820s, the city of Fortaleza began to grow into an important seaport. In response to this growth, in 1875 a plan was commissioned to transform Fortaleza—a la Haussmann in Paris—into a city of broad boulevards overlaying a functional grid. Unfortunately, little of that initial city planning remains.

These days the city's major industry is tourism, as Dutch, Portuguese, and other foreigners land en masse on the beaches again, this time armed with cameras and bathing suits and a fierce will to enjoy the sun and ocean. What sets

Fortaleza's beaches apart from Brazil's other 8,000km (4,960 miles) of coastline is the combination of colorful cliffs and huge sand dunes.

ESSENTIALS

ARRIVING

BY PLANE   Natal is served by **TAM, Vasp, Varig,** and **Gol.** All flights arrive at **Aeroporto Internacional Pinto Martins,** Av. Senador Carlos Jereissati 3000 (© **085/477-1200**). Taxis from the airport are inexpensive, about R$20 to R$30 (U$7–US$10) to the beaches or downtown.

BY BUS   Long-distance buses arrive at the **Rodoviária Eng. João Tomé,** Av. Borges de Melo s/n, Fatima (© **085/256-2100**).

GETTING AROUND

BY BUS   Most visitors use the bus to go between the beach neighborhoods and Centro. In Meireles or Mucuripe you catch the bus on the street parallel to the beach (Av. Abolição). Look for buses marked MEIRELES, CAÇA E PESCA, or GRANDE CIRCULAR. Fare is R$1.40 (45¢)

BY TAXI   Taxis can be hailed almost anywhere. To order a taxi ahead of time call **Disque Taxi** (© **085/287-7222**). A taxi from Meireles to Centro costs approximately R$15 (US$5), from Mucuripe to Praia de Iracema R$20 (US$7).

BY CAR   Within Fortaleza a car is likely a nuisance; however, to explore the outlying beaches a car is ideal. See "Fast Facts," below, for car-rental information.

VISITOR INFORMATION

Fortaleza's **airport** has a 24-hour tourist information center (© **085/477-1667**) in the arrivals hall. The state tourist information center (Centro de Turismo do Ceará) is located downtown at Rua Senador Pompeu 350 (© **085/488-7411**) and at Mucuripe Beach, Rua Vicente de Castro s/n (© **085/263-1115**). Both are open Monday to Saturday from 7am to 5pm.

CITY LAYOUT

Located just east of the Ceará River, the commercial heart of Fortaleza—called *Centro*—is small and quite walkable, though the traffic and sidewalk vendors can make the area seem quite unruly and disorganized. Starting from the waterfront **Fortaleza N. S. de Assunção,** Centro stretches inland in a grid pattern. An easy stroll to the east of Centro is the beach neighborhood **Praia de Iracema,** the first of a long string of beaches that line the waterfront, connected together by the **Avenida Beira Mar.** (Unfortunately, none of the urban beaches are recommended for bathing.) Iracema is very much the party beach. You'll find lots of restaurants and bars along the sea wall, and the **Rua Tabajaras** that runs parallel to the beach is packed with nightlife and restaurants. Heading east from Iracema, the beach and Avenida Beira Mar enter a bit of a quiet zone, until after a kilometer or so you come to the next beach neighborhood, **Meireles.** From here onward, the beachside boulevard becomes a pleasure to walk. It's nice and wide with shade and plenty of kiosks for a drink or snack. The nightly **crafts market** (see below) always attracts large crowds. Although the border is impossible to see, **Mucuripe** beach is considered another neighborhood to the east of Meireles. At the end of Mucuripe beach there's a small colony of fishermen and a fish and seafood market where the catch of the day is sold fresh off the boat.

FAST FACTS   To exchange money, try **Banco do Brasil,** Av. Barão do Rio Branco 1515, Centro (© **085/254-2122**), which also has an ATM, or **Acctur Câmbio,** Av. Mons Tabosa 1600, Meireles (© **085/248-8900**). The **American**

Express office is inside the Via Scala Shopping, Av. Beira Mar 3960 (© **085/ 452-5400;** Mon–Fri 9am–3pm).

The **post office** on Av. Beira Mar 4452 (© 085/248-7519) doubles as an Internet cafe. Cost is R$7.50 (US$2.50) per hour. To rent a car for exploring the beaches outside of Fortaleza contact **Localiza** (© 085/477-5050), **Avis** (© 085/477-1303), or **Hertz** (© 085/477-5055).

WHAT TO SEE & DO

Fortaleza's main attractions are the beaches outside of the city, including the **Morro Branco** with its multicolored cliffs, the glorious sand dunes of **Canoa Quebrada,** and the stunningly beautiful and rustic **Jericoacoara.** The city itself has a small **historic center** that's only worth a visit if you're already here and have a day to spare, but it's certainly not worth the trip by itself. The best way to get out and see the beaches is to head out on a day trip to Morro Branco or Canoa Quebrada; both are only a short distance from Fortaleza. These beaches are playgrounds for adults and children alike. Buggy tours, sandboarding, sand tobogganing, parasailing, boat rides—you name it and you can experience it, all under a hot tropical sun.

To enjoy Jericoacoara you need at least three days. This isolated beach community is best known for its vast Sahara-like sand dunes, plus its laid back casual atmosphere, stunning white beaches, and warm waters.

THE TOP ATTRACTIONS

Morro Branco 🌴 Best known for its colored sand cliffs, Morro Branco is located 85km (53 miles) east of Fortaleza. The beach is nice enough, but most visitors come to see the maze of colored sand cliffs close to the beach. A closer look at these cliffs will reveal the incredible variations in color, ranging from almost pure white to yellow, gold, pink, orange, red, and purple. You can't miss the region's best-known souvenir, the sand-filled glass bottles with amazing intricate designs made out of variously colored sands. Local guides in Morro Branco (who work for a donation, anything from R$5–R$10/US$1.65–US$3.35) is appreciated) will take you through the maze of cliffs, showing off the spots with the best colors.

From Fortaleza there is only 1 main highway, the CE 040. Take the CE 040 to Beberibe, then take the turnoff for Morro Branco (it's approximately 4km/2½ miles from the main junction to the beach).

Canoa Quebrada 🌴🌴 *Kids* All beaches should be this beautiful—miles and miles of soft white sand, the green-blue waters framed by low red cliffs. It's an easy place to spend a day. Buggy rides are the perfect way to get a better view of the beach and the spectacular dunes. Bugreiros (buggy drivers) usually charge R$18 (US$6) per person for a tour. One of the stops is at a lagoon that looks like an oasis in the desert, the perfect stop for a swim or a cold beer. Back at the beach there are plenty of *barracas* (stalls) that rent out chairs and umbrellas, and food and drink is always close at hand. Local women will offer scalp and shoulder massages using palm oil infused with herbs (this also makes great tanning oil if your skin has gotten used to the sun). A 15- to 20-minute massage will cost R$10 (US$3.35).

Canoa Quebrada is located 156km (97 miles) east of Fortaleza. To reach the community, take Hwy. CE 040 east to Aracati. Just past Aracati there will be a turnoff for Canoa Quebrada.

Cumbuco 🌴🌴 The attraction in Cumbuco? Beach and dunes. The main activity? The dune buggy ride. Why visit? This is the best place in the Fortaleza region to experience a hair-raising ride with *emoção*. Drivers are able to take you on a roller coaster ride over the shifting sands, dropping down steep inclines, swerving over piles of sand as if they were a minor speed bump and skidding and sliding at almost vertical angles off the face of the taller dunes.

Cumbuco is located 37km (23 miles) east of Fortaleza. To reach Cumbuco follow the signs for highway CE 085. The turnoff for Cumbuco is 11km (7 miles) past Coité.

TOUR OPERATORS

Fortaleza's main tour operator, **Ernatitur,** Av. Barão de Studart 1165 (© **085/244-9363;** www.ernanitur.com.br), offers regular tours to all the destinations listed above. You can choose between a very inexpensive tour bus excursion with no English speaking guides, or a much more expensive private van service (maximum of eight people) with English-speaking guides. A half-day city tour costs R$19 (US$6) bus excursion, R$180 (US$60) private tour. Tours to Cumbuco, Morro Branco, or Canoa Quebrada range from R$19 to R$39 (US$6–US$13) for a bus excursion or R$220 to R$410 (US$73–US$137) for a private tour, maximum of eight people).

Jericoacoara 🌟🌟🌟   Jericoacoara's attraction is partially its isolation, almost 300km (175 miles) west of Fortaleza. With no direct roads, visitors can only arrive by 4×4, preferably driven by someone who knows how to navigate through the 18km (11-mile) drive through constantly shifting sands. The payoff for those who persevere? Miles and miles of unspoiled beaches, rock formations, lagoons, mangroves, palm trees, and a Sahara desert landscape of beautiful dunes, some over 30m (100 ft.) tall. The isolation used to be enough to keep out all but a hardy few, but in recent years as word has spread this formerly sleepy fishing village has gotten, if not exactly crowded, certainly much more visited. Plan your travel for the shoulder season (Aug–Nov and late Mar to June) if you can. The easiest way to travel to Jeri (as locals call it) is by package tour. These include transportation from Fortaleza and 1 or 2 nights in Jeri. Keep in mind that Jeri remains a very rustic sort of spot—there are no fancy hotels, and amenities and facilities are pretty basic. Bring plenty of cash (in small bills) as bank machines are nonexistent and credit cards are rarely accepted. For more information check www.jericoacoara.com. One company that offers excellent packages is **Ceará Adventure,** Av. Dom Manuel 497 (© **085/254-3232;** www.cearadventure.com.br).

DOWNTOWN FORTALEZA

Though not worth a trip in itself, downtown Fortaleza does have some worthwhile sights if you want to take a day off from the beach. A good place to start is the **Centro de Turismo,** Rua Pompeu 350 (© **085/488-7411;** Mon–Sat 7am–6pm). This large complex, housed in the former city jail, has more than 100 crafts stalls in addition to a tourist information booth that gives out a good free map. At the waterfront stands the **Fortaleza de N. S. da Assunção,** Av. Alberto Craveiro (© **085/255-1600;** daily 8–11am and 2–5pm). Built by the Dutch in 1649 as Fort Schoonenborch, the fort was rechristened after the Dutch were driven from Brazil in 1654.

For souvenirs check out the **Mercado Central,** Rua Alberto Nepomuceno 199, one of the best crafts markets in the city. The large circular building houses over 500 stalls and small shops selling a variety of handicrafts.

Just a short stroll from the Mercado Central is the area that the locals call *Casario,* a lovely collection of restored 19th century colonial buildings, located primarily on the **Rua Dragão do Mar** and **Rua Almirante Tamandaré.** The area really comes to life at night as most of the historic buildings house nightclubs or cafes. The new centerpiece of this square is the contemporary **Centro Cultural Dragão do Mar,** Rua Dragão do Mar 81 (© **985/488-8600;** Tues–Thurs 9am–5:30pm, Fri–Sun 2–9:30pm). The cultural center is worth a stroll, both to admire its design and for the picture perfect views it provides of the buildings below.

WHERE TO STAY

Most people choose to stay within walking distance of the city beaches of Iracema, Meireles or Mucuripe. Though none are recommended for bathing, the boulevards are very pleasant and you'll find plenty of restaurants and activity along the ocean front.

Hotel Luzeiros ✸✸✸   This is the best hotel in Fortaleza. Built in 2002, the hotel positively shines "newness." All rooms have balconies and king-size beds and are elegantly furnished with dark-wood furniture set off with gold accents. White tile floors, quality linens, and high-end finishes add an air of luxury to even the most basic rooms. The prime rooms have a full ocean view *(frente mar),* the standard rooms have partial views *(vista mar).* The amenities such as the swimming pool, business center, and fitness room are excellent.

Av. Beira Bar 2600, Meireles, Fortaleza, 60165-121 CE. © 085/486-8586. Fax 85/486-8587. www.hotelluzeiros. com.br. 202 units. R$260 (US$87) double partial ocean view; R$290 (US$97) double full ocean view; R$520 (US$173) suite. Extra person about 25%. Children under 7 stay free in parent's room. AE, DC, MC, V. Free parking. **Amenities:** Restaurant; bar; outdoor pool; business center; limited room service; laundry; nonsmoking rooms. *In room:* A/C, TV, dataport, minibar, safe.

Ibis Hotel *(Value*   The best value on Praia de Iracema. Like all other Ibis hotels, the concept is basic: All rooms are identical and accommodations are comfortable but plain. Each room has a nice firm double bed, a desk and closet space. Bathrooms are equally frills-free but are modern and spotless and come with showers only. The hotel amenities are kept to a minimum to reduce the operating costs, and breakfast is optional (R$7/US$2.35). The payoff for guests is quality accommodations in an excellent location at very reasonable rates.

Rua Dr. Atualpa Barbosa Lima 660, Praia de Iracema, Fortaleza, 60060-370 CE. © 085/219-2121. Fax 085/ 219-0000. www.accorhotels.com.br. 171 units (shower only). R$83 (US$28) double. Extra person R$15 (US$5). Children under 5 stay free in parent's room. AE, DC, MC, V. Free parking. **Amenities:** Restaurant; laundry service. *In room:* A/C, TV, fridge, safe.

Meliá Confort ✸✸ *(Value*   Properties in the Meliá chain always look much more expensive than they are, giving you great value for money. The hotel's 134 rooms are all beautifully furnished in blue and yellow tones and come with king-size beds; the bathrooms are done in beautiful marble. The smallest rooms are the standard rooms. These do not have balconies but do look out over the ocean. The deluxe rooms all have balconies and are very spacious, definitely worth the price difference.

Av. Beira Mar 3470, Mucuripe, 60165-121 CE © 0800/703-3399 or 085/466-5500. Fax 085/466-5501. www. solmelia.com. 134 units (shower only). *Note:* The highest rate is the rack rate (discounts depend on the time of year and capacity). R$130–R$230 (US$43–US$77) standard double; R$150–R$280 (US$50–US$93) deluxe double; R$260–R$470 (US$87–US$157) executive suite. Extra person about 25%. Children under 9 stay free in parent's room. AE, DC, MC, V. Free parking. **Amenities:** Restaurant; bar; large outdoor pool; fitness center; sauna; massage; business center; tour desk; 24-hr. room service; laundry, nonsmoking rooms. *In room:* A/C, TV, minibar, fridge, hair dryer.

Parthenon Golden Fortaleza   Located on the beach boulevard, this apart-hotel offers large one-or two-bedroom suites. The hotel is in the midst of a renovation. The revamped rooms are fabulous—decorated with fresh bright colors, the rooms are bright, have a kitchen and living room separate from the bedroom and luxurious bathrooms with glass-enclosed shower boxes and large mirrors. All apartments have balconies and views.

Av. Beira Mar 4260, Mucuripe, Fortaleza, 60165-121 CE. ℭ 085/466-1413. goldenfortaleza@uol.com.br. 71 units. R$150 (US$50) 1-bedroom suite; R$200–R$250 (US$67–US$83) 2-bedroom suite. Extra person R$65 (US$22). Children under 8 stay free in parent's room. AE, DC, MC, V. Free parking. **Amenities:** Excellent restaurant; small outdoor pool; Internet access in lobby; laundry. In room: A/C, TV, minibar, safe.

WHERE TO DINE IN FORTALEZA

Fortaleza's restaurants are surprisingly excellent. You will find fine dining at surprisingly low prices as well as a number of outstanding seafood restaurants. Closest to the tourist zone, **Praia de Iracema** is a fun and lively dining area. Further out, **Meireles** and **Mucuripe** beaches offer a few excellent options as well. For a fun dining scene frequented mostly by local Fortalezans, head to the newly vibrant restaurant enclave of **Aldeota.**

Al Mare 𝔊 SEAFOOD   Al Mare is as spectacular as they come. Set on Praia de Meireles, the patio and dining room wrap around the main building offering maximum views. The atmosphere is strangely formal; senior waiters in tuxedos deliver expert yet slightly stodgy service and the decor is a tad heavy on the maritime memorabilia, but the food is excellent. The most spectacular dish is the grilled seafood combination, *Grelhada Al Mare.* Two people will have plenty to eat with this platter of grilled lobster, prawns, fish, octopus, and squid.

Av. Beira Mar 3821, Meireles. ℭ **085/263-3888.** Main courses R$23–R$38 (US$9–US$13) for 2; grilled seafood platters R$72–R$85 (US$24–US$28) for 2. AE, DC, MC, V. Tues–Sun noon–3pm and 7pm–midnight.

Café Matisse 𝔊𝔊 SEAFOOD   Café Matisse offers creative cuisine at very reasonable prices. Leaning more towards seafood, the dishes are refreshingly unique. The *peixe Carmel* is a grilled fish served with a grape and caper sauce, served with caramelized mushrooms and asparagus. One of the more popular fish dishes is the *Peixe Bonne Femme*—grilled filet of fish served with a béchamel sauce with mushrooms and shrimp. The wine list offers a decent selection of wines from France, Italy, Portugal, Spain, Australia, and South America.

Rua Silva Jatahy 942, Aldeota. ℭ **085/242-1377.** Main courses R$18–R$42 (US$6–US$14). AE, DC, MC, V. Sun–Fri noon–3pm; daily 7pm–midnight.

La Bohème 𝔊𝔊 SEAFOOD   One of the most beautiful restaurants in Praia de Iracema, La Bohème combines an art gallery with restaurant and large outdoor patio. Specializing in seafood, La Bohème serves a delicious variety of lobster, grilled with catupiry cheese or sautéed in a *moqueca* stew. The prawns are definitely worth trying—one of the more interesting dishes is the flambéed prawns served in a pineapple shell. Other good choices include grilled fish as well as squid or octopus stews *a Baiana* with coconut milk and red *dendê* oil. A lively band plays nightly from 9pm onward.

Av. Rua dos Tabajaras 380, Praia de Iracema. ℭ **085/219-3311.** Main courses R$35–R$85 (US$12–US$28) for 2 (the lobster dishes are the more expensive items). AE, DC, MC, V. Mon–Sat 5pm–1am (may close later on weekends).

Moanna 𝔊𝔊𝔊 BRAZILIAN   Located on Mucuripe beach, Moanna has it all. This is high-end dining with quality ingredients, creative cuisine and excellent service, yet most dishes don't even crack the US$12 mark. One of our favorite dishes is the *frango tropical,* succulent pieces of grilled chicken breast served in mango sauce with savory crepes stuffed with leek mousse. For dessert, chocoholics may want to order the *último desejo* (the last wish), a rich combination of two slices of chocolate cookie stuffed with crème caramel served on a bed of crème anglaise with sliced strawberries and chocolate sauce.

Av. Beira Mar 4260, Mucuripe (inside the Golden Fortaleza Parthenon). ℂ 085/263-4635. R$12–R$48 (US$4–US$16) for 2. AE, DC, MC, V. Sun–Thurs noon–1am; Fri–Sat noon–2am.

SHOPPING IN FORTALEZA

Ceará is known for its quality handicrafts. The most famous souvenirs are the sand-filled glass bottles and the handmade lace. A good place to browse for crafts is the **outdoor market** that takes place nightly from 5 to 10pm in front of the **Othon Hotel** in **Meireles.** Another excellent location for buying crafts is the **Mercado Central,** Rua Alberto Nepomuceno 199 (no phone; Mon–Sat 9am–7pm, Sun 9am–noon). With over 500 stalls, the variety is good and prices very reasonable.

FORTALEZA AFTER DARK
THE PERFORMING ARTS

One of the loveliest venues in Fortaleza is the high Victorian **Teatro de Jose de Alencar,** Praça Jose de Alencar s/n, Centro (ℂ **085/452-1590**). Although often used for theater presentations, music lovers can watch for classical music performances by the Eleazar de Carvalho Chamber Orquestra. Call the box office for program details or check www.secult.ce.gov.br under "programe-se."

CLUBS & BARS

Fortaleza is known for its nightlife. Almost any day of the week one can find a good party. The most happening nightlife area is around **Praia de Iracema** and the **Casario,** the historic buildings around the **Rua Dragão do Mar** and **Rua Alm. Tamandaré,** centered on the new cultural showpiece, the **Centro Cultural do Dragão.**

On Mondays the place to be is **Piratas,** Rua dos Tabajaras 325, Praia de Iracema (ℂ **085/219-8030**). The party starts at 8pm but goes until the early hours of the morning. The house band gets things really going with their dancers and electrifying *forró, axé,* reggae, and other rhythms.

On Thursday nights, locals and tourists head out to **Praia do Futuro, southwest of Mucuripe** for a traditional evening of crab-eating or *caranguejada.* The best-known *barraca* in Praia do Futuro is **Chico do Caranguejo,** Av. Zé Diogo 4930 (ℂ **085/234-6808**). Things start to warm up after 7pm. The band usually starts around 8:30pm. Taking a taxi is recommended.

10 The Amazon: Manaus

Manaus: 3,281km (2,034 miles) NW of Rio de Janeiro, 3,156km (1,957 miles) NW of São Paulo

The largest city in the Amazon, Manaus is located on the shores of the Rio Negro, just upstream from where it joins the Rio Solimões to become the Amazon. It had its biggest period of growth near the end of the 19th century, when worldwide demand for rubber exploded. This era was when some of the city's finest buildings went up, among them the Customs house and the famous Teatro Amazonas. The city's next big boom came in 1966, when Manaus was declared a free-trade zone. Brazilians visited Manaus to stock up on cheap electronics. Nowadays, tourism is the expanding industry, most of it focused on the Amazon rainforest.

ESSENTIALS
GETTING THERE

BY PLANE   Manaus's international airport **Eduardo Gomes,** Avenida Santos Dumont (ℂ **092/652-1212**), is located 16km (10 miles) south of downtown.

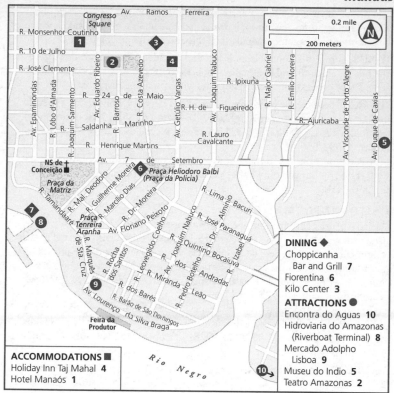

The airport is serviced by **Varig, VASP,** and **TAM** airlines. A taxi to Centro will cost about R$40 (US$13). City bus no. 306 goes to Centro; the fare is R$1.50 (50¢). There's also an Equipol shuttle to the downtown hotels for R$18 (US$6). Guests of the Hotel Tropical de Manaus (p. 365) can take the Fontur shuttle for R$12 (US$4) per person.

BY BOAT   Boats dock at the **Hidroviaria do Amazonas (Riverboat Terminal)** (© **092/621-4359**), Rua Marquês de Santa Cruz 25. Boats arrive or depart from here several times a week for downriver destinations, such as Belém at the mouth of the Amazon, and upriver destinations, such as Porto Velho in the state of Rondônia. From here, it is a short walk or taxi ride to the downtown hotels; taxi fare is usually R$8 to R$12 (US$2.65–US$4). To the Hotel Tropical, it's a 20-minute taxi ride (costing R$40/US$13) or a 40-minute bus ride on bus no. 120 from Centro.

GETTING AROUND

In downtown Manaus, all activity gravitates toward the waterfront on the Rio Negro. The main attractions for visitors are concentrated in a 20-block radius around the port and are easily accessible on foot. The downtown bus terminal is directly in front of the port. To the east of the terminal are a number of narrow parallel streets, centered on **Rua Guilherme Moreira,** that form Manaus's main downtown shopping district. The busy east-west **Avenida Sete de Setembro** marks the end of the oldest section of downtown. The only real site of interest north of here is the Teatro Amazonas, 4 blocks north on Rua Barroso. **Ponta Negra** beach, about 18km (11 miles) from downtown, is one of the more upscale neighborhoods where the beachfront has become a popular nightlife and entertainment area.

BY BUS   From the Ponta Negra beach and the Hotel Tropical to downtown, take bus no. 120; the ride will take about 35 to 40 minutes and costs R$1.50 (50¢). Once downtown, all attractions are within walking distance.

BY TAXI   Taxis can be hailed on the street or reserved by phone for a specific time. Contact **Coopertaxi** at © 092/652-1544 or 092/652-1568. In town, call **Tele-Rádio Táxi** at © 092/633-3211. In Ponta Negra, call **Ponta Negra Rádio Táxi** at © 092/656-6121.

Taxis to and from the Hotel Tropical operate on a fixed price. Officially, it's R$40 (US$13), but you can knock that down by 20% if you bargain before getting in the cab.

VISITOR INFORMATION

The city tourist information agency, **Manaustur** (© 092/622-4948; www.manaustur.com.br), Av. Sete de Setembro 157, is inconveniently located at the bottom end of Avenida Sete de Setembro in a run-down part of the port. Stop in at the airport instead. The downtown office is open Monday through Friday from 9am to 6pm. The desk at the airport in the arrivals hall (© 092/652-1120) is open daily from 7am to 11pm.

The State of Amazonas tourism agency, **AmazonasTur,** has unfortunately taken down its excellent website, but it maintains an info center at Rua Saldanha Marinho 321, Centro (© 092/233-1928). It's open Monday through Friday from 9am to 6pm.

FAST FACTS   An **American Express** office is located at Praça Adalberto Valle 17 (© 092/622-2577). To exchange currency, try **Banco do Brasil,** Rua Guilherme Moreira 315, Centro (© 092/621-5000); **Cortês Câmbio,** Av. Sete de Setembro 1199, Centro (© 092/622 4222), or **Amazonas Shopping** (© 092/642-2525)

For medical attention, go to **Pronto Socorro e Hospital dos Acidentados,** Av. Joaquim Nabuco 1755, Centro (© 092/663-2200). If you need a dentist, contact Sos Dentista, Rua 24 de Maio 220 (Rio Negro Center), Room 710, Centro © 092/9982-1133).

The **Hotel Tropical** has an Internet cafe, open daily from 9am to 10pm and charging R$18 (US$6) per hour. In Centro, a great spot is **Amazon Cyber Café,** Av. Getúlio Vargas 626, Centro (© 092/232-9068). It's open Monday through Friday from 9am to 11pm, Saturday from 10am to 8pm, and Sunday from 1 to 8pm.

WHAT TO SEE & DO IN MANAUS
THE TOP ATTRACTIONS

CIGS Zoo   It's a strange place, this zoo. It's part of the army's jungle warfare training center, and many of the animals were captured by soldiers on patrol. The animal enclosures range from the worst you've ever seen to quite sophisticated and humane habitats. The collection of wildlife is tremendous: black and spotted jaguars, cougars, various smaller cats, toucans and macaws, harpy eagles stuck in heartbreakingly small enclosures, and numerous monkeys in wide, well-done habitats. You could easily spend an hour or so browsing here.

Estrada do Ponta Negra s/n. © 092/625-2044. Admission R$2 (65¢) adults, free for children under 13. Tues–Sun 9am–4:30pm. Bus: 120.

Encontra das Aguas   The Meeting of the Waters is certainly a remarkable sight. The dark slow water of the Rio Negro meets the faster muddy brown water of the Rio Solimões, and because of differences in velocity, temperature, and salinity, the two rivers don't immediately blend but carry on side-by-side for miles. It's a classic Manaus day trip. If you're booked at a lodge downstream of Manaus you'll pass through the Meeting of the Waters on the way there and back. If you haven't there are day trips, most of which unfortunately include a trip to the detestable **Lago Janauary Ecological Park.** If you speak some Portuguese, the best idea is to go to the Porto de Ceasa or downtown waterfront and hire your own personal boat and driver. Failing that, book with a reputable agency like **Viverde,** Rua dos Cardeiros 26, Manaus (*©*/fax **092/248-9988;** www.viverde.com.br). This company also offers flight-seeing tours, which are perhaps the best way to see the Meeting of the Waters.

Mercado Adolpho Lisboa *©*   The Adolpho Lisboa is a beautiful iron-and-glass copy of the now demolished market hall in Les Halles, Paris. It's a great place to see some of the local fish, fruits, and vegetables. All the fish vendors are kept in one area; the variety of fish is overwhelming. Not for the squeamish, the vendors cut and clean the fish on the spot; though chopped in half, some of the larger catfish still wriggle. In case you want to heal thyself, stop in at one of the herb stalls. Who needs a pharmacy when the cures for diabetes, kidney failure, obesity, heart problems, and headache are all laid out in dried bunches of leaves?

Rua dos Barés 46, Centro. *©* **092/233-0469.** Mon–Sat 5am–6pm; Sun 5am–noon.

Museu do Indio   Spread out over six rooms, this museum presents the culture and social structure of the peoples of the Upper Rio Negro. Artifacts and clothing give an overview of their hunting and fishing traditions, as well as showing the spiritual rituals of a funeral and healing ceremony. The displays contain photos, drawings, a large number of artifacts, and occasionally models and replicas. All descriptions are in Portuguese, English, and German. Allow 1 hour. The gift shop downstairs run by the Salesian sisters offers a great selection of Indian crafts and souvenirs at very reasonable prices.

Rua Duque de Caxias 356, Centro. *©* **092/234-1422.** Admission R$4 (US$1.65) adults and seniors, R$1 (35¢) children 5 and up. Mon–Fri 8:30–11:30am and 2–4:30pm; Sat 8:30–11:30am.

Teatro Amazonas *©©*   This is one tourist "must-see" that is actually worth seeing. This remarkable landmark was erected in the midst of the Amazon jungle in 1896 at the peak of the rubber boom. The tour shows off the lobby of marble and inlaid tropical hardwoods, the fine concert hall, and the romantic mural in the upstairs ballroom. Even better is to see a concert (see "Manaus After Dark," below). The theater's official website has some nice contemporary and historical photos, but unfortunately no programming information.

Praça São Sebastião. *©* **092/622-1880.** www.teatroamazonas.com.br. Guided 15-min. tours in both English and Portuguese, departing every 30 min. R$6 (US$2) Mon–Sat 9am–4pm.

SHOPPING

Downtown Manaus is one big shopping area: Vendors hawk their wares, stalls clog up the sidewalks and squares, and the streets are jam-packed with little stores. The main shopping streets run behind the Praça Tenreiro Aranha, Rua Marcilio Dias, Rua Guilherme Moreira, and Rua Mal Deodoro. The church square, **Praça da Matriz** has a large market during weekdays selling everything from clothing to hair accessories and bags.

Just across from the Teatro Amazonas is **Artesanato da Amazonia,** Rua Jose Clemente 500, Loja A, Centro (*©* **092/232-3979**). It's a large souvenir shop with a good selection of native arts and crafts such as baskets, pottery, jewelry, and bags, as well as the standard T-shirts, key chains, and postcards.

Even if you have had your fill of local crafts, **Artindia,** Praça Tenreiro Aranha s/n, Centro (© **092/232-4890**), is worth checking out just for the building. A lovely wrought-iron and glass structure originally built as a tea salon in 1912, it was moved from the nearby Praça Matriz to its current location. Now, you'll find two floors stacked with Indian art and crafts. In addition to the usual trinkets, the collection contains a large number of bows and arrows, carved paddles, headdresses, spears, and masks. **Feira de Artesanato,** the crafts market located around the Artindia store, sells a wide variety of Indian crafts. There is usually a large selection of necklaces, bracelets, woodcarvings, T-shirts, baskets, and handbags. Go early in the day for a better selection.

WHERE TO STAY IN MANAUS
CENTRO
Expensive
Holiday Inn Taj Mahal   The Holiday Inn Taj Mahal is your best bet for a top-notch hotel downtown. Located within spitting distance of the Opera House, the Holiday Inn provides hard-to-find American-standard accommodations: Beds are firm, TVs large, and coffeemakers and irons come standard in every room. Standard rooms—which the Taj calls "luxo"—are of adequate size but come with a shower only and a view of nothing much. The "super-luxo" rooms are the best value; they have lots of space, a big queen bed, couches, chairs, writing table, whirlpool tub, and balcony with (for floors six and above) an excellent view of the Opera House. "Executivo" rooms have two double beds but feature only showers. Junior suites, meanwhile, feature a small sitting room, balconies, and a good-size bathroom with jetted tub. Prices are negotiable. Always ask for a discount.

Av. Getúlio Vargas 741, Centro, Manaus, 69020-010 AM. © **0800/925-333,** or ©/fax 092/627-3737. www.holidayinntajmahal.com.br. 208 units. R$190–R$450 (US$63–US$150) double. 50% corporate and group discount and in Dec–Jan low season. Extra person about 25%. Children under 15 stay free in parent's room. AE, DC, MC, V. Free parking. **Amenities:** Rooftop restaurant; rooftop pool; weight room; business center; salon; 24-hr. room service; laundry. In room: A/C, TV, dataport, minibar, coffeemaker, hair dryer, iron, safe.

Moderate
Hotel Manaós   Situated cater-cornered from the Opera House, the Manaós provides something rare in the Amazon—basic clean accommodations at a moderate price. Rooms come in two flavors: two singles, or a double and a single. The price is the same for both. Bathrooms are extremely clean and bright (consider wearing your shades in the shower). Best of all for those in the know, room nos. 304 through 311 and 204 through 211 provide the kind of view of the Opera House for which other hotels charge hundreds extra.

Av. Eduardo Ribeiro 881, Centro, Manaus, 69010-001 AM. © **092/633-5744.** Fax 092/232-4443. manaos@argo.com.br. 39 units (shower only). R$160 (US$53) double. 10% discount for stays of more than 1 day. Extra person R$30 (US$10). Children under 7 stay free in parent's room. AE, DC, MC, V. Free parking. **Amenities:** Restaurant; 24-hr. room service; laundry. In room: A/C, TV, minibar.

PONTA NEGRA
Nineteen kilometers (12 miles) from downtown, Ponta Negra beach is a popular nightlife district on the bank of the Rio Negro. Access to Manaus is quick by bus or taxi, and the hotel has a regular shuttle as well; all excursions and tours include hotel pickup, and many boat tours depart from the dock of the Hotel Tropical. Out of all the hotels in Brazil, this one is definitely worth the splurge.

Hotel Tropical de Manaus 𝕱𝕱𝕱   After the Copacabana Palace, this is the most famous hotel in Brazil. Built on the shores of the Rio Negro, within its own little patch of rainforest, the Tropical is a destination in itself. The amenities are absolutely unsurpassed (zoo, large pool complex, children's play area, archery range). The original wing, built in 1975, is referred to as *ala colonial;* the second phase is referred to as *ala moderna.* Where you stay is more a matter of preference than quality. The colonial rooms have more character, decorated with beautiful dark wood furniture and hardwood floors. They can also be a bit musty. The modern wing is pleasantly furnished with carpets and contemporary decor in light colors. All rooms are of a good size with high ceilings and large windows, and the bathrooms are spacious and modern with showers and bathtubs. The deluxe rooms come with a balcony and even more space than the superior and standard rooms. The junior suites are not that great a deal, especially compared to the spacious deluxe rooms.

Av. Coronel Texeira 1320, Ponta Negra, Manaus, 69029-120 AM. © 0800/701-2670 or 092/659-5000. Fax 92/658-5026. www.tropicalhotel.com.br. 601 units. R$465 (US$155) standard double; R$558 (US$186) superior double; R$651 (US$217) deluxe double; R$930 (US$310) junior suite. There is usually a 20%–40% discount on these rates; inquire about discounts for Varig ticket holders and Amex cardholders. Extra person 25%. Children under 11 stay free in parent's room. AE, DC, MC, V. Bus: 120. **Amenities:** 3 restaurants; 2 bars; disco; large pool complex; tennis courts; health club; spa; sauna; watersports rental; children's program; game room; tour desk; concierge; car rental; business center; shopping arcade; salon; 24-hr. room service; massage; babysitting; laundry; dry cleaning; nonsmoking rooms or floors. *In room:* A/C, TV, dataport, minibar, fridge, hair dryer, safe.

ELSEWHERE
Mango Guest House 𝕱   The Mango is a nice small guesthouse located (unfortunately) in a boring walled-off suburb about halfway between downtown and Ponta Negra. Rooms here are simple, small, and pleasant, with tile floors, firm single or double beds, and clean functional bathrooms with super-hot showers. All rooms have a small veranda that looks out on a grassy courtyard and small pool. There is no public transit, and the guesthouse is a R$20 (US$7) ride from either Ponta Negra or downtown. Tell taxi drivers the guesthouse is in Kissia Dois, off Rua Jacira Reis, which runs off Rua Darcy Vargas.

Rua Flavio Espirito Santo 1, Kissia II, 69040-250 AM. © 092/656-6033. Fax 92/656-6101. www.naturesafaris. com.br. 10 units. R$150 (US$50) standard double. Extra person 25%. AE, DC, MC, V. No public transit. **Amenities:** Bar; small outdoor pool; free shared Internet terminal. *In room:* A/C, fridge.

WHERE TO DINE
CENTRO
Choppicanha Bar and Grill 𝕱 CHURRASCO   The food is fine, the beer is cold, and the location magic—on a pier on the edge of the Amazon, overlooking the riverboats of the new Hidroviaria do Amazonas. Cuisine is standard Brazilian *churrasco* fare—picanha and other beef cuts, plus chicken and, thanks to the location, local fish including *tambaqui* and *piraruçu.* The restaurant is on the patio at the end of the concrete pedestrian overpass.

Rua Marques de Santa Cruz 25, Centro. © 092/631-1111. Main courses R$18–R$22 (US$7.50–US$11). AE, DC, MC, V. Mon–Sat 11am–3pm and 6–11:30pm; Sun 11am–4pm.

Fiorentina ITALIAN   After days of eating fish, pasta may come as a welcome change. Manaus's best (and only) Italian spot offers pizzas, lasagnas, and stuffed pastas such as ravioli. On Sunday there's a huge buffet.

Praça da Polícia s/n Centro. © 092/215-2255. www.fiorentina.com.br. Main courses R$12–R$21 (US$4–US$7). AE, MC, V. Mon–Fri 11am–3pm and 6–10:30pm; Sat–Sun 11:30am–3pm and 6–10pm.

Amazonian Cuisine

Amazonian cuisine uses lots of ingredients available only locally. The star attraction is fish. It's worth visiting the market in Manaus just to see what some of these creatures look like. Make sure you try the *tucunaré*, one of the prime fishes with meat so tasty it's best served plainly grilled. *Pirarucú* is known as the cod of the Amazon. *Tambaqui* and *paçu* also have delicious firm flesh that works well in stews and broths.

Tacacá is a delicious local soup made with the yellow *tucupí* cassava, *murupí* peppers, garlic, onion, and dried shrimp. You'll often find it for sale on the streets, traditionally served in a gourd. All Amazon dishes are usually served with some cassava, a drier version of the *farofa* you find in Rio and São Paulo.

The region is also very rich in fruits, many of which are found only in the Amazon. The citruslike *bacuri* has soft spongelike skin and white flesh; like Christmas mandarins, you can't have just one. The *cupuaçu* is a large round fruit, like a small pale coconut but with an odd taste of sweet and sour. It's usually served in desserts and juices. *Tucumã* is a small and hard fruit like an unripe peach. Locals eat slices of it on bread. *Açai* is a popular fruit, but it can't be eaten raw; the berries are first soaked and then squashed to obtain the juice. You will find it in juices and ice cream. Some people also eat the dark purple pulp with a bit of sugar and manioc *(açai na tijela)*. In the jungle, you'll come across fruits that you don't even see in the markets in Manaus. Our favorite is the *mari-mari*, a snakelike vine about as long as your arm, that when opened with a quick twist reveals a row of green, round, and juicy fruits, full of vitamins.

Kilo Center KILO/BUFFET A great lunch spot, located just 2 blocks off Getúlio Vargas. The selection is quite varied; international dishes include pasta, Stroganoff, and great salads. The buffet also gives you the opportunity to try various local fish dishes, stews *(caldeirada)*, and beans. Codfish lovers (we know you're out there) will love the Friday lunch menu.

Rua 10 de Julho 203, Centro. ℂ 092/622-6948. Main courses R$21 (US$7) per kilo (2¼ lb.). AE, MC. Mon–Sat 11am–3pm.

ELSEWHERE

Peixaria Moronguêtá ⋌⋌ SEAFOOD This lovely small restaurant overlooking the Porto de Ceasa serves fresh local Amazon fish in a astonishing variety of ways. The best include *tambaqui, tucanaré, dourado, matrichã,* piranha, and *camarão.* These can all be prepared in Bahian moquecas or stewlike calderadas, served grilled with banana, cooked with coconut milk, and fried on a hot grill with spicy peppers. There's lots of good Brazilian beer and excellent local fruit juices.

Rua Jaith Chaves s/n, Porto de Ceasa. ℂ 092/615-3362. Main courses R$18–R$30 (US$6–US$10). MC, V. Daily Mon–Sat 11am–11pm.

MANAUS AFTER DARK

Better than just touring the **Teatro Amazonas,** Praça São Sebastião s/n, Centro (ℂ **092/622-2420;** www.teatroamazonas.com.br), is actually sitting back in the plush chairs and taking in a performance. The theater has a resident philharmonic orchestra, choir, and dance group who perform regularly. Tickets are eminently affordable, usually around R$15 (US$5).

In downtown Manaus, the best spot for an evening drink is **Bar do Armando,** Rua 10 de Julho 593 (© **092/232-1195**). Located on the square in front of the opera house, this venerable small drinking spot is the nighttime home of Manaus's artists, intellectuals, journalists, and other interesting ne'er-do-wells.

One more reason to stay at the Hotel Tropical is its easy access to the city's most happening nightlife spot, **Ponta Negra beach.** People stroll up and down the wide boulevard; there are regular concerts and events at the amphitheater, and a number of bars have entertainment and live music in the evening. Close to the waterfront, you'll find a whole bunch of *botequins.* Most places open at 5 or 6pm on weekdays and stay open until at least 1 or 2am. On weekends, many bars and restaurants open at 11am and stay open until 3 or 4am. The Hotel Tropical also has a happening club; the **Studio Tropical Night** (© **092/659-5000**), open Thursday through Saturday, hosts concerts every now and then and has deejays on most nights. Two popular gay bars can be found in Centro: **Enigma's Bar,** Rua Silva Ramos 1054 (© **092/234-7985**), and **Turbo Seven,** Rua Vivaldo Lima 33 (© **092/232-6793**). Both are open Thursday through Saturday from 10pm onwards.

THE AMAZON

There are many ways of exploring the Amazon. What suits you best depends on how much time you have and how comfortable you want to be. Most people choose to stay at a lodge within a few hours by boat from Manaus. Lodges vary in luxury and size, but the programs offered are pretty similar. Another comfortable way of seeing the Amazon is by boat. The vessel serves as your home base, and you take excursions in canoes up the smaller channels. Specialized operators offer expedition-style trips where the emphasis is on truly experiencing the rainforest. You don't need to be in top shape for these; you just have to be able to hike or paddle a boat, and be willing to forego amenities like minibars and hot showers for a more hands-on jungle experience. One excellent adventure outfitter is **Amazon Mystery Tours** (see below).

LODGES

Lodges are a popular way of experiencing something of the Amazon while keeping comfort levels high. Most lodges are within a 3-hour boat ride from Manaus. Lodge tours are pretty much standardized. There'll be an introductory jungle tour, a sunset and/or sunrise tour, a forest hike, a visit to a native village, an evening of caiman hunting, and an afternoon of piranha fishing. What distinguishes one lodge from another is the size, the quality of the surrounding forest, and the quality of the guides.

To book a stay at a lodge, you can contact the lodges directly or contact a tour operator. In Manaus, contact the travel experts at **Viverde,** Rua dos Cardeiros 26, Manaus (©/fax **092/248-9988;** www.viverde.com.br). Their excellent website offers detailed information on tours and the Amazon in general. In the United States and Canada, contact **Brazil Nuts** at © **800/553-9959** or visit their website at www.brazilnuts.com.

Amazon Village Lodge ☆☆   Amazon village offers one of the best quality rainforest experiences. The lodge is set by the edge of a pristine rainforest reserve, which is in turn surrounded by areas that have seen a lot of deforestation. The lodge consists of a main building with a large lounge, bar, and dining room, all constructed with local wood, high ceilings, and a palm-frond roof. The rooms are small and clean with private toilets and showers. There is no hot water, and electricity is limited to the evening hours. There's a guide assigned to each party, whether that's a family of four, a couple or two, or someone traveling alone. Because Amazon Village pays better than most other lodges, the guides tend to be more senior and more knowledgeable. Forest hikes explore the lodge's reserve of pristine rainforest. The food is excellent, and the staff are very friendly.

Rua Ramos Ferreira 1189, Sala 403, Manaus. (© 092/633-1444. Fax 092/633-3217. www.internext. com.br/avillage. 36 units (shower only). 3-day packages from $440 per person. AE, DC, MC, V. **Amenities:** Restaurant; bar.

Amazonat ☆☆☆ If you like space to move around, you will love the Amazonat, set on its own 900-hectare (2,223-acre) reserve of *terra firme*. Located 160km (98 miles) east (downstream) of Manaus, Amazonat is surrounded by extensive walking trails that you can roam at will on your own.; there is a lake with a beach for swimming and an orchid park with over 1,000 specimens to see and sniff and wonder at. The lodge itself is set in beautiful lush jungle gardens and the chalets are more than comfortable. The basic 3-day package includes a number of guided walks and a river trip on the Urubu for bird-watching, as well as plenty of time to explore on your own. The 4-day package includes all of the above plus a full day on the Amazon River and a visit to the Opera House and the Meeting of the Waters. The owners have done an excellent job setting up a variety of specialized programs for those who want to experience more of the jungle: the Jungle Trekker package includes a number of longer hikes and two overnight stays at a jungle camp. All packages include airport transfers, all meals (the food is fabulous) and excellent guides on all excursions.

Caixa Postal 1273, Manaus, AM 69006-970. (© 092/328-1183 hotel, or (©/fax 092/633-3227 reservations office. www.amazonat.com.br. 20 units (showers only). 3-day packages from $275 (for 2 people), 4-day packages $395 (for 2 people). Children 6–12 25% of rate, 13–16 50% of rate. AE, DC, MC, V. **Amenities:** Restaurant; bar; pool. *In room:* Fan, minibar, no phone.

Ariaú Jungle Towers *(Overrated* Avoid this place. The Ariaú is the Disneyland Ford Factory of jungle lodges. While the marketing photos of treehouses and boardwalks suggest a kind of Swiss Family Robinson adventure, what the Ariaú delivers is theme-park style mass-market tourism, with hundreds of guests getting trundled each day along a set tourist route that already has been trodden literally tens of thousands of times. Repetition is a factor at any lodge, but the Ariaú has a serious problem of scale—there are nearly 300 units in place and another 100 under construction—combined with a management fixation on minimum expense and maximum profit. Group size runs from 15 to 25. Trips are always in motorized canoes, equipped with "go-devil" motors—noisy, fume-spewing two-strokes with the engine mounted on the propeller shaft. Little Evinrude outboards would be quieter and less polluting, but are apparently too expensive. And although Ariaú charges top price, it has never seen fit to hire a lodge biologist—to give evening nature talks, for example—or open an on-site interpretation center. Instead, in keeping with its McDonald's approach, Ariaú pays its guides less than almost any other local lodge. Not surprisingly, Ariaú guides are younger, less knowledgeable, sometimes bitter, and often on the verge of quitting. Their poor pay may explain the high-pressure commission sales approach to "add-on" tours.

Rua Leonardo Malcher 699, Manaus. (© 0800/925-000 or 092/2121-5000. Fax 092/233-5615. www.ariau.tur.br. 309 units (shower only, cold water). 3-day packages from $315, 4-day packages $375. Suites are $500 extra per package, regardless of the number of nights; Tarzan house $1,000 extra per package. Prices are negotiable; suites can be had for as little as $200 per package when occupancy is low. AE, DC, MC, V. **Amenities:** Restaurant; bar; pool; laundry service; Internet room (intermittent connection). *In room:* A/C, fridge, no phone.

Jungle Palace ⟨☆⟩ Appropriately named, the Jungle Palace is a floating hotel with all the modern conveniences. There is nothing rustic or rainforest-like about this lodge. It floats on a steel barge on the left bank of the Rio Negro at Lago do Tatu, about 50km (30 miles) upstream from Manaus. Rooms are sparsely furnished with one double and one single bed, but come with big-city amenities like telephones, dataports, and of course, hot showers. All rooms have balconies overlooking the river. The lodge also has a swimming pool, observation deck, lounge, bar, and restaurant. It's a peculiar kind of feeling, being in the lap of luxury in the middle of the rainforest. The palace offers the usual outings.

Rua Saldonha Marinho 700, Manaus. ⟨✆⟩ **092/633-6200.** Fax 092/234-0029. www.junglepalace.com.br. 20 units (shower only). 3-day packages $257 per person, 4-day packages $392. AE, DC, MC, V. **Amenities:** Restaurant; bar; pool; laundry. *In room:* A/C, TV, dataport, minibar, fridge, safe.

BOAT TRIPS

There are numerous operators that run boat trips out of Manaus. If you go with a package tour you will get a similar experience to that of a lodge: excursions on the small side channels, sunset and sunrise tour, caiman spotting, piranha fishing, and a visit to a *caboclo* (river peasant) settlement. The big difference is that in the time you're not on an excursion, you're moving on the river. There is always something to see, even if it's just the vastness of the river itself.

Viverde, Rua dos Cardeiros 26, Manaus (⟨✆⟩/fax **092/248-9988;** www.viverde. com.br), can arrange boat voyages or charters. Their website has photos and descriptions of the better Manaus-based touring boats.

Amazon Clipper Cruises (⟨✆⟩ **092/656-1246;** www.amazonclipper.com.br) has three old-style Amazon riverboats—the *Amazon Angler, Selly Clipper,* and *Selly Clipper II*—which make regular 3- and 4-day trips departing from the Hotel Tropical. The 3-day tour ($395) stays on the Solimões River; the 4-day tour ($550) goes up the Rio Negro.

If you want to set your own agenda, **Amazon Nut Safaris** (⟨✆⟩ **092/234-5860;** www.amazon-safaris.com) has two small traditional Amazon riverboats available for charter, complete with guide and crew. The *Iguana* has four cabins and one aluminum motor canoe. It charters for $462 per day. The *Cassiquiari* has eight cabins and six motor canoes, and charters for $1,050 per day. The price includes food, soft drinks and water, and activities such as piranha fishing and forest walks.

Swallows and Amazons ⟨☆⟩ One of the better-run companies in the Manaus adventure-tour market, Swallows and Amazons is run by New Englander Mark Aitchison and his Brazilian wife, Tania. The company's core trip is a 7-day package that spends a day in Manaus and then sets off up the Rio Negro to explore the territory around the Anavilhanas Archipelago. Transportation is on company-owned traditional wooden riverboats, while exploration is done either on foot or by canoes. Accommodations are either on the riverboat or in a comfortable but basic lodge near the Anavilhanas Archipelago. Maximum group size on any trip is eight. Cost for any of them is about US$100 per day if you book directly. These trips run year-round; check the website for timing and availability. In recent years the company has tried to expand into more off-the-beaten-track **adventure trips,** involving combinations of bush plane, motor-canoe, and hiking, sometimes to spots quite deep in the Amazon. Because demand is limited there are no regularly scheduled adventure trips; these have to be arranged through prior contact with the company.

Rua Quintino Bocaiuva 189, 2nd floor. ⟨✆⟩ **092/622-1246.** www.swallowsandamazonstours.com.

RIDING THE RIVERBOATS

The old-style wood or steel hull riverboats that ply the Amazon basin are about transport, not seeing wildlife. They stick to deeper channels, taking passengers and goods up and down the Amazon. Popular routes include Manaus-Belém, Manaus-Porto Velho, and Manaus-Santarém; these are all multiple-day trips. Most boats have several categories of cabins, or you just sling your hammock on deck. The ticket price includes basic meals; water and beer can be bought on board.

To book passage, go down to the new **Hidroviaria do Amazonas** in the middle of downtown at Rua Marquês de Santa Cruz 25. The **Agência Rio Amazonas** (© **092/621-4359**), which now enjoys a monopoly on riverboat tickets, has an information desk inside the front door where you can find out about arrival and departure times. By purchasing here, you can be sure you will not be cheated. Boats for **Belém** normally depart Monday, Wednesday, and Friday. Cost of a first-class hammock spot (on the upper deck) is R$236 (US$79). The trip takes 3 days. Boats for **Santarem** normally depart Tuesday and Thursday. The cost is R$115 (US$38) for first-class hammock. The trip takes about 40 hours. *Note:* Boats are BYOH (bring your own hammock).

DEEPER INTO THE AMAZON: EXPEDITIONS

Amazon Indian Tours *Value*   Amazon Indian provides a quality but no-frills introduction to the Amazon rainforest. Getting to its jungle camp involves a 3-hour drive followed by a 2-hour motorboat journey upriver. Using a simple hammock camp as a base, participants paddle out with a guide in small boats, or go for jungle walks of 3 to 4 hours in duration. The company owner and most guides are indigenous. Cost is $45 per person per day, meals and transport included.

Rua dos Andrades 311, Centro. ©/fax **092/633-5878**.

Amazon Mystery Tours *Value*   If you want to really explore the jungle, this is the company to go with; Amazon Mystery has the skills and experience to bring you deep into the rainforest, make your time there safe, comfortable, fun, and informative, and then get you back to town again. The company's core adventure is kayak descents of Amazon tributary rivers upstream of Manaus. A typical day includes a few hours of paddling, followed by a delicious lunch of fresh fish, followed by a hike to a waterfall or hidden cavern that few have ever seen. At night, you head out with a spotlight to search for caiman or other jungle creatures. Participants need a basic level of physical ability—for example, you should be able to hike and paddle a small boat—but no special skills. The camping is very comfortable, and the food is excellent (always important). You sleep in hammocks. On some of the trips, it's possible to practice **arborism**—tree climbing—where you hoist yourself 60m or 70m (197–230 ft.) up into the tops of the trees the way rainforest canopy researchers do. This is truly magic (arborism does cost extra). All trips have two professional guides, but with advance notice the company can also arrange specialized itineraries geared to a particular interest (for example, orchids or birdlife) accompanied by a scientist accredited on that particular topic.

Av. Djalma Batista 385, Sala 103, Manaus. © **092/633-7844**. Fax 092/233-2780. www.amazon-outdoor.com.

11 The Pantanal

Cuiabá: 1,978km (1,226 miles) NW of Rio de Janeiro, 1,608km (997 miles) NW of São Paulo; Campo Grande: 1,414km (877 miles) NW of Rio de Janeiro, 992km (615 miles) NW of São Paulo

The best place in South America to see wildlife is not the Amazon but the Pantanal, a France-size wetland on the far western edge of Brazil that is bursting

The Pantanal

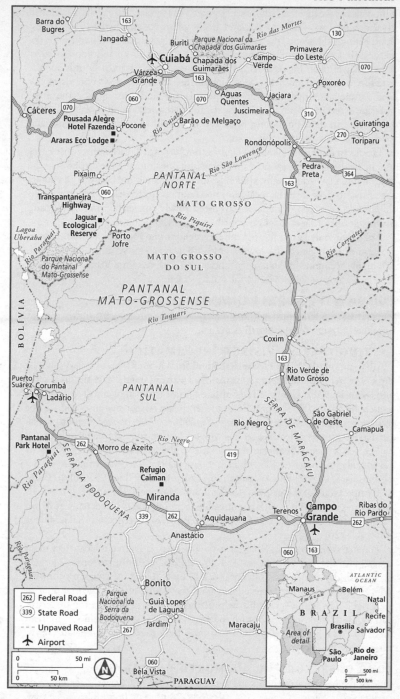

with animals—capybaras, caimans, jaguars, anacondas, giant otters, colorful Hyacinth macaws, kites, hawks, and flocks of storks and herons. The largest flood plain in the world, the Pantanal's rhythm is governed by the rivers. In the wet season, from November through April, the rivers fill up and flood to cover a vast alluvial plain for months. Millions of birds are attracted by this aquatic paradise, and the mammals take refuge on the remaining few mounds of dry land. As the water drains from May onwards, the land dries up, and the situation slowly reverses: Animals are attracted to the few remaining water pools. Fish get trapped in these pools, and birds and mammals alike gather for water and food as they wait for the rains to start.

Thanks to this yearly cycle, the land cannot be farmed intensively. Most farms use the land for cattle grazing in the dry season only, moving the cattle when the fields flood. Few roads of any kind exist in the Pantanal; the best way to explore the area is to make like the locals and head out on horseback. Many of the cattle *fazendas* (ranches) in the area have been slowly converting over to tourism. Staying at one of these lodges is your best option for exploring the area.

Tip: If you only have a limited time to spend in the Pantanal, we recommend seeing the North Pantanal; allow for at least 3 days at a lodge, and 4 days is ideal. We highly recommend Araras Eco Lodge (p. 374); accommodations are basic, but the territory is fabulous and the guides excellent.

CUIABÁ & THE NORTH PANTANAL

Cuiabá is a modern town without much to see. Still, the city makes a great jumping-off point for the North Pantanal.

GETTING THERE & VISITOR INFORMATION

Cuiabá's airport, **Aeroporto Marechal Rondon,** is located 6km (4 miles) south of the city center in the adjacent municipality of Varzea Grande. The airport is serviced by **Varig, VASP, Gol,** and **TAM** airlines. A taxi to downtown will cost approximately R$24 (US$8). The only buses to Centro are regular city buses and are not recommended for travelers with luggage. *Note:* If you have booked a tour to a Pantanal lodge, check with your operator whether airport transfers are included.

The very efficient **bus terminal** of Cuiabá, Av. Marechal Deodoro s/n, is in Alvodarada just north of the city center. Cuiabá is a long way from anywhere: To Brasília, it's 1,098km (682 miles), to São Paulo, 1,597km (992 miles). Buses to Campo Grande, the gateway to the South Pantanal, take approximately 10 hours. An overnight bus with comfortable reclining chairs leaves daily at 8 and 9:30pm. Contact **Motta** at © **065/621-1159;** www.motta.com.br). The fare is R$60 (US$20).

The main tourist office, **Secretaria de Turismo,** is located on Cuiabá's main square, the Praça da República 131 (© **065/624-9060**); it's open Monday through Friday from 8am to noon and 2 to 6pm. There is no sign on the outside; enter the lovely heritage building, and the tourist office is the first door to your right. The staff is incredibly helpful and has tons of information on lodges and tour operators. The state of Mato Grosso is pouring money into its tourism industry, and it offers excellent information. Check the website for details: **www.turismo.mt.gov.br**.

TOUR OPERATORS IN THE NORTH PANTANAL

One of the best tour operators is Pantanal **Explorer,** Av. Governador Ponce de Arruda 670, Varzea Grande (© **065/682-2800;** fax 065/682-1260; www.araraslodge.com.br). Stays in the Pantanal are at the excellent Araras Eco-Lodge.

In addition, the company offers trips to the Chapada dos Guimarães, boat trips in the Pantanal, as well as ecotours to the Mato Grosso part of the Amazon rainforest. Another well-known tour operator is **Anaconda Turismo,** Av. Isaac Póvoas 606, Centro (© **065/624-4142;** www.anacondapantanal.com.br). This operator works with a large number of fazendas and *pousadas* and can customize a package according to your interests. It also operates in the Chapada dos Guimarães (see "A Side Trip to Chapada dos Guimarães," below). If you want to reserve your Pantanal package before arriving in Brazil, you can contact **Brazil Nuts** (© **800/553-9959** or 914/593-0266; www.brazilnuts.com) or **4StarBrazil** (© **866/464-7827;** http://4starbrazil.com).

Most packages—including transportation, English-speaking guides, accommodations, and meals—cost around R$450 (US$150) per day per person, depending on the time of year and number of people in your party.

THE TRANSPANTANEIRA

Despite the name, this gravel road stops dead at Porto Jofre, 143km (89 miles) from where it began, and at least that far from the far edge of the Pantanal. Had it been completed, it would likely have destroyed the Pantanal by totally skewing the ecosystem's drainage pattern, but in its unfinished state, it has become one of the great wildlife-viewing areas in the world. The ditches on either side of the roadbed have become favorite feeding grounds for kingfishers, egrets, jabiru storks, and more than four varieties of hawks and three different kinds of kites. Beneath the many rickety bridges are small rivers or pools where *jacaré* gather by the hundreds. Spend but a day on the Transpantaneira, and you'll see more wildlife than you'd see in a week in the Amazon.

To reach the Transpantaneira, take highway BR-163 west from Cuiabá. After about 18km (11 miles), turn southwest on highway MT-060 and follow it for 75km (46 miles) to the small town of Poconé. Follow the signs through the small downtown to the beginning of the Transpantaneira on the far side of town.

WHERE TO STAY IN CUIABA

Many lodges will pick you up right at the airport, sparing you the need to stay in Cuiabá.

Expensive

Eldorado Hotel 🌟 Though it's the only luxury hotel in Cuiabá, the rooms at the Eldorado are fairly standard (certainly not as nice as the apartments in the Soleil; see below). They're comfortably furnished with a desk, armchair, and table; the colors and decor are slightly dated, but the bathrooms are modern and come with bathtubs. However, it's in the amenities that you get what you pay for. The Eldorado is the only joint in town that offers a business center, room service, a spacious swimming pool, and a sun deck.

Av. Isaac Póvoas 1000, Cuiabá 78045-640, MT. © 065/624-4000. Fax 065/624-1480. www.hoteiseldorado. com.br. 147 units. R$140–R$255 (US$70–US$128) double; R$230–R$425 (US$115–US$213) suite. Extra person R$50 (US$25). Children under 11 stay free in parent's room. AE, DC, MC, V. Free parking. **Amenities:** Restaurant; bar; outdoor pool; business center; 24-hr. room service; laundry service. *In room:* A/C, TV, dataport, minibar, fridge, hair dryer, safe.

Le Soleil 🌟🌟 *(Kids)* Le Soleil offers by far the best accommodations in Cuiabá, provided you don't need amenities such as a pool, business center, or room service. The hotel was built as an apartment building, so every unit is a full suite; all are spacious with complete kitchens and lots of closet space. To splurge, go for a duplex penthouse. There are four of them on the top floor, and they are huge! On the top floor, there's a sitting room, kitchen, and large deck with a barbecue; down the spiral staircase are two spacious bedrooms and two bathrooms. As nice as the duplex suites are, the regular one-bedroom suites are nothing to sneeze at: Nicely furnished, with the spacious sitting room, dining area, fully equipped kitchen, and bedroom, you will have more space than in any hotel room in town.

Av. S. Sebastião 2622, Goiabeiras, Cuiabá, MT. ℂ 065/623-0433. Fax 065/623-0803. 22 units (shower only). R$172 (US$86) 1-bedroom double; R$228 (US$114) duplex suite. Up to 30% discount in low season. Extra person 25%. Children under 11 stay free in parent's room. Over 10, R$20 (US$10). AE, DC, MC, V. Free parking. **Amenities:** Laundry service. *In room:* A/C, TV, dataport, kitchen.

LODGES IN THE NORTH PANTANAL

Araras Eco Lodge 🌟🌟🌟   Araras Lodge is situated right on the Transpantaneira Highway, making it one of the best spots for exploring the Pantanal. With only 14 rooms, the lodge is pleasantly small and rustic. No fancy rooms or amenities; each guest room comes with a private bathroom and a hammock outside on the veranda. The guides that Araras works with are excellent, either university trained or with many years of experience with the local animals and birdlife. Unlike other lodges, where guests are lumped together into one big group, Araras assigns each party its own guide, even if there are only two of you. Activities include long hikes to the lodge's lookout tower. One afternoon, as we watched the sun set over the Pantanal, a group of five Hyacinth macaws flew right over us. Other excursions include boat or canoe trips on a small local river known for large hawks and giant river otters. On drives along the Transpantaneira, even in a 3-hour time span, you'll lose track of the number of birds you'll see. Horse lovers and experienced riders will be in heaven riding through the flooded fields. All meals are included, and though simply cooked, the food is delicious and plentiful, often including excellent local fish.

Transpantaneira Hwy. Reservation office: Av. Governador Ponce de Arruda 670, Varzea Grande, MT. ℂ 065/ 682-2800. Fax 065/682-1260. www.araraslodge.com.br. 15 units (shower only). R$1,500–R$1,800 (US$500– US$600) per person for a 3- or 4-day package w/all meals and guided activities. Extra person about 25%. Children under 11 stay free in parent's room. AE, DC, MC, V. Free parking. **Amenities:** Restaurant; bar; outdoor pool; laundry. *In room:* A/C, no phone.

Jaguar Ecological Reserve 🌟🌟   Wildlife viewing is always a matter of luck and patience, particularly when it comes to large predators like jaguars. But one of the best ways of improving your odds is to visit this lodge—the centerpiece of a private ecological reserve—where an astonishing one in four guests sees one of these huge South American cats. It's a very long way 110km (68 miles) down the bumpy Transpantaneira, and the accommodations are expensive and only basic, but for a view of that big cat it may be worth it. For the 75% of guests who do not see jaguars, there is still the usual vast array of caiman and colorful birds, so rare in the rest of the world, so common in the Pantanal. Stays at the JER are coordinated though the U.S. agency Focus Tours (www.focustours.com).

Transpantaneira, Km 110, Poconé, MT. ℂ 505/466-4688 in the U.S., or 065/9968-6154 in Brazil. www.focus tours.com. 7 units (shower only). R$375 (US$125) per person, all meals included. Free parking. Transfer not included in price. **Amenities:** Wildlife-viewing. *In room:* No phone.

A SIDE TRIP TO CHAPADA DOS GUIMARÃES

In one sense, the Chapada dos Guimarães is an integral part of the Pantanal. Some of the water that covers the Pantanal flows from these highlands. More important, their low jagged red cliffs prevent any water from flowing north or east, with the result that the Pantanal yearly turns into a kind of giant bathtub. In appearance, the Chapada has much in common with the desert buttes of Arizona or Utah.

There are weird and wonderful formations of bright red rock, and long beautiful canyons. The vegetation is dry and scrubby, except where the many rivers channel, and then you get waterfalls streaming down into basins lush with tropical vegetation. Hiking is excellent; trails are clear even if—as ever in Brazil—they're completely without markers or signage. Most trails end at a view point, a waterfall, or a natural pool. Sometimes, you get all three. Wildlife is obviously not up to the standard set by the Pantanal, but in the Chapada, you do have the opportunity of seeing the gorgeous red macaw, oftentimes playing in the thermals by a cliffside. Finally, Chapada is a quiet, laid-back place with a very slight counterculture feel. Over the years, the geodesic center of Brazil, located in the Chapada, has attracted a fair sampling of New Agers, some of whom have settled in the area and started up restaurants or *pousadas* or the inevitable crafts shop.

The tourist office will have you believe that you could easily spend a week here, but we figure 2 days is plenty. The best time to visit is May through September, when the weather is dry and sunshine almost guaranteed. The heavy rains in the summer (Dec–Apr) can make some of the trails treacherous and the dirt roads inaccessible. The best hikes include **Cachoeira Veu de Noiva,** the tallest waterfall in the park; **Mirante da Geodesia,** a fabulous lookout over the lowlands below the Chapada, with Cuiabá in the distance; **Cidade de Pedra (City of Stone),** which is named after the eroded formations that appear to form structures and look like ruins of buildings; and **Morro São Jerônimo,** the highest point in the Chapada. Morro São Jerônimo can be reached by a 4-hour hike; bring lots of water and sunscreen, as you will be exposed to the hot sun most of the way.

If you're staying overnight, there are a couple of good options. **Pousada Laura Vicuña,** Rodovia Emanuel Pinheiro, Km 62, Chapada dos Guimarães (© 065/ 301-2313; www.pousadalauravicuna.com.br), is perfect for those traveling with kids. The large leisure area has an outdoor swimming pool and a second pool with water slides. The *pousada* also offers bicycles, a volleyball court, and soccer fields; short trails leading to a waterfall start just behind the *pousada.* The accommodations are very basic—just clean and cool rooms with a double bed and bunk bed. The three chalets sleep four people comfortably and provide a bit more privacy. Rooms cost R$130 to R$155 (US$43–US$52); seasonal discounts are available. Located in town, **Hotel Turismo,** Rua Fernando Correa da Costa 1065, Centro (© 065/301-1176; www.chapadadosguimaraes.com.br/ hotelturismo), offers 35 simply furnished rooms with a double and a single bed. The *pousada* offers a hearty breakfast and has two small outdoor swimming pools. Rooms cost R$75 to R$110 (US$25–US$37).

To stuff yourself silly on a variety of regional dishes, head to **O Mestrinho,** Rua Quinco Caldas 119, Centro (© 065/301-1181), one of the most popular lunch spots in town. Dishes include chicken and beef stews, beans, *farofa,* and grilled fish. It's open daily from 11am to 5pm. Perched on the edge of the plateau and overlooking the plains below the Chapada is **Morro dos Ventos** ⊛, Chacara Morro dos Ventos via Estrada do Mirante (© 065/301-1030). The menu offers regional home cooking. Dishes are huge and serve at least three people. A good choice is the chicken stew with okra served in a heavy cast-iron pot with generous side dishes of beans, salad, *farofa,* and rice. It's open daily from 9am to 6pm.

GETTING THERE   The Chapada is 72km (45 miles) north of Cuiabá. By car, follow the MT 251 to the park and the town of Chapada. Direct buses leave from Cuiabá's *rodoviária,* take about 1 hour, and cost R$6 (US$2). **Viação Rubi** (© 065/624-9044) has daily departures at 9, 10:30am, 2, and 6:30pm.

The **tourist office** is at Rua Quinco Caldas s/n (© **065/301-2045**). The park visitor center (© **065/301-1133**) is located on highway MT-251 about 8km (5 miles) past the park entrance, about 15km (9 miles) before the town of Chapada dos Guiamarães. An excellent local tour operator, **Ecoturismo Cultural,** Praça Dom Wunibaldo 464 (© **065/301-1393;** www.chapadadosguimaraes. com.br), arranges day trips with guides and transportation and can assist with accommodations.

CAMPO GRANDE & THE SOUTH PANTANAL

Campo Grande is a fairly new town; established at the end of the 19th century, it is an important transportation hub for the region. The Pantanal in Mato Grosso do Sul is a little less wild, a little more given over to cattle ranching, and significantly harder to access.

GETTING THERE & VISITOR INFORMATION

Campo Grande's **airport** is located 6km (4 miles) west of downtown on Avenida Duque de Caxias (© **067/368-6093**). The airport is serviced by **VASP, Varig, TAM,** and **Gol** airlines. Your best option to get from the airport to downtown is by taxi—the fare is R$21 (US$7).

The **bus station** in Campo Grande is located at Rua Dom Aquino and Rua Joaquim Nabuco (© **067/383-1678**), just a block from the main avenue, Avenida Afonso Pena. Buses connect Campo Grande to Cuiabá (approximately 10 hr.), Bonito (5 hr.), and Corumbá (7 hr.). **Motta** (© **067/324-3242;** www.motta. com.br) provides service between Campo Grande and Cuiabá. **Viação Cruzeiro do Sul** (© **067/382-9170**) offers daily service between Campo Grande, Bonito, and Corumbá.

The main **tourist information office** is on Av. Noroeste 5140, at the corner of Avenida Afonso Pena (© **067/324-5830**). It's open Tuesday through Saturday from 8am to 7pm and Sunday from 9am to noon. They've got great maps, excellent brochures, and contacts for Pantanal lodges and Bonito packages.

TOUR OPERATORS IN THE SOUTH PANTANAL

Located in Campo Grande, **Open Door** has some excellent packages. A tour at a Pantanal lodge for 3 nights including all meals and activities, with transfer from and to Campo Grande airport, starts at $350. Contact Open Door at Rua Barão do Rio Branco, Campo Grande (© **067/721-8303;** www.opendoortur. com.br). The agency is very quick in responding to e-mail.

N & T Japantour, Av. Afonso Pena 2081, Room 20, Campo Grande (© **067/ 782-9425;** www.japantour.com.br), provides packages to several Pantanal lodges. Including your transfer from Campo Grande, a 3-day stay will cost R$675 to R$1,120 (US$225–US$370) and a 4-day stay R$825 to R$950 (US$275– US$1,425) depending on the lodge.

LODGES IN THE SOUTH PANTANAL

Pantanal Park Hotel 🐾🐾   Located on the shores of the Paraguay River, the Pantanal Park Hotel takes full advantage of the wild Pantanal territory of the Corumbá-Paraguay area. (Transportation from Campo Grande can be arranged at an additional cost of R$600/US$200 for two people.) The lodge is a wonderful comfortable retreat. Common areas include a large outdoor pool and sun deck, and lovely common building. Accommodations are in smaller chalet buildings, with four apartments per building. Ecotourists have the option of horseback riding, bird spotting, piranha fishing, nighttime caiman spotting trips and, in the daytime and with luck, jaguar spotting (there are cats in the area and sightings do happen, but they aren't everyday affairs). Fishing fiends will be in heaven as the lodge specializes in fishing trips; *paçu, barbado, pintado,* and more are abundant. All meals are included.

Contact for reservations: Rua Hipólito Jose da Costa 229, Presidente Prudente SP. ℭ **018/231-5332.** Fax 018/231-1333. Hotel contact: ℭ 067/9987-3267. www.pantanalpark.com.br. 41 units (shower only). 3-day package R$375 (US$125) per person. Children 5–10 R$252 (US$84). Children under 5 stay free in parent's room. AE, DC, MC, V. Free parking. Access from either Corumbá or Campo Grande: Take Andorinha bus and get off at Port Morinho where the lodge will pick you up by boat. **Amenities:** Restaurant; bar; pool; laundry. *In room:* A/C, TV, fridge, no phone.

Refugio Caiman ☆☆   The most luxurious lodge in the Pantanal, the Refugio Caiman is set on a huge cattle ranch outside the town of Miranda, about 250km (155 miles) from Campo Grande. The land is not as rugged as what you'll see in the North Pantanal; the refugio is still very much a working cattle ranch, and that in itself provides some interest. The lodge and its package of activities are very safe, very "soft adventure"—perfect for families with young children. Avid horseback riders may want to avoid this place; no trotting or cantering are allowed. Excursions head out well after breakfast and are perfect for those who lack the fitness level for longer hikes or expeditions. The food is outstanding, and the accommodations in an old hacienda with a new central pool are positively luxurious. The lodge has an excellent library and video collection on the Pantanal.

Reservations: Rua Campos Bicudo 98-112, Itaim São Paulo. ℭ **011/3079-6622.** www.caiman.com.br. 29 units (shower only). R$450–R$600 (US$150–US$200) double. Extra person about 25%. Children under 11 stay free in parent's room. AE, DC, MC, V. Free parking. **Amenities:** Restaurant; bar; outdoor pool; game room; laundry. *In room:* A/C, no phone.

12 Iguaçu Falls

1,421km (881 miles) SW of Rio de Janeiro, 1,019km (632 miles) SW of São Paulo

Anyone who's ever seen *The Mission* will instantly recognize the falls of Iguaçu. The Rio Iguaçu—which here forms the border between Brazil and Argentina—roars over a sheer precipice 5km (3 miles) wide and 81m (270 ft.) high. The fine mist tossed up by the falls precipitates down and creates a pocket microclimate of rainforest lushness, filled with tropical birds and an abundant population of glorious tropical butterflies. Aside from the falls, there's not a lot to see in Foz do Iguaçu. For those with an air pass, Iguaçu Falls makes a perfect 2-day stopover. Those without one may want to consider whether the falls—glorious as they truly are—are worth a 998km (620-mile) trip from Rio or São Paulo.

ESSENTIALS
GETTING THERE
BY PLANE   The **Aeroporto Internacional Foz do Iguaçu** (ℭ **045/521-4276**) is located on BR-469 halfway between downtown and the national park. The airport is serviced by **Varig, TAM,** and **VASP.** The 13km (8-mile) taxi ride to downtown Foz do Iguaçu will cost R$30 to R$40 (US$10–US$13). A city bus connects the airport to downtown and takes 45 minutes and costs R$1.50 (50¢).

BY BUS   Long-distance buses arrive at the **Terminal Rodoviário,** Av. Costa e Silva s/n (ℭ **045/522-2590**). The station is 4km (2½ miles) northeast of downtown. For buses to and from Rio de Janeiro or São Paulo, contact **Pluma** at ℭ **045/522-2515.** Pluma also has buses to Buenos Aires.

GETTING AROUND
Foz do Iguaçu (normally just called Iguaçu) is a small modern city of 250,000 people. To the south of the city lies the Iguaçu River and beyond it, Argentina.

The falls are a 27km (17-mile) drive southeast from downtown on the Avenida das Cataratas (Hwy. BR-469). There are quite a few good hotels and some other attractions and restaurants along this road. About 6km (4 miles) from downtown, there's a turnoff for the Ponte Tancredo Neves, which crosses into Argentina. The city's downtown is small and easy to navigate, but except for some decent shopping, it offers few attractions.

BY BUS   City buses begin and end their routes at Avenida Juscelino Kubitschek (Av. J. K.) at the corner of Avenida República Argentina. Buses to the falls are marked CATARATAS (R$2/65¢) or PARQUE NACIONAL (R$1/35¢). They run every 20 minutes until 6:40pm. The trip to the park gate and visitor center takes 45 minutes. From the park gate, a shuttle bus takes you the rest of the way to the falls.

BY TAXI   A trip across town will cost around R$10 (US$3.35), while a trip from the city center to a hotel on the Avenida Cataratas will cost between R$15 and R$30 (US$5–US$10), depending how far along the road you are. **Coopertaxi** (© **0800/524-6464** or 45/529-8821) has cabs available 24/7.

VISITOR INFORMATION

The main **tourist information center** is at Praça Getúlio Vargas (Av. J. K and Rua Rio Branco) (© **045/521-1125;** www.fozdoiguacu.pr.gov.br). It's open Monday through Friday from 9am to 5pm. There are also tourist information booths at the airport and bus station (see "By Plane" or "By Bus," above). You can also call the Iguaçu tourist information service **Teletur** (© **0800/451-516** toll-free within Brazil). The service operates daily from 7am to 11pm. Attendants speak excellent English and have up-to-date and accurate information.

FAST FACTS   The American Express agent is STTC Turismo (inside the Hotel Bourbon) Av. das Cataratas, Km 2.5 (© **045/529-8580**). To exchange currency, go to **Banco do Brasil,** Av. Brasil 1377 (© 045/521-2525), or **Omegatur Turismo e Cambio,** Av. Juscelino Kubitschek 245 (© 045/572-2837).

For medical attention, go to **Hospital Internacional,** Av. Brasil 1637 (© 045/ 523-1404). If you have a dental emergency, contact the **Clinica Odontologica** at © 045/523-5965; it's open 24 hours a day.

For Internet access try **NetPub** (© **045/572-5773**), at Rua Rui Barbosa 549 (corner of Av. J. K.); it's open daily 10am to 10pm. Access costs R$5 (US$1.65) per hour.

WHAT TO SEE & DO
THE TOP ATTRACTIONS

For hassle-free visits of the falls, a number of tour operators can organize transportation and guides. Trips can be customized to include visits to other Iguaçu attractions such as the bird park, Macuco Safari, or the Itaipu Dam. The most popular service is the 1-day guided visit to the Argentine falls, which at most agencies costs around R$220 to R$250 (US$73–US$83) total for up to four people. Reputable companies include **Conveniotur,** Rua Rui Barbosa 820 (© **045/ 523-3500;** www.conveniotur.com.br), and **STTC Turismo** (© 45/529-6464; www.sttcturismo.com.br). **Central Tur** (© 45/521-4258; www.centraltur.com.br) is the only company that will offer transfer to the Argentine falls without the expensive and frankly completely unnecessary tour guide. Cost is R$120 (US$40) for a minivan that seats up to seven people.

Itaipu Dam ⟨⟨⟨   The world's largest hydroelectric project stands 10km (6 miles) upriver from Foz do Iguaçu on the Río Paraná. Whatever your thoughts

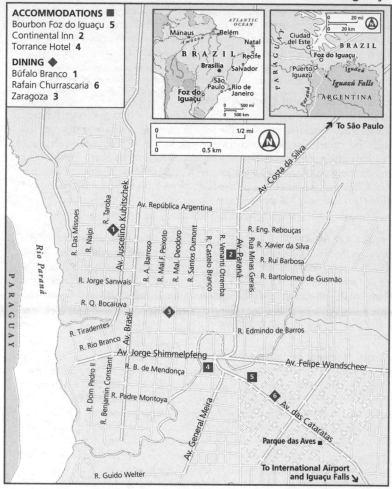

Foz do Iguaçu

ACCOMMODATIONS ■
Bourbon Foz do Iguaçu **5**
Continental Inn **2**
Torrance Hotel **4**

DINING ◆
Búfalo Branco **1**
Rafain Churrascaria **6**
Zaragoza **3**

on dams, the long curving concrete barrage is indeed a beautiful sight. Visitors to the dam are shown a deeply biased 30-minute film offering a very limited amount of information on the fascinating construction of the dam, and none at all on its environmental impacts. Then you board a bus that crosses to an observation platform in the midpoint of the dam. Special Tours (which include a visit to the Production Building) and Technical Tours (where you go inside the dam to see the turbines) are still available, but dam authorities now require more lead time and will ask many more questions before granting permission.

Av. Tancredo Neves 6702. ☎ **045/520-5252.** www.itaipu.gov.br. Free admission. Regular 1½-hr. guided tours Mon–Sat at 8, 9, 10am, 2, 3, and 4pm. Special 2-hr. tours by prior arrangement only. Bus: 110 or 120.

Macuco Boat Safari ☆☆ Macuco participants pile aboard 7.5m (25-ft.) Zodiacs, the guide fires up twin 150hp outboards, and you're off up the river, bouncing over wave trains, breaking eddy lines, powering your way up the surging current until the boat's in the gorge, advancing slowly towards one of the (smaller) falls. As the boat nears, the mist gets thicker, the roar louder, the passengers wetter and more and more thrilled (or terrified), until the Zodiac peels away, slides downstream, and hides in an eddy till everyone's caught their breath. Then you do it all again. Allow 2 hours for the entire trip.

Parque Nacional do Iguaçu. ℂ 045/574-4244. Fax 045/574-4244. www.macucosafari.com.br. R$60 (US$20) per person. Mon 1–5:30pm; Tues–Sun and holidays 8am–5:30pm. Bus: Parque Nacional or Cataratas.

Escalada Rappel and Climbing Park 🐵🐵

The highlight of this climbing park opposite the Tropical Hotel is an extraordinary **Iguaçu Gorge Rappel,** from a gangway cantilevered over the edge of the gorge all the way down to the rocks by the edge of the Iguaçu river. Once at the bottom those with some climbing experience (and their own gear) can rock-climb back up. Also on sight is a climbing wall and an elevated 15-part high-wire obstacle course. Construction of the park was just being finished as of press time; prices for the rappel and obstacle course have not yet been set.

Parque Nacional do Iguaçu. ℂ 045/529-9175. Daily 9am–5:30pm. Bus: Parque Nacional or Cataratas.

Parque das Aves 🐵🐵

For the best bird-watching in Iguaçu, visit the Parque das Aves. Set in 5 hectares (12 acres) of lush subtropical rainforest, the Parque das Aves (Bird Park) displays more than 180 species, many of the them local Iguaçu species. A large number of birds are in huge walk-through aviaries, some 24m (80 ft.) tall and at least 60m (200 ft.) long. Expect to spend 2 hours here.

Rodovia das Cataratas, Km 11, 300m (984 ft.) before the National Park entrance. ℂ 045/529-8282. www. parquedasaves.com.br. R$24 (US$8), free for children under 9. Daily 8:30am–5:30pm. Bus: Parque Nacional or Cataratas.

Parque Nacional do Iguaçu 🐵🐵🐵

The Brazilians and Argentines are deeply competitive about which side offers the best vantage point for viewing the falls. The Argentines do have one bit of logic in their favor—more of the falls *are* on their side—but the best view point is from the Brazilian side. Starting at the visitor center, you board a shuttle bus and set off down the parkway for the falls. (Private vehicles are not allowed in the park.) Starting in front of the Tropical das Cataratas hotel, a little view point is where you get your first magic view of the falls. From here, a pathway zigs and zags down the side of the gorge and trundles along the cliff as you look across the narrow gorge at water cascading down in a hundred different places. At the end of the trail, there's an elevator that lifts you up to the Canoas restaurant by the edge of the falls. Before going up, however, take the elevated walkway leading out *in front* of one of the falls. The wind and spray coming off the falls are deeply exhilarating and, unless you've brought a raincoat, it's guaranteed to have you soaked in less than 30 seconds. You can easily spend a half-day looking at the falls and exploring the park. For more about the falls from the Argentine side, see "Puerto Iguazú & Iguazú Falls" in chapter 4.

Rodovia dos Cataratas, Km 18. ℂ 045/572-2261. www.cataratasdoiguacu.com.br. Admission R$18 (US$6) adults, R$12 (US$4) children under 7, includes transportation inside the park. Parking R$6 (US$2). Mon 1–6pm; Tues–Sun and holidays 8am–6pm (summer until 7pm). Bus: Cataratas or Parque Nacional.

SHOPPING

Iguaçu's Centro is a popular shopping district. Most shops are concentrated around the Avenida Brasil, Rua Barbosa, Rua Almirante Barroso, and Quintino Bocaiuva. You'll find excellent leather goods such as jackets and purses. The one and only souvenir shop worth visiting is **Tres Fronteiras,** BR 469 Rodovia das Cataratas Km 11, just before the turnoff for Argentina (ℂ **045/523-1167;** www.tresfronteiras.com.br). Tres Fronteiras sells crafts and souvenirs from all of

Brazil. The deli sells a selection of Brazilian wines, coffees, sweets, and delicious handmade chocolates from Rio Grande do Sul. The shop is open daily from 9am to 8pm.

WHERE TO STAY
CENTRO

Continental Inn ★★ *Finds*   Completely renovated in 1998, the Continental Inn is a real gem. All rooms have been redone and are very comfortable, but the suites are truly outstanding and worth the small surcharge of R$40 (US$20) for a regular suite or R$90 (US$45) for a master suite. The suites have beautiful hardwood floors and modern blond wood furniture, a separate sitting area, a desk, a table, and a bathroom with a large round bathtub. Rooms for travelers with disabilities are available.

Av. Paranà 1089, Foz do Iguaçu, 85852-000 PR. ⓒ 045/523-5000. www.continentalinn.com.br. 113 units (102 rooms shower only). R$130 (US$43) double; R$250 (US$83) suite; R$350 (US$117) master suite. In low season 20% discount. Children under 5 stay free in parent's room. Over 5 R$30 (US$15). AE, DC, MC, V. Free parking. **Amenities:** Restaurant; large pool; exercise room; sauna; game room w/video arcade; business center; 24-hr. room service; laundry. *In room:* A/C, TV, dataport, minibar, fridge, hair dryer, safe.

Torrance Hotel *Value*   The Torrance has the look and amenities of a more expensive hotel: Nice location, nice patio with good pool, a restaurant, and such, but at a price that (almost) puts it in competition with a youth hostel. So what's the catch? Well, the rooms aren't exactly cramped, but they're not sizable either. Some clever architecture with interesting floor plans and small balconies make what actually are fairly cozy spaces seem larger than they are. As long as sight-seeing's what you're here for, the Torrance could be your best option.

Rua Manêncio Martins 108, Foz do Iguaçu, 85853-130 PR. ⓒ 045/523-2124. Fax 045/523-2149. www.torrance hotel.com.br. 93 units (shower only). R$100 (US$33) double. 30% discount in off season. Extra person about 25%. Children under 6 stay free in parent's room. AE, DC, MC, V. Free parking. **Amenities:** Restaurant; bar; adult's pool and small children's pool; game room; 24-hr. room service; massage; laundry. *In room:* A/C, TV, dataport, minibar, hair dryer.

ON THE PARK ROAD

Bourbon Foz do Iguaçu ★★★ *Kids*   An outstanding resort hotel, the Bourbon's rooms are beautifully appointed; those in the original wing are pleasantly decorated in light colors and look out over the front of the hotel and entrance, and superior rooms have a veranda. The 10-year-old newer wing houses the master suites, which are really just a room, but with panorama windows and newer, more modern furnishings. But don't count on spending a lot of time in your room; the real draw of the Bourbon is its leisure space. Three kilometers (2 miles) of trails in the woods behind the hotel loop through orchards, a tree nursery, and gardens. The vast outdoor pool area includes three large pools, and in high season, activity leaders organize all-day children's activities.

Rodovia das Cataratas, Km 2.5, Foz do Iguaçu, 85863-000 PR. ⓒ 0800/701-8181 or 045/529-0123. www. bourbon.com.br. 311 units. R$295–R$327 (US$98–US$109) standard, superior, or master double. Extra person R$75–R$100 (US$25–US$33). AE, DC, MC, V. Free parking. Bus: Parque Nacional or Cataratas. **Amenities:** 3 restaurants; huge pool complex (3 outdoor pools, 1 small indoor pool); outdoor tennis courts lit for evening play; sauna (dry and steam); children's programs; game room; tour desk; concierge; car rental; business center; shopping arcade; salon; 24-hr. room service; massage; laundry service; nonsmoking rooms. *In room:* A/C, TV, dataport (master suites only), minibar, fridge, hair dryer, safe.

Tropical das Cataratas ★★   The only hotel allowed inside the national park, the Tropical is built in a style similar to that of the Tropical in Manaus: a low building with long hallways, elegant lounges, and rooms in colonial style, with lovely jacaranda wood everywhere. You can hear the falls, but you can't see them from the hotel. Rooms are spread out over a number of wings, connected by spacious long corridors. The deluxe rooms all have beautiful hardwood floors and dark wood furniture; desks and tabletops are finished with light granite, and the bathrooms have large bathtubs. The bathrooms in the superior rooms were recently renovated, and now feature large granite countertops, shower and tub combos, and bright, movable makeup mirrors. The only potential drawback to staying at the Tropical is that it is very far from town.

Parque Nacional do Iguaçu, Foz do Iguaçu, 85863-000 PR. ⓒ **0800/701-2670** or 045/521-7000. www.tropical hotel.com.br. 200 units. R$496–R$595 (US$165–US$198) double superior; R$694 (US$231) double deluxe. Children under 10 stay free in parent's room. AE, DC, MC, V. Free parking. Take the road to Iguaçu Falls, go straight toward the gate; do not turn left into the visitor area. Identify yourself at the gate. Reservations recommended. **Amenities:** 2 restaurants; bar; large outdoor pool; tennis court; game room; tour desk; concierge; children's programs; business center (24-hr. Internet access); shopping arcade; salon; 24-hr. room service; laundry service. *In room:* A/C, TV, minibar, fridge, hair dryer, safe.

WHERE TO DINE

For the best *feijoada* in town, visit the colonial dining room of **Itaipu** restaurant, in the Hotel Tropical (ⓒ **045/574-1688**), on Saturday afternoon, of course. A large feast is served up Carioca-style with white rice, *farofa,* fried banana, green cabbage, slices of orange, and all the black beans and meat you can eat.

As an alternative to beef, **Zaragoza,** Rua Quintino Bocaiúva 882 (ⓒ **045/ 574-3084;** www.restaurantezaragoza.com.br), offers excellent seafood with a strong Spanish flavor. The menu is particularly strong on prawns, lobster, and local fish served grilled or broiled. On Sunday, people come from far and wide to savor the paella for lunch.

Rafain Churrascaria, Av. das Cataratas 1749, Km 6.5 near the Hotel Bourbon (ⓒ **045/523-1177**), is best known for its evening folklore show. Monday through Saturday from 9 to 11pm, the restaurant hosts a tacky but fun variety show with artists who present songs and dances from Argentina, Paraguay, Mexico, and Brazil. Highlights include the Xena-esque bolo woman and the tacky tango presentation. The food is surprisingly good. There's a large selection of cold salads, appetizers, fish, chicken, and all-you-can-eat *churrasco.*

In town the best *churrascaria* is **Búfalo Branco,** Rua Rebouças 530, Foz do Iguaçu (ⓒ **045/523-9744**). Certainly not touristy like the Rafain, the restaurant offers a good selection of cold dishes, salad, dessert, and of course *churrasco.* In addition to the succulent, well-prepared cuts of beef, the waiters also serve up grilled fish such as surubim.

Outside of town, **Clube Maringá,** Rua Dourado 111 (ⓒ ⓒ **045/527-9683**), serves a prix-fixe fish dinner (R$30/US$10) including unlimited access to a reasonable self-service buffet, plus a calderão (thick soup) of piranha, and three fresh fish dishes. Offerings change daily, but often include *piapara* fish grilled in a banana leaf, barbecued *dourado,* or *surubi* sautéed in butter. To get there, take Av. Cataratas to Av. General Meira, turn right at the Maringá billboard and follow the street about 3km (1¾ miles) to the very end.

7

Chile

by Haas Mroue & Kristina Schreck

Chile is called "the country of contrasts," and it's no wonder: Stretching 4,300km (2,700 miles) from tip to tail (about the same distance from New York to Los Angeles), the country's lengthy, serpentine shape incorporates the earth's driest desert, the Atacama; the fertile Central Valley with its Mediterranean-like climate; the volcanoes and forests of the Lake District; and the vast plains, glaciers, and granite cathedrals of Patagonia. The country is hemmed in on both sides by the forbidding Andes chain and the Pacific Ocean, and in no part does the country exceed 240km (150 miles) in width. Chile also claims Easter and Robinson Crusoe islands in the Pacific Ocean, as well as a slice of Antarctica.

These geological curiosities provide Chile with the widest variety of adventure-travel activities in South America. The hundreds of rivers that descend from the Andes provide anglers with phenomenal fly-fishing opportunities, not to mention some of the planet's wildest white-water rafting. Snowy peaks and volcanoes provide excellent terrain for skiing and mountain climbing. The northern desert's eerie land formations and high-altitude salt flats are as easily explored by vehicle as by mountain bike. The country's prize gem, the national park Torres del Paine, offers hiking, backpacking, and ice climbing. And there are kayak trips through emerald fiords and slogs through junglelike rainforest.

Magnificent landscapes and thrilling adventures are just the beginning. There are plenty of low-key activities here as well, including fiord cruises and scenic drives, soaks in hot springs, or just kicking back on a beach. Chileans themselves are proud people whose culture has been curiously defined by the geographical barriers that isolate them from the rest of South America. A staggeringly long coastline provides the country with what is perhaps the most varied seafood in the world. A thriving capital city, a strong economy, and a modern infrastructure promise high-quality amenities and services.

Chances are you've heard about ex-dictator Pinochet in the news and the attempts to bring him to trial for crimes committed during his reign. Chile has traveled a long, sorrowful road to get to where it is today, but now the country enjoys a firmly entrenched democracy, and it is one of the safest countries in South America. Corruption is relatively unheard of here, unlike in its neighbors Argentina and Peru.

Chile's well-defined high season dictates price jumps in lodging and more, leaving the question, when should you go? And better yet, *where* should you go? How expensive is it, and what level of value can you expect? You'll find the answers to these questions and more in this chapter.

1 The Regions in Brief

Chile's long, narrow shape means it's necessary to fly from point to point if you plan to visit several destinations in one trip; thankfully, frequent air service and efficient transfers make this a viable option. However, if you have only a week to spare, you won't be able to visit more than two regions of the country. Visitors with 7 to 10 days who travel to Patagonia or any remote lodge with a long transfer time should be able to squeeze in a night or two in Santiago and maybe a quick day visit to the coast or the wine country, but little else. You may consider skipping more remote destinations to sample two widely different regions in Chile—for example, spend several days in the Atacama Desert (all you'll need, really), then enjoy a few days in the Lake District. This would allow time for a day trip to the coast from Santiago. You might also consider a weeklong loop through the adjacent lake districts of both Chile and Argentina. (For information on Argentina's Lake District, see chapter 4.) Visitors with 7 to 10 days to work with, and who plan their trip carefully, will be able to drive the Carretera Austral; just fly directly to Puerto Montt, and then head back to Santiago at Coyhaique (or vice versa). Travelers with 2 to 3 weeks will have the freedom and the time in their schedules to pick and choose destinations at will.

NORTHERN CHILE   This region claims the world's driest desert, a seemingly unearthly "wasteland" set below a chain of purple and pink volcanoes and high-altitude salt flats. The sun-baked region is flecked with oases such as **San Pedro de Atacama,** an adobe-built pueblo typical of the region, as well as plentiful and well-preserved Indian ruin sites. The arid climate and the geological forces at work in this region have produced far-out land formations and superlatives such as the highest geyser field in the world.

SANTIAGO & CENTRAL CHILE   The central region of Chile, including Santiago and its environs, features a mild, Mediterranean climate. This is Chile's breadbasket, with fertile valleys and rolling fields that harvest a large share of the country's fruit and vegetables; it also is the site of Chile's wineries. Santiago's proximity to ski resorts, beach resorts, and the idyllic countryside, with its campestral and ranching traditions and colonial estates, allows it to offer a distinct variety of activities.

LAKE DISTRICT   Few destinations in the world rival the magnificent scenery of Chile's Lake District. This region is packed with a chain of conical, snowcapped volcanoes, glacier-scoured valleys, several national parks, thick groves of native forest, hot springs, jagged peaks, and, of course, many shimmering lakes. Temperatures during the summer are idyllic, but winter is characterized by months of drizzling rain. It's an outdoor-lover and adventure-seeker's paradise, especially in **Pucón** and **Puerto Varas.**

CHILOE   The island of Chiloé is as attractive for its picturesque bays and colorful wooden churches as it is for the folkloric culture that developed here after 300 years of geographic isolation from mainland Chile. When it's not raining, Chiloé makes for fine sightseeing drives, and Chiloé National Park offers ample opportunity for hiking along the island's untamed coastal rainforest.

THE CARRETERA AUSTRAL   Across the sound from Chiloé sits Chile's "frontier" highway, commonly known as the Carretera Austral, a dirt road that stretches nearly 1,000km (620 miles) from **Puerto Montt** in the north to beyond **Coyhaique** in the south. Along the way, this relatively new road passes through virgin territory visited by few travelers: tiny villages separated by thick, untouched

Chile

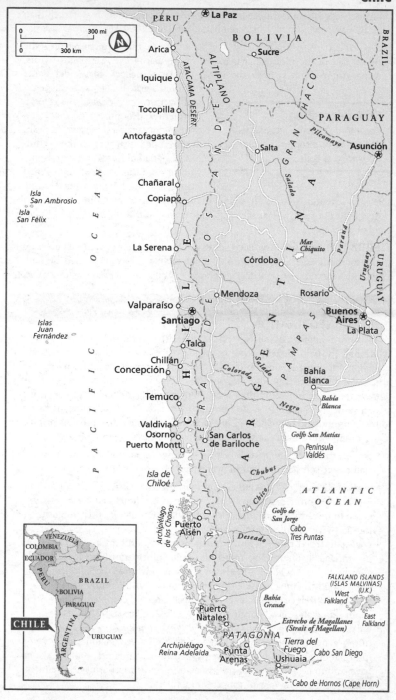

0 ___ 300 mi
0 ___ 300 km

PERU

La Paz

BOLIVIA

Arica

Sucre

ATACAMA DESERT

ALTIPLANO

Iquique

A N D E S

GRAN CHACO

Pilcomayo

PARAGUAY

Tocopilla

Antofagasta

Salta

Asunción

Salado

Chañaral

Copiapó

Isla
San Ambrosio

Isla
San Félix

C O R D I L L E R A   D E   L O S

Mar
Chiquito

Paraná

La Serena

Córdoba

URUGUAY

Uruguay

P A C I F I C   O C E A N

Mendoza

Rosario

Valparaíso

Santiago

**Buenos
Aires**

La Plata

Islas
Juan
Fernández

Talca

A R G E N T I N A

P A M P A S

Chillán

Concepción

Colorado

Salado

Bahía
Blanca

Temuco

Negro

Bahía
Blanca

Valdivia

Osorno

Puerto Montt

San Carlos
de Bariloche

Golfo San Matías

Península
Valdés

Isla de
Chiloé

Chubut

A T L A N T I C
O C E A N

Archipiélago
de los Chonos

Puerto
Aisén

Chico

Deseado

Golfo de
San Jorge

Cabo
Tres Puntas

C O R D I L L E R A

**FALKLAND ISLANDS
(ISLAS MALVINAS)**
(U.K.)

West
Falkland

East
Falkland

Puerto
Natales

Bahía
Grande

Estrecho de Magallanes
(Strait of Magellan)

Archipiélago
Reina Adelaida

PATAGONIA

Tierra del
Fuego

Punta
Arenas

Ushuaia

Cabo San Diego

Cabo de Hornos (Cape Horn)

BRAZIL

VENEZUELA
COLOMBIA
ECUADOR
PERU
BRAZIL
BOLIVIA
PARAGUAY
CHILE
ARGENTINA
URUGUAY

385

rainforest; rugged peaks that rise from crystal-clear lakes; and more waterfalls than you can reasonably count. This could be one of Chile's best-kept secrets.

PATAGONIA   Also known as the Magellanic Region, this dramatic region at the southern end of the continent has soared in popularity over the past 10 years, drawing visitors from all over the world to places such as **Torres del Paine National Park.** Patagonia is characterized by vast, open *pampa,* the colossal Northern and Southern ice fields and their mighty glaciers, the rugged peaks of the Andes as they reach their terminus, a myriad of fiords and sounds that wind around thousands of uninhabited islands, and wind, wind, wind. Getting here is an adventure—it usually takes 24 hours if you're coming directly from the United States or Europe. But the long journey pays off in the beauty and singularity of the region.

Shameless Plug

For more in-depth coverage of Chile, pick up a copy of *Frommer's Argentina & Chile.*

TIERRA DEL FUEGO   Situated across the Strait of Magellan, this archipelago at the southern extremity of South America is, like Patagonia, shared by both Chile and Argentina. It's similar in geography to Patagonia, if even less hospitable.

2 Planning Your Trip to Chile

VISITOR INFORMATION

You'll find a municipal tourism office in nearly every city and a **Sernatur (National Tourism Board)** office in major cities. The quality of service and availability of printed matter, such as maps and brochures, varies from office to office. Double-check any information you receive from these offices, as many representatives do not verify their facts, and they will sometimes give a wrong answer rather than admit they do not know. Outside of Chile, you won't find a tourism promotion board, but Chile's consulates sometimes provide printed material and visitor information. Some helpful websites are listed below.

- **www.sernatur.cl**   Sernatur's helpful website has enough general information to get you started planning your trip; however, it is in Spanish.

- **www.chile.com**   Chile's largest and most comprehensive website, featuring everything from regional and travel information, hotel and car rentals to a guide to investment. The majority is in Spanish, however their English section has very complete information.

- **www.chiptravel.com**   This comprehensive site is run by a group of expats in Santiago. It offers good travel ideas and information, but it is not religiously updated. The informed reviews and essays are especially enlightening. Good first-timer's guide to history, politics, and cultural issues.

- **www.andesweb.com**   This great website offers complete information about skiing and snowboarding in Chile and Argentina.

- **www.visit-chile.org**   The *Corporación Promoción Turística* offers a site featuring general information in English about Chile, including travel and information about hotels, restaurants, and tour companies, most of whom have paid to be a member of the association (most top businesses are members). Good overall view of top sites in Chile.

- **www.turistel.com**   This popular Chilean road guide series has a website, and although it is in Spanish, you can download complete route maps of

Telephone Dialing Info at a Glance

In Chile, each telephone carrier has a separate prefix, which you must dial when placing national and international long-distance calls. Telephone centers use their own prefix, and there is a list of prefixes in telephone booths—all charge virtually the same rates when calling from a phone booth. The prefixes are CTC (188), Entel (123), BellSouth (181), and Chilesat (171), among others.

- **To place a call from your home country to Chile,** dial the international access code (011 in the U.S. and Canada, 0011 in Australia, 0170 in New Zealand, 00 in the U.K.) plus the country code (56), plus the Chilean area code, followed by the number. For example, a call from the United States to Santiago would be 011+56+2+000+0000.
- **To place a call within Chile,** dial a carrier prefix, then the area code, and then the number. (To place a collect call, dial a prefix and then 182 for an operator.)
- **To place a direct international call from Chile,** dial a carrier prefix followed by 0, then the country code of the place you are calling, plus the area code and the local number.
- **To reach an international long distance operator,** dial © 800/800-288 for AT&T; © 800/207-300 (using CTC) and 800/360-180 (using Entel) for MCI; © 800/360-777 for **Sprint.**

Chile by clicking on *mapas ruteras.* These maps are more detailed than maps found on www.visit-chile.org.

- **www.samexplo.org**   The South American Explorer's Club produces and excellent website that includes up-to-date information about health and political crises, as well as frequently asked questions, travelogues, and catalogs and books for sale.
- **www.chilevinos.com**   Every aspect of the Chilean wine industry is covered at this excellent Spanish-language website, such as winemaker and winery profiles, a glossary, and online ordering.

ENTRY REQUIREMENTS
All visitors to Chile must carry a valid **passport. Please note that citizens of the following countries must pay a reciprocity fee when entering the country, and only U.S. dollars are accepted:** United States $100, Canada $55, and Australia $33. New Zealanders do not pay a fee. Before entering Chile, you'll need to fill out a tourist card that allows visitors to stay for 90 days. You'll need to present this tourist card to Customs when leaving the country. Also, many hotels waive Chile's 18% sales tax applied to rooms when the guest shows this card and pays with U.S. dollars. The easiest (and free) way to renew your 90-day stay is to cross the border and return. However, tourist cards can be renewed (for another 30 days only) at the **Extranjería,** Agustinas 1235, 2° piso, in Santiago (© **2/550-2400),** open Monday to Friday 8:30am to 2pm, or at any Gobernación Provincial office in the provinces, but it's expensive at $100. Bring the original card and passport, and photocopies of the two.

Chile requires children under 18 traveling alone, with one parent, or with a third party to present written authorization by the absent parent(s) or legal guardian granting permission to travel alone, with one parent, or with a third party. The authorization must be notarized before a Chilean consulate officer in your home country. For more details, contact your embassy or consulate.

LOST DOCUMENTS

Report lost tourist cards at the nearest police station or, in Santiago, at the **Policía Internacional,** Departamento Fronteras, General Borgoña 1052 (© 2/ **690-1010**), open Monday to Friday 8:30am to 12:30pm and 3 to 6pm. If you lose your passport, contact your embassy for a replacement. It is imperative that you carry a photocopy of your passport with you and another form of ID to facilitate the process.

CHILEAN EMBASSY LOCATIONS

In the U.S.: 1732 Massachusetts Ave. NW, Washington, DC 20036 (© **202/ 785-1746;** fax 202/887-5579; www.chile-usa.org)

In Canada: 1413-50 O'Connor St., Ottawa, ON K1P 6L2 (© **613/235-4402;** fax 613/235-1176; www.chile.ca)

In the U.K.: 12 Devonshire St., London W1G 7DS (© **020/7580-6392;** fax 020/7436-5204; www.echileuk.demon.co.uk)

In Australia: 10 Culgoa Circuit, O'Malley, ACT 2600 (© **02/6286-2430;** fax 02/6286-1289; www.embachile-australia.com)

In New Zealand: 19 Bolton St., Wellington (© **04/471-6270;** fax 04/472-5324; www.embchile.co.nz)

CUSTOMS

Any travel-related merchandise brought into Chile, such as personal effects or clothing, is not taxed. Visitors entering Chile may also bring in no more than 400 cigarettes, 500 grams of pipe tobacco, or 50 cigars, and 2.5 liters of alcoholic beverages per adult.

MONEY

The unit of currency in Chile is the **peso.** The value of the peso held steady at 700 pesos to the dollar throughout 2001 and 2002, however at press time a weak dollar places the rate at 650 pesos. Bills come in denominations of 500, 1,000, 2,000, 5,000, 10,000, and 20,000 pesos. There are currently six coins in circulation, in denominations of 1, 5, 10, 50, 100, and 500 pesos; however, it's unusual to be issued 1 peso or even 5. In slang, Chileans commonly call 1,000 pesos a *luca.*

Chile levies a steep, 19% **sales tax,** called IVA *(Impuesto al Valor Agregado),* on all goods and services. Foreigners are supposedly exempt from the IVA tax when paying in dollars for hotel rooms, car rentals, and some tourism-oriented shops; however, this is not the case with inexpensive hotels. A few hotels will list prices in pesos and IVA-exempt dollars, but in fact, the peso rate is cheaper when factoring in the fluctuating exchange rate, so do a little math before paying. The prices given in this book are listed in dollars (adjusted per a 650-pesos-to-the-dollar rate), due to the ambiguous nature of the IVA tax.

Dollars and traveler's checks can be exchanged at a *casa de cambio* (money-exchange house) for a small charge; casas de cambio are generally open Monday through Friday from 9am to 6pm (closing 1–3pm for lunch), and Saturday until

1pm. Some banks exchange money, although most charge a steep fee. By far the best exchange rates are given when retrieving money from an **ATM,** identifiable by the name "RedBanc" posted on a maroon-and-white sticker.

Most hotels and restaurants in Chile accept credit cards such as Visa, Master Card, Diners Club, and American Express. In the event of a lost or stolen credit card, call the following numbers (in Santiago): Visa/MasterCard at © **2/631-7003,** American Express at © **800/361002,** and Diners Club at © **800/220220.**

WHEN TO GO

PEAK SEASON   The peak season for South American vacationers is during the austral summer from December 15 to the end of February, as well as the last 2 weeks in July and Holy Week *(Semana Santa),* the week preceding Easter Sunday. The volume of tourists in popular destinations such as Pucón or Viña del Mar during the summer can be overwhelming. During this time, most hotel rooms nearly double in price, and reservations are sold out sometimes months in advance. Most North Americans and Europeans come between late September and early December or between March and mid-May; both seasons have pleasant weather, and the views are less crowded. It is, in fact, preferable to visit the extreme regions of Chile during these "off seasons." For example, in San Pedro de Atacama, the summer heat is a killer, and in Patagonia, the fierce wind blows most consistently from December to February.

CLIMATE   Chile's tremendous length incorporates a variety of climates, and in many areas, there are microclimates, pockets of localized weather that can completely alter the vegetation and landscape of a small area.

The northern region of Chile is so dry that some desert areas have never recorded rain. Summer temperatures from early December to late February in this region can top 100°F (38°C), then drop dramatically at night to 30°F (−1°C). Winter days, from mid-June to late August, are crisp but sunny and pleasant, but as soon as the sun drops, it gets bitterly cold. Along the coast, the weather is mild and dry, ranging from 60°F to 90°F (16°C–32°C).

The Santiago and Central Valley region features a Mediterranean climate, with rain during the winter only and temperatures that range from 32°F to 55°F (0°C–13°C) in the winter, and 60°F to 95°F (16°C–35°C) during the summer. Farther south, the Lake District and the Carretera Austral are home to very wet winters, and sometimes even summers, especially in the regions around Valdivia and Puerto Montt.

The Magellanic Region presents unpredictable weather patterns, especially during the summer, with extraordinary, knockout windstorms that can reach upwards of 120kmph (75 mph), and occasional rain. The windiest months are mid-December to late February, but it can blow any time between October and April. Winters are calm, with irregular snowfall and temperatures that can dip to 5°F (−15°C).

PUBLIC HOLIDAYS   Chile's national holidays are New Year's Day (Jan 1), Good Friday, Labor Day (May 1), Remembrance of the War of the Pacific Victory (May 21), Corpus Christi (June 29), Asunción de la Virgen (Aug 15), Independence Day and Armed Forces Day, perhaps the largest holidays of the year (Sept 18–19), Indigenous Day (Oct 12), All Saint's Day (Nov 1), Feast of the Immaculate Conception (Dec 8), and Christmas (Dec 25).

It's important to note that national and local elections bring about a virtual standstill from midnight to midnight as Chileans cast their obligatory votes. Alcohol is not sold on this day.

HEALTH CONCERNS

Chile poses few health risks to travelers, and no special vaccinations are required. In fact, there are no poisonous plants or animals in Chile to worry about, either. Nevertheless, standard wisdom says that travelers should get tetanus and hepatitis boosters.

Few visitors to Chile experience anything other than run-of-the-mill traveler's stomach in reaction to unfamiliar foods and any microorganisms in them. Chile's tap water is clean and safe to drink; however, a small percentage of travelers with very delicate stomachs report intestinal upsets from tap water. You'll often hear that the water has a "high mineral content," but by and large most travelers experience no symptoms at all. Do not under any circumstances drink tap water while in San Pedro de Atacama. It contains trace amounts of arsenic.

Altitude sickness, known as *soroche* or *puna,* is a temporary yet often debilitating affliction that affects about a quarter of travelers to the northern *altiplano,* or the Andes at 2,400m (7,872 ft.) and up. Nausea, fatigue, headaches, shortness of breath, and sleeplessness or spaciness are the symptoms, which can last from 1 to 5 days. If you feel as though you've been affected, drink plenty of water, take aspirin or ibuprofen, and avoid alcohol and sleeping pills.

The shrinking ozone layer is a serious problem in southern Chile; several years ago the ozone hole opened *completely* for several days over Punta Arenas—the first time it had ever happened. If you are planning to travel to Patagonia, keep in mind that on "red alert" days (typically Sept–Nov), it's possible for your skin to burn in *10 minutes.* If you plan to be outdoors, you need to protect yourself with sunblock, a long-sleeved shirt, a wide-brimmed hat, and sunglasses.

GETTING THERE
BY PLANE

Santiago's Comodoro Arturo Merino Benítez Airport is the international arrival point for Chile. Travelers pay a $26 departure tax for all international departures.

FROM NORTH AMERICA   The country's national air carrier **LanChile** (© 800/735-5526; www.lanchile.com) has daily flights to Santiago from New York and Los Angeles, and nonstop flights from Miami. You can register on their website for last-minute deals. **American Airlines** (© 800/433-7300; www. americanairlines.com) has daily nonstop flights from Miami and Dallas–Fort Worth, with connections from Vancouver, Toronto, and Montreal. **Delta** (© 800/221-1212; www.delta.com) offers nonstop daily flights from Atlanta. Costa Rica's **Lacsa** airline, of the parent company Taca (© 800/535-8780; www.taca.com), has flights from San Francisco, Los Angeles, New York, or Miami. Air Canada now offers nonstop service from Toronto to Santiago (© 888/247-2262).

FROM AUSTRALIA & NEW ZEALAND   Qantas (© 13 13 13 in Australia, or 9/357-8900 in New Zealand; www.qantas.com) works in conjunction with LanChile, offering three flights per week from Sydney and Auckland to Santiago. **Aerolíneas Argentinas** (© 1800/222-215 in Australia, or 0800/650-881 in New Zealand; www.aerolineas.com.ar) has two weekly direct flights from Sydney and Auckland to Buenos Aires, Argentina, with a connecting flight to Santiago aboard LanChile.

FROM THE U.K.   LanChile (© 1293/596607 in the U.K.; www.lanchile.com) serves London to Santiago via Madrid, in partnership with Iberia and British Airways, or try booking directly with **Iberia** (© 800/772-4642 in the U.S., or 020/7830-0011 in London; www.iberia.com). **Air France** (© 0845/0845 111;

www.airfrance.com/uk) has two to five daily flights from London to Santiago via Paris.

BY CRUISE SHIP

There are now quite a few 11- to 15-day cruises that sail around the Cape Horn, beginning in Buenos Aires and ending in Valparaíso, Chile, or vice versa, and usually with a stop in Montevideo, Uruguay. Ports of call include Chile's Puerto Montt, Puerto Chacabuco, and Punta Arenas; Argentina's Ushuaia, Puerto Madryn, and sometimes the Falkland Islands. Sailing through the southern region's fjords is truly remarkable. Several cruise operators that provide this trip are **Norwegian Cruises** (© 800/327-7030; www.ncl.com), **Celebrity Cruises** (© 800/722-4951; www. celebrity-cruises.com), **Silverseas Cruises** (© 800/722-9955; www.silversea.com) and **Princess Cruises** (© 800/PRINCESS; www.princesscruises.com). Most offer the Cape Horn trip in both directions, and some add-on stops in northern Chile and Brazil.

GETTING AROUND
BY PLANE

The drawn-out geography of Chile makes flying the most reasonable way to get around. **LanChile,** and its subsidiary **LanExpress** (© 800/735-5526 in the U.S., or 2/526-2000 in Santiago; www.lanchile.com), is the only domestic carrier in Chile, with daily flights to all major destinations. To get to smaller cities using an air taxi, see information in individual destination chapters.

BY BUS

Chile has a very efficient and inexpensive bus system, with three types of service. Standard buses go by the name *clásico* or *pullman* (no relation to the giant bus company Pullman); an *ejecutivo* or *semi-cama* offers lots of legroom, and seats that recline farther; and the *salón cama* features seats that fold out into beds. Think long and hard before booking a 30-hour ride to the desert north, or any comparable distance; it's an excruciatingly long time to be on the highway. For popular destinations, especially during weekends or holidays, buy a round-trip ticket as far in advance as possible.

BY CAR

Travelers seeking the independence to explore at their own pace might consider renting a car. To make a reservation from the United States, call **Alamo** (© 800/ GO-ALAMO; www.alamo.com), **Avis** (© 800/230-4898; www.avis.com), **Budget**

Tips Recommended Maps

Copec, the popular gas station chain, now sells Automapa's *Rutas de Chile* road maps at most of their stations. **Sernatur** might have road maps, but don't count on it. **Turistel** guidebooks, which are sold at most bookstores and a few kiosks on popular intersections, or from their office directly at Av. Santa María 0120 in Providencia (© 800/200-0000), are in Spanish but provide detailed road maps, city maps, and visitor information—you can even download and print them from www.turistel.cl before you leave for your trip. **JLM's** regional maps highlight major routes, towns, points of interest, and hiking trails, and are available at shops that sell outdoor gear or at tourism-oriented shops.

(© 800/527-0700; www.budget.com), **Dollar** (© 800/800-3665; www.dollar. com), or **Hertz** (© 800/654-3131; www.hertz.com). If renting once you're already in Chile, don't overlook a few of the local car-rental agencies for cheaper prices; you sometimes find better quality with the smaller operations.

The police, or *carabineros,* are allowed to stop motorists without reason, which they occasionally do under the guise of "traffic control." They usually just ask to see your driver's license, and then let you pass through their checkpoint.

Driving in Santiago is maddening, with congested streets and speedy, aggressive drivers—*especially* bus drivers. Chile recently inaugurated the new four-lane Panamericana Highway, which charges tolls either at the on-ramp or on the highway itself. Expect to pay between 50¢ and $5.50 at a tollbooth. The **Automóvil Club de Chile** offers services to its worldwide members. For more information, contact their offices in Santiago at Av. Andrés Bello 1863 (© **2/431-1000;** emergency breakdown service 600/6000 600; www.aclub.cl). Car-rental agencies provide emergency road service. Be sure to obtain a 24-hour number before leaving with your rental vehicle.

BY FERRY

If you've got the time and you're headed to southern Chile, consider arriving by ferry, which takes travelers through a verdant wonderland of fiords and islands. **Navimag, Transmarchilay,** and the upscale **Skorpios** offer ferry trips between Puerto Montt and Puerto Chacabuco, near Coyhaique, with a stop at the magnificent Laguna San Rafael Glacier. Navimag also offers a spectacular 3-day cruise between Puerto Montt and Puerto Natales, near Torres del Paine National Park. **Andina del Sud** offers a picturesque cruise across Lago Todos los Santos in Vicente Pérez Rosales National Park near Puerto Varas, which connects with the company Cruce de Lagos for the final leg to Bariloche, Argentina. The **Terra Australis** offers memorable one-way and round-trip cruises from Punta Arenas to Ushuaia. See individual regional listings for more information.

TIPS ON ACCOMMODATIONS

Chile has accommodations to suit the tastes and budgets of all travelers, from five-star luxury hotels to *hospedajes* (also known as *residenciales*), which are simple rooms in someone's private home. The hotel industry has remained stagnant for the past few years, and many establishments are maintaining or dropping prices in an effort to draw in business. The prices listed in this book are **rack rates,** but most hotels will offer a much cheaper rate or promotion deal—always ask for a discount, especially during the off season, or check their website for special offers. Every hotel listed in this book includes **breakfast** in the price, unless otherwise noted. Hotels might charge a "midseason" rate during November and March. Rates during the December-to-February high season are pricey in resort areas such as Pucón or Viña del Mar; however, some hotels drop their prices by as much as 50% during the off season. **Price ranges listed in hotel write-ups reflect low to high season;** for example, $50 to $75 double would mean $50 March to November and $75 December to February. Always verify high-season dates with your hotel.

TIPS ON DINING

Chances are you will not return from your trip raving about the cuisine in Chile. There are, however, many excellent dining options in Santiago, inside major hotels, and in towns that see a fair share of tourism. When ordering lunch, ask whether the restaurant has a *menú del día* or *menú ejecutivo*, a fixed-price lunch for $4 to $7 that usually includes an appetizer, main course, beverage or wine, coffee, and dessert. Oftentimes, the *menú* is a cheaper and tastier alternative to anything listed on the *carta* (menu). Chile is known for its seafood and the weird and wonderful shellfish found up and down the length of the country. All seafood and shellfish are free from any intoxicating elements, but do not collect or eat shellfish on your own.

TIPS ON SHOPPING

The only place where bargaining for goods is accepted is at stalls in central markets that sell arts and crafts, jewelry, regional goods and clothing, and the like. If the price is already ridiculously cheap, you might want to refrain from bargaining, as the income generated from these sales is all these handicraft sellers make. Otherwise, expect to pay the full marked price for any goods in regular shops and malls. Buying wine by the case is not always an economically sound idea considering the cost of shipping it home, so check prices first.

FAST FACTS: Chile

American Express Operates out of **Turismo Cocha,** Av. El Bosque Norte 0430, in Santiago's Las Condes neighborhood (© 2/464-1000; Mon–Fri 9:30am–5pm; for 24-hr. bilingual service © 800/361002).

Business Hours Banks are open Monday to Friday from 9am to 2pm, and are closed on Saturday and Sunday. Commercial offices close for a long lunch hour, which can vary from business to business. Generally, hours are Monday through Friday from 10am to 7pm, closing for lunch around 1 or 1:30pm and reopening at 2:30 or 3pm.

Doctors Many doctors, especially in Santiago, speak basic English; for a list of English-speaking doctors, call your embassy.

Drug Laws Possession and use of dangerous drugs and narcotics are subject to heavy fines and jail terms.

Electricity Chile's electricity standard is 220 volts/50Hz. Electrical sockets have two openings for tubular pins, not flat prongs, so you'll need a plug adapter available from most travel stores.

Embassies/Consulates The only U.S. representative in Chile is the **U.S. Embassy** in Santiago, located at Av. Andrés Bello 2800 (© 2/232-2600). The **Canadian Embassy** is at Nueva Tajamar 481, 12th floor, Torre Norte (© 2/362-9660). The **British Embassy** can be found at El Bosque Norte 0125 (© 2/231-3737). The **Australian Embassy** is at Isidora Goyenechea 3621 (© 2/550-2500). The **New Zealand Embassy** is at Av. Golf 99, no. 703 (© 2/290-9802).

Emergencies Obviously, you'll want to contact the staff if something happens to you in your hotel. Otherwise, for a police emergency, call © **133.** For fire, call © **132.** To call an ambulance, dial © **131.**

Hospitals *Clínicas* and private hospitals are always better than a town's general hospital. The cost of medicine and treatment is expensive, but most hospitals and pharmacies accept credit cards. Many doctors, especially in Santiago, speak basic English; for a list of English-speaking doctors and medical specialists in Santiago, call your embassy. The best hospitals in Santiago are **Clínica Las Condes** at Lo Fontecilla 441 ((_C_) **2/210-4000**) and **Clínica Alemana** at Vitacura 5951 ((_C_) **2/212-9700**).

Internet Access No matter where you are in Chile, you should find an Internet station, either in a cafe or at telephone centers CTC or Entel. Most hotels, even hostels, have their own Internet service; if they don't, they'll be able to point out where to find one. Expect to pay $2 to $4 per hour.

Language Spanish is the official language of Chile. Many Chileans in the tourism industry and in major cities can speak basic English, but don't count on it. Try to learn even a dozen basic Spanish phrases before arriving; there are several excellent phrase books on the market, and they will facilitate your trip tremendously. See also "Appendix: Useful Terms & Phrases," at the back of this book.

Liquor Laws The legal drinking age in Chile is 18. Alcohol is sold every day of the year, except during elections.

Newspapers & Magazines The largest and most respected newspaper in Chile is the right-leaning *El Mercurio*, although *La Tercera, La Crónica,* and *El Metropolitano* are popular. *La Segunda* and *El Cuarto* are both tabloids. Newspapers and magazines are sold from kiosks; those in major cities usually carry *Time* and *Newsweek* in English editions, as well as other English-language magazines.

Police Police officers wear olive-green uniforms and are referred to as *carabineros* or colloquially as *pacos*. Dial (_C_) **133** for an emergency.

Restrooms Many low-cost hotels and restaurants will ask that you deposit used toilet paper in a wastebasket because of poor plumbing. It's a good idea to carry a small stash of toilet paper because occasionally an establishment will not supply any.

Safety Santiago is probably the safest major city in South America. Serious violent crime is not unheard of, but it's not common either. A visitor's principal concern will be pickpockets, but even then your chances of being robbed are rare.

Telephone For more information, see "Telephone Dialing Info at a Glance," earlier in this chapter. To place a collect call, dial a carrier prefix and then 182 for an operator. The country code for Chile is **56**. A local phone call requires 100 pesos, and better rates are to be had with a phone card sold from kiosks, but verify that a particular company's phone card works with any phone and not only with its own public phone. Cellular phones are prefixed by **09**, and are more expensive to call.

Time Chile is 4 hours behind Greenwich mean time (GMT) from the first Sunday in October until the second Sunday in March; the country is 6 hours behind during the rest of the year. Or think of it as the same time zone as New York from the second Sunday in March to the second Sunday in October and 2 hours ahead of New York the rest of the year.

Tipping Diners leave a 10% tip in restaurants. In hotels, tipping is left to the guest's discretion. Don't tip taxi drivers.

3 Santiago

Santiago, one of South America's most sophisticated cities, is a thriving metropolis that is home to five million people, or nearly a third of Chile's entire population. On a clear day, Santiago's main attraction is its spectacular location at the foot of the snowcapped Andes, which rise majestically over the city's eastern limits. It's a breathtaking sight, one that is unfortunately hidden behind a dense layer of smog that often shrouds the city. The smog is at its eye-burning worst in the winter, unless a rainstorm comes along and washes the air clean. During the summer, light breezes and an exodus by vacationers combine to greatly alleviate the condition.

Nevertheless, Santiago is an intriguing city, and there's certainly plenty to see and do here. It is the historic, economic, and cultural center of Chile, and its restaurants, art centers, and theaters are the best in the country. It also makes a convenient base for exploring a number of great destinations outside the city limits—including beaches, ski resorts, and wineries. If you're planning a visit to Chile, you'll inevitably spend at least 1 night here on your way into or out of the country, but if you have the time, you should try to spend 2 or 3 days here, more if you plan to visit those outlying areas.

The city is a curious mix of old and new: A glitzy skyscraper towers over a 200-year-old stone building, and a charming cobblestoned street dead-ends at a tacky 1970s shopping gallery. Santiago's unchecked development has led to a lack of architectural uniformity, and the contrasts can often be amusing. Some neighborhoods look as though they belong to entirely different cities. Bear in mind that your opinion of Santiago can easily be shaped by the neighborhood you're staying in.

ESSENTIALS
GETTING THERE
BY PLANE Santiago's **Comodoro Arturo Merino Benítez Airport** (© 2/ 690-1900; www.aeropuertosantiago.cl) is served by the Chilean national carrier LanChile and most major international carriers. Once you pass through Customs, there is a small **currency-exchange** kiosk, but it is recommended that you exchange larger sums downtown at a bank for better rates. Men in olive jumpsuits at the arrival and the outdoor-departure curb work as airport bellhops, and they will assist you with your luggage for a 300- to 500-peso tip (40¢–75¢).

Depending on traffic, your Santiago destination, and how you get there, the city can be reached in 20 to 45 minutes. Most hotels have transfers either free of charge or for about $20. A **taxi** to Santiago costs $12 to $18; just outside the glass gate wait registered taxis, and cheaper city taxis that have just dropped someone off wait outside the terminal near the curb. **TransVip** (© 2/677-3000) operates door-to-door minivan "transfers" for $5 to $7 for shared vans, or you can rent one for a group of up to seven for $25, and you can even book online at www.transvip.cl. TransVip reps await passengers at the gate, but their desks are at the arrival area if you can't find a rep. The **Centropuerto** blue bus (© 2/601-9883) costs $1.25 and leaves every 30 minutes from the curb outside arrivals, stopping in Santiago first at the San Borja bus station, then the Estación Central, followed by Los Heroes Metro station.

BY BUS Travel by bus is very popular in Chile. There are three principal **bus stations** in Santiago. For international arrivals and departures to and from destinations

in southern Chile, use the **Terminal Santiago,** Alameda O'Higgins 3850 (© 2/
376-1750; Metro: Universidad de Santiago). The **Terminal Alameda** (© 2/270-
7500) next door at Alameda O'Higgins 3712 is the terminal for the Pullman and
Tur Bus companies, two well-respected, high-quality services. For departures to
northern and central Chile, use the **Terminal San Borja,** Alameda O'Higgins 3250
(© 2/776-0645; Metro: Estación Central). The smaller **Terminal Los Héroes,**
Tucapel Jiménez 21 (© 2/420-0099; Metro: Los Héroes), has service to a variety
of destinations in both northern and southern Chile.

ORIENTATION

Santiago incorporates 32 *comunas,* or neighborhoods, but you'll spend your time
in just two or three of these areas. **Downtown,** or *el centro,* is the thriving financial, political, and historic center of Santiago, although many businesses have
now relocated to **Providencia** and **Las Condes.** These two upscale, attractive
neighborhoods are residential areas centered on a bustling commercial strip.
Santiago is bisected by the Río Mapocho; on one side rises Cerro San Cristóbal,
a large, forested park. Below is the artists' neighborhood **Bellavista,** with dozens
of bars and restaurants.

GETTING AROUND

Santiago is beset with congested traffic during the day. Therefore, the Metro is
the quickest way from point A to point B. Taxis are also a good bet, except during rush hour from 5 to 7pm.

BY METRO   The Metro is clean, safe, efficient, and inexpensive (about
30¢–50¢, depending on the time of day). There are three Metro lines. Line 1
runs from Providencia to downtown along Avenida O'Higgins. This line will
take you to most major attractions. Line 2 runs from Cal y Canto (near the Mercado Central) to Lo Ovalle (near the Palacio Cousiño). Line 5 runs from La
Florida to Baquedano. The Metro runs from 6am to 11pm Monday through
Saturday, and 8am to 10am Sunday.

BY BUS   City buses, or *micros,* are tricky in Santiago because there aren't any
route maps available. Each bus lists its general direction on a sign on its windshield, but it's better to stick with the Metro or taxis.

BY TAXI   Taxis are identifiable by their black exterior and yellow roof, and
they are plentiful and moderately priced. You do not tip a taxi driver. Do not
confuse taxis with *colectivos* (shared taxis with fixed routes), which are similar
in appearance but without the yellow roof. For a "radio taxi" that will pick you
up at your door, check out the yellow pages or try **Centro** (© 2/695-4148) or
Apoquindo (© 2/225-3064).

BY RENTAL CAR   It is totally unnecessary to rent a car in Santiago unless
you plan to drive to any of the peripheral areas, such as Viña del Mar or the
Andes—and even then, buses and shuttles are very convenient. Driving in Santiago can be a hair-raising experience due to maniacal, swerving buses; drivers
who do not confine their cars to one lane; and absolutely phenomenal traffic
jams, especially between 5 and 7pm.

CAR RENTALS   At the airport, you'll find most international rental agencies,
such as **Alamo** (© 2/690-1370), **Avis** (© 2/690-1382), local agency **Bert** (© 2/
690-1317), **Budget** (© 2/362-2000), **Dollar** (© 2/202-5510), **Hertz** (© 2/
690-1029), and **Localiza** (© 2/362-3200). All agencies also have downtown or
Providencia offices. The most economical car rental costs between $175 and
$300 per week (taxes and insurance included), depending on the season.

PARKING   Most hotels offer parking on their own property or in a nearby lot. Downtown parking is nearly impossible on the street, unless you can find a lot. In Providencia, along Providencia Avenue, there is a series of underground lots. Commercial and downtown streets are manned by meter maids. Chile is also home to the parking *cuidador,* where unofficial "caretakers" stake out individual blocks and "watch" your car for you. They are everywhere, even at grocery store lots, and they expect a small tip, about 50 to 200 pesos (10¢–50¢), when you leave. *Cuidadores* in busy commercial areas are very aggressive.

ON FOOT   When you have a map in hand, Santiago is fairly easy to figure out, especially if you stick close to major streets. Pedestrians should be alert at all times and should not stand on curbs, as buses roar by dangerously close to sidewalks. Also, drivers do not always give the right of way to pedestrians, and therefore you should get across the street as quickly as possible.

VISITOR INFORMATION

The **National Tourism Service (Sernatur)** has its main office at Av. Providencia 1550 (© **600/SERNATUR;** www.sernatur.cl; Metro: Manuel Montt), and is open Monday through Friday from 9:30am to 6:30pm, Saturday and Sunday from 1:30 to 6:30pm. Sernatur also has an information center at the airport. Sernatur is plagued by inconsistent service and often depleted of brochures after the high season in March. It does, however, have a bilingual staff that can answer general questions about Santiago. There's also an **Oficina de Turismo** downtown, inside the Casa Colorada at Merced 860 (© **2/632-7783**). A private concession operates a tourism **kiosk** at the intersection between Paseo Ahumada and Paseo Huérfanos pedestrian walkways in the city center, with tours, brochures, and other information.

FAST FACTS   **Banks** are open from 9am to 2pm, closed on Saturday and Sunday. ATMs are referred to as "RedBancs" and can be identified by the maroon-and-white logo sticker. Downtown casas de cambio, such as Exprinter or Afex, can be found around Paseo Huérfanos and Agustinas. In Providencia, money-exchange houses are around Avenida Pedro de Valdivia and Avenida Providencia.

For a **police emergency,** call © 133. For **fire,** call © 132. To call an **ambulance,** dial © 131. If you need medical attention, the American Embassy can provide a list of medical specialists in Santiago. The best hospitals in Santiago are private: **Clínica Las Condes,** Lo Fontecilla 441 (© **2/210-4000**), **Clínica Alemana,** Vitacura 5951 (© **2/212-9700**), and **Clínica Santa María** (© **2/461-2000**).

Virtually every hotel and telephone center in Santiago has Internet access. Hours for phone centers and cafes are typically 9am to 11pm. In Providencia, try **Café Phonet,** General Holley 2312, Providencia (© **2/335-6106**), or **CyberCafé** at Pedro de Valdivia 037 (© **2/283-3083**). In Las Condes, there's a site at San Sebastián 2815.

The main **post office** is on the Plaza de Armas (Mon–Fri 8am–7pm; Sat 8am–2pm). There are other branches at Moneda 1155 in downtown and Av. 11 de Septiembre 2239 in Providencia.

WHAT TO SEE & DO

Even if you have just 1 day in Santiago, you should be able to pack in a sizable amount of the city's top attractions. It's a push, but nearly all attractions lie within a short walk or taxi ride from each other, which makes it easy to pick and choose according to your interests.

DOWNTOWN HISTORIC & CIVIC ATTRACTIONS

Begin your tour of Santiago at the historic heart of the city, the **Plaza de Armas** 🕃🕃🕃, which can be reached by taking the Metro to Estación Plaza de Armas. The plaza was founded by Pedro de Valdivia in 1541 as the civic nucleus of the country, and its importance was such that all distances to other parts of Chile were, and still are, measured from here. The plaza is not only a wonderful place to sit, relax, or read, but it is also a great place to watch the colorful characters milling about and downtown workers hurrying to and fro.

Catedral Metropolitana & Museo de Arte Sagrado 🕃   The Metropolitan Cathedral is the fifth cathedral to have been erected at this site. The cathedral began construction in 1748 but was completed in 1780 by the Italian architect Joaquín Toesca, who gave the building its neoclassical-baroque facade. The central nave holds the cathedral's ornate altar, brought from Munich in 1912 and made of marble, bronze, and lapis lazuli. There's also the Museo de Arte Sagrado, where you'll find a collection of paintings, furniture, antique manuscripts, and silverwork handcrafted by Jesuits.

Paseo Ahumada, on the west side of the plaza. No phone. Free admission. Mon–Sat 9am–7pm; Sun 9am–noon. Metro: Plaza de Armas.

Palacio de la Real Audiencia/Museo Histórico Nacional 🕃🕃   Sandwiched between the post office and Santiago's municipal building is the Palacio de la Real Audiencia, built between 1804 and 1807 by a student of Toesca who followed his preference for neoclassical design. The building has undergone several transformations, but the facade is still intact. The Palacio is the historic site of the first Chilean congressional session that followed independence. Today, it holds the fascinating National History Museum, which displays a grab bag of more than 70,000 items from the colonial period, including clothing, suits of armor, weapons, home appliances, industrial gadgets, flags, money, and medallions through the years, and an interpretive timeline and photo montage of Chilean history.

Plaza de Armas 951. ✆ 2/6381411. Admission 75¢ adults, 35¢ under 18; free Sun and holidays. Tues–Sun 10am–5:30pm. Metro: Plaza de Armas.

Casa Colorada & Museo de Santiago 🕃🕃   The Casa Colorada is a half block from the Plaza de Armas; the antique structure is made of stone, whose color gives it its name—"The Red House." It's widely regarded as the best-preserved colonial structure in Santiago, built between 1769 and 1779 as a residence for the first president of Chile, Mateo de Toro y Zambrano. Today, the Casa Colorada operates as the Santiago Museum, depicting the urban history of the city until the 19th century. The museum is small and somewhat interesting, more than anything to visit and marvel at the architecture and browse through the museum's bookstore. A **visitor center** with information about Santiago is also located in the Casa Colorada.

Merced 860. ✆ 2/633-0723. Admission 75¢. Tues–Fri 10am–6pm; Sat 10am–5pm; Sun 11am–2pm. Metro: Plaza de Armas.

Basílica de la Merced 🕃   One block from the Casa Colorada on Merced at the corner of MacIver sits this intriguing, neo-Renaissance-style church and museum. Built in 1735, the church boasts a magnificent Bavarian baroque pulpit and arched naves. The museum has a collection of Easter Island art, including wooden Moai sculptures. There are also 78 wood and ivory Christ Child figures, among other religious artifacts.

MacIver 341, corner of Merced. No phone. Admission 70¢ adults, 20¢ students. Tues–Fri 10am–1pm and 3–6pm; Sat 10am–1pm. Metro: Plaza de Armas.

Museo Chileno de Arte Precolombino ✫✫✫   Heading back on Merced and past the plaza to Bandera, you'll find the excellent Museo Chileno de Arte Precolombino, housed in the old 1807 Royal Customs House. This is one of the better museums in all of Chile, both for its collection of pre-Columbian artifacts and its inviting design. There are more than 1,500 objects on display here, including textiles, metals, paintings, figurines, and ceramics spread throughout seven exhibition rooms. It's not a stuffy old museum, but a vivid exhibition of indigenous life and culture before the arrival of the Spanish. The material spans from Mexico to Chile, incorporating all regions of Latin America divided into four areas: Mesoamérica, Intermedia, Andina, and Surandina. Downstairs there's a patio cafe and a well-stocked bookstore that also sells music, videos, and reproductions of Indian art, textiles, and jewelry.

Bandera 361. ✆ 2/688-7348. www.precolombino.cl. Admission $3 adults, free for students; free for everyone Sun and holidays. Tues–Fri 10am–6pm; Sat–Sun and holidays 10am–2pm. Metro: Plaza de Armas.

PLAZA CONSTITUCION & THE COMMERCE CENTER

The Plaza Constitución, located between calles Agustinas, Morandé, Moneda, and Teatinos, is an expansive plaza used primarily as a pedestrian crossway. It's also the site of the famous **Palacio de la Moneda** ✫✫, the Government Palace and site of the September 11, 1973, coup d'état led by Augusto Pinochet, who shelled and bombed the building until President Salvador Allende committed suicide. The building, the largest erected by the Spanish government during the 18th century, was the focus of much criticism for being too ostentatious, but today it's considered one of the finest examples of neoclassical architecture in Latin America. Visitors are allowed to enter the courtyard and walk around. Try also to catch the impressive **changing of the guard** ✫✫, when hundreds of soldiers march in step in front of the palace, every other day at 10am. Across Alameda is the **Plaza Bernardo O'Higgins.** His remains are buried under the monument dedicated to him in the center of the plaza.

ATTRACTIONS OFF THE ALAMEDA

Calle Dieciocho & Palacio Cousiño ✫   Heading west on Avenida Bernardo O'Higgins (the Alameda), past the giant Entel tower, will put you at Calle Dieciocho and what used to be an elegant neighborhood of mansions built by wealthy families at the turn of the 20th century. The neighborhood is certainly scruffier these days, but it is possible to picture the area during its heyday. The first few homes are on the corners of Dieciocho and Alameda, including the 1873 Palacio Errázuriz, now home to the Brazilian Embassy; the 1917 Palacio Ariztía; and the Iglesia San Vicente de Paul. These palaces were designed using beautiful European architectural styles, especially French.

The crème de la crème is the Palacio Cousiño, located several blocks down Calle Dieciocho, today a museum and testament to the obscene wealth of one of Chile's most successful entrepreneurial dynasties, the Goyenechea-Cousiño family. To get here, you'll have to walk (it's 8 blocks from the Plaza Bernardo O'Higgins), take a taxi, or ride the Metro to Estación Toesca.

Barrio París Londres ✫   This charming, singular neighborhood with its narrow cobblestoned streets was built between the 1920s and 1930s on the old gardens of the Monastery of San Francisco. The neighborhood consists of small mansions, each with a different facade, that today house artists, students, and cultural centers. The neighborhood was designated a national monument in 1982, and its streets are now pedestrian walkways.

The streets between Prat and Santa Rosa, walking south of Alameda O'Higgins.

Iglesia, Convento y Museo de San Francisco 🏃🏃   The Church of San Francisco is the oldest standing building in Santiago, and although this landmark has been renovated over the years, the main structure has miraculously survived three devastating earthquakes. The highlights are the museum and the convent, the latter with an idyllic patio planted with flora brought from destinations as near as the south of Chile and as far away as the Canary Islands. The garden is so serene, you'll find it hard to believe you're in downtown Santiago, with horrifying traffic racing by just outside. The museum boasts 54 paintings depicting the life and death of San Francisco, one of the largest and best-conserved displays of 17th-century art in South America.

Av. Bernardo O'Higgins. 📞 2/638-3238. Admission convent and museum 50¢ adults, 25¢ children. Tues–Sat 10am–1pm and 3–6pm; Sun and holidays 10am–2pm.

CERRO SANTA LUCIA & PLAZA MULATO GIL DE CASTRO

Cerro Santa Lucía is an idyllic hilltop park located steps from the Biblioteca Nacional on Alameda and Santa Lucía. It's open daily September through March from 9am to 8pm, April through August from 9am to 7pm; free admission. The Mapuches called this rocky hill *Huelén* (Curse) until Pedro de Valdivia renamed it Santa Lucía in 1540. The hill offers leafy walkways that lead to lookout points with a sweeping view of Santiago. At the staircase, you'll also find the **Centro de Exposición de Arte,** with a large assortment of Indian-influenced crafts, clothing, and jewelry on display and for sale.

PARQUE FORESTAL

This slender, well-manicured park, built in 1900 and lined with rows of native and imported trees, skirts the perimeter of the Río Mapocho from the Metro station Baquedano to the park's terminus at the Mapocho station. If the air is clear, the path that meanders through this park makes for a pleasant stroll, and you can stop along the way at the **Palacio de Bellas Artes** 🏃🏃, José Miguel de la Barra (📞 2/632-7760; Tues–Fri 11am–7pm, Sat–Sun 11am–2pm). The Palacio de Bellas Artes houses both the Fine Arts and Contemporary Art museums (with separate entrances and admissions) in a regal, neoclassical, 1910 building. The importance of the permanent installations in the Fine Arts museum may be debatable, but they occasionally host great temporary exhibitions. The Contemporary Museum features more than 2,000 paintings, sculptures, and other works by well-known Latin artists.

Mercado Central 🏃🏃 *Kids*   Just before reaching the Estación Mapocho, you'll pass the colorful, chaotic world of the Mercado Central. This lively market sells fruits and vegetables, handicrafts, and rows and rows of slippery fish and shellfish displayed on chipped ice, some familiar, others odd fruits of the sea that can be found only off the shores of Chile. Depending on your perspective, the barking fishmongers and waitresses who harangue you to choose *their* zucchini, *their* sea bass, *their* restaurant, can be entertaining or somewhat annoying. Either way, don't miss it, especially for the market's lofty, steel structure that was prefabricated in England and assembled here in 1868.

Vergara and Av. 21 de Mayo. No phone. Daily 7am–3pm (restaurants open until 8pm). Metro: Cal y Canto.

BARRIO BELLAVISTA & PARQUE METROPOLITANO (CERRO SAN CRISTOBAL)

These two attractions lie next to one another, so it makes sense to see both in one visit. But here's a word of caution: The extensive views that come with an ascent to the top of Parque Metropolitano (Cerro San Cristóbal) can be ruined if it is a particularly smoggy day. But if the air is clear, this attraction rates as one of the best in the city, offering a breathtaking panorama of sprawling Santiago and its city limits that stop just short of the Andes.

The **Parque Metropolitano** ★★★ is a 730-hectare (1,803-acre) park and recreation area with swimming pools, walking trails, a botanical garden, a zoo, picnic grounds, restaurants, and children's play areas. The park is divided into two sectors, Cumbre and Tupahue, both of which are accessed by car, cable car, funicular, or foot. In Bellavista, head to the end of Calle Pío Nono to Plaza Caupolican, where you'll encounter a 1925 **funicular** that lifts visitors up to a lookout point, open Monday from 1pm to 8pm, Tuesday through Friday from 10am to 8pm, Saturday and Sunday from 10am to 8:30pm; tickets cost $1.75 adults, $1 children. The lookout point is watched over by a 22m (72-ft.) high statue of the **Virgen de la Inmaculada Concepción.** Below the statue is the ***teleférico*** (cable car) that connects the two sections of the park, open Monday 2:30pm to 7pm, Tuesday through Friday from 10:30am to 8pm, Saturday and Sunday from 10:30am to 8:30pm. Tickets cost $2.25 adults, $1 children; ticket combinations with the funicular cost $3 adults, $1.50 children. There are also buses that go up Pío Nono and down Avenida Pedro de Valdivia. Admission for vehicles is $2. It's also possible to take a taxi up, but you'll need to pay the park entrance fee as well as the fare. The Parque Metropolitano's hours are daily from 8:30am to 9pm, cars until 10pm.

La Chascona ★★★ This is one of three homes once owned by the nationally adored, Nobel Prize–winning poet Pablo Neruda. It was built for his third wife, Matilde, and its name refers to her unruly hair. As with Neruda's other two homes, La Chascona was built to resemble a ship, with oddly shaped rooms that wind around a compact courtyard. It's fascinating to wander through Neruda's quirky home and observe his collection of precious antiques and whimsical curios collected during his travels. Neruda's library is especially interesting, and it holds the antique encyclopedia set he purchased with a portion of his earnings from the Nobel Prize. The home is headquarters for the Fundación Pablo Neruda, which provides the guided tours.

Fernando Márquez de la Plata 0192. ✆ **2/777-8741.** Admission $5 for tour in English, $3 in Spanish. Tues–Sun 10am–1pm and 3–6pm.

ESPECIALLY FOR KIDS

Santiago is home to many kid-friendly attractions, some of which are just as appealing to adults. At **Parque Bernardo O'Higgins,** reached by taxi or Metro to Estación Parque O'Higgins, there's an amusement park called Fantasilandia (✆ **2/689-3035**); admission is $7.50 adults, $6.50 children. In winter, it's open Saturday, Sunday, and holidays from 11am to 8:30pm; in summer, Tuesday through Friday from 2 to 8pm, Saturday and Sunday from 11am to 8pm. There are also two museums, the **Museo de Insectos y Caracoles** (✆ **2/556-1937;** Mon–Sun 10am–8pm), with a collection of more than 1,500 mounted butterflies, beetles, and snails; and the **Museo del Huaso** (✆ **2/556-5680;** Tues–Fri 10am–5pm, Sat–Sun 10am–2pm), which highlights the culture and typical dress of the Chilean cowboy.

There is a cluster of museums located within the idyllic **Parque Quinta Normal,** located at 502 Matucana and accessible via a short taxi ride. The **Museo Nacional de Historia Natural** ★ (✆ **2/680-4600;** Tues–Sat 10am–5:30pm, Sun noon–5:30pm) has a fairly interesting collection of native flora and fauna, and anthropological exhibits. More worthwhile is the **Artequín Museum** ★★ at Av.

Portales 3530 (℃ 2/681-8687; Tues–Sun 10am–5pm; admission $1.25 adults, 50¢ students), which is housed in a cast-iron building built for the Chilean exhibition at the 1889 Parisian centenary of the French Revolution, and then shipped here. The museum strives to introduce visitors to the art world through 120 reproductions of well-known works by artists from Picasso to Monet. The **Museo de Ciencia y Tecnología**℗ (℃ 2/681-6022; admission $1 adults, 50¢ students) has interactive displays, and the **Museo Ferroviario** (℃ 2/681-4627) has exhibits that include 14 steam engines and railway carriages; both are open Tuesday through Friday from 10am to 5:30pm and Saturday and Sunday from 11am to 6pm.

ORGANIZED TOURS

Cocha Tours (℃ 2/464-1000; www.cocha.com) and **First Premium** (℃ 2/258-2000; www.firstpremium.cl) can plan city tours, winery tours, and other excursions, although most hotels can arrange a tour for you. An interesting option for visitors to Santiago is the *Culinary Tour of Historic Santiago Centro,* run by an American chef. The tour features an architectural walking tour, a visit to an open-air market with an introduction to native Chilean foods, followed by a gourmet lunch (℃ 2/681-1799; www.tercerchakra.com; $50 per person).

SPECTATOR SPORTS & RECREATION

GYMS Try **Fisic** at Tobalaba 607 in Providencia (℃ 2/232-6641; $8 per visit), Pacific Club at Isidora Goenechea 2852 (℃ 2/333-1260), or **Bio Acción** at Av. Providencia 065 near the Baquedano Metro station (℃ 2/634-7282).

HORSE RACING Two racetracks hold events on either Saturday or Sunday throughout the year: the recommended **Club Hípico** at Blanco Encalada 2540 (℃ 2/683-9600) and the **Hipódromo Chile** at Avenida Vivaceta in Independencia (℃ 2/270-9200).

SOCCER *(FUTBOL)* Top games are held at three stadiums: **Estadio Monumental,** Avenida Grecia and Marathón; **Universidad de Chile,** Camp de Deportes 565 (both are in the Ñuñoa neighborhood); and **Universidad Católica,** Andrés Bello 2782, in Providencia. The most popular teams, Colo Colo, Universidad Católica, and Universidad Chile, play at these stadiums. Check the sports pages of any local newspaper for game schedules.

SHOPPING

Santiago is home to two American-style megamalls: **Parque Arauco,** Av. Kennedy 5413 (Mon–Sat 10am–9pm, Sun and holidays 11am–9pm) and **Alto Las Condes,** Av. Kennedy 9001 (Mon–Sun 10am–10pm). Public transportation is difficult, so take a cab.

Crafts markets can be found around Santiago either as permanent installations or weekly events. The best is at **Las Condes Los Domínicos** at Av. Apoquindo 9085 (℃ 2/245-4513; Tues–Sun 10:30am–7pm), designed to resemble a colonial village, and where you'll find everything from hand-knit sweaters to lapis lazuli to quality art to live pheasants. Also try the **Galería de Exposición de y Ventas Bellavista** at Avenida Bellavista 0357 (℃ 2/777-9429; Mon–Sun 10am–7pm, Sat 10am–6pm), or the **Centro Artesanal Santa Lucía** across the street from Cerro Santa Lucía, which sells copperware, textiles, wooden items, jewelry, and clothes (and plain old junk).

Antiques lovers will find a large selection in **Barrio Brasil** around Parque de los Reyes at calles Brasil and Matucana and Brasil and Providencia (reachable only by taxi). In the neighborhood Providencia, at the corner of Bucharest and Avenida Providencia, dozens of galleries sell everything from paintings to china

Finds Lapis Lazuli, a Gem of a Gift

Looking for that special something to bring home to your loved ones? Try lapis lazuli, a stone that can be found in only two places in the world: Afghanistan and Chile (although there are spotty reserves in Russia). The color of lapis ranges from a bright royal blue to a violet-navy blue and is used primarily for jewelry, but also for sculptures and even counter tile. Lapis has been used for 6,500 years and was considered the most valuable gem until the Middle Ages. The best place to shop for lapis is in the **Bella-vista** neighborhood, where a dozen stores are clustered along Calle Bella-vista between Pío Nono and Arzobispo Casanova. Here, you'll find jewelry, chess sets, figurines, picture frames, and more, all fabricated from lapis. Most arts and crafts shops sell lapis lazuli.

to furniture. If you're a bargain hunter, you might give the chaotic **Bío Bío Market** a try; it's located around calles Bío Bío and Franklin and open Saturday and Sunday from 9am to 7pm. There's an intriguing selection of antique furniture and other odds and ends, especially at Calle Bío Bío, but you might have to look through a lot of cast-offs to find it.

Wine shops have been popping up all over Santiago, including **El Mundo de Vino** at Av. Isidora Goyenechea 2931 (✆ 2/244-8888), open Monday through Sunday from 10:30am to 8pm, which has a wide selection and a knowledgeable staff. Also on Avenida Isidora Goyenechea at 3520 is **La Vinoteca** (✆ 2/334-1987), open Monday through Saturday from 9:30am to 9pm. Most shops will ship for you. Note that most supermarkets offer a wide selection, and often at cheaper prices, too. If you can't make it to a wine shop, there is one at the airport.

WHERE TO STAY

The most economical lodging can be found downtown. Keep in mind that visitors are quickly linked to downtown attractions from Providencia and Las Condes via the Metro. Parking at Santiago hotels is free unless otherwise indicated in the review.

DOWNTOWN SANTIAGO
Very Expensive

Hotel Carrera ✸✸✸ *Moments*   Santiago is now home to a dozen five-star hotels, but the history and old-fashioned splendor of the Carrera make it one of the more unique choices for lodging. Built between 1937 and 1940, and for decades the social center of Santiago's elite, the building's lobby features crystal chandeliers from Bohemia and an enormous glass mural depicting the arrival of the Spanish to the New World. The hotel sits directly on the Plaza Constitución, cater-cornered from the presidential building, Palacio de la Moneda (site of Pinochet's coup in 1973). Rooms are spacious and have been completely remodeled; the executive Carrera Club rooms on the fifth and sixth floors are the best in the hotel. Rooms have a richly textured English decor with classic floral and striped wallpaper and Oriental carpets. Those facing the neighboring Ministerio de Hacienda are dark; instead, opt for a room facing Calle Agustinas or the plaza. A highlight at the Carrera is its glitzy rooftop pool, where you can gaze out above the rooftops and watch the hustle and bustle of downtown below. Standard rooms do not include breakfast. Inquire about promotions because prices here can often drop as low as $198 for a Carrera Club room, $150 for a

Downtown Santiago

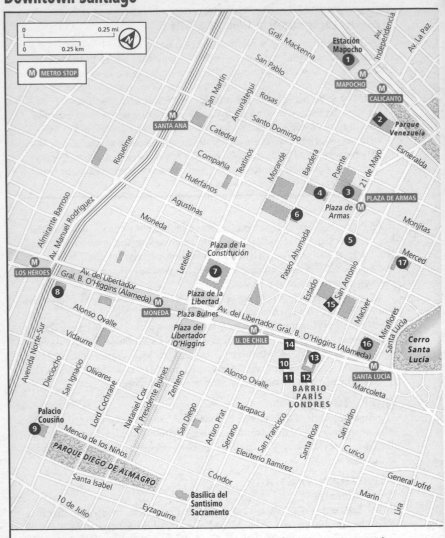

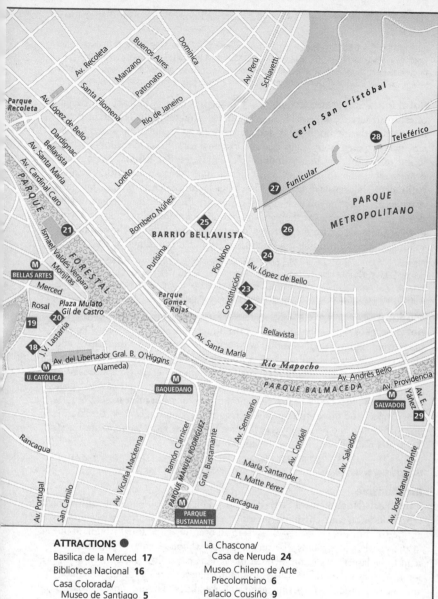

ATTRACTIONS ●

Basílica de la Merced **17**

Biblioteca Nacional **16**

Casa Colorada/
Museo de Santiago **5**

Catedral Metropolitana/
Museo de Arte Sagrado **4**

Estación Mapocho **1**

Funicular **27**

Iglesia San Francisco **13**

Jardín Zoológico **26**

La Chascona/
Casa de Neruda **24**

Museo Chileno de Arte
Precolombino **6**

Palacio Cousiño **9**

Palacio de Bellas Artes **21**

Palacio de la Moneda **7**

Palacio de la Real Audencia/
Museo Historico Nacional **3**

Palacio Errázuriz **8**

Teleférico **28**

standard—sometimes even lower. The Copper Room Bar is a great spot for a cocktail.

Teatinos 180. ⓒ 2/698-2011. Fax 2/672-1083. www.carrera.cl. 331 units. $140 deluxe; $170 Carrera Club junior suite; $360 suite. AE, DC, MC, V. Metro: Estación Moneda. **Amenities:** 3 restaurants; bar; outdoor pool; racquetball court; gym; sauna; whirlpool tub; concierge; business center; gift and floral shops; salon; room service; massage; babysitting; laundry service; photo service; conference rooms. *In room:* A/C, TV, minibar.

Hotel Plaza San Francisco 😺😺😺 This elegant hotel with its clubby design offers smart service, impeccable rooms, and a central location. The decor is traditional and the interior lighting dark, with low, wood ceilings supported by pillars, richly colored fabric wallpaper, and Oriental rugs. Relax in the lobby to the sound of the tinkling indoor fountain, or enjoy the Bar Bristol's all-you-can-drink happy hour from 6 to 9pm. Guest rooms are spacious, with sparkling bathrooms and classic furniture. The hotel is conveniently located on busy Avenue Alameda, but you won't hear the din of traffic due to double-paned windows. The hotel has a wine shop and an indoor pool hidden downstairs in a windowless room. Apart from executives, plenty of travelers choose the Plaza when visiting Santiago, including the Dalai Lama, who has stayed here twice.

Alameda O'Higgins 816. ⓒ 2/639-3832. Fax 2/639-7826. www.hotelsanfrancisco.cl. 160 units. $130–$145 double; $175–$190 junior suite; $215–$245 executive suite. AE, DC, MC, V. Parking available. Metro: Universidad de Chile. **Amenities:** Award-winning restaurant; bar; indoor pool; gym; whirlpool; concierge; LanChile office; business center; room service; massage; laundry service; art gallery. *In room:* A/C, TV, minibar.

Moderate

Hotel Foresta 😺 If you can get past the dungeonlike lobby, the Hotel Foresta offers comfortable, spacious rooms with leafy views of Cerro Santa Lucía, and an excellent location. Doubles come with a sitting room, and each room is decorated with an eclectic mix of furniture from seemingly every era and design—one room has floral bedspreads; the next, green wallpaper and smoked glass tables. It's an older hotel, and its funkiness makes for a fun place to stay. Singles are cramped, and those with interior views are disappointingly dark. Breakfast is not included in the price. Always ask for a room that faces Cerro Santa Lucía. There is a rooftop restaurant with panoramic windows.

Victoria Subercaseaux 353. ⓒ 2/639-6261 or 2/639-4862. Fax 2/632-2996. 35 units. $48 double. AE, DC, MC, V. Parking available. Metro: Santa Lucía. **Amenities:** Restaurant; bar. *In room:* TV, minibar.

Inexpensive

Hotel París/Nuevo Hotel París 😺 *Value* This is a good budget hotel with a central location and charming interiors, especially within the newer annex's antique rooms. Budget backpackers from all over the world usually bunk in one of the simple, older rooms. (Be sure to ask for a room with a TV because they tend to be larger.) It's recommended that guests pay a little extra here and opt for a room in what's referred to as the Hotel Nuevo París, as rooms are quieter and include Oriental rugs and mahogany moldings. These rooms are darker, though not unappealingly so, and a few rooms even come with a glass-enclosed alcove or tiny outdoor terrace; they are the same price and worth asking for. Continental breakfast costs $2.

París 813. ⓒ 2/664-0921. Fax 2/639-4037. carbott@latinmail.com. 40 units. $26 double new wing; $23 double. AE, DC, MC, V. Parking across the street $3–$5 per day. Metro: Universidad de Chile. **Amenities:** Cafe; laundry service. *In room:* TV (not all rooms).

Residencial Londres 😺😺 *Value* Residencial Londres is simply the best choice for travelers on the cheap in Santiago, and it is patronized by everyone from backpackers to businesspeople on a budget. Rooms are admittedly very basic, with foam mattresses and bare bulbs, but the hotel is decorated with antiques and has gorgeous parquet floors. Some rooms have French doors and armoires, tables, and chairs. Golden light floats through the lobby in the afternoon, and there's a TV lounge off to the side. Four floors wrap around an interior patio; during the summer, travelers use the patio to store gear and dry out tents. A toast-and-coffee breakfast is available for $1.50.

Londres 54. Ⓒ/fax 2/638-2215. 25 units. $21 double w/private bathroom; $19 double w/shared bathroom. No credit cards. Metro: Universidad de Chile. *In room:* No phone.

PROVIDENCIA
Very Expensive

Ritz-Carlton Santiago 🏠🏠🏠   The brand-new Ritz is the first in South America, and it is one of the finest five-star hotels in the city. Conveniently located near shops, restaurants, and the thriving economic hub of Santiago, the Ritz-Carlton's bland brick exterior belies its handsome interiors. The hotel's lobby, which has a two-story rotunda and floors made of imported marble with a Mediterranean-style black and gold inlay, features a lounge with frequent drink and appetizer service, and there is a plush wine bar. Their Restaurant Mediterráneo has a terrace for outside dining. The guest rooms have been decorated in floral designs in blues, greens, and reds, all made of plush silk and brocade and with custom-made South American furnishings. Club-level rooms are accessible only by elevator key and feature upgraded amenities. Of course, the Ritz-Carlton provides noteworthy service, with a multilingual staff and sharp attention to detail. The state-of-the-art gym and whirlpool deserves special mention for its location on the top floor and beneath a tremendous glass dome, offering a spectacular view of the city and the Andes.

El Alcalde 15. Ⓒ 800/241-3333 in the U.S., or 2/362-9619. Fax 2/362-9640. www.ritzcarlton.com. 205 units total, 49 club level rooms, 3 club suites, 12 executive suites, 1 Ritz-Carlton suite. $160 deluxe; $260 junior suite; $320 club suite. AE, DC, MC, V. Metro: El Golf. **Amenities:** 4 restaurants; bar; indoor rooftop pool; gym; sauna; whirlpool; concierge; car rental; business center; salon; room service; massage; babysitting; laundry service; valet service. *In room:* A/C, TV, minibar, hair dryer, safe.

Santiago Park Plaza Hotel 🏠🏠   The Park Plaza is easily confused with the Plaza Hotel downtown, and indeed their styles are quite similar. This exclusive brick hotel also caters predominately to traveling executives and diplomats, although its discreet location tucked away on Calle Lyon in Providencia is more tranquil. The Park Plaza is a boutique hotel designed in the European style, with classic furniture and rich fabrics; adjoining the lobby is a small restaurant serving excellent French cuisine. All rooms have plenty of space and good light. The hotel is conveniently located near shops and a block from the Metro, but what really stands out is the Park Plaza's impeccable service. The Park Plaza has a second hotel around the corner, the **Park Suite Apartments** (Lota 2233; $100 one-bedroom, $180 two-bedroom), with 20 fully furnished guest rooms featuring spacious kitchenettes and living areas. Prices for these apartments are reduced for multiple-day stays.

Ricardo Lyon 207. Ⓒ 2/372-4000. Fax 2/233-6668. www.parkplaza.cl. 104 units. $125 standard double; $250 junior suite. Parking available. Metro: Los Leones. **Amenities:** Restaurant; bar; indoor pool; city tours and transfers to tennis and golf courts; gym; sauna; business center; room service; babysitting; laundry service; Internet. *In room:* A/C, TV, minibar, hair dryer, safe.

Sheraton Santiago 🏠🏠🏠   The gala Sheraton Santiago offers more room sizes and amenities than are possible to list in this description, especially since they added on the San Cristóbal Tower with conference centers and luxury executive rooms. The Sheraton sits apart from the city, facing the Río Mapocho and backing the Cerro San Cristóbal mountain; psychologically you're cut off from the city, but it's just 5 blocks from downtown Providencia. Anything over the 10th floor offers spectacular views. The rooms at the Sheraton vary according to their location within the hotel, but all are well appointed with the same high-quality linens and attractive furnishings. The new executive guest rooms and suites in the Tower complex are truly top-notch; each floor has its own butler, and there's a private lounge for breakfast or tea on the 21st floor. The Neptune Pool & Fitness Center is unbelievable, with a turquoise pool surrounded by murals and softly lit by skylights. With its crystal chandeliers and marble floors, the Sheraton is all about glamour whereas the Park Plaza is low-key elegance. Take note that the entire Sheraton can be sold out for a week at a time due to visiting conventioneers. Call or check their website for promotions.

Av. Santa María 1742. © **800/335-3535** in the U.S., or 2/233-5000. Fax 2/234-1066. www.sheraton.cl. 379 units. $125 double standard; $155 executive suite. San Cristóbal Tower: $190 executive double; $450 suite. AE, DC, MC, V. Metro: Pedro de Valdivia. **Amenities:** 3 restaurants; bar; outdoor and indoor pools; tennis courts; sauna; whirlpool; concierge; travel agency; car-rental agency; business center; shopping gallery; salon and barber; massage; babysitting; laundry service. *In room:* A/C, TV, minibar, hair dryer, safe.

Expensive

Hotel Orly ★★ *Finds* This irresistible boutique hotel is one of my favorites in Santiago, and it is close to absolutely everything. The Orly is housed in a renovated mansion with French-influenced architecture. The lobby has a few nooks with reading lights for relaxing and a small, glass-covered patio; there's also a bar and an eating area for breakfast. The interiors are white and accented with contemporary art and glowing light. Room sizes vary; doubles come with two twins or a full-size bed and are of average size; singles are claustrophobic. All rooms have desks, and suites have a sitting area within the same room. If you need peace and quiet, request a room in the back. One of the high points here is the hotel's friendly service.

Av. Pedro de Valdivia 027. © **2/231-8947.** Fax 2/252-0051. www.orlyhotel.com. 32 units. $77–$98 double; $100–$124 suite. AE, DC, MC, V. Metro: Pedro de Valdivia. **Amenities:** Cafe; bar; laundry service. *In room:* A/C, TV, minibar, safe.

Moderate

Hotel Club Presidente ★★ *Value* The Hotel Club Presidente is one of the best values in this category. The rooms here are fresh, tidy, and comfortable, although a little on the small side and slightly dark. The Presidente is a small hotel but doesn't skimp on friendly, professional service. Past the compact, white foyer, a hall leads to a restaurant and a idyllic patio draped in foliage and serenaded by a bubbling fountain. The hotel is located on a residential street just a 3-minute walk away from the subway, about halfway between Providencia and downtown. This is another hotel that offers airport transfer service, and the price is just unbeatable. The Club Presidente also owns the **Apart-Hotel Club Presidente** in Las Condes at Luis Thayer Ojeda 558 (© **2/233-5652**), with double rooms of the same quality as this hotel, plus a full kitchen—a great deal for extended stays in Santiago. Rates for a two-bedroom apartment run from $72 to $83.

Av. Eliodoro Yañez 867. © **2/235-8015.** Fax 2/235-9148. www.presidente.cl. 50 units. $50–$55 double. Parking available. Metro: Salvador. **Amenities:** Restaurant; bar; room service; laundry. *In room:* A/C, TV, stereo, minibar, safe.

LAS CONDES
Very Expensive

Hyatt Regency Santiago ★★★ Ten years ago, the Hyatt brought a whole new concept in five-star luxury to Santiago: 310 spacious, opulent rooms, hip

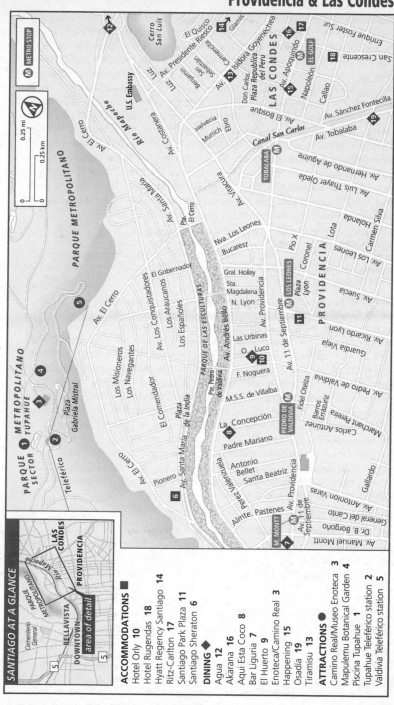

Providencia & Las Condes

SANTIAGO AT A GLANCE

Cementerio General

PARQUE METROPOLITANO

Río Mapocho

LAS CONDES

PROVIDENCIA

DOWNTOWN

BELLAVISTA

area of detail

ACCOMMODATIONS
Hotel Orly **10**
Hotel Rugendas **18**
Hyatt Regency Santiago **14**
Ritz-Carlton **17**
Santiago Park Plaza **11**
Santiago Sheraton **6**

DINING
Agua **12**
Akarana **16**
Aqui Esta Coco **8**
Bar Liguria **7**
El Huerto **9**
Enoteca/Camino Real **3**
Happening **15**
Osadia **19**
Tiramisu **13**

ATTRACTIONS
Camino Real/Museo Enoteca **3**
Mapulemu Botanical Garden **4**
Piscina Tupahue **1**
Tupahue Teleférico station **2**
Valdivia Teleférico station **5**

Metro Stop

PARQUE METROPOLITANO

Av. El Cerro

U.S. Embassy

Río Mapocho

Cerro San Luis

El Quisco

Av. Presidente Riesco

Glamis

Enrique Foster Sur

Isidora Goyenechea

Plaza Republica del Peru

LAS CONDES

El Golf

San Crescente

Napoleón

Callao

Av. Apoquindo

Don Carlos

San Sebastián

Benjamin

Luz

Carmencita

Av. El Bosque

Av. Sánchez Fontecilla

Helvecia

Munich

Ebro

Canal San Carlos

Av. Tobalaba

TOBALABA

Av. Hernando de Aguirre

Av. Luis Thayer Ojeda

Av. Santa María

Av. Costanera

Av. Vitacura

Pte. El Cerro

PARQUE DE LAS ESCULTURAS

Nva. Los Leones

Bucarest

Gral. Holley

Sta. Magdalena

N. Lyon

LOS LEONES

Plaza Lyon

Coronel

Pio X

PROVIDENCIA

Holanda

Carmen Silva

Av. Los Leones

Lota

Suecia

El Gobernador

Av. Los Conquistadores

Los Araucanos

Los Españoles

Av. El Cerro

Av. Andrés Bello

Av. Providencia

Las Urbinas

O. Luco

F. Noguera

Av. 11 de Septiembre

Av. Ricardo Lyon

Guardia Vieja

Av. Pedro de Valdivia

Los Misioneros

Los Navegantes

El Comendador

Plaza de la India

Av. Santa María

Pte. Pedro de Valdivia

M.S.S. de Villalba

PEDRO DE VALDIVIA

Fidel Oteiza

Carlos Antúnez

Marchant Pereira

Barros Errázuriz

Av. Pedro de Valdivia

Oteiza

La Concepción

Padre Mariano

Antonio Bellet

Santa Beatriz

Pionero

Av. El Cerro

Av. Peréz Valenzuela

Almte. Pastenes

Av. Providencia

Av. Antonio Varas

General del Canto

Gallardo

Dr. B. Borgoño

Av. 11 de Septiembre

MANUEL MONTT

Av. Manuel Montt

Plaza Gabriela Mistral

Teleférico

PARQUE SECTOR

METROPOLITANO

TUPAHUE

0.25 mi

0.25 km

Providencia & Las Condes

restaurants, a plethora of services, and sky-high prices. The Hyatt is a 24-story atrium tower with two adjacent wings and four glass elevators that whisk guests up to their split-level rooms and terraced suites. Inside it feels as spacious as an airport hanger. Unfortunately, for this reason the Hyatt can't help feeling somewhat antiseptic, a fact exacerbated by bland, uniform brown stone interiors. Nevertheless, guests are usually wowed by this behemoth and always rave about the flawless service provided by the staff and the panoramic views. The palm-and-fern–fringed pool and fully staffed gym are superb. The Hyatt's standard rooms are accented with weathered blond wood and richly colored furnishings. They're as large as average suites, meaning the executive suites are enormous. All rooms have sumptuous bathrooms. The lounge hosts daily tea, complete with a buffet of mouth-watering cakes, that is open to the public. The Hyatt's three restaurants are considered some of the finest in Santiago. To get around from here, you'll always need to take a taxi, because the location at the head of a crazy traffic loop makes it difficult to reach any destination on foot.

Av. Kennedy 4601. ℂ 2/218-1234. Fax 2/218-3155. www.santiago.hyatt.com. 336 units. $165–$185 double; $450 suite. AE, DC, MC, V. **Amenities:** 3 restaurants; bar; outdoor pool; tennis courts; gym; sauna; whirlpool; concierge; American Airlines office; Hertz car-rental office; business center; shopping arcade; salon; room service; massage; babysitting; laundry service; solarium; valet service; billiards room (suites only). *In room:* A/C, TV, minibar, hair dryer, safe.

Expensive

Hotel Rugendas 🐟🐟   The Hotel Rugendas is a good choice in Las Condes for its cozy accommodations and plentiful amenities. The hotel is housed in a tall brick building on a leafy residential street about 2 blocks from busy Avenida Apoquindo. The top floor is encased with glass; here, you'll find a game room with card tables and a billiards table, not to mention a breathtaking view. The Rugendas's state-of-the-art gym is open 24 hours a day, and there is a sauna. Thick, golden curtains and bedspreads, a country decor, and large wooden headboards accent each room. Rooms on the upper floors have great views of the Andes, and a few have terraces. A Tuscan-style restaurant serves wonderful cuisine and an abundant breakfast buffet; there's also outdoor seating under large canvas umbrellas. Professional service and frequent promotions round out this premium hotel.

Callao 3121. ℂ/fax 2/655-1881. www.rugendas.cl. 48 units. $145 double; $155 junior suite; $185 suite. AE, DC, MC, V. Metro: El Golf. **Amenities:** Restaurant; bar; gym; sauna; game room; concierge; business center; laundry. *In room:* A/C, TV, minibar, hair dryer, safe.

WHERE TO DINE

Santiago's gastronomic scene has undergone a revolution, and diners can now expect to find dozens of innovative restaurants that have discovered new takes on Chilean cuisine, as well as many ethnic restaurants. Many restaurants are concentrated along several streets in neighborhoods such as Bellavista, Las Condes (Av. El Bosque, in particular), and Providencia (especially Calle Suecia and General Holley). You could just head over to these areas and stroll around until something strikes your fancy. Don't forget that most major hotels, notably the Hyatt and the Hotel Plaza San Francisco, have outstanding restaurants.

DOWNTOWN

There are a cluster of restaurants around the tiny plaza Mulato Gil de Castro, really your best bet for evening dining if you are staying downtown and don't feel like going far. However, almost everything is closed on Sunday. In addition to restaurants listed below, at the plaza try **La Pérgola de la Plaza** (ℂ 2/639-3604; Mon–Sun 8am–4pm), a pretty cafe with a good fixed-price lunch menu, or **"R"**

(① **2/664-9844;** Mon–Sat 12:30–4:30pm and 7:30pm–1:30am), a cozy spot for wine and conversation. For food to go, try **Chez Henry** on the Plaza de Armas (① **2/696-6612;** daily 9am–11pm).

Expensive
Le Due Torri ⚡ ITALIAN/INTERNATIONAL   Set back from busy Calle San Antonio, the classic Le Due Torri serves more than 20 kinds of pasta and other Italian favorites, as well as international fish and meat entrees. It offers excellent service and great food to match. For a light lunch, try the vast, colorful antipasto bar that offers one trip around for $10. Walls made of wood and river rock create a warm atmosphere. This is an expensive, semiformal setting that sees many executives during the lunch hours, usually wining and dining clients.

San Antonio 258. ① 2/639-7609. Main courses $7–$15. AE, DC, MC, V. Mon–Fri 12:30–11pm.

Squadritto ⚡⚡ ITALIAN/INTERNATIONAL   Squadritto is on a charming, leafy street near the Plaza Mulato Gil de Castro, and its Tuscan-style dining room is a preferred setting for businesspeople in the area. It's semiformal, with a warm interior filled with plants and twinkling lights—and a choice restaurant if you're looking for fine cuisine and a special place to dine. The fresh pastas are superb, with items such as salmon ravioli in a bay-shrimp sauce, but there's lots else on offer, including grilled fish, beef, chicken seasoned with herbs or a light sauce, and an extensive wine list.

Rosal 332. ① 2/632-2121. Reservations recommended. Main courses $7–$12. AE, DC, MC, V. Daily 1–3pm and 7:30–11pm.

Moderate
Gatopardo ⚡ MEDITERRANEAN/CHILEAN   Tasty nouvelle cuisine has made this restaurant a local favorite. During lunch, executives head over for a fixed-price menu that can include pork loin in herb and curry sauce or for a run through the fresh salad bar, which, with the wine and dessert included, makes $8 seem like a steal. Gatopardo mixes Chilean, Mediterranean, and Bolivian specialties that might include spinach-ricotta ravioli with chopped walnuts in a Roquefort sauce. Bar appetizers are varied, from tacos and quesadillas to steamed mussels. The light, airy interior has mustard-colored walls and an atrium supported by giant oak trunks felled by an earthquake in the south of Chile.

Lastarria 192. ① 2/633-6420. Main courses $8–$15. AE, DC, MC, V. Mon–Fri 12:30–3:30pm and 7:30pm–midnight; Sat 7:30pm–1am.

27 de Nueva York ⚡ INTERNATIONAL   Located in the heart of the financial district, the 27 de Nueva York is an ideal place to stop for lunch if you are around the Bolsa de Comercio or Plaza de Armas. A warm, attractive dining area is a favorite with businessmen and women. The restaurant serves grilled meats, fish, and salads, and it also offers an *autoservicio,* or self-serve, restaurant next door, which is recommended if you're in a hurry.

Nueva York 27. ① 2/699-1555. Reservations recommended. Main courses $5–$9. AE, DC, MC, V. Mon–Fri 8am–11pm.

BELLAVISTA & PROVIDENCIA
Expensive
Aquí Está Coco ⚡⚡⚡ SEAFOOD   This one-of-a-kind restaurant not only serves superb seafood, it's also a fun place to dine. Housed in a 140-year-old home with more nooks and crannies than one can reasonably navigate, the restaurant is owned by one charismatic Jorge "Coco" Pacheco, who gave the place its name: "Here's Coco." Jorge traveled the world for 3 years and brought back

boxes of crazy knickknacks and a wealth of tantalizing recipes, both of which give Aquí Está Coco its unique flavor. Nearly every kind of seafood is offered, including trout stuffed with crab, hake, swordfish, cod, sea bass, and more, served with sauces such as caper, black butter, or tomato-wine. The appetizers are mouth-watering, such as crab cakes or broiled scallops in a barnacle sauce.

La Concepción 236. © 2/235-8649. Main courses $9–$16. AE, DC, MC, V. Mon–Sat 1–3pm and 8–10:30pm.

Astrid y Gastón ✺✺✺ INTERNATIONAL/CHILEAN   Frequently rated as one of the top three eateries in Santiago, Astrid y Gastón is named for the Peruvian and German couple who own and run this wonderful restaurant with such care. Beyond the outstanding food served here, the service is truly impeccable, and they have an on-site sommelier and a lengthy wine list (for variety, it is tied with Kilometre 11680). The chef uses the finest ingredients, combined so that each plate bursts with flavor and personality; here you'll find French, Spanish, Peruvian, and Japanese influences. Dessert orders are usually placed early, so they can make each one specially. Try the duck salad, the glazed pork, or the tuna filet bathed in a honey sauce.

Antonio Bellet 201. © 2/650-9125. Reservations required. Main courses $10–$15. AE, DC, MC, V. Mon–Sat 1–3:30pm and 8pm–midnight.

Moderate

Azul Profundo ✺✺ SEAFOOD   If you love seafood, the "Deep Blue" is the place to come. Salmon, conger eel, swordfish, sea bass, and more come grilled, or *a la plancha* (it comes sizzling out of the kitchen on a cast-iron plate), and are served alone or with tantalizing sauces. Everything on the menu is appealing; therefore, decisions are not easily made, so try getting started with an appetizer of one of eight different kinds of ceviche. The cozy, nautical-themed ambience includes a wooden siren hanging from a mock ship's bow, as well as bathroom doors that look like they lead to a sailor's bunk.

Constitución 111. © 2/738-0288. Main courses $7–$13. DC, MC, V. Daily 1–4pm and 8:30pm–midnight.

Kilometre 11860 ✺✺ FRENCH BISTRO   The two French wine lovers who own Kilometre came to Chile to sample its varietals and ended up opening this bistro to offer what is possibly the best wine list in town. There are nearly 150 varieties of Chilean wine on the menu, including export varieties you won't find in stores. Each week they choose a special, expensive wine by the glass to try so you won't have to buy an entire bottle. The food includes French staples such as foie gras, baked goat cheese, duck confit, tarte tatin, fish, and meats. Lunch is only available on Friday, when there is a fixed-price menu for $11. The terrific patio has an outdoor seating area and a bar.

Dardignac 0145. © 2/777-0410. Main courses $10–$17. AE. Mon–Thurs and Sat 8pm–1am; Fri lunch only noon–4pm.

Inexpensive

Bar Liguria ✺✺ *Finds* CHILEAN BISTRO   Tremendously popular, the Bar Liguria now has several restaurants around the city, yet this flagship is still the most vibrant and "in" spot in Providencia for actors, businesspeople, and young people in the area. It's a great restaurant with tiny alcoves and corners to hide in, and a long wooden bar for dining and drinking. The menu is bistro-style, with about 15 entrees and a selection of soups and sandwiches. The walls are covered with kitsch: movie posters, street signs, pictures of soccer stars, advertisements, and so on. Good service is provided by plentiful waiters in black bow ties. In the evening, you might have to wait for a table. It's a great place for outdoor dining, but get here early. If you're looking for a fun place for food and nightlife, this is your spot.

Av. Providencia 1373. ℭ 2/235-7914. Main courses $4–$9. No credit cards. Mon–Wed 10am–noon; Thurs–Sat 10am–2am. Metro: Pedro de Valdivia.

Caramaño ℛ CHILEAN   They call themselves the "anti-restaurant," and they're probably right. The Caramaño is totally anonymous from the street, and diners used to miss it until they put a sign up this year. Just ring the front bell to enter. Inside, graffiti-scrawled walls are something of a contrast to the tables filled with men and women in suits. Service is casual, and the food classic Chilean: inexpensive and good.

Purísima 257. ℭ 2/737-7043. Main courses $3–$9. AE, DC, MC, V. Daily 1–4pm and 7pm–12:30am.

El Huerto ℛ VEGETARIAN   Some call the popular El Huerto the best vegetarian restaurant in Santiago, and with good reason: The chefs whip up creative, appetizing dishes, from burritos to pasta to Chinese stir-fries. Add one of their fresh apple, raspberry, or peach juices, and it makes for a wonderful meal. Prices have risen slightly recently, and the owners have opened up a more economical cafe, *La Huerta,* next door (at the left), with a limited but good menu and fixed-price lunch. The softly lit, mellow dining room of El Huerto is a cool place to relax on a summer day. The restaurant also has a shop that sells books, postcards, and arts and crafts.

Orrego Luco 054. ℭ 2/233-2690. Main courses $4–$10. AE, DC, MC, V. Mon–Thurs 12:30pm–midnight; Fri–Sat 12:30pm–1am. Cafe opens at 9am.

LAS CONDES (EL BOSQUE NORTE)/VITACURA

The street El Bosque has it all: Chilean, French, seafood, steakhouses, fast-food courts, and more. For American fare, there's a **T.G.I. Friday's** with the usual menu at Goyenechea 3275 (ℭ 2/234-4468; Sun–Thurs noon–1:30am, Fri–Sat noon–2:30am), and **New York Bagel,** Roger de Flor 2894 (ℭ 2/246-3060). The best place for breakfast is the **Cafe Melba,** Don Carlos 2898 (ℭ 2/232-4546; opens at 7:30am on weekdays, 8:30 weekends). You'll need a cab to reach restaurants in Vitacura but they're well worth seeking out.

EXPENSIVE

Agua ℛℛℛ FUSION   Agua is the chic place to be seen, and for good reason: the hip, minimalist design of concrete and glass is as fashionable and tasteful as the fusion cuisine. The young chef at Agua has catapulted to culinary fame in Santiago for his creations, such as tuna, either tartare or rolled with king crab and served over an avocado and shrimp relish. Agua is known for its extensive and noteworthy seafood dishes, but dishes such as pork loin stuffed with mushrooms and foie gras are outstanding as well. The wine list is superb.

Nueva Costanera 3467. ℭ 2/263-0008. Reservations recommended. Main courses $8–$15. AE, DC, MC, V. Mon–Sat 1–3:30pm and 8pm–midnight.

Happening ℛℛ ARGENTINE/CHILEAN   If you're in the mood for steak, this Argentine-owned restaurant (there's another Happening in Buenos Aires) is your place. The grilled meat selection is endless, cooked on an enormous indoor barbecue and served in a refined, attractive ambience. There's also a variety of salads, fish, and pastas to choose from. It's housed on a busy corner in a large, gray building. You can bring your clients here for lunch or enjoy a candlelit dinner in the evening.

Av. Apoquindo 3090. ℭ 2/233-2301. Reservations recommended. Main courses $7–$13. AE, DC, MC, V. Mon–Sat noon–4pm and 8pm–midnight.

Osadía 🏃🏃🏃 FUSION   One of Santiago's newest and most unique restaurants, Osadía boasts a fantastical design of semi-demolished brick walls painted white and dripping with candles. The food is as out-there as the restaurant's decor, with high-concept blends of flavors and complicated presentations that can often be difficult to figure out how to eat. It's elegant yet fun, and they serve exquisite dishes such as rabbit cooked with tarragon and beer and served with spaetzle; crab ravioli with mushroom sauce; and smoked mussels in a cilantro vinaigrette. Save room for dessert.

Tobalaba 477. ⓒ 2/232-2732. Reservations recommended. Main courses $9–$15. AE, DC, MC, V. Mon–Fri 1–4pm and 8pm–midnight; Sat 8pm–midnight.

MODERATE

Akarana 🏃🏃 *Finds* FUSION   Akarana was opened recently by the owner of the Cafe Melba, who is from New Zealand. She has created a menu that reflects the tastes from her home country, fusing Asian cuisine with New Zealand specialties to create a wonderful feast for the palate. Sample dishes include gingery egg rolls and tempura, grilled, herbed sea bass with radish puree and aioli, designer pizzas, and steak with portobello mushrooms and Parmesan mashed potatoes. The white interiors are fresh and airy, and the wraparound patio dining area offers undoubtedly the most pleasant outdoor seating in the area.

Reyes Lavalle 3310. ⓒ 2/231-9667. Reservations recommended. Main courses $6–$10. AE, DC, MC, V. Daily noon–midnight.

INEXPENSIVE

Tiramisu 🏃 PIZZA   Come to Tiramisu for big, thin-crust pizzas baked in a stone oven and served in a delightful atmosphere. With dozens and dozens of combinations from traditional to arugula with shaved Parmesan and artichokes, you'll have a hard time choosing. There are fresh, delicious salads, too, and desserts that of course include tiramisu. Outdoor seating is available. Tiramisu is very popular with the lunch crowd.

Av. Isidora Goyenechea 3141. ⓒ 2/335-5135. Main courses $4–$7. AE, DC, MC, V. Mon–Sun 1–4pm and 7pm–midnight.

SANTIAGO AFTER DARK

There are plenty of theaters, nightclubs, and bars to keep your evenings busy in Santiago. Like Buenos Aires, Santiago adheres to a vampire's schedule, dining as late as 11pm, arriving at a nightclub past midnight, and diving into bed just before the sun rises. It can take a little getting used to, and there are many early-hour nighttime attractions if you can't bear late nights. Several newspapers publish daily listings of movies, theater, and live music as well as Friday weekend-guide supplements: *El Mercurio*'s "Wiken" is the best, or try *La Tercera*'s "Guía Fin de Semana."

THE PERFORMING ARTS

Santiago is known for its theater, from large-scale productions to one-person monologues put on at a local cafe. Ask around for recommendations, either from the hotel staff or at a visitor information center, such as the kiosk at Paseo Ahumada and Paseo Huérfanos, which typically have complete theater listings and can suggest particular acts.

The following are some of the more well-established theaters in Santiago. Four theaters in Bellavista offer contemporary productions and comedies in an intimate setting: **Teatro Bellavista** at Dardignac 0110 (ⓒ 2/735-2395), **El Conventillo** at Bellavista 173 (ⓒ 2/777-4164), **Teatro La Feria** at Crucero Exeter 0250 (ⓒ 2/737-7371), and **Teatro San Ginés** at Mallinkrodt 76 (ⓒ 2/738-2159). As the name implies, the nearby **Teatro La Comedia** at Merced 349 (© 2/639-1523) hosts comedy, but it is better known for cutting-edge productions. In Las Condes, try the **Teatro Apoquindo** at Av. Apoquindo 3384 (© 2/231-3560). The cultural center **Estación Mapocho** at the Plaza de la Cultura s/n (© 2/361-1761) hosts a large variety of theater acts, often concurrently.

If symphony music, ballet, or opera is your thing, you won't want to miss a performance at the historic downtown **Teatro Municipal** at Agustinas 749 (© **2/639-0282**). The National Chilean Ballet performs here, with contemporary productions that might be danced to the tunes of tango, Chilean folklore, or Janis Joplin. Visiting orchestras and the Fundación Beethoven play at the **Teatro Oriente** at Avenida Pedro de Valdivia between Avenida Providencia and Avenida Andrés Bello (© **2/251-5321**), from May to late September; the ticket and information office can be found at Av. 11 de Septiembre 2214, #66. **Teatro Universidad de Chile** at Av. Providencia 043 (© **2/634-4746**) hosts ballet and symphony productions, both national and international, throughout the year.

THE BAR & CLUB SCENE

Crowd-pulling national and international megabands typically play in the **Estado Nacional** or the **Estación Mapocho**. You'll find listings for these shows in the daily newspaper. If you're looking for something mellower, **Bellavista** is a good bet for jazz, bolero, and folk music that is often performed Thursday through Saturday in several restaurants/cafes. **La Tasca Mediterráneo**'s next-door cafe at Purísima 161 (© **2/735-3901**) hosts mostly jazz acts in a cozy atmosphere, but it can get crowded as the night wears on.

Also in Bellavista, there are four similar cozy bars at Antonia López and Mallinkrodt. **La Casa en el Aire** at Antonia López de Bello 0125 (© **2/735-6680**) has a great ambience lit by candlelight, and is known for poetry readings and live music. Across the street at Antonia López de Bello 0126 is **El Perseguidor** (© 2/777-6763), a literary cafe with jazz performances every evening Thursday through Sunday. For salsa dancing, try the **Habana Salsa** at Dominica 142 (© 2/737-1737). Despite the hokey exterior of faux building facades, it's where many salsa fanatics spend their weekend nights. For a younger salsa crowd, head to **Delirio Caribeño**, at Bucarest 117 (© **2/231-8029**). In Providencia try **Vitamina** at Paseo Orrego Luco 42, with an outdoor courtyard, and the fun, vibrant neighborhood staple, **Bar Liguria** at Manuel Montt 1373.

There are dozens of music venues spread across the city, but several are concentrated in the Ñuñoa neighborhood, about a 5- to 10-minute taxi ride from downtown and Providencia. **La Batuta** at Jorge Washington 52 (© 2/274-7096) is a dance club on Saturday; the rest of the week it's a great spot to check out a wide variety of international and national contemporary and folk bands. The atmosphere is underground, but the crowd profile depends on who's playing.

The **Club de Jazz** at José Pedro Alessandri 85 (© **2/274-1937**) is one of the city's most traditional places (Louis Armstrong once played here), and every Thursday, Friday, and Saturday beginning at 11pm, several excellent bands get together and jam for the audience.

In Providencia, **Tomm** at General Holley 2366 has live music and a changing crowd depending on the music that evening.

Santiago's club scene typically caters to an 18- to 35-year-old crowd, and it all gets going pretty late, from midnight to 6am, on the average. If you like electronica music, you might check out "fiestas" publicized in the weekend entertainment sections of newspapers that list 1-night-only raves and live music, or, in Bellavista, try **La Feria** at Constitución 275, in an old theater. **Blondie** at

Alameda 2879 (© **2/681-7793**) is like spending a night in 1985, with an '80s revival scene and music to match. Harder to get to (semilong cab ride) is the **Skuba** club in Paseo San Damian (Av. Las Condes 11271; © **2/243-1108**), a European-style disco that attracts Chilean jet setters.

4 Around Santiago & the Central Valley

Santiaguinos often say the best thing about their city is its proximity to attractions such as beaches, nature preserves, hot springs, wineries, and ski resorts. These destinations are an alleviating escape when Santiago is smoggy; and all excursions are within several hours' drive from the city, which means it is possible to pack a lot of action into just a few days.

South of Santiago is the nation's breadbasket, the Central Valley. Most Chilean wineries can be found in this region, as well as country restaurants along the highway and, farther south, the popular resort Termas de Chillán.

Destinations around Santiago can all be explored on day trips. You might find an overnight stay in Viña del Mar or Valparaíso an attractive option; it will allow for more time for exploring the area. If you use Santiago as a base, rental cars are obviously handy but not entirely necessary, as public transportation—from minivans to buses—is efficient and inexpensive.

VIÑA DEL MAR & VALPARAISO

These popular coastal destinations are less than a 2-hour drive from the capital. Viña del Mar is a fashionable seaside resort located 120km (74 miles) northwest of Santiago, and is built of manicured lawns, lush gardens, a bustling little downtown, and a waterfront lined with towering apartment buildings, restaurants, hotels, nightclubs, and a casino. Some refer to the town as Chile's Riviera, but most simply call it "Viña"—you'll call it chaos if you come during the high season between December and late February. There are plenty of fine beaches here, but the Humboldt Current that runs the length of Chile to Antofagasta makes for cold swimming conditions, even during the summer.

Viña is quite a contrast to the ramshackle streets of Valparaíso; indeed, it is difficult to believe the two cities are just 15 minutes from one another. Valparaíso is Viña's blue-collar sister, with a history and vibrant culture that speaks strongly of the golden days before the Panama Canal, when every ship on its way around the Cape stopped here for supplies. The features of Valparaíso, with its multicolored jumble of clapboard homes and weathered Victorian mansions, sinuous streets, steep hills, and rollicking seafront bars, is enchanting, fascinating even—although it might not capture you at first. Valparaíso can be a little scary to first-time visitors, but give it a chance and allow the city to work its magic on you.

ESSENTIALS
Getting There
BY BUS   Both **Tur Bus** (© 2/270-7500) and **Pullman Bus** (© 2/560-3700) offer service to Viña and Valparaíso, leaving every 15 minutes. Tur Bus leaves from its terminal at 3750 Alameda O'Higgins, and Pullman leaves from the Terminal Alameda at Alameda O'Higgins 3712. (Both terminals are near the Metro stop University de Santiago.) The fare is about $4 one-way. It is wise to purchase a round-trip ticket on weekends and holidays.

BY CAR   To get to Viña del Mar and Valparaíso from Santiago, take Alameda O'Higgins west until it changes into Ruta Nacional 68, 10km (6 miles) from the coast, and follow the signs to Valparaíso. Street parking is plentiful; in Valparaíso

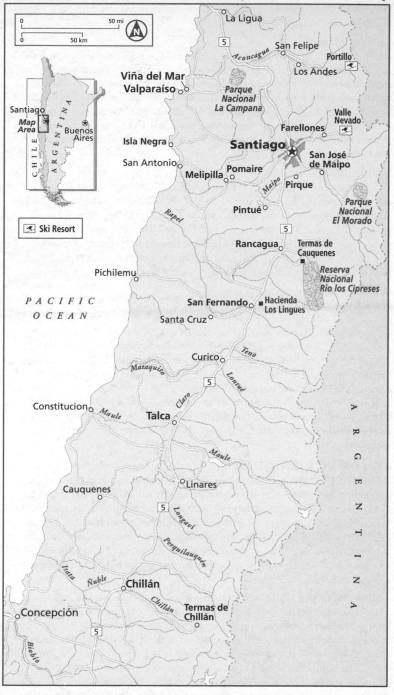

0 | 50 mi
0 | 50 km

Santiago
Map Area
Buenos Aires

CHILE
ARGENTINA

Ski Resort

La Ligua

San Felipe

Aconcagua

Portillo

Los Andes

Viña del Mar
Valparaíso

Parque Nacional La Campana

Valle Nevado

Farellones

Isla Negra

Santiago

San José de Maipo

San Antonio

Pomaire

Melipilla

Maipo

Pirque

Pintué

Parque Nacional El Morado

Rapel

Rancagua

Termas de Cauquenes

Pichilemu

Reserva Nacional Rio los Cipreses

PACIFIC OCEAN

San Fernando

Hacienda Los Lingues

Santa Cruz

Teno

Curico

Mataquito

Lontué

Claro

Constitucion

Maule

Talca

Maule

ARGENTINA

Cauquenes

Linares

Longaví

Perquilauquén

Itata

Ñuble

Chillán

Chillán

Concepción

Termas de Chillán

Bío Bío

there is a central parking garage on Calle Errázuriz, across from the Plaza Sotomayor and near the visitor center.

Getting Around

Walking is really the only way to see Valparaíso. Viña can be managed by foot, and there is a pleasant beachfront promenade for a stroll. The easiest way to travel between both towns is by **taxi** or aboard the **commuter train** "Merval," which runs every 30 minutes from its stations in Viña (at Francisco Vergara between calles Bohn and Alvarez) and Valparaíso (the train's final stop is at Estación Puerto, near the visitor center at the pier). The train runs from about 6:30am to 10pm and costs 35¢ to 75¢. Taxis can be hailed in the street, or your hotel can call one.

Visitor Information

The **Oficina de Turismo de Viña** is located on Plaza Vergara, next to the post office near avenidas Libertad and Arlegui (© **800/800830,** toll-free in Chile). Summer hours are Monday through Saturday from 9am to 9pm (closed 2–3pm); off-season hours are Monday through Friday from 10am to 7pm (closed 2–3pm), and Saturday from 10am to 2pm. A helpful staff (including a few who speak basic English) can provide visitors with accommodations information, but without ratings. It's also a good place for information about where to go to rent a temporary apartment.

FAST FACTS: VINA DEL MAR   Most major **banks** can be found on Avenida Arlegui, and although they're open Monday through Friday from 9am to 2pm only, nearly all have 24-hour ATMs (RedBancs). Casas de cambio (money-exchange houses) are open in the summer Monday through Friday from 9am to 2pm and 3 to 8pm, Saturday from 9am to 2pm; in the winter, Monday through Saturday from 9am to 2pm and 4 to 7pm, Saturday from 9am to 2pm. Several cambios can be found along Avenida Arlegui.

If you need to reach the **police** in an emergency, dial © 133. For **fire,** dial © 132. To call an **ambulance,** dial © 131. For medical attention, go to **Hospital Gustavo Fricke** on calles Alvarez and Simón Bolívar (© 32/675067, or 32/675267 for emergencies).

EXPLORING VIÑA DEL MAR

BEACHES   The **Playa Caleta Abarca** beach is located in a protected bay near the entrance to Viña del Mar, next to the oft-photographed "flower clock" and the Cerro Castillo. Northeast and fronting the rows of terraced high-rise apartment buildings, you'll find **Playa Acapulco, Playa Mirasol,** and **Playa Las Salinas.** (The latter is near the naval base.) These beaches all see throngs of vacationers and families in the summer. The *in* spot for beaches is just north of Viña at Reñaca—it's close enough to take a taxi, or grab a bus numbered 1, or bus Nañdú at Avenida Libertad and Avenida 15 Norte.

Casino Municipal   Built in 1930, the Casino Municipal was the most luxurious building in its day and is worth a visit even if you're not a gambler. The interior has been remodeled over time, but the facade has withstood the caprices of many a developer and is still as handsome as the day it opened. Semiformal attire (that is, no T-shirts, jeans, or sneakers) is required to enter the gaming room. The casino also holds temporary art exhibits on the second floor.

Plaza Colombia between Av. San Martín and Av. Perú. © **32/500600** or 32/500700. Admission $6 (charged only to enter game room). Hours vary, but generally: Game room daily 6pm–4am (Sun–Thurs winter hours are 6pm–2am); slot machines daily noon–4am; bingo daily 4pm–4am. Weekends open 24 hr.

Quinta Vergara Park/Museum of Fine Art ★★   One of the loveliest parks in central Chile, the Quinta Vergara is also home to a large amphitheater that holds Viña's yearly Song Festival as well as the Museum of Fine Art. The Quinta, whose area is naturally fenced in by several steep hills, was once the residence of Portuguese shipping magnate Francisco Alvarez and his wife, Dolores, who created the park, planting a multitude of native and other exotic species. The museum is housed in the ornate **Palacio Vergara,** which was built by Francisco's great-granddaughter, and the collection includes art from the family collection and other works from collectors in Viña.

Near Plaza Parroquia. Museum © 32/252481. Park: Free admission; daily 7am–6pm (until 7pm in summer). Museum: Admission 60¢ adults, 30¢ children; Tues–Sun 10am–2pm and 3–6pm.

Museo de Arqueología e Historia Francisco Fonck ★★ *(Kids)* This museum boasts a large collection of indigenous art and archaeological items from Easter Island, with more than 1,400 pieces and one of the six Moai sculptures outside Easter Island (the others are in England, the U.S., Paris, Brussels, and La Serena in Chile). There is also a decent archaeological exhibition of Mapuche pieces and other items from the north and central zones of Chile. The Museum of Natural History is on the second floor, featuring birds, mammals, insects, and fossils.

Av. 4 Norte 784. © 32/686753. Admission $1.60 adults, 30¢ children. Tues–Fri 9:30am–6pm; Sat–Sun 9:30am–2pm.

Museo Palacio Rioja ★   This enormous 1906 Belle Epoque stone mansion is worth a visit for a peek into the lives of the early-20th-century elite in Viña del Mar. Built by Spaniard Fernando Rioja, a banker, and originally spanning 4 blocks, the palace took opulence to a new level, with a stone facade featuring Corinthian columns and a split double staircase. Interiors are made of oak and stone, with enough salons to fit a family of 20. Although a fraction of what it once was, the palm-fringed garden surrounding the house is idyllic.

Quillota 214. © 32/689665. Admission 60¢ adults, 20¢ children. Tues–Sun 10am–1pm and 3–5:30pm.

EXPLORING VALPARAISO

Museo Naval y Marítimo ★★   This fascinating museum merits a visit even if you do not particularly fancy naval and maritime-related artifacts and memorabilia. The museum is smartly designed and divided into four salons: the War of Independence, the War against the Peru-Bolivia Confederation, the War against Spain, and the War of the Pacific. Each salon holds interesting artifacts, such as antique documents, medals, uniforms, and war trophies. Of special note is the Arturo Prat room, with artifacts salvaged from the *Esmeralda,* a ship that was sunk during the War of the Pacific.

Paseo 21 de Mayo, Cerro Artillería. © 32/283749. Admission 90¢ adults, 35¢ children under 12. Tues–Sun 10am–5:30pm.

La Sebastiana ★★★   La Sebastiana is one of poet Pablo Neruda's three homes that have since been converted into museums honoring the distinguished Nobel laureate's work and life. Neruda called himself an "estuary sailor"— although terrified of sailing, he nevertheless was fascinated by the sea, and he fashioned his homes to resemble boats, complete with porthole windows. There are self-guiding information sheets that explain the significance of important documents and items on display, as well as Neruda's whimsical collection of eccentric knickknacks culled from his journeys through the Americas and abroad. A cultural center has been built below the house, with a gallery and a gift shop. Don't miss this fascinating attraction.

The walk from Plaza Victoria is a hike, so you might want to take a taxi. From Plaza Ecuador, there's a bus, Verde "D." Or you might opt to take *La Cintura* **(The Waist),** a bus route that takes riders up and down and around the snaking streets of Valparaíso and eventually stops a block or so from Neruda's house (be sure to tell the driver that's your final destination because the bus continues on). To take this route, board Bus Verde "O" at Plaza Echaurren near the Customs House (La Aduana).

Calle Ferrari 692. (C) **32/256606.** Admission $2.50 adults, $1.25 students. Mar–Dec Tues–Fri 10:30am–2pm and 3:30–6pm, Sat–Sun 10:30am–6pm; Jan–Feb Tues–Sun 10:30am–6pm; closed Mon.

WALKING TOURS OF VALPARAISO

The best walk here treats visitors to rides aboard the city's famed *ascensores,* followed by a stroll through the narrow, picturesque streets that wind erratically through Valparaíso's most charming neighborhoods, Cerro Alegre and Cerro Concepción.

Pick up a city map at the visitor center at Muelle Prat, and head toward Plaza Sotomayor, Valparaíso's civic center until 1980. Here, you'll encounter the **Monument to the Heroes of Iquique,** under which the remains of Prat, Condell, and Serrano, heroes of the War of the Pacific, are buried. To the left of the plaza, next to the Palacio de Justicia, ride the Ascensor Peral (ca. 1902) for 10¢ to the top of Cerro Alegre, and there you'll find the **Paseo Yugoslavo,** a terrace walkway built by Pascual Baburizza in 1929, whose **Palacio Baburizza** now houses the Fine Arts Museum (closed for renovation). The walkway curves to the right around a tiny plaza; follow it until you reach Calle Alvaro Besa. Take the shortcut down **Pasaje Bavestrello,** a cement stairway at the left. Continue until you reach Calle Urriola, which you'll cross; then walk up to another stairway, Pasaje Gálvez. At Calle Papudo, climb the stairway and turn left into **Paseo Gervasoni,** lined with stately, 19th-century mansions. This street looks out onto the port of Valparaíso. Here, you'll also find the **Museo de Casa Lukas,** an exhibition of hundreds of illustrations made by Renzo Pecchenino, cartoonist and satirist for the newspaper *El Mercurio,* open Tuesday through Sunday from 11am to 8pm; admission is 70¢. From here, descend via Ascensor Concepción or continue around Gervasoni until you reach Papudo. At Paseo Atkinson, you'll find another pedestrian walkway, bordered by antique English homes. Continue down the pedestrian stairway until you reach Calle Esmeralda, and the end of the walk. You can also descend by doubling back and riding the Ascensor Concepción to Calle Prat.

OTHER SHORT WALKS

THE PORT NEIGHBORHOOD Begin at the **Aduana (Customs House),** the grand, colonial American–style building built in 1854 and located at the north of town at Plaza Wheelwright at the end of Cochrane and Calle Carampangue. To the right, you'll find the **Ascensor Artillería,** built in 1893 (and it shows); it costs 10¢. The wobbly contraption is a delight, and it takes visitors to the most panoramic pedestrian walkway in Valparaíso, **Paseo 21 de Mayo.** This lovely promenade has a lookout gazebo from which it is possible to take in the town's bustling port activity. Follow the walkway until you reach the **Museo Naval y Marítimo** (see "Exploring Valparaíso," above). To return, double back and descend via the *ascensor,* or head down the walkway and take a left at Calle Carampangue.

PLAZA VICTORIA/MUSEO A CIELO ABIERTO/LA SEBASTIANA (PABLO NERUDA'S HOUSE)   In the late 1880s, Plaza Victoria was the elegant

Valparaíso

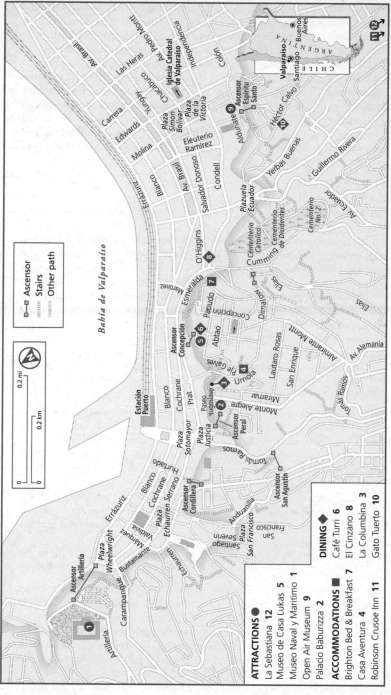

Bahía de Valparaíso

0.2 mi
0.2 km

Ascensor
Stairs
Other path

ARGENTINA
Buenos Aires
CHILE
Valparaíso Santiago

ATTRACTIONS ●
La Sebastiana **12**
Museo de Casa Lukas **5**
Museo Naval y Marítimo **1**
Open Air Museum **9**
Palacio Baburizza **2**

ACCOMMODATIONS ■
Brighton Bed & Breakfast **7**
Casa Aventura **4**
Robinson Crusoe Inn **11**

DINING ◆
Café Turri **6**
El Cinzano **8**
La Columbina **3**
Gato Tuerto **10**

center of society, as is evident by the grand trees, trickling fountain, and sculptures imported from Lima that recall that era's heyday. From the plaza, head south on Calle Molina to Alduante for the **Open Air Museum,** which features more than 20 murals painted on cement-retainer and building walls along winding streets. The project features murals conceived by well-known Chilean painters and carried out by students. Begin at the steep stairway at Calle Alduante and turn left at Pasaje Guimera, and left again at the balcony walkway that leads to **Ascensor Espíritu Santo.** (You can ride the funicular up and backtrack this route, walking down.) Continue along Calle Rudolph until you reach Calle Ferrari. Head down Ferrari all the way to Edwards and Colón. Note that the Open Air Museum runs through an interesting but grubby, somewhat rough neighborhood, and for that reason might not appeal to everyone.

WHERE TO STAY
In Viña del Mar

Hotel del Mar 👁👁👁   This brand-new, five-star hotel opened in 2003, and it is Viña's most upscale luxury lodging option. The Hotel del Mar is owned by and located next to the casino and overlooks the sea; it's an ideal location close to everything. Double standard and superior rooms have balconies and panoramic views of the ocean and the casino gardens, as do all suites. All rooms are quite spacious, and decorated in handsome, rich linens and curtains. The complete Salute Health Center is the highlight, located inside a semicircular building that overlooks the ocean and features a state-of-the-art gym, beauty center, and indoor lap pool. There's also a terrace that overlooks the sea. Lodging includes free entrance to the casino and shows.

Av. San Martín 199. ⓒ 600/700-6000. Fax 32/500601. www.casino.cl. 60 units. $200–$250 double standard; $330–$390 suite. AE, DC, MC, V. Valet parking. **Amenities:** 4 restaurants; bar; indoor pool; gym; sauna; children's game room; business center; room service; massage; babysitting; laundry service; solarium; art gallery. *In room:* A/C, cable TV, DVD and CD player, safe.

Hotel Monterilla 👁👁👁 *(Finds* This appealing boutique hotel is one of the best in Chile. Warm, personal service and a central location are definite draws, but the chic, contemporary design is what really makes the Monterilla special. The interiors feature white carpet, cushy orange chairs, and walls adorned with colorful postmodern art. The rooms are not huge, but they are elegant and comfortable, and several have kitchenettes. There's a cafe/restaurant that serves snacks and an excellent daily breakfast buffet. A small common area has several sofas for reading or relaxing. The Monterilla is a family-run hotel, and service is friendly and personal. This is a great value, with a convenient location near the beach and the casino.

Dos Norte 65, Plaza México, Viña del Mar. ⓒ 32/976950. Fax 32/683576. www.monterilla.cl. 20 units. $80 double; $90 apt. AE, DC, MC, V. **Amenities:** Cafeteria; bar; office services; laundry service. *In room:* Cable TV, minibar.

Hotel Oceanic 👁👁   The Oceanic enjoys a splendid location on a rocky promontory with dramatic views of Valparaíso and the ocean crashing against the shore. The hotel is warm and friendly and full of places to sit and relax to the soothing sound of the sea. During the summer, the pebbled terrace with its oceanside pool and lounge chairs is the best around. The cozy rooms come with comfortable beds, wooden beams, and rose-colored drapes. (Some have sea views, and some look out to the busy road to Reñaca.) A few "attic" rooms are especially spacious and come with a breakfast nook and great views. The plant-filled restaurant is popular, but the views are a tad more noteworthy than the cuisine. The Oceanic is a short taxi ride away from most restaurants and points of interest.

Av. Borgoño 12925, Viña del Mar. © 32/830006. Fax 32/830390. www.hoteloceanic.cl. 28 units. $115–$125 oceanview double. AE, DC, MC, V. **Amenities:** Restaurant; bar; outdoor pool; sauna; salon; laundry service. *In room:* Cable TV, minibar.

Hotel O'Higgins *(Overrated* This traditional hotel, a stone landmark constructed in the heart of Viña in 1934, has sadly begun to show its age. Minor renovations, including new hallway carpet and fresh drapes and bedspreads, have improved its image somewhat, but a stale lobby, dark hallways, and worn furniture reveal that the glory days of the O'Higgins are over. Nevertheless, it's an interesting place to spend the night, if not for its historical appeal then for its downtown location (close to shops but on a noisy plaza), outdoor pool, and complete services, including two restaurants and Harry's Bar. Ask to see the accommodations if at all possible, as the quality varies from room to room, and those facing the main plaza are nicer than side rooms. The O'Higgins often stages conventions and weddings in one of its 10 salons. Ask for price specials when booking.

Plaza Vergara, Viña del Mar. © 32/882016. Fax 32/883537. www.panamericanahoteles.cl. 265 units. $53–$83 double. AE, DC, MC, V. Free parking. **Amenities:** 2 restaurants; bar; outdoor pool; kids' recreation room; car-rental agency; 24-hr. room service; babysitting; laundry. *In room:* TV.

Offenbacher hof Residencia ☆☆ Housed in a lovely Victorian building perched high atop Cerro Castillo, the Offenbacher has sweeping views of Viña del Mar and an exquisite patio cafe. Still, it is the friendly German-Chilean owners of the Offenbacher that make this bed-and-breakfast really special. The interiors are older, and in some rooms you might find the furnishings a tad worn, but most rooms are spacious. Each features a different style, from romantic to masculine. The attic rooms are well lit, but slightly smaller. Breakfast is served in the antique dining room downstairs or underneath an umbrella at a patio table outside. You'll be wowed by the view, so be sure to get a room that has one. There's also a sauna, solarium, and hydromassage whirlpool for an extra price.

Balmaceda 102, Cerro Castillo, Viña del Mar. © 32/621483. Fax 32/662432. residoff@chilesat.net. 15 units. $35–$45 double. AE, DC, MC, V. **Amenities:** Cafe; bar; sauna; laundry service; sightseeing tours. *In room:* Cable TV.

In Valparaíso

The majority of travelers lodge in Viña del Mar and visit Valparaíso by day; however, there are a few charming places to spend the night in Valparaíso, and some travelers prefer the rough-and-tumble charm of the city as opposed to the predictable resort ambience of Viña.

Brighton Bed & Breakfast ☆☆☆ *(Moments* This is one of the prettiest places to spend the night in Valparaíso, offering one of the most exceptional locations of any hotel in Chile. A big yellow Victorian perched high atop Cerro Concepción, this B&B offers stunning, sweeping views of the harbor and the city center below. The cozy rooms have had an update recently, and they are decorated with pale linens, antiques, and cream-colored wallpaper. Because this is a converted home, room sizes vary; try booking the "suite" (really a large double) with a balcony and sea view. There's also a cafe on the first floor with checkered black-and-white floors and two terrace patios—an unbeatable location for lunch or coffee. On weekends, the cafe has live bolero and tango music, and it stays open until 4am. To get here, take the Ascensor Concepción and go left.

Paseo Atkinson 151–153, Cerro Concepción, Valparaíso. ©/fax 32/223513. www.brighton.cl. 6 units. $42 double w/o bathroom, $50 double w/bathroom; $57 double w/bathroom and ocean view. AE, DC, MC, V. **Amenities:** Cafe.

Casa Aventura 🦎 *Value*   This tiny gem of a *hostal* has a picturesque, central location; clean, colorful interiors and Spanish-language courses and excursions. With just five rooms (two triples, two with a double bed, and one quad), the atmosphere is quiet and intimate, with a sunny living area and couches for just hanging out. The German-Chilean couple owns Casa Aventura, and they typically cater to budget travelers and students who take part in their on-site, optional Spanish courses. If your group doesn't fill the room, you might end up sharing with a stranger. Beds have fluffy down comforters, but the only rooms that are sunny and bright are the two triples. Guests have kitchen and laundry privileges. Spanish courses should preferably be reserved in advance by e-mail; average cost for a private class is $10 per hour, or $14 total for two students.

Pasaje Gálvez 11, Cerro Alegre, Valparaíso. ⓒ/fax 32/755963. www.casaventura.cl. 5 units. $9 per person. No credit cards. **Amenities:** Self-service laundry; kitchen facilities.

Robinson Crusoe Hotel 🦎🦎🦎 *Finds*   They don't have a website, nor do they seem to want much publicity, which makes this little bed-and-breakfast the best find in Valparaíso. The Robinson Crusoe is a stylish inn topped with a terrace lounge that offers a knockout view of the city. The inn was once a collection of several run-down homes; the remodeled hotel now features dark wood, ceramic floors, winding stairways, and walls painted in rich plums and ornamented with arts and crafts and nautical decor. The old-fashioned tall doors, stained glass, and high windows all lend an antique splendor to the inn. The rooftop restaurant/lounge has captivating views of the port and the colorful streets that plummet toward it. An excellent breakfast is another highlight. The hotel is about a 15-minute walk to downtown Valparaíso, and a climb back, so you might find yourself taking a taxi. Close to the Pablo Neruda museum.

Héctor Calvo 389, Valparaíso. ⓒ 32/495499. robinsoncrusoeinn@hotmail.com. 14 units. $60–$78 double. AE, DC, MC, V. **Amenities:** Restaurant. *In room:* TV.

WHERE TO DINE
In Viña del Mar

Diego's Pizzas 🦎 *Kids* PIZZA   Diego's creative, artistic pizzas stand out from Domino's and Pizza Hut down the road for their dozens and dozens of far-out toppings, more than 50 kinds of empanadas, and wonderful, fresh salads. Every pizza has a name; the biggest seller at Diego's is the "Four-Season Pizza," with shrimp, mussels, smoked salmon, razor clams, onion, mozzarella, and tomato.

Av. San Martín 636. ⓒ 32/689512. Individual pizzas $5–$8; salads $6. AE, DC, MC, V. Daily 10am–2am.

Fellini 🦎 INTERNATIONAL/CHILEAN   The extensive menu offered at Fellini is simply incredible—virtually anything and everything is offered, making this a great place for a group that can't agree on what to eat. The offerings include dozens of rich, homemade pastas; fresh seafood; grilled meats served draped in sauces such as Roquefort and cognac; stuffed crepes; vegetarian and low-fat plates; and the list goes on. Everything is made fresh here, even ice cream. The dining area is semielegant and warm, and the tables are well appointed. You can't miss Fellini: The pea-green exterior is visible a block away.

Av. 3 Norte 88. ⓒ/fax 32/975742. Main courses $7.50–$11. AE, DC, MC, V. Daily 1–4pm and 7:30pm–midnight.

Las Delicias del Mar 🦎 SEAFOOD   This Basque-influenced restaurant serves wonderfully sumptuous seafood dishes that are matched by sharp, attentive service. Las Delicias is known for its paella (which can be ordered for one or two people), but the fish dishes are really the most savory. This is one of the few Chilean restaurants to actually put time and thought into preparing a dish, and the results are mouthwatering: sea bass, salmon, or conger eel under a rich cream-mushroom-shrimp sauce and topped with freshly grated Parmesan, baked golden brown; or sole stuffed with cheese and prawns. Tangerine-colored walls and leafy plants make for a warm, comfortable atmosphere.

Av. San Martín 459. ℭ **32/901837.** Main courses $10–$12. AE, DC, MC, V. Daily 12:30–4pm and 7:30pm–midnight.

Ristorante San Marco ★★ SOUTHERN ITALIAN   San Marco is one of the best restaurants in the area, and has been since it opened its doors in 1957. Everything is made fresh daily here, from the pasta to the tiramisu. Most of the pastas are traditional and served with typical sauces, such as bolognese or Alfredo, but you can have your fettuccine or tortellini with seafood or creamy basil sauce. San Marco offers an extensive list of rich, homemade desserts and a reasonably priced wine list. The simple dining area has wraparound windows festooned with hanging vines and tables draped with white linen tablecloths.

Av. San Martín 597. ℭ **32/975304.** Fax 32/884872. Main courses $6–$10. AE, DC, MC, V. Daily noon–4pm and 8pm–midnight.

Savinya ★★ INTERNATIONAL/CHILEAN   The brand-new Hotel del Mar is home to one of Viña's best restaurants, Savinya, the only restaurant in town that combines high-quality ingredients, an elegant dining area, attentive service, and a gorgeous panoramic view of the ocean. Offerings include a wonderful marinated king crab with shiitake mushrooms and apples, and fresh trout stuffed with a razor clam souffle and an abalone sauce. The menu is predominately seafood, but there are meat options as well. There are two other restaurants in the Hotel del Mar, **Sushiyana,** a Japanese restaurant, and **La Barquera,** with gourmet pizzas and a more informal atmosphere.

San Martín 199, Viña del Mar. ℭ/fax **32/500600.** www.casino.cl. Main courses $8–$18. AE, DC, MC, V. Daily noon–4pm and 8pm–1am.

In Valparaíso
Café Turri ★★ (Moments   Regionally famous, Café Turri is one of the best restaurants in the city. Fine food, gorgeous views, and an attentive waitstaff make this an enjoyable gastronomic experience, especially when it is sunny and you dine on the terrace. Housed in a converted home built a century ago by an English immigrant, the restaurant sits high atop the Cerro Concepción and occupies three floors. Café Turri's specialty is seafood, but they also serve a variety of meat and chicken dishes. The remarkably extensive menu includes sea bass, salmon, congrio, albacore tuna, and more, each cooked 24 different ways, as well as exquisite appetizers and desserts.

Calle Templeman 147 (Cerro Concepción; take the Concepción lift). ℭ **32/259198.** Dinner reservations recommended for outdoor seating. Main courses $5–$15. AE, DC, MC, V. Mon–Fri 9am–midnight; Sat–Sun 9am–2am.

El Cinzano ★ CHILEAN   Since 1896, this classic yet kitschy restaurant has been the popular hangout for poets, intellectuals, musicians, and the like, who come for late-night *chorrillanas,* a Valparaíso specialty of steak, eggs, onions, and french fries, tossed together and heaped on a platter. During lunch and dinner, waiters in smart black jackets and bow ties serve typical Chilean seafood fare and grilled meats, as well as their other specialty: *vino arreglado,* or "fixed" wine with strawberry, peach, or *chirimoya* (custard apple). In the evening, the Cinzano has one of the liveliest ambiences around, with customers serenaded to the sounds of live tango singers.

Aníbal Pinto 1182. ℭ **32/213043.** Main courses $3.50–$8. AE, DC, MC, V. Daily 10am–1am (until 4:30am Thurs–Sat).

Gato Tuerto 🐾🐾 SEAFOOD/INTERNATIONAL   This restaurant is housed within the vividly painted lemon yellow and blue Victorian that hovers over Plaza Victoria. The Gato Tuerto is part of the Foundation Valparaíso, which is dedicated to renovating antique structures such as the old home the restaurant is housed in. The ambience is enchanting, due to the view and the service. The menu serves about 20 dishes from a dozen different countries, ranging from Moroccan to Thai to Indonesian, such as Nasi Goreng, a dish with shrimp, red pepper, squash, and almonds, served with rice.

Héctor Calvo 205 (Espíritu Santo Funicular). ⓒ 32/593156. Main courses $5–$8. AE, DC, MC, V. Daily noon–midnight.

La Columbina 🐾🐾🐾 *Moments* INTERNATIONAL/CHILEAN   This terrific restaurant occupies three floors of a beautiful Victorian building and includes a tearoom with stained-glass windows and a panoramic view; a restaurant/pub with parquet floors and a pretty terrace shaded by striped awnings; and a more formal dining area with linen tablecloths, antiques, and smartly dressed waiters. The antique building is an old servants' quarters for the nearby Palacio Baburizza. In the evening, the pub offers an additional menu of appetizers, including Mexican and Thai platters, as well as excellent, artfully prepared entrees, such as filet mignon marinated in dark beer and fresh herbs. Wood-burning stoves, sumptuous views, a colorful, amicable staff, and live jazz, tango, and bolero music on Friday and Saturday make for a great atmosphere.

Pasaje Apolo 91–77. ⓒ 32/236254. Main courses $5–$10. No credit cards. Tues–Sat 9am–4pm, 4–8pm (tearoom only), and 8pm–midnight (Fri–Sat until 2am); Sun–Mon 9am–4pm.

VALPARAISO AFTER DARK

Most restaurants and bars do not adhere to a set closing hour, but instead close "when the candles burn down." Try **El Cinzano** (see "Where to Dine," above), which hosts dinner dances and spotlights tango music and singers in a wonderful, early-20th-century ambience. **La Columbina** (ⓒ 32/236254) is frequented by the 30-and-up crowd for its comfortable ambience, live jazz and bolero music, and glittering view. **La Piedra Feliz,** Errázuriz 1054 (ⓒ 32/256788), has wooden floors and a tranquil atmosphere—until they fire up live music in the evening from Tuesday to Sunday.

CAJON DE MAIPO

Cajón de Maipo is a quick city escape that puts visitors in the middle of a rugged, pastoral setting of towering peaks and freshly scented forest slopes along the Río Maipo. A highlight in this area is **El Morado National Park** (see below), but it is certainly not a requisite destination. Cajón de Maipo offers a wide array of outdoor activities, such as rafting, horseback riding, hiking, climbing, and more, but it also offers a chance to linger over a good lunch or picnic, stroll around the area, and maybe even lay your head down for the night in one of the cabañas that line the valley.

To get there, take one of the buses that leave from the Metro station Parque O'Higgins toward San José de Maipo every 15 minutes from 6am to 11:30pm, and every half-hour for San Alfonso. Your hotel should be able to arrange a private minivan tour to Cajón de Maipo. By car, head south on Avenida Los Leones in Providencia, a road that changes names twice to España and then Macul. Take a left at the fork at Puente Alto.

EXPLORING THE AREA & STAYING ACTIVE

EL MORADO NATIONAL PARK   This 3,000-hectare (7,410-acre) park is 90km (56 miles) from Santiago, and features a rugged alpine landscape that seems hundreds of miles away from the city. The views at El Morado are impressive, and a great spot to take in all this beauty is the attractive, gingerbread-style mountain lodge **Refugio Alemán at Lo Valdés.** The *refugio* (cabin) serves a tasty fixed-price lunch and dinner, and they offer clean, bunk bed–style accommodations should you decide to spend the night. Per-person rates are $30; full-board rates are $50; ⓒ **09/220-8525.**

The raggedy little village of Baños Morales features several hot spring pools open daily from 8:30am to 8pm during the summer and from 10am to 4pm April through September, but in truth they are not particularly inviting, and are packed during the peak of summer. There are more hot springs at **Termas de Colina,** rock pools located in an outstanding Alpine setting, with fascinating clay pools. To get there by car, continue past Lo Valdés up a semipaved dirt road for about 12km (7½ miles). If you don't have a car, try **Manzur Expediciones** (ⓒ **2/777-4284**), which has trips on Wednesday, Saturday, and Sunday. These hot springs can get crowded during weekends. There are also transport services to Termas de Colina at Baño Morales. Admission is $5 per adult, $2.25 kids.

RAFTING   Rafting the Maipo River is very popular among Santiaguinos and foreigners alike. Although the season runs from September to April, the river really gets going from November to February, when rafters can expect to ride class III and IV rapids. Two reliable companies offer half-day rafting excursions: **Cascada de las Animas** (ⓒ **2/861-1777;** www.cascada-expediciones.cl) arranges rafting trips from its tourism complex (see "Where to Stay & Dine in Cajón de Maipo," below) in San Alfonso, but it's best to reserve beforehand. Another highly respected outfitter is **Altué Expediciones,** in Santiago, Encomenderos 83 (ⓒ **2/232-1103;** www. altue.com).

HORSEBACK RIDING   Visitors to El Morado can rent horses with a guide at Baños Morales or Termas de Colina for about $6 to $15 per person, depending on group size and duration. Cascada Expediciones has horseback riding through its own private chunk of the Andes. This ride is suitable for families.

WHERE TO STAY & DINE IN CAJON DE MAIPO

Cascada de las Animas ⓚ is a tourism center that's run by long-time residents who own a tremendous amount of acreage outside San Alfonso, part of which is used for excursions and 80 campground and picnic sites scattered about a lovely, wooded hillside (San Alfonso s/n; ⓒ **2/861-1303;** www.cascadalasanimas.cl; $62 cabaña for two; no credit cards). The complex includes nine enchanting log cabins with fully equipped kitchens and wood-burning stoves—but they're not cheap. They offer kayaking, rafting, and horseback-riding excursions, and there is a full-service restaurant. The ambience is a cross between outdoorsy and New Age, as the owners also offer meditation and spiritual retreats.

There's also **La Bella Durmiente** ⓚ (Calle Los Maitenes 115, San Alfonso; ⓒ **2/861-1525;** www.labelladurmiente.cl; $55 double; no credit cards), with fairy-tale cabins nestled among a grove of trees that surround a small restaurant and pool. All come with kitchens; three are dark, and two have sunny patios. There are cabins for two to six guests, with full pension or without.

Trattoria Calypso 🍴🍴 serves wonderful homemade pasta and, Saturday and Sunday only, stone oven–baked pizzas (Camino el Volcán 9831; ℂ **2/871-1498;** Thurs–Sun 12:30pm–10pm; no credit cards). Everything is made using organic and local farm ingredients, and there's outdoor seating. If you don't eat at **Casa Bosque** 🍴, stop here anyway to admire the fabulously outlandish architecture: polished, raw tree trunks left in their natural shape form zany door frames, ceiling beams, and pillars. Casa Bosque is a *parrilla* (grill), serving grilled meats paired with fresh salads and other accompaniments. Good food, great atmosphere, but horrible service (Camino el Volcán 16829; ℂ **2/871-1570;** Mon–Thurs 12:30pm–6pm, Fri–Sat 12:30pm–midnight; American Express, Diners Club, MasterCard, and Visa accepted). **La Petite France** 🍴 serves mouthwatering French bistro classics and Chilean and international dishes, as well as incredible pastries (Camino el Volcán 16096; ℂ **2/861-1967;** Tues–Sun noon–midnight; no credit cards). This is a good place for afternoon tea.

NEARBY WINERIES

Many "classic" wineries can be found within 35km (20 miles) of Santiago, south toward the Central Valley, close enough to take a radio-taxi. Prominent wine-growing valleys outside Santiago limits that you will hear of are the Aconcagua, Maule, or Curicó, yet it is the Rapel Valley and its smaller Colchagua Valley that offer the best full-day/overnight wine-tasting trip, including the organized Ruta del Vino. For wineries in the Colchagua Valley (3 hr. from Santiago), rent a car or join a bilingual tour. **Ace Turismo** specializes in custom-made wine country and culture trips (ℂ **2/335-6309;** www.aceturismo.cl), or try **Chip Tours,** with a variety of day tours to the Maipo and Colchagua Valley (ℂ **2/735-9044;** www.chiptravel.cl). Nearly all the travel agencies listed under "Santiago," earlier in this chapter, offer day trips and/or transportation.

Prominent wine-growing valleys outside Santiago limits that you will hear of are the Aconcagua, Maule, or Curicó, yet it is the Rapel Valley and its smaller Colchagua Valley that offer the best full-day/overnight wine-tasting trip, including the organized **Ruta del Vino** (see below). Visitors to the Ruta del Vino typically lodge at the **Hotel Santa Cruz Plaza** 🍴🍴, an attractive, four-star hotel with an excellent restaurant and swimming pool (Plaza de Armas 286; ℂ **72/ 821010;** www.hotelsantacruzplaza.cl; $105–$115 double; all major credit cards accepted). While in Santa Cruz, you won't want to miss one of Chile's best museums, the **Museo de Colchagua** (no phone; Mon–Sun 10am–6pm; admission $4). One of the loveliest places to spend the night in wine country is Santa Rita winery's picturesque 19th-century hotel, **Hotel Viña Santa Rita** 🍴🍴🍴, Camino Padre Hurtado 0695, Alto Jahuel (ℂ **2/821-9966;** www.santarita.cl; $220 double). This hotel boasts an outstanding restaurant and is very close to Santiago.

Many "classic" wineries can be found within 35km (20 miles) of Santiago, south toward the Central Valley, close enough to take a radio-taxi.

Concha y Toro 🍴🍴   Chile's most popular winery produces the lion's share of wines, from inexpensive table reds to some of Chile's priciest cabernet sauvignons. Like Cousiño-Macul, the winery itself is part of the attraction, with expansive gardens that have eight full-time gardeners, and antique bodegas whose interiors are part of your tour. Concha y Toro is also close enough to Santiago to get there by cab.

Av. Virginia Subercaseaux 210, Pirque. ℂ 2/821-7069. www.conchaytoro.com. Tours in English Mon–Fri 11:30am and 3pm; Sat 10am and noon. Tours in Spanish Mon 10:30am and 4pm; Fri 10:30am and 3:30pm; Sat 11am. Reservations required. Tour is $4, but you take your wineglass w/you.

Cousiño-Macul 👁️👁️👁️   If you have time to visit just one winery while in Chile, make it the Cousiño-Macul. This winery is more traditional than eating empanadas on Sunday; in fact, the first vines in Chile were planted here in 1546. The beautiful estate and its lush, French-designed gardens are as impressive as the winery's Antiguas Reservas traditional red, and it's just a cab ride away from Santiago.

Av. Quilín 7100, Peñalolen, Santiago. ✆ 2/284-1011. www.cousinomacul.cl. Free admission. Wine tasting $1 per glass. Bilingual tours Mon–Sat 11am; reservations required.

La Ruta del Vino del Valle de Colchagua 👁️👁️ *(Finds* This half- or full-day tour takes you to several up-and-coming wineries, many of them good to excellent, including Viña Montes, Viña Bisquertt, Casa Lapostolle, Viu Manent, and more. A full-day tour includes two wineries and the **Museo de Colchagua** or visits to three wineries. You may use your own rental vehicle and hire a guide to accompany your group, or you can join their shuttle van, which leaves from the plaza, typically from the Hotel Santa Cruz Plaza. The included lunch for the full-day tour is at the Hotel Santa Cruz.

Plaza de Armas 6, 2nd floor. ✆ 72/823199. www.rutadelvino.cl. Reservations required 24 hr. in advance. Bilingual tours per person full day $65; parties of 2 (includes lunch) half-day $40; 6 guests full day $41, half-day $23. Maximum 16 guests.

Viña Santa Rita 👁️👁️   Santa Rita will not only let you sample their wine, they'll let you spend the night in their former estate house, which has been converted into an elegant inn. Because this winery is about an hour's drive from Santiago, it makes for a pleasant day trip and a good base for exploring the Central Valley. The wine-tasting room where you'll sample your Casa Real cabernet sauvignon is a national monument.

Hendaya 60, no. 202, Las Condes, Santiago. ✆ 2/362-2594 or 2/362-2520. Fax 2/228-6335. www.santarita. com. Bilingual tours (reservations required) Tues–Fri 10:30, 11:30am, 12:15, 3, and 4pm; Sat–Sun 12:30 and 3:30pm (lunch required). Tours $4 per person.

HITTING THE SKI RESORTS

Every year, hundreds of Americans and Europeans head to Chile from mid-June to mid-October to ski or snowboard the Andes at one of Chile's famed ski resorts. The reason? The terrain is awesome, offering everything from easy groomers to frightening steeps; the season runs during the Northern Hemisphere's summer, and some come escaping the heat back home; parents can take their kids with them because they are on summer vacation; and ski and snowboard classes are a little over half the price back home, meaning aficionados can come and improve their technique at "summer camp."

The major resorts in Chile are top-notch operations with modern equipment and facilities. Resorts centered on the Farallones area, such as Valle Nevado, La Parva, and El Colorado, can be reached in a 1- to 2-hour drive from Santiago or the airport. At a little over 2 hours from Santiago, the venerable, world-renowned Portillo is a very viable option, too, and anyone thinking of skiing for several days or a week might consider bunking in its all-inclusive hotel. Rates shown for resorts below are 2003 prices, and are expected to rise about 3% for 2004.

GETTING TO THE RESORTS   Two companies offer transfer service to the resorts near Farallones. **Ski Total** (✆ 2/246-6881) offers minivan transfers for around $10 per person. You must come to their offices at Av. Apoquindo 4900, #40 (in the Omnium shopping mall in Las Condes—the best way to get there is by taxi) for one of their 8 or 8:30am shuttles; if your hotel is reasonably close, they'll pick you up. For downtown pickups, call **Manzur Expediciones** (✆ 2/ 777-4284). Manzur requires a reservation and might charge extra for hotel pickup, but in general the cost is around $15 round-trip. Call for more information. For transportation to Portillo, see below for their transportation service.

Ski Portillo ☆☆☆ *(Kids)* For 54 years, the world-renowned Portillo Ski Resort has hosted everyone from the U.S. Ski Team to Fidel Castro, and it continues to entertain a veritable Who's Who in skiing and snowboarding. The sunflower-yellow Portillo is set in a magnificent setting high in the Andes on the shore of Lake Inca, 2 hours from Santiago and near the Argentine border. Although open to the public for day skiing, Portillo really operates as a weeklong, package-driven resort that includes lodging, ski tickets, all meals, and use of their plentiful amenities. There are no other hotels in the area, ensuring no lift lines and lots of untracked powder. The resort encompasses a variety of terrain, from beginner to some of the steepest runs found anywhere in the world. There's heliskiing too, and probably the most reliable snowfall of any resort in South America.

What makes Portillo unique is its maximum of 450 people, which makes visitors feel much like they are skiing in their own private resort. The atmosphere is very intimate, and many guests make friends and enjoy themselves so much they make Portillo a yearly trip. In early July, the resort is popular with families (Portillo offers day care, activity programs, and a superb kids' ski school); from late July to September there's a more adult crowd. Special weeks include Chilean Wine Week, Friends & Singles Week, and Gastronomic Week.

The grand yet rustic hotel forgoes glitz for a more relaxed atmosphere encouraged by its American owners. Rooms are on the small side but entirely comfortable. The sixth floor doubles are recommended for their decks.

The resort sells Saturday to Saturday ski packages, which are recommended for the Portillo "experience," although during slower weeks and last minute you can usually book shorter stays.

There are 12 lifts, including five chairs, eight T-bars, and a unique Va et Vient "slingshot" lift that leaves skiers at the top of vertiginous chutes. The terrain is 43% beginner and intermediate, 57% advanced/expert. Lift tickets are $27 adults, $20 kids 12 and under; the first and last 3 weeks of the season, two kids under 12 per family ski free.

Hotel Portillo's 7-day packages include lodging, lift tickets, four meals per day, and use of all facilities. Per person rates are: double with lake view $970 to $2,045, suites $1,550 to $3,275; family apartments (minimum four people) $840 to $1,760. Children under 4 stay free, kids 4 to 11 pay half price, and kids 12 to 17 pay about 25% less than adults. The **Octagon Lodge** features four bunks to a room (you may have to share with strangers), and includes the same amenities as above for $620 to $1,100. The **Inca Lodge,** another bunkhouse, popular with 20-somethings, charges $390 to $450.

Renato Sánchez 4270, Santiago. © 800/829-5325 in the U.S., 800/514-2579 in Canada, or 2/263-0606. Fax 2/263-0595. www.skiportillo.com. Lift tickets $30 adults, $22 children under 13. AE, DC, MC, V. **Amenities:** Restaurant; cafeteria; bar; outdoor heated pool; fitness center; sauna; child-care center; game room; salon; room service; massage; laundry; ski tuning and repair; ski rental; full-court gymnasium; disco; cybercafe; theater.

Valle Nevado ☆☆ *(Kids)* Valle Nevado is a 9,000-hectare (22,230-acre) full-service ski resort featuring three hotels, seven restaurants, a condominium complex, and dozens of shops squeezed into one compact village straddling a ridge overlooking a plunging canyon. It is French-designed, somewhat like the St. Moritz of Chile, and though it is not as steep as Portillo, it offers plenty of groomed, intermediate runs. The resort hosts the FIS Snowboard World Cup every season, they have developed a world-class half-pipe and terrain park, and they offer heliskiing.

Many head to Valle Nevado for the day, meaning it can get very busy on weekends. The ski resort has 27 runs serviced by three chairlifts and six T-bars. The terrain is 15% expert, 30% advanced, 40% intermediate, and 15% beginner.

Valle Nevado offers all-inclusive packages that include lodging, ski tickets, breakfast, and dinner, which can be taken in any one of the resort's restaurants. Verify what's open toward the end of the season as two of the three hotels close and only one restaurant remains open. Prices are per person, double occupancy, and the range reflects low to high season. The most upscale option is the **Hotel Valle Nevado,** which features full amenities and a ski-in, ski-out location for $175 to $320 per night. There's also a piano bar, glass-enclosed gym, sauna, cozy lounge, and more.

The four-star **Hotel Puerta del Sol,** which is the most popular among North Americans and Europeans, consists mostly of suites that go for $145 to $375 a night, which isn't that much more than a double. Amenities at the Puerta del Sol include cable TV, sauna, game room, piano bar, Internet cafe, and gym.

Hotel Tres Puntas has many bunk-bed rooms; each features a minibar, cable TV, and a full bathroom. This hotel is frequented by a younger crowd and has the liveliest bar; room prices range from $100 to $192 per night.

Office at Gertrúdis Echenique 441, Santiago. (✆ 2/206-0027. Fax 2/208-0695. www.vallenevado.com. Lift tickets $30 adults, $20 children under 13. AE, DC, MC, V. **Amenities:** In addition to amenities mentioned for each specific hotel, the following amenities are offered for all hotels: outdoor heated pool; full-service spa w/fitness gym; whirlpool; massage and sauna; child-care center; game room; room service; laundry; cinema. For the public, there's a bank; high-end boutiques; and a minimarket. *In room:* TV.

La Parva ⭐⭐
This resort is the smallest and most exclusive of the group, and is a great place to ski, with decent terrain that doesn't see the crowds that flock to Valle Nevado. For a few bucks more, you can ski the two with an interconnecting ticket. La Parva is somewhat like a private club for well-heeled families from Santiago, most of whom have a condo here. There are few lodging options for the outside visitor.

The resort's terrain breaks down into 10% expert, 30% advanced, 45% intermediate, and 15% beginner. There are four chairs and 10 surface lift runs, such as T-bars. There are a few very good restaurants at the base and slope side.

La Concepción 266, no. 301, Santiago. (✆ 2/264-1466 (in Santiago), or 2/220-9530 (direct). Fax 2/264-1575. www.laparva.cl. Lift tickets low to high season: $25–$30 adults, $17–$22 children 5–12 and seniors, $6.50–$9 children under 5. Interconnect tickets w/Valle Nevado $35–$40 adults, $22–$27 children under 13. A 20% discount is offered to women on Wed and students on Thurs.

El Colorado ⭐⭐
El Colorado is a very popular resort for its versatility, both because of its location just 39km (24 miles) from Santiago and its large size. El Colorado has an advantage over the other resorts in that the snow conditions always seem better and there are fewer people than at Valle Nevado. The resort is actually made of up of two villages, Villa Farellones and Villa Colorado, that are connected by two ski lifts.

Farellones is the older, more economical option located just slightly downhill from Colorado, and is popular with beginning skiers, tobogganers, snowman builders, and the like. El Colorado's modern center is really the hub of the resort, and skiers generally come directly here. The 1,000-hectare (2,470-acre) resort has five chairlifts and 17 surface lifts, such as T-bars. There's a bit of off-piste skiing, and there are 22 runs: 4 for experts, 3 advanced, 4 intermediate, and 11 beginner.

Apoquindo 4900, no. 47–48 (Edificio Omnium). (✆ 2/246-3344. Fax 2/206-4078. www.elcolorado.cl. Lift tickets low to high season: $25–$32 adults, $16–$20 children 5–12, $6 seniors and children under 5. Prices $18–$24 on Wed for women, Mon for students. AE, DC, MC, V. Ski rental available.

THE CENTRAL VALLEY & CHILLAN

South of Santiago the scenery unfolds into wide fields of grapevines, a testament to the nation's thriving wine industry. Less than one-tenth of Chile's land is arable, and a good chunk of it can be found here. The region has both rich soil and a Mediterranean climate conducive to agriculture, and the fresh fruits and vegetables grown here can be bought from one of the many food stands and country restaurants that dot the Panamericana Highway.

Beyond the central valley is one of Chile's largest and most deluxe ski and summer resorts, Termas de Chillán.

A VISIT TO CHILE'S OLDEST HOTEL

Hacienda Los Lingues ★★★ *Moments*   About 125km (78 miles) south of Santiago and nestled among poplar-lined country fields and rolling hills is the Hacienda Los Lingues, one of the oldest and best-preserved haciendas in Chile that is now run as a splendid, full-service hotel as a member of the exclusive Relais & Châteaux group. Hacienda Los Lingues is also a working ranch and home to one of the most prestigious horse-breeding farms in Latin America, where the horses are all descendants of the horses brought over by Spanish conquistadors. A visit here is like taking a step back in time to colonial Chile.

This beautiful estate has remained in the same family for 400 years, though most of the buildings, all of which have been superbly maintained, were built around 250 years ago. From the ruby-red French salon to the classic, formal sitting room, every room is accented with crystal chandeliers, Oriental rugs, and antique furniture, and is brimming with decorative pieces, family photos, collector's items, and fascinating odds and ends that you could spend hours observing and admiring. The guest rooms are decorated individually with antiques, fresh flowers, and a bucket of champagne. A bountiful breakfast is served to you in bed.

The hotel offers day tours that include a welcome cocktail, a tour of the hacienda, lunch in the cavernous wine bodega, a horse demonstration, and optional use of a swimming pool. There's also horseback riding at an additional cost. To get there, the Hacienda charges a steep $320 for a private van for a day trip for one to eight people, and $400 for the van if you spend the night. The cheaper alternative is to rent a car or take a bus to San Fernando (in Santiago, ride to the Universidad de Santiago Metro stop for the bus terminal), then take a taxi to the hotel.

Reservations in Santiago: Av. Providencia 1100, no. 205. ℂ 2/235-5446. Fax 2/235-7604. www.loslingues.com. 21 units. $236 double w/breakfast; $452 double w/full board. Day tours $46. AE, DC, MC, V. **Amenities:** Outdoor pool; 2 clay tennis courts; game room; room service; horseback riding; fly-fishing.

CHILLAN & TERMAS DE CHILLAN RESORT

Chillán is a mid-size city located 406km (252 miles) south of Santiago, and is the gateway to the popular **Termas de Chillán,** one of South America's largest and most complete ski and summer resorts. A tidy city of 145,000, with five attractive plazas and tree-lined streets, Chillán is a pleasant enough place to spend an afternoon, but it really offers little of interest to the foreign visitor. If you're driving south to the Lake District, you might consider spending the night here.

Chillán is divided into two sectors: the downtown area and Chillán Viejo, or Old Chillán. The town's history is one of relocations and disasters, specifically the 1939 earthquake that destroyed 90% of the city and killed 15,000 of its residents. Today, the city's principal highlight is the **Feria de Chillán** ★★, one of the largest and most colorful markets in Chile, where you'll find baskets, *huaso* clothing and saddles, chaps and spurs, pottery, knitwear, and more. The market is open every day.

Essentials

GETTING THERE   By Air   Chillán is served by the **Aeropuerto Carriel Sur** in Concepción, about an hour away. There are direct flights here from Santiago several times daily from **LanChile.** If you've made hotel reservations in town or in Termas de Chillán, their transfer service will pick you up. If not, you must take a taxi to the bus terminal, where buses for Chillán leave every 20 minutes.

By Bus   Línea Sur and **Tur Bus** offer daily service from most major cities, including Santiago. The trip from Santiago takes about 5 to 6 hours and costs $11 one-way. The bus terminal in Chillán is located at Av. O'Higgins 010, and from there you can grab a bus for the Termas.

VISITOR INFORMATION   Sernatur can be found at 18 de Septiembre 455 (© 42/223272); it's open Monday through Friday from 8:30am to 1:30pm and 3 to 6pm, and closed on weekends. It has a large amount of published material.

Where to Stay & Dine in Chillán

The best hotel in Chillán is the **Hotel Las Terrazas** at Constitución 664 (© 42/ 227000; www.lasterrazas.cl; $45 double weekday, $57 double weekend; American Express, Diners Club, MasterCard, and Visa accepted), with comfortable rooms and great views of Chillán Volcano. The city's traditional hotel, the **Gran Hotel Isabel Riquelme,** on the plaza at Arauco 600 (© 42/213663; $54 double; American Express, Diners Club, MasterCard, and Visa accepted), is still a good bet, but others have since surpassed the hotel in quality, even though its rooms are remarkably spacious.

Dining options in Chillán are few. If you're looking for local color and cheap prices, go to the **Municipal Market** across the street from the Feria de Chillán, where simple restaurants prepare seafood and regional dishes. The **Café París** at Arauco 666 (© 42/223881; daily 8am–2am) is the most popular restaurant in town, and the **Fuente Alemán** across the street (© 42/21720) is popular for sandwiches, quick meals, and food to go. For more upscale dining, try the **Gran Hotel Isabel Riquelme** (see above), although it tends to close its dining area during the winter.

TERMAS DE CHILLAN

Termas de Chillán ★★ *Kids*   About 80km (50 miles) from the city is Termas de Chillán, a full-season resort that is principally known for skiing, but offers great hiking, biking, and horseback riding opportunities in the summer. Most visitors to Chile head to Pucón, Puerto Varas, or even Patagonia for those kinds of summer-season activities because the locations are more uniquely beautiful than Chillán. However, you might find a hot springs spa and the 5-hour distance from Santiago to be more appealing.

The resort is nestled in a forested valley under the shadow of the 3,212m (10,535-ft.) Chillán Volcano. The resort has 28 runs, 3 chair lifts, and 5 T-bars, as well as heli-skiing, dog sledding, an international ski school, equipment rental, and restaurants.

But what really makes the Termas stand out from the pack are its spa facilities. There are nine thermal pools, steam baths in caves, and three state-of-the-art spa

---

Tips **Get Your Funds in Order Before You Arrive**

Note that there are no ATMs anywhere in Termas de Chillán or Las Trancas, so do your banking beforehand.

centers that offer hydrotherapy, aromatherapy, mud baths, and massages. It is possible to visit the thermal pools and spa for the day, for an extra charge (depending on which pools and services you opt for). Contact the hotel for updated prices.

There are two hotels here: the newer, upscale **Gran Hotel Termas de Chillán** with 120 rooms, and the three-star **Hotel Shangri-La** with 48 rooms. Rooms are everything you'd expect in terms of comfort, and rates include breakfast and dinner, ski tickets, and spa facilities (low to high season: $815–$1,605 per week, per person). The Shangri-La is the older unit, but it's comfortable and wraps around an outdoor thermal pool (rates include the same amenities as the Gran Hotel; low to high season: $595–$1,095). The complex has several restaurants, as well as a squash court, gym, three outdoor pools, a game room, and a disco.

Lift tickets are about $40 adults, $25 children, but prices fluctuate throughout the season. For more information, contact the resort at © **42/223887** (in Chillán) or 2/233-1313 (in Santiago).

Av. Libertad 1042, Chillán. © **42/223887** (in Chillán), or 2/233-1313 (in Santiago). www.termaschillan.cl. Average lift tickets $40 adults, $25 children. AE, DC, MC, V. **Amenities:** Restaurant; bar; squash court; gym; state-of-the-art spa; child-care center; game room; salon; room service; laundry. *In room:* TV.

5 The Desert North

SAN PEDRO DE ATACAMA

Quaint, unhurried, and built of adobe brick, San Pedro de Atacama sits in the driest desert in the world 1,674km (1,040 miles) north of Santiago, a region replete with bizarre land formations, including giant sand dunes, jagged canyons, salt pillars, boiling geysers, and a smoking volcano. Better to call it a moonscape than a landscape. For adventure seekers, the region offers hiking, mountain biking, and horseback riding—but sightseeing and visiting the Atacama Indian ruins around the area are as exciting, as is simply wandering the streets and admiring the town's colonial architecture. The town has fomented somewhat of a bohemian ambience, but with the variety of activities and lodging options, the region appeals to just about everyone. To visit the major sites here, you'll need 3 or 4 days, a few more to see everything including the outlying villages or the Chuquicamata mine. Unless you're a desert freak, you might find more than a week to be too much. From October to March, the presence of gringos can be overwhelming. Somehow, however, San Pedro maintains its mellow charm.

GETTING THERE

The town of **Calama** is not a destination in itself, but it is the gateway to San Pedro de Atacama. Calama is also a convenient jumping-off point to several attractions such as the Chuquicamata mine, the colonial village **Chiu Chiu,** and the Indian ruins **Pukará de Lasana,** although these last two attractions can be visited on the way back to Calama from San Pedro via the Tatio Geysers, if you've rented your own vehicle.

BY PLANE Calama's **Aeropuerto El Loa** (no phone) is served by LanChile. A taxi to Calama costs around $2. To get to San Pedro de Atacama, hire one of the transfer services outside for around $10 per person, or take a taxi for about $35—and be sure to fix a price before leaving the airport.

BY BUS It takes around 22 hours to reach Calama by bus. **Tur Bus** leaves from Santiago's Terminal Alameda at O'Higgins 3750 (© **2/270-7500**), and **Pullman Bus** leaves from the Terminal Norte at the Central Station (© **800/320320**). For

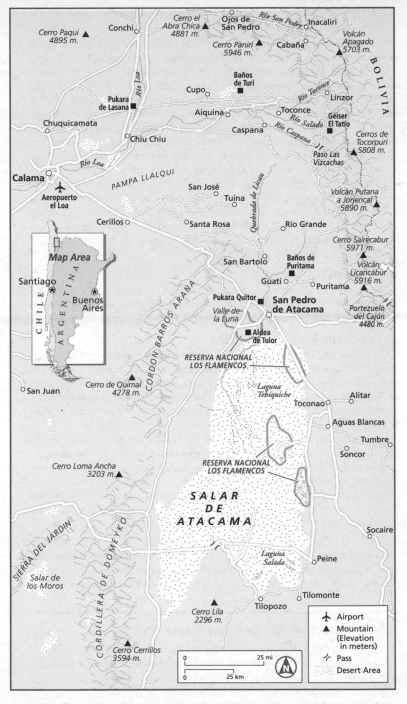

Cerro Paqui 4895 m.

Conchi

Cerro el Abra Chica 4881 m.

Ojos de San Pedro

Río San Pedro

Inacaliri

Cerro Paniri 5946 m.

Cabaña

Volcán Apagado 5703 m.

B O L I V I A

Cupo

Baños de Turi

Río Toconce

Linzor

Pukara de Lasana

Aiquina

Toconce

Río Salado

Géiser El Tatío

Chuquicamata

Chiu Chiu

Caspana

Río Caspana

Cerros de Tocorpuri 5808 m.

Paso Las Vizcachas

Calama

Río Loa

PAMPA LLALQUI

San José

Quebrada de Lican

Volcán Putana a Jorjencal 5890 m.

Aeropuerto el Loa

Tuina

Cerro Sairécabur 5971 m.

Cerillos

Santa Rosa

Río Grande

Map Area

CHILE

ARGENTINA

Santiago

Buenos Aires

San Bartolo

Baños de Puritama

Guati

Puritama

Volcán Licancábur 5916 m.

Pukara Quitor

San Pedro de Atacama

Valle de la Luna

Portezuelo del Cajón 4480 m.

Aldea de Tulor

CORDON BARROS ARANA

RESERVA NACIONAL LOS FLAMENCOS

San Juan

Cerro de Quimal 4278 m.

Laguna Tebiquiche

Toconao

Alitar

Aguas Blancas

Tumbre

Soncor

Cerro Loma Ancha 3203 m.

RESERVA NACIONAL LOS FLAMENCOS

S A L A R   D E   A T A C A M A

Socaire

SIERRA DEL JARDIN

CORDILLERA DE DOMEYKO

Salar de los Moros

Laguna Salada

Peine

Cerro Lila 2296 m.

Tilopozo

Tilomonte

Cerro Cerrillos 3594 m.

0   25 mi

0   25 km

N

✈ Airport

▲ Mountain (Elevation in meters)

⤙ Pass

Desert Area

service from Calama to Atacama, try **Buses Frontera,** Antofagasta 2041 (© 55/318543), which offers 8 trips daily for about $2.

BY CAR Most attractions must be reached by vehicle, and some visitors find it convenient to rent a car in Calama to explore at their own pace rather than go with a tour. Consider renting a 4×4 if you really plan to explore along poorly maintained roads. Car-rental companies in Calama: **Avis** at Pedro Lyon Gallo 1883 (© **55/363120,** or 55/363325 airport); **Budget** at Granaderos 2875 (© **55/361072**); and **Hertz** at LaTorre 1510 (© **55/341380**). There are also rental-agency kiosks at the airport. To get to San Pedro from Calama, head southeast on the route marked SAN PEDRO DE ATACAMA and continue for 98km (61 miles).

If you decide to rent a car, it is imperative that you consider safety first. Road service can be hard to come by, so ask your rental agency about procedures for road emergencies and breakdowns. Bring plenty of water and extra food, as well as sunscreen, sunglasses, warm clothing, and even a blanket (in the event you have to spend a chilly night on the road). Always double-check the state of any spare tires. Check the weather forecast; this is the driest desert in the world, but some areas are prone to flash floods, known as the Bolivian Winter, which can strike between December and early March.

VISITOR INFORMATION

Sernatur operates a small visitor center at the plaza on the corner of Antofagasta and Toconao (© **55/85-1420**). Hours are Saturday through Thursday from 9:30am to 1:30pm and 3 to 7pm.

ATTRACTIONS NEAR CALAMA

CHUQUICAMATA COPPER MINE Ghost towns dot the northern desert from Chile's nitrate-mining days, but the copper-mining industry is alive and well, as is evident by Calama's **Chuquicamata mine,** the largest open-pit mine in the world at 810m (2,700 ft.) deep. Few wonders generate the visual awe a visitor experiences when gazing into this gigantic hole in the ground. The mine is so big, in fact, that it can be seen from space.

Tours run every day, except holidays (© **55/321861** for information). There's just one tour a day, at 8:30am; there's limited space, so arrive early. To get there, take a taxi from the main plaza in Calama on Calle Abaroa to the company mining town, and sign up for the tour at the Sede de Chuqui Ayuda a la Infancia Desvalida at José Miguel Carrera and Tocopilla streets. There is no admission price; however, they do accept donations. For safety reasons, it is recommended that visitors wear pants and long-sleeved shirts and closed shoes.

COLONIAL VILLAGES & PUKARAS Chiu Chiu *ββ* is a charming colonial village founded by the Spanish in the early 17th century, and it boasts the most picturesque church in the north, the **Iglesia San Francisco** *ββ*, open Tuesday through Sunday from 9am to 1pm and 3 to 7pm. The whitewashed

---

Tips **Important Info to Know Before Arriving in San Pedro**

There are no banks or pharmacies in town, and medical service is limited to a small clinic. San Pedro is at 2,438m (7,997 ft.) above sea level, and a small percentage of visitors may be affected by the high altitude.

adobe walls of this weather-beaten beauty are 120 centimeters (47 in.) thick, and its doors are made of cedar and bordered with cactus, displaying a singular, Atacamanian style. North of Chiu Chiu is a similar village, **Caspana** 😊, that appears sunken into the earth and is surrounded by a fertile valley cultivated in a step formation. In the center, visitors will find a tiny museum dedicated to the culture of the area, and the **Iglesia de San Lucas** 😊, built in 1641 of stone, cactus, and mortar and covered in adobe. The church is not officially open, but if you find the caretaker, he will unlock the door for you.

Another fascinating attraction near Calama is the **Pukará de Lasana** 😊😊, a 12th-century Indian fort and national monument that was restored in 1951. You'll want to spend some time wandering the labyrinthine streets that wind around 110 two- to five-story ancient building remains.

Near Caspana is the **Pukará de Turi** 😊, which was the largest fortified city of the Atacama culture, built in the 12th century, and widely believed to be an Inca administrative center. The size of these ruins is impressive, with wide streets, circular towers, and buildings made of volcanic stone and adobe.

EXPLORING SAN PEDRO

Museo Arqueológico Padre le Paige 😊😊😊

This tiny museum is one of Chile's best, offering a superb collection of pre-Columbian artifacts gathered by Padre le Paige, a Belgian missionary who had a fondness for archaeology. What makes this museum especially unique is the well-preserved state of the artifacts, due to the arid conditions of the region. Ceramics, textiles, tablets used for the inhalation of hallucinogens, and other tools are displayed according in timelines; most intriguing of all are the mummies with their skin and hair nearly intact, and the skulls that show the creepy ancient ritual of cranial deformation.

Admission $2. Jan–Feb daily 10am–1pm and 3–7pm; rest of the year Mon–Fri 9am–noon and 2–6pm, Sat–Sun 10am–noon and 2–6pm.

Outdoor Attractions

Travelers fill their days with outdoor activities and excursions, and visits to archaeological ruins. The following tour operators offer excursions to all the sites highlighted here: **Cuna Expeditions,** Domingo Atienza 388 (© **55/851825;** www.cuna.cl); **Desert Adventure,** corner of Tocopilla and Caracoles (©/fax **55/851067;** www.desertadventure.cl); or Atacama Connection at the corner of Caracoles and Toconao (© **55/851424;** atacamaconnection@entelchile.net). The average price for the tour to Valle de la Luna is $6, and the Tatio Geysers about $20, which includes the entrance fee at the thermal baths. Several points of interest can be reached by foot or bike.

Some 15km (9 miles) from town is the **Valle de la Luna (Valley of the Moon)** 😊😊, where you can view eerie land formations and a mountainous sand dune. A good time to visit is in the evening, when the sun sets, or especially during a full moon, when ghostly light enhances the landscape's peculiarities. Bike or drive west on Caracoles and turn left on the signed, dirt road (the old road to Calama).

The **Atacama Salt Flat,** a gigantic mineralized lake that is covered in many parts by a weird, putty-colored crust, is also home to a **flamingo reserve.** There's also an interpretive center (no phone); it's open September through May daily from 8:30am to 8pm, and June through August daily from 8:30am to 7pm. Drive south toward Toconao, 33km (20 miles) from San Pedro, and once you've passed through the town of Toconao, watch for the entrance to the flamingo reserve signed "Laguna Chaxa."

A memorable, recommended full-day trip is to the **Geysers del Tatio** ★★★, the highest geysers in the world. Most tours leave before dawn to see the fumaroles in their most active state, and end the trip at the **Baños de Puritama** ★★, a hot-springs oasis run by Hotel Explora (see "Where to Stay in San Pedro," below). The geysers are 95km (59 miles) north of San Pedro. Drivers need to pay sharp attention to the often-confusing road and signs. Ask for a detailed map and directions at your car-rental agency. The hot springs are 60km (37 miles) from the geysers, and cost $10 to enter, although tours normally include the entrance fee in their price. Tour companies leave around 4 to 5am for the 2½-hour journey to Tatio. Drivers can continue on to Calama from here, but be sure to have someone clearly map the route for you.

Two interesting archaeological sites are near town: the 12th-century, pre-Inca defensive fort **Pukará de Quitor** ★ and the **Aldea de Tulor** ★★, the Atacama's oldest pueblo (dating from 800 B.C.). The Quitor is about 3km (2 miles) from San Pedro; to get there, walk, bike, or drive west up Calle Tocopilla and continue along the river until you see Quitor at your left. The Aldea de Tulor is a bike ride or drive 9km (5½ miles) southwest of San Pedro.

Sports Activities

BIKING Visitors can mountain bike regions such as the Quebrada del Diablo (Devil's Gorge) or ride across the flat desert to visit sites such as Tulor. **Azimut 360,** Caracoles 195 (✆ **55/851469**), rents mountain bikes for $5.50 for 4 hours, and they have route maps and plan excursions such as a descent from the *altiplano.*

HORSEBACK RIDING **Rancho Cactus,** Toconao 568 (✆ **55/851506;** ranchocactus@sanpedrodeatacama.com), has guided horseback rides for about $6 an hour or $40 for the day (includes lunch). They also plan multiday, full-service excursions.

VOLCANO ASCENTS Climbing one of the four volcanoes in the area requires total altitude acclimatization and a good physical state—previous mountaineering experience wouldn't hurt either. The most popular volcanic ascent is up Láscar Volcano to 5,400m (17,712 ft.). Many tour companies offer this excursion; try **Azimut 360,** Caracoles 195 (✆ **55/851469**), which rents mountain bikes for $5.50 for 4 hours, or **Cuna Expeditions,** Domingo Atienza 388 (✆ **55/851825;** www.cuna.cl).

WHERE TO STAY & DINE IN CALAMA

The **Park Hotel** ★★ is a good bet for travelers seeking dependable, high-quality accommodations (Camino Aeropuerto 1392; ✆ **55/319900;** fax 55/319901; www.parkplaza.cl; $120 double standard, $150 double superior; American Express, Diners Club, MasterCard, and Visa accepted). Their circular, outdoor pool makes for a refreshing desert respite; and there's a sauna, a gym, tennis courts, car rental, and planned excursions. The hotel also has a good restaurant and bar. Or try the interesting **Hotel El Mirador** ★, which is furnished with antiques and old photos, and has a plant-filled patio (Calle Sotomayor 2064; ✆/fax **55/340329;** $49 double; American Express, MasterCard, and Visa accepted).

If you're looking for hearty Chilean cuisine, try **Bavaria** at Sotomayor and Abaroa (✆ **55/341496**); it serves barbecued meats, seafood, and sandwiches. Calama locals' favorite for Chinese is **Tong Fong,** Calle Vivar 1951 (no phone). For fine dining and international cuisine, head to the **Park Hotel** at Camino Aeropuerto 1392 (✆ **55/319990**).

WHERE TO STAY IN SAN PEDRO

Hotel Explora ✦✦✦   Like its counterpart in Patagonia, the luxury Hotel Explora in Atacama is elegant yet unpretentious, a somewhat cubist-design hotel with a freestanding lobby, bar, and restaurant and 52 linked one-story rooms that extend in an angular ring from the main unit. The minimalist exterior is painted entirely white, with splashes of pale blue and yellow. Inside, the lounge and guest rooms are tastefully decorated with local art and painted in quiet, primary tones. Cut-out window displays hold Atacama Indian artifacts found when the hotel broke ground. The lounge, with soaring ceilings, is enormous, stretching the length of the building and scattered with plush couches and wicker chairs draped in sheepskin. Ceiling fans and cool ceramic floors make this a soothing respite from the searing heat. The rooms have ultracomfortable beds made with crisp linens and fluffy down comforters; each bathroom comes with a whirlpool tub. Each room has a window that stretches the length of the building—if you can, try to get a room facing the Licancabúr Volcano. Above the main building is an open deck with an outstanding view of the desert, and the four swimming pools, designed to resemble irrigation ditches, each with their own sauna.

Explora operates as an all-inclusive hotel, offering 3-, 4-, and 7-night packages that include transfers, four meals per day, an open bar, and all excursions. Every evening, one of their full-time bilingual guides meets with guests to plan daily excursions. The international cuisine here is as outstanding as the view from the dining room. They also have a weekly on-site barbecue.

Domingo Atienza s/n (main office: Américo Vespucio Sur 80, Piso 5, Santiago). ✆ 55/851110 (local), or 2/206-6060 in Santiago (reservations). Fax 2/228-4655, 800/858-0855 (U.S.), or 800/275-1129 (Canada). www.explorachile.com. 52 units. Double occupancy, all-inclusive, per-person rates: 3 nights, $1,296; 4 nights, $1,706; 7 nights, $2,441. Reduced tariffs available for guests under 20. AE, DC, MC, V. **Amenities:** Restaurant; bar; 4 outdoor pools; sauna; massage; babysitting; laundry service; mountain bikes; horseback riding; TV room; library.

Hotel Tambillo ✦ *Value*   The Tambillo is the best option in this price range. The 12 rooms are lined along both sides of a narrow, attractive pathway inlaid with stone; rooms have arched windows and doors. Rooms come with no decoration other than two boldly striped bedspreads, but it's not unappealing—on the contrary, the atmosphere is fresh and clean. There's a large restaurant that serves breakfast, lunch, and dinner, and a tiny sheltered patio. It's a 4-block walk to the main street.

Gustavo Le Paige s/n. ✆/fax 55/851078. tambillo@sanpedroatacama.com. 12 units. $48 double. No credit cards. **Amenities:** Cafeteria. *In room:* No phone.

La Aldea ✦✦   This chic adobe hotel is owned by two architects, who have bestowed great taste to its interiors. The principal drawback here is the 5-minute dusty walk to the center of town, which can be a bother. The welcoming lobby, lounge, and restaurant are built of stone, adobe walls, cinnamon-colored wood, ironwork, and thatched roofs. A curving stairwell leads to a game room and lounge. Several rooms branch off from the main unit, and although they are slightly dark, they have a cooling effect on a hot day. They are also spacious enough to give some breathing room. Perhaps the best rooms are in the separate cabañas for three, which are cylindrical two-stories with fresh white walls and lots and lots of light; two of them are brand-new. Outside is a turquoise pool, surrounded by a pebbled courtyard.

Solcor s/n. ✆/fax 55/851247 or 55/851333. www.hotelaldea.cl. 9 units, 3 cabañas. $96 double; $138 3-person cabaña. AE, MC, V. **Amenities:** Restaurant; outdoor pool; room service; laundry service; TV room; bicycles; horseback riding.

Lodge Terrantai 🌟🌟 *Finds*   If the prices at the Explora are a little beyond your budget, but you're looking for something of comparable quality, you might try this appealing little hotel near the main street. The Terrantai is in a 100-year-old home that was renovated by two well-known Chilean architects who preserved the building's flat-fronted facade, adobe walls, and thatched roof. The style is pure minimalism, and every inch of the interior hallways and the rooms is made of stacked rock. The rooms are very comfortable, with down comforters, linen curtains, soft reading lights, and local art. Most rooms have large floor-to-ceiling windows that look out onto a pleasant garden patio. The Terrantai has a small restaurant; dinner is served here during the summer only, which means that prices are slightly cheaper during the off season. Hotel rates include daily excursions with Atacama Desert Expeditions.

Tocopilla 411. ⒸⒸ **55/85-1045.** Fax 55/85-1037. www.terrantai.com. 14 units. $137 double; all-inclusive, English-guided package doubles, per person: 2-night $542, 3-night $733, 4-night $870, 5-night $1,018. MC, V. **Amenities:** Restaurant; outdoor pool (more like a soak tub); laundry service; daily excursions w/bilingual guides.

WHERE TO DINE IN SAN PEDRO

For a quick, inexpensive bite to eat, try the **Café Buena Tierra** at Caracoles s/n (daily 9am–10:30pm), with vegetarian, whole-meal empanadas made from scratch while you wait, as well as sandwiches and breakfast.

Adobe CONTEMPORARY CHILEAN 🌟   This is one of the best choices in San Pedro, both for the good food and even better ambience. The Adobe is a popular place for eating, drinking, or just hanging out in front of the bonfire that blazes every evening in the semi-enclosed outdoor area. The Adobe is known for its fixed-price breakfasts, which can include pancakes, eggs, a fruit salad, and espresso, but really any meal is quite good here.

Caracoles 211. Ⓒ **55/851132.** www.cafeadobe.cl. Main courses $5–$8. AE. Daily 8am–1am.

La Casona 🌟 CHILEAN   La Casona is a newly renovated restaurant/bar housed in an old colonial building with soaring ceilings and a crackling fire as a centerpiece of the dining area. Candelit, wooden tables adorned with a few sprigs of flowers set a quieter ambience. There's also a pool table and pub in the rear room that can get fairly lively, as can the outdoor bar, featuring music and a roaring fire, as well as three computers for use to check e-mail. The owner is from Finland, but the menu is typically Chilean, with appetizers such as a *palta reina* (avocado stuffed with tuna) or *palta york* (stuffed with chicken) and main dishes such as grilled tenderloin in a creamy pepper sauce. They also serve pastas, vegetarian dishes, and *picoteos* (appetizer plates).

Caracoles 195. Ⓒ **55/851004.** www.restaurantlacasona.com. Reservations not accepted. Main courses $5–$9; sandwiches $1.50–$4. AE, DC, MC, V. Daily 9am–11pm.

La Estaka 🌟 INTERNATIONAL/CHILEAN   La Estaka is part hip, part hippie, and one of the most popular restaurants in San Pedro, especially in the evening when the music is turned up and the wine starts to flow. The plentiful yet simple menu offers both meat and vegetarian dishes, including omelets, pasta, salads, and even sushi in a funky ambience that features semioutdoor seating with a netlike roof, dirt floor, and molded banquettes, and a spacious indoor eating area with lofty ceilings and large wood tables. The lunch hour is quite mellow, but at night the bar gets pretty loud. There's a deejay Fridays and Saturdays.

Caracoles 259. Ⓒ **55/851201.** www.laestaka.cl. Reservations not accepted. Main courses $5–$10; sandwiches $2–$4.50. AE, DC, MC, V. Daily 8:30am–1:30am.

6 The Chilean Lake District ⭒⭒⭒

The region south of the Río Biobío to Puerto Montt is collectively known as the Lake District, a fairy-tale land of emerald forests, snowcapped volcanoes, frothing waterfalls, and hundreds of lakes and lagoons that give the region its name. It is one of the most popular destinations in Chile, not only for its beauty, but for the diverse outdoor and city-themed activities available and a well-organized tourism structure that allows travelers to pack in a lot of action and yet rest comfortably and well fed in the evening.

Summers can be balmy, but the rest of the year, this region sees a tremendous amount of rain and subsequent flooding. In the Puerto Montt and Valdivia region, rain often falls even during summer. It's a good idea to bring clothing that will keep you dry.

EXPLORING THE REGION

The Lake District is composed of the **Región de la Araucania,** which includes the city **Temuco** and the resort area **Pucón,** and the **Región de los Lagos,** where you'll find the port cities **Valdivia** and **Puerto Montt, Puerto Varas** and **Frutillar,** and the island **Chiloé.** There's plenty more to see and do outside these principal destinations, including hot springs, boat rides, adventure sports, and miles of bumpy dirt roads that make for picturesque drives through enchanting landscapes. Towns such as Puerto Varas and Pucón are excellent bases from which to take part in all of these activities. Most visitors will find they need 3 to 4 days to explore each destination, more if planning to backpack, fish, or really get out and see everything. You may consider crossing into the equally beautiful Argentine Lake District, which can be done by vehicle from Pucón or by boat from Puerto Varas.

TEMUCO

With the introduction of air service directly to Pucón from Santiago during the peak season in January and February, Temuco, once the year-round gateway to Pucón, will undoubtedly lose a fair share of tourism during the upcoming years. Still, Temuco is home to a regional highlight, the **Mercado Municipal** ⭒⭒, a vibrant, crafts-filled market. For information about getting to Temuco, see "Getting There" under "Pucón," below.

The Mercado can be found at Portales and Aldunate and is open Monday through Saturday from 8am to 8pm, Sunday and holidays from 8:30am to 3pm; from April to September, the market closes at 6pm Monday through Saturday. Rows of stalls sell everything from high-quality woven ponchos, knitwear, textiles, woodwork, hats, and silver Mapuche jewelry, to assorted arts and crafts. Around the perimeter, fishermen and food stalls aggressively vie for business while butchers in white aprons hawk their meats from behind dangling sausages.

WHERE TO STAY

You'll find the most character and history at the **Hotel Continental** ⭒ at Antonio Varas 708 (© **45/238973;** fax 45/233830; turismochile.cl/continental). Inaugurated in 1889, the Continental is the oldest hotel in Chile, and its guest book has registered many well-known names, such as Pablo Neruda. Virtually nothing has changed, including the antique wooden bar, the dining room, and the period bronze chandeliers; however, neither have the stark rooms or the beds (all singles), which are hilariously springy and wobbly. Doubles go for about $46 with a bathroom, $31 shared. For predictability and a little more comfort than the Continental, try the **Holiday Inn Express,** located a half block from an

American-style shopping mall at Ortega 1800 (© **800/366666** or 45/223300). Doubles go for $65, and children under 18 stay free in parent's room. There's also a small outdoor pool.

WHERE TO DINE

The **Mercado Municipal** has a dozen casual food stalls and restaurants selling inexpensive fare (see above). An excellent spot for an inexpensive, casual meal is **Quick Biss** at Antonio Varas 755 (© **45/211219;** daily 10am–11pm; America Express, Diners Club, MasterCard, and Visa accepted). This modern cafeteria-style restaurant operates as a self-service buffet at lunch, but there's also a menu. The **Continental Hotel's restaurant** is still the traditional favorite in town for dining (Antonio Varas 708; © **45/238973;** daily noon–3pm and 8–11:30pm; American Express, Diners Club, MasterCard, and Visa accepted), with a vast, century-old dining area lit by enormous bronze chandeliers. The fare is simple and Chilean, with a few choice highlights such as crab stew. Meat lovers will find two of Chile's best parrillas in Temuco.

PUCON

789km (489 miles) S of Santiago, 25km (16 miles) E of Temuco

Nationally and internationally known as the **"Adventure Capital of Chile,"** Pucón offers every outdoor activity imaginable: fly-fishing, rafting the Río Trancura, hiking Huerquehue and Conguillío national parks, and skiing the slopes of Volcán Villarrica—or even climbing to its bubbling crater. Yet there's also an abundance of low-key activities, such as hot-spring spas and scenic drives through spectacular landscapes. You could just hang out on the beach and sun yourself, as hundreds do during the summer. Pucón is almost entirely dependent on tourism, and during the summer season, particularly December 15 to the end of February, as well as Easter week, the town is jam-packed with tourists. Hotel and business owners gleefully take advantage of this and jack up their prices, sometimes doubling their rates.

ESSENTIALS

GETTING THERE By Plane Visitors normally fly into Temuco's **Manquehue Airport** (ZCO), and then arrange transportation for the 1- to 1½-hour ride into Villarrica or Pucón. Most hotels will arrange transportation for you, although it's usually at an additional cost. **Transfer & Turismo de la Araucania** (© 45/339900), a minivan service at the airport, will take a maximum of six guests to Pucón for $42, or Temuco for $6. Direct air service to Pucón is available during the summer only from **LanChile Express** (© 600/526-2000); to get downtown, take a short taxi ride.

By Car Most tour companies offer transportation to all attractions; however, renting a car gives you the freedom to stop and sightsee according to your whims. The Temuco airport has rentals with Hertz and Avis, and downtown locations in Temuco: **Hertz** can be found at Las Heras 999 (© 45/318585); **Avis** at Vicuña Mackenna 448 (© 45/238013). In Pucón, try **Christopher** in front of the supermarket (© 45/449013). From the Panamerican Highway south of Temuco, follow the signs for Villarrica onto Ruta 199, then for Pucón. If coming from Valdivia, take 205 to the Panamericana Norte (Hwy. 5). Just past Loncoche, continue east, following signs for Villarrica and Pucón.

By Bus TurBus (© 2/270-7500; www.TurBus.cl) offers service to Pucón from destinations such as Santiago, stopping first in Temuco and Villarrica. The

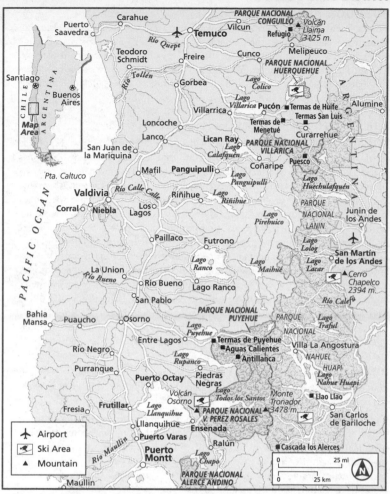

Airport
Ski Area
Mountain

trip is about 9 to 11 hours and generally a night journey; the cost is about $19 for an economy seat and $31 for an executive seat. **Buses JAC** has service from Temuco every half-hour from its terminal at Bustamante and Aldunate.

By Train EFE (② **2/632-2802** in Santiago, or 45/233416 in Temuco; www. efe.cl) has service to Temuco with economy, salon, and sleeper coaches. EFE's "La Frontera" has daily service to Santiago, leaving at 9pm and arriving at 8:45am; return trips leave Santiago at 9:30pm arriving in Temuco at 9:15am. The train station in Temuco is at Barros Arana and Lautaro; in Santiago, the station is at Bulnes 582. Tickets are $17 sleeper, $14 economy.

VISITOR INFORMATION In Pucón, **Sernatur** (② 45/443338) operates a helpful tourism office at the corner of calles Brasil and Caupolican; it's open daily from 8:30am to 10pm December through March, and from 8:30am to 8pm the rest of the year. Pucón has an excellent tourism website at www. pucon.com.

OUTDOOR ACTIVITIES

With so many outdoor adventures available here, it's no wonder there's a surplus of outfitters eager to meet the demand. When choosing an outfitter in Pucón, remember that you get what you pay for, and be wary of those that treat you like just another nameless tourist. You want a memorable experience for the fun you've had, not for the mishaps and accidents. Most outfitters include insurance in the cost of a trip, but first verify what their policy covers.

For more things to see and do in this area, see "Hot Springs Outside of Pucón" and "Natural Attractions Outside of Pucón," below.

TOUR OPERATORS **Politur,** O'Higgins 635 (© **45/441373;** www.politur. com), is a well-respected tour company that offers fishing expeditions, Mapuche-themed tours, and sightseeing trips around the Seven Lakes area, in addition to volcano ascents. **Aguaventura,** Palguín 336 (© **45/444246;** www. aguaventura.com), is run by a competent, dynamic French trio and specializes in snowboarding in the winter with a shop that sells and rents boards, boots, and clothing. In the summer, the focus is on rafting and kayaking, with canyoneering and rappelling excursions and horseback rides. **Trancura,** O'Higgins 211-c (© **45/441189;** www.trancura.com), operates a variety of excursions, but it's known for rafting and volcano climbs. Trancura offers just about everything, including ski rental at several locations along the main strip. Prices are low here, but service is often unsatisfactory. Still, they're the only tour agency that offers wild-boar hunting. **Sol y Nieve,** O'Higgins and Lincoyán (© **45/441070;** www.chile-travel.com/solnieve.htm), has been on the scene for quite a while, offering rafting and volcano ascents, as well as fishing, airport transfers, and excursions in other destinations around Chile.

BIKING Several outfitters on O'Higgins, the main street, rent bicycles by the hour and provide trail information and guided tours. Bicycle rentals run an average of $8 for a half-day.

CLIMBING THE VOLCANO ★★ An ascent to the percolating, fuming crater of Volcán Villarrica is perhaps the most thrilling excursion available here—but you've got to be in okay shape to tackle it. (Those in great physical shape might consider this an easy excursion.) The trip begins early in the morning, and climbers are outfitted with clothing, crampons, and ice-axes. The descent is a combination of walking and sliding on your behind in the snow. Volcán Villarrica is on the verge of erupting, and sometimes trips are called off during periods of heavy rumbling. Tour companies that offer this climb are **Aguaventura, Politur, Sol y Nieve,** and **Trancura** (see "Tour Operators," above). The average cost is $35 and does not include lunch.

FISHING You can pick up your fishing license at the visitor center at Caupolican and Brasil. Guided fishing expeditions typically go to the Río Trancura or the Río Liucura. See a list of outfitters above for information, or try **Off Limits,** Fresia 273 (© **45/441210**).

GOLFING Pucón's private, 18-hole Peninsula de Pucón golf course is open to the playing public. For information, call © **45/441021,** ext 409. The cost is $42 for 18 holes.

HIKING The two national parks, Villarrica and Huerquehue, offer outstanding hiking trails that run from easy to difficult. An average excursion with an outfitter to Huerquehue, including transportation and a guided hike, costs about $22 per person.

HORSEBACK RIDING   The **Centro de Turismo Huepil** (© 09/643-2673) offers day and multiday horseback rides, including camping or a stay at the Termas de Huife, from a small ranch about a half-hour from Pucón. (Head east out of Pucón and then north toward Caburgua; take the eastern road toward Huife and keep your eyes open for the signs to Centro de Turismo Huepil.) You'll need to make a reservation beforehand. All-inclusive multiday trips cost about $95 per person, per day. Contact a tour agency for day rides in Villarrica Park, which go for about $60 for a full day. Tour agencies will also organize rides that leave from the **Rancho de Caballos** (© 45/441575) near the Palguín thermal baths.

RAFTING   Rafting season runs from September to April. The two classic descents in the area are the 14km (8½-mile) Trancura Alto, rated at class III to IV, and the somewhat gentler Trancura Bajo, rated at class II to III. Both trips are popular and can get crowded in the summer. The rafting outfitter **Trancura** (see "Tour Operators," above) also offers an excursion rafting the more technical Río Maichin, which includes a barbecue lunch. The 3-hour rafting trip on the Trancura Alto averages $20; the 3-hour Trancura Bajo costs an average of $8.

SKIING   The **Centro Esquí Villarrica** is one of Chile's largest resorts, although the owners, **The Grand Hotel Pucón,** rarely open more than two of its five chairs. (They'll offer a lame excuse, but it's slacker city here and laziness is closer to the truth.) Still, how often can you ski the slopes of a smoking volcano? You'll need to take a chairlift to the main lodge, which means that non-skiers too can enjoy the lovely views from the lodge's outdoor deck. There's a restaurant, child-care center, and store. The Centro has a ski school and ski-equipment rental; there are slightly cheaper rentals from Aguaventura, Sol y Nieve, and Trancura, among other businesses along O'Higgins. Lift tickets vary according to season and day of the week; the average price is $23. Most tour companies offer transport to and from the resort.

WHERE TO STAY

Pucón is very busy during the summer, and advance reservations for accommodations are required for the high season from December to the end of February. Prices listed below show the price range from low to high season, but verify each hotel's exact dates. Off-season rates can drop almost 50%. Private parking or ample street parking is available and free for all hotels.

For inexpensive lodging, try one of the following pleasant hostels: **¡école!** ℛ at General Urrutia 592 (©/fax **45/441675;** www.ecole.cl) has small but clean rooms with beds that come with goose-down comforters for $12 to $14 per person. It has a great restaurant and an outdoor patio with picnic tables, lots of reading material, and an ecology center and tour desk that plans day trips to outlying areas. The showers are bad, but the price is nice. **La Tetera** ℛ next door at Urrutia 580 (©/fax **45/441462;** www.tetera.cl) has rooms that are simple but meticulously clean, and a sunny reading area, outdoor deck, cafe, and tour desk. Double rooms run $20 to $33.

Hotel Antumalal ℛℛℛ *Finds*   The minute you arrive here, you know you've come upon something special. Perhaps it is the Antumalal's unique Bauhaus design and its lush, beautiful gardens, or perhaps it's the sumptuous view of the sunset on Lake Villarrica seen nightly through the hotel's picture windows or from its wisteria-roofed deck. Either way, this is simply one of the most unique hotels in Chile. Low slung and literally built into a rocky slope, the Antumalal was designed to blend with its natural environment. The lounge features walls made of glass and slabs of araucaria wood, goat skin rugs, tree-trunk lamps, and couches built of iron and white rope. It's retro-chic and exceptionally cozy, and the friendly, personal attention provided by the staff heightens a sense of intimacy with your surroundings. The rooms are all the same size, and they are very comfortable, with panoramic windows that look out onto the same gorgeous view, as well as honey-wood walls, a fireplace, and a big, comfortable bed. All the bathrooms were reno-vated in 2003 and boast new fixtures and tile. Lovely, terraced gardens zigzag down the lake shore, where guests have use of a private beach. All fit for a queen—indeed, Queen Elizabeth graced the hotel with her presence several decades ago. The hotel's restaurant serves some of the best cuisine in Pucón.

Camino Pucón-Villarrica, Km 2. ⓒ 45/441011. Fax 45/441013. www.antumalal.com. 16 units. $153–$212 dou-ble. Rates include full breakfast. AE, DC, MC, V. **Amenities:** Exquisite restaurant; beautiful bar area; kidney-shaped outdoor pool; tennis court; room service; massage; laundry service.

Hotel del Lago 🍴 *(Kids)* Pucón's sole full-service luxury hotel boasts a casino, the only cinema in town, and amenities galore. Attractively designed and recently built, the Hotel del Lago is airy and bright, with a lobby covered by a lofty glass ceiling. There's a certain amount of excitement here in the lobby as a result of the constant hustle and bustle; the front doors seem almost perpetually in motion. All the hotel's furnishings were imported from the United States, and the spacious rooms have wood trim made of faux-weathered pine, iron head-boards, crisp linen, and heavy curtains colored a variety of creamy pastels, all very light and bright. The bathrooms are made of Italian marble and are a decent size, as are double-size rooms—note that a double standard comes with two twins. The Suite Volcán has the volcano view, but rooms facing west enjoy the late afternoon sun. The concierge can plan a variety of excursions for guests, as well as transport to the ski center.

Miguel Ansorena 23, Pucón. ⓒ 45/291000. Fax 45/291200. www.hoteldellago.cl. 122 units. $120–$240 double; $200–$300 suite. AE, DC, MC, V. **Amenities:** 2 restaurants; bar; small indoor pool; large outdoor pool; state-of-the-art health club; spa; sauna; children's programs; game room; concierge; room service; babysit-ting; dry cleaning; laundry service. *In room:* TV, minibar, safe.

Hotel Huincahue 🍴 *(Finds)* Pucón's newest hotel sits right on the main plaza and has an elegant homey feel to it. From the cozy lobby lounge with a fireplace and adjoining library to the peaceful pool in the lovely garden, this place feels more like a private mansion than a hotel. Rooms have pleasant beige carpets, and nice wrought iron and wood furniture, and a few have spectacular views of the volcano (no. 202 is best). Second-floor rooms have small balconies. The marble bathrooms are large and many have windows, as well. The staff tries hard to accommodate, but their English is minimal, so be patient.

Pedro de Valdivia 375. ⓒ/fax 45/443540 or 45/442728. www.hotelhuincahue.cl. 20 units. $85–$120 double. Rates include continental breakfast. AE, MC, V. **Amenities:** Restaurant; bar; lovely outdoor pool; room service; massage; babysitting; laundry service. *In room:* TV.

Cabañas

Cabañas are independent units that come with a kitchen or kitchenette. Here is the best, but consult the tourism office or www.pucon.com for more options.

Almoni del Lago Resort 🍴🍴 has a superb location on the lapping shores of Lake Villarrica and is backed by lush grounds (Camino Villarrica-Pucón, Km 19; ⓒ 45/262252; fax 45/442304; www.almoni.cl; $47–$90 cabaña for two). The cabañas are a 5-minute drive from town, and come with an outdoor pool, tennis courts, and barbecues.

WHERE TO DINE

¡école! VEGETARIAN *(Value* This vegetarian restaurant includes one salmon dish among heaps of creative dishes like calzones, quiche, pizza, burritos, chop suey, and more. Sandwiches come on homemade bread, and breakfast is good, featuring American breakfast as well as Mexican and Chilean. ¡école! uses locally and organically grown products and buys whole wheat flour and honey from a local farm. There are also fresh salads. There's a lovely outdoor patio where you can dine under the grapevine in good weather. The service is slightly disorganized; they usually offer a shorter menu during the winter.

General Urrutia 592. ℂ/fax 45/441675. Main courses $3–$6. MC, V. Daily 8am–11pm.

Hotel Antumalal *(★★ (Moments* INTERNATIONAL   The Hotel Antumalal's restaurant serves some of the most flavorful cuisine in Pucón, with innovative dishes that are well prepared and seasoned with herbs from an extensive garden. In fact, most of the vegetables used here are local and organic; the milk comes from the family's own dairy farm. Try thinly sliced beef carpaccio followed by chicken stuffed with smoked salmon, or any one of the pastas. There's a good selection of wine and an ultracool cocktail lounge for an after-dinner drink. It's worth a visit for the view of Lake Villarrica alone, and you can soak it in from inside the attractive dining area or, better yet, from a terrace patio. There is often an abbreviated menu during slow winter months.

Camino Pucón-Villarrica, Km 2. ℂ 45/441011. Fax 45/441013. Reservations required. Main courses $5–$12. AE, DC, MC, V. Daily noon–4pm and 8–10pm.

La Maga STEAKHOUSE   Pucón's newest parrilla opened in the fall of 2002 and is proving very popular with locals. It originated in the beach town of Punta del Este, Uruguay. The food is excellent, especially the meat, chicken, and fish grilled on the giant barbecue on the patio. Order a bottle of wine and a large fresh salad and watch the people go by the large picture windows overlooking the street. Try the grilled salmon with capers, if you're in the mood for fish. But, really, the best cuts here are the beef filets, known as *lomos,* served with mushrooms, Roquefort, or pepper sauce. The *bife de chorizo* (New York strip steak) is thick and tender. For dessert, the flan here is excellent.

Fresia 125. ℂ 45/444277. Main courses $5–$9. No credit cards. Daily noon–4pm and 7pm–midnight.

Marmonhi *(★ (Finds* CHILEAN   The food here is typically Chilean, prepared by the amiable Elena, who runs a tight ship. Many of Pucón's residents stop by here to pick up lunch or dinner for their families, although the simple dining room is pleasant for a leisurely meal and there's a small patio for outdoor dining in good weather. Specials change daily, according to what Elena finds at the market. Vegetable or beef empanadas are a great start to the meal. Then order a big Chilean salad (fresh tomatoes and lots of sweet onion) and one of the special chicken or fish dishes. They're simply yet deliciously prepared: marinated and grilled and served with vegetables and rice. There's excellent baked lasagna, as well. For dessert, have one of the decadent tarts that locals rave about but skip the coffee, which is instant and tasteless.

Ecuador 175. ℂ 45/441972. Main courses $3–$8. No credit cards. Daily noon–4pm and 7–10:30pm.

PUCON AFTER DARK

Pucón's **casino** can be found inside the five-star Hotel del Lago (see "Where to Stay," above), with three gaming rooms and a bingo hall. The bar here is good and appeals to all ages; it's open very late. The Hotel del Lago also has the town's only **cinema** (© **45/291000**); check the newspaper or call for schedules. For bars, **Bar Bazul,** Lincoyán 361 (no phone), has food and outdoor seating, and **El Living,** at the corner of Colo Colo and O'Higgins (no phone), has sushi by day and techno music by night; it's open very late.

HOT SPRINGS OUTSIDE OF PUCON

All the volcanic activity in the region means there's plenty of *baños termales,* or hot springs, that range from rustic rock pools to full-service spas with massage and saunas. Nothing beats a soothing soak after a long day packed with adventure, or on a rainy day. Below is my favorite. To find others, consult www.pucon.com.

Termas de Huife 🍂   Nestled in a narrow valley on the shore of the Río Liucura, Huife operates as a full-service health spa for day visitors and guests who opt to spend the night in one of their cabañas or suites. The accommodations are cozy and the landscaping is quite beautiful, featuring river-rock hot springs pools flanked by bamboo and palm fronds. The complex features two large outdoor thermal pools and a cold-water pool, as well as private thermal bathtubs, individual whirlpools, and massage salons arranged around an airy atrium. There are four-person cabañas and double suites, and all come with wood-burning stoves; the bathrooms have Japanese-style, sunken showers and baths that run thermal water.

The service is friendly, but the food (fried, heavy fare without variety) could stand to be revamped. Otherwise, it's a great place to unwind. To get here, head east out of Pucón toward Lago Caburgua until you see a sign for Huife, and follow the signs.

Road to Huife, 33km (20 miles) east from Pucón. ©/fax **45/441222**. www.termashuife.cl. 10 units. $118–$135 double. Day use: $9 adults, $4.30 children under 13. AE, DC, MC, V. Thermal baths daily 9am–8pm, year-round. **Amenities:** Restaurant; cafeteria; 3 outdoor pools; exercise room; Jacuzzi; sauna; game room. *In room:* TV, minibar.

NATURAL ATTRACTIONS OUTSIDE OF PUCON
PARQUE NACIONAL HUERQUEHUE

Parque Nacional Huerquehue boasts the best short-haul hike in the area, the **Sendero Los Lagos.** This 12,500-hectare (30,875-acre) park opens as a steeply walled amphitheater draped in matted greenery and crowned by a forest of lanky araucaria trees. There are a handful of lakes here; the first you come upon is Lago Tinquilco, upon whose shore sits a tiny, ramshackle village built by German colonists in the early 1900s.

GETTING THERE & BASICS   The park is 35km (22 miles) from Pucón. There is no direct bus service to the park, but most tour companies offer minivan transportation and will arrange to pick you up later, should you decide to spend the night. If you're driving your own car, head out of Pucón on O'Higgins toward Lago Caburga, until you see the sign for Huerquehue that branches off to the right. From here, it's a rutted, dirt road that can be difficult to manage when muddy. Conaf charges $5 for adults and $1 for kids to enter, and is open daily 8:30am to 6pm.

PARQUE NACIONAL VILLARRICA

This gem of a park is home to three volcanoes: the show-stealer Villarrica, Quetrupillán, and Lanín. It's quite a large park, stretching 61,000 hectares (150,670 acres) to the Argentine border and that country's Parque Nacional Lanín, and is blanketed with a thick, virgin forest of araucaria and evergreen and deciduous beech. A bounty of activities are available year-round, including skiing and climbing to the crater of the volcano (see "Outdoor Activities" under "Pucón," earlier in this chapter), hiking, horseback riding, bird-watching, and more.

The park has three sectors, but most visitors to the park head to **Sector Rucapillán.** There are two trails here, the 15km (9-mile) **Sendero Challupén** that winds through lava fields and araucaria, and the 5km (3-mile) **Sendero El Glaciar Pichilancahue,** which takes visitors through native forest to a glacier. The park ranger booth at the entrance can point out how to get to the trail heads.

VALDIVIA ⚐
839km (520 miles) S of Santiago

Valdivia is often referred to as one of Chile's most beautiful cities. Though most visitors will certainly find that assertion quite dubious, the city does have a port town's ramshackle charm and enough history, colonial German architecture, great museums, and ancient forts to warrant a day visit or overnight stay. (It's about a 2-hr. drive from Pucón.) The town is divided by a series of narrow rivers that wrap around the city's downtown area, providing a lively waterfront where fishmongers peddle the fresh catches of the day and pleasure boats disembark for a variety of journeys. The incongruity of the architecture here, encompassing seemingly every style invented since 1800, gives Valdivia a weary appearance—but part of the fascination with Valdivia is its ability to tenaciously bounce back after every attack, flood, and fire that has beset the city over the past 4 centuries, including the disastrous earthquake of 1960 that nearly drowned the city under 3m (10 ft.) of water. Valdivia is to a considerable extent now a college town due to the Universidad Austral de Chile that is located here.

ESSENTIALS
GETTING THERE   By Plane   Valdivia's Aeropuerto Pichoy, ZAL (© 63/272294) is about 30km (19 miles) northeast of the city, and is served by Lan-Chile Express. A taxi to town costs about $12, or take one of Transfer Valdivia's minibuses for $2.50.

By Bus   The bus terminal can be found at Anwanter and Muñoz, and nearly every bus company passes through here; there are multiple daily trips from Pucón and Santiago. (The average cost for a ticket from Santiago to Valdivia is $10; from Pucón to Valdivia, $3.50.)

By Car   From the Panamericana Highway, take Ruta 205 and follow the signs for Valdivia. A car is not really necessary in Valdivia, as most attractions can be reached by boat, foot, or taxi. It's about a 2-hour drive from Pucón to Valdivia. For car rentals, try **Assef y Méndez Rent A Car** at General Lagos 1335 (© 63/213205), and **Hertz** at Ramón Picarte 640 (© 63/218316); both have airport kiosks.

VISITOR INFORMATION   Sernatur's **Oficina de Turismo** is near Muelle Schuster at Arturo Prat 555 (© 63/215739), and is open March to November, Monday through Friday from 8:30am to 1pm and 2:30 to 6:30pm; December to February, Monday through Sunday from 9am to 7pm. There's also an information kiosk at the bus terminal open daily from 8am to 9pm.

BOAT TRIPS ⚐
Valdivia's myriad waterways make for an enjoyable way to explore the region, and there are a variety of destinations and boating options that leave from the pier Muelle Schuster at the waterfront, including yachts, catamarans, and an antique steamer. Tours are in full swing during the summer, and although there's

---

Tips Planning with a Personal Touch

If you require more personal assistance planning your trip, contact Elisabeth Lajtonyi at **Outdoors Chile** (© **63/253377;** www.outdoorschile.com). She can arrange for your entire trip, from reserving hotels to airport transfers and personalized sightseeing tours; she can also put together an all-outdoor adventure itinerary. Although based in Valdivia, Elisabeth works with out-fitters, fishing guides and hotels throughout the Lake Region.

---

limited service during the off season, it is possible for a group to hire a launch for a private trip. The most interesting journeys sail through the **Carlos Anwanter Nature Sanctuary** to the **San Luis de Alba de Cruces Fort** and to **Isla Mancera** and **Corral** to visit other 17th-century historic forts; both tours run about 5 to 6 hours round-trip and usually include meals.

The easiest way to find an inexpensive tour is to head down to the pier. Several companies that offer service are **Orión III** (© **63/210533;** hetours@telsu.cl), which also includes a stop at the Isla Huapi Natural Park ($25 per person); and the nicer **Catamarán Extasis** (© **63/295674**), which offers Isla Mancera and Corral tours and evening dinner cruises, both at a cost of about $28 per person. The *Collico* (© **09/319-3284**) is a completely restored 1907 German steamer; there's a required minimum of 10 guests (or a negotiated fee), and reservations must be made at least 48 hours in advance ($30 per person).

OTHER ATTRACTIONS

The bustling **Mercado Fluvial** ✿ at Muelle Schuster (Av. Prat at Maipú) is the principal attraction in Valdivia, and is worth a visit for the dozens of fishermen who hawk their catches under the watchful eyes of lanky pelicans and enormous sea lions that bark for handouts.

A block up from the waterfront, turn right on Yungay and head south until the street changes into **General Lagos** at San Carlos, where you'll find stately, historic homes built by German immigrants between 1840 and 1930. At General Lagos 733 is the **Centro Cultural El Austral,** commonly known as the Casa Hoffman for the Thater-Hoffman family, who occupied the home from 1870 until 1980. It's open Tuesday through Sunday from 10am to 1pm and 4 to 7pm; admission is free. The first floor of this handsome building has been furnished to re-create the interior as it would have looked during the 19th century. At the junction of General Lagos and Yerbas Buenas, you'll find the **Torreón Los Canelos,** a 1781 defensive tower built to protect the southern end of the city.

Across the bridge in the neighborhood known as Isla Teja, visitors will find the splendid history museum, the **Museo Histórico y Antropológico Mauricio van de Maele** (© **63/212872;** Mon–Sun 10am–1pm and 2–8pm Dec 15–Mar 15, Tues–Sun 10am–1pm and 2–6pm the rest of the year; admission $2 adults, 50¢ children under 13). To get there, cross the Pedro de Valdivia bridge, walk up a block, turn left, and continue for half a block. The museum is housed in the grand family home of Karl Anwanter, brewery owner and vociferous supporter and leader of German immigrants. The museum is a collection of antiques, photos, letters, everyday objects, and more culled from local well-to-do families, historical figures, Mapuche Indians, and Spanish conquistadors. It's worth at least an hour's visit, and an hour longer if you plan to carefully peruse the photos and letters.

WHERE TO STAY

There's no luxury hotel in Valdivia yet. The city's oldest and most venerable hotel, The **Pedro de Valdivia,** Carampangue 190, Valdivia (© **63/212931;** fax 63/203888; www.pedrodevaldivia.com), is closing its doors sometime in the spring of 2004 to make way for an entirely new hotel to be built in the same fantastic location on the river, right in the center of town. When it finally reopens in 2005 or 2006, the Pedro de Valdivia is forecast to be the city's most modern and luxurious hotel with pool, health club, restaurant, cafe, bar, and a wealth of new amenities in its plush rooms that will all come with a view of the river.

Airesbuenos International Hostel 🐦 *Value*   This beautiful house is a historical monument in Valdivia and dates from 1890. The young and friendly owner, Lionel Brossi, has meticulously restored the entire house and oversees the day-to-day operation of the hostel. There's a special touch everywhere, which is rare when it comes to budget accommodations. A vintage staircase leads to eleven rooms of varying sizes, all with beautiful (and original) hardwood floors. Some of the rooms have bunk beds and are the top choice for traveling European and American backpackers; the bathroom in the hallway is clean and spacious. The five rooms with private bathrooms are pleasant and bright; the front room even has a balcony with river views. All beds come with cute blue-and-gold cotton sheets. There's Internet access for guests in the foyer, and the owner will arrange free transportation from the bus station if you give him advance notice. The hotel is located about a 15-minute walk from the market and most restaurants.

General Lagos 1036, Valdivia. ©/fax **63/206304.** www.airesbuenos.cl. 11 units. $8.50 per person in a shared room; $40 double w/private bathroom. Rates include breakfast. No credit cards. **Amenities:** Lounge; Internet access.

Hotel Naguilán 🐦 *Moments*   Although it sits about a 20-minute walk from the edge of downtown, the Hotel Naguilán, now part of Best Western, boasts a pretty riverfront location and solid, attractive accommodations. The hotel is housed in an interesting structure (ca. 1890) that once held a shipbuilding business. All rooms face the Río Valdivia and the evening sunset; from here it's possible to watch waterfowl and colorful tugs and fishing skiffs motor by. The rooms are divided into 15 newer units in a detached building and 17 in an older wing. The newer "Terrace" units sit directly on the riverbank and feature contemporary floral design in rich colors, classic furniture, ample bathrooms, and a terrace patio. The older wing is more economical and features a few dated items, such as 1960s lime-green carpet, but the entire hotel is impeccably clean.

General Lagos 1927, Valdivia. © **63/212851.** Fax 63/219130. www.valdivianet.com/naguilan. 32 units. $78 standard double (older units); $89 double (newer units); from $120 suite. AE, DC, MC, V. **Amenities:** Restaurant; bar; outdoor pool; game room; concierge; room service; laundry service. *In room:* TV, minibar.

Puerta del Sur *Overrated* *Kids*   This quiet resort just across the bridge on Isla Teja offers all the amenities a guest would expect from a full-service hotel but its drab decor and mediocre service don't quite live up to expectations. However, it does boast a gem of a location on the shore of the Nature Sanctuary. It's about a 7-minute walk to downtown, but you'll feel miles away. All rooms come with views of the river and are fairly comfortable; double superiors are roomy, as are the sparkling bathrooms. This is one of the few hotels in Chile to offer doubles with either a queen-size or two full-size beds instead of singles. The suites come with giant, triangular picture windows, but are not much larger than a double superior.

Outside, a path winds past the pool and whirlpool to a private dock where guests can be picked up for boat tours or launch one of the hotel's canoes. There are also bikes available for guests at no extra charge.

Los Lingues 950, Isla Teja, Valdivia. © 63/224500, or 2/633-5101 for reservations (in Santiago). Fax 63/211046. www.hotelpuertadelsur.com. 40 units. $90–$114 double; from $162 suite. AE, DC, MC, V. **Amenities:** Restaurant; bar; large outdoor pool; tennis court; Jacuzzi; sauna; game room; room service; babysitting; laundry service. *In room:* TV.

WHERE TO DINE

Valdivia's two classic cafes, Café Haussman and Entre Lagos, are excellent spots for lunch. **Café Haussman,** at O'Higgins 394 (© **63/202219;** Mon–Sat 8am–9pm; no credit cards) has been serving *crudos* (steak tartare) since 1959, and the tiny, old-fashioned diner is ideal for a sandwich and local color. **Entre Lagos,** at Pérez Rosales 622 (© **63/212047;** daily 9am–1:30pm and 3:30–8pm; American Express, Diners Club, MasterCard, and Visa accepted), is famous throughout Chile for its chocolate and marzipan, and now it serves equally delicious crepes, juicy sandwiches, heavenly cakes, and cappuccinos.

La Calesa *(Finds* PERUVIAN/INTERNATIONAL   Owned and operated by a Peruvian family, the cozy La Calesa features spicy cuisine served in the old Casa Kaheni, a gorgeous, 19th-century home with high ceilings, wood floors, and antique furnishings. The menu features Peruvian fare along with several international dishes. Standouts include grilled beef tenderloin and sea bass in a cilantro sauce; *ají de gallina,* a spicy chicken and garlic stew with rice; or any of the nightly specials. The pisco sours are very good, as is the wine selection.

Yungay 735. © **63/225437.** Dinner reservations recommended. Main courses $9–$12. Daily 1–3:30pm and 8pm–midnight.

New Orleans *(Kids* INTERNATIONAL   This is Valdivia's most popular restaurant, tucked away on a side street a few streets in from the river, and it seems to always be busy. There's a pleasant outdoor patio with tables very close together and a charming dining room with more spacious seating. The food here is consistently good and fresh and the menu changes often. Main courses often include pastas, grilled salmon or tuna, chicken, and steak. This is a loud, boisterous place, often filled with families with children early in the evening. Later, the atmosphere is more publike.

Esmeralda 682. © **63/218771.** Dinner reservations recommended. Main courses $9–$10. AE, DC, MC, V. Mon–Fri noon–4pm and 7pm–midnight; Sat–Sun 5pm–midnight.

FRUTILLAR *(*

58km (36 miles) S of Osorno, 46km (29 miles) N of Puerto Montt

Frutillar offers a rich example of the typical architecture popular with German immigrants to the Lago Llanquihue area, and it is situated to take advantage of the dynamite view of the Osorno and Calbuco volcanoes. The town is smaller than, though as charming as, its neighbor Puerto Varas. It makes a great day trip, and the coastal dirt road that connects the town and its other neighbor, Puerto Octay, is especially beautiful, with clapboard homes dotting an idyllic countryside. You might even consider staying in Frutillar, which has a good supply of attractive lakeside hotels and bed-and-breakfasts. Note that the town is split in two: "Alto" and "Bajo," meaning "high" and "low," respectively. Skip Frutillar Alto, and stay in Frutillar Bajo.

ESSENTIALS

GETTING THERE   By Bus   Frequent, inexpensive bus service leaves from the bus terminal in Puerto Montt (try Cruz del Sur or one of the small, white minibuses with signs for Frutillar that are parked alongside larger charter buses). From Puerto Varas, take one of the small buses labeled FRUTILLAR that leave from the corner of Walker Martínez and San Bernardo. Bus service in Puerto Varas is confusing, so if you're having trouble, ask for help at the Puerto Varas visitor center.

By Taxi   Taxis will take you to Frutillar for a relatively inexpensive fee ($18–$26), but make sure you bargain and set a price before setting off.

By Car   From Puerto Montt or Puerto Varas, head north on the Panamericana Highway and look for signs for Frutillar. Remember to continue down to Frutillar "Bajo" (along the lakeshore) instead of getting off at Frutillar "Alto."

VISITOR INFORMATION   The **Oficina de Información Turística** is located along the coast at Costanera Philippi (© **65/421080**); it's open January to March daily from 8:30am to 1pm and 2 to 9pm; April to December, Monday through Friday from 8:30am to 1pm and 2 to 5:45pm.

EXPLORING FRUTILLAR

The two most-visited attractions in town are the **Museo de la Colonización Alemana de Frutillar** and the **Reserva Forestal Edmundo Winkler.** The museum (© **65/421142**) is located where Arturo Prat dead-ends at Calle Vicente Pérez Rosales. Admission is $2 adults, 70¢ children 12 and under; it's open April to November, Monday through Sunday from 10am to 1:30pm and 3 to 6pm, and December to March, from 9:30am to 1:30pm and 3 to 7pm. It features a collection of 19th-century antiques, clothing, and artifacts gathered from various immigrant German families around the area. It's quite interesting if you have 30 minutes to spare.

The Reserva is run by the University of Chile and features a trail winding through native forest, giving visitors an idea of what the region looked like before immigrants went timber-crazy and chopped down a sizable percentage of trees in this region. It's open year-round, daily from 10am to 7pm; admission costs 75¢ for adults and 35¢ for kids. To get there, you'll have to walk 1km (½ mile) up to the park from the entrance at Calle Caupolican at the northern end of Avenida Philippi.

WHERE TO STAY

Private parking or ample street parking are available and free for all hotels.

Hotel Ayacara *Finds*   The Ayacara is a top choice in Frutillar, housed in a superbly renovated, 1910 antique home on the coast of Lago Llanquihue. The interior of the hotel is made of light wood and this, coupled with large, plentiful windows, translates into bright accommodations. The rooms come with comfy beds, crisp linens, wood headboards, country furnishings, and antiques brought from Santiago and Chiloé. The Capitán room is the largest and has the best view. An attractive dining area serves dinner during the summer, and there's a small, ground-level outdoor deck and a TV/video lounge. The staff can arrange excursions around the area; fly-fishing excursions are their specialty.

Av. Philippi 1215, Frutillar. ©/fax 65/421550. www.hotelayacara.com. 8 units. $42–$60 double; $85–$110 Capitán double. Rates include full breakfast. AE, DC, MC, V. **Amenities:** Restaurant (summer only); bar; tour desk.

Hotel Elun ⟨⟩ This decent, azure-colored hotel is a good bet for anyone seeking modern accommodations, a room with a view, and a quiet, forested location. The hotel, opened in 1999, is made almost entirely of light, polished wood, and was designed to take full advantage of the views. The lounge, bar, and lobby sit under a slanted roof that ends with picture windows; there's also a deck should you decide to lounge outside. Double standard rooms are decent size and feature Berber carpet and spick-and-span white bathrooms. The superiors are very large and come with a comfy easy chair and a table and chairs. Room no. 24 looks out over Frutillar. The hotel is attended by its owners, who will arrange excursions.

200m (656 ft.) from start of Camino Punta Larga, at the southern end of Costanera Phillipi, Frutillar. ⟨⟩ 65/ 420055. www.hotelelun.cl. 14 units. $54–$80 double. Rates include continental breakfast. DC, MC, V. **Amenities:** Restaurant (summer only); lounge; mountain bike rental; tour desk; room service; laundry service. *In room:* TV.

Hotel Villa San Francisco *Moments* The Villa San Francisco sits high on a cliff, with rooms that all face the lake, some with a view of the volcano. All of the rooms are identical, decorated with simple but attractive furnishings that include comfortable beds and wicker headboards. Some guests might find the rooms a little on the small side, but most come with a terrace and four have corner windows. The new owners of this hotel have invested a great deal in idyllic gardens that surround the property.

Av. Philippi 1503, Frutillar. ⟨⟩/fax 65/421531. iberchile@telsur.cl. 15 units. $57–$64 double. AE, MC, V. **Amenities:** Restaurant; bar. *In room:* TV.

WHERE TO DINE

You'll find much better restaurants in Puerto Varas, and that town's proximity makes it feasible to plan on dining there. Otherwise, the traditional **Club Alemán** ⟨⟩, San Martín 22 (⟨⟩ **65/421249;** daily noon–4pm and 8pm–midnight; American Express, Diners Club, MasterCard, and Visa accepted), serves Chilean and German specialties. **La Selva Negra,** Antonio Varas 24 (⟨⟩ **65/421164;** daily noon–midnight; American Express, Diners Club, MasterCard, and Visa accepted), is perhaps the best bet in town, with innovative international and Chilean dishes served in a hutlike replica of a German dry-goods bodega. For smoked meats, game, and standard Chilean fare, try **El Ciervo,** San Martín 64 (⟨⟩ **65/420185;** daily noon–10pm; American Express, Diners Club, Master Card, and Visa accepted).

PUERTO VARAS ⟨⟩⟨⟩
20km (12 miles) N of Puerto Montt, 996km (618 miles) S of Santiago

Puerto Varas is on the shore of Lago Llanquihue, and is also an adventure-travel hub and gateway to the **Parque Nacional Vicente Pérez Rosales** (see "Parque Nacional Vicente Pérez Rosales & the Lake Crossing to Argentina," later in this chapter, for more information). It is a tidy little town, with quaint architecture and a bustling center, and it extends more services to its visitors than Frutillar, including a spanking-new casino, tour operators, and more. Puerto Varas doesn't see the crowds that Pucón sees, but then the weather here is unpredictable, with occasional rain during the summer. The city was founded by German immigrants and later became an important exit port for goods being shipped to Puerto Montt. Today, Puerto Varas relies heavily on tourism, but it is also a residential community for many who work in Puerto Montt.

ESSENTIALS

GETTING THERE **By Plane** El Tepaul (PMC) airport (© 65/252019) lies an almost equal distance from Puerto Montt and Puerto Varas; it's about 25km (16 miles) from the airport to Puerto Varas. A taxi from the airport costs $14 to $24, or you can arrange a transfer with **Andina del Sud** (© 65/257797; www.andinadelsud.com) for about $6 per person. LanChile Express serves the El Tepaul airport with five to six daily flights from Santiago; Sky Airline operates two to three nonstops from Santiago. See "Essentials" under "Puerto Montt," below. Always ask your hotel about transfers, as those may be sometimes included in the accommodations package.

By Bus The following buses offer service to and from major cities in southern Chile, including Santiago: **Buses Cruz del Sur,** San Pedro 210 (© 65/233008); **Buses Tas Choapa,** Walker Martínez 230 (© 65/233831); and **Buses Lit,** Walker Martínez 227-B (© 65/233838). Buses Tas Choapa and **Andesmar** (© 65/252926) both offer daily service to Bariloche, Argentina.

By Car Puerto Varas is just 20km (12 miles) north of Puerto Montt and 88km (55 miles) south of Osorno via the Panamericana. There are two exits leading to Puerto Varas, and both deposit you downtown. To get to Frutillar, you need to get back on the Panamericana, go north, and take the exit for that town.

GETTING AROUND **By Bus** There are also cheap, frequent minibuses to the bus terminal in Puerto Montt that leave from the corner of San Bernardo and Walker Martínez. Puerto Varas is small enough to see by foot.

By Car You might consider renting a car for a sightseeing drive around Lake Llanquihue. Try **Adriazola Turismo,** Santa Rosa 340 (© 65/233477); or **Travi Viajes,** Camino Ensenada, Km 1 (© 65/257137). Hertz and Avis have rentals at the airport.

VISITOR INFORMATION The **Oficina de Turismo Municipal** at San Francisco 441 is open from December 15 to March 15 Monday through Sunday from 8am to 9pm, and the rest of the year Monday through Friday from 8am to 4:45pm (© 65/232437; www.puertovaras.cl).

For event and excursion information (in Spanish), a good website to check is www.puertovaras.org.

A WALK AROUND TOWN

Puerto Varas is compact enough to explore by foot, which is really the best way to view the wooden colonial homes built by German immigrants from 1910 until the 1940s. Eight of these homes have been declared national monuments, yet there are dozens more clustered around town.

Walk up San Francisco from Del Salvador until reaching María Brunn, where you turn right to view the stately **Iglesia del Sagrado Corazón de Jesús,** built between 1915 and 1918 and modeled after the Marienkirche in the Black Forest. Continue along María Brunn and turn right on Purísima, where you'll encounter the **Casa Gasthof Haus** (1930), then **Casa Yunge** (1932), just past San Luis on the left, and on the right, **Casa Horn** (1925), and finally **Casa Kaschel** at Del Salvador, where you turn left. If you'd like to see more, walk to Calle Doctor Giesseler and turn right, following the train tracks for several blocks.

On the other side of town, near the park and lookout point at **Parque Phillippi,** are many shingled homes, including **Casa Juptner** (1910) on the

Calle Nuestra Señora del Carmen, and the **Casa Kuschel** (1910) at the corner of Klenner and Turismo. Pick up a map of the homes at the visitor center.

OUTDOOR ACTIVITIES

TOUR OPERATORS & OUTFITTERS Puerto Varas has a few competent outfitters and tour operators offering excursions around the region, and even as far away as the Aisén region along the Carretera Austral. Perhaps the most difficult, and thrilling, excursion in this region is an ascent up Volcán Osorno. This excursion requires adequate physical fitness and a guided tour company that can provide necessary gear such as ropes and crampons. **Tranco Expediciones,** Santa Rosa 580 (© 65/311311), offers this climb. **AlSur Expediciones,** Del Salvador 100 (©/fax 65/232300; www.puertovaras.com/alsur), and **Aquamotion Expediciones,** San Pedro 422 (© 65/232747; fax 65/235938; www.aquamotion.cl), offer rafting, sea kayaking, horseback riding, photo safaris, and more.

For city tours and sightseeing tours around the Lake District, including trips to Frutillar, Puyehue, Chiloé, and Parque Nacional Alerce Andino, try **Andina del Sud,** at Del Salvador 72 (© 65/232811; www.andinadelsud.com). Andina del Sud is the company that provides boat excursions on Lago Todos los Santos and the Chilean leg of the lake crossing to Argentina (for information, see "Parque Nacional Vicente Pérez Rosales & the Lake Crossing to Argentina," below).

BOATING For a sailing cruise around Lago Llanquihue, try **Motovelero Capitán Haase** (© 65/235120; fax 65/235166; captain@chilesat.net). Mr. Haase, the amicable owner and captain, offers four daily cruises aboard his yacht, which was modeled after the antique versions that used to sail the lake.

FISHING This region is noted for its excellent fly-fishing opportunities, namely along the shores of Río Puelo, Río Maullín, and Río Petrohue. Many hotels will set up tours with guides, but the central hub for information, gear, and fishing licenses is at **Gray's Fly-Fishing Supplies,** which has two shops at San José 192 and San Francisco 447 (© 65/310734; www.grayfly.com). Gray's has a roster of fly-fishing guides who will arrange outings to all outlying areas, for river and lake fishing.

HORSEBACK RIDING **Campo Aventura,** San Bernardo 318, Puerto Varas (© 65/232910; www.campo-aventura.coml), offers horseback riding October 15 to April 15, leaving from a camp in Valle Cochamó, south of the national park, with day and multiday trips. **AlSur** (see "Tour Operators & Outfitters," above), can arrange horseback-riding day trips in Vicente Pérez Rosales National Park.

RAFTING Few rivers in the world provide rafters with such stunning scenery as the Río Petrohue, whose frothy green waters begin at Lago Todos los Santos and end at the Reloncaví Estuary. The river is class III and suitable for nearly everyone, but it is not a slow float, so timid travelers might consult with their tour agency before signing up. The tour operators listed above offer rafting, but AlSur is the best bet.

WHERE TO STAY

There's no truly luxurious hotel in town; the Yan Kee Way lodge (see below) about a 40-minute drive outside of town, is your best if you're looking for the best of the best in this area.

Private parking or ample street parking are available and free for all hotels.

Colonos del Sur ★★ Boasting a waterfront location next door to the new casino and charming German colonial architecture, the Colonos del Sur is a standard favorite among travelers to Puerto Varas, and it is one of the nicer hotels in town. It was built with a tremendous amount of wood, all of it native species such as alerce and beech. The common areas are large and plentiful, including a tea salon and lounge, and feature a quaint yet handsome decor sprinkled with various antique furnishings and objects such as foot-operated sewing machines. The tea salon is one of the best in Puerto Varas, both for its rich cakes and its waterfront location. The rooms are not especially noteworthy but do offer solid quality. Doubles with a lake view are slightly larger, for the same price; others face the casino.

Del Salvador 24, Puerto Varas. © 65/233369, or 65/233039 for reservations. Fax 65/233394. www.colonosdel sur.cl. 54 units. $75–$110 double; from $132 suite. AE, DC, MC, V. **Amenities:** Restaurant; bar; indoor pool; exercise room; Jacuzzi; sauna; business center; room service; babysitting; laundry service. *In room:* TV, minibar, safe.

Hotel Cabañas del Lago 🛋 (Kids)

Not the height of luxury, but with its sweeping views of Puerto Varas and Volcán Osorno, the Hotel Cabañas del Lago is the highest quality lodging available in town. The lake-view and park suites are plushly appointed and colossal in size; one could get lost in the bathroom alone. A junior suite is a slightly larger double, and might be worth booking for the larger windows and better decoration. Doubles are not overly spacious, and have cramped bathrooms, but curtains and bedding have been updated. Doubles with a lake view are the same price as rooms that overlook the cabañas.

The hotel takes advantage of its location with lots of glass in its attractive lounge and restaurant, which, like all the rooms, sports a country decor. The common areas have the feel of a mountain lodge, complete with deer antler chandeliers. There's also a large sun deck.

Klenner 195, Puerto Varas. © 65/232291. Fax 65/232707. www.cabanasdellago.cl. 65 units, 21 cabañas. $100–$114 double; $124–$136 junior suite; $95–$130 cabañas for up to 4 people. Rates include buffet breakfast. AE, DC, MC, V. **Amenities:** Restaurant; bar; lounge; indoor heated pool; sauna; game room; room service; babysitting; laundry service. *In room:* TV.

Hotel Licarayén (Value)

This is one of Puerto Varas's best values, for its comfortable accommodations, waterfront views, and central location. The lobby and rooms are cheery and well lit, and the double standard rooms are average-size. Double superior rooms come with lake views, balconies, and whirlpool tubs. Superiors are also substantially larger than standards and come with big, bright bathrooms. Only a few standards have lake views, so ask for one; suites are ample, and come with a couch. The hotel may not have the antique character of Colonos del Sur (see above), but the rooms are just as good, if not better. There's a pleasant dining area for breakfast, again with lake views.

San José 114, Puerto Varas. © 65/232305. Fax 65/232955. 23 units. $70 double standard. Rate includes continental breakfast. AE, DC, MC, V. **Amenities:** Sauna; room service. *In room:* TV.

WHERE TO DINE

Unless otherwise indicated, reservations are not required for the restaurants listed here. Beyond the restaurants listed below, **Café Mamusia** 🛋, San José 316 (© 65/237971; in summer daily 8:30am–2am, in winter daily 9am–10:30pm), has inexpensive, good fixed-price lunches, but this cafe is locally renowned for its mouthwatering cakes, pastries, and *kuchen* that fill the entryway.

Ibis 🛋 INTERNATIONAL/CHILEAN   This popular restaurant is one of the best in Puerto Varas, namely for its creative cuisine and vast menu featuring everything from meat to pasta to sushi. Menu highlights include the flambéed Ecuadorian shrimp in cognac; pistachio salmon; beef filet in a sauce of tomato, garlic, and chipotle pepper; and lamb chops with mint sauce. To begin, you might try a salad such as endive and Roquefort, and end the meal with crêpes suzette. The eating area is small but warm, and is decorated with crafts-oriented art; there's also a bar. The wine list also merits mention for its variety.

Av. Vicente Pérez Rosales 1117. © 65/232017. Main courses $7–$12. AE, DC, MC, V. Mon–Sat 12:30–3pm and 8pm–midnight.

Kika's 🅡🅡 *Finds* CHILEAN/INTERNATIONAL   This is one of the newest and most charming eateries in town and it's tucked away in a lovely old house, a few blocks in from the lake. The bright dining room has hard wood floors, a beautiful fireplace, and lots of plants. There's a very young and casual atmosphere, but the food is quite sophisticated. The fresh seafood is outstanding and Kika's is known for its combination plates, such as the salmon and congrio eel with crab sauce or the jumbo shrimp served with a tender filet mignon. There are also several duck and wild game choices, depending on the season. To drink with your dinner, choose from over 60 award-winning Chilean wines. Desserts are heavenly—try the delicate raspberries baked with orange liquor.

Walker Martínez 584. © 65/234703. Main courses $7–$12. AE, DC, MC, V. Daily 9am–11pm.

Mediterráneo *Moments* INTERNATIONAL   Boasting an excellent location right on the Costanera, this new restaurant has a glass-enclosed terrace with water views. The cheerful orange tablecloths add to its brightness as does the pleasant waitstaff. Mediterráneo is known for its imaginative dishes (think Chilean-Mediterranean fusion) that change weekly. The owners use mostly local produce, including spices bought from the Mapuche natives. Here, you'll find big fresh salads mixing such ingredients as endives, Swiss cheese, anchovies, olives, and local mushrooms. For the main course, the venison here is excellent, served with a yummy zucchini gratin. Other standouts are the fresh sea bass with a caper white-wine sauce and a delicious lamb cooked in a rosemary wine reduction and served with roasted potatoes. For dessert, try one of the yummy fruit sorbets.

Santa Rosa 068, corner of Portales. © 65/237268. AE, DC, MC, V. Main courses $11–$14. Daily noon–3:30pm and 7:30–11pm.

Merlin 🅡🅡 *Finds* CHILEAN   Merlin is arguably the finest restaurant in the center of town, located on a hillside just a block up from the lake. It is also one of the only restaurants in Chile that has managed to take Chilean cooking to a new level by exchanging the same tired recipes for creative dishes while still using only local (and mostly organic) ingredients. The setting is elegant, with hardwood floors, and a lovely view overlooking a small park (from the back dining area). The front dining room overlooks the street. The German chef who has been running this restaurant for 10 years changes the menu seasonally. A few examples include sea bass ceviche, crawfish bisque, smoked-salmon-and-chive ravioli, rabbit with asparagus and olive risotto, and curried scallops, shrimp, and vegetables served with almond rice. The wine list also deserves mention for its selection of fine varietals not usually seen in this region.

Imperial 0605. © 65/233105. Reservations recommended. Main courses $11–$13. AE, DC, MC, V. Daily noon–3pm and 7pm–midnight.

PARQUE NACIONAL VICENTE PEREZ ROSALES & THE LAKE CROSSING TO ARGENTINA 🅡🅡

About 65km (40 miles) from Puerto Varas is Chile's oldest national park, Vicente Pérez Rosales, founded in 1926. It covers an area of 250,000 hectares (617,500 acres), incorporating the park's centerpiece, Lago Todos los Santos, and the Saltos de Petrohue and three volcanoes: Osorno, Tronador, and Puntiagudo. The park is open during the summer from 9am to 8pm, and during the winter from 9am to 6pm; admission to the Saltos de Petrohue is $3. Conaf's **information center** (no phone) can be found near the Hotel Petrohue; the center adheres loosely to these hours: December to February from 8:30am to 8pm, March to November from 8:30am to 6:30pm.

By far the most popular excursions here are boat rides across the unbelievably emerald waters of **Lago Todos los Santos,** which **Andina del Sud** offers as a day trip, or with an overnight in the Peulla Hotel; from here, guests return or continue on to Bariloche with the Argentine company Cruce de Lagos. Andina del Sud has a ticket office at the pier and an office in Puerto Varas, at Del Salvador 72 (© **65/232811**). The boat ride to Bariloche is one of the biggest tourist draws to this region, and it is indeed a spectacular journey to sail through the Andes. However, some travelers have complained that 1-day trips to Bariloche are not worth the money on stormy days.

For more information check out the website www.lakecrossing.com.

There are relatively few hiking trails here. A short and popular trail to the **Saltos de Petrohue** (located just before the lake; admission $3) takes visitors along a walkway built above Río Petrohue; from here, it is possible to watch the inky-green waters crash through lava channels formed after the 1850 eruption of Volcán Osorno. If you're into backpacking, pick up a copy of the JLM map *Ruta de los Jesuitas* for a description of longer trails in the park. Day hikes take visitors around the back of Volcán Osorno.

GETTING THERE

If you have your own vehicle, take the coastal road east out of Puerto Varas toward Ensenada and follow the signs for the park. In Puerto Varas, you'll find minibuses at the intersection of San Bernardo and Martínez that go to Ensenada, Petrohue, and Lago Todos los Santos every day at 9:15, 11am, 2, and 4pm. **Andina del Sud,** Del Salvador 72 (© **65/232811;** www.andinadelsud.com), has daily trips to this area as well.

WHERE TO STAY NEAR THE PARK

Private parking or ample street parking are available and free for all hotels.

Hotel Peulla *Moments*   Passengers on the 2-day journey to Bariloche stop for the night at this giant lodge, which sits on the shore of Lago Todos los Santos. It's possible to spend several days here if you'd like, to take part in trekking, fishing, and kayaking in the area. The lodge's remoteness is perhaps its biggest draw, surrounded as it is by thick forest and not much else. The Peulla features an enormous dining room and roaring fireplaces, and there's also a large patio and lawn. Room rates are lower if you reserve through a travel agency.

Lago Todos los Santos. ©/fax 2/889-1031 in Santiago. 78 units. $131 double. AE, MC, V. **Amenities:** Restaurant, bar; watersports equipment; game room. *In room:* TV.

Yan Kee Way *Finds*   The name "Yankee Way" is a play on words, a gringo's pronunciation of Llanquihue, and is owned by the American who began Digital Systems. The outdoorsy lodge complex is luxury at its finest; from the minute you arrive at the circular driveway, you know that no expense has been spared to make this lodge stand apart from any other in Chile (the reason it is patronized by Chilean and foreign VIPs). The lodge is nestled in a forest on the lakeshore, with an astounding view of the volcano in front of the lodge.

There are two chalets, eight bungalows, five two-bedroom suites, and four standard hotel rooms. Prices for each vary and can often be negotiated, especially when it comes to high and low season; there are also all-inclusive packages. Each lodging type has the same first-class decor: dark green walls, ebony leather couches, sunken bathtubs, copper-detailed showers, and contemporary art. The hotel's main bar and restaurant are detailed with marble and brass chandeliers, fireplaces made of volcanic rock, and orangey leather chairs; there's a basement "cave" for wine-tasting and a cigar bar that sells Havanas. The hotel began as a fishing lodge—there are five staff guides—but now offers a wide variety of activities, including the region's only sailcraft for floating on the lake. You might consider stopping here for lunch in its exquisite restaurant, Latitude 42, the finest in southern Chile.

Road to Ensenada east of Puerto Varas, Km 42. ℂ 65/212030. Fax 65/212031. www.southernchilexp.com. 18 units. $100–$150 double; from $250 1-bedroom chalet; $318 per person all-inclusive package, per day. Package includes all meals and house wines w/dinner. MC, V. **Amenities:** Outstanding restaurant w/lake views; bar; lounge; spa; Jacuzzi; sauna; exercise room; watersports equipment; room service; massage; laundry service; wine-tasting cellar; cigar bar. *In room:* Fridge, hair dryer, safe.

PUERTO MONTT
1,016km (630 miles) S of Santiago, 20km (12 miles) S of Puerto Varas

This port town of roughly 110,000 residents is the central hub for travelers headed to lagos Llanquihue and Todos los Santos, Chiloé, and the national parks Alerce Andino and Pumalín. It is also a major docking zone for dozens of large cruise companies circumnavigating the southern cone of South America and several ferry companies with southern destinations to Laguna San Rafael National Park and Puerto Natales in Patagonia.

The town presents a convenient stopover point for travelers, but it is not as attractive as Puerto Varas or Frutillar, due to its mishmash of office buildings and its scrappy industrial port. The small downtown is pleasant enough, however, and the city offers great restaurants and a huge outdoor market that sells Chilean handicrafts and clothing. Puerto Montt is the capital of Chile's Región X.

ESSENTIALS
GETTING THERE   By Plane   Puerto Montt's **El Tepaul** (PMC) airport (ℂ 65/252019) is served by **LanChile/LanChile Express,** San Martín 200 (ℂ 65/253141), with six to eight daily flights to Santiago; two to four daily flights to Punta Arenas; three daily flights to Balmaceda; and once-weekly flights to Valdivia and Temuco. **Sky Airlines,** a new privately owned company, began services in early 2003 using a small fleet of Boeing 737 jets. As of this writing, it operated two flights a day between Santiago and Puerto Montt; it doesn't yet have an office in Puerto Montt or a website for purchasing tickets but you can make reservations by calling ℂ 600/6002828 toll-free from within Chile, or 2/353-3169; you can check on flight schedules at www.skyairline.cl. Tickets are sold at the airline's counter at the airport. **Aero Met,** Urmeneta 149 (ℂ 65/252523), has two or three daily flights from Chaitén and the cost is $100

⟮*Tips*⟯ Flying from Puerto Montt to San Carlos de Bariloche

Lan Chile has just announced it plans to begin operating a once-weekly flight from Puerto Montt to San Carlos de Bariloche in Argentina. This is very welcome news for travelers who wish to cross the lake to the other side but want a quick way back to catch onward flights. As of this writing, schedules were not yet available; check the airline's website for up-to-the-minute information at **www.lanchile.com**.

round-trip. A bus from the airport to the city's downtown bus terminal costs $1; a taxi costs $8.50. Agree on the fare before getting into the cab. There are several car-rental agencies at the airport, including Hertz and Avis.

By Bus   Puerto Montt's main terminal is at the waterfront, about a 10-minute walk from downtown, and there are taxis. Service to and from major cities is provided by **Cruz del Sur** (© 65/254731), **Tur Bus** (© 65/253329), **Tas Choapa** (© 65/254828), and **Bus Norte** (© 65/252783).

By Car   The Panamericana Highway ends at Puerto Montt.

GETTING AROUND   By Foot   The city center is small enough to be seen on foot. The crafts market and fish market in Angelmó are a 20-minute walk from the center, but you can take a cab. You'll need a taxi to reach the Pelluco district.

By Bus   Buses Cruz del Sur (© 65/252783) leaves for Puerto Varas 15 times daily from the bus terminal, and so do the independent, white shuttle buses to the left of the coaches; look for the sign in the window that says PUERTO VARAS. Cruz del Sur also serves Chiloé, including Castro and Ancud, with seven trips per day. **TransChiloé** (© 65/254934) goes to Chiloé 11 times per day from the terminal.

VISITOR INFORMATION   The municipality has a small **tourist office** in the plaza at the corner of Antonio Varas and O'Higgins (© 65/261700; Dec–Mar daily 9am–9pm; Apr–Nov Mon–Fri 9am–1pm and 2:30–6:30pm, Sat–Sun 9am–1pm). There is also an office in the bus terminal on the second floor, and two new kiosks on the pedestrian street Calle Talca near Calle Urmeneta.

FAST FACTS   For currency exchange, try **Turismo Los Lagos,** Talca 84; **Trans Afex,** Av. Diego Portales 516; **Inter/Cam,** O'Higgins 167, first floor; **La Moneda de Oro,** in the bus terminal, office no. 37; and **Eureka Tour,** Antonio Varas 445. **Hospital de la Seguridad** is at Panamericana 400 (© 65/257333). Get online at **Mundo Sur Cibercafé,** San Martín 232; **Tetris Entel,** Antonio Varas 529; and **Travellers Center,** Av. Angelmó 2456 (© 65/262099).

TOUR OPERATORS & TRAVEL AGENCIES   **Ace Turismo** at Antonio Varas 445 (© 65/254988) offers just about everything, including tours to Vicente Pérez National Park, the Termas de Puyehué, Chiloé, sightseeing tours around the circumference of Lago Llanquihue, 2-night treks around Volcán Osorno with an overnight in a family home, and more.

   Petrel Tours at Benavente 327 (© 65/251780) is a full-service travel agency and offers city tours and sightseeing excursions around the area and to the Vicente Pérez Rosales National Park. **Andina del Sud** at Antonio Varas 447 (© 65/257797) is another agency offering classic trips such as city tours and sightseeing journeys, and has a transportation service to attractions, as well as the monopoly on Lago Todos los Santos for the lake crossing to Bariloche.

ATTRACTIONS IN PUERTO MONTT
Museo Juan Pablo II   This museum contains a medley of artifacts culled from this region. There's an interesting interpretive exhibit of the Monte Verde archaeological dig that found bones estimated to be 12,000 years old. There's also an open-air railway exhibit next to the museum. Truthfully, the museum really holds little of interest, but if you're in the area, it's worth a quick stop. It won't take you more than 30 minutes to breeze through it.

Av. Diego Portales 991. No phone. Admission 70¢. Mar–Dec daily 9am–noon and 2–6pm; Jan–Feb daily 9am–7pm.

> ### Tips Renting a Car for Local Trips & for the Carretera Austral
>
> Local car-rental agencies in Puerto Montt include **Hertz** at Antonio Varas 126 (© **65/259585**; www.hertz.com), **Avis** at Urmeneta 1037 (© **65/253307**; www.avis.com), **First** at Av. G. Gallardo 211 (© **65/252036**), and **Econo Rent** at Av. G. Gallardo 450 (© **65/254888**). A typical rental (taxes and insurance included) runs $400 to $650 per week, with an expensive $500 to $600 drop-off fee if you decide to leave the car in Coyhaique. Some companies insist that you rent a truck with 4×4, but during the summer a 4×4 is really not necessary. Call or visit the websites to see if you can work out a deal, especially in the low season.

SHOPPING

Puerto Montt is a great place to pick up souvenirs. On Avenida Angelmó, from the bus terminal to the fish market, is the **Feria Artesanal de Angelmó** (daily 9am–7pm), with dozens of stalls and specialty shops that peddle knitwear, ponchos, handicrafts, jewelry, regional foods, and more from areas around the Lake District, including Chiloé. It's about a 15-minute walk from the plaza, or you can take a taxi.

WHERE TO STAY

Private parking or ample street parking are available and free for all hotels.

Gran Pacífico 🏖🏖   Opened in late 2001, the Gran Pacífico is the city's only luxurious full-service hotel, and its imposing seven-story structure towers over the waterfront. The Art Deco lobby is sleek and modern with lots of wood and marble. The rooms follow the same motif and are spacious, modern, and very bright. They have wood headboards, off-yellow wallpaper, and large-screen TVs. Those overlooking the water have breathtaking views (request an upper-level oceanview floor when you check in). The marble bathrooms are a tad small but the size of the room makes up for it. For such a high-caliber hotel, the staff is not too efficient nor do they speak much English, so be patient.

Urmeneta 719, Puerto Montt. © 65/482100. Fax 65/482110. Reservas@hotelpacifico.cl. 48 units. $95–$160 double. AE, DC, MC, V. **Amenities:** Restaurant; bar; lounge; exercise room; sauna; room service; laundry service. *In room:* TV, dataport, minibar, safe.

Hotel Viento Sur 🅕inds   The main body of this appealing B&B-style hotel is within an 80-year-old home clinging to a cliff, with a decade-old, added-on wing below that keeps with the architectural uniformity of the establishment. The hotel has luminous, blonde-wood floors and is brightly lit by a generous supply of windows that look out over Puerto Montt's bay. The rooms are unique, each with a folk-art and nautical theme, but simple and not luxurious at all. The upstairs rooms in the old house have tall ceilings, the rooms in the lower wing have the cozy feel of a ship's cabin, and rooms on the fourth floor have terraces or balconies. Doubles come in standard and superior, and nearly all have a view of the bay. A large patio juts out from the front of the hotel.

Ejército 200, Puerto Montt. © 65/258701. Fax 65/258700. www.hotelvientosur.cl. 27 units. $75–$90 double standard; $85–$98 double superior. Rates include buffet breakfast. AE, DC, MC, V. **Amenities:** Restaurant; sauna; laundry service. *In room:* TV.

WHERE TO DINE

Puerto Montt is Chile's **seafood capital,** offering the widest variety of shellfish and fish found anywhere in the country. It'd be a crime if you left here without sampling at least a few delicacies. And where better to see, smell, and taste these fruits of the sea than the **Fish Market of Angelmó,** located at the end of Avenida Angelmó where the artisan market terminates; it's open daily from 10am to 8pm. Like most fish markets, it's a little grungy, but it's a colorful stop nevertheless, and there are several restaurant stalls offering the freshest local specialties around.

Balzac ⊛ CHILEAN/FRENCH   Balzac is one of the best restaurants in Puerto Montt, and is accordingly popular with local residents and tourists alike. The idea behind Balzac is to create innovative dishes with a French flavor, using only fresh, regional products and ingredients. Plenty of Chilean specialties abound, such as garlic shrimp *pil pil* or conger eel with a caper or chardonnay sauce. You'll see a few French classics here, such as *boeuf bourguignon,* but the emphasis is seafood, of which there's a large variety, including albacore tuna or a *curanto* stew for two. The brightly painted interior is an attractive surrounding for enjoying your meal. The wine list features fine Chilean varieties.

Calle Urmeneta 305. ✆ 65/313251. Main courses $7–$9. No credit cards. Mon–Fri noon–3:30pm and 8–11:30pm; Sat–Sun 8–11:30pm.

Sherlock ⊛ *Finds* CHILEAN/PUB   The newest and most happening place in Puerto Varas is this centrally located pub, cafe, and restaurant all rolled into one. There's lots of charm, a nice bar, and wood furniture, and it fills with locals at all hours of the day. This is a good place to get some local color, and they serve excellent homemade Chilean cuisine and delicious sandwiches. Try the albacore steak with a Chilean tomato and onion salad or the Sherlock sandwich with beef strips, tomato, corn, cheese, bacon, and grilled onion ($5).

Antonio Varas and Rancagua 117. ✆ 65/288888. Main courses $6–$10; sandwiches $3–$5. No credit cards. Daily 9am–2am.

GETTING THERE

If you're driving, head south on Ruta 7, winding past tiny villages on a gravel road until you reach Chaica, about 35km (22 miles) from Puerto Montt, where a sign indicates the road to the park entrance at the left. The park ranger station is open from 9am to 5pm. There is no direct bus service to the park. For tours to either of the park's sectors, try **Andina del Sud,** in Puerto Varas at Antonio Varas 437 (✆ **65/257797**; www.andinadelsud.com); the company also has an office in Puerto Montt, at Del Salvador 72 (✆ **65/232811**).

WHERE TO STAY

Alerce Mountain Lodge ⊛ *Finds*   This quiet, remote lodge sits on the shore of a small lake—which must be crossed by a hand-drawn ferry—at the edge of the national park, and is surrounded by dense stands of stately, 1,000-year-old alerce trees.

The lodge is about a 1-hour drive from Puerto Montt (it provides transportation from there), and is built almost entirely of handcrafted alerce logs, with giant trunks acting as pillars in the spacious, two-story lobby. The woodsy effect continues in the cozy rooms, which are decorated with local crafts and feature forest views. The cabins have a view of the lake and come with a living room and two bedrooms, and accommodate a maximum of five guests. One of the highlights at this lodge is that the surrounding trails are not open to the general public, so you have them practically to yourself. Bilingual guides lead horseback rides and day hikes that can last as long as 7 hours or as little as a half-hour.

Carretera Austral, Km 36. ©/fax 65/286969. www.mountainlodge.cl. 11 units, 3 cabañas. All-inclusive packages run per person, double occupancy: 1 night/2 days $230; 3 nights/4 days $680. Inquire about other packages and off-season discounts. AE, DC, MC, V. **Amenities:** Restaurant; bar; Jacuzzi; sauna; game room; laundry service.

7 Patagonia ★★★

Few places in the world have captivated the imagination of explorers and travelers like Patagonia and Tierra del Fuego. The region's harsh, wind-whipped climate and its geological curiosities have produced some of the most beautiful natural attractions in the world: the granite towers of Torres del Paine and Los Glaciares national parks, the Southern and Northern ice fields with their colossal glaciers, the flat pampa broken by multicolored sedimentary bluffs, the emerald fiords and lakes that glow an impossible sea-foam blue. In the end, this is what compels most travelers to plan a trip down here, but Patagonia's seduction also lies in the "remote"—the very notion of traveling to The End of the World.

EXPLORING THE REGION

For the region's tremendous size, Patagonia and Tierra del Fuego are surprisingly easy to travel, especially now that most destinations have opened airports. Travelers can plan a circuit that loops through, for example, Ushuaia, Punta Arenas, Torres del Paine, and then El Calafate and El Chaltén. If you're planning a trip to Chile or Argentina, you'll really want to include a visit to this region if possible—there's so much to see and do here, you'd be missing out if you went home without putting foot in this magical territory. How long you stay depends on what you'd like to see and how you plan to see it. Some come to backpack for 2 weeks in just one national park, others take a weeklong cruise; and still others visit a variety of destinations, spending several days in each.

Argentine Patagonia

For coverage of destinations on the Argentine side of Patagonia and Tierra del Fuego, see chapter 4.

PUNTA ARENAS

Punta Arenas is the capital of the Magellanic and Antarctic Región XII, and it is Patagonia's most important city, with a population of 110,000. Upon arrival, it seems unbelievable that Punta Arenas is able to prosper as well as it does in such a forsaken location on the gusty shore of the Strait of Magellan, but its streets hum with activity and its airport and seaports bustle with traffic passing through the strait or in transit to Antarctica. Punta Arenas's streets are lined with residential homes with colorful, corrugated rooftops, business offices and hotels downtown, and an industrial port—all characteristically weather-whipped, and attractive in their own way.

Punta Arenas's history, extreme climate, and position overlooking the renowned Strait of Magellan make for a fascinating place to explore. There's enough to do here to fill a day, and it's much easier to plan on spending 1 night here, even if your plans are to head directly to Torres del Paine.

ESSENTIALS
Getting There

BY PLANE Punta Arenas's **Aeropuerto Presidente Ibáñez** (PUQ; no phone) is 20km (12 miles) north of town, and, depending on the season, it's serviced with

Patagonia

PACIFIC
OCEAN

Cochrane

Lago Buenos Aires

Villa O'Higgins

Lago O'Higgins

Parque
Nacional

Puerto Edén

ISLA WELLINGTON

▲ Cerro Chaltén/
Fitz Roy

Lago San Martín

Lago Cardiel

Gobernador
Gregores

Bernardo O'Higgins

Parque Argentino
Los Glaciares

Lago Viedma

Lago Argentina

Chico

Glaciar
Perito Moreno ■

✈ El Calafate

C H I L E

A R G E N T I N A

Santa Cruz

Puerto
Santa Cruz

Parque Nacional
Torres del Paine

Cueva de Milodon ■

Bahía Grande

Reserva
Nacional
Alacalufes

Puerto Natales ✈

Coig

Gallegos

Río Gallegos

Aguas
Calientes ■

[9]

Punta Delgada

*ATLANTIC
OCEAN*

Reserva Nacional
Magallanes

Penguin
colony ■

Isla Magdalena

Seno Otway ✈
Punta Arenas

Estrecho de Magallanes

Reserva Nacional
Laguna Parrillar

Fuerte
Bulnes

Porvenir ✈

Camerón

*ISLA
GRANDE
DE
TIERRA
DEL
FUEGO*

Río Grande

*GRANDES
VENTISQUEROS*

Parque
Nacional

Alberto
de Agostini

Parque Nacional
Tierra del Fuego

Mar Chileno

Ushuaia ✈

Puerto Williams ✈

Parque Nacional
Cabo de Hornos

Cabo de Hornos

✈ Airport
▲ Mountain

0 ___ 50 mi
0 ___ 50 km

Map Area inset

PACIFIC
OCEAN

Santiago ✱

CHILE

ARGENTINA

Buenos
Aires ✱

Map
Area

three to five daily flights from Santiago (all stop in Puerto Montt) by **LanChile/ LanChile Express,** Lautaro Navarro 999 (© **600/661-3000** or 61/241100). There's also one flight a week (usually on Sat) from Balmaceda. The airline **Aerovías DAP,** O'Higgins 891 (© **61/223340;** www.aeroviasdap.cl), has flights to and from Ushuaia every Wednesday and Friday from October to March, and Wednesday only from April to September; it also has daily service to Porvenir and the only air service to Puerto Williams and Cape Horn. To get to Punta Arenas, hire a taxi for about $8 or take one of the transfer services there (which can also arrange to take you back to the airport): **Ecotour** (© **61/223670**) and **Buses Transfer** (© **61/229613**) have door-to-door service for $5 per person; Buses Transfer has bus service to and from its office for $3 per person.

BY BUS From Puerto Natales: **Bus Sur** at José Menéndez 565 (© 61/244464) has four daily trips; **Buses Fernández** at Armando Sanhueza 745 (© 61/242313) has seven daily trips; **Buses Transfer** at Pedro Montt 414 (© 61/229613) has two daily trips; and **Buses Pacheco** at Av. Colón 414 (© 61/242174) has three daily trips. The cost is about $5 and the trip takes 3 hours.

To and from Ushuaia, Argentina: **Buses Tecni Austral** and **Buses Ghisoni** at Lautaro Navarro 975 (© **61/222078**) leave Punta Arenas Tuesday, Thursday, Saturday, and Sunday and return from Ushuaia on Monday, Wednesday, and Saturday. **Buses Pacheco** at Av. Colón 900 (© **61/242174**) has service to Ushuaia on Monday, Wednesday, and Friday and returns on Tuesday, Thursday, and Saturday. Buses cross through Porvenir or Punta Delgada. Bus fare is about $19 and the trip takes 12 hours, sometimes longer depending on the border crossing delays.

BY CAR Ruta 9 is a paved road between Punta Arenas and Puerto Natales. Strong winds often require that you exercise extreme caution when driving this route. To get to Tierra del Fuego, there are two options: Cross by ferry from Punta Arenas to Porvenir, or drive east on Ruta 255 to Ruta 277 and Punta Delgada for the ferry crossing there.

CAR RENTAL Try **Hertz** at O'Higgins 987 (© 61/248742), **Lubac** at Magallanes 970 (© 61/242023), **Budget** at O'Higgins 964 (© 61/241696), **Emsa** at Roca 1044 (© 61/241182), **First** at O'Higgins 949 (© 61/220780), or **Rus** at Av. Colón 614 (© 61/221529).

Visitor Information

There's an excellent **Oficina de Turismo** (© **61/200610**) inside a glass gazebo in the Plaza de Armas that also sells a wide range of fascinating historical and anthropological literature and postcards. The office is open from October to March, Monday through Friday from 8am to 8pm, Saturday from 9am to 6pm, and Sunday from 9am to 2pm. From April to September, it's open Monday through Friday from 8am to 7pm, and is closed weekends.

FAST FACTS Your currency exchange options are **La Hermandad,** Lautaro Navarro 1099 (© 61/248090); **Cambios Gasic,** Roca 915, no. 8 (© 61/242396); **Cambio de Moneda Stop,** José Nogueira 1168 (© 61/223334); or **Scott Cambios,** corner of Avenida Colón and Magallanes (© 61/245811). Casas de cambio are open Monday through Friday from 9am to 1pm and 3 to 7pm, and Saturday from 9am to 1pm.

For medical attention, go to **Hospital de las Fuerzas Armadas Cirujano Guzmán,** Avenida Manuel Bulnes and Guillermos (© 61/207500), or the **Clínica Magallanes,** Av. Manuel Bulnes 1448 (© 61/211527).

ACCOMMODATIONS ■
Hostal Calafate I **6**
Hotel Finis Terrae **7**
Hotel Isla Rey Jorge **2**
Hotel José Nogueira **5**

DINING ◆
La Pérgola **4**
Remezón **1**
Restaurante
  Hotel Finis Terrae **7**
ATTRACTIONS ●
Instituto de
  Patagonia **9**
Museo Naval
  y Marítimo **3**
Museo Salesiano **8**
Palacio Sara Braun **5**

✚ Hospital
✉ Post office

For Internet access, try **Telefónica,** Bories 798 (✆ **61/248230**) or **Calafate,** Magallanes 22 (✆ **61/241281**). Internet service costs an average of $3 per hour.

The central **post office** is at José Menéndez and Bories (✆ 61/222210); hours are Monday through Friday from 9am to 6pm and Saturday from 9am to 1pm.

EXPLORING PUNTA ARENAS

You might begin your tour of Punta Arenas in **Plaza Muñoz Gamero,** in whose center you'll find a bronze sculpture of Ferdinand Magellan, donated by José Menéndez on the 400-year anniversary of Magellan's discovery of the Strait of Magellan. From the plaza on Avenida 21 de Mayo, head north toward Avenida Colón for a look at the newly renovated Teatro Municipal, designed by the French architect Numa Mayer and modeled after the magnificent Teatro Colón in Buenos Aires. Head down to the waterfront and turn south toward the pier to watch the shipping action. At the pier is a 1913 clock imported from Germany that has complete meteorological instrumentation, hands showing the moon's phases, and a zodiac calendar.

City Cemetery   They say you can't really understand a culture until you see where they bury their dead, and in the case of the cemetery of Punta Arenas, this edict certainly rings true. Opened in 1894, inside this necropolis lies a veritable miniature city, with avenues that connect the magnificent tombs of the region's founding families, settlers, and civic workers and a rather solemn tomb where lie

Cruising from Punta Arenas to Ushuaia, Argentina

Cruceros Australis operates an unforgettable journey from Punta Arenas to Ushuaia and Ushuaia to Punta Arenas aboard its new ship, the M/V *Mare Australis*. This cruise takes passengers through remote coves and spectacular channels and fiords in Tierra del Fuego and then heads into the Beagle Channel, stopping in Puerto Williams on Isla Navarino and later Ushuaia, Argentina. The trip can be done as a 7-night, 8-day round-trip journey, a 4-night one-way from Punta Arenas, or a 3-night, one-way journey from Ushuaia. More than a few guests aboard the *Mare Australis* plan their entire trip to South America around this cruise.

Guides give daily talks about the region's flora, fauna, history, and geology. The accommodations are comfortable, ranging from suites to simple cabins. All-inclusive, per-person prices (excluding cocktails) for a midrange cabin range from $785 to $1,903 one-way from Punta Arenas and $1,152 to $2,537 round-trip. This cruise operates from late early October to April. For reservations or information, contact their offices in Santiago at Av. El Bosque Norte 0440 (© **2/442-3110;** fax 2/203-5025) or in Punta Arenas at Av. Independencia 840 (© **61/224256;** www. australis.com).

the remains of the last Selk'nam Indians of Tierra del Fuego. Just as interesting are the cypress trees that line the walkways, which have been trimmed into tall bell shapes.

Av. Manuel Bulnes and Angamos. No phone. Free admission. Daily 7:30am–8pm.

Instituto de Patagonia/Museo del Recuerdo   The Instituto de Patagonia/ Museo del Recuerdo is an engaging exhibit of colonial artifacts, and antique machinery and horse-drawn carts are displayed around the lawn and encircled by several colonial buildings that have been lifted and transported here from ranches around the area. There's a library on the premises with a collection of books and maps on display and for sale. To get into the colonial buildings, you'll need to ask someone in the museum's office to unlock them for you. The museum is about 4km (2½ miles) out of town, so you'll need to take a taxi and figure in about an hour's visiting time. The Zona Franca (a duty-free shopping center) is just down the street, so you could tie in a visit to the two.

Av. Manuel Bulnes 01890. © **61/217173.** Admission 70¢. Mon–Fri 8:30–11am and 2:15–6pm; Sat 8:30am–12:30pm.

Museo Salesiano Maggiorino Borgatello ⓡ   This fascinating museum is well worth a visit, offering insight into the Magellanic region's history, anthropology, ecology, and industrial history. The first room you enter is a dusty collection of stuffed and mounted birds and mammals that at times feels almost macabre. It's an old collection, and some specimens are in desperate shape; nevertheless, it allows you to fully appreciate the tremendous size of the condor and the puma. Several rooms in the museum hold displays of Indian hunting tools, ritual garments, jewelry, an Alacalufe bark canoe, and colonial and ranching implements. Plan on spending about 1½ hours here.

Av. Manuel Bulnes and Maipú. © **61/221001.** Admission $2. Tues–Sun 10am–12:30pm and 3–6pm.

Palacio Sara Braun & Museo Regional Braun Menéndez ✮ *Moments*

These two attractions are testament to the staggering wealth produced by the region's large-scale, colonial-era sheep and cattle *estancias* (ranches). The museums are the former residences of several members of the Braun, Nogueira, and Menéndez families, who believed that any far-flung, isolated locale could be tolerated if one were to "live splendidly and remain in constant contact with the outside world." The Palacio Sara Braun is now partially occupied by the Hotel José Nogueira. The Museo Regional Braun Menéndez is the former residence of Mauricio Braun and Josefina Menéndez, a marriage that united the two largest fortunes in the Magellanic region.

The homes are national monuments and both have been preserved in their original state. European craftsmen were imported to craft marble fireplaces and hand-paint walls to resemble marble and leather. The interior fixtures and furniture include gold and crystal chandeliers, tapestries from Belgium, stained-glass cupolas, English and French furniture, hand-carved desks, and more. A couple of hours should give you ample time to view both.

Palacio Sara Braun: Plaza Muñoz Gamero 716. (© 61/248840. Admission $1.50 adults; free for under 16. Tues–Sat 11am–1pm and 6–8pm. Museo Regional Braun Menéndez: Magallanes 949. (© 61/244216. Admission $1.15; Sun and holidays free. Mon–Fri 10:30am–5pm; Sat–Sun 10:30am–2pm.

SHOPPING

Punta Arenas is home to a duty-free shopping center called the **Zona Franca,** with several blocks of shops hawking supposedly cheaper electronics, imported foodstuffs, sporting goods, perfumes, clothing, booze, cigarettes, and more. The savings here are negligible, except for on alcohol, and the selection isn't what you'd hope for, although there certainly is a lot on offer, including a few supermarkets. The Zona Franca is located on Avenida Manuel Bulnes, just outside town. Take a taxi or grab any *colectivo* that says ZONA FRANCA on its sign. It's open Monday through Saturday from 10am to 12:30pm and 3 to 8pm, and is closed Sunday and holidays.

For regional crafts, try the great selection available at **Chile Típico,** Carrera Pinto 1015 (© 61/225827); or **Artesanía Yoyi,** Av. 21 de Mayo 1393 (© 61/229156). Both have knitwear, woodcarvings, lapis lazuli, postcards, and more.

EXCURSIONS OUTSIDE PUNTA ARENAS
Tour Operators

Many tour operators run conventional city tours and trips to the Seno Otway colony and Fuerte Bulnes, as well as short visits and multiday, all-inclusive trekking excursions to Torres del Paine National Park. However, more and more adventure-travel outfitters are popping up around town, offering day- and week-long trips to Tierra del Fuego, including all-inclusive kayaking, mountaineering, hiking, fly-fishing, and horseback-riding combination trips.

Turismo Yamana, Av. Colón 568 (© 61/240056; www.turismoyamana.cl), offers half- and full-day kayak trips on the Strait of Magellan, and multiday trips to Lago Blanco in Tierra del Fuego for trekking, horseback riding, and fishing. If you're a bird-watcher, they can put you in touch with an English-speaking ornithologist guide. The tour company **VientoSur,** Fagano 585 (© 61/226930; www.vientosur.com), offers all conventional tours, as well as tours to Torres del Paine and Porvenir.

Penguin Colonies at Seno Otway & Isla Magdalena

One of the highlights of a visit to Punta Arenas is a trip to the **penguin colonies** at Seno Otway and Isla Magdalena. At both colonies, visitors are allowed to watch the amusing Magellanic penguins (also called Jackass penguins for their characteristic bray) at their nesting sites, whisking out sprays of sand or poking their heads out of their burrows. Every morning around 10am and in the afternoon around 5pm, the penguin couples change shifts—one heads out to fish, the other returns from fishing to take care of their young. When this changing of the guard begins, the penguins politely line up and waddle to and from the sea. Viewing takes place from September to late March, but they're best viewed from November to February.

Seno Otway is a smaller colony, with an estimated 3,000 penguins, and it's accessible by road about 65km (40 miles) from Punta Arenas. A volunteer study group has developed the site with roped walkways and lookout posts. Tours are offered in four languages, and there is a tiny cafe here, too. Admission is $3.50; hours are September to April from 8am to 8:30pm. Both **Buses Transfer,** Pedro Montt 966 (© **61/229613**) and O'Higgins 1055 (© **61/243984**), and **Eco Tour Patagonia,** Lautaro Navarro 1091 (© **61/223670**), offer transportation to Seno Otway, leaving at 4pm daily. (Most tour companies also have similar trips.) The cost, not including the entrance fee, is $12. If you drive here in your own vehicle, come for the morning shift-change, when the crowds are thinner. Take Ruta 9 toward Puerto Natales, then turn left on the dirt road that branches out near the police checkpoint.

Isla Magdalena ☆☆ is much larger than Seno Otway, with an estimated 150,000 penguins sharing nesting space with cormorants. These penguins are more timid than those at Seno Otway, but the sight of so many of these birds bustling to and fro is decidedly more impressive. To get here, you need to take a ferry, which makes for a pleasant half-day afternoon excursion. **Turismo Comapa,** Av. Independencia 830, second floor (© **61/225804**), puts this tour together. Its boat, the *Barcaza Melinka,* leaves from the pier at 3:30pm, returning at 8:30pm on Tuesday, Thursday, and Saturday from December to February ($28 for adults, $13 children under 12).

SKIING IN THE AREA

Punta Arenas has a ski resort that operates from mid-June to mid-September: the **Centro de Esquí Cerro Mirador,** situated at the border of the Reserva Nacional Magallanes. If you're here during the season, this little resort is a fun place to spend the afternoon, notable more than anything for its view of the Strait of Magellan, Tierra del Fuego, and—on a clear day—Dawson Island. During the summer, it often runs its only chairlift to carry you to the top of the peak, or you can hike the hill yourself. The resort has 10 runs, ski rental, and a cafeteria. Ski-lift tickets cost about $18. The resort (© **61/241479**) is very close to town; to get here, take a taxi.

WHERE TO STAY

There is no large luxury hotel in Punta Arenas. The Hotel José Nogueira (see below) is the best in town. For all hotels, parking is either free, or street parking is plentiful.

Hotel Finis Terrae ☆   This hotel is very popular with foreigners, especially Americans, and it's part of the Best Western chain. The well-lit accommodations here are quite comfortable, with king-size beds in double rooms and a softly hued decor in peach and beige, with wood trim and wooden headboards. And although Richard Gere stayed here in November 2002 (he chose the spacious 5th-floor suite with a whirlpool tub and minibar) on his way to Antarctica to film a documentary, the rooms are by no means luxurious. The singles here are tiny, so be sure to ask for a larger double for the single price, which they will likely agree to, especially during slower months.

Av. Colón 766, Punta Arenas. ℂ 61/228200. Fax 61/248124. www.hotelfinisterrae.com. 66 units. $149–$179 double; $189–$290 superior suite. Rates include buffet breakfast. AE, DC, MC, V. **Amenities:** Restaurant; lounge; room service; laundry service. *In room:* TV.

Hotel Isla Rey Jorge ⋆ *(Finds)*

This hotel is housed in an antique English-style mansion, 2 blocks from the plaza. There's a compact lounge lit by a pergola-like glass ceiling, decorated with a blue country-style theme. Altogether it's a lovable little hotel, especially since the wallpaper and bedspreads were changed in 2002. The snug rooms with angled eaves are just slightly dark, but kept toasty warm. Rooms have a classic, executive-style decor, in navy blue and burgundy offset with brass details. The junior suites are the most spacious, with king-size beds and whirlpool tubs. The friendly staff let it be known that they rarely charge the advertised price, so ask for a discount.

Av. 21 de Mayo 1243, Punta Arenas. ℂ/fax 61/248220. www.Islareyjorge.com. 25 units. $146 double; from $189 junior suite. Rates include buffet breakfast. AE, DC, MC, V. **Amenities:** Restaurant; pub; room service; laundry service. *In room:* TV.

Hotel José Nogueira ⋆⋆ *(Moments)*

The best hotel in town is in this partially converted neoclassical mansion once owned by the widow of one of Punta Arenas's wealthiest entrepreneurs; half of the building is still run as a museum. The mansion was built between 1894 and 1905 on a prominent corner across from the plaza, with materials imported entirely from Europe. The José Nogueira is appealing for its historical value, but also offers classic luxury. The rooms here are not as large as you would expect, but high ceilings accented by floor-to-ceiling curtains compensate for that. All are tastefully decorated, either in rich burgundy and navy blue–striped wallpaper or rose and cream combinations, Oriental rugs, and lithographs of local fauna; the marble bathrooms are sparkling white.

Bories 959, Punta Arenas. ℂ 61/248840. Fax 61/248832. www.hotelnogueira.com. 28 units. $119–149 double; from $199 suite. Rates include buffet breakfast. AE, DC, MC, V. **Amenities:** Restaurant; bar; room service; laundry service. *In room:* TV, minibar.

WHERE TO DINE

La Pérgola ⋆ *(Moments)* REGIONAL

La Pérgola is located inside the glass-enclosed, vine-draped "winter garden" that once was part of the stately mansion owned by Sara Braun, now part of the Hotel José Nogueira. The ambience is as lovely as the cuisine. The menu provides photos of each dish, including king crab quiche, curried lamb with glazed carrots, filet mignon in three sauces, and pork loin in a cherry sauce. There's even salmon sashimi. An ample wine list and desserts such as tiramisu round out the menu. Small tables make this restaurant unsuitable for large groups.

Bories 959. ℂ 61/248840. Main courses $9–$13. AE, DC, MC, V. Daily noon–3:30pm and 7:30pm–midnight.

Remezón ⋆⋆ *(Finds)* CONTEMPORARY REGIONAL

One of the best restaurants in the region, Remezón breaks from the traditional mold with a warm, intimate dining area decorated with a jumble of art and slightly kitsch items that are as personal as the chef's daily changing menu. The food is, in a word, divine: not too pretentious but always prepared with fresh, regional vegetables, seafood, and meats seasoned to delicious perfection. The menu features five appetizers and as many main dishes handwritten on a chalkboard; usually the chef approaches your table and explains each item to diners before ordering. Sample dishes include delicious garlic soup; broiled Parmesan scallops; calamari, zucchini, and avocado salad; goose marinated in pisco and lemon; and crepes stuffed with king crab and cream. There's always a vegetarian dish on offer, such as vegetable *pastel de choclo,* a casserole topped with a corn crust. Remezón is located on the edge of town in a somewhat grungy neighborhood so taking a taxi here would be best.

Av. 21 de Mayo 1469. © 61/241029. Main courses $8–$13. AE, DC, MC, V. Daily noon–3pm and 7:15pm–midnight. Closed Mon Apr–Sept.

Restaurant Hotel Finis Terrae CHILEAN/INTERNATIONAL   This restaurant is located on the top floor of the Hotel Finis Terrae. The food is not as good as what you'll find at the other two restaurants mentioned in this section, but it's decent; what makes this restaurant unique are the sweeping views seen through enormous arched windows that wrap around the dining area. This is a great place for breakfast, and it opens early, at 6:30am. The ambience leans toward the casual, and the menu has enough options to satisfy anyone, from beef stuffed with king crab in an herb sauce to sea bass with mussels and spinach; there are also soups and sandwiches for a light lunch and a variety of pasta dishes. For dinner, there's usually a $15 fixed-price meal—your choice of an appetizer, main course, and dessert. There's a decent wine list, as well.

Av. Colón 766. © 61/228200. Main courses $6–$13; fixed-price 3-course meal $15. AE, DC, MC, V. Daily 6:30am–11pm.

PUNTA ARENAS AFTER DARK

One of the most popular pubs for all ages is in the **La Taberna** (© 61/248840) cellar bar, below the Hotel José Nogueira at the corner of Bories and Sequel across from the plaza; it serves a long list of appetizers. Another popular spot is the **Pub 1900** (© 61/242759), at the corner of Avenida Colón and Bories; yet another pub is **El Galeón** at Av. 21 de Mayo 1243, below the Hotel Isla Rey Jorge (© 61/248220). The cinema **Commercial Cine Magallanes,** at Plaza Muñoz Gamero 765 across from the tourism kiosk at the plaza (© 61/223225), has one screen; call or check newspaper listings for what's playing.

PUERTO NATALES ✿

Puerto Natales is a rambling town of 15,000, spread along the sloping coast of the Señoret Canal between the Ultima Esperanza Sound and the Almirante Montt Gulf. This is the jump-off point for trips to Torres del Paine, and most visitors will find themselves spending at least 1 night here. The town itself is nothing more than a small center and rows and rows of weather-beaten tin and wooden houses, but it has a certain appeal, and it boasts a stunning location with grand views out onto a grassy peninsula and the glacier-capped peaks of the national parks Bernardo O'Higgins and Torres del Paine in the distance. Along the Costanera, elegant black-necked swans drift along the rocky shore. From May to September, the town virtually goes into hibernation, but come October, the town's streets begin to fill with travelers decked out in parkas and hiking boots on their way to the park.

ESSENTIALS
Getting There & Getting Around

BY PLANE   The tiny Puerto Natales airport (no phone) has only one scheduled flight per day and that is a nine-passenger propeller plane from El Calafate. Contact **Aerovías DAP,** in Punta Arenas, at O'Higgins 891 (© 61/223340; www.aeroviasdap.cl), for information and reservations. At this writing, the one-way fare is $50 for the short hop to Argentina. Note that this service is frequently canceled because of high winds. A taxi from Puerto Natales to the airport costs $1.50 and is only a 5-minute drive.

BY BUS   Puerto Natales is the hub for bus service to Torres del Paine National Park and El Calafate, Argentina. For information about bus service to and from Torres del Paine, see "Parque Nacional Torres del Paine," later in this chapter. There are frequent daily trips between Punta Arenas and Puerto Natales. In Puerto Natales each bus company leaves from its own office.

To & from Punta Arenas   **Buses Fernández,** Eberhard 555 (© **61/411111**), has seven daily trips; **Bus Sur,** Baquedano 558 (© **61/411325**), has six daily trips; **Buses Pacheco,** Baquedano 244 (© **61/414513**), has six daily trips (and the most comfortable buses); and **Transfer Austral,** Baquedano 414 (© **61/412616**), has three daily trips. The trip takes about 3 hours and the cost is $5 one-way.

To El Calafate, Argentina   **Buses Zaahj,** Arturo Prat 236 (© **61/412260**), leaves at 9am; **Bus Sur,** Baquedano 534 (© **61/411325**), leaves at 9am; and **Cootra,** Baquedano 244 (© **61/412785**), leaves at 6:30am. The cost is $22 one-way. The trip takes 5 to 6 hours, depending on the traffic at the border crossing. Note that most of this voyage is on unpaved dirt roads.

BY CAR   Ruta 9 is a paved road that heads north from Punta Arenas. The drive is 254km (158 miles) and takes about 2½ to 3 hours. If you're heading in from El Calafate, Argentina, you have your choice of two international borders: Cerro Castillo (otherwise known as Control Fronterizo Río Don Guillermo) and Río Turbio (otherwise known as Controles Fronterizos Dorotea y Laurita Casas Viejas). Cerro Castillo is the preferred entry point for its easier access. Both are open 24 hours from September to May, and from 8am to 11pm the rest of the year.

Car rentals in Puerto Natales are offered by **Motorcars** at Baquedano 380, no. 3 (© 61/413593), **EMSA** (an Avis representative) at Av. Manuel Bulnes 632 (© 61/410775), and **Bien al Sur** at Av. Manuel Bulnes 433 (© 61/414025). Bien al Sur also rents bicycles, but the wind will probably dissuade you from pedaling.

BY BOAT   **Navimag** runs a popular 3-night ferry trip, departing every Friday morning at 4am, between Puerto Natales and Puerto Montt, passing through the southern fiords of Chile. If you have the time, this is an excellent way to reach the Lake District. Navimag's offices can be found next to the Hotel Costa Australis at Pedro Montt 262 (© **61/414300;** www.navimag.com).

Visitor Information

The **Sernatur** office is on the Costanera at Pedro Montt and Philippi (© **61/412125;** www.sernatur.cl); it's open October to March, Monday through Friday from 8:30am to 8pm, Saturday and Sunday from 9:30am to 1pm and 2:30 to

---

(Tips Where to Rent Camping Equipment

If you don't feel like lugging your own gear down here, there are several agencies that rent equipment. Typical daily rental prices are two-person tents $5 to $6, sleeping bags $2, stoves $1.50, sleeping mats $1.50, and backpacks $3. During the high season, it's best to reserve these items. The following companies rent equipment: **Casa Cecilia,** Tomás Roger 60 (© **61/411797;** redcecilia@entelchile.net); **Onas,** Eberhard and Blanco Encalada (© **61/412707;** onas@chileaustral.com); and **Fortaleza Aventura,** Arturo Prat 234 (© **61/410595;** monofortaleza@hotmail.com).

6:30pm; April to September, it's open Monday through Friday from 8:30am to 1pm and 2:30 to 6:30pm, closed Sunday and holidays. Tour operators are really the best sources of information about the park (see "Tour Operators & Adventure Travel Outfitters," below).

SAILING TO PARQUE NACIONAL BERNARDO O'HIGGINS 🔍

This park is unreachable except by boat tours to the glaciers Balmaceda and Serrano. There are several boat excursions that leave from Puerto Natales, sailing first through the Ultima Esperanza Sound and eventually docking near the narrow Serrano Glacier. The best way is to leave Torres del Paine via one of the Zodiac services that drops riders off at the Serrano Glacier, where you take the boat back to Puerto Natales, or vice versa (see "Getting There & Away" under "Parque Nacional Torres del Paine," below).

There are two companies that offer the excursion. The cutter *21 de Mayo* with offices at Eberhard 560 (© 61/411978; www.turismo21demayo.cl) leaves at 8am and arrives at the Serrano Glacier at 11:30am, where it stays for 1½ hours, returning at 5pm. The cost is $30 per person, not including lunch. A new service offered by **Aventour** at Av. Manuel Bulnes 689 (© 61/410253; www.aventouraventuras. com) takes visitors along a similar route aboard its wooden yacht *Nueva Galicia*, leaving at 7:30am and arriving at the Serrano Glacier at 11am for a half-hour, then crossing the adjoining river to its lodge, the Hostería Monte Balmaceda (see below). The cost for this trip is $55 per person.

Hostería Monte Balmaceda *(Moments)* This *hostería* sits along the Río Serrano and across from the glacier of the same name—a remote, stunning location that is reached by boat. Although the site provides a direct view of the glacier as it tumbles down the mountain, it unfortunately cannot be viewed from any of the rooms. Why the owner decided to design the rooms in three rows like army barracks that face each other can only be explained by the fact that he is an ex-military man. Nevertheless, the circular, separate restaurant is lovely (and comes with views), and the self-guided trail they've built around the property is really a delight, giving visitors lots of space to quietly walk and enjoy nature; there are fishing opportunities here as well. The rooms are not noteworthy, but they're brand-new and spacious enough.

Aventour's office in Puerto Natales, Av. Manuel Bulnes 689. © 61/410253. Fax 61/410825. www.aventour aventuras.com. 16 units. $45 May–Sept; $100 Oct and Apr; $145 Nov–Mar. AE, DC, MC, V.

TOUR OPERATORS & ADVENTURE TRAVEL OUTFITTERS

The glut of tour operators in Puerto Natales can be divided into two groups: conventional sightseeing day tours and adventure travel outfitters that arrange multiday, all-inclusive excursions to Torres del Paine and Bernardo O'Higgins national parks. Keep in mind that it's very easy to arrange your own trekking journey in Torres del Paine; the bonus with outfitters is that they carry tents and food.

CONVENTIONAL DAY TOURS These tours are for people with a limited amount of time in the area. Tours typically leave at 7:30am and return around 7:30pm, and cost about $28 per person, not including lunch or park entrance fees. Try **Turismo Mily,** Blanco Encalada 183 (© 61/411262); **Turismo María José,** Av. Manuel Bulnes 386 (© 61/414312); and **Turismo Zaahj,** Arturo Prat 236 (© 61/412260); Zaahj includes a stop at the Cueva de Milodón.

ADVENTURE TRAVEL Apart from the local guiding outfitters, several American and Chilean companies offer well-planned trekking excursions in Torres del Paine. **Bigfoot Expeditions,** Blanco Encalada 226 (© 61/414611; www.bigfoot patagonia.com), is the leader of the pack here in Puerto Natales; in Santiago, its office is at Helvecia 210 (© 2/335-1796; fax 2/335-1798). Bigfoot offers a variety of multiday trekking journeys through the park, kayaking the Río Serrano, trekking through the Sarmiento Mountain Range, and sailing through the Canal of the Mountains. They'll also arrange custom tours. **Onas,** Blanco Encalada and Eberhard (©/fax **61/412707;** www.onaspatagonia.com), offers trekking excursions in Torres del Paine and a 2-day kayak trip down the Río Serrano. (Onas has a half-day Zodiac trip down the Río Serrano; see "Getting There & Away" under "Parque Nacional Torres del Paine," below.) **Aventour,** Av. Manuel Bulnes 689 (© **61/410253;** www.aventouraventuras.com), works mainly out of Parque Nacional Bernardo O'Higgins.

WHERE TO STAY

Many homes large enough to rent out a few rooms have hung an HOSPEDAJE sign above their door—these simple, inexpensive accommodations can be found everywhere, and quality is about the same. The high season in Puerto Natales runs from October to April, and the price range shown reflects this. For all hotels, parking is either free, or street parking is plentiful.

For inexpensive lodging, try **Casa Cecilia** ⓐ at Tomás Roger 60 (©/fax **61/411797;** redcecilia@entelchile.net), which has a kitchen, clean rooms, a tour desk, and equipment rental; a double room costs $20 to $32, less for a shared bathroom. Another good, popular *hostal* is **Concepto Indigo** at Ladrilleros 105 (© **61/413609;** www.conceptoindigo), which has simple rooms that are noteworthy only for their incredible view. A double here costs $40.

Hostal Los Pinos *(Value)*   The Hostal Los Pinos is a great value for the price. It's tucked behind two cypress trees, across from the local high school and 3 blocks from the plaza. The friendly owners make you feel at home, especially while relaxing in the ample living area. Oriental rug runners lead to squeaky clean rooms with enough details here and there that bring them a step above most moderate accommodations found in town. The bathrooms aren't huge, but they'll do. The new mattresses and TVs, added in 2002, round out this excellent value.

Philippi 449, Puerto Natales. © 61/411735. Fax 61/411326. 12 units. $32 double. Rates include continental breakfast. No credit cards. **Amenities:** Lounge. *In room:* TV.

Hotel CostAustralis ⓐ   This hard-to-miss, sunflower-yellow hotel on the coast offers the highest caliber lodging in Puerto Natales. Floor-to-ceiling windows face out onto the sound, which means that whether you're in the bar, the restaurant, or the lounge, you always have sweeping views and a splendid evening sunset. The CostAustralis is the town's largest hotel, but it retains a certain coziness with its grasscloth wallpaper offset by wooden trim and ceilings, stiff potted palms, and soft light. Unfortunately, the coziness translates to also being able to hear your neighbor's plumbing upstairs, so try to request a top-floor room. Spacious doubles come with a sea view or a truly depressing view of the buildings in the back; all feature glossy wood paneling and attractive furnishings. The hotel has two restaurants, one for breakfast, and a semiformal dining area for dinner (see "Where to Dine," below) and is popular with European tour groups.

Pedro Montt 262, Puerto Natales. © 61/412000. Fax 61/411881. www.australis.com. 50 units. $75–$181 double. Rates include buffet breakfast. AE, DC, MC, V. **Amenities:** 2 restaurants; bar; room service; laundry service. *In room:* TV.

WHERE TO DINE

Concepto Indigo *(Finds)* VEGETARIAN   This cozy and happening eatery is one of the few in town with a water view. The menu here is on the vegetarian side; the only meat item is a ham sandwich. The menu is simple, with grilled or sautéed salmon, scallops, king crab, pastas, and spongy pizzas. The sandwiches are served on wagon-wheel bread, and are hefty enough for a dinner. The bar is a good place for a late evening drink, and there's a computer with Internet access in the adjoining lounge.

Ladrilleros 105. Ⓒ 61/413609. Main courses $3.50–$7. AE, DC, MC, V. Daily 11am–11pm; bar closes at 1am. Closed May–Aug.

El Living ★★ *Value* CAFE/VEGETARIAN If you're looking for a friendly, comfortable place to kick back and spend the evening, then look no further. At El Living, recently opened by a British expatriate couple, you can lounge on a comfortable sofa with a pisco sour or have an excellent vegetarian dinner at one of their handmade wooden dining tables. The menu is simple and inexpensive but fresh and delicious. The Sweet and Sour Red Salad is a perfect mix of beets, red cabbage, kidney beans, and onion; the veggie burger is delicious and served on a whole-wheat baguette. This is the only place in Chile that serves a peanut-butter-and-jelly sandwich. There's also French toast with fried bananas, a divine toasted banana sandwich, and a variety of cakes baked daily. A full bar and wine list round out this excellent place.

Arturo Prat 156. Ⓒ 61/411140. Main courses $2.50–$3.75. No credit cards. Daily 11am—11pm.

Hotel CostAustralis ★★ *Moments* INTERNATIONAL This is as close as you'll get to fine dining in Puerto Natales. If you're looking for tasty cuisine and a wonderful ambience, look no further. The sunset views from the picture windows in combination with your candlelit table make for a sumptuous environment. The new chef is very talented and tries hard to maintain the regional angle in the menu. A good example is the lamb and potato stew typical of this region but not easy to find in restaurants. Salmon and conger eel are usually the fresh catches of the day. Other specialties include wild hare marinated in red wine and herbs, and pork loin with mustard and whiskey. Top off your dinner with the apricots and peaches stewed in syrup and served with cream of wheat, or minty pears poached in wine with chocolate ice cream.

Pedro Montt 262. Ⓒ 61/412000. Main courses $8–$13. AE, DC, MC, V. Daily noon–3pm and 7:30–11pm.

PARQUE NACIONAL TORRES DEL PAINE ★★★

This is Chile's prized jewel, a national park so magnificent that few in the world can claim a rank in its class. The park is made of granite peaks and towers that soar from sea level to upward of 2,800m (9,184 ft.); golden pampas and steppes that are home to guanacos and more than 100 species of colorful birds, such as parakeets and flamingos; electric-blue icebergs that cleave from glaciers descending from the Southern Ice Field; and thick, virgin beech forest. The park is not something you visit; it is something you experience.

Although it sits next to the Andes, **Parque Nacional Torres del Paine** is a separate geologic formation created roughly 3 million years ago when bubbling magma pushed its way up, taking a thick sedimentary layer with it. Glaciation and severe climate weathered away the softer rock, leaving the spectacular Paine Massif whose prominent features are the *Cuernos* (which means "horns") and the one-of-a-kind Torres—three salmon-colored, spherical granite towers. *Paine* is the Tehuelche Indian word for "blue," and it brings to mind the varying shades found in the lakes that surround this massif—among them the milky, turquoise waters of lakes Nordenskjold and Pehoe.

This park is a backpacker's dream, but just as many visitors find pleasure staying in lodges here and taking day hikes and horseback rides—even those with a short amount of time here are blown away by a 1-day visit.

WHEN TO GO & WHAT TO BRING

This is not the easiest of national parks to visit. The climate in the park can be abominable, with wind speeds that can peak at 161kmph (100 mph) and rain and snow even in the middle of summer. The period in which your chances are highest of avoiding wind and rain are early October to early November and mid-March to late April, but keep in mind that the only thing predictable here is the unpredictability of the weather. Spring is a beautiful time for budding flowers and birds; during the fall, the beech forests turn striking shades of crimson, orange, and yellow. The winter is very cold, with relatively few snowstorms and no wind—but short days. Summer is ironically the worst time to come, especially late December to mid-February, when the wind blows at full fury and crowds descend upon the park. When the wind blows it can make even a short walk a rather scary and often frustrating experience—just try to go with it.

Equip yourself with decent gear (especially hiking boots if you plan to do any trekking), weatherproof outerwear, and warm layers, even in the summer. The ozone problem is acute here, so you'll need sunscreen, sunglasses, and probably a hat.

GETTING THERE & AWAY

Many travelers are unaware of the enormous amount of time it takes to get to Torres del Paine. There are no direct transportation services from the airport in Punta Arenas to the park, except with package tours and hotels that have their own vehicles. If you're relying on bus transportation (as most do), it's only logical that you will need to spend the night in Punta Arenas or Puerto Natales.

BY BUS   Several companies offer daily service from October to April. During the low season, only two companies, Bus Sur and JB, offer service to the park. Buses to Torres del Paine enter through the Laguna Amarga ranger station, stop at the Pudeto catamaran dock, and terminate at the park administration center. If you're going directly to the Torres trail head at Hostería Las Torres, minivan transfers waiting at the Laguna Amarga station charge $3 one-way. The return times given below are when the bus leaves from the park administration center; the bus will pass through the Laguna Amarga station about 45 minutes later.

JB at Arturo Prat 258 (© **61/412824**) leaves at 7, 8am, and 2:30pm and returns at 1, 2:30, and 6:30pm; **Fortaleza Aventura** at Arturo Prat 234 (© **61/410595**) leaves at 7am and 2pm, returning at 2 and 6pm; **Buses Paori** at Eberhard 577 (© **61/411229**) leaves at 7:30am, returning at 2pm; **Turismo María José** at Av. Manuel Bulnes 386 (© **61/414312**) leaves at 7:30am, returning at 2pm; and **Andescape** at Eberhard 599 (© **61/412592**) leaves at 7am, returning at 12:15pm. The cost is about $8 one-way.

BY CAR   Heading north on Pedro Montt out of town, follow the dirt road for 51km (32 miles) until you reach Cerro Castillo. From here, the road turns left and heads 47km (29 miles) toward the park. (Keep your eyes open for another left turn that is signed TORRES DEL PAINE.) You'll come to a fork in the road; one road leads to the Lago Sarmiento Conaf station, another to the Laguna Amarga station.

CROSSING LAGO PEHOE BY CATAMARAN   At some point, you'll likely cross Lago Pehoe on a catamaran, either at the beginning or end of your trip. Several crossings per day are timed to meet all buses; the cost is an expensive $14 one-way. Times are posted outside the Refugio Pehoe, and every *refugio* in the park has a time schedule.

GETTING TO THE PARK BY BOAT   Few are aware that they can arrive by a Zodiac-catamaran combination that takes visitors from Puerto Natales through the Ultima Esperanza Sound and up the Río Serrano, or vice versa. The Zodiac takes visitors past the glaciers Tyndall and Geike, and eventually to the Serrano Glacier. Here, you disembark for a walk up to the ice, then board another boat for a 3½-hour ride to Puerto Natales. The trip runs about $60 to $90 per person, depending on the season. Two companies also offer a 2-night, 3-day kayak descent down the Río Serrano, meeting the boat for the ride to Puerto Natales. For address and telephone numbers, see "Tour Operators & Adventure Travel Outfitters," above. **Onas** is the oldest-running company with Zodiac service, leaving at 8:30am from the administration office. (They'll pick you up from longer distances for an extra charge.) Two companies, **Aventour** and **21 de Mayo,** also take guests down the Río Serrano. Aventour includes an additional stop at its lodge and offers round-trips up and down the river that start from its lodge near the Serrano Glacier. The Zodiacs are not roofed.

VISITOR INFORMATION   The park's administration and visitor center can be reached at ⓒ 61/691931.

WHERE TO STAY & DINE IN TORRES DEL PAINE
Hotels & *Hosterías*
Hostería Lago Grey   This spruce little white *hostería* is tucked within a beech forest, looking out onto the beach at Lago Grey and the astounding blue icebergs that drift to its shore. It's well on the other side of the park, but they have a transfer van and guides for excursions to all reaches of the park. The 20 rooms are spread out from the main common area, with a restaurant and lounge area. The rooms are comfortable, but the walls are a tad thin. Also, when the wind whips up, this side of the park is colder, but the location is more tranquil than that of Las Torres, and there are plenty of trails that branch out from here, including the stroll along the beach out to the Pingo Valley and the strenuous hike up to Mirador Ferrier. The transfer van will pick you up from anywhere in the park.

Office in Punta Arenas, Lautaro Navarro 1061. ⓒ 61/410172. 20 units. Oct–Apr $200 double; May–Sept $85 double. Rates include buffet breakfast. AE, DC, MC, V. **Amenities:** Restaurant; lounge.

Hostería Las Torres   This *hostería* sits at the trail head to the Torres on an estancia that still operates as a working cattle ranch. The complex includes a ranch-style hotel, a large campground, and a hostel, meaning there's a fair amount of traffic coming in and out daily. The main building has a restaurant, a bar, and half the guest rooms; the other half of the rooms are located in a brand-new separate unit, but the newer rooms are identical to the old. The superior rooms are slightly larger than the standard, and they come with central heating; other than this, the difference is slight. The rooms are not especially noteworthy, but they are comfortable, and there's a relaxing lounge with couches and game tables for guests only. The entire building is made of terra-cotta–colored logs, situated on an idyllic grassy expanse that is backed by the Paine Massif. The *hostería* offers guided excursions and horseback rides. The *hostería's* restaurant deserves special note for its delicious evening buffet dinner for $24.

Office in Punta Arenas, Magallanes 960. ⓒ/fax 61/226054. 20 units. $195 double superior; $135 standard. Rates include buffet breakfast. AE, DC, MC, V. **Amenities:** Restaurant; lounge; tour desk; room service; laundry service.

Hotel Explora Salto Chico ✸✸✸ *(Moments*   Few hotels in Chile have garnered as much fame as the Hotel Explora, and deservedly so. The Explora's location is simply stunning, looking out over the blue waters of Lago Pehoe and directly at the dramatic Cuernos formation. The hotel was designed by several renowned Chilean architects to take full advantage of its location, with a band of picture

> **Tips** **Advance Planning**
>
> It's not easy to arrange for your own accommodations before arriving here; phones sometimes are inoperable, there's no e-mail, and the wind wreaks havoc with the postman. If you are trying to set up your trip in advance, e-mail or call Alfonso Lopez Rosas, manager of the largest tour operator in the park. Through his office in Puerto Natales, he'll secure whatever you need, contact the hotels, and even arrange for your transportation. Path@ gone Travel is at Ebarhard 595, Puerto Natales (© **61/413291**; pathgone@ entelchile.net). Alfonso can sometimes negotiate lower hotel rates at the park's *hosterías* as well as arrange for everything from camping equipment to horseback riding trips.

windows that wrap around the full front of the building and large windows in each room. Explora's style is relaxed elegance, with softly curving, blonde-wood interiors, soft lighting, chintz sofas that line the drawn-out lounge, and several cozy nooks for curling up fireside. The rooms are superb, with checkered linens, handsome slate-tiled bathrooms, powerful showers, and warming racks for drying gear. Explora operates as a full-service lodge with packages that include direct airport transfers, meals, open bar, and excursions. Every evening, guides meet with guests to discuss the following day's excursions, which range from easy to difficult. The set menu is limited to two choices, generally a meat dish and a vegetarian dish, and it must be said that the food quality is often uneven—never bad, but not as outstanding as you would expect from a hotel of this caliber. Americans make up a full 50% of the guests, who typically leave thrilled with their visit.

In Santiago, Américo Vespucio Sur 80, Piso 5. © **22/066060**. Fax 2/228-4655. www.explora-chile.com. 31 units. Packages per person, double occupancy: 3 nights/2 days $1,234; 4 nights/3 days $1,624; 7 nights/6 days $2,323. Rates include all meals. AE, DC, MC, V. **Amenities:** Restaurant; bar; lounge; large indoor pool; outdoor Jacuzzi; sauna; massage.

Refugios & Albergues

These cabinlike lodging units can be found at the base of trails or in the backcountry. They are moderately priced options for those who are not interested in pitching a tent, and although most have bedding or sleeping bags for rent, your best bet is to bring your own. All come with hot showers, a cafe, and a common area for hiding out from bad weather. Simple meals and sandwiches are sold, or you can bring your own food and cook in their kitchens. Each *refugio* has rooms with two to six bunks, which you'll have to share with strangers when they're full. Per-person rates average $16. During the high season, you'll need to book a bed at least 2 days in advance, but busier *refugios* can book up 4 to 5 days ahead. All agencies in Puerto Natales take reservations, or you can call or e-mail (see below). There is a *refugio* near the park administration center, but you must sleep on the floor on the second floor. This *refugio* is on a first-come, first-served basis. Every travel and tour agency in Puerto Natales books *refugio* reservations. Except for Pehoe, these *refugios* are open from September to April, but they'll arrange to open for a large group from May to August.

The following *refugios* can be reserved by calling or faxing © **61/226054**. These three are open from September to April; call if you have a group outside the season.

- **Refugio Chileno:** Probably the least-frequented *refugio* for its position halfway up to the Towers. (Most do the trail as a day hike.) Still, it's nicer to stay in this pretty valley than down below.

- **Albergue Las Torres:** This albergue sits near the Hostería Las Torres, with a full-service restaurant. Horseback rides can be taken from here.
- **Refugio Los Cuernos:** The park's nicest *refugio*, at the base of the Cuernos.

The following cabinlike *refugios* can be reserved by faxing **61/412592.** Pehoe is open year-round, Grey and Dickson September to April.

- **Refugio Grey:** Tucked in a forest on the shore of Lago Grey, this *refugio* is a 10-minute walk to the lookout point for the glacier.
- **Refugio Dickson:** Another less-frequented *refugio* (it's on the other side of the park) that boasts a fantastic location with a glacier view.
- **Refugio Pehoe:** This *refugio* is the hub for several of the trail heads as well as the docking site for the catamaran. It is, therefore, constantly busy, and service is notoriously bad here.

CAMPING IN TORRES DEL PAINE

Torres del Paine has a well-designed campground system with free and concession-run sites. All *refugios* have a campground, and all concession sites charge $4 per person, which includes showers, water, and bathrooms. Free campgrounds are run by Conaf, and they can get a little dingy, with deplorable outhouses. Beginning in March, mice become a problem for campers, so always leave food well stored or hanging from a tree branch. The JLM hiking map (available at every bookstore, kiosk, and travel agency and at the park entrance) denotes which campgrounds are free and which cost a fee. Camping Los Perros has a few rooms for let, though it is not a full-service *refugio*.

TRAILS IN TORRES DEL PAINE

There are a multitude of ways to hike or backpack in Torres del Paine. All are determined by how much time you have here and what kind of walking you're up for. You'll want to pick up one of JLM's Torres del Paine maps (sold everywhere) to plan your itinerary. Walking times shown below are average. The minimum amount of days shown means walking 4 to 8 hours a day, and if you want to take it easy, plan for extra days and maybe another day or two for bad weather.

LONG-HAUL OVERNIGHT HIKES

There are essentially two long-haul overnight hikes, the "W" and the **Circuit.** The "W" is so called because hikers are taken to the park's major geological features along a trail that forms a **W.** It's the preferred multiday hike for its relative short hauls and time frame that requires 4 to 5 days, and hikers can sleep at the various *refugios* along the way. Most hikers begin at Hostería Las Torres; if you begin here, you'll end the trip with catamaran across Lago Pehoe to an awaiting bus back to Puerto Natales.

The Circuit is a spectacular, long-haul backpacking trip that takes hikers around the back side of the Paine Massif. It can be done in two ways: with the "W" included or without. Including the "W," you'll need 8 to 11 days; without it, from 5 to 7 days. The Circuit involves several difficult hikes up and down steep, rough terrain and over fallen tree trunks. But you'll be rewarded for your effort with dazzling views of terrain that varies from grassy meadows and winding rivers to virgin beech forest, snowcapped peaks, and the awe-inspiring view of Glacier Grey seen from atop the John Garner Pass. Always do this trail counterclockwise for easier ascents and with the scenery before you.

DAY HIKES & TRIPS

Las Torres (The Towers) is the classic hike to the granite formations that give the park its name. The 6-hour, moderate-to-difficult hike leaves from the Hostería

Las Torres. The **Valle Francés (French Valley)** trail takes hikers into a granite amphitheater and past Paine Grande mountain and its hanging glacier. The trail is moderate to difficult and can be reached from Refugio Los Cuernos, Refugio Pehoe or, in a push, by including a round-trip catamaran trip across Lago Pehoe. The trail to the face of **Glaciar Grey** is the same: the trail begins at Refugio Pehoe and can be completed, in a push, in 1 day by crossing the lake by catamaran.

The easiest walk in the park is also one of the most dramatic for the gigantic blue icebergs that rest along the shore of **Lago Grey.**

Another easy day hike, **Lago Nordenskjold,** ends at a lookout point with dramatic views of the French Valley and the Cuernos, looking over Lago Nordenskjold. The trail begins near the Pudeto catamaran dock, at the Salto Grande waterfall.

OTHER OUTDOOR ACTIVITIES IN THE PARK

A horseback ride in Torres del Paine can be one of the most enjoyable ways to see the park, especially from the Serrano pampa for big, bold views of the Paine Massif. Contact **Path@gone Travel** in Puerto Natales, Eberhard 595 (© 61/ 413291; pathgone@entelchile.net). They can arrange a wide variety of trips across the Serrano pampa to Lago Grey and excursions around the Laguna Amarga and Laguna Azul sectors. They also offer multiple-day trips that include camping and stays in *refugios*. The cost depends on the number of riders (10 maximum), but averages $28 to $50 per person for 1- to 3-hour rides. Most trips require prior experience. **Hostería Las Torres** has horseback riding to Refugios Chileno and Los Cuernos; its Punta Arenas office is at Magallanes 960 (©/fax **61/226054**). The full-day trips cost $75 per person, and they leave from the hotel.

There is nothing as thrilling as a walk across Glacier Grey. Trips begin from the Refugio Grey at 9am and return at 5pm, with an hour walk to the entrance site and then back to the *refugio*. Guests are provided with full equipment, including crampons, ice axes, ropes, and harnesses, and are given basic ice-climbing instructions. Visitors who have taken this hike have consistently given rave reviews for the chance to peer into deep blue crevasses and explore the glacier's otherworldly contours up close. **Bigfoot Expeditions** runs this concession, and reservations are recommended, although there is often space for walk-ins. You need to spend the previous night at the Refugio Grey or in its campsite; the office in Puerto Natales is at Blanco Encalada 226 (© **61/414611;** www.bigfootpatagonia.com). The cost is $60 per person, which includes a box lunch; credit cards are accepted at their concession site at Refugio Grey.

8

Ecuador

by Haas Mroue

When my Ecuadorian friends heard that I was writing about Ecuador, they all had the same reaction: They begged me to tell you that Ecuador is so much more than the Galápagos Islands. I happen to agree with them. Yes, it's true that the opportunity to get up close to wild animals in the Galápagos is a once-in-a-lifetime experience. But it would be a real pity to fly all the way to Ecuador and miss out on what the rest of the country has to offer.

Quito is one of the oldest cities in the Americas. When you walk along the cobblestone streets and visit 16th-century churches, you really feel as though you have taken a trip back in time. Within a couple of hours of Quito, you can climb to the top of the highest active volcano in the world or shop for handicrafts in one of the largest and most colorful markets in South America.

Guayaquil may be South America's most up-and-coming city, a booming metropolis (it's Ecuador's largest city) that is making tremendous changes to its old image of an uninteresting, even drab destination—and it's been hugely successful. The new Malecón 2000 is a beautiful stretch of riverfront boardwalk complete with great galleries, new museums, and hip restaurants.

Then there's the jungle. Hop on a quick flight from Quito and you'll find yourself in one of the most biologically diverse tropical rainforests in the world. Early in the morning, you can watch parrots and macaws gathering for breakfast. As you take canoe trips down the river, you might spot an anaconda curled up on the rocky shores, waiting patiently for its prey, or perhaps you'll catch a glimpse of playful dolphins frolicking in the river. If you're lucky, you may hear a jaguar howling in the night. You can also visit local villages in the jungle, where the people live very much the same way their ancestors did hundreds of years ago.

Cuenca is a must for history (and culinary) buffs. Before the Spanish arrived, this was the second-most important city in the Inca empire. Many of the city's majestic churches were built over the foundations of Inca palaces. But even before the Incas arrived, the area was inhabited by the sophisticated Cañaris culture. Just outside the city, you can visit Ingapirca, an important archaeological site that was sacred for both the Cañaris and the Incas. In the city itself, there are several excellent restaurants serving Ecuadorian specialties not found elsewhere in the country.

Ecuador is small enough that if you have 2 weeks, you can see the best of everything. If you only have time to visit the Galápagos, you certainly won't be disappointed. But if you travel through the mainland, you will have the chance to discover the diverse wonders of this tiny country.

1 The Regions in Brief

The Republic of Ecuador sits near the northwestern corner of South America. It's bordered by Colombia to the north, Peru to the south and east, and the Pacific Ocean to the west. The Galápagos Islands, which straddle the equator, are located about 966km (600 miles) to the west in the Pacific Ocean. The country covers an area of 272,046 sq. km (105,037 sq. miles), making it roughly the same size as Colorado.

If you want to visit the Galápagos, it's tough to see the rest of Ecuador in the span of 1 week. You have two options: You can spend your whole trip in the Galápagos on a 7-day tour, or you can see the highlights of the Galápagos on a 3- or 5-day tour and spend the rest of your time visiting the mainland. Ideally, I would recommend spending as much time in the Galápagos as you can. You can see all the Quito highlights in 1 day and spend an additional day shopping in Otavalo and Cotacachi. If you have 2 weeks, you can also spend several days on a jungle tour. Instead of hanging loose in Quito and Otavalo, physically adventurous travelers should consider climbing one of Ecuador's volcanoes; the trek to the top of Cotopaxi is one of the most popular excursions. Archaeology buffs should focus on Cuenca and Ingapirca and those interested in a more urban experience should consider spending at least a couple of days in Guayaquil.

QUITO ⓡ   Situated at more than 2,700m (9,000 ft.), Quito is the second-highest capital city in the world (after La Paz, Bolivia). It may be the capital of Ecuador, but it's only the second-most populous city in the country, after Guayaquil. The city is a major transportation hub, so most visitors begin and end their trips to Ecuador here. Fortunately, no one seems to mind—Quito is one of the most charming cities in South America. Its Old Town, with its wonderfully preserved colonial-style buildings, was declared a Cultural Patrimony of Mankind by UNESCO. The New Town is a lively cosmopolitan area, with all the modern amenities you would expect to find in a world-class destination.

Quito is ideally situated. A quick 2-hour journey north will take you to **Imbabura Province,** where you can explore the colorful markets in Otavalo. The crater lakes and volcanoes make this area a nature lover's paradise. Drive 2 hours to the east, and you will find yourself in a **cloud forest,** which is great for hiking and bird-watching. **Cotopaxi National Park** is a little more than an hour south of Quito; here, active travelers can climb to the summit of the highest active volcano in the world.

THE CENTRAL HIGHLANDS ⓡ   The Central Highlands cover the area just south of Quito. Baños and Riobamba are the main attractions in this part of the country. Travelers head to Baños mainly to relax and enjoy its natural resources. The city, which is nestled at the bottom of the active Tungurahua Volcano, offers great hiking and biking opportunities. You can also take a soothing soak in one of the hot springs, go white-water rafting in the nearby rivers, or arrange a trip to some of Ecuador's most interesting rainforests (3–8 hr. away). Riobamba is more of an industrial city. There's not much to do here besides catching the tourist train, which involves a spectacular journey along the switchbacks known as the **Nariz del Diablo (Devil's Nose).**

THE SOUTHERN HIGHLANDS ⓡⓡ   **Cuenca** is the largest and most interesting city in the Southern Highlands. Like Quito, it was declared a Cultural Patrimony of Mankind by UNESCO. Cuenca was the second-most important city in the Inca empire (after Cusco). Nearby, you can explore **Ingapirca,** an archaeological site with both Inca and pre-Inca ruins. Cajas National Park is located only an hour outside of the city.

GUAYAQUIL & THE COAST   Guayaquil is Ecuador's largest city. Chiefly a port and industrial city, the city is reinventing itself at a dizzying pace. Several new museums and parks and a dozen new restaurants were scheduled to open in 2004. The airport is being renovated; crime is down and tourism is up. **Machalilla National Park,** on the central part of the coast, is known as the "Poor Person's Galápagos." The sleepy town of Puerto López is a gateway to **Isla de la Plata,** which is home to a rich variety of wildlife (similar to what you'd find in the Galápagos).

EL ORIENTE   The eastern region of Ecuador, known as El Oriente, is home to the Amazon basin and jungle area of the country. For the most part, the indigenous people in this region escaped domination by both the Incas and the Spanish, so they have been able to hold on to their ancient rituals and traditions. Most visitors explore this area by staying at a jungle lodge, some of which are surprisingly comfortable. English-speaking guides will take you to local villages, as well as show you the incredible diversity of wildlife here.

THE GALAPAGOS ISLANDS 𝒜𝒜𝒜   The Galápagos Islands, located about 966km (600 miles) off the coast of Ecuador, are one of nature's most unique outdoor laboratories. The unusual wildlife here helped Charles Darwin formulate his "survival of the fittest" theory. Fortunately for modern-day visitors, not much has changed since Darwin's time, and the islands still offer visitors the chance to get up close and personal with a wide variety of endemic and local species, including giant tortoises, marine iguanas, penguins, sea lions, albatrosses, boobies, and flightless cormorants. The best way to explore the area is on a tour ship. You should note, however, that this is not your typical cruise destination—trips here involve some seriously strenuous activity. A more relaxing option would be to base yourself at a resort in Santa Cruz (the most populated island in the Galápagos) and take select day-trips to the islands of your choice.

2 Planning Your Trip to Ecuador

VISITOR INFORMATION
The Ecuadorian Ministry of Tourism has very limited resources. There are virtually no government-sponsored tourist offices outside of Ecuador. However, the Ecuadorian embassy in Washington, D.C., has an excellent website at **www. ecuador.org**. For general travel information about Ecuador, www.ecuador explorer.com, www.ecuaworld, and www.thebestofecuador.com provide the best information. If you're looking for last-minute deals, log onto **www.toppsa.com**.

For specific travel-related information, your best bet is to contact travel agencies that specialize in trips to Ecuador. Here is a list of some of the best:

- **Adventure Associates,** 13150 Coit Rd., Dallas, TX 75240 (© **800/527-2500;** info@adventure-associates.com). This is the North American representative for Metropolitan Touring, one of the oldest and best established full-service travel agencies in Ecuador.
- **Condor Journeys and Adventures,** 1 Valley Rise, Mill Bank, Sowerby Bridge HX6 3EG, U.K. (© **01422/822-068;** www.condorjourneysadventures.com). This British company offers tour packages and active vacations throughout South America.

Ecuador

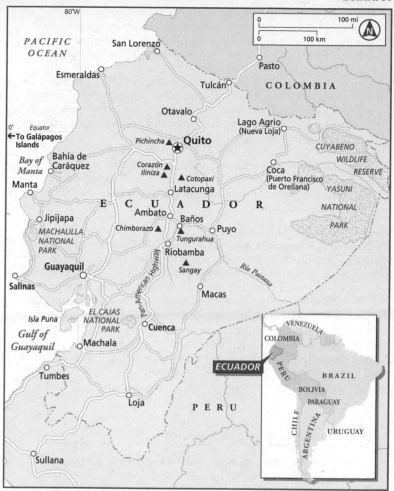

- **Bahía Dolphin Tours,** Calle Bolívar 10004, Manabi, Ecuador. ℂ **09/ 9754-773**; www.bahiadolphin.com). Patricio Tamariz, the owner of this excellent agency, used to be the manager of tourism for the coastal region of Ecuador. He knows the country like the back of his hand and is especially knowledgeable about ecoadventure vacations.
- **Latin American Expeditions** ℱ, 6251 SW 57th St., South Miami, FL 33143 (ℂ **888/368-9929;** www.canodros.com). This company is the North American representative for Canodros and Asiri. (Canodros owns and operates the cruise ship *Galapagos Explorer II,* as well as the high-end jungle lodge, Kapawi. Asiri is the best-run travel agency in Ecuador.) The staff can arrange tailor-made trips throughout the country.
- **Latin American Reservations Center** ℱ, PO Box 1435, Dundee, FL 33838 (ℂ **800/327-3573;** www.larc1.com). If you're traveling from the U.S. to Ecuador, this should be your first phone call. Judy Martin who runs

this excellent operation has the best deals with many of the hotels we recommend and knows firsthand some of the best guides in the country.

- **Naturetrek,** Cheriton Mill, Cheriton, Alresford, Hampshire S024 0NG, U.K. (© **01962/733-051;** www.naturetrek.co.uk). This company specializes in bird-watching trips to Ecuador.

- **Quasar Náutica,** 7855 NW 12th St., Miami, FL 33126 (© **800/247-2925;** www.quasarnautica.com). This is one of the most high-end Ecuadorian travel agencies. Their boats are considered some of the best in the Galápagos. Their North American representatives can arrange cruise packages as well as tours throughout the mainland.

- **Zenith Ecuador Travel** ☎, Juan León Mera 453 and Roca #202, Quito (© **593-2/2529-993;** www.zenithecuador.com). This excellent Quito-based agency can arrange for some of the least expensive Galápagos cruises and land tours in Ecuador. They are also the only travel agency to offer all-gay cruises in the Galápagos.

ENTRY REQUIREMENTS

A valid passport is required to enter and depart Ecuador. Visas are not required if you're a citizen of the United States, the United Kingdom, Canada, Australia, New Zealand, South Africa, France, Germany, or Switzerland. Upon entry, you will automatically be granted permission to enter for 90 days. Technically, to enter the country you need a passport that is valid for more than 6 months, a return ticket, and proof of how you plan to support yourself while you're in the country, but I've never seen a Customs official ask for the last two requirements. If you plan on spending more than 90 days here, you will need to apply for a visa at your local embassy. Requirements include a passport valid for more than 6 months, a police certificate with criminal record from the state or province in which you currently live, a medical certificate, a return ticket, and two photographs.

Telephone Dialing Info at a Glance

- **To place a call from your home country to Ecuador,** dial the international access code (011 in the U.S. and Canada, 0011 in Australia, 0170 in New Zealand, 00 in the U.K.), plus the country code (593), plus the Ecuadorian area code minus the 0 (for example, Quito 2, Cuenca 7, Guayaquil 4, the Galápagos 5, Baños 3, Otavalo 6), followed by the number. For example, a call from the U.S. to Quito would be 011+593+2+0000+000.

- **To place a call within Ecuador,** you must use area codes if you're calling from one province to another. Note that for all calls within the country, area codes are preceded by a 0 (for example, Quito 02, Cuenca 07, Guayaquil 04, the Galápagos 05, Baños 03, Otavalo 06).

- **To place a direct international call from Ecuador,** dial the international access code (001), plus the country code of the place you are dialing, plus the area code and the local number.

- **To reach an international operator,** dial © 116. Major long distance company access codes are as follows: **AT&T** © 1800/225-528; **Bell Canada** © 999-175; **British Telecom** © 999-178; **MCI** © 999-170; **Sprint** © 999-171.

ECUADORIAN EMBASSY LOCATIONS

In the U.S.: 2535 15th St. NW, Washington, DC 20009 (© **202/234-7200;** fax 202/667-3482; www.ecuador.org)

In Canada: 50 O'Connor St., Suite 113, Ottawa, ON K1P 6L2 (© **613/563-8206;** fax 613/235-5776; www.ncf.carleton.ca/ecuador)

In the U.K.: 3 Hans Crescent, Knightsbridge, London, SW1X OLS (© **020/7584-8084;** fax 020/7823-9701)

In Australia: 11 London Circuit, first floor, Canberra ACT 2601 (© **628/11009**)

CUSTOMS

Visitors to Ecuador are legally permitted to bring in up to $1,250 worth of items for personal use, including cameras, portable typewriters, video cameras and accessories, tape recorders, personal computers, and CD players. You can also bring in up to 2 liters of alcoholic beverages and 200 cigarettes (one carton).

MONEY

As of September 2000, the official unit of currency in Ecuador is the **U.S. dollar** (US$). You can use American or Ecuadorian coins, both of which come in denominations of 1¢, 5¢, 10¢, 25¢, and 50¢. Otherwise, all the currency is in the paper form of American dollars, in denominations of 1, 5, 10, 20, 50, and 100. It's very hard to make change, especially for any bill over $5. If you are retrieving money from an ATM, be sure to request a denomination ending in 1 or 5 (most ATMs will dispense money in multiples of $1) so that you won't have to worry about breaking a large bill. If you are stuck with big bills, try to use them in restaurants to make change.

Here's a general idea of what things cost in Quito: a taxi within the center of town, $2; a double room at a budget hotel with private bathroom, $20 to $30; a double room at a moderate hotel with private bathroom, $40 to $65; a double room at an expensive hotel, $100 to $160; a small bottle of water, 25¢; a 36-exposure roll of film, $4; lunch at local restaurant, $2 to $5; and a three-course dinner for one, $9 to $14.

ATMs   ATMs are ubiquitous in Ecuador. You'll even find them in remote areas such as the Galápagos. Some of the major banks include **Banco de Guayaquil** and **Banco del Pacífico.** Most ATMs accept cards from the **Cirrus** network (© **800/424-7787**), but they can't deal with PINs that are more than four digits. Before you go to Ecuador, make sure that your PIN fits the bill. *Tip:* If you're unable to use ATMs for any reason, you can get a cash advance from inside the bank. To do this, you must provide the bank with a photocopy of your passport.

TRAVELER'S CHECKS   You can't change American Express traveler's checks at the American Express offices in Ecuador. (Yes, I know that sounds strange, but it's true.) These offices only allow you to make a cash advance on your Amex card. If you're traveling with traveler's checks, your best bet is to exchange them at a *casa de cambio* (money-exchange house) or a bank. Most upscale hotels and restaurants will accept traveler's checks. For lost American Express traveler's checks, you must call collect to the United States at © **801/964-6665.**

CREDIT CARDS   MasterCard and Visa are accepted most everywhere. American Express and Diners Club are less common, but still widely accepted. To report lost or stolen credit cards, you must call collect to the United States. For **MasterCard,** call © 314/542-7111; for **Visa,** © 410/581-9994; and for **American Express,** © 910/333-3211.

WHEN TO GO

PEAK SEASON & CLIMATE   The peak seasons for travelers in Ecuador last from mid-June to early September and from late December through early January, because most American and European visitors have vacation time during these months. Cruises in the Galápagos will be booked solid during these times of year. But since Ecuador is hardly Disney World, you'll always be able to find a room (or a berth on a ship), and the country never feels overcrowded. I find that Ecuador is great throughout the year, so whenever you visit, you won't be disappointed.

There are four distinct geographical zones in Ecuador that are all subject to their own weather patterns. In the Galápagos, from June through September, the air and water are chilly and the winds can be a bit rough. From October through May, the air and water temperatures are warmer, but you can expect periodic light rain almost daily. On the coast, the rainy season lasts from December through May; this season is marked by hot weather and humidity. The cooler air temperature from June through September attracts whales and dolphins to the waters off the coast. In Quito and the highlands, the weather is coolest from June through September (the dry season), but it's only a few degrees colder than the rest of the year. Keep in mind that although Quito is practically on the equator, the temperature can get quite cool because it's at such a high altitude (more than 2,700m/9,000 ft. above sea level); the city has an average high of 67°F (19°C) and an average low of 50°F (10°C). In the jungle area, it rains year-round, but especially hard from December through April. The temperature in the jungle can reach 80°F to 90°F (27°C–32°C) during the day; it's a bit cooler at night.

PUBLIC HOLIDAYS   Official holidays in Ecuador include New Year's Day (Jan 1), Easter, Labor Day (May 1), National Day (Aug 10), Guayaquil Independence Day (Oct 9), All Souls' Day (Nov 2), Cuenca Independence Day (Nov 3), and Christmas (Dec 25). The country also closes down on some non-official holidays including Carnaval (Mon and Tues prior to Ash Wednesday), Battle of Pichincha (May 24), Christmas Eve (Dec 24), and New Year's Eve (Dec 31). Foundation of Quito (Dec 6) is observed as a holiday only in Quito.

HEALTH CONCERNS

COMMON AILMENTS   Travelers to Ecuador should be very careful about contracting **food-borne illnesses.** Always drink bottled water. Never drink beverages with ice unless you are sure that the water for the ice has been previously boiled. Be very careful about eating food purchased from street vendors. I recommend taking supplements such as super bromelain, which helps aid in the digestion of parasites; consult your doctor to find out whether this is a good option for you. If you do contract a case of diarrhea, rehydration supplements such as Tesalia (the Ecuadorian version of Gatorade) and Pedialyte are readily available.

If you plan on visiting the highlands of Ecuador—Quito, Otavalo, Baños, and Cuenca—you don't have to worry about **malaria.** There have been outbreaks of malaria in rural areas on the coast and in the jungle area. If you plan to travel to these areas, you will be at risk if you spend a significant amount of time here. To prevent malaria, the Centers for Disease Control and Prevention (CDC) recommends taking the drugs mefloquine, doxycycline, or Malarone; consult your doctor for more information. Also be sure to bring plenty of insect repellent.

Of concern in areas of high altitude is **altitude sickness.** Common symptoms include headaches, nausea, sleeplessness, and a tendency to tire easily. The most common remedies include taking it easy, abstaining from alcohol, and drinking lots of bottled water. To help alleviate these symptoms, you can also take the drug acetazolamide (Diamox); consult your doctor for more information.

The **sun** can also be very dangerous in Ecuador, especially at high altitudes. Be sure to bring plenty of high-powered sunblock and a wide-brimmed hat. It gets cold in Quito, but don't let this fool you into complacency—even when it's cold, the sun can inflict serious damage on your skin.

In general, the health care system in Ecuador is good enough to take care of mild illnesses. For a list of hospitals in Quito, see "Hospitals" in "Fast Facts: Ecuador," below.

VACCINATIONS   No inoculations or vaccines are required for visitors to Ecuador. Fortunately, since mosquitoes can't live in high altitudes, malaria is not a risk in Quito, Cuenca, Baños, the Galápagos, or Otavalo. But because there is a small risk of malaria for travelers who plan on spending time in the jungle area, the CDC recommends that travelers who plan on visiting these areas protect themselves by taking the drugs mefloquine, doxycycline, or Malarone. The CDC also recommends that visitors to Ecuador be vaccinated against hepatitis A.

GETTING THERE
BY PLANE

There are two international airports in Ecuador. All flights into Quito land at the **Aeropuerto Internacional Mariscal Sucre** (© 02/2430-555). Most international flights also touch down in Guayaquil's **Aeropuerto Internacional Simón Bolívar** (© 04/2282-100). If you plan to go to the Galápagos immediately after you arrive in Ecuador, it's best to fly into Guayaquil. All international passengers leaving by air from Ecuador must pay a $25 departure tax.

FROM NORTH AMERICA   **American Airlines** (© 800/433-7300; www. aa.com), **Continental Airlines** (© 800/231-0856; www.continental.com), and **LanChile/LanEcuador** (© 866/LANCHILE; www.lanchile.com) are the only airlines that offer direct service to Ecuador from North America. American has two flights daily leaving from Miami; Continental's flights depart from Houston and Newark. (The flight from Newark makes a stop in Bogotá along the way.) LanChile/LanEcuador offers direct service from JFK in New York to Guayaquil and direct service from Miami to Quito. **Copa Airlines** (© 800/359-2672; www.copaair.com) offers daily flights from both Los Angeles and Miami to Ecuador with a quick stop in Panama City. Presently, there are no direct flights from Canada to Ecuador, so Canadians will have to take a connecting flight via the United States.

FROM THE U.K.   There are no direct flights from the United Kingdom to Ecuador. British travelers can fly to the United States (Miami, Houston or New York), and then hook up with a direct flight (see "From North America," above). **KLM** (© 08705/074-074; www.klmuk.co.uk) offers service from many cities in England to both Guayaquil and Quito via Amsterdam and Bonaire. **Iberia** (© 0845/601-2854; www.iberia.com) offers the only non-stop flight from Europe (Madrid) to Quito; convenient connections are available from London Heathrow daily.

FROM AUSTRALIA & NEW ZEALAND   To get to Ecuador from Australia or New Zealand, you'll first have to fly to Los Angeles and then on to Miami or Houston, where you can connect with an American Airlines, Continental or LanChile/LanEcuador flight to Ecuador. See "From North America," above, for more information.

BY BUS

It is possible to travel by bus to Ecuador from Peru. (We don't recommend traveling from Colombia due to kidnapping incidents near the border.) From Peru, the most popular border crossing is from Tumbes to Huaquillas in Ecuador. As you exit Peru, you will need to disembark from the bus and walk across the border. Peruvian buses don't usually cross into Ecuador, so to continue your journey, you will need to catch an Ecuadorian bus. **Panamericana** (© 02/ 2570-425) and **Flota Imbabura** (© 02/2236-940) are two of the more reliable companies in Ecuador.

GETTING AROUND

Because Ecuador is one of the smallest countries in South America, traveling from one end of the country is not much of a challenge. The bus routes are comprehensive. However, the roads can be a bit rough, and the buses are often hot and crowded. If you're short on time, I really recommend flying, which is cheap and efficient. If you're traveling only a short distance, however, say from Quito to Otavalo (a little more than 2 hr.) or Riobamba (almost 4 hr.), the bus is your best bet.

BY PLANE   Tame (© 02/2909-900 or 02/2509-375 in Quito, or 04/2310-305 or 04/2560-778 in Guayaquil; www.tame.com.ec) is the national airline of Ecuador, managed by the Air Force. It's a tedious, aging airline plagued with delays and I highly recommend you fly either Icaro or Aerogal (see below) before resorting to Tame. That said, Tame has routes to almost every corner of the country, and airfares generally aren't expensive. (Expect to pay about $50–$60 for a one-way ticket.) The exceptions are flights to the Galápagos, which are relatively outrageously priced. During the low season—mid-September through May, not including December—a round-trip ticket costs $336. In the high season, expect to pay about $396. In Quito, Tame's offices are located at Av. Amazonas 1354, near the corner of Colón. In Guayaquil, the office is at Pedro Icaza 434 and General Córdova.

Two airlines have emerged to give Tame a run for its money. **Icaro** (© 800/ 883-567; www.icaro-air.com) flies from Quito to Guayaquil, Cuenca, Coca (in the Oriente), Manta, and Loja. They also fly from Guayaquil to Cuenca and Loja. **Aerogal,** short for Aerogalápagos (© 800/237-6425; aerogal@ andinanet.net), flies from Quito and Guayaquil to San Cristóbal airport in the Galápagos. The fare is identical to that of Tame's. But Aerogal offers much superior service and will expand its network in the coming months to include Cuenca and possibly Baltra in the Galápagos.

Neither Icaro nor Aerogal has a city ticket office. But you can buy tickets from their airport offices located across from the national terminal at the Quito airport. Tickets can also be bought at the airlines' ticket counters in Cuenca and Guayaquil and the other airports they serve. Fares on both airlines are generally equal to or just a few dollars less than Tame's.

BY BUS   In Ecuador, all roads lead to Quito. From Quito, you can find a bus to every corner of the country. But don't expect to get anywhere quickly. Locals never board buses at the actual bus terminals. Instead, buses leave the station empty, and then drive very slowly through the outskirts of town, picking up passengers along the way. This adds at least an hour onto every bus ride. Still, for relatively short distances, buses are your best option. The journeys between Quito and Riobamba, Baños, Otavalo, and Cotopaxi are best served by bus, which leave frequently for these destinations. The road between Cuenca and Guayaquil is also a popular bus route. Some of the best bus companies include **Flota Imbabura** (© 02/2236-940) and **Panamericana** (© 02/2570-425).

BY CAR   I don't recommend renting a car in Ecuador. For the most part, the roads are in terrible condition, and since signs are nonexistent, it's very easy to get lost. For short-distance journeys, it's much more economical to take a taxi. (For the 2-hr. trip from Quito to Otavalo, for example, a taxi will cost about $40.) Nevertheless, if you're an adventurous type and you want to see the country from the privacy of your own car, you can rent a car from Localiza or Budget. Because the roads are poorly maintained, you definitely should rent a 4×4. At **Localiza** (© 800/562-254; www.localiza.com.ec), 4×4s cost between $57 and $130 per day, including 100km (62 miles) free and basic insurance. Localiza has offices in Quito at the airport and at Veintimilla E8-124 (at the corner of 6 de Diciembre). In Guayaquil and Cuenca, there are Localiza offices at the airport. To rent a car, you must be at least 23 years old, have a driver's license for at least 2 years, and have a credit card. **Budget** (© 02/2237-026; www.budgetrentacar.com.ec) also has offices at the airports in Quito and Guayaquil, as well as on Avenida Colón and Amazonas in Quito. Prices are similar to Localiza's, but you must be at least 25 years old to rent a car.

BY TRAIN   Train service is a rarity in Ecuador. There's a tourist train from Riobamba to Alausí that travels along switchbacks known as the Nariz del Diablo (Devil's Nose). For a real thrill, most tourists ride on the roof of the train. It leaves Riobamba on Wednesday, Friday, and Sunday. If you only have a few days in Ecuador, I wouldn't recommend the trip. But if you plan on spending 2 weeks or more here, it is exciting to wend your way up the Devil's Nose.

TIPS ON ACCOMMODATIONS

You'll find a whole range of accommodations in Ecuador but the only truly world-class luxury resort is the Royal Palm in the Galápagos. The only Relais & Châteaux hotel in Ecuador is La Mirage Garden Hotel & Spa, just outside of Otavalo (p. 525). In Quito and Guayaquil, high-class business hotels will cater to all your needs. In Cuenca you'll find several beautiful renovated colonial homes that have been turned into small, elegant hotels.

In general, inexpensive accommodations are easy to find. In Quito, you can rent a clean room with private bathroom and television for little more than $20; in smaller towns, you can find a bed for as little as $10 a night.

Recently, some 200-year-old haciendas have been opening their doors to overnight guests. The antique furnishings and cozy rooms will make you feel as though you are an Ecuadorian aristocrat living in the 18th century. These are by far some of the most romantic places to stay in the country (my favorite is Hacienda Cucin near Otavalo). On the other end of the spectrum are jungle lodges, usually built in the style of structures typical to the Amazon basin (thatched roofs, bamboo walls, and so on). Accommodations are usually basic; the more expensive ones such as Kapawi Ecolodge & Reserve (p. 528) have private bathrooms, but hot showers are a rarity.

In the Galápagos, most visitors spend their nights sleeping on ships. The general rule is that if you don't pay a lot, you won't get a lot. The least expensive

---

Heads Up
When hotels quote prices, they rarely include the hefty tax. Expect to pay an additional 22% in taxes on the prices quoted by hotels and listed in this chapter, unless otherwise noted.

---

boats have dorm-style common sleeping rooms and one shower for everyone onboard. However, even the more expensive ships have a small berth; oftentimes the rooms are wide enough only for bunk beds. The M/V *Galapagos Explorer II* is the only ship with good-size cabins (p. 555).

TIPS ON DINING

In major cities such as Cuenca, Guayaquil, and Quito, you'll find tons of Ecuadorian restaurants, as well as an excellent selection of international cuisines. In Quito, there is everything from Mongolian barbecue to Thai food to sushi. Throughout the country, you'll also be able to find authentic pizza joints.

But while you're in Ecuador, you really should definitely try *comida típica* (typical food). *Ceviche de camarones* (shrimp cooked in a tangy lemon juice and served with onions and parsley) is one of the most popular dishes in Ecuador—you'll find it on almost every menu. *Ceviche* is also served with a side of salty popcorn, fried corn, and fried plantains. The salt complements the tart lemon flavor. Other local specialties include *seco de chivo* (goat stew in a wine sauce), *empanadas de verde* (turnovers made with fried green bananas and filled with cheese), *tortillas de maíz* (small round corn pastries, served with avocado), and *humitas* (a sweet corn mush mixed with eggs, served in a corn husk). In the highlands area, where it can get very cold, locals often have a soup called *locro de papas* (a creamy potato soup with cheese). In Cuenca, *mote pillo con carne* (huge potato-like pieces of corn, mixed with onions and eggs, served with a fried piece of meat and *tortillas de papa*—the Ecuadorian version of potato pancakes) is one of the more popular local dishes.

Fixed-price lunches *(almuerzo del día)* are also common in smaller restaurants. For about $1.50, you will get soup, a main course, dessert, and fresh juice. The main course often includes *menestra* (rice with a lentil sauce). However, the quality of the meat is usually not the best, and you can't choose what you want to eat. (The menu is preselected.)

Prices on menus don't include tax or tip. Expect to pay an extra 22% in taxes on the prices listed on menus and in this chapter.

TIPS ON SHOPPING

It's impossible to leave Ecuador empty-handed. Local artisan traditions have been thriving here for thousands of years. Take a trip up to the market in Otavalo (one of the best local handicraft markets in all of South America), and you'll find an amazing array of hand-woven goods, including alpaca scarves, gloves, sweaters, colorful bags, tapestries, and ceramics. In the neighboring towns, you can buy leather goods and beautifully crafted hand-carved wood products. Keep in mind that Ecuadorians are not hagglers. At the markets, the prices are never fixed, but don't expect to spend hours negotiating. In the first few minutes, you can convince the seller to lower the price by a few dollars, but that's it. When vendors say that the price is final, it's usually not going to go any lower.

Cuenca is the largest producer of Panama hats in the world. These aren't your typical Panama Jack hats—these are stylish beauties worn by the likes of Julia Roberts and Queen Elizabeth. Ceramics are also a specialty in Cuenca.

In Quito, you can find most everything from handcrafted silver jewelry to pre-Columbian masks. The Ecuadorian artists have done an excellent job of using traditional techniques to create products that appeal to modern-day tastes.

FAST FACTS: Ecuador

American Express There are two American Express travel offices in Ecuador—one in Quito, the other in Guayaquil—both run by Ecuadorian Tours. Unfortunately, they offer limited services for cardholders: You can't exchange traveler's checks here, and you can only make cash advances on your Amex card. In **Quito,** the office is located on Amazonas 329 and Jorge Washington (© 02/2560-488). In **Guayaquil,** the office is located on Av. 9 de Octubre 1900 (© 04/2394-984).

Business Hours In general, business hours are weekdays from 9am to 1pm and 2:30 or 3 to 6:30pm. In Quito and Guayaquil, most banks stay open all day from about 9am to 5pm, but some still close in the middle of the day, so it's best to take care of your banking needs early in the morning. Most banks, museums, and stores are open on Saturday from 10am to noon. Everything closes down on Sunday.

Doctors If you need an English-speaking doctor, your best bet is to look for one in Quito. See "Hospitals," below, for hospitals in Quito with English-speaking doctors.

Drug Laws If you're caught possessing, using, or trafficking drugs in Ecuador, expect severe penalties, including long jail sentences and large fines. If you're arrested in Ecuador, you should also prepare yourself for a lengthy delay in prison before your case is tried before a judge. It's not uncommon to detain prisoners without bail.

Electricity The majority of outlets in Ecuador are 110/120V AC (60 Hz).

Embassies & Consulates In Quito: **United States,** at the corner of Avenida 12 de Octubre and Avenida Patria, across from the Casa de la Cultura (© 02/2562-890, ext. 480); **Canada,** Av. 6 de Diciembre 2816 and Paul Rivet (© 02/2232-114); and **United Kingdom,** Avenida Naciones Unidas and República de El Salvador, Edificio Citiplaza, 14th floor (© 02/2970-800). There is no Australian Embassy in Ecuador, but there is an **Australian Honorary Consul** in Guayaquil, in the Kennedy Norte neighborhood on Calle San Roque and Avenida Francisco de Orellana (© 04/2680-823).

Emergencies In case of an emergency, call © 911 or 101 for the police only.

Hospitals The three best hospitals in Quito are **Hospital Metropolitano,** avenidas Mariana de Jesús and Occidental (© 02/2261-520 or 02/2269-030); **Hospital Voz Andes,** Villalengua 278 (© 02/2262-142); and **Clínica Internacional,** Av. América 2530 and Atahualpa (© 02/2521-140 or 2529-488). They're also where you are most likely to find English-speaking doctors. For hospitals in other cities, see the "Fast Facts" for each individual city.

Internet Access Internet service is available almost everywhere in Ecuador, including the Galápagos. But don't expect to see anything resembling a computer in the jungle. Connections in major cities cost 80¢ to $1 per hour. In smaller towns such as Baños, the connection can cost up to $3 an hour. In the Galápagos, the Internet moves at a snail's pace and costs about $4 an hour.

Language Spanish is the language most commonly used in business transactions. Indigenous languages such as Quechua are also widely spoken throughout the country. Shuar is common in the Amazon basin. It's best to come to Ecuador with a basic knowledge of Spanish. Outside of the major tourist sights, it's hard to find someone who speaks English.

Liquor Laws The official drinking age in Ecuador is 18. At discos, you often need to show a picture ID for admittance.

Newspapers & Magazines At the airports in Quito and Guayaquil and at the high-end business hotels, you can find the latest edition of the *Miami Herald* for only 50¢. English-language copies of *Time* or *Newsweek* are also available at some newsstands in the most touristy areas of Quito.

Police Throughout Ecuador, you can reach the police by dialing © **101** in an emergency. The tourist police can also help sort out your problems. In Quito, the number for the tourist police is © 02/2543-983.

Post Offices/Mail Most post offices in Ecuador are open Monday through Friday from 8am to 12:30pm and 2:30 to 6pm, and Saturday from 8am to 2pm. It costs 80¢ to mail a letter to the United States or Canada, and 95¢ to Australia and Europe. From time to time, you can buy stamps at kiosks and newsstands. But your best bet is to mail your letter and buy your stamps from the post office itself, especially since there are no public mailboxes.

Restrooms The condition of public facilities is surprisingly good in Ecuador. In museums, the toilets are relatively clean, but they never have toilet paper. If you have an emergency, you can also use the restrooms in hotel lobbies without much of a problem. Note that most buses don't have toilet facilities, and when they stop at rest stops, the facilities are often horrendous—usually smelly squat toilets. It's always useful to have a roll of toilet paper handy.

Safety Pickpocketing is a problem in all large cities. But if you keep an eye on your belongings at all times, you should be fine. Never put anything valuable in your backpack. Also be careful on the Trole (trolley). At night, Quito can be dangerous, especially in the touristy areas—take a taxi, even if you're only going a short distance. Because the streets in Quito are often deserted at night, I recommend walking in the middle of them to prevent someone from jumping at you from a hidden doorway. Guayaquil used to hold the award for being the most dangerous city in Ecuador, but in the past few years, the city has cleaned up its act. Cuenca is the safest city in Ecuador and residents routinely walk around at night, especially on weekends. Report all problems to the tourist police office located on Roca and Reina Victoria, © 02/2543-983.

Telephone & Fax Most high-end hotels in Quito, Guayaquil, and Cuenca have international direct-dial and long-distance service, and in-house fax transmission. But these calls tend to be quite expensive, especially since hotels often levy a surcharge, even if you're calling a toll-free access number.

The least expensive way to make international phones is to go to one of many, many "Andinatel or BellSouth" offices in every Ecuadorian town. There, you'll have a private booth where you can make all your call and pay the attendant after you are done. You must pay in cash as they don't accept credit cards. Cost is roughly 30¢ per minute to the U.S. and 45¢ to the U.K. Post offices also offer a similar service.

To make local calls from a public phone, you need a phone card, which you can buy at any kiosk on the street. With the $3 BellSouth phone card, you can call the United States and talk for about 7 minutes; phone cards come in denominations of $3, $5, or $10.

For tips on dialing, see "Telephone Dialing Info at a Glance" on p. 486.

Time Zone Mainland Ecuador is on Eastern Standard Time, 5 hours behind Greenwich mean time (GMT). The Galápagos Islands are on Central Standard Time, 6 hours behind GMT. Daylight savings time is not observed.

Tipping Restaurants in Ecuador add a 10% service charge to all checks. It's common to add 5% to 10% on top of this. Taxi drivers don't expect tips. Hotel porters are typically tipped 50¢ to $1 per bag.

Water Always drink bottled water in Ecuador. Most hotels provide bottled water in the bathroom. You can buy bottles of water on practically any street corner. Small bottles cost about 25¢. The better restaurants use ice made from boiled water, but always ask, to be on the safe side.

3 Quito

Sebastián de Benalcázar founded Quito in 1534. If he were to return today, he would probably feel right at home. In the Old Town, many of the original colonial structures have been wonderfully preserved and restored. Quito was and still is a city of grand churches with wildly detailed hand-carved facades, and a place where 500-year-old buildings open onto medieval-style courtyards, complete with columned archways. Even the highly active Pichincha Volcano, which dominates the western side of the city, has failed to destroy this living testimonial to Quito's colonial past.

But that's only one side of Quito. If Benalcázar were to venture a couple of miles north, the glass skyscrapers, electric trolleys, and early-20th-century mansions would make his head spin. Quito is a city of wonderful juxtapositions. It's a place where you can travel to the past, while still enjoying a life of modern-day comforts. The living museums in the Old Town nicely complement the modern art and archaeology museums in the New Town. Spend two leisurely days here and you'll see the best of what the city has to offer. Then you can travel to colorful indigenous markets, a unique cloud forest, or to the glaciers of the world's highest active volcano—all within 2 hours of the city.

Remember that at 2,804m (9,348 ft.) above sea level, Quito is one of the highest capital cities in the world, and the air is much thinner up here. Fortunately, this is a great place for taking it easy.

Quito

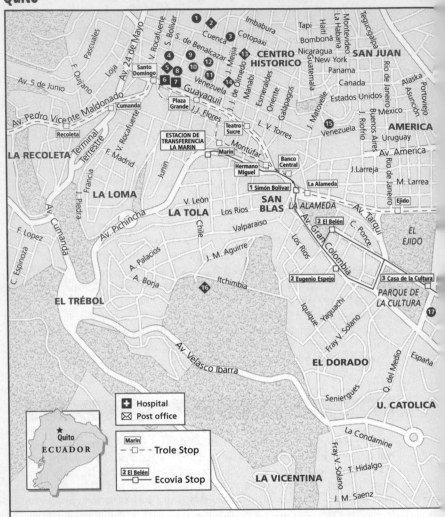

ACCOMMODATIONS ■
Apart-Hotel Antinea **28**
Cayman Hostal **29**
Hilton Colón Quito **18**
Hostal Fuente de Piedra I **26**
Hostal Jardin del Sol **30**
Hostal La Rábida **31**
Hostal Santa Bárbara **37**
Hotel Café Cultura **19**
Hotel Dann Carlton **44**
Hotel Real Audienca **6**
Hotel San Francisco de Quito **7**

Hotel Vieja Cuba **34**
JW Marriott Hotel **32**
La Cartuja **20**
Mansión del Angel **24**
Swissôtel Quito **35**

DINING ◆
Café Mosaico **16**
El Nispero **36**
El Patio Trattoria **13**
La Bodequita de Cuba **33**
La Querencia **43**

Las Redes **22**
Los Troncos Steak House **45**
The Magic Bean **25**
Mare Nostrum **27**
Mea Culpa **14**
Paragon **38**
Pavarotti Pizzeria **39**
Red Hot Chile Peppers **23**
Rest-Cafetería
  Agroecologia y Cultura **5**
Rincón la Ronda Restaurant **40**
Tianguez **2**

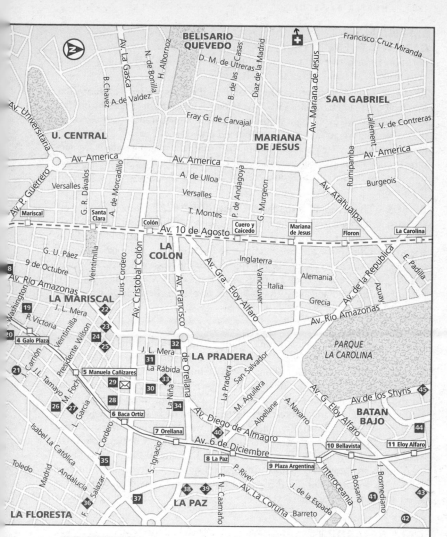

ESSENTIALS
GETTING THERE

For more information on arriving in Quito, see "Getting There" in "Planning Your Trip to Ecuador," earlier in this chapter.

BY PLANE   All flights into Quito land at the **Aeropuerto Internacional Mariscal Sucre** (© 02/2430-555). The airport is about 8km (5 miles) from the heart of the New Town. Right before you exit the international terminal, you'll find several information desks. I recommend ordering and paying for your taxi here, then taking your receipt to one of the many taxis waiting outside the terminal. Taxis shouldn't cost more than $6. Unfortunately, there are no information desks in the national terminal, but it's easy to find a yellow taxi as you exit the airport.

BY BUS   The **Terminal Terrestre de Cumandá** (© 02/2570-529), located on the edge of the Old Town, is the main bus station in Quito. A long line of taxis is usually waiting at the arrivals area. A taxi to the New Town should cost $4 to $5; to the Old Town, the fare should only be $1. If you don't have a lot of luggage, you can also take the Trole (trolley) into the heart of Quito. From the terminal, you have to walk up a serious set of stairs to the Cumandá Station. To get to both the Old and New Town, be sure to get on the Trole going toward "La Y."

ORIENTATION

Quito is a long and thin city. It runs 35km (22 miles) from north to south and 5km (3 miles) from east to west. If you were to combine the most visited areas, that area would measure only about 1.5km (1 mile). Most of the city's attractions are located in two main areas: the Old Town and the New Town. The **Old Town,** at the south end of the city, is where you'll find most of the historic churches, museums, and colonial architecture. **Plaza de la Independencia** is in the heart of the Old Town. From here, you can walk to all the main attractions. The Old Town can be dangerous at night; it's best to sleep in the **New Town** (also known as the **Mariscal**), which is north of Parque El Ejido. Most of the city's hotels are located here. You'll also find a host of good restaurants, Internet cafes, bars, and nightclubs in this part of town. New Town's main commercial street is **Avenida Amazonas,** where most of the banks and travel agencies are located.

GETTING AROUND

BY TAXI   The streets of Quito are swarming with yellow taxis, and they're my preferred means of transport here. Taxis are cheap, costing only $1 to $2 for a ride within the Old or New Town and $3 to $4 for longer distances. Drivers are required by law to use a meter, but it's obviously not a strict law because few taxis use them. Try to negotiate a price with your driver before you get in a cab. I usually don't ask how much the fare is; instead I pay what I think the driver deserves (see prices above), and I've never had a problem with this. Quito can be dangerous at night, so it's best to take a taxi wherever you go, no matter how short the distance. The staff at most restaurants, hotels, and bars will be happy to call a cab for you. In case you need to call one yourself, dial © 02/2222-222.

BY TROLE/ECOVIA   There are two electric trolley lines that wind their way through Quito, connecting the Old Town with the New Town. In the New Town, the **Trole** runs along Avenida 10 de Agosto, which is a few blocks west of Avenida Amazonas. When it reaches the Old Town, it travels along Avenida

Guayaquil. To reach Plaza de la Independencia, be sure to get off at the Plaza Grande stop. The **Ecovía** is much more convenient if you want to start your journey in the New Town; it runs along Avenida 6 de Diciembre, which is one of the major streets. Unfortunately, when it reaches the Old Town, it stops along Avenida Gran Colombia, which is a bit of a hike from the main square. Both the Trole and Ecovía cost 25¢ for a one-way trip. The turnstiles accept only exact change, but fortunately, all stations have change machines.

BY BUS   Quito has an extensive and very complicated system of city buses. In the New Town, buses run along Avenida Amazonas and Avenida 12 de Octubre. If you're only going a short distance along these streets, it's easy to hop on a bus (just flag it down). However, beware: Once you pass Avenida Colón, the buses go off in many convoluted directions. Short rides cost 25¢. But overall, it's much easier to travel through Quito by taxi. They only cost $1 to $4 and they will take you exactly where you need to go.

VISITOR INFORMATION

The nonprofit **South American Explorers** ★★, Jorge Washington 311 and the corner of Leonidas Plaza (© 02/2225-228; www.saexplorers.org/quito.htm), is the best source for visitor information. The offices are staffed by native English speakers who seem to know everything about Ecuador. Membership costs $50 a year. As a member, you will have access to trip reports (reviews of hotels, restaurants, and outfitters throughout Ecuador written by fellow travelers) and a trip counselor. If you aren't a member, the staff can give you basic information that will get you on your way.

The government-sponsored **Ministerio de Turismo** information center on Eloy Alfaro N32-300, third floor (at the corner of Carlos Tobar), is woefully inadequate. The staff is always too busy to help visitors. You can buy a few maps, but don't expect to find much else here.

Since the Ministerio de Turismo has proved to be useless, a group of hotel and tour operators have banded together to create **Tourist Information Centers** (www.captur.com). There is a useful kiosk in the New Town at Av. 6 de Diciembre 1424 (© **02/2509-860**); in the Old Town, the information center is located half a block from the Plaza de la Independencia on Calle Venezuela near the corner of Chile (© **02/2954-044**). *Note:* Both TIC locations are closed on the weekend.

There are also several travel agencies that serve as informal information centers. **Metropolitan Touring,** which has offices at Amazonas and 18 de Septiembre (© **02/2506-654**) and at Av. República de El Salvador N36-84 (© **02/2464-780**), offers daily city tours for $12 per person. **ASIRI,** Portugal 448 and Catalina Aldaz (© **02/2442-801**), is also extremely helpful.

Tips If You Want a Guide

If you'd like ultrapersonalized service, an English-speaking guide, a private car, and even a bodyguard or two to accompany you while you visit the city or the highlands, then contact **Turisvision,** Ultimas Noticias N37-97 and El Espectador, Quito (© **02/2246-756**; fax 02/224-5741; www. turisvision.com). They will take care of you from the moment you arrive at Quito airport until the moment you depart.

FAST FACTS There is one **American Express** office in Quito, on Av. Amazonas 329 and Jorge Washington (© **02/2560-488**). Unfortunately, you can only make travel arrangements and get cash advances on your Amex card here. The office is open Monday through Friday from 8:30am to 5pm. You can exchange traveler's checks nearby at **Vaz Cambios,** Avenida Amazonas close to the corner of Roca (no phone), for a 1.8% commission ($2 minimum). The office is open Monday through Friday from 8am to 6pm and Saturday 9am to 1pm. The **Banco del Pacífico,** Avenida Amazonas near the corner of Ramírez Dávalos (no phone), also changes American Express traveler's checks and foreign currency for a $5 commission. (You can change $200 maximum.) The exchange office is downstairs and is open Monday through Friday from 8:30am to 4pm.

In case of an **emergency,** call © 911. You can reach an **ambulance** at © 09/9739-801 or 02/2442-974; for **police assistance** call © 101. For the **tourist police** call © 02/2543-983; the headquarters are located at Roca and Reina Victoria. For information about doctors and hospitals in Quito, see "Fast Facts: Ecuador" on p. 493. **Fybeca** is the largest chain of pharmacies in Ecuador. You can call Fybeca's toll-free line (© **800/392-322**) 24 hours a day for home delivery. The most centrally located Fybeca is at Avenida 6 de Diciembre and Cordero. **Rey de Reyes** (© **02/2557-357**) is a 24-hour pharmacy located at Jorge Washington 416 near the corner of 6 de Diciembre.

Internet cafes are ubiquitous in Quito; there seems to be one on every block in the New Town. Fast connections can be found at **El Choque** on the corner of Reina Victoria and Calama. **Cyber Coffee,** on Calama between Reina Victoria and Juan León Mera, is also good and the only Internet cafe in Quito with a CD burner. Most Internet cafes have access to Net2Phone, which allows you to make international calls at a reasonable price.

The most conveniently located **post office** is on the ground floor of the Ecuatoriana Building on the corner of Colón and Reina Victoria. It's open Monday through Friday from 7:30am to 7:30pm and Saturday 8am to 2pm.

The cheapest way to make international calls is to use the phones at an Internet cafe. For local and long-distance calls, you can buy a BellSouth Phone card (in denominations of $3, $5, and $10) at many kiosks along the street. You can also make calls from the **Andinatel** office on Av. Colón E4-284 (a half block up from Amazonas; © **02/2256-1900**). Calls from the Andinatel office to the United States only cost 30¢ per minute, and the quality is far superior to the calls made from Internet cafes.

WHAT TO SEE & DO

You can easily visit all of Quito's main attractions in 1 day. I recommend that you spend the morning touring Old Town highlights such as Iglesia de San Francisco, La Compañía de Jesús, and Casa Museo María Augusta Urrutia, and then head over to Fundación Guayasamín in the afternoon. However, you should note that most attractions close down from about noon to 3pm, so if you only have 1 day and you want to see everything, it's imperative that you start sightseeing around 8:30am. During the midday break, you could head up to El Panecillo for panoramic views of the city.

IN THE OLD TOWN

La Basílica Work on the basilica began in 1883 and is still unfinished to this day. Yet, visitors are permitted inside of this concrete marvel, which is modeled on Notre-Dame de Paris. Most people come here for the spectacular aerial views of the Old City and to see the Winged Virgin in the distance. For the best views,

---

Fun Fact   Colorful Quito

When a smallpox epidemic hit Quito in 1756, the government declared that all buildings must be painted with white limestone, which was then believed to be a disinfectant. From then until the late 1980s, all buildings in Quito were white. Everything changed when the mayor of Quito surveyed the local people and discovered that most *Quiteños* felt that the Old Town was *too* white. Out came the art historians, who did extensive research, uncovering the true colors of all the colonial structures in the city. Now all the buildings have been restored to their pre-1756 luster.

---

you have to climb 90m (300 ft.) to the top of the towers. Note that the elevators don't always work and that the "ladders" that climb to the top are very narrow and quite steep. As you cross the bridge to enter the towers, look for the carved condors—the stonework is impressive and the condors look as though they are about to fly away. The basilica is also famous for its mystical gargoyles in the form of local Ecuadorian icons such as pumas, monkeys, penguins, tortoises, and condors. There is a cafe on the third floor—a good place to catch your breath after taking in the breathtaking views.

At the corner of Calle Venezuela and Carchí. Admission $2. Daily 9:30am–5:30pm.

Casa Museo María Augusta Urrutia   It's hard to have a favorite sight in the Old Town—there are just so many amazing things to see. But this museum, which provides a nice break if you've been visiting churches all morning, ranks high on my list. It allows modern-day visitors to envision what it must have been like to live in a 19th-century Spanish-style mansion in the Old Town. When you enter the house, you immediately find yourself in a gorgeous courtyard. Not much has been changed since Doña María Augusta Urrutia lived here, so the dramatic entry that you experience is probably what the pope and many other important world leaders also experienced when visiting this home. The house is surprisingly modern, with a full bathroom and modern kitchen appliances; but there are also a cold storage room, a wood-burning stove, and the oldest grain masher in Ecuador. The interior is unbelievable, featuring antique European furniture, a bed that belonged to General Sucre, hand-painted wallpaper, stained-glass windows, handcrafted moldings, murals on the walls, and Belgian tiles. There is also an incredible collection of Ecuadorian art.

Note: Guided tours are available in English. Just ask for a guide when you enter. Allow about 40 minutes to visit the whole house.

García Moreno 760, between Sucre and Bolívar. © 02/2580-107. Admission $2.50. Tues–Sun 9am–5pm.

El Centro Cultural Metropolitano   Few museums in the world can boast that they were once both a prison and a university. This museum is one of them. Instead of prisoners or students, however, this 400-year-old complex now displays a variety of art. The galleries on the main floor are used for temporary exhibitions. Upstairs, the museum houses an impressive collection of colonial art, which you can visit only by a 45-minute guided tour. (English-speaking guides are available.) The guide will also take you to the old Jesuit residences and the basement area that used to house the prisoners. This mildly interesting museum is worth a visit if you love colonial art; otherwise, I recommend a visit here only if you have an extra hour on your hands.

Corner of Espejo and García Moreno. Free admission. Tues–Sun 9am–5pm.

La Compañía de Jesús ⓐ   This Jesuit church is one of the great baroque masterpieces in South America. It took 160 years to complete all the work (1605–1765). The facade won't fail to impress you—the carvings are unbelievably detailed. Notice the Solomonic columns, which are symbolic of the Catholic doctrine that life's journey starts at the bottom (on earth), but by following the holy path, it ends at heaven.

Almost every inch of the interior has intricate decorations. When you enter La Compañía, look for the symbols of the sun in both the main door to the church and the ceiling. The sun was a very important Inca symbol, and the Spanish thought that if they decorated the entryway with indigenous symbols, it might encourage local people to join the church. The walls and ceilings of La Compañía are very typical of Moorish design—you will only see geometric shapes, no human forms. The building has been under renovation for the past several years, and some of the gold leaf on the ceiling and walls has been restored to its natural luster. Natural sunlight and candlelight really bring out an angelic brilliance.

If you happen to be in Quito on November 1 (the Day of the Dead), you can also visit the catacombs here.

On García Moreno near Sucre. Admission $2. Mon–Fri 10am–1pm and 2–5pm; Sat 10am–1pm.

Iglesia de la Merced   It's believed that after the expulsion of the Moors from Spain in 1492, many Moorish artists sought refuge in South America. The current Iglesia de la Merced, a delightful example of Moorish design, only dates from 1737, but it was originally built in 1538. The resplendent gold-leaf altar, designed by the great Bernardo de Legarda, is pure baroque. Many of the oil paintings are by Víctor Mideros, one of the greatest Ecuadorian artists of the 20th century. If you have the time (and it's still early in the morning), you can head around the corner to visit the convent, which dates back to the early 16th century and still houses the church's priests. Some of the highlights include the Neptune sculpture in the stone fountain and the 17th-century sun clock above the dome. The convent is open Monday through Saturday from 8 to 10:30am; the entrance is on Mejía near the corner of Cuenca.

Chile, near the corner of Cuenca. Free admission. Mon–Fri 6:30am–noon and 3–6pm; Sat 6:30am–noon.

Museo Histórico Militar "Casa de Sucre"   This museum will appeal to both history and military buffs. The house dates from the 17th century, but the house's namesake, the Independence hero Mariscal Antonio José de Sucre, lived here from 1828 until his death in 1830. On the ground floor, in the Sala de Armas, you can see swords, pistols, and bayonets that all belonged to Sucre. There is also an old stable with old-fashioned saddles on display. On the second floor, you can visit the original brick kitchen with two cold storage rooms. The *archivo* is where Sucre received visitors; the desk is original. Sucre's bedroom doesn't contain his original bed, but look at the walls—you'll notice that they have slats, allowing Sucre to move the walls of his room closer together in order to preserve heat. In general, most of the tours here are in Spanish. But even if you can't understand your guide, you can get a good picture of what it must have been like to live in a home on the Old Town in the 19th century. Plan on spending about 45 minutes here.

Venezuela 573 at the corner of Sucre. ⓒ 02/2952-860. Admission $1. Tues–Sat 8:30am–4:30pm.

El Panecillo/Virgin Monument *(Moments)*   From a distance, the hill that hosts a huge statue of the winged virgin does indeed look like a panecillo (small bread roll). Since it's directly south of the city, this hill was an ideal spot to construct the 45m-high (148-ft.) *La Virgen de Quito,* a copy of Bernardo de Lagarda's *La Virgen de Quito* sculpture that is on display on the main altar in the San Francisco church. The panecillo stands at about 3,000m (9,840 ft.), so you can also see the sculpture from the center of Quito.

The significance of the panecillo hill dates back to Inca times, when it was known as *Shungoloma* ("hill of the heart"). Before the Spanish arrived, the local people used this hill as a place to worship the sun. Afterward, the Spanish used this site to construct a fortress between 1812 and 1815 and to control what was going on down below. These days, most people come up here for the 360-degree views of Quito. For the best views, try to get here early in the morning (around 10am) before the clouds settle in around the nearby mountains. On a clear day, you can see Cotopaxi in the distance. It'll take you about 25 minutes to get here and half an hour is all you'll need to take in the sights.

South of the city; it's best to take a taxi (round-trip from the Old Town back to a hotel in the New Town should cost about $5). Admission to enter the grounds $1; admission to climb to the top of the monument $1. Mon–Fri 9am–6pm; Sat–Sun 9am–5pm.

La Plaza de la Independencia ★★   This became the main square of Quito in the 16th century. The Spanish were afraid that the Incas might poison their water supply, so the Spanish set up their own protected well here, and this plaza subsequently became the social center of town. The plaza also served as a central market and bullfighting area. Today, Old Town's main square is bordered by the Government Palace on the west, City Hall to the east, the Archbishop's Palace on the north, and the Cathedral to the south.

The **Government Palace** ★ is the most interesting building on the plaza. Don't be intimidated by the chain-link fence in front of the palace; everyone is welcome to walk inside the main area—just tell the guard that you're a curious tourist. Once you walk into the main entry area, you can get a sense of the Spanish/Moorish architecture. If you look straight ahead, you'll see the impressive 1966 mural by Guayasamín of Orellana discovering the Amazon.

The **City Hall** is probably the least impressive structure on the plaza. It was built in 1952, in the Bauhaus style. The **Archbishop's Palace** was built in 1852; it was formerly the mayor's house. Currently, you can walk inside and see the Andalusian and Moorish-inspired courtyard; note that the floor of the courtyard is made from the spines of pigs. This area is now an informal crafts market. The **cathedral** dates from the 16th century. Inside, there is a good collection of art from the Quiteña school, including works by Caspicara and Manuel Samaniego. You can visit the cathedral Monday through Saturday from 6am to 10am. The square is beautiful when all the buildings light up after dark.

To get to the Plaza de la Independencia from the Trole, get off at the Plaza Grande stop and walk 1 block on either Calle Espejo or Chile. The plaza is bordered by Calle Venezuela on the bottom (east), García Moreno on the west, Chile on the north, and Espejo to the south.

El Sagrario   This 17th-century church was once part of the nearby cathedral. It's a mishmash of different architectural styles, from baroque to neoclassical. The Solomonic columns on the outside are both Ionic and Gothic. Inside, you can see the Moorish influence in the painted domes. As you enter El Sagrario, look down—you will see crypts. (Those with crossbones mean that the body buried there died of smallpox.) The second door is regarded as a colonial-era masterpiece. It was painted with liquid gold leaf and is designed with vegetables and fruits, including pineapples, which is considered to be an indigenous

welcome symbol. The intricately designed rococo altarpiece is also impressive—it took 12 years to build, and the fine details are quite lovely.

Around the corner from the cathedral on García Moreno near Espejo. Free admission. Mon–Sat 8am–noon and 2–5:30pm.

Iglesia de San Francisco ✶✶✶ San Francisco is the first church built in Quito. Construction began in 1535, just 1 month after the Spanish arrived here. (It took more than 100 years to finish it.) You'll notice that Plaza San Francisco is distinctly sloped; for several hundred years, it was assumed that it followed the shape of the Earth. However, a group of archaeologists recently discovered that San Francisco was built over an Inca temple, which is the reason why the actual church is much higher than other structures in Quito. As you walk up the stairs from the plaza to the church, you can't help but realize how wide the stairs are. Supposedly, the architects designed the stairs this way so that as you approached the church, you had to keep your eyes on your feet to watch where you were going—in other words, it forced you to bow your head in respect.

Like La Compañía, San Francisco is an important baroque church, but San Francisco is much larger and, for some reason, feels much more somber. The ceilings have a beautiful Moorish design. In the entryway, like in La Compañía, you will notice all the images of the sun, which were used to lure indigenous people into the Christian religion. You will also find important mixtures of indigenous and Catholic symbols inside the church. For example, the interior of the church is decorated with angels in the shape of the sun—and the faces of these angels have distinct Indian characteristics.

The baroque altar in the front of the church has three important sculptures: The top is the *Baptism of Jesus;* the bottom is a representation of *Jesús de Gran Poder;* and the middle is probably one of the most important sculptures in Ecuador, the original *La Virgen de Quito,* designed by Bernardo de Legarda. (*La Virgen de Quito* was the model for the huge winged angel on the Panecillo; see p. 502.)

Plaza San Francisco. Free admission. Mon–Sat 7–11:30am and 3–5:30pm; Sun 7am–noon.

San Francisco Museum and Convent (Museo Fray Pedro Gocial) This museum, which is attached to the San Francisco church, allows visitors to see the convent as well as the church's choir. Tour guides also will show you some of the pieces of the church's fantastic colonial art collection. I highly recommend a visit to the choir. Here, you can see the church's original wood ceiling, as well as a beautiful wood inlaid "lyric box" that was used to hold up the music for the singers in the choir. Plus, you will also experience Manuel Chile Caspicara's famous "crucifix," which dates back to 1650 to 1670. It is said that Caspicara tied a model to a cross to learn how to realistically represent Christ's facial and body expressions; the glass eyes are piercing.

⟮*Tips* Touring Iglesia de San Francisco

In the morning, the San Francisco church closes down at noon, earlier than most of the other churches in the Old Town, and it doesn't open again until 3pm. So if you're trying to see everything in the Old Town in one morning, be sure to visit San Francisco first. If you can't make it before 11:30am, you can always visit Museo Fray Pedro Gocial, the museum connected to the church (see above).

Plaza San Francisco. Admission $2. Mon–Sat 9am–6pm; Sun 9am–1pm. Visits only by guided tour, which leave on an as-needed basis. (Most of the tours are in English.)

IN THE NEW TOWN

Fundación Guayasamín 𝒢   This powerful museum displays the works and art collections of Oswaldo Guayasamín, one of Ecuador's most famous artists. The museum has three sections. **El Museo Arqueológico** houses Guayasamín's collection of pre-Columbian art. The artist once said, "I paint from three or five thousand years ago." It's interesting to see both his collection and his inspiration. Keep an eye out for the sitting shamans and tribal chiefs, and the jugs with the intricately carved faces.

Across the courtyard is the **Museo de Arte Moderno** 𝒢, which displays Guayasamín's own art. Most impressive is his work from the period 1964 to 1984 entitled "La Edad de la Ira" (the Age of Anger), which represents his anger against violence in the world, and in South America in particular. One of the most dramatic pieces is the three-paneled *Homenaje a Víctor Jara* (Homage to Víctor Jara). Jara was a Chilean guitarist and Communist Party supporter who was tortured and killed by General Pinochet's army after the 1973 military junta. Military officers cut off his hands to try to stop his protest songs, but it took a machine gun to silence him. The images of a skeleton playing a guitar have a tremendous impact.

In the **Museo de Arte Colonia,** you can view Guayasamín's incredible collection of colonial art. The majority of the pieces are from the Quiteña school; they give viewers a good idea of the art created by the first inhabitants of Quito. The collection contains more than 80 different crucifixes.

There is also a nice patio (with a great view) and a cafe on the premises. It doesn't take more than an hour to explore the whole museum.

Calle José Bosmediano E 15-68 Bellavista (Batán). Take a taxi to get here (about $1 from the heart of the New Town). ℂ 02/2465-265. Admission $3. Mon–Fri 9am–1:30pm and 3–6:30pm.

Capilla del Hombre

A few blocks from the Fundación Guayasamín (see above), this is the latest museum dedicated to Oswaldo Guayasamín who died in 1999 at the age of 90. It was the artist's dream to open a museum on the first day of the new century, but financial problems delayed its opening until November 2002. Dedicated to "man's progress through art," the museum houses many of the artists' paintings and will add a collection of colonial art, archaeological finds, and a wing focused entirely on contemporary art in coming years. Basically, it's a more condensed collection similar to the one found in the sprawling Fundación (see above). It's worth a trip only if you're really interested in Guayasamín's work and it'll take you about an hour to view the collection.

Corner of Mariano Calvache and Lorenzo Chávez, Bellavista. ℂ 02/2465-266. Admission $3. Tues–Sun 10am–5pm.

Museo Jacinto Jijón y Caamaño

This tiny museum holds the personal collection of Jacinto Jijón y Caamaño, an Ecuadorian who did extensive archaeological excavations in South America in the 20th century. In my opinion, the most interesting artifacts are the *fardos funerarios* that he discovered in Lima in 1925. You will see mummies and all sorts of jewelry and learn about pre-Columbian funeral rituals. Also impressive is the display of exquisite colonial furnishings. You can see the entire collection in about 30 minutes.

Av. 12 de Octubre and Roca (on the 3rd floor of the Edificio de la Biblioteca). Admission $1. Mon–Fri 8:30am–4pm.

Museo Nacional del Banco Central del Ecuador ⊕   This enormous and enormously rich museum offers visitors an opportunity to learn about the evolution of Ecuadorian art. When you see all the artifacts and works of art displayed chronologically, you begin to understand how pervasive pre-Columbian art techniques and symbols are in the colonial, Republican, and contemporary art of Ecuador. To see everything in this massive museum, you really need at least 4 hours; I recommend taking a guided tour.

If you visit the museum from beginning to end, you will start at the **Archaeological Gallery.** On display are artifacts dating from 11,000 B.C. You can learn a lot about the beliefs of some of the most important pre-Columbian cultures from their artwork. The **Golden Court** ⊕⊕ is my favorite exhibit. Because many indigenous groups worshipped the sun, they used gold to create masks, chest decorations, and figurines that were all used to represent the sun. The fine details are really amazing—many of the pieces in this gallery are a sight to behold.

You can see the influence of both the importance of the sun and the veneration of women in the artwork in the **Colonial Art Gallery,** which displays pieces from 1534 to 1820. Much of the colonial art here combines the rich ornamentation popular in pre-Columbian art with the severe polychrome style of European art. You'll also probably notice that a lot of pieces in this gallery are quite bloody and gory—all an attempt to scare the indigenous people into believing in God.

After independence from Spain, Ecuadorian artists began to eschew religious art. In the **Republican Art Gallery,** you can see this switch. Instead of gory religious art and paintings of the Virgin, you'll find very lifelike portraits of Ecuador's independence heroes. One of my favorites is *Retrato de Simón Bolívar* (Portrait of Simón Bolívar).

The art in the **Contemporary Art Gallery** is on a whole different plane. You'll see peaceful landscapes as well as representations of anger by Oswaldo Guayasamín. In addition to the above galleries, the museum also hosts temporary art exhibits. And in the same building, there is a **Museum of Musical Instruments,** which is a lot of fun if you're traveling with kids.

Av. Patria, between 6 de Diciembre and 12 de Octubre. © 02/2223-258. Adults $2, students 50¢. Tues–Fri 9am–5pm; Sat–Sun 10am–4pm. Free guided tours in English given Tues–Fri 2–5pm.

SPORTS & OUTDOOR ACTIVITIES

Quito itself is a large sprawling city, so it's hard to do anything outdoorsy within the city limits. But if you travel an hour or two outside the city, you'll find an abundance of outdoor pursuits.

CLIMBING, HIKING & TREKKING   Quito is right in the heart of the "Avenue of the Volcanoes." Within an hour either north or south of the city, hiking and trekking opportunities abound. One of the most exciting and rigorous treks is up the glacier-covered Cotopaxi Volcano. **Safari,** Calama 389 and Juan León Mera (© 02/2552-505; www.safari.com.ec), is one of the best hiking and climbing outfitters in the country. In addition to organizing treks up Cotopaxi, the company also arranges over 15 varieties of day trips to Cayambe Volcano, Mindo (for bird-watching), the lakes near Otavalo, the Quiltoa Crater, and small-town markets. Day trips cost between $40 and $65. **SURTREK,** Av. Amazonas 897 and Wilson (© 02/2231-534; www.surtrek.org), specializes in 2- to 6-day hikes.

MOUNTAIN BIKING Biking down Cotopaxi from the *refugio* (not the summit) is one of the most popular biking trips in the area. Other routes include biking to Mindo (for bird-watching) or Papallacta Hot Spring. **Arie's Bike Company,** Wilson 578 and Reina Victoria (© 02/2906-052; www.ariesbike company.com), and **Biking Dutchman,** Foch 714 and Juan León Mera (© 02/ 2568-323; www.biking-dutchman.com), are the two best outfitters in Quito.

SOCCER Soccer season in Quito lasts March through December. All games take place at the **Estadio Olímpico Atahualpa** on 6 de Diciembre and Avenida Naciones Unidas (© 02/2247-510). Game day is usually Saturday or Sunday. General admission seats cost $2; the good seats go for $10. You can buy tickets at the stadium on the day of the game. Once a month, an international tournament is held in Quito. Tickets for these matches cost between $10 and $70. They go on sale 5 days before the match. You can also buy tickets at the sports store **Almacenes de Maratón,** located in shopping malls. To get to the stadium, take the Ecovía line to the Estadio stop.

WHITE-WATER RAFTING & KAYAKING The rivers near Quito are usually most rapid in October, November, and December, but it is possible to go white-water rafting year-round. **ECO ADVENTOUR** ⚡, Foch 634 and Reina Victoria (© 02/2223-720; www.ecoadventour.com), is the best kayaking and rafting outfitter in Quito. You can arrange 1-day tours on the Toachi and Blanco rivers (class III–III+); or the Quijos River (class IV–IV+). Longer rafting trips in the jungle and other rivers are also available. The company uses high-quality equipment and certified guides. **Yacu Amu Rafting** on Baquedano E5-27 and Juan León Mera (© 02/2236-844; www.yacuamu.com) is another excellent outfitter. One-day trips start at $70; overnight trips cost about $190 per person.

SHOPPING

Shopping in Quito mainly consists of shopping for folksy handicrafts (alpaca sweaters, tapestries, figurines, pottery, hats, and jewelry) made by indigenous Ecuadorian artists. Some of the stuff you'll find is mass-produced or of poor quality. But if you know where to go (and I'll tell you), there are some great shops, which support local indigenous groups. In addition to the stores listed below, there is a fun arts-and-crafts market on Saturday and Sunday at Parque El Ejido.

A note on store hours: Unless noted below, all stores close for a siesta from 1:30 to 3pm, and most are closed on Sunday.

Exedra This nonprofit community of stores helps support scholarships for poor children. You'll find a variety of artwork here, including ceramics, acrylics, books, lithographs, painted furniture, and tapestries. There are also several antiques stores and a cafe. Carrión 243 and Plaza. © 02/2224-001.

Galería Aymara This beautiful jewelry store features a wide selection of fantastic rings, bracelets, earring, and necklaces. Most of the jewelry is silver with semiprecious stones, and most of the designs are unique to this store. Reina Victoria 1110 and Cordero. © 02/2549-088.

Galería Latina Like Olga Fisch (see below), Galería Latina specializes in high-quality handicrafts. Here, you will find great pottery and a nice selection of alpaca sweaters, in addition to silver and gold jewelry, textiles, and even some antiques. Open Sunday. Juan León Mera N23-69 (833), between Baquedano and Wilson. © 02/2540-380.

LaPosta Art Forum   Quito is known as a center for artists in South America. At this gallery, you can see firsthand what local artists are producing in the form of jewelry, paintings, sculptures, pottery, and photos. Juan León Mera N23-106 and Wilson (across the street from Libri Mundi). ⓒ 02/2544-185.

Libri Mundi   This is the best bookstore in Quito; it features a wide selection of English books about Ecuador. Juan León Mera N23-83. ⓒ 02/2234-791.

Olga Fisch Folklore *Finds*   We have Olga Fisch to thank for recognizing and inspiring the creation of high-quality, locally made handicrafts. As an artist, Fisch had a very keen eye, and she worked with indigenous groups to create carpets, figurines, jewelry, and decorative arts based on their own traditional understanding of the arts. Everything here is displayed in a gorgeous showroom. There is also a nonprofit museum here that supports the development of these arts in indigenous communities. I suggest that you visit the museum first to get an idea of the local artisan traditions—it will help you understand what you are looking at when you shop in the showroom. Open during siesta. Av. Colón E10-53 and Caamaño. ⓒ 02/2541-315.

Punto en Blanco *Finds*   A gorgeous linen store. You'll find beautiful lace place mats, towels, pillowcases, and wonderful baby clothing, all handmade. Closed Saturday and Sunday. Veintimilla 560 and Av. 6 de Diciembre. ⓒ 02/2541-843.

Tianguez *❋❋*   Tianguez showcases products very similar to those you'll find at Olga Fisch and Galería Latina, including masks, ceramics, and all sorts of pieces inspired by pre-Columbian artisan traditions. *Tianguez* means "market" in Quechua, and it's an especially appropriate name because the store is housed in a sprawling old market in the Old Town under the San Francisco church. It feels like the catacombs in Rome. A nonprofit organization, Sinchi Sacha, runs Tianguez and supports indigenous and mestizo artisan groups. Open Sunday and during siesta. Plaza San Francisco. ⓒ 02/2230-609.

WHERE TO STAY
IN THE NEW TOWN
Expensive

Hilton Colón Quito *❋* *Overrated*   In 1967 when the Hilton Colón opened (under a different name and on a much smaller scale—there were only 20 rooms), it must have been the height of fashion. But that was then, and this is now. These days, its age is showing, and it has nothing on the new, flashy, upscale hotels that have opened in Quito in the past decade or so (specifically the Swissôtel and the JW Marriott Hotel). The two main towers here were built in the past 16 years, and all rooms were renovated in 1999, but unfortunately, the Soviet-style cement architecture doesn't add much to the hotel's allure. The deluxe rooms are on the small side, with tiny marble bathrooms to match. The superior rooms are a bit larger and more modern, but the real benefit of these rooms is access to the business center (which includes a free continental breakfast and Internet service). The junior suites are similar to the superior rooms, except they have a breakfast table, and two sinks in the bathroom. Suites have a separate sitting area and both a tub and shower in the bathrooms. The service here is also a bit erratic. Clearly, this isn't my first choice in Quito, but the hotel does offer the amenities of a large hotel, and it's very conveniently located (near Parque El Ejido, Casa de la Cultura, and the business center of the city). Be sure to ask about promotional rates; doubles here are frequently discounted to just below $100 so don't hesitate to bargain.

Av. Amazonas and Patria, Quito. ℂ **800/221-2424** or 02/2560-666. Fax 02/2563-903. www.hiltoncolon. com. 395 units. $180 deluxe; $220 superior; $300–$800 suite. AE, MC, DC, V. **Amenities:** 2 restaurants; bar; lounge; midsize outdoor pool; small health club; Jacuzzi; sauna; concierge; tour desk; business center; shopping arcade; salon; 24-hr. room service; in-room massage; babysitting; same-day dry cleaning; laundry service; nonsmoking floors; executive/club floor; casino; free airport shuttle. *In room:* A/C, TV, minibar, hair dryer, safe.

Hotel Dann Carlton ✶ *Finds*   The 6-year-old Dann Carlton is probably the only high-rise in all of Quito to have more brick than glass. It's not brash or flashy; rather, it looks like one of the subtly luxurious hotels built in the 1920s in the United States. The Dann Carlton bills itself as a boutique hotel because it offers all the charm and personal service that you'd find at a small hotel. The rooms are quite spacious and come with dark wood furnishings, built-in closets, CD players, and subtle green, earthy tones. The marble bathrooms are sparkling. Only two floors currently have air-conditioning (so make your request at check-in), but the hotel will be adding this amenity floor by floor in the next two years. Rooms in back of the hotel have sumptuous views of the city, El Panecillo, Parque La Carolina, and the volcanoes. The location is a bit out of the way, but the neighborhood is nice and the huge Parque La Carolina is just outside the door. Guests get 30 minutes of free daily Internet use in the business center.

Av. República de El Salvador N34-377 and Irlanda, Quito. ℂ 02/2249-008. Fax 02/2448-807. www. hotelesdann.com. 130 units. $160 double; $180 suite. AE, MC, DC, V. **Amenities:** Restaurant; bar; miniscule exercise room; Jacuzzi; sauna; concierge; business center; salon; limited room service; massage; same-day dry cleaning; laundry service; nonsmoking floors. *In room:* TV, dataport, minibar, fridge, hair dryer, safe.

JW Marriott Hotel ✶✶✶ *Value*   The newest and most luxurious hotel in Quito is only 5 years old, so compared to the 36-year-old Hilton, it seems like paradise. Service is top-notch, the restaurants are fantastic, and the large pool area makes you feel as if you've escaped to a tropical resort. You enter each room through a carved wooden door that looks like it should open on to an old-fashioned den. But instead of a den, you'll find a large room with colorful bedspreads, heavy wood furniture, and comfy chairs. Most rooms offer views of either the city or the volcanoes. (If you can, opt for the volcano view; my least favorite rooms have views of the glass-enclosed lobbies.) The large marble bathrooms are wonderful; all with separate tub/shower. La Hacienda restaurant offers delicious local specialties and a sumptuous lunch buffet for $15 per person. The weekend rates (valid Thurs–Sun) begin at $99 for a double—and for the luxury and excellent service you get, this makes the JW Marriott the best luxury hotel value in Quito.

Orellana 1172 and Amazonas, Quito. ℂ **800/228-9290** or 02/2972-000. Fax 02/2972-050. www.marriott hotels.com. 257 units. $99–$155 deluxe; $119–$179 executive; $139–$199 suite. AE, MC, DC, V. **Amenities:** 2 restaurants; sushi bar; bar; humongous pool w/waterfalls; health club; Jacuzzi; sauna; concierge; tour desk; business center; shopping arcade; salon; 24-hr. room service; massage; babysitting; same-day dry cleaning; laundry service; nonsmoking floors; executive/club floor. *In room:* A/C, TV, dataport, minibar, hair dryer, iron, safe.

Mansión del Angel ✶✶ *Finds*   Mansión del Angel feels more like a friend's home than a hotel. In fact, after you stay here for a few days, you will probably meet the owner, who will indeed become a friend. Everything here comes with a personal touch. The staff distributes fresh flowers throughout the hotel daily, so everything smells lovely. The sitting areas on the first floor are full of gorgeous antiques, handmade wood furniture, unique art, crystal chandeliers, and gilded mirrors. All the rooms have brass canopy beds, hand-carved moldings, Oriental carpets, and plush bedspreads. The bathrooms are not especially spacious; none have tubs, but they all have very large showers. The larger rooms on the top floor have a separate sitting area. Since the rooms in the back of the hotel don't face the street, they are a bit quieter. The breakfast, served on the enclosed rooftop terrace, includes freshly baked breads, and at night, the smell of baking bread permeates the entire hotel. Delicious!

Wilson E5-29 and Juan León Mera, Quito. © **800/327-3573** in the U.S., or 02/2557-721. Fax 02/2237-819. www.larc1.com. 10 units (shower only). $95–$120 double. Rates include breakfast. MC, V. **Amenities:** Enclosed rooftop breakfast terrace; afternoon tea; laundry service. *In room:* TV, hair dryer, safe.

Swissôtel Quito 🌟 This is the second-best hotel in town, after the JW Marriott. It may be a Swissôtel, but the rooms here have much more of a Danish feel. In the past 2 years 70% of the rooms were renovated; the rest will be completed by 2005. (Since the hotel is hardly ever full, you'll most likely get one of the newly renovated rooms—but double check when you arrive.) The new rooms are very modern with a touch of classic Danish design: sleek blond wood paneling, cream-colored striated wallpaper, and stylish wood desks, dressers, and closets. The bathrooms are very spacious with double sinks and brand-new fixtures. The pool area is attractive but it's so tiny that only a few lounge chairs are available on the grass outside and on weekends there's hardly a vacant spot in which to stretch out. You can expect all the services that you would normally find at a high-end business hotel here, although beware that the service is spotty and a number of the staff members don't speak a word of English. Another complaint: Not only does the Swissôtel have the highest room rates in the city, but it also charges an exorbitant amount for breakfast. Expect to dish out an extra $20 for breakfast (compared to $9 at the Marriott). The hotel is about 12 years old, so it doesn't feel as hip as the Marriott, but it does have a good location, a handful of excellent, if overpriced, restaurants, and the best hotel health club in Quito.

Av. 12 de Octubre 1820 and Luis Cordero, Quito. © **800/637-9477** in the U.S., or 02/2567-600. Fax 02/2568-080. www.swissotel.com. 250 units. $160–$280 standard; $200–$310 deluxe; $230–$1,600 suite. AE, MC, DC, V. **Amenities:** 5 restaurants; bar; small pool (½ indoors, ½ outdoors); 1 outdoor tennis court; racquetball and squash courts; state-of-the-art health club; spa; Jacuzzi; sauna; concierge; tour desk; business center; shopping arcade; salon; 24-hr. room service; massage; babysitting; same-day dry cleaning; laundry service; nonsmoking floors; executive/club floor. *In room:* A/C, TV, dataport, minibar, coffeemaker, hair dryer, iron, safe.

Moderate

Hostal La Rábida 🏆 Hostal La Rábida is in an old home on a quiet street, away from the fray of the Mariscal neighborhood. The rooms are lovely if a bit small, with brass or iron beds (one even has a canopy) and luxurious white down comforters. The spacious bathrooms come complete with old-fashioned wooden sinks and antique fixtures. Room no. 11 has a patio and beautiful blue-and-white wallpaper; no. 2 has a large balcony. The beautiful breakfast room/restaurant opens onto a small garden. Overall, the hotel has a very English feel—the walls are covered with botanical prints and old maps, Oriental carpets complement the hardwood floors, and every evening a fire burns in the very cozy living room.

La Rábida 227 and Santa María, Quito. © 02/2222-169. larabida@uio.satnet.net. 11 units (shower only). $53 double; $64 triple. AE, MC, DC, V. **Amenities:** Restaurant and bar; limited room service; laundry service. *In room:* TV.

Hostal Santa Bárbara Here's an Ecuadorian hotel with Gothic trappings. The hotel is housed in a mansion from the 1930s, and guests can enjoy some of the old-fashioned details that the owners left behind. The rooms have hardwood or elegant parquet floors, dark wood paneling, detailed moldings, archways, iron chandeliers, bay windows, and dark-hued furniture. Some of the rooms even have decorative stone fireplaces or sloped ceilings. All the rooms are large and very comfortable; the bathrooms have good proportions and great showers. Room no. 23, with its enormous balcony and views of both the garden and the city, is one of my favorites. Room no. 20 is gigantic with a kitchen, sink, and refrigerator. The rooms in the front of the hotel tend to be a bit noisy.

Av. 12 de Octubre N26-15 and Coruña, Quito. ©/fax **02/2225-121** or 02/2564-382. santabarbara@ porta.net. 16 units (3 w/tubs). $65 double; $78 triple. AE, DC, MC, V. **Amenities:** Restaurant; bar; laundry service. *In room:* TV.

Hotel Café Cultura ★★ *Finds*   In the heart of the New Town, the Café Cultura is definitely one of the most unique and interesting hotels in Quito. What used to be the French Cultural Center, this old but beautifully renovated house is now the hippest hotel in the city. It's truly an inner-city retreat, complete with a lush garden with resident hummingbirds and doves. All of the rooms have hand-painted designs on the walls and their own personal touches. For example, no. 25 has a tree growing through it; no. 1 has a fireplace, French doors, painted furniture, and a claw-foot tub. Several of the rooms have sloped wooden ceilings; many were renovated in 2003 and all the windows have been soundproofed. In general, the bathrooms are also sights to behold; however, there are some rooms where only a curtain separates the bathroom from the rest of the room. Note that all the rooms are nonsmoking. The charming owner, Laszlo Karolyi, has done a great job of making this hotel feel like a real home. It's also the only hotel in the city not to charge the full 22% service fee but adds only the minimum tax of 12% to your bill. There's a lovely cafe adjacent to the lobby, complete with hardwood floors and flickering candles, that attracts many of the young, hip residents of Quito. This is a great place in which to linger and get a glimpse into the local scene.

Robles and Reina Victoria, Quito. ©/fax **02/2224-271** or 02/2504078. www.cafecultura.com. 26 units (5 w/tubs). $69 double; $79 triple and junior suite; $89 suite. AE, DC, MC, V. **Amenities:** Restaurant; activities desk; limited room service; laundry service; free airport pickup if you book online. *In room:* Safe.

Hotel Vieja Cuba ★ *Finds*   This lovely old colonial house was renovated in 2002 to house the city's newest hotel. The owner, a Cuban immigrant, has spared no expense in the redesign: A soothing fountain in the courtyard and gleaming hardwood floors lead to cozy rooms with exposed brick and modern wooden beds. The rooms are simple but rustic and comfortable. The bathrooms have nice mosaic tile, brand-new everything, and showers with great pressure. Everything is very clean and very new. The larger doubles come with either a sitting area or a fireplace; suite no. 11 has a nice sitting area downstairs and a loft bedroom upstairs with a small balcony. And for $85, it's a great bargain. The attractive restaurant downstairs offers homemade Cuban dishes and great mojitos.

Diego de Almagro 1212 and La Nina, Quito. © **02/2906-729.** Fax 02/2520-738. Viejacuba@andinanet.net. 24 units. $55 double; $70 large double w/sitting area or fireplace; $85 suite. Rates include breakfast. MC, V. **Amenities:** Restaurant; bar; laundry service; massage. *In room:* TV, dataport, hair dryer.

Inexpensive

Hostal Fuente de Piedra I *Finds*   Not to be confused with the less charming Hostal Fuente de Piedra II, this is a great find on a quiet street close to everything. A serene courtyard with a trickling fountain leads to small, simply furnished rooms with exposed stone in some and large picture windows in others. The bathrooms are clean and good-size, though none have tubs. There's a small balcony with reading chairs for guests on the second floor and a very cozy restaurant with fireplace on the ground floor. A three-course meal for lunch costs $3. Although this hotel has been open for 10 years, the management still tries hard to please its guests. This is the only hotel in Quito to offer an alcoholic welcome drink (a kind of orangey mojito) to its guests at check-in.

Wilson 211 and Tamayo, Quito. © **02/2525-314.** Fax 02/2559-775. www.ecuahotel.com. 19 units (shower only). $40 double. Rates include breakfast. AE, MC, V. **Amenities:** Restaurant; bar; lounge. *In room:* TV.

Hostal Jardín del Sol *Value*   The "garden of the sun" hotel offers inexpensive and basic accommodations and is conveniently located close to many of the New Town's bars and restaurants. The friendly staff will welcome you with a smile and seem to genuinely care to make your stay as pleasant as possible. Rooms are small but clean and simply furnished with wooden beds and tiny bathrooms with newly tiled floors. Some rooms have balconies with limited views of Quito. Some have yellow walls as bright as the sunshine (thus the hotel's name). Next to the lobby, there's a computer room with free Internet access for guests. Another nice touch is the complimentary transfer from the airport if you book directly with the hotel—but be sure to call the day before to confirm that you are being met.

Jose Calama 166 and Diego de Almagro, Quito. © **02/2230-941.** Fax 02/2230-950. www.hostaljardin delsol.com. 22 units (shower only). $28 double. Rates include breakfast. AE, MC, V. **Amenities:** Restaurant; laundry service. *In room:* TV, dataport.

IN THE OLD TOWN

I really don't recommend this area for an overnight stay. There are no decent hotels in Old Town and that's mostly due to the fact that this area is not very safe at night. As a result, there hasn't been much hotel development here; if you're looking for good quality accommodations, you won't find much here. Additionally, if you stay in the Old Town, you might feel isolated because everything closes down at night, and most hotels don't recommend strolling through the area after dark.

That said, the most reliable hotel here is the **Hotel Real Audiencia,** Bolívar 220 and Guayaquil (© **02/2952-711;** fax 02/2580-213; www.realaudiencia. com). The rooms feel old and musty, but they are clean and spacious. Some rooms, such as no. 301, have great views of the city. Doubles cost $34, triples and suites $42; rates include breakfast.

Alternatively, you can stay in a true colonial home. The **Hotel San Francisco de Quito,** Sucre 217 and Guayaquil (© **02/2287-758;** fax 02/2951-241; hsfquito@andinanet.net), is housed in a 17th-century building with a charming old-fashioned stone courtyard. Overall, the rooms are quite musty with hard beds, ugly blue comforters, and walls that are in desperate need of a paint job; still, this hotel is one of the only options in this area. There are also mini-apartments available with kitchens and fireplaces. Doubles cost $18 to $22; triples, $28; quads, $36; and rooms for five to six people, $36 to $44. Mini-apartments cost $32 to $37. Rates include breakfast.

WHERE TO DINE
IN THE NEW TOWN

Most locals consider **La Vina,** Isabel La Católica and Cordero (© **02/2566-033;** Tues–Sat noon–3pm and 7:30–10:30pm) to have the best overall service and highest quality international cuisine in the city. I have not included a full review below because they were closed for vacation the entire month of August when I was last in Quito.

Moderate

El Nispero 🌟🌟 *Finds* NEW ECUADORIAN   This hip newcomer on the Quito dining scene has taken the locals by storm. Ask any bigwig where the best Ecuadorian restaurant is and they'll most likely tell you to come here. The restaurant is housed in a charming old home that was totally renovated last year with hardwood floors and blue and yellow walls; a serene, quiet atmosphere prevails throughout. Service is gracious; and unlike other good restaurants in town this one has a young, hip waitstaff (as opposed to old and stuffy). And the food is very good. The specialty is traditional recipes with a twist: The roast pork is served with figs and a mint sauce; the fresh prawns with coconut sauce come with an Ecuadorian nut called *tocte;* pancakes are made from yuca flour and the *humitas* (a kind of corn mush) are served like a pudding, in a bowl. For dessert, try the Oritas—small Ecuadorian bananas drizzled with local honey. The house (Chilean) sauvignon blanc is good and reasonably priced at $2.50 a glass. If you like ice cream, be sure to ask about the *helado* special of the day—it's delicious.

Valladolid N24-438 and Cordero. © 02/2226-398. Main courses $7–$12. AE, DC, MC, V. Tues–Sat noon–4pm and 7 to 11pm; Sun–Mon noon–4pm.

La Querencia 🌟 *Finds* ECUADORIAN   La Querencia offers delicious local food in a beautiful setting. If you're looking to try Ecuadorian specialties such as *seco de chivo* (a lamb stew) or *ceviche* (white fish cooked by contact with acidic citrus juices rather than heat), but you're a bit apprehensive about venturing into a hole-in-the-wall restaurant, La Querencia is for you. From the outside, you can immediately tell that this is a place for wheelers and dealers. On the inside, you'll find large picture windows, which open on to a garden; brightly colored walls decorated with typical Ecuadorian crafts; a fireplace; and charming, large-planked hardwood floors. I recommend starting your meal with *empanadas de verde* and *tortillas de maíz.* **Note:** The locals eat the *empanadas* with their hands, so don't be bashful about using yours. The *seco de chivo* is outstanding, as is the *ceviche.* Other unique dishes include *papas con cuero* (pork skins with potatoes in a peanut sauce) and *arroz con menestra* (a juicy filet served with rice, lentils, and fried bananas). This is definitely the best restaurant in Quito for high-quality local dishes.

Eloy Alfaro 2530 and Catalina Aldaz. © 02/2446-654. Main courses $5–$22. AE, DC, MC, V. Mon–Sat 11am–11pm; Sun 11am–5pm.

Los Troncos Steak House ARGENTINE STEAKHOUSE   This is where Ecuadorian businesspeople meet for power lunches, and where families come to sample some of the best grilled meat in town. When you walk into the restaurant, you'll pass the huge grilling area, where juicy steaks, pork loin, chicken breasts, sausages, and other savory meat specialties are roasting over hot coals. I recommend that you order the *parrillada* (grilled) special, so that you can sample everything on the menu, including the aforementioned meats, plus *riñón* (kidney) and *morcilla* (blood pudding). You can also order everything individually. Because everything is grilled over a coal fire, all the meat has a delicious charcoal flavor. Vegetarians can eat here too—there's a large selection of pasta, soup, and salad (including an impressive salad bar).

Av. de los Shyris 1280 and Portugal. © 02/2437-377. Main courses $6–$14. AE, DC, MC, V. Mon–Sat 10am–11pm; Sun 10am–5pm.

Mare Nostrum 🌟🌟 SEAFOOD   This dimly lit restaurant with a distinctly medieval feel is the best (and most expensive) place in Quito to enjoy fresh seafood. You won't find *ceviche* on the menu; instead, the offerings have more of a European flair. Specialties of the house include bouillabaisse, paella, and other seafood stews. *Arroz del capitán* (rice, prawns, mussels, clams, squid, octopus, and any other fresh seafood available that day mixed with coriander, soy sauce, and onions) is the only Ecuadorian dish on the menu. However, the coconut shellfish dish uses local tropical flavors. Also available are Chilean mussels, lobster, calamari, and fresh fish. The sea bass in a butter and garlic sauce is succulent. Whatever you order, you probably won't be disappointed—the chef has a knack for throwing together different flavors from the sea. Landlubbers beware: Tripe is the only nonseafood dish available.

Mariscal Foch E10-5 and Tamayo. ℂ 02/2528-686. Main courses $7–$21. AE, DC, MC, V. Daily noon–6pm and 7–11:30pm.

Rincón La Ronda Restaurante ⭐ *Overrated* ECUADORIAN This restaurant takes its name from one of the most historic streets in the Old City, with colorful colonial buildings and old-time charm. The restaurant feels very Spanish colonial, with thick white stucco walls, red carpeting, sloped wood ceilings, brick archways, dark wood high-back chairs, and iron chandeliers. But tour buses bring hordes of diners here nightly; very few locals come here. If you're looking to mingle with *Quiteños,* I suggest you skip this place and head to El Nispero (see above). That said, the food here is excellent if slightly lacking in imagination. Highlights of the high-quality Ecuadorian cuisine include *langostinos del Pacífico* (Pacific jumbo shrimp in garlic or tarragon sauce), *brocheta mixta con lomo, pollo, y chancho* (grilled kabob with beef, chicken, and pork), and *pernil con llapingachos, mole, salsa de maní, y aguacate* (roasted leg of pork with mashed potatoes and cheese in a peanut sauce with avocados). For appetizers, I recommend the *ceviche,* chicken *tamales,* and famous Ecuadorian soup *locro de papas con queso y aguacate* (creamy potato soup with cheese and avocado).

Belo Horizonte 400 and Almagro. ℂ 02/2540-459. Main courses $6–$17. AE, DC, MC, V. Daily noon–11pm.

Inexpensive
Las Redes ⭐ SEAFOOD This restaurant serves the best *ceviche* in Quito. I'm not the only one with this opinion; all my local *Quiteño* friends agree. Here, you can order any type of *ceviche* from clams to octopus to fish or shrimp. The chefs here also do an excellent job with all sorts of seafood. One of the specialties includes the *gran mariscada,* which is an enormous beautiful platter of an assortment of sizzling seafood. The *arroz con mariscos* (yellow rice with peppers, onions, mussels, clams, shrimps, calamari, octopus, and crayfish) is also delicious. Even though Las Redes is on one of the busiest streets of Quito, the simple wood tables and fishnets hanging from the ceilings make you feel as though you are at a local seafood joint on the coast.

Av. Amazonas 845 and Veintimilla. ℂ 02/2525-691. Main courses $5–$9. DC, MC, V. Tues–Sat 11am–10pm; Sun 10am–4pm.

The Magic Bean *Kids* BREAKFAST/SANDWICHES The Magic Bean reminds me of a cozy cafe you would find in your hometown. It's not fancy, but it has a pleasant setting with shaded outdoor tables. Expect to see most of the city's expatriates at breakfast and lunch during the week; very few people seem to come here for dinner. The fare is typical cozy cafe food—pancakes, French toast, sandwiches, bagels, omelets, fresh fruit drinks, salads made with organic lettuce, and freshly brewed coffee. Overall, the food is quite good. Just beware: The pancakes are enormous! Clearly, the Magic Bean caters to foreigners, but it's comforting to find a place in Ecuador that reminds you of your favorite little spot at home.

Mariscal Foch 681 (E5-08) and Juan León Mera. ℂ **02/2566-181.** Main courses $2–$6. AE, DC, MC, V. Daily 7am–10pm.

Pavarotti Pizzería *Kids* PIZZA/ITALIAN   Even if you don't like pizza, come here for the view of Quito. The booths have picture-perfect windows, and you can see the whole city and the volcanoes in the distance. The crisp, brick-oven thin-crust pizza is delicious. There are 26 different types, ranging from the basic Margherita (tomato and mozzarella) to the *alle mele* (with tomato, bacon, mint, and apple). Other toppings include tuna, artichokes, chopped meat, prosciutto, Roquefort or Gorgonzola cheese, pineapple, ham, salami, capers, and anchovies. Besides pizza, there is a nice selection of pasta, seafood (including several different preparations of shrimp), chicken, and steak. During the day, you can enjoy the views and pizza in an outdoor patio area.

Whimper N28-39 and Coruña. ℂ **02/2564-616.** Pizzas $4–$7. AE, DC, MC, V. Daily noon–3:30pm and 6:30–11pm.

Red Hot Chile Peppers *Value* MEXICAN   When you've had enough of *ceviche* and *empanadas*, head to this no-frills restaurant for great fajitas and margaritas. The place has only a few wood tables, has graffiti on the walls, and is usually full of foreigners early in the evening; but the food is tasty and flavored with pungent Ecuadorian spices. Besides fajitas, you can also order burritos and other typical Mexican fare.

Mariscal Foch 713 and Juan León Mera. ℂ **02/2557-575.** Main courses $4–$7. No credit cards. Mon–Sat noon–10:30pm.

IN THE OLD TOWN

Only 2 years ago there wasn't a single good restaurant in Old Town. But things are changing fast as the area becomes a bit safer. But if you do come at night, I suggest taking a taxi directly here and then asking the restaurant to call you a taxi for your ride back to your hotel. Strolling on the Plaza de la Independencia after dark is relatively safe as it's the only place in the Old Town where people linger late into the evening, but I don't recommend venturing into any of the side streets at night.

Moderate

El Patio Trattoria *Finds* ITALIAN   Tucked away a few steps from the Plaza de la Independencia, this new restaurant opened in the summer of 2003 and is the only Italian eatery in Old Town. Come here for lunch to enjoy the lovely outdoor area shaded by a giant Magnolia tree and ringed with palm trees. If the weather is bad, the indoor dining room is quite charming with gleaming hardwood floors, high ceilings and live music on the weekends. The food is typically Italian: risotto with shrimp, asparagus and saffron; mussels marinara; and scaloppini Marsala. The most interesting (and yummy) dish is the beef tenderloin with caramelized onions and raisins in a port-wine sauce. For dessert, try the apple turnover drizzled with caramel sauce.

Calle Mejia Oe5-36 (enter from Benalcázar and García Moreno). ℂ **02/2288-140** or 09/9819-533. Main courses $8–$9.50. DC, MC, V. Tues–Sat 11am–11pm; Sun 11am–5pm.

Mea Culpa *Moments* INTERNATIONAL   This grand old restaurant opened in 2003 to much acclaim as it commands one of the most beautiful settings in Old Town. On the second floor of a building that overlooks the Plaza de la Independencia, Mea Culpa is by far the grandest restaurant in the entire city. So grand in fact, that they require "Business Casual" attire if you decide to dine here and if you're caught trying to sneak in with tennis shoes you will be politely thrown out (it happened to me, so I should know!). Dress up if you come here and call ahead for reservations and specify that you want a table by the window. Everybody comes here for the view and not the food. The pricey and mediocre appetizers include a seafood salad, prawn flambé, a cold salmon terrine, frittata mea culpa (like a quesadilla filled with octopus, shrimp, mussels, and calamari). Main courses are rather bland and unimaginative: pastas, filet mignon, and shrimp crepes. Stick to the simplest of dishes and you'll be fine. Remember: You're here for the setting, not the food!

On the Plaza de la Independencia, Venezuela Oe4-22. © 02/2951-190. Reservations recommended. Main courses $10–$16. AE, DC, MC, V. Mon–Fri 12:15–3:30pm and 7–11pm; Sat 7–11pm.

Inexpensive

Café Mosaico ✦✦✦ *Finds* INTERNATIONAL   Much more than a cafe and more like an elite gathering place, Mosaico is hands down, the most spectacular eatery in Ecuador. Set in an old house high up on a hill overlooking the Old Town, Mosaico was opened in 2003 by an Ecuadorian-Greek-American family. The view is beyond belief—the entire city stretched at your feet and the place filled with the crème de la crème of Ecuadorian society. Settle into your beautiful table, inlaid with hand-painted mosaic tiles, and take in the view. Many people come here only for cocktails or dessert and coffee but the food is surprisingly good. The Greek moussaka is delicious, as is the tender souvlaki. The vegetarian lasagna is divine and there's a good selection of delicious sandwiches including a turkey club. This is the only place in Ecuador to serve real New York cheesecake. Reservations are not accepted and this place fills up fast; be prepared to wait for a table. Best time to come here is late afternoons during the week before the after-work crowd arrives; that way you'll score a table fast, get to see the place during the day and also take in the incredible view as the city lights up after dark.

Manuel Samaniego N8-95 and Antepara, Itchimbia. © 02/2542-871. A taxi from the Old Town costs $1.50; $4 from the New Town. Main courses $4–$6. No credit cards. Mon–Wed 4–8pm; Thurs–Sat 11:30am–9:30pm.

Café Tianquez ✦ *Value* ECUADORIAN   This is the perfect place in which to have a quick meal when you're spending the day in Old Town visiting the sights. Just below the Iglesia de San Francisco, the large outdoor cobblestone patio has a sweeping view of the Plaza de San Francisco. The indoor dining room is very small and it can get quite cozy when it's full as you sit elbow to elbow with your neighbors; but the atmosphere is friendly and convivial and the staff works hard to keep everybody happy. The food here is simple and delicious. Order a *plato típico* and you'll get a sampling of local specialties: *empanadas, humitas,* fried yuca, and fried pork. For something lighter, there's a good selection of large salads and sandwiches and freshly squeezed fruit juices.

Plaza de San Francisco. © 02/2954-326. Main courses $2.50–$5. No credit cards. Daily 9:30am–6:30pm.

QUITO AFTER DARK

Bars and clubs abound in Quito; unfortunately, the diversity of nightlife tends to be a bit skimpy. In general, you have either British-style pubs or run-of-the-mill bars and dance clubs. On the plus side, since the locals are extremely friendly, it's not uncommon to make new Ecuadorian friends at a raucous bar or club.

In August 2001, the city government issued a new law stating that all bars and clubs must close at midnight on weekdays, 2am on weekends, so don't expect to party all night long. You should also remember that, at night, Quito can be very dangerous, especially near the bars and clubs. Take a cab, even if it's only for a few blocks; bartenders can call a taxi for you. If you have a cellphone, dial © 02/2222-222 for a taxi 24 hours a day.

BARS & PUBS   One of the most happening places is the **Kama Sutra Bar & Café** ଙ୍ଗ, Calama 380 and Juan León Mera, which fills up with the after-work crowd and stays hopping until after midnight. This is where most *Quiteños* gather with their friends for drinks before dinner or, on weekends, before heading to the disco. **El Pobre Diablo,** Isabel La Católica 1206 near the corner of F. Galaviz (1 block behind the Swissôtel), is a good low-key bar. It's popular with local bohemian types. The **Reina Victoria Pub,** Reina Victoria 530 (between Carrión and Roca), caters to the English-speaking set (expect a nice big "Hello" when you enter). This is one of the few pubs in Quito that serves beer on tap, from a Canadian-owned local brewery. Once you have a fresh-brewed beer in hand, relax by the cozy fireplace or practice your dart game. The **Turtle's Head** on La Niña between Amazonas and Juan León Mera has a similar atmosphere to Reina Victoria, except it also has a pool table and occasional live music. Right next door, also on La Niña, is **Séptimo Cielo** (it doesn't have a sign, but it's a white house with gold-colored columns and black doors; you have to knock to get in), which is one of the few bars in Quito that somehow managed to excuse itself from the curfew law; it stays open quite late but it doesn't attract the most hip of clientele.

DANCE CLUBS   On weekends, everybody heads to the new **Papillon Disco** ଙ, on Pinezón and Colón. There's no cover charge and the music is quite good—a mix of American and Latin pop and some techno. It's the most popular dance club in town and attracts a healthy mix of people, from late teens to early forties. If you're looking for a typical frat-style bar/dance club, **No Bar** on Calama 380 and Juan León Mera is your best bet. The cover charge is $2 and includes a free drink. Music varies from "techno Titanic" to pop Latino music. Even though the bar is in the heart of the tourist area, the crowd is surprisingly local. **Seseribó** ଙ, on Veintimilla and 12 de Octubre (in the basement of the Edificio El Girón), is the best place in town for salsa; there's no cover.

LIVE MUSIC   You can hear live Cuban and Ecuadorian music Wednesday through Saturday at **Varadero,** Reina Victoria 1721 and La Pinta. Note that on Thursday nights, the dancing moves next door to **La Bodeguita de Cuba** ଙ (the crowd sometimes spills out onto the sidewalk; Thurs is the night to come here for sure).

PERFORMING ARTS   The **National Symphony** performs weekly in different venues around town, including some colonial churches; call © 02/ 2256-5733 for up-to-date information. Every Wednesday at 7:30pm, the **Ballet Andino "Humanizarte"** performs traditional Andean dances at the Fundación Cultural "Humanizarte," located on Leonidas Plaza N24-226 and Lizardo García (© 02/226-116). The **Ballet Folkórico Nacional Jacchigua** performs traditional dances and songs on Wednesday and Friday nights at 7:30pm at the Teatro Aeropuerto. Tickets cost $12, and it's easiest to buy them through Metropolitan Touring, which has offices on Amazonas and 18 de Septiembre (© 02/2506-654) and at Av. República de El Salvador N36-84 (© 02/2464-780).

COTOPAXI NATIONAL PARK ☆☆

At 5,897m (19,347 ft.), Cotopaxi is the world's highest continuously active volcano. Your first encounter with the almost perfectly cone-shaped and snow-covered Cotopaxi might be from overhead in a plane. I've been on planes that have flown terrifyingly close to the volcano, where I almost felt I could reach out and touch it. From up above, it's hard to determine where the clouds end and where the glaciers begin. The snow glimmers in the sunlight and magically mixes in with the bright blue sky—what a sight! On a clear day in Quito, even if you're not airborne, it's easy to see Cotopaxi standing high and mighty above the clouds.

Looking down at a volcano from a plane is one thing—climbing it is a whole different animal. But every year, thousands of intrepid climbers take out their ice axes, strap on their crampons, and head out to conquer the summit. From what I've heard, the climb is not terribly complicated. However, I have met several experienced climbers who have been severely affected by the altitude and were forced to turn back early. Be sure to spend several days in Quito acclimating before you attempt Cotopaxi, and even if you're feeling fine at 2,800m (9,184 ft.), remember that the air will feel a whole lot thinner at 5,000m (16,400 ft.), especially if you're exerting a lot of energy. You should also note that the climb typically starts at about 1am and you will be going uphill on glaciers for about 8 hours straight before you reach the top. This way, you reach the crater before the clouds settle in.

Fortunately for the less adventurous, you really don't need to climb Cotopaxi to enjoy it. Several outfitters in Quito organize day trips to the volcano. Some day trips take you on a long and bumpy journey to the parking lot, which is actually a lot more interesting that you might expect. The parking lot is 4,500m (14,760 ft.) above sea level—at this altitude, the air is quite thin and it's not uncommon to feel lightheaded. Plus, the wind is mighty strong up here and can knock you over. From the parking lot, you can walk about 45 minutes to the *refugio* (4,723m/15,744 ft.); if you still have some steam after you reach the *refugio,* you can forge ahead for about another hour to the point where the glaciers begin. In a day trip, this is about as far as you can get to the top. The views are phenomenal, and once you get accustomed to the thin air, you might even a feel a bit giddy. Be sure to bring warm clothes and good hiking shoes. The terrain is rough and the wind can be bitter.

ORGANIZING A CLIMB TO THE TOP   It's very important to make sure that you're climbing Cotopaxi with an experienced guide and good equipment. The best companies provide one guide for every two climbers. The best and most experienced outfitter is **Safari,** Calama 389 and Juan León Mera (© **02/2552-505**). The trip costs $165 per person for 2 days and 1 night; food, equipment, and one guide for every two climbers are included.

DAY TRIPS   Almost every travel agency in Quito offers a similar day trip to Cotopaxi, which includes a hike from the parking lot to the *refugio.* For $40, **Safari,** Calama 389 and Juan León Mera (© 02/2552-505), will organize day hikes in the area. **Metropolitan Touring,** Amazonas and 19 de Septiembre (© 02/2506-654), arranges panoramic tours, where you may or may not reach the parking lot. (You definitely will *not* have time to hike up to the *refugio.*) The tour does, however, include lunch at a typical hacienda. If you want to hike around Cotopaxi, be sure to ask your organizer what exactly the tour includes. *Note:* On all tours, you will have to pay an additional $10 national park fee.

Alternatively, you can also organize a day trip to Cotopaxi on your own. You can hire a taxi in Quito for about $50 to $60 round-trip. The ride from Quito to the parking lot takes about 1½ hours. Once you reach the parking lot, you can then hike up to the *refugio* or glacier at your own pace, while the taxi waits for you. This is my preferred way of visiting Cotopaxi.

MOUNTAIN BIKING   Most mountain-biking trips start at the parking lot and head down a windy, bumpy, and windy road. You will bike through a dense pine forest, where you will have the opportunity to see a variety of birds and stop at some beautiful lakes. **Arie's Bike Company,** Wilson 578 and Reina Victoria (© 02/2906-052; www.ariesbikecompany.com), and **Biking Dutchman,** Foch 714 and Juan León Mera (© 02/2568-323; www.ecuadorexplorer.com/dutchman), arrange biking trips for $40 per person—the price includes a box lunch, equipment, and protective gear. **ECO ADVENTOUR,** Foch 634 and Reina Victoria (© 02/2223-720; www.ecoadventour.com), also arranges biking trips in the area.

BELLAVISTA CLOUD FOREST RESERVE 🐦🐦

Bellavista is one of the most exciting side trips you can take from Quito. Within 2 hours, you will escape the city and find yourself in a cloud forest—or, more technically, in the Choco bioregion, which is one of the most diverse places on earth. As you explore the 720-hectare (1,800-acre) Bellavista Reserve, you will have the opportunity to hike to waterfalls, bird-watch (there are about 275 different bird species in the area, including the giant antpitta, Tanager finch, oscillated tapaculo, and my personal favorite, the plate-billed mountain toucan), and enjoy an incredible diversity of flora (including bromeliads, orchids, mosses, and an unbelievable variety of flowers).

Since Bellavista is only about 2 hours from Quito, you can easily come in the morning and leave in the afternoon, but I recommend staying overnight in the dome-shaped **Bellavista Hotel,** one of the most unique places to stay in the world. It's not fancy, but the views over the forest canopy are dramatic, the food is excellent, and the nature guides will open up your eyes to a whole different world. The rooms in the thatched-roof bamboo dome all have their own balconies and picture-perfect views of birds and the surrounding mountainside. Ten rooms have private bathrooms and hot showers. There is also a dormitory-style room with a shared bathroom. You can arrange a 2-day/1-night special package, which includes accommodations, transportation, one guided tour, and four meals for $134 per person. For the dormitory, the package costs $99 per person. If you don't want to pay for transportation, food and lodging cost $58 per person per night. Day trips cost about $64 per person and include breakfast and lunch, round-trip transportation, and a guided tour. For more information, you can contact Bellavista's office in Quito at Jorge Washington E7-23 between 6 de Diciembre and Reina Victoria (© **02/2232-313** or 02/2901536; www.ecuadorexplorer.com/bellavista/home).

GETTING THERE   If you're staying at the hotel, you can sign up for a package that includes transportation, or arrange private transportation in a taxi from Quito for $45 to $50 each way. It's a little more complicated to travel to Bellavista on your own: You have to take a 2-hour bus ride from Quito to Nanegalito, where you can arrange for a truck (ask around for Raúl Chaneusi) to take you on the 45-minute ride to Bellavista. The ride costs about $15 (for the whole vehicle, not per person).

4 Otavalo & Imbabura Province

Otavalo: 95km (59 miles) N of Quito, 515km (319 miles) NE of Guayaquil, 537km (333 miles) N of Cuenca

Imbabura Province, and the town of Otavalo in particular, is a shopper's paradise. The locals, known as *Otavaleños,* have been famous for their masterful craftsmanship for centuries. The market in Otavalo is the area's best-known attraction and one of the most popular markets in Ecuador. In Otavalo's main plaza, the local people still wear their traditional clothing as they sell their exquisite handicrafts. Saturday is the main market day, and this is when the town bursts with life. But luckily for travelers with tight schedules, the market has become so popular that it now takes place on the other 6 days of the week, though on a much smaller scale. In addition to shopping at Otavalo's market, you can also explore the back roads of the province and visit local studios. Some of the smaller towns specialize in specific crafts: Cotacahi is known for leather work, San Antonio de Ibarra for its age-old woodcarving techniques.

Even nonshoppers will love Otavalo and its surroundings. The town has an almost perfect setting. It's nestled in the Sunrise Valley in the shadow of two protective volcanoes, Cotacachi and Imbabura. According to local legend, Cotacachi is the area's symbolic mother; Imbabura is the father, standing watch. To feel the inspirational powers of Mother Nature, I recommend spending a few days exploring the area, breathing in the fresh air, gazing at the dark blue waters of the local crater lakes, and standing in awe of the snow-covered volcanoes. After you find the perfect alpaca sweater, you can wear it as you take a stroll around Cuicocha Lake or a hike in the mountains; then you can soothe your sore muscles by trying out the ancient health remedies at one of the several traditional spas in the area.

ESSENTIALS
GETTING THERE

Every hotel listed in this section provides a **private shuttle** from Quito directly to the hotel; prices range from $40 to $50 for two to four people. You can also take a **taxi** from Quito to the Otavalo area; the state-mandated price for the 1½-hour ride is $35. If you're heading for the market, I recommend taking a taxi. **Buses** are the least expensive and most hectic option—they leave every 15 minutes from about 4am to 6:30pm, and a one-way ticket costs $2. You'll want to catch the bus to Ibarra and get off in Otavalo; the ride takes about 2½ hours. The bus station in Otavalo is located on Quito and Atahualpa, about a 15-minute walk from Plaza de los Ponchos.

GETTING AROUND

There is little reason to spend much time in Ibarra, the capital of Imbabura Province. If you're looking for "big city" action, you should base yourself in Otavalo. It's not quite a thriving metropolis, but it does have a decent infrastructure for tourists (lots of gringo-style restaurants, Internet cafes, travel agencies, and of course, the huge artisan market on Sat). Additionally, most of the best hotels are outside of Otavalo; you can easily take a taxi for $4 or $5 between the hotels and the highlights of the area.

It's not difficult to travel around Imbabura Province. Taxis aren't expensive—for example, from Otavalo to Cotacachi or San Antonio de Ibarra, taxis only cost about $3 to $4 each way. You can also hop on a bus in Otavalo at the bus terminal, which is located on the corner of Ordoñez and Atahualpa, and ask the driver to drop you off at towns or hotels anywhere between Otavalo and Ibarra

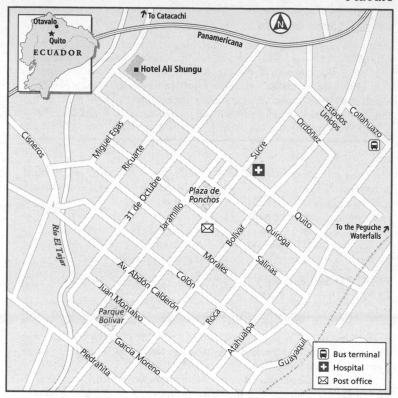

or in the Lago San Pablo area. A short bus jaunt generally costs about 25¢. Hotels can also arrange transportation for you; rates range from $4 an hour for a taxi to $15 to $20 an hour for a van.

VISITOR INFORMATION

There is no formal visitor information center in Otavalo, but all the travel agencies are extremely friendly and give out general information for free. My favorite is **Runa Tupari Native Travel** 𝒢, located right on Plaza de los Ponchos between Sucre and Quiroga (𝒞 **06/925-985;** www.runatupari.com). This agency is the only nonprofit travel agency in Otavalo and it supports rural indigenous communities. **Dicency Viajes,** on the corner of Sucre and Colón, is also helpful.

FAST FACTS Banks aren't abundant in Otavalo, but the **Filanbanco** on Sucre between Colón and Calderon has an ATM. You can exchange money or cash traveler's checks at **Banco del Pichincha,** which is just north of Plaza de los Ponchos on Sucre between Quiroga and Quito. **Vaz Cambios,** Plaza de los Ponchos at Juan Jaramillo and Saona, also changes money.

If you need a hospital, head to **Hospital San Luis** (𝒞 **06/920-144**) on Calle Sucre and Quito. Pharmacies work on a *turno* system, which means that each pharmacy periodically takes responsibility for being open 24 hours. The **Farmacia Otavalo** (𝒞 **06/920-716**) at Colón 510 between Sucre and Juan Jaramillo is very helpful.

┌───
Tips **Sunny Otavalo**

Otavalo is practically on the equator. It's also located at about 2,700m (9,000 ft.) above sea level. The sun here is extremely powerful. To top it all off, in the main market, there is not one single ounce of shade. Be sure to bring plenty of sunscreen and a brimmed hat, and carry water with you at all times. It gets very hot, so dress appropriately—light pants and a short-sleeved shirt will be fine. If you plan on heading out to Cuicocha Lake, you'll also need a sweatshirt (it gets cold up there).
└───

It's easy to find an Internet cafe in Otavalo. Fast connections can be found at **Internet Native** on Sucre between Colón and Morales. The **post office** is adjacent to Plaza de los Ponchos on the corner of Salinas and Sucre. It's on the second floor of a dreadful building that is constantly under construction. Yes, it looks as though the building has been condemned, but it hasn't, so head up the stairway and walk past the mini–construction site to the post office. For telephone calls, your best bet is to head to one of the Internet cafes.

WHAT TO SEE & DO
EXPLORING THE AREA

Imbabura Province is most famous for the Saturday market in Otavalo. The market is indeed a must-see, but shoppers shouldn't stop there—the whole area is well known for its artisan traditions. Outside of Otavalo, you can visit weavers' studios in Peguche, leather shops in Cotacachi, and woodcarving workshops in San Antonio de Ibarra.

Nature lovers should also take note: With the snow-covered Cayambe overhead and green mountains in the distance, Imbabura is a place of stunning beauty. There are several excellent hikes in the area, including one from Otavalo to the Peguche Waterfalls or the 4-hour hike around Cuicocha, the crater lake. Several travel agencies in Otavalo can arrange hiking, trekking, and horseback-riding excursions to some of the most beautiful and off-the-beaten path spots in the area.

If you have limited time, it is possible to see the highlights of Imbabura Province in 1 day. But, frankly, it's a tiring trip from Quito for just 1 day. Plan to spend at least one or two nights here. It's best if you explore the area with a guide—you'll be able to visit indigenous communities or hike on trails that are a bit off-the-beaten path. (*Note:* Many tour companies will try to convince you to spend some time at San Pablo Lake, but the lake is nothing too special, and your time will be better spent at some of the attractions listed below.) **Runa Tupari Native Travel** , located right on Plaza de los Ponchos between Sucre and Quiroga (© **06/925-985;** www.runatupari.com), and **Dicency Viajes,** on the corner of Sucre and Colón (© **06/921-217**), are the two best agencies in town. Runa Native uses native guides for all their tours, including a trip to the sacred sites of the area.

OTAVALO MARKET The market at Otavalo presents some of the best bargains in Ecuador and, just as important, some of the best people-watching. On Saturday, the city becomes one big shopping area. It's not just for tourists; Ecuadorians come here too, from miles away, to peddle and buy high-quality handmade goods. The *Otavaleños* are extremely friendly and helpful, and they wear beautiful traditional clothing. Overall, this is one of the most colorful markets in Ecuador and the handicrafts are of excellent quality.

Some of the most interesting buys include handmade alpaca sweaters, soft alpaca scarves, wool fedoras, colorful straw bags, hand-embroidered blouses, ceramics, tapestries, fresh pineapple, and llamas. Yes, llamas. Early in the morning on Saturday, there is an animal market, where you can exchange your cow for a llama or simply buy a dozen chickadees. To get to the animal market from the main plaza, walk down Sucre or Bolívar to Morales. Take a right on Morales and walk straight for about 5 blocks and cross over the bridge. Turn right after the bridge and then take a left at the next main street. The animal market is about half a block up. Get here early (around 7 or 8am) because the market closes down at 10am. There is also an excellent fresh produce market in Plaza 24 de Mayo.

Saturday is market day, but there is a small market every day in Plaza de los Ponchos. Whatever day of the week you visit, you'll find the same great crafts on sale here, and the same beautiful people selling them. I find that the Saturday market is a bit overwhelming—I prefer coming on a weekday, when I don't have to visit millions of stands to be sure that I have found the most perfect bag or hat.

Shoppers should expect to do some bargaining, but I've found that prices will only drop a dollar or two (or 10% at most). Don't worry—the asking price is usually quite low, and everything here is already a bargain.

CUICOCHA LAKE *✿* Cuicocha is a sparkling blue crater lake, formed about 3,000 years ago when the crater of the volcano collapsed onto itself during an eruption. The crater was covered with snow and when the snow melted, this lake was born. When the Incas came here, they thought that the island in the middle looked like a *cuy* (guinea pig), hence the name Cuicocha (guinea pig lake). You can take a motorized boat ride out to the island in the middle of the lake—you'll see *totora* (the reed used in this area for making baskets and floor coverings), ducks, and a primary forest. The ride costs $2 per person. Be sure to bring a warm sweater, because the wind here can be vicious.

Cuicocha Lake also happens to be situated in one of the most dramatic settings in Ecuador. A trail loops around the crater—it takes about 4 hours to circle the whole thing. But even if you walk along it for only 5 minutes, you'll be able to see Otavalo, Cotacachi, Cayambe, and all the volcanoes of Imbabura Province.

There is no public transportation available from Otavalo to Cuicocha; it's best to hire a taxi in Otavalo. A round-trip ride costs about $12, and the journey takes about 30 minutes each way.

COTACACHI Cotacachi is a sleepy little pueblo with incredible vistas. From here, you can see the snow-covered Cayambe and the lush green mountains in the distance. But no one comes here for the views (because Cuicocha, about 10 min. up the road, offers the best views in all of Imbabura Province). Cotacachi is famous for its leather stores that line Avenida 10 de Agosto. The quality varies widely, but if you search hard enough, you are bound to find some great bargains. Cotacachi is about 15 minutes from Otavalo; you can easily take a public bus from the station in Otavalo, or hire a taxi for about $5 each way.

PEGUCHE Peguche is home to some of the best weavers in Ecuador. It's a tiny town located about 10 minutes outside of Otavalo (a $3 taxi ride). If you stop in the main square, you can visit the galleries and studios of José Cotacachi, a master weaver. If you visit the town on a guided tour (which I highly recommend), you will explore the back streets of Peguche and visit the homes of some of the town's best weavers and learn about the whole old-fashioned process of spinning wool. Peguche is also famous for its musical instruments.

SAN ANTONIO DE IBARRA Cedar wood is abundant in Imbabura Province. Take a trip to San Antonio de Ibarra and you can see how local wood-carvers transform this raw wood into high art. The town is full of galleries selling wood figurines in almost every shape and size that you could ever imagine. They are all beautifully hand-painted. The best stores are on the main street, 25 de Noviembre. I recommend stopping in at **Galería de Arte Gabriel Cevallos** and **Pájaro Brujo.** To get here, you can take a public bus from the main terminal in Otavalo. Otherwise, a taxi should cost about $6 each way for the 30-minute trip.

MOJANDA LAKES About 30 minutes outside of Otavalo, you will find the Mojanda Lakes, which you can explore in a day of hiking. Mount Fuya Fuya stands majestically above the lakes, creating a beautiful setting. This is a great spot for bird-watching—more than 100 species of birds fly in the area, including the giant hummingbird and the endangered Andean condor. A taxi here costs about $12 each way.

OUTDOOR ACTIVITIES

Hiking trails abound. One of my favorite hikes is the 4-hour trek around Cuicocha Lake; robberies have been reported in the area, so it's best to do the trail with a guide. You can also hike from Cuicocha to the Mojanda Lakes, up Coctachi Volcano, or around the Mojanda Lakes and up Mount Fuya Fuya. Both **Dicency Viajes** (© 06/921-217) and **Runa Tupari Native Travel** (© 06/925-985; www.runatupari.com) can provide experienced guides and help organize your hiking excursions.

Dicency Viajes also specializes in **horseback-riding** trips. One of the most popular is the trail around Cuicocha Lake. A half-day trip costs $40 per person. If you stay at Hacienda Pinsaquí (p. 525), you can also take guided trips of the area for $12 an hour.

WHERE TO STAY

If you want to stay in the town of Otavalo itself, try the **Hotel Ali Shungu** (© 06/920-750; www.alishungu.com) on Calle Quito and Miguel Egas. The rooms aren't fancy at all, but they are all large and decorated with local handicrafts; doubles cost $40. (If you book through the hotel's website you can usually score at 20% discount off the above price.) This is the best hotel in town. But when I'm in Otavalo, I prefer the solitude and tranquillity of the hotels outside of the city. Here are a few of my favorites.

EXPENSIVE

Hacienda Cucin ★★★ *(Finds* This 17th-century hacienda is my favorite in the Otavalo area, especially if you're looking for a mix of luxury and history. Englishman Nicholas Millhouse bought the property some 12 years ago and has lovingly restored it to its past grandeur, paying particular attention to the magnificent landscaping. Cucin sits on over 4 hectares (10 acres) of lush gardens and cobblestone courtyards overflowing with bougainvillea, orchids, and palm trees. Rooms are located in the renovated one-story hacienda and come with antique furnishings and high ceilings. The garden cottages are newly constructed but have a wonderfully rustic feel; they're scattered throughout the lush grounds and come with working fireplaces and wooden bed and armoires. The owner's suite is large enough for a family of four. All units have spacious bathrooms with lovely blue tile. The friendly staff can help you arrange a myriad of activities including the popular overnight horseback riding trip to the Imbambura volcano. Spanish language classes are available also. The restaurant serves a wonderful dinner by candlelight so there's no need to leave the property after dark. There's a computer with Internet access for guests to use at the reception.

San Pablo del Lago, Otavalo. © **06/918-013.** Fax 06/918-003. www.haciendacucin.com. 42 units. $105 double; $120 triple; $140 quad; $120 garden cottages; $200 owner's suite. AE, DC, MC, V. **Amenities:** 2 restaurants; bar; game room; activities desk. *In room:* No phone.

Hacienda Pinsaquí ✿ *Moments*   The Hacienda Pinsaquí is one of the great historic hotels of Ecuador. The 200-year-old hacienda is a feast for the senses. The antique floors have the seasoned scent of old wood. The homey smell of well-worn fireplaces permeates the air. The narrow, old-fashioned hallways are filled with flowers fresh from the outdoor gardens. And the rooms are sumptuous; each one is unique, but all have a touch of old-fashioned country elegance. Room no. 8 has a magnificent canopy bed, beautiful antique furniture, and a Jacuzzi, as well as a separate sitting area where you can gaze out onto the property's wonderfully landscaped gardens. In general, though, the bathrooms aren't perfect: The blue toilets and sinks don't mesh well with the classic decor. On the plus side, some do have charming claw-foot tubs. Once you leave the comfort of your cozy room, you can walk around the property's gardens or explore the area by horseback. (The hotel offers guided riding tours.)

Panamericana Norte, Km 5, Otavalo. © **06/946-116.** Fax 06/946-117. www.pinsaqui.com. 20 units. $99 double; $110 triple; $122 quad. Rates include tax and breakfast. AE, MC, DC, V. **Amenities:** 2 restaurants; original 17th-c. bar; horseback riding; limited room service; laundry service. *In room:* No phone.

La Mirage Garden Hotel & Spa ✿✿✿   If you're looking for luxury, you won't find any better hotel in the highlands than this one. It's owned by the same guy who owns Mansión del Angel in Quito; clearly, interior design and landscaping are his specialty. All the rooms are essentially suites, with separate sitting areas and fireplaces. Every one of them could be featured in the pages of *House & Garden.* Some rooms have brass canopy beds; others have antique wood frames. Crystal chandeliers brighten the rooms, while plush Oriental carpets decorate the floors. The spacious bathrooms come with extra-large showers. All the rooms have sloped wood ceilings, which gives them a rustic feeling. Reina Sofía of Spain stayed in stately no. 114, and I'm sure she must have felt right at home. Room no. 109 overlooks a garden with a handful of colorful peacocks. You will surely be spoiled here: Turndown service consists of lighting the fire in your private fireplace and slipping two hot water bottles in your bed. The spa here was the first one to open in Ecuador and it's a real classic. You can indulge in clay baths and body massages, or treat yourself to a full-body purification performed by a local female shaman. The outdoor gardens are also magnificent. The outstanding restaurant offers the only fine dining experience in the region.

At the end of Calle 10 de Agosto, Cotacachi. © **800/327-3573** in the U.S., or 06/915-237. Fax 02/915-065. www.larc1.com. 23 units (shower only). $220–$280 double; $300–$550 suite. DC, MC, V. Rates include breakfast and dinner. **Amenities:** 2 restaurants; bar; pristine indoor pool; tennis court; tiny exercise room; full spa; limited room service; dry cleaning; laundry service. *In room:* TV, hair dryer, safe.

MODERATE
Casa Mojanda ✿   Ever wondered what it would be like to stay in the middle of nowhere? Stay at the Casa Mojanda and you'll find out. The hotel is located

only about 10 minutes outside of Otavalo, but the isolated 7.2-hectare (18-acre) property is nestled in a valley surrounded by mountains and rolling green hills. The vistas are phenomenal, unspoiled by any man-made structures. The cabins are rustic chic; all of them have either tile or hardwood floors, antique dressers, small reed floor coverings, and tons of personal touches. Several have their own personal fireplaces. You can enjoy the spectacular views from the comfort of your own bed. Room no. 6 is great for families—it has a kitchenette, a separate living room, and separate bedrooms. The gorgeous dining area, filled with antiques and local crafts, serves as the heart of the hotel. This is where you can enjoy scenic vistas as well as divine home-cooked meals, all made with food grown in the hotel's gardens. The English-speaking owners are charming.

Casilla 160, Otavalo. (C) 09/731-737. Fax 09/731-737. www.casamojanda.com. 10 units. $60 per person. Rates include breakfast and dinner. No credit cards. **Amenities:** Restaurant; Jacuzzi; game room; laundry service; library. *In room:* No phone.

WHERE TO DINE

There aren't any great restaurants in Otavalo itself. The recommended hotels (see "Where to Stay," above) serve the best food in the area. La Mirage has the only fine dining restaurant in the region. Casa Mojanda, Hacienda Pinsaqui, and Hacienda Cucin all have excellent restaurants featuring local specialties. (Dinner is included in the price of a room at Casa Mojanda and La Mirage).

If you're in Otavalo shopping for the day, I recommend having lunch at the restaurant of the **Hotel Ali Shungu** ((C) **06/920-750;** www.alishungu.com) on Calle Quito and Miguel Egas. It's nothing fancy but has good homemade Ecuadorian dishes. Nothing costs more than $7.

The food at **Casa Mojanda** (F) is outstanding. The menu is mainly vegetarian, but they occasionally offer a fish dish. All of the food served here is fresh from the hotel's garden, and that freshness makes all the difference in the world. As an added bonus, the dining room is nestled into the side of a mountain; the views are phenomenal. Lunch or dinner here costs $15. The hotel is located about 10 minutes outside of Otavalo on the road to Mojanda (a taxi here should cost about $4).

If you're looking for somewhere with a view, then I suggest dining at a restaurant overlooking the largest lake in Ecuador, Lago San Pablo. The restaurant of the **Hostería Puerto Lago,** Lago San Pablo and Panamerican Hwy., Km 5/12, Otavalo ((C) **06/920-920**), sits right on the lake and serves delicious fresh grilled trout in addition to the usual Ecuadorian and Continental offerings. Almost every table has a lake view with the magnificent Imbabura volcano in the background. Main courses are $6 to $8 and MasterCard and Visa are accepted. The restaurant is open daily from 7:30am to 9pm.

5 El Oriente (F)(F)

Lago Agrio: 259km (160 miles) NE of Quito, 674km (418 miles) NE of Guayaquil, 700km (434 miles) NE of Cuenca

The vast territory of Ecuador that stretches from the eastern slopes of the Andes all the way to the border with Peru is known as El Oriente (the east). It's commonly called the Amazon region because the rivers here—created by melting snow coming down from the Andes—flow into the Amazon. The junglelike landscape and the rainforest have been home to Native American groups for thousands of years. Because of the Andes, the people here have lived in almost complete isolation. Some tribes have only had contact with the "outside world" since the 1970s. Their languages and lifestyle are markedly different from those who live on the other side of the mountains. In order to adapt to the somewhat harsh conditions of the region, they have developed a special relationship with the natural resources of the area. When you take a trip to El Oriente, you will have the opportunity to meet with these people, who will share their land with you and teach you some of their age-old secrets.

In addition to learning about the local cultures, you will also have the opportunity to explore the incredible biodiversity that exists here. Fifty-seven percent of all mammals in Ecuador live here in the Amazon basin, and there are more than 15,000 different species of plants in Ecuador's tropical rainforest. You'll have the chance to see almost 300 different species of tropical birds, dolphins, 11 different species of monkeys, sloths, anacondas, boas, giant otters, turtles, and if you're very lucky, the rare and elusive jaguars.

A healthy ecotourism business has developed here over the past 10 years. There are several excellent jungle lodges, built to blend in with the natural environment. Naturalist guides from these lodges will take you on all sorts of excursions: walks through the forest to learn about the medicinal properties of the local plants; fishing trips where you will try to catch piranhas; early-morning bird-watching expeditions to see parrots, macaws, and other tropical birds; visits to traditional villages; canoe rides at night in search of caimans; and outings where you can paddle down river in an old-fashioned canoe. Just be sure to bring plenty of mosquito repellent!

ESSENTIALS
GETTING THERE

All of the jungle lodges listed below arrange their own transportation. Because many of these lodges are extremely isolated and difficult to find, I strongly encourage you to book your trip in Quito. Depending on where you're staying, the journey usually involves a commercial flight to Coca or Lago Agrio. Flights on **Icaro** (© 800/883-567; www.icaro-air.com) cost about $120 round-trip. From there, your lodge will pick you up and take you the rest of the way in a motorized canoe. For extremely out-of-the-way places such as Kapawi, you can only reach the lodge via a charter flight on a tiny plane. The views of Ecuador as you pass from the Andes to the jungle are phenomenal.

ORIENTATION

El Oriente consists of six different provinces, but it is generally divided up into two general areas: the **northern Oriente** and the **southern Oriente.** The northern part has been hit hard by the oil industry and the lack of security close to the border with Colombia. In fact, the State Department has issued a travel advisory warning against travel to the northernmost regions of Ecuador. I suggest sticking to the areas closer to Coca in the southern Oriente which aren't as developed, partly because there hasn't been much oil exploration in the area. These areas are also the safest parts of the jungle.

JUNGLE LODGES

Trips to the jungle usually last 4 or 5 days. In general, the 4-day trips leave on Friday and return on Monday. The 5-day trips run from Monday through Friday.

In addition to Kapawi (see below), I recommend **La Selva Jungle Lodge** (www.laselvajunglelodge.com), with its own butterfly farm and physically challenging Amazon Light Brigade program, where you spend your whole trip in the outdoors sleeping in tents. The offices in Quito are located on Av. 6 de Diciembre 2816 y Paul Rivet (© **02/2550-995**). Another excellent option is **Sacha Lodge** (www.sachalodge.com) located right on Pilchicocha Lake, 2 hours by canoe from Coca. This beautiful lodge has a unique observation tower—40m (131 ft.) high—that allows for sweeping views of the rainforest and excellent bird-watching. Tours for both properties include transportation to the lodges and three delicious meals per day and are similarly priced: around $575 per person for 4 days and $725 for 5 days. The Chef at Sacha Lodge can whip up excellent vegetarian meals if advance notice is given. Their offices in Quito are located at Julio Zaldumbide 375 and Toledo (© **02/2566-090**).

Kapawi Ecolodge & Reserve ★★★   In the late 1980s, the tropical rain-forests of the Amazon River basin were being destroyed at a rate of approximately 51,800 sq. km (20,000 square miles) per year. If it weren't for people like the ones who run Kapawi, all may have been lost. But Kapawi is a bright example of sustainable tourism. This lodge has been developed with the cooperation and participation of the local Achuar community; in the year 2011, Canodros (the owners of Kapawi) will hand over the lodge to them. In the meantime, the company is paying a monthly rent for the use of the land and training the community in the areas of business and tourism.

All of the structures here were built using traditional methods and environ-mentally friendly technology. The 20 cabins are rustic in a handsome way and extremely comfortable, with polished wood floors, thatched roofs, and bamboo walls. After a hard day of hiking or canoeing, you can relax in a hammock on your own balcony as you gaze down at the river below. The bathrooms are small, but the showers have solar-heated hot water (a rarity in the jungle). The food here is so good that it's hard to believe that you're in the middle of the jungle.

Beyond the accommodations, the excursions are well organized and loads of fun. Two guides—a local from the Achuar community and an English-speaking naturalist—lead the trips and will point out wildlife and discuss the local trees and plants. When you visit the local village, don't worry—the Achuar people won't be offended if you don't drink the *chicha* (an alcoholic beverage made from corn by the local women; when they chew on the corn, their saliva works to ferment it). Spend a few days at Kapawi and you will leave with memories that last a lifetime.

6251 SW 57th St., South Miami, FL 33143. © **305/662-2965.** Fax 305/662-2953. www.kapawi.com. 20 units (shower only). $600–$820 double for 3 nights; $720–$975 double for 4 nights; $1,100–$1,495 double for 7 nights. Airfare is an additional $200 per person. Rates include accommodations, all meals, guide services, and all excursions. AE, DC, MC, V. **Amenities:** Restaurant and bar; library.

6 Cuenca ★★

442km (274 miles) S of Quito, 250km (155 miles) SE of Guayaquil, 254km (157 miles) S of Riobamba

Cuenca is Ecuador's third-largest city, but it feels much more like a charming small town. UNESCO designated Cuenca a World Heritage Site in 1999. Once you're here, you'll immediately understand why. Much of the city's colonial architecture remains intact. Even before the Spanish arrived here, however, Cuenca was the second-largest city in the Inca empire (after Cusco). The foun-dations of former Inca palaces later became foundations for the city's churches. Amazingly enough, before the Incas conquered the area, the Cañaris, a mysteri-ous culture from no one knows where, lived in the area. The Incas used stones from the Cañaris structures to build their palaces.

Cuenca

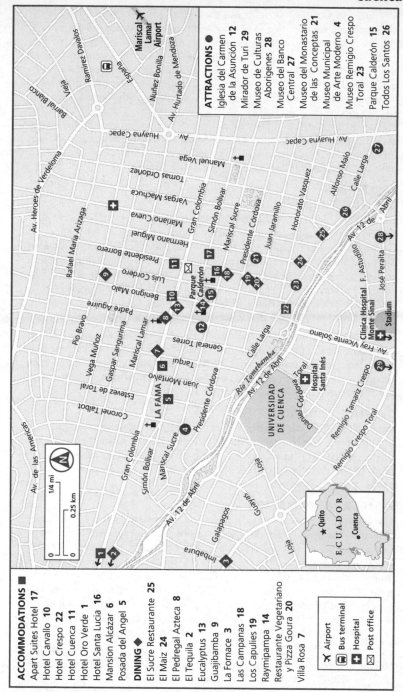

ATTRACTIONS ●

Iglesia del Carmen de la Asunción **12**
Mirador de Turi **29**
Museo de Culturas Aborígenes **28**
Museo del Banco Central **27**
Museo del Monasterio de las Conceptas **21**
Museo Municipal de Arte Moderno **4**
Museo Remigio Crespo Toral **23**
Parque Calderón **15**
Todos Los Santos **26**

ACCOMMODATIONS ■

Apart Suites Hotel **17**
Hotel Carvallo **10**
Hotel Crespo **22**
Hotel Cuenca **11**
Hotel Oro Verde **1**
Hotel Santa Lucía **16**
Mansion Alcázar **6**
Posada del Angel **5**

DINING ◆

El Sucre Restaurante **25**
El Maíz **24**
El Pedregal Azteca **8**
El Tequila **2**
Eucalyptus **13**
Guajibamba **9**
La Fornace **3**
Las Campanas **18**
Los Capulies **19**
Raymipampa **14**
Restaurante Vegetariano y Pizza Goura **20**
Villa Rosa **7**

✈ Airport
🚌 Bus terminal
✚ Hospital
⊠ Post office

ECUADOR
★ Quito
● Cuenca

Visitors to Cuenca will be treated to a quick history lesson. Many of the museums here are dedicated to the city's rich past. The Museo del Banco Central sits right next to the archaeological site, Pumapungo, which was an Inca palace. Not only can you see artifacts on display in the museum, but you can also put all the pieces together as you wander around the site. A few blocks away, the Todos Los Santos archaeological site literally symbolizes the three layers of history—in one single area, you will see structures with Cañaris, Inca, and Spanish influences.

One day is enough to explore all of Cuenca, but you'll need another couple of days to enjoy the surrounding area. Ingapirca, Ecuador's most impressive Inca ruins, are only 2 hours away; Cajas National Park, which is full of scenic hiking trails and peaceful blue lagoons, is an hour north of the city.

ESSENTIALS
GETTING THERE
BY PLANE   Tame (© 02/2909-900; www.tame.com.ec) and **Icaro** (© 800/883-567; www.icaro-air.com) offer daily flights to Cuenca from Quito and Guayaquil. One-way tickets cost $50 to $58. All planes arrive at the Aeropuerto Mariscal LaMar, which is only 1.5km (1 mile) outside of town. The renovations of the terminal should be complete by late 2004, when the airport will officially become "international." Flights from Tumbes and Piura (both Peruvian border cities) are planned to commence at that time.

Taxis from the airport to the center of town cost about $3.

BY BUS   The Cuenca bus terminal is on Avenida España, about 1.5km (1 mile) northeast of the center of town. The 9-hour ride from Quito costs $11. Buses leave in the morning, midafternoon, and around 8pm. Buses from Guayaquil take about 5 hours and cost $8. The buses that run between Quito and Cuenca stop in Baños and Riobamba along the way.

GETTING AROUND
Parque Calderón is the commercial heart of Ecuador. From here, you can walk to all the banks, travel agencies, hotels, and attractions in town.

Most of the sights in Cuenca are within easy walking distance of the main plaza. To visit the Mirador de Turi, you'll need to take a taxi. It's easy to find one on the street, but hotels can also call one for you.

VISITOR INFORMATION
The main tourist office is located on Mariscal Sucre on the south side of Parque Calderón. The friendly staff can give you maps and help you get your bearings. But for the best visitor information in all of Ecuador, you should head to **TerraDiversa** ⋒ on Calle Hermano Miguel 4-46, about a quarter of a block in from Calle Larga (© 07/823-782). The owners are former tour guides who know all of Ecuador like the back of the their hands. The staff can answer your questions and organize tours in the area. (They have connections with all the best travel agencies in Cuenca.) **Hualambari Tours** ⋒, on Av. Borrero 9-67 next to the post office (© 07/848-768), is also an excellent resource.

FAST FACTS   ATMs are ubiquitous in Cuenca but most of them accept MasterCard and Visa with the Cirrus link only. However, **Banco del Pacífico**, Benigno Malo 9-75 near Gran Colombia (© 07/831-144), has an ATM where you can use most types of bank cards. From 8:30am to 4pm, you can also exchange traveler's checks here (on the 2nd floor, way in the back); the limit is

$200 a day and the fee is $5. **Vaz Cambios** on the corner of Luis Cordero and Gran Colombia also changes traveler's checks; there is a 1.8% commission for all transactions.

Clínica Hospital Monte Sinai, M. Cordero 6-111 and Av. Solano (© 07/ 885-595), is the best hospital in Cuenca. Also good are **Hospital Santa Inés,** Augustín Cueva and Daniel Córdova (© **07/817-888**), and **Clínica Santa Ana,** Av. Manuel J. Calle 1-104 (© **07/817-564**). **Fybeca** is the only 24-hour pharmacy in Cuenca; there are two convenient locations: one at Av. Huayna Capac 6-15 on the corner of Juan Jaramillo (© **07/844-501**), the other on the corner of Gran Colombia and Unidad Nacional (© **07/839-871**). **Farmacia Los Andes** at Borrero 7-57 (© **07/839-029**) is a little closer to the center of town.

For laundry service, your best and cheapest bet is **La Química Automática** located at Borrero 7-34, on the corner of Daniel Córdova. Internet cafes are abundant in Cuenca; two of my favorites are **@lfnet,** on the corner of Borrero and Honorato Vásquez, and **Hol@net,** located at Borrero 5-90 and Juan Jaramillo. The latter also provides relatively cheap international phone service via the Internet. You'll find the **post office** on the corner of Borrero and Gran Colombia. It's open Monday through Friday from 8am to 12:30pm and 2:30 to 6pm, and Saturday from 9am to noon.

WHAT TO SEE & DO
PARQUE CALDERON & NEARBY ATTRACTIONS
Parque Calderón is the historical heart of Cuenca and the center of the action. Here, you'll find both the Catedral Nueva and the Catedral Vieja. The **Catedral Vieja** 🞂🞂, also known as the Iglesia del Sagrario, is the oldest construction in the city. It dates from 1557 and was built over a Pumapungo (Inca) castle. Because cities can't have two cathedrals, once the New Cathedral opened in 1967, the old one went out of business. It's still closed, but by 2005 it will reopen as a museum of religious art. Construction began on the **Cathedral Nueva,** also known as the Catedral de la Inmaculada Concepción, in 1885, but it wasn't completed for almost another 80 years. It has a mix of styles— Romanesque on the outside with Gothic windows. It is modeled on the Battistero (Baptistery) in Florence. The floors are made of white marble imported from Italy. The stained-glass windows have a mix of Catholic and indigenous symbols (the sun and the moon, for example). In 1985, when the pope visited this cathedral and saw the Renaissance-style main altar (which is modeled on the one in St. Peter's in Rome), he looked confused and asked, "Am I in Rome?" The cathedral is open Monday through Friday from 7am to 4:30pm and Saturday from 9am to noon.

Around the corner on Padre Aguirre and Sucre is the **Iglesia del Carmen de la Asunción.** The church is not open to the public, but from the outside you should take note of its unique stone entrance. The church faces the delightful and colorful **Mercado de las Flores (Flower Market).** In the early part of the 20th century, women weren't allowed to work. To create a diversion for them, the men of the city decided to set up this market for the use of women only. Nowadays, anyone can wander around the fresh-smelling market. Ecuador is one of the world's largest exporters of flowers, and there are some real beauties here. And some bargains, too: 25 long-stemmed roses cost $1! Nearby, on Presidente Córdova and Padre Aguirre, is the **Iglesia y Mercado de San Francisco.** At the market, you'll find folk remedies for all sorts of illnesses.

MUSEUMS & OTHER POINTS OF INTEREST

If you're interested in archaeological finds, stop by the **Museo de las Culturas Aborígenes** ⍟⍟ at Av. 10 de Agosto 4-70 and Rafael Torres Beltrán (© 07/ 880-010; Mon–Fri 8:30am–noon and 1–6pm, Sat 8:30am–12:30pm). This amazing private collection includes more than 5,000 Ecuadorian archaeological pieces dating as far back as 500 B.C. Some of the most interesting are the pre-Inca urns that were used to bury the dead in an upright position and the flutes made from the bones of different animals. Downstairs, there's an excellent gift shop and a cafe and bakery serving traditional Ecuadorian snacks.

Todos Los Santos is an archaeological site discovered in 1972. There are influences here from the Cañaris, Inca, and Spanish cultures. The site is located at the intersection of Calle Large and Avenida Todos Los Santos (a few blocks down from the Museo del Banco Central). Todos Los Santos is an open-air museum, with no gates or guards standing by. You can visit it whenever you want, free of charge.

For a bird's-eye view of Cuenca, take a taxi up to the **Mirador de Turi.** In Quechua, *turi* means twins, and from this sight you can see twin mountains in the distance. A taxi here should cost about $3 each way.

Museo del Banco Central   Locals in Cuenca like to think that this is one of the best museums in Ecuador. I beg to differ. It does have some excellent archaeological exhibits, which help visitors understand the history of Cuenca. But it also has some hokey salons dedicated to reconstructed homes typical of local cultures in Ecuador. The **Tomebamba Hall** ⍟ is the highlight. The museum was constructed over the ruins of an Inca palace—Pumapungo—and in this room, you will learn the history of the Incas in Cuenca, as well as see archaeological artifacts found in the area. Afterwards, you can exit and walk behind the museum to see the actual archaeological site. Other exhibits in the museum are dedicated to 19th-century art, coins, and the different cultures of Ecuador. The museum is huge, but it will take less than an hour to see the best of what the museum has to offer.

Calle Larga and Av. Huayna Capac. © 07/831-255. Admission $1. Mon–Fri 9am–6pm; Sat 9am–1:30pm.

Museo del Monasterio de la Conceptas ⍟   This small museum was a former monastery and is a classic colonial structure, dating back to the 18th century. The nun's rooms are now all wonderfully curated art galleries; the theme is religious art. One of the highlights includes an impressive collection of gruesome crucifixes by local artist Gaspar Sangurima.

Calle Hermano Miguel 6-33 (between Presidente Córdova and Juan Jaramillo). No phone. Admission $2. Mon–Fri 9am–5:30pm; Sat 10am–1pm.

Museo Municipal de Arte Moderno   It's hard to predict what type of art you'll see when you visit this museum—there are no permanent exhibits. But the museum does display the best of Ecuadorian modern art—previous shows have included works by Guayasamín, Tábara, and Oswaldo Muñoz Mariño. The museum is also famous for hosting the **Bienal Internacional de Pintura,** a biannual exposition of Ecuadorian and American art. Even if you're not into art, it's nice to come here and relax in the peaceful colonial courtyard.

Calle Sucre 15-27 and Coronel Tálbot. © 07/831-027. Free admission. Mon–Fri 8:30am–6:30pm; Sat 9am–1pm.

Museo Remigio Crespo Toral   The exhibits here focus on the history of Cuenca and of Ecuador in general. The museum possesses 18,000 archaeological pieces, and the exhibits are constantly changing to highlight different time periods. The museum also houses a coin collection and a good selection of colonial art. This small museum, housed in a neobaroque French-style palace, is great if you're a history buff, but it's not much different from any other archaeological museum in Ecuador.

Calle Larga 7-27 and Presidente Borrero. No phone. Free admission. Mon–Fri 8:30am–1pm and 3–6:30pm; Sat 10am–1pm.

SPORTS & OUTDOOR ACTIVITIES

Cuenca may be Ecuador's third-largest city, but if you venture just a few miles outside of the city center, you'll find yourself at one with nature. For the best hiking in the area, you should head to Cajas National Park (see "Side Trips from Cuenca," later in this chapter). **MontaRuna Tours** on Gran Colombia 10-29, between Padre Aguirre and General Torres (© 07/846-395), specializes in organizing horseback-riding expeditions through the mountains, stopping at small towns along the way. Trip duration ranges from 3 hours to 10 days. Three-hour tours cost $35 per person; full-day tours are $55, including a guide, transportation, and food.

SHOPPING

Cuenca is a shopper's paradise. Ceramics and Panama hats are the best buys here, but in general, you can find an excellent selection of folksy handicrafts.

CERAMICS   For hundreds of years, Cuenca has been a center for ceramics. Walk into any museum in the area, and you'll see examples of beautiful pre-Inca jugs and vases. **Artesa** 𝒜𝒜, Gran Colombia and the corner of Luis Cordero (© 07/842-647), keeps the tradition alive. This is the best place in Cuenca for hand-painted ceramics. **Yo Ceraturo,** at Borrero 5-41 and Juan Jaramillo, also has an excellent selection of pottery. For a more personalized experience, visit the studio (there's an adjoining gallery with items for sale) of Cuenca's famous ceramic artist **Eduardo Vega** 𝒜𝒜, Via a Turi 201, next to the Mirador de Turi (a taxi will cost $3). I suggest phoning ahead to make the gallery is open (© 07/881-407).

ARTS & CRAFTS   Walk down any street in the center of Cuenca and you are sure to find scads of stores specializing in handmade crafts. **Tejemujeres** 𝒜, on Hermano Miguel and Presidente Córdova, sells beautiful handcrafted sweaters. **Altare,** at Hermano Miguel 6-87, specializes in handmade glass products. **Galería de Arte 670,** at Hermano Miguel 6-70, showcases works of local artists. **E. Vega** 𝒜𝒜, which is located right in front of the Mirador de Turi, is a workshop/gallery offering murals, handicrafts, and wonderful jewelry.

PANAMA HATS   Here's a newsflash for you: Panama hats are originally from Ecuador. In 1910, when the Panama Canal was being built, these hats became popular among the workers. These workers returned to the United States and called them Panama hats. But they have always been made in Ecuador: For generations, the indigenous people on the coast have been using local straw to create finely woven hats. The trade has moved inland, and Cuenca is now the major hub for the production of Panama hats. **Homero Ortega P. & Hijos** 𝒜𝒜 makes the highest quality Panama hats in the world; fans include the queen of England. You can visit the factory and learn how the hats are made. Afterward, you can browse in the elegant boutique. The store is located a few minutes outside the center of town at Av. Gil Ramírez Dávalo 3-86 (© 07/809-000; www.homeroortega.com). **Sombreros Barranco,** at Calle Larga 10-41 between

General Torres and Padre Aguirre (© **07/831-569**), also sells these finely crafted hats.

WHERE TO STAY
EXPENSIVE
Hotel Oro Verde ✪   Oro Verde means "green gold" in Spanish. It refers to bananas, which are a major industry in Ecuador (the largest exporter of bananas in the world). At the Oro Verde in Cuenca, there is no lack of bananas, but the true green gold here is the huge garden area and the grassy paths that surround the hotel's private lagoon. Unfortunately, since the heart of Cuenca is mostly stone, the owners of this 21-year-old hotel had to head outside of town to find greener pastures. That's my main complaint—you can't walk to the center of Cuenca from the Oro Verde. Fortunately, a taxi costs only about $3. This hotel is perfect, however, if you're looking for something more of a country retreat. The hotel offers some of the largest rooms in Cuenca, all decorated with local pieces of art and with a separate nook where you can enjoy views of the lagoon, which is home to lively swans and ducks. The executive suite is appropriately named—it has a conference table, large desk, and fax machine. Free airport pickup can be arranged if you contact the hotel a day before. Discounts abound here so be sure to ask for "promotional rates" when making your reservations.

Av. Ordoñez Lazo (several kilometers outside of the center of town—take a taxi), Cuenca. © **07/831-200.** Fax 07/832849. www.oroverdehotels.com. 79 units. $112 double; $160 suite. Rates include breakfast. AE, DC MC, V. **Amenities:** 2 restaurants; deli; small outdoor pool; small health club; sauna; business center w/secretarial services; limited room service; massage; babysitting; same-day dry cleaning; laundry service. *In room:* TV, minibar, hair dryer, safe.

Mansión Alcázar ✪✪   This is an elegant oasis in the heart of Cuenca, a meticulously renovated 1870s house that once belonged to the president of Ecuador. Behind a large closed gate you'll enter into a world of old colonial living. A beautifully tiled enclosed courtyard with a fountain leads to plush rooms on two floors. Each room is different in size and decor but they all have one thing in common: Every piece of furniture was made in Cuenca. Elegant antiques and fine objets d'art give the rooms that old colonial feel. The suites have wrought-iron four-poster beds; no. 207 has a mural of angels on its ceiling. Bathrooms have Cuencan marble and each one has different hand-painted walls. There's a lovely garden ringed with palm trees and filled with lavender and rose bushes; a few resident hummingbirds complete the picture. The beautiful dining area overlooks the garden and there are a few tables outside for alfresco dining on warm days. The elaborate breakfast includes rolls and fruitcakes baked on the premises. The affable owners are welcoming and friendly and will help make your stay as comfortable as possible.

Calle Bolívar 12-5 and Tarquí, Cuenca. © **07/823-918.** Fax 07/823-554. www.mansionalcazar.com. 14 units. (only 3 w/tubs). $100 double; $150 suite. Rates include American breakfast and afternoon tea. AE, DC, MC, V. **Amenities:** Restaurant; bar; lounge; limited room service; laundry service. *In room:* TV, hair dryer, safe.

MODERATE
Hotel Carvallo ✪   Opened in late 2002, the Carvallo is full of understated elegance. Yet another lovingly restored old house, this one boasts cozy rooms with blue walls and armoires made from local black walnut wood. Some come with terrific views of the city; no. 303 has a lovely view of the red-tiled rooftops of Cuenca. The bathrooms are small but spanking new and very clean. If you request a bathrobe at check-in, they'll deliver one to your room. The honeymoon suite is a great bargain at $80 and comes with a king-size bed, plush

comforter, and giant candelabra. The hotel is linked to the hip Eucalyptus restaurant (see "Where to Dine," below) across the street and they'll deliver snacks or meals to your room if you're too tired to venture out.

Gran Colombia 9-52 and Padre Aguirre, Cuenca. ☎ **07/832-063.** Fax 07/840-749. Carvallo@etapaonline. net.ec. 30 units. $75 double; $80 suite. Rates include American breakfast. MC, V. **Amenities:** Limited room service; laundry service. *In room:* TV, minibar, hair dryer.

Hotel Crespo   This hotel is a real classic. The original building is more than 140 years old, and although it's been a hotel since 1942, it still feels like a small home. The rooms have an old-fashioned charm, with wood paneling, classic green walls, dark furniture, and colorful hand-painted moldings. The ceilings are charming too—they are designed to look like antique tin ceilings. The rooms in the back of the hotel have views of the river down below, and the bathrooms are nice, with marble tiles and lots of counter space. Room no. 408 is my favorite as it has both river and mountain views. Overall, this is a good choice but not nearly as elegant nor as intimate as Mansión Alcázar or the Santa Lucía. One hour of free Internet use is included in the price of a room. Book online and receive a 25% discount.

Calle Larga 7-93, Cuenca. ☎ **07/842-571.** Fax 07/839-473. www.hotel-crespo.com. 40 units. $70 double; $80 triple. Rates include breakfast. AE, DC MC, V. **Amenities:** Restaurant; bar; business center; limited room service; dry cleaning; laundry service. *In room:* TV, minibar, hair dryer.

Hotel Santa Lucía ⭐⭐ *Finds*   In 2002, after a 2-year renovation of this enchanting 1859 house, the lovely Hotel Santa Lucía was awarded the prize of "best restoration of a historical building" by the city of Cuenca. What you can expect here is a meticulous attention to detail—in both the decor and the service. The owner hails from an old Cuenca family and he will go out of his way to make sure your stay is as exquisite as possible. The large enclosed courtyard that comes with a 100-year-old magnolia tree and beautiful baby palms, leads to spacious, comfortable accommodations. Rooms have the amenities of a large, luxury hotel; the suites have sleeping lofts and hardwood floors; no. 212 has a view of the cathedral. All but four of the spacious bathrooms have tubs. On the second floor, there's a huge private salon with a fireplace for guests to gather around; antiques adorn the hallways and fresh flowers are arranged daily. The airy Trattoria restaurant serves authentic Italian cuisine while the cozy Bacus Café is very popular for its inexpensive Ecuadorian meals.

Antonio Borrero 8-44 and Sucre, Cuenca. ☎ **07/828-000.** Fax 07/842-443. www.santaluciahotel.com. 20 units (4 w/shower only). $70 double; $90 triple; $90 suite. Rates include American breakfast. AE, DC, MC, V. **Amenities:** 2 restaurants; lounge; limited room service; dry cleaning; laundry service. *In room:* TV, minibar, hair dryer, safe.

INEXPENSIVE
Posada del Angel *Value*   If you're looking for a bit of charm at rock-bottom rates, then this is the hotel for you. After an extensive renovation of the 120-year-old large colonial house, the Posada del Angel is a whimsical, airy place. Bright yellow and blue colors are the theme here. You enter through a large enclosed courtyard to the rooms scattered on two floors; they are all different shapes and sizes. But all are simply furnished, very clean and all but three have beautiful hardwood floors. Some rooms have wrought-iron lamps made in Cuenca and attractive wooden armoires. The tiled bathrooms are tiny but sparkling. Free Internet access is available for guests in the reception area. Be sure to ask about the "promotional rates" if you book directly with the hotel—those are usually $3 to $4 lower than the regular rates listed below. Single room

rates here go for as little as $20 so this is a good option if you're traveling alone on a tight budget.

Bolívar 14-11 and Estévez de Toral, Cuenca. © **07/840-695.** Fax 07/821-360. Hdaniel@cue.satnet.net. 19 units (shower only). $31 double; $42 triple; $52 quad. Rates include breakfast. MC, V. **Amenities:** Laundry service. *In room:* TV.

WHERE TO DINE

Cuenca has excellent restaurants and wonderful bakeries so you'll eat well here. In addition to the restaurants below, and if you're feeling particularly adventurous, you may want to sample the typical Cuencan guinea pig roasted on a spit. The best place to sample this local delicacy is **Guajibamba,** Luis Cordero 12-32 (© **07/831-016**); a whole guinea pig (feeds several people) is $17. They're open Monday to Saturday 11am to 3pm and 6pm to midnight.

If you get hungry while you're exploring the sights around the main plaza, pop into **La Fama** ⚔, on Bolívar 128 and Montalvo. This Cuencan family-run institution has been serving the same delicious pulled pork sandwiches for over 50 years. You'll need to order at least two (they're tiny), and eat them like the locals with a little garlic sauce. This place is so popular they serve nothing else besides the pork sandwiches (90¢ per sandwich) and juice (70¢). They're open Monday to Saturday 10am to 1:30pm and 3pm to 9pm (they close at 8pm on Sat).

MODERATE

Villa Rosa ⚔⚔⚔ *Finds* ECUADORIAN/INTERNATIONAL   The loveliest restaurant in Cuenca is owned and managed by the friendly Berta Vintimilla. The setting is divine: The enclosed courtyard of an old Cuencan home elegantly refurbished into a restaurant. Crisp white tablecloths and comfortable wooden chairs (with armrests) may feel more like a restaurant in Paris than in Cuenca but rest assured that the food has its roots in Ecuador. Mrs. Vintimilla bakes the delicious *empanadas* herself and they are excellent as an appetizer; the recipes for many of the Ecuadorian specials come from her family's rich history of cooking. If you're in the mood for something really hearty, try the amazingly good *locro de papas* (potato soup served with a slice of avocado). Main courses include sea bass with crab sauce served with rice and vegetables, tender tenderloin of beef and a variety of daily specials. The service is excellent, the wine list is reasonable, and every ingredient used in the kitchen is of the highest quality. Note that the restaurant is closed on weekends.

Gran Colombia 12-22 and Tarquí. © **07/837-944.** Reservations recommended. Main courses $5.50–$12. AE, DC, MC, V. Mon–Fri noon–2:30pm and 7–10:30pm.

INEXPENSIVE

El Maíz ⚔ ECUADORIAN   Cuenca's newest restaurant is very attractive and has a lovely outdoor patio for alfresco dining. Yet another renovated old house, El Maíz specializes in traditional Ecuadorian cuisine. The attractive dining indoor dining room feels like somebody's house with wood floors, red tablecloths, and a gracious waitstaff. There are two outdoor seating areas: a lower patio with colorful tiles overlooking a courtyard full of plants and an upper terrace with a lovely view of the green hills. Appetizers include the usual offerings of *humitas, empanadas,* and *locro de papas.* The main courses are terrific and unique. My two favorite are the fried trout with rice and yuca salad and hornado cuencano (roasted pork served with llapingachos—mashed potatoes with cheese). For dessert, try the *almíbar de babaco* (a compote of a local fruit, tart and sweet).

Calle Larga 1-279 and Calle de los Molinos. ✆ **07/840-224**. Main courses $4–$7. MC, V. Mon–Sat 11:30am–10:30pm.

El Pedregal Azteca ⊛ MEXICAN   This could very well be the best Mexican restaurant in Ecuador. Since 1989, Maria and Juan Manuel have welcomed diners into their cozy restaurant with a smile. Here, everything is homemade—even the tortillas are baked here (the owners bring some of the ingredients back from Mexico to ensure the highest quality). The enchilada de mole is delicious, as are the tacos that are filled with your choice of stuffing. The huge burrito comes with spicy sausage and egg, based on an old Mexican recipe. For dessert, the *arroz con leche* (rice pudding) is divine and comes with fresh vanilla and plump raisins. There's live music here on Friday and Saturday night and the place fills with a youngish crowd, but it's very quiet here on weekday nights.

Gran Colombia 10-29 and Padre Aguirre. ✆ **07/823-652**. Main courses $4–$8. MC, V. Mon–Sat 12:30–3pm and 6–11pm.

El Tequila ⊛ (Value CUENCA   The locals flock to this simple place that serves the best roasted pork in the city. If you're looking for a taste of true Cuencan cuisine, not diluted for foreign tastes, then this place is for you. You'll dine in a simple room with red tile, wooden tables and chairs, and bright yellow walls. Outside, the local women roast the pork on the grill along with baby potatoes and fava beans. Here's how it works: You order a serving of pork and choose several sides to share with your dining companions. Sides include fresh steamed corn on the cob, *tamales,* fresh local cheese, and mashed potatoes. Do like the locals and order a Canelazo (warm wine and cinnamon drink) to round out your meal.

Gran Colombia 20-59 and León. ✆ **07/822-807**. Main courses $4–$8. No credit cards. Mon–Sat noon–11pm.

Eucalyptus (Finds TAPAS/INTERNATIONAL   Opened in late 2002, this has fast become Cuenca's hippest and most happening restaurant and bar. The crème de la crème of the city's yuppies flock here (especially on weekend nights) to gather for drinks and appetizers. The food here is tapas; most people order several appetizers and share them. Selections are truly international (more than 50 dishes from 20 different countries) and include hot Cuban sandwiches, cheese quesadillas, French bread with tapenade, and stuffed peppers with rice, raisins, and parsley. This is the only place in the city to offer sushi and sashimi, though I recommend you stick with the hot appetizers; the quality here is not consistent. Eucalyptus has the only draft beer in the city; try the Llama Negra that's made in Quito (a dark stout beer like a Guinness).

Gran Colombia 9-41 and Benigno Malo. ✆ **07/849-157**. Tapas $4–$9. AE, DC, MC, V. Mon–Fri 11am–midnight; Sat–Sun 5pm–midnight.

Los Capulies ⊛ ECUADORIAN   If you're looking for tasty local food and live Ecuadorian music, it's hard to find any restaurant better than Los Capulies. The restaurant is housed in the courtyard of a gorgeous and restored colonial mansion, complete with a working stone fountain and hand-painted archways. The food is definitely very Ecuadorian. For example, one of the specialties is *mote pillo con carne* (huge potato-like pieces of corn, mixed with onions and eggs, served with a piece of fried meat and *tortillas de papa*—the Ecuadorian version of potato pancakes). The *tamales* (mashed corn pancakes with peppers, eggs, and raisins) are also a local treat. However, not everything on the menu is a local specialty—you can also order old favorites such as chicken with rice. You

can enjoy live music with your dinner on Thursday, Friday, and Saturday nights (starting at about 8:30pm).

Located on the corner of Presidente Córdova and Presidente Borrero. © 07/832-339. Main courses $4.25–$6.50. AE, DC, MC, V. Daily noon–midnight.

Restaurante Vegetariano y Pizza Goura VEGETARIAN   The owners of this restaurant emphasized to me that the food here has a Hindu flair. But the menu mainly consists of dishes such as spaghetti, soy-based beef, vegetarian paella, and pizza. However, hand-dyed batiks do cover most of the walls. The restaurant is adorable, with a junglelike mural in the front and small wood tables everywhere (including the balcony). The buffet at lunch is both delicious and endless with all sorts of pizzas, pastas, and mock meat dishes. *Note:* The restaurant does serve dairy food, but no eggs.

Juan Jaramillo 7-27 (between Borrero and Cordero). No phone. Main courses $1–$2; buffet lunch $1.25. No credit cards. Mon–Fri noon–8pm.

CUENCA AFTER DARK
Cuenca used to be a sleepy little town, but in the past few years, young people have woken up and turned this into a mini–party city. **Wunderbar Café** ♣, right off the stairs below Calle Larga and Hermano Miguel, and **El Cafecito,** Honorato Vásquez 7-36, are both popular spots for foreigners. If you're looking to go dancing, **La Fábrica** on Presidente Córdova and Manuel Vega is one of the best discos in town. For live music, you should head to **Cava San Angel** on Hermano Miguel at the corner of Presidente Córdova. It's open Thursday through Saturday nights. **La Mesa,** Gran Colombia between Machuca and Ordóñez, is the best place in town for salsa. The 20- and 30-something who's who of Cuenca gather at **Eucalyptus** (see "Where to Dine," above), which serves the only draft beer in the city.

Note: The above venues are open Wednesday to Saturday. Sunday, Monday and Tuesday are very quiet nights in Cuenca and hardly anybody ventures out late.

SIDE TRIPS FROM CUENCA
If you happen to be in Cuenca on a Sunday, you should hop on a bus at the main terminal for **Sigsig, Chordeleg,** or **Gualaceo.** They all host lively Sunday markets where you can buy some very high-quality handicrafts.

PARQUE NACIONAL CAJAS ♣
After you've seen the museums and historic sights in Cuenca, it's great to get away from the city and immerse yourself in the natural wonders that this area has to offer. Cajas is only about 32km (20 miles) northeast of the city (about a 1-hr. drive), but it feels worlds away. Unlike many other areas in Ecuador, the park was formed by glaciers, not volcanic activity. The park covers about 29,000 hectares (72,000 acres) and has 232 lakes. One of my favorite hikes is up **Tres Cruces,** which offers spectacular views of the area and the opportunity to see the Continental Divide. I also recommend the hike around the Laguna Quinoa Pato. The vistas of the lake are impressive, and as you walk on the trails, you'll have a good chance of spotting some ducks. From the main visitor center, you can walk around and explore the flora of the humid mountain-forest climate— mosses, orchids, fungi, and epiphytes are common. The forest is full of polylepis trees, one of the few trees in the world that grow at about 3,000m (9,840 ft.). *Note:* Wear warm clothing, as it can get extremely cold here.

GETTING THERE   Cajas is huge and it's easy to get lost among the many trails. I highly recommend exploring the park with a guide. **Hualambari Tours** 👁👁 at Borrero 9-67, next to the post office (© **07/848-768**), is the best travel agency in Cuenca. Their guides do an excellent job of showing you the highlights of the park. If you want to go on your own, catch a **Turismo Occidental Bus** in the direction of Molleturo. Ask to be dropped off at La Toreadora. Buses leave daily at 6, 6:20, and 10:20am from Mariscal Lamar and Octavio Cordero.

INGAPIRCA 👁👁

Ingapirca is the Machu Picchu of Ecuador. It is the largest pre-Columbian architectural complex in Ecuador, and it's definitely the most interesting. The Incas arrived here around 1470. Before then, the Cañaris, a mysterious culture, inhabited the area. It's believed that the Cañaris used Ingapirca as a religious site. When the Incas conquered the area, they ordered all Cañaris men to move to Cusco. In the meantime, the Incas sent in men of their own to live with the Cañaris women to subtly impose their beliefs on the local culture. It was common for the Incas to build their own religious palaces over the ruins of the conquered culture. So what you have here is a mix of Cañaris and Inca influences. For example, many of the structures here are round or oval-shaped, which is very atypical of the Incas. In fact, Ingapirca is home to the only oval-shaped sacred Inca palace in the world. One of the highlights of the site is **El Adoratorio/Castillo,** the elliptical structure, which is believed to be a temple to the sun. It is built from east to west, and if you're here on the June 21, you can watch as the sun projects light on certain symbols. Nearby are the **Aposentos,** rooms made with tight stonework, thought to have been used by the high priests. Most of the remains from the Cañaris culture have been found at **Pilaloma** at the south end of the site (where you first enter). Pilaloma means "small hill" and some archaeologists surmise that this was a sacred area, especially because it is the highest point in the area. Eleven bodies (mostly women) have been found here—perhaps the circle of stones were some sort of tomb.

GETTING THERE   The site is open daily from 7:30am to 6:30pm; admission is $6. If you want to go to Ingapirca on your own, you can catch a bus from the main bus terminal in Cuenca. **Transporte Cañar** operates buses that stop at the site; they depart at 9am and 1pm, and the 2½-hour ride costs $6. When you get to Ingapirca, ask for Rafael—he's the only English-speaking guide at the site. Alternatively, I recommend visiting the site with an experienced guide. Contact **Hualambari Tours** 👁 at Borrero 9-67, next to the post office (© **07/848-768**), for more information.

7 Guayaquil

250km (155 miles) NW of Cuenca, 420km (260 miles) SW of Quito, 966km (600 miles) east of the Galápagos

Guayaquil is the St. Louis of Ecuador: Both are important river ports and both have seen a renaissance and a drop in crime in the downtown area in the past few years. Most importantly, both are gateways to the west—Guayaquil is the gateway to the Galápagos Islands, about 966km (600 miles) west of the city.

Most visitors to South America don't stop off in Guayaquil—the major urban center and economic capital of Ecuador—unless they are heading to the Galápagos or doing business here. But that is changing slowly as this up-and-coming city reinvents itself at a dizzying pace, adding tourist attractions and infrastructure, renovating its aging airport and repaving (and landscaping) entire avenues and boulevards.

Although Guayaquil was founded in 1537, you won't find the colonial architecture here that you find in Quito—a great fire ravaged the city in 1896. More than 100 years after the great fire, the development and the huge investment in the Malecón 2000 (the city's long-neglected riverfront) is a symbol of the city's rebirth.

As recently as 1998, crime was rampant in Guayaquil; in the past few years, things have changed for the better thanks to the new dynamic mayor. The city is safer, more visitor-friendly, and the new planned neighborhoods have an abundant (and visible) tourist police presence.

ESSENTIALS
GETTING THERE
BY PLANE   Tame (© 02/2909-900; www.tame.com.ec), **Icaro** (© 800/883-567; www.icaro-air.com), and **Aerogal** (© 800/2376-425; aerogal@andinanet.net) offer daily flights to Guayaquil from Quito and Cuenca. One-way tickets range from $48 to $60.

All planes arrive at the newly renovated international **Simón Bolívar Airport** (© 04/2282-100), which is located about 10 minutes north of downtown Guayaquil. If your hotel doesn't provide a shuttle service from the airport, it's incredibly easy to catch a taxi. As you exit the Customs area in the international arrivals area, there is a desk with friendly staff who will arrange a taxi for you. You pay at the desk and receive a voucher, which you then present to a driver, who will be waiting for you once you exit the terminal. A taxi to the downtown area should cost no more than $6.

BY BUS   The bus station, **Terminal Terrestre** (© 04/2232-422), is a few minutes north of the airport. Buses from Cuenca leave on a very frequent schedule; the 5-hour bus ride costs $7. From Quito, buses leave every half-hour for Guayaquil; the 8-hour ride costs $9. **Flota Imbabura** (© 04/2295-389) is one of the best bus companies in Ecuador, providing service throughout the country.

GETTING AROUND
Guayaquil is a compact city. Avenida 9 de Octubre is the main street, running in the Malecón 2000 (the huge pedestrian mall on the river) where you'll find all the major shops and travel agencies. Most of the museums are located within a block or two of the Malecón 2000.

In Guayaquil, taxis are the cheapest and most efficient way to get around. It's easy to find them on any street corner. Rides within the center of the city cost only $2 to $3.

VISITOR INFORMATION
The tourist information office is located on Pedro Icaza 203 (between Pedro Carbo and Panamá), on the sixth floor (© 04/2568-764). The office is open Monday through Friday from 8:30am to 5pm. The city maintains an excellent website crammed with information at www.guayaquil.gov.ec. An English version will be available by 2004.

FAST FACTS   The **American Express** office is located at Av. 9 de Octubre 1900 (© 04/2394-984). Unfortunately, you can't exchange traveler's checks here—you can only make a cash advance on your Amex card. Most banks in Guayaquil are clustered around the intersection of Pedro Icaza and General Córdova.

The best hospital in Guayaquil is the **Hospital Clínica Kennedy,** located north of the city in the Mall Policentro on Av. del Periodista (© 04/2286-963);

ACCOMMODATIONS ■
Grand Hotel Guayaquil **10**
Hilton Colón Guayaquil **6**
Hotel Oro Verde **2**
Hotel Sol de Oro **9**
Tangara Guest House **4**

DINING ◆
El Patio Cafeteria/Spice Grill **3**
Ensalada de Frutas **14**
La Canoa **13**
LA PROA **19**
Lo Nuestro **1**

✚ Hospital
✉ Post office

ATTRACTIONS ●
Cementerio General **7**
Malecón 2000 **16**
Museo Antropológico y
de Arte Contemporanea
(M.A.A.C.) **18**
Museo Arqueológico
del Banco del Pacifico **17**
Museo Municipal
de Guayaquil **11**
Museo Nahim Isaías B **15**
Parque Centenario **8**
Parque Historico **5**
Parque Seminario **12**

the hospital runs a 24-hour pharmacy. If you need a 24-hour pharmacy in town, try **Farmacia Victoria** on 9 de Octubre and Rumichaca (© **04/2534-020**). Directly across the street is **Farmacia Fybeca** (© **04/2530-290**).

You can make relatively cheap international telephone calls and use the Internet at **SCI Cyber Center,** adjacent to Parque Seminario at the intersection of Clemente Ballén and Chile (© **04/2323-308**). You can also log onto the Internet at **CyberTek** on the corner of Baquerizo Moreno and 9 de Octubre. The main **post office** is located on Clemente Ballén and Pedro Carbo.

WHAT TO SEE & DO

Construction is continuing at a frenzied pace in the city; roads are ripped open as new sidewalks are built; major avenues are being repaved and landscaped. Two new museums are expected to open in the city by 2006. The huge **Museo Antropológico y de Arte Contemporáneo** (known simply as the **MAAC**) at the end of the Malecón 2000 will focus on archaeological finds (including some very recent discoveries from the coast) from Ecuador as well as a big collection of contemporary art—both Ecuadorian and international. When the museum if fully operational, it will house the largest collection of archaeological pieces in South America. This museum has already been built and is just receiving the final touches and should be open right after this book goes to press. The already open festival hall attached to the museum is home to several annual events, including the popular Guayaquil Jazz Festival every October; the 400-seat theater will be the home of film festivals and special screenings of noncommercial movies.

If You're Short on Time

Many visitors find themselves with only a few hours in Guayaquil as they connect to or from the Galápagos. If you fall into that category, don't despair: You can still get a good feel for the city in a few hours.

Grab a cab (or walk, if you're close) from your hotel to the Malecón. The Malecón 2000 area is best enjoyed on foot so prepare yourself for a good 3.2km (2-mile) hike and bring protection from the sun. It's best to begin at the southern end, the corner of the Malecón and Av. Olmedo. Here you can browse the shops selling local artifacts, and the boardwalk is breezy and airy on this end. As you walk north, you'll find many food shops (and more people). Take a break halfway; most of the food stalls here sell freshly squeezed juice that makes an excellent pick-me-up; small bottles of water are also readily available and there are impressively clean public restrooms here too. At the end of the Malecón, just past the MAAC, you'll find **Las Penas** neighborhood—a narrow street filled with art galleries and funky shops. After you walk around Las Penas, climb up the 456 stairs to the top of **Cerro Santa Ana** 🐊🐊, to get a fantastic view of the entire city, the river and the surrounding countryside. (Cerro Santa Ana is where the city of Guayaquil was first established in the mid-1500s.) The chapel of Santa Ana is also at the top, along with a beautiful lighthouse—both were built in 2002. The Cerro Santa Ana is still being finished—restaurants and cafes are just beginning to open and a marine museum is being built toward the top. You'll find many places to eat and drink on the stairs leading up to the top. This is one of the safest areas in the city as specially trained tourist police patrol the stairs day and night.

A Marine Museum is under construction towards the top of Cerro Santa Ana (with a great view of the river) and will focus on everything to do with boats, ships, and the Ecuadorian navy over the years.

Check with the tourist office (see above) when you arrive, for the latest museum openings.

The **Malecón 2000 (Dos Mil)** 🐊🐊🐊 is the shining star of the new and improved Guayaquil. It's impressive to enter the Malecón 2000 from Avenida 9 de Octubre, where you are greeted by a 1937 statue of the independence heroes Simón Bolívar and San Martín shaking hands. On either side of the statue, you can climb up lookout towers, which afford impressive views of the city and the river. Walk south and you'll hit the Moorish Clock Tower, Glorious Aurora's Obelisk, a McDonald's, a mini-mall, and tons of inexpensive food stalls. As you walk in this direction, look across the street: You'll see the impressive neoclassical Palacio Municipal. If you walk north from the Bolívar/Martín statue, you'll come across a lively playground and an exercise course.

In addition to the Malecón 2000 and the museums listed below, there are a few parks and an interesting cemetery to visit. **Parque Seminario** 🐊 dates from 1880, and is adjacent to the neo-Gothic cathedral (from 1948). **Parque Centenario** is in the middle of the city; it's a pleasant place to relax and people-watch. The **Cementerio General** is north of the downtown area, and has some impressive aboveground Italian-style marble tombs.

Museo Arqueológico del Banco del Pacífico ✸   This is my favorite museum in Guayaquil. Unlike at the two museums listed below, *all* the exhibits here have explanations both in English and Spanish. The museum is small, but it does a good job of showing what life must have been like in the coastal areas of Ecuador thousands of years before Europeans arrived there. You will learn about food, clothing, tools, music, and the use of hallucinogenic drugs in pre-Columbian cultures. The most interesting artifacts come from the Chorrera Period (1000–300 B.C.). Keep an eye out for the double-chambered whistling bottle and the descriptive figurines from this period.

Pedro Icaza 113 and Pichincha. ✆ 04/2566-010. Free admission. Mon–Fri 9am–6pm; Sat–Sun 11am–1pm.

Museo Municipal de Guayaquil   If you're wondering about the history of Guayaquil, head to this museum. It starts off with pre-Columbian history, displaying artifacts similar to those found in the Museo Nahim Isaías B (see below). Then, as you move through the museum, you'll learn about colonial history, the independence movement, the republic, and the 20th century. On display are pistols, army uniforms, coins, and an old-fashioned car. *Note:* The exhibits are in Spanish, although there are some pamphlets available in English.

Sucre between Chile and Pedro Carbo. ✆ 04/2524-100. Free admission. Tues–Sat 9am–5pm; Sun 10am–2pm.

Parque Histórico Guayaquil ✸✸ *(Moments*   This brand-new historical theme park is a great place to spend an afternoon and learn more about southern Ecuador. Here, you can walk in a large "forest" filled with regional flora (including some endangered plants and trees) and rows of different banana plants, some endemic only to Ecuador (remember Ecuador is the world's largest banana exporter). There's a traditional country house built to replicate how rural farmers lived and what farming utensils they used. In the courtyard of a beautiful old hacienda, plays are staged twice daily depicting life on a farm in the 19th century. The boardwalk here is dubbed Malecón 1900 and gives you a glimpse into how the city looked 100 years ago. An old trolley completes the picture. A large pirate ship is expected to start offering rides from the Malecón 2000 to the Malecón 1900 in the near future. Check with the tourist office when you arrive, if you're interested. I suggest coming here on a weekday—weekends are very crowded as this theme park is becoming extremely popular with Ecuadorian families. There's also an old-fashioned bakery and cafe serving traditional dishes in a lovely outdoor setting.

Vía Samborondón, avs. Esmeraldas and Central. ✆ 04/2833-807. Tues–Sat $3 adults; $1.50 children under 12; Sun and public holidays $4.50 adults, $3 children. Tues–Sun 9am–4:30pm.

Museo Nahim Isaías B   Welcome to the wonderful world of pre-Columbian artifacts. This small museum displays some amazing treasures found in coastal areas near Guayaquil; some date as far back as 4200 B.C. You'll see ceramic jugs, wonderfully expressive figurines, gold jewelry, and—my personal favorite—carved seashells in the shape of fish. On the second floor is colonial art from the Quito school.

Clemente Ballén and Pichincha. Free admission. Mon–Sat 10am–5pm.

SHOPPING

The **Malecón** shopping center is the newest and most frequented by visitors. It's located on the Malecón and Calle Junín. As a throbbing metropolis, Guayaquil is full of modern shopping malls that make you feel as if you're in California. The best one is located close to the Hilton and the airport: **Mall del Sol,** av.

Juan Tanca Marengo and Joaquin Orrantia, no phone. (If you're staying at the Hilton you can ask for a free shuttle ride here and back.) There are over 250 shops here.

The **Mercado Artesanal,** Baquerizo Moreno (between calles Loja and Juan Montalvo), is the best place to find local handicrafts. Over 280 local artisans sell everything from vegetable ivory statues to place mats and ceramics.

WHERE TO STAY

In addition to the hotels listed below, and if you're looking for an inexpensive but charming place, your best bet is the **Tangara Guest House,** Ciudadela Bolivariana, Manuela Saenz and O'Leary Block F, House 1 (℃ 04/2284445; fax 04/ 2284039). Doubles go for $58 including continental breakfast.

The following three American chain hotels are a good choice if there's no space at the hotels below, or if you prefer a certain name brand: **The Hotel Ramada** (℃ 04/2565-555; www.hotelramadaecuador.com) is located on the Malecón 2000; the **Hampton Inn** (℃ 800/HAMPTON; www.hampton.com. ec) is conveniently located not far from the Ramada; and the **Four Points Sheraton** (℃ 04/2691-888; www.sheraton.com) is the closest hotel to the airport.

VERY EXPENSIVE

Hilton Colón Guayaquil ✫✫✫   This 6-year-old hotel is housed in a modern high-rise and it's definitely the best hotel in the city. It has a gracious air about it and is extremely comfortable. The hotel has become an institution in Guayaquil—its restaurants, banquet halls and bars are frequented by the crème de la crème of Ecuadorian society. The rooms are large with big windows—some rooms offer views of planes taking off and landing at the nearby airport. The corner suites are the most desirable—they have a lovely balcony with a great view. All rooms have coffeemakers—a rarity in Ecuador. The marble bathrooms are huge and sparkling. The beautiful outdoor pool has a swim-up bar and a snack bar for alfresco dining. The coffee shop serves excellent Ecuadorian specials at reasonable prices and the Portofino restaurant is the best and most elegant Italian eatery in Guayaquil. Several airline offices, including LanChile and KLM, are located in the shopping arcade adjacent to the hotel lobby. The Hilton Colón is located less than 5 minutes from the airport, which makes it an ideal place for people trying to catch an early flight to the Galápagos. Complimentary airport transportation is available upon request—contact the hotel 24 hours before arrival to arrange for pickup.

Av. Francisco de Orellana, Guayaquil. ℃ 800/221-2424 in the U.S., or 04/2689-000. Fax 04/2689-149. www. guayaquil.hilton.com. 294 units. $205 double; $460–$1,880 suite. AE, DC, MC, V. Free parking. **Amenities:** 4 restaurants; 2 bars; beautiful large pool; exercise room; Jacuzzi; sauna; concierge; business center; shopping arcade; salon; 24-hr. room service; massage; babysitting; same-day dry cleaning; laundry service; nonsmoking floors; executive/club floors. *In room:* A/C, TV, dataport, minibar, coffeemaker, hair dryer, safe.

Hotel Oro Verde ✫ *Overrated*   The Oro Verde commands a central location and is located right next to the U.S. consulate (complete with armed vehicles and cordoned-off alleyways). It looks and feels like a typical high-end business hotel. The public areas, cafes, and restaurants are attractive and the service is excellent. Unfortunately, the hallways and rooms are aging fast and are in desperate need of renovations. Most rooms are spacious and have recessed lighting, moldings on the wall, and smallish marble bathrooms with leaky showers that need new fixtures. Suites come with two bathrooms, an extra sitting room, and personal fax machines (it's free to receive a fax); some even have a kitchenette. But everything is aging and tired. This is not a good hotel for light sleepers;

windows are not soundproofed and the walls are thin. Rooms facing the street come with the roar of buses and windows on the other side of the hotel face a loud bar above the pool, where live bands often play until midnight (and beyond). For business travelers working downtown, the location of Oro Verde is good, but if you want to visit the Malecón 2000 or some of the museums, you'll have to walk about 15 blocks or take a quick taxi ride. My first choice would be to stay at the Hilton since you'll be cabbing it most everywhere from here, too. All guests receive 30 minutes free daily use of the Internet at the Business Center and the excellent health club offers inexpensive massages—1 hour for $26. There's an hourly complimentary shuttle to the airport.

Av. 9 de Octubre and García Moreno, Guayaquil. ℂ **04/2327-999**. Fax 04/2329-350. www.oroverdehotels. com. 242 units. $260 double; from $320–$400 suite. AE, DC, MC, V. Free parking. **Amenities:** 4 restaurants; 2 bars; bakery; tiny outdoor pool; modern exercise room w/new machines; Jacuzzi; sauna; concierge; business center; 24-hr. room service; massage; babysitting; same-day dry cleaning; laundry service; nonsmoking floors; executive/club floors. *In room:* A/C, TV, minibar, hair dryer, safe.

MODERATE

Grand Hotel Guayaquil ⓖ
There are two reasons to stay at this hotel. First, the location: It's only a few blocks from the Malecón 2000 and close to all the major attractions in the downtown area. Second, the gorgeous swimming pool: Take one look at the magnificent waterfall cascading into the clear blue water and you'll feel as though you are in a tropical resort. It provides a great escape from the heat, noise, and pollution of Guayaquil. Unfortunately, the rooms aren't as fancy as the pool, but they are comfortable and of a generous size. The walls are a bit thin, so to avoid hearing your neighbors as they traipse through the hallway, try to request a room as far from the elevator as possible. This hotel is not luxurious (it feels a bit dated), especially compared to the Hilton Colón, but it does offer similar amenities, and for the price, it's a great deal.

Boyacá and 10 de Agosto, Guayaquil. ℂ **04/2329-690**. Fax 04/2327-251. www.grandhotelguayaquil.com. 175 units. $85–$125 double; from $150 suite. AE, DC, MC, V. **Amenities:** 3 restaurants; 2 bars; nice pool; 2 air-conditioned squash courts; exercise room; Jacuzzi; sauna; massage; small business center; salon; 24-hr. room service; laundry service; nonsmoking floors; executive/club floors. *In room:* A/C, TV, fridge, hair dryer, safe.

INEXPENSIVE

Hotel Sol de Oro ⓥalue
This unassuming hotel offers a lot of bang for your buck. It's a bit off the beaten path; street vendors selling all sorts of seemingly useless wares crowd the surrounding sidewalks. But you're only a few blocks from the refreshing Parque Centenario, and you can easily walk from the hotel to Parque Seminario. The lobby is a bit stifling (no air-conditioning), but don't let this deter you. The rooms are large and bright with huge windows, and the bathrooms are spacious too. The hotel tries to keep air-conditioning use to a minimum, so every time you return to your room, you'll have to wait for it to cool down. The rooms are clean, but the humidity leaves a musty pall in the air. But for $28 for a double, it's easy to turn on the air conditioner and forget all about that pesky humidity. Try to request a corner room, where you can enjoy great views of the city.

Lorenzo de Garaicoa 1243 and Clemente Ballén, Guayaquil. ℂ **04/2532-067**. Fax 04/2532-068. 30 units. $28 double; $32 triple. Rates include breakfast. AE, DC, MC, V. Free parking. **Amenities:** Restaurant; limited room service. *In room:* A/C, TV, minibar.

WHERE TO DINE

New restaurants are opening in Guayaquil at a dizzying pace. Restaurants seem to come into fashion for a few months and then fade away. The restaurants

An Alternative to the Galápagos

If you don't have the time or the money to visit the Galápagos Islands, you should consider visiting **Machalilla National Park.** At the park's main attraction, Isla de la Plata, which sits 37km (23 miles) off the coast of Ecuador, you will have the chance to see albatrosses; blue-footed, masked, and red-footed boobies; frigate birds; and sea lions, all of which also live in the Galápagos. There are also some colorful snorkeling spots here. From June through September, it's common to see whales as you make your way out to the island. But be careful—the boats are small and rickety, and the sea is often rough. If you're prone to seasickness, be sure to take Dramamine before you board the boat.

Isla de la Plata is the best-known attraction in Machalilla, but if you have a few days, you can also explore some archaeological sites (this area of the coast was home to a thriving pre-Columbian civilization) and hike along Los Frailes, a 3-hour trail that will reward you with breathtaking views of the coast.

Most visitors to Machalilla base themselves in Puerto López, a tiny little coastal town. From Quito, a bus leaves daily at 7:30am and arrives in Puerto López around 5pm. You can also take a bus or flight from Quito to Portoviejo; from Portoviejo, you travel by bus to Puerto López via Jipijapa. If hot, antique buses aren't your thing, you can also take a taxi from Portoviejo for about $50. **Tame (© 02/2909-900; www.tame.**

reviewed below are the solid favorites. But if you're looking for an in-place, I just heard of a good restaurant on the Malecón: **La Proa** (just next to the MAAC) was opened recently by an Ecuadorian-American guy and serves international cuisine.

You'll also find tons of restaurants, cafes, and fast-food places on the Malecón and on the stairs of the Cerro Santa Ana.

As in many South American cities, local bigwigs dine at the restaurants in the major hotels. The Italian restaurant, **Portofino,** at the Hilton Colón (see "Where to Stay," above), is considered to be among the finest restaurants in all of Ecuador. It's also one of the most romantic restaurants in the city.

If you're wandering around Parque Seminario or visiting a museum and you need a quick break, head to **Ensalada de Frutas,** Pedro Carbo 711 and Aguirre. The place isn't fancy, but you can sit at one of the clean tables and enjoy a refreshing fruit shake (with fresh fruit and milk), sandwiches, or *humitas* (corn mush—better than it sounds).

El Patio Cafeteria ECUADORIAN   Okay, so when you walk into El Patio, it's hard to forget that you're in a hotel restaurant. But the food is surprisingly good, and this is your chance to sample true Ecuadorian cuisine. If you come for dinner, opt for the $14 buffet, which is a great value. (Dessert is included!) This isn't your typical hotel buffet. A wide array of fresh seafood, chicken, beef, and baby goat are displayed on the table. Once you've picked out whatever tickles your fancy, you then choose your spices, vegetables, and rice or pasta. And then, right before your eyes, a chef mixes it all together. Soup, cold cuts, salad, and prepared foods are also available at the buffet table. If you want to order com.ec) offers daily flights from Quito to Portoviejo for about $100 round-trip.

The national park has licensed 14 tour companies in Puerto López. These companies are all located on the town's main street, and they all offer exactly the same services. Tours cost $30, including round-trip boat transportation and lunch; the entry fee to the park is an additional $25.

The most charming lodging in Puerto López is the **Mantaraya Lodge** ★★ (© **02/2448-985;** www.advantagecuador.com/mantaraya), which sits on top of a hill overlooking the ocean. Opened in 2003, the Mantaraya offers 15 simply furnished but elegant suites done in bold yellow and blue colors. The breathtaking pool is the centerpiece of this hotel and you can have drinks and meals taking in the magnificent view. Doubles cost $85 to $140.

A less expensive option is the **Hostería La Terraza** (© **05/604-235**), which sits a half mile above town. The rooms are basic, but spotless; the views of the crashing surf below are wonderful. Doubles cost $25.

In addition to the restaurant at the Mantarraya Lodge, **Delfín Mágico** serves the best seafood in the area. It's located about 10 minutes outside of Puerto López in Salango, the next town over. The owner will drive you back to Puerto López for free.

from the menu, you won't be disappointed—options include several types of *empanadas,* fresh seafood, pasta, and grilled meat. Shrimp is big here. Live music from the Lobby Bar drifts into the restaurant, adding some zest to the sterile atmosphere.

In Oro Verde Hotel, Av. 9 de Octubre and García Moreno. © **04/2327-999.** Lunch $5–$9; dinner $7–$21. AE, DC, MC, V. Sat–Thurs 5am–1am; Fri 5am–2am.

La Canoa ★★ ECUADORIAN   Unlike El Patio Cafeteria (see above), you'll have a hard time believing that La Canoa is attached to a hotel. This 28-year-old restaurant looks like a typical diner, but at lunchtime, it's the most happening place in town. Locals come here for the inexpensive but very satisfying Ecuadorian food. Recommended dishes include *seco de chivo, humitas, ceviche,* grilled chicken, and delicious milkshakes. Before noon, you can choose from a large selection of breakfast specialties. If you're not ready for baby goat, there's also a large selection of soups, salads, and sandwiches. This restaurant is a great place to take a break if you're seeing the sights of Guayaquil—it's close to most of the museums and only a few blocks from the Malecón 2000.

In Hotel Continental, Chile and 10 de Agosto. © **04/2329-270.** Lunch and dinner $4–$8. AE, DC, MC, V. Daily 24 hr.

Lo Nuestro ★★ *Finds* ECUADORIAN   The best Ecuadorian restaurant in the city is located 10 minutes from downtown a (taxi will cost about $3) and is a small, elegant eatery, its walls filled with historical photos of Guayaquil. Service is a bit stuffy—all the waiters are old and not very friendly—but the food is divine. Always ask what the fresh fish is: Seafood reigns supreme here. *Ceviches* make for the best appetizers and the grilled sea bass with crab sauce is my favorite main course. There's a myriad of daily specials but traditional favorites include a variety of homemade *empanadas, seco de chivo,* and shrimp prepapered several different ways. Everything is of the highest quality—and meticulously prepared. This is the kind of place where you enjoy a 3-hour meal and where the waiters wheel down a liquor tray to offer you an after-dinner drink. Certainly don't come here if you're pressed for time!

Av. Estrada 903 and Higueras. ⓒ 04/2386-398. Main courses $6–$13. MC, V. Mon–Thurs noon–3:30pm and 7pm–midnight; Fri–Sun noon–1am.

8 The Galápagos Islands ⭐⭐⭐

966km (600 miles) W of continental Ecuador

The Galápagos Islands offer some of the best wildlife viewing in the world, not only because the animals themselves are beautiful and interesting, but also because they are virtually fearless. Through a quirk of evolution, large predators failed to evolve here, with the result that all the islands' wild residents are endowed with a unique sense of security. This means that the famous blue-footed boobie will perform its awkwardly elegant two-stepped mating dance right under your nose, oblivious to your camera. Mockingbirds will hop onto your shoes. Adolescent sea lions will do figure eights to show off their swimming prowess as you snorkel among them. The local penguins (the only tropical species of penguin in the world) are, admittedly, a bit aloof, but even they aren't above using a snorkeler as a human shield as they attempt to sneak up on schools of tasty fish. In the Galápagos, you don't have to get downwind and peer through the bushes to get a glimpse at the wildlife. You do, however, have to be careful not to step on sleeping sea lions on the beach as you back up for a better photo, as responsible guides will remind you.

It's not easy to get to the Galápagos—at press time, only two airlines were making the flight from the mainland—and fares are certainly not cheap. The best way to see the islands is to book a berth in a local cruise ship, which vary widely in quality. My advice is to spend as much money as you can afford. But even if you can't afford the best, you won't be disappointed. The wildlife here, which so beguiled Charles Darwin and Herman Melville in the 19th century, is no less astonishing now than it was 150 years ago.

ESSENTIALS
GETTING THERE
You can only reach the Galápagos Islands by plane. **Tame** (ⓒ **02/2909-900;** www.tame.com.ec) offers daily flights to the **Baltra Airport,** right off Santa Cruz Island, and three weekly flights to **Puerto Baquerizo Moreno** on San Cristóbal Island. The majority of tours to the Galápagos fly into Baltra. During the low season (mid-Sept through mid-Dec and mid-Jan through mid-June), flights from the mainland cost around $336 round-trip. In the high season, they hover just below $400. As of now, Tame is the only carrier with service to Baltra. **Aerogal** (ⓒ **800/2376-425;** aerogal@andinanet.net) offers three weekly flights to San Cristóbal with fares identical to Tame's, but the service it offers is far superior to Tame's. Aerogal is also hoping to launch service to Baltra in the next year or so.

If you have already booked a tour before you arrive, you can expect someone to pick you up at the airport. If you're traveling on your own, I don't recommend flying into San Cristóbal Island. There is very little tourist infrastructure here,

and very few boats leave from this port. Instead, you should book a flight to Baltra. Once you land at the airport, a free shuttle bus will take you to a ferry crossing to Santa Cruz Island. The ferry costs 50¢. A regular bus will be waiting for you on the other side. From here to Puerto Ayora (the largest town on the island), the ride takes about 40 minutes and costs $1.50.

All flights from the mainland stop in both Quito and Guayaquil. If you are planning on flying to the Galápagos the day after you arrive in Ecuador, I recommend spending the night in Guayaquil. The flights leave Quito early in the morning and then stop for more than an hour to pick up passengers in Guayaquil. You will save more than 2 hours (and gain precious sleep time) if you board the plane there.

GETTING AROUND

The Galápagos Islands are an archipelago that consists of 13 big islands, six small islands, and more than 40 islets. **Santa Cruz** is the most populated island; its main town, Puerto Ayora, is the major city in the Galápagos. From here, you can arrange last-minute tours around the islands, day trips, and scuba-diving excursions. Santa Cruz is also home to the Darwin Research Station, where you can see giant land tortoises. **San Cristóbal** is the second-most populated island. Several tour boats begin their journeys from the port here, Puerto Baquerizo Moreno; the town is small, and there's not much to see on this island. I don't recommend staying here to try to find a last-minute trip—you'll have a much better chance of finding one on Santa Cruz. **Isabela** is the largest island, but

Tips Organizing a Last-Minute Trip to the Galápagos

There's no way around it—trips to the Galápagos are expensive. But if you book a cruise at the last minute, you can save up to 50% off of the regular rates. Unfortunately, it's not easy to find a last-minute price. During the high season (June–Sept and late Dec to early Jan), you shouldn't even waste your time looking for one. Even during the low season, you shouldn't expect to come to Ecuador and immediately find a boat that's leaving the next day. In some cases, you may have to wait a week to 10 days before you find an opening. If you have the time, here is a list of travel agencies and tour operators that you should contact once you arrive in Ecuador.

Websites

- **TOPPSA** ☆, also known as Travel Opportunities South America (www.toppsa.com), manages a website that specializes in offering last-minute trips throughout Ecuador (including the Galápagos). If you're planning to travel to Ecuador within the next 60 days, it's worth a look to see whether special offers are available.
- **Ecoventura** ☆, operates three first-class yachts in the Galápagos. Through the Miami office website, it sometimes offers last-minute deals at reduced rates (6303 Blue Lagoon Dr., Suite 140, Miami; © **800/633-7972** or 305/262-6264; www.ecoventura.com). If there are no special discounts on the website, do call the number above and talk to Doris, the friendly sales manager, who will try and do her best to get you a great deal.

Travel Agencies In Quito
Note: **Galasam** on Avenida Amazonas and Cordero specializes in wildly inexpensive last-minute trips to the Galápagos. But I have heard

only the third-most populated. In general, most visitors only stop here on a guided tour. For more information about individual islands in the Galápagos, see "Exploring the Galápagos" on p. 551.

To see the best of what the Galápagos have to offer, I recommend exploring the islands by boat. There are more than 100 tourist ships that ply the seas. All boats need a permit and must register with the national park, so it's very difficult to use your own private craft. If you're prone to seasickness, you can take day trips from Puerto Ayora to Santa Fe, Plaza Island, North Seymour, and Bartolomé.

Flights between the islands aren't frequent, but the Galápagos Airline **EMETEBE** (© 05/526-177; mtbgal@gye.satnet.net) offers service on tiny propeller planes between Santa Cruz, San Cristóbal, and Isabela islands. Fares are $80 for each flight sector.

VISITOR INFORMATION

The main tourist information office in the Galápagos is located in Puerto Ayora on Avenida Charles Darwin, close to the corner of Charles Binford. It is open Monday through Friday from 8am to noon and 2 to 5:30pm.

complaints about the level of service and the inefficiency on its ships. The prices are low, but so is the quality.

- **Zenith Ecuador Travel** ★★, Juan León Mera 452 and Roca (© 02/2529-993; www.zenithecuador.com), has access to information about 100 boats that ply the waters around the Galápagos Islands. Give the staff your dates and your requirements, and they'll talk to their contacts and try to find you a special last-minute deal. Ask to speak to the owner, Mr. Marcos Endara, and tell him you are a Frommer's reader.
- **Angermeyer's Enchanted Expeditions,** Foch 726 near the corner of Amazonas (© 02/2569-960; www.angermeyer.com), operates four boats in the Galápagos. If there's space, you won't have trouble negotiating a discounted last-minute price.

Travel Agencies in Puerto Ayora

- Bargain hunters should make **Moonrise Travel Agency,** Av. Charles Darwin 00160 near the corner of Charles Binford (© 05/526-402; www.galapagosmoonrise.com), their first stop. It specializes in booking last-minute trips on a number of different vessels (all classes and all sizes).
- Many boat companies have their own offices here. It's worth a shot to stop in and see what might be available. The *Galapagos Explorer II* has a last-minute booking office in the Red Mangrove Adventure Inn on Avenida Charles Darwin. If you're looking for luxury, stop in at **Quasar Náutica's** office on Avenida Charles Darwin, near the corner of Avenida Los Piqueros.

FAST FACTS   You can exchange traveler's checks or use the ATM at **Banco del Pacífico** on Avenida Charles Darwin (near the corner of Charles Binford).

The hospitals in the Galápagos offer less than adequate service. If you need a pharmacy, try **Farmacia Edith** (© 05/526-487) or **Farmacia Vanessa** (© 05/526-392) on Avenida Padre Juil Herrera, about 2 blocks up from Avenida Charles Darwin.

Internet access is slow and expensive. (It costs about $5 per hour.) The most reliable Internet cafe is **Sharknet** on Avenida Charles Darwin, right across from the Tame office. The **post office** is located at the far end of Avenida Charles Darwin, right across from the main dock.

For scuba divers, there is now a decompression chamber on Santa Cruz. Call **Henry Schaefer** at © 05/526-544 for more information.

EXPLORING THE GALAPAGOS
WHEN TO GO

There's never a bad time to visit the Galápagos. The peak season lasts from mid-June through early September and from mid-December through mid-January. It's almost impossible to find a last-minute deal at these times. The national park limits the number of visitors to each island, so the Galápagos will never feel like

Disney World. But if you visit in the summer, you are less likely to feel a sense of solitude and isolation. Here is a quick summary of the seasons to help you decide what time of year is best for you:

DECEMBER THROUGH MAY   During this time of year, the water and the air are warmer, but this is also the rainy season. It drizzles almost daily for a short period of time. Ironically, this is also the sunniest time of year. The end of December and the beginning of January is still the high season, so expect more crowds than during the rest of the year.

Because the water is warm, the idea of swimming and snorkeling is enticing. On the flip side, there aren't as many fish to see as there are later in the year. This is also the breeding season for land birds, so it's a good opportunity to watch some unusual mating rituals. If you're into turtles, this is best time of year to come; you can watch sea turtles nesting on the beach, and from March through May, you can often see the land tortoises wandering around the lowland areas of the islands as they make their way down from the highlands in search of a mate. Sea lions also mate in the rainy season—it's entertaining to watch as the males fight it out for the females. Around March and April, you'll see the adorable newborn pups crawling around the islands.

In February, March, and April, as the rains dissipate, flowers start to blossom and the islands are awash in bright colors. Another benefit of traveling to the Galápagos at this time of year: The sea is much calmer, so there is less chance of getting seasick.

JUNE THROUGH NOVEMBER   From June through November, the Humboldt Current makes it way up to the Galápagos from the southern end of South America. The current brings cold water and cold weather, but it also brings water rich in nutrients and plankton, which attracts fish and birds. During this season there always seem to be clouds in the air, but it rarely rains. It's also quite windy, and the seas tend to be rough.

Experienced divers claim that this is the best time of year to visit the Galápagos. Unfortunately, to see the wide variety of underwater marine life, you have to brave the cold water. Because there are more fish in the sea at this time of year, there are also more seabirds searching for these fish. Albatrosses arrive on Española in June and stay until December. Penguins also like the cold water and abundance of fish, so you're more likely to see them here during this season. On Genovesa, the elusive owls mate in June and July, and you have the best chance of spotting one during this time. Blue-footed boobies also mate during this time of year, so it won't be difficult to witness their beautiful mating ritual known as the "sky point."

If you decide to visit the Galápagos during this time of year, be prepared for cool weather. If you have a wet suit, I highly recommend bringing it with you.

THE ISLANDS IN BRIEF

Every island in the Galápagos has its own special allure. The more time you have, the richer your experience, but even if you only have a few days, if you plan your vacation right, you'll come home with a lifetime of memories. When you're choosing a tour operator, you should always examine the itinerary. Note that 7-day trips often make frequent stops at Santa Cruz or San Cristóbal to collect and drop off passengers. The best trips head out to far-flung places, such as Genovesa, Española, and Fernandina, and spend only 1 day docked in Puerto Ayora on Santa Cruz Island. To help you decide which trip might be best for you, here's a list of what each island has to offer.

BARTOLOME *(Moments)*   Bartolomé is famous for its dramatic vistas and barren volcanic landscape. You can climb more than 200 steps to reach the top of an extinct volcano. From here, you can look out over the ocean and see the oddly shaped Pinnacle Rock. Many snorkelers have spotted penguins off this island.

GENOVESA (TOWER) ⋒   Almost every Galápagos tourist brochure has a picture of a frigate bird puffing up its red neck in an attempt to attract females. Here on Genovesa, you'll have ample opportunities to see these birds in action. This island is also home to the largest colony of red-footed boobies. The snorkeling here is excellent. In the afternoon, you'll explore the other side of the island, where you can see masked boobies and storm petrels. If you're lucky, you might spot the elusive short-eared owl—since these guys don't have predators, they are the only owls in the world that are diurnal. It's easiest to see them in June and July.

CERRO DRAGON   Cerro Dragon (Dragon Hill) is on the north side of Santa Cruz. Here, you will have the opportunity to see land iguanas that don't exist anywhere else in the world.

ESPAÑOLA ⋒⋒   Española is enchanting. From May through December, albatrosses settle down here to mate and take care of their young. In May and June, if you arrive early in the morning, you can witness the beak-cracking mating ritual of the albatross. Later in the season (Sept–Dec), you can see the little chicks. There must be some sort of aphrodisiac on this island because this is also the best place to see blue-footed boobies doing their mating dance, known as the "sky point," where the male extends his wings and lifts his beak as he howls at his prospective mate. If the female likes what she sees, she will mimic her suitor.

FERNANDINA ⋒   The largest colony of marine iguanas live here on Fernandina. These cold-blooded animals hug and cuddle with each other to warm up after swimming in from the ocean. Flightless cormorants also inhabit the island; even though these birds can't fly (they are the only flightless cormorants in the world), they still dry their wings in the sun, just like their flying ancestors used to do millions of years ago.

ISABELA   This is the largest island in the Galápagos. Darwin's Lake provides an excellent backdrop for dramatic photos of the sea. You'll also see lots of land iguanas here, and you can take a long hike to a scenic point, where you can see for miles around. When you first arrive on the island, you'll be able to examine graffiti that dates all the way to 1836. Some tour companies offer *panga* (dinghy)

⋒ Tips Scuba Diving Trips

The waters surrounding the Galápagos offer some of the best diving in the world. If you want to dive here, you have two options: You can arrange a tour on a dive boat, and dive every day, or you can take a non-diving cruise and then spend a couple of extra days in Puerto Ayora and arrange diving excursions from there. Two of the best diving outfitters are **SCUBA Iguana** (www.scuba-iguana.com), located at the Hotel Galápagos on Avenida Charles Darwin, right below the Darwin Research Station, and **Sub-Aqua** (www.galapagos-sub-aqua.com) on Avenida Charles Darwin and Avenida 12 de Febrero.

rides around Tagus Cove, where you will enter an underwater cave and have the opportunity to see the Galápagos penguins.

SAN CRISTOBAL   Most boats only stop on San Cristóbal to pick up and drop off passengers. There's not much to see or do here. If your trip begins on this island, you will probably stop at Cerro Brujo, a beach with sea lions, red crabs, and colorful lava gulls. You will also pass through Kicker Rock—a unique rock formation set about 1.5km (1 mile) offshore.

SANTA CRUZ   You will most likely begin and end your trip to the Galápagos on Santa Cruz. If you plan on arranging your trip on your own, you should use Santa Cruz as your base. If you're looking for a luxury getaway, this island offers the only such choice: The Royal Palm Hotel. This island is also home to the Charles Darwin Research Center, where you can observe tortoises firsthand. Tours of the island also include stops at Los Gemelos (The Twins), two sinkholes that stand side by side. As you walk around Los Gemelos, you will have a good chance of spotting the beautiful vermilion flycatcher. Some companies will take you to a farm in the highlands, where you can see tortoises in the wild. It's exciting to see these enormous creatures crawling about, but I must warn you, it's either hot and sunny up here or cool and drizzly (depending on the seasons). After you see the tortoises, the tour continues on a long, boring hike to a small, unattractive lake. If you can, try to turn back after you see the tortoises. Finally, most trips make a stop at the lava tubes, where you can wander though underground tunnels created by the movement of hot lava.

SANTIAGO   Most of the sea lions in the Galápagos are California sea lions. But on this island, you will have the chance to see the only endemic species of sea lions in the Galápagos, the fur sea lion. After you see the fur sea lions, you will have an opportunity to take advantage of the excellent snorkeling here. Expect to see sea turtles. The island is also full of coastal birds such as great blue herons, lava herons, oystercatchers, and yellow-crowned night herons.

RABIDA 𝒻   Rábida has a beautiful red-sand beach. In my opinion, the waters off of Rábida offer the best snorkeling in the islands. You may even find yourself swimming with penguins.

CHOOSING A BOAT TOUR

Hundreds of companies offer trips through the Galápagos. Trying to sift through all the tourist brochures is a daunting task. First and foremost, let me warn you that in the Galápagos, you get what you pay for. There are four classes of boats: economic, tourist class, first class, and luxury. The **economic** boats have shared dormitories and bathrooms, inexperienced (and non-English-speaking) guides, and mediocre food. On a **tourist class boat** you may have your own private quarters, but expect them to be cramped. You probably won't have air-conditioning or hot water, and your guide won't have a good command of the English language. **First-class** ships have excellent guides, small but private cabins with hot water and air-conditioning, and passable food. The main difference between first-class and **luxury** service is the food; some luxury boats also have swimming pools, but the cabins are not necessarily much bigger. The *Galapagos Explorer II* is the one exception: All the rooms are large suites, the biggest in the Galápagos Islands.

Another warning for you: Don't expect your cruise in the Galápagos to be a typical pleasure cruise. The boats are used mainly for lodging and transportation purposes. During the day, small dinghies, known as *pangas,* will transport you to the actual islands. Once you're on land, the excursions often involve long, uphill hikes. The Galápagos are not a place for taking it easy—expect to partake in strenuous activities.

You should also note that although the lower cabins are dark, with portholes, these cabins are also the most stable. (In other words, it's easier to get seasick when you're sleeping up top.) You should also try to request a cabin in the back of the boat—in the front, the dropping of the anchor and the humming of the motor can be disturbing, especially in the middle of the night.

Trips to the Galápagos venture out to the high seas, and the waters can be rough. Be sure to bring Dramamine or another antiseasickness medication with you. You'll definitely need it. Candied ginger also helps settle small stomach upsets and is an alternative to medication. The big cruise boats don't provide more stability than the small ones.

RECOMMENDED TOUR OPERATORS

In addition to the companies below, I also recommend **Metropolitan Touring**'s 90-passenger *Santa Cruz* and its exquisite 40-passenger *Isabela II*. Additionally, Metropolitan organizes a land-based program in the Galápagos, where you sleep in Puerto Ayora but take day trips to the nearby islands. For more information, contact **Adventure Associates** at © 800/527-2500 in the United States, or log on to www.metropolitan-touring.com.

Quasar Náutica 🌟🌟🌟 operates eight of the most luxurious yachts in the Galápagos. The company also has four luxurious sailboats, as well as two fully equipped dive boats. For more information in the United States, call © 800/247-2925 or check out the website www.quasarnautica.com.

Angermeyer's Enchanted Expeditions (© 02/2569-960; www.angermeyer. com) offers the best tourist-class boats. Their fleet includes two sailboats (one 10-passenger and one 12-passenger), a 16-passenger motorized yacht, and the first-class 16-passenger Beluga yacht.

Ecoventura *(Moments* FIRST CLASS   In my opinion, a successful trip to the Galápagos depends on your guide. A great tour guide will share the secrets of the islands with you, spot the rare animals, and treat you like a friend. You can expect this and more from the guides on Ecoventura's boats. The company operates four ships: the 16-passenger dive boat M/Y *Sky Dancer,* and the three identical 20-passenger boats M/Y *Eric, Flamingo I,* and *Letty.* The latter three have two guides for every 20 people, a large sun deck, bar, two sea kayaks and snorkeling equipment. The *Sky Dancer* is one of the best boats in the islands for scuba diving; the crew includes a dive instructor and two dive masters. In addition to providing personalized service, Ecoventura is also environmentally conscious. The Rainforest Alliance has awarded them a "green seal of approval" for their conservation efforts in the Galápagos. Don't expect high-class service, luxurious cabins, or great food but you can count on this operation having the most experienced guides in the islands.

6303 Blue Lagoon Dr., Miami, FL 33126. © 800/633-7972. Fax 305/262-9609. www.ecoventura.com. 4 boats. *Eric, Flamingo,* and *Letty:* 7 nights $2,195–$2,495 per person based on double occupancy. *Sky Dancer:* 7 nights $2,695–$2,895 per person; 10 nights $3,795–$3,995 per person. Rates include accommodations, all meals, nonalcoholic beverages, guide services, snorkeling equipment, wet suits, sea kayaks, and transfers between the dock and airport.

M/V *Galapagos Explorer II* 🌟🌟 LUXURY   When you book a trip on the *Explorer II,* you can rest assured that you're on the most luxurious ship in the Galápagos. This 100-passenger cruise ship offers all the amenities you could ever want: swimming pool, Jacuzzi, bars, first-class cruise food, elevator, research center, nightly naturalist lectures, library, game room, and even medical center. Most important, this is the one boat where you don't have to cram yourself into a tiny little cabin. All the accommodations are suites, with small sitting areas, a minibar, and a TV/VCR. But in my opinion, when you're on a ship like this, you're sacrificing personal attention for comfort. I'm just not a big fan of the large-cruise-ship experience in the Galápagos. When you're exploring the islands with 100 other people, the islands lose some of their mystique. Plus, you always feel a bit rushed, because there is always a group behind you, waiting for you to continue on your way. It's all a matter of taste. If you like big cruise ships, you'll love the *Galapagos Explorer II*. But if you want linger on the islands and ask your guide questions, you'll be better off on a smaller ship.

6251 SW 57th St., South Miami, FL 33143. (℃ 305/662-2965. Fax 305/662-2953. www.galapagosexplorer. com. 3 nights $1,080–$1,725 per person; 4 nights $1,435–$2,295 per person; 7 nights $2,395–$3,825 per person. Rates include accommodations, all meals, nonalcoholic beverages, glass of wine at dinner, guide services, and transfers between the dock and airport. Snorkeling equipment is $5 extra.

KLEIN Tours ⋨ FIRST CLASS   KLEIN Tours is one of the oldest companies operating boats in the Galápagos, and their experience shows. The company maintains three ships: the 20-passenger M/Y *Coral*, the 26-passenger M/Y *Coral II*, and the 90-passenger M/V *Galapagos Legend*. The smaller boats offer similar services to the small boats in Ecoventura's fleet, but KLEIN Tours's food is better. The guides are excellent and knowledgeable. The *Legend* has large cabins, a swimming pool, massage service, a 24-hour coffee bar, and a jogging track. I prefer the intimate feel of the smaller boats, but on the *Legend*, you won't be lacking for any personal comforts. *Note:* KLEIN Tours's boats don't stop on Genovesa, so you may not have the opportunity to see red-footed boobies.

Av. Eloy Alfaro and Catalina Aldaz, Quito. (℃ 888/50-KLEIN in the U.S. Fax 02/2442-389 in Ecuador. www. kleintours.com. *Coral* and the *Coral II*: 3 nights $815–$1,050 per person; 4 nights $1,167–$1,400 per person; 7 nights $1,825–$2,400 per person. Rates include accommodations, all meals, nonalcoholic beverages, guide services, snorkeling equipment, and transfers between the dock and airport.

PUERTO AYORA

Puerto Ayora is the largest town in the Galápagos. If you're arriving on your own, this is a good place to base yourself and organize your trip. The **Moonrise Travel Agency,** Av. Charles Darwin 00160 near the corner of Charles Binford (℃ 05/526-402; www.galapagosmoonrise.com), will be your best source of information. The staff is friendly and they can help you arrange a last-minute cruise of the Galápagos and independent tours around the islands.

WHERE TO STAY

In addition to the Royal Palm and Finch Bay below, the **Hotel Silberstein** (formerly the Hotel Angermeyer), Avenida Charles Darwin and Piqueros (℃ 05/526-277), is a good choice in the center of Puerto Ayora. The 22 rooms are large, with sparkling white tiles and built-in wooden beds. All the rooms are positioned around a pretty outdoor swimming pool. Plus, the hotel's travel agency can arrange excursions. Doubles cost $103 a night. The **Red Mangrove Adventure Inn,** Avenida Charles Darwin (℃ 05/526-564; www.redmangrove. com), is more aesthetically pleasing. Many of the rooms have views of the bay, and they all have funky colorful furnishings and adobe platform beds. One major flaw: None of the bathrooms have doors; curtains are the only thing that comes between the bedroom and the toilet. Doubles cost $130 to $197 a night. For more inexpensive but perfectly adequate rooms, try **Hotel Palmeras** on

Tomás de Berlanga and Bolívar Naveda (© **05/526-139**; hotelpalmeras@ hotmail.com). Doubles cost $28 to $36 a night.

Finch Bay Hotel ✦✦ *Moments*   The only beachfront hotel in Santa Cruz opened in 2003 and is a 5-minute boat ride from Puerto Ayora. Secluded and serene among the mangroves with a magnificent pool and private beach, the Finch Bay also boasts over 30 species of resident birds including red-footed boobies. Rooms are tastefully decorated with yellow walls and attractive wooden blinds; bathrooms are large and have spacious showers with good water pressure (rare in the islands). The hotel prides itself on being environmentally friendly with solar power and a policy of conservation. There's a Zen garden where yoga is offered in the mornings; bikes, kayaks, and snorkeling equipment are available for guests. The friendly staff can organize day trips to the islands and scuba-diving excursions. The excellent restaurant serves three meals a day with emphasis on healthy, organic ingredients; vegetarian offerings are also available. There's a computer with Internet access for guests to use for free. Be sure to ask about promotional rates when making your reservations. None of the rooms have TVs, but there's a lounge with satellite TV. To get here, grab a water taxi from the dock; it'll cost you 50¢.

Punta Estrada, Isla Santa Cruz. © **05/5526-297**. Fax 02/2463-681. Finchbayhotel@spsinter.net. 21 units. $134 double. Rates include American breakfast. AE, DC, MC, V. **Amenities:** Excellent restaurant; 2 bars; lounge; large outdoor pool; Jacuzzi; watersports equipment; bike rental; tour desk; limited room service; laundry service. *In room:* A/C, dataport, safe.

Royal Palm Hotel ✦✦✦ *Finds*   The newest and most exclusive resort in Ecuador sits on 200 lush hillside hectares (500 acres), a 20-minute drive from Puerto Ayora. Already, the Royal Palm is attracting a healthy dose of celebrities seeking the privacy and personalized service that this resort offers. There are 10 beautiful villas scattered on the hillside, 4 veranda studios, and 3 spectacular suites. The villas all have separate living/dining area, a bedroom with a king-size bed and CD player, and a huge bathroom with large shower, dressing area, and a separate room with a Jacuzzi tub; all villas come with gleaming hardwood floors and leather sofas. Windows face the serene countryside and the ocean at the bottom of the hill. The three suites are all different—the two-bedroom, two-bathroom Imperial comes with its own Jacuzzi hidden in a private garden and the Royal has a four-poster bed and an indoor sauna. The studios are the simplest (and least expensive) units but have charming patios with hammocks and spacious bathrooms with Jacuzzi tubs. Service is exquisite, friendly and not at all stuffy. Anybody staying here will be made to feel like a VIP, from the special greeting at the airport to the private speedboat used to transfer guests from Baltra to Santa Cruz. If you want to feel like royalty without pomp and circumstance, this is the place for you.

Via Baltra, Km 18, Isla Santa Cruz. © **800/528-6069** for reservations in the U.S., or 05/5527-409. Fax 05/ 5527-408. www.royalpalmhotel.net. 17 units. $310 studio; $420–$500 suite; $550 villa for 2; $800 Imperial suite. Rates include American breakfast. AE, DC, MC, V. **Amenities:** Restaurant; bar; beautiful outdoor swimming pool; 2 outdoor tennis courts; exercise room; sauna; concierge; large business center; 24-hr. room service; massage; same-day dry cleaning; laundry service. *In room:* TV/VCR, fax, dataport, minibar, hair dryer, safe, Jacuzzi (in suites and villas).

WHERE TO DINE

The restaurant at the **Royal Palm Hotel** (see above) is the best place to dine on the island. Specialties include both Ecuadorian and International dishes and creations by the very talented 28-year-old chef. If you're not staying at the resort, call ahead for reservations. Main courses are $12 to $18. The **Finch Bay** (see above) also has an excellent restaurant. For lunch and dinner there's always an $18 per-person buffet; you can opt to dine outdoors around the pool in good weather; you can also order a la carte, and main courses are $3 to $10.

In town, the place with the best food and best atmosphere is Restaurant **La Garrapata,** Barrio Pelican Bay, Avenida Charles Darwin (© **05/5526-264**). This is where the local expats eat—and all the foreign guides who work on the ships. There's a great selection of fresh juices and sandwiches. There's usually a *menú del día* (menu of the day) with soup, main course, and dessert for less than $5. Sandwiches are $5 and juices are $1.50.

AFTER DARK

The **Bongo Bar** is the most happening place in town at night. It's located just behind Restaurant La Garrapata (see "Where to Dine," above) and usually gets busy after 8pm. Across the street, the **Limón Café** is popular early in the evening and you can check e-mail from several computers with Internet access. The **Angermeyer Bar** has the best view; it overlooks the harbor. To get there, grab a water taxi for 50¢ from the main dock—the trip takes all of 3 minutes. There's a restaurant here too but the food is overpriced and mediocre. I recommend coming here for a drink, then going back to your hotel or to the Garrapata for dinner.

9

Peru

by Neil E. Schlecht

When Francisco Pizarro, the Spanish conquistador, and his fortune-hunting cronies descended on Peru in 1528, they discovered the vast riches they were searching for and a highly sophisticated culture. The Spaniards soon overpowered the awed and politically weakened Inca empire, but they didn't find the Incas' greatest secret: the imperial city of Machu Picchu, hidden high in the Andes. Machu Picchu is acclaimed as the pinnacle achievement of the continent's pre-Columbian societies, yet it is only one of the exhilarating discoveries that await visitors to Peru.

Peru has a habit of turning virtually every visitor into an amateur archaeologist. Ruins fire the imagination and outstanding museum collections weave an intricate tale of complex cultures through ceramics, spectacular textiles, and remarkably preserved mummies. You can see the Lord of Sipán in all the glory of the jewels and rituals that accompanied his burial, as well as the frozen corpse of Juanita the Ice Maiden, an Inca princess sacrificed on a mountain ridge more than 500 years ago.

Peru has few peers when it comes to physical beauty and diversity. Its landscapes will delight anyone with an appreciation for the outdoors: the rugged, cloud-ringed Andes; the brilliant azure water of Lake Titicaca; great canyons graced by giant condors; and a teeming Amazon jungle that possesses one of the world's richest repositories of plant and animal life. Peru is fast becoming South America's top destination for mountain climbing, river rafting, bird-watching, river cruises, and rainforest treks. Urban Peru is a mix of laid-back and elegant colonial towns, a chaotic and cosmopolitan capital, and the surprisingly lively Cusco, a grand 16th-century city that rocks to the beat of a young crowd of global backpackers.

Peru's history of suffering—political mayhem and corruption, surprise attacks from homegrown Maoist "Shining Path" terrorists, cocaine trafficking, and violent street crime—is well documented. In the late 1980s and early 1990s, Peruvians fled the capital and the countryside, and understandably, few travelers were brave enough to plan vacations in Peru. With the 2001 election of Alejandro Toledo, the nation's first president of native Indian origin, many Peruvians were hopeful that the country had finally turned a corner. However, Toledo's presidency has been beset by continued economic strife, widespread strikes and continued unease, amid rumors of a Shining Path resurgence. Peru remains desperately poor, but on the whole the country is still safer and more welcoming than it has been in many years. Too many unfortunate years of corrupt politicians, lawlessness, and economic disarray clouded though never eclipsed the beauty of this fascinating Andean nation.

1 The Regions in Brief

Peru, which lies just below the equator, is the third-largest country in South America, covering an area of nearly 1,300,000 sq. km (500,000 sq. miles). Peru shares borders with Ecuador and Colombia to the north, Brazil and Bolivia to the east, and Chile to the south. Peruvians like to say that their country consists of three distinct geological components: coast, *sierra* (highlands), and *selva* (jungle). Though Lima lies on the coast, the bold Andes mountain range and Amazon rainforest, which makes up nearly two-thirds of Peru, dominate the country. Its considerable size, natural barriers, and a lack of efficient transportation options make Peru a somewhat difficult and time-consuming place in which to get around.

Unless you have at least 3 weeks or a month to spend in Peru, a real danger is trying to do too much in a short period. In a single week, there's really only enough time to see the best of Lima, Cusco, Machu Picchu, and the Sacred Valley's main sights—and even that is really pushing it. Even 2 or 3 weeks in Peru involves making a few hard choices. The first week could be spent as above, though it may be necessary to scale back on the Sacred Valley or passing entirely on the capital, Lima, if you're intent on seeing another part of the country. During the second week, head south to Lake Titicaca, arranging an overnight stay at one of the lake's islands, and then head to Arequipa and Colca Canyon to see the giant condors, or fly north for a jungle lodge excursion from Iquitos. Physically adventurous travelers should consider either the 4-day Inca Trail to Machu Picchu or the 2-day trek (if you do the latter, you'll have more time for other activities in the Sacred Valley, such as river rafting), as well as a jungle lodge or camping excursion, flying from Cusco to explore the Manu Biosphere Reserve or Tambopata Reserve Zone in the Southern Amazon Basin.

LIMA & THE CENTRAL COAST   The Pacific coastal region is a narrow strip that runs from one end of the country to the other (a distance of some 2,254km/1,400 miles) and is almost entirely desert. Lima lies about halfway down the coast. To the south in one of the driest areas on earth are **Pisco, Ica,** and **Nasca,** cradle of several of Peru's most important ancient civilizations, as well as the famously mysterious **Nasca Lines** and the **Ballestas Islands,** promoted locally as "Peru's Galápagos" for their diverse indigenous fauna.

SOUTH CENTRAL PERU   The dramatic Andes mountains contain the country's most famous sights, including the former Inca capital of **Cusco** and scenic highland villages that run the length of the beautiful **Sacred Valley.** The valley is dotted with singularly impressive Inca ruins, of which **Machu Picchu** (and the **Inca Trail** leading to it) is undoubtedly the star.

SOUTHERN PERU   Massive **Lake Titicaca,** shared with Bolivia, is the largest lake in South America and the world's highest navigable body of water. **Puno,** at the edge of Lake Titicaca, is a rough-and-tumble town that hosts some of Peru's liveliest festivals. The elegant colonial city of **Arequipa** is gorgeously situated at the base of three snowcapped volcanoes, and nearby is **Colca Canyon,** twice as deep as the Grand Canyon and perhaps the best place in South America to view the regal condor.

Shameless Plug

For more in-depth coverage of Peru, pick up a copy of *Frommer's Peru.*

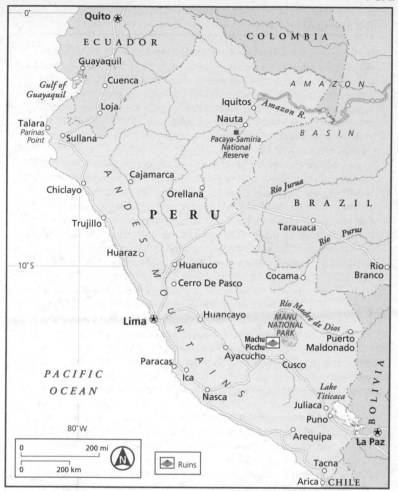

NORTH CENTRAL HIGHLANDS The mountain ranges north of Lima are among the highest in Peru. Within **Huascarán National Park,** the Cordillera Blanca stretches for 200km (124 miles) and contains a dozen peaks over 5,000m (16,400 ft.) high. The region is a favorite of trekkers and outdoor adventure travelers. The main jumping-off point for these activities is the town of **Huaraz.** In valleys east of the capital is **Chavín de Huantar,** one of Peru's oldest archaeological sites.

NORTH COAST & NORTHERN HIGHLANDS Peru's north is much less visited than the south, even though it possesses some of the country's most outstanding archaeological sights. **Trujillo, Chiclayo,** and **Cajamarca,** a lovely small city in the highlands, are the main colonial towns of interest. Near Trujillo and Chiclayo are **Chan Chan, Túcume,** and **Sipán,** extraordinary adobe cities, pyramids, and royal tombs and treasures that vastly predate the Incas.

THE AMAZON BASIN & THE JUNGLE Though about 60% of Peru is Amazon rainforest, only about 5% of the country's human inhabitants reside

Off the Beaten Path

Northern Peru is vastly underappreciated; in fact, most of the region is virtually unknown to foreigners who travel to Peru. The few travelers who get to know the north are mainly those with a specific interest in ancient Peruvian cultures or hikers and adventurous travelers looking to get out into the country, beyond the reach of the majority of gringos who trod well-beaten paths in the Andes and southern Peru. If you make it to this part of Peru, you may be in for the not-unwelcome treat of being one of the few.

You wouldn't know it from the paucity of foreign visitors, but the northern coastal desert of Peru holds some of the country's greatest archaeological treasures: Chan Chan, the great adobe city of the Chimú civilization; 1,500-year-old Moche temples; and the royal tomb that brought the great Lord of Sipán to the world's attention in 1987—Peru's very own King Tut. Northern beaches draw surfers to some of the best waves off of South America, and nestled in the *sierra* is one of the country's most charming and beautiful mountain towns, Cajamarca, a mini-Cusco of the north.

Where gringos of a particular ilk and style of outdoor performance gear do make it in significant numbers is the Cordillera Blanca, home to some of the most beautiful peaks in South America and some of the finest trekking on the continent. Huaraz is the primary base for excursions into the valleys and mountain ranges of the northern Andes. For years, the destination has been favored principally by sports and adventurer travelers, especially hard-core hikers, but the range of activities is opening up and appealing more and more to average travelers who also want a taste of Peru's great outdoors.

Aero Continente (© 01/242-4242; www.aerocontinente.net) and AeroCondor (© 01/442-5215; www.aerocondor.com.pe) fly daily to Trujillo and Cajamarca from Lima; Aero Continente and Aviandina (© 01/447-8080) fly daily from Lima to Chiclayo. Agencies offering standard city and archaeological tours in Trujillo include Guía Tours, Jr. Independencia 580 (© 044/245-170); Chacón Tours, Av. España 106 (© 044/255-212); and Trujillo Tours, Diego de Almagro 301 (© 044/233-091).

Traveling by bus from Lima, or from other points along the north coast or the northern Andes, is the only way to get to Huaraz. For the 7- to 8-hour journey from Lima, major companies offering daily service are CIVA (© 01/428-5649), Cruz del Sur (© 01/225-6163), and Movil Tours (© 044/722-555 in Huaraz). For mountaineering and trekking information, consult the respected Casa de Guías de Huaraz, Parque Ginebra 28 (© 044/721-811).

For a full discussion of the attractions of northern Peru, pick up a copy of *Frommer's Peru*.

there. For the visitor, there are two primary jungle destinations. The northern jungle, of which **Iquitos** is the principal gateway, is the most explored and has the most facilities. Much less trafficked and more controlled is the Madre de

Dios department (one of the administrative districts into which Peru is divided) in the south, which contains **Manu National Park** (and its Biosphere Reserve), **Puerto Maldonado,** and **Tambopata.**

2 Planning Your Trip to Peru

VISITOR INFORMATION

Peru doesn't maintain national tourism offices abroad, so your best official source of information before you go is the **PromPerú** (Commission for the Promotion of Peru) website at **www.peru.org.pe.** Peruvian embassies and consulates usually offer some brochures and other information on traveling to Peru, but it's probably best not to expect too much. Additional websites of interest include:

- **www.peruemb.org**: The website for the Peruvian Embassy in Washington, D.C.
- **www.perurail.com**: Peru Rail's official site with routes and services
- **www.saexplorers.org**: The South American Explorers Club website, especially good for trekking and adventure travel
- **www.traficoperu.com/english**: An online travel agency with information on flights, hotels, and special deals

IN PERU

Visitor information is not handled by a single, centralized government agency across Peru. PromPerú works alongside Mitinci (Ministry of Industry, Tourism & International Business Negotiation) and several private entities. The result is that tourism information is confusingly dispersed among sometimes poorly equipped small municipal offices and is often limited to regional or local information. Occasionally, private travel agencies are more adept at dispensing information, though their goal is, of course, to hawk their services.

PromPerú operates a 24-hour information booth (© **01/574-8000**) in the international terminal of Lima's Jorge Chávez International Airport. The

---

Telephone Dialing Info at a Glance

- **To place a call from your home country to Peru,** dial the international access code (011 in the U.S. and Canada, 0011 in Australia, 0170 in New Zealand, 00 in the U.K.), plus the country code (51), plus the Peruvian area code, followed by the number. For example, a call from the United States to Lima would be 011+51+1+000+0000.
- **To place a local call within Peru,** you do *not* need to dial the city area code (for example, 01 for Lima); dial only the number. To place a long-distance call within Peru, dial 0 plus the city code and the number. For information, dial © 103.
- **To place a direct international call from Peru,** dial the international access code (00), plus the country code of the place you are dialing, plus the area code and the local number.
- **To reach an international operator,** dial © 108. Major long-distance company access codes are as follows: **AT&T** © 0800/50-000; **MCI** © 0800/50-010; **Sprint** © 0800/50-020.

Tourist Protection Bureau (Indecopi) operates a 24-hour traveler's assistance line that handles complaints and questions about consumer rights; call © **01/224-7888** in Lima, or 0800/42-579 (toll free) in other cities. The Tourist Protection Bureau's Lima office is at Calle La Prosa 138, San Borja (© **01/224-8600**); for local branch numbers, see "Fast Facts" in the individual city sections in this chapter.

ENTRY REQUIREMENTS

Citizens of the United States, Canada, Great Britain, South Africa, New Zealand, and Australia require valid passports to enter Peru as tourists. Citizens of any of these countries conducting business or enrolled in formal educational programs in Peru also require visas.

Tourist (or landing) cards, distributed on arriving international flights or at border crossings, are good for stays of up to 90 days. Keep a copy of the tourist card for presentation upon departure from Peru. (If you lose it, you'll have to pay a $4 fine.) A maximum of three extensions of 30 days each, for a total of 180 days, is allowed.

PERUVIAN EMBASSY LOCATIONS

In the U.S.: 1700 Massachusetts Ave. NW, Washington, DC 20036 (© **202/833-9860;** www.peruvianembassy.us)

In Canada: 130 Albert St., Suite 1901, Ottawa, Ontario K1P 5G4 (© **613/238-1777;** emperuca@magi.ca)

In the U.K.: 52 Sloane St., London SW1X 9SP (© **020/7235-1917;** www.peruembassy-uk.com)

In Australia: 43 Culgoa Circuit, O'Malley, ACT 2606 (© **02/6286-9507;** www.embaperu.org.au)

In New Zealand: Cigna House, 40 Mercer St., Level 8, Wellington (© **04/499-8087;** embassy.peru@xtra.co.nz)

CUSTOMS

You are allowed to bring 3 liters of alcohol and 400 cigarettes or 50 cigars into Peru duty-free. New items for personal use, including camera equipment and sports gear such as mountain bikes and kayaks, are allowed. Travelers may bring in up to $300 in varied gifts, as long as no individual item exceeds $100. To avoid the possibility of having to fill out forms or pay a bond, it's best not to draw attention to expensive, new-looking items that officials might believe you are intent on reselling. (In other words, take new items out of their original boxes.)

Exports of protected plant and endangered animal species—live or dead—are strictly prohibited by Peruvian law and should not be purchased. This includes headpieces and necklaces made with macaw feathers, and even common "rain sticks," unless authorized by the Natural Resources Institute (INRENA). Vendors in jungle cities and airports sell live animals and birds, as well as handicrafts made from insects, feathers, or other natural products. Travelers have been detained and arrested by the Ecology Police in Lima for carrying such items.

It is also illegal to take pre-Columbian archaeological items, antiques, and artifacts from precolonial civilizations (including ceramics and textiles), and colonial-era art out of Peru. Reproductions of many such items are available, but even their export may cause difficulties at Customs or with overly cautious international courier services if you attempt to send them home. To be safe, look for the word REPRODUCCION or an artist's name stamped on reproduction ceramics, and keep business cards and receipts from shops where you have purchased these items. Particularly fine items may require documentation from Peru's National Institute of Culture (INC) verifying that the object is a reproduction and may be exported. You may be able to obtain a certificate of authorization from the INC kiosk at Lima's Jorge Chávez International Airport or the **INC office** in Lima at the National Museum Building, Sixth Floor, Av. Javier Prado Este 2465, San Borja (© **01/476 9900**).

MONEY

Peru's official currency is the **nuevo sol** (S/), divided into 100 centavos. Coins are issued in denominations of 5, 10, 20 and 50 centavos, and bank notes of S/10, 20, 50, 100, and 200. The U.S. dollar is the second currency; many hotels post their rates in dollars, and plenty of shops, taxi drivers, restaurants, and hotels across Peru accept U.S. dollars for payment. It is often difficult to pay with large bank notes (in either soles or dollars). Try to carry denominations of 50 and lower in both.

Counterfeit bank notes and even coins are common, and merchants and consumers across Peru vigorously check the authenticity of money before accepting payment or change. (The simplest way: Hold the banknote up to the light to see the watermark.) Many people also refuse to accept bank notes that are not in good condition (including those with small tears, those that have been written on, and even those that are simply well worn) and visitors are wise to do the same when receiving change to avoid problems with other payments. Do not accept bills with tears (no matter how small), and refuse taped bills.

Here's an idea of what things cost in Peru: a short taxi ride, $2 to $3; a double room at a budget hotel, $20; a double room at a moderate hotel, $40 to $80; a double room at an expensive hotel, $80 to $150; coffee or a soft drink, 50¢; a movie, $3; lunch, $2 to $10; dinner, $5 to $20.

CURRENCY EXCHANGE & RATES   At press time, the rate of exchange was approximately 3.5 soles to the U.S. dollar. (Rates are pretty consistent across the country.) If you pay in dollars, you will likely receive change in soles, so be aware of the correct exchange rate. Currencies other than U.S. dollars receive very poor exchange rates. Money can be exchanged at banks; with money changers (legal in Peru), often wearing colored smocks with "$" insignias, on the street; and at rarer *casas de cambio* (money-exchange houses). Money changers offer current rates of exchange, but you are advised to count your money carefully (you can simplify this by exchanging easily calculable amounts, such as $10 or $100) and make sure you have not received any counterfeit bills.

ATMs   Peru is still very much a cash society. In villages and small towns, it may be impossible to cash traveler's checks or use credit cards. Make sure you have cash (in both soles and U.S. dollars) on hand. ATMs, which are the best way of getting cash in Peru, are found in most towns and cities, though certainly not on every street corner. Screen instructions are in English as well as Spanish. Some bank ATMs dispense money only to those who hold accounts there, and lines can be frustratingly long. Peruvian banks include Banco de Crédito, Banco Wiese, Interbank, Banco Central de Reserva, Banco de Comercio, and Banco Continental. Look for the symbols of major international networks, **PLUS** (© **800/843-7587**) and **Cirrus** (© **800/424-7787**). Your personal identification number (PIN) should contain four digits.

TRAVELER'S CHECKS   Traveler's checks in Peru are exchanged at fewer places and at a considerably lower rate (often 2%) than cash. If you use traveler's checks, **American Express** is the brand most easily exchanged. Replacing traveler's checks outside of Lima can be very problematic, if not impossible. Keep a record of check numbers and the original bill of sale in a safe place. To report lost or stolen traveler's checks, call American Express at ℭ **01/330-4484.**

CREDIT CARDS   Many establishments accept the major international credit cards, including **Visa, MasterCard, Diners Club,** and **American Express.** Visa is the most widely accepted card in Peru. However, many shops and restaurants charge the consumer an additional 10% for paying with a credit card; ask about this practice before you pay. When using a credit card, be careful to check the amount you are being charged. In rural areas and small towns, cash is essential for payment. At the very least, you should carry a supply of dollars in these areas.

To report lost or stolen credit cards, call Visa at ℭ **01/441-2112;** MasterCard at ℭ **01/444-1891;** American Express at ℭ **01/330-4484;** and Diners Club at ℭ **01/221-2050.**

WHEN TO GO

PEAK SEASON   Peru's high season for travel coincides with the driest months: May through September, with the greatest number of visitors in July and August. May and September are particularly fine months to visit much of the country. Airlines and hotels also consider mid-December through mid-January to be peak season.

From June through September in the *sierra,* days are clear and often spectacularly sunny, with nights chilly or downright cold, especially at high elevations. For trekking in the mountains, including the Inca Trail, these are by far the best months. This is also the best time of the year to visit the Amazon basin: Mosquitoes are fewer, and many fauna stay close to the rivers (although some people prefer to travel in the jungle during the wet season, when higher water levels allow more river penetration). Note that Peruvians travel in huge numbers around July 28, the national independence day, and finding accommodations in popular destinations can be difficult.

CLIMATE   Generally speaking, May through October is the dry season, and November through April is the rainy season. The wettest months are January through April; in mountain areas, roads and trek paths may become impassable. Peru's climate, though, is markedly different among its three vastly different regions. The coast is predominantly arid and mild, the Andean region is temperate to cold, and the eastern lowlands are tropically warm and humid.

PUBLIC HOLIDAYS   National public holidays in Peru include New Year's Day (Jan 1); Día de los Reyes (Jan 6); Maundy Thursday and Good Friday; Labor Day (May 1); Fiestas Patrias (Independence; July 28–29); Battle of Angamos (Oct 7); All Saints' Day (Nov 1); Feast of the Immaculate Conception (Dec 8); Christmas Eve (Dec 24); and Christmas (Dec 25).

HEALTH CONCERNS

COMMON AILMENTS   As a tropical South American country, Peru presents certain health risks, but major concerns are limited to those traveling outside urban areas and to the Amazon jungle. The most common ailments for visitors to Peru are common **traveler's diarrhea** and altitude sickness, or **acute mountain sickness (AMS),** called *soroche* locally. Cusco sits at an elevation of about 3,300m (11,000 ft.), Lake Titicaca, 3,900m (13,000 ft.). At these heights, shortness of breath and heart pounding are normal, given the paucity of oxygen. Some people may experience headaches, loss of appetite, extreme fatigue, and nausea. Most symptoms develop during the first day at high altitude, though occasionally travelers have delayed reactions. The best advice is to rest on your first day in the highlands and eat frugally. Drink plenty of liquids, including the local remedy *mate de coca,* or coca leaf tea (perfectly legal), and avoid alcohol. Give yourself at least a day or two to acclimatize before launching into strenuous activities. Many hotels in Cusco offer oxygen for those severely affected with headaches and shortness of breath. If symptoms persist or become more severe, seek medical attention. People with heart or lung problems and persons with sickle cell trait may develop serious health complications at high altitudes; consult your doctor before visiting Peru.

VACCINATIONS   Though no vaccinations are required of travelers to Peru, it's wise to take certain precautions, especially if you are planning to travel to jungle regions. A yellow fever vaccine is strongly recommended for trips to the Amazon. As recently as July 2001, the Ministry of Health reported an outbreak of 13 deaths from yellow fever in Peru, part of the highest number of cases reported across South America since 1998. The Centers for Disease Control and Prevention (CDC) warn that there is a risk of malaria and yellow fever in all departments except Arequipa, Moquegua, Puno, and Tacna, though Lima and the highland tourist areas (Cusco, Machu Picchu, and Lake Titicaca) are not at risk; consult your doctor about malaria prophylaxes and other preventative treatments.

The CDC also recommends hepatitis A or immune globulin (IG), hepatitis B, typhoid, and booster doses for tetanus-diphtheria and measles, though you may wish to weigh your potential exposure before getting all of these. For additional information on travel to tropical South America, see the CDC website at www.cdc.gov/travel/tropsam.htm (and specifically, www.cdc.gov/travel/yb/countries/Peru.htm).

HEALTH PRECAUTIONS   Other recommendations for safe and healthy travel in Peru: Drink only bottled or boiled water (and plenty of it, both at high altitudes and in hot and humid areas); eat only thoroughly cooked or boiled food or fruits and vegetables you have peeled yourself; avoid eating food from street vendors; bring insect repellent containing DEET (diethylmethyltoluamide) if you are traveling to the jungle; and avoid swimming in fresh water.

It is also advisable to get a thorough check-up and take out health insurance before your trip, and to take sufficient supplies of all required medicines.

GETTING THERE
BY PLANE
All flights from North America and Europe arrive at Lima's **Jorge Chávez International Airport** (© 01/575-1434). International flights to Iquitos in the northern Amazon region may be resumed at some point in the near future.

The airport tax on domestic flights is S/18 ($5.15); on international flights, S/98 ($28). The tax must be paid in cash before boarding.

FROM NORTH AMERICA   From the United States, there are direct flights to Lima from Miami, New York, Newark, Houston, Dallas, and Atlanta. The major carriers are **American** (© 800/433-7300; www.aa.com), **Continental** (© 800/231-0856; www.continental.com), **United** (© 800/538-2929; www.united.com), **LanPeru** (© 800/735-5590; www.lanperu.com), and **LanChile** (© 800/735-5526; www.lanchile.com).

From Canada, **American, Continental,** and **United** all fly to Peru, making stops at their hubs in the United States first. **Air Canada** (© 888/247-2262; www.aircanada.ca) makes connections with other carriers at U.S. stops, usually Miami. **LanPeru** and **LanChile** partner with other carriers to the United States, making stops in New York, Miami, or Los Angeles on the way to Lima.

FROM THE U.K.   There are no direct flights to Lima from London or any other part of the United Kingdom or Ireland; getting to Peru involves a layover in either another part of Europe or the United States. **American** (© 020/8572-5555 in London, or 08457/789-789), **Continental** (© 0800/776-464), and **United** (© 0845/844-4777) fly through their U.S. hubs (Dallas, Houston, and Miami) on the way to Lima. European carriers make stops in continental Europe; they include **Iberia** (© 0845/601-2854; www.iberia.com); **KLM** (© 08705/074-074; www.klm.com); and **Lufthansa** (© 0845/7737-747; www.lufthansa.com).

FROM AUSTRALIA & NEW ZEALAND   You can fly to Buenos Aires on **Aerolíneas Argentinas** (© 800/22-22-15; www.aerolineas.com.au) and then connect to Lima, or you can go through Los Angeles or Buenos Aires on **Qantas** (© 0800/808-767; www.qantas.com) or **Air New Zealand** (© 0800/737-000; www.airnz.co.nz). **LanPeru** (© 02/9321-9333 in Australia, and 09/912-7435 in New Zealand;) and **LanChile** (© 1-300-361-400 in Australia, 09/309-8673 in New Zealand; www.lanchile.com) also make stops in Los Angeles on the way to Lima.

BY BUS

You can travel overland to Peru through Ecuador, Bolivia, or Chile. Though the journey isn't short, Lima can be reached from major neighboring cities. If you're traveling from Quito or Guayaquil, you'll pass through the major northern coastal cities on the way to Lima. From Bolivia, there is frequent service from La Paz and Copacabana to Puno and then on to Cusco. From Chile, most travel from Arica to Tacna, making connections either to Arequipa or Lima.

GETTING AROUND

Because of its size and natural barriers, including difficult mountain terrain, long stretches of desert coast, and extensive rainforest, Peru is not easy to get around. Train service is limited, and many trips can take several days by land. Many visitors with limited time fly everywhere they can. Travel overland, though very inexpensive, can be extremely time-consuming if not altogether uncomfortable. However, for certain routes, intercity buses are your only real option.

BY PLANE

Flying to major destinations within Peru is the only practical way around the country if you wish to see several places in a couple of weeks or less. Some places in the jungle can only be reached by airplane. Flying to major destinations, such as Lima, Cusco, Arequipa, Puerto Maldonado, and Iquitos, is relatively simple and relatively inexpensive; one-way flights to most destinations cost between $59 and $89. Puno (and Lake Titicaca), however, requires passengers to fly first to Juliaca before continuing by land the rest of the way—a reality that prompts many to take a direct train or bus from Cusco to Puno.

Peru's carriers include **Aero Continente** (© 01/242-4242; www.aerocontinente.com), **AeroCondor** (© 01/442-5215; www.aerocondor.com.pe), **LanPeru** (© 01/213-8200; www.lanperu.com), **Taca Peru** (© 01/213-7000;

www.grupotaca.com), and **TANS** (℗ 01/213-6000; www.tansperu.com). Lan-Peru and Aero Continente fly to most major destinations in Peru. TANS flies to Cusco, Iquitos, and Pucallpa. AeroCondor flies to Cajamarca and Trujillo. Flight schedules and fares are apt to change frequently and without notice. Flights should be booked several days in advance, especially in high season, and it's very important to reconfirm airline tickets in advance (for local flights, reconfirm 48 hr. in advance; for international flights, 72 hr.). You should also make sure you get to the airport at least 45 minutes before your flight to avoid being bumped.

BY TRAIN

Peru's national railway network was privatized in 1999. The four tourist or passenger train routes operated by Peru Rail (owned by Orient Express) are all very popular and scenic journeys. One is the **Titicaca-Cusco Route,** round-trip from Cusco to Puno, on the shores of Lake Titicaca (two classes of service: first class $89 one-way, and Tourist $14). By far the most popular train routes in Peru are the **Cusco–Machu Picchu** and **Sacred Valley–Machu Picchu** routes, which link Cusco and the Sacred Valley, traveling from the old Inca capital to Ollantaytambo, Urubamba, and the world-famous ruins of Machu Picchu. From Cusco to Machu Picchu, there are three classes of service: the new luxury Hiram Bingham, $350 round-trip; Vistadome, $89 round-trip; and Backpacker $60 round-trip. From Cusco to the Sacred Valley, prices are Vistadome $69 round-trip and Backpacker $48 round-trip. Two antique coaches running the **Puno (Lake Titicaca)-Arequipa** route in southern Peru are now available by charter only.

Luggage theft has long been a problem on Peruvian trains; if possible, purchase a premium-class ticket that limits access to ticketed passengers. For additional information, call **Peru Rail** at ℗ **01/9953-5802** in Lima, 084/238-722 in Cusco, or 054/215-350 in Arequipa, or visit www.perurail.com.

BY BUS

Buses are the cheapest and most popular form of transportation in Peru. A complex network of private bus companies crisscrosses Peru, with a number of competing lines covering the most popular routes. Many companies operate their own bus stations, and their locations, dispersed across many cities, can be endlessly frustrating to travelers. Theft of luggage is an issue on many buses, and passengers should keep a watchful eye on their carry-on items and pay close attention when bags are unloaded. Only a few long-distance buses have luxury buses comparable in comfort to European models (bathrooms, reclining seats, movies). These premium-class ("Royal" or "Imperial") buses cost up to twice as much as regular buses, though for many travelers the additional comfort and services are worth the difference in cost (which remains inexpensive). For many short distances (such as Cusco to Pisac), *colectivos* (smaller buses without assigned seats) are the fastest and cheapest option.

Ormeño (℗ **01/472-1710** or 01/427-5679) and **Cruz del Sur** (℗ **01/428-2570** or 01/424-1005) are the top two bus companies with the best reputations for long-distance journeys and the most extensive coverage of Peru. **Civa** (℗ **01/426-4926**) is also a reputable company with service to most parts of the country, though its buses are generally a notch down from Ormeño and Cruz del Sur. Given the mercurial and extremely confusing nature of bus companies, terminals, and destinations, it's always best to approach a local tourism information office or travel agency (most of which sell long-distance bus tickets) with a destination in mind and let them direct you to the terminal for the best service.

BY CAR

Getting around Peru by means of a rental car isn't the easiest or cheapest option for most travelers. Distances are long, roads are often not in very good condition, Peruvian drivers are aggressive, and accident rates are very high; the U.S. State Department also warns against driving in Peru at night or alone on rural roads. A 4×4 vehicle would be the best option in many places, but trucks and jeeps are exceedingly expensive for most travelers. However, if you want maximum flexibility and independence in a particular region (say, to get around the Sacred Valley outside of Cusco, or to visit Colca Canyon beyond Arequipa) and have several people to share the cost, a rental car could be a decent option. By no means plan to rent a car in Lima and head off for the major sights across the country; you'll spend all your time in the car. It is much more feasible to fly or take a bus to a given destination and rent a car there.

The major international rental agencies are found at Lima's airport and around the city, and a handful of international and local companies operate in other cities, such as Cusco and Arequipa. Agencies in Lima include **Avis** (© 01/434-1111 or 01/434-1034); **Budget** (© 01/442-8703); **Dollar** (© 01/444-3050); **Hertz** (© 01/445-5716); **Inka's Rent A Car** (© 01/447-2129); **InterService Rent A Car** (© 01/442-2256); **National** (© 01/433-3750); and **Paz Rent A Car** (© 01/436-3941). An economy-size vehicle costs about $30 to $50 a day, plus 18% for insurance. To rent a car, you'll need to be at least 25 years old and have a valid driver's license and passport. Deposit by credit card is usually required. For mechanical assistance, contact the **Touring y Automóvil Club del Peru (Touring Club of Peru)** at © **01/221-3225** in Lima, or 084/224-561 in Cusco.

TIPS ON ACCOMMODATIONS

A wide range of accommodations exists in Peru, including world-class luxury hotels, affordable small hotels in colonial houses, rustic rainforest lodges, and inexpensive budget inns. Midrange options have expanded in recent years, but the large majority of accommodations still court budget travelers and backpackers. Accommodations go by many names in Peru: "Hotel" generally refers to comfortable hotels with a range of services, but *hostal* is used for a wide variety of smaller hotels, inns, and pensions. At the lower end are mostly *hospedajes, pensiones,* and *residenciales.* However, these terms are often poor indicators of an establishment's quality or services. Luxury hotels are rare outside of Lima and Cusco; budget accommodations are plentiful, and many of them are quite good for the price.

Advance reservations are strongly recommended during high season (June–Oct) and at times of national holidays and important festivals. This is especially true of hotels in the middle and upper categories in popular places such as Cusco and Machu Picchu. Many hotels quote their rates in U.S. dollars. If you pay in cash, the price will be converted into soles at the going rate. Note that at most budget and many midrange hotels, credit cards are not accepted. Most published rates can be negotiated and travelers can often get greatly reduced rates outside of peak season simply by asking.

Hotel taxes and service charges are an issue that has caused some confusion in recent years. Most upper-level hotels add an 18% general sales tax (IGV) and a 10% service charge to the bill. However, foreigners who can demonstrate they live outside of Peru are not charged the 18% tax (although they are responsible for the 10% service charge). In practice, hotels sometimes either mistakenly or purposely include the IGV on everyone's bill; presentation of a passport is sufficient to have the tax deducted from your tab. Many hotels—usually those at the midlevel and lower ranges—simplify matters by including the tax in their rates; at these establishments, you cannot expect to have the tax removed from your charges. At high-end hotels, be sure to review your bill and ask for an explanation of additional taxes and charges. Prices in this chapter do not include taxes and service charges unless otherwise noted.

Safety is an issue at many hotels, especially at the lower end, and extreme care should be taken with regard to personal belongings left in the hotel. Leaving valuables lying around is asking for trouble. Most hotels have safety-deposit boxes (only luxury hotels have room safes). Place your belongings in a carefully sealed envelope. Also, if you arrive in a town without previously arranged accommodations, you should be wary of taxi drivers and others who insist on showing you to a hotel. Occasionally, they will provide excellent tips, but in general, they will merely be taking you to a place where they are confident they can earn a commission. A final precaution worth mentioning is the electric heater found on many shower heads: These can be dangerous, and touching them while functioning can prompt an unwelcome electric jolt.

TIPS ON DINING

Peruvian cuisine is among the best and most diverse cuisines found in Latin America, and it's one of the most important contributors to the wave of Pan-Latino restaurants gaining popularity in many parts of the world. Peruvian cooking differs significantly by region, and subcategories mirror the country's geographical variety: coastal, highland, and tropical. The common denominator among them is a blend of indigenous and Spanish (or broader European) influences, which has evolved over the past 4 centuries. In addition to Peruvian cooking, visitors will also find plenty of international restaurants, including a particularly Peruvian variation: the *chifa* (Peruvian-influenced Chinese, developed by the large immigrant Chinese population), a mainstay among many non-Chinese Peruvians. *Chifas* are nearly as common as restaurants serving *pollo a la brasa* (spit-roasted chicken), which are everywhere in Peru.

Traditional Peruvian coastal cooking is often referred to as *comida criolla,* and it's found across Peru. Coastal preparations concentrate on seafood and shellfish, as might be expected. The star dish is *ceviche,* a classic preparation of raw fish and shellfish marinated in lime or lemon juice and hot chile peppers, served with raw onion, sweet potato, and toasted corn. Coastal favorites also include *escabeche* (a tasty fish concoction served with peppers, eggs, olives, onions, and prawns), scallops *(conchitas),* and sea bass *(corvina).* Land-based favorites are *cabrito* (roast kid) and *ají de gallina* (a tangy creamed chicken and chile dish).

Highlanders favor a more substantial style of cooking. Meat, served with rice and potatoes, is a mainstay of the diet, as is trout *(trucha). Lomo saltado,* strips of beef mixed with onions, tomatoes, peppers, and french-fried potatoes and served with rice, seems to be on every menu. *Rocoto relleno,* a hot bell pepper stuffed with vegetables and meat; *papa rellena,* a potato stuffed with veggies and then fried; and *papa a la huancaína,* boiled potatoes served with a cheese sauce and garnished with hard-boiled eggs and a lettuce leaf, are just as common (but are occasionally extremely spicy). *Cuy* (guinea pig) is considered a delicacy in many parts of Peru; it comes roasted or fried, with head and feet upturned on the plate.

In the Amazon jungle regions, most people fish for their food, and their diets consist almost entirely of fish such as river trout and *paiche* (a huge river fish). Restaurants feature both of these, with accompaniments such as *yuca* (a root), *palmitos* (palm hearts) and *chonta* (palm-heart salad), bananas and plantains, and rice *tamales* known as *juanes*. Common menu items such as chicken and game are complemented by exotic fare: caiman, wild boar, turtle, monkey, and piranha.

Drinking is less of an event in Peru. Peruvian wines and beers can't compare with superior examples found elsewhere on the continent. Yet one indigenous drink stands out: pisco, a powerful white grape brandy. The pisco sour (a cocktail mixed with pisco, egg whites, lemon juice, sugar, and bitters) is Peru's margarita: tasty, refreshing, and ubiquitous. Peruvians everywhere drink *chicha*, a tangy fermented brew made from maize and inherited from the Incas. Often served warm in huge glasses, it is unlikely to please the palates of most foreign visitors, though it's certainly worth a try if you come upon a small, informal place with the *chicha* flag flying (literally—it means something akin to "fresh *chicha* available inside") in a rural village. The potent *chicha* is not to be confused with another drink popular in Peru: *chicha morada*, a nonalcoholic refreshment made from blue corn.

Restaurants range from the rustic and incredibly inexpensive to polished places with impeccable service and international menus. Set three-course menus (*menú económico* or *menú ejecutivo*) can sometimes be had for as little as $2. In general, you should ask about preparation of many Peruvian dishes, as many are quite spicy. Informal eateries serving Peruvian cooking are frequently called *picanterías* and *chicherías*. Fancy restaurants may add service charges of 10% and an additional tax of up to 18%. Less expensive restaurants usually charge either a 5% tax or no additional tax or service charge.

TIPS ON SHOPPING

Peru is one of the top shopping destinations in Latin America, with some of the finest and best-priced crafts anywhere. Its long traditions of textile weaving and colorful markets have produced a dazzling display of alpaca wool sweaters, blankets, ponchos, shawls, scarves, typical Peruvian hats, and other woven items. Peru's ancient indigenous civilizations were some of the world's greatest potters, and reproductions of Moche, Nasca, Paracas, and other ceramics are available.

Lima and Cusco have the lion's share of tourist-oriented shops and markets, but other places may be just as good for shopping. Locals in Puno and Taquile Island on Lake Titicaca produce spectacular textiles, and Arequipa is perhaps the best place in Peru to purchase very fine, extremely soft baby alpaca items. The Shipibo tribe of the northern Amazon produces excellent textiles and ceramics. You'll also see items in the jungle made from endangered species, including alligator skins and turtle shells, but purchasing these items is illegal.

There are scores of *artesanía* shops in many tourist centers, and prices may not be any higher than what you'd find at markets. At both stores and in open markets, bargaining—gentle, good-natured haggling over prices—is accepted and even expected. However, when it gets down to ridiculously small amounts of money, it's best to recognize that you are already getting a great deal on probably handmade goods and relinquish the fight over a few soles.

FAST FACTS: Peru

Addresses   "Jr." doesn't mean "junior;" it is a designation meaning *jirón*, or street, just as "Av." (sometimes "Avda.") is an abbreviation for *avenida*, or avenue. Perhaps the most confusing element in street addresses is "s/n," which frequently appears in place of a number after the name of the street. "S/n" means *sin número,* or no number.

American Express There's an office in Lima at Jr. Belén 1040 (© **01/330-4485**); it's open Monday through Friday from 9am to 5pm. There is another office at Pardo y Aliaga 698, San Isidro, Lima (© **01/222-2525**). Both offices are housed with Lima Tours travel agencies. They will replace stolen or lost travelers' checks and sell American Express checks with an Amex card, but they do not cash their own checks.

Business Hours Most stores are open Monday through Friday from 9 or 10am to 12:30pm and from 3 to 5 or 8pm; banks are generally open Monday through Friday from 9:30am to 4pm, though some stay open until 6pm. In major cities, most banks are also open Saturday from 9:30am to 12:30pm.

Doctors & Hospitals Medical care is of a generally high standard in Lima and adequate in other major cities, where you are likely to find English-speaking doctors. Medical care is of a lesser standard in rural areas and small villages, and it's much less likely that you'll find an English-speaking physician in these locales. Many physicians and hospitals require immediate cash payment for health services, and they do not accept U.S. medical insurance (even if your policy applies overseas). You should check with your insurance company to see if your policy provides for overseas medical evacuation.

It's best to get vaccinations and obtain malaria pills before arriving in Peru, but if you decide at the last minute to go to the jungle and need to get a vaccine in the country, you may go to the following Oficinas de Vacunación in Lima: Calle Independencia 121, Breña (next to the Hospital del Niño); Jorge Chávez International Airport, Second Floor; International Vaccination Center, Dos de Mayo National Hospital, Avenida Grau, block 13.

Drug Laws Cocaine and other illegal substances are perhaps not as ubiquitous in Peru as one might think, though in Lima and Cusco, they are commonly offered to foreigners. This is especially dangerous; many would-be dealers also operate as police informants, and some are said to be undercover narcotics officers. Penalties for possession and use of or trafficking in illegal drugs in Peru are strict; convicted offenders can expect long jail sentences and substantial fines. Peruvian police routinely detain drug smugglers at Lima's international airport and land border crossings. Since 1995, three dozen U.S. citizens have been convicted of narcotics trafficking in Peru. If arrested on drug charges, you will face protracted pre-trial detention in poor prison conditions.

Electricity All outlets are 220 volts, 60 cycles AC (except in Arequipa, which operates on 50 cycles), with two-prong outlets that accept both flat and round prongs. Some large hotels also have 110-volt outlets.

Embassies & Consulates In Lima: **United States,** Avenida La Encalada, Block 17, Monterrico (© 01/434-3000); **Australia,** Victor A. Belaúnde 147/ Vía Principal 155, Building 3, Office 1301, San Isidro (© 01/222-8281); **Canada,** Libertad 130, Miraflores (© 01/444-4015); **United Kingdom** and **New Zealand,** Torre Parque Mar, Av. Jose Larco 1301, Floor 22, Miraflores (© 01/617-3000).

Emergencies In case of an emergency, call the **traveler's hot line** (℃ 01/574-8000) or the **tourist police** (℃ 01/225-8698 in Lima, or 01/225-8699). The general **police** emergency number is ℃ 105. The **INDECOPI** 24-hour hot line can also assist in contacting police to report a crime (℃ 01/224-7888 in Lima, 01/224-8600, or toll free 0800/42579 from any private phone).

Guides Officially licensed guides are available at many archaeological sites and other places of interest to foreigners. They can be contracted directly, though you should verify their ability to speak English if you do not understand Spanish well. Establish a price beforehand. Many cities are battling a scourge of unlicensed and unscrupulous guides who provide inferior services or, worse, cheat visitors. As a general rule, do not accept unsolicited offers to arrange excursions, transportation, and hotel accommodations.

Internet Access Public Internet booths, or *cabinas,* have proliferated throughout Peru, especially in major cities like Lima, Cusco, and Arequipa. Most cities have several to choose from, but few are of the cybercafe variety. Most are simple cubicles with terminals; occasionally, printers are available. The average cost for 1 hour is $1 or less. Many *cabinas* now feature software to make very inexpensive international phone calls via the Internet.

Maps Good topographical maps are available from the **Instituto Geográfico Nacional (IGN),** located at Av. Aramburú 1190, San Isidro, Lima (℃ 01/475-9960). Hiking maps are available from the **South American Explorers Club,** Piura 135, Miraflores, Lima (℃ 01/445-3306) and Choquechaca 188, Apto. 4, Cusco (℃ 084/245-484).

Language Spanish is the official language of Peru. The Amerindian languages Quechua and Aymara are spoken primarily in the highlands. English is not widely spoken but is understood by those affiliated with the tourist industry in major cities and tourist destinations. Learning a few key phrases of Spanish will help immensely.

Newspapers & Magazines If you read Spanish, *El Comercio* and *La República* are two of the best daily newspapers. Look for *Rumbos,* a glossy Peruvian travel magazine in English and Spanish with excellent photography. In Lima, you will find copies (although rarely same-day publications) of the *International Herald Tribune* and the *Miami Herald* as well as *Time, Newsweek,* and other special-interest publications. Top-flight hotels sometimes offer free daily fax summations of the *New York Times* to their guests. Outside of Lima, international newspapers and magazines are hard to come by.

Police Peru has special tourist police forces (Policía Nacional de Turismo) in all major tourist destinations, such as Lima, Cusco, Arequipa, and Puno, as well as a dozen other cities. You are more likely to get a satisfactory response, not to mention someone who speaks some English, from the tourist police, who are distinguished by their white shirts. See "Fast Facts" in individual city sections for contact information.

Post Offices/Mail Peru's postal service is reasonably efficient, especially now that it is managed by a private company (Serpost S.A.). Post offices are open Monday through Saturday from 8am to 8pm; some are also open Sunday from 9am to 1pm. Letters and postcards to North America take between 10 days and 2 weeks to arrive and cost S/3.30 (95¢); to Europe, S/4.20 ($1.20). If you are purchasing lots of textiles and other handicrafts, you can send packages home from post offices, but it's not inexpensive— more than $100 for 10 kilograms (22 lb.), similar to what it costs to use DHL, where you're likely to have an easier time communicating. UPS is found in several cities, but its courier services cost nearly three times as much as DHL.

Restrooms Public toilets are rarely available except in railway stations, restaurants, and theaters. Peruvian men tend to urinate outside in full view; don't emulate them. Use the bathroom in a bar, cafe, or restaurant. Public restrooms are labeled WC (water closet), *Damas* (Ladies), and *Caballeros* or *Hombres* (Men). Toilet paper is not always provided, and when it is, establishments ask patrons to throw it in the wastebasket rather than the toilet to avoid clogging.

Safety Peru has not earned a great reputation for safety among travelers, although the situation is quickly improving. Simple theft and pickpocketing remain fairly common; assaults and robbery are rare. Most thieves look for moments when travelers, laden with bags and struggling with maps, are distracted.

Although most visitors travel freely throughout Peru without incident, warnings must be heeded. In downtown Lima and the city's residential and hotel areas, the risk of street crime remains high. Carjackings, assaults, and armed robberies are not unheard of; occasional armed attacks at ATMs occur. However, in most heavily touristed places in Peru, a heightened police presence is noticeable. Use ATMs during the day, with other people present.

Street crime is prevalent in Cusco, Arequipa, and Puno, and pickpockets are known to patrol public markets. In Cusco, "strangle" muggings (in which victims are choked unconscious and then relieved of all belongings) were reported in years past, particularly on streets leading off the Plaza de Armas, the San Blas neighborhood, and near the train station. This form of violent assault seems to have subsided, but you should still not walk alone late at night on deserted streets.

In major cities, taxis hailed on the street can lead to assaults. (I highly recommend using telephone-dispatched radio taxis, especially at night.) Ask your hotel or restaurant to call a cab, or call one from the list of recommended taxi companies in the individual city sections below.

Travelers should exercise extreme caution on public city transportation, where pickpockets are rife, and on long-distance buses and trains (especially at night), where thieves employ any number of strategies to relieve passengers of their bags. You need to be supremely vigilant, even to the extreme of locking backpacks and suitcases to luggage racks. Be extremely careful in all train and bus stations.

In general, do not wear expensive jewelry; keep expensive camera equipment out of view as much as possible; use a money belt worn inside your pants or shirt to safeguard cash, credit cards, and passport. Wear your daypack on your chest rather than your back when walking in crowded areas. The time to be most careful is when you have most of your belongings on your person—such as when you're in transit from airport or train or bus station to your hotel. At airports, it's best to spend a little more for official airport taxis; if in doubt, request the driver's official ID. Don't venture beyond airport grounds for a street taxi. Have your hotel call a taxi for your trip to the airport or bus station.

Although the large-scale terrorist activities of the local groups Sendero Luminoso and MRTA were largely stamped out in the early 1990s, there have been reports of a possible resurgence. Neither group is currently active, however, in any of the areas covered in this book.

Taxes A general sales tax (IGV) is added automatically to most consumer bills (18%). In some upmarket hotels or restaurants, service charges of 10% are often added. At all airports, passengers must pay a S/98 ($28) departure tax for international flights, S/18 ($5.15) for domestic flights.

Telephone & Fax Peru's telephone system has been much improved since it was privatized and acquired by Spain's Telefónica in the mid-1990s. (There are now several additional players in the market, including Bell South.) It's relatively simple to make local and long-distance domestic and international calls from pay phones, which accept coins and phone cards *(tarjetas telefónicas)*. Most phone booths display country and city codes and contain instructions in English and Spanish.

You can also make international calls from Telefónica offices and hotels, though surcharges levied at the latter can be extraordinarily expensive. A new and very inexpensive way to make international calls is through Internet software such as Net2Phone, which more and more Internet booths in Peru are featuring. Rates are as low as 20¢ per minute to the United States. Reception, however, can be spotty.

Fax services are available at many hotels, but they are expensive, especially for international numbers ($3 per page and up).

Time Zone All of Peru is 5 hours behind GMT (Greenwich mean time). Peru does not observe daylight savings time.

Tipping Most people leave about a 10% tip for the waitstaff in restaurants. In nicer restaurants that add a 10% service charge, many patrons tip an additional 5% for good service. Taxi drivers are not usually tipped unless they provide some additional service. Bilingual tour guides should be tipped $1 to $2 per person for a short visit, $5 per person or more for a full day.

Water Do not drink tap water, even in major hotels. Visitors should drink only bottled water, which is widely available. Try to avoid drinks with ice. *Agua con gas* is carbonated; *agua sin gas* is still.

3 Lima

Lima was the richest and most important city in the Americas in the 17th century and was considered the most beautiful colonial settlement in the region. Today, the capital of Peru is a sprawling, chaotic, and mostly unlovely metropolis, and many visitors dart through it as quickly as possible or bypass it altogether. Peru's blistering poverty is more apparent here than perhaps anywhere else: Depressing shantytowns called *pueblos jóvenes* lacerate the outer rings of the

Downtown Lima

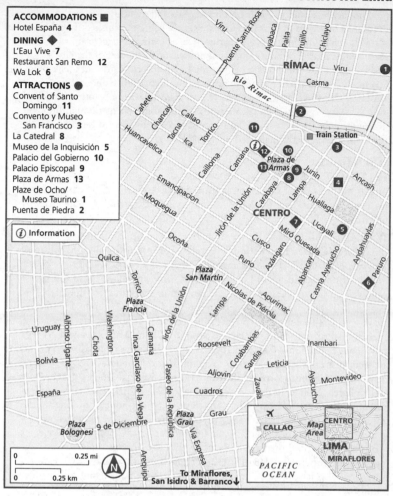

ACCOMMODATIONS ■
Hotel España **4**

DINING ◆
L'Eau Vive **7**
Restaurant San Remo **12**
Wa Lok **6**

ATTRACTIONS ●
Convent of Santo
  Domingo **11**
Convento y Museo
  San Francisco **3**
La Catedral **8**
Museo de la Inquisición **5**
Palacio del Gobierno **10**
Palacio Episcopal **9**
Plaza de Armas **13**
Plaze de Ocho/
  Museo Taurino **1**
Puenta de Piedra **2**

ⓘ Information

city, and the despair of a large segment of the largely migrant and mestizo population contrasts uncomfortably with the ritzy apartment and office buildings in the residential suburbs. If that's not enough, for most of the year an unrelenting gray cloud called the *garúa* hangs heavy overhead, obscuring the coastline and dulling the city's appearance. The sun comes out in Lima only from December to April; the rest of the time, Lima makes London look like Lisbon.

With a population of eight million—about one-third of Peru's total population—and as the seat of the national government and headquarters of most industry, Lima thoroughly dominates Peru's political and commercial life. But for many visitors, Lima demands too much effort to sift beneath the soot and uncover the city's rewards, especially when such extraordinary treasures hover over the horizon in the Andes and the Amazon jungle. So why come to Lima except to beeline it to Cusco or elsewhere? If you skip Lima altogether, you'll miss a vital part of what is Peru today. Lima has calmed down since its days as a cauldron of chaos in the 1980s and 1990s. The country's best museums are here, and so are its best restaurants and nightlife. Many of the classic colonial buildings in the old *centro* are slowly being refurbished. But the city still feels schizophrenic; outer suburbs such as Barranco are relatively gentle oases, worlds apart from the congestion and grime of the rest of the city.

Even if you have only a day or two for Lima, the city's art and archaeology museums serve as perfect introductions to the rich history and culture you'll encounter elsewhere in the country. If you also squeeze in a tour of colonial Lima, dine at a great *criollo* restaurant, soak up some energetic nightlife, and browse the country's best shops, you may just come away from Lima pleasantly surprised, if not exactly enamored of the city.

ESSENTIALS
GETTING THERE
Lima is the gateway for most international arrivals to Peru; see "Getting There" in "Planning Your Trip to Peru," earlier in this chapter, for more detailed information.

BY PLANE   All overseas flights from North America and Europe arrive at Lima's **Jorge Chávez International Airport.** For international flight information, call ⓒ 01/575-1712; for domestic flights, call ⓒ 01/574-5529.

To get from the airport to Lima—either downtown, about 16km (10 miles) southwest of the airport, or Miraflores, San Isidro, and Barranco (the major residential neighborhoods and sites of most tourist hotels), about 45 minutes away—you can take a taxi or private bus. **Taxis** inside the security area at the international arrivals terminal charge around $20 to Miraflores and $15 to downtown Lima (Lima Centro). You can try bargaining or head just beyond the security area, where prices drop to about $10 to Miraflores and $8 to Lima Centro. The **Urbanito Airport shuttle** service delivers passengers to the doors of their hotels. Stop by its desk in the international terminal; buses to downtown ($6) and Miraflores and San Isidro ($8) leave every half-hour or so. The shuttle stops by the hotel of each passenger; at peak hours, if there are many fellow passengers, this may not be the fastest way from the airport. Unless you're alone, it's also probably not the cheapest. Call a day ahead to arrange a pickup for your return to the airport (ⓒ **01/814-6932**). Private **limousine taxis** (*taxis ejecutivos* or *remises*) also have desks in the airport; their fares range from $27 to $45 round-trip.

BY BUS   The multitude of bus companies serving various regions of the country all have terminals in Lima. Many are located downtown, though several companies have their bases in the suburbs. Most bus terminals have nasty reputations for thievery and general unpleasantness; your best bet is to grab your things and hop into a cab pronto.

BY TRAIN   Lima is the starting point of the **Ferrocarril Central Railroad,** the highest railway in the world (up to 4,781m/15,685ft). However, the passenger train to and from Huancayo departs only once a month. It leaves downtown Lima at the **Desamparados station,** Jr. Ancash 201 (ⓒ **01/441-2222**), just behind the Government Palace. A taxi from the station to your downtown hotel costs S/3 to S/4 ($1), to Miraflores, S/10 ($3).

ORIENTATION
The city beyond central Lima (**Lima Centro**) is a warren of ill-defined neighborhoods; most visitors are likely to set foot into only a couple of them. Several of Lima's top museums are in **Pueblo Libre,** a couple of miles southwest of Lima

Centro, while **San Borja,** a couple of miles directly south of Lima Centro, holds two of the finest collections in all of Peru. **San Isidro** and **Miraflores,** the most exclusive residential and commercial neighborhoods, and also where most tourist hotels are located, are farther south toward the coast. **Barranco,** a former seaside village now known primarily for its nightlife, is several miles farther out along the ocean.

GETTING AROUND

Navigating Lima is a complicated and time-consuming task, made difficult by the city's sprawling character (many of the best hotels and restaurants far from downtown, spread among three or more residential neighborhoods), heavy traffic and pollution, and a chaotic network of confusing and crowded *colectivos* and unregulated taxis.

BY TAXI   Taxis hailed on the street are a reasonable and relatively quick way to get around in Lima. However, taxis are wholly unregulated by the government and do not use meters: All anyone has to do to become a taxi driver is get his hands on a vehicle—of any size and condition, though most are the tiny Daewoo "Ticos"—and plunk a cheap TAXI sticker inside the windshield. He is then free to charge whatever he thinks he can get—with no meters, no laws, and nobody to answer to besides the free market. I counsel visitors to be a bit wary taking taxis in Lima, though I personally have never had problems greater than a dispute over a fare. (If you're not fluent in Spanish, and even if you are but you have an obviously non-Peruvian appearance, be prepared to negotiate fares.) Limeños tell enough stories of theft and even the occasional violent crime in unregistered cabs to make hailing one on the street inadvisable for seniors or for those with little command of Spanish or little experience traveling in Latin America. Taxi drivers themselves have told me that if you hail a taxi on the street, try to pick out older drivers; many contend that young punks are almost wholly responsible for taxi crime. If the issue of getting into quasi-official cabs makes you nervous, by all means call a registered company from your hotel or restaurant—especially at night (even though the fare can be twice as much).

Registered, reputable taxi companies—the safest option—include **Taxi Amigo** (© **01/349-0177**), **Taxi Móvil** (© **01/422-7100**), or **Taxi Seguro** (© **01/275-2020**). Whether you call or hail a taxi, you'll need to establish a price beforehand—be prepared to bargain. Most fares range from $2 to $5. From Miraflores to downtown, expect to pay S/8 to S/14 ($2.25–$4); from Miraflores to San Isidro, about S/5 ($1.50); San Isidro to downtown, S/5 to S/7 ($1.50–$2); Miraflores to Museo de Oro, S/8 to S/10 ($2.25–$3); Miraflores to Barranco, S/5 ($1.50).

BY BUS   Local buses are of two types: *micros* (large buses) and *combis* (minibuses or vans). They're both quite crowded, with a reputation for pickpockets, and can be hailed at any place along the street without regard to bus stops. Routes are more or less identified by signs with street names placed in the windshield, making many trips confusing for those unfamiliar with Lima. Some do nothing more than race up and down long avenues. (For example: TODO AREQUIPA means it travels the length of Av. Arequipa.) For assistance, ask a local for help; most Limeños know the incredibly complex bus system surprisingly well. Because they make so many stops, trips from the outer suburbs to downtown can be quite slow. Most *micros* and *combis* cost S/1 (35¢), slightly more after midnight and on Sunday and holidays. When you wish to get off, shout *"Baja"* (getting off) or *"Esquina"* (at the corner).

BY FOOT   Lima can be navigated by foot only a neighborhood at a time. (And even then, congestion and pollution strongly discourage much walking.) Lima Centro and Barranco are best seen by foot, and while large, Miraflores is also walkable. Between neighborhoods, however, a taxi or bus is essential.

VISITOR INFORMATION

A 24-hour tourist information booth, **iperu** (© **01/574-8000**) operates in the international terminal at the Jorge Chávez International Airport. The municipal **Oficina de Información Turística** is helpful and well located a block off the Plaza de Armas at Los Escribanos 145 in Lima Centro (© **01/427-6080**); it's open Monday through Friday from 9am to 6pm, Saturday and Sunday from 10am to 5pm. Two other offices are found in Miraflores: One is a small booth in Parque Central that's open daily from 9am to 9pm (but not always according to schedule); the other is at Av. Larco 770 (© **01/446-2649**), and it's open Monday through Friday from 8:30am to 5pm. One of the best private agencies for arrangements and city tours as well as general information is **Fertur Peru,** Jr. Junín 211 and Azángaro 105, within the Hotel España (© **01/427-1958**). Also well worth a visit, especially for members, is the Lima office of the **South American Explorers Club,** Piura 135, Miraflores (© **01/445-3306;** www. saexplorers.org).

FAST FACTS   Peruvian and international **banks** with currency exchange bureaus and ATMs are plentiful throughout central Lima and especially in the outer neighborhoods, such as Miraflores, San Isidro, and Barranco, which are full of shopping centers, hotels, and restaurants. Money changers, almost always wearing colored smocks (sometimes with obvious "$" insignias), patrol the main streets off Parque Central in Miraflores and Lima Centro with calculators and dollars in hand.

   English-speaking medical personnel and 24-hour emergency service are available at the following hospitals and clinics in Lima: **Clínica Anglo-Americana,** Alfredo Salazar, 3rd block, San Isidro (© 01/221-3656); **Clínica San Borja,** Guardia Civil 337, San Borja (© 01/475-4000); and **Maison de Sante,** Calle Miguel Adgouin 208–222, near the Palacio de Justicia (© 01/428-3000, or emergency 01/427-2941). For an ambulance, call **Alerta Médica** (© 01/470-5000) or **San Cristóbal** (© 01/440-0200).

   The **Policía Nacional de Turismo (National Tourism Police)** has an English-speaking staff and is specifically trained to handle needs of foreign visitors. The main office in Lima is next to the Museo de la Nación at Av. Javier Prado Este 2465, 5th floor, San Borja (© 01/225-8698 or 01/476-9879).

   Internet *cabinas* are everywhere in Lima. Rates are S/2 to S/3 (50¢–$1) per hour, and most are open daily from 9am to 10pm or later. Lima's main **post office (Central de Correos)** is located on the Plaza de Armas, Camaná 195 (© 01/427-0370). The Miraflores branch is on Petit Thouars 5201 (© 01/445-0697), the San Isidro branch, Calle Las Palmeras 205 (© 01/422-0981). A **DHL/Western Union** office is located at Nicolás de Piérola 808 (© 01/424-5820). The principal **Telefónica** office, where you can make long-distance and international calls, is on Plaza San Martín (Carabaya 937) in Lima Centro.

WHAT TO SEE & DO

Many visitors to Lima are merely on their way to other places in Peru. But, since everything goes through the capital, most people take advantage of layovers to see what distinguishes Lima: its colonial old quarter, once the finest in the

Americas, and several of the finest museums in Peru, all of which serve as magnificent introductions to Peruvian history and culture.

Much of the historic center has suffered from sad neglect; the municipal government is committed to restoring the aesthetic value, but with limited funds it faces a daunting task. Today, central Lima has a noticeable police presence and is considerably safer than it was just a few years ago. A full day in Lima Centro should suffice; depending on your interests, you could spend anywhere from a day to a week traipsing through Lima's many museum collections, many of which are dispersed in otherwise unremarkable neighborhoods. Few people, however, spend more than a couple of days in the capital.

LIMA CENTRO: COLONIAL LIMA

Lima's grand **Plaza de Armas** 𝒢 (also called the Plaza Mayor), the original center of the city and site where Francisco Pizarro founded the city in 1535, is essentially a modern reconstruction. The disastrous 1746 earthquake that initiated the city's decline leveled most of the 16th- and 17th-century buildings in the old center. The oldest surviving element of the square is the central bronze fountain, which dates from 1651. Today the square, while perhaps not the most beautiful or languid in South America, is still rather distinguished beneath a surface level of grime and bustle (and it has been named a UNESCO World Heritage Site). On the north side of the square is the early-20th-century **Palacio del Gobierno (Presidential Palace),** where a changing of the guard takes place daily at noon. The **Municipalidad de Lima (City Hall)** is on the west side of the plaza. Across the square is the **Catedral** (cathedral), rebuilt after the earthquake, and the **Palacio Episcopal (Archbishop's Palace),** distinguished by an extraordinary wooden balcony next to it.

A block north of the Plaza de Armas, behind the Presidential Palace, is the Río Rímac and a 17th-century Roman-style bridge, the **Puente de Piedra** (literally, "stone bridge"). It leads to the once-fashionable **Rímac** district, today considerably less chic—some would say downright dangerous—though it is the location of a few of Lima's best *peñas,* or live *criollo* music clubs. The **Plaza de Acho** bullring, once the largest in the world, and decent **Museo Taurino** (bullfighting museum) are near the river at Hualgayoc 332 (© **01/482-3360**). The ring is in full swing during the Fiestas Patrias (national holidays) at the end of July; the regular season runs from October to December.

Five blocks southwest of Plaza de Armas is Lima Centro's other grand square, **Plaza de San Martín.** This stately square with handsome gardens, inaugurated in 1921, was recently renovated. At its center is a large monument to the South American liberator José de San Martín.

Lima's **Barrio Chino,** the largest Chinese community in South America (200,000-plus), is visited by most folks to get a taste of the Peruvian twist on traditional Chinese cooking at the neighborhood's *chifas.* The official boundary of Chinatown is the large gate, Portada China, on Jirón Ucayali.

Catedral 𝒢   Lima's baroque cathedral, an enlargement of an earlier one from 1555, was completed in 1625. It suffered damages in earthquakes in 1687 and was decimated by the big one in 1746. The present building, though again damaged by tremors in 1940, is an 18th-century reconstruction of the early plans. Twin yellow towers sandwich an elaborate stone facade. Inside are several notable Churrigueresque altars and carved wooden choir stalls, but the cathedral is best known for the chapel where Francisco Pizarro lies. The founder of Lima and killer of Inca chieftain, Atahualpa, was himself assassinated in the Plaza de

Armas in 1541, but his remains weren't brought to the cathedral until 1985. (They were discovered in a crypt in 1977.) Look closely at the mosaic on the far wall of the chapel; it depicts his coat of arms, Atahualpa reaching into his coffer to cough up a ransom in the hopes of attaining his release, and other symbols of Pizarro's life. The cathedral also houses a small **Museo de Arte Religioso,** which has a few fabulous painted glass mirrors from Cusco, a collection of unsigned paintings, and a seated sculpture of Jesus, with his chin resting pensively on his hand—it's as bloody a figure of Christ as you're likely to see.

Plaza de Armas. ℂ 01/427-5980. Admission to cathedral and museum S/5 ($1.50) adults, S/3 ($1) students. Guides available in English and Spanish (voluntary tip). Mon–Sat 10am–5pm.

Convento y Museo de San Francisco ✷✷   Probably the most spectacular of Lima's colonial-era churches, the Convent of St. Francis is a strikingly restored 17th-century complex that survived the massive earthquake in 1746. The facade is a favorite of thousands of pigeons, who rest on rows of ridges that rise up the towers—so much so that from a distance it looks like black spots add an unexpectedly funky flavor to this baroque church. Cloisters and interiors are lined with beautiful *azulejos* (glazed ceramic tiles) from Seville; carved *mudéjar* (Moorish-style) ceilings are overhead. The mandatory guided tour takes visitors past the cloisters to a fine museum of religious art, with beautifully carved saints and a series of portraits of the apostles by the studio of Francisco Zurbarán, the famed Spanish painter. For many, though, the most fascinating component of the visit is the descent into the catacombs, which were dug beginning in 1546 as a burial ground for priests and others. (As many as 75,000 bodies were interred here before the main cemetery was built.) Also of great interest are the church, outfitted with an impressive neoclassical altar, and a fantastic 17th-century library, which was the second-most important of its time in the Americas (after one in Quito) and holds 20,000 books (many date from the earliest years after Lima's foundation). A breathtaking carved Moorish ceiling over a staircase is a reconstruction of the original from 1625.

Plaza de San Francisco (between Lampa and Ancash). ℂ 01/427-1381. Admission S/5 ($1.50) adults, S/2.50 (75¢) students. Guides available in English and Spanish. Daily 9am–4:45pm.

Museo de la Inquisición *Finds*   This magnificent mansion across the street from the House of Congress once belonged to the family that was considered the founders of Lima, but it became the tribunal for the notorious Spanish Inquisition. Today, it is a museum that soberly addresses religious intolerance from the Middle Ages through colonial times. The handsomely restored house itself is worth a visit, since it's a fine peek at the elegant *salas* of a prominent 16th-century colonial home (including the intricately carved ceiling of the Tribunal room). But its unfortunate history is plainly evident in the catacombs, which served as prison cells; on view are several instruments of torture. At least 32 Peruvians died here during the Inquisition, which persisted until 1820.

Plaza Bolívar (Junín 548). ℂ 01/427-5980. Free admission. Guided tours in English, Spanish, French, and Portuguese. Daily 10am–6pm.

THE TOP MUSEUMS
Museo Arqueológico Rafael Larco Herrera ✷✷   Founded in 1926, this is the largest private collection of pre-Columbian art in the world. It concentrates on the Moche dynasty, with an estimated 45,000 pieces—including incredibly fine textiles, jewelry, and stonework from several other ancient cultures—all housed in an 18th-century colonial building. Rafael Larco Hoyle, the author of the seminal study *Los Mochicas,* is considered the founder of Peruvian

archaeology; he named the museum after his father. The Moche (A.D. 200–700), who lived along the northern coast in the large area near present-day Trujillo and Cajamarca, are credited with achieving one of greatest artistic expressions of ancient Peru. The pottery gives clues to all elements of their society: diseases, curing practices, architecture, transportation, dance, agriculture, music, and religion. The Moche are also celebrated in the modern world for their erotic ceramics. The Sala Erótica is removed from the general collection, like the porn section in a video store. The Moche depicted sex in realistic, humorous, moralistic, and religious—but above all, explicit—terms. If you're traveling with kids, expect giggles or questions about the ancient Peruvians' mighty phalluses.

Av. Bolívar 1515, Pueblo Libre. ✆ 01/461-1312. http://museolarco.perucultural.org.pe. Admission S/20 ($6) adults, S/10 ($3) students. Private guides available in English and Spanish (tip basis, minimum S/10/$3). Daily 9am–6pm. Take a taxi or the "Todo Brasil" *colectivo* to Av. Brasil and then another to Av. Bolívar. If you're coming from the Museo Nacional de Arqueología, Antropología e Historia del Perú (see below), walk along the blue path.

Museo de la Nación ✮✮✮ (Kids)   Peru's ancient history is exceedingly complicated. Peru's pre-Columbian civilizations were among the most sophisticated of their times; when Egypt was building pyramids, peoples in Peru were constructing great cities. Lima's National Museum, the city's biggest and one of the most important in Peru, guides visitors through the highlights of overlapping and conquering cultures and their achievements, seen not only in architecture (including scale models of most major ruins in Peru) but also, highly advanced ceramics and textiles. The exhibits, spread over three rambling floors, are ordered chronologically—very helpful for getting a grip on these many cultures dispersed across Peru. In case you aren't able to make it to the archaeology-rich north of Peru, pay special attention to the facsimile of the Lord of Sipán discovery, one of the most important in the world in recent years. Explanations accompanying the exhibits are usually in both Spanish and English. Allow 2 to 3 hours to see it all.

Av. Javier Prado Este 2465, San Borja. ✆ 01/476-9878. Admission S/6 ($1.75) adults, S/3 ($1) seniors, S/1 (30¢) students. Guides in several languages can be contracted. Tues–Sun 9am–5pm. You can get here by *colectivo* along Av. Prado from Av. Arequipa, but it is much simpler to take a taxi from Lima Centro or Miraflores/San Isidro.

Museo Nacional de Arqueología, Antropología e Historia del Perú
With such a mouthful of an official name, you might expect the National Museum of Archaeology, Anthropology, and History to be the Peruvian equivalent of the Met. It's not, but it's a worthwhile and enjoyable museum that covers Peruvian civilization from prehistoric times to the colonial and republican periods. There are ceramics, carved stone figures and obelisks, metalwork and jewelry, lovely textiles, and mummies in the fetal position wrapped in burial blankets. There's also a selection of erotic ceramics from the Moche culture, but not nearly as extensive as that of the Rafael Larco Herrera museum (p. 582). Individual rooms are dedicated to the Nasca, Paracas, and Moche and Chimú cultures. Toward the end of the exhibit, which wanders around the central courtyard of the handsome 19th-century Quinta de los Libertadores mansion (once lived in by South American independence heroes San Martín and Bolívar), is a large-scale model of Machu Picchu. Basic descriptions throughout the museum are mostly in Spanish, though some are also in English. Allow about an hour for your visit.

From the museum, you can follow a walking path along a painted blue line to the Rafael Larco Herrera museum. It's about 1.5km (1 mile), or 20 minutes,

All That Glitters Ain't Necessarily Gold

The privately held **Museo de Oro del Perú (Gold Museum),** Av. Alonso de Molina 1100, Monterrico (🕐 **01/345-1292**), was for decades the most visited museum in Peru. But that was before National Institute of Culture and the Tourism Protection Bureau declared just about everything in the museum—some 7,000 or more pieces—to be fake. The massive collection, mainly consisting of supposed pre-Columbian gold, was assembled by one man, Miguel Mujica Gallo—who, curiously enough, died just days before the investigation into his collection was launched. Although the museum was expensive and poorly organized, all that glittering gold—augmented by hundreds (if not thousands) of ceremonial objects, tapestries, masks, ancient weapons, clothing, several mummies, and military weaponry and uniforms from medieval Europe to ancient Japan—certainly caught many a visitor's eye over the years. It's pretty difficult to recommend visiting such a fraudulent collection today; however if you still want to pay a visit, a taxi is the most direct and timesaving way to get here. It's open daily from 11am to 7pm; admission costs S/25 ($7) for adults, S/10 ($3) for students.

straight into traffic on Antonio de Sucre (make sure you turn at the Metro supermarket on Leguia Melendes).

Plaza Bolívar s/n, Pueblo Libre. 🕐 **01/463-5070.** Admission S/10 ($3) adults, S/5 ($1.50) students. Private guides available in English and Spanish (tip basis, minimum S/10/$3). Tues–Sat 9:15am–5pm; Sun 10am–5pm. Take a taxi here, or take the "Todo Brasil" *colectivo* to Av. Vivanco and then take a 15-min. walk.

SHOPPING

Lima has the greatest variety of shopping in Peru, from tony boutiques to artisan and antiques shops. In Lima, you can find handicrafts from across Peru; prices are not usually much higher and the selection may be even better than in the regions where the items are made. One exception is alpaca goods, which are better purchased in the areas around Cusco, Puno, and Arequipa, both in terms of price and selection. Miraflores is where most shoppers congregate, though there are also several outlets in Lima Centro and elsewhere in the city.

LIMA CENTRO   The best spot for handicrafts from around Peru is the **Santo Domingo** *artesanía* **arcades** across the street from the Santo Domingo convent on Conde de Superunda and Camaná. Lima Centro's crowded **Mercado Central** is south of the Plaza Mayor, at the edge of Chinatown (at the corner of Ayacucho and Ucayali). The **Feria Artesanal** on Avenida de la Marina in Pueblo Libre has a wide variety of handicrafts of varying quality but at lower prices than most tourist-oriented shops in Lima Centro or Miraflores. Haggling is a good idea.

SUBURBS   Miraflores houses the lion's share of Lima's well-stocked shops overflowing in handicrafts from around Peru, including weavings, ceramics, and silver. Several of the largest malls are here, and several dozen large souvenir and handicrafts shops are clustered on and around Avenida Ricardo Palma (look for **Artesanías Miraflores,** no. 205) and Avenida Petit Thouars (try **Artesanía Expo Inti,** no. 5495). Other handicraft shops in Miraflores include **Agua y Tierra,** Diez Canseco 298 (🕐 01/445-6980); and **Silvania Prints,** Diez

Canseco 378 (© 01/242-0667). Alpaca sweaters and other items can be had at **Alpaca 111,** Av. Larco 671 (© 01/447-1623); **Alpaca Perú,** Diez Canseco 315 (© 01/241-4175); **Mon Repos,** Tarata 288 (© 01/445-9740); and **All Alpaca,** Av. Schell 375 (© 01/427-4704). Look for silver jewelry and antiques along Avenida La Paz. *Platerías* and *joyerías* (silver and jewelry shops) worth a visit are **Ilaria,** Av. Larco 1325 (© 01/444-2347); and **El Tupo,** La Paz 553 (© 01/444-1511). Antiques shops include **El Almacén de Arte,** Francia 339 (© 01/445-6264); and **Porta 735,** Porta 735 (© 01/447-6158).

For fine *retablos* (gradines) and artisanship typical of Ayacucho (which produces some of Peru's most notable pieces), visit the **Museo-Galería Popular de Ayacucho,** Av. Pedro de Osma 116 (© 01/247-0599), in Barranco. There are small handicrafts markets, open late to catch bar and post-dinner crowds, in the main squares in both Miraflores and Barranco.

WHERE TO STAY

Lima Centro has its share of hotels and budget inns, but most people head out to Miraflores, San Isidro, and, to a lesser extent, Barranco. These barrios have little in the way of sights, but they are more convenient for nightlife and shopping and probably safer, if not necessarily much quieter, than Lima Centro.

LIMA CENTRO
Inexpensive

Hotel España ⭐ *Finds*   Near the Convento de San Francisco and just 4 blocks from Plaza de Armas, this extremely popular budget hostel has a funky flair and communal atmosphere. If you're looking to hook up with backpackers from around the globe and set off to explore Peru, you can't do better than Hotel España. It occupies a rambling colonial building bursting with paintings, ceramics, faux Roman busts, plants, and even the occasional mummy and skull. A maze of rooms, most with shared bathrooms, are up a winding staircase. The rooms themselves are simple, with concrete floors but brightly colored walls. The leafy rooftop garden terrace, with views of San Francisco, is a good place to hang out and trade travel tales. Some complain that security is a little lax, so lock up your stuff in the lockers. Hot water goes to the early bird. The place can be noisy, but that's part of its charm.

Azángaro 105, Lima. ©/fax **01/428-5546.** www.hotelespanaperu.com/ingles. 30 units, 6 w/private bathroom. $9 double w/o bathroom, $12 w/bathroom. No credit cards. **Amenities:** Cafe; tour desk; laundry service. *In room:* No phone.

MIRAFLORES
Very Expensive

Miraflores Park Hotel ⭐⭐⭐   Perhaps Lima's most elegant hotel, the Park Hotel bathes business executives and upscale tourists in unsurpassed luxury. It hugs the malecón, the avenue flush with parks that traces the Lima coastline. From the cozy, library-like lobby and handsome restaurant to the tastefully appointed, plush rooms (including marble and granite bathrooms most New Yorkers would give their left arms to live in), the hotel is a distinguished address. All rooms are suites with comfortable king-size beds and sitting areas. Many rooms have ocean views—at least on the few days of the year when one can see the coast in Lima.

Av. Malecón de la Reserva, 1035 Miraflores, Lima. © **01/242-3000.** Fax 01/242-3393. www.mira-park.com. 81 units. $295 deluxe double; from $340 suite. AE, DC, MC, V. **Amenities:** Restaurant; cafe; bar; small outdoor rooftop pool; squash court; exercise room; sauna; concierge; extensive business center and executive services; salon; room service; laundry service. *In room:* A/C, TV/VCR, fax, dataport, minibar, hair dryer.

Expensive

Hotel Antigua Miraflores ★★★ *Value* This charming early-20th-century mansion, full of authentic Peruvian touches and color, calls itself "a hidden treasure in the heart of Miraflores." As many return visitors know, that's not just hype. The hotel is owned and operated by a North American who's a long-time Lima resident. The house is elegant and tasteful, lined with colonial Peruvian art and built around a leafy courtyard. The staff is exceptionally helpful and friendly. Rooms range from huge suites with large Jacuzzis and kitchenettes to comfortable double rooms with handcrafted furniture and good-quality beds. Most bathrooms are quite luxurious, with colonial tiles, brass fixtures, and bathtubs. The public rooms look more like an art gallery than a hotel lobby (the paintings are for sale).

Av. Grau 350, Miraflores, Lima. ℂ **01/241-6116.** Fax 01/241-6115. http://peru-hotels-inns.com. 35 units. $74–$89 double; $104 suite. Rates include taxes and a nice selection of breakfasts. AE, DC, MC, V. Free parking. **Amenities:** Restaurant; bar; small gym; Jacuzzi; tour desk; room service; laundry service. *In room:* A/C, TV, minibar, hair dryer.

Sonesta Posada del Inca Miraflores ★★ *Value* The Miraflores branch of a chain with a handful of hotels across Peru, this small modern hotel is efficient and professionally run. Centrally located just 2 blocks from Parque Central (Parque Kennedy), it's within easy walking distance of Miraflores's many nightclubs, restaurants, and shops. The well-appointed rooms are large with very comfortable beds, good-size bathrooms, and an ocher-and-deep-green color scheme with plaid bedspreads.

Alcanfores 329, Miraflores, Lima 18. ℂ **800/SONESTA,** or 01/241-7688 or 01/222-4777. Fax 01/447-8199. www.sonesta.com/peru_miraflores. 28 units. $70 double; $94 suite. Rates include taxes, service charge, and breakfast buffet. AE, DC, MC, V. Free parking. **Amenities:** 24-hr. cafe and bar; fitness center (½ block from hotel); concierge; business center; room service; babysitting; laundry service; nonsmoking rooms. *In room:* A/C, TV, minibar, hair dryer on request, safe.

Moderate

San Antonio Abad ★ Named for a saint, this clean and very friendly neighborhood hotel aims high. Its goal is to be welcoming and comfortable, and it succeeds. The colonial building, near the commercial center of Miraflores and several parks, has a garden terrace, fireplace, and sitting room. The rooms, which are simply decorated but ample, have private bathrooms. Because of street noise, ever present in Lima, you might ask for a room with an interior courtyard view.

Av. Ramón Ribeyro 301, Miraflores, Lima. ℂ **01/447-6766.** Fax 01/446-4208. www.hotelsanantonio abad.com. 24 units. $55 double; $120 suite. Rates include taxes and breakfast buffet. AE, DC, MC, V. Free parking. **Amenities:** Restaurant; bar; room service; laundry service. *In room:* A/C, TV, minibar, hair dryer on request, safe.

Inexpensive

Inkawasi Backpacker ★ *Kids* Designed to appeal to backpackers, this pleasant bed-and-breakfast is a step up from most Peruvian hostels. It features an airy and comfortable homelike atmosphere in a secure part of Miraflores, just a few blocks from supermarkets, shops, restaurants, banks, and cinemas. There are two fully equipped kitchens available to guests, an interior patio and garden, and a roof garden and barbecue area. All rooms have private bathrooms, and suites have a queen-size bed, desk, kitchenette with microwave, and cable TV. The inn is especially family-friendly; kids can enjoy a play area with toys and children's videos.

Miraflores

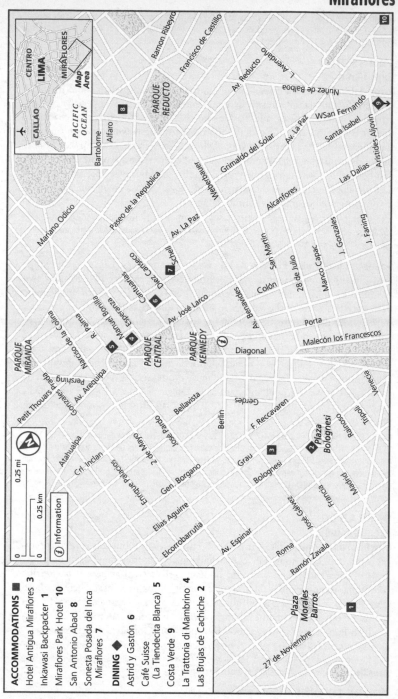

ACCOMMODATIONS ■
Hotel Antigua Miraflores **3**
Inkawasi Backpacker **1**
Miraflores Park Hotel **10**
San Antonio Abad **8**
Sonesta Posada del Inca
Miraflores **7**

DINING ◆
Astrid y Gastón **6**
Café Suisse
(La Tiendecita Blanca) **5**
Costa Verde **9**
La Trattoria di Mambrino **4**
Las Brujas de Cachiche **2**

ⓘ Information

0.25 mi
0.25 km

Alfredo Salazar 345, Miraflores, Lima. ℂ/fax **01/422-7724**. www.inkawasi.com. 10 units. $10 per person, or $25–$35 double; $45 suite. Rates include taxes and continental breakfast. Use of kitchen $2 a day; extra bed $5; children's bed $2. **Amenities:** Laundry service. *In room:* TV, kitchenette in suites, minibar, no phone.

SAN ISIDRO
Expensive
Hotel Libertador ☆☆ *(Value*   Smack in the middle of the San Isidro financial district, the Libertador is relatively unassuming and tranquil, especially considering the more imposing and flashier hotels nearby. Still, that's its charm. It doesn't try too hard, but it gets the job done for guests who are both business travelers and tourists. Part of a very well-run Peruvian chain of upscale hotels, this midsize offering is handsomely decorated with modern art, some kilim rugs, and bold colors—eschewing the typical blandness of business hotels—and has a nice top-floor restaurant and bar with good views. Quite a good value, especially if you can get an upgrade to a junior suite.

Los Eucaliptos 550, San Isidro, Lima. ℂ **01/421-6666**. Fax 01/442-3011. www.libertador.com.pe. 54 units. $80 double; $150–$235 suite. AE, DC, MC, V. Valet parking. **Amenities:** Restaurant; bar; gym; Jacuzzi; sauna; concierge; laundry service. *In room:* A/C, TV, minibar.

Sonesta Lima Hotel El Olivar ☆☆ *(Value*   The Sonesta chain's upscale property, aimed squarely at visiting business travelers, is named for the historic Olive Grove Park, which it faces. This seven-story hotel is well located for its clientele, in a peaceful section of the San Isidro business district of the city. The rooms, a step up from the more rustic decor in the chain's Posada del Inca, are quite large, with boldly colored fabrics and beige marble bathrooms. Service is friendly and efficient, and the amenities outdo those of most hotels in the city. Business travelers on a tighter budget who nonetheless wish to stay in San Isidro should also check out the Sonesta Posada del Inca, an easygoing sister property whose guests are allowed to use the pool and gym at El Olivar. It's located just a few blocks away at Av. Conquistadores 490 (ℂ **01/222-4373;** $105 double including taxes).

Pancho Fierro 194, San Isidro, Lima. ℂ **01/221-2121**. Fax 01/221-2141. www.el-olivar.com.pe. 134 units. $125–$160 double; $200–$400 suite. Rates include breakfast buffet. Children under 8 stay free in parent's room. Weekend deals $99 per night. AE, DC, MC, V. Free parking. **Amenities:** 2 restaurants; cafe; cocktail lounge; bar; fitness center w/rooftop outdoor pool; Jacuzzi; sauna; concierge; business and conference center; salon; massage; babysitting; 24-hr. laundry service; nonsmoking rooms. *In room:* A/C, TV/VCR w/pay movies, minibar, hair dryer, safe.

BARRANCO
Inexpensive
Mochileros ☆ *(Finds*   The name means "backpackers," but this isn't your typical youth hostel. It's housed in a great-looking 1903 postcolonial mansion in the heart of Lima's most laid-back and bohemian district, Barranco. It has terrific communal rooms, painted in vibrant colors with high ceilings. There are both large shared rooms and a handful of private doubles and singles. Shared bathrooms are outside the main building, but they have hot water all day. The on-site Irish Pub, Dirty Nelly's, is good fun and open Monday through Saturday.

Av. Pedro de Osma 135, Barranco, Lima. ℂ **01/477-4506**. Fax 01/247-6089. www.backpackersperu.com. 10 units. $10 per person in shared room; $30 double. No credit cards. Rates include breakfast. Free parking. **Amenities:** Restaurant; bar; bike rental. *In room:* No phone.

WHERE TO DINE
As you might expect, Lima offers the most cosmopolitan dining in Peru, with restaurants for all budgets serving a wide range of cuisines. Sometimes, there are

entire streets and neighborhoods specializing in a single type of food: In Lima Centro, you can visit the *chifas* of Chinatown (**Wa Lok** at Jr. Paruro 864 is probably the best known), and in Miraflores, a pedestrian street off Parque Central is referred to as "Little Italy" for its scores of look-alike pizzerias and Italian restaurants.

LIMA CENTRO
Moderate

L'Eau Vive ✿ *Finds* FRENCH/PERUVIAN If you're feeling helpless and obscenely rich in this impoverished country, you'll do a tiny bit of good by eating here. The restaurant, run by a French order of nuns, donates its proceeds to charity. In a colonial palace 2 blocks from the Plaza de Armas, it features several large dining rooms with high ceilings. If you come for the cheap lunch set menu, though, you'll have to sit in the simpler front rooms. The "a la carte" dining rooms are considerably more elegant. Though the lunch menu is a deal, you get a pious show free with dinner: The nuns sing "Ave María" promptly at 9:30pm. The French menu includes items such as prawn bisque, trout baked in cognac, and grilled meats; it also incorporates some international dishes from around the globe—chiefly the many countries from which the order's nuns come.

Ucayali 370. ✆ 01/427-5612. Reservations recommended on weekend evenings. Main courses S/9–S/43 ($2.50–$12); set lunch menus S/8–S/12 ($1.25–$3.50). AE, MC, V. Mon–Sat 12:30–3pm and 7:30–9:30pm.

Restaurant San Remo PERUVIAN On one of central Lima's more appealing streets near the Plaza de Armas, this efficient eatery has an appealing terrace with outdoor tables. Popular with local businesspeople and travelers who trickle out of the tourism information office next door, it offers particularly good deals at lunch. The evening menu lists plenty of *criollo* and seafood plates from the Peruvian coast, including gourmet dishes with pre-Columbian influences. At lunch, though, most people sit down to more standard fare such as grilled trout and fettuccine Alfredo, served with a salad and beverage.

Los Escribanos 137–141. ✆ 01/427-9102. Reservations recommended on weekend evenings. Main courses S/10–S/28 ($3–$8); set lunch menus S/20–S/24 ($6–$7). MC, V. Mon–Thurs 9am–9pm; Fri–Sat 9am–midnight.

MIRAFLORES & SAN ISIDRO
Very Expensive

Astrid y Gastón ✿✿✿ PERUVIAN/INTERNATIONAL Hidden discreetly behind a nonchalant facade on a busy side street leading to Parque Central is this warm and chic modern colonial dining room and cozy bar. The restaurant has high white peaked ceilings and orange walls decorated with colorful modern art, the products of local students. In back is an open kitchen where one of the owners, Gastón, can be seen cooking with his staff. The place is sophisticated but low-key, a description that could fit most of its clients, who all seem to be regulars. The menu might be called *criollo*-Mediterranean: Peruvian with a light touch. Try spicy roasted kid or the excellent fish called *noble robado,* served in miso sauce with crunchy oysters. The list of desserts is nearly as long as the main course menu. At evening's end, Astrid (the other member of the husband–wife team) often takes a seat and chats with customers at their tables.

Cantuarias 175, Miraflores. ✆ 01/444-1496. Reservations recommended. Main courses S/39–S/59 ($11–$17). AE, DC, MC, V. Mon–Sat 12:30–3:30pm and 7:30pm–midnight.

Las Brujas de Cachiche ✿✿ PERUVIAN/CRIOLLO The "Witches of Cachiche" celebrates 2,000 years of local culture with a menu that's a tour of the "magical" cuisines of pre-Columbian Peru. The chef even uses ancient recipes and ingredients. The extensive menu includes classic Peruvian dishes, such as *ají de gallina* (creamed chicken with chiles), but concentrates on fresh fish and shellfish and fine cuts of meat with interesting twists and unusual accompaniments. Brujas de Cachiche sole is prepared with Asian and *criollo* spices and served with peas and bell peppers sautéed in soybean sauce. A steak in pisco (grape brandy) butter sauce is served with braised mushrooms. Among the excellent desserts, several continue the indigenous theme, such as *mazamorra morada* (purple corn pudding and dried fruit). The restaurant, in a sprawling old house with several warmly decorated dining rooms, is popular both night and day with well-heeled Limeños, expat businesspeople, foreign government officials, and tourists; it's exclusive and it's expensive, but it's worth the splurge. A lunch buffet is served every day but Monday and Saturday from 11am to 4pm.

Jr. Bolognesi 460, Miraflores. ⓒ 01/447-1883. Reservations recommended. Main courses S/30–S/62 ($9–$18); lunch buffet $33, including 2 glasses of wine. AE, DC, MC, V. Mon 1pm–midnight; Tues–Sat 11am–midnight; Sun noon–5pm.

Moderate

Café Suisse (La Tiendecita Blanca) SWISS/INTERNATIONAL   This
classic old-style cafe, a Lima institution founded in 1937, is decorated with cool enamel doors and staffed by waitresses in folkloric red and white dresses. It's best known for its exquisite gourmet food shop, but "the little white store" is also a good little restaurant, perfect for lunch and even breakfast. Choose from fresh-baked quiches, *empanadas* (stuffed savory pastries), and sandwiches, or go Swiss with a fondue for two. There's a daily lunch *menú de la casa* for $10. Of course, if you spot that long counter bursting with homemade desserts, you may be unable to resist spoiling your meal.

Av. Larco 111, Miraflores. ⓒ 01/445-9797. Reservations not accepted. Main courses S/19–S/34 ($5–$10). AE, DC, MC, V. Daily 8am–10pm.

La Trattoria di Mambrino ⭐ ITALIAN   One of Lima's most popular and
enduring Italian eateries is this attractive bistro, owned by an Italian gentleman who makes the rounds most evenings. Decorated in warm Roman tones, the restaurant is often packed with families and young couples. La Trattoria bakes its own delicious rustic bread—with a bit of olive oil, it's an appetizer in itself. Among the many excellent homemade pastas are several stuffed versions, such as the anglotti with rabbit, pork, and beef. There are daily specials such as ragout of rabbit over pappardelle and stuffed peppers with prawns. Pizzas from the wood-burning oven and large, fresh salads round out the menu.

Manuel Bonilla 106, Miraflores. ⓒ 01/446-7002. Reservations recommended. Main courses S/20–S/55 ($6–$16). AE, DC, MC, V. Daily 1–3:15pm and 8–11:15pm.

Segundo Muelle ⭐ Ⓥalue SEAFOOD/CEVICHE   At the top of most peo-
ple's lists of favorite Peruvian dishes is *ceviche,* and you won't have trouble finding a *cevichería* anywhere along the coast. This informal, lunch-only place in San Isidro, popular with local office workers, is one of the most reasonable options in Lima for excellent fresh fish and *ceviche* plates without any fuss. If you're new to *ceviche,* you can't go wrong with the *mixto* (white fish, octopus, prawns, snails, scallops, and squid). There is a long list of other fish dishes, including sole, salmon, seafood pasta, and varied rice and seafood plates. Top off your meal with *chicha morada,* a sweet and delicious purple corn beverage made with pineapple and lemon. Kids' plates are available for S/12 ($3.50). There's a second branch in San Isidro at Av. Conquistadores 490 (ⓒ **01/421-1206**).

Av. Canaval y Moreyra 605 (at the corner of Pablo Carriquirry), San Isidro. © 01/224-3007. www.segundo muelle.com. Reservations not accepted. Main courses S/18–S/30 ($5–$8.50). MC, V. Daily noon–5pm.

BARRANCO
Very Expensive
Costa Verde 🌟🌟 *Overrated* SEAFOOD   Any time a restaurant in Peru lists all prices in dollars, you know it's not going to be cheap. Costa Verde, perched on a promontory jutting out into the ocean along the "green coast" south of Miraflores, is probably as expensive a meal as you'll have in Peru, but it's also good enough to draw a decent number of Limeños celebrating special occasions. It draws a bigger share of foreigners, as evidenced by the touristy little national flags the hostess places on everyone's table. (I suggest telling her you're from Iceland or Zimbabwe, just to see how well stocked they are in miniature flags.) The restaurant is attractive enough, but it's the big-time seafood buffet that makes everyone's eyes bulge. There's a daily lunch buffet and also a huge gourmet dinner buffet (60 bucks a head—in Peru!), which the restaurant claims is registered in the *Guinness Book of Records*. The regular menu seems not to have changed in more than 3 decades of business, but you can't really argue with sea bass with wild mushrooms and morel sauce with scallop mousse, or basil and ricotta gnocchi with river shrimps in saffron sauce. Not in the mood for fish? Try the pork loin in beer and honey sauce. Sit in the glass-enclosed atrium to hear the sound of waves crashing against the shore, and you'll feel far indeed from the chaos and commotion of downtown Lima.

Circuito de Playas (Playa Barranquito), Barranco. © 01/227-1244. Reservations recommended. Main courses $13–$29. AE, DC, MC, V. Daily 11am–midnight.

Expensive
Manos Morenas 🌟🌟🌟 PERUVIAN/CRIOLLO   In a beautiful early-1900s house on a quiet, leafy street in Barranco, this is one of the coolest restaurants in Lima. The name makes reference to the country's small but culturally potent Afro-Peruvian population and its traditions, influences crucial to both the menu and the lively, costumed music and dance shows that the restaurant has become famous for. The main dining room is very appealing, with handsome wooden chairs and tables and art for sale on the elegant yellow walls. A nice bar greets you at the entrance in case you have to wait for a table. The kitchen, staffed by women dressed like the restaurant's logo of a black woman in a head wrap, creates excellent versions of Peruvian standards such as *lomo saltado* (beef strips with onions, tomatoes, peppers, and french-fried potatoes, served with rice), *ají de gallina* (creamed chicken in chile sauce), *tamales,* and *piqueos* (assorted appetizers). *Corvina Manos Morenas* is sea bass served with mashed potatoes, spinach, prawns, and a béchamel sauce. The restaurant charges a substantial cover for the live shows.

Av. Pedro de Osma 409, Barranco. © 01/467-0421. Reservations recommended. Main courses S/17–S/48 ($5–$13). Live show cover Tues–Sat S/40 ($12). AE, DC, MC, V. Mon–Sat 12:30–4pm and 7pm–1am.

Moderate
Antica Trattoria 🌟🌟 *Value* ITALIAN   This is a charming and laid-back Italian restaurant that perfectly suits the surrounding Barranco barrio. It has a number of small, separate dining rooms decorated with a rustic and minimalist masculinity: stucco walls, dark wood-beamed ceilings, country-style wood tables, and simple, solid chairs. The house specialty is gourmet pizza from the wood-fired ovens, but the menu has several tempting ideas to lure you away from pizza, such as homemade pasta and osso buco or delicious *lomo fino a la*

tagliata, buried under a mound of arugula. The relaxed environment makes this a great date place, as well as the perfect spot for dinner before hitting one of Barranco's live music or dance clubs.

San Martín 201, Barranco. (℃ 01/247-5752. Reservations recommended. Main courses S/19–S/35 ($5.50–$10). AE, DC, MC, V. Daily noon–midnight.

LIMA AFTER DARK

As its largest city, Lima certainly has Peru's most varied nightlife scene. The best after-dark scenes are in Miraflores and particularly Barranco.

PEÑAS   You should check out at least one *peña,* a *criollo*-music club that quite often inspires rousing participation. **Caballero de Fina Estampa,** Av. del Ejército 800, Miraflores (℃ 01/441-0552), is one of the chicest, with a large colonial salon and balconies. **De Rompe y Raja,** Manuel Segura 127, Barranco (℃ 01/247-3099), is a favorite of locals. Look for the popular Matices Negros (an Afro-Peruvian dance trio). **Las Guitarras,** Manuel Segura 295, Barranco (℃ 01/479-1874), is a cool spot where locals go to play an active part in their *peña.* It's open Friday and Saturday only. **Brisas del Titicaca,** Jr. Wukulski 168 at the first block of Avenida Brasil, Lima Centro (℃ 01/332-1901), is a cultural institution with *noches folklóricas* Thursday through Saturday and some of the best shows in Lima.

THE BAR & CLUB SCENE   **Freiheit,** Lima 471, Miraflores (℃ **01/247-4630**), is a warmly decorated bar in the style of a German tavern. The dance floor is separate from the bar area. There's a drink minimum on weekends. **O'Murphy's Irish Pub,** Shell 627, Miraflores (℃ 01/242-1212), is a longtime favorite drinking hole. Expect a pool table, darts, Guinness on tap, and Brits and Irish hoisting it. **Son de Cuba,** Bulevar San Ramón 277, Miraflores (℃ **01/ 445-1444**), is on the pedestrian street called "Little Italy" by locals, but the club focuses on the rhythms and drinks of the Caribbean Tuesday through Sunday.

My vote for best live music club in Lima is **La Noche,** Bolognesi 307, Barranco (℃ **01/477-5829**); despite its prosaic name, this sprawling multilevel club feels like a swank treehouse, with a great stage and sound system and good bands every night of the week that run the gamut (though frequently jazz), plus a hip mixed Limeño and international crowd. The Monday night jam sessions are particularly good and have no cover charge; otherwise, covers range from S/5 to S/15 ($1.50–$4). **El Ekeko,** Av. Grau 266, Barranco (℃ 01/247-3148), is a two-level place with live music Wednesday through Saturday; most acts fall within the Latin category, often Cuban. Covers range from S/10 to S/20 ($3–$6). **La Estación de Barranco,** Pedro de Osma 112 (℃ 01/247-0344), is another nice place with live music Tuesday through Saturday and a slightly more mature crowd. **Satchmo,** Av. La Paz 538, Miraflores (℃ 01/444-4957), is a classy joint with a variable roster of live bands; it's a good date spot. Covers are S/20 to S/45 ($6–$13).

Many of Lima's discos are young and wild affairs. Check out **Deja-Vu Trattoria & Bar,** Av. Grau 294, Barranco (℃ **01/247-3742**), whose decor is based on TV commercials. The music trips from techno to trance; it's a dancefest Monday through Saturday. **Kitsch,** Bolognesi 743, Barranco (℃ **01/ 247-3325**), is one of Lima's hottest bars—literally, as it sometimes turns into a sweatbox—with over-the-top decor (flowery wallpaper and a fish tank in the floor) and recorded tunes that range from 1970s and 1980s pop to Latin and techno.

AN EXCURSION FROM LIMA: THE NASCA LINES ✦✦✦

The unique Nasca Lines remain one of the great enigmas of the South American continent. The San José desert, bisected by the great Pan-American Highway that runs the length of Peru, is spectacularly marked by 70 giant plant and animal line drawings, as well as a warren of mysterious geometric lines, carved into the barren surface. Throughout the Nasca Valley, an area of nearly 1,000 sq. km (386 sq. miles), there are at least 10,000 lines and 300 different figures. Most are found alongside a 50km (30-mile) stretch of the Pan-American Highway. Some of the biggest and best-known figures are about 21km (13 miles) north of the town of Nasca. Most experts believe they were constructed by the Nasca (pre-Inca) culture between 300 B.C. and A.D. 700, though predecessor and successor cultures—the Paracas and Huari—may have also contributed to the desert canvas. The lines were discovered in the 1920s when commercial airlines began flights over the Peruvian desert. From the sky, they appeared to be some sort of primitive landing strips.

As enigmatic as they are, the Nasca Lines are not some sort of desert-sands Rorschach inkblot; the figures are real and easily identifiable from the air. With the naked eye from the window of an airplane, you'll spot the outlines of a parrot, hummingbird, spider, condor, dog, whale, monkey with a tail wound like a top, giant spirals, huge trapezoids, and, perhaps oddest of all, a cartoonish anthropomorphic figure with its hand raised to the sky that has come to be known as the "Astronaut." Some figures are as much as 300m (1,000 ft.) long, while some lines are 30m (100 ft.) wide and stretch more than 9km (6 miles).

Questions have long confounded observers. Who constructed these huge figures and lines and why? Apparently, the Nasca people, over many generations, removed hard stones turned dark by the sun to "draw" the lines in the fine, lighter colored sand. The incredibly dry desert conditions—it rains only about 20 inches a year on average—preserved the lines and figures for more than 1,000 years. Why the lines were constructed is more difficult to answer, especially considering that the authors were unable to see their work in its entirety without any sort of aerial perspective. A scientist who dedicated her life to study of the lines was a German mathematician, María Reiche. She concluded that the lines formed a giant astronomical calendar, crucial to calculating planting and harvest times. According to this theory, the Nasca were able to predict the arrival of rains, a valuable commodity in such barren territory. Other theories, though, abound. Nasca is a seismic zone, with 300 fault lines beneath the surface and hundreds of subterranean canals; an American scientist, David Johnson, proposed that the trapezoids held clues to subterranean water sources. Some suggest that the lines not only led to water sources, but that they were pilgrimage routes, part of the Nasca's ritual worship of water. Notions of extraterrestrials and the Nasca's ability themselves to fly over the lines have been dismissed by most serious observers.

By far the most convenient—although certainly not the cheapest—way to see the lines is as part of a 1-day round-trip package from Lima with **AeroCondor,** Jr. Juan de Arona 781, San Isidro (© **01/422-4214**). The package includes an overflight of the Nasca Lines, lunch, and a short sightseeing tour of Ica; it costs $140 per person, with a minimum of two people. Overflights organized in Nasca run about $50 per person. The small aircraft seats between three and five passengers; if you're prone to airsickness, you should note that these flights take some stomach-turning dips and dives. (Only 10 min. into one recent flight, the four French travelers onboard with me were all tossing their *petits déjeuners* into the white plastic bags that had been thoughtfully provided.)

4 Cusco ★★★

1,153km (715 miles) SE of Lima

As the storied capital of the Inca dynasty and the gateway to Machu Picchu, Cusco is one of the highlights of South America. Paved with stone streets and building foundations laid by the Incas more than 5 centuries ago, the town is also remarkably dynamic, enlivened by throngs of travelers who have transformed the historic center around the Plaza de Armas into a mecca for South American adventurers. Cusco is one of those rare places that seems able to preserve its unique character and enduring appeal despite its prominence on the international tourism radar.

Cusco looks and feels like the very definition of an Andean capital. It's a fascinating blend of pre-Columbian and colonial history and contemporary mestizo culture. Cusco's highlights include Inca ruins and colonial-era baroque and Renaissance churches and mansions. The heart of the historic center has suffered relatively few modern intrusions, and despite the staggering number of souvenir shops, travel agencies, hotels, and restaurants overflowing with visitors soaking up the flavor, it doesn't take an impossibly fertile imagination to conjure the magnificent capital of the 16th century.

Today, Cusco thrives as one of the most vibrant expressions of Amerindian and mestizo culture anywhere in the Americas. Every June, the city is packed during Inti Raymi, the celebration of the winter solstice and the sun god, a deeply religious festival that is also a magical display of pre-Columbian music and dance. Thousands trek out to Paucartambo for the riveting Virgen del Carmen festival in mid-July. Other traditional arts also flourish. Cusco is the handicrafts center of Peru, and its streets teem with merchants and their extraordinary textiles, many hand-woven using the exact techniques of their ancestors.

Spectacularly cradled by the southeastern Andes Mountains, Cusco sits at a daunting altitude of 3,400m (11,000 ft.). The air is noticeably thinner here than in almost any other city in South America, and the city, best explored on foot, demands arduous hiking up precipitous stone steps, leaving even the fittest of travelers gasping for breath. It takes a couple of days to get acclimatized before moving on from Cusco to explore the mountain villages of the Inca's Sacred Valley, the Amazon basin, and, of course, Machu Picchu, but many visitors find Cusco so seductive that they either delay plans to explore the surrounding region, or add a few days to their trip to allow more time in the city. Increasingly, travelers are basing themselves in one of the lower-altitude villages of the Sacred Valley, but there is so much to see and do in Cusco that an overnight stay is pretty much required of anyone who hasn't previously spent time in the area.

ESSENTIALS
GETTING THERE
BY PLANE   Most visitors arrive by plane from Lima (a 1-hr. flight). In high season, flights arrive by the dozens from Lima as well as Arequipa, Puerto Maldonado, and La Paz, Bolivia, at **Aeropuerto Internacional Velasco Astete** (© **084/222-611**). See "Getting Around" in "Planning Your Trip to Peru," earlier in this chapter, for more flight information. Flights are occasionally delayed by poor weather.

Transportation from the airport to downtown Cusco, about 20 minutes away, is by taxi or private hotel car. Taxis are plentiful and inexpensive. (A less convenient *combi*, or small bus, passes outside the airport parking lot and goes to Plaza San Francisco; unless you have almost no baggage and your hotel is right

Cusco

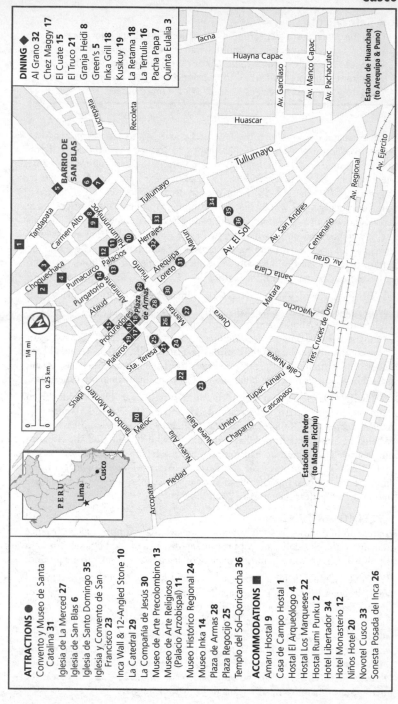

DINING ◆
Al Grano **32**
Chez Maggy **17**
El Cuate **15**
El Truco **21**
Granja Heidi **8**
Green's **5**
Inka Grill **18**
Kusikuy **19**
La Retama **18**
La Tertulia **16**
Pacha Papa **7**
Quinta Eulalia **3**

ATTRACTIONS ●
Convento y Museo de Santa
  Catalina **31**
Iglesia de La Merced **27**
Iglesia de San Blas **6**
Iglesia de Santo Domingo **35**
Iglesia y Convento de San
  Francisco **23**
Inca Wall & 12-Angled Stone **10**
La Catedral **29**
La Compañía de Jesús **30**
Museo de Arte Precolombino **13**
Museo de Arte Religioso
  (Palacio Arzobispal) **11**
Museo Histórico Regional **24**
Museo Inka **14**
Plaza de Armas **28**
Plaza Regocijo **25**
Templo del Sol–Qoricancha **36**

ACCOMMODATIONS ■
Amaru Hostal **9**
Casa de Campo Hostal **1**
Hostal El Arqueólogo **4**
Hostal Los Marqueses **22**
Hostal Rumi Punku **2**
Hotel Libertador **34**
Hotel Monasterio **12**
Niños Hotel **20**
Novotel Cusco **33**
Sonesta Posada del Inca **26**

595

A Safety Note

Over the years, Cusco has earned a reputation for being rather unsafe for foreign visitors, especially at night when violent muggings have been known to occur on empty streets. Do not walk alone late at night; have restaurant or bar staff call a taxi to transfer you to your hotel. Please refer to "Safety" in "Fast Facts: Peru" on p. 575 for more details.

on that square, it's not worth the few soles you'll save to take a *combi.*) Most hotels, even less expensive hostels, are happy to arrange airport pickup. If you take a taxi, note that the fare is likely to drop precipitously if you merely refuse the first offer you get (likely to be S/15–S/20 or $4–$5.50). Taxi fare to Cusco is generally S/8–S/10 ($2–$3) from the airport to the center. When you exit with your luggage, you will be besieged with offers from taxi and tour-company representatives, many of whom will pretend to have your name on their "arrivals list" just to take you into town and try to score a commission from one of hundreds of tour operators. If you have arranged for your hotel to pick you up, be certain that you are dealing with someone authorized by the hotel and who possesses your exact arrival information.

BY BUS   Buses to Cusco arrive from Lima, Arequipa, Puno/Juliaca, and Puerto Maldonado in the Amazon basin. From Lima to Cusco is 26 hours by land; from Puno, 7 hours; and from Arequipa, 12 hours. There is no central bus terminal in Cusco. Buses arrive at either a terminal on Avenida Pachacutec or (more commonly) at the newer **Terminal Terrestre,** at the end of Avenida El Sol (several miles from the city center). Buses from the Sacred Valley use small, makeshift terminals on Calle Huáscar and Calle Intiqhawarina, off Tullumayo.

BY TRAIN   There are two main Perurail train stations in Cusco. Trains from Puno and Arequipa arrive at **Estación de Huanchaq** (also spelled "Wanchac"), Av. Pachacutec s/n (℃ **084/238-722** or 084/221-931), at the southeast end of Avenida El Sol. Trains from Ollantaytambo, Machu Picchu, and the Amazon jungle arrive at **Estación de San Pedro,** Calle Cascaparo s/n (℃ **084/221-352** or 084/221-313), southwest of the Plaza de Armas. Thieves operate in and around both stations, but visitors should be particularly cautious at San Pedro station, which is near the crowded Mercado Central.

GETTING AROUND

Getting around Cusco is straightforward and relatively simple, especially since so many of the city sights are within walking distance of the Plaza de Armas in the historic center. You will mostly depend on leg power and taxis to get around.

BY TAXI   Unlike in Lima, taxis are regulated in Cusco and charge standard rates (although they do not have meters). Taxis are inexpensive (S/2 or 50¢ for any trip within the historic core during the day, S/3 or $1 after 10pm) and a good way to get around, especially at night. Hailing a cab in Cusco is considerably less daunting than in Lima, but you may still wish to call a registered taxi when traveling from your hotel to train or bus stations, going to the airport, and when returning to your hotel late at night. Licensed taxi companies include **Okarina** (℃ **084/247-080**) and **Aló Cusco** (℃ **084/222-222**). Taxis can be hired for return trips to nearby ruins or for half or full days.

BY BUS   Most buses—called variously *colectivos, micros,* and *combis*—cost S/1 (30¢), slightly more after midnight, on Sunday, and on holidays. You aren't likely to need buses often in the city, though the *colectivos* that run up and down Avenida El Sol are also a useful option for some hotels, travel agencies, and shopping markets. A bus departs from Plaza San Francisco to the airport, but it isn't terribly convenient.

BY CAR   Renting a car in the Cusco region—more than likely to visit the beautiful Sacred Valley mountain villages—is a more practical idea than in most parts of Peru. Rental agencies include **Avis,** Av. El Sol 808 (© **084/248-800**), and **Localiza,** Av. Industrial J-3, Urbanización Huancaro (© **084/233-131**). Rates range from $40 per day for a standard four-door to $65 per day for a Jeep Cherokee 4×4.

BY FOOT   Most of Cusco is best navigated by foot, though because of the city's high elevation and steep climbs, walking is demanding. Allow extra time to get around and carry a bottle of water. You can walk to the major ruins just beyond the city—Sacsayhuamán and Q'enko—but you should be fit to do so.

VISITOR INFORMATION

As the top tourist destination in Peru, Cusco is well equipped with information outlets. There's a branch of the **Oficina de Información Turística** (© **084/380-145**) at the Velasco Astete Airport in the arrivals terminal; it's open daily from 6:30am to 12:30pm. The principal Oficina de Información Turística is located on Mantas 117-A, a block from the Plaza de Armas (© **084/263-176**). It's open Monday through Friday from 8am to 6pm and Saturday from 9am to noon. It's very helpful and efficient, and it sells the essential boleto turístico (tourist ticket; see "Cusco's Boleto Turístico" on p. 599). Another information office is located in the **Terminal Terrestre de Huanchaq** train station, Av. Pachacutec s/n (© **084/238-722**); it's open Monday through Saturday from 8am to 6:30pm.

FAST FACTS   Most Peruvian and international **banks** with money-exchange bureaus and ATMs are located along Avenida El Sol. Money changers, usually wearing colored smocks, patrol the main streets off the Plaza de Armas.

In a **police emergency,** call © 105. The **National Tourist Police** are located at Portal de Belén, Plaza de Armas (© **084/221-961**). You can also try the **Tourist Protection Bureau,** Portal Carrizos 250, Plaza de Armas (© **084/252-974**). If you have a medical emergency, contact **Tourist Medical Assistance** at Heladeros 157 (© **084/260-101**). English-speaking medical personnel are available at the following hospitals and clinics: **Hospital Essalud,** Av. Anselmo

---

Tips Acclimatization

You'll need to take it easy for the first few hours or even couple of days in Cusco to adjust to the elevation. Headaches and shortness of breath are the most common ailments. Drink plenty of water, avoid heavy meals, and do as the locals do: Drink *mate de coca,* or coca-leaf tea. (Don't worry, you won't get high or arrested, but you will adjust a little more smoothly to the thin air.) If that doesn't cure you, ask whether your hotel has an oxygen tank you can use for a few moments of assisted breathing. And if that doesn't do the trick, it may be time to seek medical assistance; see "Fast Facts," above. Those who think they may have an especially hard time with the altitude might consider staying the first couple of nights in the Sacred Valley (Urubamba or Ollantaytambo).

Cusco = Cuzco = Q'osqo

Spanish and English spellings derived from the Quechua language are a little haphazard in Cusco, especially since there's been a linguistic movement to try to recuperate and value indigenous culture. Thus, you may see Inca written Inka; Cusco written Cuzco, Qosqo, or Q'osqo; Qoricancha as Coricancha or Koricancha; Wanchac as Huanchac or Huanchaq; Sacsayhuamán as Sacsaywaman; and Qenko as Kenko, Q'enko, or Qenqo. There are others, all used interchangeably.

Alvarez s/n (© 084/237-341); **Clínica Pardo,** Av. de la Cultura 710 (© 084/624-186); **Hospital Antonio Loren,** Plazoleta Belén s/n (© 084/226-511); **Hospital Regional,** Av. de la Cultura s/n (© 084/231-131); and **Clínica Paredes,** Lechugal 405 (© 084/225-265).

Internet *cabinas* are everywhere in the old section of Cusco. Rates are generally S/2.50 (75¢) per hour and S/1 (30¢) for 15 minutes. Most keep very late hours, opening at 9am and staying open until midnight or later. Cusco's main **post office,** Av. El Sol 802 (© 084/225-232), is open Monday through Friday from 8am to 1:30pm and 3 to 8pm, and Saturday from 8am to 1pm and 3 to 7pm. A **DHL/Western Union** office is located at Av. El Sol 627-A (© 084/244-167). The principal **Telefónica del Perú** office, for long-distance and international calls, is at Av. El Sol 382 (© 084/241-114).

WHAT TO SEE & DO

The stately **Plaza de Armas** ✶✶, lined by arcades and carved wooden balconies and framed by the Andes, is the focal point of Cusco. Next to Machu Picchu, it is one of the most familiar sights in Peru. You will cross it, relax on the benches in its center, and pass under the porticoes that line it with shops, restaurants, travel agencies, and bars innumerable times during your stay in Cusco. The plaza—which was twice its present size in Inca days—has two of Cusco's foremost churches and the remains of original Inca walls on the northwest side of the square, thought to be the foundation of the Inca Pachacutec's palace.

The Incas designed their capital in the shape of a puma, with the head at the north end, at Sacsayhuamán (even its zigzagged walls are said to have represented the animal's teeth). This is difficult to appreciate today; even though much of the original layout of the city remains, it has been engulfed by growth. Still, most of Cusco can be seen on foot, certainly the best way to appreciate this historic mountain town.

Many principal sights within the historic quarter of Cusco and beyond the city are included in the boleto turístico (see box, below), but a few very worthwhile places of interest, including the Temple of the Sun, are not.

AROUND THE PLAZA DE ARMAS

Catedral ✶✶   Built on the site of the palace of the Inca Viracocha, Cusco's cathedral is a beautiful religious and artistic monument. Until 2005, however, it will be undergoing massive restoration, so at this writing much of it is under wraps. The central nave looks like a construction site, entirely supported by wooden beams. Completed in 1669 in the Renaissance style, the cathedral possesses some 400 canvases of the distinguished Cusqueña School, painted from the 16th to 18th centuries. There are also amazing woodcarvings, including the spectacular cedar choir stalls. The main altar—which weighs more than 882 pounds and is fashioned from silver mined in Potosí, Bolivia—features the patron saints of Cusco. To the right of the altar is a particularly Peruvian painting of the Last Supper, with the apostles drinking *chicha* (fermented maize beer) and eating *cuy* (guinea pig). The **Capilla del Triunfo** (the 1st Christian church in Cusco) is next door, to the right of the main church. It holds a painting by Alonso Cortés de Monroy of the devastating earthquake of 1650 and an altar adorned by the locally famous "El Negrito" (El Señor de los Temblores, or Lord of the Earthquakes), a brown-skinned figure of Christ on the cross that was paraded around the city by frightened residents during the 1650 earthquake (which, miracle or not, ceased shortly thereafter).

The entrance to the cathedral and ticket office, where you can purchase the boleto turístico, is actually at the entrance to the **Capilla de la Sagrada Familia,** to the left of the main door and steps.

Plaza de Armas (north side). Admission included in boleto turístico. Mon–Sat 10–11:30am and 2–5:30pm; Sun 2–5pm.

La Compañía de Jesús ★   Cater-cornered to the cathedral is this Jesuit church, which rivals the cathedral in grandeur and prominence on the square (an intentional move by the Jesuits, and one that had Church diplomats running back and forth to the Vatican). Begun in the late 16th century, it was almost entirely demolished by the quake of 1650, rebuilt, and finally finished 18 years later. Like the cathedral, it was also built on the site of the Inca Huayna

---

⟨Value⟩ Cusco's Boleto Turístico

Cusco's municipal tourism office sells an excellent tourist ticket that is your admission to 16 of the most important places of interest in and around Cusco, including some of the major draws in the Sacred Valley of the Incas. You cannot get into some churches and museums without it. The full ticket costs $10 for adults and $5 for students and children, is valid for 10 days, and is available at the tourism office at Mantas 117-A (© 084/263-176), open Monday through Friday from 8am to 6:30pm and Saturday from 8am to 2pm. The boleto allows admission to the following sights: La Catedral, Museo de Arte Religioso, Iglesia de San Blas, Municipal Palace Museum, Qoricancha Archaeological Museum, Museo Histórico Regional, Convento y Museo de Santa Catalina, and the Inca ruins of Sacsayhuamán, Q'enko, Pukapukara, Tambomachay, Pisac, Ollantaytambo, Chinchero, Pikillacta, and Tipón.

Not all of these are indispensable, and while you can buy a partial ticket ($6) that allows entry to a handful of attractions, I don't recommend it because chances are you'll want to see a combination of all Cusco has to offer, even if you don't end up checking off absolutely everything on your color photo–coded boleto. Make sure you carry the ticket with you when you're planning to make visits, as guards will demand to see it so that they can punch a hole alongside the corresponding picture. Students must also carry their International Student Identification Card (ISIC), as guards often demand to see that ID to prove that they didn't fraudulently obtain a student boleto and thus cheat the city out of five bucks.

The Magic of Inca Stones: A Walking Tour

The ancient streets of Cusco are lined by dramatic Inca walls, mammoth granite blocks so exquisitely carved that they fit together, without mortar, like jigsaw puzzle pieces. The Spaniards razed many Inca constructions but built others right on top of the original foundations. (Even hell-bent on destruction, they recognized the value of good engineering.) Colonial architecture has, in many cases, not stood up nearly as well as the Incas' bold structures, designed to withstand the immensity of seismic shifts common in this part of Peru.

Apart from the main attractions detailed in this section, a brief walking tour will take you past some of the finest Inca constructions that remain in the city. East of the Plaza de Armas, **Calle Loreto** is one of the best-known Inca thoroughfares. The massive wall on the left-hand side, composed of meticulously cut rectangular stones, was once part of the Acllahuasi, or the "House of the Chosen Maidens," the Inca's Virgins of the Sun. This is the oldest surviving Inca wall in Cusco, and one of the most distinguished. Northeast of the Plaza de Armas, off of Calle Palacio, is **Hatunrumiyoc,** a cobbled street lined with impressive walls of polygonal stones. Past the Archbishop's Palace on the right side is the famed **12-angled stone** (now appropriated as the symbol of Cuzqueña beer and appearing on its labels), magnificently fitted into the wall. Originally, this wall belonged to the palace of the Inca Roca. Although this large stone is impressively cut, the Incas almost routinely fitted many-cornered stones (with as many as 32, as seen at Machu Picchu, or even 44 angles) into structures. From Hatunrumiyoc, make your first right down another pedestrian alleyway, Inca Roca; about halfway down on the right side is a series of stones said to form the shape of a **puma,** including head, large paws, and tail. It's not all that obvious, so if you see someone else studying the wall, ask him or her to point out the figure. Other streets with notable Inca foundations are Herrajes, Pasaje Arequipa, and Santa Catalina Angosta. Only a couple of genuine Inca **portals** remain. One is at Choquechaca 339 and another at Romeritos 402, near Qoricancha.

Not every impressive stone wall in Cusco is Inca in origin, however. Many are transitional period (postconquest) constructions, performed by local masons under the service of Spanish bosses. Peter Frost's *Exploring Cusco* (available in local bookstores) has a good explanation of what to look for in distinguishing an original from what amounts to a copy.

Capac (said to be the most beautiful of all the Inca rulers' palaces). Inside, it's rather gloomy, but the gilded altar is stunning, especially when illuminated. The church possesses several important works of art, including a picture of St. Ignatius de Loyola by the local painter Marcos Zapata, and the Cristo de Burgos crucifixion by the main altar. Also of note are the paintings to either side of the entrance, which depict the marriages of St. Ignatius's nephews; one is the very symbol of Peru's mestizo character, as the granddaughter of Manco Inca wed the man who captured the last Inca, Tupac Amaru, leader of an Indian uprising.

Plaza de Armas (southeast side). Free admission. Mass Mon–Sat 7am, noon, and 6pm; Sun 7:30, 11:30am, 6, and 7pm. Variable opening hours for visits; enter whenever open between Masses.

Convento y Museo de Santa Catalina ⭐⭐

A small convent located a couple of blocks west of the Plaza de Armas, Santa Catalina was built between 1601 and 1610 on top of the Acllawasi, where the Inca sequestered his chosen Virgins of the Sun. The convent contains a museum of colonial and religious art. The collection includes an excellent collection of Cusqueña School paintings, featuring some of the greatest works of Amerindian art—a combination of indigenous and typically Spanish styles—in Cusco. The interior of the monastery is quite beautiful, with painted arches and an interesting chapel with baroque frescoes of Inca vegetation. Other items of interest include very macabre statues of Jesus and an extraordinary trunk that, when opened, displays the life of Christ in 3-D figurines (it was employed by the Catholic Church's traveling salesmen, used to convert the natives in far-flung regions of Peru). The main altar of the convent church is tucked behind steel bars.

Santa Catalina Angosta s/n. ⓒ 084/223-245. Admission included in boleto turístico. Daily 8am–6pm.

Museo Inka ⭐

Housed in the impressive Admirals Palace, this museum contains artifacts designed to trace Peruvian history from pre-Inca civilizations and Inca culture, including the impact of the conquest and colonial times on the culture. On view are ceramics, textiles, jewelry, mummies, architectural models, and an interesting collection (reputed to be the world's largest) of Inca drinking vessels *(qeros)* carved out of wood, many meticulously painted. The museum is a good introduction to Inca culture, and there are explanations in English. The palace itself is one of Cusco's finest colonial mansions, with a superbly ornate portal indicating the importance of its owner; the house was built on top of yet another Inca palace at the beginning of the 17th century. In the courtyard is a studio of women weaving traditional textiles.

Cuesta del Almirante 103 (corner of Ataúd and Tucumán). ⓒ 084/237-380. Admission not included in boleto turístico; S/5 ($1.50) adults, S/2 (50¢) students. Mon–Fri 8am–5pm; Sat 9am–4pm.

SOUTH & EAST OF THE PLAZA DE ARMAS

Templo del Sol–Qoricancha (Temple of the Sun) & Iglesia de Santo Domingo ⭐⭐⭐

Qoricancha and Santo Domingo together form perhaps the most vivid illustration in Cusco of Andean culture's collision with Western Europe. Like the Great Mosque in Córdoba, Spain—where Christians dared to build a massive church within the perfect Muslim shrine—the temple of one culture sits atop and encloses the other. The extraordinarily crafted Temple of the Sun was the most sumptuous temple in the Inca Empire and the apogee of the Inca's naturalistic belief system. Some 4,000 of the highest-ranking priests and their attendants were housed here. Dedicated to worship of the sun, it was apparently a glittering palace straight out of El Dorado legend: Qoricancha means "golden courtyard" in Quechua, and in addition to hundreds of gold panels lining its walls, there were life-size gold figures, solid gold altars, and a huge golden sun disc. The sun disc reflected the sun and bathed the temple in light. During the summer solstice, the sun still shines directly into a niche where only the Inca chieftain was permitted to sit. Other temples and shrines existed for the worship of lesser natural gods: the Moon, Venus, Thunder, Lightning, and the Rainbow. Qoricancha was the main astronomical observatory for the Incas.

After the Spaniards ransacked the temple and emptied it of gold, the exquisite polished stone walls were employed as the foundations of the Convent of Santo Domingo, constructed in the 17th century. The baroque church pales next to the fine masonry of the Incas—and that's to say nothing about the original glory of the Sun Temple. Today all that remains is Inca stonework. Thankfully, a large section of the cloister has been removed, revealing four original chambers of the temple, all smoothly tapered examples of Inca trapezoidal architecture. Stand on the small platform in the first chamber and see the perfect symmetry of openings in the stone chambers. A series of Inca stones displayed reveals the fascinating concept of male and female blocks and how they fit together. The 6m (20-ft.) curved wall beneath the west end of the church, visible from the street, remains undamaged by repeated earthquakes and is perhaps the greatest example of Inca stonework. The curvature and fit of the massive stones is astounding.

After the Spaniards had taken Cusco, Juan Pizarro was given the eviscerated Temple of the Sun. He died soon after, though, at the battle at Sacsayhuamán, and he left the temple to the Dominicans, in whose hands it remains.

Plazoleta Santo Domingo. ℂ **084/222-071.** Admission not included in boleto turístico; S/4 ($1) adults, S/2 (50¢) students. Mon–Sat 8am–5pm; Sun 2–4pm.

Museo de Arte Religioso (Palacio Arzobispal) On the corner of one of Cusco's most extraordinary streets, Hatunrumliyoc, the Museum of Religious Art is housed in a handsome colonial palace that previously belonged to the Archbishop of Cusco (and before that, was the site of the palace of Inca Roca and then the home of a Spanish marquis). Inside is a nice collection of colonial religious paintings, notable for the historical detail they convey, but the house itself—with its impressive portal, balcony, and small chapel—is nearly the main draw.

Corner of Hatunrumiyoc and Palacio. ℂ **084/222-781.** Admission included in boleto turístico. Mon–Sat 8–11:30am and 3–5:30pm.

Barrio de San Blas 𝕽𝕽 Cusco's most atmospheric and picturesque neighborhood, San Blas, a short but increasingly steep walk from the Plaza de Armas, is lined with artists' studios and artisans' workshops, as well as a good number of tourist haunts—bars and restaurants and a surfeit of hostels. It's a great area to wander around—many streets are pedestrian-only—though you should exercise caution with your belongings, especially at night. The neighborhood also affords some of the most spectacular panoramic vistas in the city. In the small plaza at the top and to the right of Cuesta San Blas is the little white **Iglesia de San Blas** 𝕽𝕽, said to be the oldest parish church in Cusco (admission by boleto turístico). Though a simple adobe structure, it contains a marvelously carved, Churrigueresque cedar pulpit. It's carved from a single tree trunk; some have gone as far as proclaiming it the finest example of woodcarving in the world. The pulpit comes with an odd story, and it's difficult to determine whether it's fact or folklore: It is said that the carpenter who created it was rewarded by having his skull placed within his masterwork (at the top, beneath the feet of St. Paul) upon death. Also worth a look is the baroque gold-leaf main altar.

Museo de Arte Precolombino ⭐⭐   A new addition to the Cusco cultural landscape is this archaeological museum run by and featuring part of the vast collection of pre-Columbian works belonging to the Rafael Larco Herrera Museum in Lima. Housed in an erstwhile Inca ceremonial court and later mansion—now handsomely restored—of the Conquistador Alonso Díaz are 450 pieces (about 1% of the pieces in storage at the museum in Lima), dating from 1250 B.C. to A.D. 1532. Halls exhibit gold and precious metal handicrafts, jewelry, and other artifacts depicting the rich traditions from the Nazca, Moche, Huari, Chimú, Chancay, and Inca cultures. The museum is especially worthwhile for anyone unable to visit the major museums in Lima.

Plaza de las Nazarenas s/n, San Blas. (🕿 084/233-210. Admission S/16 ($4) adults, S/7.50 ($2) students. Daily 9am–10pm.

SOUTHWEST OF THE PLAZA DE ARMAS

La Merced ⭐   Erected in 1536 and rebuilt after the great earthquake in the 17th century, La Merced ranks just below the cathedral and La Compañía in importance. It has a beautiful facade and lovely cloisters with a mural depicting the life of the Merced Order's founder. The sacristy contains a small museum of religious art, including a fantastic solid gold monstrance swathed in precious stones. In the vaults of the church are the remains of two famous conquistadors, Diego de Almagro and Gonzalo Pizarro.

Calle Mantas s/n. (🕿 084/231-821. Admission S/3 ($1) adults, S/2 (50¢) students. Mon–Sat 8:30am–noon and 2–5pm.

Museo Histórico Regional   The colonial home of Garcilaso de la Vega, a prominent historian of the Incas and colonial Cusco, is the appropriate setting for this museum, which presents a survey of Peruvian history, from pre-Inca civilizations to the Inca and colonial periods. If you don't plan on visiting the bigger and better museums in Lima, this will serve as a good enough historical and archaeological overview of cultures such as the Chavín, Chancay, Moche, and Nasca. In addition to ceramics, textiles, and mummies, there are Cusco School art and colonial-era furniture. The museum isn't well labeled, though, so for some, the handsomely rebuilt colonial mansion may ultimately prove more interesting.

Plaza Regocijo, at the corner of Garcilaso and Heladeros. (🕿 084/223-245. Admission included in boleto turístico. Mon–Sat 8am–5:30pm.

Iglesia y Convento de San Francisco   This large and austere 17th-century convent church extends the length of the plaza of the same name. It is best known for its collection of colonial artwork, including paintings by Marcos Zapata and Diego Quispe Tito, both of considerable local renown. A monumental canvas (12m by 9m/39 ft. by 30 ft.) that details the genealogy of the Franciscan family (almost 700 individuals) is by Juan Espinoza de los Monteros. The Franciscans also decorated the convent with ceiling frescos and a number of displays of skulls and bones.

Plaza de San Francisco s/n. (🕿 084/221-361. Admission S/3 ($1) adults, S/2 (50¢) students. Mon–Sat 9am–4pm.

INCA RUINS NEAR CUSCO

The best way to see the following set of Inca ruins just outside of Cusco is on a half-day tour. The hardy may want to approach it as an athletic archaeological expedition: If you've got 15km (9 miles) of walking and climbing at high altitude in you, it's a beautiful trek. Otherwise, you can walk to Sacsayhuamán and nearby Q'enko (the climb from the Plaza de Armas is strenuous and takes 30–45 min.) and take a *colectivo* or taxi to the other sites. Alternatively, you can take a Pisac/Urubamba minibus (leaving from the bus station at Calle Intiqhawarina, off Av. Tullumayo, or at Huáscar 128) and tell the driver you want to get off at the ruins farthest from Cusco, Tambomachay, and work your way back on foot. Some even make the rounds by horseback. (You can easily and cheaply contract a horse at Sacsayhuamán, but know that you'll walk to all the sites alongside a guide.) Visitors with less time in Cusco or interest in taxing themselves may wish to join a guided tour, probably the most popular and the easiest way of seeing the ruins. Virtually any of the scads of travel agencies and tour operators in the old center of Cusco offer them. Well-rated traditional agencies with a variety of city programs include **Gatur Tour,** Puluchapata 140 (© 084/223-496); **Milla Turismo,** Av. Pardo 689 (© 084/231-710); **SAS Travel,** Portal Panes 143, Plaza de Armas (© 084/237-292; www.sastravel peru.com); and **Top Vacations,** Portal Confituria 265, Plaza de Armas (© 084/ 263-278).

Admission to the following sites is by boleto turístico, and they are all open daily from 7am to 6pm. Official and unofficial guides hover around the ruins; negotiate a price or decide on a proper tip. There are other Inca ruins on the outskirts of Cusco, a couple of which even appear on the boleto, but the ones discussed below are the most interesting.

These sites are generally safe, but at certain times of day—usually dawn and dusk before and after tour groups' visits—several ruins are said to be favored by thieves. It's best to be alert and, if possible, go accompanied.

SACSAYHUAMAN ⟨⟨⟨⟩⟩⟩   The greatest and nearest to Cusco of the ruins, Sacsayhuamán reveals some of the Incas' most extraordinary architecture and monumental stonework. Usually referred to as a garrison or fortress—it was constructed with forbidding, castlelike walls—it was probably a religious temple (though most experts also believe it had military significance). The festival Inti Raymi (June 24) is celebrated here annually, and it's a great spectacle.

The ruins cover a huge area, but they constitute perhaps one-quarter of the original complex. Surviving today are the astounding outer walls, constructed in a zigzag formation of three tiers. Many of the base stones employed are almost unimaginably massive; some are twice as tall as a 1.8m (6-ft.) man, and one is said to weigh 300 tons. Like all Inca constructions, the stones fit together perfectly without the aid of mortar. After victory here, the Spaniards made off with the more manageable blocks to build houses and other structures in Cusco. It's easy to see how hard it would have been to attack these ramparts with 22 distinct zigzags; the design would automatically expose the flanks of an opponent.

Above the walls are the circular foundations of three towers—used for storage of provisions and water—that once stood here. The complex suffered such extensive destruction that little is known about the actual purpose Sacsayhuamán served. What is known is that it was the site of one of the bloodiest battles between the Spaniards and native Cusqueños. More than 2 years after the Spaniards had initially marched on Cusco and installed a puppet government, the anointed Inca (Manco Inca) led a seditious campaign that took back Sacsayhuamán and nearly defeated the Spanish in a siege of the Inca capital. Juan Pizarro and his vastly outnumbered but superior armed forces stormed Sacsayhuamán in a horrific battle in 1536 that left thousands dead. Legend speaks of their remains as carrion for giant condors in the open fields here.

Can't Leave Well Enough Alone

The Peruvian authorities are notorious for messing with ruins, trying to rebuild them rather than let them be what they are: ruins. You'll notice at Sacsayhuamán and other Inca sites that unnecessary and misleading restoration has been undertaken. The grotesque result is that small gaps where original stones are missing have been filled in with obviously new and misplaced garden rocks—a disgrace to the perfection pursued and achieved by Inca masons.

A flat, grassy esplanade separates the defense walls from a small hill where you'll find the "Inca's Throne" and large rocks with well-worn grooves, used by children (and almost as frequently, adults) as slides. Nearby is a series of claustrophobia-inducing tunnels (pass through them if you dare).

Night visits to the ruins are now permitted from 8 to 10pm. Under a full moon in the huge star-lit Andean sky, Sacsayhuamán is so breathtaking that you'll instantly grasp the Incas' worship of the natural world, in which both the sun and moon were considered deities. If you go at night, take a flashlight and a few friends; security is a little lax, and assaults on foreigners have occurred.

Walking directions: It's a steep 2km (1¼-mile) walk from the center of Cusco. There are a couple of paths. Head northwest from the Plaza de Armas. You can take Palacio (behind the cathedral) until you reach stairs and signs to the ruins, or at the end of Suecia, climb either Huaynapata or Resbalosa (the name means "slippery") until you come to a curve and the old Inca road. Past the San Cristóbal church at the top, beyond a plaza with fruit-juice stands, are the ruins.

Q'ENKO 🎔 The road from Sacsayhuamán leads past fields, where Cusqueños play soccer and have cookouts on weekends, to the temple and amphitheater of Q'enko (*ken-koh*); it's a distance of about 1km (½ mile). A large limestone outcrop was hollowed out by the Incas and in the void they constructed a cavelike altar. (Some have claimed the smooth stone table inside was used for animal sacrifices.) You can also climb on the rock and see the many channels cut into the rock, where it is thought that either *chicha* or, more salaciously, sacrificial blood coursed during ceremonies.

PUCA PUCARA A small fortress (the name means "red fort") just off the main Cusco-Pisac road, this may have been some sort of storage facility or lodging. It is probably the least impressive of the sites, but it has nice views of the surrounding countryside.

TAMBOMACHAY 🎔 About 8km (5 miles) from Cusco on the way to Pisac (and a short, signposted walk off the main road) is this site, known as Los Baños del Inca (Inca Baths). Water still flows across a system of aqueducts and canals in the small complex of terraces and a pool, but these were not baths as we know them—they were most likely a place of water ceremonies and worship.

SHOPPING

Cusco is Peru's acknowledged center of handicraft production, especially of hand-woven textiles, and its premier shopping destination. Many Cusqueño artisans still employ ancient weaving techniques, and they produce some of the finest textiles in South America. From tiny one-person shops to large markets with dozens of stalls, there are few better places to shop than Cusco for excellent-value Andean handicrafts. Items to look for include alpaca wool sweaters, shawls, gloves, hats, scarves, blankets, and ponchos; antique blankets and textiles, beautiful but pricey; woodcarvings, especially nicely carved picture frames; fine ceramics and jewelry; and Cusqueña School reproduction paintings.

The barrio of **San Blas,** the streets right around the **Plaza de Armas** (particularly calles Plateros and Triunfo), and **Plaza Regocijo** are the best and most convenient haunts for shopping outings. You won't have to look hard for whatever it is that interests you, but a bit of price comparison is always helpful. If merchants think you've just arrived in Peru and don't know the real value of items, your price is guaranteed to be higher. Although bargaining is acceptable and almost expected, merchants in the center of Cusco are confident of a steady stream of buyers, and as a consequence are often less willing to negotiate than their counterparts in markets and more remote places in Peru. Most visitors will find prices delightfully affordable, though, and haggling beyond what you know is a fair price when the disparity of wealth is so great is generally viewed as bad form.

For a general selection of *artesanía,* **Galería Latina,** Calle San Agustín 427 (© **084/246-588**), has a wide range of top-end antique blankets, rugs, alpaca wool clothing, ceramics, jewelry, and handicrafts from the Amazon jungle in a large shop near the Hotel Libertador. About a block away from the Plaza de Armas on Plateros and also at Triunfo 393, you'll find good-size markets of crafts stalls. **Centro Artesanal Cusco,** at the end of Avenida El Sol, across from the large painted waterfall fountain and Hotel Savoy, is the largest indoor market of handicrafts stalls in Cusco, and many goods are slightly cheaper than they are closer to the plaza.

San Blas is swimming with art galleries, artisan workshops, and ceramics shops. You'll stumble upon many small shops dealing in reproduction Cusqueña School religious paintings and many workshops where you can watch artisans in action. Several of the best ceramics outlets are also here. Check out **Artesanías Mendivil,** Plazoleta San Blas 619 (© 084/233-247), known for saint figures with elongated necks; the **Juan Garboza taller** (studio), Tandapata 676/ Plazoleta San Blas (© 084/248-039), which specializes in pre-Inca style ceramics; and **Artesanías Olave,** Triunfo 342 (© 084/252-935), a high-quality crafts shop.

Several shops feature wool or alpaca *chompas,* or jackets, with Andean designs (often lifted directly from old blankets and weavings). **Artesanías Quipu Cancha,** Plateros 321 (© 084/223-369), has by far the most stylish and best quality jackets, but they're also the most expensive. For other upscale alpaca fashions— mostly sweaters and shawls—try **Alpaca 3,** Calle Ruinas 472 (© 084/226-101); **Alpaca 111,** Herladeros 202 (© 084/243-233); or **Royal Alpaca,** Santa Teresa 387 (© 084/252-346). **Werner & Ana,** a Dutch-Peruvian design couple, sell stylish clothing in fine natural fabrics such as alpaca. They have a shop on Plaza San Francisco 295-A at Calle Garcilaso (© 084/231-076).

For jewelry, **Ilaria** deals in fine silver and unique Andean-style pieces and has two branches in Cusco: one at Hotel Monasterio, Calle Palacios 136 (© 084/ 221-192), and another at Portal Carrizos 258, Plaza de Armas (© 084/246-253). The contemporary jewelry designer **Carlos Chaquiras,** Triunfo 375 (© 084/227-470), is an excellent craftsman; many of his pieces feature pre-Columbian designs. Lots of shops have hand-carved woodwork and frames, but the best spot for handmade, baroque frames (perfect for your Cusqueña School reproduction or religious shrine) is **La Casa del Altar,** Mesa Redonda lote A (© 084/244-712), not far from the Plaza de Armas. In addition to frames, they make *retablos* and altars.

Cusco's famous, frenzied **Mercado Central** (near the San Pedro rail station) is shopping of a much different kind—almost more a top visitor's attraction than a shopping destination. Its array of products for sale—mostly produce, food, and household items—is dazzling, and even if you don't come to shop, this rich tapestry of modern and yet highly traditional Cusco still shouldn't be missed. Don't take valuables (or even your camera), though, and be on guard, as it is frequented by pickpockets on the lookout for tourists.

WHERE TO STAY

In recent years, the number of lodgings has really blossomed in Cusco, now numbering in the hundreds. Still, advance reservations in high season (June–Sept) in Cusco are essential, especially around the Inti Raymi and Fiestas Patrias festivals at the ends of June and July, respectively. Outside of high season, look for bargains, as hotel rates come down considerably. Most of the city's most desirable accommodations are very central, within walking distance of the Plaza de Armas. The San Blas neighborhood is also within walking distance, though many hotels and hostels in that district involve very steep climbs up the hillside. (The upside is that guests are rewarded with some of the finest views in the city.) Many hotels and inns will arrange free airport transfers if you communicate your arrival information to them in advance. Hot water is an issue at many hotels, even those that swear they offer 24-hour hot showers.

Several of the hostels below are cozy, family-run places, but travelers looking for even greater contact with a Peruvian family might want to check out the very inexpensive inns belonging to the **Asociación de Casas Familiares (Family Home Association),** which operates a website (www.cusco.net/familyhouse) with listings of guesthouses with one or more rooms available for short- or long-term stays.

NEAR THE PLAZA DE ARMAS
Very Expensive

Hotel Libertador ★★★   One of Cusco's top two hotels, the Libertador, could just as easily be called the Conquistador. Directly across from the Inca Temple of the Sun and built on the foundations of the "Aclla Huyasi," where the Inca chief kept maidens, this elegant traditional hotel occupies a historic house once inhabited by Francisco Pizarro. The handsome art- and antiques-filled hotel is built around a dramatic colonial courtyard marked by perfect arches, terra-cotta tiles, and a Spanish-style fountain; the swank lobby has a massive pyramidal skylight and exposed Inca walls. Guest rooms are spacious and refined; furnishings have rustic colonial touches, and the marble bathrooms are large and well equipped. Many rooms have small terraces. But the Libertador perhaps most distinguishes itself with attentive and very professional service. The fine but pricey restaurant, Inti Raymi, named for Cusco's important winter solstice festival, is built around the edges of the courtyard and features a nightly dance and music show.

Tips **No Sleeping In**

Most Cusco hotels have annoyingly early checkout times—often 9 or 9:30am—due to the deluge of early-morning flight arrivals to the city. At least in high season, hotels are very serious about your need to rise and shine, but you can always store your bags until later.

Calle San Agustín 400 (Plazoleta Santo Domingo 259), Cusco. ℂ **084/231-961.** Fax 01/233-152. www.summithotels.com. 254 units. $185 deluxe double; $215–$260 suite. Rates include taxes. AE, DC, MC, V. **Amenities:** Restaurant; coffee shop; fitness center; sauna; concierge; business center and executive services; salon; room service; laundry service. *In room:* A/C, TV/VCR, fax and dataport in some units, minibar, hair dryer, safe.

Hotel Monasterio ✹✹✹   Perhaps Peru's most extraordinary place to stay, this beautiful hotel occupies the San Antonio Abad monastery, constructed in 1592 on the foundations of an Inca palace. The Monasterio—converted into a hotel in 1995—exudes grace and luxury. While checking in, you relax in a lovely hall while sipping coca tea. (Altitude-challenged guests can also immediately hook up to an oxygen tank.) As much a museum as a hotel, it has its own opulent, gilded chapel and 18th-century Cusqueña School art collection. The hotel makes fine use of two courtyards with stone arches; one is set up for lunch—about as beautiful a setting as there is to be found in Cusco. Rooms are impeccably decorated in both colonial and modern styles; the accommodations off the first courtyard are more traditionally designed and authentic-feeling. For a special treat, consider one of the two-story suites. The Tupay Restaurant is housed in the original vaulted refectory of the monastery; early risers, many on their way to Machu Picchu, enjoy a terrific buffet breakfast serenaded by Gregorian chants. There are travelers who prefer the Libertador (see above) and have had reservations about the service at the Monasterio, but for me, the historic quarters and splendid grounds at the latter take the prize.

Calle Palacios 136 (Plazoleta Nazarenas), Cusco. ℂ **084/241-777.** Fax 084/237-111. http://monasterio.orient-express.com. 122 units. $275 deluxe double; $360–$535 suite. Rates include buffet breakfast. AE, DC, MC, V. **Amenities:** 2 restaurants; cafe; bar; concierge; room service; laundry service. *In room:* A/C, TV/VCR, minibar, hair dryer, safe.

Expensive

Novotel Cusco ✹   Cusco's newest hotel, a member of the French Novotel chain, is built around the guts of a 16th-century colonial building with a handsome courtyard, but the majority of rooms are in new sections. Opened in 2001, the hotel is modern and dependable, with good services and amenities, though in most regards, it's a notch below the city's two top-flight luxury hotels. Rooms are well equipped and brightly colored, but are otherwise standard accommodations. The hotel, a short distance from the Plaza de Armas, features a nice garden-side restaurant serving French fare, and a warm bar with a fireplace.

Palacio San Agustín 239 (corner of Pasaje Santa Mónica), Cusco. ℂ **084/228-282.** Fax 084/228-855. www.novotel.com. 99 units. $150 double. Rate includes taxes and breakfast. AE, DC, MC, V. **Amenities:** Restaurant/cafe; sauna; concierge; business facilities; salon; room service; babysitting; laundry service. *In room:* AC, TV, minibar, hair dryer.

Moderate

Hostal El Arqueólogo *Finds* *Kids*   It takes a little bit of effort to uncover this hostel, named for the profession responsible for discovering so much of Peru's pre-Columbian past and owned by a Frenchman who's a longtime Cusco resident. Down a stone alleyway and tucked behind the unprepossessing facade of a late-19th-century house, it certainly doesn't jump out at you, but once inside, you'll find a lovely, sunny garden—with ample space for kids to play—and rooms that run along a corridor overlooking the patio. Rooms are simply furnished but comfortable. More rooms are being added in the colonial courtyard of an attached house. The French restaurant, La Vie en Rose, is fairly upscale and surprisingly good for an inn of this size.

Ladrillos 425, Cusco. ℭ **084/232-569.** Fax 084/235-126. www.hotelarqueologo.com. 20 units. $42–$52 double. Rates include taxes and breakfast buffet. MC, V. **Amenities:** Restaurant; travel agency; room service; laundry service. *In room:* No phone.

Sonesta Posada del Inca ⓧ *Value*   Like the rest of the hotels belonging to this small and very well-run Peruvian group, the Posada del Inca is extremely cozy, cheery, and a very good value. Best of all, it's sandwiched between the Plaza de Armas and Plaza Regocijo—about as centrally located as you can be in Cusco, without the additional all-night noise of being right on the plaza. Rooms are of a good size and comfortable, and the homey lounge has a fireplace. Several rooms have excellent views of the city. Deals are often available ($80 double), including one with the possibility of staying 1 night at this hotel and another night at the chain's lovely place in the Urubamba valley (in Yucay) for a slightly discounted rate.

Portal Espinar 142, Cusco. ℭ **084/227-061.** Fax 084/233-091. www.sonesta.com. 40 units. $90 double. Rate includes taxes and breakfast buffet. AE, DC, MC, V. **Amenities:** Cafe/restaurant; concierge; business facilities; room service; babysitting; laundry service. *In room:* TV, minibar, hair dryer.

Inexpensive

Hostal Los Marqueses *Finds*   This hostel, housed in a 1590 mansion, is loaded with colonial character. It's perfect for people who want a step up from a budget inn but not manufactured flavor. Rooms are huge and simply furnished; some beds and other furnishings are in definite need of updating, while others are cool colonial pieces. The magnificent arcaded courtyard, the breakfast room that looks like a 17th-century parlor, and the grand suite (no. 7)—which features a sitting room, a canopy bed, carved wooden doors, and a huge dose of yesteryear—are sure to appeal to travelers in search of the romantic side of Cusco. However, be forewarned that some rooms are rather dark and unappealing; it's best to have a look at several rooms before committing. Discounts are available for 3- or 4-night stays.

Garcilaso 256, Cusco. ℭ **084/257-819.** marqueseshotel@hotmail.com. 30 units. $30 double. Rate includes taxes and continental breakfast. No credit cards. **Amenities:** Laundry service. *In room:* No phone.

Hostal Rumi Punku ⓧ   A glance at the name or address of this idiosyncratic family-owned hostel will give you an indication of its strong connection to Cusco's Inca roots. The massive portal to the street is a fascinating original Inca construction of perfectly cut stones, once part of a sacred Inca temple. (The door is one of only three belonging to private houses in Cusco, and elderly residents of the city used to do the sign of the cross upon passing it.) Inside is a charming, flower-filled colonial courtyard with a cute little chapel and gardens along a large Inca wall. The clean bedrooms are ample, with hardwood floors and Norwegian thermal blankets. The top-floor dining room, where breakfast is served, has excellent panoramic views of Cusco's rooftops. The hostel is on the way up to Sacsayhuamán, but only a short walk from the Plaza de Armas. Rumi Punku, by the way, means "door of stone" in Quechua.

Choquechaca 339, Cusco. ℭ **084/221-102.** Fax 084/242-741. www.rumipunku.com. 24 units. $35–$40 per person. Rates include taxes and continental breakfast buffet. MC, V. **Amenities:** Restaurant; laundry service. *In room:* No phone.

Niños Hotel ⭑⭑⭑ *Kids* *Value*   The Dutch owners of the charming "Children's Hotel" say they have a story to tell, and it's an inspirational one. Jolanda van den Berg and her partner, Titus Bovenberg, in just 4 short years in Peru, have mounted a small empire of goodwill: They adopted 12 Peruvian street children; constructed an extremely warm and inviting hotel in the old section of Cusco that puts all its profits toward their foundation to care for needy children; constructed a learning center and restaurant for 125 such kids; and are in the process of creating a second center with athletic facilities and additional medical attention for another 125 disadvantaged youth of Cusco.

The good news for travelers is that, should they be lucky enough to get a room here (reserve about 6 months in advance), they won't have to suffer for their financial contribution to such an important cause. The hotel, in a restored colonial house just 10 minutes from the Plaza de Armas, is one of the finest, cleanest, and most comfortable small inns in Peru. The large rooms—named for the couple's adopted children—are very nearly minimalist chic, with hardwood floors and quality beds, and they ring a lovely sunny courtyard, where breakfast is served. The hotel also has four terrific apartments for longer stays, ideal for small families, in the first of the children's learning and day-care facilities.

Meloq 442, Cusco. ⓒ 084/231-424. www.targetfound.nl/ninos. 20 units. $30 double w/bathroom; $24 double w/shared bathroom. Rates include taxes and continental breakfast. No credit cards. **Amenities:** Restaurant/cafe; laundry service. *In room:* No phone.

SAN BLAS & BEYOND
Moderate
Casa de Campo Hostal 🌟🌟 *Value*   Lodged in the hills of the traditional neighborhood of San Blas, Casa de Campo means "country house," and the air up here, high above Cusco, has the freshness of country air. An organic complex, its chalet-style rooms appear to have sprouted one from the other. An exceptionally friendly and comfortable place, it's nonetheless not for everyone, especially not those who are tired of climbing the steps of Inca ruins. The climb up to the hotel is taxing enough, but once inside the gate, guests must use their remaining reserves to amble up several more flights of stone steps. Once there, though, they're rewarded with nice gardens and several terraces with unparalleled sweeping views of the city and surrounding mountains, as well as a cozy lounge with a large fireplace. Rooms are not overly large, but they have good firm beds and are rustically decorated, with exposed wood beams and thick wool blankets. One special room has a fireplace (for the same price as a regular room); another is like a cottage towering above the city. The staff will build a fire in the bar on request, and arrange a free city tour in Cusco.

Tandapata 296, San Blas, Cusco. ⓒ 084/243-069. Fax 084/244-404. www.hotelcasadecampo.com. 25 units. $35–$40 double. Rates include taxes, breakfast buffet, and airport pickup. AE, MC, V. **Amenities:** Restaurant; laundry service. *In room:* No phone in some units.

Inexpensive
Amaru Hostal 🌟   Popular with legions of backpackers, this hostel, in a pretty colonial-republican house in the midst of the San Blas artist studios and shops, has a lovely balconied patio, with a very nice garden area that tends to attract sunbathers and with good views of Cusco. Rooms are very comfortable, attractively decorated, and a good value. Several have colonial-style furnishings and lots of natural light. (Ask to see several rooms if you can.) A very friendly and relaxed place.

Cuesta San Blas 541, San Blas, Cusco. ⓒ/fax 084/225-933. www.cusco.net/amaru. 16 units. $25 double w/bathroom; $16 double w/shared bathroom. Rates include taxes, continental breakfast, and airport pickup. No credit cards. **Amenities:** Coffee shop; laundry service. *In room:* No phone.

WHERE TO DINE

Visitors to Cusco have a huge array of restaurants and cafes at their disposal; eateries have sprouted up even faster than hostels and bars, and most are clustered around the main drags leading from Plaza de Armas. The large majority of them are economical, informal places favored by backpackers and adventure travelers—some offer midday three-course menus for as little as S/6 or S/7 ($2)—though there are a number of upscale dining options as well, which tend to be excellent values. Calle Procuradores, which leads off the Plaza de Armas across from the Compañía de Jesús church, is sometimes referred to as "Gringo Alley," but it could just as easily be called "Restaurant Row" for the cheap eateries that line both sides of the narrow passageway. Many are pizzerias, and Cusco has become known for its wood-fired, crispy-crusted pizzas.

Few restaurants in Cusco accept credit cards; many of those that do, especially the cheaper places, will charge a 10% surcharge to use plastic, so you're better off carrying cash (either soles or dollars). Top-flight restaurants often charge both a 10% service charge and 18% sales tax.

EXPENSIVE

El Truco ✩ PERUVIAN In a 17th-century *casona* that operated as a mint for the Spanish vice-regency and later as a gambling house, this restaurant combines good Peruvian cooking and *platos típicos* with a loud and lively *peña* show each night (8:30–10:30pm). The restaurant, virtually an institution now that it's been around for 40 years, has an attractive colonial interior and offers a daily lunch buffet of Peruvian specialties. At night, it's a la carte only. Dishes include pork *tamales,* roasted pork, roasted lamb, and stuffed *rocoto* peppers. The lively music and dance show, along with consistently good food, make El Truco very popular with upscale tour groups.

Plaza Regocijo 261. ✆ 084/235-295. Reservations recommended. Main courses S/16–S/32 ($4.50–$9); daily lunch buffet $10. AE, DC, MC, V. Mon–Sat noon–11pm.

Inka Grill ✩✩✩ PERUVIAN A large and attractive modern two-level place right on the Plaza de Armas, the distinguished Inka Grill serves what might be called *nuevo andino* fare and is one of Cusco's finest dining experiences. Start with a bowl of yummy *camote* (sweet potato) chips and green salsa. The best dishes are Peruvian standards such as sautéed alpaca tenderloin served over *quinoa* (a grain) and *ají de gallina* (shredded chicken with nuts, cheese, and chile peppers), and desserts such as coca-leaf crème brûlée. The extensive menu also features a wide range of international dishes, including pizza, pasta, and risotto.

Portal de Panes 115. ✆ 084/262-992. Reservations recommended. Main courses S/18–S/45 ($5–$13). AE, DC, MC, V. Mon–Sat 11am–midnight.

La Retama ✩✩ PERUVIAN/INTERNATIONAL Overlooking the Plaza de Armas from a huge second-floor space, La Retama is one of Cusco's most enduring favorites. The views and nightly folklore shows bring in the tour groups, but the food is good enough to warrant a visit even by those who fear long tables with group leaders and interpreters. The menu focuses on classic Peruvian dishes, such as pink trout and king fish from Lake Titicaca, *seco de cordero* (lamb), *anticucho de lomo* (beef brochette), *cuy,* and trout *ceviche.* International dishes include chicken curry and trout Florentine. The restaurant's walls are lined with the art and handicrafts of Peru, and there's also a gift shop. Folklore shows begin nightly at 8pm.

Portal de Panes 123, 2nd floor. ✆ 084/226-372. Reservations required. Main courses S/14–S/30 ($4–$8.50). AE, DC, MC, V. Mon–Sat noon–midnight.

Cusco's *Quintas*

When the day warms up under a huge blue sky in Cusco, you'll want to be outside. Cusco doesn't have many sidewalk cafes, but it does have a trio of *quintas,* traditional open-air restaurants that are most popular with locals on weekends. These are places to get large portions of good-quality Peruvian cooking at pretty reasonable prices. Among the dishes they all offer are *tamales, cuy chactado* (fried guinea pig) with potatoes, *chicharrón* (deep-fried pork, usually served with mint, onions, and corn), alpaca steak, *lechón* (suckling pig), and *costillas* (ribs). You can also get classics such as *rocoto relleno* (stuffed hot peppers) and *papa rellena* (potatoes stuffed with meat or vegetables). Vegetarian options include *sopa de quinoa* (grain soup), fried yuca, and *torta de papa* (potato omelet). *Quintas* are open only for lunch (noon–5 or 6pm), and most people make a visit their main meal of the day. Main courses cost between S/15 and S/45 ($4–$13).

Quinta Eulalia ⭐, Choquechaca 384 (℃ **084/224-951**), is Cusco's oldest *quinta* (open since 1941). From a lovely colonial courtyard, there are views of the San Cristóbal district to the surrounding hills from the upper eating area. It's a great place on a sunny day, and the Andean specialties are reasonably priced. **Pacha Papa,** Plazoleta San Blas 120 (℃ **084/241-318**), is in a beautiful courtyard across from the small church in San Blas. In addition to Andean dishes, you'll find sandwiches. The house specialty, *cuy,* must be ordered 1 day in advance. Alpaca steak is served in several varieties, including alpaca goulash and alpaca kabob.

MODERATE

Greens ⭐⭐⭐ *(Value* INTERNATIONAL   In the heart of San Blas, on an atmospheric street just off the *plazoleta,* Greens is one of Cusco's most stylish and romantic restaurants. The intimate space has deep green walls, modern art, an open kitchen, and a handful of tables with candlelight mixed with hipster sofas for more informal dining. The soundtrack of laid-back dance beats; the creative, funky menu; and the reasonable prices appeal to a cool young crowd. On the menu, you'll find steaks, chicken, and curries, all excellent. Try the beef tenderloin in red wine–and-onion sauce, served with raisin rice; or the tropical chicken curry with bananas, peaches, and strawberries. On Sunday, the restaurant features a roast—by reservation only—that has become locally famous: chicken, roast potatoes, veggies, and homemade apple pie. Happy hour (two-for-one) is every evening from 6:30 to 7:30pm. Check out breakfast, too; an outdoor table overlooking the San Blas plaza on a sunny morning is heaven.

Tandapata 700. ℃ 084/243-820. Reservations recommended. Main courses S/10–S/30 ($3–$9). No credit cards. Daily noon–3pm and 6pm–midnight.

Kusikuy ⭐ ANDEAN/INTERNATIONAL   If you've resisted trying the Andean specialty that makes most foreigners recoil or at least raise an eyebrow, this could be the place to get adventurous. The restaurant's name in Quechua means "happy little guinea pig," so *cuy al horno* is, of course, the house dish. The rest of the menu focuses on other typical Peruvian dishes and adds stuff for gringos, such as pasta and basic chicken and meat dishes. It also serves a good-value lunch menu. The good-looking restaurant on busy Plateros is warmly decorated with hardwood tables, black-and-white tile floors, and a mix of antiques and musical instruments from the Amazon.

Plateros 348. ℂ **084/262-870.** Reservations not accepted. Main courses S/12–S/38 ($3.50–$11). MC. V. Mon–Sat 8am–midnight.

INEXPENSIVE

Al Grano ASIAN   A quiet corner cafe with lots of natural light, decorated with Andean textiles, and featuring exposed Inca stonework, this little place doesn't specialize in standard *criollo* fare, as you might expect, but in all manner of Asian dishes. On the menu are items from Indonesia, India, Pakistan, and Sri Lanka, including chutneys, vegetarian curries, and lamb in spices and yogurt. Most dishes are pretty mild. There's a very cheap daily fixed-price menu, served until 3pm, as well as daily specials. The cafe also has a range of great baked goods for dessert (try the brownie or spice cake) and good coffee and tea.

Santa Catalina Ancha 398 (at San Agustín). ℂ **084/228-332.** Reservations not accepted. Main courses S/6–S/18 ($1.75–$5); daily menu S/7.50 ($2). No credit cards. Mon–Sat 10am–9pm.

Chez Maggy ITALIAN/PERUVIAN   This bustling little joint, which has been around for 25 years and spawned a couple of branches in other parts of Peru, has a bit of everything, from trout and alpaca to homemade pasta to Mexican food, but most people jam their way in for the freshly baked pizza. Made in a traditional wood-burning brick oven, it's some of the best in Cusco. Chez Maggy is usually packed in the evenings, and there's often live *andina* music when roaming street musicians pop in to entertain diners. The restaurant is a long corridor with shared bench tables full of gringos—a good way to meet other travelers, since you'll be jockeying for elbow space with them. A second location is on Procuradores, better known as Gringo Alley. If you want a pizza on the terrace of your hostel, Chez Maggy will deliver for free.

Plateros 339. ℂ **084/234-861.** Reservations not accepted. Main courses S/12–S/30 ($4–$9). MC, V. Daily 6–11pm.

El Cuate ⭐ MEXICAN   I'm usually very wary about trying out Mexican restaurants while traveling in countries other than Mexico, since they almost always serve a crummy imitation of Tex-Mex. But this animated hole-in-the-wall on Gringo Alley is Cusco's first Mexican restaurant, and it dishes out pretty authentic Mexican food for scores of backpacker types. El Cuate's success has spawned several imitators who've felt compelled to add Mexican dishes to their Peruvian and Italian menus. But if you're sure you want Mexican, this is still the place to come. It has a number of bargain menus offering six courses for S/25 ($7) or S/15 ($4), or five items for just S/10 ($3), offered at lunch and dinner, and dishes such as *enchiladas suizas* (cheese enchiladas), Mexican soup, tacos, and burritos. With long bench tables, often shared, it's a jovial place.

Procuradores 386. ℂ **084/227-003.** Reservations not accepted. Main courses S/10–S/25 ($3–$7). MC. Daily 11am–midnight.

Granja Heidi ⭐ *(Finds)* HEALTH FOOD/VEGETARIAN   A healthy new addition to the Cusco dining scene is this cute upstairs place in San Blas serving great breakfasts and very good-value fixed-price menu meals. With a high ceiling and the airy, sun-filled look of an art studio, it's perfect for the neighborhood. Run by a German woman who also has a farm of the same name outside of Cusco, the restaurant features fresh ingredients and products, such as yogurt, cheese, and quiches, that taste like they came straight from the farm. The daily menu offers vegetarian and nonvegetarian choices, and might start with pumpkin soup, followed by lamb or a veggie stir-fry, fruit salad, and tea. Don't pass on dessert or you'll miss excellent home-baked cakes, such as the cheesecake or the irresistible Nelson Mandela chocolate cake.

Cuesta San Blas 525. (℄ 084/233-759. Reservations not accepted. Main courses S/7–S/20 ($2–$6); daily menu S/7.50 ($2). No credit cards. Daily 8am–9:30pm.

La Tertulia *Value* BREAKFAST/CAFE FARE   A classic Cusco spot for breakfast or other light meals, this little restaurant is a gringo hangout *par excellence.* The name means "discussion," which is fitting because people gather here to read newspapers and foreign magazines, and to exchange books and advice on hiking the Inca Trail and other far-flung adventures across South America. Many come to fuel up as early as 6:30am before setting out on one of those trips, and the superb breakfast buffet does the trick. It's all-you-can-eat eggs, fruit salads, yogurt, granola, amazing homemade whole-meal bread, French toast, *tamales,* fresh juices, and coffee—truly the breakfast of champions and an excellent value. The breakfast menu also features 16 types of crepes. There is a fixed-price lunch deal and a nice salad bar, as well as pizza, sandwiches, and fondue. If you feel bad about stuffing yourself at breakfast, you can feel good about the fact that La Tertulia donates one sol of each buffet to a Peruvian orphanage.

Procuradores 44, 2nd floor. (℄ 084/241-422. Reservations not accepted. Main courses S/8–S/20 ($2–$6); buffet breakfast S/12 ($3). MC. V. Daily 6:30am–3pm and 5–11pm.

CUSCO AFTER DARK

Most first-time visitors to Cusco, discovering an Andean city with such a gentle, pervasive Amerindian influence and colonial feel, are surprised to find that it has such a rollicking nightlife. It's not as diverse as Lima's, true, but if you like your nights full of predominantly young and rowdy patrons in the latest trekking gear, Cusco's your kind of place. I have heard countless young backpackers from countries across the world exclaim, in universal MTV lingo and with pisco sour in hand, "Cusco rocks!" Perhaps the best part is that, even though the city is inundated with foreigners many months of the year, it isn't just gringoland in the bars. Locals (and Peruvians from other cities, principally Lima, and other South Americans) tend to make up a pretty healthy percentage of the clientele. Clubs are in close range of each other—in the streets just off the Plaza de Armas and to a lesser extent in San Blas—and virtually everyone seems to adopt a pub-crawl attitude, bopping from one bar or disco to the next, often reconvening with friends in the plaza before picking up a "free drink ticket" and free admission card from any of the many girls on the square handing them out

---

Tips Raw Fish: A Cure for What Ails You

If you hang out so much and so late in Cusco that you wind up with a wicked hangover, adopt the tried-and-true Andean method of reviving yourself. For once, the solution is not coca leaf tea—it's *ceviche* that seems to do the trick. Something about raw fish marinated in lime juice and chiles delivers a nice slap in the face. When I lived in Ecuador (a country that fights with Peru not only over boundaries, but also for credit for having invented *ceviche*), late Sunday mornings at the *cevichería* were part of the weekly routine for pale-faced folks hiding behind sunglasses.

and moving on to the next club. It's rare that you'll have to pay a cover charge in Cusco.

For those who are saving their energy, there are less rowdy options, such as Andean music in restaurants, more sedate bars, and English-language movies every night of the week.

BARS & PUBS Bars are often very crowded with gringos hoisting cheap drinks and trading information on the Inca Trail or latest jungle or rafting expedition. They're generally open from 11am or noon until 1am or 2am. Most have elongated or frequent happy hours with half-price drinks, making it absurdly cheap to tie one on. **Cross Keys,** Portal Confiturias 233, Plaza de Armas, second floor (no phone), is one of the oldest pubs in town, owned by the English honorary consul and owner of Manu Expeditions. It's especially popular with Brits who can play darts or catch up on European soccer on satellite. **Los Perros,** Tecsicocha 436 (© 084/226-625), is one of the coolest bars in Cusco, a funky lounge with sofas, good food, and drinks (including hot wine), as well as live jazz on Sunday and Monday nights. **Norton Rat's Tavern,** Loreto 115, Plaza de Armas (© 084/246-204), is American-owned and sometimes it can feel like you're in Ohio, hanging with bikers—there's pool and lots of sports on the tube. **Paddy Flaherty's,** Triunfo 124, Plaza de Armas (© 084/246-903), is a cozy, relaxed, and often crowded Irish bar. **Rosie O'Grady's,** Santa Catalina Ancha 360, around the corner from the Plaza de Armas (© 084/247-935), is fancier digs in which to down your (canned) Guinness.

LIVE MUSIC Live music starts around 11pm in most clubs. By far the best place in Cusco for nightly live music is **Ukukus,** Plateros 316, 2nd floor (© 084/227-867). The range of acts extends from bar rock to Afro-Peruvian, and the crowd jams the dance floor. Often the mix is half gringo, half Peruvian. It's open until the wee hours (5am), and there's pizza and 24-hour Internet. Pick up a pass for free entrance so you don't get stuck paying a cover. **Kamikase,** Plaza Regocijo 274, second floor (© 084/233-865), is a two-level bar and a live music area with tables and funky decor. Music ranges from "rock en español" to reggae. **Rosie O'Grady's** (see "Bars & Pubs," above) also has live music on weekends (usually Peruvian, jazz, and blues).

DISCOS A young crowd of both backpackers and Peruvians is lured to the discos by the free drink cards handed out on the Plaza de Armas. Popular and often full and sweaty, **Mama América,** at the corner of Calle Triunfo and Santa Catalina Angosta, just off the Plaza de Armas (Portal Belén 115, 2nd floor; © 084/241-979), spins a good international dance mix of Latin, reggae, rock, and techno, as does its not-exactly-amicable spinoff, **Mama Africa** (Portal Harinas 191; © 084/241-979). Both are decent downscale spots for cheap drinks. **Eko,** Plateros 334, Second Floor (no phone), is the hottest dance club. It throbs with a variety of rock and techno; for those who need a break, there's a cool and laid-back lounge out back. With two bars and a fleet of what seems like dozens of young girls enticing visitors with free drink cards, **Bar Xcess,** Portal de Carnes 298 (© 084/240-901), swarms with one of Cusco's youngest crowds.

TRADITIONAL PERUVIAN MUSIC You can catch Peruvian bands with a beat at Ukukus and Rosie O'Grady's (see "Live Music," above), but for a traditional folklore music–and–dance show, you'll need to check out one of the restaurants featuring nightly entertainment. In addition to **El Truco** (p. 611) and **La Retama** (p. 611), **Tunupa,** Portal de Confituria 233, Plaza de Armas (© 084/252-936), has a pretty good traditional music and dance show.

MOVIES Probably the best selection of films, mostly American, shows at **The Film Movies & Lounge,** Procuradores 389, second floor (no phone); it has a nice little bar and serves food. Other screens showing movies, usually daily, can be found at **Ukuku's,** Plateros 316, and **Andes Grill,** Portal de Panes, Plaza de Armas.

5 The Sacred Valley of the Incas

The Urubamba Valley, better known as the Valle Sagrado or Sacred Valley of the Incas, is a relaxed stretch of villages and ancient ruins spread across a broad plain and the gentle mountain slopes northwest of Cusco. Through the valley rolls the revered Río Urubamba, a pivotal religious feature of the Incas' cosmology. With the river as its source, the fertile valley was a major center of agricultural production for the Incas, who grew native Andean crops such as white corn, coca, and potatoes. Along with Cusco and Machu Picchu, the Valle Sagrado is one of the highlights of Peru—if you're visiting either of the former, it would be a shame not to spend at least a couple of days in the valley. The magnificent ruins found from Pisac to Ollantaytambo and beyond are testaments to the region's immense ceremonial importance. The Incas built several of the empire's greatest estates, temples, and royal palaces between the sacred centers of Cusco and Machu Picchu. Today, the villages of the Sacred Valley remain starkly, charmingly traditional. Quechua-speaking residents work the fields and harvest salt with methods unchanged since the days of the Incas, and market days—although now conducted to attract the tourist trade as well as intervillage commerce—remain important rituals.

If you have the time, a good way to explore the valley is to advance town by town toward Machu Picchu or vice versa, starting out from Machu Picchu and returning piecemeal towards Cusco. Seeing the valley's highlights on a daylong guided bus tour is certainly doable, but it can't compare to a leisurely pace that allows you an overnight stay and the chance to soak up the area's immense history, relaxed character, stunning scenery and, in the dry season, equally gorgeous springlike weather. Not only that, the valley is about 500m (1,640 ft.) lower than Cusco, making it much more agreeable for those potentially afflicted with altitude-related health problems. More and more visitors are now spending several days in the valley, choosing to base themselves in Pisac, Urubamba, or Ollantaytambo rather than the capital of the department, Cusco.

ESSENTIALS
GETTING THERE & AROUND
BY GUIDED TOUR Nearly every Cusco travel agency offers a 1-day Sacred Valley tour for as little as $20 per person, and most provide English-speaking guides. The tours tend to coincide with market days (Tues, Thurs, and Sun) and generally include Pisac, Ollantaytambo, and Chinchero.

BY TRAIN The only spots in the Sacred Valley you can reach by train are Urubamba and Ollantaytambo, roughly midway on the Cusco–Machu Picchu route. All trains traveling from Cusco to Machu Picchu stop at Ollantaytambo. Passengers traveling just from Ollantaytambo to Machu Picchu, or the reverse, take either the **Vistadome** ($69 adults round-trip) or **Backpacker** ($48 adults round-trip) train.

Trains depart Cusco from **Estación San Pedro,** Calle Cascaparo s/n (© **084/ 221-352** or 084/221-313), and arrive in Ollantaytambo about 2 hours later. The train station in Ollantaytambo is a long 15-minute walk from the main square. Besides the Inca Trail, the train is the only option for traveling from Ollantaytambo to Machu Picchu.

BY BUS Local buses (often small *combis* or *colectivos*) are the easiest and cheapest way to get around the Sacred Valley. They are often full of color if not comfort. (Tall people forced to stand will not find them much fun, however.) Buses to and from the Sacred Valley use terminals on Calle Huáscar and Calle Intiqhawarina, off Tullumayo, in Cusco. They leave regularly throughout the day, departing when full. Fares are generally S/2 to S/3 (about $1 or less). The trip to Pisac takes about an hour; for Urubamba, just over 2 hours from Cusco, you can go via Pisac or via Chinchero. To travel to Ollantaytambo, you'll need to change buses at the terminal in Urubamba. The train is a simpler option if you don't plan on intermediate stops in the valley.

In **Pisac,** buses leave for Cusco and other parts of the valley from the main street just across the river (about 3 blocks west of the main square). In **Urubamba,** buses for Cusco and Chinchero leave from the Terminal Terrestre about 1km (½ mile) from town on the main road to Ollantaytambo (just beyond and across from the Incaland Hotel). *Combis* for other points in the valley depart from the intersection of the main road at Avenida Castilla. In **Ollantaytambo,** buses for Cusco depart from Avenida Estación, the main street leading away from the rail terminal.

BY TAXI You can hire a taxi for a daylong tour of the Sacred Valley or any of the valley towns; expect to pay about S/50 ($14). While a taxi to Pisac on your own may cost $10, it is often possible to go by private car for as little as S/3 (75¢) per person. Taxis from Ollantaytambo to Cusco generally charge about $20.

VISITOR INFORMATION

You're best off getting information on the Sacred Valley before leaving Cusco at the helpful main Tourist Information Office (see "Visitor Information," earlier in this chapter). Cusco's **South American Explorers Club,** Choquechaca 188, Apto. 4 (© **084/245-484;** www.saexplorers.org), is also an excellent source of information, particularly on the Inca Trail and other treks, mountaineering, and white-water rafting in the valley. Inquire there about current conditions and updated transportation alternatives. In the valley itself, you may be able to scare up some limited assistance in Urubamba (Av. Cabo Conchatupa s/n), Ollantaytambo (the CATCO museum, off Principal), and Yucay (office of Turismo Participativo, Plaza Manco II 103; © **084/201-099**). Beyond that, the best sources of information are hotels.

FAST FACTS You can exchange dollars—in cash—with small shops in Pisac or Ollantaytambo; in Urubamba, there are ATMs on either side of the main road to Yucay.

In a medical emergency, contact **Centro de Salud,** Av. Cabo Conchatupa s/n, Urubamba (© 084/201-334), or **Hospital del Instituto Peruano de Seguridad Social,** Avenida 9 de Noviembre, Urubamba (© 084/201-032). For the police, contact **Policía Nacional,** Calle Palacio s/n, Urubamba (© 084/201-092).

Urubamba has one of the best Internet *cabinas* in all of Peru, with a good supply of machines and fast connections. **Academia Internet Urubamba,** begun with the help of an American exchange student, is 2 blocks northeast of the Plaza de Armas, on the corner of Jirón Belén and Jirón Grau. The **post office** in Pisac is on the corner of Comercio and Intihuatana, in Ollantaytambo and Urubamba on their respective Plazas de Armas.

The Sacred Valley

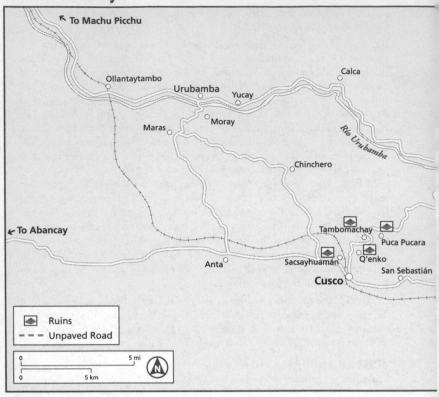

PISAC ⋆⋆

The pretty Andean village of Pisac lies at the eastern end of the valley, 32km (20 miles) from Cusco. Though the town seems to be prized principally for its Sunday artisan market, Pisac should be more widely recognized for its splendid Inca ruins, which rival Machu Picchu. Perched high on a cliff is the largest fortress complex built by the Incas. The commanding distant views from atop the mountain, over a luxuriously long valley of green patchwork fields, are breathtaking.

Pisac's famed **market** draws hundreds of visitors on Sunday mornings in high season, when it is without doubt one of the liveliest in Peru. (There are slightly less popular markets on Tues and Thurs as well.) Hundreds of stalls crowd the central square and spill down side streets. Sellers come from many villages, many of them remote places high in the Andes, and wear the dress typical of their village. Dignitaries from the local villages usually lead processions after Mass (said in Quechua), dressed in their versions of Sunday finery. The goods for sale at the market—sweaters, ponchos, rugs—are familiar to anyone who's spent at least a day in Cusco, but prices are occasionally lower on selected goods such as ceramics. The market begins at around 9am and lasts until midafternoon.

The Pisac **ruins** ⋆⋆⋆ are some of the finest in the entire valley. The best but most time-consuming way to see the ruins is to climb the hillside, an extraordinary

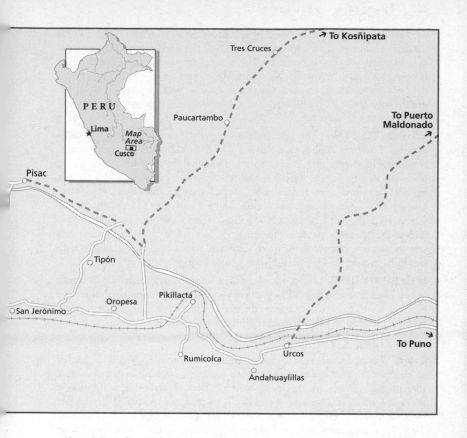

path and slice of local life. Trudging along steep mountain paths is still the way most Quechua descendants from remote villages get around these parts; many people you see at the Pisac market will have walked a couple of hours or more to get there. To reach the site on foot (about 5km/3 miles, or about 90 min.), you'll need to be pretty fit and/or willing to take it very slowly. Begin the ascent at the back of the main square, to the left of the church. The path bends to the right through agricultural terraces. There appear to be several competing paths; all of them lead up the mountain to the ruins. When you come to a section that rises straight up, choose the extremely steep stairs to the right (the path to the left is overgrown and poorly defined). If an arduous trek is more than you've bargained for, you can also hire a taxi in Pisac (easier done on market days) to take you around the back way. If you arrive by car or *colectivo* rather than by your own power, the ruins will be laid out the opposite of the way they are described below. The ruins are open daily from 7am to 5:30pm; admission is by boleto turístico (see "Cusco's Boleto Turístico" on p. 599).

From a semicircular terrace and fortified section at the top, called the **Quori-huayrachina,** the views south and west are spectacular. The Pisac nucleus was both a fortress and ceremonial center, and its delicately cut stones are some of the best found at any Inca site. The most important component of the complex is the **Templo del Sol (Temple of the Sun),** one of the Incas' most impressive examples of masonry, found on the upper section of the ruins. There you'll find the **Intiwatana,** the so-called "hitching post of the sun," which looks to be a sundial but, in fact, is an instrument that helped the Incas determine the arrival of important growing seasons. Nearby (just paces to the west) are another temple, thought to be the Temple of the Moon, and a ritual bathing complex, fed by water canals. Continuing north from this section, as you pass along the eastern edge of the cliff, you'll arrive at a tunnel, which leads to a summit look-out at 3,400m (11,200 ft.).

WHERE TO STAY   The best place to stay in Pisac is **Hotel Royal Inka Pisac** ⟨R⟩, Carretera Pisac Ruinas Km 1.5 s/n (✆ **084/222-284** for reservations; www.royalinkahotel.com), about a 15-minute walk from the village along a road up to the Inca ruins. The hotel has a surprising array of facilities and activities, including a tennis court, indoor pool, sauna, horseback riding, and mountain-bike rentals. The ample and comfortable double rooms cost $64 to $70. A good alternative is the small, pleasant **Hotel Pisaq,** Plaza Constitución 333 (✆ **084/ 203-062;** htpisaq@mail.cosapidata.com.pe). The warm little inn has a sauna and an attractive courtyard; the nicely decorated rooms cost $10 per person with shared bathroom, $13 per person with private bathroom.

WHERE TO DINE   For good trout dishes from the river, check out **Samana Wasi,** Plaza Constitución 509. Another good bet is the excellent **bakery** on Mariscal Castilla, a short walk from the plaza. The bakery serves excellent vege-tarian *empanadas* and breads from traditional adobe ovens.

URUBAMBA & YUCAY

Centrally located Urubamba (77km/48 miles northwest of Cusco) is the busiest of the Sacred Valley towns. Although the town itself doesn't have much more than magnificent mountain scenery to offer visitors, several of the best hotels in the region are located between it and Yucay, an attractive colonial village backed by a sophisticated system of agricultural terraces and irrigation canals, about 3km (1¾ miles) down the road. The area is a fine base from which to explore the Sacred Valley region.

The main square of Urubamba, the Plaza de Armas, is handsomely framed by a twin-towered colonial church and *pisonay* trees. Dozens of *mototaxis,* a funky form of local transportation not seen in other places in the valley, buzz around the plaza in search of passengers. Worth visiting in town is the beautiful home and workshop of **Pablo Seminario,** Calle Berriozábal 111 (✆ **084/201-002**), a ceramicist whose whimsical work features pre-Columbian motifs and is sold throughout Peru. The grounds are a minizoo, with llamas, parrots, nocturnal monkeys, falcons, rabbits, and more.

About 6km (3½ miles) down the main road toward Ollantaytambo is the amazing sight of the **Salineras de Maras** ⟨RR⟩, thousands of individual ancient salt pans that form unique terraces in a hillside. The mines, small pools thickly coated with crystallized salt like dirty snow, have existed in the same spot since Inca days and are still operable. Families pass them down like deeds and con-tinue the backbreaking and poorly remunerated tradition of salt extraction (crystallizing salt from subterranean spring water). To get to the salt pans, take a taxi to a point near the village of Tarabamba. (You can either have the taxi wait for you or hail a *combi* on the main road when you return.) From there, it's a lovely 45-minute walk along a footpath next to the river. There are no signs; cross the footbridge and bend right along the far side of the river and up through

Extreme Sacred Valley

The Sacred Valley region is one of the best in South America for white-water rafting, mountain biking, trekking, hang gliding, and paragliding. River runs are extremely popular, and justifiably so: Peru has some of the world's wildest rivers. The most popular activity is, of course, hiking the Inca Trail to Machu Picchu, but there are plenty of other adventure opportunities. Many tour operators in Cusco organize adventure trips. Participants range from novices to hard-core adventure junkies; no experience is required for many trips, but make sure you sign up for a program appropriate for your level of interest and ability. Extreme sports being what they are, thoroughly check out potential agencies and speak directly to the guides, if possible. Hunting for bargains in this category is not advisable; quality equipment and good English-speaking guides are fundamental for safety considerations.

WHITE-WATER RAFTING   There are some terrific Andean river runs near Cusco, ranging from mild class II to moderate and world-class IV and V. Recommended agencies include **Amazonas Explorer** (© 084/236-826 or 084/225-284; www.amazonas-explorer.com); **Apumayo Expediciones** (© 084/246-018; www.cuscoperu.com/apumayo); **Eric Adventures** (© 084/228-475; www.ericadventures.com); **Instinct Travel** (© 084/233-451; www.instinct-travel.com); **Loreto Tours** (© 084/236-331); and **Mayuc** (© 084/232-666; www.mayuc.com).

TREKKING   In addition to the groups that organize Inca Trail hikes (see "Hiking the Inca Trail" on p. 630), the following agencies handle a wide variety of trekking excursions: **Apu Expeditions** (© 084/652-975); **Aventours** (© 084/224-050; www.aventours.com); **Manu Expeditions** (© 084/226-671; www.manuexpeditions.com); **Mayuc** (© 084/232-666; www.mayuc.com); and U.S.-based **Andean Treks** (© 800/683-8148 or © 617/924-1974; www.andeantreks.com/peru.htm).

MOUNTAIN BIKING   Mountain biking is just really beginning to catch on, and tour operators are rapidly expanding their services and equipment. **Amazonas Explorer, Apumayo Expediciones, Eric Adventures, Instinct Travel** (see "White-Water Rafting," above), and **Manu Ecological Adventures** (© 084/261-640; www.cbc.org.pe/manu) offer 1- to 5-day organized mountain biking excursions ranging from easy to rigorous.

BALLOONING & PARAGLIDING   **Globos de los Andes** (© 084/232-352; www.globosperu.com) has been on-again and off-again in past years, but if you want aerial panoramas of the Sacred Valley, Inca ruins, and the majestic Andes, they're the only outfit doing such trips. You might also check around Cusco for posters advertising tandem paraglider flights over the Sacred Valley.

the mountains toward the salt pans. As you begin the gentle climb up the mountain, stick to the right to avoid the cliff-hugging, inches-wide trail that forks to the left.

WHERE TO STAY   One of the best hotels in the region is the handsome, ranch-style **Sonesta Posada del Inca** ⍟, Plaza Manco II de Yucay 123, Yucay (© **084/201-107;** www.sonesta.com). Originally a monastery in the late 1600s and then a hacienda, it is now a colonial village–like complex with great character, great mountain views, and relaxed comfort. Double rooms cost $90.

Closer to Urubamba is the charming and rustic **Hotel San Agustín Monasterio de la Recoleta** ⍟, Calle Recoleta s/n, off the main road to Ollantaytambo (© **084/201-420;** fax 084/201-004). Less polished and luxurious than Posada del Inca, it has far simpler rooms for $65 to $70. Ask for a room in the old part of the convent and climb up to the bell tower above the old chapel for great views of the valley. In Huicho, 2km (1¼ mile) west of Urubamba, **Hotel Sol y Luna** ⍟⍟ (©/fax **084/201-620;** www.hotelsolyluna.com) is a French- and Swiss-owned cluster of 14 invitingly decorated, circular bungalow-style rooms (including four family bungalows) with private terraces, surrounded by beautifully landscaped gardens and gorgeous mountain views. The hotel has a nice if small pool and restaurant and pub, and there's also an adventure club offering all sorts of outdoor activities in the region. Opened in 2000, Sol y Luna is one of the nicest spots in the valley. Doubles cost $105; a family bungalow runs $155.

WHERE TO DINE   **Hotel Sol y Luna** (see above) has a fine restaurant, open for lunch and dinner. The best restaurant in Urubamba—and the entire Sacred Valley—is **La Casa de la Abuela** ⍟⍟, Bolívar 272 (© **084/622-975**), a charming, warm house a couple of blocks from the Plaza de Armas. Specializing in wood-fired pizza, pasta, and tasty home-cooked Peruvian dishes (such as delicious trout), the restaurant has several dining rooms and an inviting living room/bar area. People flock here for the Carnaval fiestas and *noches criollas,* when there's *peña* music. Sadly, the owner recently fell ill and she now opens only by advance arrangement (have your hotel call ahead to inquire).

Chez Mary, Plaza de Armas (at the corner of Comercio and Grau; © **084/ 201-280**), is a funky two-story pub/restaurant that features good soups and sandwiches, as well as *ceviche* and grilled or garlic trout. At night, it is more hip music pub than restaurant. Out on the main road going toward Yucay, **Quinta Los Geranios,** Av. Cabo Conchatupa s/n (© **084/201-093**), is a good open-air restaurant, set around a garden. It gets hit midday with tour buses but still manages to concoct fine versions of Peruvian standards such as *rocoto relleno* (stuffed hot peppers) and a number of indigenous soups. The three-course lunch menu is a good value.

OLLANTAYTAMBO ⍟⍟⍟

A tongue twister of a town, this lovely little place 97km (60 miles) northwest of Cusco is affectionately called Ollanta (oh-*yan*-tah) by locals. Plenty of outsiders who can't pronounce it fall in love with the town, too. The scenery around Ollantaytambo is some of the loveliest in the region. The snowcapped mountains that embrace the town frame a much narrower valley here than at Urubamba or Pisac, and both sides of the gorge are lined with Inca *andenes,* or agricultural terraces. Most extraordinary are the precipitous terraced ruins of a massive temple-fortress built by the Inca Pachacutec. Below the ruins, Ollantaytambo's old town is a splendid grid of streets lined with adobe brick walls, blooming bougainvillea, and perfect canals, still carrying rushing water down from the mountains. Except for the couple of hours a day when tour buses deposit large groups at the foot of the fortress (where a handicrafts market habitually breaks out to welcome them), the town is quiet.

The Inca elite adopted Ollantaytambo, building irrigation systems and a crowning temple designed for worship and astronomical observation. The **ruins** *★★* represent one of the Incas' most formidable feats of architecture. Rising above the valley and an ancient square (Plaza Mañaraki) are dozens of rows of stunningly steep stone terraces carved into the hillside. They appear both forbidding and admirably perfect. The Incas were able to successfully defend the site against the Spanish in 1537, protecting Manco Inca after his retreat here from defeat at Sacsayhuamán. The complex was in all probability more a temple than a citadel to the Incas. The upper section—reached after you've climbed 200 steps—contains typically masterful masonry of the kind that adorned great Inca temples. A massive and elegant doorjamb indicates the principal entry to the temple; to its left is a series of 10 niches. On the next level are six huge pink granite blocks, amazingly cut, polished, and fitted together, which appear to be parts of rooms never completed. On the stones, you can still make out faint, ancient symbolic markings in relief. Across the valley is the quarry that provided the stones for the structure; a great ramp descending from the hilltop ruins was the means by which the Incas transported the massive stones from several kilometers away. The ruins are open daily from 7am to 5:30pm; admission is by boleto turístico (see "Cusco's Boleto Turístico" on p. 599). To see the ruins in peace before the tour buses arrive, get there before 11am. Early morning is best of all, when the sun rises over mountains to the east and then quickly bathes the entire valley in light.

A footpath winds up the hill behind an outer wall of the ruins to a clearing and wall with niches that have led some to believe prisoners were tied up here— a theory that is unfounded. Regardless of the purpose, the views south over the Urubamba Valley and of the snowcapped peak of Verónica are outstanding. At the bottom of the terraces, next to the Patacancha River, are the **Baños de la Ñusta (Princess Baths),** a place of ceremonial bathing. Wedged into the mountains facing the baths are granaries built by the Incas. Locals like to point out the face of the Inca carved into the cliff high above the valley. (If you can't make it out, ask the guard at the entrance to the ruins for a little help.)

The **Old Town** *★★*, below the ruins and across the River Patacancha, is the finest extant example of the Incas' masterful urban planning. Many original residential *canchas,* or blocks, each inhabited by several families during the 15th century, are still present; each *cancha* had a single entrance opening onto a main courtyard. The finest streets of this stone village are directly behind the main square. Get a good glimpse of community life within a *cancha* by peeking in at Calle del Medio (Calle Chautik'ikllu), where a couple of neighbor houses have a small shop in a courtyard and their ancestors' skulls displayed as shrines on the walls of their living quarters. The entire village retains a solid Amerindian air, unperturbed by the crowds of gringos who wander through, snapping photos of children and old women. It's a traditional place, largely populated by locals in colorful native dress and women who pace up and down the streets or through fields absentmindedly spinning the ancient spools used in making hand-woven textiles.

On the edge of the old town, 2 blocks northwest of the Plaza Mayor, is an enjoyable and well presented but not indispensable **CATCO** (Centro Andino de Tecnología y Cultural de Ollantaytambo) **Ethnographic and History**

Museum. It's open Tuesday through Sunday from 10am to 1pm and 2 to 4pm; admission is S/5 ($1.50).

WHERE TO STAY   El Albergue 𝒢, located next to the railway station platform in Ollantaytambo (𝒞/fax **084/204-014;** www.bed42.com/elalbergue), is a homey hostel owned by a longtime American resident of Ollantaytambo. With large, comfortable, and nicely—if austerely—furnished rooms, great gardens, a wood-fired sauna, three Labrador retrievers roaming the grounds, and a spot right next to the train to Machu Picchu, it's usually full. Rooms with shared bathrooms cost $30. On the road from the train station to town, **Hotel Pakaritampu** 𝒢𝒢, Av. Ferrocarril s/n, Ollantaytambo (𝒞 **084/204-020;** www. pakaritampu.com), is quite upscale for unassuming Ollantaytambo. Rooms are very tasteful, with sturdy, comfortable furnishings, and there's a nice restaurant/bar. Double rooms cost $104. Sandwiched between the main square of the village and the CATCO museum, **Hostal Sauce,** Calle Ventiderio 248, Ollantaytambo (𝒞 **084/204-044**), is a modern and comfortable free-standing building with a smattering of very clean, nicely equipped rooms, which cost $69 ($59 cash). Some rooms have superb views of the ruins. Budget travelers gravitate toward **Hostal Las Orquídeas** (𝒞 **084/204-032**), which has clean and simple rooms with shared bathrooms for $20; and **Hostal La Ñusta,** Carretera Ocobamba (𝒞 **084/204-032**), a clean and friendly place with good views from the balcony. Rooms with shared bathrooms are $10 per person.

WHERE TO DINE   Kusicoyllor, Plaza Araccama s/n (𝒞 **084/204-103**), is a cool cafe/bar right next to ruins, so you might expect it to be a tad touristy and overpriced, which it is—but it's still nice. It serves standard Peruvian and predominantly Italian dishes and offers a fixed-price menu ($7). Breakfast is especially good, making it a fine stop after an early-morning tour of the ruins. **Restaurant El Mirador,** Calle Convención s/n (no phone), is a great place for a simple lunch of *lomo saltado* or a basic chicken dish. You'll be tempted to sit for hours drinking beer, gazing at the mountains, and toasting your good fortune of having time to relax on your own in Ollantaytambo. **Bar-Restaurant Tunupa,** Av. Estación s/n (no phone), is an inexpensive family-run terrace joint between the main plaza and the ruins, and it has a very agreeable open-air atmosphere. It serves breakfast, lunch, and dinner, and has a surprisingly wide-ranging menu and great views of the ruins. **El Alcázar Café,** Calle Medio (𝒞 **084/204-034**), is an informal but reliable little place mostly open for lunch only. You can get a good home-cooked meal at the hostel by the train station, **El Albergue** (see "Where to Stay," above). Other cheap restaurants, such as **Bar Ollantay** and **Fortaleza,** ring the main square.

MACHU PICCHU 𝒢𝒢𝒢

The Incas hid Machu Picchu so high in the clouds that the empire-raiding Spaniards never found it. It is no longer lost, of course, and you can now zip there by high-speed train as well as by a more traditional 2- or 4-day trek, but Machu Picchu retains its great sense of mystery and magic. No longer overgrown with brush, as it was when it was discovered—with the aid of a local farmer who knew of its existence—by the Yale historian Hiram Bingham in 1911, it still cannot be seen from below. The majestic setting that the Incas chose for it is unchanged. And when the early morning sun rises over the peaks and methodically illuminates the ruins' row by row of granite stones, Machu Picchu leaves visitors as awestruck as ever.

Machu Picchu

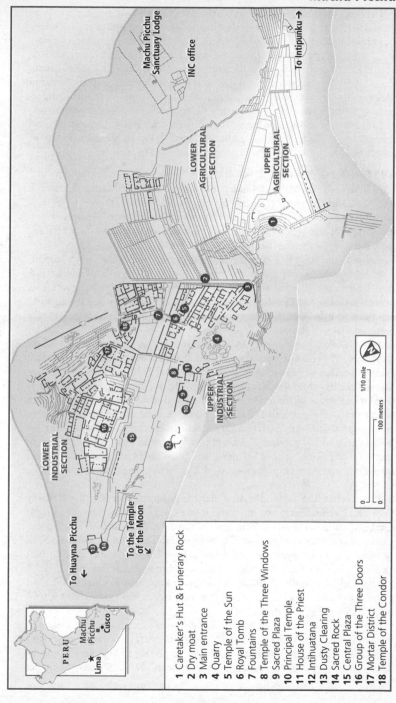

To Huayna Picchu →

To the Temple of the Moon ↓

Machu Picchu Sanctuary Lodge

INC office

To Intipunku →

LOWER AGRICULTURAL SECTION

UPPER AGRICULTURAL SECTION

UPPER INDUSTRIAL SECTION

LOWER INDUSTRIAL SECTION

1 Caretaker's Hut & Funerary Rock
2 Dry moat
3 Main entrance
4 Quarry
5 Temple of the Sun
6 Royal Tomb
7 Fountains
8 Temple of the Three Windows
9 Sacred Plaza
10 Principal Temple
11 House of the Priest
12 Intihuatana
13 Dusty Clearing
14 Sacred Rock
15 Central Plaza
16 Group of the Three Doors
17 Mortar District
18 Temple of the Condor

PERU

Lima ★

Machu Picchu ■

Cusco ■

1/10 mile

100 meters

The great majority of visitors to Machu Picchu still do it as a day trip from Cusco, but many people feel that a few hurried hours to the ruins at peak hours, amidst throngs of people following guided tours, simply do not suffice. By staying at least 1 night, either at the one upscale hotel just outside the grounds of Machu Picchu or down below in the town of Aguas Calientes (also called Machu Picchu Pueblo), you can remain at the ruins later in the afternoon after most of the tour groups have gone home, or get there for sunrise—a dramatic, unforgettable sight. Aguas Calientes is a tiny tourist trade town where weary backpackers rest up and celebrate their treks along the Inca Trail over cheap eats and cheaper beers. There are some additional good hikes in the area, but most people head back to Cusco after a couple of days in the area.

GETTING TO MACHU PICCHU

BY TRAIN   The 112km (69-mile) train from Cusco to Machu Picchu is a truly spectacular journey. It zigzags up Huayna Picchu and then through lush valleys hugging the Río Urubamba, with views of snowcapped Andes peaks in the distance. There are three tourist trains from Cusco to Machu Picchu, taking just under 4 hours: the **Backpacker,** the slowest and least expensive; the **Vistadome,** the faster first-class service; and the top-of-the-line, newly inaugurated luxury line **Hiram Bingham** (named after the discoverer of Machu Picchu). The tourist trains, all of which now belong to Orient-Express, depart from Cusco's **Estación San Pedro** on Calle Cascaparo; it's open Monday through Friday from 5am to 3pm, Saturday and Sunday from 5am to 12:30pm. Hiram Bingham trains depart from Poroy station, a 15-minute drive from Cusco, 6 days a week in high season (Apr–Oct) and 4 days a week in low season (Nov–Mar). Tickets may also be purchased at **Estación Huanchaq** on Avenida Pachacutec; it's open Monday through Friday from 8:30am to 5:30pm, Saturday and Sunday from 8:30am to 12:30pm. The Backpacker departs Cusco at 6:15am and arrives in Aguas Calientes at 10:10am; the Vistadome leaves at 6am and arrives at 9:40am; and the Hiram Bingham starts out at 9am and arrives at 12:30pm. Fares are $60 round-trip for Backpacker, $89 round-trip for Vistadome, and $350 round-trip for Hiram Bingham (which includes brunch, afternoon tea, guided tour of the ruins, and cocktails and dinner on the return trip). For the best views on the way to Machu Picchu, sit on the left side of the train.

Travelers based in the Urubamba Valley can go by the **Sacred Valley Railway** to Machu Picchu. Vistadome-class service originates in Urubamba (departing at 6am) and Ollantaytambo (departing at 7:05 and 10:30am, and 2:05pm); Backpacker-class service originates in Ollantaytambo. The journey takes 2 hours, 20 minutes from Urubamba and 90 minutes from Ollantaytambo. Trains depart Urubamba at 6am and Ollanta at 7:05am, arriving in Aguas Calientes (Machu Picchu Pueblo) at 7:40, 10:40am, and 4:55pm. Returning to Ollanta, the train leaves at 8am, 2:05, and 5:20pm. The trip costs $69 in Vistadome class and $48 in Backpacker class round-trip.

Train schedules and names and classes of service have changed frequently in the past few years, so verify hours and fares before you go. It's wise to make your reservation at least a day (or more) in advance, especially in high season. For the luxury service, reservations several weeks or more in advance are recommended.

BY HELICOPTER   All helicopter flights to Machu Picchu have been suspended indefinitely, due to environmental concerns.

(Tips Package Visits to Machu Picchu

One-day Machu Picchu tour packages that include a round-trip train ride from Cusco to Aguas Calientes (Machu Picchu Pueblo), a bus to the ruins, admission, a guided tour, and sometimes lunch at Machu Picchu Sanctuary Lodge, can be purchased from travel agencies in Cusco. They generally cost between $90 and $110; it's worth shopping around for the best deal. Try **Gatur Tour,** Puluchapata 140 (© **084/223-496**); **Milla Turismo,** Av. Pardo 689 (© **084/231-710**), or any of the tour agencies that organize Inca Trail treks (see "Hiking the Inca Trail" on p. 630). Packages that include overnight accommodations can also be arranged.

BY BUS   You can't travel from Cusco to Machu Picchu by bus, but if you walk the Inca Trail or ascend the slope to the ruins from the town of Aguas Calientes, you can take one of the frequent buses that depart from the railroad tracks. The buses wend their way up the mountain, performing exaggerated switchbacks for 15 minutes before suddenly depositing passengers at the entrance to the ruins. The cost is $9 round-trip. There's no need to reserve; just purchase your ticket at the little booth in front of the lineup of buses. Buses begin running at 6:30am and come down all day, with the last one descending at dusk. Some people choose to purchase a one-way ticket up and walk down (30–45 min.) to Aguas Calientes.

BY FOOT   The celebrated **Inca Trail (Camino del Inca)** is almost as famous as the ruins themselves, and the trek is rightly viewed as an attraction in itself. See "Hiking the Inca Trail" on p. 630 for more details.

EXPLORING MACHU PICCHU

Since its initial exploration by American archaeologists from 1911 to 1915, Machu Picchu has resonated far beyond the status of a mere archaeological site. Reputed to be the legendary "lost city of the Incas," it is deeply steeped in mystery and folklore. The ruins of the complex—the only significant Inca site to escape the ravenous appetites of the conquistadors in the 16th century—rank as the top attraction in Peru, arguably the greatest in South America, and for my money, one of the world's most stunning sights. Countless glossy photographs of the ruins, gently positioned like a saddle between two massive peaks swathed in cottony clouds, can't do it justice.

Invisible from the Urubamba Valley below, Machu Picchu lay dormant for more than 4 centuries, nestled nearly 2,400m (8,000 ft.) above sea level under thick jungle and known only to a handful of Amerindian peasants. Never mentioned in the Spanish chronicles, it was seemingly lost in the collective memory of the Incas and their descendants. Its unearthing raised more questions than it answered, and experts still argue over its purpose. Was it a citadel? An agricultural site? An astronomical observatory? A ceremonial city or sacred retreat for the Inca emperor? Or some combination of all of these? Adding to the mystery, this complex city of exceedingly fine architecture and masonry was constructed, inhabited, and abandoned all in less than a century—a flash in the 4,000-year history of Andean Peru. It was very probably abandoned even before the arrival of the Spanish, perhaps a result of the Incas' civil war. Or perhaps it was drought that drove the Incas elsewhere.

Yale historian Hiram Bingham had thought Machu Picchu to be the lost city of Vilcabamba, the last refuge of the rebellious Manco Inca. Machu Picchu is not that lost city, which exists deeper in the jungle, at Espíritu Pampa. Most believe that the Inca Pachacutec, who founded the Inca Empire, had Machu Picchu built sometime in the mid-1400s. It appears that the complex was both a ceremonial and agricultural center. Never looted by the Spanish, many of its architectural features remain in excellent condition—even if they do little to advance our understanding of the exact nature of Machu Picchu.

One thing is certain: Machu Picchu is one of the world's great examples of landscape art. The Incas revered nature, worshipping celestial bodies and more earthly streams and stones. The spectacular setting of Machu Picchu reveals just how much they reveled in their environment. Steep terraces, gardens, granite and limestone temples, staircases, and aqueducts seem to be carved directly out of the hillside. Forms echo the very shape of the surrounding mountains, and windows and instruments appear to have been constructed to track the sun during the June and December solstices. Machu Picchu lies 300m (1,000 ft.) lower than Cusco, but you'd imagine the exact opposite, so nestled are the ruins among mountaintops and clouds.

Appreciating Machu Picchu for its aesthetic qualities is no slight to its significance. The Incas obviously chose the site for the power of its natural beauty. They, like we, must have been in awe of the snowcapped peaks to the east; the rugged panorama of towering, forested mountains and the sacred cliff of Putukusi to the west; and the city sitting gracefully like a proud saddle between two huge peaks. It remains one of the most thrilling sights in the world. At daybreak, when the sun's rays creep over the jagged silhouette, sometimes turning the distant snow peaks fiery orange and then slowly casting brilliant light on the ruins building by building and row by row, it's enough to move some observers to tears and others to squeals of delight.

Visiting the Ruins

From May to September, as many as 1,000 visitors a day visit the ruins. Even that number, though, is rarely overwhelming. The place is large enough to escape most tour group bottlenecks, though people fearful of the crush should plan to arrive before 11am and/or stay past 3pm. Perhaps the worst time to visit is from July 28 to August 10, when Peruvian national holidays bring untold numbers of school groups and families to Machu Picchu.

The ruins are open from dawn to dusk; the first visitors, usually those staying at the hotel next door or arriving from the Inca Trail, enter at 6am. Everyone is ushered out by 6pm. The entrance fee is $20 (half-price with an ISIC card). You will be given a map of the ruins, which gives the names of the individual sections, but no detailed explanations. The numbers indicated in brackets below follow our own map on p. 625. For a detailed guide of the ruins and their history, Peter Frost's *Exploring Cusco,* available in Cusco bookstores, is quite excellent.

English-speaking guides can be independently arranged on-site. Most charge around $15 to $20 for a private 2-hour tour. You can also join a tour group for little more than $2 or $3 per person.

Inside the Ruins

After passing through the ticket booth, you can either head left and straight up the hill, or down to the right. The path up to the left takes you to the spot above the ruins, near the **Caretaker's Hut** and **Funerary Rock** [1], which affords the classic postcard overview of Machu Picchu. If you are here early enough for sunrise (6:30–7:30am), by all means go here first. The hut overlooks rows and rows of steep agricultural terraces. From this vantage point, you can see clearly the full layout of Machu Picchu, which had clearly defined agricultural and urban zones; a long **dry moat** [2] separates the two sectors. A population of perhaps 1,000 lived here at the high point of Machu Picchu.

Head down into the main section of the ruins, past a series of burial grounds and dwellings and the **main entrance to the city** [3]. A section of stones, likely a **quarry** [4], sits atop a clearing with occasionally great views of the snowcapped peaks (Cordillera Vilcabamba) to the southwest.

Down a steep series of stairs is one of the most famous Inca constructions, the **Temple of the Sun** [5] (also called the Torreón). The rounded, tapering tower has extraordinary stonework, the finest in Machu Picchu; its large stones fit together seamlessly. From the ledge above the temple, you can appreciate the window perfectly aligned for the June winter solstice, when the sun's rays come streaming through at dawn and illuminate the stone at the center of the temple. The temple is cordoned off, and entry is not permitted. Below the temple, a cave carved from the rock, is a section traditionally called the **Royal Tomb** [6], even though no human remains have been found there. Inside is a meticulously carved altar and series of niches that produce intricate morning shadows. To the north, just down the stairs that divide this section from a series of dwellings called the **Royal Sector,** is a still-functioning water canal and series of interconnected **fountains** [7]. The main fountain is distinguished both by its size and excellent stonework.

Back up the stairs to the high section of the ruins (north of the quarry) is the main ceremonial area. The **Temple of the Three Windows** [8], each a trapezoid extraordinarily cut with views of the Andes in the distance across the Urubamba gorge, is likely to be one of your lasting images of Machu Picchu. It fronts one side of the **Sacred Plaza** [9]. To the left, if you're facing the Temple of the Three Windows, is the **Principal Temple** [10], which has masterful stonework in its three high walls. Directly opposite is the **House of the Priest** [11]. Just behind the Principal Temple is a small cell, termed the **Sacristy** and renowned for its exquisite masonry. It's a good place to examine how amazingly these many-angled stones (one to the left of the doorjamb has 32 distinct angles) were fitted together by Inca stonemasons.

Up a short flight of stairs is the **Intihuatana** [12], popularly called the "hitching post of the sun." It looks to be a ritualistic carved rock or sort of sundial, and its shape echoes that of the sacred peak Huayna Picchu beyond the ruins. The stone almost certainly functioned as an astronomical and agricultural calendar. It appears to be powerfully connected to mountains in all directions. The Incas built similar monuments elsewhere across the empire, but most were destroyed by the Spanish (who surely thought them to be instruments of pagan worship). The one at Machu Picchu survived in perfect form until 2001, when authorities

---

Tips **Come Prepared**

Take a bottle of water in a knapsack to Machu Picchu (not to mention a good sun hat and sunscreen), no matter how long you plan to stay. It gets very warm and the sun is incredibly strong at this elevation, and there's nowhere to go for refreshment (and few places to find shade) besides the hotel at the entrance.

allowed the filming of a Cuzqueña beer commercial here and the crew sneaked in a 1,000-pound crane, which fell over and chipped off the top section of the Intihuatana. All to sell more beer!

Follow a trail down through terraces and past a small plaza to a **dusty clearing** [13] with covered stone benches on either side. Fronting the square is the massive sculpted **Sacred Rock** [14], whose shape mimics that of Putukusi, the sacred peak that looms due east across the valley. This area likely served as a communal area for meetings and perhaps performances.

To the left of the Sacred Rock, down a path, is the gateway to **Huayna Picchu,** the huge outcrop that serves as a dramatic backdrop to Machu Picchu. Though it looks forbidding, it can be climbed by anyone in reasonable shape. The steep path up takes most visitors about an hour or more, though some (including me) have ascended the peak in less than 25 minutes. Guards at a small booth require visitors to sign in and out; the path is open from 7am to 1pm and you must return before 3pm, or they'll come looking for you. The views from the very top, of Machu Picchu below and the panorama of forested mountains, are spectacular. The climb is highly recommended for all energetic sorts. (I've seen octogenarians climb the path at an enviable clip.) In wet weather, you may want to reconsider, as the stone steps can get very slippery and dangerous.

Returning back down the same path (frighteningly steep at a couple points) is a turnoff to the **Temple of the Moon,** usually visited only by Machu Picchu completists. Cleaved into the rock at a point midway down the peak, it almost surely was not a lunar observatory, but it is a strangely forlorn and mysterious place of caverns and niches and enigmatic portals. It has some terrific stonework. The path takes about an hour round-trip from the detour.

Continuing back into the complex, enter the lower section of the ruins, separated from the spiritually oriented upper section by a **Central Plaza** [15]. The lower section was more prosaic in function, mostly residential and industrial. Eventually, you'll come to a series of cells and quarters, called the **Group of the Three Doors** [16] and the **Mortar District** or Industrial Sector [17]. By far the most interesting part of this lower section is the **Temple of the Condor** [18]. Said to be a carving of a giant condor, the rock above symbolizes the great bird's wings. You can actually crawl through the cave at the base of the rock.

HIKING THE INCA TRAIL ★★★

The Incas conceived of both Machu Picchu and the great trail leading to it in grand artistic and spiritual terms. Hiking the Inca Trail—the ancient royal highway—is hands-down the most authentic and scenic way to visit Machu Picchu and get a clear grasp of the Incas' overarching architectural concept and supreme regard for nature. As impressive as Machu Picchu itself, the trail traverses a 325-sq.-km (125-sq.-mile) national park designated the Machu Picchu Historical Sanctuary. The zone is replete with extraordinary natural and man-made sights: Inca ruins, exotic vegetation and animals, and dazzling vistas.

There are two ways to walk to Machu Picchu: either along an arduous 4-day, 3-night path, or as part of a more recently opened 2-day, 1-night trail. You can hire porters to haul your packs or suck it up and do it the hard way, but **you must go as part of an organized group arranged by an officially sanctioned tour agency** (see "New Inca Trail Regulations," below). Independent trekking on the Inca Trail, without an official guide has been prohibited since June 2001. However, a couple or small number of people can organize their own group if they are willing to play higher prices for the luxury of not having to join an ad-hoc group. The classic 4-day route is along hand-hewn stone stairs and through sumptuous mountain scenery, amazing cloud forest, and dozens of Inca ruins. The zone is inhabited by rare orchids, 300-plus species of birds, and even the indigenous spectacled bear. The trek begins at Qorihuayrachina, more easily described as Km 88 of the railway to Aguas Calientes. The 43km (27-mile) route passes three steep mountain passes, including the dreaded "Dead Woman's Pass," to a maximum altitude of 4,200m (13,700 ft.). Virtually all groups enter the ruins of Machu Picchu at sunrise on the fourth day.

Others choose to take the 2-day trek, a reasonable alternative if time or fitness are lacking. This trail begins closer to Machu Picchu, at Km 104, and circumvents much of the finest mountain scenery and ruins. Groups spend the night near the ruins of Wiñay Wayna before arriving at Machu Picchu for sunrise on the second day. More and more people of all ages and athletic abilities are tackling the Inca Trail; the Peruvian government, in addition to adopting more stringent regulations governing its use, also placed flush toilets in campsites in 2003 in an attempt to make the trail cleaner and more user-friendly.

Either way you go, it is advisable to give yourself a couple of days in Cusco or the Sacred Valley to acclimatize to the high elevation. Cold- and wet-weather technical gear, a solid backpack, and comfortable, sturdy hiking boots are musts (also needed: sleeping bag, flashlight, and sunblock). Above all, respect the ancient trail and its environment. Whatever you pack in, you must also pack out. You must also choose your dates extremely carefully. The dry season (June–Sept) is the most crowded time on the trail but excellent in terms of weather. May is perhaps best, with good weather and low numbers of trekkers. Other months are simply too wet for all but the hardest-core trail vets. The entire trail is now closed for maintenance and conservation during the entire month of February—which was one of the rainiest and least appealing months for trekking to Machu Picchu anyway.

The Peruvian government has sought to limit numbers of trekkers on the Inca Trail but also to maximize revenue from one of its foremost attractions. Thus, the cost of hiking the trail has steadily climbed: It now costs about three times what it did just 3 years ago. Standard-class treks, the most common and economical service, cost between $240 and $300 per person, including entrance fees ($50 for adults, $25 for students, free for children under 11) and return by tourist train ($35). Independent trekkers generally join a mixed group of travelers; groups tend to be between 12 and 16 people with guaranteed daily departures. The cost includes a bus to Km 88 to begin the trek, an English-speaking guide, tents, mattresses, three daily meals, and porters who carry all common equipment. Tips for porters or guides are extra. Personal porters, to carry your personal items, can be hired for about $50 for the 4 days. Premium-class services generally operate smaller group sizes (a maximum of 10 trekkers), and you generally get an upgrade on the return train. Prices for premium group treks, organized for private groups, range from $275 to as much as $650 per person.

Prices vary for trail packages based on services and the quality and experience of the agency. In general, you get what you pay for. Rock-bottom prices will probably get you a guide who speaks little English, food that is barely edible, camping equipment on its last legs, and a large, rowdy group. Especially important is the ability of an agency to guarantee departure even if its desired target number of travelers is not filled. Never purchase Inca Trail (or, for that matter,

New Inca Trail Regulations

For decades, individuals trekked the Inca Trail on their own, but hundreds of thousands of visitors—as many as 75,000 a year—left behind so much detritus that not only was the experience compromised for most future trekkers, but also the very environment was placed at risk. The Peruvian government has finally instituted changes and restrictions designed to lessen the human impact on the trail and on Machu Picchu itself. In the first couple of years, regulations were poorly enforced, but the government recently announced its intentions to fully and strictly enforce them.

All trekkers are now required to go accompanied by a guide and group. In addition, prices for both the trail and the ruins were tripled ($17–$50 adults, $9–$25 students); the overall number of trekkers permitted on the trail was significantly reduced, to 220 per day; only professionally qualified and licensed guides are allowed to lead groups on the Inca Trail; the maximum loads porters can carry has been limited to 20 kilograms (44 lb.); tourists are no longer permitted to travel on the local train from Aguas Calientes to Machu Picchu (or vice versa); and all companies must pay porters the minimum wage (about $30).

These changes have cut the number of trekkers on the trail in half and have made reservations essential in high season. Guarantee your space on the trail by making a reservation at least 1 week in advance of your trip (but 1 month or more in advance for June–Sept; reservations can be made as much as a year in advance). Travelers willing to wing it *might* still find available spots a couple of days before embarking on the trail, perhaps even at discounted rates, but waiting is a huge risk if you're really counting on doing the Inca Trail.

any tour) packages from anyone other than officially licensed agencies, and be careful to make payments (and get official receipts) at the physical offices of the agencies. If you have questions about whether an agency is legitimate or is authorized to sell Inca Trail packages, ask for assistance at the main tourism information office in Cusco.

Recommended agencies (all based in Cusco) for organizing treks along the Inca Trail include **Andean Life,** Plateros 372 (© 084/249-410; www.andeanlife.com); **Big Foot Tours,** Plateros 335 (© 084/238-568; www.bigfootcusco.com); **Explorandes,** Portal de Panes 236/Plaza de Armas (© 084/244-308; www.explorandes.com); **Q'Ente,** Garcilaso 210 (© 084/238-245; www.qente.com); **SAS Travel,** Portal Panes 143, Plaza de Armas (© 084/237-292; www.sastravelperu.com); **Top Vacations,** Portal de Panes 143/Plaza de Armas (© 084/263-278); and **United Mice,** Plateros 351 (© 084/221-139; unitedmice@andeantravelweb.com)

To guarantee a spot with an agency (which must request a trek permit for each trekker) it is imperative that you make a reservation and pay for your entrance fee at least 15 days in advance (at least 1 month in advance if you plan to go during peak months of May–Sept). Reservations can be made as much as a year in advance. Gone are the days when trekkers could simply show up in Cusco and organize a trek on the fly. Changing dates once you make a reservation is difficult if not impossible. If spots remain on agency rosters, they are offered on a first-come, first-served basis.

WHERE TO STAY IN AGUAS CALIENTES

The **Machu Picchu Sanctuary Lodge** ✿✿ is a newly transformed luxury lodge next to the ruins (© **084/246-419;** www.orient-express.com). Rooms are not especially large, but they have a good deal of Peruvian character, and one-third of them have views of the ruins. Rooms cost $547 to $575 for a double, $646 for a suite (rates include three meals a day); even at those prices, you must reserve 3 months in advance during high season (May–Sept), and you must also hold a reservation in Cusco at the Hotel Monasterio. Easily the best place to stay if you can't get into the Machu Picchu Sanctuary Lodge (or are understandably scared off by its prices and restrictions) is the **Machu Picchu Pueblo Hotel** ✿✿, Avenida Imperio de los Incas (© **800/442-5042,** or 084/211-032 for reservations; www.inkaterra.com). This rustic 10-year-old hotel, a compound of Spanish-colonial bungalows, is craftily set into lush gardens, and it offers orchid tours, bird-watching, and guided ecological hikes. The large, comfortable rooms cost $195 to $270 for a double, $300 to $390 for a suite.

    Gringo Bill's Hostal ✿, Colla Raymi 104, Plaza de Armas (©/fax **084/211-046**), was started by an American expat and has been a backpacker's institution since the early 1980s. The comfortable and clean rooms have good beds, and many have great views of the Upper Amazon tropical rainforest. Double rooms with shared bathrooms cost $35 to $40. **Hostal Machupicchu,** Av. Imperio de Los Incas s/n (© **084/211-065;** fax 084/212-034), is one of the best midrange options in Aguas Calientes. Restored and redecorated in 1999, it has very clean, well-furnished, and airy rooms, some painted in funky colors. Double rooms with shared bathrooms cost $30. One of the best of the inexpensive hostels along the main drag and railroad tracks, **Hostal Continental,** Av. Imperio de Los Incas 177 (© **084/211-034**), is very tidy, and you won't lack for hot water. Rooms aren't large, but the beds are pretty decent for a budget backpacker; $28 will get you a double with a shared bathroom.

WHERE TO DINE IN AGUAS CALIENTES

Scores of small and friendly restaurants line the only two streets in Aguas Calientes, Avenida Imperio de Los Incas and Avenida Pachacutec. Many are fairly generic, serving decent, cheap *menús* and pizza from wood-fired ovens. If you're just looking for pizza, **El Fogón de las Mestizas** and **Chez Maggy** (on Pachacutec) and **Incawasi, Inti Killa, Pizzería Su Chosa,** and **Pachamama** (all on Av. Imperio de los Incas) are all dependable. Menu hawkers, often the kids of the cook or owner, will try to lure you in with very cheap menu deals. If you're just looking for lunch during visits to the ruins, you have two choices: the overpriced buffet lunch at Machu Picchu Sanctuary Lodge, or a sack lunch. I recommend the latter (pick one up at Gringo Bill's or assemble one from your hotel's buffet breakfast). Other good dining options include **Indio Feliz** ✿✿, Calle Lloque Yupanqui 112 (© **084/211-090**), Aguas Calientes's best restaurant, serving Peruvian and French cuisine; **Pueblo Viejo,** Av. Pachacutec s/n (© **084/211-193**), a simple and cozy restaurant specializing in grilled meats; and **Restaurant Manu,** Av. Pachacutec 139 (© **084/211-101**), a relaxed and friendly spot featuring lots of international and Peruvian items, including pizza, homemade pasta, baked trout, and grilled chicken.

6 The Southern Amazon: Manu & Tambopata ⟨★⟨★⟨★

Puerto Maldonado: 500km (310 miles) NE of Cusco

More than half of Peru is Amazon rainforest, and the country has some of the richest biodiversity on the planet. Not surprisingly, jungle ecotourism has exploded in Peru. The jungle regions are now more accessible, even though some areas remain complicated and time-consuming to get to, and there are more lodges and eco-options than ever.

Cusco is the gateway to the southeastern jungle and some of Peru's finest Amazon rainforest. Two of Peru's top three jungle sites—and two of the best in South America—are found in the southern Amazon. The region's two principal protected areas, the **Manu Biosphere Reserve** and the **Tambopata Reserve Zone,** differ in terms of remoteness and facilities. Manu is complicated to visit; most expeditions last a minimum of 4 days and involve both overland and air (not to mention river) travel. The jungle frontier city of Puerto Maldonado, a half-hour flight from Cusco, is the jumping-off point to explore Tambopata. Travelers without the time or budget to accommodate Manu may find Tambopata a worthy alternative.

For both destinations, airfare from Cusco to Puerto Maldonado or Boca Manu (the gateway to the Manu Biosphere Reserve) is usually extra. Cheaper tours travel overland, stay at lesser lodges (or primarily at campsites), and may travel on riverboats without canopies. Independent travel to Tambopata and two-way overland travel to either are options only for those with a lot of time and patience on their hands. Organizing your trip with one of the lodges or specialized tour operators listed below is highly recommended. Most have fixed departure dates throughout the year. Do not purchase any jungle packages from salespeople on the streets of Cusco; their agencies may not be authorized to enter restricted zones, and last-minute "itinerary changes" are likely.

Dry season (May–Oct) is the best time for southern jungle expeditions; during the rainy season, rivers overflow and mosquitoes gobble up everything in sight. But intense heat and humidity are year-round constants in the jungle.

MANU BIOSPHERE RESERVE

Manu is the least accessible and explored jungle in Peru, and about as close as you're likely to come to virgin rainforest anywhere in the world. Manu, a UNESCO World Heritage Site and the largest protected area in Peru (and one of the largest in the world), has a surface area of more than 1.5 million hectares (4 million acres) of varied habitats, including Andes highlands, cloud forests, and lowland tropical rainforests. Manu is unparalleled for its wealth of wildlife, which includes more than 1,000 species of birds, 1,200 butterfly species, 15,000 plants, and 13 species of primates. Bird-watchers thrill at the prospect of glimpsing bird populations that account for 10% of the world's total, more than those found in all of Costa Rica. Other Manu fauna include jaguars, tapirs, spectacled bears, ocelots, and giant otters. Manu is also home to untold quantities of reptiles, amphibians, and insects, as well as dozens of native tribes, some of which have contact with the modern world.

Only a handful of travel agencies in Cusco are authorized to organize excursions to the Manu Biosphere Reserve. Visitors can enter two of three separate zones of the reserve. Access to the **Reserve Zone,** up the River Manu northwest of Boca Manu, is by permit and accompanied by an authorized guide only. The other sector of the park, the **Cultural Zone,** is home to traditional nomadic

> ### *Tips* Wildlife Viewing
>
> Peru's Amazon jungle regions have some of the greatest recorded biodiversity and species of plants and animals on earth. However, you will be disappointed if you go expecting a daily episode of *Wild Kingdom*. An expedition to the Amazon is not like a safari to the African savanna. Many mammals are extremely difficult to see in the thick jungle vegetation, and though the best tour operators employ guides skilled in ferreting them out, there are no guarantees. Even in the most virgin sections, after devoting several patient days to the exercise, you are unlikely to see many mammals, especially the rare large species such as tapirs, jaguars, and giant otters. If you spot even a couple, your jungle expedition can be considered a roaring success. In Manu and Tambopata, you are much more likely to see plenty of jungle birds (including fabulous macaws), butterflies, insects, and some monkeys.

groups, but the zone is open to all visitors; many tour operators in Cusco offer a variety of tours to lodges.

Getting to Manu is itself an eco-adventure. Overland access to the Manu Reserve Zone from Cusco is a stunning 2-day journey through 4,000m (13,120-ft.) mountains and cloud forest before descending into lowland rainforest. Because the reserve is so isolated and access is so restricted, Manu visits are fairly expensive, ranging from $500 to $1,500 per person for a 5- to 8-day trip.

MANU TOUR OPERATORS

Only about a dozen tour companies are permitted to run organized expeditions to the Manu Biosphere Reserve (and they are limited to 30 travelers each per week). The best of the firms listed below are closely involved with conservation and local development programs.

- **Tropical Nature Travel (TNT),** P.O. Box 5276 Gainesville, FL 32627-5276 (© **877/827-8350** toll-free in the U.S.; www.tropicalnaturetravel.com). Perhaps the most serious and sophisticated outfit operating ecotourism trips in the Peruvian Amazon, TNT is the private travel operator of the nonprofit conservation organization Tropical Nature (www.tropicalnature.org) and is partnered with the local nonprofit, Peru Verde. Trips are offered to four different lodges, including **Manu Wildlife Center** ☆☆☆; **Cock of the Rock Lodge,** good for birders; **Sandoval Lake Lodge** ☆, easily accessible from Puerto Maldonado and on an oxbow lake; and the newest, the remote **Heath River Wildlife Center,** situated near the Bolivian border and owned and staffed by the Ese'Eja Sonene people. Packages range from 4 days, 3 nights at Sandoval Lake Lodge for $260 to 5 days, 4 nights at Manu Wildlife Center for $1,050.

- **Manu Expeditions,** Av. Pardo 895, Cusco (© **084/226-671;** www.manu expeditions.com). This is one of the pioneering ecotourism operators in the Manu Biosphere Reserve, organizing rainforest tours for nearly 2 decades. Tours include stays at the **Manu Wildlife Center** ☆☆☆, of which the group is part owner, next to the famed macaw clay lick, and a safari camp facility deep within the Manu Biosphere Reserve. The Wildlife Center is considered the best lodge in Peru for birding. Four-, 6-, and 9-day tours range from $940 to $1,600 per person.

- **Manu Nature Tours,** Av. Pardo 1046, Cusco (© **084/252-721;** www. manuperu.com). A professional outfit with 15 years' experience in Manu, it operates the well-known and comfortable **Manu Lodge,** the oldest lodge within the Reserve Zone (4-, 5-, and 8-day trips, $1,440–$1,990), and the new **Manu Cloud Forest Lodge** in the Cultural Zone (2- and 3-day trips, $180–$270). Add-on options include mountain biking, rafting, and tree canopy climbs.
- **Pantiacolla,** Plateros 360, Cusco (© **084/238-323;** www.pantiacolla.com). An initiative of a Dutch biologist and local conservationist, the agency operates the small **Pantiacolla Lodge** ⟨★ at the edge of the Manu National Park. It's favored by budget travelers, offering camping and lodge trips ranging from $725 for 5 days to $985 and up, depending on the number of travelers, for Cultural Zone lodge tours.

Other reputable Manu tour companies include **Manu Ecological Adventures,** Plateros 356, Cusco (© **084/261-640;** www.manuadventures.com); and **SAS Travel,** Portal Panes 143, Plaza de Armas, Cusco (© **084/237-292;** www.sastravelperu.com), a well-run and popular all-purpose agency that offers varied programs to both Manu and Tambopata and stays at various lodges.

TAMBOPATA RESERVE ZONE

Upstream from Puerto Maldonado, Tambopata is a massive tract 1.5 million hectares (3.7 million acres) of tropical rainforest in the department of Madre de Dios. Visits to jungle lodges are more accessible (by boat) than those in Manu. Although man's imprints are more noticeable here, the area is one of superb environmental diversity, with a dozen different types of forest. Many environmentalists claim that Tambopata has one of the greatest diversities of wildlife recorded, owing to a location at the confluence of lowland Amazon forest with three other ecosystems. At least 13 endangered species are found here, including the jaguar, giant otter, ocelot, harpy eagle, and giant armadillo. The **Manu Macaw Lick (Colpa de Guacamayos)** within the reserve is one of the largest natural clay licks in Peru and perhaps the wildlife highlight of the country. Thousands of brilliantly colored macaws and parrots arrive daily at the cliffs to feed on mineral salts.

Flights to Puerto Maldonado from Cusco are about $60 each way. (Flights are often included in packages.) To get to the Tambopata-Candamo Reserve, you must then hop a boat from Puerto Maldonado. Packages begin with 2-day, 1-night arrangements, but 3-day, 2-night packages are better. Lodge stays generally allow visitors to see a large variety of trees, plants, and birds, but few wild mammals apart from monkeys. Rare species such as the jaguar or tapir are rarely seen.

TAMBOPATA TOUR OPERATORS & LODGES

- **Peruvian Safaris,** Alcanfores 459, Miraflores, Lima (© **01/447-8888;** www.peruviansafaris.com). About 3 hours upriver from Puerto Maldonado along the River Tambopata, at the edge of the Tambopata Reserve Zone, **Explorer's Inn** ⟨★ is a comfortable 25-year-old lodge that hosts both tourists and scientists. It's excellent for fauna, particularly jungle birds. Prices range from $180 for 2 nights to $495 for 4 nights.
- **Rainforest Expeditions,** Av. Aramburú 166-4B, Miraflores, Lima (© **877/ 905-3782** toll-free in the U.S., or 01/421-8347; www.perunature.com). This veteran ecotourism company promotes tourism with environmental education, research, and conservation and operates two Tambopata lodges.

The **Posada Amazonas** ✦✦, about 2 hours up the Tambopata River from Puerto Maldonado, is owned jointly with an indigenous community and is very good for inexpensive, introductory nature tours. It has an eagle nest site and observation tower. Prices are $190 to $280 for 3- to 4-day trips. The **Tambopata Research Center** ✦✦ is more remote (8 hr. upriver from Puerto Maldonado), located at the Manu Macaw Lick, and better for in-depth tours and wildlife. It's the place to see flocks of colorful macaws. Prices are $690 to $870 for 5- to 7-day trips.

- **Andean Treks,** 32 Russell Ave., Watertown, MA 02472, and Pardo 705, Cusco (© 800/683-8148 in the U.S., or 084/225-701; www.andeantreks. com). Among a number of South American outdoor adventures, the company operates the **Libertador Tambopata Jungle Lodge,** a private reserve lodge on the Río Tambopata (4 hr. from Puerto Maldonado). It has several trails nearby and offers overnight trips to the macaw clay lick. Prices range from $270 for 3 days to $660 for 5 nights.

Lodges nearer to Puerto Maldonado are generally cheaper and less time-consuming to get to, but because they are located in secondary jungle and not nearly as remote, they serve as introductory visits to the Amazon. Several of the best easily accessible lodges are: **Sandoval Lake Lodge** ✦✦, run by Tropical Nature Travel/Inkanatura (see above); **Cusco Amazónico Lodge** (© 01/422-6574 in Lima; http://perudiscover.com/hotel/reserva_amazonica.htm); and **Eco Amazonia Lodge,** Calle Garcilazo 210, Of. 206, Cusco (© 084/236-159; www.ecoamazonia.com.pe), with tours available through **Adventure Life Journeys,** 1655 S. 3rd St. W., Missoula, MT 59801 (© 800/344-6118 toll-free in the U.S., or 406/541-2677; www.adventure-life.com/peru/ecoamazonia.html).

7 Puno & Lake Titicaca

388km (241 miles) S of Cusco

Puno, founded in the late 17th century following the discovery of nearby silver mines, is a messy, ramshackle town that draws numbers of visitors wholly disproportionate to its innate attractions. A mostly unlovely city on a high plateau, it has one thing going for it that no other place on earth can claim: Puno hugs the shores of fabled Lake Titicaca, the world's highest navigable body of water, a sterling expanse of deep blue at 3,800m (12,540 ft.) above sea level. The magnificent lake straddles the border of Peru and Bolivia; many Andean travelers move on from Puno to La Paz, going around, or in some cases over, Titicaca. Before leaving Puno, though, almost everyone hops aboard a boat to visit at least one of several ancient island-dwelling peoples. A 2-day tour takes travelers to the Uros floating islands, where Indian communities consisting of just a few families construct tiny islands out of *totora* reeds; there are two inhabited natural islands, Amantani and Taquile.

Though dry and often brutally cold, Puno is known for its warmly celebrated festivals. In fact, the unassuming town, where the people descended from the Aymara from the south and the Quechua from the north, is reputed to be the capital of Peruvian folklore. Its traditional fiestas, dances, and music are without argument among the most vibrant in Peru. Among those worth planning your trip around are the Festival de la Virgen de la Candelaria (Candlemas), February 2 to 15; San Juan de Dios, March 8; Fiesta de las Cruces Alasitas, May 8; San Juan, San Pedro, and San Pablo, June 24 to 29; Apóstol Santiago, July 25; and Puno Week, November 1 to 7. Of these, Candlemas and Puno Week (especially Nov 5) are the most exceptional.

ESSENTIALS
GETTING THERE

BY PLANE   Puno does not have an airport; the nearest is **Aeropuerto Manco Capac** (② 054/322-905) in Juliaca, about 45km (28 miles) north of Puno. **Aero Continente, LanPeru,** and **TANS** fly daily from Lima and Arequipa to Juliaca. Flights are generally available for $59 to $89 (depending on the season) one-way. Flights were recently suspended from Cusco to Juliaca, so be sure to check if they have been reinstated by the time you are ready to travel. Tourist buses run from the Juliaca airport to Puno (a 1-hr. trip), depositing travelers on Jirón Tacna.

BY BUS   Road service from Cusco to Puno has greatly improved, and many more tourists now travel by bus, which is faster and cheaper than the train. The trip between Puno and Arequipa by bus continues to be tortuous: 12 hours of winding mountain roads—about the same as the train, but less expensive.

From Cusco, executive- or imperial-class buses make the trip in less than 7 hours. **Imexso** (② 084/240-801; $14) and **First Class** (② 051/365-192; www.firstclassperu.com; $25) operate buses with videos and English-speaking tour guides. **Inka Express** (② 051/365-654) has daily 8am departures of regular-class service between Cusco and Puno (10 hr.). **Cruz del Sur** (② 051/ 622-626) offers night service to Puno (10 hr.). Regular buses are as cheap as S/12 ($3.50), but they are uncomfortable, have no restrooms or videos, and are potentially dangerous.

From Arequipa to Puno, buses generally travel all night, leaving around 5 or 6pm and arriving at 5am. **Cruz del Sur** (② 051/622-626) and **Ormeño** (② 051/352-321) make the trip for around $10.

Given the confusing number of bus companies and services, it's wise to make bus reservations with a travel agent; see "Puno Travel Agencies & Tour Operators" on p. 643.

BY TRAIN   The Titicaca Route journey from Cusco to Puno, along tracks at an altitude of 3,500m (11,500 ft.), is one of the most scenic in Peru, though it is slow (9–10 hr. and prone to late arrivals) and has experienced its share of onboard thievery. Keep a careful eye on your bags and, if possible, lock backpacks to the luggage rack; keep valuables close to your person. Trains from Cusco to Puno depart from **Estación Huanchaq** (② 084/238-722), at the end of Avenida Sol. Service to Puno is Monday, Wednesday, Friday, and Saturday, departing at 8am and arriving at 6pm. First class costs $89 one-way, tourist (local) class, $14.

Train service from Arequipa to Puno is now available by charter only, though it may be revived sometime in the near future; check www.perurail.com for the latest information.

On the trains themselves, but especially at rail stations, travelers are advised to pay close attention to their belongings, even going so far as to lock them to luggage racks. The routes have earned a reputation as havens for thieves; for this reason, safer Inka-class seats are recommended.

GETTING AROUND

Few visitors spend much time in Puno, and the little getting around that needs to be done in town is either on foot or by taxi. Taxis are inexpensive and plentiful, easily hailed on the street and best used at night and to get back and forth from the hotels out on the banks of Titicaca. Most trips in town cost no more than S/3 (75¢). Taxis can also be hired for return trips to nearby ruins or for

---

Take It Easy

Puno's elevation of 3,300m (10,900 ft.) is nearly as high as Cusco, and unless you've already spent time in the Andes, you'll almost certainly need to rest for at least a day to acclimatize. See "Health Concerns" in "Planning Your Trip to Peru," earlier in this chapter, for further information on how to address altitude sickness.

---

half- or full days. Visits to Lake Titicaca and its islands, as well as the ruins on the outskirts of town, are best done by organized tour; see "Puno Travel Agencies & Tour Operators" on p. 643.

VISITOR INFORMATION

A small, poorly equipped, and not very helpful **tourist information office** is located at Pasaje Lima 549 (no phone), the pedestrian-only main drag of Puno, though you're probably better off going to one of the travel agencies that organizes Titicaca and area trips, such as All Ways Travel or Edgar Adventures. See "Puno Travel Agencies & Tour Operators" on p. 643.

For those crossing into Bolivia who need visas or other information, the **Bolivian Consulate** is located at Jr. Arequipa 120 (© **051/351-251**). North Americans and Europeans do not need a visa to enter Bolivia, but the border is a historically problematic one (it was closed for more than a month in 2001), so you may need to check on the status of the crossing before traveling to Bolivia.

FAST FACTS   You'll find **banks** and **ATMs** located along Jirón Lima (also called Pasaje Lima), just before the tourist information office. Money changers can generally be found along Jirón Tacna, where most bus stations are located, and the market near the railway and Avenida de los Incas.

For medical attention, go to **Clínica Puno,** Jr. Ramón Castilla 178–180 (© 051/368-835), or **Hospital Regional Puno** (© 051/369-696). The **tourist police** are located at Jr. Deusta 538 (© 051/357-100).

Pretty fast Internet connections are available at **Qoll@internet,** Jr. Oquendo 340 (Parque Pino). It's open Monday through Saturday from 8am to midnight and Sunday from 3 to 9pm; rates are S/2 (50¢) per hour. Other Internet *cabinas* are located along Pasaje Lima. Cusco's main **post office** is located at Moquegua 267; it's open Monday through Friday from 8am to 6pm and Saturday from 8am to 1pm. The **Telefónica del Perú** office is on the corner of Moquegua and Arequipa. An international calling center is also located on Parque Pino.

WHAT TO SEE & DO IN PUNO

Puno itself is a rather bleak and unimpressive place if you don't count its enviable geography. The top attractions in Puno are outside the city: Lake Titicaca and the ancient Sillustani ruins. What there is to see in Puno doesn't delay most visitors more than a half-day or so. However, if you stumble upon one of Puno's famously colorful festivals, you may want to linger.

The large **cathedral,** on the west side of the Plaza de Armas (at the end of Jr. Lima), is the focal point of downtown Puno. The 18th-century baroque church is big, but no great shakes; the elaborate exterior is much more impressive than the spartan, spacious, chilly interior. On the plaza is the **Casa del Corregidor,** Deustua 576, purportedly Puno's oldest house, with an impressive Spanish balcony; it now houses a lovely "cultural" cafe and is the best spot in town for a breather. Nearby, the **Museo Municipal Carlos Dryer,** Conde de Lemos 289, is the town's principal (but small) museum. It has a decent selection of pre-Inca ceramics and textiles, as well as mummies with cranial deformations, but it's not very well illuminated. It's open Monday through Friday from 7:30am to 3:30pm; admission is S/3.5 ($1). For a view of Lake Titicaca and a vantage point that makes Puno look more attractive than it is, climb the steep hill to **Huajsapata Park,** about 10 minutes southwest of the main square. On top is a statue of Manco Capac, the first Inca.

Back down below, Jirón Lima is a pedestrianized mall that runs from the Plaza de Armas to **Parque Pino,** a relaxed square populated by locals. Puno's seedy **central market** is 2 blocks east, and it spills across several streets. Although not attractive, it's a realistic look at the underbelly of the Peruvian economy. Beyond the railroad tracks is a **market** targeting tourists with all kinds of alpaca and woolen goods, often much cheaper than those found in Cusco and other cities.

LAKE TITICACA 𝒜𝒜𝒜

Lake Titicaca has long been considered a sacred place among indigenous Andean peoples. According to Andean legend, Lake Titicaca was the birthplace of civilization. Viracocha, the creator deity, lightened a dark world by having the sun, moon, and stars rise from the lake and occupy their places in the sky. The people who live in and around the lake consider themselves descendants of Mama Qota (Sacred Mother), and they believe that powerful spirits live in the lake's depths.

Lake Titicaca is a dazzling sight, worthy of such mystical associations: Its deep azure waters seemingly extend forever across the altiplano at more than 3,800m (12,540 ft.). The lake covers more than 8,500 sq. km (5,300 sq. miles); it is 176km (109 miles) long and 50km (31 miles) wide. The sun is extraordinarily intense at this altitude, scorching off 600 cubic m (21,000 cubic ft.) of water per second. Daybreak and sunset, as the sun sinks low into the horizon, are particularly stunning to witness.

Lake Titicaca has been inhabited for thousands of years. *Totora* reed boats roamed the lake as early as 2500 B.C. Titicaca's islands—both man-made and natural—are home to several communities of Quechua and Aymara Indians, groups with remarkably different traditions and ways of life. Visiting them, and staying overnight on one of the islands if you can, is one of the highlights of Peru and one of the most unique experiences in South America.

The most convenient way to visit is by an inexpensive and well-run guided tour, arranged by one of several travel agencies in Puno; see "Puno Travel Agencies & Tour Operators" on p. 643. Although it is possible to arrange

---

Tips Traveling to Bolivia

Plenty of travelers continue on to Bolivia, which shares Lake Titicaca with Peru, from Puno; several travel agencies in Puno sell packages and bus tickets. The most common and scenic route is from Puno to La Paz via Yunguyo and Copacabana. The trip to La Paz takes 7 or 8 hours by bus. You can also go by a combination of overland travel and hydrofoil or catamaran, a unique but very time-consuming journey (13 hr.). At the border, visitors get an exit stamp from Peru and a tourist visa (30 days) from Bolivia. Foreigners are commonly tapped for phony departure and entry fees; resist the corrupt attempts. For more information on Bolivia, see chapter 5.

independent travel, the low cost and easy organization of a group don't encourage it. Even if you go on your own, you'll inevitably fall in with groups, and your experience won't differ radically. You can go on a half-day tour of the Uros Floating Islands or a full-day tour that combines Taquile Island, but the best way to experience Lake Titicaca's unique indigenous life is to stay at least 1 night on either Taquile or Amantani, preferably in the home of a local family.

UROS FLOATING ISLANDS (LAS ISLAS FLOTANTES) ✦

As improbable as it sounds, the Uros Indians of Lake Titicaca live on floating "islands" made by hand from *totora* reeds that grow in abundance in the shallow waters of Lake Titicaca. This unique practice has endured since the time of the Incas, and today, there are some 45 floating islands in the Bay of Puno. The islands first came into contact with the modern world in the mid-1960s, and their inhabitants now live mostly off of tourism. Many visitors faced with this strange sight conclude that the Uros can't possibly still live on the islands, that it must be a show created for their benefit. True, they can seem to be little more than floating souvenir stands; the communities idly await the arrival of tourist boats and then seek to sell them handmade textiles and reed-crafted items while the gringos walk gingerly about the springy islands—truly a strange sensation—photographing the Uros's houses and children.

But it's not just a show. A couple hundred Uros Indians continue to live year-round on the islands, even if they venture to Puno for commercial transactions. The largest island, Huacavacani, has homes and a floating Seventh-Day Adventist church, a candidate for one of the more bizarre scenes you're likely to find in Peru. Others islands have schools, a post office, and souvenir shops. Only a few islands are set up to receive tourists, though. The vast majority of the Uros people live in continued isolation and peace, away from camera lenses.

The Uros, who fled to the middle of the lake to escape conflicts with the Collas and Incas, long ago began intermarrying with the Aymara Indians, and many have now converted to Catholicism. Fishers and birders, the Uros live grouped by family sectors, and entire families live in one-room, tentlike, thatched huts constructed on the shifting reed island that floats beneath. They build modest houses and boats with fanciful animal head bows out of the reeds, and continually replenish the fast-rotting mats that form their fragile islands. Visitors might be surprised, to say the least, to find some huts outfitted with TVs powered by solar panels (donated by the Fujimori administration after a presidential visit to the islands).

Inexpensive tours that go only to the Uros Islands last about 3 hours and include hotel pickup, an English-speaking guide, and motorboat transportation to the islands. Unless you're unusually pressed for time, it's best to visit the Uros as part of a wider tour to the natural islands of Amantani or Taquile.

TAQUILE ISLAND (ISLA TAQUILE) ✦✦✦

Taquile is a fascinating and stunningly beautiful island about 4 hours from Puno. The island is only 1km (½ mile) wide and about 6km (3 miles) long. It rises to a high point of 264m (870 ft.), and the hillsides are laced with formidable Inca stone agricultural terraces. The island is a rugged ruddy color, which contrasts spectacularly with the blue lake and sky. Taquile is littered with Inca and pre-Inca stone ruins.

The island is as serene as the views. Taquile has been inhabited for 10,000 years, and life remains starkly traditional; there is no electricity and no vehicles, and islanders (who number slightly more than 1,000) quietly go about their business. Taquile natives allow tourists to stay at private houses (in primitive but not uncomfortable conditions), and there are a number of simple restaurants near the central plaza. Though friendly to outsiders, the Quechua-speaking islanders remain a famously reserved and insular community. Their dress is equally famous—Taquile textiles are some of the finest in Peru. Men wear embroidered, woven red waistbands *(fajas)*, and embroidered, wool stocking caps that indicate marital status: red for married men, red and white for bachelors. Women wear layered skirts and black shawls over their heads. Taquile textiles are much sought-after for their hand-woven quality, but they are considerably more expensive than mass-produced handicrafts in other parts of Peru. There's a cooperative shop on the main plaza, and stalls are set up during festivals. Locals are more reluctant to haggle than artisans in other parts of Peru.

If you are lucky enough to catch a festival on the island, you will be treated to a festive and traditional pageant of color, with picturesque dances and women twirling in circles, revealing as many as 16 layered, multicolored skirts. Easter, Fiesta de Santiago (July 25), August 1 and 2, and New Year's are the best celebrations. Any time on the island, though, is a splendid and unique experience—especially once the day-trippers have departed and you have the island and incomparable views and stars virtually to yourself. Taquile then seems about as far away from modernity and "civilization" as you can travel on this planet.

Access to the island from the boat dock is either by a long path that wends around the island or by an amazingly 533-step stone staircase that climbs to the top, passing through two stone arches with astonishing views of the lake. Independent travelers sign in and pay a nominal fee. Those wishing to spend the night can arrange for a family-house stay; expect to rough it a bit without proper showers. Many islanders do not speak Spanish, and English is likely to be met with blank stares.

Most single-day tours of the Uros and Taquile islands depart early in the morning and stop at the islands of Uros for a half-hour en route. For most visitors, a day trip—which allows only 1 or 2 hours on the island and 8 hours of boat time—is too grueling and insufficient to appreciate the beauty and culture of Taquile Island.

AMANTANI ISLAND (ISLA AMANTANI) 🐸🌟
Amantani, a circular island about 4½ hours from Puno (and about 2 hr. from Taquile), is home to a very different but equally fascinating Titicaca community. Also handsomely terraced and home to farmers, fishers, and weavers, in many ways Amantani is even more rustic and unspoiled than Taquile. It is a beautiful place, with a handful of villages composed of about 800 families and ruins clinging to the island's two peaks, Pachatata and Pachamama (Father Earth and Mother Earth). The islanders, who for the most part understand Spanish, are more open and approachable than natives of Taquile.

Amantani is best visited on a tour that allows you to spend the night (visiting the Uros islands en route) and travel the next day to Taquile. Tour groups place groups of four or five travelers with local families for overnight stays. Not only will the family prepare your simple meals, you will be invited to a friendly dance in the village meeting place. Most families dress up their guests in local outfits—women in layered, multicolored, embroidered skirts and blouses, and the men in wool ponchos—for the event. Though the evening is obviously staged for tourists' benefit, it's low-key and charming rather than cheesy. It's a good idea to bring small gifts for your family on Amantani, since they make little from stays and must alternate with other families on the island. Pens, pencils, and batteries all make good gifts. The tour price normally includes accommodations, lunch and evening meal on the first day, and breakfast the following morning.

SILLUSTANI RUINS 🕿

Just beyond Puno are mysterious pre-Inca ruins called *chullpas* (funeral towers). The finest sit on the windswept altiplano on a peninsula in Lake Umayo at Sillustani, 32km (20 miles) from Puno. The Colla people—a warrior tribe who spoke Aymara—buried their elite in giant cylindrical tombs, some as tall as 12m (40 ft.). The Collas dominated the Titicaca region before the arrival of the Incas. After burying their dead along with foodstuffs, jewels, and other possessions, they sealed the towers. The stone masonry is exquisite; many archaeologists and historians find them more complex than and superior to Inca engineering. The structures form quite an impression on such a harsh landscape.

The best way to visit Sillustani is by guided tour, usually in the afternoon; see "Puno Travel Agencies & Tour Operators," below. Dress warmly, as the bitter gusts make the wind of a wintry day on Lake Michigan look like a gentle spring breeze.

PUNO TRAVEL AGENCIES & TOUR OPERATORS

Most travel agencies in Puno handle the conventional tours of Lake Titicaca and Sillustani, along with a handful of other ruins programs. Two of the best agencies are **All Ways Travel,** Jr. Tacna 234 (📞 051/355-552; awtperu@terra. com.pe), run by the very friendly and helpful Víctor Pauca and his daughter Eliana, and offering progressive cultural trips in addition to the standard tours; and **Edgar Adventures,** Jr. Lima 328 (📞 051/353-444; edgaradventures@ terra.com.pe), run by a Peruvian husband-and-wife team. Both can arrange bus and air travel as well, including travel to Bolivia. Another agency worth checking out for travel arrangements is **Highland Travel Experts,** Jr. Tacna 273 (📞 051/365-737; hightravel@latinmail.com). Uros Islands trips cost about $6 per person; full-day Uros Floating Reed Islands/Taquile Island trips, $9 to $10 per person; 2-day, 1-night Uros, Amantani, and Taquile islands trips, $15 per person; and 3-hour Sillustani tours, $5 to $7 per person.

WHERE TO STAY

Puno doesn't exactly overflow with hotel options. The majority continue to be geared toward a budget backpacker crowd; even the best of those are very basic, and many are noisy dives with fleeting hot water, so if you're looking at the bottom end, check the place out first. If you don't mind relying on taxis to get back and forth, the best options are on Lake Titicaca.

EXPENSIVE

Hotel Libertador Puno 🕿   Ensconced in splendid isolation on the shore of a small island 5km (3 miles) from Puno, overlooking the expanse of Lake Titicaca, this hotel takes full advantage of its privileged—or inconvenient, depending on your perspective—location. Part of the luxury Libertador chain, the hotel's rooms are spacious if a little bland, and about half have panoramic views of the lake. Service is excellent, and the large white-block hotel has soaring ceilings, but it doesn't have as much character as the better value Posada del Inca (see below), which has views that are almost as good. The hotel is linked to the mainland by a causeway, and the only way back and forth to Puno is by taxi (about $3 each way).

Isla Esteves s/n, Lake Titicaca. 📞 054/367-780. Fax 054/367-879. www.libertador.com.pe. 123 units. $150 deluxe double; $215–$240 suite. Rates include breakfast buffet. AE, DC, MC, V. **Amenities:** Restaurant; bar; fitness center; sauna; concierge; room service; laundry service. *In room:* A/C, TV, minibar, hair dryer, safe.

Sonesta Posada del Inca ★★ *Kids* *Value*   Like the Libertador, Posada del Inca is perched on the shores of Titicaca, but it fits more sensitively into its enviable surroundings. The newest hotel in Puno (opened in 1999), it is imaginatively designed, with warm colors and Peruvian touches, including bright modern art and folk artifacts. Rooms are large and comfortable, and bathrooms are also large and nicely equipped. The restaurant and many rooms look over the lake; other rooms have views of the mountains. The relaxed lobby has a cozy fireplace. Service is friendly, and the staff can arrange visits to Titicaca's islands. Children will enjoy the miniversion of a floating lake community on the grounds by the lake.

Sesquicentenario 610, Sector Huaje, Lake Titicaca. © 051/364-111. Fax 051/363-672. www.sonesta.com. 62 units. $82–$91 double. Children under 8 stay free in parent's room. Rates include breakfast buffet. AE, DC, MC, V. **Amenities:** Restaurant; cocktail lounge; concierge; business center; room service; laundry service. *In room:* A/C, TV, minibar, hair dryer, safe.

MODERATE

Hotel Colón Inn ★ *Value*   A small and charming Belgian-owned hotel (but affiliated with Best Western) in the heart of busy Puno, the Colón inhabits a 19th-century republican-era building on a corner. Built around an airy, sky-lit, colonial-style lobby, it has three floors of good-size and comfortably appointed rooms with marble bathrooms and desks. The cozy, top-floor pub is advertised for its panoramic views, but in reality, all you see are the tops of concrete buildings. The two restaurants, Sol Naciente and Pizzeria Europa, are a couple of the better places in Puno for lunch or dinner.

Calle Tacna 290, Puno. ©/fax 051/351-432. www.titicaca-peru.com. 21 units. $53 double. Rate includes taxes and breakfast buffet. AE, DC, MC, V. **Amenities:** 2 restaurants; bar; room service; laundry service. *In room:* TV, minibar, safe.

Hotel Italia   A modest little hotel in the midst of Puno's hubbub, the Italia is homey and well maintained, and it has an attractive small restaurant and breakfast room. The rooms are clean, of a decent size, and for the most part tastefully decorated, though many are marred by scary circular fluorescent lights. The staff is very friendly and helpful. An unusual feature for a small, moderately priced hotel: free porn on channel 39 (more a feature of local cable than of this otherwise modest hotel, I'm guessing).

Jr. Teodoro Valcarcel 122, Puno. © and fax 051/352-521. www.hotelitaliaperu.com. 21 units. $44 double. Rate includes taxes and continental breakfast. MC. **Amenities:** Restaurant; cafe/bar; concierge; laundry service. *In room:* TV.

INEXPENSIVE

Hostal Los Uros   One of the most popular Puno hostels targeting backpackers, Los Uros represents a good value at the low end. The very basic rooms are clean, beds are pretty decent, the place is quiet, and if you get chilly, the staff will dole out extra wool blankets. Rooms have either private or shared bathrooms. Your best bet for hot water is in the evening. Breakfast is available at the simple cafeteria.

Jr. Teodoro Valcarcel 135, Puno. © 051/352-141. 14 units. $10 double w/private bathroom; $8 w/shared bathroom. Rates include taxes. No credit cards. **Amenities:** Cafeteria. *In room:* No phone.

WHERE TO DINE

Most of Puno's more attractive restaurants, popular with gringos, are located on the pedestrian-only main drag, Jirón Lima. In addition to those listed below, check out the two restaurants at Hotel Colón Inn (see above).

MODERATE

Apu Salkantay PERUVIAN/INTERNATIONAL   A cozy, two-level lodge-like place, this Quechua-named restaurant seems to attract more people for drinks next to the fireplace-stove. The menu has standard offerings such as soups, pizza, pasta, and basic fish (king fish and trout), but they also serve up Peruvian specialties such as *cuy,* alpaca steak with *quinoa* rice, and alpaca *piqueo* with fries, onions, tomatoes, and peppers. Deftly targeting tourists, the cafe/bar also has Internet facilities. The daily *menú* includes a soft drink, bread, and main course.

Jr. Lima 357. ℂ 051/363-955. Reservations not accepted. Main courses S/17–S/22 ($5–$6); daily *menú* S/22 ($6). DC, MC, V. Daily 9am–10pm.

Incabar ✿ NEW PERUVIAN/INTERNATIONAL   Awfully stylish and down-right funky for rough-around-the-edges Puno, this new lounge bar/restaurant aims high. The menu is much more creative and flavorful than other places in town (even if dishes don't always succeed), with interesting sauces for lake fish and alpaca steak and artful presentations. For a recent meal, I had a spinach-and-tomato cream soup and *atravezados de pollo*—chicken rolls marinated in sesame, ginger, and garlic and served with pineapple, peppers, and rice. There are two inexpensive fixed-price menus daily. Incabar is also a good place to hang out, have a beer or coffee, and write postcards—the back room has comfortable sofas. Breakfast is also served (S/10/$3).

Jr. Lima 356. ℂ 051/368-865. Reservations recommended. Main courses S/12–S/17 ($3.50–$5); daily *menú* S/15–S/20 ($4–$5.75). DC, MC, V. Daily 9am–10pm.

La Casona ✿ PERUVIAN/INTERNATIONAL   Puno's best and most popu-lar eatery calls itself a "museum-restaurant." In a town such as Puno, with rela-tively few attractions, that's fair enough. La Casona ("big house") has traditional, rather old-style Spanish charm, with lace tablecloths. The three dining rooms are filled with antiques and large religious canvases, but it retains a decidedly informal appeal. Its specialty is Lake Titicaca fish, such as trout and king fish *(pejerrey),* served La Casona style, with an everything-but-the-kitchen-sink preparation of rice, avocado, ham, cheese, hot dog, apple salad, french fries, and mushrooms. Chicken and beef are prepared the same way. If that's a little over-whelming for you, go with the simple trout served with mashed potatoes. In the evening, make a point about asking for the *menú del día,* the fixed-price meal that is offered and is a great deal (essentially half price) but not advertised. Service can be a little slow, but there's not much to do in Puno anyway.

Jr. Lima 517. ℂ 051/351-108. Reservations recommended. Main courses S/12–S/32 ($3.50–$9); *menú* S/13 ($3.75). DC, MC, V. Daily 9am–10pm.

INEXPENSIVE

Pizzería El Buho *Value* PIZZA/ITALIAN   A cozy little place, with red check-ered tablecloths, a high vaulted ceiling, wood-burning oven/chimney, and a lofty perch upstairs, the "Owl Pizzeria" feels like a spot where you'd duck in from the cold at a ski lodge. It's extremely popular with both gringos and locals, and it serves the best pizza in Puno. The menu also lists a good number of pastas and handful of soups, but I swear I've never seen anyone have anything other than pizza.

Jr. Lima 347. ℂ 051/363-955. Reservations not accepted. Main courses S/8–S/14 ($2.25–$4); pizza S/8–S/22 ($2.25–$6). DC, V. Daily 4:30–10:30pm.

8 Arequipa

1,020km (632 miles) SE of Lima; 521km (323 miles) S of Cusco; 297km (184 miles) SW of Puno

The southern city of Arequipa, the second-largest in Peru, may well be the country's most handsome. Founded in 1540, it retains an elegant historic center constructed almost entirely of *sillar* (a porous, white volcanic stone), which gives the city its distinctive look and nickname *la ciudad blanca,* or the white city. Colonial churches and the sumptuous Santa Catalina convent gleam beneath palm trees and a brilliant sun. Ringing the city are three delightfully named snowcapped volcanic peaks: El Misti, Chachani, and Pichu Pichu, all of which hover around 6,000m (20,000 ft.).

Arequipa has emerged as a favorite of outdoors enthusiasts who come to climb volcanoes, raft on rivers, trek through the valleys, and above all, head out to Colca Canyon—twice as deep as the Grand Canyon and the best place in South America to see giant condors soar overhead. Suiting its reputation as an outdoor paradise, Arequipa has weather that is Southern California perfect: more than 300 days a year of sunshine, huge blue skies, and low humidity. Arequipa looks very much the part of a desert oasis.

The commercial capital of the south, Arequipa not only looks different, but it also feels dissimilar from the rest of Peru. Arequipeños have earned a reputation as aloof and distrusting of the centralized power in Lima. Relatively wealthy and a place of prominent intellectuals, politicians, and industrialists, Arequipa has a haughty air about it—at least to many Peruvians who hail from less distinguished places.

As beautiful and confident as it is, Arequipa has not escaped disaster. A devastating earthquake (which registered 8.1 on the Richter scale) struck the city and other points farther south in June 2001. Though international reports at the time painted a picture of a city that had caved in on itself, thankfully, that wasn't the case. Poorly constructed housing in some residential districts was destroyed, but the colonial core of the city survived intact. The major damaged structure, the cathedral on the Plaza de Armas, is still undergoing repair, its asymmetry of towers no doubt a serious aesthetic offense in this stately city.

ESSENTIALS
GETTING THERE
BY PLANE **Aeropuerto Rodríquez Ballón** (© **054/443-464** or 054/ 443-458) is about 7km (4 miles) northwest of the city. There are daily flights to and from Lima, Juliaca, and Cusco on **Aero Continente** (© 01/242-4242), **LanPeru** (© 01/213-8200), and **TANS** (© 01/213-6000).

From the airport, transportation is by taxi ($3–$5) or shared *colectivo* service (about $2 per person) to downtown hotels.

BY BUS The main **Terminal Terrestre** is about 4km (2 miles) south of downtown Arequipa; nearby is a newer station, **Nuevo Terrapuerto.** Both stations are on Av. Andrés Cáceres (Parque Industrial). A huge number of bus companies travel in and out of Peru's second city from across the country, and you'll need to ask if leaving Arequipa by bus whether it departs from Terminal or Terrapuerto. From Lima (16 hr.), recommended companies include **Ormeño** (© 01/472-1710), **Cruz del Sur** (© 01/428-2570), **Civa** (© 01/428-5649), and **Oltursa** (© 01/476-9724 or 054/426-566); from Puno and Juliaca (10–12 hr.), **Civa** (© 054/426-563), **Cruz del Sur** (© 054/622-626), and **Julsa** (© 054/430-843

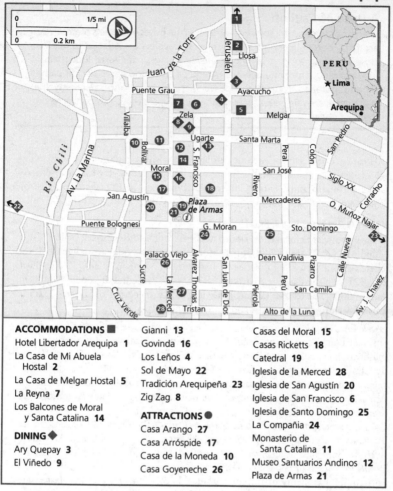

ACCOMMODATIONS ■
Hotel Libertador Arequipa **1**
La Casa de Mi Abuela
    Hostal **2**
La Casa de Melgar Hostal **5**
La Reyna **7**
Los Balcones de Moral
    y Santa Catalina **14**

DINING ◆
Ary Quepay **3**
El Viñedo **9**

Gianni **13**
Govinda **16**
Los Leños **4**
Sol de Mayo **22**
Tradición Arequipeña **23**
Zig Zag **8**

ATTRACTIONS ●
Casa Arango **27**
Casa Arróspide **17**
Casa de la Moneda **10**
Casa Goyeneche **26**

Casas del Moral **15**
Casas Ricketts **18**
Catedral **19**
Iglesia de la Merced **28**
Iglesia de San Agustín **20**
Iglesia de San Francisco **6**
Iglesia de Santo Domingo **25**
La Compañia **24**
Monasterio de
    Santa Catalina **11**
Museo Santuarios Andinos **12**
Plaza de Armas **21**

or 054/331-952); from Cusco (12–15 hr.), **Cruz del Sur** (© 054/221-909); and from Chivay/Colca Canyon (3–4 hr.), **Reyna** (© 054/426-549), and **Cristo Rey** (© 054/213-094).

BY TRAIN   The Arequipa rail station is at Av. Tacna y Arica 200, 8 blocks south of the city center (© **054/215-640,** or 054/223-600 for reservations). Puno-to-Arequipa trains are now available only by private charter for groups; check www.perurail.com for the latest information.

GETTING AROUND

Arequipa is compact, and most of its top attractions can easily be seen on foot. Taxis are inexpensive and plentiful, easily hailed on the street, and best used at night. Most trips in town cost no more than S/3 (75¢). To call a taxi at night, try **Taxi Seguro** (© 054/450-250), **Taxi Sur** (© 054/465-656), **Master Taxi** (© 054/220-505), or **Ideal Taxi** (© 054/288-888).

A Note of Caution

Arequipa's bus and rail stations—as well as the buses and trains themselves—are fairly notorious for attracting thieves. Travelers are advised to pay very close attention to their belongings, even going so far as to lock them to luggage racks. The route between Arequipa and Puno especially has earned a bad reputation. It's best to opt for more exclusive and safer, as well as more expensive, first-class seats on the more upscale bus companies recommended above.

A car isn't necessary in Arequipa unless you wish to explore the countryside, especially Colca and/or Cotahuasi canyons, independently. Try **Lucava Rent-A-Car,** Aeropuerto and Centro Comercial Cayma no. 10 (© 054/663-378); or **Avis,** Aeropuerto (© 054/443-576) and Palacio Viejo 214 (© 054/282-519).

VISITOR INFORMATION

There's a **tourist information booth** at the Aeropuerto Rodríquez Ballón, Calle Moral 316 (© **054/444-564**), open Monday through Friday from 9am to 4pm. There's also a very helpful office at Portal de la Municipalidad 112 (© **054/211-021**), on the Plaza de Armas across from the cathedral; it's open daily from 8am to 6pm. The **tourist police,** Jerusalén 315 at the corner of Ugarte (© **054/239-888**), also give out maps and tourism information.

FAST FACTS   You'll find ATMs in the courtyards of the historic Casa Ricketts, San Francisco 108, now the offices of **Banco Continental.** Other banks in the historic center include **Banco Latino** at San Juan de Dios 112, and **Banco de Crédito** at San Juan de Dios and General Morán 101. Money changers can generally be found waving calculators and stacks of dollars on the Plaza de Armas and major streets leading off the main square. There are several *casas de cambio* (money-exchange houses) near the Plaza de Armas.

In an emergency, call **Policía Nacional** at © 054/254-020 or **Policía de Turismo** at © 054/239-888. For medical attention, go to **Clínica Arequipa,** Avenida Bolognesi at Puente Grau (© 054/253-416), or **Hospital General,** Peral/Don Bosco (© 054/231-818).

Arequipa has plenty of Internet *cabinas.* Two of the cheapest and fastest are **La Red,** Jerusalén 306B (© 054/286-700), and **TravelNet,** Jerusalén 218 (© 054/205-548). Most *cabinas* are open daily from 8am to 10pm, charge S/2 (50¢) per hour, and have Net2Phone or other programs allowing very cheap Web-based international phone calls.

The main **post office** is located at Calle Moral 118 (© 054/215-246); it's open Monday through Saturday from 8am to 8pm and Sunday from 9am to 2pm. There's a **DHL** office at Santa Catalina 115 (© 054/220-045). The **Telefónica del Perú** main offices are located at Av. Los Arces 200 B, Cayma district (© 054/252-020).

WHAT TO SEE & DO
THE TOP ATTRACTIONS

Monasterio de Santa Catalina ✶✶✶ *Kids*   Arequipa's stellar and serene Convent of Santa Catalina, founded in 1579 under the Dominican order, is the most important and impressive religious monument in Peru. This is not just another church complex; it is more like a small, labyrinthine village, with narrow cobblestoned streets, plant-lined passageways, pretty plazas and fountains, chapels, and cloisters. Tall, thick walls, painted sunburned orange, faded blue, and brick red, hide dozens of small cells where more than 200 sequestered nuns once lived. Built in 1569, the convent remained a mysterious world unto itself until 1970, when local authorities forced the sisters to install modern infrastructure, a requirement that led to opening the convent for tourism. Today, only a couple of dozen cloistered nuns remain, out of sight of the hundreds of tourists who arrive daily to explore the huge and curious complex.

Santa Catalina feels like a small village in Andalucía, Spain, with its predominantly *mudéjar* (Moorish-Christian) architecture, intense sunlight and shadows, and streets named for Spanish cities. In all, it contains three cloisters, six streets, 80 housing units, a square, an art gallery, and a cemetery. Though the nuns entered the convent having taken vows of poverty, they lived in relative luxury, having paid a dowry to live the monastic life amid servants (who outnumbered the nuns), well-equipped kitchens, and art collections. Today, the convent has been nicely restored, though it retains a rustic appeal. Visitors are advised to wait for an informative guided tour (in English and other languages), though it's also fun just to wander around. Of particular note are the Orange Tree Cloister, with mural paintings over the arches; Calle Toledo, a long boulevard with a communal *lavandería* at its end, where the sisters washed their clothes in halved earthenware jugs; the 17th-century kitchen with charred walls; and the rooms belonging to Sor Ana, a 17th-century nun at the convent who was beatified by Pope John Paul II and is on her way to becoming a saint. Visitors can enter the choir room of the church, but it's difficult to get a good look at the main chapel and its marvelous painted cupola. To see the church, slip in during early morning Mass (daily at 7:30am); the cloistered nuns remain secluded behind a wooden grille.

Santa Catalina 301. ⓒ 054/229-798. www.santacatalina.org.pe. Admission S/25 ($7). Daily 9am–4pm.

Museo Santuarios Andinos ★★ (Kids)   The Museum of Andean Sanctuaries has a number of fascinating exhibits, including mummies and artifacts from the Inca Empire, but it is dominated by one small girl: Juanita, the Ice Maiden of Ampato. The victim of a ritualistic sacrifice by Inca priests high on the volcano Mount Ampato and buried in ice at more than 6,000m (20,000 ft.), "Juanita" was discovered in almost perfect condition in 1995 after the eruption of a volcano melted ice on the peak. Only Inca priests were allowed to ascend to such a high point, where the gods were believed to have lived. Juanita, who became famous worldwide through a *National Geographic* report on the find, died from a violent blow to the head; she was 13 or 14 at the time of her death. Her

---

⟨Tips⟩ A Safety Note

Arequipa has earned a reputation as one of Peru's more unsafe cities, mostly in terms of pickpocketing, though locals continue to talk about tourist robberies and even "strangle muggings." I've never had a problem in Arequipa, but I do think that late at night, you should be especially cautious exiting bars and restaurants in the historic center, and, as always, leave unnecessary belongings in your hotel. Some taxi drivers in Arequipa also warn about their colleagues who set up tourists for ambushes. They suggest either calling for a cab or getting into taxis with older drivers, since most of the crimes have been perpetrated by younger drivers.

remarkable preservation has allowed researchers to gain great insights into Inca culture by analyzing her DNA. Today, she is kept in a glass-walled freezer chamber here, less a mummy than a frozen body nearly 600 years old. Displayed nearby are some of the superb doll offerings and burial items found alongside the corpse. Guided visits are mandatory.

Santa Catalina 210. © **054/200-345.** Admission S/15 ($4.25) adults, S/5 ($1.50) students, free for seniors. Mon–Sat 9am–5:45pm; Sun 9am–3pm.

Plaza de Armas 🐱🐱 Arequipa's grand Plaza de Armas, an elegant and symmetrical square of gardens and a central fountain lined by arcaded buildings on three sides, is the focus of urban life. It is one of the loveliest main squares in Peru, though its profile suffered considerable damage when the great earthquake of 2001 felled one of the cathedral's two towers and whittled the other to a delicate pedestal. The 17th-century neoclassical **Catedral,** previously devastated by fire and other earthquakes, is likely to remain closed through at least 2004 to repair the damage, though it remains an impressive sight, occupying one entire side of the main square.

La Compañía 🐱🐱, just off the plaza at the corner of San Francisco and Morán, opposite the cathedral, is a splendid 17th-century Jesuit church with an elaborate (plateresque) facade carved of *sillar* stone. The magnificent portal, one of the finest in Peru, shows the end date of the church's construction, 1698, more than a century after work began on it. The interior holds a handsome carved cedar main altar, bathed in gold leaf, and two impressive chapels: the Capilla de San Ignacio, which has a remarkable painted cupola, and the Capilla Real, or Royal Chapel. Painted murals in the sacristy feature a jungle motif in brilliant colors. Next door to the church are the stately Jesuit cloisters, of stark *sillar* construction, now housing upscale boutiques (enter on Calle Morán). Climb to the top for good views of the city's rooftops and distant volcanoes. The church is open Monday through Saturday from 9am to noon and 3 to 7pm.

Monasterio de la Recoleta 🐱 Across the Río Chili from the historic center of town, distinguished by its tall brick red–and–white steeple, is the Recoleta convent museum. It's only a 10-minute walk or short cab ride from the Plaza de Armas. Founded in 1648 and rebuilt after earthquakes, the peaceful Franciscan convent contains impressive cloisters with *sillar* columns and lovely gardens; today, just four of the original seven remain. The convent museum comprises several collections. In one room is a collection of pre-Inca culture artifacts, including funereal masks, textiles, and totems; in another are mummies and a series of paintings of the 12 Inca chieftains. At the rear of the convent is a small Amazonian museum,

---

⌢Tips Arequipa's Colonial Churches

Arequipa has a wealth of colonial churches that are well worth a visit if you have the time. They include **Iglesia de San Francisco** (Zela 103), built of *sillar* and brick in the 16th century with an impressive all-silver altar; **Iglesia de San Agustín** (at the corner of San Agustín and Sucre), with a superbly stylized baroque facade, an excellent example of 16th- and 17th-century mestizo architecture (it was rebuilt in 1898 after earthquake damage); **Iglesia de Santo Domingo** (at Santo Domingo and Piérola), and **Iglesia de La Merced** (La Merced 303).

House Tour: Arequipa's Other Colonial Mansions

Arequipa possesses one of the most attractive and harmonious colonial nuclei in Peru. Several extraordinary seigniorial houses were constructed in white *sillar* stone. They are predominantly flat-roofed single-story structures, a design that has helped them withstand the effects of frequent earthquakes that would have toppled less solid buildings. Most of these houses have attractive interior patios and elaborately carved facades. Best equipped for visitors is the recently restored **Casa del Moral** (see below), but several others are worth a look, especially if you have an interest in colonial architecture.

Just off the main square, **Casa Ricketts** (also called Casa Tristán del Pozo; San Francisco 108), a former seminary and today the offices of Banco Continental, is one of the finest colonial homes in Arequipa. Built in the 1730s, its beautiful portal, perhaps Arequipa's finest expression of colonial civil architecture, has delicate representations of the life of Jesus. Inside are two large, beautiful courtyards with gargoyle drainage pipes. On the other side of the cathedral, **Casa Arróspide** (also called Casa Iriberry; at the corner of Santa Catalina 101 at San Agustín), built in the late 18th century, is one of the most distinguished *sillar* mansions in the city. Now the **Cultural Center of San Agustín University** (© 054/204-482), it hosts temporary exhibits of contemporary art and photography; you'll also find an art shop and nice cafe with a terrace and great views over the top of the cathedral. Other colonial houses of interest include **Casa Arango** (Consuelo at La Merced), a squat and eclectic 17th-century home; **Casa Goyeneche** (La Merced 201), now the offices of Banco de Reserva; and **Casa de la Moneda** (Ugarte at Villaba).

stocked with curious items collected by Franciscan missionaries in the Amazon basin. The missionaries were understandably fascinated by prehistoric-looking fish, crocodiles, and piranhas, and the clothing of indigenous communities. Those souvenirs pose an interesting contrast to the Dominicans' fine library containing some 20,000 volumes, including rare published texts from the 15th century. Guides (tip basis) are available for 1-hour tours in English, Spanish, and French.

Recoleta 117. © 054/270-966. Admission adults S/5 ($1.50), students S/3 (75¢), free for seniors. Mon–Sat 9am–noon and 3–5pm.

Casa del Moral 🐾   An extraordinary mestizo-baroque mansion, built at the beginning of the 18th century by a Spanish knight and nicely restored with period detail in 1994, Casa del Moral offers one of the best windows onto colonial times in Arequipa. Named for an ancient mulberry tree—the *moral* found in the courtyard—the home is also distinguished by a magnificent stone portal with heraldic emblems carved in *sillar*. Handsome furnishings, carved wooden doors, and Cusco School oil paintings decorate large salons, built around a beautiful courtyard in the largest of the colonial residences in the city. Look for 17th-century maps that depict the borders and shapes of countries quite differently from their usual representations today. A second courtyard, painted cobalt blue, was used as the summer patio. Climb to the rooftop for a great view of Arequipa and the surrounding volcanoes. Visits are by guided tour (at no extra cost).

Calle Moral 318 (at Bolívar). © 054/210-084. Admission S/5 ($1.50) adults, S/3 (75¢) students. Mon–Sat 9am–5pm; Sun 9am–1pm.

SHOPPING

Arequipa is one of the best places in Peru to shop for top-quality baby alpaca, vicuña, and woolen goods. Many items are considerably more expensive than the lesser-quality goods sold in other parts of Peru. In Arequipa, you'll find nicer designs and export-quality knit sweaters, shawls, blankets, and scarves. Arequipa also has good leather goods and several excellent antiques shops featuring colonial pieces and even older items (remember, though, that these antiques cannot legally be exported from Peru).

Three general areas are particularly good for alpaca items. One is the cloisters next to La Compañía church at General Morán and San Juan de Dios, housing several alpaca boutiques and outlets. Another is Pasaje Catedral, the pedestrian mall just behind the cathedral. A third is Calle Santa Catalina. Shops with fine alpaca items include **Millma's Baby Alpaca,** Pasaje Catedral 177 (© 054/205-134); **Baby Alpaca Boutique,** Santa Catalina 208 (© 054/206-716); **Anselmo's Souvenirs,** Pasaje Catedral 119 (no phone); and an outlet store of the chain **Alpaca 111,** Calle Zela 212 (© 054/223-238).

For antiques, Calle Santa Catalina and nearby streets have several antiques shops. I found lots of items I wished I could have taken home at **Curiosidades,** Zela 207 (© 054/952-986); **Alvaro Valdivia Montoya**'s two shops at Santa Catalina 204 and Santa Catalina 217 (© 054/229-103); and **Arte Colonial,** Santa Catalina 312 (© 054/214-887).

There is a general handicrafts market with dozens of stalls in the old town jail, next door to the Plazuela de San Francisco (between Zela and Puente Grau). For handmade leather goods, stroll along Puente Bolognesi, which leads west from the Plaza de Armas, and you'll find numerous small stores with handbags, shoes, and other items.

A good bookstore with art books and English-language paperbacks is **Librería El Lector,** San Francisco 221 (no phone).

WHERE TO STAY

Arequipa has an ample roster of hotels and hostels at all levels. Several occupy historic houses in the old quarter. The area north of the Plaza de Armas is nicer and less chaotic and commercial than the streets south of the square. If you hop in a taxi from the airport or bus or train station, insist on going to the hotel of your choice; taxi drivers will often claim that a particular hotel is closed in order to take you to one that will pay them a commission.

EXPENSIVE

Hotel Libertador Arequipa ★★ *Kids*   Arequipa's swankest hotel near the historic center is in this handsome 1940s colonial-style building. In the midst of quiet Selva Alegre, the largest park in Arequipa, the midsize hotel is about a 15-minute walk from the main square. It maintains a colonial theme throughout, with soaring ceilings, historical murals, and dark-wood period furnishings in expansive, elegantly appointed rooms. The rooms, equipped with marble bathrooms, are about as large as you're likely to find. The hotel has a lovely outdoor pool (unheated) among nice gardens and tall palm trees. Families will appreciate the outdoor recreation and game area for children.

Plaza Bolívar, Selva Alegre, Arequipa. ⒸΦ 054/215-110. Fax 054/241-933. www.libertador.com.pe. 88 units. $115 deluxe double; $150–$185 suite. Rates include taxes. AE, DC, MC, V. **Amenities:** 2 restaurants; bar; large outdoor pool; fitness center; Jacuzzi; sauna; concierge; room service; laundry service. *In room:* A/C, TV, minibar, safe.

La Maison d' Elise ⓖ *Finds*   A nondescript facade hides this small gem of a hotel. Across from the park on the other side of Puente Grau, just beyond the historic center, this 10-year-old hotel is like a small Mediterranean village. Ochre and white villas are clustered around courtyards ripe with cacti and colorful flowering plants. Double rooms are very large and comfortably furnished; matrimonial suites have a lower-level sitting room. There are also apartments with private terraces. The hotel has a small pool with a rock waterfall, and a notable and nicely decorated restaurant. Deals are sometimes available. This hotel is less luxurious overall than the Hotel Libertador, but it's also quirkier and much cheaper.

Av. Bolognesi 104, Yanahuara, Arequipa. Ⓒ 054/256-185. Fax 054/253-343. www.aqplink.com/hotel/ maison. 88 units. $70 double; $78–$96 suite. Rates include taxes. AE, DC, MC, V. **Amenities:** 2 restaurants; bar; pool; room service; laundry service. *In room:* A/C, TV, safe.

MODERATE

La Casa de Melgar Hostal ⓖⓖ *Value*   A spectacular colonial house made of white *sillar* (volcanic stone), this charming small hotel is one of the nicest in Peru, and one of the best values. Just 3 blocks from the Plaza de Armas, the lovingly restored 18th-century mansion—the former residence of the bishop of Arequipa—has massive, thick walls, three courtyards, and is decorated in rich brick red and blue. The ample rooms have good beds. Some rooms—especially those on the ground floor that have high vaulted brick ceilings—exude colonial character; if the hotel isn't full, ask to see a couple of them. The staff is very friendly. Breakfast is served in the neat little cafe next door in one of the courtyards. Advance reservations are a must in high season.

Melgar 108, Cercado, Arequipa. Ⓒ/fax 054/222-459, or 01/446-8343 for reservations. www. lared.net.pe/lacasademelgar. 23 units. $35–$45 double. Rates include taxes and breakfast. V. **Amenities:** Restaurant; bar; laundry service. *In room:* No phone.

La Casa de Mi Abuela Hostal ⓖ   One of the friendliest and best-run small hotels in Peru, "My Grandmother's House" is tucked behind a security gate but welcomes everyone with open arms and an easygoing atmosphere. An organic place that has grown from a tiny B&B into a very popular 50-room hotel, it is still family-run. Today, it's a self-contained tourism complex, with a restaurant, live-music *peña* bar, Internet access, book exchange, travel agency, and beautiful gardens with views of El Misti. Some rooms have roof terraces, others balconies. Many rooms are plainly decorated and cramped, but the hostel is still a very good deal given the level of services, facilities, and security. The hostel is about a 10-minute walk (6 blocks) north of the main square. It's often filled, so make advance reservations. They serve nice breakfasts in the garden (extra charge).

Jerusalén 606, Cercado, Arequipa. Ⓒ 054/241-206. Fax 054/242-761. www.lacasademiabuela.com. 50 units. $44 double. Rate includes taxes. DC, MC, V. **Amenities:** Restaurant; bar; pool; game room; laundry service. *In room:* TV, minibar, safe.

INEXPENSIVE

La Reyna *Value*   One of the most popular budget inns in town, La Reyna is smack in the middle of the historic center, just a block from the famed Santa Catalina monastery and paces away from plenty of bars and restaurants. The hostel's many rooms feed off a labyrinth of narrow staircases that climb up three floors to a roof terrace, a popular spot to hang out. There are simple, rock-bottom dormitory rooms for zero-budget travelers and a couple of rooftop *casitas* that have private bathrooms and their own terraces with awesome views of the mountains and the monastery below—they're something akin to back-packer penthouse suites. Room no. 20 is worth reserving if you can. The hostel, though a little haphazardly run, organizes lots of canyon treks and volcano climbing tours, and even offers Spanish classes.

Zela 209, Arequipa. ©/fax 054/286-578. 20 units. S/24 ($7) double w/o bathroom, S/35 ($10) double w/bathroom; S/12 ($3.50) per person in shared rooms. Rates include taxes. No credit cards. **Amenities:** Laundry service. *In room:* No phone.

Los Balcones de Moral y Santa Catalina ☆ (*Value* This inviting small hotel
is very comfortable and well furnished, a nice step up from budget hostels. In the heart of the old quarter, it's only a couple of blocks from the Plaza de Armas. Half of the house is colonial (1st floor); the other is republican, dating from the 1800s. The house is built around a colonial patio with a sunny terrace. Furnishings are modern, with wallpaper and firm beds. Eleven of the good-size rooms have large balconies with nice views of the city and hardwood floors; the other rooms are carpeted and less desirable (though quieter). All have good, tiled bathrooms.

Calle Moral 217, Arequipa. © 054/201-291. Fax 054/222-555. www.losbalconeshotel.com. 17 units. S/90 ($26) double. Rate includes taxes. MC, V. **Amenities:** Restaurant; laundry service. *In room:* TV.

WHERE TO DINE
Several restaurants in the historic quarter specialize in traditional Arequipeño cooking, though two of the best are a short taxi ride beyond downtown.

MODERATE
Ary Quepay ☆ PERUVIAN   A relaxed, rustic restaurant with a gardenlike dining room under a bamboo roof and skylights, Ary Quepay specializes in traditional Peruvian cooking. Starters include *choclo con queso* (corn on the cob with cheese), stuffed avocado, and *sopa a la criolla* with beef, noodles, and eggs. The main dishes are classic: *rocoto relleno* (stuffed peppers), *adobo* (pork stew with *ají*), and *escabeche de pescado* (spicy fish stew). There are a number of dishes for vegetarians, as well as good breakfasts, juices, and milkshakes. In the evenings, there's often live folkloric music.

Jerusalén 502. © 054/672-922. Main courses S/10–S/25 ($3–$7). DC, MC, V. Daily 8am–10pm.

El Viñedo ☆ ARGENTINE/GRILLED MEAT   Hard to say whether this restaurant would satisfy the purist carnivore instincts of my friends from Buenos Aires, but for Peru, this rustic yet refined restaurant is a winner. It does a good enough job with its *parrilladas* (mixed grills) to convince this gringo. There are also "Argentine" pizza (topped by ingredients such as grilled chorizo and served on wood boards) and pasta. A bonus for those who can only eat so much meat: a free salad bar. The interior is sprawling and candlelit, with a tango music soundtrack, a half dozen separate dining rooms, and a garden courtyard that a waiter told me is perfect for couples. The wine list may not earn the restaurant's name ("The Vineyard"), but it's pretty good for Peru, if a little expensive. Connected to the restaurant is El Jayari, a restaurant serving Peruvian dishes (and sharing the same chef and kitchen).

San Francisco 319-A. © 054/205-053. Reservations recommended on weekends. Main courses S/10–S/25 ($3–$7). AE, DC, MC, V. Daily 1pm–midnight.

Gianni *(Kids)* *(Value)* ITALIAN   A very popular, amiable trattoria on Arequipa's restaurant row, this bustling little place is often filled with more locals and families than gringos—always a good sign. Gianni serves standard but well prepared Italian fare: gnocchi, ravioli, cannelloni, and lasagna, as well as trout and other fish and steak. There's seating on the second floor above the bar, or downstairs under a vaulted ceiling. Service is fast and friendly.

San Francisco 304. ✆ 054/287-138. Reservations recommended. Main courses S/9–S/24 ($2.50–$7). DC, MC, V. Mon–Sat 6pm–1am.

Sol de Mayo *(★★★)* *(Value)* PERUVIAN   A 5-minute taxi ride from downtown Yanahuara, the city's nicest residential neighborhood, this longtime stalwart (which has been around more than a century) is the standard-bearer for Arequipeño cooking. A favorite of upscale locals and tourists alike, it is perhaps the most delightful of the city's restaurants. The colonial tables are set around the edges of a breezy, picture-perfect courtyard with thick grass, geraniums, cacti, a small pool and cascading waterfall, and strolling altiplano musicians. There are also indoor dining rooms inside the brick red–and–yellow *sillar* stone building, but nothing beats eating outdoors here. Peruvian specialties are Sol de Mayo's calling card: *chicharrón de chancho* (fried pork), ostrich, fresh shellfish, and a tantalizing lineup of *ceviches*. Starters include a yummy mixed salad of *choclo* (white corn), tomato, and avocado. The pisco sours are a must to start off your meal. Even for budget-oriented backpackers, this would be the place in Arequipa to splurge.

Jerusalén 207, Yanahuara. ✆ 054/254-148. Reservations recommended. Main courses S/12–S/30 ($3.50–$8.50). AE, DC, MC, V. Daily 11am–10pm.

Tradición Arequipeña *(★★)* *(Value)* PERUVIAN   It's a few miles outside of town in the Paucarpata district, so you'll need to grab a taxi to get to this classic open-air restaurant. Elegantly set amid beautiful gardens with stunning views of snowcapped El Misti from the upper deck, it's open only for lunch (although you could also squeeze in an early dinner at 5 or 6pm). Most encouraging is how popular it is among tourists and locals alike. It serves large portions of classic Peruvian dishes, such as *cuy, adobo,* and *ceviche,* but they're more carefully prepared here than in many other *comida típica* restaurants. A good starter is the combination fried cheese and fried yuca with *picante* sauce and *salsa verde* (green sauce). Meals are very affordable for such a refined place.

Av. Dolores 111, Paucarpata. ✆ 054/426-467. Reservations recommended on weekends. Main courses S/8–S/32 ($2–$9). AE, DC, MC, V. Daily noon–7pm.

Zig Zag *(★★)* PERUVIAN/GRILLED MEAT   This is one of my favorite restaurants in Arequipa. Zig Zag is both chic and comfortable, equally welcoming to families and young people on dates. It's also unique: The house specialty is stone-grilled ostrich. The owners have an ostrich farm with 4,000 ostriches, and they educate their customers about ostrich as a healthy alternative to other meats. Inside the leather-bound menu is a chart illustrating how low in cholesterol, calories, and fat the great bird is. (Alpaca is healthier still.) Try the ostrich carpaccio in lemon or ostrich stone-grilled with Swiss-style hash browns (or get any other meat, such as lamb, beef, or alpaca, prepared in a similar fashion). Other favorites are fondue and pasta. Big-time meat eaters should order the *piedra criolla* (stone-grilled chorizo, beef, lamb, pork, hearts, intestines, and gizzards with potatoes and chimichurri sauce), a world-class bargain for just S/27 ($8). The two-level restaurant plays hip music and has attentive service. A couple of tables upstairs are perched on a ledge overlooking the attractive Plazuela San Francisco.

Calle Zela 210. ℂ **054/206-020.** Reservations recommended. Main courses S/12–S/30 ($3.50–$8.50). AE, DC, MC, V. Daily 6pm–midnight.

INEXPENSIVE

Govinda VEGETARIAN/INDIAN   A good all-around vegetarian restaurant, Govinda—part of a chain across Peru, with the original in London—has a pleasant outdoor garden dining area and good-value fixed-price menus and dishes. It serves vegetarian Italian, Asian, and Peruvian items, as well as pizza, pasta, soup, salad, and yogurt dishes, a nice reprieve from many travelers' overdose of chicken, pork, and alpaca in Peru. The daily fixed-price menus are very cheap, though the self-service buffet is not all-you-can-eat and its lineup of vegetarian dishes isn't the most creative you've ever seen. It's a good place for breakfast, with muesli, brown bread, fruit salad, and juice.

Santa Catalina 120. ℂ **054/285-540.** Reservations not accepted. Main courses S/5–S/15 ($1.50–$4.25); *menú* S/6–S/15 ($1.75–$4.25); buffet S/11 ($3). No credit cards. Daily 7am–9:30pm.

Los Leños PIZZERIA   This is a charming cave of a pizza place, where diners share long wooden tables, and the footprints of many hundreds of travelers carry on in the graffiti that covers every square inch of stone walls up to a vaulted ceiling. The house specialty is pizza from the wood-fired oven; among the many varieties, the Leños house pizza is a standout: cheese, sausage, bacon, ham, chicken, and mushrooms. Those who've had their fill of pizza can go for other standards, such as lasagna and a slew of other pastas. Los Leños opens early; you can choose from among 20 different "American breakfasts."

Jerusalén 407. ℂ **054/289-179.** Reservations not accepted. Main courses S/6–S/13 ($1.75–$3.75); *menú* S/6–S/15 ($1.75–$4.25); buffet S/11 ($3). No credit cards. Daily 7am–11pm.

AREQUIPA AFTER DARK

Arequipa has a pretty hopping nightlife in the old quarter, with plenty of bars, restaurants, and discos catering both to gringos and locals. Sunday through Wednesday is usually pretty quiet, with things heating up on Thursday night.

Las Quenas, Santa Catalina 302 (ℂ **054/281-115**), is a *peña* bar and restaurant featuring live Andean music Monday through Saturday from 9pm to midnight and special dance performances on Friday and Saturday nights. There's a nominal cover charge of S/5 ($1.50). It's a cozy little place that serves pretty good Peruvian dishes. You can also catch *peña* music at **El Tuturutu,** Portal San Agustín 105 (ℂ **054/201-842**), a restaurant on the main square. Another spot for folkloric music is **La Troica,** Jerusalén 522 (ℂ 054/225-690), a tourist-oriented restaurant in an old house.

As for pubs and bars, **Siwara,** Santa Catalina 210 (ℂ **054/626-218**), is a great-looking beer tavern that spills into two patios in the building of the Santuarios Andinos museum, across from the Santa Catalina monastery. Fashionable young people spill out of **La Leña,** Zela 202 (no phone), a pub with good music and drinks, open until the wee hours. Another good spot for a drink is **Montreál Le Café Art,** Santa Catalina 300B (no phone), which features live music Wednesday through Saturday and has happy hours between 5 and 11pm. **La Casa de Klaus,** Zela 207 (ℂ **054/203-711**), is a simple and brightly lit tavern popular with German, British, and local beer drinkers.

For a little more action, check out **Forum Rock Café,** San Francisco 317 (ℂ **054/202-697**), a huge place that is equal parts restaurant, bar, disco, and concert hall. It sports a rainforest theme, with jungle vegetation and "canopy walkways" everywhere. Live bands (usually rock) take the stage Thursday through Saturday. Just down the street, **Déjà Vu,** San Francisco 319 (© **054/ 221-904**), has a good bar with a mix of locals and gringos, a lively dance floor, and English-language movies on a big screen every night at 8pm. **Kibosh,** Zela 205 (© **054/626-218**), is a chic, upscale pub with four bars, a dance floor, and live music (ranging from Latin to hard rock) Wednesday through Saturday.

AN EXCURSION FROM AREQUIPA: COLCA VALLEY

The primary day trips and overnight excursions from Arequipa are to Colca Canyon, where the highlight is Cruz del Cóndor, a lookout point where giant South American condors soar overhead; and trekking, rafting, and mountaineering expeditions through the valley. Tour agencies have mushroomed in Arequipa, and most offer very similar city, canyon, countryside *(campiña),* and adventure trips. Going with a tour operator is economical and by far the most convenient option—public transportation is poor and very time-consuming in these parts. Only a handful of tour operators in Arequipa are well run, however, and visitors need to be careful when signing up for guided tours to the canyon and valley. Avoid independent guides who don't have official accreditation. Adventure and sports enthusiasts should contact one of the specialist agencies listed below. A minimum of 2 or 3 days is needed to see a significant part of the valley.

COLCA CANYON 👣👣👣

Mario Vargas Llosa, novelist and the most famous Arequipeño, described Colca as "The Valley of Wonders." That is no literary overstatement. Colca, located 165km (102 miles) north of Arequipa, is one of the most scenic regions in Peru, a land of imposing snowcapped volcanoes, artistically terraced agricultural slopes, narrow gorges, arid desert landscapes and vegetation, and remote traditional villages, many visibly scarred by seismic tremors common in southern Peru.

The Río Colca, the origin of the mighty Amazon, cuts through the canyon, which remained largely unexplored until the 1970s, when rafting expeditions descended to the bottom of the gorge. Reaching depths of 3,400m (11,152 ft.)— twice as deep as the Grand Canyon—the Cañón del Colca forms part of a volcanic mountain range more than 100km (62 miles) long. Among the great volcanoes, several of which are still active, are Mount Ampato, where a sacrificed Inca maiden was discovered frozen in 1995, and Mount Coropuna, Peru's second-highest peak at 6,425m (21,200 ft.).

Dispersed across the Colca Valley are 14 colonial-era villages that date from the 16th century, distinguished primarily by their small but often richly decorated churches. Local populations, descendants of the Collaguas and Cabanas, pre-Inca ethnic groups, preserve ancient customs and distinctive traditional dress. Ethnic groups can be distinguished by their hats; some women wear hats with colored ribbons; others have elaborately embroidered and sequined headgear. The valley's meticulous agricultural terracing, even more extensive than the terraces of the Sacred Valley, were first cultivated more than 1,000 years ago. Colca villages are celebrated for their vibrant festivals, as authentic as any in Peru, throughout the year.

Most organized tours of the region are very similar if not identical. The road that leads out of Arequipa and into the valley, bending around the Misti and Chachani volcanoes, is poor and unbearably dusty. It passes through the **Salinas and Aguada Blanca Nature Reserve,** where you'll usually have a chance to see vicuñas, llamas, and alpacas from the road. The altiplano landscape is barren and bleak. Most tours stop at volcano and valley lookout points along the way before arriving in Chivay.

The gateway to the region is **Chivay,** the Colca's main town on the edge of the canyon, a little more than 3 hours from Arequipa. This easygoing market town lies at an altitude of 3,600m (11,520 ft.). From here, many organized tours embark on short treks in the valley and visit the wonderfully relaxing hot springs of **La Calera,** about 4km (2½ miles) from Chivay. Evening visits to the hot springs allow visitors to bathe in open-air pools beneath a huge, starry sky; artificial light in the valley is almost nonexistent. Charming colonial villages in the valley often visited by tours include Yanque, Coporaque, Maca, and Lari.

Most 2-day tours head out early the following morning for **Cruz del Cóndor,** a lookout point quickly growing in fame. At a spot 1,200m (3,960 ft.) above the canyon river, crowds gather, zoom lenses poised, to witness a stunning wildlife spectacle. Beginning around 9am, Andean condors—the largest birds in the world, with wingspans of 3.5m (12 ft.)—begin to appear, circling far below in the gorge and gradually gaining altitude with each pass, until they soar silently above the heads of awestruck admirers. Condors are such immense creatures that they cannot lift off from the ground; instead, they take flight from cliff perches. Each morning, the condors glide and climb theatrically before heading out along the river in search of prey. To witness the condors' majestic flight up close is a mesmerizing sight, capable of producing goose bumps in even the most jaded travelers. The condors return late in the afternoon, but fewer people attend the show then.

GETTING THERE   The great majority of travelers to the Colca Valley visit on guided tours, arranged in Arequipa. Conventional travel agencies offer day trips to Cruz del Cóndor, leaving at 3 or 4am, with brief stops at Chivay before returning to Arequipa ($15–$20 per person)—it's an awful lot to pack into a single day, especially at high altitude. Two-day tours ($35–$50) are much more enjoyable. The best all-purpose agencies in Arequipa are **Giardino Tours,** Calle Jerusalén 604-A (© 054/241-206); **Santa Catalina Tours,** Santa Catalina 219 (© 054/216-994); and **Illary Tours,** Santa Catalina 205 (© 054/220-844).

Local buses travel from Arequipa to Cabanaconde, near the Cruz del Cóndor, with stops in Chivay. **Reyna,** Terminal Terrestre (© 054/426-549), and **Cristo Rey,** San Juan de Dios 510 (© 054/213-094), make these runs.

OUTDOOR ADVENTURES IN COLCA VALLEY

The countryside around Arequipa is some of the best in Peru for outdoor adventure travel. Trails crisscross the Colca Valley, crossing mountain ridges, agricultural terraces, and curious rock formations, and passing colonial towns and fields where llamas and vicuñas graze. The most common pursuits are river running, treks through the canyon valleys, and mountain climbing on the volcanoes just beyond the city. Many tour agencies in Arequipa offer 2- and 3-day visits to the Colca and Cotahuasi canyons, as well as longer, more strenuous treks through the valleys. (Some of the most interesting, but most time-consuming and difficult, expeditions combine rafting and trekking.) Your best bet for organizing any of these activities is with one of the tour operators below; several in Arequipa focus solely on eco- and adventure tourism.

Cusipata Viajes y Turismo, Jerusalén 408-A (© **054/203-966**), is the local specialist for Chili and Colca rafting and kayaking (including courses), and its guides frequently subcontract out to other agencies in Arequipa. **Ideal Tours,**

Urbanización San Isidro F-2, Vallecito (© 054/244-433), handles Chili and Majes rafting, as well as Colca and other standard tours. **Apumayo Expediciones,** Garcilaso 265 Int 3, Cusco (© 084/246-018; www.cuscoperu.com/apumayo), is good for long trekking/rafting expeditions to Cotahuasi and Colca, as is **Amazonas Explorer,** Zela 212 (© 054/212-813; www.amazonas-explorer.com), an international company that organizes hardy multisport trips to Cotahuasi and Colca (which can be combined with tours to Cusco, the Inca Trail, and Machu Picchu). **Apu Expediciones,** Portal Comercio 157, Cusco (© 084/652-975), arranges rafting trips to Majes and Colca, among other adventure options.

Colca Trek, Jerusalén 401-B (© 054/224-578), and **Peru Trekking,** Jerusalén 302-B (© 054/223-404), are two other local outfits that offer canyon treks of 3 to 5 days or more and a number of other adventure activities, such as horseback riding, mountain biking, rafting, and climbing.

For mountain climbing, one agency stands out: **Zárate Aventuras,** Santa Catalina 204, no. 3 (© 054/202-461; fax 054/263-107; www.zarateadventures.com), which is run by Carlos Zárate, perhaps the top climbing guide in Arequipa (a title his dad held before him). He can arrange any area climb and has equipment rental and a 24-hour mountain rescue service. Climbing expedition costs (per person) are El Misti, $50; Chachani, $70; and Colca Canyon, $75. They also organize rafting and mountain biking adventures.

9 Iquitos & the Northern Amazon

1,860km (1,153 miles) NE of Lima

Iquitos, the gateway to the northern Amazon, is Peru's largest jungle town and the capital of its largest department, Loreto (which occupies nearly a third of the national territory). Though you must fly to get here—unless you have a full week to kill for hot and uncomfortable river travel—the pockets of jungle down- and upriver from Iquitos are the most accessible of the Peruvian Amazon basin. Some of the best jungle lodges in the country are located just a few hours by boat from Iquitos. Because the region is the most trafficked and developed of the Peruvian Amazon, costs are lower for most jungle excursions than they are in the more exclusive Manu Biosphere Reserve.

Founded by Jesuits in the 1750s, Iquitos lies about 3,220km (2,000 miles) upriver from the mouth of the Amazon River. Its proximity to South America's greatest rainforest and its isolation from the rest of Peru have created a unique tropical atmosphere. In the late 1860s and 1870s, pioneering merchants got rich off the booming rubber trade and built ostentatious mansions along the river. Today, though, those great homes are faded monuments to the city's glory days, and just blocks from the main square lies the fascinating Belén district, where families live in a squalid pile of ramshackle wooden houses on the banks of the river. Some houses are propped up by spindly stilts, while others float, tethered to poles, when the river rises 6m (20 ft.) or more. Belén looks Far Eastern, and Iquitos seemingly has more in common with steamy tropical Asian cities than the highlands of Peru. Like a South American Saigon, the air is waterlogged, and the streets buzz with unrelenting waves of motorcycles and *motocarros* (or *mototaxis*). Locals speak a languid, mellifluous Spanish unmatched in other parts of the country, and they dress not in alpaca sweaters and shawls, but in flesh-baring tank tops and short skirts.

Iquitos has an intoxicating feel that's likely to detain you for at least a couple of days. But for most visitors, the lure of the Amazon rainforest is the primary attraction. Virgin rainforest, though, is hard to find. To lay eyes on exotic wildlife, such as pink dolphins, caiman, and macaws, you have to get at least 80km (50 miles) away from Iquitos and onto secondary waterways. Options for rainforest excursions include lodge visits, river cruises, and independent guided treks.

ESSENTIALS
GETTING THERE
BY PLANE   Iquitos's **Aeropuerto Francisco Secada Vigneta** (© 065/260-151) was until recently an international airport; flights from Miami were suspended in 1999. **Aero Continente** (© 01/242-4242), **Aviandina** (© 01/242-4242 or 01/484-1177), and **TANS** (© 01/213-6000) fly daily from Lima and other cities in the Loreto department.

The airport is usually chaotic when flights arrive, with dozens of representatives of tour operators and countless touts competing for your attention. Do not let anyone take your bags, and don't let anyone you don't know hop in a cab with you. To downtown Iquitos, an automobile taxi costs about S/10 ($3), by *motocarro*, S/7 ($2).

BY BOAT   Arriving by boat is an option only for those with the luxury of ample time; it takes about a week when the river is high (and 3–4 days in the dry season) to reach the capital city of Loretos upriver along the Amazon from Pucallpa or Yurimaguas. The Iquitos port, **Puerto Masusa,** is about 3km (2 miles) north of the Plaza de Armas. To travel to Colombia or Brazil by boat, your best bet is by river cruise (p. 665). Cruises to Manaus, Santarém, and Belém in Brazil are offered by Amazon Tours and Cruises (see below). Direct service all the way to Manaus has been suspended.

GETTING AROUND
BY TAXI/*MOTOTAXI*   Motorcycle buggies or rickshaws *(motocarros)* are everywhere in Iquitos; if you don't mind the noise and wind in your face (and aren't worried about accidents), it's a great way to get around. In-town fares are S/1.5 (40¢). Regular car taxis are only slightly less ubiquitous; most trips in town cost S/2 (60¢).

BY BUS   *Combis* (minivans) and *ómnibuses* (buses) travel principal routes, but are much less comfortable and not much less expensive than more convenient *motocarros*.

BY FOOT   Though the city is spread over several square kilometers, the core of downtown Iquitos is compact and easy to get around on foot, and even the waterfront Belén district is easy to walk to. Some hostels and hotels are a distance from the main square, though, requiring the occasional use of inexpensive *motocarros*.

VISITOR INFORMATION
A municipal **tourism information booth** is located in the arrivals terminal at the airport (© 065/235-621). It maintains a chart of hotels and prices, and the staff is happy to dispense information about the various jungle tour and lodge operators. One of Peru's most helpful tourism information offices is at Napo 226 on the north side of the Plaza de Armas (© 065/235-621). The English-speaking staff offers free maps and lists of all recommended hotels and tour operators (including photo albums of lodges) and will try to sort through the (often intentionally) confusing sales pitches of jungle tour companies. The office is open

ATTRACTIONS ●
Barrio de Belén
(market & port) **17**
Casa de Fierro **10**
Iglesia Matriz **7**
Malecón Tarapacá **11**
Museo Amazónico **13**
Plaza de Armas **8**

ACCOMMODATIONS ■
El Dorado Plaza Hotel **6**
Hospedaje El Sitio **16**
Hospedaje La Pascana **2**
Hotel Amazon Garden **1**
Hotel Victoria Regia **15**
Real Hotel Iquitos **9**

DINING ◆
El Huaralino **14**
El Nuevo Mesón **3**
Fitzcarraldo **4**
Montecarlo **5**
Regal (Casa de Fierro) **10**
Restaurant Gran Maloca **12**

Monday through Saturday from 8am to 8pm, as well as occasional Sunday mornings.

FAST FACTS   Banks and ATMs are located along Putumayo and Próspero, on the south side of the Plaza de Armas. Two banks that exchange traveler's checks and cash are **Banco de Crédito,** Putumayo 201, and **Banco Continental,** Sargento Lores 171. Money changers can usually be found hanging about the Plaza de Armas and along Putumayo and Próspero, but figure the exchange beforehand and count your money carefully.

If you're planning to cross into Brazil or Colombia, I suggest you make contact with your embassy in Lima or even at home before traveling to Peru. For questions about border-crossing formalities for jungle travel to and from Brazil and Colombia (regulations have been known to change frequently), contact the **Migraciones** office at Malecón Tarapacá 382 (© 065/235-371).

In a medical emergency, call **Cruz Roja (Red Cross)** at © 065/241-072. For medical attention, visit **Clínica Ana Stahl,** Av. la Marina 285 (© 065/252-535);

Essalud, Av. la Marina 2054 (© 065/250-333); or **Hospital Regional,** Av. 28 de Julio s/n, Punchana (© 065/251-882). The **tourist police** office is located at Sargento Lores 834 (© 065/242-081).

There are several **Internet** *cabinas* near the Plaza de Armas, particularly on Próspero and Putumayo. The one next to the entrance to the Casa de Fierro is pretty dependable. Most stay open late, and rates are about S/2 (50¢) per hour. Iquitos's **post office** is located at Arica 403, at the corner of Morona (© 065/231-915); it's open Monday through Friday from 8am to 6pm, and Saturday from 8am to 3pm. The **Telefónica del Perú** office is at Arica 276.

WHAT TO SEE & DO
IN IQUITOS

The Plaza de Armas, while perhaps not Peru's most distinguished, is marked by an early-20th-century, neo-Gothic **Iglesia Matriz** (parish church) and the **Casa de Fierro.** The walls, ceiling, and balcony of this Gustave Eiffel–designed house (for the 1889 Paris Exhibition) are plastered in rectangular sheets of iron. Said to be the first prefabricated house in the Americas, it was shipped unassembled from Europe and built on-site where it currently stands.

One block away from the plaza, facing the Amazon River, the riverfront promenade known as the **Malecón Tarapacá** was recently enlarged and improved with fountains, benches, and street lamps, making it the focus of Iquitos's urban life. It is lined with several exquisite 19th-century mansions; the most spectacular is probably **Casa Hernández,** no. 302–308. The **Museo Amazónico,** Malecón Tarapacá 386, has occasionally interesting exhibits of Amazon folklore and tribal art, as well as a curious collection of 76 Indian statues made of fiberglass but fashioned as if they were bronze. It's open Monday through Friday from 9am to 1pm and 3 to 7pm, Saturday from 9am to 1pm; admission is S/3 (85¢). Other houses worth checking out are **Casa Fitzcarrald,** Napo 200–212, an adobe house belonging to a famed rubber baron; **Casa Cohen,** Próspero 401–437; **Casa Morey,** Brasil, first block; and the **Logia Unión Amazónica,** Nauta 262.

The waterfront **Barrio de Belén** 🀄🀄, about a 15-minute walk south along the malecón, is Iquitos's most interesting quarter. Known for its sprawling and odiferous open-air market, where you'll find a bounty of strange and wonderful Amazon fish, fauna, and fruit, Belén's residential district is a seedy but endlessly fascinating shantytown. Houses are constructed above the waters of the Amazon, and when the river is high, transportation is by canoe. You are free to walk around in dry season (or take a locally arranged canoe trip during much of the year), but you should go in a group and only during the day.

JUNGLE LODGES & TOURS

Though the town itself holds a kind of sultry fascination, ecotourism is the primary draw for visitors to Iquitos, and the giant Amazon River system just beyond the city holds a wealth of natural wonders: rustic jungle lodges, canopy walks, and opportunities for bird-watching, piranha fishing, visits to Indian villages, and wildlife-spotting (as well as less-standard activities, such as shaman consultations and *ayahuasca* drug ceremonies). The mighty Amazon reaches widths of about 4km (2½ miles) beyond Iquitos, and the river basin contains some 2,000 species of fish; 4,000 species of birds; native mammals such as anteaters, tapirs, marmosets, and pink dolphins; and 60 species of reptiles, including caiman and anacondas. Your options for exploring the jungle are lodge stays (which include jungle activities such as treks and canoe excursions), river cruises, or more adventurous guided camping treks. Don't expect to spend your time in the jungle checking off a lengthy list of wildlife sightings, though; no matter where you go, your opportunities for viewing more than a couple of these birds, fish, and mammals will be severely limited. The northern Amazon basin within reach of Iquitos has been explored and popularly exploited far longer than the more remote southern jungle areas of Manu and Tambopata.

For a quick and simple experience, you can stay at a lodge only an hour or two by boat from Iquitos, in secondary jungle. You're likely to see more fauna and have a more authentic experience in primary rainforest, but you'll have to travel up to 4 hours by boat and pay quite a bit more for the privilege. Generally speaking, you'll have to trade comforts for authenticity. A true foray into virgin jungle, far from the heavy footsteps of thousands of guides and visitors, requires at least a week of demanding camping and trekking. Hard-core ecotypes may wish to contract private guides to go deep into the *selva* and camp; ask at the tourism information office for a list of licensed, official guides. (They also have a list of blacklisted guides.)

Prices for lodges and tours vary tremendously. Costs are directly related to distance from Iquitos; the farther away, the more expensive they are. For conventional lodges contracted in Iquitos, lodge tours average around $40 to $50, going up to $100 or more per person per day for lodges located farthest from the city. Some budget lodges offer bargain rates, as little as $25 to $30 per day (in most cases, you get what you pay for), and independent guides may charge as little as $15 a day. Costs include transportation, lodging, buffet-style meals, and guided activities. (Beverages are extra.)

Beware: There are many look-alike lodges and tours. Hustlers and con artists abound in Iquitos, and you need to exercise a certain amount of caution before handing over your money for a promised itinerary. The local tourism office (© **065/235-621**) works hard to ferret out guides, tours, and lodges with bad reputations. If you're making a tour decision on the ground in Iquitos, it's a good idea to visit the office first for the most up-to-date information.

Jungle Lodges

Most jungle lodges have either individual thatched-roof bungalows or main buildings with individual rooms; communal dining areas; hammock lounges; covered plank walkways; toilets; and hot- or cold-water sinks and showers. A few lodges have extras such as swimming pools, lookout towers, canopy walkways, and electricity. Guests are taken on guided day- and nighttime excursions, including jungle walks, piranha fishing, and canoe and motorboat trips to spot birds, caimans, and dolphins. Many lodges offer cheesy visits with local Indian tribes, staged for your pleasure, and some host *ayahuasca* rituals (with the privilege of

---

Tips Eco-nomizing

You can almost certainly get a better deal by going door-to-door to the lodge and tour sales offices in Iquitos and comparing programs and prices than you would by contracting one in Lima or from your home country prior to stepping foot in Peru. However, you risk not getting the tour you want when you want it. For many travelers, the extra hassle and uncertainty may not be worth the dollars saved. Prices quoted on websites and through travel agents may be quite negotiable if you contact operators directly, depending on season and occupancy rates.

taking a natural hallucinogenic potion prepared by an "authentic" Indian shaman at $15 a shot—the local version of taking peyote with Don Juan).

The following tour operators and lodges have good reputations, though the list is not by any means exhaustive.

- **Explorama Tours** ✆, Av. la Marina 340 (✆ **800/707-5275** in the U.S. and Canada, or 065/252-530; www.explorama.com). The most established jungle tour company in Iquitos and owned by an American, Explorama operates three lodges and a campsite, ranging from 40km to 160km (25–100 miles) downriver from Iquitos. Near **Explornapo** (the lodge deepest in the jungle), there's a splendid canopy walkway high above the treetops. Explorama owns the jungle's most luxurious lodge, **Ceiba Tops,** a jungle resort hotel with air-conditioning, pool, and Jacuzzi. Prices range from $225 for a 2-day, 1-night trip to $1,135 for an 8-day, 7-night trip. There are no discounts, but 3-day weekend Explornapo specials cost $395.

- **Muyuna Amazon Lodge,** Putumayo 163-B (✆ **065/242-858;** www. muyuna.com). This small and attractive bungalow lodge is located 120km (74 miles) upriver; it's friendly and popular with young travelers. A 3-day, 2-night trip costs $300.

- **Paseos Amazónicos,** Pevas 246 (✆ **065/231-618;** p-amazon@amauta. rcp.net.pe). This company operates three well-run camps upriver. The farthest (Tambo) is 180km (112 miles) from Iquitos; the other two are much closer in and focus on quick in-and-out tours. They offer pretty good budget to midrange standard tours in rustic shared lodges. A 4-day, 3-night trip costs $175.

- **Tahuayo Lodge** ✆✆✆, Amazonia Expeditions, 10305 Riverburn Dr., Tampa, FL (✆ **800/262-9669** in the U.S.; www.perujungle.com). One of the finest lodges in the northern Amazon, this 7-year-old low-impact ecoproperty, associated with the Rainforest Conservation Fund, lies on the shores of the River Tahuayo. *Outside* magazine has touted it as one of the top-10 travel finds in the world. It is the only lodge with access to the Tamshiyacu-Tahuayo Reserve, a splendid area for primate viewing. The 15 cabins are open year-round, and the lodge offers an excellent schedule of excursions ranging from the rugged (jungle survival training) to relaxed; most enticing are zip-line canopy ropes for tree-top viewing. A 7-day, 6-night trip is $1,295 per person.

- **Yacumama** ✆✆, Sargento Lores 149 (✆ **800/854-0023** in the U.S. and Canada, or 065/235-510; www.yacumama.com). This is an American-owned, first-class lodge with solar power and ecosensitive flush toilets deep in the Amazon—186km (110 miles) upriver on Río Yarapa—on an excellent 7,000-hectare (17,290-acre) forest reserve with a 10-story canopy tower. It's been in operation since 1993, and the company dedicates a percentage of its profits to conservation efforts. Good jungle treks and dolphin sightings. A 4-day, 3-night trip costs $750; discounts may be available in Iquitos.

- **Yarapa River Lodge** ✆✆ (✆ **800/771-3100;** www.yarapariverlodge.com). Associated with Cornell University (which built a field lab for students and faculty here), this attractive conservation-minded lodge is 186km (110 miles) upriver on the Yarapa. It features composting, full solar power, and flush toilets with a waste management system. A 4-day, 3-night trip runs $600 per person; 7 days, 6 nights, $1,050 to $1,200 per person. Travelers can opt for an overnight in the remote Pacaya-Samiria National Park Reserve, 4 hours away by boat.

CRUISES

Riverboat cruises down the Amazon and along its tributaries don't allow you to see much in the way of fauna or pristine jungle, though you will likely spot lots of birds and dolphins. Cruises are best for people who don't want to rough it too much and like the romance of traveling the Amazon by boat. Many cruises stop off at reserves for jungle walks and visits to local villages.

- **Amazon Tours and Cruises,** Requena 336 (© **800/423-2791** in the U.S. and Canada, or 065/233-931; www.amazontours.net). This American-owned company has been active in the northern Amazon for 4 decades. Its midlevel cruises are aboard older, air-conditioned fleets that aren't as nice or as expensive as those of Junglex (see below). They offer 3- and 6-night Río Amazonas cruises, as well as river trips to Colombia (Leticia) and Manaus, Santarém, and Belém (Brazil). A 7-night journey to Manaus costs $1,595 (per person in double room). It may offer discounts.

- **Jungle Expeditions** ✪, Av. Quiñones 1980 (© **065/261-583;** www.junglex.com). This company offers luxury river cruises on a fleet of six elegant boats, and cruises upriver along the Río Ucayali. Prices range from $1,500 to $2,700 for 7- and 8-day expeditions. They only accept passengers through their Lima booking office (© 01/241-3232) or International Expeditions (© 800/633-4734; www.internationalexpeditions.com) in the United States, which offers air-inclusive packages and programs with Cusco and Machu Picchu extensions.

SHOPPING

The most intriguing shopping option is the Belén open-air market, though it's likely you'll find more to photograph and smell than actually buy. For local artisans' goods, there aren't many options; try the sparsely populated market downstairs from the malecón (**Centro Artesanal Anaconda**) or the larger market (**Mercado Artesanal**) with stalls selling hammocks, woodcarvings, and paintings on Avenida Quiñones on the way out to the airport (about 3km/2 miles from downtown). Some of the best crafts, including textiles and pottery, come from the Shipibo Indian tribe.

WHERE TO STAY

Iquitos has fewer good hotels than its environs have attractive jungle lodges—which is perhaps logical, since the jungle is where most of the tourist attention is placed. All but the cheapest will arrange for a free airport transfer if you pass on your arrival information ahead of time.

EXPENSIVE

Hotel El Dorado Plaza ✪✪ With a privileged location on the Plaza de Armas, the El Dorado Plaza has filled a gaping hole in the Iquitos hotel scene—the city never before had a bona fide high-end hotel. A modern high-rise, with a soaring lobby, good restaurant, and bar, this is clearly the finest hotel in town. Rooms are large and nicely outfitted, if not quite at the upper-echelon levels found in Lima or Cusco. Guests have a view of either the main square or the pool. The hotel has quickly become popular with foreigners who come to Iquitos for top-of-the-line jungle tours. The staff is very friendly and helpful. Deals are frequently available—occasionally as much as half the rack rate.

Napo 258 (Plaza de Armas), Iquitos. © **065/222-555.** Fax 065/224-304. www.eldoradoplazahotel.com. 65 units. $150 double. Rate includes breakfast buffet. AE, DC, MC, V. **Amenities:** Restaurant; coffee shop; 2 bars; excellent outdoor pool; fitness center; Jacuzzi; sauna; concierge; room service; laundry service. *In room:* A/C, TV, minibar, hair dryer, safe.

MODERATE

Real Hotel Iquitos *Value*   The former (and formerly grand) state-owned Hotel de Turistas is now a curious hotel with a unique appeal for those who shy away from perfectly run, internationally flavored chain hotels. Part of a Peruvian group with a half dozen hotels spread across the country, this midsize entry seems larger and emptier than it is. Some of the rooms are surprisingly expansive, and a few have enviable balconies overlooking the malecón and the river. If you score such a room (ask to see a few first), you'll have yourself a deal. (No. 312 is huge and has its own terrace.) They're simply furnished, though with some unique touches, such as red curtains and green walls—kind of cool in an offbeat way, though I admit it's not the place for folks in search of great air-conditioning and top-shelf service. No other hotel, though, can boast these river views—and the Amazon is why you came to Iquitos, isn't it? Interior rooms, with no view and considerably smaller, are half as expensive as the larger accommodations.

Malecón Tarapacá s/n, Iquitos. ⓒ/fax **065/231-011.** 54 units. $45 double w/view; S/80 ($23) double w/o view. Rates include continental breakfast. MC, V. **Amenities:** Restaurant/bar; laundry service. *In room:* A/C, TV.

Victoria Regia ⭐ *Value*   An extremely comfortable and friendly midsize hotel, the Victoria Regia—named for the lily found throughout the Amazon—is the choice of both independent travelers and business execs with long-term affairs to attend to in Iquitos. It's a modern block hotel on a busy residential street about 10 minutes from the main square. The rooms are built around an indoor pool and are just a notch below the El Dorado in terms of comfort, although they have air-conditioning that really cranks.

Av. Ricardo Palma 252, Iquitos. ⓒ/fax **065/231-983,** or 01/421-9195 for reservations. www.victoriaregia hotel.com. 65 units. $60–$70 double; $70–$90 suite. Rates include breakfast buffet. AE, DC, MC, V. **Amenities:** Restaurant/bar; covered pool; small business center; laundry service. *In room:* A/C, TV, minibar, safe.

INEXPENSIVE

Hospedaje El Sitio   In the midst of several of the city's busiest streets, El Sitio—its name means "the place" or "the site"—doesn't aspire to much more than good, clean budget accommodations. Rooms are simple, cheap, and humid, though they have ceiling fans, private bathrooms, and cable TV. Rooms on the bottom floor are somewhat larger than those upstairs.

Ricardo Palma 541, Iquitos. ⓒ **065/234-932.** Fax 065/233-466. pascana@tsi.com.pe. 20 units. S/35 ($10). Rate includes taxes. No credit cards. **Amenities:** Cafeteria; room service. *In room:* TV.

Hospedaje La Pascana *Value*   One of the better budget inns in Iquitos, the Pascana is a small, friendly place with rooms built around a long, plant-lined, open-air courtyard. Rooms are very simple but not uncomfortable, and they have fans rather than air-conditioning. The place is quiet and peaceful, and just a 2-minute walk from the malecón and the Plaza de Armas—reasons why it's often full and popular with small budget-level groups. Don't expect much hot water at this price, though you probably won't care in the sweltering heat.

Calle Pevas 133, Iquitos. ⓒ **065/231-418.** Fax 065/233-466. pascana@tsi.com.pe. 18 units. $14. Rate includes taxes and continental breakfast buffet. No credit cards.

WHERE TO DINE

Easygoing restaurants in Iquitos are a good place to sample dishes straight out of the Amazon, such as turtle meat soup, *paiche* (a huge fish), hearts of palm salad, and *juanes* (rice *tamales* made with chicken or fish). Although protected species are not supposed to appear on menus, they often do. If you venture into the Belén market, you'll see even more exotic foodstuffs, such as monkey and lizard meat.

EXPENSIVE

Montecarlo ★★ *Value* INTERNATIONAL/PERUVIAN The exterior of this restaurant in Iquitos, behind the cheesy, glittering gold lights of a casino, doesn't look too auspicious. Yet upstairs from the gaming tables is an elegant restaurant that produces the most refined dining in this jungle city. It's perhaps the only place where you'll sit down to a full set of silver and wine and water glasses. The decor goes for a high-end treetop look, with ferns, wood-beamed ceilings, jungle murals, and a little Disneyesque Indian hut in the corner. Montecarlo however, serves exquisitely prepared seafood and jungle specialties such as turtle stew and tropical gator. If you can't bear to bite into an endangered species, try the *pescado a la diabla,* lightly fried John Dory fish drenched in squid and shrimp and topped with a spicy ginger-and-tomato sauce, hearts of palm stuffed with shrimp, or daily specials such as *cazuela de pescado y marisco* (fish and seafood casserole). There are also some appetizing steaks and pastas.

Napo 140 (2nd floor). ✆ 065/232-246. Reservations recommended. Main courses S/17–S/35 ($5–$10). AE, DC, MC, V. Daily noon–3:30pm and 6pm–midnight.

Regal (Casa de Fierro) INTERNATIONAL/PERUVIAN In the famed Iron House on the Plaza de Armas, this British pub and hangout is also a reputable restaurant exuding a desultory colonial atmosphere. There are great views from the wraparound iron balcony, with its slowly rotating old-style ceiling fans. It's a good place to try local dishes such as *paiche,* which is served any number of ways, or the house specialty, Regal *lomo fino* (beef tenderloin in port-wine sauce), served with salad, Greek rice, a peach stuffed with Russian salad, and french fries. Some find that the food suffers in comparison with the general ambience, so you might opt just to kick back with the expat Brits around the bar for a pint.

Putumayo 182, Plaza de Armas (2nd floor). ✆ 065/222-732. Reservations recommended. Main courses S/16–S/30 ($4.50–$8.50). AE, DC, MC, V. Daily noon–10pm.

Restaurant Gran Maloca *Value* PERUVIAN/AMAZONIAN One of Iquitos's most celebrated traditional restaurants, located in a grand, tile-covered (and air-conditioned!) 19th-century house, Gran Maloca serves both *platos de la selva*—jungle dishes—and standard upscale fare. Try Amazon-style venison (with cilantro, coconut, and yuca), tropical alligator, or less risky items such as filet mignon, tenderloin with mushroom risotto, or chicken a la Maloca (chicken breast stuffed with ham and baked in white wine). The split personality of the restaurant is present in the decor: The would-be formal trappings and pastel color scheme coexist with a large collection of colorful butterflies adorning the walls. (If you like those, wait until you get a load of the framed Amazonian bugs, tarantulas, and other creepy crawlers in the bathrooms.) Gran Maloca serves a cheap three-course daily lunch special for just S/12 ($3.50).

Sargento Lores 170. ✆ 065/233-126. Reservations recommended. Main courses S/18–S/30 ($5–$8.50). AE, DC, MC, V. Daily noon–10pm.

MODERATE

El Huaralino *Finds* PERUVIAN A lunch-only affair worth seeking out, this family-oriented place is in the heart of the Iquitos commercial district, about 15 minutes from the Plaza de Armas. More popular with locals than tourists, the pleasant, airy restaurant with stucco walls and yellow trim serves Peruvian *comida criolla*. Excellent, large-portioned dishes include *paiche* served with salad, rice, and beans; spicy duck *(pato de ají)*; *cuy*; and *asado* (grilled meats). The service is personal and very friendly. The only thing to detract from an easygoing meal here is the inevitable, incessant noise of passing *mototaxis*. (The restaurant is open to the street.)

Huallaga 490. ℂ 065/233-126. Reservations not accepted. Main courses S/14–S/20 ($4–$6). AE, DC, MC, V. Daily 11am–5pm.

El Nuevo Mesón PERUVIAN   Open to the passing parade of people, souvenir sellers, and curious locals on the malecón, this lively restaurant is a good place for an introduction to regional specialties and the city itself. If you come on a weekend night, you'll be entertained not only by altiplano musicians inside, but also by all kinds of locals hovering near the sidewalk tables, some gawking at your meal. (Several kids jostled for the rights to my leftovers; disadvantaged people often hang around outside restaurants hoping for part of a meal.) Service can be a little haphazard, but most dishes are pretty well prepared. Try regional dishes such as the ubiquitous *pescado a la Loretana* (fish filet with yuca, fried bananas, and *chonta*) and freakier fare such as alligator crisps with fried manioc or curried turtle. There's a long list of fish, dominated by *dorado* (a kind of flaky white catfish), served in a variety of styles (such as "poor boy," with potatoes, salad, bananas, eggs, and rice), as well as steaks and *mariscos* (shellfish).

Malecón Tarapacá 153. ℂ 065/231-837. Reservations recommended for groups. Main courses S/15–S/26 ($4–$7.50). MC, V. Daily noon–midnight.

Fitzcarraldo INTERNATIONAL   This popular joint right on the malecón has a diverse menu to appeal to tourists of all stripes and appetites. You can go light, choosing from a number of salads such as *chonta* with avocado and tomato, or regular dinners including *pescado a la Loretana,* or even turtle in ginger sauce with manioc. There are also pizzas, sandwiches, and hamburgers. The restaurant is a convivial, lively place in an open-air house with views of the Amazon, good music, sidewalk tables, and underpowered ceiling fans.

Napo 100 (at Malecón Tarapacá). ℂ 065/243-434. Reservations recommended for groups. Main courses S/6–S/38 ($1.75–$11). MC, V. Daily noon–midnight.

IQUITOS AFTER DARK

More locals than gringos usually make it to the coolest spot in Iquitos, **Café-Teatro Amauta,** Nauta 250 (ℂ 065/233-366), a bar with great bohemian flavor, a romantic interior, and sidewalk tables. Calling itself *"El Rincón de los Artistas"* (The Artists' Corner), it supports live music of diverse types (Peruvian, Latino, and Amazon sounds) Monday through Saturday from 10pm until 3am. Along the malecón are a couple of lively bars with good views of the river. **Arandú Bar** is particularly hopping, a good place for a pitcher of sangria. Locals hang out at **Noa-Noa,** a rock bar near the Plaza de Armas at Pevas 298.

10

Uruguay

by Shane Christensen

The second-smallest nation in South America, Uruguay is a little place that makes a big impression. With an impressive living standard, high literacy rate, large urban middle class, and excellent social services—including the best medical care system in South America—it has become a model for other developing countries in the region.

Despite its homogeneous population of 3.2 million (mostly of European descent), Uruguay reveals splendid contrasts. This is a land of dusty colonial towns and sparkling beach resorts, of rough-and-ready gauchos and subtle artists and festive plazas. Uruguay is a place where soccer (*fútbol*) is worshipped without reserve, where the sun shines brightly and the air stays warm, where few question the dignity of their homeland. And despite the economic troubles of recent years, Uruguay remains a proud and peaceful nation.

1 The Regions in Brief

Uruguay's origins as a country rest firmly in Europe; the indigenous people inhabiting the region were displaced by the colonizing Portuguese and Spaniards in the late 17th and early 18th centuries. You will find the European influence most evident among the historic treasures of **Colonia,** where the Portuguese first entrenched themselves, and amid the rich architecture of **Montevideo,** where the Spaniards landed. Montevideo is the cultural heartland of the country, a place where you will discover the bold accomplishments of Uruguay in music, art, and literature. Among the several internationally accomplished artists are Pedro Figari, who inspired a school of painters; José Enrique Rodó, Uruguay's famed essayist from the early 20th century; and Mauricio Rosencof, the politically active playwright from recent decades. Outside the capital, miles of pastureland and rolling hills draw your attention away from the capital's urban existence to a softer, quieter life. But this rural lifestyle stops at the coast, where world-class resorts centered on **Punta del Este** lure the continent's rich and famous.

2 Planning Your Trip to Uruguay

VISITOR INFORMATION

The Internet is an excellent source of information on Uruguay. Try **www.turismo.gub.uy** or **www.uruguaynatural.com** for official visitor information. Additional countrywide tourist information can be found at **www.visit-uruguay.com**.

ENTRY REQUIREMENTS & CUSTOMS

Citizens of the United States, the United Kingdom, Canada, and New Zealand need only a passport to enter Uruguay (for tourist stays of up to 90 days). Australian citizens must get a tourist visa before arrival.

A helpful Customs information guide for Uruguay can be found at **www. euro-trans.com/customs/uruguay.asp**.

URUGUAYAN EMBASSY LOCATIONS

In the U.S.: 2715 M St. NW, Third Floor, Washington, DC 20007 (© **202/ 331-1313;** fax 202/331-8142; www.embassy.org/uruguay)

In Canada: 130 Albert St., Suite 1905, Ottawa, ON K1P 5G4 (© **613/234- 2727;** fax 613/233-4670; www.iosphere.net/~uruott)

In the U.K.: 140 Brompton Rd., second floor, London SW3 1HY (© **207/ 589-8835)**

MONEY

The official currency is the **Uruguayan peso** (designated NP$, $U, or simply $); each peso is comprised of 100 **centavos.** Uruguayan pesos are available in $10, $20, $50, $100, $200, $500, $1,000, and $5,000 notes; coins come in 10, 20, and 50 centavos, and 1 and 2 pesos. The Uruguayan currency devalued by half in July 2002, and the exchange rate as this book went to press was approximately 28 pesos to the dollar. The value of the peso fluctuates greatly with inflation, so all prices in this chapter are quoted in U.S. dollars.

Traveler's checks are accepted only at some currency-exchange houses. The most widely accepted **credit cards** are Visa and MasterCard; you'll have less luck with American Express and Diners Club. To report a lost or stolen credit card, call the following numbers: for **American Express,** © 0411/008-0071; for **MasterCard,** © 636/722-7111 (collect call to the U.S.); and for **Visa,** © 0411/ 940-7915.

Telephone Dialing Info at a Glance

Uruguay's national telephone company is called ANTEL. You can buy a telephone card from any kiosk or ANTEL *telecentro* location. You can also make domestic and international calls from *telecentro* offices— they are located every few blocks in major cities—but be warned that international calls are very expensive, especially during peak hours.

- **To place a call from your home country to Uruguay,** dial the inter- national access code (011 in the U.S., 0011 in Australia, 0170 in New Zealand, 00 in the U.K.) plus the country code (598), plus the city or region area code (for example, Montevideo 2, Punta del Este 42, Colonia del Sacramento 11) followed by the number. For example, a call from the United States to Montevideo would be 011+598+2+000+0000.
- **To place a domestic long-distance call within Uruguay,** dial a 0 before the area code, and then the local number.
- **To place a direct international call from Uruguay,** dial the interna- tional access code (00), plus the country code of the place you are dialing, plus the area code and the number.
- **To reach an international long distance operator,** dial © 000-410 for **AT&T;** © 000-412 for **MCI;** or © 000-417 for **Sprint.**

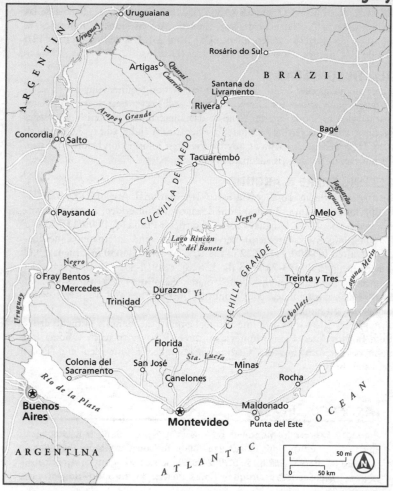

ATMs ATMs on the Cirrus network are widely available in Montevideo and Punta del Este. If you travel to Colonia or elsewhere outside these cities, you should bring Uruguayan pesos.

WHEN TO GO

PEAK SEASON & CLIMATE The best time to visit Uruguay is October through March, when the sun shines and temperatures are mild. (Remember that seasons are reversed from the Northern Hemisphere.) Punta del Este overflows with tourists from Argentina in summer; if you're seeking a more relaxed time to visit the beaches of the coast, consider going between October and December. Average temperatures are 62°F (17°C) in spring, 73°F (23°C) in summer, 64°F (18°C) in autumn, and 53°F (12°C) in winter.

PUBLIC HOLIDAYS National holidays include New Year's Day (Jan 1), Día de los Reyes (Jan 6), Carnaval (the days leading up to Ash Wednesday), Easter,

Desembarco de los 33 Orientales (Apr 19), Labor Day (May 1), Batalla de las Piedras (May 18), Natalicio de José Gervasio Artigas (June 19), Jura de la Constitución (July 18), Independence Day (Aug 25), Día de la Raza (Oct 12), Día de los Difuntos (Nov 2), and Christmas (Dec 25).

HEALTH CONCERNS

There are no specific health concerns or vaccination requirements for travel to Uruguay. The **Centers for Disease Control and Prevention** does recommend that travelers to South America be up-to-date on tetanus-diphtheria and measles vaccines, as well as getting vaccinated for hepatitis A and B and typhoid. Check the CDC's website at **www.cdc.gov** for the latest information before your trip. Health care in Uruguay is adequate to excellent.

GETTING THERE & AROUND

International flights land at **Carrasco International Airport** (© **02/604-0386**), located 19km (12 miles) from downtown Montevideo. A taxi to downtown costs about $15. Uruguay's national carrier is **Pluna** (© **0800/118-811** or 02/604-4080; www.pluna.aero), serving domestic and international destinations. **United** (© **800/241-6522** in the U.S., or 02/902-4630 in Uruguay) and **American** (© **800/433-7300** in the U.S., or 02/916-3929 in Uruguay) offer connecting service from the United States. **Aerolíneas Argentinas** (© **02/901-9466**; www.aerolineas.com) connects Buenos Aires and Montevideo; the flight takes 50 minutes.

Punta del Este has its own international airport; the majority of flights arrive from Buenos Aires. From Montevideo, the easiest way to reach Colonia and Punta del Este is by bus (see "Getting There" under "Montevideo" and "Punta del Este," below).

FAST FACTS: Uruguay

American Express In Montevideo, American Express Bank is located at Rincón 477, Eighth Floor (© **02/916-0000**). Turisport Limitada, Calle San José 930 (© **02/902-0829**; fax 02/902-0852), acts as an agent of American Express Travel Services in Uruguay; hours are Monday through Friday from 9am to 5pm.

Business Hours In general, businesses stay open weekdays from 9am to 6:30 or 7pm, with a 2-hour break for lunch around noon. Retail outlets keep similar hours and are usually open a half-day on Saturday as well. Banks are open weekdays from 1 to 5pm.

Electricity Electricity in Uruguay runs on 220 volts, so bring a transformer and adapter along with any electrical appliances. Note that most laptops operate on both 110 and 220 volts. Some luxury hotels may supply transformers and adapters.

Embassies & Consulates In Montevideo: U.S., Lauro Muller 1776 (© **02/418-7777**; http://uruguay.usembassy.gov); **U.K.**, Marco Bruto 1073 (© **02/623-3630**); and **Canada**, Plaza Independencia 749, Office 102 (© **02/902-2030**; www.dfait-maeci.gc.ca/uruguay).

Emergencies The general emergency number is © **911**. Outside Montevideo, dial © 02-911 to connect with Montevideo Central Emergency

Authority. The following numbers also work: police ℂ **109;** ambulance ℂ **105;** fire department ℂ **104.**

Internet Access Cybercafes are commonly found around Montevideo and other Uruguayan cities. Many hotel business centers have Internet access, as do the guest rooms in high-end hotels.

Post Offices/Mail Post offices are generally open Monday through Friday from 8am to 6pm and Saturday from 8am to 1pm. You can buy stamps there or in mailing centers in shopping malls.

Restrooms It's permissible to use the toilets in restaurants and bars without patronizing the establishment; offer a nice smile on the way in. Nobody should bother you unless they're having a bad day.

Safety Uruguay is one of the world's safest countries, although petty crime in Montevideo has risen in recent years. Outside the capital, cities and beach resorts such as Punta del Este are considered safe. Travelers visiting Uruguay are advised to take common-sense precautions and avoid large gatherings where crowds have congregated to demonstrate or protest.

Taxes Value-added tax is called IVA in Spanish. IVA is 14% for hotels and restaurants and 24% for general sales tax; the tax is almost always included in your bill. The departure tax when leaving the country is $12.

Telephones See "Telephone Dialing Info at a Glance," above.

Time Zone Uruguay is 1 hour ahead of Eastern Standard Time.

Tipping A 10% to 15% tip is common in restaurants. For taxis, round up to the nearest peso. Tip bellhops 50 cents per bag.

Water Locals swear that the drinking water in Uruguay is perfectly healthy; in fact, Uruguay was the only country in the Americas (along with the nations of the Caribbean) to escape the cholera pandemic of the early 1990s. If you are concerned, stick with bottled water (*agua mineral sin gas*).

3 Montevideo

Montevideo, the southernmost capital on the continent, is home to half the country's population. Born on the banks of the Río de la Plata, Montevideo first existed as a fortress of the Spanish empire and developed into a major port city in the mid–18th century. European immigrants, including Spanish, Portuguese, French, and British, influenced the city's architecture, and a walk around the capital reveals architectural styles ranging from colonial to Art Deco. Indeed, the richness of Montevideo's architecture is unrivaled in South America.

Although Montevideo has few must-see attractions, its charm lies in wait for the careful traveler. A walk along La Rambla, stretching from the Old City to the neighborhood of Carrasco, takes you along the riverfront past fishermen and their catch to parks and gardens where children play and elders sip *mate* (a tealike beverage). Restaurants, cafes, bars, and street performers populate the port area, where you will also discover the flavors of Uruguay at the afternoon and weekend Mercado del Puerto, or Port Market. Many of the city's historic sites surround Plaza Independencia and can be visited in a few hours.

ESSENTIALS
GETTING THERE
BY PLANE To get to Montevideo by plane, see "Getting There & Getting Around," above. A private, unmetered taxi or *remise* (radio taxi) from the airport to downtown costs about $15.

BY BOAT OR HYDROFOIL **Buquebús,** Calle Río Negro 1400 (© 02/916-8801 or 130), operates three to four hydrofoils per day between Montevideo and Buenos Aires; the trip takes about 2½ hours and costs about $75 round-trip. Montevideo's port is just over 1.5km (1 mile) from downtown. If you have taken a ferry to Colonia, you can get connecting bus service to Montevideo.

BY BUS **Terminal Omnibus Tres Cruces,** General Artigas 1825 (© 02/409-7399), is Montevideo's long-distance bus terminal, connecting the capital with cities in Uruguay and throughout South America. Buses to Buenos Aires take about 8 hours. **COT** (© 02/409-4949) offers the best service to Punta del Este, Maldonado, and Colonia.

For roadside emergencies or general information on driving in Uruguay, contact the **Automóvil Club de Uruguay,** Colonia 1251 (© **1707**), or the **Centro Automovilista del Uruguay,** E. V. Haedo 2378 (© **02/408-2091**).

ORIENTATION
Montevideo is surrounded by water on three sides, a testament to its earlier incarnation as an easily defended fortress for the Spanish Empire. The Old City begins near the western edge of Montevideo, found on the skinny portion of a peninsula between the Rambla Gran Bretaña and the city's main artery, Avenida 18 de Julio. Look for the Plaza Independencia and the Plaza Constitución to find the center of the district. Many of the city's museums, theaters, and hotels reside in this historic area, although a trip east on Avenida 18 de Julio reveals the more modern Montevideo with its own share of hotels, markets, and monuments. Along the city's long southern coastline runs the Rambla Gran Bretaña, traveling 21km (13 miles) from the piers of the Old City past Parque Rodó and on to points south and east, passing fish stalls and street performers along the way.

GETTING AROUND
It's easy to navigate around the city center on foot or by bus. Safe, convenient buses crisscross Montevideo if you want to venture outside the city center (for less than $1 per trip). Taxis are relatively inexpensive, but can be difficult to hail during rush hour. One recommended company is **Remises Carrasco** (© **094/405-473**). To rent a car, try **Thrifty** (© **02/204-3373**).

VISITOR INFORMATION
Uruguay's **Ministerio de Turismo** is at Av. Libertador 1409 and Colonia (© **02/908-9105**). It assists travelers with countrywide information and is open daily from 8am to 8pm in winter, from 8am to 2pm in summer. There's also a branch at Carrasco International Airport and Tres Cruces bus station. The **municipal tourist office,** Explanada Municipal (© **1950**), offers city maps and brochures of tourist activities and is open weekdays 11am to 6pm, weekends 10am to 6pm. It also organizes cultural city tours on weekends.

FAST FACTS To exchange money, try **Turisport Limitada** (the local Amex representative) at San José 930 (© **02/902-0829**); **Gales Casa Cambiaria,** Av. 18 de Julio 1046 (© **02/902-0229**); or one of the airport exchanges. ATMs are

Montevideo

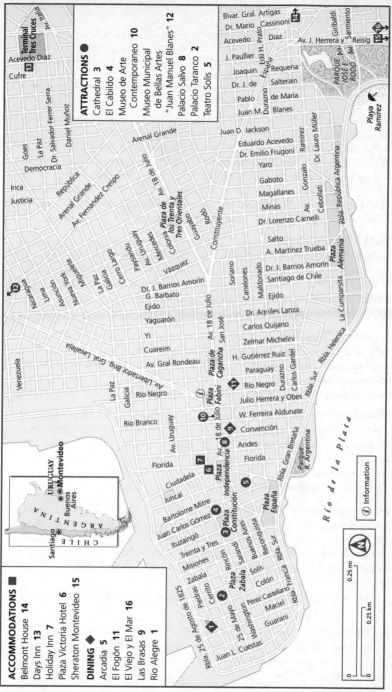

ATTRACTIONS ●
Cathedral **3**
El Cabildo **4**
Museo de Arte
  Contemporaneo **10**
Museo Municipal
  de Bellas Artes
  "Juan Manuel Blanes" **12**
Palacio Salvo **8**
Palacio Taranco **2**
Teatro Solis **5**

ACCOMMODATIONS ■
Belmont House **14**
Days Inn **13**
Holiday Inn **7**
Plaza Victoria Hotel **6**
Sheraton Montevideo **15**

DINING ◆
Arcadia **5**
El Fogón **11**
El Viejo y El Mar **16**
Las Brasas **9**
Rio Alegre **1**

ⓘ Information

Safety Note

Although Montevideo remains very safe by big city standards, street crime has risen in recent years. Travelers should avoid walking alone, particularly at night, in Ciudad Vieja, Avenida 18 de Julio, Plaza Independencia, and the vicinity around the port. Take a taxi instead.

plentiful (most have access to the Cirrus network); look for **Bancomat** and **Redbrou** banks.

For medical attention, go to the **British Hospital,** Av. Italia 2420 (© **02/ 487-1020**). For additional emergency numbers, see "Fast Facts: Uruguay," above.

Internet cafes appear and disappear faster than discos, but you won't walk long before coming across another spot in the city center. Reliable cybercafes include **El Cybercafé,** Calle 25 de Mayo 568; **Arroba del Sur,** Guayabo 1858; and **El Cybercafé Softec,** Santiago de Chile 1286. The average cost is $2 per hour.

WHAT TO SEE & DO

Catedral 🖈 Also known as Iglesia Matriz (parish church), the cathedral was the city's first public building, erected in 1804. It houses the remains of some of Uruguay's most important political, religious, and economic figures, and is distinguished by its domed bell towers.

Calle Sarandí at Ituzaingó. Free admission. Mon–Fri 8am–8pm.

El Cabildo (Town Hall) 🖈 Uruguay's constitution was signed in the old town hall, which also served as the city's jailhouse in the 19th century. Now a museum, the Cabildo houses the city's historic archives as well as maps and photos, antiques, costumes, and artwork.

Juan Carlos Gómez 1362. © 02/915-9685. Free admission. Tues–Sun 2:30–7pm.

Museo de Arte Contemporáneo 🖈 Opened in 1997, this museum is dedicated to contemporary Uruguayan art and exhibits the country's biggest names. To promote cultural exchange across the region, a section of the museum has been set aside for artists who hail from various South American countries. Allow an hour for your visit.

Av. 18 de Julio 965, 2nd floor. © 02/900-6662. Free admission. Daily noon–8pm.

Museo Municipal de Bellas Artes Juan Manuel Blanes 🖈 The national art history museum displays Uruguayan artistic styles from the beginning of the nation to the present day. Works include oils, engravings, drawings, sculptures, and documents. Among the great Uruguayan artists exhibited are Juan Manuel Blanes, Pedro Figari, Rafael Barradas, José Cúneo, and Carlos Gonzales. Plan to spend an hour here.

Av. Millán 4015. © 02/336-2248. www.montevideo.gub.uy/museoblanes. Free admission. Tues–Sun noon–6pm.

Palacio Salvo Often referred to as the symbol of Montevideo, the Salvo Palace was once the tallest building in South America. Although its 26 stories might not impress you, it remains the city's highest structure.

Plaza Independencia.

Palacio Taranco 🖈 Now the decorative arts museum, the Taranco Palace was built in the early 20th century and represents the trend toward French architecture during that period. The museum displays an assortment of Uruguayan furniture, draperies, clocks, paintings, and other cultural works; they've recently added a small section exhibiting Islamic art, including a collection of ancient Egyptian statuettes. An hour should give you enough time to see it all.

Calle 25 de Mayo 379. © 02/915-1101. Free admission. Tues–Sat 10am–6pm.

Plaza Independencia 😊😊 Originally the site of a Spanish citadel, Independence Square marks the beginning of the Old City and is a good point from which to begin your tour of Montevideo. An enormous statue of General José Gervasio Artigas, father of Uruguay and hero of its independent movement, stands in the center.

Bordered by Av. 18 de Julio, Florida, and Juncal.

Teatro Solís 😊😊 Montevideo's main theater and one of South America's prized opera houses, opened in 1852, completed an extensive renovation a few years back. It hosts Uruguay's most important cultural events, as well as concerts and ballet performances, and is the site of the Museo Nacional de Historia Natural (National Museum of Natural History).

Calle Buenos Aires 652. © 02/916-0908. Free admission. Museum Mon–Fri 2–6pm.

SHOPPING

Shopping in Montevideo is concentrated in a few downtown shops and in three major shopping centers. In Uruguayan stores, expect to find leather goods, jewelry, and local crafts and textiles—including sweaters, cardigan jackets, ponchos, coats, and tapestries made of high-quality wool (Uruguay is the world's largest exporter of wool). International stores carry American and European products. Montevideo's most fashionable mall is the **Punta Carretas Shopping Center,** Calle Ellauri and Solano, located on the site of a former prison next to the new Sheraton hotel. Downtown, the **Montevideo Shopping Center,** Av. Luis Alberto de Herrera 1290, is the city's original mall with more than 180 stores and a 10-screen theater. **Portones de Carrasco,** avenidas Bolivia and Italia, is another recommended shopping center in the Carrasco neighborhood.

MARKETS The **Villa Biarritz fair** at Parque Zorilla de San Martín-Ellauri takes place Saturday from 9:30am to 3pm and features handicrafts, antiques, books, fruit and vegetable vendors, flowers, and other goodies. The **Mercado del Puerto (Port Market)** 😊 opens afternoons and weekends at Piedras and Yacaré, letting you sample the flavors of Uruguay, from small *empanadas* to enormous barbecued meats. Saturday is the best day to visit, when cultural activities accompany the market. **Tristán Narvaja,** Avenida 18 de Julio in the Cordón neighborhood, is the city's Sunday flea market (6am–3pm), initiated more than 50 years ago by Italian immigrants. **De la Abundancia/Artesanos** is a combined food and handicrafts market. It takes place Monday through Saturday from 10am to 8pm at San José 1312.

WHERE TO STAY

Montevideo's hotel infrastructure is improving, and hotel rates have fallen since the currency devalued in July 2002. Prices are jacked up during Carnaval time in February and when major conventions come to town, however. A 14% tax will be added to your bill; parking is included in the rates of most Uruguay hotels.

EXPENSIVE

Belmont House 😊😊😊 *(Finds* A boutique hotel in Montevideo's peaceful Carrasco neighborhood, Belmont House offers its privileged guests intimacy and luxury. Small elegant spaces with carefully chosen antiques and wood furnishings give this place the feeling of a wealthy private home. The beautiful guest rooms feature two- or four-poster beds; rich, colorful linens; and marble bathrooms with small details like towel warmers and deluxe toiletries. Many of the rooms feature balconies overlooking a pretty courtyard and pool, and two of the rooms have Jacuzzis. Belmont House is a skip and a jump away from the beach, golf, and tennis. Gourmands will find an excellent international restaurant, afternoon tea, and a *parrilla* (grill) open weekends next to the pool. The gracious staff assists guests with outdoor activities and local itineraries.

Avda. Rivera 6512, 11500 Montevideo. © 02/600-0430. Fax 02/600-8609. www.belmonthouse.com.uy. 28 units. $155 double; from $180 suite. AE, DC, MC, V. Rates include gourmet breakfast. **Amenities:** 2 restaurants; bar; beautiful outdoor pool; small fitness center and sauna; discounts for nearby tennis and golf; business center; room service; babysitting; laundry service; dry cleaning. *In room:* A/C, TV, minibar, hair dryer.

Radisson Montevideo Victoria Plaza Hotel ⭐⭐
The Victoria Plaza has long been one of Montevideo's top hotels. The European-style hotel stands in the heart of the financial district (next to Plaza Independencia) and makes a good base from which to do business or explore the capital. Its convention center and casino also make it the center of business and social activity. Ask for a room in the new tower, built in 1996 adjacent to the original Plaza Victoria Hotel, housing spacious guest rooms and a number of executive suites with classic French-style furnishings and panoramic city or river views. The busy hotel has a large, multilingual staff that attends closely to guest needs. If you plan to stay on a weekend, inquire about one of the special spa packages. Victoria Plaza is famous for its casino, with French roulette tables, blackjack, baccarat, slot machines, horse races, and bingo. There are two lobby bars, in addition to the casino bars. **Arcadia** (see "Where to Dine," below) on the 25th floor is the city's most elegant dining room.

Plaza Independencia 759, 11100 Montevideo. © 02/902-0111. Fax 02/902-1628. www.radisson.com/ Montevideouy. 255 units. $80–$180 double; from $180 suite. AE, DC, MC, V. Rates include breakfast at rooftop restaurant. **Amenities:** Restaurant; 2 bars; excellent health club w/skylit indoor pool, fitness center, aerobics classes, Jacuzzi, sauna, and massage; concierge; travel agency; business center w/high-speed Internet access; room service; laundry service; dry cleaning; executive-level floors. *In room:* A/C, TV, dataport, minibar, hair dryer, safe.

Sheraton Montevideo ⭐⭐
Opened in 1999, the Sheraton Montevideo has replaced Victoria Plaza as Montevideo's most luxurious hotel. A walkway connects the hotel to the Punta Carretas Shopping Center, formerly a jail during the military dictatorship and now one of the city's best malls, located just next door. The hotel, which lies a few miles from downtown, was actually built on the grounds of the old jail's soccer field—but you won't detect any of this today. The spacious guest rooms have imported furniture, king-size beds, sleeper chairs, marble bathrooms, 25-inch televisions, and works by Uruguayan artists. Choose between views of the Río de la Plata, Uruguay Golf Club, or downtown Montevideo, with views from the 20th through 24th floors being the most impressive. Rooms on the top two executive floors feature Jacuzzis and individual sound systems. Hotel service is excellent, particularly for guests with business needs. The main restaurant, Las Carretas, serves Continental cuisine with a Mediterranean flair; don't miss the dining room's spectacular murals by contemporary Uruguayan artist Carlos Vilaro. Next door, the lobby bar is a popular spot for casual business meetings and afternoon cocktails.

Víctor Soliño 349, 11300 Montevideo. © 02/710-2121. Fax 02/712-1262. www.sheraton.com. 207 units. $85–$195 double; from $200 suite. Rates include buffet breakfast. AE, DC, MC, V. Free parking. **Amenities:** Restaurant; bar; deluxe health club w/fitness center, indoor pool, sauna, and massage; concierge; car-rental desk; business center and secretarial services; salon; room service; babysitting; laundry service; dry cleaning; executive-level floors. *In room:* A/C, TV, dataport, minibar, hair dryer, safe.

INEXPENSIVE

Days Inn Obelisco (Value) The modern Days Inn caters to business travelers looking for good-value accommodations. The hotel is located next to the "Tres Cruces" bus station and not far from downtown or the airport. Rooms are comfortable and modern, if not overly spacious. Free local calls are permitted.

Acevedo Díaz 1821, 11800 Montevideo. ⊘ 02/400-4840. Fax 02/402-0229. www.daysinn.com. 60 units. From $70 double. Rates include buffet breakfast. AE, DC, MC, V. Free parking. **Amenities:** Coffee shop; small health club; business center; room service. *In room:* A/C, TV, minibar, hair dryer.

Holiday Inn Montevideo (⋆) This colorful Holiday Inn is actually one of the city's best hotels, popular with tourists and business travelers. It's situated in the heart of downtown, next to Montevideo's main square. A bilingual staff greets you in the marble lobby, attached to a good restaurant and bar. Guest rooms have simple, contemporary furnishings typical of an American chain, with red being the dominant color. Because the hotel doubles as a convention center, it can become very busy.

Colonia 823, 11100 Montevideo. ⊘ 02/902-0001. Fax 02/902-1242. www.holidayinn.com.uy. 137 units. From $51 double. Rates include buffet breakfast. AE, DC, MC, V. **Amenities:** Restaurant; bar; heated indoor pool; fitness center; sauna; business center; room service; laundry service; dry cleaning. *In room:* A/C, TV, minibar, safe.

WHERE TO DINE

Restaurants in Montevideo serve steak—just as high quality as Argentine beef— and usually include a number of stews and seafood selections as well. You will find the native barbecue, in which beef and lamb are grilled on the fire, in any of the city's grill restaurants, referred to interchangeably in Spanish as parrillas or *parrilladas*. Sales tax on dining in Montevideo is a whopping 23%. As in Argentina, there's usually a table cover charge, called the *cubierto,* as well—usually about 25 pesos ($1) per person.

MODERATE

Arcadia (⋆⋆) (Moments) INTERNATIONAL Virgil and Homer wrote that Arcadia was a quiet paradise in ancient Greece; this elegant restaurant atop the Plaza Victoria is a quiet paradise in Montevideo. Tables are nestled in semiprivate nooks with floor-to-ceiling bay windows. The classic dining room is decorated with Italian curtains and crystal chandeliers; each table has a fresh rose and sterling silver place settings. For such grandeur, however, dishes are priced very reasonably. Creative plates such as terrine of pheasant marinated in cognac are followed by grilled rack of lamb glazed with mint and garlic, or duck confit served on a thin strudel pastry with red cabbage. You won't find a better restaurant in Montevideo.

Plaza Independencia 759. ⊘ 02/902-0111. Main courses $6–$10. AE, DC, MC, V. Daily 7pm–midnight.

El Fogón (⋆) URUGUAYAN The brightly lit parrillada and seafood restaurant is popular with Montevideo's late-night crowd. The extensive menu includes calamari, salmon, shrimp, and other fish, as well as generous steak and pasta dishes. Food here is inexpensive and prepared with care. The express lunch menu comes with steak or chicken, dessert, and a glass of wine. Waiters, dressed in long white shirts, look suspiciously like medical doctors, and service is fairly reserved. Giant mirrors covering the walls give you an opportunity to inspect

yourself; the large painting of two horses and a deserted wagon might spark a new table conversation.

San José 1080. © 02/900-0900. Main courses $5–$9. AE, DC, MC, V. Daily noon–4pm and 7pm–1am.

El Viejo y el Mar 🦀 SEAFOOD   Resembling an old fishing club, El Viejo y el Mar is located on the riverfront near the Sheraton hotel. The bar is made from an abandoned boat, while the dining room is decorated with dock lines, sea lamps, and pictures of 19th-century regattas. You'll find every kind of fish and pasta on the menu, and the restaurant is equally popular for evening cocktails. An outdoor patio is open most of the year.

Rambla Gandhi 400. © 02/710-5704. Main courses $5–$7. MC, V. Daily noon–4pm and 8pm–1am.

Las Brasas 🦀🦀 URUGUAYAN   When Hillary Clinton visited the restaurant, her photographer took 220 pictures of her with the staff. One of the images hangs proudly on the wall, and the waiters talk about her visit as though it happened yesterday. This casual parrillada resembles one you'd find in Buenos Aires—except that this restaurant also serves an outstanding range of *mariscos* (seafood) such as the Spanish paella or *lenguado Las Brasas* (a flathead fish) served with prawns, mushrooms, and mashed potatoes. From the parrilla, the *filet de lomo* is the best cut—order it with Roquefort, mustard, or black pepper sauce. The restaurant's fresh produce is displayed in a case near the kitchen.

San José 909. © 02/900-2285. Main courses $5–$8. AE, DC, MC, V. Daily 11:45am–3:30pm and 7:30pm–midnight.

INEXPENSIVE

Río Alegre 🦀 *Value* LIGHT BITES   This casual, inventive lunch stop specializes in quick steaks off the grill. Ribs, sausages, and most cuts of beef are cooked on the parrilla and made to order. Río Alegre is a local favorite because of its large portions, good quality, and cheap prices. Order a tall beer to wash it all down.

Pérez Castellano and Piedras, at the Mercado del Puerto, Local 33. © 02/915-6504. Main courses $2–$3. No credit cards. Daily 11am–3pm.

MONTEVIDEO AFTER DARK

As in Buenos Aires, nightlife in Montevideo means drinks after 10pm and dancing after midnight. For earlier entertainment, ask at your hotel or call directly for performance information at the **Teatro Solís,** Buenos Aires 652 (© 02/916-0908), the city's center for opera, theater, ballets, and symphonies. **SODRE,** Av. 18 de Julio 930 (© 02/901-2850), is the city's "Official Radio Service," which hosts classical music concerts from May to November.

Gamblers should head to the **Plaza Victoria casino,** Plaza Independencia (© 02/902-0111), a fashionable venue with French roulette tables, blackjack, baccarat, slot machines, horse races, and bingo. It opens at 2pm and keeps going through most of the night.

Many of the city's most popular bars are located in the coastal areas of Carrasco and Pocitos. **Mariachi,** Gabriel Pereira 2964 (© 02/709-1600), is one of the city's top bars and discos, with live bands or deejay music Wednesday to Sunday after 10pm. **Café Misterio,** Costa Rica 1700 (© 02/600-5999), is another popular bar, while **New York,** Mar Artico 1227 (© 02/600-0444), mixes a restaurant, bar, and dance club under one roof and attracts a slightly older crowd. Montevideo's best tango clubs are **La Casa de Becho,** Nueva York 1415 (© 02/400-2717), where composer Gerardo Mattos Rodríguez wrote the famous "La Cumparsita," and **Cuareim,** Zelmar Michelini 1079, which offers both tango and *candombe,* a lively dance indigenous to the area. La Casa de Becho is open Friday and Saturday after 10:30pm; Cuareim, Wednesday, Friday, and Saturday after 9pm. The tourist office can give you schedule information for Montevideo's other tango salons.

4 A Side Trip to Colonia del Sacramento

242km (150 miles) W of Montevideo

The tiny gem of Colonia del Sacramento, declared a World Heritage City by UNESCO, appears untouched by time. Dating from the 17th century, the old city boasts beautifully preserved colonial artistry down its dusty streets. A leisurely stroll from the Puerta de Campo into the **Barrio Histórico** (Old, or Historic, Neighborhood) leads under flower-laden windowsills to churches dating from the 1680s, past exquisite single-story homes from Colonia's time as a Portuguese settlement and on to local museums detailing the riches of the town's past. The Barrio Histórico contains brilliant examples of colonial wealth and many of Uruguay's oldest structures. Yet while the city resides happily in tradition, a mix of lovely shops, delicious cafes, and thoughtful museums make the town more than a history lesson.

ESSENTIALS
GETTING THERE
Many people make Colonia a day trip from Buenos Aires, catching a morning ferry and returning in the late afternoon. The easiest way to reach Colonia from Buenos Aires is by ferry. **FerryLíneas** (© 02/900-6617) runs a fast boat that arrives in 45 minutes and a slower 3-hour bus. **Buquebús** (© 02/916-1910) also offers two classes of service. Prices range from $10 to $35 each way.

Colonia can also easily be visited from Montevideo, and is a good stopping-off point if you're traveling between Buenos Aires and Montevideo. **COT** (© 02/409-4949 in Montevideo) also offers bus service from Montevideo and from Punta del Este.

VISITOR INFORMATION
The **Oficina de Turismo,** General Flores and Rivera (© 052/27000 or 27300), is open daily from 8am to 8pm. Speak with someone at the tourism office to arrange a guided tour of the town.

WHAT TO SEE & DO
A WALK THROUGH COLONIA'S BARRIO HISTORICO
Your visit to Colonia will be concentrated in the **Barrio Histórico (Old Neighborhood),** located on the coast at the far southwestern corner of town. The sights, which are all within a few blocks, can easily be visited on foot in a few hours. Museums and tourist sites are open daily (except Wed) from 11am to 5:45pm. For less than $1, you can buy a pass at the Portuguese or Municipal museum that will get you into all the sights.

Start your tour at **Plaza Mayor,** the principal square that served as the center of the colonial establishment. To explore Colonia's Portuguese history, cross Calle Manuel Lobo on the southeastern side of the plaza and enter the **Museo Portugués,** which exhibits European customs and traditions that influenced the town's beginnings. Upon exiting the museum, turn left and walk to the **Iglesia Matriz,** among the oldest churches in the country and an excellent example of 17th-century architecture and design.

Next, exit the church and turn left to the **Ruinas Convento San Francisco.** Dating from 1696, the San Francisco convent was once inhabited by Jesuit and Franciscan monks, two brotherhoods dedicated to preaching the gospel to indigenous people. Continue up Calle San Francisco to the **Casa de Brown,** which houses the **Museo Municipal.** Here you will find an impressive collection of colonial documents and artifacts, a must-see for history buffs.

For those with a more artistic bent, turn left on Calle Misiones de los Tapes and walk 2 blocks to the **Museo del Azulejo,** a unique museum of 19th-century European and Uruguayan tiles housed in a gorgeous 300-year-old country house. Then stroll back into the center of town along Calle de la Playa, enjoying the shops and cafes along the way, until you come to the **Ruinas Casa del Gobernador.** The House of the Viceroy captures something of the glorious past of the city's 17th- and 18th-century magistrates, when the city's port was used for imports, exports, and smuggling. After exploring the opulent lifestyle of colonial leaders, complete your walk with a visit to the **UNESCO-Colonia** headquarters, where exhibits on the city's Historic Heritage of Humanity status will place your tour in the larger context of South American history.

WHERE TO STAY & DINE

Few people stay in Colonia, preferring to make a day trip from Buenos Aires or a stop along the way to Montevideo. If you'd rather get a hotel, however, your best bets are the colonial-style **Hotel Plaza Mayor,** Calle del Comercio 111 (© **052/ 23193**), and **Hotel La Misión,** Calle Misiones de los Tapes 171 (© **052/26767**), whose original building dates from 1762. Both hotels charge from $90 for a double room. Parking is included in the rates of most Uruguayan hotels.

For dining, **Mesón de la Plaza,** Vasconcellos 153 (© **052/24807**), serves quality international and Uruguayan food in a colonial setting, while **Pulpería de los Faroles,** Calle Misiones de los Tapes 101 (© **052/25399**), in front of Plaza Mayor, specializes in beef and bean dishes and homemade pasta.

5 Punta del Este

140km (87 miles) E of Montevideo

Come late December, Punta del Este is transformed from a sleepy coastal village into a booming summer resort. For the next 2 months, there seem to be more *Porteños* (as residents of Buenos Aires are called) in "Punta" than in Buenos Aires itself, and anyone left in Argentina's Federal Capital is deemed to be clearly *declassé.* Without a doubt, this coastal strip that juts into the southern Atlantic is the favorite summer getaway for Argentines, a resort with beautiful white-sand beaches and perfect swimming, world-class hotels and restaurants, and an inexhaustible list of outdoor activities—including golf, tennis, horseback riding, biking, bird-watching, and numerous watersports. Browsing Punta's elegant boutiques offers the one respite from an endless sun, and the shopping here is world-class. You'll have no problem finding an excellent restaurant for dinner, and nightlife in Punta del Este beats just about anywhere else in South America in summer.

ESSENTIALS
GETTING THERE

BY PLANE   International flights arrive at **Aeropuerto Internacional de Laguna del Sauce,** 24km (15 miles) east of Punta del Este. **Pluna** (© **0800/118-881** or 042/490-101; www.pluna.aero) and **Aerolíneas Argentinas** (© **042/444-343;**

www.aerolineas.com) fly between Buenos Aires and Punta. The flight takes 50 minutes. A taxi or *remise* from the airport into town will run about $14.

BY BUS   The **Terminal de Buses Punta del Este,** Rambla Artigas and Calle Inzaurraga (© **042/489-467**), has buses connecting to Montevideo, Colonia, and other cities throughout Uruguay. **COT** (© **042/486-810,** or 02/409-4949 in Montevideo) offers the best service to Montevideo. The trip takes 1½ to 2 hours and costs about $15 round-trip.

BY CAR   If you are driving from Montevideo, you can reach Punta in 1½ hours by taking Route 1 east past Atlántida and Piriápolis to the turnoff for Route 93.

ORIENTATION
Punta del Este is both the name of the famous resort city and the broader region taking in Punta Ballena and Maldonado. The Rambla Artigas is the coastal road that winds its way around the peninsula past the enticing beaches. Calle Gorlero is the main street running through the center of Punta, where you find most of the restaurants, cafes, and boutiques.

GETTING AROUND
If you want to explore the region by car, you can visit **Avis** at the airport (© **042/559-065**) or at Calle 31 and Calle Gorlero (© **042/442-020**). **Budget** also has a branch at the airport. **Hertz** rents cars at the airport (© **042/559-032**) and in the Conrad Hotel (© **042/492-109**).

VISITOR INFORMATION
The **Oficina de Turismo** at Parada 24 (© **042/230-050**) is open daily 9am to 10pm (shorter hours in winter). You should also be able to obtain visitor information from your hotel staff and from the **Centro de Hoteles y Restaurantes de Punta del Este,** Plaza Artigas on Avenida Gorlero (© **042/440-512**).

WHAT TO SEE & DO
OUTDOOR ACTIVITIES
In Punta itself, the main beaches are **Playa Mansa** (on the Río de la Plata) and **Playa Brava** (on the Atlantic). The two beaches are separated by a small peninsula only a few blocks wide. **La Barra del Maldonado,** a small resort 5km (3 miles) east of Punta del Este, also boasts clean, beautiful beaches.

In summer, you will find vendors offering watersports from parasailing and windsurfing to water-skiing and snorkeling on both Playa Mansa and Playa Brava. If you're staying at the Conrad Resort & Casino (see "Where to Stay," below), a full-time staff is dedicated to helping you arrange outdoor activities. For boating or fishing expeditions, contact the **Yacht Club Punta del Este,** Puerto de Punta del Este (© **042/441-056**).

Golf courses include **Club de Golf** (© **042/482-127**) in Punta itself, and **Club del Lago** (© **042/578-423**) in Punta Ballena. Horseback riding can be arranged through **Hípico Burnett,** Camino a La Laguna, Pinares 33 (© **042/230-375**). Tennis fans should call **Médanos Tennis,** avenidas Mar del Plata and Las Delicias (© **042/481-950**).

SHOPPING
Punta has world-class shopping, with Uruguayan shops and European boutiques lining **Calle Gorlero,** the principal street bisecting this resort town. **Punta Shopping Mall,** Avenida Roosevelt at Paradas 6 and 7, has 100 stores on three levels and a 12-screen cinema. A weekend crafts market takes place from 5pm to midnight at Plaza Artigas.

WHERE TO STAY

Prices listed below are for summer peak season and are often half that in the off season. **Semana Santa** (Dec 24–31) is the busiest, most expensive week. Reserve well ahead of your visit, as all of Buenos Aires seems to flee to Punta del Este during summer vacation. Parking is free and available at all hotels in Punta.

VERY EXPENSIVE

Conrad Resort & Casino ☆☆☆ The spectacular Conrad dominates social life in Punta del Este. It's the first choice of the international jet set—mostly from Argentina—that descends on this Atlantic resort in summer. The hotel's elegance stands in stark contrast to the city's other hotels, and guests look as though they've dressed for an afternoon on Rodeo Drive rather than the beach. Luxurious rooms have balconies overlooking Playa Mansa and Playa Brava, and the professional staff is highly attentive to guest needs. Personal trainers can assist you with your favorite sport, from tennis to golf to horseback riding. The outdoor pool and gardens are gorgeous, and there's an excellent health club for the truly motivated. Conrad's casino and showrooms are focal points for Punta nightlife. If you're going to spend the money to visit Punta del Este, you might as well stay here.

The Conrad is a year-round party with nonstop entertainment, from fashion shows and Las Vegas–style reviews to music, dance, and magic shows. Open 24 hours per day, the enormous casino features 560 slots and 63 tables for baccarat, roulette, blackjack, poker, dice, and fortune wheel. There are five restaurants, from refined dining to poolside barbecues. Two excellent beaches are located in front of the resort.

Parada 4, Playa Mansa, 20100 Punta del Este. © **042/491-111.** Fax 042/489-999. www.conrad.com.uy. 302 units. From $300 double. AE, DC, MC, V. **Amenities:** 5 restaurants; golf; 2 lit tennis courts; deluxe health club w/fitness center, temperate-water pool, sauna, and massage; concierge; business center and secretarial services; room service; laundry service; dry cleaning; executive-level floors. *In room:* A/C, TV, dataport, minibar, hair dryer, safe.

EXPENSIVE

L'Auberge ☆☆ *Finds* This exclusive boutique hotel lies in the quiet residential neighborhood of Parque de Golf and is 2 blocks from the beach. Formerly an 18th-century water tower, the hotel today houses beautiful guest rooms decorated with antiques and a dedicated staff committed to warm, personalized service. The colorful gardens and pool will draw you outside, and the staff can help you arrange horseback riding, golf, tennis, or other outdoor sports in the surrounding parks. The sophisticated resort has an elegant European tearoom overlooking the gardens, famous for its homemade waffles. An evening barbecue is offered by the pool.

Barrio Parque del Golf, 20100 Punta del Este. © **042/482-601.** Fax 042/483-408. www.lauberge.com.uy. 40 units. From $160 double; from $350 suite. Rates include continental breakfast. AE, DC, MC, V. **Amenities:** Outdoor pool; golf; tennis court; fitness center; spa; concierge; business center and secretarial services; room service; babysitting; laundry service; dry cleaning. *In room:* TV, minibar, hair dryer, safe.

MODERATE

Best Western La Foret ☆ *Kids* Opened in 2000, La Foret offers spacious guest rooms 1 block from Playa Mansa. The amenities are impressive given the price, and the hotel is a nice option for families (children under 17 stay free, and there's a children's playground and babysitting services). There's also a good international restaurant and coffee shop with a multilingual staff.

Calle La Foret, Parada 6, Playa Mansa, 20100 Punta del Este. © **042/481-004.** Fax 042/481-004. www. bestwestern.com. 49 units. From $70 double. Rates include buffet breakfast. AE, DC, MC, V. **Amenities:** Restaurant; bar/lounge; pool; Jacuzzi; sauna; concierge; business services; babysitting. *In room:* TV, minibar, dataport, hair dryer, safe.

Days Inn Punta del Este 🌟🌟 *(Value)*   Opened in 1999, this atypical Days Inn sits on the waterfront. It's an excellent value for its location, featuring simple but modern rooms, many with ocean views. The Conrad Resort & Casino is next door, along with restaurants, cinemas, and excellent beaches. This is the best midrange hotel in Punta.

Rambla Williman, Parada 3, Playa Mansa, 20100 Punta del Este. ℂ 042/484-353. Fax 042/484-683. www.daysinn.com. 38 units. From $80 double. Rates include buffet breakfast. AE, DC, MC, V. **Amenities:** Bar/lounge; indoor heated and outdoor pool; room service; babysitting; laundry service. *In room:* TV, minibar, dataport, hair dryer, safe.

WHERE TO DINE

Punta's dining scene is seasonal, with restaurants packed in summer and fairly dead in winter. Not surprisingly, restaurant hours vary depending on the season, and some establishments close altogether from April to October. Expect considerably higher prices here than elsewhere in Uruguay, a consequence of Punta's jet-set clientele.

EXPENSIVE

La Bourgogne 🌟🌟🌟 *(Moments)* FRENCH   Jean-Paul Bondoux is the top French chef in South America, splitting his time between La Bourgogne in Punta del Este and its sister restaurant tucked inside the Alvear Palace Hotel, in Buenos Aires. A Relais & Châteaux member, La Bourgogne is an unforgettable dining experience. The cuisine is inspired by Bondoux's Burgundy heritage. Traditional main course such as rack of lamb, breast of duck, rabbit with mustard sauce, and veal cutlet are chef's favorites, while fresh vegetables, fruits, herbs, and spices from the owner's private farm accentuate the menu. Delicious French bread, baked in-house, is available for takeout from the restaurant's small bakery. Ask for a table inside the elegant dining room or amid the jasmine-scented garden. Service is impeccable, as is the wine list featuring French and South American labels.

Pedragosa Sierra (Maldonado). ℂ 042/482-007. Reservations recommended. Main courses $15–$25. AE, DC, MC, V. Open for lunch and dinner (call ahead for hours). Closed July and Mon–Wed Apr 12–Nov 30.

MODERATE

Andrés 🌟🌟 INTERNATIONAL   This father-son establishment enjoys an excellent reputation across the board. Its setting along the Rambla, with most tables outside, makes for a perfect summer night out. Dishes, ranging from grilled meats to baked fish and fresh vegetable soufflés, are prepared with considerable care. Service is friendly and professional; ask for assistance matching a South American wine with your meal.

Edificio Vanguardia, Parada 1. ℂ 042/481-804. Main courses $8–$15. AE, MC, V. Daily 11am–midnight in summer; rest of the year Wed–Sat only.

Lo de Tere 🌟🌟 *(Finds)* URUGUAYAN   Among the first restaurants in Punta del Este, this cozy establishment has a staff that makes you feel at home, offering graceful, cheerful service. Lo de Tere sits right on the water, with a beautiful view of the harbor. The specialties are fresh fish and pasta, which vary depending on the catch and the chef's inspiration. The restaurant transforms from festive and relaxed at lunch to more refined at dinner. Three-course menus are available for $16 to $32.

Rambla del Puerto and Calle 21. ℂ 042/440-492. Main courses $6–$15. AE, DC, MC, V. Summer daily 12:30–6pm and 9pm–3am; winter daily noon–3:30pm and 8pm–midnight.

Yacht Club Uruguayo 🌟 URUGUAYAN   This popular restaurant, with tables inside and on the outdoor terrace, looks across the water to Gorriti Island.

The dining room's marine theme prepares you for an evening of seafood, with octopus, hake, and swordfish among the favorites. Waiters, dressed in proud white shirts, offer attentive service.

Rambla Artigas and Calle 8. ℭ 042/441-056. Main courses $8–$20. AE, DC, MC, V. Summer daily noon–2am; winter daily noon–3:30pm and 7:30pm–midnight.

INEXPENSIVE

Los Caracoles ⭑ *Value* URUGUAYAN   The town's most recommended parrillada also serves excellent seafood, including Spanish-style paella. A good salad bar accompanies the hearty selection of meats and fish, and there are a number of homemade pastas to choose from as well. Packed with 70 tables, the rustic dining room is casual and boisterous.

Calle Gorlero 20. ℭ 042/440-912. Main courses $4–$7. AE, DC, MC, V. Summer daily noon–6pm and 8pm–3am; winter daily noon–4pm and 7pm–1am.

PUNTA DEL ESTE AFTER DARK

The **Conrad Resort & Casino,** Parada 4, Playa Mansa (ℭ **042/491-111**), is the focal point for evening entertainment in Punta, featuring Las Vegas–style reviews and other music, dance, and magic shows—sometimes around the torch-lit swimming pools. The enormous 24-hour casino has 450 slots and 63 tables for baccarat, roulette, blackjack, poker, dice, and fortune wheel.

Bars and discos come and go with considerable frequency in Punta, often changing names from one season to the next. The concierge at Conrad Resort & Casino (p. 684) is a good source for what's hot in town. The best bar is **Moby Dick,** located at Rambla de la Circunvalación (ℭ **042/441-240**), near the yacht harbor. Punta's bronzed Latin bodies then make their way to **Gitane** and **La Plage** (ℭ **042/484-869**), two discos next to each other on Rambla Brava, Parada 12. The Conrad Hotel's own disco, **La Boite,** is another upscale club free for hotel guests and $10 to enter for outsiders (this $10 can be redeemed for chips in the casino).

11

Venezuela

by Eliot Greenspan

From snowcapped Andean peaks to white-sand Caribbean beaches, from the Orinoco river basin to the skyscrapers of Caracas, and from the mysterious mesas of the Gran Sabana to the flooded plains of Los Llanos, Venezuela has an amazing variety of must-see sites, attractions, and natural wonders. It has some of the richest oil reserves in the western hemisphere and was a founding member of OPEC. Thanks to the oil, it is one of the most modern and industrialized countries in Latin America. However, an estimated 80% of the population lives below the poverty line. Widespread unemployment, underemployment, and crippling poverty spur high levels of crime and violence. Venezuela is a nation whose politics have historically been marked by corruption and tyrannical rule, and whose current leader is a military man regarded as everything from a populist hero to an autocratic dictator.

Nevertheless, Christopher Columbus, on his third voyage to the New World, was inspired enough to call Venezuela "paradise on earth." If you stay away from the urban and industrial areas, you may agree with him. Venezuela is exceptionally rich in biological diversity and pure natural beauty. With 43 national parks and a score of other natural monuments and protected areas, it's a fabulous destination for nature lovers, bird-watchers, and adventure travelers. There's great windsurfing, scuba diving, fishing, mountain biking, mountain climbing, hiking, trekking, and river rafting. Venezuela has the world's tallest waterfall, Angel Falls; the world's highest and longest tramway in the Andean city of Mérida; and miles and miles of white-sand Caribbean beaches.

Venezuela is the closest South American country to the United States, with some of the most frequent and affordable air connections to both the United States and Europe, and thus easily accessible to international tourists. Most of the country is connected by an excellent network of paved roads and a good internal commuter air system. Still, Venezuela is largely undiscovered by tourists. This chapter covers the principal tourist destinations—Caracas, Isla de Margarita, Los Llanos, Mérida and Los Andes, Los Roques, and Canaima and Angel Falls—and will guide you to some unforgettable experiences.

1 The Regions in Brief

Venezuela lies between 1° and 12° south latitude and goes from sea level to 5,007m (16,423 ft.)—giving it everything from steamy equatorial jungles to perennially snowcapped mountains. There are dry barren deserts and lush tropical rainforests. More than 90% of the population lives in cities located in the northern part of the country. Bordered by the Caribbean Sea, Colombia, Brazil, and Guyana, Venezuela is 916,445 sq. km (352,144 sq. miles) in area and is divided into 23 states.

Given the wide range of destinations, attractions, and adventures offered in Venezuela, the itinerary you choose will greatly depend on your particular interests and needs. Business travelers in Caracas with a free day or two should head to Isla de Margarita for some fun in the sun, or to Los Roques for a chance to go fishing or scuba diving. Adventure travelers should visit Mérida and the Andes. Bird-watchers and nature lovers should not miss Los Llanos. Families looking for an all-inclusive resort vacation with plenty of activities to keep the kids busy should choose Isla de Margarita. And anyone looking for an adventurous tour through some of South America's most stunning scenery should head to Canaima and Angel Falls.

CARACAS Caracas is an overcrowded, inhospitable, and famously violent city. The city center occupies a flat valley surrounded by high mountains and hillsides. Urban sprawl has covered most of these hillsides with dense *ranchitos* (shantytowns). A total of some six million inhabitants, or *Caraqueños,* make up the greater metropolitan area. Despite the widespread poverty and overcrowding, Caracas is one of the more cosmopolitan and architecturally distinctive cities in Latin America, with a vibrant and active population.

THE URBAN BELT From Maracaibo in the west to Cumaná and Maturín in the east is a more or less linear belt of urban development, much of it based around major petroleum, mining, and agricultural centers, and most of it on or close to the Caribbean coast. Major cities include Maracaibo, Barquisimeto, Valencia, Maracay, and Caracas. An estimated 80% of the country's population lives within this relatively narrow urban belt. In fact, Venezuelans refer to almost all the rest of the country as "the interior."

THE CARIBBEAN COAST & THE ISLANDS Venezuela has 3,000km (1,850 miles) of coastline and hundreds of coastal islands, most of them uninhabited. The largest of the islands, **Isla de Margarita,** is Venezuela's most popular tourist destination. **Los Roques,** an archipelago of 42 named islands and 200 sand spits, mangrove islands, and tiny cays, is also very popular. The coastal region closest to Caracas, known as **El Litoral,** was devastated in 1999 by massive landslides and flooding, which left an estimated 200,000 dead and many more homeless. This region is still showing the effects of the disaster. However, the coastal areas further east and west of El Litoral still offer scores of relatively undiscovered and undeveloped beaches for the more intrepid and independent travelers. The climate all along the coast and on the Caribbean islands is hot and tropical, and much drier than the rest of the country.

THE ANDES The great South American mountain chain, the Andes, runs through Venezuela from the Colombian border in a northeasterly direction through the states of Táchira, Mérida, and Trujillo. The mountains here, in three major spines—the Sierra Nevada, Sierra de La Culata, and Sierra de Santo Domingo—rise to more than 5,000m (16,000 ft.). The principal city here is **Mérida,** a picturesque and bustling college town nestled in a narrow valley. However, there are many small mountain towns, as well as some interesting indigenous villages, that are scattered about and worth exploring. This is a prime area for hiking, trekking, and a wide range of adventure sports.

LOS LLANOS Located on plains that roll on for hundreds of miles south and east of the Andes, **Los Llanos** is an area of flat, mostly open cattle ground, punctuated with some isolated stands of forest. During the latter part of the rainy season (July–Nov), the plains are almost entirely flooded, with only a few raised highways and service roads passable in anything that doesn't float. In the

Venezuela

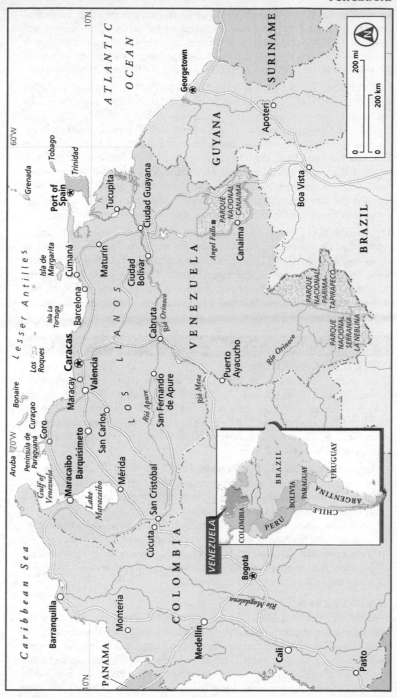

dry season, the land reemerges and wildlife congregates in dense herds and mixed flocks around the ponds and creeks that are left behind. The quantity and variety of wildlife visible at the nature lodges located in Los Llanos is truly phenomenal—anaconda, caiman, capybara, deer, and even wildcat are commonly sighted. This is one of the top spots on the planet for bird-watching.

SOUTHERN VENEZUELA & THE GRAN SABANA   Southern Venezuela is a largely uninhabited and wild region of tropical forests and jungle rivers. The region is home to several ancient indigenous tribes, including the Piaroa, Pemón, and Yanomami, who still live an often-nomadic lifestyle based on hunting and gathering. This area is home to vast expanses of forest, including **Canaima National Park,** the largest national park in Venezuela, and the sixth largest in the world, as well as **Angel Falls,** the highest waterfall on the planet, and a series of stunning steep-walled flat mesas called *tepuis.* Much of this region is also known as the Gran Sabana, or "Great Plains," as it features large stretches of flat savanna broken up only by these imposing *tepuis.*

THE ORINOCO DELTA   The eastern end of Venezuela comprises the largely uninhabited Orinoco Delta. Second in size and import to the Amazon (both as a river and river basin), the Orinoco Delta is a vast area of shifting rivers, tributaries, mangroves, rainforests, and natural canals. The area is also known as the Delta Amacuro, after a smaller river that empties into the basin and forms part of the border with Guyana. This area is just starting to develop as a destination for naturalists and ecotourists.

2 Planning Your Trip to Venezuela

VISITOR INFORMATION
Good tourist information on Venezuela is hard to come by. The country's tourism institute, **INATUR** (see "In Venezuela," below), is an overwhelmingly rudderless bureaucracy that does very limited outreach and promotional work. Your best bet is to search the Internet, contact the nearest Venezuelan embassy or consulate (p. 692), or deal directly with hotels and tour operators working in Venezuela. Some useful websites:

- **http://lanic.utexas.edu/la/venezuela**: The University of Texas Latin American Studies Department's database features an extensive list of useful links.
- **http://think-venezuela.net**: "Think Venezuela" is perhaps the best all-around general tourism site on Venezuela.
- **www.embavenez-us.org**: The website for the embassy of Venezuela in the United States has current information and a small section of links.
- **www.cantv.net**: This Spanish-language site belongs to the country's principal telecommunications and Internet company, and features links to online white and yellow-page phone directories.

IN VENEZUELA
INATUR (© **0800/462-8871** or 0212/576-9032; www.inatur.gov.ve) is the national tourism institute. Its main office, located on the 35th floor of the Torre Oeste (West Tower) of the Parque Central (near the Caracas Hilton), is open weekdays during business hours. The staff can give you a basic map and some brochures for hotels and attractions, but I find the view here more worthwhile than the information available. Most bookstores and many hotel gift shops around the country stock a small selection of maps and useful books on Venezuelan history, culture, and tourism, some in English.

ENTRY REQUIREMENTS

You need a valid passport to enter Venezuela. Upon arrival, citizens and residents of the United States, Canada, Great Britain, Australia, and New Zealand who enter by air or cruise ship are issued a free tourist card valid for 90 days. You can extend your tourist card for up to 60 days at the Caracas office of the national immigration agency, **Dirección de Identificación y Extranjería (DIEX; ✆ 0212/483-2070;** www.onidex.gov.ve). In theory, you can apply for two consecutive extensions. The extensions cost between $20 and $25, depending on the length of time you apply for.

Common advice is that you should make photocopies of your passport and stamped tourist card and keep them in a separate, safe place, while carrying the originals with you. I personally recommend that unless you need your passport for a bank transaction, you should keep it and other valuables in a hotel safe and carry a photocopy of the first page of your passport with you. Note that you will have to present your tourist card upon departure.

If you plan to enter Venezuela by sea or land, it is advisable to try to obtain a tourist card or visa in advance from your nearest Venezuelan embassy or consulate, although, in practice, this is usually not necessary. Tourist cards are free, although I've heard reports that you may face an arbitrary charge of between $3 and $10 at some of the border crossings along the Colombian and Brazil borders. You will be charged between $30 and $40 for a tourist visa depending on the processing fees and policies of your local embassy or consulate.

Venezuela requires children under 18 traveling alone, with one parent, or with a third party to present a copy of their birth certificate and written, notarized

---

Telephone Dialing Info at a Glance

Venezuela's phone system features a standardized system of seven-digit local numbers, with three-digit area codes. Note that you must add a zero before the three-digit area code when dialing from within Venezuela, but not when dialing to Venezuela from abroad.

- **To place a call from your home country to Venezuela,** dial the international access code (011 in the U.S. and Canada, 0011 in Australia, 0170 in New Zealand, 00 in the U.K.), plus the country code (58), plus the three-digit Venezuelan area code (Caracas 212, Isla de Margarita 295, Mérida 274), plus the seven-digit phone number.
- **To place a local call within Venezuela,** dial the seven-digit local number. To call another area within Venezuela, you must add a 0 before the three-digit area code. For information, dial ✆ 113; to place national collect calls, dial ✆ 101.
- **To place a direct international call from Venezuela,** dial the international access code (00), plus the country code, plus the area code and local number of the other party.
- **To reach an international operator,** dial ✆ 122. Major long-distance company access codes are as follows: **AT&T** ✆ 800/100-1120; **Bell Canada** ✆ 800/100-1100; **British Telecom** ✆ 800/100-1440; **MCI** ✆ 800/11-140; **Sprint** ✆ 800/100-1110.

authorization by the absent parent(s) or legal guardian granting permission to travel alone, with one parent, or with a third party. For more details, contact your embassy or consulate.

VENEZUELAN EMBASSY LOCATIONS

In the U.S.: 1099 30th St. NW, Washington, DC 20007 (© **202/342-2214;** fax 202/342-6820; www.embavenez-us.org)

In Canada: 32 Range Rd., Ottawa, ON KIN 8J4 (© **613/235-5151;** fax 613/235-3205; www.misionvenezuela.org)

In the U.K.: 1 Cromwell Rd., London SW7 2HW (© **020/7581-2776;** fax 020/7589-8887; www.venezlon.demon.co.uk)

In Australia & New Zealand: 7 Culgoa Circuit, O'Malley, Canberra, ACT 2606 (© **02/6290-2967;** fax 02/6290-2911; www.venezuela-emb.org.au)

CUSTOMS

You may bring in to Venezuela all reasonable manner of electronic devices and items for personal use (including cameras, personal stereos, and laptop computers). Officially, you may bring in up to $1,000 worth of miscellaneous merchandise—tobacco, liquor, chocolate, and the like. However, this is only loosely enforced. The guiding rule is to try to not attract the interest of immigration officials. Once their interest is piqued, they could decide to give you a hard time, if the mood strikes.

MONEY

The Venezuelan unit of currency is the **bolívar,** popularly referred to as *bolos,* and abbreviated as "Bs." Paper bills come in denominations of 5, 10, 20, 50, 100, 500, 1,000, 2,000, 5,000, 10,000, 20,000, and 50,000 bolivares. There are coins of 5, 10, 20, 50, 100, and 500 bolivares. There are even coins for céntimos (fractions of a bolívar), but the currency has devalued so much in recent years that all coins are virtually meaningless and increasingly rare. Many taxis, small shops, and restaurants are reluctant (and sometimes unable) to change larger denomination bills, so it's always good to try to keep a few 1,000 and 2,000 notes on hand.

Here's a general idea of what things cost in Caracas: a taxi from the airport to the center of town, $11 to $18; a double room at a very expensive hotel, $150 to $200; a double room at an expensive hotel, $60 to $100; a double room at a budget hotel, $20 to $40; dinner for one at a moderate restaurant (without wine), $8; a Coca-Cola, 50¢; a roll of 36-exposure color film, $3.50; a movie ticket, $2 to $4.

CURRENCY EXCHANGE & RATES In January 2002, the government fixed the official exchange rate at 1600Bs to the U.S. dollar. It also made it virtually impossible for Venezuelan citizens and businesses, as well as tourists, to exchange bolivares for dollars. This has led to a thriving black market, where the real exchange rate hovers around 2500Bs to the dollar as of press time. The most common place to exchange dollars for bolivares at the black market rate is the Simón Bolívar International airport. While this is technically illegal, and you should be careful about whom you deal with, I nevertheless recommend changing dollars at the black market rate, as it will make your dollars go considerably further. Note, if you are dealing with a Venezuelan-based tour agency, be sure to ask if they would be willing to buy your dollars at a more favorable rate. Since it is so hard for Venezuelan companies to get dollars, they are usually willing and able to exchange them for you, and this takes some of the risk out of dealing with an unknown entity at the airport.

Prices in this book are listed at the official exchange rate. Most restaurants, tour agencies, and attractions set their prices in bolivares. On the other hand, many hotel prices, particularly at the higher end hotels, as well as tours and car rentals, are quoted in and pegged to the U.S. dollar. It is always best to inquire in advance if the price you are being quoted is in bolivares or dollars. If it is in bolivares, you will be saving some serious money by exchanging dollars at the black market rate. Given this situation, it is currently recommended to bring cash and plenty of it, as all credit card purchases and ATM withdrawals are charged at the much less favorable official exchange rate.

Most banks do not exchange foreign currencies, and those that do often make the process cumbersome and unpleasant. But there are currency exchange offices in most major cities and tourist destinations, as well as 24-hour exchange offices in both the national and international airport terminals at the Simón Bolívar International Airport; however, they only exchange money at the official rate.

ATMs   ATMs are readily available in Caracas and most major cities and tourist destinations. **Cirrus** (© **800/424-7787**; www.mastercard.com) and **PLUS** (© **800/843-7587**; www.visa.com) are the two most popular networks; check the back of your ATM card to see which network your bank belongs to. Use the toll-free numbers to locate ATMs in your destination. It might take a few tries, but you should be able to find one connected to either, or both, the PLUS and Cirrus systems that will allow you to withdraw bolivares against your home bank account. However, these will be sold to you at the official exchange rate.

TRAVELER'S CHECKS   In an era of almost universally accepted bank and credit cards, traveler's checks are becoming less and less common. The security they offer will soon not justify the cost and hassle of using them. Most hotels, restaurants, and shops that cater to foreign tourists will still accept and cash traveler's checks, some will actually change them for you at or near the going black market exchange rate, but most will only change them at the official exchange rate, and they often exact a surcharge as well. Money-exchange houses will only change traveler's checks at the official rate and usually charge an additional 1% to 5% fee.

To report lost or stolen traveler's checks, see "Credit Cards," below.

CREDIT CARDS   Credit cards are widely accepted at most hotels, restaurants, shops, and attractions in all but the most remote destinations. American Express, MasterCard, and Visa have the greatest coverage, with a far smaller number of establishments accepting Diners Club.

To report lost or stolen credit cards or traveler's checks, call the following numbers: **American Express,** © 0212/206-0222 or 0212/206-0333; **Diners Club,** © 0212/503-2461; **MasterCard,** © 0800/100-2902; and **Visa,** © 0800/100-2167 or 0212/285-2510.

WHEN TO GO

PEAK SEASON   November through February, when it's cold and bleak in Europe and North America, is the peak season in Venezuela, but you can truly enjoy the country any time of year. Venezuelans travel a lot within the country on holidays and during the school break lasting from late July through early September. It is extremely hard to find a hotel room or bus or airline seat during Christmas and Easter vacations. April through June is a fabulous time to enjoy great deals, deserted beaches, and glorious solitude in the more popular destinations.

CLIMATE   Venezuela has two distinct seasons: rainy (June–Oct) and dry (Nov–May). The rainy season is locally called *invierno* (winter), while the dry season is called *verano* (summer). However, temperatures vary principally according to altitude. Coastal and lowland areas are hot year-round, and temperatures drop as you rise in altitude.

Set at an altitude of some 1,000m (3,000 ft.), Caracas has an average temperature of 72°F (22°C), with little seasonal variation. Daytime highs can reach around 90°F (32°C) on clear sunny days. Nights get a little cooler, but you'll rarely need more than a light jacket or sweater.

PUBLIC HOLIDAYS Official public holidays celebrated in Venezuela include New Year's Day (Jan 1); Carnaval (the Mon and Tues before Ash Wednesday); Easter (Thurs and Fri of Holy Week are official holidays); Declaration of Independence (Apr 19); Labor Day (May 1); Battle of Carabobo (June 24); Independence Day (July 5); Birth of Simón Bolívar (July 24); Discovery Day, or *Día de la Raza* (Oct 12); Christmas Day (Dec 25).

HEALTH CONCERNS

COMMON AILMENTS Your chances of contracting any serious tropical disease in Venezuela are slim, especially if you stick to the major tourist destinations. However, malaria, dengue fever, yellow fever, hepatitis, and leptospirosis all exist in Venezuela, so it's a good idea to be careful and consult your doctor before a trip here.

Malaria is found predominantly in the jungle areas of the Amazonas and Bolívar states, as well as in the Orinoco Delta. Malaria prophylaxes are often recommended, but several have side effects and others are of questionable effectiveness. Consult your doctor as to what is currently considered the best preventive treatment for malaria. Be sure to ask whether a recommended drug will cause hypersensitivity to the sun; it would be a shame to travel here for the beaches and then have to hide under an umbrella the whole time. If you are in a malarial area, wear long pants and long sleeves, use insect repellent, and either sleep under a mosquito net or burn mosquito coils (similar to incense but with a pesticide).

Of greater concern may be **dengue fever,** which reached epidemic proportions in 2001 and again in 2003. Dengue fever is similar to malaria and is spread by an aggressive daytime mosquito. This mosquito seems to be most common in lowland urban areas, although dengue outbreaks have been reported throughout the country. Dengue is also known as "bone-break fever" because it is usually accompanied by severe body aches. The first infection with dengue fever will make you very sick but should cause no permanent damage. However, a second infection with a different strain of the dengue virus can lead to internal hemorrhaging and may be life-threatening. Take the same precautions as you would against malaria.

Although **cholera** exists in Venezuela, your chances of contracting cholera while you're here are very slight. Avoid tap water and all unpeeled fruits and vegetables in more remote areas and at any hotels, restaurants, or public facilities that are obviously unsanitary.

The most common health concern for travelers to Venezuela is a touch of **diarrhea.** The best way to protect yourself from diarrhea is to avoid tap water and drinks or ice made from tap water. Those with really tender intestinal tracts should avoid uncooked fruits and vegetables likely to have been washed in tap water, unless you can peel and prepare them yourself.

VACCINATIONS No specific vaccinations are necessary for travel to Venezuela, although it is recommended that you be up-to-date on your tetanus, typhoid, and yellow-fever vaccines. It is also a good idea to get a vaccination for hepatitis A and B.

HEALTH PRECAUTIONS Staying healthy on a trip to Venezuela is predominantly a matter of being a little cautious about what you eat and drink, and using common sense. Know your physical limits and don't overexert yourself in the ocean, on hikes, or in athletic activities. Respect the tropical sun and protect yourself from it. Also try to protect yourself from biting insects, using a combination of repellent and light, loose, long-sleeved clothing. I recommend buying and drinking bottled water or soft drinks, although the water in Caracas and in most of the major tourist destinations is reputed to be safe to drink.

GETTING THERE
BY PLANE
The **Simón Bolívar International Airport** (© 0212/303-1526; www.aero puerto-maiquetia.com.ve) in Maiquetía, 28km (17 miles) north of Caracas, is the gateway to Venezuela and the point of entry for most visitors to the country. There is an airport departure tax of 48,500 Bs ($25), paid in either bolivares, or the current official exchange in dollars. This fee is sometimes included in the airline ticket price, so be sure to ask before paying twice.

FROM THE U.S. Miami, which is only around 3 hours and 15 minutes away by air, is the principal gateway to Caracas. **American Airlines** (© 800/433-7300; www.aa.com) has several daily direct flights between Miami and Caracas, and **Aeropostal** (© 888/990-2527; www.aeropostal.com) has one daily direct flight from Miami. **Continental** (© 800/525-0280 or 800/231-0856; www.continental.com) has a daily direct flight from Houston, and a once weekly direct flight from Newark; **Delta Airlines** (© 800/221-1212; www.delta.com) has a daily flight from Atlanta; and **American** also has a daily direct flight from Dallas–Fort Worth. **Mexicana** (© 800/531-7921; www.mexicana.com) and **Grupo Taca** (© 800/535-8780; www.grupotaca.com) have flights from Los Angeles connecting through Mexico City, Mexico, and San José, Costa Rica, respectively.

FROM CANADA **American, Continental,** and **Mexicana,** have flights from Montréal, Toronto, and Vancouver to Caracas, connecting through Miami, Los Angeles, or New York (Newark).

There are numerous charter flights from Toronto and Montréal to Isla de Margarita, particularly during the winter months. Ask your travel agent, check online, or look in the Sunday travel section of your local newspaper to find them.

FROM THE U.K. **British Airways** (© 0845/773-3377; www.british-airways.com) has three weekly regular direct flights to Caracas from Heathrow. **Air Europa, Air France, Alitalia, KLM, Iberia,** and **Lufthansa** also offer regular service to Venezuela, often with connections from London.

FROM AUSTRALIA & NEW ZEALAND To fly to Venezuela from either Australia or New Zealand, you will almost certainly have to connect via Los Angeles. **Air New Zealand** (© 0800/737-000 in New Zealand, or 13-24-76 in Australia; www.airnewzealand.com) and **Qantas** (© 13-13-13 in Australia, or 0800/808-767 in New Zealand; www.qantas.com) are the two main carriers. Both fly into Los Angeles with connections to Caracas.

BY BUS
Venezuela is serviced by international bus routes via Colombia to the west and Brazil to the south. In general, crossings from Colombia are considered dangerous, due to guerrilla and drug-cartel activity. The only road route between Brazil

and Venezuela connects Boa Vista, Brazil, and Santa Elena de Uairén, Venezuela. Two recommended companies are **Bus Ven** (© **0212/953-8441;** www.busven. com) and **Expreso Internacional Ormeño** (© **0212/471-7205**).

BY BOAT

There are ferry services between several Caribbean islands and Isla de Margarita, Venezuela. Routes and schedules vary seasonally and change on short notice. Islands with the most consistent connections include Barbados, St. Vincent, and Trinidad and Tobago.

GETTING AROUND

BY PLANE   As distances are relatively long and land travel time consuming, Venezuela has an excellent network of commuter airlines servicing the entire country and all major tourist destinations. Fares run $30 to $150 each way, depending on destination, distance, availability, and demand. On any internal flight, you have to pay an airport tax of $1 to $5, depending on the specific destination. For the names and contact information of individual commuter airlines, see "Getting There" in each destination section in this chapter.

BY BUS   Regular and inexpensive buses service all of terrestrial Venezuela. Most popular destinations are also serviced by *expreso* (express), *ejecutivo* (executive), and/or *de lujo* (luxury) buses. In most cases, it's worth the few extra dollars for the *expreso, ejecutivo,* or *de lujo* options. Some reputable luxury lines are **Aeroexpresos Ejecutivos** (© **0212/226-2321;** www.aeroexpresos.com.ve), **Expresos Los Llanos** (© **0212/243-6140**), and **Rodovías** (© **0212/577-6622;** www.rodovias.com.ve). There are two principal bus terminals in Caracas, Terminal La Bandera and Terminal del Oriente, although depending on the route, destination, and bus line, you may embark at either of these or a private terminal.

BY CAR   I do not recommend a rental car as a means of exploring Venezuela. Many of the top destinations—Los Roques, Canaima, and Angel Falls, for example—are inaccessible by car. (*Note:* The only two destinations included in this chapter where a car would come in handy are Isla de Margarita and Mérida. In both cases, you'd be better off flying to the destination and renting a car there for the duration of your stay.) Venezuelan drivers are quite aggressive and ignore most common traffic laws and general rules of road safety. Moreover, roads are not well marked, distances between destinations are considerable, and you run the risk of becoming a target for one of many robbery schemes. If you do decide to rent a car, all of the major international agencies operate in Venezuela, with offices in Caracas (often with a branch at the airport) and in most major cities and tourist destinations. Rates run $40 to $85 per day.

Your best bet for renting a car, both in terms of rates and reliability, is to choose one of the major international agencies and book in advance from your home country. **Avis** (© **800/230-4898** in the U.S., or 0212/355-1190 in Venezuela; www.avis.com), **Budget** (© **800/527-0700** in the U.S., or 0800/ 283-4381 in Venezuela; www.budget.com.ve), **Dollar** (© **800/800-3665** in the U.S., or 0212/993-2469 in Venezuela; www.dollar.com), and **Hertz** (© **800/ 654-3131** in the U.S., or 0212/905-0411 in Venezuela; www.hertz.com) all have offices both in Caracas and at Simón Bolívar International Airport.

One amazing upside of driving around Venezuela is that gas is amazingly cheap, around 60Bs to 90Bs (2¢–5¢) per liter, or 225Bs to 340Bs (14¢–21¢) per gallon.

BY ORGANIZED TOUR   Considering the current state of affairs, organized tours are a reasonable way to go in Venezuela. The country is still a bit inhospitable and unused to freewheeling independent exploration. The tourism industry here was built top-down, with lots of big hotels and big operations that almost seem to not want to waste their time on independent travelers. In many cases, tour operators and wholesalers are able to get better rates on rooms, tours, and transfers than you'd be able to find on your own. Many of them use the hotels and local tour operators recommended in this book.

Akanan Travel & Tours ★★ (© 0212/234-2103 or 0212/234-2323; www. akanan.com) is one of my favorite operators on the ground in Caracas. It offers a wide range of tour options. **Lost World Adventures** ★★ (© 800/999-0558 in the U.S., or 0212/577-0303 in Caracas; www.lostworldadventures. com) is an excellent operator and a pioneer in Venezuelan travel. It offers a wide range of tour options and can customize a trip to your needs and specifications.

Geodyssey ★ (© 020/7281-7788; www.geodyssey.co.uk) is a British operator with a fair amount of experience in Venezuela. **Journey Latin America** (© 020/8747-3108; www.journeylatinamerica.co.uk) is a large British operator specializing in Latin American travel. It often has excellent deals on airfare.

TIPS ON ACCOMMODATIONS

You'll find hotel rooms in all price ranges, although in general, the country's strong suit is in upper-end and business-class hotels, and room rates are high. There are a dozen or so large, all-inclusive resorts on Isla de Margarita. However, there is a major glut of hotel rooms throughout the country, and competition is getting fierce. The tourism industry is reeling from major declines in the number of visitors over the past years. Few hotels actually charge their published and advertised rack rate. You can get especially good deals in the off season and midweek. It always pays to bargain, especially if you book directly by phone, fax, or the Internet.

When booking a room, if you ask for a double *(doble),* you may be given a room with two twin beds. If you want a double or queen-size bed, be specific and ask for a *cama matrimonial.*

TIPS ON DINING

Although both Caracas and Isla de Margarita have a wide range of restaurants serving a whole gamut of international cuisines, your choices will be much more limited throughout most the rest of the country. Venezuelan cuisine is neither very distinctive nor noteworthy. Most meals consist of a meat or chicken dish (either fried, grilled, or in a stew), accompanied by some stewed vegetables, rice, and the ubiquitous *arepa,* the traditional cornmeal patty that's a kind of cross between a tortilla and a biscuit. Vegetarians may have a particularly hard time. If you are vegetarian, try to coordinate your meals in advance with hotels and tour agencies.

For those with a sweet tooth, be sure to try a piece of the national cake, *bienmesabe,* a soft sponge cake soaked in a sweet coconut cream sauce. (Its name literally means "Tastes good to me!") Also be sure to sample some of the fresh fruit drinks, or *batidos.* These are made with whatever ripe tropical fruits are on hand. My favorite *batido* is made of mango, but *parchita,* or passion fruit, runs a close second.

TIPS ON SHOPPING

Outside of the massive malls in Caracas, which have all the standard international designer stores you could ask for, shopping is far from rewarding in Venezuela. Your best bet is to look for and stick to local and indigenous arts and crafts. Masks are particularly attractive and varied. Keep an eye out for the local hammocks, called *chinchorros*, which are an intricate weave of thin strands of rough natural fibers. You'll also find a variety of woven baskets, hats, and handbags, as well as simple ceramic wares. Despite its duty-free status, Isla de Margarita is unlikely to be of much interest for international shoppers. Prices and selection are comparable to what most folks can find at home.

Outside of department stores, hotel gift shops, and malls, you should bargain. In many cases, street merchants and sellers at outdoor markets and souvenir shops can easily be bartered down by 25% to 30%.

FAST FACTS: Venezuela

American Express There is an office in Caracas at Torre Corporación Banca, Avenida Blandin, La Castellana (© 0212/206-0333); it's open Monday through Friday from 8am to noon and 2 to 4:30pm. For Global Assist, call © 0212/285-5809, or call collect 715/343-7977 in the United States.

Business Hours Most businesses open between 8am and 9am, and close between 5 and 6pm. Many businesses and stores close down for an hour or more for a lunch break between noon and 2:30pm. On Saturday, most shops are open and most businesses are closed. On Sunday, only shops in malls and major shopping districts are open. Most banks are open Monday to Friday from 8:30am to 3:30pm; however, banks and exchange houses in some of the major malls are open during shopping hours, which often include the early evenings and weekends.

Doctors & Dentists Medical and dental care is generally of acceptable to high quality in Venezuela. If you need care while in the country, contact your embassy, ask at your hotel, or look in the *Daily Journal*. In the event of a medical emergency, contact one of the clinics listed under "Essentials: Fast Facts" in "Caracas," later in this chapter.

Drug Laws Venezuelan drug laws are strict, and punishment, especially for foreigners, is severe. Do not try to smuggle, buy, or use illegal drugs in Venezuela.

Electricity Electric current is 110 volts AC (60 cycles). U.S.-style flat-prong plugs are used. However, three-prong grounded outlets are not universally available. It's helpful to bring a three-to-two prong adapter.

Embassies & Consulates In Caracas: **Canada,** avenidas Francisco de Miranda and Sur, Altamira (© 0212/600-3000; fax 0212/261-8741; www.dfait-maeci.gc.ca/caracas); **New Zealand,** Torre KPMG, 7th floor, Av. Francisco de Miranda, Chacao (© 0212/277-7961); **United Kingdom,** Torre La Castellana, Avenida Principal La Castellana, Piso 11 (© 0212/263-8411; fax 0212/267-1275; www.britain.org.ve); and the **United States,** calles F and Suapure, Colinas de Valle Arriba (© 0800/100-5154, or 0212/975-7831; fax 0212/975-8991; http://embajadausa.org.ve).

Emergencies Venezuela has an integrated emergency network (police, fire, ambulance). To reach it, dial © 171. The call is free; you can dial 171 from any pay phone, without using a calling card. Don't expect the operator to speak English.

Internet Access There are Internet cafes all over Venezuela, particularly in tourist destinations. Rates run $1 to $4 per hour.

Language Spanish is the official language of Venezuela. Although most hotels and tourist destinations have staff and guides with at least some command of English, it is not widely spoken amongst the general population.

Liquor Laws The official drinking age in Venezuela is 18, although it is rarely enforced.

Newspapers & Magazines There are around a dozen daily newspapers and tabloids. The main Spanish-language newspapers are *El Nacional* (http://el-nacional.com) and *El Universal* (www.el-universal.com). The *Daily Journal* is a small English-language daily newspaper available at most newsstands and stocked by many hotels.

Police Venezuela has a host of overlapping police departments but no specific tourist police. Depending on the circumstances, you may encounter metropolitan police (policía metropolitana), municipal police (policía municipal), investigative police (policía técnica judicial), the National Guard (guardia nacional), or transit police (policía de tránsito). Their uniforms and specific responsibilities vary. Corruption and indifference is widespread. Venezuela has an integrated emergency network (police, fire, ambulance). To reach it, just dial ☎ 171. The call is free—you can dial 171 from any pay phone, without using a calling card. However, don't expect the operator to speak English.

Post Offices/Mail Ipostel is the national mail service. It is considered neither swift nor secure for international correspondence. Generally, a letter or postcard takes 10 to 20 days to reach most parts of the United States and Europe. There are branch post offices in most cities and tourist destinations, and some of the malls even have Ipostel offices. Still, your hotel is usually your best bet for buying stamps and mailing a letter. Feel free to mail home postcards and letters, but avoid using Ipostel for anything of value or importance.

In the event that you need to mail anything of value or personal import, call any of the following international courier services: **DHL** (☎ 0800/225-5345 or 0212/205-6000; www.dhl.com), **FedEx** (☎ 0800/463-3399 or 0212/205-3333; www.fedex.com), or **UPS** (☎ 0212/241-6454; www.ups.com).

Restrooms There are few readily available public toilets in Venezuela. Your best bet is a restaurant, hotel, or service station. Some of these establishments (particularly service stations and roadside restaurants) will actually charge you a small fee for the use of the facilities. It's always a good idea to carry a small amount of toilet paper with you, especially on the road, as the facilities at many service stations—and at lower-end restaurants and hotels—might not have any.

Safety Venezuela has developed quite a reputation for its violence and crime, much of it deserved. *Caraqueños* talk about muggings, car thefts, and burglaries with amazing candidness and regularity. The greatest danger to travelers is theft. If you use common sense and standard precautions, you should have no problems. Keep a tab on your belongings, use hotel safes whenever possible, and don't carry large sums of money with you or wear obviously expensive clothing or jewelry. Stick to the well-worn tourist parts of Caracas and other major cities. Avoid the *ranchitos* and poorer *barrios*. Take reputable taxis whenever possible and definitely avoid strolling around cities at night. If you have a rental car, always leave it in guarded parking and never leave anything of value inside it unattended.

Taxes There is a 16% sales tax on all purchases, including both goods and services. There is also a 1% tourism tax applied to all tourism-related purchases (hotel rooms, plane tickets, tours, and so on). In both cases, since government enforcement is lax, the tax is sometimes not charged, especially on cash transactions and at budget and lower-end establishments.

Telephone & Fax There are public phones all around most cities and major tourist destinations. You'll even find public phones in places as remote as Canaima and Los Roques. Most work with magnetic-strip calling cards that are readily available in stores all over the country. Look for signs or stickers advertising CANTV calling cards. The cards come in denominations of 3,000Bs and 5,000Bs; international cards of 5,000Bs and 10,000Bs are also available. A local call costs 37Bs to 60Bs (2¢–3¢) per minute. Your hotel is usually your best bet for sending and receiving faxes, although they may charge exorbitant rates for international faxes.

For tips on dialing, see "Telephone Dialing Info at a Glance" on p. 691.

Time Zone Venezuela is 4 hours behind Greenwich mean time (GMT), and does not observe daylight savings time.

Tipping Most restaurants automatically add a 10% service charge. If you feel the service was particularly good, you should leave an additional 5% to 10%. Tip the hotel staff as you would at home. Since most taxi drivers do not use meters and are almost always overcharging foreigners, it is not customary to tip them. If you feel you are getting an extremely good deal, or beyond-the-call-of-duty treatment, by all means, tip your driver.

Water Although the water is considered safe to drink in most urban areas, I recommend that visitors stick to bottled water to be on the safe side. Ask for *agua mineral sin gas* (noncarbonated mineral water).

3 Caracas

Caracas is one of the more cosmopolitan cities in Latin America, with a vibrant and active population. Architecturally, Caracas is also one of the most modern and distinctive cities in Latin America. Concrete and plate glass reign supreme, much of it showing the bold forms and sleek lines of the Art Deco and postmodern architectural currents of the past half century. Aficionados will enjoy works of Carlos Raúl Villanueva, a local architect who often integrated into his designs large kinetic sculptures by such renowned figures as Alexander Calder and Jesús Soto. The Universidad Central de Venezuela (Central University of Venezuela) is Villanueva's crowning achievement.

Caracas, and the international airport in Maiquetía, is the de facto hub for travel around Venezuela. If you plan on visiting several destinations in the country, you will most probably be passing through Caracas as part of your itinerary. You can easily get a good feel for the city and its major attractions in a couple of days.

ESSENTIALS
GETTING THERE
Simón Bolívar International Airport (© **0212/303-1526;** www.aeropuerto-maiquetia.com.ve) in Maiquetía, 28km (17 miles) north of Caracas, is the gateway

> **Tips Safety First**
>
> It's not just hype: Caracas is one of the most violent and dangerous cities in Latin America. On Monday mornings, one of the prime statistics published in all the papers is the number of homicides registered over the weekend. The number averages around 35 to 45 in Caracas alone. Be very careful about where you walk, what you wear, and with whom you associate. Don't wear fancy jewelry or flash lots of cash, and keep close watch on your personal belongings. Take a well-marked taxi, or one called by your hotel, whenever possible. Be wary of unofficial cabs, or *piratas*. And, finally, don't get too adventurous at night.

to Venezuela and the point of entry for most visitors to the country. *Note:* The airport is most commonly referred to as the Maiquetía Airport by locals, travel agents, and taxi drivers. For information on arriving by plane, see "Getting There" in "Planning Your Trip to Venezuela," earlier in this chapter.

A taxi from the airport should cost between 18,000Bs and 25,000Bs (US$11–US$16), depending on where in the city you are going. Official fares are slightly higher after 5pm. Use the official airport taxi companies (© **0212/355-2770**). They have several prominent booths in both the national and international terminals. You buy a ticket at the booth for a predetermined fee depending on the hour and specific destination. Although you may be offered a slightly better fare by one of the informal or "pirate" *(pirata)* taxi drivers that hang around the airport, there have been reports of mistreatment and muggings of tourists by these operators. The downside of the official companies, however, is that they use a fleet of Ford Explorers. In fact, it was the high accident and death rates caused by rollovers and tire-tread separations of Ford Explorers in Venezuela that first drew attention to safety problems with this model.

Por puestos (private buses and vans) run between the airport and the Gato Negro metro station. The fare is 2,500Bs (US$1.50); however, note that you should not use this option at night or if you have much luggage. There are regular free shuttles between the national and international terminals at Maiquetía.

ORIENTATION

Of greatest interest to travelers are the **Capitolio** area around **Plaza Bolívar,** the historic center of Caracas, and **Parque Central,** a modern zone of high-rise office towers and home to several important museums and theaters. The **Sabana Grande** is an open-air pedestrian mall of small shops and street vendors that stretches on for nearly a mile, between the Plaza Venezuela and Plaza Chacaito. However, the Sabana Grande area has become increasingly seedy and dangerous. Today, shoppers and affluent *Caraqueños* tend to favor modern malls and the more exclusive areas of **Altamira, El Rosal,** and **Las Mercedes.** The latter three zones are the principal upscale residential, business, and shopping districts, respectively—they all have a mix of hotels, restaurants, cafes, shops, and private residences.

GETTING AROUND

BY METRO   Caracas has a clean, relatively safe, and efficient metro system (© 0212/507-4211; www.metrodecaracas.com.ve). The main line of the system crosses the city from Palo Verde in the east to Propatria in the west. A couple of new spurs head off to the south, and a couple more are in the works.

Caracas

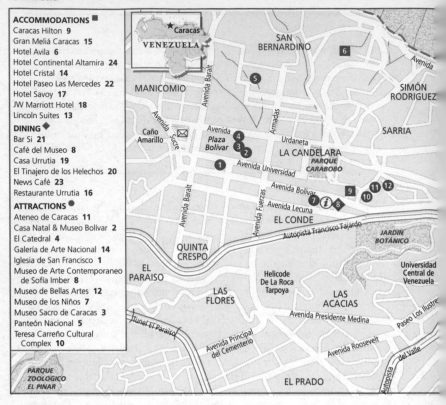

Ticket prices vary slightly according to the number of stations you travel before your final stop, but in general, a one-way fare costs 260Bs to 350Bs (16¢–23¢). You can buy a 10-trip ticket for 2,500Bs ($1.60). Even if you buy a one-way fare, keep your ticket handy because you have to pass it through the electronic turnstiles upon entering and exiting each station. The metro operates daily from 5:30am to 11pm. Although the metro is generally safe, be wary of pickpockets and muggings at either very busy or very desolate times and stations.

BY BUS   There are two parallel bus systems in Caracas. The **Metrobús** (© **0212/ 507-4211;** www.metrodecaracas.com.ve) is a traditional urban bus system that, in theory, can be used in conjunction with the metro. More common are the *por puestos,* private buses or vans running fixed routes servicing most of the metropolitan area. Fares on both systems are extremely inexpensive, but I don't recommend them as the transportation of choice because there's little rhyme or reason to the routes and, in the case of the *por puestos,* no readily available maps or guides. Moreover, crowded buses are prime haunts of pickpockets and petty thieves.

BY TAXI   Most taxis in Caracas do not have meters. Most rides within the city limits should cost you 3,000Bs–5,000Bs ($1.90–$3.10). There are a host of different taxi companies. Some are based in certain zones, others at specific hotels and malls. In general, taxis based at a hotel or mall will charge more than a typical cab hailed on the street. However, given the current economic environment, the difference is often inconsequential. As a traveler, you will likely be a target

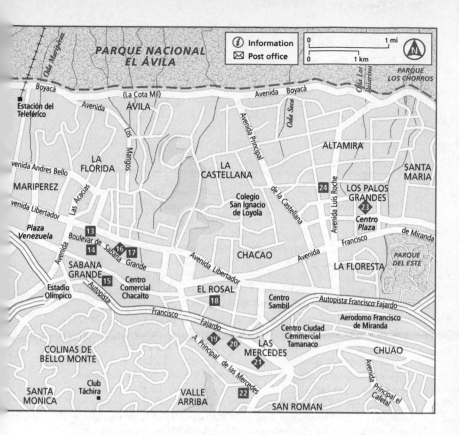

for overcharging. Always try to ask hotel staff or other locals what a specific ride should cost and negotiate in advance with the driver. Taxi drivers are legally allowed to charge an additional 20% after 6pm.

If you can't flag a cab in the street, or if your hotel can't or won't call one for you, try **Taxiven** (© 0212/985-5715), **Taxitour** (© 0212/794-1264), or **Tele Taxi** (© 0212/753-3289).

BY FOOT   Caracas is not particularly amenable to exploration by foot. Street crime is a real problem in all but a few neighborhoods. In fact, almost no place is absolutely safe. The safest neighborhoods to walk around are Las Mercedes, El Rosal, Los Palos Grandes, and Altamira. With care, you should also be fine during the daytime around the Capitolio, Sabana Grande, and Parque Central areas, although their popularity as tourist destinations attracts pickpockets.

VISITOR INFORMATION

INATUR (© **0800/462-8871** or 0212/576-9032; www.inatur.gov.ve) is the national tourism institute. Its main office, located on the 35th floor of the Torre Oeste (West Tower) of the Parque Central (near the Caracas Hilton), is open weekdays during business hours. The staff can give you a basic map and some brochures for hotels and attractions, but I find the view here more worthwhile than the information available.

Most bookstores around town and many hotel gift shops stock a small selection of maps to Caracas and the rest of the country. The best bookshop for

English-language materials is the **American Book Shop,** Centro Plaza, Nivel Jardín, Avenida Francisco de Miranda, Los Palos Grandes (© **0212/286-2230**).

FAST FACTS   There are a couple of currency exchange offices, including an **Italcambio** branch, at the airport, as well as scores of money-exchange houses around town. Many hotels will change dollars and traveler's checks, although usually at slightly below the official exchange rate. Although most banks won't change money, they often have ATMs.

Simón Bolívar, El Libertador

The great hero of Latin American independence, Simón Bolívar, was born in Caracas on July 24, 1783, into a *criolla* family of the city's commercial *cacao* elite. The second of four children, young Simón lost both parents by the time he was 9 years old. Raised by an uncle and schooled in private schools in both Venezuela and Europe, Bolívar was well-educated and erudite. In 1802, while in Europe, he met and married María Teresa Rodríguez del Toro, a Spanish aristocrat. However, Maria Teresa died of yellow fever just a few months later, soon after the couple's return to Venezuela. Despondent, Bolívar sought solace in travel.

His travels following the death of his wife brought him into direct contact with the leaders and results of both the French and American revolutions. In Europe, he also met famed scientist and explorer Alexander von Humbolt, who further sowed the seeds of Bolívar's revolutionary work. Humbolt allegedly told Bolívar that South America was ripe for freedom but lacked a charismatic leader to lead the struggle.

Upon his return to Venezuela, Bolívar began political opposition to Spanish rule and, soon after that, armed struggle. By 1812, he had taken over the Venezuelan independence movement and spent most of the next 20 years in armed combat. Bolívar mounted a series of impressive long-range campaigns against Spain that are still admired and studied. He ultimately liberated the area comprising modern-day Venezuela, Colombia, Panama, Ecuador, Peru, and Bolivia. However, his dream of a united "Gran Colombia" never took hold, and Bolívar himself fell quickly out of political favor following the defeat of the Spanish.

Bolívar may have set the model for military men seizing and dictating political power throughout Latin America. He was an eloquent and stirring orator. In private, he was also renowned for his saucy tongue and numerous affairs. His most famous lover, Manuela Sáenz, was an Ecuadorian woman who saved him from an assassination attempt. Their story is immortalized in Gabriel García Márquez's *The General in His Labyrinth*.

Bolívar died of tuberculosis on December 17, 1830, in Santa Marta, Colombia, nearly broke and on his way to live in self-imposed exile in Europe. Twelve years later, in 1842, his remains were interred in Caracas. In 1876, they were ceremoniously transferred to the Panteón Nacional. Today, his presence and legacy are omnipresent in Venezuela: The principal public park in every town and city bears his name, as does the country's currency.

Venezuela has an integrated **emergency** network (police, fire, ambulance). To reach it, just dial Ⓒ 171. Don't expect the operator to speak English. In the event that you need medical care, consult with your hotel first or head to the **Hospital de Clínicas de Caracas,** Avenida Panteón, San Bernardino (Ⓒ 0212/574-2011); the **Policlínica Las Mercedes,** Avenida Principal Las Mercedes and Calle Monterrey (Ⓒ 0212/993-5944); or the **Clínica El Avila,** Avenida San Juan Bosco and 6th Transversal, Altamira (Ⓒ 0212/208-1111).

Internet cafes are located all over town, and most hotels either have their own Internet cafe or can refer you to the closest option. Rates run 50¢ to $2 per hour.

Ipostel is the national mail service. The main **post office,** or *correo,* is located at Avenida Urdaneta and Norte 4 (Ⓒ **0800/476-7835;** www.ipostel.gov.ve), near the Plaza Bolívar, and is open weekdays from 8am to 6pm, closing an hour earlier on weekends. There are quite a few branch post offices around town and in the suburbs, and several of the modern malls have Ipostel offices; many of these have a reduced schedule. Your hotel is usually your best bet for getting stamps and mailing a letter.

You'll find public phones all around Caracas. Most phones work with magnetic-strip calling cards that are readily available in stores and hotels all over the city. You can send and receive faxes and make credit card international calls from the **CANTV Centro Plaza** office (Ⓒ **0212/285-6788;** fax 0212/286-2261), on Avenida Francisco Miranda in Los Palos Grandes, 2 blocks east of the Altamira metro station.

WHAT TO SEE & DO
ATTRACTIONS
Plaza Bolívar & El Capitolio

Pigeons, pedestrians, park benches, and a towering bronze statue of El Libertador on his sturdy steed are the hallmarks of this square city block, which was once the heart of colonial Caracas. Within a 4- or 5-block radius, you will find several important museums and cathedrals, as well as the birthplace of Simón Bolívar, the national Congress (El Capitolio), and the Panteón Nacional, the country's most important mausoleum. Using common sense and caution, this area is relatively safe to be explored during the day, but I would definitely avoid it after dark.

Catedral ⟨★⟩   Anchoring the eastern end of Plaza Bolívar, this is the national cathedral. The present-day church was built between 1665 and 1713, after the original building was destroyed in the 1641 earthquake. It's home to the private Bolívar family chapel and features a painting by Rubens. Adjoining the cathedral is the **Museo Sacro de Caracas,** which has a modest collection of religious art and sculpture, as well as colonial-era dress and relics and a delightful little cafe.

Plaza Bolívar. Cathedral Ⓒ **0212/862-4963;** museum Ⓒ 0212/861-5814. Free admission to cathedral; admission to museum 500Bs (31¢) adults, 400Bs (25¢) children. Cathedral daily 7am–1pm and 3–6pm; museum Tues–Sun 10am–5pm. Metro: Capitolio.

Iglesia de San Francisco ⟨★★⟩   Not as large or ornate as La Catedral, this is the church where Bolívar was proclaimed El Libertador in 1813, and the site of his massive funeral in 1842—the year his remains were brought back from Colombia, some 12 years after his actual death. Begun in 1575, the church bears the architectural influences of various periods and styles but retains much of its colonial-era charm. The gilded altars and religious paintings are worthy of a 20-minute stroll through the building.

Av. Universidad and Norte 2. Ⓒ 0212/484-5172. Free admission. Mon–Fri 7am–noon and 2–5pm; Sat–Sun 10am–5pm. Metro: Capitolio.

Casa Natal & Museo Bolívar
These side-by-side attractions comprise the restored birthplace of Simón Bolívar and a small museum of memorabilia and historic items related to El Libertador—his life, death, and military and political campaigns. A place of pilgrimage for many Venezuelans, the simple house where Bolívar was born on July 24, 1783, sits in stark contrast to the modern city surrounding it.

Av. Universidad and Norte 1. © 0212/545-9828. Free admission. Tues–Sun 9am–noon and 2:30–5:30pm. Metro: Capitolio.

Parque Central & Bellas Artes
Galería de Arte Nacional & Museo de Bellas Artes 👁 Making up an
area popularly known as the Plaza de los Museos, these side-by-side and loosely connected institutions house a broad collection of Venezuelan art, ranging from the fine arts and modern masters to folk art and crafts, dating from the colonial period to the present. One of the nicer features here is the shady sculpture garden, which borders Parque Los Caobos. The Bellas Artes gift shop has a small, but nice, selection of mostly high-end artworks and indigenous crafts.

Plaza Morelos, beside the Parque Los Caobos, in front of the Caracas Hilton. © 0212/578-1818. www.wtfe.com/gan. Free admission. Tues–Fri 9am–5pm; Sat–Sun 10am–5pm. Metro: Bellas Artes.

Museo de Arte Contemporáneo de Sofía Imber 👁👁 The 13 *salas* here
form a minimaze covering several floors of the angular concrete architecture of Parque Central. The permanent collection features a good representation of the conceptual works of Venezuelan star Jesús Soto, as well as a small but high quality collection of singular works by such modern masters as Picasso, Red Grooms, Henry Moore, Joan Miró, and Francis Bacon. The museum regularly hosts traveling exhibits of international stature. The small sculpture garden here is nowhere near as lovely as that found at the nearby Bellas Artes, but the elegant museum cafe is one of the nicer casual dining spots on this side of town.

Parque Central. © 0212/573-7289. www.maccsi.org.ve. Free admission. Tues–Fri 9am–noon and 2–5pm; Sat–Sun 10am–5pm. Metro: Bellas Artes.

Museo de los Niños (Children's Museum) 👁ᵏⁱᵈˢ It's nothing truly spectac-
ular, but this museum is a great place to pass a couple of hours if you've got children with you. A wide range of interactive and participatory exhibits cover the natural sciences, physics, medicine, and more. This place is often quite crowded with school groups during the week and families on weekends.

Av. Bolívar, between the 2 towers of Parque Central. © 0212/575-3022. Admission 5,000Bs ($3.15) adults, 4,000Bs ($2.50) children. Mon–Fri 9am–6:30pm; Sat–Sun 9am–5pm. Metro: Bellas Artes.

SPORTS & OUTDOOR ACTIVITIES
BASEBALL Baseball is the number-one sport in Venezuela. Venezuelans follow the sport with devotion and fervor. It's hard to find pickup games, but if you're in town for the season, you might want to catch a game. The local professional season runs October through January; as this is the off-season for U.S. major league baseball, some professional and minor-league players play here to stay in shape. There are a couple of professional teams in Caracas, as well as teams in most major cities around the country. The main Caracas team is *Los Leones;* another popular team (formerly of Caracas, but currently based out of Valencia) is *Los Magallanes.* The Leones-Magallanes rivalry is quite heated. You can get tickets to most games rather easily for 3,000Bs to 20,000Bs ($1.90–$13). I'd recommend splurging for the more expensive seats, as they often provide protection

from the sun, the rain, and the rowdier crowds. Los Leones play at the Estadio Universitario de Caracas (at the university). Tickets can be purchased by calling ℂ 0212/762-1211, or visit www.ticketcentro.com.

BIKING Caracas is a terrible city for bicycling. Biking is prohibited inside the Parque del Este, which is perhaps the only suitable spot. If you're interested in doing some mountain biking in **Parque Nacional El Avila,** contact one of the tour agencies listed in "Excursions from Caracas," later in this chapter.

HIKING The place to go for hiking around Caracas is **Parque Nacional El Avila** ⭐, located on the northern edge of the city and encompassing some 82 hectares (203 acres) of the coastal mountain range separating the city from the Caribbean Sea. There are dozens of trails through the park as well as a well-developed network of restrooms, ranger stations, and campsites. The park and its trails get crowded on weekends. You should be able to reach **Pico El Avila** (2,153m/7,062 ft.) in 2 to 4 hours of semistrenuous hiking, depending on the pace and route you choose. The highest peak here, **Pico Naiguatá,** rises to 2,765m (9,070 ft.). Be prepared for wide ranges in temperatures and the possibility of late afternoon rains on the forested slopes of the park. It's best to hike in groups of at least four persons, as some robberies and muggings have been reported in the park. The most popular access to the park is from the northern end of the Altamira district, at the end of Avenida San Juan Bosco, and from all along Avenida Boyaca. You can take the metro to the Altamira stop, although it's a steep 10-block walk uphill from both the metro station and from the San Bernardino area to the entrance to the park. Admission to the park is 200Bs (12¢).

EL TELEFERICO ⭐ Another, much less strenuous, way to reach Pico El Avila is via the restored and reopened *teleférico.* This modern cable car system stretches from the Maripérez station on the northern edge of the city. The 3.4km (2 miles) ride to the top of El Avila takes between 12 and 15 minutes, where you'll find a skating rink, rock climbing wall, telescopes, simple restaurants, souvenir shops and snack stands, and the dormant 14-story Hotel Humbolt. Plans include the reopening of this landmark hotel, a modern casino, and further development of the peak's recreational facilities. The restoration and reopening of the tramway section down to the coastal city of La Guaira is still far off.

When the weather is clear, there are fabulous views over both Caracas and down the coastal mountains to the Caribbean sea. At the summit, you can also hire a taxi to take you to one of the dozen or so restaurants in and near the small mountain village of Galipán. These restaurants range from simple roadside shacks, to fine dining establishments serving everything from Mexican to French cuisine.

The *teleférico* (ℂ 0212/793-5129) is open Tuesday to Sunday from 10am to 8pm, and Monday from noon to 8pm. The round-trip cost is 15,000Bs ($9.40) for adults, 8,000Bs ($5) for children. A light sweater or windbreaker is recommended, as it can get chilly up top. To get here, just ask a taxi to take you to *el terminal Maripérez del teleférico.*

Safety Advice

Although outwardly inviting, I recommend that you avoid Parque El Calvario Park, which lies on the western end of the Capitolio area. In recent years, it's garnered a reputation as a dangerous and unprotected area.

(Finds) Parque del Este

This large **urban oasis** ⭐⭐ is a favorite spot for *Caraqueños*. Joggers, yoga and tai chi enthusiasts, tennis players, and people looking for pickup soccer and basketball games fill this park on most mornings and throughout the weekend. You can take part in any of the aforementioned activities or just stroll the paths, sit on a bench, or visit the tiny zoo. On weekends you can catch one of the shows at the Humbolt Planetarium here. The park is open Tuesday through Sunday from 5am to 5pm, Monday from 5am to 8am. Admission is 200Bs (12¢). Metro: Parque del Este.

JOGGING   Joggers should definitely head to either **Parque del Este** for more or less flat terrain, or **Parque Nacional El Avila** (see "Hiking," above) for more challenging mountainous terrain.

SHOPPING

Venezuelans—and most visitors—tend to shop at one of the many modern malls that have been built around Caracas over the past 20 years. Of these, the **Centro Comercial Sambil** ⭐, Avenida Libertador (Metro: Chacao), is perhaps the most popular. Reputed to be the largest mall in South America, it features everything from a multiplex cinema to gourmet restaurants to a performing arts space to a mini-amusement park. Other prominent malls include the **Centro Comercial Ciudad Tamanaco (CCCT),** Autopista Francisco Fajardo and Calle La Estancia (no metro); and the **Centro Lido,** Avenida Francisco de Miranda, El Rosal (Metro: Chacaito).

Las Mercedes ⭐ is an upscale district of restaurants, shops, nightclubs, and art galleries, which makes it the choice spot for a leisurely afternoon of browsing and buying.

If you're looking for arts and crafts, you can head to the **Mercado Guajiro** ⭐, Paseo Las Flores near the western end of Plaza Chacaito, a collection of 30 shops featuring indigenous and other arts and crafts. However, perhaps the best shopping for Venezuelan arts and crafts is to be found in El Hatillo at the **Hannsi Centro Artesanal** ⭐⭐, Calle Bolívar 12 (© 0212/963-7184; www.hannsi.com.ve). This huge indoor bazaar has everything from indigenous masks to ceramic wares to woven baskets. The selection is broad and covers everything from trinkets to major pieces of fine craftsmanship.

WHERE TO STAY

Hotel rates in Caracas are crazy. Business travelers fill almost every room in the city Monday through Thursday, and hotels slash their rates on weekends. Moreover, the high occupancy and heavy corporate traffic has made rack rates at most Caracas hotels almost meaningless. Very few hotels actually charge their published and advertised rack rate. It always pays to ask for a corporate or special rate, and if that fails, try to bargain at all but the truly top-end hotels.

VERY EXPENSIVE

Caracas Hilton ⭐   Long the city's hotel and meeting place of choice, the Hilton has been steadily losing ground to the newer luxury options in town. Although the rooms are all comfortable enough, they can't compare—at similar prices—to those at the other high-end entries listed here. The furnishings are dated and most of the bathrooms too cramped for this price range. Aside from the excellent views that most rooms feature, the best thing going for the Hilton is its proximity to several worthwhile museums, as well as the Teresa Carreño Theater complex. This is also the closest downtown hotel to the airport, so if you're looking for a quick overnight stay as part of a longer itinerary, this hotel will do. The Hilton is extremely popular with business and conference travelers, and it has all the facilities to accommodate them, and it's still the most common choice for visiting dignitaries and heads of state.

Av. Libertador and Sur 25 (Apdo. 6380), Caracas. (℃ **800/223-1146** in the U.S., or 0212/503-5000 in Venezuela. Fax 0212/503-5003. www.hilton.com. 738 units. $160–$250 double; $250–$500 suite; $1,200 Presidential suite. AE, MC, V. Parking $11. **Amenities:** 3 restaurants; 2 bars; lounge; small outdoor pool; 2 lighted outdoor tennis courts; small health club; concierge; business center; executive floors; shopping arcade; salon; 24-hr. room service; laundry service/dry cleaning; nonsmoking rooms. *In room:* A/C, TV, minibar, hair dryer, safe.

Gran Meliá Caracas ★★★   This luxury hotel probably has the most impressive facilities in town, although it's in a somewhat sketchy neighborhood. Still, the rooms, amenities, and general ambience here are all top-notch. The lobby is opulent and grand, with marble floors, massive Persian rugs, and plenty of gold trim and varnished wood accents. The rooms are large and modern, and feature a high-tech all-in-one bedside control panel for lights, television, air-conditioning, and alarm clock. There are bidets in every bathroom, and all of the tubs feature Jacuzzi jets. The upper five floors house the executive-level rooms, with private check-in and checkout service, rotating complimentary buffets, butler service, and other perks. There's a modern commercial mall just next door, and while the open-air pedestrian mall of Sabana Grande is just a block or so away, it's become increasingly unsafe for visitors. The spa here is one of the best in the city. The Gran Meliá also has an additional 236 one- and two-bedroom apartments for longer stays.

Av. Casanova and El Recreo, Sabana Grande, Caracas. (℃ **0212/762-8111.** Fax 0212/762-3737. www.solmelia. com. 432 units. $110–$220 double; $295–$450 suite; $1,350 presidential suite. AE, MC, V. Self-parking $8, valet parking $20. **Amenities:** 5 restaurants; 3 bars; lounge; large outdoor pool w/landscaped waterfall; well-equipped health club and spa; concierge; tour desk; car-rental desk; business center; salon; 24-hr. room service; massage; babysitting; laundry service/dry cleaning. *In room:* A/C, TV, dataport, minibar, coffeemaker, hair dryer, safe.

JW Marriott Hotel ★★★   This new luxury hotel caters primarily to businessmen, and while it's not quite as opulent as the Gran Meliá, it's in a decidedly nicer neighborhood. The rooms are all very comfortable and spacious, with lush furnishings and decor, and sleek marble bathrooms. There are two towers here, and one is entirely suites. The regular deluxe rooms all come with separate tubs and showers, although oddly some of the suites only have a tub/shower combo. The large "spa suites" come with a private Jacuzzi tub. Most rooms, particularly those on higher floors, have wonderful views, but the best view to be found is on the 17th-floor bridge connecting the two towers. Service is attentive and accommodating. Dining options in the hotel are somewhat limited, but there are several very good restaurants within a couple of blocks, and the hotel's principal restaurant "Sur" serves up excellent *Nuevo Latino* cuisine.

Av. Venezuela and Calle Mohedano, El Rosal, Caracas. (℃ **0212/957-2222.** Fax 0212/957-1111. www.marriott. com. 269 units. $155–$175 double; $185–$215 suite. AE, MC, V. Free valet parking. **Amenities:** Restaurant; bar; coffee shop; outdoor pool; small, well-equipped health club; concierge; tour desk; car-rental desk; 24-hr. business center; small shopping arcade; salon; 24-hr. room service; massage; laundry service/dry cleaning; nonsmoking rooms; executive floors. *In room:* A/C, TV, dataport, minibar, coffeemaker, hair dryer, iron, safe.

MODERATE

In addition to the hotels listed in this section, the **Hotel Paseo Las Mercedes** ★, Centro Comercial Paseo Las Mercedes (℃ **0212/993-6644;** www.hotelpaseo lasmercedes.com), is a business-class hotel located in the heart of the fashionable

Las Mercedes shopping and dining district. I find this hotel a much better choice in this area than the neighboring Tamanaco Inter-Continental (☎ **0212/909-7111;** www.intercontinental.com), which has suffered from age and inconsistent maintenance.

Hotel Avila ⊊ *Finds*   The aged grande dame of Caracas hotels, this place still is worth considering. Built by Nelson Rockefeller in 1942, the hotel is a quiet oasis located about 15 minutes from downtown on the flanks of Mount Avila. The lush grounds and flowering gardens are a welcome change from the cold concrete and glass that characterize most of Caracas. The hotel is showing its age but still retains a certain dignity and charm, if not glamour. Most of the rooms are comfortable and spacious, with high ceilings, new carpeting, and rattan furnishings, although most do not have air-conditioning. The suites are a mixed bag: Some are quite nice, while others are less appealing than the standard rooms. The Tower and Executive suites are the best rooms in the house. Meals are served in the poolside dining area and adjacent open-air dining room. A taxi from the hotel to downtown will cost you around 4,000Bs ($2.50).

Av. Washington, San Bernardino, Caracas. ☎ 0212/555-3000. Fax 0212/552-3021. www.viajes-venezuela. com/hotelavila. 113 units. $45–$65 double; $70 junior suite; $85–$95 suite. Rates include full breakfast. AE, MC, V. Free parking. **Amenities:** Restaurant; bar; lounge; small oval outdoor pool; 6 lighted tennis courts; small health club; concierge; tour desk; salon; limited room service; massage; laundry service. *In room:* TV, safe.

Lincoln Suites   This modern, midrange option caters to Venezuelan businesspeople and international travelers alike. Located right on the principal Sabana Grande pedestrian mall, and just 1 block from the metro station, the Lincoln Suites features many of the facilities and amenities of the more expensive options in town. The rooms are carpeted and comfortable, and most have been recently remodeled. More than half the units are classified as suites or junior suites, and even the standard rooms are very spacious. However, the suites do come with a very large sitting area/living room.

Av. Francisco Solano between Los Jabillos and San Jerónimo, Sabana Grande, Caracas. ☎ 0212/761-2727. Fax 0212/762-5503. www.lincoln-suites.com.ve. 126 units. $85–$100. AE, MC, V. Parking nearby. Metro: Sabana Grande. **Amenities:** Restaurant; bar; tour desk; modest business center; salon; limited room service; babysitting; laundry service/dry cleaning. *In room:* A/C, TV, dataport, fridge, safe.

INEXPENSIVE

There's a host of inexpensive options in Caracas catering to backpackers and budget travelers, particularly in the Sabana Grande area. One of the best of the bunch is the **Hotel Cristal,** Pasaje Asunción and Calle Real de Sabana Grande (☎ **0212/761-9131;** fax 0212/763-2118), which is a good bet if the Savoy (see below) is full or if you want to spend even less.

Hotel Savoy *Value*   This long-time favorite is probably your best budget choice in the Sabana Grande area. The rooms are clean and comfortable and come with air-conditioning, cable television, and a small refrigerator. The rooms aren't particularly large, but some have a small private balcony. The Savoy is just a block off the main pedestrian mall of Sabana Grande, close to a score of restaurants, and about 4 blocks from the nearest metro stop. The hotel staff is friendly and helpful.

Av. 2 Las Delicias, Sabana Grande, Caracas. ☎ 0212/762-1971. Fax 0212/761-7154. 95 units. $25–$45 double. AE, MC, V. Parking nearby. Metro: Chacaito. **Amenities:** Restaurant; limited room service; laundry service. *In room:* A/C, TV, fridge.

NEAR THE AIRPORT

Years after *La tragedia de Vargas* (the Vargas tragedy) the coastal area near Venezuela's principal airport is just beginning to come back to life. In December

1999, heavy rains caused massive landslides all along El Litoral, killing as many as 200,000 and leaving many, many more homeless. Somehow, the international airport at Maiquetía survived, but almost all of the hotels and towns in the area were wiped out or severely damaged. The towns and cities of Catia La Mar, Maiquetía, La Guaira, Macuto and Caraballeda were devastated, and the heavy runoff, debris, and detritus have left the beaches here decidedly unappealing.

Nevertheless, in the past year or so several options have opened within a 15-minute radius of the airport. It is once again feasible to stay near the airport and thus avoid Caracas all together, a good option if your travel plans are predominantly built around the natural wonders and beautiful beaches found further afield. In addition to the option listed below, there is also a brand-new **Hampton Inn and Suites** , Avenida La Armada, Urbanización 10 de Marzo, Maiquetía (© 800/426-7866 in the U.S., or 0212/331-7111 in Venezuela; www.hamptoninn.com), located just 2 minutes from the terminals at the Simón Bolívar International Airport. This hotel is surrounded by empty lots and barren ground, but if you arrive late and leave early the next morning, it's a good choice. If you're looking for a budget option in the area, try **Il Prezzano,** Avenida Principal de Playa Grande, Catia La Mar (© **0212/351-5306;** fax 0212/351-3144; il-prezzano@cantv.net).

Moderate
Hotel Olé Caribe ★★   This is by far the most comfortable option on the coast near the airport. A comfortable and well-maintained luxury hotel, the Olé Caribe is filling the void left by the closings of the nearby Sheraton and Meliá properties. The rooms are all clean, bright, and well maintained, and feature a handful of amenities to be expected in this class. Most of the rooms have ocean views. Those that don't, face the coastal mountains behind the hotel. The Olé Caribe is a bit inland from the sea and there are no really worthwhile beaches close by; however, the pool area and surrounding landscaped grounds are quite tropical and inviting. Located 15-minutes from the airport, this is becoming the prime choice of local and international tour operators who are increasingly having their guests bypass Caracas.

Avenida Intercomunal, El Playón Macuto. © 0212/331-1133. Fax 0212/331-4393. www.hotelolecaribe.com. 122 units. $100–$120 double; $190 suite. AE, MC, V. Free parking. **Amenities:** 3 restaurants; 2 bars; large outdoor pool w/landscaped waterfall and children's pool; 1 unlit tennis court; 1 squash court; small gym; concierge; tour desk; car-rental desk; business center; salon; 24-hr. room service; massage; laundry service/dry cleaning. *In room:* A/C, TV, minibar, hair dryer.

WHERE TO DINE
Caracas has a lively restaurant scene. The local upper and middle classes support a host of fine restaurants and trendy joints. World and fusion cuisines are the rage, along with sushi bars and upscale steakhouses. New places open and close with the frequency and fanfare worthy of New York City. If you're serious about delving into the local restaurant scene, pick up a copy of the latest edition of Miro Popic's *Guía Gastronómica de Caracas/Caracas Restaurants Guide* ★★ (www.miropopic.com), a comprehensive, accurate, and bilingual guide to metropolitan restaurants, cafes, and nightspots.

In addition to the places listed below, **Chez Wong,** Plaza La Castellana (© **0212/266-5015**), is widely considered the best Chinese restaurant in town, while **Da Guido,** Avenida Francisco Solano, Sabana Grande (© **0212/763-0937**), and **Vizio** , Avenida Luis Rocha, bottom floor of the Casa Rómulo Gallegos, Altamira (© **0212/285-5675**), are recommended for Italian cuisine.

On a more popular level, simple *arreperías* and informal *fuentes de soda,* the local equivalent of diners, are ubiquitous. Be sure to stop in to one or two of them for a light meal and a bit of local color. Given the prevalence and popularity of huge modern malls, you can usually count on finding a wide selection of restaurants, as well as an assortment of U.S.-based and -styled fast food chains, in most of them.

EXPENSIVE

Bar Si ⍟⍟ PAN-ASIAN   This is hands-down the best Pan-Asian restaurant in the country. The heart of the menu is Thai and Vietnamese, but there is also a wide selection of Japanese dishes, including a small sushi bar with a long list of offerings. Try the *Ho Mog Pla,* a Thai dish of grouper in a coconut-milk curry with fresh mango, all served in a banana leaf. Or you could opt for the ostrich steak in a honey curry with basil. The low ceilings and low lighting give this place an intimate, sometimes claustrophobic feel. The exposed heating ducts remind me of the film *Brazil,* although the overall experience is much more uplifting. The bar here is extremely popular on weekends. The food is expensive, but definitely top-notch.

Calle Madrid, between Veraruz and Caroní, Las Mercedes. ✆ 0212/993-9124. Reservations recommended. Main courses $8–$22. AE, MC, V. Mon–Wed noon–3pm and 7–11pm; Thurs–Sat noon–3pm and 7pm–midnight; Sun noon–3pm.

Restaurante Urrutia ⍟⍟ SPANISH   This has been one of the most popular restaurants in Caracas for more than 40 years. The place has an intimate family feel, with low ceilings and dark wood beams. Start with a carpaccio of beef or salmon, or a *tapa* of Spanish tortilla (a potato-and-egg omelet). Although everything's delicious, one specialty here is the *piquillo* peppers stuffed with your choice of grouper, squid, or *bacalao* (cod) in a tomato-based Vizcaina sauce. If you make it through the extensive menu with room to spare, try the homemade *membrillo* jam with Manchego cheese for dessert. They have another branch, **Casa Urrutia** (✆ 0212/ 993-9526) in the Las Mercedes district, at Calle Madrid and Calle Monterrey.

Av. Francisco Solano and Los Manguitos, Sabana Grande. ✆ 0212/7763-0448. Reservations recommended. Main courses $6–$20. MC, V. Mon–Sat noon–11pm; Sun noon–5pm.

MODERATE

News Café ⍟⍟ INTERNATIONAL   This multifaceted joint tries to do it all, and does a great job on all counts. Part bookstore, part cafe, part jazz club, and full-time restaurant, they serve breakfast, lunch, and dinner daily. There are several rooms and environments, including an open-air rooftop terrace with heavy marble tables under white canvas umbrellas, a second-floor balcony space, and a vibrant main dining room with cracked-tile mosaic floors. The food is simple and straightforward, with a host of interesting sandwiches served on fresh baked baguettes, mixed with a selection of salads, crepes, bruschettas, and pastas. More substantial entrees include medallions of beef in a white wine, porcini and cream sauce, or, my favorite, Salmon al Matteotti, which is served in a champagne and almond reduction. There's live music most afternoons for lunch, as well as Thursday through Saturday evenings.

1st Transversal de los Palos Grandes and 1st Av. Quinta d'Casa. ✆ 0212/286-5096. Reservations recommended for dinner. Sandwiches $4–$7.50; main courses $5–$11. AE, MC, V. Mon–Fri 10am–1am; Sat–Sun 8am–1am.

INEXPENSIVE

El Fogón ⍟ *Finds* VENEZUELAN   Take a table on the second-floor open-air balcony of this popular local joint. Hanging ferns and wind chimes give the place an air of sophistication, but the food is as traditional as it comes. Order an *arepa* to start things off, or try a *cachapa*—a sweet corn pancake folded over your choice of filling. The *asado* here is excellent, and they almost always have *halla-cas*, the local equivalent of tamales, cornmeal paste stuffed with chicken, pork, olives, raisins, boiled egg, and other goodies, wrapped in a banana leaf, and boiled or steamed. For dessert, have some fried *churros*.

Calle La Paz, El Hatillo. (*C*) 0212/963-1068. Reservations recommended on weekends. Main courses $2–$5. No credit cards. Tues–Fri 9am–8pm; Sat–Sun 8am–10pm.

El Tinajero de los Helechos ⟨ VENEZUELAN   There are several reputable steakhouses in Caracas, but this is my favorite—as much for the casual vibe as for the fine meats and side dishes. There's an extensive selection of meat dishes, and nearly as many fish and chicken choices. The *pabellón criollo* and *asado negro* are both excellent. If you want something less traditional, try the chateaubriand or medallions of sirloin in a port sauce. A wide range of traditional Venezuelan appetizers and sides are available as well. There are four rooms of differing sizes here. A large U-shaped bar takes up much of one of them. Indigenous craftworks hang against the brick or pastel-painted walls.

Av. Rio de Janeiro, between Caroní and New York, Las Mercedes. (*C*) 0212/993-3581. Reservations recommended. Main courses $4–$10. AE, DC, MC, V. Daily 11:30am–midnight.

SNACKS & CAFES

For a good view of the passing spectacle of bustling Caracas, you can grab a table at any one of the many covered sidewalk cafes lining the Sabana Grande. In addition to the News Café (see above) another nearby coffeehouse worth checking is the **Café Arábica** ⟨, Avenida Andres Bello between 1st Transversal and Avenida Francisco Miranda ((*C*) **0212/285-3469**), an upscale place on the ground floor of the Multicentro Los Palos Grandes mall that roasts its own beans bought from local producers.

If you're hungry for a quick bite and there's a *fuente de soda* handy—the local equivalent of a diner or deli—you should definitely try an *arepa*, the traditional cornmeal patty that usually comes stuffed with meat, cheese, or chicken.

CARACAS AFTER DARK

Caracas is a big, cosmopolitan city, and your nighttime options are many and varied. It's advisable to stick to the more upscale and relatively safe neighborhoods such as Altamira, El Rosal, and Las Mercedes.

The **Juan Sebastián Bar** ⟨⟨, Avenida Venezuela, El Rosal ((*C*) **0212/951-5575**), is a popular restaurant and bar—and the most consistent place in the city to catch live jazz. Expatriates, locals, and tourists alike enjoy the **TAZ Sports Bar,** Avenida Principal Las Mercedes and Calle New York ((*C*) **0212/992-0343**). The name of this raucous bar is an acronym that stands for "Typical American Zoo," which says it all. Rockers head to **Greenwich** ⟨, Avenida San Juan Bosco, Altamira ((*C*) **0212/267-1760**), a small place with live bands; or **Little Rock Café,** Avenida 6 between 3rd and 4th Transversal, Altamira ((*C*) **0212/267-8337**), a knock-off of the Hard Rock chain that also has live bands on most nights.

El Maní Es Así ⟨, Avenida Francisco Solano and Calle El Cristo, Sabana Grande ((*C*) **0212/763-6671**), is one of the more popular salsa and Latin dance spots. Open every night except Monday from 5pm until around 5am, they charge no cover and always have a live band. **Planet Bar,** Avenida Principal and Calle New York, Las Mercedes ((*C*) **0212/992-8312**), and **Masai,** Centro Commercial

San Ignacio (© **0212/267-6703**), are two other good dance spots, with more modern musical selections.

Located just across from the Caracas Hilton, the **Teresa Carreño Cultural Complex** (© **0500/67372** or 0212/574-9122; www.teatroteresacarreno.com) and the **Ateneo de Caracas** (© **0212/573-4400**) are the places to go for live performances. Top-notch popular and classical concerts take place in the Teresa Carreño, while film series and modern theater are often on tap at the Ateneo. The **Trasnocho Cultural** ⍟, Centro Comercial Paseo Las Mercedes (© **0212/993-1910;** www.trasnochocultural.com), is a new and popular option with a beautiful theater and a couple of cinemas offering a steady diet of live music, theater, and avant-garde cinema. Check the local papers or ask at your hotel for a performance schedule. Ticket prices range from 2,000Bs to 30,000Bs ($1.25–$19).

EXCURSIONS FROM CARACAS

Caracas-based tour companies offer a host of **tour options,** from guided city tours and adventure activities to longer excursions to destinations such as Los Roques and Angel Falls (see below). Some of the more popular day-tour options from Caracas include trips to Colonia Tovar and mountain-bike or jeep tours through Parque Nacional El Avila. Prices for day tours range from $40 to $90 per person. A half-day guided tour to El Hatillo usually runs around $30 per person. **Akanan Travel & Tours** ⍟⍟ (© 0212/234-2103 or 0212/234-2323; www.akanan.com) and **Cacao Expeditions** ⍟ (© **0212/977-1234;** www.cacao travel.com) are both reputable local operators offering a wide range of single and multiday options.

EL HATILLO ⍟⍟   This neocolonial town, located 15km (9 miles) southeast of downtown, is a great place to spend a few leisurely hours and grab a meal. You'll want to spend most of your time strolling around, but be prepared—it's hilly here. Moreover, the narrow streets have even narrower sidewalks, so beware of car traffic. Window-shop the many crafts and artisan jewelry stores and be sure to sample some homemade sweets at one of the many local pastry and candy shops. You'll find a good selection of restaurants, cafes, and bars here. Stop in for a coffee or a light bite at **Croquer,** Calle Bolívar 17 (© **0212/961-4269**). After admiring the memorabilia, try to grab one of the third-floor tables under canvas umbrellas on the open-air terrace.

Buses run between Caracas and El Hatillo at regular intervals throughout the day. *Por puestos* leave from Avenida Humbolt near the Chacaito metro stop; the fare is 300Bs (20¢). Metro bus route 202, beginning near the Altamira metro station, also goes to El Hatillo; the fare is 360Bs (25¢). A taxi to El Hatillo should cost around 7,000Bs ($4.40).

COLONIA TOVAR   This small mountain village located 65km (40 miles) to the west of Caracas was founded and settled in 1843 by German immigrants. A paved road to the isolated hamlet wasn't laid until 1963. The town was so iso-lated for so long that it still feels almost a world apart, although its sudden and amazing popularity also gives it a little bit of an Epcot feel. German food, Ger-man architecture, and German dress are the norm here. You can wander around town, or hike through the nearby forests and fields. On weekends, the town fills up with *Caraqueños* looking for a cool getaway. In fact it gets downright crowded. I prefer to visit on weekdays. If you want to spend a night or two here, check out the **Hotel Selva Negra** (© **0244/355-1415;** selvanegra@cantv.net), or the **Posada Don Elicio** ⍟(© **0244/355-1254;** www.posadadonelicio.com).

Por puestos leave Caracas from the corner of Avenida Lecuna and Sur 9. Take the *por puesto* marked "El Junquito"; in El Junquito, you'll have to switch to another *por puesto* for the rest of the ride. The entire trip should take around 2 hours and cost around 1,600Bs ($1) each way. A taxi to Colonia Tovar costs between 100,000Bs and 120,000Bs ($62–$75) for up to four people. This should be a round-trip fare; you may have to negotiate, depending on how long you want the driver to wait for you or to drive you around Colonia Tovar.

LOS ROQUES 😊😊 Perhaps the most popular excursions from Caracas are to Los Roques, a gorgeous archipelago of small islands around a calm saltwater lagoon in crystal-clear Caribbean waters. **Aerotuy** 😊 (© **0212/761-6231;** www. tuy.com) is by far the most established and professional operator offering trips to Los Roques. The cost for a full-day trip is $141 per person. Children are roughly half-price, and rates are slightly lower during the low season and midweek. For more information, see "Los Roques National Park," later in this chapter.

PARQUE NACIONAL HENRI PITTIER 😊 Venezuela's first national park, founded in 1937, is named after a Swiss botanist who pioneered efforts to create the nation's national park system. The park covers much of the northern state of Aragua, running from the Caribbean sea almost to the city of Maracay. The park encompasses a wide range of ecosystems, from coastal lowlands to cloud forest to rainforest, with mountains inside the park rising to more than 2,000m (6,000 ft.). The flora and fauna here is extremely rich and diverse, and Henri Pittier is one of the world's prime bird-watching spots, with more than 550 resident and migratory species recorded. The park is the gateway to the tourist towns of Choroní and Puerto Colombia and a string of isolated and beautiful Caribbean beaches. The area can be reached by bus and taxi from Maracay, or as part of a tour from Caracas (see above).

CANAIMA & ANGEL FALLS 😊😊 You may actually see advertisements for or be offered a day tour to Canaima and Angel Falls. However, given the distance, travel time, and outstanding natural beauty of the area, I highly recommend a longer trip. See "Canaima, Angel Falls & the Gran Sabana," later in this chapter, for more information.

4 Isla de Margarita 😊

40km (25 miles) N of Cumaná

Isla de Margarita is Venezuela's most popular destination. Venezuelans come here in droves to take advantage of the island's status as a duty-free port, while Canadian, European, and Latin American travelers come to enjoy the warm sun, white sands, and turquoise waters of this small Caribbean island. Margarita remains relatively undiscovered and unexplored by Americans.

Margarita is really two islands joined in the middle by a stretch of sand, mangrove, and marsh that make up **La Restinga National Park.** The western side, called the **Peninsula de Macanao,** is largely undeveloped. It's an extremely arid and dry area, crisscrossed with rugged dirt roads and horse trails, and home to the endemic yellow-headed and yellow-shouldered Margaritan parrot. Almost all development is found on the larger, eastern side, which boasts three principal cities—**Porlamar, Pampatar,** and **La Asunción**—and a couple dozen different beaches and resort areas. The island has two national parks and three nature reserves, as well as several colonial-era forts and churches.

Fun Fact **Twin Peaks**

Whether you arrive by air or by ferry, one of the first sights most visitors have upon approaching Isla de Margarita are two rounded hills that are officially and affectionately known as **Las Tetas de María Guevara** (María Guevara's Tits). A transplant from the mainland who moved to Margarita in the early 19th century, María Guevara became a local icon important in the growth of Punta de Piedras. Regardless of whether you're told she was a groundbreaking feminist or a successful brothel owner, she clearly inspired local fishermen to christen the prominent landmarks that guided them home in her honor. Today, the hills are a national monument.

Margarita's climate is hot and tropical, with ample sunshine and very little rainfall year-round. You're most likely to encounter some rain during the months of July and August and between November and January.

ESSENTIALS
GETTING THERE
BY PLANE   Several international airlines and dozens of charter carriers have service to Margarita from major European cities, as well as from Toronto, Montréal, Miami, and New York. Many of these are sold as package tours.

From Caracas, there are a couple dozen flights to Margarita throughout the day. **Aeropostal** (© 0800/284-6637 or 0212/708-6211; www.aeropostal.com), **Aserca** (© 0800/649-8356; www.asercaairlines.com); **Avior** (© 0212/202-5811, or 0501/ 284-67737; www.avior.com.ve), **Lai** (© 0212/355-2322; fax 0212/355-1296), and **Laser** (© 0800/237-3200 or 0212/232-6533; www.laser.com.ve) all fly between Caracas's Simón Bolívar International Airport and Isla de Margarita. Fares vary radically according to season and day of the week, ranging $30 to $75 each way. Midweek and low-season fares are considerably less expensive. Conversely, seats sell out well in advance and at a premium on weekends and holidays and during the high season. Flight schedules and travel agents refer to the airport as Porlamar (PMV), although it is around 20km (13 miles) from the city, on the southern part of the island near the beach of El Yaque.

BY FERRY   Although losing ground to air traffic, ferry service has and continues to be Margarita's principal link to the mainland. Visitors, residents, cars, buses, and most of the island's goods and merchandise travel by sea. The main ferry station is at Punta de Piedras on the southern end of the island. The main departure points for ferries to Margarita are La Guaira on the coast about 30 minutes from Caracas, and Puerto La Cruz and Cumaná on the northern coast of Venezuela several hours east of Caracas. There are numerous public buses throughout the day from Caracas to both Puerto La Cruz and Cumaná. The bus trip runs about 5 hours from Caracas to Puerto La Cruz (fare $4–$7), and 7 to 8 hours to Cumaná (fare $3–$6). You can also try the **Unión Conductores de Margarita,** Terminal Oriente, Caracas (© **0212/541-0035** or 0295/287-0931), which has a direct combined trip that costs around $20 each way.

Basically, there are two types of ferries running from Puerto La Cruz and Cumaná: the older regular ferries, which take between 3 and 4 hours each way, and the newer "express" ferries, which make the crossing in around 2 hours. **Conferry** has finally opened regular express service between La Guaira (just outside of Caracas) and Margarita, although it only runs on Tuesday and Thursday.

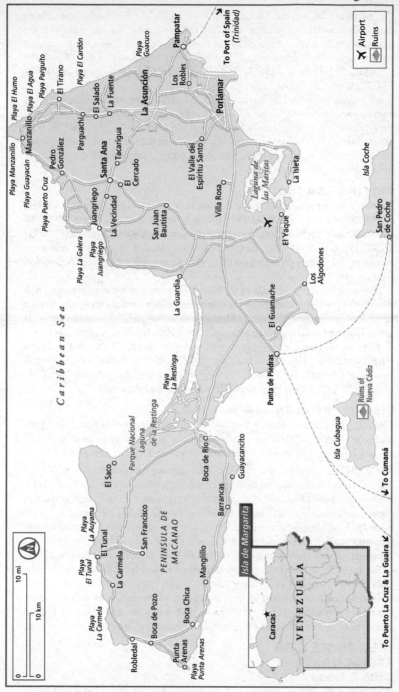

Isla de Margarita

Airport
Ruins

To Port of Spain
(Trinidad)

Pampatar

Playa Guacuco

La Asunción

Los Robles

Porlamar

El Tirano

El Salado

La Fuente

Playa El Cardón

Playa Parguito

Playa El Agua

Playa El Humo

Playa Guayacán

Playa Manzanillo

Manzanillo

Parguachi

Santa Ana

Tacarigua

El Cercado

El Valle del Espíritu Santo

Isla Coche

Playa Puerto Cruz

Pedro González

Juangriego

La Vecindad

San Juan Bautista

Villa Rosa

Laguna de las Maritas

La Isleta

San Pedro de Coche

Playa La Galera

Playa Juangriego

El Yaque

Los Algodones

La Guardia

Caribbean Sea

Playa La Restinga

El Guamache

Punta de Piedras

To Cumaná

Parque Nacional Laguna de la Restinga

Boca de Río

Guayacancito

Barrancas

Isla Cubagua

Ruins of Nueva Cádiz

El Saco

Isla de Margarita

Playa La Auyama

El Tunal

San Francisco

Mangillo

PENINSULA DE MACANAO

VENEZUELA

Playa El Tunal

La Carmela

Boca Chica

Caracas

Playa La Carmela

Robledal

Boca de Pozo

Punta Arenas

Playa Punta Arenas

To Puerto La Cruz & La Guaira

10 mi

10 km

0

0

N

The crossing takes around 5 hours to or from La Guiara. Ferry schedules change drastically according to season and demand, and even the set schedules are sometimes somewhat flexible. Many of the car ferries will leave only when they are completely full. For current ferry schedules and fares, contact **Conferry** (© **0212/782-8544** or 0295/261-6397), or **Gran Cacique Express** (© **0800/ 227-2600** or 0295/239-8339).

It's recommended to try buying tickets in advance on weekends and during high season. Costs range from $5 to $15 per person and $20 to $40 per car on most ferries. The cost difference for passengers is often tied to the "class" of your ticket. Splurge for the higher-class fares, which will get you a seat in an enclosed and air-conditioned lounge deck. The cost is $40 per car and $25 per person on the modern express ferries.

GETTING AROUND

Renting a car is not essential, but it does make it easier around Margarita. **Budget** (© **0800/283-4381** or 0295/269-1047; www.budget.com.ve), **Hertz** (© **0800/ 800-0000** or 0295/905-0400; www.hertz.com), and **Margarita Rentals** (© **0295/ 263-2711**) all have offices at the airport. It costs $30 to $70 per day to rent a car. Several outfits around the island rent scooters and mopeds for between $20 to $35 per day.

Por puesto buses service most of the island. They are a very inexpensive and reliable way to get around, although the going can be slow, as they often stop to pick up and discharge passengers at maddeningly short intervals. Typical service hours are daily from 6am to 8pm. Fares range from 250Bs to 1000Bs (15¢–63¢).

Taxis are also readily available. It will cost you around 10,000Bs ($6.25) to travel between the airport and Porlamar; 3,000Bs ($1.90) between Porlamar and Pampatar; 12,000Bs ($7.50) between Playa El Agua and either Porlamar or Pampatar; and 18,000Bs ($11) between Playa El Agua and the airport.

VISITOR INFORMATION

There is a simple, very basic information desk at the airport in Porlamar. However, you're better off heading to one of the scores of tour agencies to be found around Porlamar and Pampatar and at most major hotels on the island.

FAST FACTS   You'll find a couple of **currency exchange** offices at the airport and a dozen or more money-exchange houses in Porlamar and around the island. Most major hotels here will change money for you as well, although usually at slightly unfavorable rates. There are scores of **banks** on Isla de Margarita. They often have ATMs connected to PLUS or Cirrus systems that will advance you bolivares against your home account. You'll find ATMs in both Porlamar and Pampatar, as well as at all the large malls and some of the large resort hotels.

In case of any medical emergency, consult with your hotel first, or head to the **Luis Ortega Hospital** in Porlamar (© 0295/261-1101).

Internet cafes are located in most malls and major resorts, as well as in Porlamar, in Pampatar, and along Playa El Agua. For regular mail, there are **Ipostel** offices in both Porlamar and Pampatar. Most hotels will also post mail for you.

WHAT TO SEE & DO
ATTRACTIONS
Cities & Towns

Porlamar is the largest city and the commercial hub of the island. Founded in 1536, Porlamar was granted its duty-free status in the 1970s. It's not particularly attractive, and these days the majority of shoppers are heading to large, modern malls built on the outskirts of the city. The city center is a chaotic jumble of shops and small department stores. Still, Porlamar has the highest concentration of shops, restaurants, bars, and discos on Margarita.

Pampatar, about 10km (6 miles) northeast of Porlamar, is much more picturesque and calm. Founded in 1535 around the island's most protected deep-water harbor, Pampatar still retains much of its colonial-era flavor and architecture. The main attraction here is the **Castillo de San Carlos Borromeo** ✹, a 17th-century fort that protected the town and harbor from foreign and pirate attacks. The fort's thick stone walls and bronze cannons still watch over the beach, harbor, and Caribbean Sea. The fort is open Monday through Saturday; admission is free. Across from the fort, you'll find the **Iglesia de Santísimo Cristo del Buen Viaje,** a church of great importance to the sailors and fishermen of Margarita. Legend has it that the crucifix here was left as a last resort, when the colonial-era vessel transporting it was unable, after repeated attempts, to leave the harbor. At the eastern end of the harbor are the ruins of the **Fortín de la Caranta,** which offers excellent views of the town and bay.

> **(Fun Fact You Don't Say!**
>
> Both Porlamar and Pampatar are rough contractions of their original monikers, Pueblo de la Mar and Puerto Royal de Mampatare, respectively.

Located on a hillside, inland from Pampatar, **La Asunción** is the capital of the island and of the entire state of Nueva Esparta. The city's church, **La Catedral de Nuestra Señora de la Asunción** ✹, is said to be the oldest in Venezuela. A few minutes from the center of town is the **Castillo de Santa Rosa,** another of the island's historic and battle-worn forts.

In between Porlamar and Pampatar is the area known as **Los Robles.** Here, you'll find the colonial-era **Iglesia El Pilar de Los Robles,** whose statue of the Virgin Mary is reputed to be of solid gold.

On the road north of La Asunción is the town of **Santa Ana.** In 1816, Simón Bolívar signed the proclamation of the Third Republic in the small church here. It's now best known as the hub for a series of small artisan villages and roadside crafts shops.

Finally, on the northern coast of the island is the popular fishing village and bay of **Juangriego** ✹. This spot is becoming increasingly popular, particularly for **sunsets** ✹✹. The small **Fortín La Galera,** on a bluff on the northern end of the bay, is probably the most sought-after spot for sunsets on the island. Arrive early if you want a prime table and viewing spot at one of the small open-air restaurants and bars here.

The Beaches ✹✹

Isla de Margarita is ringed with dozens of white-sand beaches. Some have huge modern resorts and facilities, others are home to a handful of fishermen and locals, and some are entirely undeveloped and deserted. Perhaps the most popular beach on the island is **Playa El Agua,** a long, broad, straight stretch of white sand with moderate surf, backed by palm trees and a broad selection of restaurants and shops. In the past year or so, neighboring **Playa Parguito** has begun to rival El Agua in terms of popularity. Both of these beaches can get packed on weekends and during peak periods. To the south and north of Playa El Agua, you'll find beaches such as **Manzanillo** ✹, **El Tirano** ✹, **Cardón,** and **Guacuco,** all very nice and less developed. Manzanillo and El Tirano are my favorites, because they are the least developed and often quite deserted. Manzanillo is a great place to watch sunsets. Playas Parguito and El Tirano are the best surf breaks on the island. Close to Porlamar, folks head to **Playa Bella Vista** and **Playa Morena,** although I'm not particularly taken by the vibe or water quality at either.

On the northern coast of Margarita you will find a string of excellent and less-developed beaches, including **Playa Caribe** ⟨★⟩, **Playa Pedro González,** and **Playa Puerto Viejo.** These are some of my favorite beaches on Margarita, and they are building up fast. Those looking for solitude should head to the still-undeveloped beaches that ring the Macanao Peninsula.

National Parks
LA RESTINGA NATIONAL PARK ⟨★⟩   This 10,700-hectare (26,429-acre) park encompasses a zone of mangroves, marshland, sandbar, and coral-sand beaches making a natural land bridge between the two islands that today are Isla de Margarita. A visit to the park usually involves a boat tour through the mangroves, followed by some beach time on the 10km (6-mile) stretch of beach that forms the isthmus uniting the two sides of Margarita. You'll find some simple beachside restaurants and souvenir stands here. The bird-watching is excellent in the mangroves, and the park's beach is renowned for its supply of seashells. To reach La Restinga, take a taxi or the Línea La Restinga *por puesto* out of Porlamar. At the park entrance you'll have to pay a $1 entrance fee and then walk to the nearby pier, where there are scores of boats waiting to take you on a tour. The boats charge $4 to $10 per person, depending on the size of your group. The trip through the mangroves usually lasts between 30 minutes and 1 hour, at which point you will be left at the beach. Have the boatman wait, or arrange a firm pickup time and place for your return to the pier.

CERRO EL COPEY NATIONAL PARK ⟨★⟩   This 7,130-hectare (17,611-acre) park occupies the high ground in the center of Isla de Margarita, near La Asunción. The mountainous terrain is some of the lushest on the island, somewhere between tropical cloud and rainforest. There are several hiking trails through the park, a lookout near the park entrance, and even better views at Las Antenas (920m/3,017 ft.), the highest point on Margarita. If you're lucky, you'll see some white-faced capuchin monkeys.

Islas Coche & Cubagua
The entire state of Nueva Esparta is made up of Isla de Margarita and two much smaller neighboring islands, **Isla Coche** and **Isla Cubagua.** The pearl beds off these two islands were major sources of wealth during the colonial period. Both islands are popular destinations for day cruises, which bring folks to their pristine and nearly deserted beaches. Isla Coche has some development and rolling hills, while Isla Cubagua is mostly barren, flat, and undeveloped. One of the only attractions here are the ruins of Nueva Cádiz. Founded on Isla Cubagua in 1528, this was the first Spanish town formally established in the Americas. However, its heyday was short-lived: An earthquake and tidal wave destroyed the town in 1541.

(*Tips* **Get Comfortable**

On most of the more popular beaches, you can rent a lounge chair and beach umbrella for $2 to $4 per day. A worthwhile investment, if you want some comfort, cool shade, and additional protection from the sun.

Day tours by small cruise ships and converted fishing boats are common. The full-day tour usually includes round-trip transportation from your hotel to the marina, continental breakfast, a buffet lunch, an open bar, beach chairs, umbrellas, and organized activities on the island. Prices range from $30 to $65 per person. *Be forewarned:* There's a real cattle-car feel to most of these tours.

There's also a daily Conferry vessel leaving at 6am from the Punta de Piedras pier for Isla Coche and returning at 6pm. The cost is $1 per person, $6 per car.

OUTDOOR ACTIVITIES
In addition to the activities mentioned below, jet skis and WaveRunners are available at many beaches and resorts around the island, as are parasail flights.

AMUSEMENT PARKS   **Parque El Agua,** Avenida 31 de Julio, El Cardón, on the way to Playa El Agua (© **0295/234-8559;** www.parqueelagua.com), is a new water park with an assortment of pools, slides, and rides. The park is open daily from 10am to 6pm. Admission is $9 for adults, $4.50 for children.

Diverland, Isla Aventura near Pampatar (© **0295/262-5545;** www.parque diverland.com), is a combination amusement park and water park, with a wide range of attractions and rides. It's open from 10am to 11pm daily throughout the high season and most weekends the rest of the year. Operating days and hours are much more limited during the week and low season. Admission is $5 for adults and $3 for children for unlimited use of the rides and pools. This place offers both dolphin and seal shows, as well as the chance to swim with captive dolphins, but I have some serious doubts about the environmental and humanitarian standards of their operation.

BIKING   The stunning scenery and combination of off-road and paved highway possibilities make Margarita a good place to rent a bike for exploring. Be careful, though: The sun can be brutal, and the distances between towns and beaches can quickly become more daunting than you might expect. The best place for mountain biking is the Macanao Peninsula.

CRUISES & SAILBOAT CHARTERS   The most popular day cruises from Margarita are to the islands of Coche, Cubagua, and Los Frailes. Trips cost from $30 to $65 per person for a full-day tour with lunch. See "Islas Coche & Cubagua," above, and "Scuba Diving & Snorkeling," below, for more information.

With the constant trade winds and translucent turquoise waters, Margarita is a great place to sail. A host of charter vessels anchor in the Pampatar harbor and other protected anchorages and bays around Margarita. The fleet fluctuates seasonally, but a sailboat is always available for a day cruise or multiday charter. Day tours cost from $45 to $100 per person. Rates for all-inclusive multiday charters range from $100 to $200 per person per day, with a minimum of four people. Contact **Explore Yachts** (© **0414/287-7554;** www.explore-yachts.com), which manages a fleet of vessels.

FISHING   The waters off Isla de Margarita are excellent fishing grounds. A day's catch might include any combination of tuna, dorado, marlin, and sailfish. You can hire a guide and a boat for the day, with lunch and beverages, for between $300 and $1,200, depending on the size of the boat, number of fishermen, and game sought; check with your hotel, or call **Explore Yachts** (© **0414/ 287-7554;** www.explore-yachts.com).

GOLF   There's currently only one working 18-hole course on the island. The **Isla Margarita Golf Club** (© **0295/265-7371**) at the Hesperia Isla Margarita is a 70-par links course. The course is fairly flat and open, with few trees, little rough, and inconsistent groundskeeping. This isn't a popular golf destination, so tee times generally aren't required, but it wouldn't hurt to make a reservation. Greens fees are free for guests at both Hesperia hotels on the island and $36 for visitors. The new Margarita Golf & Country Club project, located near the Hilton, is fairly projected to open sometime in early 2004.

HORSEBACK RIDING   Whether you fancy a ride on the beach, through the forested hills of the Cerro El Copey, or over the barren desertlike landscape of the Macanao Peninsula, there are great opportunities for horseback riding all over Margarita. Inquire at your hotel, or contact **Cabatucan Ranch** (© 0416/ 681-9348), which specialize in tours of the Macanao Peninsula.

JEEP TOURS   Small 4×4 jeeps are the ideal transport for a full-day tour taking in a wide range of the sights and scenery of Isla de Margarita. The tours usually include pickup at your hotel, a trip to the top of Cerro El Copey, visits to a couple of churches and forts, a boat ride through La Restinga, stops at several beaches, and lunch and an open bar. The prices range from $40 to $65 per person. Contact **Highberg Jeep Tours** (© 0295/264-0145; info@purelifetours.com) or **Walter's Tours** (© 0295/274-1265; www.margaritaislandguide.com).

SCUBA DIVING & SNORKELING   As this is the Caribbean, count on some good snorkeling and scuba diving on and around Isla de Margarita. Conditions immediately around the island can be a little too rough and murky. Two of the more popular dive sites close to Margarita are **Los Frailes,** a group of small rock islands about 11km (7 miles) offshore that are good for both snorkeling and scuba, and the **Cueva el Bufón,** a small cave near Pampatar thought to be a hiding place for pirate loot that can only be visited with scuba gear. Off **Isla Cubagua,** you can dive the wreck of a sunken ferry, with intact cars still aboard.

Snorkel trips average between $40 and $60 per person for a full-day tour with lunch, and scuba tours cost between $55 and $85 for a two-tank dive trip. Contact **Atlantis Diving Center** (© 0295/249-1325; www.scubadiving-venezuela.info) or **Margarita Divers** (© 0295/262-1280; www.margaritadivers.com).

SURFING   If the swell is right, you can find ridable surf on the island. **Playa Parguito,** just south of Playa El Agua, and **El Tirano,** a little further south, are the principal breaks on Margarita.

ULTRALIGHT FLIGHTS   Several pilots and companies offer ultralight flights over and around the island leaving from the old municipal airport in Porlamar and from Playa El Agua. You can either ask at your hotel, head directly to the dirt airstrip at Playa El Agua, or call **Fun Flight Margarita** (© 0295/262-8863).

WINDSURFING   Although you can rent a Windsurfer on many of the beaches on Margarita, **Playa El Yaque,** on the southern end of the island near the airport, is windsurf central. A handful of small hotels here cater specifically to windsurfers, usually with a wide selection of boards and sails for rent. **El Yaque Paradise** (© 0295/263-9418; www.hotelyaqueparadise.com) and **El Yaque Motion** (©/fax 0295/263-9742; www.elyaquemotion) are both good options here.

SHOPPING

Venezuelans and visitors alike take advantage of the island's status as a duty-free port, although I'm not sure the selection or deals are all that special. The downtown heart of Porlamar is a chaotic jumble of shops and small department stores selling everything from perfume to lingerie to electronics and appliances to liquor and foodstuffs. In 2002, the Puerto de la Mar pier was opened for cruise ship traffic, allowing cruise passengers to disembark in downtown Porlamar, just blocks from the aforementioned jumble of shops and stores. In recent years, however, large malls have been attracting shoppers away from the downtown options. The biggest of the bunch is the new **Centro Sambil Margarita,** Avenida Jovito Villalba, Pampatar. Other popular malls include the **Centro Comercial Rattan Plaza,** Avenida Jovito Villalba, Los Robles; and **Centro Comercial Jumbo,** Avenida 4 de Mayo.

For better bargains and a more local feel, head to **El Mercado de los Conejeros.** Located on the northwestern outskirts of Porlamar, it's a sort of permanent flea market of food, crafts, and dry-goods stalls. It's open daily from the wee hours of the morning until around 2pm.

At shops and roadside stands around the island, you will come across locally produced jewelry and ceramic wares of varying quality. One of the nicer and more readily available handicrafts for sale on Margarita are the local hammocks, or *chinchorros,* which are an intricate weave of thin strands of rough natural fibers. You'll also find woven baskets, hats, and handbags. The town of Santa Ana and the roads that form a triangle between Santa Ana, Pedro González, and Juangriego are prime hunting grounds for crafts shops and galleries.

WHERE TO STAY

Isla de Margarita has hundreds of hotels and thousands of rooms. Visions of a tourist mecca led to the construction of massive resorts in the style of Cancún and the Dominican Republic. The tourists never arrived in large enough numbers, and the current political climate has further affected the industry. There's a glut of rooms, construction has been halted on a number of big projects, and several hotels have folded in recent years. The glut and desperate competition to fill beds is good news for travelers.

In general, all-inclusive packages here are a good bet and can often come quite cheap. Charter packages to Margarita from the United States, Canada, and even Europe, including round-trip airfare can cost as little as $800 per person for a full week. I've heard of even better deals on Internet auction sites. Another alternative is to book your tour in bolivares through a Venezuelan-based tour agency. Margarita hotels are struggling to attract national tourists and offering very attractive all-inclusive packages, including round-trip airfare from Caracas. If you pay in cash, and exchange dollars on the black market, this can be a very inexpensive way to go. Try **Akanan Travel & Tours** ✪✪ ((℗ **0212/234-2103** or 0212/234-2323; www.akanan.com), or **Cacao Expeditions** ✪ ((℗ **0212/977-1234;** www.cacaotravel.com).

The prices listed below are the hotels' published rack rates. These tend to be the highest rate applicable, and as in Caracas, most hotels here sell very few rooms at the actual rack rate. Prices fluctuate radically according to season and demand. If you book direct, feel free to bargain—it may pay off with some deep discounts.

EXPENSIVE

Hesperia Isla Margarita ✪✪   This luxury resort is located on the northern end of the island, near Pedro González. The hotel has the only operational 18-hole golf course on the island, a well-equipped and luxurious spa, and a lovely little section of semi-private beach. The central lobby is a large hexagonal area heavily draped in ferns and tropical plants that reach up five stories to a skylight. The rooms are quite large, with dark wood floors, high ceilings, rattan furnishings, and comfortable bathrooms. A large wall of windows lets in plenty of light. Around

70% of the rooms have an ocean view. The best are those that look out over the pool and golf course to the sea; those with the least impressive views face inland over the mostly barren landscape.

The hotel is about a 30- to 35-minute taxi ride from either Porlamar or the airport, although they do provide a twice-daily shuttle to Porlamar. At press time, plans for a casino were still up in the air.

Playa Bonita, Pedro González, Isla de Margarita. ℭ 0295/400-7111. Fax 0295/265-7211. www.hesperiaisla margarita.com. 312 units. $90–$164 double; $190–$264 suite. Rates include buffet breakfast. All-inclusive plans available. AE, DC, MC, V. Free self-parking. **Amenities:** 4 restaurants; 3 bars; 2 lounges; large rectangular pool w/children's pool; 18-hole links golf course and pro shop; 2 lighted tennis courts; well-equipped health club and spa; watersports equipment rental; children's programs; concierge; tour and activities desk; car-rental desk; modest business center; shopping arcade; salon; 24-hr. room service; in-room massage; babysitting; laundry service; nonsmoking rooms. *In room:* A/C, TV, minibar, hair dryer, safe.

Hilton Margarita ☆☆
This is the foremost luxury hotel on Margarita. It has a slightly more elegant feel than the all-inclusive resorts that dominate the island. The rooms and facilities are all up to snuff, and there's a good range of restaurants and shops, both on the grounds and nearby. All the rooms come with a small private balcony and an angular view to the sea. The end units on the north tower, however, have larger balconies and full-on ocean views. Although the rooms themselves are spacious, the bathrooms are on the small side. Moreover, if beach time is what you're after, head elsewhere. The Hilton is located on a decidedly mediocre patch of beach, so you'll probably want to spend more time around one of the pools than on the sand and in the sea. The casino here is one of the largest and swankiest on the island, and the hotel is a quick taxi ride away from both Porlamar and Pampatar. This hotel is extremely popular with business travelers, and it's often packed with conferences, conventions, and trade groups.

Calle Los Uveros, Costa Azul, Isla de Margarita. ℭ 800/HILTONS in the U.S., or 0295/262-3333. Fax 0295/ 262-0810. www.hilton.com. 336 units. $140–$230 double; $250–$290 suite. AE, DC, MC, V. Valet parking $10. **Amenities:** 3 restaurants; 2 bars; 2 outdoor pools connected by a faux-river channel; children's pool; 2 lighted tennis courts; exercise room; watersports equipment rental; children's programs; concierge; tour and activities desk; car-rental desk; small business center; shopping arcade; salon; 24-hr. room service; in-room massage; laundry service; nonsmoking rooms. *In room:* A/C, TV, minibar, hair dryer, safe.

Laguna Mar ☆☆ (Kids)
This massive resort has the most extensive and impressive facilities on the island. From the wave pool to the water-slide pool to the private watersports lagoon, the installations here make it a great choice for families with children and anyone looking for constant activity. The rooms are spacious and cool, with plenty of light. Although the bathrooms all have bidets, some are a bit cramped. Some rooms have private balconies, and the best of the lot have ocean views and balconies. The hotel is located on a long stretch of beautiful beach, which can get a bit rough at times. Free jitneys circulate constantly to take you around the extensive grounds. With a steady flow of European all-inclusive travelers, Laguna Mar's bars, disco, and casino stay fairly lively. Most of the meals are served buffet style. Reserve early if you want to eat at either Carusso's or La Troje, the two a la carte dinner options, serving Italian and Mexican cuisine, respectively. The resort sells a mix of all-inclusive packages and timeshares, and there are future plans for a golf course.

Pampatar, Isla de Margarita. ℭ 0295/264-1854. Fax 0295/262-0963. www.lagunamar.com.ve. 406 units. $80–$120 per person double occupancy standard; $130–$240 per person suite. Rates are all-inclusive. AE, DC, MC, V. Free self-parking. **Amenities:** 4 restaurants; snack bar; 4 bars; 6 outdoor pools and several children's pools; 9 lighted tennis courts; exercise room; 3 Jacuzzis; watersports equipment rental; children's programs; tour and activities desk; car-rental desk; small business center; shopping arcade; salon; laundry service; disco; midsize casino. *In room:* A/C, TV, safe.

MODERATE

Hesperia Playa Agua 🦋 This all-inclusive resort has a bit of a small village feel. Rooms are either in small duplex or triplex bungalows, or one of the hotel's four seven-story towers. All the rooms are clean, comfortable, and recently remodeled. Rooms in the towers have private balconies, some of which have ocean views. The hotel is located just across the street from a nice central section of Playa El Agua. Buffet meals are served in the large, central dining area; at the beachside Frailemar restaurant; or around the main pool. There are nightly entertainment reviews and a variety of organized activities throughout the day. This hotel doesn't have near as many facilities as Laguna Mar or some of the other large all-inclusives, but it does have a great location, plenty to keep you busy, and is much less expensive.

Playa El Agua, Isla de Margarita. © 0295/249-0433. Fax 0295/249-0466. www.hesperiaplayaelagua.com. 355 units. $46–$77 per person standard double; $51–$87 per person suite. Rates are all-inclusive. AE, DC, MC, V. Free self-parking. **Amenities:** 2 restaurants; 2 bars; 4 outdoor pools; 3 lighted tennis courts; limited watersports equipment rental; children's programs; tour and activities desk; car-rental desk; laundry service; outdoor nightly entertainment review and disco. *In room:* A/C, TV, fridge, safe.

INEXPENSIVE

In addition to the hotels listed below, there is a growing range of small posadas, inns, and bed-and-breakfasts, particularly at the popular beaches. For these more intimate options, try contacting **Asopet** (© **0295/261-6269;** www.asopet.org), the local association and booking service.

Hotel María Luisa This seven-story hotel is the most popular budget choice in Porlamar. The rooms vary in size, but all feature white-tile floors, painted pink wainscoting, air-conditioning, a desk, and a tiny television. The "family" rooms located at the ends of each floor are larger, and some even have nice ocean views. The beach, which is located just across the street, is not one of the island's nicest, but it'll do in a pinch. There's a small restaurant in the hotel, but unfortunately, the hotel's main restaurant, Bahía, which is set right on the beach, was closed when I last visited.

Bulevar Raúl Leoni, Sector Bella Vista, Porlamar, Isla de Margarita. © 0295/261-0564. Fax 0295/263-5979. hotmarlu@telcel.net.ve. 98 units. $25–$40 double. AE, MC, V. Free parking. **Amenities:** Restaurant; bar; tiny outdoor pool; tour desk; laundry service. *In room:* A/C, TV.

Miramar Village *Value* This is one of the better budget options on the island. The rooms are located in two long, two-story buildings separated by a cool central passageway. The rooms are all clean and comfortable, with bamboo beds and furnishings. The bathrooms even feature bidets. The hotel is located just next door to the Hesperia Playa El Agua, and it's directly across the street from the same wonderful stretch of Playa El Agua.

Playa El Agua, Isla de Margarita. © 0295/249-1797. Fax 0295/249-1453. www.miramarvillage.com. 49 units. $25–$55 double. Rates include full breakfast. MC, V. Free self-parking. **Amenities:** Restaurant; bar; tiny outdoor pool; tour desk; laundry service. *In room:* A/C, fridge, hair dryer, safe.

WHERE TO DINE

Despite the fact that most visitors to Isla de Margarita stay at all-inclusive resorts, there are a host of restaurants around the island. Many of the beaches have simple restaurants on or close to the sand; they're great options for a lunch of fresh fish, lobster, or *pabellón,* the Venezuelan national dish consisting of shredded beef, rice, beans, and fried plantain.

In addition to the places listed below, **El Rancho de Pablo,** Avenida Raúl Leoni, Porlamar (© **0295/263-1121**) and **El Pescador de la Marina,** Avenida

Raúl Leoni, Porlamar (© **0295/264 6374**) are two excellent open-air waterfront restaurants specializing in fresh local seafood, while **Café Mediterráneo,** Calle Campos, Porlamar (© **0295/264-0503**), **Il Positano,** Calle Fermín and Calle Tubores, Porlamar (© **0295/264-1110**), and **La Scala,** in the Hilton Margarita (© **0295/262-4111**) are all recommended options for Italian.

El Pacífico ⭐ VENEZUELAN/SEAFOOD   This is probably the best of the bunch among the strip of beachside joints lining Playa El Agua. Get a table near the large windows overlooking the sea, or live dangerously and dine at a table under one of the tall coconut palms. Start things off with the *plato de pescado ahumado* (plate of smoked fish) and follow it with the fresh grilled red snapper or *langostinos al parchita* (jumbo shrimp in passion-fruit sauce). The elegant presentation of plates garnished with swirled sauces and parsley flakes contrasts nicely with the plastic lawn furniture with worn tablecloths.

Playa El Agua. © **0295/249-0749.** Reservations recommended during high season. Main courses $5–$12; lobster $11–$25. AE, MC, V. Daily 9am–11pm.

Nikkei ⭐⭐ JAPANESE/PERUVIAN/FUSION   Elegant, yet not pretentious, Nikkei serves up a wide-ranging blend of traditional and fusion creations from the cuisines of Peru, Japan and a smattering of other Asian countries. The second-floor dining room is actually a large loft, with walls of solid glass on all sides and heavy natural wood beams supporting a red tile roof overhead. There's a tiny three-seat sushi bar in one corner, and a quiet lounge and bar taking up the first floor. The service is attentive and friendly. Start things off with a Salad Nikkei, a small bowl of fresh mixed greens and seaweed in a ginger, honey-mustard vinaigrette, where bits of fried salmon skin take the place of croutons. From here the choices are nearly endless, as the menu is positively huge. I'd recommend mixing and matching dishes for a Pan-Asian/Peruvian feast. Don't let the small sushi bar fool you; the sushi here is excellent. Chef Julio Ikeda is also the force behind Nikkei's popular sister restaurant **Tambo,** Avenida Francisco Miranda, Torre Europa, Campo Alegre (© **0212/952-4243**), in Caracas.

Avs. Bolívar and Gómez, in the La Samanna Hotel. © **0295/262-2222.** Reservations recommended during high season. Main courses $6–$13; sushi $1–$2; rolls $3.75–$8.75. AE, MC, V. Daily noon–4pm and 7–11pm.

ISLA DE MARGARITA AFTER DARK

Given its status as a vacation getaway, Isla de Margarita has its fair share of bars, discos, and nightclubs; however, the recent downturn in tourism has seen the closing of some of the islands more popular and long-standing clubs. Many visitors stick to their all-inclusive resort, which usually features a small collection of bars and a disco and nightly entertainment revue. Others like to barhop sections of Avenida 4 de Mayo and Avenida Santiago Mariño.

Señor Frogs (© **0295/262-0451**), the popular Mexican chain, has a lively restaurant and bar in the Centro Comercial Costa Azul, near the Hilton, which turns into a raging disco most evenings after 11pm. In the Sambil mall, **A Granel** ⭐ (© **0295/260-2491**) is a new restaurant and cafe that often features live jazz or bolero outfits.

Casino gaming is an option on Margarita, with modern and well-fitted casinos at the Margarita Hilton, Laguna Mar and Marina Bay hotels. The casino at the Hilton is by far the swankiest and most popular.

There are cinemas in Porlamar and Juangriego, as well as in several of the larger malls. They mostly show the standard Hollywood fare, with an occasional Venezuelan, Mexican, or Argentine film to round out the bill.

EXCURSIONS FROM ISLA DE MARGARITA

Perhaps the most popular excursions from Margarita are to either **Los Roques** or **Canaima** and **Angel Falls.** By far the most established and professional operator making trips to both destinations is **Aerotuy** ✇ (© **0295/263-0307;** www.tuy.com). The cost for the Los Roques day trip is $199 per person; to Canaima and Angel Falls, the cost is $240 per person. The fares for children are roughly half-price, and rates are slightly lower during the low season and midweek. See the sections on each destination below for more information.

5 Los Roques National Park ✶✶

166km (103 miles) N of Caracas

Hundreds of deserted little islands of soft white sand surrounded by crystal-clear turquoise waters are making Los Roques one of the prime vacation getaways in Venezuela. About 42 named islands—only a couple of which are inhabited—and 200 sand spits, mangrove islands, and tiny cays surround a 400-sq.-km (156-sq.-mile) central lagoon. Barrier reefs protect the rest of the perimeter, making this the premier dive spot in the country. Near-constant trade winds from the northeast also make this a great place to sail and windsurf.

Although the islands were originally a transient camping site for ancient fishermen, ceramic shards found here suggest that they may have also held some religious significance for the indigenous peoples of the Caribbean basin. By the end of the 19th century, Los Roques was primarily inhabited by fishermen from Isla de Margarita who found it a handy base from which to expand their fishing grounds.

Declared a national park in 1972, Los Roques protects vast areas of sea-grass beds, mangroves, and coral reef. The park is an important sea-turtle nesting ground. Of the 92 recorded bird species here, you are likely to see brown- and red-footed boobies, as well as scores of pelicans, gulls, terns, and other assorted shorebirds.

ESSENTIALS
GETTING THERE
BY GUIDED TOUR One of the most popular ways to visit Los Roques is on a day tour from Caracas or Isla de Margarita. These trips are sold by almost every travel agent and tour company in Caracas and are aggressively hawked at the airport. **Aerotuy** ✇ (© **0212/761-6231;** www.tuy.com) is by far the most established and professional operator on the archipelago, with a fleet of catamarans anchored at Gran Roque. The tour generally leaves between 6am and 8am, arriving on Gran Roque in less than an hour. Soon after arrival, you'll board one of the catamarans for a sail to one or more of the nearby cays, with one or more stops for beach time and snorkeling, as well as a buffet lunch onboard the vessel. You'll return to Gran Roque in the late afternoon for your flight back to Caracas. The cost is $141 per person from Caracas, $199 from Margarita (prices are slightly lower midweek and during the low season). Although there is a slight cattle-car feel to the operation, the organization is tight, and the bilingual guides tend to be helpful, knowledgeable, and cheerful. However, Los Roques is so isolated and enchanting, you'll definitely wish you had spent the night . . . or two.

BY PLANE There are several daily flights to Los Roques from both Caracas and Isla de Margarita, with extra scheduled and charter flights on weekends and during peak periods. **Aerotuy** (© **0212/761-6231;** www.tuy.com) has two daily

---

Fun Fact **You Don't Say! (Redux)**

The interesting names of many of the cays are the result of a process of rough transliteration of the original English names into Spanish. Thus, Northeast Key becomes Nordisquí, Sailor's Key becomes Selesquí, and Spanish Key becomes Espenquí.

---

flights leaving Caracas at 8:30am and 5pm, returning from Los Roques at 9am and 6pm, respectively. **Avior** (© **0212/202-5811** or 0501/284-67737; www.avior.com.ve), **Transaven** (© **0212/355-1179;** www.transaven.com), and **Aero Ejecutivos** (© **0212/991-7942;** www.aeroejecutivos.com.ve), also offer regular service to Los Roques.

Round-trip airfare from Caracas or Margarita costs from $70 to $110. Prices fluctuate a little seasonally, and you can sometimes get good deals midweek or on afternoon flights to Los Roques.

All visitors to Los Roques must pay a 15,000Bs ($9.35) one-time entrance fee for the national park, good for the duration of your stay.

GETTING AROUND

There are no cars on Gran Roque—just a garbage truck, a water truck, and a couple of golf carts. You can walk from one end of the town of Gran Roque to the other in less than 10 minutes; you can hike to the more distant spots on the island in under an hour.

The only permanent settlement is on the main island of Gran Roque. There are some private vacation homes and fishermen shacks on some of the other islands, but for all intents and purposes, a visit to Los Roques implies a visit to Gran Roque.

Four crushed-coral and sand streets run lengthwise through the town, beginning at the airstrip on the eastern end of the island. The small Plaza Bolívar is just a block or so from the airstrip. The public dock is on the southern side of the island nearly smack-dab in the middle of town. The Inparques office and Sesto Continente pretty much define the western edge of things.

VISITOR INFORMATION

Los Roques is not particularly hospitable to independent travelers. Almost all visitors come as part of an organized tour or an all-inclusive stay at one of the *posadas* (inns) on Gran Roque. Given the isolation and limited number of hotel rooms, you should make firm reservations before arriving, particularly on weekends and during the high season.

Independent travelers can purchase, a la carte, all the typical tours and activities offered on the islands. Inquire at your hotel or at one of the small information/tour desks beside the airstrip.

FAST FACTS   There is actually a branch of the **Banesco** (© **0237/221-1265**) bank on Gran Roque, but it is of limited use to tourists, as it does not have an ATM and will not change money. However, it will do in a pinch if you need a cash advance off of your credit card. There are no official money exchange offices on Los Roques. Moreover, most hotels and shops are reluctant to change money, and quite a few do not accept credit cards. Many will accept dollars for payment, but it's best to bring a sufficient supply of bolivares for your stay.

If you have a medical emergency, you will have to be air-evacuated on the next scheduled flight or special charter. Local dive shops often have dive masters and instructors schooled in first aid.

Currently, there aren't any Internet cafes on Los Roques. This should change, as land-based phone lines have been installed. In the meantime, ask if your hotel will let you check e-mail. Also, note that there is no Ipostel office on the island—you'll have to mail your postcards and letters from the mainland. A handful of public phones operate on calling cards available at one of the few general stores on Gran Roque.

WHAT TO SEE & DO

Most of the fun to be had here is either on or below the surface of the water. The most popular activity on Los Roques is to take a day trip to one of the nearby uninhabited cays. If your hotel doesn't include excursions to the outer islands and cays, you can hire a *peñero* (small boat) at the main docks for between $5 and $20 per person, depending on the distance to the cay chosen and the number of people in your party. You should pack a lunch, bring plenty of drinks, and try to secure a beach umbrella for shade. Make sure you firmly arrange a pickup time and place for your return to Gran Roque.

OUTDOOR ACTIVITIES

In addition to the activities discussed below, you should be able to find a Windsurfer and/or Hobie Cat to rent for a few hours or the day. Ask at your hotel or around town.

HIKING   Two volcanic humps mark the western end of Gran Roque and give the archipelago its name. The tallest of these is just 130m (426 ft.) above sea level. There's an active lighthouse on the farthest hump, as well as an abandoned lighthouse on a high hill towards the center of the island. Both make nice little hikes, providing wonderful views of the Caribbean Sea, turquoise lagoon, and surrounding islands.

SNORKELING & DIVING   The diving and snorkeling around Los Roques is some of the best in the Caribbean. Barrier reefs surround the archipelago, with sheer walls on the southern and eastern flanks dropping off steeply to depths of as much as 900m (3,000 ft.).

Almost all of the hotels and local operators will include snorkel equipment (or help arrange rental) as part of their day tours to the outlying cays. A knowledgeable guide will be able to point you to many excellent shallow reefs for great snorkeling.

There are several dive operators on the island: **Sesto Continente** (©/fax 0212/632-9411; www.scdr.com) and **Ecobuzos** (© 0237/221-1235; www. ecobuzos.com) are my two recommendations. Sesto Continente is by far the larger operator, with the best equipment and boats, although you might get a slightly better deal at Ecobuzos. Rates run between $80 and $90 for a full day of diving (up to three dives in some instances), including guide, tanks, weights, regulator, and vest. Your hotel will most likely pack you a bag lunch. Both of the dive operators also offer package tours and certification courses.

Tips Protect Yourself

The sun is brutally hot on Los Roques. Moreover, there is little shade available on the outer cays. Be sure to use copious amounts of sunscreen. Also, bring along a wide-brimmed hat and some light, long-sleeved clothing, and drink plenty of water. Many of the hotels and tour operators will provide a beach umbrella for your outings to the cays; if not, you can rent one in town.

Tips **BYOM**

Although all of the dive and snorkel operators will provide equipment, either free of charge or for a small fee, I highly recommend you bring your own mask. If you plan to snorkel or dive, a good mask that properly fits your face is your most important piece of equipment and a worthwhile investment. Nothing will ruin a day of snorkeling more than a leaky mask.

Scuba divers will have to pay a one-time 2,000Bs ($1.25) national park's dive fee, in addition to the parks entrance fee paid upon arrival.

FISHING   Bonefish *(pez ratón)* is the primary game fish here. They are stalked in the shallow waters and grass flats all over the archipelago. Offshore fishing options include tuna, dorado, marlin, and sailfish.

You can hire a guide and a boat for the day, with lunch and beverages, for between $150 and $300 for bonefishing, and up to $1,200 for offshore fishing, depending on the size of the boat, number of fishermen, and game sought. Most hotels either have their own fishing guides, or will hook you up with one. Alternately, you could look into staying at a specialized fishing operation such as **Pez Ratón Fishing Lodge** (© **800/245-1950** in the U.S., or 0414/257-0167 in Venezuela; www.pezraton.com), which works out of the Posada Mediterráneo, listed below in "Where to Stay."

SAILING   A host of charter vessels anchor in the Gran Roque harbor. With the constant trade winds and flat water, Los Roques is an ideal place to sail. The fleet fluctuates seasonally, but there's always a sailboat available for a day cruise or multiday charter. Rates range from $100 to $170 per person per day, all-inclusive, for multiday charters with a minimum of four people. Day tours cost $45 to $90 per person. Contact **Explore Yachts** (© **0414/287-7554**; www.explore-yachts.com), which manages a fleet of vessels.

WHERE TO STAY

Given its status as a national park, building is extremely regulated and limited on Los Roques. There are some 50 or so posadas on Gran Roque; all of the posadas are small, usually between 4 and 10 rooms. A great majority of the posadas are owned and managed by Italians, to the point that you might imagine you're in Sardinia. Rooms are at a high premium, and the posadas fill up fast on weekends and during holiday periods.

In general, Los Roques is expensive—I'd say overpriced. There is nothing approaching true luxury on the island, but you wouldn't know it from the prices. The lodge and restaurant owners blame it on the cost of importing all the basic goods, but they're just charging what the market will bear, given the limited number of rooms and high demand.

Most of the posadas on Los Roques are all-inclusive, which means they provide breakfast and dinner at the lodge, as well as a day trip to one of the outlying cays, with a bag lunch. In some cases, alcoholic beverages are included in the price; in others, they can be included for an extra fee. Many posadas offer a 2-day/1-night package, taking advantage of the early flights in and late-afternoon departures out of Gran Roque. With this package, you'll get lunch and a tour on both days.

VERY EXPENSIVE

Macanao Lodge 🏕 This is arguably the nicest lodge on Los Roques, but I'm not sure it's worth $400 per day for a double. The rooms have wood floors, heavy wood doors, and attractive wood latticework above the windows. All have high ceilings, ceiling fans, two twin beds, and mosquito netting over the beds. Room nos. 8, 9, and 10 have ocean views. It's a pet peeve of mine, but I strongly prefer a real queen- or king-size bed over two twin beds pushed together, which is what you get here. The large central courtyard, with its seagrape trees and fountains, is the nicest feature. There's also a comfortable rooftop terrace for enjoying the sea views and sunsets. The restaurant serves a mix of Italian and Venezuelan cuisine.

Los Roques. ℂ 0237/221-1301. Fax 0237/221-1040. www.macanaolodge.com. 8 units. $190–$220 per person per day, all-inclusive. AE, MC, V. **Amenities:** Restaurant; bar, lounge. *In room:* No phone.

EXPENSIVE

Posada Acuarela 🏕 Artistic touches abound in this popular posada. The walls are inlaid with hand-painted tile, bits of colored glass and shell, and whole bottles. Each of the rooms features an original painting or two by the owner, Angelo Belvedere. The nicest room has a small private rooftop terrace up a steep flight of stairs. Meals are served family-style in the common dining room. Five of the rooms feature air-conditioning.

Los Roques. ℂ 0237/221-1456 or 0212/781-9635. www.posadaacuarela.com. 11 units. $135–$195 per person per night, double occupancy. Rates include meals and nonalcoholic drinks. AE, MC, V. **Amenities:** Restaurant; bar, lounge. *In room:* No phone.

Posada Arrecife 🏕 If you want a phone and DIRECTV in your room, albeit on a tiny television, this is your best—and only—choice on Gran Roque. The rooms have high ceilings, polished concrete floors, and heavy wood beds; the bathrooms feature ceramic sinks. A couple of the rooms here even have modern swamp cooler units, which the hotel bills as air-conditioning—they do cool things down. Meals are served family-style in a comfortable common dining room. These folks also work in conjunction with the nearby **Posada Terramar** (ℂ 0237/221-1203; posada_terramar@hotmail.com), which is another nice, slightly less expensive option.

Los Roques. ℂ 0237/221-1066. Fax 0237/221-1024. 6 units. $150–$180 per person per night, double occupancy. Rates include meals, nonalcoholic drinks, and day tour. AE, MC, V. **Amenities:** Restaurant; bar; lounge. *In room:* TV, safe.

Posada Mediterráneo 🏕🏕 This chic little posada provides personal attention, with an eye to the small details. Rough stucco walls are whitewashed, and the firm orthopedic beds are built-in. Louvered windows open onto the central hallway, and the ceiling fan is usually enough to cool the room at night. There's a nice little rooftop terrace with a bar. Delicious dinners are served family-style, either on the roof or around a large table on the front porch. The personalized service, excellent meals, and owners' sense of style give this place an edge over most of the other similarly priced posadas.

Los Roques. ℂ/fax 0237/221-1130. www.posadamediterraneo.com. 6 units. $120–$150 per person per night double occupancy. Rates include meals, nonalcoholic drinks, and day tour. AE, MC, V. **Amenities:** Restaurant; bar; lounge. *In room:* A/C, safe, no phone.

Posadas LTA 🏕 Aerotuy, or LTA (Línea Turística Aerotuy), is the main package tour operator on Los Roques, and they have four posadas here: Las Palmeras, La

Plaza, Macabi, and Vistamar. All are clean and comfortable, and painted in colorful Caribbean colors. Each posada has a rooftop terrace. Vistamar, which is located right beside the public dock, is the nicest, and even has a couple of rooms with an ocean view. Only seven of their 47 rooms have double beds, so if you are a couple, be sure to request one or you'll get two twin beds, some of which are built-in and can't be pushed together. Buffet-style meals are served in the El Muelle restaurant, which overlooks the sea. Daily sun, sand, and snorkel tours are conducted aboard one of Aerotuy's catamarans, and fishing and diving tours are also available.

Los Roques. ℂ 0212/761-6231. Fax 0212/762-5254. www.tuy.com. 47 units. $140–$195 per person per night double occupancy. Rates include meals, nonalcoholic drinks, and a full-day sailboat tour. AE, MC, V. **Amenities:** Restaurant. *In room:* No phone.

MODERATE
Posada Gremary *(Value* This popular midrange hotel is considered a budget choice in Los Roques. You'll find more of a hostel feel here than you will in most other places, perfect if you're a backpacker looking to meet and hang with fellow travelers. In recent years, they've been making improvements and upping the price accordingly, but it's still one of the best deals on the island. Definitely try to check out a room or two before settling in, as some are quite a bit nicer than others. As at most hotels here, there's a rooftop terrace for hanging out.

Los Roques. ℂ/fax 0212/462-3115. pollon24@hotmail.com. 11 units. $70–$85 per person per night double occupancy. Rates include meals, nonalcoholic drinks, and day tour. AE, MC, V. **Amenities:** Restaurant. *In room:* No phone.

Posada Guaripete *(Value* This economical posada has a slightly funky feel, but I mean that in a good way. The clean rooms feature Italian tile floors and built-in beds. Hanging shell and driftwood mobiles decorate the building. The rooftop terrace here is partially covered for shade and features a bar. The homemade Italian meals are served family-style in the common lounge and living area. At press time they were planning to buy the house next door and expand.

Los Roques. ℂ 0237/221-1368 or 0414/204-1258. info@posadaguaripete.com. 7 units. $80–$90 per person per night double occupancy. Rates include meals, drinks, and day tour. AE, MC, V. **Amenities:** Restaurant, bar. *In room:* No phone.

INEXPENSIVE
There are few true budget options on Los Roques. A couple of rather rustic posadas around the Plaza Bolívar charge between $30 and $50 double occupancy for just the room. **Posada Doña Magalis** (ℂ 0237/221-1497; www. magalis.com) and **Posada Doña Carmen** (ℂ 0414/938-2284) are your best bets in this category.

If you're really looking to visit Los Roques on a tight budget, you can camp on Gran Roque and a few of the other cays. You'll need a permit, which is issued free by **Inparques** from its office at the western end of town. A few of the isolated cays are open to campers; ask at Inparques for the current list. *Be forewarned:* The few shops and general stores on Gran Roque have very limited supplies and often run out of even the most basic goods. If you plan on camping, come prepared. If you camp on any other island, you'll have to bring all of your own food and water and make firm arrangements in advance to be picked up at a specific time on a specific day. Also, remember, it gets very hot here, and many tents only increase the heat.

WHERE TO DINE
As mentioned above, most visitors to Los Roques come as part of a package tour or stay at an all-inclusive posada. There are, in fact, very few independent restaurants

on Gran Roque. If you're not staying at an all-inclusive posada, or if you want to broaden your culinary horizons on the island, stop in at the **Bar & Restaurant Acuarena** ⨂, which is on the water between the airstrip and Plaza Bolívar. You can grab a table on the sand and order up some fresh grilled fish, or just spend the night working through their extensive list of cocktails. They also have good breakfasts and lunches, as well as a little gift shop. The restaurant is open daily from 6:30am to 11pm.

LOS ROQUES AFTER DARK
There are a couple of small bars around the Plaza Bolívar. Of these, the **Rasquatekey Bar** and **Bora El Mar** are the nicest and most popular. You could also stop in at **La Plaza Pizza Pub** or **El Canto de la Ballena.** If you're looking for a mellower vibe, try **Bar & Restaurant Acuarena** (see "Where to Dine," above). In general, hours of operation for bars are 4pm to midnight, although some will stay open as long as there are customers buying drinks.

6 Mérida, the Andes & Los Llanos ⨂⨂
680km (422 miles) SW of Caracas

Mérida is a picturesque and bustling college town nestled in a narrow valley between two mountain rivers, the Albarregas and Chama rivers, and flanked by two high Andean ridges, the Sierra Nevada and Sierra La Culata. Mérida's narrow streets and colonial architecture make it a great city to wander at your leisure, while the roaring rivers and rugged mountain terrain make it a prime base for some serious adventure. Thanks to the presence of the Universidad de los Andes (ULA), along with the budding tourist industry, Mérida has a great assortment of cafes, restaurants, bars, and discos.

Despite the imposing snow-covered peaks that surround it, Mérida enjoys a mild, springlike climate year-round. Days are generally warm, although you'll probably need a light sweater or jacket at night. May through November is the rainy season, with August and September being the wettest months.

ESSENTIALS
GETTING THERE
BY PLANE   There are more than a dozen commuter flights daily to Mérida from Caracas's Simón Bolívar International Airport. The principal airlines serving this route are **Avior** (© **0212/202-5811** or 0501/284-67737; www.avior.com.ve), **Lai** (© **0212/266-6379,** or 0274/263-7815 in Mérida), and **Santa Bárbara** (© **0212/204-4000,** or 0274/262-0381 in Mérida; www.santabarbaraairlines. com). Fares range from $45 to $65 each way, depending on season and demand. Flight time is 1 hour and 20 minutes.

Mérida's **Alberto Carnevalli Airport** is located about 5 minutes southwest of downtown. There are frequent *por puesto* minibuses that pass right in front of the airport and will take you into downtown for 15¢. A taxi to the center will cost around $1.50 to $2.

BY BUS   Several bus lines (**Expresos Occidente, Expresos Mérida, Expresos Flamingo**) have daily service between Caracas and Mérida. Almost all depart between 6:30 and 10pm and drive through the night. The trip takes 12 to 14 hours and costs around $10 to $15. Most buses leave from La Bandera Terminal, near La Bandera metro stop, although Expresos Flamingo has opened a new terminal near the Parque del Este. The bus station in Mérida is located about

3km (2 miles) southwest of downtown on the Avenida Las Américas, and is connected to downtown by regular *por puestos* and inexpensive taxis.

BY CAR The fastest route to Mérida from Caracas is via Barinas. It's mostly flat to Barinas, after which you rise quickly and dramatically into the Andes, passing through Santo Domingo, Apartaderos, and Mucuchies. This route takes between 10 and 12 hours. For a more scenic tour through the Andes, you can turn off at Guanare and head up to Trujillo. From Trujillo, the Trans-Andean highway passes through Valera, Timotes, and Paseo El Aguila (Eagle Pass), before heading into Mérida. If you come this way, you can drive to the summit of **Pico Aguila;** at 4,007m (13,416 ft.); it's the highest point in Venezuela you can reach in a car.

GETTING AROUND
Mérida is a town of many parks and plazas. The two most important are the **Plaza Bolívar,** which is the de facto center of town, and the **Plaza Las Heroínas** (located about 5 blocks south of Plaza Bolívar), which is the town's tourism hub and site of the tramway's first station.

You can easily walk to most destinations and attractions in downtown Mérida. Taxis are relatively plentiful and inexpensive. Most rides in town will run you $1.50 to $3. There's also a good system of local buses and buses to nearby towns, which is a good way to get around for next to nothing.

Both **Budget** (© 0274/263-1697 or 0274/263-1768; www.budget.com.ve) and **Dávila Tours** (© 0274/266-1711) have offices at the airport and rent cars for $45 to $90 per day.

VISITOR INFORMATION
Cormetur, the Mérida Tourism Corporation (© 0800/637-4300), has a half dozen information booths around town, including locations at the airport, bus terminal, and on the Plaza Las Heroínas. Office hours vary slightly according to location, but most are open Monday through Saturday from 8am to 6pm. Their main office is beside the airport on Avenida Urdaneta and Calle 45, but you can get a copy of the map they distribute and their list of hotels and tour operators at any of their branches.

Some useful websites you might visit before coming to Mérida are **www.merida web.com** and **www.andesholidays.com**, which is the English-language sister to the slightly more up-to-date and extensive **www.andes.net**.

FAST FACTS There's an **Italcambio** branch at the airport, and several currency-exchange houses and a host of banks around town. Although most banks won't change money, they often have ATMs connected to PLUS or Cirrus systems.

If you need medical attention, ask at your hotel, or head to **Centro Clínico** on Avenida Urdaneta, opposite the airport (© 0274/263-9611). It has an emergency room and a variety of doctors on staff with offices nearby. Or you can contact the bilingual doctor **Giotto Guillén** (© 0274/244-6519).

There are scores of Internet cafes all over town. Rates run between 50¢ and $2 per hour. One of the nicest is **La Abadía** ⟨, Avenida 3 between calles 17 and 18 (© 0274/251-0933; www.grupoabadia.com), a well-equipped Internet cafe and restaurant with a host of different spaces, ranging from small intimate alcoves and semiprivate rooms to an open-air second-floor restaurant. Some of the spaces are quasi-galleries, and there are paintings and murals throughout the joint, as well as the occasional interior courtyard and garden. This place even features live music most weekends.

Mérida

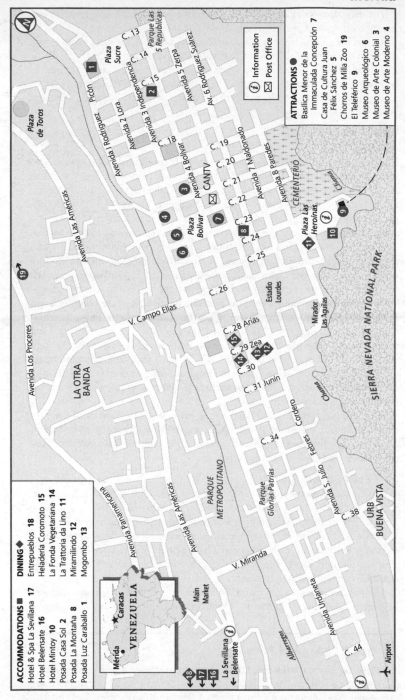

ATTRACTIONS ●
Basílica Menor de la
  Immaculada Concepción **7**
Casa de Cultura Juan
  Félix Sánchez **5**
Chorros de Milla Zoo **19**
El Teleférico **9**
Museo Arqueológico **6**
Museo de Arte Colonial **3**
Museo de Arte Moderno **4**

ACCOMMODATIONS ■
Hotel & Spa La Sevillana **17**
Hotel Belensate **16**
Hotel Mintoy **10**
Posada Casa Sol **2**
Posada La Montaña **8**
Posada Luz Caraballo **1**

DINING ◆
Entrepueblos **18**
Heladería Coromoto **15**
La Fonda Vegetariana **14**
La Trattoria da Lino **11**
Miramilindo **12**
Mogombo **13**

SIERRA NEVADA NATIONAL PARK

Plaza de Toros

LA OTRA BANDA

VENEZUELA
Caracas
Mérida

Main Market

Airport

The main **Ipostel** office is on Calle 21 between avenidas 4 and 5; there's also a branch office at the main bus terminal.

Mérida is a great place to brush up on your high school Spanish or take a crash course in the language. **The Iowa Institute,** Avenida 4 and Calle 18 (© **0274/252-6404;** fax 0274/244-9064; www.iowainstitute.com), runs programs of between 1 week and up to 6 months. Class sizes are small, and home stays can be arranged. Costs average $120 per week for classes, $105 per week for room and board with a local family.

WHAT TO SEE & DO
ATTRACTIONS

Mérida's principal church, the **Basílica Menor de la Inmaculada Concepción** 𝒶𝒶, took more than 150 years to complete, but the effort paid off in one of the most impressive and eclectic cathedrals in Venezuela. Originally based on the design of the 17th-century cathedral in Toledo, Spain, work was begun in 1803. A couple of earthquakes and several distinct periods of construction have left it a mixed breed, with artistic and architectural touches representing various epochs.

Within a 4-block radius of Plaza Bolívar, you'll find a handful of local museums. The small but interesting **Museo de Arte Moderno (Museum of Modern Art)** 𝒶, Avenida 2 and Calle 22, is housed within the city's new Cultural Arts Complex, where you can often find out what concerts, exhibits, and performances are happening around town, if none are happening in the complex's own performing arts center. The nearby **Casa de Cultura Juan Félix Sánchez,** Avenida 3 and Calle 23 (© **0274/252-6101**), has rotating exhibits of local and popular artists. The **Museo Arqueológico,** Edificio del Rectorado at the Universidad de los Andes, Avenida 3 and Calle 23, has a small collection of archaeological relics, and the **Museo de Arte Colonial,** Avenida 4 and Calle 20, has a decent collection of art and crafts, including many religious works, from the colonial period.

Finally, about 3km (2 miles) northeast of town, you'll find the small **Chorros de Milla Zoo,** at the end of Avenida Chorros de Milla (© **0274/244-3864**). I always find small zoos even sadder than large zoos, and this is no exception, but the grounds and gardens here are quite nice.

EL TELEFERICO 𝒶𝒶

With a final stop on the summit of Pico Espejo at 4,765m (15,629 ft.), the *Teleférico* is the world's highest cable car system. At 13km (7¾ miles), it is also the longest. The tramway is actually divided into four stages, beginning at the Plaza Las Heroínas. The entire trip without missing a connection takes about 1 hour each way. At the end of each stage, you'll have a brief break to walk around while awaiting the next car. If you want, you can skip a car and stay longer. Small snack bars are located at each station.

The trip begins with a quick and high crossing over the Río Chama, followed by a steep ascent over lush forests. The montane forests turn to cloud forest as

---

Tips A Change of Pace

At the top of the third stage, Loma Redonda, you'll see a small stable with a dozen or so mules. The mules can be hired for the 4- to 5-hour trip to Los Nevados (see "Excursions from Mérida," later in this chapter). The cost is around $5 to $8 per person, plus another $5 for a guide.

you gain altitude. The flora changes quickly, and soon you'll see the scrub pines and distinctive velvety-leafed *frailejones* of the paramo. By the final stage, you've left the paramo and are above tree line over barren mountain, with traces of snow on the highest peaks. At the top, you'll be greeted by a statue of the Virgen de las Nieves (Virgin of the Snows), and if the clouds permit, a good view of **Pico Bolívar,** the highest mountain in Venezuela.

During peak periods and on weekends, the *Teleférico* can get very crowded, and the lines to buy tickets and board a car can get quite long. Your best way to avoid the crowds and the wait is to buy your ticket in advance (© **0274/252-5080;** www.telefericodemerida.com) and get to the base at around 6:30am. Leaving early will also give you your best odds of clear skies, although visibility is extremely variable here. Alternately, you could book a trip with a tour agency, which will handle the ticket purchase and should have a guide staking out a place online. Don't forget to bring warm clothes and put them on in layers. For a couple of dollars, you can rent wool gloves and a wool hat from a variety of stands at the base of the tram. For a few dollars more, they'll rent you a ski parka.

A health note: Visitors in poor physical shape or with heart conditions should seriously consider stopping at the end of the third stage at Loma Redonda at 4,045m (13,268 ft.). The high altitude and thin oxygen can take their toll.

Typically, the *Teleférico* makes outbound trips Wednesday through Sunday from 7am through noon. The last car returning from Pico Espejo usually leaves around 2pm. During peak periods, the hours are sometimes stretched a little, and they often open every day of the week. During the low season, the operation may be shut down during normal working hours. The ticket you buy at the base is good for the first three stages. If you decide to continue on to the top, you must purchase a separate ticket at Loma Redonda for the final stage. During the high season, tickets cost 21,000Bs ($13) for the first three stages and 4,000Bs ($2.50) for the final stage. The rates are slightly lower in the off season, and children under 13 pay roughly half price.

OUTDOOR ADVENTURES & TOURS

There are a score of tour agencies and adventure tour companies in and around Mérida. You'll find the greatest congregation of them around the Plaza Las Heroínas. The competition is cutthroat and you can often find good deals by shopping around. However, be careful, as some of them are real fly-by-night operations. I personally highly recommend the companies mentioned below, as their level of service, quality of guides and equipment, and safety standards are consistent and dependable. Whatever tour company you choose, be absolutely sure that you feel confident about the competence of the guides and the quality of the equipment.

Arassari Treks ★★, Calle 24 no. 8-301, behind the *Teleférico* (©/fax **0274/ 252-5879;** www.arassari.com), and **Natoura Adventure Tours** ★★, Calle 24 no. 8-237 (© **0274/252-4216;** fax 0274/252-4075; www.natoura.com), are the two most established and trustworthy tour companies in town. Both companies offer most of the outdoor adventure options listed below, and then some. Both can help you with onward tours and trips to Los Llanos and most other destinations in Venezuela. U.S.-based operator **Lost World Adventures** (© **800/999-0558** in the U.S., or 0212/577-0303 in Caracas; www.lostworldadventures.com) has a lot of experience in and around Mérida, with a good local operation, as well.

CANYONEERING   This is a relatively new adventure sport here, and only **Arassari Treks** (see above) offers it. The tour, which consists of a mix of hiking, sliding, and rappelling down a river canyon, is full of thrills and chills. No experience is necessary, but you should be prepared to get very wet. A 6.3m (21-ft.) natural water slide is just one of the highlights. The cost for the full-day tour, with a snack and late lunch at the end (around 4pm), is $40 per person.

CLIMBING & TREKKING   At 5,007m (16,423 ft.), **Pico Bolívar** is Venezuela's highest peak. Crowned with a statue of its namesake hero, it's the most popular summit for visiting climbers. Although the simplest routes are not technically difficult, the sheer altitude and variable weather conditions make a summit climb here plenty challenging. Only experienced climbers in good shape should attempt it. There are also more challenging routes over steep rock and ice for die-hard climbers. One of the nicest things about climbing Pico Bolívar is that you have the option of riding the *Teleférico* down.

Other high Andean summits here include **Pico Humbolt** (4,944m/16,216 ft.), **Pico La Concha** (4,922m/16,144 ft.), **Pico Bonpland** (4,883m/16,016 ft.), and **Pico El Toro** (4,755m/15,596 ft.). Several of these peaks can be combined into a multiday trek. Some require ropes, crampons, and ice-climbing gear. All should be attempted only with a guide, proper conditioning, and proper acclimation.

For those looking for less adrenaline and a touch of culture, multiday treks of the high paramo that visit several small towns and Andean villages can also be arranged. Bird-watchers can also hire specialized guides for day hikes and multiday treks. Although you can see hundreds of species in the area, one of the most sought-after sightings is that of a giant Andean condor.

Prices for climbing and treks range from $40 to $60 per person per day, depending on group size, season, itinerary, and equipment rentals. Porters can be hired for around $20 per day.

HORSEBACK RIDING   If walking or biking don't strike your fancy, you can saddle up and tour the area on horseback. Prices range from around $25 for a half-day tour to between $35 and $50 for a full-day tour. Overnight and multiday tours are also available.

MOUNTAIN BIKING   The same Andean peaks and paramo that make this such a great area for mountain climbing and trekking also make it a prime area for mountain biking. A variety of options are available, from simple half-day jaunts to multiday adventures. Tours can be designed to suit your skill level, experience, and conditioning. Prices range from $30 to $50 per person per day. Rental of a decent bike should cost between $8 and $10 per day.

PARAGLIDING   The high mountain walls of the Andes and near-constant thermal wind currents make the Mérida valley perfect for paragliding. You may not see a condor, but you will get a condor's-eye view of things. Experienced paragliders will want to fly solo, but beginners can also enjoy the thrill, strapped into the front of a double harness with an experienced pilot behind them. If conditions are right, air time can exceed 90 minutes. A typical 3-hour tour, with 20 to 40 minutes in the air, will cost $40 to $60 per person.

TROUT FISHING   Several of the high-altitude lakes and streams up here, including Laguna Mucubají and Laguna La Victoria, are well stocked with brown and rainbow trout. The season runs from mid-March through September. You'll need to get a permit from the **Ministry of Agriculture and Renewable Resources (MARN),** Avenida Urdaneta near the airport (© **0274/263-2981**), for around $25. For a modest service charge, most tour companies in town can get the permit for you, saving you some hassle.

> ## (Moments Pendulum Plunge, Anyone?
>
> I still don't know what possessed me, but if you crave adrenaline, you might consider jumping off the Miranda bridge in Mérida. Not exactly a bungee jump, this "pendulum" plunge still requires you to jump off a 30m (98-ft.) bridge, attached by 25m (82 ft.) of rope. The folks at **Arassari Treks** twisted my arm and somehow got me to do it, but you might need less cajoling. The price is $20 per jump.

WHITE-WATER RAFTING   Rafting here is possible year-round, but the high season for it is May through November. Rafting is conducted down in the lower elevations near Barinas, so a hefty car or van ride is involved, and the trips are generally a minimum of 2 days. The rivers run include the Acequias, upper Canagua, and Sinigui rivers, and they range in difficulty from Class I to Class V. Arassari is the main rafting operator, and in 2002 they opened a lovely little lodge on the banks of the Acequias River to make the trips even more enjoyable. Prices run around $100 per person for a 3-day, 2-night adventure.

WHERE TO STAY

A backpacker and adventure tourist hot spot, you'll find some real bargains in and around Mérida. In fact, even the most upscale options here come in at under $50 per night double. There are scores of very inexpensive posadas geared towards backpackers in Mérida. Many are congregated in close proximity to the Plaza Las Heroínas and the tramway start-point. Most charge $5 to $10 per person. My favorite budget options are listed below, but if you're in the mood, it's quite easy to comparison shop and check out a handful before committing.

In addition to the places listed below, **Natoura Adventure Tours** (see above) was well along on the construction of a charming downtown hotel, **Posada Casa Sol** (© 0274/252-4164; www.posadacasasol.com), which should be another excellent budget option, with a reputable adventure tour operator running the show.

Hotel & Spa La Sevillana (Finds)   Located up a winding narrow road in the foothills above Mérida, this small spa is a great getaway. The place feels as much like a cozy B&B as a spa. The rooms are all comfortable and well equipped and come with either two twin beds or one king-size bed. Flowering gardens, small ponds, and little waterfalls fill the grounds. There are nice views of the surrounding cloud forest from the shared verandas of the second-floor rooms, and there's great bird-watching all around. The spa is small but well equipped and offers a wide range of very fairly priced treatment options. There's a comfortable lounge and bar area, with a central stone fireplace and spinet piano. A taxi here from the airport or downtown will cost around $4 to $7; the ride takes around 20 minutes.

Sector Pedregosa Alta, Mérida. © 0274/266-3227. Fax 0274/266-2810. www.andes.net/lasevillana. 12 units. $46 double. Rates include full breakfast. No credit cards. Free parking. **Amenities:** Restaurant; bar/lounge; small spa w/sauna, Jacuzzi, and hydrotherapy; laundry service. *In room:* TV, coffeemaker, hair dryer, iron, no phone.

Hotel Belensate   This miniresort is located in a quiet, residential community southwest of downtown. Probably the most upscale option in the city, it's far from luxurious. The hotel is a short taxi ride ($1–$2) from most of the restaurants, attractions, and action. The rooms are all simply furnished but spacious and clean. Depending on their size, the suites can accommodate up to six people, and some come with microwave ovens and minifridges. The more formal restaurant here serves good Italian cuisine at moderate prices, but I prefer the open-air, informal restaurant near the pool for most occasions.

Urbanización La Hacienda, Mérida. ©/fax **0274/266-2963.** www.hotelbelensate.com. 82 units. $26–$35 double; $35–$50 suite. AE, MC, V. Valet parking. **Amenities:** 2 restaurants; bar; midsize outdoor pool w/children's pool and Jacuzzi; laundry service. *In room:* TV.

Posada La Montaña *(Value* This simple posada is the best of the backpacker bunch near the Plaza Las Heroínas. It's a little bit more expensive than the rock-bottom options, but hey, the beds are firm—and you even get a tiny television with cable. The rooms are located on two floors on either side of a narrow interior hallway heavily hung with ferns. The red-tile floors, yellow stucco walls, heavy wooden banisters, and blue trim give the place some colonial charm. The restaurant is a popular hangout for international travelers, and there's a comfortable second-floor lounge.

Calle 24, no. 6-47, between avs. 6 and 7, Mérida. © **0274/252-5977.** Fax 0274/252-7055. posadalamontana@ hotmail.com. 17 units. $20–$25 double. AE, DC, MC, V. **Amenities:** Restaurant; laundry service. *In room:* TV, safe, no phone.

Posada Luz Caraballo   Located on the charming little Plaza Milla (Sucre) at the northeast end of town, this is another solid budget option with plenty of colonial flavor. The rooms are spread over three floors connected by interior courtyards and verandas. Rooms are simple and clean; a few have mattresses a little too thin and soft for my back, others have comfortable new beds. If possible, request no. 30 or 35; both have great views over tile roofs, over the plaza, and onto the Andes. As at Posada La Montaña, you also get a tiny television with cable here. The simple restaurant is popular and inexpensive.

Av. 2, no. 13-80, in front of Plaza Milla, Mérida. © **0274/252-5441.** 36 units. $16–$26 double. No credit cards. Limited free parking. **Amenities:** Restaurant; laundry service. *In room:* TV, no phone.

WHERE TO DINE

There are dozens of inexpensive Venezuelan restaurants around town—and almost as many pizza places. Most are pretty good. Walk around and choose one whose menu and ambience strike your fancy. If there's trout on the menu, it's likely to be fresh and local. For Italian cuisine check to see if **La Trattoria da Lino,** Pasaje Ayacucho 25–30, Vía Teleférico, in front of El Seminario (© **0274/252-9555**), is open. Vegetarians should head to **La Fonda Vegetariana,** Calle 29, between avenidas 3 and 4 (© **0274/252-2465**). Finally, there are a couple of excellent options a bit farther afield. Both **Cabañas Xinia & Peter** 👉👉 (© **0274/ 283-0214**) and **Casa Solar** 👉 (© **0416/674-5653**) serve up excellent international fare in elegant and intimate settings.

An interesting note: In Mérida, and throughout much of the Andes region, *arepas* are made with wheat flour instead of the traditional cornmeal.

Moments Heladería Coromoto

The **Heladería Coromoto** 👉👉, Avenida 3 and Calle 29, in front of the Plaza El Llano, holds the Guinness world record for the most ice cream flavors. Adventurous souls can sample smoked trout, garlic, beer, avocado, or squid. The eclectic and *long* list takes up two walls in the joint. The count currently exceeds 750 flavors, with roughly 100 choices available on any given day. Open Tuesday through Sunday from 2 to 10pm.

Entrepueblos ★★ *Finds* INTERNATIONAL This tiny little restaurant serves up some of the most creative and eclectic fare in the region. Generous cuts of meat, chicken and fresh fish come in a wide range of preparations with sauces based on everything from green peppercorns to prunes. There are daily chalkboard specials and tempting desserts. Six small tables are crowded into the main dining room. However, I prefer the two tables on the front porch, even though they are roadside. This place has a sister restaurant on the road to Jají, which is only open on weekends and during holiday periods.

Av. 2 Bolívar, no. 8-115. La Parroquia. © 0274/271-0483. Reservations recommended. Main courses $3–$7. AE, DC, MC, V. Mon and Wed–Fri noon–10:30pm; Fri–Sat noon–11pm; Sun noon–6pm.

Miramilindo ★ SPANISH This semiformal little restaurant is the most refined option in Mérida. The menu changes regularly, but you'll always find a broad mix of meat, fish, and poultry entrees and house specialties, deftly prepared. The steak in a port-and-fresh-mushroom sauce is a favorite here, as is the trout in saffron with crispy rice. For dessert, try the homemade *tejas* of chocolate, in the shape of a classic roof tile, served with chocolate mouse. The atmosphere is subdued and quiet. I love the lighting in the small attached atrium at night, but I find it a bit too bright during the day. These folks also run a nice little sushi bar, just next door.

Inside the Hotel Chama, Av. 4 and Calle 29. © 0274/252-9437. Reservations recommended. Main courses $4–$12. AE, MC, V. Mon–Sat noon–3pm and 7–11pm; Sun noon–3pm.

Mogombo INTERNATIONAL/CAFE With old saxophones and photos of jazz artists on the wall, this simple bistro is at once elegant, comfortable, and lively. The menu ranges from sandwiches to fajitas to fondue. The *mero en salsa verde*, a fresh fish filet in a parsley-based green sauce, is excellent. There are good salads and delicious desserts. Live music on weekends makes this a great alternative to the discos and rowdy bar scene.

Av. 4 and Calle 29. © 0274/252-5643. Sandwiches $2–$4. Main courses $2–$8. AE, MC, V. Daily 8–10am and 7–11pm.

MERIDA AFTER DARK

This is both a college town and a popular backpacker and adventure tourism destination, so you'll find a relatively active nightlife here. In general, the bars get going around 9pm and shut down around midnight to 2am. Discos get cranking around 10pm and close their doors between 3 and 4am. None of the bars in town charge a cover; some of the discos will occasionally charge $2 to $5 admittance, but it will usually get you one or two drinks.

La Cucaracha, Centro Comercial Las Tapias, and El Bodegón de Pancho, Centro Comercial Mamayeya, are both multienvironment establishments and two of the more popular nightspots in town. Birosca Carioca, Avenida 2 and Calle 24, is another popular meeting place and dance spot with Brazilian flair. Gradas Sports Bar, Avenida 4 and Calle 19, is somewhere between a traditional U.S.-style sports bar and a local dive. And La Vía, Centro Comercial Mamayeya, is one of the city's more established gay bars.

EXCURSIONS FROM MERIDA

Mérida is surrounded by picturesque mountain towns and villages. These can be visited in a rental car or as part of guided tours. Most have quaint little *posadas* for overnight stays, and some even have pretty nice lodges and hotels.

Los Nevados ★, a tiny, isolated mountain village, is one of the more popular destinations. Trips here are often done in a circuit, with one leg conducted by

Isolated Lodges or *Hatos*

Hato is the local term for a very large expanse of land. It designates a ranch or farm much larger than a *finca* or a hacienda. With the recent boom in ecotourism, *hato* has also become the local term for an isolated nature lodge. *Hatos* in Los Llanos range from almost luxurious lodges with boats for river and lagoon excursions and large, open-air safari-style trucks for land tours, to basic camps with a zinc shelter over a concrete slab where hammocks are hung inside mosquito nets. Tours at the more basic *hatos* are usually conducted by foot or horseback and, occasionally, in boats.

jeep and the other by mule and the *Teleférico*. **Mucuchies** is best known for its namesake breed of dog. On the road just outside of Mucuchies, on the way to Barinas and Los Llanos, is the beautiful little stone church of **San Rafael de Mucuchies** ⟨⟩, built by Juan Félix Sánchez. Another stone church, also built by Sánchez, can be seen in **El Tisure**. Other popular towns include **Tabay, Jají** ⟨⟩, and **Mucutuy.** The trails, lakes, and waterfalls of the **Mucubají** ⟨⟩⟨⟩ section of the **Sierra Nevada National Park** make a great destination for a day trip.

WHERE TO STAY IN THE MOUNTAIN TOWNS AROUND MERIDA

If you are tripping around the mountain towns outside of Mérida, there are several pleasant options for spending a night or two. One of the nicest is the intimate **Cabañas Xinia & Peter** ⟨⟩⟨⟩, La Mucuy Baja, Tabay (© **0274/283-0214;** www.andes.net/cabanasxiniaypeter), a delightful and artistically done retreat about 20 minutes outside of Mérida. Close to Jají, is the rustic **Hacienda El Carmen** (© **0414/632-7383;** www.haciendaelcarmen.com), a former coffee plantation that retains the ambience of its working past. Located about 60km (37 miles) outside of Mérida, **Casa Solar** ⟨⟩, Apartaderos (© **0416/674-5653;** www.casasolar.info), is a small little lodge that bears the distinction of being the highest hotel in Venezuela at 3,500m (11,500 ft.). Finally, on the road to Barinas, near the town of Santo Domingo, you'll find **La Trucha Azul** (© **0274/ 898-8066;** www.latruchaazul.com), a modern resort-style hotel very popular with well-to-do Venezuelans.

A SIDE TRIP TO LOS LLANOS ⟨⟩⟨⟩

Located on plains that roll on for hundreds of miles south and east of the Andes, **Los Llanos** is an area of flat, mostly open cattle ground, punctuated with some isolated stands of gallery forest. During the latter part of the rainy season (July–Nov), the plains are almost entirely flooded, with only a few raised highways and service roads passable in anything that doesn't float. In the dry season, the land reemerges and wildlife congregate in dense herds and mixed flocks around the ponds and creeks left behind. Traditionally agricultural land, Los Llanos have, in recent years, garnered fame as a destination for wildlife lovers and bird-watchers.

The quantity and variety of wildlife visible at the nature lodges located in Los Llanos is truly phenomenal—anaconda, caiman, capybara, deer, and even wildcats are commonly sighted.

GETTING THERE

Most folks visit Los Llanos as part of a package tour out of either Mérida or Caracas. In this case, your transportation will be taken care of. It is possible to reach the gates, or at the least, nearby towns of most of the *hatos* by bus as well, but since you have to coordinate your arrival time and pickup with the lodge, it is best that you coordinate any independent travel closely with the lodge beforehand.

Note: It's hot in Los Llanos year-round, and in the dry season, the sun can be downright brutal. Definitely bring sunscreen, but also make sure that you've got a wide-brimmed hat. Mosquitoes and other insects can also be plentiful here. Although repellent is recommended, I often prefer using lightweight long-sleeved shirts and pants. Also, be sure to bring glasses or sunglasses on the safari-style tours. When the trucks pick up a bit of velocity, particularly around dusk or on the night tours, you'll find your corneas attracting insects like a semi's windshield.

WHAT TO SEE & DO

Folks come to Los Llanos to **see and photograph wildlife** ⋆⋆⋆. And for that, they are richly rewarded. From pink river dolphins to giant anaconda, this is a wildlife lover's dream come true. Hundreds of bird species are also to be seen, many in massive flocks. Among the highlights are the Jabiru and wood stork; scarlet macaw; numerous species of hawks, herons, and parrots; and large flocks of scarlet ibis. The Hoatzin is one of the more bizarre and louder members of the avian world. Common mammals include the white-tailed deer, red howler *(araguato)* and capuchin monkeys, giant anteater, gray fox, peccary, and giant river otter. Although difficult to spot (and far from guaranteed), jaguars, pumas, and ocelots are relatively common in Los Llanos. However, you are guaranteed to see large families of capybara *(chigüire)*, as well as dozens of spectacled caiman *(baba)*.

Tours are conducted year-round, with a much higher percentage of boat tours in the rainy season, of course.

WHERE TO STAY & DINE

In addition to the two lodges listed below, many of the tour agencies in Mérida arrange trips to the Llanos. Price wars wage on the streets of Mérida, however, by opting for the cheapest options you may find yourself in an overcrowded van and sleeping in very rustic conditions. That said, 4-day, 3-night tours from Mérida run between $100 and $300 per person; the price includes transportation, meals, and a variety of tours. The price range generally reflects the level of luxury you'll find in transportation and accommodations.

Hato El Cedral ⋆   There are so many capybara, caiman, and anaconda here that it feels like a zoo. More than 340 species of birds have been recorded. The newer rooms here are quite large, with two double beds and a hammock hung indoors. The older rooms are somewhat smaller, have only one double and one twin bed, and feature lower ceilings, although they do have larger bathrooms. All of the rooms feel a bit spartan and could use some decorative touches to spruce things up. Buffet-style meals are served in a common dining room, and there's usually a concert of local *llanero* music after dinner. There are some 140km (87 miles) of roads, a couple of rivers and streams, and some forest trails within this massive *hato,* so you'll have plenty of options for tours and adventures.

Fun Fact **Man Versus Man-Eater**

In the rainy season when the rivers rise, you can fish for piranha. Stick a piece of raw meat on the end of a simple hook and toss it in. Be very careful once you land one—their teeth really are razor sharp. If your catch is big enough, you can have it cooked for you back at the lodge.

Tips Choosing Your *Hato*

Both **Hato Piñero** and **Hato El Cedral** (see above) are well-run nature lodges, with capable and friendly bilingual guides offering a steady stream of wildlife-watching tours. At each, you will see enough birds, mammals, and reptiles to keep you pinned to your binoculars and reeling off rolls of film. However, they are different: In a nutshell, Piñero will give you greater diversity (of species), while El Cedral will give you greater density. Piñero is considered a better spot for spotting jaguar and other wild-cats, although their spotting is far from guaranteed. You can sometimes spot as many as 100 different species of birds in 1 day at Piñero. On the other hand, the sheer number of capybara at El Cedral—more than 50,000—is mind-boggling. Moreover, El Cedral is perhaps the best spot for spotting anaconda, particularly in the dry season.

Near Mantecal. Mailing address: Av. La Salle, Edificio Pancho, Piso 5, PH, Los Caobos, Caracas. ℭ **0212/781-8995** or ℭ/fax 0212/793-6082. www.hatocedral.com. 25 units. $120–$145 per person double occupancy. Rates include 3 meals, 2 guided tours, and all nonalcoholic beverages. AE, MC, V. **Amenities:** Restaurant, lounge; postage stamp–size outdoor pool; laundry service. *In room:* A/C, no phone.

Hato Piñero 🐾   This pioneer nature lodge is the most charming of the *hatos*. A working farm and ranch, Piñero has the feel of a traditional hacienda. Rooms are comfortable but rustic, with cold-water showers, polished concrete floors, and two built-in twin beds. The best features here are the high ceilings, whitewashed walls, and blue-trimmed wooden windows opening up to the outdoors and an interior hallway. Four rooms have air-conditioning, but only one, which is a sort of minisuite, has a double bed. Buffet-style meals are served in a common dining area, and guests congregate in the small lounge and bar. However, the nicest place to hang, when you're not out on a horseback- or safari-style tour, is the large, open-air veranda at the entrance to the lodge. You'll also want to check out the library and biological exhibitions at the lodge's own biological research center. Early on, Piñero declared much of its property a biological preserve, and they've maintained a steady stream of invited scientific researchers, student groups, and interns, who have their own residence and basic research facilities.

El Baúl. Mailing address in the U.S.: Poba International N. 156, P.O. Box 521308, Miami, FL 33152-1308. ℭ **0212/991-8935.** Fax 0212/991-6668. www.branger.com. 11 units. $95–$130 per person double occupancy. Rates include 3 meals, 2 guided tours, all beverages, and taxes. Transportation by car from Caracas costs $190–$212 round-trip for up to 4 persons. AE, MC, V. **Amenities:** Restaurant; lounge; laundry service. *In room:* No phone.

---

7 Canaima, Angel Falls & the Gran Sabana ★★

725km (450 miles) SE of Caracas

The southeastern section of Venezuela is home to one of the nation's principal tourist attractions: **Angel Falls,** the world's tallest waterfall. In addition to Angel Falls and hundreds of other tropical jungle waterfalls, this area is marked by distinct geological formations, or *tepuis*—massive steep-walled and flat-topped mesas that inspired Sir Arthur Conan Doyle's *The Lost World*. A large chunk of this region, more than 3 million hectares (7 million acres), is protected within **Canaima National Park,** the largest national park in Venezuela and the sixth largest in the world.

The small Pemón Indian village and tourist enclave of Canaima is the gateway to Angel Falls and much of this region. Set on the edge of a black-water lagoon ringed with soft, pink-sand beaches; fed by a series of powerful waterfalls; and surrounded by miles of untouched jungle, the word "idyllic" doesn't do this spot justice.

This region is also known as the Gran Sabana, or "Great Plains," as it features large stretches of flat savanna broken up only by these imposing *tepuis*. However, the area around Canaima itself is mostly hilly and thickly forested. The true Gran Sabana is located in the southeastern (and much less visited) section of Canaima National Park.

ESSENTIALS
VISITOR INFORMATION & TOURS   Almost all visitors to Canaima come as part of a prearranged package that includes meals, accommodations, and tours. These packages can be arranged with either the local lodges listed below or any number of agencies and operators in Caracas or abroad. It's best to deal directly with the lodges, cutting out the middleman. Given the remote location, lack of roads, and limited accommodations, you should make reservations prior to your arrival. If you decide to visit on your own, there are usually several local tour agencies waiting for incoming flights at informal information desks at the small airport. Independent travelers can quickly shop around and try to arrange the best price and timing for a trip to Angel Falls, as well as local accommodations, which can range from a hammock under a simple roof to one of the nicer lodges mentioned below. Although their prices tend to be a little higher, **Canaima Tours** ⭐⭐ (© **0286/962-0559;** www.canaimatours.com) historically has had the best guides and captains and the most reliable boats and engines working this area, although any of the hotels and operators listed below can generally be trusted.

WHEN TO GO   Because Canaima is such a popular destination, it can get quite busy during the high season, particularly from July to August and from November to January. During peak periods, prices can get inflated, and the river, lagoon, and waterfall tours seem downright crowded.

Although flyovers are conducted year-round, trips to Angel Falls itself are only possible during the rainy season, when the water level is high enough in the rivers to reach its base. The unofficial season for tours to the foot of Angel Falls runs from June through November. October and November are regarded as the best months to visit, since the rains are winding down but the water level remains high. Depending on the river level, trips can sometimes be made as late

---

Fun Fact The *Tepuis*
Formed over millions and millions of years, the sandstone *tepuis* of the Gran Sabana are geological and biological wonders. With vertical edges that plunge for thousands of feet, most are unclimbed and unexplored. The highest, Roraima, at 2,810m (9,217 ft.), towers over the savanna below. Auyántepui, or "Devil's Mountain," is some 700 sq. km (275 sq. miles) in area—roughly the size of Singapore. Given their age and isolation, the *tepuis* host an astounding number of endemic species, both flora and fauna. In some cases, as much as half of all species of flora and fauna on a given *tepui* will be endemic.

as December and even January. August and September are definitely the rainiest months to visit, and although the falls are thick and impressive, visibility may be limited. Although there are no organized trips to Angel Falls in the dry season (Jan–May), this is also a good time to take advantage of low-season bargains and the relative desolation of Canaima. The dry season is actually a good time to visit the region as a beach destination, as the many pink- and white-sand beaches that line the rivers' edges throughout the dry season all but disappear during the rainy season.

GETTING THERE

BY CAR   There are no year-round serviceable roads into Canaima, and even in the dry season, the road here is so long and arduous as to be an unviable option for travelers.

BY PLANE   Most visitors to Canaima come on package tours that include the air transport. If you decide to book your travel by yourself, be forewarned that flight schedules to and from Canaima change frequently and seasonally. Given the isolation and distance, it's recommended that you book your return flight with a confirmed departure out of Canaima, so as to not find yourself waiting standby for several days for an open seat out.

Avior (© 0212/202-5811 or 0501/284-67737; www.avior.com.ve) offers four flights a week between Caracas and Canaima. **Rutaca** (© 0285/632-2195; www.rutaca.com) flies to Canaima each day from Ciudad Bolívar. Flights cost between $90 and $150 each way from Caracas, and between $50 and $95 each way from Ciudad Bolívar. If you get to Ciudad Bolívar or Puerto Ordaz, you can usually find a tour or charter company with a trip heading to Canaima, although the scheduling and costs can vary immensely depending on demand.

If you need to overnight in Ciudad Bolívar, be sure to check in to the **Posada Angostura** (0212/977-1234; www.cacaotravel.com), a simple, yet lovely little hotel in the colonial center of the city.

Aerotuy (© 0212/761-6231; www.tuy.com) runs daily day tours ($240 per adult, $120 per child) to Canaima from Isla de Margarita, including a flyover of Angel Falls and a visit to Salto El Sapo. It also uses this flight to bring people to and from its Arekuna Lodge (see below). The flight leaves Margarita at 8am and departs Canaima around 3:30pm. The hours are subject to change, as it often juggles its itinerary to Canaima and Arekuna with a stop in Ciudad Bolívar.

All visitors to Canaima must pay the 8,000Bs ($5) park entrance fee. The fee is collected at the airport upon arrival and is good for the duration of your stay.

GETTING AROUND

Besides the few dirt tracks that ring the eastern edge of the lagoon and define the tiny village of Canaima, there are virtually no roads in this region. Transportation is conducted primarily by boat in traditional dugout canoes called *curiaras*. From Canaima, numerous tours are arranged to a half-dozen waterfalls, including Angel Falls, and neighboring indigenous communities. Aside from strolling around the small village of Canaima and walking along the edge of the lagoon or to the lookout over Ucaima Falls, you will be dependent upon your lodge or tour operator for getting around.

FALLS, FALLS & MORE FALLS: WHAT TO SEE & DO IN CANAIMA

ANGEL FALLS ★★★

With an uninterrupted drop of 807m (2,648 ft.) and a total drop of 979m (3,212 ft.), Angel Falls is an impressive sight—and as you are already aware, the

Fun Fact **Jimmy Angel**

Angel Falls are named after American bush pilot and gold-seeker Jimmy Angel, who first spotted the falls in 1935. Although earlier anecdotal reports exist about them, and certainly the local Pemón people knew of them, Jimmy Angel gets most of the credit. In 1937, Angel crash-landed his plane on the top of Auyántepui. No one was injured, but the pilot, his wife, and two companions had to hike for 11 days to descend the *tepui* and reach safety. For decades, the silver fuselage of "El Río Coroní" could be seen on the top of Auyántepui. In 1970, it was salvaged by the Venezuelan Air Force. The plane was restored and is currently on display at the airport in Ciudad Bolívar.

tallest waterfall on earth. The vast majority of tourists who visit Angel Falls get to see it only from the window of their airplane. Almost all flights to Canaima, both commercial and charter, attempt a flyover of the falls. However, given the fact that Angel Falls is located up a steep canyon that is often socked in with clouds (especially in the rainy season), the flyovers are sometimes either aborted or offer limited views. Moreover, even on a good day, when the plane makes a couple of passes on each side, the view is somewhat distant and fleeting. If for some reason your flight doesn't make the pass in front of Angel Falls, you can arrange for a quick flyover for $40 to $80 per person, with a minimum of four persons. Ask at your hotel or check at the airport. *Be aware:* If you choose to purchase a flyover trip to Angel Falls, operators will *not* refund your money even if you don't catch the slightest glimpse of the falls.

If you want to really enjoy the splendor of Angel Falls, you'll have to take a trip there in a boat. Almost all of the hotels and tour agencies in Canaima offer 1-, 2-, and 3-day tours to Angel Falls. As the route and distance traveled are the same, the only difference is the amount of time you actually spend at the falls— and whether or not you spend a night or two in a hammock at one of the rustic camps, either at the base of the falls or on Isla Orquídea. Typically the tour begins at 5am with a pickup at your hotel and transfer to the tiny port atop Ucaima Falls. From here, you travel up the Carrao River, with a portage around some particularly rough rapids, to Isla Orquídea or another camp for a breakfast stop. After breakfast, it's back into the boats and on to the narrow Churún River, which snakes up Cañón del Diablo (Devil's Canyon) and over scores of rapids to Isla Ratoncito (Little Mouse Island) at the base of the falls. Overall, the upriver journey takes 4 hours. Keep your eyes peeled and you might see a toucan, cock-of-the-rock, or some howler monkeys. Once at the base, you'll still need to hike for another hour uphill through tropical forest to reach the pools at the foot of the falls. The hike is a little strenuous and can be slick and muddy, but a swim in the refreshing pool at the foot of the massive falls makes it worth the effort. Back on Isla Ratoncito, you'll have lunch before boarding the boats once again for the trip back to Canaima. With the current, the trip is a bit faster and you should even get to visit Salto El Sapo before being dropped back off at your hotel around sunset.

Multiday tours sometimes leave later in the morning or afternoon, sacrificing a visit to the falls on the first day. However, once there, you get to spend a longer time at the foot of the falls, and/or visit the falls on consecutive days. Day tours from Canaima range from $100 to $200 per person. Two-day, 1-night tours to

Angel Falls can cost between $150 and $250. Be careful about trying to save a few dollars: Paying more for a respectable operator will often get you a boat with two working engines (required by law, but not always the case in practice), a more experienced captain (important, given the nature of the rivers), and a better and truly bilingual guide.

OTHER AREA FALLS 𝕬𝕬

Several distinct and impressive falls work together to form the Canaima lagoon. All of these are easily visited in organized boat trips out of town. The most popular of these falls is **Salto El Sapo,** which is located on the backside of small Anatoly's Island, on the north end of the lagoon. A visit to Salto El Sapo includes a 15-minute hike across the island, from the foot of Hacha Falls to the base of Salto El Sapo. After a swim in the pool here, you are led along a path that passes behind the falls (be prepared to get wet), then up around the other side, with a visit to the smaller El Sapito Falls, and then (when the water level permits) across the top. Tours to Salto El Sapo often include lunch, or at the very least a refreshment.

Hacha, Golondrina, and **Ucaima falls** are located in a neat row fronting the lagoon. They can be observed and enjoyed from just about any point along the edge of the lagoon or by dugout canoe. At a 15-minute hike uphill from the small village, you'll find a little lookout built as part of the small hydroelectric plant on the top of Ucaima Falls. It's not Niagara, but it's a pretty good view. A 10-minute drive and then a 15-minute boat ride downstream are the wide and roaring **Yuri Falls.** A visit to Yuri Falls usually includes a short but interesting walk through the forest. All of the hotels and tour operators in town offer trips to all of these waterfalls, in half- and full-day combinations, which often include a little bit of hiking, a little bit of swimming, and lunch and/or refreshments. Prices range from $20 to $45 for a half-day tour, and from $50 to $90 for a full-day tour.

OUTDOOR ADVENTURES

Few organized adventure sports are regularly practiced in this region. Despite the scores of rivers, with ample rapids and white water, no one yet is offering any rafting or kayaking in the area. Aside from the relatively soft adventures mentioned above, multiday treks around the region, including climbs of Auyántepui and Roraima, are possible. If you're interested in a multiday trek you can ask one of the local tour operators in Canaima, or try contacting **Akanan Travel & Tours** 𝕬𝕬 (✆ **0212/234-2103** or 0212/234-2323; www.akanan.com) or **Lost World Adventures** 𝕬𝕬 (✆ **800/999-0558** in the U.S., or 0212/577-0303 in Caracas; www.lost worldadventures.com).

Finally, Auyántepui and Angel Falls have become a coveted destination for base jumpers. If you're a member of this adrenaline-starved group, **Jungle Rudy**

Tips Swimming Safety

Be careful when the cool, inviting waters of Canaima lagoon beckon. Given the presence of so many strong waterfalls, there are some treacherous currents. There's a small roped-off swimming area in front of Campamento Canaima. If you want to swim elsewhere, it's always best to check with your guide or hotel before venturing in, and make sure you choose a safe and calm spot for swimming. Be especially careful when swimming anywhere near any of the falls.

Campamento (see "Where to Stay & Dine," below) has hosted several teams of base jumpers and could probably help you with arrangements.

SHOPPING

There are several gift shops located in and around the small village of Canaima. By far the best of the bunch is **Makunaima Arte Indígena** ⚘ (© **0286/621-5415**), located just beyond Waku Lodge. Open daily from 8am to 6pm, this place has a broad and reasonably priced selection of local indigenous crafts, including Pemón blowguns, Yanomami baskets, and Piaroa masks, as well as quality jewelry, ceramics, and woodwork. Another good option—but with a much more limited selection—is the **Kayarinwa Gallery** (no phone), located right in the small village of Canaima. Unless you need toothpaste or some basic goods from their attached general store, avoid the **Canaima Souvenir Shop,** which has a broad but over-priced selection of crafts.

WHERE TO STAY & DINE

As previously mentioned, most visitors here come on prearranged packages that include transportation, meals, and tours. All of the lodges listed below offer packages, but package prices vary greatly depending on whether or not you visit Angel Falls and the duration of your stay. Basic per-night rates are listed below, with the various tours as add-ons.

Finally, budget travelers can find several options for hanging a hammock, or sleeping in a rented hammock, for $5 to $10 per person per night. Your best bet for this option is to ask around the information desks at the airport upon arrival, or try to get to the rustic **Campamento Tomás Bernal** (© **0414/854-8234;** bernaltours@terra.com.ve) on Anatoly Island. Usually, a representative of Bernal Tours is at the airport.

Campamento Parakaupa   This lodge is located on a small hill about 720m (2,400 ft.) inland from the lagoon. You can see the Hacha, Golondrina, and Ucaima falls from the grounds here, but the lagoon is mostly blocked by forest. The rooms are clean and comfortable, with indigenous crafts hanging on the walls and varnished woven-thatch ceilings. Meals are served family-style in the common dining area, and there's a new large, open-air restaurant and lounge, with changing rooms for day-trippers. Parakaupa offers all the standard tours around the area.

Canaima (Sector Laguna de Canaima, Gran Sabana, Edificio Bolívar). ©/fax **0286/961-4963**. www. canaima.net. 14 units. $110–$145 per person per day. Rates include 3 meals (but no beverages), taxes, and airport transfers. MC, V. **Amenities:** Restaurant; lounge; laundry service. *In room:* No phone.

Jungle Rudy Campamento ⚘⚘ *(Finds*   Located a short boat ride up the Río Carrao above Ucaima Falls, this small and simple nature lodge is a wonderful and romantic retreat. The lodge was founded and built up over a period of decades by the late, legendary Rudy Truffino. The rooms are simple but clean, with indige-nous artifacts and wildlife photos on the walls. Although most have wonderful river views, only a few have double beds—the rest come with either two or three twin beds. You should definitely ask for no. 9, which used to be Rudy's and, in addition to having one of the few double beds, has a small private veranda just a few feet from the river's edge. Tasty meals are served family-style in the open-air dining room. There are well-tended gardens and grounds, and two riverside swimming nooks formed by natural and sculpted rock formations. All of the standard tours are offered, including to Salto El Sapo, Yuri Falls, and Canaima lagoon. Tours cost $35 to $100 per person, depending on the destination and length of the outing. A full-day tour to Angel Falls costs $140 per person, with a $70 add-on for an overnight at their rustic camp on the Churún River.

Canaima (Parque Nacional Canaima, Sector Laguna de Canaima, Gran Sabana, Edificio Bolívar). ©/fax **0286/ 962-2359** in Canaima, or 0212/693-0618 in Caracas. www.junglerudy.com. 14 units. $140–$180 per person per day. Rates include 3 meals, welcome cocktail, and airport transfers. AE, MC, V. **Amenities:** Restaurant; bar; laundry service. *In room:* No phone.

Waku Lodge 🏵🏵   Set right on the banks of the Canaima lagoon, with a straight on view of the Hacha and Ucaima falls, this new lodge is run by the folks at Canaima Tours. The rooms are all comfortable, clean and spacious, and feature a front patio with a couple of chairs and a hammock looking out over the grounds and towards the lagoon. The restaurant is housed in a large, open-air structure with a thatched roof, and their lounge area even features a television with DIRECTV hookup. Canaima Tours is one of the best and longest-running tour operators in the area, with a wide range of tour options available.

Canaima (Parque Nacional Canaima, Sector Laguna de Canaima, Gran Sabana, Edificio Bolívar). © **0286/ 962-0559.** www.canaimatours.com. 15 units. $120–$160 per person per day. Rates include 3 meals, a quick boat tour around the lagoon, and airport transfers. AE, MC, V. **Amenities:** Restaurant; bar; laundry service. *In room:* No phone.

A NEARBY NATURE LODGE

Arekuna Lodge 🏵🏵   Run by Aerotuy, this rustically luxurious nature lodge is located a 10-minute flight away from Canaima on the banks of the Caroní River. Fifteen duplex bungalows are spread around the base, and up the flanks, of a small but steep hill. The rooms are quite large, with massively high ceilings, although much of the floor space is taken up by the three twin beds and indoor hammock. With huge screened windows and dormers, these units get plenty of ventilation. The nicest touch here is the petroglyph reproductions around the grounds and in the rooms. Family-style meals and spectacular sunsets are enjoyed in the large open-air dining room and bar that crowns the hill. In the daytime, this perch affords great views of the river, surrounding jungles, and Guariche Tepui. Most of the bungalows have river views, but the best views can be had in the Apouwa (which also is one of the few units with double beds), Caroní, and Yurwan duplexes. Available tours include visits to local indigenous communities, as well as Baba and Guariche falls and ancient petroglyphs (in the dry season). However, river trips to Angel Falls are not conducted from Arekuna.

On the edge of Canaima National Park. © **0212/761-6231.** Fax 0212/762-5254. www.tuy.com. 30 units. $150 per person per day. Rates include 3 meals, all nonalcoholic beverages, and 2 tours daily. A 2-day, 1-night package from Margarita, including airfare, costs $375 per person double occupancy. Lower rates in the off season and for children. AE, MC, V. **Amenities:** Restaurant; bar; laundry service. *In room:* No phone.

12

Difficult Destinations: Antarctica & Colombia

by Kristina Schreck

They are worlds apart, but they both rank as South America's most difficult destinations: Antarctica and Colombia. As anyone knows, Antarctica is its own continent, but the hook of the Antarctic Peninsula is closest to the tip of South America, and therefore, the traveling majority departs from Ushuaia, Argentina. Why is Antarctica difficult? Distance, cost, and capricious weather patterns—but these factors have bred mystique for this unique destination and are, therefore, part of its allure.

Colombia, on the other hand, presents grave political and social problems that make us question the advisability of sending readers there. In this chapter, we will provide you with some background on this war-torn nation's history, culture, and political situation and offer tips and warnings for the intrepid traveler planning a visit there.

1 Antarctica

It's the coldest spot on the planet, but it's a hot destination for travelers seeking the next great adventure. Antarctica is home to exotic wildlife and landscapes that are equally savage and beautiful. Be prepared for ice like you've never seen it: monumental, peacock-blue icebergs shaped in surreal formations, craggy glaciers that crash into the sea, sheer ice-encrusted walls that form magnificent canals, and jagged peaks that jut out of icy fields. A major highlight here are the penguins—colonies of several hundred thousand can be found nesting and chattering away throughout the area. Humpback, orca, and minke whales are often spotted nosing out of the frigid water, as are elephant, Weddell, leopard, and crabeater seals. Bird-watchers can spend hours studying the variety of unique seabirds, including petrels and albatrosses.

Most important, Antarctica sits at the "End of the World," and this reason alone is enough to compel many people to travel here. Like the early explorers who first visited this faraway continent in the 1800s, travelers today revel in the chance to venture to a pristine region where relatively few humans have stepped foot before. But Antarctica's remoteness comes with a toll: No matter how you get here, it's not cheap, and the tediously long traveling time and sometimes-uncomfortable conditions are also part of the price you'll pay. Nevertheless, many of Antarctica's 14,000 yearly visitors would agree that the effort is worth it.

A BRIEF HISTORY

The history of exploration and the discovery of the Antarctic continent are littered with claims, counter claims, tall tales, intrigue and suffering. Captain James Cook discovered the South Sandwich and South Georgia islands in 1773, but he never spotted the Antarctic continent. He did, however, set off a seal-hunting

frenzy after providing reports of the large colonies he found there, and it's estimated that sealers discovered around a third of the islands in the region. Two
sealers were the first to actually step foot on the continent: the American John
Davis at Hughes Bay in 1821, and the British James Weddell at Saddle Island in
1823. During a scientific expedition in 1840, the American navy lieutenant
Charles Wilkes finally concluded that Antarctica was not a series of islands and
ice packs but rather a contiguous landmass.

The South Pole was not reached until 90 years later, on December 4, 1911,
by Norwegian Roald Admudsen and his well-prepared five-man team. Though
Amundsen's arrival at the pole accounted for one of the most remarkable expeditions ever to be completed by man, his feat at the time was eclipsed by the
tragic finale of an expedition led by his rival, the British captain Robert Scott.
Scott arrived at the pole 33 days later, only to find Amundsen's tent and a note.
Scott and his party, already suffering from scurvy and exposure, finally froze to
death on their return trip, just 18km (11 miles) from their ship.

No other destination has held such an adventurous cachet for explorers. One
of the greatest adventures ever recorded was in 1915, led by the Irish explorer
Ernest Shackleton, who pronounced Antarctica "the last great journey left to
man." Shackleton attempted to cross the Antarctic continent but never achieved
his goal: Pack ice trapped and sank his boat. The entire party miraculously survived for 1 year on a diet of penguin and seal before Shackleton sailed to South
Georgia Island in a lifeboat to get help.

Today, 27 nations send personnel to Antarctica to perform seasonal and
year-round research. The population varies from 4,000 people in the summer
to roughly 1,000 in the winter. There are a total of 42 stations that operate year-
round, and an additional 32 that operate during the summer only. The stations
study world climactic changes, and in 1985, researchers at the British Halley station discovered a growing hole in the ozone layer.

PLANNING YOUR TRIP TO ANTARCTICA
VISITOR INFORMATION
A number of websites offer helpful information about Antarctica. A few of the
best:

- **www.iaato.org**: This is the official website of the International Association
  Antarctic Treaty Organization, the only governing body in Antarctica
  (although it is more akin to a gentleman's treaty between all nations with
  bases here). It is important that your tour group be a member of the IAATO.
  Statistics, general information, and news can be found on the website.
- **www.70south.com**: This site includes links to other Antarctica-oriented
  websites, as well as weather and event information and message boards.
- **www.antarcticconnection.com**: This site offers travel information, tour
  operator links, and items for sale, including maps and videos.

ENTRY REQUIREMENTS
No single country claims Antarctica as its territory, so visas are not necessary, but
you will need a passport for unscheduled stops and your first stop either in
Argentina or Chile (see chapter 3 for information about entry requirements).

WHEN TO GO
Tours to Antarctica are conducted between November and March—after March,
temperatures dip to lows of –100°F (–38°C) and the sun disappears until September. The opposite is true of the summer, and visitors can expect sunlight up

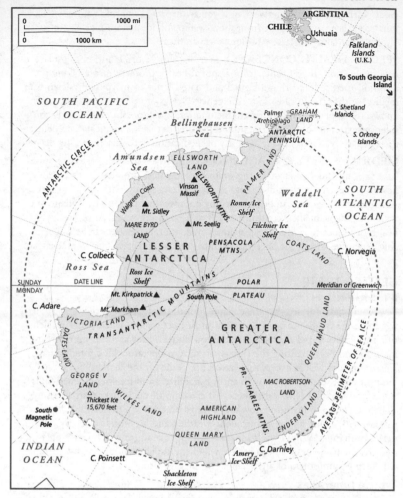

to a maximum of 18 to 24 hours a day, depending on where you are in Antarctica. Summer temperatures near the Antarctic Peninsula vary between lows of 5°F to 10°F (−15°C to −12°C) and highs of 35°F to 60°F (2°C–16°C).

What you see during your journey may depend on when you go. November is the mating season for penguins and other birds, and visitors can view their offspring in December and January. The best time for whale-watching is during February and March.

SAFETY

EXTREME WEATHER   Cold temperatures, the windchill factor, and perspiration all conspire to prohibit the body from keeping itself warm. Travelers, therefore, need to outfit themselves in the highest-quality outdoor clothing available. Tour operators are constantly amazed at how under-prepared visitors to Antarctica are, and they therefore will provide you with a packing checklist that will include items such as rubber boots; ask your tour company if it provides its guests with waterproof outerwear, or if you are expected to bring your own. The thin ozone layer and the glare from snow, water, and ice make a high-factor sun-screen, a hat, and sunglasses absolutely imperative.

SPECIAL HEALTH CONCERNS   *Everyone* should bring anti–motion sick-ness medication. If you suffer from a special health problem or are taking pre-scription medication, bring a signed and dated letter from your physician for medical authorities in case of an emergency. Delays of up to 4 weeks have been known to happen on guided trips to the interior, so visitors should seriously con-sider the extremity of such a trip, submit themselves to a full medical exam before their departure, and bring the quantity of medication necessary for a long delay.

MEDICAL SAFETY & EVACUATION INSURANCE   All passenger ships have an onboard physician in the event of a medical problem or emergency; however, passengers should discuss an evacuation policy with each operator. Emergency evacuation can be hindered by poor weather conditions, and anyone with an unstable medical condition needs to keep this in mind. Also, check your health insurance to verify that it includes evacuation because it can be unbeliev-ably expensive—from the Shetland Islands alone, it costs $35,000 to evacuate a person.

GETTING THERE
BY SHIP

Few would have guessed that the collapse of the Soviet Union in the early 1990s would be the catalyst to spawn tourism in Antarctica. But when Russian scien-tific ship crews found themselves without a budget, they spruced up the ships' interiors and began renting the vessels out to tour operators on a rotating basis. These ships (as well as others that have since come on the market) are specially built for polar seas, complete with antiroll stabilizers and ice-strengthened hulls. A few of these ships have icebreakers that can chip through just about anything.

Before you go, it helps to know that a tour's itinerary is a rough guide of what to expect on your journey. Turbulent weather and ice conditions can cause delays or detours. Wildlife sightings may prompt your group to linger longer in one area than the next. The ship's crew and the expedition leader of your tour will keep you informed of any changes to the program.

Typical Itineraries

A journey's length is the determining factor for which stops are made. Tour companies offer roughly similar trajectories for cruises to Antarctica, with the exception of a few over-the-top cruises. (Got 2 months and $50,000? Quark Expe-ditions conducts a full circumnavigation of Antarctica.) Apart from the destina-tions listed below, cruises attempt a landing at research stations when convenient. Most Antarctic cruises leave from Ushuaia, Argentina, although a tiny fraction leave from New Zealand. The Ushuaia departure point is covered in chapter 4, and it is the quickest way to reach Antarctica. Although Chile used to be a departure site for Antarctica, few (if any) travelers now leave from Chile; those who do, make the journey aboard a military ship. Plan to leave from Ushuaia.

Remember to factor in 2 days (4 in total for the return trip if traveling to the Antarctic Peninsula) to cross the Drake Passage, during which time you'll not do much more than hang out, relax, take part in educational lectures, and suffer through occasional bouts of seasickness. Cruises typically last 8 to 13 days for the Antarctic Peninsula, and 18 to 21 days for journeys that include the Sub-antarctic Islands. Seasoned travelers have frequently said that 8-day trips are not much of a value; consider tacking on 2 extra days for a 10-day trip.

THE ANTARCTIC PENINSULA   This is the easiest site to visit in Antarctica, and due to its rich variety of wildlife and dramatic scenery, it makes for a magnificent introduction to the "White Continent." If you have a short amount of time and/or a limited budget, these trips are for you.

All tours stop at the **South Shetland Islands.** Historically, sealers and whalers used these islands as a base; today they're home to research stations, colonies of elephant seals, and a variety of nesting penguins and sea birds. Popular sites here are **King Island, Livingston Island,** and **Deception Cove,** a collapsed, active volcanic crater with bubbling pools of thermal water.

Tours continue on to the eastern side of the Antarctic Peninsula, with a variety of stops to view wildlife such as Weddell and leopard seals and vast colonies of Adélie, chinstrap, and Gentoo penguins. At the peninsula, sites such as the **Lemaire** and **Neumayar** channels afford camera-worthy views of narrow, sheer-walled canals made of ice and rock. At **Paradise Harbor,** calving icebergs theatrically crash from the harbor's main glacier, and throughout the area, outlandishly shaped gigantic icebergs float by. Other popular stops include **Port Lockroy,** a former British base that is now run as a museum; **Cuverville** and **Rongé** islands, with their penguin colonies; and **Elephant Island,** named for the huge, sluglike elephant seals that inhabit it.

THE POLAR CIRCLE   Ships with ice-breaking capabilities can transport guests past the Antarctic Circle and into the zone of 24-hour sunlight. The highlight here is **Marguerite Bay,** with its abundant orca, minke, and humpback whales, and multitudinous Adélie penguins. Cruises typically stop for a fascinating tour of research stations, both ultramodern and abandoned ones.

THE WEST SIDE & THE WEDDELL SEA   Longer tours to the peninsula might include visits to its west side, known as "iceberg alley" for the mammoth, tabular chunks of ice floating slowly by. Stops include the rarely visited **Paulet Island,** an intriguing crater island, and **James Ross** and **Vega** islands, known for their nesting colonies of Adélie penguins.

An even longer trip (or simply a different itinerary) takes travelers to the distant **Weddell Sea,** which is blanketed with a vast expanse of pack ice, looking much like a frozen sea. But that's just one of the highlights here; the real reason visitors pay extra time and money to reach this white wonderland is because of the colonies of emperor penguins that reside here. Rugged mountains and glaciers are also part of the view.

SUBANTARCTIC ISLANDS   Tours to the Subantarctic Islands begin or end with a trip to the Antarctic Peninsula and the Shetland Islands, which is the reason these tours run 18 to 21 days. A few of these faraway islands are little-visited by tourists, and they instill a sense of adventure in the traveler for their remoteness and fascinating geography, not to mention their important historical aspects.

The first stop is usually the **Falkland (Malvinas) Islands,** to view birdlife, especially king penguins, and to tour the Victorian port town of Stanley. Some tours fly directly from Santiago, Chile, to the Falklands and begin the sailing journey there.

South Georgia Island is surely one of the most magnificent places on earth, and it is therefore a highlight of this trip. The island is home to a staggering array of wildlife and dramatic landscapes made of rugged peaks, fiords, and beaches. South Georgia Island is also subject to unpredictable weather, and therefore, trip landings here are at risk of being canceled far more frequently than at other sites.

Some tours tack on visits to the **South Orkney Islands** and the **South Sandwich Islands.**

Tour Operators

Prices vary depending on the length of the trip, the company you choose, and the sleeping arrangements you require. A 9-day journey in a room with three bunks and a shared bathroom runs about $3,100 per person, and a 21-day journey with lodging in a corner-window suite is about $12,000 per person. Shop around to find something to suit your needs and budget.

Prices include passage, meals, guides, and all excursions. Some tours offer scuba diving, kayaking, overflights, or alpine trekking, usually at an additional cost. When researching trips, also consider the size of the ship: Tour companies offer space for anywhere from 50 to *600* passengers. Most travelers like to share their space with fewer people; although some enjoy the camaraderie of a crowd, more than 100 to 150 guests is just too many. The International Association Antarctic Treaty Organization limits landings to 100 people, meaning large ships must conduct landings in turns.

A few well-known tour operators include:

- **Abercrombie & Kent,** 1520 Kensington Rd., Suite 212, Oak Brook, IL 60523-2141 (© **800/544-7016** or 630/954-2944; fax 630/954-3324; www.abercrombiekent.com). Like Quark, A&K offers deluxe journeys, with trips that run from 14 to 18 days.
- **Aurora Expeditions,** 182A Cumberland St., The Rocks, NSW 2000, Australia (© **02/9252-1033;** fax 02/9252-1373; www.auroraexpeditions.com.au). This is an Australian company with a variety of educational, photographic, and climbing tours for small groups.
- **Geographic Expeditions,** 2627 Lombard St., San Francisco, CA 94123 (© **800/777-8183** or 415/922-0448; fax 415/346-5535; www.geoex.com). Tours vary between 11 and 28 days, with small boat cruising, trekking, and climbing options.
- **Lindblad Expeditions,** 720 Fifth Ave., New York, NY 10019 (© **800/397-3348** or 212/765-7740; www.expeditions.com). This venerable, Swedish-run company was the first to bring tourists to Antarctica. It offers 11- to 28-day tours, with trekking.
- **Mountain Travel Sobek,** 1266 66th St., Emeryville, CA 94608 (© **888/687-6235** or 510/594-6000; fax 510/525-7710; www.mtsobek.com). This well-respected company has been operating Antarctic tours for 15 years. They offer 11- to 21-day tours, with Zodiac rides.
- **Oceanwide Expeditions,** 15710 JFK Blvd., Suite 850, Houston, TX 77032 (© **800/453-7245;** fax 281/987-1140; www.ocnwide.com). This Dutch company operates a variety of journeys aboard its own ship.
- **Peregrine Adventures,** 258 Lonsdale St., Melbourne, VIC 3000, Australia (© **1300/854444** in Australia; 03/9662-2700 outside Australia; fax 03/9662-2442; www.peregrine.net.au). This Australian company is the only operator that doesn't charge solo travelers a single supplement.
- **Quark Expeditions,** 980 Post Rd., Darien, CT (© **800/356-5699** or 203/656-0499; www.quarkexpeditions.com). This highly esteemed company offers the industry's most outrageous trips.

Reduced Fares

Several travel agencies in Ushuaia offer reduced fares for last-minute bookings made 15 to 20 days before a cruise's departure date, with prices 10% to 50%

lower than the advertised rate. Two agencies to try are: **Rumbo Sur,** Av. San Martín, Ushuaia, Argentina (© **2901/421139;** fax 2901/434788; www.rumbo sur.com.ar); and **All Patagonia,** Juana Fadul 26, Ushuaia, Argentina (© **2901/ 433622;** fax 2901/430707; www.allpatagonia.com).

BY PLANE

Apart from working for a research station, one of the few ways to get out and really explore the Antarctic continent is by plane, and there are a handful of companies that offer a small selection of astonishing and out-of-this-world journeys to the Antarctic interior and beyond.

Flights to the Antarctic can be divided into two distinct categories: flights that access man-made airstrips on certain islands close to the peninsula, and flights that penetrate the frigid interior, relying on natural ice and snow runways for landing areas. The logistics involved in flying to the Antarctic are complicated to say the least, and fuel becomes an issue. Make no mistake, air travel to the Antarctic is a serious undertaking; however, the rewards can be unforgettable.

From Punta Arenas, King George Island on the peninsula is the preferred destination. The island houses a number of research stations, some of which you can visit, and it boasts extraordinary wildlife and sightseeing opportunities. The average stay is 1 or 2 days, but weather delays can alter itineraries.

The severity of the landscape and the remoteness of the interior of the Antarctic continent call for special considerations when planning and preparing for an unexpected prolonged stay. All travelers attempting a trip to the interior should be aware of the extreme climatic conditions. Travel delays caused by severe weather are the norm. These trips however represent adventure travel in its purest form.

Tour Operators

Prices vary depending on the company and the destination. In general, flights to the Peninsula are much cheaper than those to the interior. As expected these all-inclusive trips can cost anything from $11,000 to $30,000 per person, depending on the destination. Logistical support for extended expeditions can easily run to over $40,000. Prices typically include transportation, meals, and guides.

- **Adventure Network International,** 4800 N. Federal Hwy., Suite 307D, Boca Raton, FL 33431 (© **866/395-6664** or 561/347-7523; fax 561/ 347-7523; www.adventure-network.com). This company began as a private plane service for climbers headed for Vinson Massif, the highest peak in Antarctica. They now include several 7- to 22-day tours, such as flights to the South Pole and the Transantarctic and Ellsworth mountain ranges, an emperor penguin safari, and a 60-day ski trip to the South Pole. Activities planned during these trips can include hiking, skiing, and skidoo trips; overnight camping; and ice hockey, igloo building, and just about anything else related to ice.

- **Aerovías DAP,** O'Higgins, Punta Arenas (© **61/223340;** fax 61/221693; www.aeroviasdap.cl). This small Chilean airline specializes in flights to the peninsula, in particular King George Island.

2 Colombia

Anyone who has kept up with the news knows that Colombia is a perpetual cycle of unrest and violence. Drug running, guerrilla warfare, right-wing death squads, kidnappings, and devastating earthquakes plague this midsize South

American country, and bombings, once only seen in the countryside, now rock major cities such as Bogotá. But Colombia is a bewildering paradox, and bad news is just one part of the story.

If you were to look at the country purely from a travel point of view, you might be surprised to find that Colombia is one of South America's gems, a country bestowed with magnificent landscapes as diverse as Caribbean and Pacific beaches, tropical rainforest, and snowcapped Andean peaks that tower over fertile valleys. From a historical standpoint, few Latin countries boast better museums or more handsome colonial architecture. Colombians are proud of their long-standing cultural and intellectual tradition that has produced noted writers such as Gabriel García Márquez and artists such as Fernando Botero. The country has wonderful cuisine, a rich variety of native musical styles, and a population that is ethnically diverse, somewhat sentimental, and always ready to greet you with a warm smile.

And herein lies the paradox. How could a country with so much to offer find itself torn by such violent terror and poverty? Should you as a traveler risk visiting such a country, and if so, where and how should you go? For the answers to these questions, it helps to have an understanding of historical and current events that have shaped, and disfigured, this enigmatic nation.

THE COUNTRY & ITS PEOPLE

Colombia sits in the northwest corner of South America and shares borders with Ecuador and Peru in the south, Brazil and Venezuela in the east, and Panama in the north. The juxtaposition of landscapes within the country is striking, and it makes for cumbersome domestic travel. This, in effect, has led to isolation and inequity that has affected all spheres of society.

The country is dominated by three Andean *cordilleras* (mountain ranges) that fan out from Ecuador like fingers. The central cordillera is a chain of volcanoes that divides two valleys, the Magdalena and Cauca, the latter known for its coffee and sugar plantations. The coastal shoreline meets both the Pacific Ocean and the Caribbean Sea and is separated by Panama's twiglike isthmus. To the east, the Andes plunge to an immense flatland that is sparsely populated and dominated by the *llanos,* a savanna-like terrain, and the tropical rainforest of the northern Amazon region. Because it lies on the equator, Colombia experiences virtually no change in seasonal temperature; however, there are noticeable differences in climate between the cooler Andes and the hot and humid coastal and flatland areas.

Colombia has a population of about 40 million people. The majority of Colombians, about three-fifths of the population, are *mestizo,* a mix of Indian and European blood. One-fifth of the population is classified as "white," from European descent, and another fifth are *mulato,* a mix of African and European blood, or *zambo,* a mix of African and Indian. Only about 2% of the population is pure Indian, although it is estimated that more than 100 indigenous languages are still spoken today. Colombians have, to a great degree, preserved the linguistic purity of Castilian Spanish, their official language.

The social class system in Colombia is a carryover from 16th-century Spain, with pronounced status differences and few chances to climb the social ladder. As Colombia heads into the 21st century and people increasingly migrate to urban areas with a larger middle class, this rigid status system has softened somewhat. Still, only 5% of the country owns the majority of the country's wealth.

Around 95% of the population is Roman Catholic, with the remaining 5% a collective group of Protestant and Jewish faiths. As with most Latin countries, the church wields heavy influence over the decision-making process in government.

Colombia

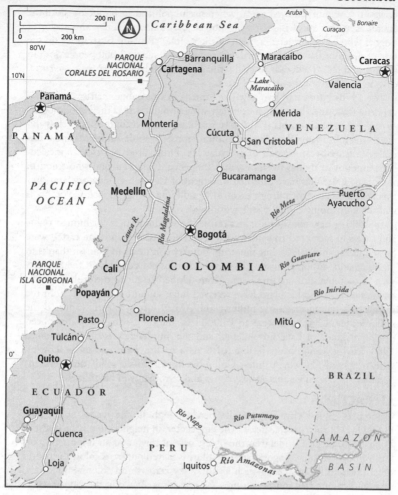

HISTORY & POLITICAL TURBULENCE

Before the arrival of the Spanish, Colombia was populated by various sub-Andean and Caribbean indigenous groups, including the highly developed Chibcha. Colombia's independence was carried out by Simón Bolívar, who in 1819 liberated *Gran Colombia* (Great Colombia), which included present-day Venezuela, Panama, and Ecuador. In 1830, Venezuela and Ecuador split off, and the remaining territory was renamed New Granada. From this arose two predominant political parties: the **conservatives,** who believed in a central government and strict religious doctrine, and the **liberals,** who favored federalism, anticlericalism, and social reforms. Few countries have experienced a two-party system that was—and still is—as mutually destructive as Colombia's. Civil wars between the two factions were the norm, and the country underwent no fewer than 25 revolutions during the next century.

In 1903, Colombia suffered deep humiliation when Panama declared and won independence with assistance from the United States. From 1903 to 1948, however, Colombia enjoyed a relatively peaceful political atmosphere—until the fateful assassination of the left-wing liberal Jorge Eliécer Gaitán, the mayor of Bogotá who was considered a "man of the people." Pent-up frustrations on the side of the poor flared into a terrifying riot that left nearly 3,000 people dead in Bogotá and set off a decade of civil strife and martial law known as *la violencia,* costing hundreds of thousands of lives.

The 1970s introduced two new phenomena in Colombia: the rise of the illegal drug trade and the emergence of left-wing groups such as the Revolutionary Armed Forces of Colombia (FARC). In response, members of the upper class and government formed right-wing paramilitary forces to snuff out leftists and criminals. Violence became a part of everyday life. Drug cartels amassed an incalculable amount of money, weapons, and influence, killing anyone who stood in their way. Guerrillas have captured one-third of Colombia's territory, and they finance their cause with drugs, extortion, and kidnapping. In fact, Colombia is still the kidnapping capital of the world.

In 1990, a new constitution was ratified to ensure respect for human rights and access to social security and health care. The Medellín and Cali cartels were busted in the mid-1990s, but the drug industry continues to flourish thanks to high demand, although dusting has reduced crops considerably in the past few years. Colombia's current president, Alvaro Uribe, has pledged to rid the country of violence, and his plans have received huge support from the U.S. in the form of $2 billion in mostly military aid. Armed forces recently captured the senior leader of FARC; more than 16,000 left- and right-wing troops have been caught or killed or have surrendered; and the murder rate is the lowest since 1986, leaving Colombians feeling safer. As a result, the economy is showing signs of growth. However, unless Colombia implements a solid rural-development strategy, lasting gains against drugs and terrorism will be unlikely.

ATTRACTIONS

Colombia's capital city, **Bogotá** sits perched high in the Andes at 2,598m (8,660 ft.). Most travelers stick to the city center, in neighborhoods such as the **Zona Rosa,** or **La Candelaria,** the oldest part of town and an important stop for its historical value. Bogotá's strange allure is played out in its colorful, chaotic street life, and its contrasts—such as glitzy skyscrapers and colonial buildings, upscale communities and poor slums—are startling. Walking the city streets is part of the attraction, but for safety reasons, be sure to have your hotel hire a reliable guide to accompany you. Highlights in Bogotá include the **Museo del Oro,** one of the best pre-Columbian museums in the world, and the **Iglesia de Santa Clara** and the **Iglesia de San Ignacio,** two splendid colonial churches.

Thankfully, one of Colombia's best and most beautiful attractions, **Cartagena,** is still relatively safe for travelers. (Some take a direct flight to Cartagena, avoiding Bogotá altogether, and many international cruise ships make a stop here.) Cartagena sits on the Caribbean coast and is a wonderfully picturesque, walled-in fishing village of pastel-painted buildings, fine cathedrals, and plenty of Spanish colonial architecture and 17th-century forts that allow you to steep yourself in history. The white-sand beaches are sublime, the restaurants are excellent, and lodging comes in all styles and prices.

Two other safe destinations (because they are offshore islands) are **San Andrés** and **Providencia.** These sun-kissed Caribbean islands have attracted tourism for their beaches, which are lapped by crystal-clear water and offer great snorkeling, fishing, and boating opportunities. The islands are actually closer to Nicaragua, and can be reached by a flight from Bogotá or San José, Costa Rica.

PLANNING YOUR TRIP TO COLOMBIA
VISITOR INFORMATION

Tourist information is limited to a few general websites and to information issued by Colombian consulates. The Colombian Embassy in Washington has a website at **www.colombiaemb.org**, with travel, business, health, and visa information. For insight into Colombia's conflicts and general information about the country, **www.colombiaupdate.com** is an excellent resource. The site **www.virtualtourist.com** has a hotel and destination guide for Colombia. It is important that you keep abreast of the ongoing conflicts in Colombia before you go, and you can do so by consulting a news service such as CNN at **www.cnn.com** or government travel warnings (see "Safety," below).

ENTRY REQUIREMENTS

Travelers need a valid passport and proof of return or onward travel. No visas are required for stays of up to 60 days. If your passport is lost or stolen, you must obtain a new passport from the local embassy and present it, together with a police report, to the main immigration office in Bogotá to obtain permission to depart. There is an airport departure tax of $25 to $31, depending on your destination. Visitors who have stayed longer than 2 months must pay an additional tax of $19. Ask for a tax stamp when you arrive to reduce your exit tax.

Colombia requires children under 18 traveling alone, with one parent, or with a third party to present a copy of their birth certificate and written authorization by the absent parent(s) or legal guardian granting permission to travel alone, with one parent, or with a third party. The authorization must be notarized before a Colombian consulate officer in your home country. For more details, contact your local Colombian embassy or consulate.

Colombian Embassy Locations

In the U.S.: 2118 Leroy Place NW, Washington, DC 20008 (© **202/387-8338;** fax 202/232-8643; www.colombiaemb.org)

In Canada: 360 Albert St., Suite 1002, Ottawa, ON K1R 7X7 (© **613/230-3760;** fax 613/230-4416; www.embajadacolombia.ca)

In the U.K.: Flat 3A, 3 Hans Crescent, London SW1X 0LN (© **020/7589-9177;** fax 020/7581-1829; mail@colombianembassy.co.uk)

In Australia: 101 Northbourne Ave., Turner, ACT 2612 (© **02/6257-2027;** fax 02/6257-1448; emaustralia@dynamite.com)

SAFETY

Plenty of travelers, Europeans especially, continue to travel to safer areas in Colombia without incident, but keep in mind that Colombia is the kidnapping capital of the world, and car bombs have detonated in cities such as Bogotá, which is a relatively new phenomenon.

The U.S. State Department and the Canadian Department of Foreign Affairs continue to gravely warn against travel to Colombia. Check for updated advisories on their websites at **http://travel.state.gov** and **http://voyage.dfait-maeci.gc.ca**, respectively. Travel advice is also available from the British Foreign & Commonwealth Office (**www.fco.gov.uk/travel**) and the Australian Department of Foreign Affairs (**www.dfat.gov.au/consular/advice**). Although many a seasoned globetrotter will scoff at these warnings as exaggerations, there's no denying that these are dangerous times for Colombia-bound travelers. This is especially true if you're an American, due to the United States's Plan Colombia and the perception that money used to eradicate drugs kills legitimate crops in the process, and might be used to fund paramilitary death squads or other nefarious political activities.

FOREIGN EMBASSIES IN COLOMBIA   It is recommended that you check in with your embassy upon arrival. In the event of an emergency, you'll need the reassurance that they have a copy of your travel itinerary on hand. International representatives in Colombia include: **U.S.,** Calle 22D-Bis no. 47–51, Bogotá (© 1/315-0811 or 315-2109 on weekends and weekdays after 5pm); **Canada,** Carrera 7, no. 115-33 (at Calle 116), Bogotá (© 1/657-9800); **U.K.,** Edificio ING Barings, Carrera 9, no. 76-49, Piso 9, Bogotá (© 1/317-6423). **Australian citizens** may go to the Australian consulate at Carrera 18, no. 90-38, Bogotá (© 1/218-0942).

KIDNAPPINGS, CRIME & SCAMS   Colombia is the only Latin American country still embroiled in a full-scale civil war. There are not one but two guerrilla groups (FARC and ELN) that have elevated kidnapping to a fine art. Last year, more than 3,700 people were taken for ransom, meaning more people are kidnapped in Colombia than anywhere else in the world. Colombian business executives are the main targets; however, foreigners are also targeted, mostly in rural areas. On September 12, 2003, ELN guerrilla rebels kidnapped eight foreign backpackers who had been trekking to a ruin site in the north called the Lost City; all were released by late December 2003 (one hostage had escaped shortly after the kidnapping).

Hijackings, bombings, and kidnappings are real dangers, but a tourist's principal concern is street crime, especially at night. Major cities are rife with pickpockets and thugs. Do not call attention to yourself by wearing flashy clothing or jewelry, and do not carry expensive items with you. At night, keep your amount of time on the streets to a minimum, or don't go out at all.

Scam artists have been known to lace drinks, cigarettes, and gum with *burundanga,* a narcotic drug that causes its victim to lapse into unconsciousness long enough to be robbed of everything. Keep a wary eye open if a stranger pays you undue attention, regardless of how well dressed or legitimate the person appears to be. The same could be said for police officers, who often are as corrupt as the criminals they're hired to arrest. Some tourists have reported cases of phony policemen who have "confiscated" their possessions and disappeared. If a policeman stops you, always ask that he return to your hotel with you to clear matters up there.

DRUGS   Colombia produces an estimated 80% of the world's supply of cocaine, and accordingly, drugs are cheap and plentiful here. The Colombian drug industry is ruthless, and it goes without saying no traveler should accept or attempt to buy illegal drugs. The danger of getting mixed up in a serious situation here is almost guaranteed.

MEDICAL SAFETY & EVACUATION INSURANCE   Colombia's rural areas are home to cholera, yellow fever, malaria, and typhoid. Short-term visitors who confine their stays to the coast or major cities are not at risk for these diseases, but always double-check with a medical specialist for updates. A tetanus shot and hepatitis A and B inoculations are often recommended. To protect yourself from intestinal bacteria, always drink bottled water, and eat only vegetables and fruit that are cooked or can be peeled.

Hospitals and clinics in major cities are good, but service in rural areas can be limited or poor. Review your medical insurance to verify that you're covered, and search for a comprehensive evacuation plan that can get you out of the country in a hurry.

GETTING THERE

BY CRUISE SHIP   Many cruise lines, specifically those that sail to the Caribbean and the Panama Canal, include a stop in Cartagena. Travelers are restricted to only 1 day to explore this beautiful coastal city, but shore excursions are generally conducted in safe, guided tours. **Princess** and **Carnival** cruise lines both include Cartagena in their Panama Canal itineraries. A travel agency can help you find the lowest fares on cruises.

BY PLANE   Visitors to Colombia who are not traveling by cruise ship will almost always enter Colombia by plane, usually at Bogotá's Aeropuerto El Dorado, about 11km (7 miles) east of the city. **Avianca,** Colombia's national airline, serves Bogotá, as do **American, Continental, Delta, Air France,** and the Costa Rican airline **Lacsa. British Airways** provides service from the United Kingdom. There are no direct flights from Canada or Australia; travelers will need to connect with one of the airlines above via the United States or Mexico. Arrange a transfer with your hotel or take a taxi—but always insist that a driver use the meter, or agree on a fare beforehand. The safest way to hire a taxi is with your hotel rather than by flagging one down on the street.

BY ORGANIZED TOUR   There are very few tour operators offering trips to or within Colombia. Your hotel should be able to arrange a day tour for you, or at least someone to accompany you while you walk the streets. You might give **FreeGate Tours** a try at 585 Stewart Ave., Suite 310, Garden City, NY 11530 (© **888/373-3428;** www.freegatetours.com).

GETTING AROUND

BY PLANE   Colombia is a large country, and this, coupled with dangerous travel conditions, makes flying the quickest and safest way to get around. Avianca and **SAM** offer frequent domestic flights, but you might find cheaper fares by going with **Satena** airlines. Avianca and SAM recently merged and yet are still having financial difficulties due to the devaluation of the peso. Ask about *cupones,* which Avianca often offers to foreigners if bought outside Colombia. There are three- and five-coupon deals, which cost from $165 to $200 for three coupons, and $280 to $435 for five. Prices are subject to change; contact Avianca in the U.S. at © **800/284-2622.**

BY CAR   **Avis, Hertz,** and **Dollar** have car-rental desks at the airport, but it is not recommended that you drive anywhere in Colombia, due to hold-ups, hijackings, and shady roadblocks. Additionally, the nation's highways and roads are in a wretched state.

BY BUS   Bus service in Colombia is comfortable, plentiful, and cheap, and you'll often see a backpacker or two traveling from place to place using this form of transportation. However, we really wouldn't recommend that you travel by bus—and neither does the U.S. State Department. The element of danger is lower than if you were driving your own vehicle, but air travel is still the recommended form of domestic travel.

Appendix:
Useful Terms & Phrases

Every Spanish-speaking country has its language idiosyncrasies. You'll find that the differences in Spanish spoken throughout South America are quite pronounced (no pun intended). Spanish is not widely spoken among Brazilians, but it helps if you speak at least some Spanish, as it shares a number of similarities with Portuguese, mostly in vocabulary.

1 Spanish Terms & Phrases

IDIOSYNCRASIES BY COUNTRY

Argentine Spanish has a rich, almost Italian sound, with the double "ll" and "y" pronounced with a "j" sound. So *llave* (key) sounds like "*zha*-ve" and *desayuno* (breakfast) sounds like "de-sa-*zhu*-no." *Usted* (the formal "you") is used extensively, and *vos* is a form of "you" that's even more familiar than *tú* (informal "you"). Among the peculiarly Argentine terms you may come across are: *bárbaro* (very cool); *Porteño* (a resident of Buenos Aires); *pasos* (steps in a tango); *bandoneón* (a cousin of the accordion, used in tango music); and *subte* (the Buenos Aires subway). **Uruguayan Spanish** closely resembles the Spanish spoken in Buenos Aires.

Bolivian Spanish (like Peruvian Spanish, below) is influenced by the high altitude and large indigenous culture here. Common terms include *soroche* (altitude sickness), *trufis* (minivans), and *flotas* (long-distance buses). Instead of *de nada* (you're welcome), it's common for Bolivians to say *no hay de que. Chola* refers to women who live in the cities but still wear traditional dress. Be careful when using this term; it can be considered derogatory. People who can trace their ancestors back to both Spain and pre-Columbian Bolivia are known as *mestizos*. To understand the local culture, it's important to be aware of *Pachamama* (Mother Earth), whom Bolivians hold in the highest regard.

Chilean Spanish has a singsong feel; sentences often end on a high-pitched note. Chileans habitually drop the "s" off the end of words such as *gracias* (thank you) and *más* (more), which end up sounding more like "gra-cia" and "ma." Words that end in *-ido* or *-ado* frequently drop the "d"; for example, *pesado* (heavy) is pronounced "peh-*sao*." When using the familiar *tú* verb tense, Chileans—especially younger Chileans—exchange the standard *-as* or *-es* ending for *-ai* or *-i*, so *¿Cómo estás?* (How are you?) becomes *¿Cómo estái?* Chileans add emphasis to *sí* or *no* by tacking on the suffix *-pues*, which is then shortened to *-po*, as in *¡Sí, po! Ya* is commonly used for "yes" or "okay," and *¡Ya, po!* means "Enough!" *Cachai* (You know?) is peppered through conversations. Two very Chilean sayings are *al tiro* (right away) and *harto* (a lot or many).

If you've studied Spanish in high school, you won't come across many surprises in **Ecuadorian Spanish.** When greeting strangers, be sure to always use the formal *usted;* you can switch to the informal *tú* when you get to know the person a bit better. One common phrase that is unique to Ecuador is *a la orden* (you're welcome), instead of *de nada*. It's also typical to add *no más* to commands and directions. In stores and at markets, vendors will often say *Siga no más*, which essentially means "Feel free to look around."

Peruvian Spanish is also straightforward and fairly free of the quirks and national slang that force visitors to page through their dictionaries in desperation. But you will hear people saying *chibolo* for *muchacho* (boy); *churro* and *papasito* for *guapo* (good-looking); *jato* instead of *casa* (house); *chapar* (literally to grab or get), slangier than *besar* (to kiss); *¡Que paja está!* or *¡Está buenísimo!* (It's great); and *mi pata* to connote a dude or chick from your posse. As in Bolivia, *Pachamama* (Mother Earth) tends to make it into conversation remarkably frequently.

Of course, Spanish is but one of the official languages of Peru. **Quechua** (the language of the Inca Empire) was recently given official status and is still widely spoken, especially in the highlands, and there's a movement afoot to include Aymara as a national language. A couple dozen other native tongues are still spoken. A predominantly oral language (the Incas had no written texts), Quechua is full of glottal and magical, curious sounds. As it is written today, it is mystifyingly vowel-heavy and apostrophe-laden, full of q's, k's, and y's; try to wrap your tongue around *Munayniykimanta* (Excuse me) or *Hayk' atan kubrawanki llamaykikunanmanta?* (How much is it to hire a llama?). Colorful phrases mix and match Spanish and Amerindian languages: *hacer la tutumeme* is the same as *ir a dormir*, or to go to sleep.

Given Venezuela's extensive coastline and historic ties to the Caribbean basin, **Venezuelan Spanish** is similar to that spoken throughout the islands and coastal regions. As in Cuba, the Dominican Republic, Puerto Rico, and Panama, the accent is thick, the speech is fast, and final consonants are often dropped. Venezuelans rarely use the familiar second person singular *tú* or *vos*, preferring to employ the more formal *usted* in most instances, even among friends and acquaintances. Some typically Venezuelan words and slang you may come across include *bolo* (short for Bolívar, the unit of currency); *caraqueño/a* (person from Caracas); and *tepui* or *tepuy* (distinct flat-topped mesas representative of the southern region).

BASIC WORDS & PHRASES

English	Spanish	Pronunciation
Good day	**Buenos días**	*bweh*-nohss *dee*-ahss
How are you?	**¿Cómo está?**	*koh*-moh ehss-*tah*?
Very well	**Muy bien**	mwee byehn
Thank you	**Gracias**	*grah*-syahss
You're welcome	**De nada**	day *nah*-dah
Goodbye	**Adiós**	ah-*dyohss*
Please	**Por favor**	pohr fah-*vor*
Yes	**Sí**	see
No	**No**	noh
Excuse me (to get by someone)	**Perdóneme**	pehr-*doh*-neh-meh
Excuse me (to begin a question)	**Disculpe**	dees-*kool*-peh
Give me	**Déme**	*deh*-meh

English	Spanish	Pronunciation
Where is . . . ?	¿Dónde está . . . ?	*dohn*-deh ehss-*tah*
the station	la estación	lah ehss-tah-*seown*
a hotel	un hotel	oon oh-*tel*
a gas station	una estación de servicio	*oo*-nah ehss-tah-*seown* deh sehr-*bee*-syoh
a restaurant	un restaurante	oon res-toh-*rahn*-teh
the toilet	el baño	el *bah*-nyoh
a good doctor	un buen médico	oon bwehn *meh*-thee-coh
the road to . . .	el camino a/hacia . . .	el cah-*mee*-noh ah/*ah*-syah
To the right	A la derecha	ah lah deh-*reh*-chah
To the left	A la izquierda	ah lah ees-*kyehr*-dah
Straight ahead	Derecho	deh-*reh*-choh
I would like . . .	Quisiera . . .	key-*syehr*-ah
I want . . .	Quiero . . .	*kyehr*-oh
to eat	comer	koh-*mehr*
a room	una habitación	*oon*-nah ah-bee-tah-*seown*
Do you have . . . ?	¿Tiene usted . . .?	*tyeh*-neh oos-*ted*
a book	un libro	oon *lee*-broh
a dictionary	un diccionario	oon deek-seown-*ar*-eoh
How much is it?	¿Cuánto cuesta?	*kwahn*-toh *kwehss*-tah?
When?	¿Cuándo?	*kwahn*-doh?
What?	¿Qué?	kay?
There is (Is there . . . ?)	(¿)Hay (. . . ?)	eye
What is there?	¿Qué hay?	keh eye
Yesterday	Ayer	ah-*yer*
Today	Hoy	oy
Tomorrow	Mañana	mah-*nyah*-nah
Good	Bueno	*bweh*-noh
Bad	Malo	*mah*-loh
Better (best)	(Lo) Mejor	(loh) meh-*hor*
More	Más	mahs
Less	Menos	*meh*-nohss
No smoking	Se prohibe fumar	seh pro-*hee*-beh foo-*mahr*
Postcard	Tarjeta postal	tar-*heh*-tah pohs-*tahl*
Insect repellent	Rapelente contra insectos	rah-peh-*lehn*-teh *cohn*-trah een-*sehk*-tohss

MORE USEFUL PHRASES

English	Spanish	Pronunciation
Do you speak English?	¿Habla usted inglés?	*ah*-blah oo-*sted* een-*glehss*
Is there anyone here who speaks English?	¿Hay alguien aquí que hable inglés?	eye *ahl*-gyehn ah-*key* keh *ah*-bleh een-*glehss*
I speak a little Spanish.	Hablo un poco de español.	*ah*-bloh oon *poh*-koh deh ehss-pah-*nyol*
I don't understand Spanish very well.	No (lo) entiendo muy bien el español.	noh (loh) ehn-*tyehn*-do mwee byehn el ehss-pah-*nyol*

English	Spanish	Pronunciation
The meal is good.	**Me gusta la comida.**	meh *goo*-stah lah koh-*mee*-dah
What time is it?	**¿Qué hora es?**	keh *oh*-rah ehss
May I see your menu?	**¿Puedo ver el menú (la carta)?**	*pweh*-doh vehr el meh-*noo* (lah *car*-tah)
The check, please.	**La cuenta, por favor.**	lah *kwehn*-tah, pohr fah-*vor*
What do I owe you?	**¿Cuánto le debo?**	*kwahn*-toh leh *deh*-boh
What did you say?	**¿Cómo? (colloquial expression for American "Eh?")**	*koh*-moh?
I want (to see) . . .	**Quiero (ver) . . .**	*kyehr*-oh (vehr)
a room	**un cuarto** or **una habitación**	oon *kwar*-toh, *oon*-nah ah-bee-tah-*seown*
for two persons	**para dos personas**	*pah*-rah dohss pehr-*soh*-nahs
with (without) bathroom	**con (sin) baño**	kohn (seen) *bah*-nyoh
We are staying here only . . .	**Nos quedamos aquí solamente . . .**	nohs keh-*dahm*-ohss ah-*key* sohl-ah-*mehn*-teh
one night	**una noche**	*oon*-ah *noh*-cheh
one week	**una semana**	*oon*-ah seh-*mahn*-ah
We are leaving . . .	**Partimos (Salimos) . . .**	pahr-*tee*-mohss (sah-*lee*-mohss)
tomorrow	**mañana**	mah-*nya*-nah
Do you accept . . . ?	**¿Acepta usted . . . ?**	ah-*sehp*-tah oo-*sted*
traveler's checks?	**cheques de viajero?**	*cheh*-kehs deh byah-*heh*-ro
Is there a laundromat?	**¿Hay una lavandería?**	eye *oon*-ah lah-*bahn*-deh-ree-ah
near here?	**cerca de aquí?**	*sehr*-ka deh ah-*key*
Please send these clothes to the laundry.	**Hágame el favor de mandar esta ropa a la lavandería.**	*ah*-ga-meh el fah-*vor* deh mahn-*dahr* ehss-tah *ro*-pah a lah lah-*bahn*-deh-ree-ah

POSTAL GLOSSARY

Airmail **Correo Aéreo**
Customs **Aduana**
General Delivery **Lista de Correos**
Insurance (insured mail) **Seguro (correo asegurado)**
Mailbox **Buzón**
Money Order **Giro Postal**
Parcel **Paquete**
Post Office **Oficina de Correos**
Post Office Box **Casilla**
Postal Service **Correos**
Registered Mail **Correo Registrado**
Rubber Stamp **Sello**
Special Delivery, Express **Entrega Inmediata**
Stamp **Estampilla** or **Timbre**

TRANSPORTATION TERMS

English	Spanish	Pronunciation
Airport	**Aeropuerto**	ah-eh-ro-*pwer*-toh
Flight	**Vuelo**	*bweh*-loh
Rental car	**Arrendadora de Autos**	ah-rehn-dah-*do*-rah deh *ow*-tohs
Bus	**Autobús**	ow-toh-*boos*
Bus or truck	**Camión**	kah-*myohn*
Local bus	**Micro**	*mee*-kroh
Lane	**Carril**	kah-*real*
Baggage (claim area)	**Equipajes**	eh-key-*pah*-hehs
Luggage storage area	**Custodia**	koo-*stow*-dee-ah
Arrivals gates	**Llegadas**	yeh-*gah*-dahs
Originates at this station	**Local**	loh-*kahl*
Originates elsewhere	**De Paso**	deh *pah*-soh
Stops if seats available	**Para si hay lugares**	*pah*-rah see eye loo-*gah*-rehs
First class	**Primera**	pree-*meh*-rah
Second class	**Segunda**	seh-*goon*-dah
Nonstop	**Sin Escala**	seen ehss-*kah*-lah
Baggage claim area	**Recibo de Equipajes**	reh-*see*-boh deh eh-key-*pah*-heh
Waiting room	**Sala de Espera**	*sah*-lah deh ehss-*peh*-rah
Toilets	**Baños**	*bah*-nyos
Ticket window	**Boletería**	boh-leh-teh-*ree*-ah

NUMBERS

1 **uno** (*ooh*-noh)
2 **dos** (dohss)
3 **tres** (trehss)
4 **cuatro** (*kwah*-troh)
5 **cinco** (*seen*-koh)
6 **seis** (sayss)
7 **siete** (*syeh*-teh)
8 **ocho** (*oh*-choh)
9 **nueve** (*nweh*-beh)
10 **diez** (dyess)
11 **once** (*ohn*-seh)
12 **doce** (*doh*-seh)
13 **trece** (*treh*-seh)
14 **catorce** (kah-*tor*-seh)
15 **quince** (*keen*-seh)
16 **dieciseis** (dyess-ee-*sayss*)

17 **diecisiete** (dyess-ee-*syeh*-teh)
18 **dieciocho** (dyess-ee-*oh*-choh)
19 **diecinueve** (dyess-ee-*nweh*-beh)
20 **veinte** (*bayn*-teh)
30 **treinta** (*trayn*-tah)
40 **cuarenta** (kwah-*ren*-tah)
50 **cincuenta** (seen-*kwen*-tah)
60 **sesenta** (seh-*sehn*-tah)
70 **setenta** (seh-*ten*-tah)
80 **ochenta** (oh-*chen*-tah)
90 **noventa** (noh-*behn*-tah)
100 **cien** (*syehn*)
200 **doscientos** (doh-*syehn*-tohs)
500 **quinientos** (kee-*nyehn*-tohs)
1,000 **mil** (meel)

2 Portuguese Useful Terms & Phrases

Since the Portuguese explorers introduced their language to the area now known as Brazil, the language has developed and evolved to reflect the unique culture of the country. Brazilian Portuguese has adopted many Indian and African words, and the language has softened from its original harsh sound to a more melodious speech. For a country the size of Brazil, the language is surprisingly homogenous, with just a few pronunciation differences and local slang distinguishing one region from another. *Cariocas,* residents of Rio de Janeiro, have added more "sh" sounds to the language and have almost completely done away with the hard "r," pronouncing the name of their city as "Heo." A "d" at the front of a word is pronounced like "j"—thus *dia* (day) sounds like "*jee*-a." An "m" at the end of a word is not fully enunciated (try making the "m" sound without closing your lips).

Brazilians have eliminated the *tu* and use *você* (you) instead. The accompanying verb has the same form as the third person singular; for example, *você vai* (you go) and *ele/ela vai* (he/she goes). Popular expressions include the upbeat *valeu* (cool, right on, awesome), often accompanied by a thumbs-up sign to express appreciation. *Maneiro* and *legal* both mean cool or right; to rave about something, yell out *Otimo!* ("Great!" or "Wonderful!").

BASIC WORDS & PHRASES

English	Portuguese	Pronunciation
Good day	**Bom dia**	bon *jee*-ah
How are you?	**Como vai?**	como vaye
Very well	**Muito bem**	*mooy*-too ben
Thank you	**Obrigado/obrigada** (man/woman)	oh-bree-*gah*-doo/ oh-bree-*gah*-dah
You're welcome	**De nada**	jeh *nah*-dah
Goodbye	**Tchau** or **ate logo**	*ah*-tjeh *loh*-goo
Please	**Por favor**	pohr fah-*vor*
Yes	**Sim**	seen
No	**Não**	now
Excuse me (to get by someone)	**Com licença**	con lee-*sen*-sa
Excuse me (to begin a question)	**Desculpa**	dehs-*kool*-pah
Give me	**Dáme**	*dah*-may
Where is . . . ?	**Onde está** or **Onde é . . . ?**	*ohn*-day ehss-*tah,* *ohn*-day *é* (as in "get")
the bus station	**a rodoviaria**	*ah* roh-doh-vi-*ahr*-ee-ah
a hotel	**um hotel**	oon oh-*tel*
a bed and breakfast	**a pousada**	ah pooh-*zah*-dah
a gas station	**um posto de gasolina**	oon *poh*-stoo dje gaz- oh-*leen*-ah
a restaurant	**um restaurante**	oon res-toh-*rahn*-tay
the toilet	**o banheiro**	oh ban-*hay*-roo
a good doctor	**um bom medico**	oon bon *may*-jee-coo
the road to . . .	**o caminho para . . .**	oh cah-*meen*-yo *pah*-rah
To the right	**A direita**	ah dir-*ray*-tah
To the left	**A esquerda**	ah ish-*kayr*-dah
Straight ahead	**em frente**	en *fren*-tjee
I would like	**Gostaria**	goh-stah-*ree*-a
I want . . .	**Quero . . .**	*keh*-roo
to eat	**comer**	coh-*mehr*
a room (no private bathroom)	**um quarto**	oon *kwar*-too
a room (with private bathroom)	**um apartamento**	oon ah-part-ah-*men*-too

English	Portuguese	Pronunciation
Do you have . . . ?	Você tem . . .?	voh-*say* teng
a book	um livro	oon *lee*-vroo
a dictionary	um diccionario	un di-syown-*ah*-ree-oo
How much is it?	Quanto custa?	*kwan*-too *koos*-tah
When?	Quando?	*kwan*-doo
What?	Que?	kay?
There is (Is there . . . ?)	Tem . . . ?	*teng*
What is there?	Que tem?	kay teng
Yesterday	Ontem	*ohn*-teng
Today	Hoje	*oh*-zhay (*h* is silent)
Tomorrow	Amanhã	ah-man-*yah*
Good	Bom	bon
Bad	Mal	mauh
Better (best)	(O) Melhor	oo mel-*hohr*
More	Mais	maizh
Less	Menos	*may*-nos
No smoking	Proibido fumar	pro-he-*bee*-doo foo-*mahr*
Postcard	Cartão postal	cahr-*tang* poh-*stau*
Insect repellent	Repelente contra insectos	ray-peh-*len*-tjee *kon*-tra in-*set*-oos

MORE USEFUL PHRASES

English	Portuguese	Pronunciation
Do you speak English?	Você fala Ingles?	voh-say *fah*-lah eeng-*laysh*
Is there anyone here who speaks English?	Tem alguem aqui que fala ingles?	teng al-*geng* a-*kee* kay *fah*-lah eeng-*laysh*
I speak a little Portuguese.	Falo um pouco de portugues.	*fah*-loh un *po*-koo dje por-tu-*gayse*
I don't understand Portuguese very well.	Não entendo portugues muito bem.	now en-*ten*-doo por-too-*gayse mooy*-too beng
The meal is good.	A comida esta boa.	ah ko-*mee*-dah es-*tah bo*-ah
What time is it?	Que horas são?	kay *ohr*-as sang
May I see your menu?	Posso ver o menu (cardapio)?	*poh*-soh vayr oh men-*ooh* (karh-*dap*-ee-oh)
The check, please.	A conta por favor.	ah *kon*-tah por fah-*vor*
What do I owe you?	Quanto te devo?	*kwan*-toh teh *djay*-voo
What did you say?	Como? (colloquial expression for American "What?" or "Eh?")	*ko*-moo
I want (to see)	Quero (ver)	*ker*-oo (vayr)
a room	um quarto or um apartamento	un *kwar*-too, un a-part-a-*men*-too
for two persons	para duas pessoas	*par*-ah *doo*-as pes-*soh*-as
with (without) bathroom	com (sem) banheiro	con (seng) bahn-*ayr*-oo

English	Portuguese	Pronunciation
We are staying here only . . .	Nos ficamos aqui somente . . .	nos fi-*ka*-mos a-*kee* so-*men*-tjee
one night	uma noite	uma *noi*-tjee
one week	uma semana	uma se-*mah*-na
We are leaving . . .	Vamos embora . . .	*vah*-mos em-*boh*-rah
tomorrow	amanhã	ah-man-*yah*
Do you accept . . .	Você aceita . . .	voh-*say* ah-*say*-tah
traveler's checks?	traveler's cheques?	(same in Portuguese)
Is there a laundromat (coin-operated)?	Tem uma lavanderia (self-service)?	teng uma la-van-dah-*ree*-ah (self service is the same in Portuguese)
near here?	Aqui perto?	ah-*kee* per-too
Please send these clothes to the laundry.	Por favor mande estas roupas para a lavanderia.	por fah-*vor man*-deh es-*tahs* ro-pahs *par*-ah ah la-van-dah-*ree*-ah

POSTAL GLOSSARY

Airmail   **Correio Aereo**
Customs   **Alfandega**
Insurance (insured mail)   **Seguro (Sedex)**
Mailbox   **Caixa postal**
Parcel   **Pacote**
Post Office   **Correios**
Registered Mail   **Registrado**
Stamp   **Selo**
Special Delivery, Express   **Sedex** or **expresso**

TRANSPORTATION TERMS

English	Portuguese	Pronunciation
Airport	Aeroporto	air-oo-*pohr*-too
Flight	Voo	voooo (long "o" as in hope)
Rental car	Locadora de carros	loh-kah-*doh*-rah dee *kah*-roos
Bus	Onibus	*ohn*-ee-boos
Baggage (claim area)	Bagagem	bah-*gah*-jen
Luggage storage area	Guarda volumes	*guar*-dah vall-*oo*-mes
Arrival gates	Chegadas or desembarque	shay-*gah*-das, deh-sem-*bar*-kee
Departure gates	Embarque	em-*bar*-kee
Statutory Holiday	Feriado	fayr-ee-*ah*-doo
Airport tax	Taxa de embarque	*tah*-sha dee em-*bar*-kee
Delay	Atraso	ah-*trah*-soo
First class	Primeira	pree-*may*-rah
Second class	Segunda	say-*goon*-dah
Nonstop	Sem escala	seng es-*kah*-lah
Baggage claim area	Recibo de bagagem	ray-*si*-boo dee bah-*gah*-jen
Waiting room	Sala de Espera	*sah*-lah dee es-*per*-ah
Toilets	Banheiro	ban-*hay*-roo
Ticket window	Bilheteria	beel-hay-tay-*ree*-ah

NUMBERS

1	**um** (oon)	17	**dizesete** (deh-say-*seh*-tay)
2	**dois** (doysh)	18	**dizoito** (dee-*soh*-toh)
3	**tres** (traysh)	19	**dizenove** (deh-say-*no*-vay)
4	**quatro** (*kwah*-troh)	20	**vinte** (*veen*-tee)
5	**cinco** (*seen*-koh)	30	**trinta** (*treen*-tah)
6	**seis** (sayss)	40	**quarenta** (kwah-*ren*-tah)
7	**sete** (*se*-tay)	50	**cinquenta** (seen-*kwen*-tah)
8	**oito** (*oy*-toh)	60	**sesenta** (say-*sen*-tah)
9	**nove** (*no*-vay)	70	**setenta** (say-*ten*-tah)
10	**dez** (dehsh)	80	**oitenta** (oh-*ten*-tah)
11	**onze** (*ohn*-say)	90	**noventa** (no-*ven*-tah)
12	**doze** (*doh*-say)	100	**cem** (sayng)
13	**treze** (*tray*-say)	200	**duzentos** (dos-*sehn*-tos)
14	**quatorze** (kah-*tor*-say)	500	**quinhentos** (keen-*ehn*-tos)
15	**quinze** (*keen*-say)	1,000	**mil** (meel)
16	**dizeseis** (deh-say-*says*)		

Index

FROMMER'S® COMPLETE TRAVEL GUIDES

Alaska
Alaska Cruises & Ports of Call
American Southwest
Amsterdam
Argentina & Chile
Arizona
Atlanta
Australia
Austria
Bahamas
Barcelona, Madrid & Seville
Beijing
Belgium, Holland & Luxembourg
Bermuda
Boston
Brazil
British Columbia & the Canadian
  Rockies
Brussels & Bruges
Budapest & the Best of Hungary
Calgary
California
Canada
Cancún, Cozumel & the Yucatán
Cape Cod, Nantucket & Martha's
  Vineyard
Caribbean
Caribbean Cruises & Ports of Call
Caribbean Ports of Call
Carolinas & Georgia
Chicago
China
Colorado
Costa Rica
Cuba
Denmark
Denver, Boulder & Colorado
  Springs
England
Europe
Europe by Rail
European Cruises & Ports of Call

Florence, Tuscany & Umbria
Florida
France
Germany
Great Britain
Greece
Greek Islands
Halifax
Hawaii
Hong Kong
Honolulu, Waikiki & Oahu
India
Ireland
Israel
Italy
Jamaica
Japan
Kauai
Las Vegas
London
Los Angeles
Maryland & Delaware
Maui
Mexico
Montana & Wyoming
Montréal & Québec City
Munich & the Bavarian Alps
Nashville & Memphis
Newfoundland & Labrador
New England
New Mexico
New Orleans
New York City
New York State
New Zealand
Northern Italy
Norway
Nova Scotia, New Brunswick &
  Prince Edward Island
Oregon
Ottawa
Paris

Peru
Philadelphia & the Amish
  Country
Portugal
Prague & the Best of the Czech
  Republic
Provence & the Riviera
Puerto Rico
Rome
San Antonio & Austin
San Diego
San Francisco
Santa Fe, Taos & Albuquerque
Scandinavia
Scotland
Seattle
Shanghai
Sicily
Singapore & Malaysia
South Africa
South America
South Florida
South Pacific
Southeast Asia
Spain
Sweden
Switzerland
Texas
Thailand
Tokyo
Toronto
USA
Utah
Vancouver & Victoria
Vermont, New Hampshire &
  Maine
Vienna & the Danube Valley
Virgin Islands
Virginia
Walt Disney World® & Orlando
Washington, D.C.
Washington State

FROMMER'S® DOLLAR-A-DAY GUIDES

Australia from $50 a Day
California from $70 a Day
England from $75 a Day
Europe from $70 a Day
Florida from $70 a Day
Hawaii from $80 a Day

Ireland from $80 a Day
Italy from $70 a Day
London from $90 a Day
New York from $90 a Day
Paris from $90 a Day
San Francisco from $70 a Day

Washington, D.C. from $80 a
  Day
Portable London from $90 a Day
Portable New York City from $90
  a Day
Portable Paris from $90 a Day

FROMMER'S® PORTABLE GUIDES

Acapulco, Ixtapa & Zihuatanejo
Amsterdam
Aruba
Australia's Great Barrier Reef
Bahamas
Berlin
Big Island of Hawaii
Boston
California Wine Country
Cancún
Cayman Islands
Charleston
Chicago
Disneyland®
Dominican Republic
Dublin

Florence
Frankfurt
Hong Kong
Las Vegas
Las Vegas for Non-Gamblers
London
Los Angeles
Los Cabos & Baja
Maine Coast
Maui
Miami
Nantucket & Martha's Vineyard
New Orleans
New York City
Paris

Phoenix & Scottsdale
Portland
Puerto Rico
Puerto Vallarta, Manzanillo &
  Guadalajara
Rio de Janeiro
San Diego
San Francisco
Savannah
Vancouver
Vancouver Island
Venice
Virgin Islands
Washington, D.C.
Whistler

FROMMER'S® NATIONAL PARK GUIDES

Algonquin Provincial Park
Banff & Jasper
Family Vacations in the National
  Parks

Grand Canyon
National Parks of the American
  West
Rocky Mountain

Yellowstone & Grand Teton
Yosemite & Sequoia/Kings
  Canyon
Zion & Bryce Canyon

FROMMER'S® MEMORABLE WALKS

Chicago
London

New York
Paris

San Francisco

FROMMER'S® WITH KIDS GUIDES

Chicago
Las Vegas
New York City

Ottawa
San Francisco
Toronto

Vancouver
Walt Disney World® & Orlando
Washington, D.C.

SUZY GERSHMAN'S BORN TO SHOP GUIDES

Born to Shop: France
Born to Shop: Hong Kong,
  Shanghai & Beijing

Born to Shop: Italy
Born to Shop: London

Born to Shop: New York
Born to Shop: Paris

FROMMER'S® IRREVERENT GUIDES

Amsterdam
Boston
Chicago
Las Vegas
London

Los Angeles
Manhattan
New Orleans
Paris
Rome

San Francisco
Seattle & Portland
Vancouver
Walt Disney World®
Washington, D.C.

FROMMER'S® BEST-LOVED DRIVING TOURS

Austria
Britain
California
France

Germany
Ireland
Italy
New England

Northern Italy
Scotland
Spain
Tuscany & Umbria

THE UNOFFICIAL GUIDES®

Beyond Disney
Central Italy
Chicago
Cruises
Disneyland®
England
Florida
Florida with Kids
Inside Disney

Hawaii
Las Vegas
London
Maui
Mexico's Best Beach Resorts
Mini Las Vegas
Mini-Mickey
New Orleans
New York City

Paris
San Francisco
Skiing & Snowboarding in the
  West
Walt Disney World®
Walt Disney World® for
  Grown-ups
Walt Disney World® with Kids
Washington, D.C.

SPECIAL-INTEREST TITLES

Athens Past & Present
Cities Ranked & Rated
Frommer's Best Day Trips from London
Frommer's Caribbean Hideaways
Frommer's China: The 50 Most Memorable Trips
Frommer's Exploring America by RV
Frommer's Gay & Lesbian Europe
Frommer's Best RV and Tent Campgrounds
  in the U.S.A.

Frommer's Road Atlas Europe
Frommer's Road Atlas France
Frommer's Road Atlas Ireland
Frommer's Wonderful Weekends from
  New York City
The New York Times' Guide to Unforgettable
  Weekends
Retirement Places Rated
Rome Past & Present

Booked aisle seat.

Reserved room with a view.

With a queen – no, make that a king-size bed.

With Travelocity, you can book your flights and hotels together, so you can get even better deals than if you booked them separately. You'll save time and money without compromising the quality of your trip. Choose your airline seat, search for alternate airports, pick your hotel room type, even choose the neighborhood you'd like to stay in.

Travelocity

Visit **www.travelocity.com**
or call **1-888-TRAVELOCITY**

Fly.
Sleep.
Save.

Now you can
hotels together, so y
than if you bo

Travelocity

Visit www.travelocity.com
or call 1-888-TRAVELOCIT